CAMBRIDGE LIBRARY

Books of enduring scholarly value

Classics

From the Renaissance to the nineteenth century, Latin and Greek were compulsory subjects in almost all European universities, and most early modern scholars published their research and conducted international correspondence in Latin. Latin had continued in use in Western Europe long after the fall of the Roman empire as the lingua franca of the educated classes and of law, diplomacy, religion and university teaching. The flight of Greek scholars to the West after the fall of Constantinople in 1453 gave impetus to the study of ancient Greek literature and the Greek New Testament. Eventually, just as nineteenth-century reforms of university curricula were beginning to erode this ascendancy, developments in textual criticism and linguistic analysis, and new ways of studying ancient societies, especially archaeology, led to renewed enthusiasm for the Classics. This collection offers works of criticism, interpretation and synthesis by the outstanding scholars of the nineteenth century.

The Latin Language

W. M. Lindsay, an outstanding figure of his time and one of the greatest of British Latinists, recognised a need for a 'new treatment' of Latin philology in this enduring work of 1894. Demonstrating his considerable familiarity with the voluminous texts of earlier Latin grammarians, Lindsay draws upon previous significant studies to illustrate how our knowledge of the Latin language has advanced over time. The book addresses all the key aspects of the Latin language in turn, including its alphabet, pronunciation, accentuation, the formation of noun and adjective stems, declensions, conjunctions, adverbs and prepositions. It is clearly organised to enable the reader easily to locate the topic required. Held in extremely high regard by classical scholars today, Lindsay's work condenses a vast store of learning on this large and complex topic into a single volume, and represents a major contribution to the analysis of Latin grammar.

Cambridge University Press has long been a pioneer in the reissuing of out-of-print titles from its own backlist, producing digital reprints of books that are still sought after by scholars and students but could not be reprinted economically using traditional technology. The Cambridge Library Collection extends this activity to a wider range of books which are still of importance to researchers and professionals, either for the source material they contain, or as landmarks in the history of their academic discipline.

Drawing from the world-renowned collections in the Cambridge University Library, and guided by the advice of experts in each subject area, Cambridge University Press is using state-of-the-art scanning machines in its own Printing House to capture the content of each book selected for inclusion. The files are processed to give a consistently clear, crisp image, and the books finished to the high quality standard for which the Press is recognised around the world. The latest print-on-demand technology ensures that the books will remain available indefinitely, and that orders for single or multiple copies can quickly be supplied.

The Cambridge Library Collection will bring back to life books of enduring scholarly value (including out-of-copyright works originally issued by other publishers) across a wide range of disciplines in the humanities and social sciences and in science and technology.

The Latin Language

*An Historical Account of
Latin Sounds, Stems, and Flexions*

W. M. LINDSAY

CAMBRIDGE UNIVERSITY PRESS

Cambridge, New York, Melbourne, Madrid, Cape Town, Singapore,
São Paolo, Delhi, Dubai, Tokyo

Published in the United States of America by Cambridge University Press, New York

www.cambridge.org
Information on this title: www.cambridge.org/9781108012409

© in this compilation Cambridge University Press 2010

This edition first published 1894
This digitally printed version 2010

ISBN 978-1-108-01240-9 Paperback

This book reproduces the text of the original edition. The content and language reflect
the beliefs, practices and terminology of their time, and have not been updated.

Cambridge University Press wishes to make clear that the book, unless originally published
by Cambridge, is not being republished by, in association or collaboration with, or
with the endorsement or approval of, the original publisher or its successors in title.

THE LATIN LANGUAGE

W. M. LINDSAY

THE
LATIN LANGUAGE

AN HISTORICAL ACCOUNT

OF

LATIN SOUNDS, STEMS, AND FLEXIONS

BY

W. M. LINDSAY, M.A.
FELLOW OF JESUS COLLEGE, OXFORD

Oxford
AT THE CLARENDON PRESS
1894

TO

PROFESSOR ROBINSON ELLIS

PREFACE

SINCE Corssen's great work (last edition, Leipzig, 1868-70), there has been no book devoted to a separate investigation by Comparative Philological methods of the Latin Language, its declensions, its conjugations, its formation of the various parts of speech, and the changes of its pronunciation and orthography, if we except the short summary (last edition, Nördlingen, 1889) written by Professor Stolz for the Iwan Müller Series of Handbooks of Classical Antiquity. And yet the additions to our knowledge of the subject since Corssen's time have been very great. Not only has the whole Science of Comparative Philology been, by the help of men like Johannes Schmidt, Osthoff, and Brugmann[1], set on a sounder basis, but a vast amount has been added to our knowledge of the Early Latin authors, especially Plautus, of the Umbrian, Oscan, and other dialects of ancient Italy, of Romance, and above all of the Celtic family of languages, a family closely united with the Italic group. The time has surely come for a new treatment of the subject, such as I venture to offer in the ten chapters of this volume.

I should have liked to have added to them a fuller discussion of the relation of Latin to the other languages of Italy. But I had already exceeded the generous limits

---

[1] I take this opportunity of acknowledging to the fullest extent possible my indebtedness to Brugmann, *Grundriss der Vergleichenden Grammatik* in chaps. iv–viii, and to Seelmann, *Aussprache des Latein* in chap. ii.

viii   PREFACE.

allowed by the Delegates of the Press, and it seemed to me that until more evidence is forthcoming in the shape of dialectal inscriptions certainty can hardly be attained. It is much to be desired that some of the money which is being raised every year for excavations should be devoted to this field of research. The records of peoples like the Samnites, who fought so gallantly with Rome for the rule of Italy, and whose religion and manners so greatly influenced the ruling race, should not be allowed to lie neglected. And yet, while the Latin, Greek, and Etruscan inscriptions of Italy are carefully sought after year by year, there has been practically no organized search for the remains of Oscan, Umbrian, Pelignian, and the rest. I trust that some step may be taken ere long in this direction.

It remains for me to acknowledge with gratitude the kind help which I have had from numerous correspondents, both in this country and abroad, as well as from my Oxford friends, such as my colleague, Mr. E. R. Wharton. My special thanks are due to Mr. Sweet for looking through the proof-sheets of my chapter on Latin Pronunciation, and to Professors Mommsen, Bormann, Huelsen, and Dressel for giving me access to the advance-sheets of the *Corpus Inscriptionum Latinarum*. My friend, Mr. J. A. Smith, Fellow of Balliol College, has been good enough to go over the whole book in proof, and to give me many valuable suggestions, especially on one of the most difficult problems of the language, the formation of the Perfect Tense.

OXFORD, *August*, 1894.

TABLE OF CONTENTS

	PAGE
LIST OF ABBREVIATIONS	xxvi

CHAPTER I.
THE ALPHABET.

SEC.
1. The Alphabet 1
2. The Alphabet of twenty-one letters 5
3. The letter F 5
4. X 5
5. Z 5
6. The Guttural-symbols 6
7. Y- and W-sounds 7
8. Double Consonant 8
9. Signs for long vowels 9
10. gg for ng 10
11. New Letters for Greek Sounds 11
12. Influence of Greek Orthography 12
13. Syllabic Writing 12

CHAPTER II.
PRONUNCIATION.

1. A 13
2. Description of the A-sound by Latin phoneticians . . 17
3. Interchange of a and e 17
4. Interchange of a and o 17
5. Anomalies in Romance 18
6. E 18
7. Descriptions of the E-sound by Latin phoneticians, &c. . 20
8. i for unaccented ĕ 21
9. i for ĕ in hiatus 21
10. 'Rustic' e for ĭ in hiatus 22
11. ī for ē 22
12. ĭ for unaccented ĕ 23
13. ä for ĕ 23
14. I 23
15. Descriptions of the I-sound by Latin phoneticians . . 25
16. by Grammarians 25

TABLE OF CONTENTS.

SEC.		PAGE
17.	Interchange of i and e	29
18.	i in hiatus	30
19.	Anomalies in Romance	30
20.	O	30
21.	Descriptions of the O-sound by Latin phoneticians	32
22.	Close for open o in accented syllables before certain consonant-groups	32
23.	u for unaccented ŏ	33
24.	u for ō	33
25.	Other changes of ŏ and ō	34
26.	U, Y	34
27.	Descriptions of the U-sound by Latin phoneticians	35
28.	Greek υ in Latin	36
29.	o for ŭ	37
30.	ō for ū	37
31.	Other changes of ŭ and ū	37
32.	Diphthongs	37
33.	Grammarians' account of diphthongs	39
34.	Ter. Maurus on au	40
35.	au in Romance	40
36.	u for accented au	40
37.	o and au	40
38.	a for au	41
39.	Greek transcriptions of au	42
40.	ae for au	42
41.	e for ae	42
42.	ai for ae	43
43.	Greek ει	43
44.	oe and e	44
45.	oe in Romance	44
46.	Greek ευ	44
47.	ui of cui	44
48.	J, V	44
49.	Testimony of grammarians	47
50.	j and v in early Latin	48
51.	in late Latin and Romance	49
52.	v confused with b in late Latin and Romance	49
53.	Intervocalic v dropped	52
54.	Postconsonantal v dropped	52
55.	ai, ei before a vowel	53
56.	H	53
57.	Testimony of grammarians	55
58.	h between vowels	57
59.	h in Old Latin	57
60.	Greek aspirates in Latin	57
61.	M, N	60
62.	Phonetic descriptions of normal m, n	65
63.	The Agma	65
64.	m, n before consonant	65
65.	Final m	67

TABLE OF CONTENTS. xi

SEC.		PAGE
66.	ns	69
67.	nx	69
68.	mn	69
69.	gn	70
70.	nct	70
71.	nd	70
72.	Parasitic vowel in Greek loanwords	70
73.	Tenues and mediae	71
74.	Greek tenues in loanwords	74
75.	Confusion of mediae and tenues in Latin words	75
76.	Mediae and tenues at end of word	76
77.	Mediae and tenues in the Dialects	77
78.	B, P	78
79.	Phonetic descriptions of b, p	78
80.	bs, bt	79
81.	ps, pt	79
82.	bm, mb	80
83.	b and dialectal f	80
84.	b and m	80
85.	D, T .	80
86.	Phonetic descriptions of d, t	82
87.	d and l	82
88.	d and r	82
89.	tl	83
90.	Assibilation of ty, dy	83
91.	K, C, G, QU, GU	84
92.	Phonetic descriptions of the Gutturals	86
93.	qu, gu	86
94.	c, g before narrow vowels	87
95.	ct, tt	89
96.	L, R	89
97.	Phonetic descriptions of l	91
98.	of r	91
99.	The grammarians on the pronunciation of l	92
100.	of r	92
101.	Interchange of r and l	92
102.	Parasitic vowel with l, r	93
103.	Avoidance of two r's	95
104.	rs	96
105.	r-n	96
106.	l-n	96
107.	l before consonant	96
108.	rl	97
109.	r before consonants	97
110.	final r	97
111.	Metathesis	97
112.	ly	98
113.	ry	98
114.	F	98
115.	Descriptions of the sound of f	100

TABLE OF CONTENTS.

SEC.		PAGE
116.	mf	100
117.	**S, X, Z**	101
118.	Phonetic descriptions of s, x	103
119.	Latin s in Romance	103
120.	Greek ζ, Latin z	104
121.	Old Roman z	105
122.	Old Roman s (z), later r	105
123.	Prosthetic vowel with st, &c.	105
124.	s before a consonant	107
125.	x	107
126.	Final s	108
127.	**Double consonants**	108
128.	Testimony of the grammarians	110
129.	Reduction of ll to l, ss to s, after a diphthong or long vowel	110
130.	Confusion of single and double letter in Latin	113
131.	Double consonants in Italian	118
132.	Double consonant (not l, s) after long vowel	118
133.	Final double consonant	119
134.	Final consonants	119
135.	'Sandhi' in Latin	121
136.	Latin 'Doublets'	122
137.	Dropping of final consonant in Latin	122
138.	Dropping of final consonants in Romance	124
139.	**Syllable-Division**	124
140.	Testimony of grammarians	125
141.	Quantity	126
142.	'Position'	129
143.	Shortening of long vowel before another vowel	131
144.	Change in quantity of vowel before certain consonant-groups	133
145.	r with consonant	140
146.	s with consonant	141
147.	n with single consonant	141
148.	l with consonant	142
149.	**Crasis of vowels, Synizesis, &c.**	142
150.	Vowel-contraction in compounds in the early dramatists	143
151.	Synizesis in Late and Vulgar Latin	144
152.	Other examples of vowel-contraction	144
153.	Elision	144
154.	**Parasitic vowels**	145

CHAPTER III.

ACCENTUATION.

1.	Nature of the Latin Accent	148
2.	Testimony of the grammarians. (1) On the Nature of the Latin Accent	154
	(2) On the circumflex accent	154
3.	Accentuation of Greek loanwords	155
4.	Romance Accentuation	156

TABLE OF CONTENTS.

SEC.		PAGE
5.	The Earlier Law of Accentuation	157
6.	Traces of I.-Eur. accentuation in Latin	159
7.	Secondary and main accent	159
8.	The Paenultima Law	160
9.	Testimony of the grammarians	162
10.	Exceptions to the Paenultima Law	163
11.	Vulgar-Latin Accentuation	164
12.	Accentuation of the Sentence	165
12a.	Latin Sentence-Enclitics	166
13.	Syncope	170
14.	Syncope in the Praenestine Dialect of Latin	177
15.	Syncope under the Old Accent Law	178
16.	Syncope of Final Syllable	181
17.	Syncope under the Paenultima Accent Law. (1) Pretonic	183
	(2) Post-tonic	184
18.	Change of Unaccented Vowels	185
19.	Other Examples. I. Syllables long by position	191
20.	II. Short Syllables (1) in -r	192
21.	(2) in -l or Labial	192
	The Parasitic Vowel	193
22.	in other short syllables	194
23.	(3) Diphthongs, ai, ae	195
	au	196
24.	(4) Diphthongs in Hiatus	196
25.	(5) je and ve	196
26.	(6) Later change of o to u, u to ü, i	196
27.	(7) Greek words with Vowel-change	197
28.	(8) Vowel unchanged. i. in Latin words	198
29.	ii. in Greek loanwords	198
30.	(9) Long vowels	199
31.	(10) Recomposition and Analogy	199
32.	(11) Pretonic	200
33.	(12) Assimilation, Dissimilation, and False Analogy	201
34.	(13) Shortening of Syllables long by position	201
35.	Change and Shortening of Vowel in Unaccented Final Syllable	203
	I. Loss or Syncope of Short Vowel	203
36.	Loss of -e	204
37.	II. Change of Vowel	205
38.	Change of final short vowel to ĕ	206
39.	Alternation of final e with internal i	206
40.	III. Shortening of Long Syllable	207
41.	Final long vowel in Hiatus	209
42.	Breves Breviantes	210
43.	Shortening of final -ā	210
44.	Shortening of final -ē	211
45.	Shortening of final -ō	212
46.	Shortening of final -ī	213
47.	Shortening of final -ū	213
48.	Shortening of final diphthong	213
49.	Shortening of long vowel before final Consonant	213

xiv TABLE OF CONTENTS.

SEC.		PAGE
50.	Shortening of Final Syllable long by position	214
51.	Shortening of Monosyllables	215
52.	Loss of Final Syllable with -m	216

CHAPTER IV.

THE LATIN REPRESENTATIVES OF THE INDO-EUROPEAN SOUNDS.

1.	Ā	219
2.	Latin ā for I.-Eur. ā	221
3.	Ă	221
4.	I.-Eur. ă	223
5.	Ē	223
6.	Lat. ē for I.-Eur. ē	224
7.	ĭ for ē	225
8.	E	225
9.	Latin ĕ for I.-Eur. ĕ	226
10.	ŏ for ĕ with w and l	226
11.	ĭ for (accented) e	229
12.	Ī	230
13.	Ĭ	231
14.	Other examples of Lat. ĭ for I.-Eur. ĭ	232
15.	iĕ, not iĭ	232
16.	Ō	232
17.	Ŏ	233
18.	Latin ŏ for I.-Eur. ŏ	234
19.	Latin ă for I.-Eur. ŏ, under influence of v	235
20.	ŭ for ŏ	235
21.	Ū	237
22.	Other examples of Lat. ū, I.-Eur. ū	237
23.	Ŭ	237
24.	Latin ŭ for I.-Eur. ŭ	238
25.	Latin ŭ and Latin ŏ	239
26.	The Diphthongs	239
27.	AI	241
28.	I.-Eur. ai, Latin ae (ai)	242
29.	AI, AE on Inscriptions	242
30.	AU	242
31.	Other examples	243
32.	EI	243
33.	Other examples of I.-Eur. ei	244
34.	EI and I in Inscriptions, &c.	244
35.	EU	245
36.	Other examples of I.-Eur. eu	246
37.	OU, U in Inscriptions	246
38.	OI	246
39.	Other examples of I.-Eur. oi	247
40.	OI, OE, U on Inscriptions	247
41.	OU	248
42.	Other examples of I.-Eur. ou	249

TABLE OF CONTENTS.

XV

SEC.		PAGE
43.	ū for older ovĭ, ovĕ	250
44.	The spurious diphthong ou	250
45.	ĀI	251
46.	ĀU	252
47.	ĒI	252
48.	ĒU	252
49.	ŌI	252
50.	ŌU	253
51.	Variation (Ablaut) of Vowels	253
52.	I.-Eur. and Latin ĕ and ŏ	258
53.	ĕ and ŏ	258
54.	ŏ-ă, ĕ-ă	258
55.	ă-ŏ	259
56.	ā and ă	259
57.	ĕ and ē	260
58.	ĭ and ī	260
59.	ŏ and ō	260
60.	ŭ and ū	260
61.	ĕ and ă	261
62.	ōu-ău	261
63.	Y	262
64.	I.-Eur. initial y	264
65.	I.-Eur. y preceded by a consonant	264
66.	I.-Eur. y between vowels	265
67.	Latin j	265
68.	W	265
69.	I.-Eur. initial w	266
70.	I.-Eur. w (and Latin v) between vowels	267
71.	I.-Eur. w after a consonant	267
72.	I.-Eur. w before a consonant	268
73.	M, N	268
	M	269
74.	I.-Eur. m; other examples	270
75.	n for m	270
76.	I.-Eur. ms	270
77.	I.-Eur. mr, ml	270
78.	N	271
79.	I.-Eur. n; other examples	272
80.	mn	272
81.	The M- and N-Sonants	273
82.	Other examples of the Nasal Sonants	274
83.	Other examples of am, an, mā, nā	274
84.	L, R	275
85.	L	275
86.	I.-Eur. l; other examples	276
87.	R	276
88.	I.-Eur. r; other examples	277
89.	ss for rs before consonant	277
90.	rr for rs before vowel	277
91.	n for r	278

TABLE OF CONTENTS.

SEC.		PAGE
92.	The L- and R- Sonants	278
93.	Other examples of the liquid Sonants	279
94.	Other examples of al, ar, lā, rā	279
95.	**Tenues, Mediae, and Aspirates**	279
96.	Media or aspirata assimilated to unvoiced consonant in Latin	281
97.	Tenuis assimilated to voiced consonant in Latin	281
98.	P	281
99.	Other examples of I.-Eur. p	282
100.	B	282
101.	Other examples of I.-Eur. b	282
102.	mn for bn	282
103.	BH	282
104.	I.-Eur. bh ; other examples	283
105.	T	283
106.	Other examples of I.-Eur. t	284
107.	I.-Eur. tl	284
108.	I.-Eur. tt	284
109.	D	284
110.	Other instances of I.-Eur. d, Latin d	285
111.	Latin l for d	286
112.	Latin r for d	287
113.	tr for dr	289
114.	DH	289
115.	Other examples of I.-Eur. dh	289
116.	The Gutturals	290
117.	x for Guttural with s	293
118.	ct for Guttural with t	293
119.	gn, gm for cn, cm	293
120.	Latin h dropped between vowels	294
121.	Dialectal f for h	294
122.	The Palatal Gutturals : $\hat{K}$, $\hat{G}$, $\hat{K}H$, $\hat{G}H$	295
123.	Other examples of I.-Eur. $\hat{k}$	295
124.	I.-Eur. $\hat{k}w$	296
125.	$\hat{G}$	296
126.	Other examples of I.-Eur. $\hat{g}$	296
127.	$\hat{G}H$	296
128.	Other examples of I.-Eur. $\hat{g}h$	297
129.	The Gutturals Proper : **K, G, GH, KH**	297
	K	297
130.	I.-Eur. k ; other examples	298
131.	G	298
132.	Other examples of I.-Eur. g	298
133.	GH	298
134.	I.-Eur. gh ; other examples	298
135.	Velar Gutturals with Labialisation : Q^u	299
136.	I.-Eur. q^u, Latin qu ; other examples	300
137.	c for qu	300
138.	Latin qu of other origin	301
139.	$Ģ^u$	301
140.	I.-Eur. g^u, Latin v ; other examples	301

TABLE OF CONTENTS.

SEC.		PAGE
141.	Dialectal b	302
142.	g for I.-Eur. gu̯	302
143.	ǴHu̯	302
144.	I.-Eur. ghu̯ in Latin ; other examples	302
145.	The Sibilants : S, Z	302
146.	S, Z	303
147.	I.-Eur. s, Latin s ; other examples	305
148.	Latin r for intervocalic sibilant	305
149.	Initial sibilant before consonant	306
150.	O. Latin stl, sl, scl	307
151.	Sibilant before voiced consonant in middle of word	307
152.	Sibilant before r in middle of word	308
153.	Assimilation of sibilant to preceding r, l	308
154.	Assimilation of preceding dental to the sibilant	309
155.	Latin ss for tt	309
156.	Other groups with a sibilant	309
157.	Loss of Consonant in Group	309
158.	Other examples	310
159.	Assimilation of Consonants	311
160.	Assimilation in Preposition compounded with Verb	313
161.	Other examples of Assimilation	314
162.	Lengthening by Compensation	314
163.	Assimilation of Syllables	315

CHAPTER V.

FORMATION OF NOUN AND ADJECTIVE STEMS.

1.	I. STEM-SUFFIXES	316
2.	Suffixes ending in -ŏ, -ā (Nouns and Adjectives of the First and Second Declension). -Ŏ-, -Ā-	316
3.	Latin Ŏ- and Ā-suffixes ; other examples	318
4.	-IŎ-, -IĀ-, (-YO-, -YĀ-)	318
5.	-UŎ-, -UĀ-	322
6.	I.-Eur. Stems in -wŏ-	322
7.	Latin Verbal Adjectives in -uus, -īvus, -tīvus	323
8.	-NŎ-, -NĀ-	324
9.	I.-Eur. NO-suffix	326
10.	Latin -nus	326
11.	Latin -īnus	326
12.	Latin -ānus	326
13.	-MĔNŎ-, -MĔNĀ-	327
14.	-MŎ-, -MĀ-	328
15.	Other examples	328
16.	-RŎ-, -RĀ-	328
17.	Other examples of the RO-suffix	330
18.	Examples of I.-Eur. -tĕro- and -erŏ- in Latin	330
19.	I.-Eur. -tro-	330
20.	I.-Eur. -dhro-	331
21.	-LŎ-, -LĀ-	331

TABLE OF CONTENTS.

SEC.		PAGE
22.	Adjectives formed by the LO-suffix	332
23.	Nouns denoting the Agent or the Instrument	332
24.	Diminutives	333
25.	Neuters formed with the suffix -tlo-	333
26.	The suffix -dhlo-	334
27.	-TŎ-, -TĀ-	334
28.	Participles in -tus	335
29.	Abstract Nouns in -ta (-sa)	336
30.	Neuters in -mentum	336
731.	-KŎ-, -KĀ-	336
32.	Adjectives with the KŎ-suffix	337
33.	Adjectives in -ĭcius	337
34.	Suffixes ending in Ĭ (Nouns and Adjectives of third Declension) : -Ĭ-	338
35.	Other examples of I-stems	338
36.	Adjective I-stems from O-stems	338
37.	-NI-	339
38.	Other examples of Latin -ni-	339
39.	-MI-	339
40.	-RI-, -LI-	339
41.	Other examples of Latin -li-, -ri-	340
42.	-TI-	340
43.	Other examples of the suffix -ti- in Latin	341
44.	Examples of Latin -tiŏn-	341
45.	Adjectival -ti- for -to- in Latin	342
46.	Other examples of Latin -tāt(i)-, -tūt(i), -tūdin-	342
47.	Suffixes ending in -ŭ (Nouns of fourth Decl.). -Ŭ-	342
48.	Other examples of U-stems in Latin	343
49.	Interchange of U- with O-stems	343
50.	Other examples of TU-stems	344
51.	The Suffixes -YĒ- (Nouns of fifth Decl.) and -Ī-. The Stems in -Ē-	344
52.	Other examples of Latin Fems. in -ī, -īc, &c	347
53.	-yē- and -ī-	347
54.	Suffixes ending in -n (Nouns of third Decl.). -EN-, -YEN-, -WEN-, -MEN-	348
55.	Masc. EN-stems in Latin	349
56.	Suffixes ending in -r (Nouns of third Decl.). -R-	349
57.	Neuter R-stems	349
58.	-ER- and -TER-	350
59.	Nouns of relationship	350
60.	Latin Nomina Agentis	350
61.	Suffixes ending in -t (Nouns and Adjectives of third Decl.). -T-	350
62.	Other examples of Latin T-stems	351
63.	-NT-	352
64.	Other examples of Latin -ent-	352
65.	-WENT-	352
66.	Other examples of Latin -ōsus	353
67.	Suffixes ending in -d (Nouns of third Decl.	353
68.	Other examples	354
69.	Suffixes ending in a Guttural (Nouns and Adjectives of third Decl.).	354
70.	Other examples	355

SEC.		PAGE
71.	Suffixes ending in -s (Nouns and Adjectives of third Decl.). -ES-	355
72.	Neuter ES-stems in Latin	355
73.	Adjective ES-stems	356
74.	Masc. (and Fem.) ES-stems	356
75.	Other S stems	357
76.	-YES-	357
77.	Suffixless Forms	357
78.	Suffixless stems at end of Compounds in Latin	358
79.	Latin Independent suffixless stems	358
80.	II. COMPOSITION	358
81.	Reduplicated Nouns and Adjectives in Latin	363
82.	Ā-stems	363
83.	O-stems	364
84.	I-stems	364
85.	U-stems	364
86.	N-stems	364
87.	R-stems	365
88.	Dental and Guttural Stems	365
89.	S-stems	365
90.	Stem-suffixes and Composition in Romance	365

CHAPTER VI.

DECLENSION OF NOUNS AND ADJECTIVES. COMPARISON OF ADJECTIVES. NUMERALS.

1.	I. DECLENSION OF NOUNS AND ADJECTIVES	366
2.	Nom. Sing. I. Masc., Fem.	371
3.	Nom. Sing. of Ā-stems in Latin	373
4.	RO-stems	374
5.	YO-stems	375
6.	I-stems	375
7.	S-stems	376
8.	N-stems	376
9.	Diphthong stems	377
10.	Nom., Acc. Sing. II. Neut.	377
11.	O-stems	378
12.	I-stems	378
13.	U-stems	378
14.	S-stems	378
15.	R-stems	379
16.	-S in Nom. Sg. Neut. of Adjectives	379
17.	Gen. Sing.	379
18.	Ā-stems	381
19.	Fifth Decl. Stems	382
20.	O-stems and IO-stems	383
21.	U-stems	384
22.	Consonant-stems	384
23.	Dat. Sing.	385

SEC.		PAGE
24. Ā-stems		386
25. Fifth Decl. Stems		386
26. O-stems		387
27. U-stems		387
28. Consonant-stems		387
29. Acc. Sing.		387
30. The endings -im and -em		388
31. Voc. Sing.		388
32. Other examples		389
33. Abl. Sing.		390
34. O. Latin Abl. with -d		391
35. I-stem and Cons.-stem 'Abl.' in -i and -e		392
36. Instr. Sing.		392
37. Locative Sing.		395
38. Locatives in -ī and -e in Latin		396
39. Ā-stems, &c.		397
40. Nom. Plur. I. Masc., Fem.		397
41. Ā-stems		398
42. O-stems		398
43. Ĭ-stems		399
44. Cons.-stems		399
45. Nom., Acc. Plur. II. Neut.		399
46. Gen. Plur.		401
47. -um and -orum in O-stems		402
48. Dat., Abl., Loc., Instr. Plural		402
49. Ā- and Ō-stems		403
50. Other stems		404
51. Acc. Plur.		404
52. II. THE COMPARISON OF ADJECTIVES		404
53. The Comparative Suffixes		406
54. The Superlative Suffixes		407
55. Some irregular Comparatives and Superlatives		407
56. III. NUMERALS		408
57. One		409
58. Unus		410
59. Two		410
60. Duo		411
61. Three		412
62. Tres		412
63. Four		413
64. Quattuor		414
65. Five		414
66. Quinque		414
67. Six		415
68. Seven		415
69. Eight		415
70. Nine		415
71. Ten		416
72. Eleven to Nineteen		416
73. O. Latin duovicesimus		417

TABLE OF CONTENTS.

SEC.		PAGE
74.	Twenty to Ninety	417
75.	Viginti, &c.	418
76.	The Hundreds	418
77.	Centum, &c.	419
78.	The Thousands	419
79.	Mille	420
80.	The Numerals in Romance	420

CHAPTER VII.

THE PRONOUNS.

1.	I. THE PERSONAL PRONOUNS AND THE REFLEXIVE. 1 Sing.	421
2.	Declension of ego	422
3.	2 Sing.	423
4.	Declension of tu	423
5.	Reflexive	424
6.	Declension of sui	424
7.	1 Plur.	424
8.	Declension of nos	425
9.	2 Plur.	425
10.	Declension of vos	426
11.	II. THE POSSESSIVE PRONOUNS	426
12.	Their forms	427
13.	III. DEMONSTRATIVES	429
14.	O. Latin so-	432
15.	The particle -ce	432
16.	Hic	433
17.	Iste	435
18.	Ille	436
19.	Is	437
20.	Ipse	440
21.	Idem	441
22.	The Pronominal Gen. and Dat. Sg.	442
23.	IV. RELATIVE, INDEFINITE, AND INTERROGATIVE PRONOUNS	443
24.	Stems q^{u}i- and q^{u}o-	444
25.	Case-forms	445
26.	The stem q^{u}u-	446
27.	The Possessive cujus	447
28.	Other Derivatives	447
29.	V. THE PRONOMINAL ADJECTIVES	449
30.	The Pronouns in Romance	452

CHAPTER VIII.

THE VERB.

1.	I. THE CONJUGATIONS	453
2.	Traces of the Athematic Conjugation in Latin	455

TABLE OF CONTENTS.

SEC.		PAGE
3.	II. THE TENSE-STEMS (Strong Aorist and S-formations)	459
4.	'Strong Aorist' forms in Latin	464
5.	Old Latin forms with -ss- (-s-)	465
6.	A. Present. (1) With Ĕ-grade of root and Thematic Vowel	466
7.	Other examples	467
8.	Weak grade of root	467
9.	(2) With reduplicated root	468
10.	(3) With root nasalized. i. With nasal infix. ii. With nasal affix	469
11.	Other examples of nasal infix	471
12.	Retention of Nasal throughout the Tenses	471
13.	Other examples of nasal affix	472
14.	Other Verb-stems with n	472
15.	(4) With suffix -YŎ-, -ĪYŎ-	472
16.	ĭ in the third Conjugation Presents with YŎ-suffix	475
17.	Other examples of E-grade roots	475
18.	Of weak grade roots	476
19.	Alternative forms in -o and -eo	476
20.	Of roots with -ā, -ē, -ō	476
21.	Inceptives, and other Verb-stems	476
22.	(5) Inceptives in -skŏ̂- (-skŏ-)	477
23.	Causatives and Intensives in -eyo-	477
24.	Latin Desideratives in -tŭrio	478
25.	Latin Iteratives or Frequentatives in -*tāyŏ-	478
26.	Other Derivative Verbs with the YŎ-suffix	478
27.	Other suffixes	478
28.	Other examples of Latin Inceptives	479
29.	Of Latin Causatives, &c.	481
30.	Of Latin Desideratives	482
31.	Of Latin Iteratives	482
32.	Of Latin Derivative verbs with YŎ-suffix	483
33.	Of other Verb-suffixes	486
33a.	The Conjugations in Romance	488
34.	B. Imperfect	489
35.	Fourth Conj. Impft. in -ībam	491
36.	C. Future	491
37.	Fourth Conj. Fut. in -ībo	493
38.	Third Conj. Fut. in -ēbo	493
39.	D. Perfect	494
40.	Other examples of Reduplicated forms	501
41.	Unreduplicated	501
42.	Form of Reduplication	502
43.	Assimilation of Reduplication-vowel to Stem-vowel	503
44.	Loss of Reduplication	503
45.	Co-existent Reduplicated and Unreduplicated forms	504
46.	S-Preterite	504
47.	Origin of the Perfect in -vi (-ui)	505
48.	Shortened forms of the Perfect in -vi	506
49.	Shortened forms of the Perfect in -si	508
50.	O. Latin Perfects in -ū(v)i	508
51.	Some Irregular Perfects	509

TABLE OF CONTENTS.

SEC.		PAGE
52.	E. Pluperfect	509
53.	F. Future-Perfect	510
54.	G. Tenses formed with Auxiliary Verbs.	510
55.	III. THE MOODS. A. Subjunctive. (Relics of the I.-Eur. Optative Mood in Latin.)	511
56.	Some O. Latin Subj. and Opt. forms	514
57.	B. Imperative	516
58.	Other examples of 2 Sg. Imper. with bare stem	517
59.	Other examples of Imper. in -tōd	519
60.	Imper. Pass. 2, 3 Sg. in -mĭnō	519
61.	3 Pl. Imperat.	519
62.	IV. THE VOICES	519
63.	Impersonal use of Latin Passive	521
64.	Active and Middle	521
65.	V. THE PERSON-ENDINGS	522
66.	(1) Active. 1 Sg.	524
67.	2 Sg.	525
68.	Athematic Sg. of fĕro, vŏlo	526
69.	3 Sg.	526
70.	The 3 Sg. Pft. in Latin	527
71.	1 Plur.	529
72.	2 Plur.	529
73.	3 Plur.	529
74.	3 Pl. Pres. in -nunt	531
75.	3 Pl. Perf.	531
76.	(2) Passive (Deponent). 1 Sing.	532
77.	2 Sing.	533
78.	Use of -re and -ris	533
79.	3 Sing.	534
80.	1 Plur.	534
81.	2 Plur.	534
82.	3 Plur.	534
83.	VI. THE INFINITIVE	535
84.	Pres. Inf. Act.	537
85.	Pres. Inf. Pass.	537
86.	Fut. Inf. Act.	537
87.	Fut. Inf. Pass.	538
88.	VII. THE SUPINES	538
89.	VIII. THE PARTICIPLES	539
90.	Pres. Part. Act.	540
91.	Perf. Part. Act.	541
92.	Perf. Part. Pass.	541
93.	'Truncated' Participles	543
94.	IX. THE GERUND AND GERUNDIVE	543
95.	Origin of the suffix -ndo-	544
96.	Adjectives in -bundo-, -cundo-, &c.	544
97.	Some Irregular Verbs	545
98.	Irregular Verbs in Romance	547

CHAPTER IX.

ADVERBS AND PREPOSITIONS.

SEC.		PAGE
1.	ADVERBS	548
2.	Nominative Adverb-forms	553
3.	Genitive Adverb-forms	555
4.	Accusative Adverb-forms	555
5.	Ablative (Instr.) and Locative Adverb-forms	559
6.	Adverbs in -tus	561
7.	Adverbial word-groups and compounds	562
8.	Other Adverbs	565
9.	Numeral Adverbs in -ies	567
10.	Pronominal Adverbs	567
11.	PREPOSITIONS	572
12.	Ab, ap-, po-, abs, a-, au-, af, absque	575
13.	Ab, abs, a	577
14.	Af	577
15.	Ad	577
16.	Ambi-	577
17.	An	578
18.	Ante	578
19.	Apud	579
20.	Circum, circa, circiter	579
21.	Clam, clanculum	580
22.	Com-, (cum), with, and co-	581
23.	Contra (see §§ 1,.4)	581
24.	Coram	581
25.	De	581
26.	Dis	582
27.	Endo	582
28.	Erga, ergo	583
29.	Ex, ec-, e	583
	Extra	584
30.	In	584
31.	Infra	585
32.	Inter	585
33.	Intra, intus	585
34.	Juxta	585
35.	Ob	585
36.	Palam	586
37.	Penes	586
38.	Per	586
39.	Pŏ-	588
40.	Post, pone	588
41.	Poste, posti-d, pos, pō-	589
42.	Prae	589
43.	Praeter	589
44.	Pro, por-	590
45.	Prō- and prŏ-	590

TABLE OF CONTENTS.

SEC.		PAGE
46. Procul		590
47. Prope		591
48. Propter		591
49. Re-		591
50. Secundum, secus		591
50a. Simul		592
51. Sine, se		592
52. Sub, subter, subtus		593
53. Super, supra, insuper, superne		593
54. Tenus		593
55. Trans		594
56. Uls, ultra		594
57. Usque		595
58. Versus, versum, adversus, adversum, exadversus, exadversum		595

CHAPTER X.

CONJUNCTIONS AND INTERJECTIONS.

1. CONJUNCTIONS	596
2. (1) Conjunctive.—Que, et, atque, ac, quoque, etiam	598
3. Atque, ac	599
4. (2) Disjunctive.—Ve, aut, vel, sive, seu	599
5. (3) Adversative.—At, ast, sed, autem, atqui, tamen, ceterum, verum, vero	600
6. (4) Limitative and Corrective.—Quidem, immo	602
7. (5) Explanatory.—Enim, nam, namque, quippe, nempe, nemut	603
8. (6) Conclusive.—Ergo, itaque, igitur	604
9. (7) Optative.—Ut, utinam	605
10. (8) Interrogative.—Ne, nonne, num, utrum, an, anne, cur, quare, quianam	605
11. (9) Comparative.—Ut, uti, quasi, ceu, quam	606
12. (10) Temporal.—Quum, quando, dum, donec, ut, ubi	608
13. (11) Causal.—Quum, quoniam, quod, quia, quippe	610
14. (12) Conditional.—Si, nisi, ni, sin, sive, seu, modo, dummodo	610
15. (13) Concessive.—Etsi, quamquam, quamvis, licet	613
16. (14) Final.—Ut, quo, quominus, quin, ne, neve, neu, nedum	613
17. (15) Asseverative Particles.—Ne (nae), -ne	614
18. (16) Negatives.—In-, ne-, nec, non, haud, ve-	615
19. Interjections	616
INDEX	619

LIST OF ABBREVIATIONS

A. L. L. = Archiv f. lat. Lexikographie u. Grammatik, ed. Wölfflin. Leipz. 1884 sqq.
Amer. Journ. Phil. = American Journal of Philology.
Anecd. Helv. = Anecdota Helvetica, ed. Hagen (a Supplement to the *Grammatici Latini*, ed. Keil).
Ann. Épigr. = Cagnat, *L'année épigraphique.* Paris, 1889 sqq.
Ann. Inst. = Annali dell' Instituto di corrispondenza archeologica. Rome, 1829 sqq.
Arch. Glottol., Arch. Glott. Ital. = Archivio Glottologico Italiano. Rome, 1873 sqq.
Ἀθην. = Ἀθηναῖον σύγγραμμα περιοδικόν. Athens, 1872-82.
B. B. = Beiträge z. Kunde d. Indog. Sprachen, ed. Bezzenberger. Göttingen, 1877 sqq.
B. P. W., Berl. Phil. Woch. = Berliner Philologische Wochenschrift. Berl. 1881 sqq.
Brit. Mus. = The Collection of Ancient Greek Inscriptions in the British Museum, ed. Sir Ch. Newton. Oxf. 1874 sqq.
Büch. *Umbr.* = Bücheler, *Umbrica.* Bonn, 1883.
Bull. = Bullettino dell' Instituto di corrispondenza archeologica. Rome, 1829 sqq.
Burs. Jahresber. = Jahresbericht über d. Fortschritte d. Classischen Alterthumswissenschaft, ed. Bursian. Berl. 1875 sqq.
C. G. L. = Corpus Glossariorum Latinorum, ed. Goetz und Gundermann. Leipz.
C. I. A. = Corpus Inscriptionum Atticarum. Berl. 1873 sqq.
C. I. G. = Corpus Inscriptionum Graecarum, ed. Boeckh. Berl. 1828 sqq.
C. I. L. = Corpus Inscriptionum Latinarum. Berl. 1863 sqq.
Class. Rev. = Classical Review.
Comm. Lud. Saec. = Commentaria Ludorum Saecularium, ed. Mommsen, in vol. viii of the *Ephemeris Epigraphica* (also published in the *Monumenti Antichi*, vol. i, part 3).
Comm. Ribbeck. = Commentationes Philologae . . . Ottoni Ribbeckio. Leipz. 1888.
Comm. Schweizer-Sidler = Philologische Abhandlungen Heinrich Schweizer-Sidler . . . gewidmet. Zürich, 1891.
Comm. Woelffl. = Commentationes Woelfflinianae. Leipz. 1891.
Eckinger = Eckinger, *Die Orthographie lateinischer Wörter in griechischen Inschriften.* Munich.

LIST OF ABBREVIATIONS. xxvii

Edict. Diocl. = the Edict of Diocletian (contained in the Supplement to vol. iii of the *Corpus Inscr. Lat.*).
Eph. Epigr. = Ephemeris Epigraphica. Berl. 1872 sqq. (A Supplement to the *Corpus Inscr. Lat.*).
Études G. Paris = Études romanes dédiées à Gaston Paris. Paris, 1891.
Etym. Lat. = Etyma Latina, by E. R. Wharton. Lond. 1890.
Fabr. = Fabretti, *Corpus Inscr. Italicarum antiquioris aevi*. Turin, 1867.
Fleck. Jahrb. = Jahrbücher f. classische Philologie, ed. Fleckeisen. Leipz. 1855 sqq.
Gl. Cyrill., Gl. Philox., Gl. Plac. = the Cyrillus, Philoxenus, and Placidus Glossaries (contained in vols. ii and v of the *Corpus Glossariorum Latinorum*, ed. Goetz und Gundermann).
Harv. Stud. = Harvard Studies in Classical Philology. Boston, 1980 sqq.
Herm. = Hermes. Zeitschrift f. classische Philologie. Berl. 1866 sqq.
I. F. = Indogermanische Forschungen, ed. Brugmann und Streitberg. Strassburg, 1891 sqq.
I. I. S. = Inscriptiones Graecae Siciliae et Italiae, ed. Kaibel. Berl. 1890.
I. N., I. R. N. = Inscriptiones Regni Neapolitani Latinae, ed. Mommsen. Leipz. 1852.
Journ. Hell. Stud. = Journal of Hellenic Studies.
Journ. Phil. = Journal of Philology.
K. Z. = Zeitschrift f. vergleichende Sprachforschung, ed. Kuhn. Berl. 1872 sqq.
Lex. Agr. = Lex Agraria (No. 200 in vol. i of the *Corpus Inscr. Lat.*).
Lex Repet. = Lex Repetundarum (No. 198 in the same vol.).
Lib. Gloss. = Liber Glossarum (selections from which are contained in vol. v of the *Corpus Glossariorum Latinorum*).
Mél. Arch. = Mélanges d'Archéologie et d'Histoire Paris, 1884 sqq. (The publication of the École française de Rome.)
Mem. Ist. Lombard. = Memorie dell' I. R. istituto Lombardo di scienze, lettere ed arti. Milan, 1843 sqq.
Mém. Soc. Ling., M. S. L. = Mémoires de la Société de Linguistique de Paris. Paris, 1868 sqq.
Meyer-Lübke = Meyer-Lübke, *Grammatik der romanischen Sprachen*. Leipz. 1890 sqq.
Mitth. = Mittheilungen d. kaiserlich deutschen archäologischen Instituts. Athens, 1876 sqq.
Mitth. (röm.) = ditto (römische Abtheilung).
Mon. Anc. = Res Gestae Divi Augusti : ex monumentis Ancyrano et Apolloniensi, ed. Mommsen. Berl.[2] 1883.
Mon. Antichi = Monumenti Antichi pubblicati per cura della Reale Accademia dei Lincei. Milan, 1890 sqq.
Morph. Unt., M. U. = Morphologische Untersuchungen, by Osthoff and Brugmann. Leipz. 1878 sqq.
M. S. L. (see Mém. Soc. Ling.).
Mur. = Muratori, *Novus thesaurus veterum inscriptionum*. Milan, 1739–42.
Neue = Neue, *Formenlehre d. lateinischen Sprache*. Berl. 1866 sqq.
Not. Scav. = Notizie degli Scavi di antichità (Atti della R. Accademia dei Lincei). Rome, 1876 sqq.
Or., Or. Henz. = Orelli, *Inscriptionum Latinarum Collectio*, vols. i–ii, Zürich, 1828, vol. iii (Suppl.), ed. Henzen. Zürich, 1856.

LIST OF ABBREVIATIONS.

Osthoff, *Dunkles u. helles l* (see Transactions of American Philological Association 1893, vol. xxiv, pp. 50 sqq.).

P. B. Beitr. = Beiträge z. Geschichte d. deutschen Sprache u. Literatur, ed. Paul und Braune. Halle, 1874 sqq.

Philol. = Philologus: Zeitschrift f. d klassische Alterthum. Göttingen, 1846 sqq.

Phil. Soc. Trans. = Transactions of the Philological Society.

Phonet. Stud. = Phonetische Studien: Zeitschrift f. wissenschaftliche u. praktische Phonetik. Marburg, 1887 sqq.

Probi App. = Probi Appendix (contained in vol. iv of the *Grammatici Latini*, ed. Keil).

Rev. Phil. - Revue de Philologie. Paris, 1877 sqq.

Rhein. Mus. = Rheinisches Museum f. Philologie. Frankf. am Main, 1842 sqq.

Riv. Filolog. = Rivista di Filologia. Rome, 1873 sqq.

Rossi = De Rossi, *Inscriptiones Christianae Urbis Romae*, 2 vols. Rome, 1861-1888.

S. C. Bacch. = Senatus Consultum de Bacchanalibus (No. 196 in vol. i of the *Corpus Inscr. Lat.*).

Stud. Ital. = Studi Italiani di filologia classica. Florence, 1893 sqq.

Studem. Stud. = Studien auf d. Gebiete d. Archaischen Lateins, ed. Studemund. Berl. 1873 sqq.

Suppl. Arch Glott. = Supplementi Periodici all' Archivio Glottologico Italiano, vol. i Turin, 1891.

Tab. Bant. = Tabula Bantina (No. 197 in vol. i of the *Corpus Inscr. Lat.*).

Versamml. Philolog. = Verhandlungen d. Versammlungen deutscher Philologen u. Schulmänner.

Von Planta = Von Planta, *Grammatik d. Oskisch-Umbrischen Dialekte*, vol. i. Strassburg, 1893.

Wien. Stud. = Wiener Studien: Zeitschrift f. class. Philologie. Vienna, 1879 sqq.

Wilm. = Wilmanns, *Exempla Inscriptionum Latinarum*, 2 vols. Berl. 1873.

Zv. *I. I. I.*, Zvet. = Zvetaieff, *Inscriptiones Italiae Inferioris Dialecticae*. Moscow, 1886.

In the transcription of the various I.-Eur. languages the system of Brugmann, *Grundriss d. vergleichenden Grammatik*, Strassburg, 1886 sqq. (Engl. trans.; London, 1888 sqq.) is in the main followed, though in ' I.-Eur.' forms Gutturals Proper are denoted by k, g. &c. (not as in Brugmann by q, g, &c.), and y, w often replace Brugmann's i̯, u̯, while in O. Engl. (Brugmann's ' Anglo-Saxon') words the orthography of Sweet, *History of English Sounds*, is preferred. I follow Brugmann in distinguishing the Oscan and Umbrian inscriptions written in the Roman alphabet from those written in the native alphabets by printing the former in italics, a type reserved in this book for Latin words, stems, suffixes, and sounds. (On the use of *k*, *g*, *gh* see p. 290.)

THE LATIN LANGUAGE

CHAPTER I.

THE ALPHABET[1].

§ 1. IF an alphabet is to express the sounds of a language properly, each nation must construct one for itself. But this ideal was not realized by the ancient languages of Italy. The Oscan and Umbrian stocks borrowed for the expression of their language the alphabet used by the Etruscans, who had themselves borrowed it at an earlier period from the Greeks; and so neither Oscans nor Umbrians were at first able to express in writing some common sounds of their language, such as *d* and *o*, which were wanting in the Etruscan speech (von Planta, *Osk.-Umbr. Dial.* i., p. 44). The Latin Alphabet, consisting in the later Republic of twenty-one letters, ABCDEFGHIKLMNOPQRSTVX, was borrowed from some Chalcidian colony (e.g. Cumae), to judge from the form of the letters, which more nearly resemble those of the Chalcidian inscriptions than of any other Greek stock. So few Latin inscriptions earlier than the second Punic War have been preserved, that it is difficult to trace each separate stage in the process of adapting the Greek alphabet to the exigencies of the Latin language. The symbols for the Greek aspirate mutes, Θ (the *th*-sound of our 'an*t-h*eap'), Φ (as in

---

[1] Hübner's article in Müller's *Handbuch d. Klass. Alterthumswissenschaft*, vol. i. pp. 492 sqq. 1886, gives a summary of what is known and a list of the authorities.

'up*h*ill'), Ψ (the symbol for the *kh*-sound of our 'ink*h*orn' in the Chalcidian alphabet, while X was the symbol for the *ks*-sound, Attic Ξ), were found superfluous by the Latins, in whose language these sounds were unknown, and were retained as symbols for numbers merely, Θ for 100 (later modified to C, the initial of *centum*), Ψ (later L) for 50, Φ for 1000 (later M, the initial of *mille*), while the right-hand half of the symbol, viz. D, was used for the half of 1000, *i.e.* 500, just as V, for 5, seems to have been the upper half of X (used probably in the Etruscan adaptation of the Greek alphabet for 10) (Ritschl, *Opusc.* iv. 704 and 722; Mommsen in *Hermes* xxii. 598). For the *f*-sound, the bilabial spirant, a sound which in Quintilian's time was quite unknown in Greek (Quint. xii. 10. 29), the nations of Italy seem to have taken the Greek combination of symbols FH (digamma with aspiration), a combination found in a few of the earliest Greek inscriptions to express a sound which seems to have been a development of an original *sw-* (e.g. Fhεκαδάμοε, in the proper name Hecademus, on an inscription of Tanagra (Röhl, *Inscr. Graec.* 131), and which may have been at that time some adumbration of the *f*-sound. This double letter FH, which we find in a very old Latin inscription on a brooch found at Praeneste with FHEFHAKED (=*fecit*) (*C. I. L.* xiv. 4123), in the earliest Etruscan inscriptions, e.g. vhulχenas (the proper name *Fulcinius*) (Fabr. *Suppl.* iii. 306), and in the inscriptions of the Veneti, an Illyrian tribe of N.E. Italy (Pauli, *Altitalische Forschungen* iii. p. 97 sqq.), was in the Etruscan alphabet reduced to a symbol like the figure 8 (a modification of H, the F being dropt), while in the Latin alphabet the second element of the compound was discarded, and F alone was used. The exact course of events which led to the use of the Greek symbol for the *g*-sound (in Chalcidian inscriptions written C not Γ), to express the Latin *k*-sound as well as the Latin *g*-sound, and in time to the almost total disuse of the symbol K, cannot, with the evidence at present forthcoming, be determined (for a conjecture, see ch. ii. § 75). On the very old Dvenos inscription, for example (*Annali dell' Inst.* 1880), we find FEKED (or FEKED corrected into FECED), (*fecit*), PAKARI, COSMIS (*cōmis*), VIRCO (*virgo*?) side by side. The inconvenience of this practice led in time to the use

§ 1.]   THE ALPHABET.   3

of a modified form of the symbol C to express the *g*-sound, the earliest example of which is found on the as libralis of Luceria (between 300 and 250 B.C. according to Mommsen), with *Ga.f.* (*Gai filius*) (Édon, *Écriture et Prononciation*, p. 145 sqq.). It was received into the Roman alphabet at the time possibly of Appius Claudius Caecus, censor 312 B.C., and took the place of Z, the symbol apparently for soft or voiced *s*, a sound which had by this time passed into the *r*-sound (see ch. iv. § 148). The symbols of the Greek vowels ι and υ were used not only for the Latin vowels *i* and *u*, but also for the *y*- and *w*-sounds of words like *jam*, *vos*, a confusion frequently remarked on by the grammarians (e.g. Quint. i. 4. 10 ' iam ' sicut ' etiam ' scribitur, et ' uos ' ut ' tuos '), which persisted till very late times; though on Inscriptions from the beginning of the Empire onwards we often find a tall form of I used for the *y*-sound (Christiansen, *de Apicibus et I longis*, p. 29); and the Emperor Claudius tried without success to introduce a new symbol, an inverted digamma, for the *w*-sound.

The third guttural symbol of the Greek Alphabet, Koppa, was retained for the *q*-sound of Latin, a sound at first expressed by Q, e.g. QOI (*qui*) on the Dvenos inscription, then by QV.

In the second century B.C. the cultivation of literature at Rome, in particular possibly the imitation of the quantitative verse of Greece, led to two usages, perhaps borrowed, the one from the Greek, the other (if not both) from the Oscan alphabet, viz. the doubling of a consonant to express the repeated or lengthened sound (see ii. 127), the doubling of a vowel (*a*, *e*, *u*, and *o*?) to express the long quantity[1]. The earliest example of the former is the Decree of Aemilius Paulus, 189 B.C. (*C. I. L.* ii. 5041), with POSSIDERE, &c., beside POSEDISENT, &c., for all the older inscriptions[2] write the consonant single in such cases; of the latter, the Miliarium Popillianum, 132 B.C. with PAASTORES. Ennius is mentioned as the introducer of the double consonant, while the practice of doubling the vowel is ascribed

---

[1] In Oscan this is normally confined to long vowels in the first syllable. (But trístaamentud, 'testamento').

[2] As do the oldest Oscan inscriptions and all the Umbrian inscriptions written in the native alphabet.

by the Roman tradition to the poet Accius, another of whose spelling reforms was the use of *gg* for the velar nasal followed by *g* (see ch. ii. § 63). The practice of doubling the consonant remained to the latest times, in spite of a temporary resort in the reign of Augustus to the use of the *sicīlicus*, a sickle-shaped mark placed above the single consonant, to express its repeated or lengthened sound; but the double vowel was soon discarded in favour of the *apex*, a mark placed above the single vowel, to express length, originally of a shape like a sickle, or like the figure 7, later of the form of the acute accent. The apex was much in fashion till about 130 A. D., when it came to be used at random over short and long vowels alike, but never attained so universal use as the doubled consonant. Long *i* was indicated by the tall form of I[1], a form likewise employed to denote the *y*-sound, and often also for initial *i* (Christiansen, *de Apicibus et I longis*).

In the last century of the Republic, when Greek Grammar, and even Greek Phonetics, came to be studied at Rome, the necessity was felt for the more exact expression of the sound of Greek loan words, which were more and more entering into the language especially of the upper classes. For the Greek aspirates, which had hitherto been represented by the Latin tenues T, P, C, compound symbols TH, PH, CH were introduced; and the mispronunciation of these sounds was considered as great a fault in polite society as the dropping of *h* is with us (see ch. ii. § 60). The Greek υ (earlier represented by Latin V), which had by this time the *ü*-sound (see ch. ii. § 14), was now expressed by the Greek letter itself in its Attic form Υ, just as we use Spanish ñ in loan words like 'cañon,' while for Greek ζ (formerly denoted by *s-*, *-ss-*, e. g. SETVS, for *Zethus*, *C. I. L.* i. 1047, *patrisso*, &c., Plaut.), the old symbol Z was revived. The reforms proposed by the Emperor Claudius, the use of the Greek symbol of the rough breathing for the *ü*-sound (see ch. ii. § 14), of the reversed C for the *ps*-sound of *scripsi*, *urbs*, &c. (see ch. ii. § 78), of the inverted digamma for the *w*-sound of *vos*, &c., did not survive his own reign (see Bücheler, *de Ti. Claudio Caesare grammatico*).

---

[1] Was this too borrowed from Oscan? We have flīet, 'fient,' on an Oscan inscription earlier than 211 B. C. (*Rhein. Mus.* 1888, p. 557).

§ 2. **The Alphabet of twenty-one letters.** Cicero (*Deor. Nat.* ii. 37. 93) argues against the Atomic Theory by showing the improbability of any chance combinations of the twenty-one letters of the alphabet ever producing a single line, much less an entire poem, of Ennius : 'hoc qui existimet fieri, non intellego cur non idem putet, si innumerabiles unius et viginti formae litterarum, vel aureae vel quaelibet, aliquo coiciantur, posse ex iis excussis annales Enni, ut deinceps legi possint, effici ; quod nescio an ne in uno quidem versu possit tantum valere fortuna.' This Alphabet, A to X, is often found on coins of the last century of the Republic (e. g. *C. I. L.* i. 374, c. 100 B.C.) ; and Quintilian (first cent. A. D.) speaks of *x* as the last letter of the alphabet (nostrarum ultima, i. 4. 9). But Y and Z are added on some coins (e. g. *C. I. L.* i. 393, 454, both with YZ ; 417 with Y—all belonging to the last century of the Republic).

§ 3. **The letter F.** That early Greek ϝh, a development of I. Eur. *sw-*, had some kind of *f*-sound is made not improbable by the analogy of other languages. In Old Irish, where I.-Eur. *sr* between two vowels became (like *sr-* in Greek ῥεῦμα, ῥυτός), *hr. rh*, (e. g. a 'his' prefixed to sruth, 'stream,' is pronounced *a rhoo*), I.-Eur. *sw-* when preceded by a vowel became *f*, e. g. a fiur, 'his sister' (I.-Eur. **esyo swesor*), which points to a connexion between *hw* (*wh*), and the *f*-sound. It must however be added that I.-Eur. *w-* in Irish regularly becomes *f*, e. g. fáith, 'a prophet' (cf. Lat. *vātēs*). A still better analogy is furnished by the Aberdeenshire dialect of Scotch, where the *wh-* or *hw*-sound of Scotch 'what,' 'when,' &c., appears as *f*, 'fat,' 'fan.'

§ 4. **X.** *x*, the last letter of the alphabet (Quint. i. 4. 9 : x nostrarum (litterarum) ultima, qua tam carere potuimus quam psi non quaerimus), was also written *xs* from early times (e. g. EXSTRAD for *extra*, on the S. C. de Bacchanalibus, 186 B.C. *C. I. L.* i. 196), especially at the period of the poet and grammarian, Accius (e. g. SAXSVM on an epitaph of one of the Scipios, c. 130 B. C., i. 34 ; PROXSVMEIS for *proximis*, EXSIGITO, LEXS on the Lex Bantina, bet. 133 and 118 B. C., i. 197), and is common in the Augustan age and in plebeian inscriptions of a later epoch (for examples, see Index to *C. I. L.* viii. &c.; *exsemplo* Comm. Lud. Saec. A. 26 ; and for instances in Virgil MSS., see Ribbeck, *Ind.* p. 445). Terentius Scaurus, second cent. A. D., condemns the spelling 'nuxs,' 'truxs,' 'feroxs' as an unnecessary repetition of the sibilant element of the *x*-sound. The guttural element is repeated in the spelling *cx*, e. g. VCXOR for *uxor* (a misspelling which has led to the corruption *voxor* in MSS. of Plautus, *Class. Rev.* v. 293), VICXIT (*C. I. L.* v. 5735). (For examples in Virgil MSS., see Ribbeck, *Ind.* p. 391). We also find *xc*; e. g. IVXCTA (*C. I. L.* vi. 14614), and *sx*, e. g. VISXIT (viii. 67), all various ways of expressing the same sound (a *c*-sound followed by an *s*-sound), for which we also find a more accurate expression, namely *cs*, e. g. VICSIT (vii. 5723). This last combination was used to express the sound in the Etruscan alphabet, the symbol X being retained only as a numerical symbol, for the number 10.

§ 5. **Z.** If we are to believe Velius Longus (7. 51 K), this symbol was found in the Carmen Saliare ; though whether the mysterious jumble of letters which the MSS. of Varro, *L. L.* vii. 26, offer as a fragment from this hymn, *cozeulodorieso*, &c., can be fairly quoted as an instance of Old Latin *z* is doubtful, for the reading suggests *O zeu* (Greek ὦ Ζεῦ) more than anything else ; and Varro quotes the passage as exemplifying the old use of *s* (not *z*) for later *r*. It is found on coins of Cosa [*C. I. L.* i. 14 COZANO (after 273 B.C.), where the letter should have the ordinary z-form and not the form printed in the Corpus (see Ritschl. *Opusc.* iv. 721 *n*)]. The *dzenoine* of the Dvenos inscription is too doubtful to quote; for the letters may read not only *dze noine*, 'on the ninth day,' but also *die noine*, or even *Dvenoi ne*. This old Latin *z* seems to have expressed the sound of soft or voiced *s* (but see ch. ii. § 121, the sound in our verb 'to use'; while our noun 'use' has the hard or unvoiced *s*. Between vowels in Latin *s* had once this soft sound, and was presumably written *z*; but this sound passed at an early time into the *r*-sound (c. 350 B.C., to judge from the remark of Cicero, *Fam.* ix. 21. 2, that L. Papirius Crassus, dictator 415 A.U.C. (=339 B.C.), was the first of his family to change the name from *Papisius* to *Papirius*; in the Digests (i. 2. 2. 36) Appius Claudius is mentioned as the author of the change : R litteram invenit ut pro Valesiis Valerii essent, et pro Fusiis Furii). Martianus Capella tells us that the letter was removed from the alphabet by Appius Claudius Caecus, the famous censor of 312 B.C., adding the curious reason that in pronouncing it the teeth assumed the appearance of the teeth of a grinning skull (Mart. Cap. iii. 261 : z vero idcirco Appius Claudius detestatur, quod dentes mortui, dum exprimitur, imitatur). In the Oscan language this soft *s*-sound was retained without passing into *r*. The native Oscan alphabet (derived from the Etruscan), expresses it by the letter *s*, which is also used for the hard *s*-sound, while the z-symbol denotes the *ts*-sound ; but in the later inscriptions, which are written in Latin characters, *z* is used (e.g. *eizazunc egmazum* (in Latin, *earum rerum*), on the Bantia tablet, c. 130 B.C.). (On the question whether the *z* (Latin character) of Osc. *zicolo-*, 'dieculus,' represents the soft *s*-sound or the *ts*-sound of the letter written in the Oscan alphabet like a capital I with top and bottom strokes prolonged, and in the Umbrian alphabet with the same strokes slanting instead of horizontal, and on the occasional use of the native letter for the *s*-sound, e.g. Umbr. zeřef, 'sedens,' see von Planta, *Osk.-Umbr. Dial.* p. 71.)

§ 6. **The Guttural-symbols**. A special symbol for the *g*-sound, made by adding a small stroke to the symbol C, is said by Plutarch (*Quaest. Rom.* 54 and 59 ; cf. Ter. Scaur. 7. 15 K.) to have been the invention of Sp. Carvilius Ruga c. 293 B.C., presumably because he was the first to write his name *Ruga* with the new symbol, as L. Papirius Crassus, dictator 339 B.C., was the first to conform the spelling of the family-name *Papisius* to the new pronunciation *Papirius*. The remark, however, of Martianus Capella about the action of the censor of 312 B.C., Appius Claudius Caecus, with regard to the letter Z, whose position in the Latin alphabet was occupied by the new symbol G, suggests that the differentiation of the C and G symbols was the work rather of that many-sided reformer. The exclusive use of the symbol C for the *k*-sound led to the disuse of the symbol K, which however, thanks to the conservative instinct of the Roman nation, was still retained as abbreviation for the proper name *Kaeso*, and in a few words before the vowel *a*, e.g. *Kalendae*, a common spelling on inscriptions (see *C. I. L.* i.. Index, p. 583), *interkalaris*, *kaput*, *kalumnia*. Terentius Scaurus, second cent. A.D. (p. 15 K.) tells us that the letter K was called *ka*, while the name of C was *ce*, and that these letters themselves had been before his time used to indicate the syllables represented by their names, e.g. *krus* (for *ka-rus*), *cra* (for *cera*). Velius Longus, first cent. A.D., speaks of some sticklers for old usages in his own age, who in their correspondence always spelt *karissime* with *k* not *c* (p. 53 K.) (see also Quint. i. 7. 10; Prisc. i. 12. 5 H.; Diom. 424. 29 K.; Cledonius 28. 5 K.; Maximus Victorinus 195. 19 K.; Probus 10. 23 K.; Serv. in Don. p. 422 K.; Donatus, p. 368 K. For spellings with *ka* in Virgil MSS., see Ribbeck, *Index*, p. 429; and for similar spellings elsewhere, Georges, *Lex. Lat. Wortf.* s. vv. *Carthago, caput, carus,* &c., and Brambach, *Lat. Orth.* p. 208.) The symbol C was similarly retained in its old use for the *g*-sound in the abbreviations of proper names, C. for *Gaius*, Cn. for *Gnaeus*; just as an old five-stroked form of the symbol M seems to be the original of the abbreviation for the name *Manius*, later written M with apostrophe. That it persisted in other words also to the beginning of the literary period, we see from the fact that a large number of archaic words, quoted by the grammarians from the early literature, are spelt with *c* not *g*, e. g. *acetare* for *agitare* (Paul. Fest. 17. 30 Th.). The proper spelling of these obsolete words was occasionally a subject of discussion, e. g. whether PACVNT in the XII Tables, NI ITA PACVNT, stood for *pagunt* (cf. *pepigi, pango*), or for *pacunt* (cf. *paciscor*, (Quint. i. 6. 10–11; Ter. Scaur. 7. 15 K.; cf. Fest. 330 23 Th.); and probably the μεταχαρακτηρισμός of early C to *c* and *g* was almost as fruitful a source of error as that of E to ε, η, ει, of O to ο, ω, ου in the Homeric text. Thus *frico*, not *frigo*, may be the proper form of the Old Latin verb, used by Accius *frigit saetas* (of a boar) *Trag.* 443 R., &c. (cf. Greek φρίσσω for φρικ-yω); *děcěre* (cf. δέκομαι, προσδοκάω) of Old Latin *degere*, 'expectare' (Paul. Fest. 51. 32 Th.). (On the use of C for the *g*-sound see also Mar. Victorin. p. 12 K. who quotes *Cabino, lece, acna*; Fest. 242 and 284 Th., &c.: C is invariably used for *g* on the Columna Rostrata (*C. I. L.* i. 195), an Imperial restoration which probably followed with some fidelity the spelling of the old inscription.) The letter Q often takes before *u* the place of classical Latin *c*, especially in inscriptions of the time of the Gracchi, e. g. PEQVNIA, OQVPARE, QVRA (for a list of the instances, see Bersu, *Die Gutturalen*, p. 49); though whether Ritschl (*Opusc.* iv. 492 *n*, 687), is right in his suggestion that one of the grammatical reforms of the poet Accius may have been the restriction of *k* to the *c*-sound before *a*, and of *q* to the *c*-sound before *u*, is quite uncertain. (For Accius' use of *gg* for *ng* in *aggulus*, &c., *gc* for *nc* in *agceps*, &c., in imitation of the Greek use of γ for the nasal guttural, see below). Marius Victorinus says (12. 19 K.): Q et fuisse apud Graecos, et quare desiderat fungi vice litterae, cognoscere potestis, si pontificum libros legeritis.

§ 7. **Y- and W-Sounds**: —*j* and *v* were not distinguished in Latin MSS. nor indeed in the earlier printed editions. In Italian some writers keep up the old Latin habit of using *i* for *j*, e. g. Gennaio for Gennajo (Lat. *Jānuārius*); others use *j* for *-ii*, e. g. vizj, 'vices.' Even now we generally print the texts of the older Latin writers, Plautus, Terence, &c., with *i, u*, not *j, v*, partly to give their language an archaic appearance, but mainly because a large number of words which in the Classical period, or the Empire, had the *y*- and *w*- sounds, had in earlier times the sound of the vowels (sometimes of the half-vowels); *lărua*, for example, is a trisyllable in Plautus, never a dissyllable. The minuscule forms *v* and *u* are developments of the V, of Capital, and the U of Uncial writing. The use of the tall I-form on Inscriptions for the *y*-sound has already been mentioned, as well as its use for initial *i*, and for long *ī*. How far the I-symbol (in ordinary form or tall form) might be employed for -*yi*-, or V for -*wu*, -*uw*- is very doubtful. Sittl, in *Burs. Jahresber.* 1891, p. 250, quotes abicere for *abyic-* (?), VESVIVS for *Vesuv-* (?) : cf. Brambach, *Orth.* p. 94.

On the Monumentum Ancyranum we have ɪᴠᴇɴᴛᴠᴛɪs (3. 5 M.), and in Virgil MSS. *iuenis, fluius, exuiae,* &c. (Ribbeck, *Ind.* p. 448). Equally doubtful is the occasional usage in the earlier history of the Latin alphabet of the Greek digamma-symbol (whether in the F-form or in the Etruscan form, viz. an E wanting the middle horizontal line) for the *w*-sound. Cornutus (ap. Cassiodor. 148. 8 K.: itaque in prima syllaba digamma et vocalem oportuit poni, 'Fotum,' 'Firgo,' quod et Aeoles fecerunt et antiqui nostri, sicut scriptura in quibusdam libellis declarat) implies merely that some of his grammatical predecessors made a hobby of writing F for *v* (cf. Prisc. i. 35 17 H.). The second symbol in the phrase d*enoine* on the Dvenos tablet may be a variety of this symbol in the later form *Dvenoi ne,* but it may also be *z, dze noine* or (most likely) a form of *i*. (See above.)

Cicero wrote *ii* to express the sound of the second element of an *i*-diphthong before a vowel (see ch. ii. § 55), e.g. *aiio, Maiia, Aiiax* (Quint. i. 4. 11; Vel. Long. 7. 54 K.: et in plerisque Cicero videtur auditu emensus scriptionem, qui et 'Aiiacem' et 'Maiiam' per duo i scribenda existimavit. He mentions also *Troiia,* and with three *i*'s, *coiiicit.* Cf. Prisc. i. 303 and i. 14 H., who ascribes the spelling *Pompeiii* to Julius Caesar).

On inscriptions we find ᴇɪɪᴠs and ᴇɪɪᴠs (see Weissbrodt in *Philologus,* xliii. pp. 444 sqq.), and in MSS. like the Ambrosian Palimpsest of Plautus, *eiius, aiiunt,* &c. (for examples in MSS. of Plautus and Virgil, see Studemund's *Apograph,* Ind. p. 509; Ribbeck, *Prol.* p. 138).

In the Umbro-Oscan alphabets, which are derived from the Etruscan, the *w*-sound is expressed by the digamma, in the form of a capital E wanting the middle horizontal stroke, while V expresses both the *u*- and the *o*-vowels (the Oscan alphabet came in time to discriminate the *o* sound by inserting a dot between the two arms of V). On the question whether Osc. *ii* and *i* correspond to I.- Eur. *iy* and *y* in words like Osc. heriiad and heriam, see ch. iv. § 63.

§ 8. Double Consonant. Festus in his discussion of the word *solitaurilia* (p. 412 Th.), which he derives from *taurus,* in the sense of κοχάνη, and the Oscan *sollo-* (in Latin *totus*), declares the doubling of the consonant to have been a practice introduced by the poet Ennius (239-169 B.C.) into Latin orthography in imitation of the Greek usage (per unum l enuntiari non est mirum, quia nulla tunc geminabatur littera in scribendo. quam consuetudinem Ennius mutavisse fertur, utpote Graecus Graeco more usus). The Roman tradition, which ascribes this spelling reform to Ennius, as well as the doubling of the long vowel to Accius, is supported by the dates at which these spellings are first found on inscriptions (double consonant 189 B.C., double vowel 132 B.C.); though it is quite possible that Ennius followed, not the Greeks, but the Oscans, who used double consonants much earlier than the Romans, and to whose nationality he belonged quite as much as to the Greek. We do indeed find a double consonant before 189 B.C. in the spelling ʜɪɴɴᴀᴅ (the town of Enna in Sicily), 211 B.C. (*C. I. L.* i. 530), which is a mere reproduction of the Greek spelling found on coins, e.g. ʜᴇɴɴᴀɪᴏɴ (Head, *Historia Numorum,* p. 119); but even after 189 B.C. the double consonant-sound is often written with the single letter till the time of the Gracchi, when the double letter became the established spelling (see Ritschl, *Opusc.* iv. 165 sqq.).

The *sicilicus* is only found on a few inscriptions of Augustus' time: **Mumiaes**

Sabelio *C. I. L.* v. 1361. osa x. 3743. Marius Victorinus, fourth cent. A.D., states that it was often to be seen in old MSS. (sicut apparet in multis adhuc veteribus ita scriptis libris (p. 8 K. Cf. Isidor. *Orig.* i. 26. 29).

§ 9. Signs for long vowels. No instance of *oo* for *ō* is found on the extant Latin inscriptions, though we have *uootum* on an inscription in the Faliscan dialect, whose orthography was very like the Latin : *pretod de zenatuo sententiad uootum dedet* (in Latin, 'praetor de senatus sententia votum dedit '), (Zvetaieff, *Inscr. Ital. Inf.* 70). For *ī* Accius wrote *ei* (Mar. Victorinus 8. 14 K.), either because the diphthong *ei* had by this time become identical with the *i*-sound, or in imitation of the Greek orthography (§ 12); for Greek ει had taken the same course as Latin *ei*, and expressed the same sound as original long *i* (Blass. *Griech. Aussprache*², p. 51). Lucilius prescribed rules for the use of *ei* and '*i* longa'; but instead of keeping *ei* for the original diphthong, and the single letter for the original long vowel, he used foolish distinctions [1], if we are to believe Velius Longus (56. 7 K.) such as that the double symbol was suitable for a plural, e. g. *puerei* Nom. Pl., the single symbol for a singular, e. g. *pueri* Gen. Sg. (alii vero, quorum est item Lucilius, varie scriptitaverunt, siquidem in iis, quae producerentur, alia per i longam, alia per e et i notaverunt, velut differentia quadam separantes, ut cum diceremus ' viri,' si essent plures, per e et i scriberemus, si vero esset unius viri, per i notaremus, et Lucilius in nono :—

   'iam puerei uenere ;' e postremo facito atque i,
   ut puerei plures fiant. i si facis solum,
  'pupilli,' 'pueri,' 'Lucili,' hoc unius fiet ;
item
   'hoc illi factum est uni ;' tenue hoc facies i :
   'haec illei fecere ;' adde e ut pinguius fiat.)

The same absurd reason seems to be assigned for the differentiation of *meille, meillia* and *miles, militia* ; of *pilum*, a mortar (Sing.) and *peila*, javelins (Plur.) in another fragment of Lucilius (9. 21-24 M.).

 'meille hominum,' 'duo meillia ;' item huc E utroque opus ; ' miles,'
 'militiam'; tenues i, 'pilam,' qua ludimus, ' pilum,'
 quo pisunt, tenues. si plura haec feceris pila,
 quae iacimus, addes e, 'peila,' ut plenius fiat.

Another fragment (or rather two fragments), of more doubtful reading, seems to prescribe single *i* in the Gen. Sg. of IO-stems, but *ei* in the Voc. Sg. (9. 17-20 M.) :—

(1)   porro hoc 'filius Luci ;'
   feceris i solum, ut 'Corneli,' 'Cornificique,'
(2) 'mendaci' 'Furique.' addes e cum dare, 'Furei,'
   iusseris
(unless we read '*date, Furei*,' and make the *ei*-form Voc. Plur.).

Whether the persistent use of -*i* in the Gen. Sg. of O-stems on inscriptions is due to the rule which Lucilius supports, or whether it is to be otherwise explained, is hard to say (see ch. vi. § 20). Varro, while disapproving of Lucilius' arguments, seems to have followed his practice, for Ter. Scaurus (p.

---

[1] Or should we call them mnemonic, as opposed to scientific, distinctions, meant to impress the orthographic rules on the memory of the common people for whom Lucilius wrote his book? (see Lucil. 26. 1 M.).

19 K.), after quoting the passage from Lucilius beginning 'meille hominum,' goes on to say : quam inconstantiam Varro arguens in eundem errorem diversa via delabitur, dicens in plurali quidem numero debere litterae i *e* (om. MSS.) praeponi, in singulari vero minime. But in general the spelling *ei* on Inscriptions seems to occur for any $\bar{\imath}$-sound (see the Index to *C. I. L.* i., and cf. below, ch. iv. § 34). From the time of Sulla the symbol in use is the tall I (Christiansen, p. 28), though EI shows itself even later, while from c. 130 A.D. the tall I is used at random for the short and long vowel alike (Christiansen, p. 29). This tall I may be indicated by Lucilius' phrase 'i longa,' and even by Plautus' allusion to the 'littera longa' in *Aul.* 77, where the miser's old serving-woman in a fit of despondency thinks of hanging herself :—

neque quicquam meliust mihi,
Ut opinor, quam ex me ut unam faciam litteram Longam.

(Cf. Ausonius 'iota longum,' of a hanging body, *Epigr.* cxxviii. 11.) But the absence of the long form from the Inscriptions till Sulla's time makes this doubtful, especially in the case of Plautus. The remark in the *Rudens* (v. 1305) that *mendīcus* has 'one letter more' than *mĕdĭcus* shows that the long *i* of the first word was not expressed by *ei*.

The reason which induced Accius to use EI, and not II, for the long *i*-sound was probably the fear of confusion with a common symbol for E, viz. II, in which a long vertical stroke is substituted for the three horizontal strokes. There was a similar symbol for F, viz. I¹, with a short vertical stroke ; both these by-forms of F and E being probably more used in writing than on inscriptions, though they are common enough in plebeian inscriptions of later times, along with a by-form of M with four horizontal strokes ||||. (See Hübner, *Exempla Scripturae Lat. Epigr.*).

In Greek inscriptions a double vowel is found perhaps only in the name *Marcus* and its cognates. In the second century B.C. the spelling Μααρκελλος, Μααρκιος, Μααρκος is the rule, and it is common till 50 B.C. But the αα is not found in derivatives where the Greek accent does not fall on this vowel, e.g. Μαρκιανος, Μαρκελλεινος, &c. (Eckinger, p. 8).

In the first century A.D. the use of *uu* for *ū* seems to have been affected for a time, for the spelling *nuulli* occurs on wax tablets found at Pompeii (*Notizie degli Scavi*, October, 1887), and *uu* is often found for *ū* of fourth decl. nouns in Virgil MSS. (see Ribbeck, *Ind.* p. 449), e.g. *metuus, curruus* ; also *suus* for *sūs* (cf. Probi Appendix, p. 202. 27 K.). In the Bamberg MS. of the elder Pliny *uus* is the regular spelling in the Gen. Sg. and (Nom. and) Acc. Pl. of fourth decl. nouns (see preface to Sillig's edition), so that this must have been Pliny's own practice (Probus, *Inst. Art.* 116. 33 K., refers to this spelling). Lucilius seems to have objected to Accius' rule of doubling the vowels, at least in the case of A, which, he points out, has the same quality when short and when long (see ch. ii. § 1); hence *ă* and *ā*, he argues, should be written in the same way, like Greek *ă* and *ā* (9. 4-7 M.) :—

a primum longa, et breuis syllaba. nos tamen unum
hoc faciemus, et uno eodemque ut dicimus pacto
scribemus 'pacem,' 'placide,' 'Ianum,' 'aridum,' 'acetum,'
Ἄπες, Ἄπες Graeci ut faciunt.

(On *vehemens* for *vēmens*, see ch. ii. § 56.)

§ 10. gg for ng. The guttural nasal of English 'sing' (ch. ii. § 61) was expressed before a Guttural by γ in Greek, e.g. ἄγγελος, ἀγκάλη, and was called by Greek grammarians the 'Agma.' Accius proposed to follow the example of the Greeks, and express this sound in Latin by *g* instead of *n*, e.g. 'aggulus' for *angŭlus*, 'aggens' for *angens*, 'iggerunt' for *ingĕrunt*, 'agceps' for *anceps*. (Varro ap. Prisc. i. p. 30 H. : ut Ion scribit, quinta vicesima est litera, quam vocant agma, cuius forma nulla est, et vox communis est Graecis et Latinis, ut his verbis : 'aggulus,' 'aggens,' 'agguila,' 'iggerunt.' in eiusmodi Graeci et Accius noster bina g scribunt, alii n et g, quod in hoc veritatem videre facile non est. Similiter 'agceps,' 'agcora.') The Inscriptions offer no example of this spelling (cf. *Eph. Epigr.* vii. 928) ; but a trace of its existence is perhaps found in the spelling 'ager' for *agger*, which the MSS. offer with singular persistence for a line of Lucilius (26. 81 M. ; cf. 11. 5 M.). If Lucilius and his contemporaries used *gg* for *ng*, they would be forced to use the single letter in words like *agger, aggero*, &c.

§ 11. New Letters for Greek Sounds : Y, Z, CH, PH, TH, RH. Our name for *y*, viz. 'wy,' comes from the Latin name for the letter which was 'ui' (*Mém. Soc. Ling.* vi. 79). Greek *v* is often represented by Latin *ui*, and vice versa, e. g. *quinici* for κυνικοί, and Ἀκύλας for *Aquila* (ibid. viii. 188; Eckinger, p. 123). Before the introduction of the Greek letter, Latin *u* was used in loan-words like *tumba*, &c., while at a later time *i* was employed, e. g. *cignus* ; and the Romance forms of these earlier and later-loan words indicate that these spellings represented the pronunciation of the time (see ch. ii. § 28). Y was not allowed in native Roman words (Caper vii. 105. 17 K.), though it sometimes gained a footing through a mistaken idea that a word was borrowed from the Greek, e. g. *sylva* supposed to be the Greek ὕλη, *lympha* identified with Greek νύμφη, &c. (see ch. ii. § 28). Greek ζ, if we are to believe the grammarians, was expressed in earlier times by *d* also (Prisc. i. p. 36 : y et z in Graecis tantummodo ponuntur dictionibus, quamvis in multis veteres haec quoque mutasse inveniantur, et pro *v* u, pro ζ vero ... s vel ss vel d posuisse, ut ... 'Saguntum,' 'massa' pro Ζάκυνθος, μᾶζα, ... 'Sethus' pro Ζῆθος dicentes, et 'Medentius' pro Mezentius) (see ch. ii. § 120).

The earlier expression of Greek θ, φ, χ by *t, p, c* (e. g. *adelpus, Metradati* on an inscr. of 81 B C. (?), *Not. Scav.* 1887, p. 110) remains in words like *tus*, Greek θύος, *Poeni* for Φοίνικες, *calx*, Greek χάλιξ (cf. Quint. i. 5. 20 diu deinde servatum ne consonantibus (veteres) adspirarent, ut in 'triumpis '). We find *b* for φ in Old Latin *Bruges* for Φρύγες, and in *ballaena* for φάλλαινα, the former of which was used by Ennius, and was still to be found in copies of his poems in Cicero's time (Cic. *Orat.* xlviii. 160 Ennius ... 'ui patefecerunt Bruges,' non Phryges, ipsius antiqui declarant libri), while the latter remained in current use. (*F* was not regularly used for φ till the middle of the fourth century A. D. (*Hermes* xiv. p. 70), though it is often found on plebeian inscriptions from Severus' time, and even on Pompeian graffiti we have, e. g. *Dafne, C. I. L.* vi. 680). But as early as 146 B. C. we find *th, ph, ch* in the dedicatory inscriptions[1] of the Graecizing L. Mummius (*C. I. L.* i. 546 CORINTHO (?), 146 B. C. ; i. 541 in Saturnians :

ACHAIA CAPTA CORINTO DELETO
ROMAM REDIEIT TRIVMPHANS).

The importance attached in polite society at Rome to the correct pronunciation

---

[1] They may be later restorations.

of these aspirated consonants in Greek loan-words led to their wrong use in native Latin words (ch. ii. § 60), e. g. *pulcher*, referred to Greek πολύχρους, a spelling found as early as 104 B.C. on a denarius of Claudius Pulcher (*C. I. L.* i. 380), much in the same way as 'antem' (O. Engl. antefn from Gk ἀντιφωνή through Low Lat.) has come to be written with th, ' anthem.' For Greek initial ῥ, and for -ῤῥ-, the older spelling was *r*, *rr*, e. g. *Regium*, *Burrus* (the invariable form of the name Πύρρος in Ennius, according to Cic. *Orat.* xlviii. 160'. The use of *rh* for initial ῥ· was not approved by Varro, who preferred to write ' Rodus,' ' retor ' (Varro, *L. L.* iii. fr. 57. p. 182 Wilm.).

In Oscan inscriptions similarly Greek aspirates are usually expressed by tenues, e. g. Arkiia (for 'Αρχίας), Meeilikiieís (for Μειλιχίου Gen.), and so Pelignian *Perseponas*, ' Proserpinae,' Gen., but we have also Osc. thesavreí, 'in thesauro,' Loc., &c.

§ 12. **Influence of Greek Orthography.**—The use of *g* for the guttural nasal, advocated without success by Accius (see above), was clearly borrowed from the Greeks. The spelling *ei* for the long *i*-sound, and the employment of double consonants, may possibly, as we have seen, have come from the same source. But however natural it may appear for the Romans to have adopted Greek spelling along with Greek terminology in matters of Grammar and Phonetics, there is hardly a single instance of the practice that can be established by proof (see Zarncke's attempt in *Comm. Ribbeck*, 1888).

§ 13. **Syllabic Writing.**—The remark of Ter. Scaurus (p. 15 K.) quoted above, that *k* had been employed to denote the syllable *ka*, *c* the syllable *ce*, suggests (unless indeed he is merely alluding to the common practice of abbreviating words by writing only the initial letter of each syllable), that spellings on early inscriptions like LVBS for *lubē*(*n*)*s* on a Marso-Latin inscription (*C. I. L.* i. 183), may be not really evidences of syncopated pronunciation, but rather traces of an old custom of syllabic writing (see ch. iii. § 14). The syllabaries found on Etruscan inscriptions (e. g. Fabretti 2403 and 450), as well as the use of a dot (like the Sanscrit virama), to indicate those consonants which are not followed by a vowel, in the inscriptions of the Veneti, an Illyrian tribe of N.E. Italy, are perhaps other indications that syllabic writing prevailed at an early period in the Italian peninsula.

CHAPTER II.

PRONUNCIATION[1].

§ 1. **A.** In the words 'man,' 'father,' the vowels which we are in the habit of classing roughly as 'short *a*' and 'long *a*,' are really very different from each other, and would be phonetically expressed by two distinct symbols. In Sweet's *Handbook of Phonetics*, while the second is written *a*, the first is denoted by a combination of the letters *a* and *e*, viz. æ, a symbol which implies that the vowel has something of the nature of an E-sound. If we compare our pronunciation of the words 'man,' 'hat,' with the German of 'Mann,' 'er hat,' we see that the German vowel is the same as the *a* of English 'father' or German 'Vater,' while we might say that our 'man,' 'hat,' 'bat,' have in them something of the sound of 'men,' 'bet.' Seelmann, who classifies the varieties of A as 'normal *a*,' '*a* inclined to an E-sound,' and '*a* inclined to an O-sound' (this last being something not quite so definitely an O-sound as the vowel of our words 'all,' 'awe '), is of opinion that the Latin *a* had a leaning to *e* rather than to *o*, and goes so far as to give to Latin *a* of the Imperial age the æ-sound of English 'man.' This however is not the sound of modern Italian *a*, e.g. padre, which Sweet now judges to be identical in quality with the *a* of English 'father,' though, owing

---

[1] Seelmann, *Aussprache des Latein*, Heilbronn, 1885, is the chief book on Latin Pronunciation.

to our smaller use of lip-action in utterance, the vowel has with us what he terms a more 'muffled' sound. And the evidence at our disposal is not at all strong enough to allow us to determine with precision under which class of A-sounds Latin *a* should be placed, nor yet how far its quality was altered by the consonants which accompanied it, nor even whether it had to some extent a different quality as a long and as a short vowel. On this last point indeed we have some evidence of weight. We can be sure that Latin *ă* and *ā*, if they differed at all in quality, did not differ so markedly as Latin *ĕ* and *ē*, *ĭ* and *ī*, *ŭ* and *ū*. For Lucilius (ix. fr. 4 M), in criticizing the proposal of the poet and grammarian Accius to write a single vowel for a short, a double for a long vowel (thus *a* for *ă*, *aa* for *ā*), says that the vowel *a* has the same sound in pronunciation when long as when short, and should be written in the same way, e.g. *păcem*, *plăcide*, &c., just as the Greeks write *ă* and *ā* in the same way, e.g. Ἄρες and Ἆρες (the passage is quoted on p. 10).

And his remark is borne out by the evidence of the Romance languages. In them there are no means of tracing the quantity of a Latin vowel, unless the long and the short vowel differed in quality as well as in quantity. This difference did exist in the case of other vowels, e.g. *ĭ* and *ī*; and so in the Romance languages Latin *ĭ* appears as close *e*, Latin *ī* as close *i* (e.g. Ital. misi for Lat. *mīsī*; Ital. beve for Lat. *bĭbĭt*). Latin *ă* and *ā*, however, show no divergence in any Romance language; and, when we are in doubt whether a Latin *a* was long or short, in a syllable long by position for example, we have to refer to some other family of languages, which happens to have borrowed the word at an early period from the Latin. A word like *saccus* is shown by its Welsh and Breton forms, sach, not to speak of Gothic sakkus, O. H. G. sac, O. Engl sæcc, to have had a short *a*; but this could not have been told from its Romance forms, Ital. sacco, Span. saco. Long *a* appears in a different guise in Welsh and Breton (e.g. poc, a kiss, representing Latin *pācem* in the formula of the priest at absolution, *pacem do tibi*), but not in Romance, e.g. Ital. pace, Span. paz.

The accounts of the pronunciation of *a*, given by the Latin writers on phonetics, do not much help us to determine the shade or shades of the A-sound, which the Latin vowel expressed, nor are any of their descriptions free from the suspicion of Greek bias. The evidence to be drawn from the phenomena of the language itself is equally indecisive. It is true that *a* becomes *e* in the unaccented syllable (long by position), as *aurĭfex* from *aurum* and *facis*, and in Early Latin in open syllables too, e.g. *ăbĕgit*, classical *ăbĭgit*, from *ăb* and *ăgo*, an *e* retained in classical Latin before *r*, e.g. *impĕro* from *păro*. But this was the fate of every short vowel in the unaccented syllable, and not of *a* alone, so that *e* was the natural sound which any short Latin post-tonic vowel tended to assume, unless attracted by a following Labial to an O-, U- or Ü-sound, e.g. *occŭpo* from *ob* and *căpio*, *testŭmōnium* (*C. I. L.* i. 197, 3) from stem *testi-* (see iii. 18). Varieties in the spelling of foreign names like *Sardĭca* and *Serdĭca*, *Delmătia* and *Dalmătia* prove nothing for Latin *a*. More important is the fact that *jă-*, *jaj-* seem to have tended to the pronunciation *jĕ-*, *jej-*, with open *e*. Thus *Jānuārius* became *Jēnuārius*; *jajūnus* is the Plautine form of the classical *jejūnus*. Here the change of *a* to *e* was due to the influence of the palatal *j* (our *y*) preceding, just as the *ū* of *jūnĭpĕrus* was changed to *i* by the same palatal in Vulgar Latin *jinipirus* (Probi Appendix, 199. 8 K.) (Ital. ginepro, Fr. genièvre, Span. enebro). No such influence is at work in the mispronunciation *stetim* for *stătim*, a Roman cockneyism like London 'keb' for 'cab,' mentioned by a grammarian of the fifth (?) century A.D. (Consentius, p. 392, 16 K.: per immutationem fiunt barbarismi sic: litterae, ut siquis dicat ' bobis ' pro vobis, ' peres' pro pedes, ' stetim' pro statim, quod vitium plebem Romanam quadam deliciosa novitatis affectione corrumpit). This is quoted by Seelmann as a strong argument for his assertion that Latin *a* had in Imperial times the sound of English *a* in 'man'; though on the other hand we might argue for an A-sound more inclining to *o* from Vulg. Lat. *nŏtare, a by-form of *nătare*, to swim, which ousted the *a*-form in Vulgar Latin about 100 B.C. In Plautus' time and later *văcare* was pronounced like *vocare*; the *o*-sound apparently having been produced by the influence of the labial *v* (our *w*) (cf. Κωδρατος, Κοδρατος for *Quadrātus* on Gk. inscriptions), as *e* was by the palatal *j* (our *y*) in *Jēnuārius*. In one of Phaedrus' fables (*App.* 21) a man mistakes the caw of a crow for *ave! ave!* It is worth mentioning that Oscan ú, the representative of Ind.-Eur. O, Ō, and, when at the end of a word, of Ind.-Eur. Ā, which must have had a sound something like our *a* in 'all,' 'awe,' and which is in those inscriptions which are written in Latin characters expressed by *o* (e.g. *tovto*, 'state,' 'community, Nom. Sing. of Ā-stem; *petiro-pert*, 'four times,' Acc. Pl. Neut.), rarely by *u* (e.g. *petiru-pert*), as in Greek characters by *o* (e.g. τωϝτο), is yet written by Festus and by Paulus, his epitomator, with *a*. Festus, when he mentions the Oscan word for 'four,' writes it *petora* (p. 250, l. 33 Th.); and Paulus gives *veia*, not *veio*, as the word for 'cart' (p. 560, l. 17 Th.); though Lucilius, if Festus (p. 426, l. 7 Th.) quotes him accurately, makes ŏ the Latin equivalent of the Oscan Neut. Pl. suffix in *sollŏ* (Lat. *tota*),

> uasa quoque omnino dirimit non sollo dupundi.

The evidence then of the Latin language itself points to Latin *a* having had a sound which was liable to influence in the direction of *o* as well as of *e*. Into the modifications of Latin *a* in each several Romance language, it is hardly necessary to enter, for they are as likely to be due to the vocal peculiarities of the nations conquered by the Romans, as to the nuances of sound in the language of the conquering race. French is the language where Latin *a* has been most widely replaced by *e* (e.g. chef, Lat. *căpŭt*, while in champ, Lat. *campus*, though *e* is not written, the preceding guttural has been palatalized); and in Portuguese it is something between the *a* of 'father' and the *a* of 'man,' though before *l* the sound is more guttural. But in Italy *a* has what may be called the normal A-sound, that of English *a* in 'father,' not that of *a* in 'man.' It is only in two districts, Emilia (i.e. the Po-valley), and the coast of Apulia, that it has an E-sound, while in some parts of Italy it tends to an O-sound (Meyer-Lübke, *Ital. Gram.* §§ 18-21). Speaking generally, we may say that the influence of a palatal or *r* often changes *a* into an E-sound in the Romance languages (e.g. Corsican berba), whereas an O-sound is produced under the influence of such letters as *l, v, b* (e.g. oltro for Latin *alter* in some dialects of N. Italy), while before *n* Latin *a* is in some places changed to *e*, in others to *o*. So that the evidence, taken as a whole, is rather more in favour of attributing to Latin *a* a sound which varied to some extent in character, according to the consonant which accompanied it, than of giving it definitely the E-character of our *a* in 'man.' And in the absence of more definite proof, it will be best, for practical purposes, to use in reading Latin the sound which the vowel bears in the language of the direct descendants of the Roman people, the normal A-sound of Italian padre.

§ 2. **Descriptions of the A-sound by Latin phoneticians.** The formation of the (Greek or Latin?) sound is described very cleverly by Terentianus Maurus (second cent. A.D.) (p. 328 of Keil's edition), in spite of the limitations of the difficult Sotadean metre (- - ⏑ ⏑ | - - ⏑ ⏑ | - ⏑ - ⏑ | - ᴗ́) :—

> a prima locum littera sic ab ore sumit:
> immunia rictu patulo tenere labra,
> linguamque necesse est ita pendulam reduci,
> ut nisus in illam valeat subire vocis,
> nec partibus ullis aliquos ferire dentes.

Marius Victorinus (fourth cent. A.D.) (p. 32 of Keil's edition) compresses the same description, in his usual way: a littera rictu patulo suspensa, neque impressa dentibus lingua enuntiatur. It is still further compressed by Martianus Capella (fourth or fifth cent. A.D.) (iii. 261, p. 63 of Eyssenhardt's edition in the Teubner series): A sub hiatu oris congruo solo spiritu memoramus.

§ 3. **Interchange of *a* and *e*.** *Delmătia* and *Dalmătia*: Vel. Longus, p. 73 K. placet etiam Delmatiam quoque, non 'Dalmatiam' pronuntiemus, quoniam a Delmino maxima ejusdem provinciae civitate tractum nomen existimatur. On Inscriptions, we have sometimes *a*, e.g. *Dalmat.* (*C.I.L.* vi. 1607), sometimes *e*, e.g. *Delmatia* (*C.I.L.* iii. p. 280) (see Georges, *Lex. Lat. Wortf.* s.v.). *Jĕ-*, *jej-* for *jā-*, *jaj-*:—The Vulg. Lat. name of the month was *Jenuarius* (*C.I.L.* vi. 1708, of 311–314 A.D., and other inscriptions) [see Schuchardt, *Vok.* i. 185. So in Greek inscrr. Ἰενουαρίων *C.I.G.* 9486 (Catana); Ἰεναρίων *I.I.S.* 62 (Syracuse)], which has developed into the Italian Gennajo (cf. Span. Enero), with open *e*. *Jejūnus* (with *ĕ* according to Ter. Maur. 343 K.), *jejentaculum* supplanted the older *jajūnus*, *jajentaculum*, the Plautine forms (*A.L.L.* 7. 528). *Jēnua*, for *jānua*, is indicated by Sardinian enna, genna, and is sometimes found in MSS. (see Schuchardt, *Vok.* i. p. 185.) *Jajunus* reappears in late Latin (in the Itala, e.g. *Luc.* iii. 20), and in Span. ayunar, while the shortened forms *jantăcŭlum*, *jantāre* are found in MSS. along with the usual *jentăcŭlum*, *jentāre* (see Georges, *Lex. Wortf.* s. vv.); and *jantare* is indicated by Old Span. yantar, Port. yantar. On Vulg. Lat. *jecto* for *jacto* (Ital. gettare, Fr. jeter), see *I.F.* ii. Anz. p. 35; and for other examples of *a–e*, Georges, *Lex. Wortf.* s. vv. *Sarapis*, *serracum*, *Serdica*, *metaxa*, *Sabadius*, and *Dict.* s. v. *Serranus*.

§ 4. **Interchange of *a* and *o*.** *Nătāre* is the form reflected in the languages of those countries which were earliest colonized (Sard. nadare, Span. nadar, Port.

nadar, Prov. nadar), while *nŏtāre appears in O. Fr. noer, Raet. nudar, Roum. innotá, Ital. nuotare, which shows that *notare did not find its way into Vulgar Latin till about 100 B.C. *Vŏcĭtus is the Vulg. Lat. original of Ital. voto, O. Fr. voit, 'empty,' and vŏcare, vŏc(u)us (see Georges, Lex. Wortf.) of Sard. bogare, Span. hueco. Vocatio for văcātio is found on the Lex Repetundarum of 123-2 B.C. (C.I.L. i. 198. 77 : militiaeque eis uocatio esto), and is the spelling of Julius Caesar in his Lex Municipalis of 45 B.C. (i. 206. 93 and 103 : vocatio rei militaris). Plautus puns on vŏcare, 'to be empty,' and vŏcare 'to call,' in Cas. 527 : Fac habeant linguam tuae aedes. Quid ita? Quom ueniam, uocent. Marmor (Greek μάρμαρος) follows the analogy of Nouns in -or. (For other examples of a–o, see Schuchardt, Vok. i. p. 177 sqq., and Brambach, Hülfsbüchlein s. v. Tamyris, and cf. below, ch. iv. § 55.)

§ 5. **Anomalies in Romance.** Accented Latin a sometimes shows o, sometimes e in Romance from a variety of causes. Thus Ital. chiovo, from Lat. clāvus, shows o by influence of v ; Ital. (dialectal) opre for apre, Fr. ouvrir, hardly point to Vulg. Lat. *operio for ăpĕrio, but are rather influenced by co(o)pĕrio, Fr. couvrir, Ital. coprire ; Ital. monco from Lat. mancus is due to the synonym tronco from Lat. truncus. Vulg. Lat. *grĕvis (Ital. greve and grave) may have adapted itself to lĕvis ; mēlum, not mālum, the original of the Romance words for apple (Ital. melo, &c.), seems to be the Greek form μῆλον, and is indicated by the pun in Petronius, chap. lvi. (p.37. 19 Büch.) contumelia . . . contus cum malo (leg. melo). The appearance of e for a in the unaccented syllable, e. g. Vulg. Lat. alecer (with stem alecro-) for ălăcri- (Ital. allegro, Span. alegre), ceresio- (ceresium and ɛerasium in Marc. Emp.) from *ceresus for cĕrăsus (Greek κερασός) in the Romance words for cherry (Ital. ciriegio, &c.) is due to the same law which produced consecro from sacro (ch. iii). The mispronunciations fetigo Prob. 212. 4, secratum Mar. Vict. x. 6, are to be similarly explained. (On the variation of Italian ă with I.-Eur. ĕ in words like Lat. păteo (Osc. pate-) besides Gk. πετάννυμι, see ch. iv. § 61.)

§ 6. **E.** The evidence for the pronunciation of Latin e is much stronger than the evidence at our disposal for Latin a. In the Romance languages we have clear proof that short and long e had in the parent-speech a different quality, ĕ being an open E-sound like Engl. 'men,' ē a close E-sound like Fr. été. (Our 'fail,' 'fate' have a diphthong of this close e combined with an I-sound.) These sounds are retained without a change in Italian at the present day in such words as bello (Lat. bĕllus) with open e, stella (Lat. stēlla) with close e, though in open syllables in many Romance languages open e has developed to ie (Ital. criepa, Span. crieba, from Lat. crĕpat) (cf. Schuchardt, Vok. ii. p. 328). All this harmonizes so wonderfully with the evidence we can draw from the Latin language itself, and from the statements of the Latin grammarians, as to leave little room for doubt. According to the grammarians long e is 'an E inclining to an I-sound,' precisely what phoneticians nowadays call 'close *e*' (open *e* would be 'an E inclining to an A-sound'), while short *e* approaches the sound of the Latin diphthong *æ*, which in the Romance languages is undistinguishable from Latin *ĕ* (e. g. Ital. cielo, Span. cielo, from Lat. *caelum*, exactly as Ital. criepa, Span. crieba, from Lat. *crĕpat*). Latin *ē* and *ĭ* are merged in the same way in Romance (Ital. fendo from Lat. *fĭndo*, like vendo from Lat. *vēndo*; inesso from Lat. *mĭssus*, like mesa from Lat. *mē(n)sa*; all with close *e*), being distinguished only in the oldest Romance dialect, viz. Sardinian (Sard. veru from Lat. *vērus*, but pira from Lat. **pĭra, pĭrum*, for which the Italian words are vero, pera), so that the two sounds must have become very like one another in quality at an early period of Vulgar Latin. They were not however identical, for they are clearly distinguished in Latin loanwords in other languages (e. g. Lat. *fĭdes, cēra*, loanwords of the second to the fourth cent. A.D., are in Welsh ffydd, cwyr). And so the probable history of the change of *ĕ* to *ĭ* in unaccented syllables (e. g. *eligo* from *lego*), is that the open *e* first became close *e*, and then passed into *ĭ*. Italian *e* in unaccented syllables is similarly close *e*, for example, the final *e* of diece, 'ten'; and English speakers of Italian often fail to give this sound correctly. It is only in the unaccented syllable that we find *i* substituted for *e* in the mispronunciations censured by the grammarians, *pinaria* for *penaria*, *pidato* for *pedatu*, *decim* for *decem*, &c., though on plebeian epitaphs, and the like, we find instances of *i* for accented *e*, some of which may be a mere graver's mistake of dropping a stroke of II, a common way of writing E. Before another vowel *ĕ* seems to have approached the sound of *ĭ*, to judge from the frequent confusion of suffixes like *-eus* and *-ius*, *-eolus* and *-iolus*. Before *ī*, older *ei*, the *ĭ*-sound was recognized as the correct pronunciation, or at least the correct spelling, e. g. *mieis, miis*, contracted to *mis*; *dii, diis*, contracted to *di, dis*; *ii, iis*, contracted to *i, is* in Plautus, &c. The contrary tendency, to substitute *ĕ* for *ĭ* before a vowel, was a feature of rustic Latin; and some of these 'rustic' forms, especially in names of agricultural implements and the like, have found their way into ordinary Latin, e. g. *mateola* for **matiola* (Sanscr. matyàm). Another dialectal change was to replace *ĕ* by *i* before *rc*, e.g. *stircus* for *stercus*. The remark of Quintilian (i. 4. 8) that some new letter was required to express the sound of the final vowel of *heri, here* (in 'here' neque e plane neque i auditur), is discussed in § 16.

In Oscan, as we shall see (§ 14), the short and long E-sounds seem to have corresponded to Latin ĕ, ē, in being the one open, the other close. A short E-vowel, however, when lengthened by 'compensation' or any other cause, appears to have retained the open sound; for it is expressed by doubling the symbol of the short vowel (e.g. eestínt, Lat. *exstant*; keenzstur, Lat. *censor, censōres*), and not by the symbol of the long vowel. For Latin nevertheless the evidence points to ē- for *ĕx*, -ē(*n*)*s*- for -*ĕns*- having had the close sound; for *ēvitat* is the instance given by a grammarian (see below) of the close E-sound of ordinary Latin ē, and the Romance and Celtic forms of Lat. *mensa*, mė(*n*)*sa* (Ital. mesa, Welsh mwys, &c.) point to the ordinary ē-vowel. But Vulg. Latin *Jēnuarius* (for *Jānuarius*) is shown by Italian Gennajo (with open *e*) to have had the E-sound which is most near *a*, that is, the open sound. (On *ens* see § 144.)

§ 7. Descriptions of the E-sound by Latin phoneticians, &c. Terentianus Maurus in his account (329. 116 K.) :—

> e quae sequitur vocula dissona est priori,
> quia deprimit altum modico tenore rictum,
> et lingua remotos premit hinc et hinc molares,

curiously omits all reference to the difference between short and long *e*. There must, however, have been such a reference in some part of his writings, for Pompeius, as we shall see, quotes him as an authority on this very point. Marius Victorinus, whose account always closely corresponds with his, after describing *e* as follows (33. 1 K.) : e quae sequitur, depresso modice rictu oris reductisque introrsum labiis effertur, goes on to say : o, ut e, geminum vocis sonum pro condicione temporis promit. Martianus Capella (iii. 261) has : E spiritus facit lingua paululum pressiore. More valuable are the remarks of those grammarians who give practical hints on the correct pronunciation of actual Latin words. Servius (fourth cent. A. D.) (*in Don.* 421. 17 K.) is very clear : vocales sunt quinque, a e i o u. ex his duae, e et o, aliter sonant productae, aliter correptae ... e quando producitur vicinum est ad sonum i litterae, ut 'meta ;' quando autem correptum, vicinum est ad sonum diphthongi, ut 'equus.' (By the 'diphthong' he means *ae* of *aequus*, &c.) Cautions against the confusion of 'equus' and 'aequus' occur more than once in the writings of the grammarians. Thus Pompeius (fifth cent. A.D.) says the one vowel-sound is short, the other long (285. 6 K.) : plerumque male pronuntiamus et facimus vitium, ut brevis syllaba longo tractu sonet ... siqui

§§ 7–9.] PRONUNCIATION. VOWELS. 21

velit dicere 'aequus' pro eo quod est equus, in pronuntiatione hoc fit (cf. Alcuin 295. 4 K. : ' aequitas,' 'aequus,' id est justus, . . . per ae diphthongon scribenda sunt ; ' equus,' si animal significat, per simplicem e) (see § 41). Pompeius, in another passage (102. 4 K.), ascribes the comparison of the long $\bar{e}$- to the i-sound to Terentianus Maurus : e aliter longa, aliter brevis sonat . . . dicit ita Terentianus ' quotienscumque e longam volumus proferri, vicina sit ad i litteram.' ipse sonus sic debet sonare, quomodo sonat i littera. quando dicis 'evitat,' vicina debet esse, sic pressa, sic angusta, ut vicina sit ad i litteram. quando vis dicere brevem e, simpliciter sonat. And 'Sergius' (*in Don.* 520. 27 K.) gives much the same account as Servius: vocales sunt quinque. hae non omnes varios habent sonos, sed tantum duae, e et o. nam quando e correptum est, sic sonat, quasi diphthongus, 'equus ;' quando productum est, sic sonat, quasi i, ut ' demens.'

§ 8. i for unaccented ĕ. Caper (first cent. A.D.) (93. 3 K.) : cella penaria, non 'pinaria,' dicendum ; ibid. 100. 23 K. primo pedatu, non 'pidato,' dicendum ; Velius Longus (first cent. A. D.) (76. 9 K.) : ' comprimo' quoque per i malo scribi, quamvis ' compressus ' dicatur ; et e contrario ' decem ' audacius dixerim, quamvis inde ' decies ' trahatur, quoniam, ut supra dixi, sono usitatiore gaudet auditus, referring to the form ' decim,' which is found now and then on inscriptions. (For other examples, see ch. iii. § 22.)

§ 9. i for ĕ in hiatus. The Appendix Probi censures *vinia* (198. 3 K.), *cavia* (198. 5), *brattia* (198. 6), *coclia* and *cocliarium* (198. 6), *lancia* (198. 8), *solia* (198. 10), *calcius* (198. 10), *tinia* (198. 19), *baltius* (198. 23), *lintium* (198. 31), *palliarium* (198. 9), *fassiolus* (198. 26). *Ariam* (e. g. *C. I. L.* vi. 541, of 88 A. D.), *horriorum* (e. g. vi. 8680, of 68 A. D.), are frequent spellings on inscriptions. Cf. Greek ὅρρια, ἄρια from the end of the first cent. A. D. ; πείλιον in the Edict of Diocletian, 301 A. D.; Ποτιολοι, Ποτιωλοι. Vulg. Lat. *mia for *mea*, &c., is shown by Sard. mia, O. Fr. moie, Roum. mea. Velius Longus (first cent. A. D.) says (77. 16 K.) : nostris auribus[1] placet . . . ' miis' per i, non ' meis' per e, ut Terentius :—

at enim ístoc nihil est mágis, Syre, miis núptiis aduérsum.

Our MSS. of Terence have not preserved the old spelling in this passage (*Heaut.* 699); but that it was a spelling current in the older period we see from *mieis* on one of the Scipio Epitaphs (*C. I. L.* i. 38, of 130 B. c.). In the Lex Parieti Faciendo (*C. I. L.* i. 577), a copy of an inscription of 105 B.C., we find the Abl. Pl. *ăbiegnieis*, *aesculnieis*, distinguished in spelling from Acc. Pl. *ăbiegnea* (*K.* xxx. 500). Similarly *dii*, *diis* represented the pronunciation, although spelt *dei*, *deis* to agree with the other cases, as we learn from Caper (first cent. A. D.) (109. 6 K.) : dei non ' dii ' ; nam et deabus Cicero dixit : igitur deis ratio, diis consuetudo ; and the same must hold of *ii*, *iis* (*ieis*, *C. I. L.* vi. 877, time of Augustus ; *ieis, iei*, but *eos*, &c., on the Regulations for the Ludi Saeculares of 17 B. C. (*Monumenti Antichi* i. iii)) ; cf. Caper 106. 11 K. eam (MSS. iam) semper dicendum, quia nihil est 'iam.' item non ' iamus,' sed eamus. (On the spelling of the Plur. of *is* and *deus* see Georges, *Lex. Wortf.* s. vv.) By-

---

[1] But the use of *i* may have been a mere usage of orthography to avoid the awkward collocation -eī-, which might be misread as the symbol for the long *i*-sound (i. 9), or -eei-, which might suggest the *ē*-sound (ibid.) followed by *i*.

forms in -*ea* and -*ia* are sometimes differentiated by the subtlety of grammarians, a practice very properly censured by Cornutus (ap. Cassiod. 150. 18 K.): vineas per e quidam scribendas tradiderunt, si hae significarentur, quas in agris videmus ; at contra per i, vinias, illas sub quibus latere miles solet, quod discrimen stultissimum est. nam neque aliunde vineae castrenses dictae sunt, quam quod vineis illis agrestibus similes sunt. (For other examples of -*ea*, -*eus* varying with -*ia*, -*ius*, see Schuchardt, *Vok.* i. p. 424 ; Brambach *Orth.* p. 133 ; and consult Georges, *Lex. Wortf.* s. vv. *glarea, linea, janeus, mustaceus, virgineus, vitreus, gallinaceus, cavea, urceolus, adorea, lancea, oreae, ostrea, pausea, labea, linteo, phaseolus, nauseo, coprea, cochlea, hordearius* ; and Brambach, *Hülfsbüchlein* s. vv. *balteus, solea, tinea, bractea*.) They have been explained by that tendency to change *i* and *e* in hiatus into consonantal *i* (*y*), which turned *lĭlium* &c. into 'lilyum,' *ārea* &c. into ' arya,' so that -*eus*, -*eum*, -*ius*, *ium* were merged in the same sound (see ch. iv. § 63). But they are more easily explained by the tendency to give a vowel in hiatus the close sound (§ 18).

§ 10. ' Rustic ' *e* for *ĭ* in hiatus. Varro (*R. R.* i. 2. 14) : rustici . . . viam 'veham' appellant. (The Oscan word is vía-, the Umbr. vea- and via-) ; -*eo* for -*io* is common in inscrr. of Etruria, Praeneste, &c. (Sittl, *Lok. Versch.* p. 10), e. g. Praenestine *fīleai* (*C. I. L.* i. 54) ; the Praenestine form of *cicōnia* is given by the MSS. of Plautus, *Truc.* 690, as *conea* not ' conia ' : ut Praenestinis conea est ciconia ; in Plaut. *Most.* 48 the MSS. read *āleāto* ' on garlic.' Charisius (70. 27 K.) censures the pronunciation of 'alii diserti' *aleum, doleum, palleum* ; the Appendix Probi rejects *aleum* (198. 18 K.), *lileum* (198. 19), *laneo* (197. 29), *osteum* (198. 5). [For other exx. see Georges, *Lex. Wortf.* s. vv. *alium, ascia, dolium, folium, lanio, ostium, pallium, solium, spolium* ; and Brambach, *Hülfsb.* s.vv. *feriae, lilium, sobrius*. Both *spongia* and *spongea* were used, the latter being, for example, the normal spelling in the MSS. of Martial (see Georges, s.v. and Friedländer's edition, i. p. 118). Schuchardt (*Vok.* ii. p. 37) gives a number of misspellings of the kind from MSS. and inscriptions.]

§ 11. ĭ for ē. Schuchardt (*Vok.* i. p. 227) quotes a large number of spellings from inscrr. of the fourth cent., and later in which an *i* appears for *ē*. It is not easy to decide how many represent a pronunciation of *ī* for *ē* [thus *Aurilius* (third cent.), *Cornilius* seem to represent that change of *ē* to *ī* before a syll. with *ĭ* (*y*) in hiatus, which appears in *fīlius*, with the ordinary Latin long *i*-sound (close *i*, § 14), to judge from its Romance descendants, Ital. figlio, Span. hijo, &c.; on this possible change of *ē* to *ī*, see ch. iv. § 7], how many a pronunciation of *ĭ* for *ē* (e. g. *filiciter*?), how many are dialectal (the equivalent of Lat. *ē* is an *i*-sound in several of the Italian dialects, e. g. Osc. *ligud* 'lege' ch. iv. § 5), and how many are mere mistakes. In Greek inscrr. *ī* for Lat. *ē* is late, probably dating from the time when Greek η came to take the *i*-sound ; but Αὐρίλιος (-ιλλιος) is found beside Αὐρηλιος in the second cent. (Eckinger, p. 24). The rare spelling *decreiuit* for *dēcrēvit* on an inscr. of 189 B.C. from Spain (*C. I. L.* ii. 5041) cannot be quoted as an example of the transition of *ē* to *ī*. The use of *ei* for *ĕ* in the unaccented syll. in the word *inpeirator* (for *impĕrător*) on the same inscr. suggests that *ei* in *decreiuit* may have been meant to indicate the close *e*-sound [cf. *leigibus* xiv. 2892 (Praeneste), *pleib.* (*Eph. Epigr.* i. 3)]. *Delīrus* and *delērus* are rightly explained by Velius Longus (73. 2 K.), who follows Varro : *delīrus* is the proper form, derived from *līra* a furrow, while the form *delērus* is due to a fanciful connexion of the word with Gk. ληρεῖν.

§§ 10–14.] PRONUNCIATION. VOWELS. 23

(On the comparative prevalence of the two spellings see Georges, *Lex. Wortf.* s. v., and cf. App. Probi 198. 19: delirus non 'delerus'); *torpĭdo* beside *torpēdo* (Caper 106. 8 K.) is merely the substitution of a more familiar for a less familiar suffix (cf. *grăvĭdo* for *grăvēdo*; see Georges, *Lex. Wortf.* s. v.), and the same is true of Vulg. Lat. *vĕnĭnum (Fr. venin), *Bizacĭnus* for *Byzacēnus* (App. Probi, 198. 1), *pergamīnum (Ital. pergamino, Fr. parchemin), *pullĭcīnum (Ital. pulcino, Fr. poussin) (-*ēnus*, -*ēnum* have been in fact supplanted by -*īno-* in Romance languages, e.g. Ital. Saracino, Messina, &c., Fr. serin, a canary, if from *Sīrēn*), *răcīmus (Ital. racimolo, Fr. raisin), *vervĭcem (Ital. berbice, Fr. brebis), *mantīle (Ital. mantile), &c. (See also Georges, s. vv. *crŭmēna, sēsămum, sērĭcus*; cf. App. Probi 199. 6: hermeneumata non 'erminomata.')

§ 12. ĭ for accented ĕ (see Schuchardt, *Vok.* i. p. 329 sqq.). *Bipinnis* for *bipennis*, censured in App. Probi 199. 6 K. (cf. Quint. i. 4. 12), is due to confusion of *pinna* with *penna* (cf. Caper 100. 17 K.); *carictum* beside *cărectum* (*de Dub. Nom.* v. 573. 2 K. Virgilius in bucolicis 'tu sub carecta latebas,' nunc caricta), may follow the analogy of *sălictum*, &c., but it is more likely that the true reading here is *caricea*, Plur. of *cariceum* (Nonius 21. 24 M.?), the original of Span. carrizo. On *vĭgeo* and *vĕgeo, filix* and *fĕlix, fĭber* and *fĕber, pinna* and *penna*, see ch. iv. § 11; and on *bĕnĕvŏlus* and *bĕnĭvŏlus, bĕnĕfĭcus* and *bĕnĭfĭcus*, &c., ch. iii. § 37. *Scĭda, schĭda* for *schĕda* (see Georges, s. v.) seems to follow the analogy of *scindo*; *spīcio, sĭco*, &c., of *prospĭcio, prōsĭco*, &c. The use of ĕ for ĭ is discussed in § 17. Before *ng* every Latin ĕ became by a phonetic law of the language *i* (see ch. iv. § 8), e.g. *tingo, confringo, attingo*; and other consonant-combinations may have influenced ĕ towards the close *e*-sound or the *ī*-sound (see Georges, *Lex. Wortf.* s. vv. *Vergilius, vergiliae, Verginius, hernia, segmentum, Porsenna*, and cf. § 144); *dignus* has been explained as *dec-nus* from *dĕcet*, and spellings like *frumintum* (Schuchardt, *Vok.* i. 354) may point to a modification of ĕ like that of ŏ (ch. iv. § 20) before *nt*.

§ 13. ă for ĕ. Before *rc* we find *a* for *e* in the mispronunciation *novarca* (for *nŏverca*) mentioned in the Appendix Probi (198. 34 K.); but forms like *ansar* (ib. 198. 22 and 23), *passar* (ib. 198. 33), *carcar* in the Acts of the Arval Brothers, &c. (cf. App. Prob. 197. 32), are better explained as cases of assimilation to the vowel of the accented syllable (see ch. iii. § 33); and *calandae*, the Vulg. Lat. form of *călendae* [in Greek always καλανδαι (cf. Eckinger), Welsh calan, New Year's Day, Mod. Gk. κάλαντα], may be a 1 Conj. Gerundive form. (Schuchardt, *Vok.* i. p. 206 sqq., has collected a list of examples of doubtful validity.)

§ 14. I. The Romance languages show us that Latin ĭ, ī differed in quality, like Latin ĕ, ē. Latin ĭ, as we have seen, they merge in Latin ē, while Latin ī remains *i*, e. g. Ital. beve, from Latin *bĭbĭt*, misi from Latin *mīsī*. This *i* from Latin ī is, of all Romance vowels, the least liable to change. In almost every Romance language it preserves its character unaltered, and resists every influence of neighbouring consonants, so that there is great likelihood that it has remained the same on Italian soil from Roman times till now. Italian sì will then exactly represent the vowel sound of Latin *sic*, finito of Lat. *fīnĭtus*. This Italian *i* has the close I-sound, like French si, fini, Germ. sie, our 'see' being rather a diphthong, while our *i* in 'bit,' 'fish,' 'kin,' is an open I-sound, but, according to Sweet, 'nearer *e* of "men" than *i* of German Kind, bitten.' The Latin grammarians similarly speak of the sound of *ī* as fuller (*plenior*) than that of *ĭ*, while the latter is 'a sound between *e* and *i*.' They add a third I-sound, which in the Romance languages is not distinguished from ordinary Latin *ĭ*, viz. the *ĭ* of *optimus* older *optumus*, &c., which they style 'a sound between *i* and *u*.' The natural inference is that Latin *ĭ* and *ī* differed as Latin *ĕ* and *ē*, the short vowel being open, the long close, while *ĭ* before a labial, in words like *optimus*, had some sound like that of German *ü* in schützen, Hütte. This *ü* is the same sound as Germ. *i* of 'Kind,' 'bitten,' modified by labialization, or as it is usually called, 'rounding,' i. e. lateral compression of the cheek passage, and narrowing of the lip-aperture (Sweet, *Handbook*, p. 13).

The relation of the E- and I-sounds in Oscan seems to offer a close parallel to that in Latin. I.-Eur. *ĕ* is in the Oscan alphabet e, e. g. edum (Lat. *ĕdere, esse* 'to eat'), estud (Lat. *esto*); *ī* is i, e. g. bivus (Lat. *vīvi*, Nom. Pl.). For *ē* and *ĭ* they have the same sign (except that for *ē* it is often written double to indicate length), a modification of this last, which we conventionally write í, e. g. fíísnam, a temple, Acc. Sg. (cf. Lat. *fēstus*), píd (Lat. *quĭd*). In Greek characters the three signs are ε, ι, ει; in Latin characters e, i, í. Everything points to their e having been, like Latin *ĕ*, an open E-sound, their i the close I-sound of Latin *ī*, while like the Romance languages they have merged close *e* and open *i* in one sound í. Whether the iu of Oscan últiumam (Lat. *ultimam*) indicates the Latin *ü*-sound is, with the scarcity of material at our disposal, uncertain (see ch. iv. § 23).

In rustic Latin, as we saw (§ 10), *ĭ* before a vowel was replaced by *e*, e. g. *mateola* for *matiola, while in the ordinary language accented *ĭ* before a vowel, e. g. *dies*, seems to have had the quality of long *i*. It had possibly the same quality in words like *audit*, where the *i*, originally long (e. g. *audīt*, Plaut.), has been shortened owing to the difficulty felt by the Romans in pronouncing a long vowel before final *t* (see ch. iii. § 49). Rustic Latin ē for ī in *speca*, &c., is probably a development of the old diphthong *ei*. Similarly ĕ, the old vowel of the open unaccented syllable, e.g. O. Lat. *ăbĕgit* for *ăbĭgit*, was retained in rustic Latin.

§ 15. Descriptions of the I-sound by Latin phoneticians. The phoneticians describe only the ī-sound. Terent. Maur. (329. 119 K.) :—

 i porrigit ictum genuinos prope ad ipsos,
  minimumque renidet supero tenus labello ;

Mar. Victor. (33. 2 K.) : i semicluso ore impressaque sensim lingua dentibus vocem dabit ; Mart. Cap. (iii. 261) : I spiritus (facit) prope dentibus pressis.

§ 16. by Grammarians. The *ŭ*-sound attracted a good deal of attention from Latin grammarians, and had the honour of being noticed by various rulers of the Roman Empire. Julius Caesar effected the adoption of the spelling *optimus maximus*, and the like, on State inscriptions ; his successor Augustus, we are told, reverted in these forms to the old spelling with *u* ; the Emperor Claudius took a course different from both of his illustrious predecessors, and tried to introduce into the Latin alphabet a new letter to express this particular sound. The statements of the Latin grammarians about the various sounds of Latin *i* are not always perfectly clear, and must be examined in detail. Quintilian (middle of first cent. A. D.), speaking of the letters wanting to the Latin alphabet says (i. 4. 8) that some special sign is required for the sound between *i* and *u* in words like *optimus*, and similarly for the sound between *e* and *i* in words like *hĕre* (older *hĕri*), *sĭbi*, *quăsi* (older *sĭbe*, *quăse*) [cf. *nise*, *ŭbe* in Virgil MSS., Ribbeck, *Index*, pp. 436, 451, *nise* in Lex Rubria of 49 B.C. (*C.I.L.* i. 205), and (with *ube*, *sebe*, &c.) on late inscrr. (see Georges). In the Appendix Probi (199. 16 K.) we have : nescio ubi non 'nesciocube'] : medius est quidam u et i litterae sonus ; non enim 'optumum' dicimus aut 'optimum¹,' et in 'here' neque e plane neque i auditur. In another passage he tells us that the change in spelling, *optimus*, &c., from *optumus*, &c., was made by the influence of Julius Caesar, a statement repeated by Velius Longus in the passage quoted below, and first uttered, according to Cornutus (ap. Cassiodor. 150. 11 K.) by Varro : Quint. i. 7. 21 : iam 'optimus maximus,' ut mediam i litteram, quae veteribus u fuerat, acciperent, Gai primum Caesaris inscriptione traditur factum. ' here ' nunc e littera terminamus ; at veterum comicorum adhuc libris invenio 'heri ad me uenit,' quod idem in epistulis Augusti, quas sua manu scripsit, aut emendavit, deprehenditur . . . 'sibe' et 'quase' scriptum in multorum libris est, sed an hoc voluerint auctores nescio ; T. Livium ita his usum ex Pediano comperi, qui et ipse eum sequebatur ; haec nos i littera finimus. This example, *here* and *heri*, has given rise to some doubt ; for we are accustomed to regard *hĕrĕ* and *herī* as differing in quantity, like *rure* and *ruri*, *Tibure* and *Tiburi* (the -*e* being the Cons.-stem Locative suffix -ĭ, the -ī being the I-stem Abl. suffix -īd,

---

¹ *V. l.* non enim sic 'optumum' dicimus ut 'optimum.' Perhaps, non enim sincere . . . aut. The reading of one MS., *opimum* for *optimum*, is certainly wrong. Cf. Quint. i. 7. 21, 22.

ch. iv). We have *herĕ*, for example, in Martial i. 44 est positum nobis nil here praeter aprum, but *herī* in Terence, Eun. 169 herī minas pro ambóbus uigintí dedi, often shortened by the peculiar metrical law of the comedians by which *ávē* was scanned as *ávĕ*, *cávē* as *cavĕ*, &c. (see ch. iii), as in the line, *Hec.* 329 herï némo uoluit Sóstratam íntro admíttere. Some have been led by this into the mistaken idea that what Quintilian is referring to, is that interchange of *ē* and *ī*, which we see on old inscriptions in rendering the diphthong *ei*, e. g. *ploirume* for *ploirumei*, later *plurimi*, on an epitaph of one of the Scipios (*C. I. L.* i. 32). But, as we shall see from the passages quoted from other grammarians, the phrase 'a sound between *e* and *i*' is the designation for Latin *ĭ* in such a word as *hominem*; and we may be sure that in Quintilian's time the word *heri*, as well as *here*, would invariably have in the utterance of everyday speech a short final syllable. He tells us expressly of the word *ave* (*have*) that, although it ought by right to have a long final vowel, being an Imperative of a verb of the second conjugation, like *splendē*, *audē*, it was never, except by precisians, pronounced otherwise than *havĕ* (i. 6. 21). (A fuller account of this shortening is given in ch. iii. § 40.) Velius Longus, who like Quintilian belonged to the first cent. A.D., talks of the 'exilis sonus' of the Latin vowel *ī* and, in some cases, of *ĭ*, e.g. in 3 Sg. Pres. Ind. of verbs of the fourth conjugation, *audīt*, &c. (In Plautus and the oldest literature this *i* is long. *audīt*, the shortening having been effected by the influence of the final *t*, just as with us the vowel of 'note' is shorter than the vowel of 'node.' See ch. iii. § 49.) Ordinary *ĭ*, as in 3 Sg. Pres. Ind. of the third conjugation, *ponĭt*, &c., he calls the 'latus sonus,' while the *i* of *optimus* is 'pinguis.' Of this last sound he says that the spelling and pronunciation of *u* for *i* in *optimus, manibiae*, &c., was regarded in his time as old-fashioned and countrified (49 K.): i vero littera interdum exilis est, interdum pinguis, ut in eo quod est 'prodit' 'vincit' 'condit' exilius volo sonare in eo vero quod significatur prodire vincire condire usque pinguescit ut jam in ambiguitatem cadat utrum per i quaedam debeant dici an per u ut est 'optumus maxumus.' in quibus adnotandum antiquum sermonem plenioris soni fuisse et, ut ait Cicero, rusticanum, atque illis fere placuisse per u talia scribere et enuntiare. erravere autem grammatici qui putaverunt superlativa per u enuntiari. ut enim concedamus illis in 'optimo,' in 'maximo,' in 'pulcherrimo,' in 'justissimo,' quid facient in his nominibus, in quibus aeque manet eadem quaestio superlatione sublata, 'manubiae' an 'manibiae,' 'libido,' an 'lubido'? nos vero, postquam exilitas sermonis delectare coepit, usque i littera castigavimus illam pinguitudinem, non tamen ut plene i litteram enuntiaremus. et concedamus talia nomina per u scribere iis qui antiquorum voluntates sequuntur, ne tamen sic enuntient, quo modo scribunt; and again (67 K.): varie etiam scriptitatum est 'mancupium' 'aucupium' 'manubiae,' siquidem C. Caesar per i scripsit, ut apparet ex titulis ipsius, at Augustus per u, ut testes sunt ejus inscriptiones [1]. . . . relinquitur igitur electio, utrumne per antiquum sonum, qui est pinguissimus et u elegantior occupabat, velit quis enuntiare, an per hunc, qui jam videtur eligantior, exilius, id est per i litteram, has proferat voces; and a little further on (68. 6 K.): mihi videtur nimis rusticana enuntiatio futura, si per u extulerimus. ita tamen existimo enuntiandum, ut nec nimis i littera exilis

---

[1] But the *Comm. Lud. Saec.* has *optimus maximus*.

sit, nec, u litteram si scripseris, enuntiationis sono nimis plena. Here his account of the 'sound between *i* and *u*' is perfectly clear. *Optumus* had in old times been written and pronounced with a U-sound; but such pronunciation was old fashioned and countrified in his own time, the sound used in polite circles being something between a normal U-sound and a normal I-sound. But the beginning of the first passage, where he discusses the other two kinds of I-sound, is not so intelligible. His examples are evidently carefully chosen synonyms of the third and fourth conjugations; and one cannot but suppose that he meant to contrast the *i* of *prodit* (from *prodo*), *vincit* (from *vinco*), *condit* (from *condo*), with that of the third person singular of *prodire*, *vincire*, *condire*. Keil supplies a sentence between the words *sonare* and *in eo*, and reads : exilius volo sonare, si dico ab eo quod est prodere, vincere, condere ; in eo vero quod significat prodire, &c. He refers the 'pinguescit' to the sound of *ī*, not to the *ĭ* of *optimus*, &c., understanding Velius Longus to distinguish *ĭ* from *ī* as 'exilis sonus' and 'pinguis sonus.' These words, 'exilis,' 'latus,' 'pinguis,' unfortunately lack the precision of the terminology of modern phoneticians. They remind us of Lucilius' use of 'tenuare' and 'plenius facere' some two centuries earlier, in a passage not less obscure (9. 14 M.) : —

'pilam' qua ludimus, 'pilum'
quo pisunt, tenues, si plura haec feceris pila
quae iacimus, addes e, 'peila,' ut plenius fiat;

whereas a later grammarian, Pompeius (fifth cent. A.D.), uses 'tenuis' and 'pinguis' to distinguish vocalic from consonantal *i* and *u* (103 K.) : ecce adverte, quomodo sonat u, 'unus,' ecce u vides quam tenuiter sonat. junge illam ad aliam litteram, et vide quia non sic sonat, sed pinguius sonat, 'vulnus,' 'vanus.' numquid sic sonat 'unus' quando u sola est? non, sed tenuiter sonat. 'vanus' quando dico pinguior sonus est. numquid dicis 'u-a-nus'? ergo vides quia, si ponantur solae, tenuem sonum habent, si jungantur ad alias litteras, pingues sonant. similiter et i sic patitur. 'itur,' ecce tenuius sonat; si dicas 'Titius,' pinguius sonat, et perdit sonum suum, et accipit sibilum. (*t* palatalized.) This confusion of terms must be borne in mind in reading the passage we now quote from Consentius (fifth cent. A.D. ?), a passage interesting from its account of the Gaulish and Greek mispronunciations of Latin *i* (394. 11 K.) : iotacismum dicunt vitium quod per i litteram vel pinguius vel exilius prolatam fit. Galli pinguius hanc utuntur, ut cum dicunt 'ite,' non expresse ipsam proferentes, sed inter e et i pinguiorem sonum nescioquem ponentes. Graeci exilius hanc proferunt, adeo expressioni ejus tenui studentes, ut, si dicant 'jus,' aliquantulum dè priori littera sic proferant, ut videas disyllabum esse factum. Romanae linguae in hoc erit moderatio, ut exilis ejus sonus sit, ubi ab ea verbum incipit, ut 'ite,' aut pinguior, ubi in ea desinit verbum, ut 'habui,' 'tenui'; medium quendam sonum inter e et i habet, ubi in medio sermone est, ut 'hominem.' mihi tamen videtur, quando producta est, plenior vel acutior esse ; quando autem brevis est, medium sonum exhibere debet, sicut eadem exempla, quae posita sunt, possunt declarare. Consentius here uses 'pinguis' and 'tenuis' or 'exilis' like Pompeius, not like Velius Longus, while he distinguishes long *i* as 'plenior vel acutior,' short *i* in *hominem* as 'a sound between e and i.' What he means by saying that in *habui*, *tenui*, *i* had the 'pinguis sonus,' must be that the words were pronounced in his time 'habuyi,' 'tenuyi.' (Seelmann gives quite a different explanation.)

These three accounts of Latin ĭ, ī, taken in connexion with the evidence supplied by the Romance languages, where Latin ĭ has become a close E-sound, while Latin ī is invariably close I, give us the right to suppose that the usual Latin ĭ was different in quality from Latin ī, being an open I, like Engl. 'bit' or Germ. Kind, while ī was the ordinary close I of Italian and other languages; though they suggest the further possibility of there having been a short variety of this latter *i* in such words as the 3 Sing. Pres. Ind. Act. of the fourth conjugation, *prodit, audit, condit*, where the *i*, long in the time of Plautus, was shortened through the difficulty felt by the Romans in pronouncing a long vowel before final -*t*. Seelmann is of opinion that this short variety of close *i* came gradually to replace open ĭ in the language of the educated classes at Rome in the first centuries of the Empire (postquam exilitas sermonis delectare coepit, Vel. Long.), and so explains the strange statement of the fourth century commentators on Donatus, quoted in our discussion of the sound of *e* (§ 7), that ĭ, ī, with ŭ, ū, were not distinguished like ĕ, ē, ŏ, ō; though Consentius a century later enlarges on this very distinction in the case of *i*. It is more probable that these commentators, though they refer to some Latin instances (*mĕta, dēmens, ĕquus*), are really quoting remarks of Greek phoneticians on the sounds of Greek vowels, designed to explain the presence of separate signs for long and short *e* and *o* in the Greek alphabet (ε, η, ο, ω); and, if this be so, it cannot but suggest the alarming suspicion that their phrase, 'ĕ is like the diphthong, ē like *i*,' may really mean that Greek ε had the sound of αι (as was the case in Attic Greek by the second cent. A.D.), η of ι (the itacism of modern Greek. Blass ascribes the change of η to ι to the fifth cent. A.D.).

To pass to the ü-sound of *optimus*, which in the Romance languages is merged in ordinary Latin ĭ. The statements of the grammarians we have quoted, particularly that of Velius Longus (49 K.), show us clearly that in the first century A.D. the vowel had a sound between *u* and *i*, having had at an earlier period a U-sound. Still earlier it was an *o* (see ch. iii. § 18), and we may regard it as the sound which ŭ (whether originally *o* or *u* or *a*, &c.) took in open syllables after the accent, when influenced by the presence of a labial; whereas accented ŭ remained, e.g. *cŭbo*. The passage which we now quote from Velius Longus extends the same sound to ĭ in accented syllables influenced by the labial sibilant *v*, as in *vir, virtus* (75 K.): 'aurifex' melius per i sonat quam per u. at 'aucupare' [et aucupium] mihi rursus melius videtur sonare per u quam per i; et idem tamen 'aucipis' malo quam 'aucupis,' quia scio sermonem et decori servire et aurium voluptati. unde fit ut saepe aliud scribamus, aliud enuntiemus, sicut supra locutus sum de 'viro' et 'virtute,' ubi i scribitur et paene u enuntiatur. unde Ti. Claudius novam quandam litteram excogitavit similem ei notae quam pro adspiratione Graeci ponunt, per quam scriberentur eae voces, quae neque secundum exilitatem i litterae, neque secundum pinguitudinem u literae sonarent, ut in 'viro' et 'virtute,' neque rursus secundum latum litterae sonum enuntiaretur, ut in eo quod est legere, scribere. In the last words he seems to refer to ĭ of the third conjugation, *legit, legimus, legitis*, &c., the sound of which he calls 'latus' as opposed to the 'exilis sonus' of ī, and the 'pinguis sonus' of *i/u*; and this confirms our view that in the passage first quoted from him, the same threefold distinction was

§ 17.] PRONUNCIATION. VOWELS. 29

explained between *prodit* of third conj. with 'latus sonus,' *prodit* of fourth conj. with 'exilis sonus,' and *optimus* with 'pinguis sonus.' There are a large number of references by other grammarians to this *i/u* sound (see Seelmann, p. 205). Of these we need only quote two; one from Marius Victorinus (fourth cent.), who points out that this vowel is really the Greek *v* (Latin *y*) (see § 28); and one from Priscian, who, like Velius Longus, gives this sound of Greek *v* to accented *ĭ* influenced by a preceding *v*. Mar. Victor. 19. 22 K. sunt qui inter u quoque et i litteras supputant deesse nobis vocem, sed pinguius quam i, exilius quam u. sed et pace eorum dixerim, non vident y litteram desiderari : sic enim ' gylam,' ' myserum,' ' Syllam ' (MSS. syllabam), ' proxymum ' dicebant antiqui. sed nunc consuetudo paucorum hominum ita loquentium evanuit. ideoque voces istas per u ⟨vel per i⟩ scribite. The spelling *myserum*, which is found on some inscriptions, may be explained by Greek μυσαρός, just as *silva* was spelt *sylva* through a fanciful connexion with ὕλη, and so *Sylla* for *Syrŭla* (cf. App. Probi 197. 26 crista non ' crysta'); but it is difficult to explain *gyla* (for *gŭla*) in the same way. All the Romance languages point to *gŭla* as the Vulgar Latin form (Ital. Span. gola, Fr. gueule). The ' antiqui' alluded to are merely former grammarians, whose innovation in spelling met with little favour, to judge from the instances found on inscriptions (Schuchardt, *Vok.* ii. pp. 197 sqq., 218 sqq.). Priscian i. 6 i et u vocales, quando mediae sunt, alternos inter se sonos videntur confundere, teste Donato, ut ' vir,' ' optimus,' ' quis' ; et i quidem quando post consonantem loco digamma functam Aeolici ponitur brevis, sequente d vel m vel r vel t vel x, sonum y Graecae videtur habere, ut ' video,' ' vim,' ' virtus,' ' vitium,' ' vix.' Schuchardt, *Vok.* ii. p. 221, gives a few examples of *vy-* for *vi-* in late inscriptions ; and in the Appendix Probi (198. 20 K.) we have : vir non ' vyr,' virgo non ' vyrgo,'. virga non ' vyrga,' so that the existence of this tendency to pronounce accented *i* as *ü* after *v* can hardly be doubted. (The Latin name for *y*, Greek *v*, was ' ui.' See below.) But Greek *v* does not represent Latin *i* in this position on Greek inscriptions. Other examples of accented *i/u* are *simus*, written for *sŭmus* by some purists of the Augustan age (Mar. Victor. 9. 5 K. Messala, Brutus, Agrippa pro sumus ' simus' scripserunt), and by Augustus himself (Suet. *Aug.* 87) (cf. *C. I. L.* ix. 3473. 14) ; *lŭbet* and *lĭbet* ; *clupeus* and *clipeus* (see Georges, *Lex. Wortf.* s. vv.) ; though two of these, *simus* and *lĭbet*, might be explained as enclitic words and so wanting the accent, e. g. *amatisumus, lubet-ire, quódlubet*, &c. (see iii. 12). (See also Georges, *Lex. Wortf.* s. vv. *Bruttii, cliens* (earlier *cluens*), *linter, scrūpulus*. The Romance forms point to both *sŭmus* (e. g. Fr. sommes) and *sĭmus* (e. g. Ital. siamo from *semo, O. Roum. semo). *Supparum*, with byform *siparum* (see Georges s. v.) seems to be an Oscan word (Varro, *L. L.* v. 131), and the mispronunciations ' imbilicus' (Prob. App. 198. 4 K. ; cf. Ir. imbliu), ' scoriscus' (ib. 198. 32 K.), ' arispex' (Vel. Long. 73. 9 K.) have been variously explained.) (On the *ü*-sound, see Parodi in *Studi Italiani*, i. 385.)

§ 17. Interchange of i and e. The misspellings on inscriptions testify abundantly to the close relation between *ĭ* and *e* (close *e*), e. g. *karessemo merentessemo* (*C. I. L.* ii. 2997) (see Schuchardt, *Vok.* ii. pp. 1-67) ; but *ĭ* is rarely written *e* except in Gaul and Britain, where *ō* too appears as *u*. In rustic Latin indeed such words as *spīca* were pronounced *spēca* (Varro, *R. R.* i. 48. 2) ; but it is not clear whether this was not confined to words which originally had the diphthong *ei* (cf. *vella*, Varro, *R. R.* i. 2 14). If so, the *e* is that dialectal *e* for

I.-Eur. *ei* which is found in the Umbrian language, e.g. prevo- (Lat. *prīvus*, *prīvatus*; Osc. *preivato-*), and in various parts of Italy. *Dēmidius* for *dīmidius* (App. Prob. 198. 27 K.) is due to confusion of *dē* with *dĭ-* (*dis*) [cf. *demedius*, *C. I. L.* vii. 140; x. 3428, and in MSS. (see Schuchardt, *Vok.* ii. 71). Fr. demi] ; *Serena* for *Sirēna* (App. Prob. 199. 10) to confusion with *sĕrēnus* (cf. Fr. serin, canary ?). On *dēlīrus* and *dēlērus*, see ch. iii. The vowel of the open unaccented syllable was in Old Latin *ĕ*, not *ĭ* (see iii. 18; ; and this ancient sound remained in Rustic Latin. So that *ĕ* for *ĭ* of *hŏmĭnem*, &c., as well as *ē* for *ī* of *spīca*, &c., and *ĕ* for *ĭ* in hiatus of *via*, &c., characterized the pronunciation of the country districts. Cicero often alludes to the 'rustic' substitution of the *e-* for the *i*-sound in the utterance of his friend L. Aurelius Cotta, the author of the famous jury-law, the Lex Aurelia Judiciaria of 70 B.C. : quare Cotta noster, cujus tu illa lata, Sulpici, nonnunquam imitaris, ut iota litteram tollas et *e* plenissimum dicas, non mihi oratores antiquos, sed messores videtur imitari (*de Orat.* iii. 12. 46. Cf. iii. 11. 42 ; *Brut.* xxxvi. 137 ; lxxiv. 259 ; and Quintilian xi. 3. 10).

The frequent occurrence on Greek inscriptions of ε for Lat. *ĭ* (e.g. Τεβεριος, λεντιον) may point to Greek ε having had (unlike Latin *ĕ*) the close E-sound (see Blass, *Aussprache des Griechischen²*, p. 23). But it may often be merely a retention of the early Latin spelling, of the form in which the word was first borrowed by the Greeks. This ε for *ĭ* is the usual spelling in κομετιον at all periods, while Καικελιος is replaced by Καικιλιος after 50 B.C., Καπετωλιον by Καπιτωλιον in the first cent. A.D.; Λεπεδος is the form of the Republican, Λεπιδος of the Imperial Age. (For other examples see Eckinger, p. 29 sqq., and for examples of *ĭ e* in Latin, Georges, *Lex. Wortf.* s.vv. *gillo, hibiscum, minus, minister, sinus, sine, sinapi, vindico, comissor, solidus*. On the late Lat. *emitari*, see Schuch. *Vok.* ii. 20, and cf. Prob. App. 199. 2, and 198. 22 K.)

§ 18. **i in hiatus.** The Romance forms of the word for day (Ital. dì, Sard. die, Span. dia, O. Fr. di) have all *i*, which is the normal representative of Latin *ī*; and on inscriptions we have sometimes the lengthened form of the letter, which usually denotes long *i*, e.g. DIES (*C. I. L.* vi. 7527) ; DIE (10239, also PRIVSQVAM). (On PIVS see § 143.)

§ 19. **Anomalies in Romance.** Ital. freddo, Fr. froid, from Lat. *frīgĭdus*, point to *friddus*, from *frig(i)dus* (cf. App. Probi 198. 3 K. frigida non frigda), where the *ĭ* has been referred to the analogy of *rīgidus* (but see § 127) ; *glērem* replaces *glīrem* in Celtic countries (Fr. loir, O. Prov. gles), but not elsewhere (Ital. ghiro) ; Vulg. Lat. *sŭbilo*, *sŭfilo*, beside *sībilo*, *sīfilo*, to whistle (e.g. Ital. sufilare, subillare, sibilare, O. Fr. subler, siffler), have been explained by reference to *sufflare*, or to *sŭbulo*, the Etruscan word for a fluteplayer ; Greek *ī* in χρῖσμα is treated like Latin *ĭ* in Fr. chrême, Ital. cresma.

§ 20. **O.** Having discovered that Latin *ĕ* is open E, Latin *ē* close E, we are almost entitled to infer that Latin *ŏ* will be open O, Latin *ō* close O. For each language has what phoneticians call a 'basis of articulation,' according to which all its sounds are regulated ; and if one set of sounds is treated in a particular way, any set of corresponding sounds is likely to receive a similar treatment. The Teutonic languages, for example, changed the I.-Eur. Aspirate Mediae to voiced Spirants (*dh* to *ð*, the sound of our *th* in 'this,' &c.). They correspondingly moved the Tenues to unvoiced Spirants (*t* to *th* of 'thin,' &c.); and similarly the Mediae to Tenues (*d* to *t*, &c.), a movement or gradation of sounds first discovered by Grimm, and known as 'Grimm's Law.' From detecting one sound in a language, we are thus often able to guess what other sounds will be; and we could in the absence of other evidence infer the quality of the O-sounds in Latin from that of the E-sounds. Evidence, however, is not wanting. The Romance languages, for example, show Latin *ŏ* as open O, Latin *ō* (with which Latin *ŭ* is merged) as close O. This open O is in many languages developed in open syllables to *uo* (e. g. Ital. ruota, from Lat. *rŏta*), as open E to *ie* (§ 6), while in Spanish *uo* has further developed to *ue* (e. g. ruede), a change that reminds us of the substitution of *ve-* for *vo-* in Latin words like *verto*, older *vorto*. In Italian we have molle (with open O) for Latin *mŏllis*, sole (with close O) for Latin *sōl, sōlem*, the open O having the O-sound of German voll, Stock, the close that of German so, Fr. chaud. Our 'short *o*' in 'stock,' 'folly,' is a 'lower' sound, formed with the tongue lower in the mouth, than the open O of German (our O-sound in 'oar' is nearer this), while our 'long *o*' in 'so' is a diphthong.

In unaccented syllables in Latin open O, before a Labial or *l*, seems, like open E before other consonants, to have become close, and then to have passed into a U-sound, as *e* into an I-sound, e. g. *sĕdŭlō* from *sē dŏlō, consŭlo* (Early Lat. *cosol-*). In Italian, *ŏ*, like *ĕ*, takes the close sound in syllables after the accent. This *u*, as we saw (§ 14), might sink to *ü*, e. g. *consilium*; but as a rule *o* is retained in the spelling of compounds more persistently than *e*, e.g. *accŏlo, agrĭcŏla* (*agricula*, Schuch. ii. 133). Even when accented, *ŏ* seems to have had the close sound before certain groups of consonants, such as *l* with another consonant (not *ll*), *m* or *n* with another consonant, *rn*, &c., to judge from such varieties of spelling as Old Latin *Culcides* for *Colchides* (Quint. i. 4. 16), Old Latin and Rustic Latin *frundes* for *frondes*, Vulg. Lat. *turnus* for *tornus*; and this is confirmed by the misspellings on plebeian inscriptions, and the like (collected by Schuchardt, *Vok.* ii. pp. 114,

&c.). In Celtic countries *u* is often found on Latin inscriptions instead of *ō*, e.g. *nepus* (for *nĕpōs*). (*C.I.L.* xii. 5336.)

The O-sounds of the Oscan language offer the same analogy to the Latin, as the E-sounds (§ 6). The Oscan alphabet, being borrowed from the Etruscan, had originally no sign for *o*, but only the sign for *u*. This *u*-sign was used for *ō* as well as for *u*, while for *ŏ* a modification of the sign was used, conventionally written by us ú. In Latin characters *u* expresses Oscan u, and *o* Oscan ú, though in the final syllable before a labial *u* sometimes takes its place [e.g. Osc. estud, in Latin writing *estud* (Lat. *estō*, older *estōd*), Osc. púd, in Latin writing *pod* (Lat. *quŏd*), Osc. deíkum, in Latin writing *deicum* (Lat. *dīcere*, older *deicere*), and *dolom, dolum* (Lat. *dŏlum*)]. In Greek characters Oscan u is ου, and sometimes o, Oscan ú is o. This Oscan ú, as was noticed before (§ 1), represents I.-Eur. final Ā of Nom. Sg. of Ā-stems and Acc. Pl. Neut. of O-stems, and can hardly have been anything but some form of open O.

21. Descriptions of the O-sound by Latin phoneticians. Terentianus Maurus distinguishes short from long O (vi. 329. 130-134 K.) :—

> igitur sonitum reddere cum voles minori,
> retrorsus adactam modice teneto linguam,
> rictu neque magno, sat erit patere labra.
> at longior alto tragicum sub oris antro
> molita rotundis acuit sonum labellis.

This 'tragic tone in the mouth-cavern' of *ō* is perhaps more applicable to Greek ω, which was open O (Blass, *Aussprache des Griechischen*[2], p. 26), than Latin *ō*, and the whole description is possibly, as we have seen, borrowed from Greek writers on Phonetics. Marius Victorinus (vi. 33. 3-8 K.) summarizes the older account: o, ut e, geminum vocis sonum pro condicione temporis promit ... igitur qui correptum enuntiat, nec magno hiatu labra reserabit, et retrorsum actam linguam tenebit. longum autem productis labris, rictu tereti, lingua antro oris pendula sonum tragicum dabit. The commentators on Donatus (Servius, *in Don.* p. 421. 17-19 K.) say the same: o productum quando est, ore sublato vox sonat, ut 'Roma'; quando correptum, de labris vox exprimitur, ut 'rosa'; Sergius, *in Don.* p. 520. 30-31 o quando longa est, intra palatum sonat; 'Roma,' 'orator'; quando brevis est, primis labris exprimitur: 'opus,' 'rosa.' Martianus Capella (iii. 261) says merely: O rotundi oris spiritu comparatur.

§ 22. Close for open o in accented syllables before certain consonant-groups. (See Schuchardt, *Vok.* ii. p. 114 sqq.) Before *l* and another consonant *ŏ* became *u* in classical Latin, e.g. *consulto* (early *consolto*, *C.I.L.* i. 548, latter part of second century B.C.); *pulcer* (but *Polc*[*er*], *C.I.L.* i. 552 of 131 B.C., cf. Prisc. i. 27. 12 H.); *culpa* (Old Lat. *colpa* Prisc. l.c.). Before *m* or *n* when these nasals are followed by a consonant we see the same tendency.

The classical spelling is *u* in *umbo, lumbus, unguis, uncus* (see ch. iv. § 20). Before *nd* in Vulg. Lat. *u* replaced classical *o* (K. Z. xxx. 336), as is shown by the Romance forms (e.g. Ital. risponde, with close *o*, Sard. respundit); and in Italian we have close *o* in ponte, fronte, fonte, which corresponds with Priscian's remark that *funtes, frundes,* &c., were the older forms retained in Rustic Latin. (Prisc. i. 26. 35 H. multa praeterea vetustissimi etiam in principalibus mutabant syllabis; ' gungrum' pro gongrum, 'cunchin' pro conchin, ' huminem' pro hominem proferentes, 'funtes' pro fontes, unde Lucretius in libro . tertio :—

atque ea nimirum quaecumque Acherunte profundo,

. . . quae tamen a junioribus repudiata sunt quasi rustico more dicta. Cf. Velius Longus p. 49. 15 K. unde in multis etiam nominibus variae sunt scripturae, ut fontes funtes, frondes frundes; and Charis. p. 130. 29 K.; sic ab Ennio est declinatum annalium libro vii; russescunt frundes, non frondes.) *Rumpia* is the Latin form of ῥομφαία, the long two-edged sword of the Thracians, quoted from Ennius by Gell. x. 25. 4, and read in the MSS. of Livy xxxi. 39. 11. Before *rn* a close sound of *ŏ*, and not the long vowel, is perhaps indicated by the apex on the *o* of *ornare* in some inscriptions (e.g. C. I. L. x. 6104. 1839. 6009) (a fuller discussion of this point in § 145). Greek κόθορνος is *cothurnus*; Greek τόρνος was in Vulgar Latin *turnus* (so spelt in the MSS. of Symmachus, *Epp.* v. 10), e.g. Span. tornar, Ital. torno (with close *o*). The vowel of *tornus* has been referred to the close sound of Greek *o* (while ω had the open sound) (K. Z. xxx. 336), and the *u* of *amurca* (Greek ἀμόργη), and other Greek loanwords in Latin (cf. App. Probi 198. 22 botruus not 'butro.' Cf. *Butrio, C. I. L.* ii. 668 and Sard. budrone), might be explained in the same way. But it is unlikely that the nuances of Greek vowels would be retained in words naturalized in Latin, and the tendency to give *ŏ* the close sound before these consonant-groups is visible in genuine Latin words. Perhaps *bb* is another group of the kind. *Obba* was in the time of Nonius (fourth cent. A. D.) *ubba* (Non. 146 M. obba, poculi genus, quod nunc ubba dicitur).

In Greek Inscriptions we have Μουντανος for Lat. *Montānus* (C. I. A. iii. 1138, of 174–8 A.D.; but usually Μονταvos), Βουλκαχιος, Κουρβουλων (and Κορβ-), Πουστουμιος (see Eckinger, p. 54). For other examples of *o-u* before consonant-groups in the accented syllable, see Georges, *Lex. Wortf.* s. vv. *conchis, dupundius, formo(n)sus, Corsi, Volscus, proboscis, colostra, bulbus, furnus, fornix, fornax, Fulvius, triumphus, cochlea;* and in the unaccented syllable, s. vv. *volsella, to(n)sillae, promunturium;* also Brambach, *Hülfsb.* s. vv. *furvus, formica.* For classical *-uv-* we have O. Lat. *-ov-* in *flovius, elovies* (see Georges s.vv.). *Curium* (for *corium*) on the Edict of Diocletian viii. 6 is a strange variety. The Appendix Probi censures *furmica* (197. 27 K.). *formunsus* (198. 9´, *detundo* (199. 1), *purpureticum marmur* (197. 19), as well as *torma* for *turma* (198. 4 and 28). We have *tundunt* on two rustic Calendars (C.I.L. i². p. 280) for class. *tondent.* Cf. Sard. tundere).

§ 23. u for unaccented ŏ. The mispronunciation *pulenta* for *pŏlenta* (Charis. 96. 13 K.; Caper 106. 4 K.) shows this change in the pretonic syllable. Cf. *lulligo* for *lollīgo* (Georges s.v), &c. In the post-tonic syllable the change to *u* is normal; see ch. iii. § 18.

§ 24. u for ō. These two sounds are, as was mentioned above, merged in the Romance languages. In Late Latin inscriptions the expression of *ō* by *u* is very common, e. g. *patrunus* for *patrōnus*. (Cf. App. Probi 197. 28 sobrius non 'suber.') Schuchardt, *Vok.* ii. p. 91 sqq., has collected a large number of instances from Inscriptions and MSS. (cf. *facitud, C. I. L.* i. 813). Forms like *pūmĭlio, pōmĭlio* belong to a somewhat different category; for the original sound here was *ou* (cf. *pater poumilionom* on an old Praenestine cista, *Eph. Epigr.* i. 20), and *ō* was a development of *ou*, in the same way that *ē* was of *ei* (see iv. 32). The same *ō* for *ou* seems to appear in the classical forms *rōbustus, rōbīgo,* for which we have occasional byforms *rubustus, rubigo* (see Georges s. v., and cf. Probi Append. 199. 5 K. robigo non rubigo). (This use of *ō* and *ū* for earlier *ou* is discussed in ch. iv. § 41.) (Cf. nongentos non 'nungentos,' Bede 281. 26 K.)

§ 25. **Other changes of ŏ and ō.** *Curtina*, a mispronunciation of *cortīna* (*Dub. Nom.* 575. 7 K.), may follow the analogy of *curtus*; *faeneris*, &c., for *faenŏris,* &c. (Vel. Long. 72 and 73 K.) are influenced by *gĕnĕris* and the like; *praestōlor* and *praestūlor* (Curt. Valerian. ap. Cassiodor. 157. 23 K.; Alcuin 306. 12 K.; Bede 286. 19 K.) depend on *praestō* and *praestū*; *ōstium* was in Vulg. Lat. *ūstium* (*ustei* Gen. is found in Marc. Emp. xxviii. 37) (Ital. uscio, O. Span. uzo, Fr. huis); *ōvum*, an egg, was *ŏvum (Ital. uovo, Span. huevo, O. Fr. uef); *cŏrallium* and *cūralium* are two different forms (Greek κοράλλιον and κουράλιον); and the same must be said of *ŏpilio* and *ūpilio*. (The note of Servius on Ecl. x. 19 venit et upilio, &c., implies these quantities: propter metrum ait 'upilio,'— nam opilio dicimus—et graeco usus est schemate, sicut illi dicunt οὔνομα pro eo quod est ὄνομα, et οὔρη pro eo quod est ὄρη. Cf. Caper 112 K. upilio, nunc opilio.)

§ 26. **U, Y.** The Latin grammarians do not speak so much about the difference of short and long *u* as they do about *ĭ* and *ī*, perhaps because the first distinction did not so much appeal to the ear. But in Romance *ŭ* and *ū* take quite different paths, *ŭ* being merged in *ō*, and *ū* preserved, as we found *ĭ* merged in *ē*, and *ī* preserved. Short *ŭ* and *ō* of Latin are distinguished not only in Sardinian (the only Romance language which distinguishes Latin *ĭ* and *ē*), but also in Roumanian and in the Latin element of the Albanian language, though in the two latter *ŭ* may have first become close *o*, and changed back again to *u*. (*A. L. L.* vii. 61.) They are distinguished also in Latin loanwords in Welsh.

Latin *ū* is little altered in Romance, except that in some countries it has taken a *ü*-sound, in France (lune, for Latin *lūna*), a Celtic country, and, perhaps by Greek influence, through the south-east coast of Italy. Italian *ū*, which seems to retain the sound of Latin *ū*, as Italian *ī* of Latin *ī*, has the close U-sound of Fr. sou, Germ. gut, du, while our 'two' is a diphthong ending with a *w*-sound. Our short *u*, e. g. 'full,' 'put,' is open U, the German *ŭ* of und, Lust, &c. being, according to Sweet (*Handb.* p. 28), rather closer than the English. The 'obscure vowel' of 'but,' which is sometimes carelessly spoken of as 'short u' is an entirely different vowel, not to be called a U-sound at all. In Welsh and Breton some Latin loanwords show $\bar{\imath}$ for $\bar{u}$, e.g. Bret. dīr (Lat. dŭrus), but this is probably due to the Celtic tendency to turn u-sounds into $\ddot{u}$-sounds (see however *K. Z.* xxix. 46). Vulg. Lat. *jinipirus* (e.g. Ital. ginepro) for *jŭnĭpĕrus* (Probi Append. 199. 8 K.) shows the same influence of the palatal spirant *j* (our *y*) as Vulg. Lat. *Jenuarius* for *Jānuarius* (§ 1). But there is little reason to believe that Latin $\bar{u}$ had naturally a $\ddot{u}$-sound. Plautus, *Men.* 654, compares the reiterated *tu tu* 'you! you!' to the hooting of an owl:—

Matrona. Tu tu istic inquam. *Peniculus.* Vin adferri noctuam,
    Quae 'tu tu' usque dicat tibi? Nam nos iam defessi sumus.

This seems to point to the *oo*-sound of our 'too-whoo,' though such comparisons should never have too much stress laid on them. The palatalization of *c* before $\bar{u}$ is hardly known in the Romance languages (*K. Z.* xxix. 46). The connexion between $\ddot{u}$ and close O is seen in the numerous misspellings of *o* for $\ddot{u}$ in plebeian inscriptions (Schuchardt, *Vok.* ii. 149, &c.). In unaccented syllables, as we have seen (§ 14), $\ddot{u}$ tended to the $\ddot{u}$-sound of *optŭmus, optĭmus*, which was written *u* to the time of Julius Caesar, afterwards *i*, and which in the Romance languages is not distinguished from *i*. This was the sound of Greek *υ*, which in older Latin was treated like Latin *u*, but afterwards was with more exactness spelt (and pronounced) with the Greek letter Υ (*y*); though in ordinary usage we often find it, like the $\ddot{u}$-sound of *optimus*, represented by *i*. In Oscan $\ddot{u}$ took after certain letters a *yu*-sound, e.g. tiurrí (Lat. *turrim*), Diumpaís (Lat. *lumpis, lymphis*), as in the Boeotian dialect τύχη was τιούχα, or in English 'tune' is pronounced 'tyūn;' but there is no trace of this sound in Latin[1] (see ch. iv. § 7).

§ 27. Descriptions of the U-sound by Latin phoneticians. Ter. Maur. vi. 329. 142-145 K. :—

    hanc edere vocem quotiens paramus ore
    nitamur ut u dicere, sic citetur ortus:
    productius autem coeuntibus labellis
    natura soni pressior altius meabit.

---

[1] The confusion of Carthaginian miuulec (?) with Lat. *mures* in Plaut. *Poen.* 1009 is no evidence.

Mar. Vict. vi. 33. 8–9 K. u litteram quotiens enuntiamus productis et coeuntibus labris efferemus. Martianus Capella iii. 261 U ore constricto labrisque prominulis exhibetur.

§ 28. **Greek v in Latin.** Ter. Scaurus says (vii. 25. 13 K.) y litteram supervacuam latino sermoni putaverunt, quoniam pro illa u cederet. sed cum quaedam in nostrum sermonem graeca nomina admissa sint, in quibus evidenter sonus hujus litterae exprimitur, ut 'hyperbaton' et 'hymnus' et 'hyacinthus' et similia, in eisdem hac littera necessario utimur. Y, as a Greek letter, was not allowed in Roman words (see ch. i.), for the custom of writing *gyla*, &c., never gained acceptance (Caper vii. 105. 17 K. y litteram nulla vox nostra adsciscit. ideo insultabis 'gylam' dicentibus. Cf. Bede vii. 273. 33 K.; Ter. Scaur. vii. 22–23 K.; Vel. Longus vii. 81. 5–8 K.; Mar. Victorin. vi. 33. 11 K.), unless the word was mistaken for a Greek one, e. g. *sylva* referred to Greek ὕλη, *lympha* to Greek νύμφη[1] (Cf. crista non 'crysta, App. Probi 197. 26 K.). The new letter invented by the Emperor Claudius to express the ü-sound of *optŭmus, optimus* is used for Greek v in words like *Nymphius, Bathyllus* in the Fasti Antiates written in the reign of Claudius (*C. I. L.* i². p. 247). But before the use of the Greek letter Υ, the Greek vowel was written *u* (Cassiod. 153. 11 K. Y littera antiqui non semper usi sunt, sed aliquando loco illius u ponebant : itaque in illorum quidem libris hanc scripturam observandam censeo, ' Suriam' ' Suracusas' ' sumbola ' ' sucophantas,' at in nostris corrumpi non debet ; cf. ibid. 160. 16 K.) ; and the MSS. of Plautus indicate such spellings as *Hĭlŭria* for *Illўria*, &c. *Burrus* and *Bruges* were the forms used by Ennius for *Pyrrhus* and *Phrўges* (Cicero, *Orator* xlviii. 160 ipsius antiqui declarant libri). That it was also pronounced like ordinary Latin *u* we see from the Romance forms of these earlier Greek loan-words which make no distinction (e. g. Lat. *tumba* for Greek τύμβος, is in Ital. tomba, in Sard. tumba, in Fr. tombe), not to speak of Plautus' pun on *Lўdus* and *lūdus* (*Bacch.* 129), and on *chrŷsălus* and *crŭcĭsălus* (ib. 362). After the *u*-sound of *optumus, optimus* came to be spelt with· *i*, the same letter was in ordinary usage employed for Greek v, e. g. *cignus* (Greek κύκνος), in Ital. cecero, being pronounced probably in the same way as the *i* of *optimus*, which in Romance is not distinguishable from ordinary *i*. *Tondrus* for *Tyndareus* on an old Praenestine cista (*C. I. L.* xiv. 4109) is perhaps to be explained by the *u*-sound of *o* before *nd* (ch. iv. § 20). Greek κυ is often spelt *qui*, e. g. Vulg. *quiatus* for *cyathus* (see Schuch. *Vok.* ii. p. 273 sqq. for examples), as Latin *qui* is often expressed by Greek κυ ; e. g. 'Ακυλας for *Ăquĭla*, Κυρεινος and Κυρινος for *Quĭrīnus* on Greek inscriptions (see Eckinger, p. 123). *Oe* is found for Greek ῡ in *goerus, coloephia*, byforms of *gŷrus, cōlŷphia*, &c. (see Georges s. vv., and Schuch. ii. 278). Latin *ü* is in Greek inscriptions always expressed by *o* till the beginning of the Empire, when ου takes its place. We find *v* especially in the suffixes *-ullus, -ulus, -urius*, &c. (Eckinger, p. 58 sqq.) *Sulla, Sylla* for *Sŷrula* (§ 16) is always Συλλας.

(For spellings of Greek *v* and the Latin *ü*-sound with *y, u, i*, see Schuchardt's examples from inscriptions and MSS., *Vok.* ii. p. 218 sqq., and consult Georges, *Lex. Wortf.* s. vv. *cumba, murra, myrtetum, myrtum, lympha,*

---

[1] Varro *Men.* 50 B. makes the Gen. Plur. *lymphon*. In Glossaries we have *nymphaticus* for *lymphaticus*, e. g. ' nymphaticus' arrepticius Gl. Sangall. 912 ; Ambr. B. 31 supr.

§§ 28-32.]   PRONUNCIATION. DIPHTHONGS.   37

murmillo, Thynia, Syrus, serpyllum, and Brambach, *Hülfsbüchlein* s. vv. *thynnus, syllaba, stīlus.* The Appendix Probi has: tymum non 'tumum' (199. 6); myrta non 'murta' (199. 7); Marsyas non 'Marsuas' (197. 24); clamys non 'clamus' (198. 20); gyrus non 'girus' (197. 27); Byzacenus non 'Bizacinus' (198. 1); amygdala non 'amiddula' (198. 26).)

§ 29. o for ŭ. The coincidence of Latin ŏ and ŭ in the Romance languages makes it natural that we should find *o* written for *ŭ* on late inscriptions, and in plebeian forms. Roman tiles, for example, from the *figlina Bucconiana* are in the earlier period marked *Bucconiana,* but from Diocletian's time often *Boconiana* (*C. I. L.* xv. p. 386); and Greek στύραξ appears in late Latin as *storax* (Georges s. v.). [In addition to the large number of instances of *o* for *ŭ* collected by Schuchardt, *Vok.* ii. p. 149 &c., see Georges, *Lex. Wortf.* s. vv. *columna, urceolus, cunnus, luxurio, verecundus,* and cf. App. Probi 198. 23 puella non 'poella'; 198. 12 cluaca non 'cloaca': 197. 25 columna non 'colomna' (on the last example, see § 68 and ch. iii. § 33.)]

§ 30. ō for ū. This interchange, as we have seen (§ 24), is properly confined to words which had originally the diphthong *ou,* which became in Latin a sound expressed variously by *ō* and by *ū* (ch. iv. § 41). Some examples of the interchange have been mentioned in § 24. To them may be added *bocula,* occasionally in MSS. of Virgil for *būcŭla* (Ribbeck, *Index,* p. 391), *jocundus* for *jūcundus* (Georges s. v.), and the examples (many of doubtful worth) collected by Schuchardt, *Vok.* ii. p. 181 sqq.

§ 31. Other changes of ŭ and ū. *Cŏlŭber* was in Vulg. Lat. *colober,* the *u* being assimilated to the accented *o* (see ch. iii. § 33). Hence Vulg. Lat. *colobra,* with open *o* accented before *br* (cf. ch. iii. § 11). (Sicil. culovria, Span. culebra, O. Fr. culuevre); cf. Append. Probi 199. 2 K. coluber non colober: so *colober* on inscrr. e. g. Mur. 1144. 3, and in MSS. (Schuch. ii. 149); *nŭrus* was *norus* (see Georges s. v.) or rather **nora* (cf. App. Probi 198. 34 nurus non 'nura'), with open *o* (Ital. nuora, Span. nuera), perhaps by analogy of *sŏror.* *Lūridus* was **lŭr(i)dus* (Ital. lordo, Fr. lourd); *pūmex* shows **pŭm-,* in Ital. pomice, Span. pomez, Fr. ponce); *nūptiae* was **noptia* (Ital. nozze, Fr. noces), explained by analogy of *nova nupta* (?). *Ūpilio* and *ŏpilio, cūralium* and *cŏrallium* were explained in § 25. *Aurūgo* and *aurīgo* are due to interchange of suffixes, not to transition of vowel-sound. (So *grăvīdo* and *grăvēdo,* § 10.)

A curious tendency to interchange *u-i* and *i-u* appears in Vulg. Lat. *stŭpŭla* (seen in Ital. stoppia, O. Fr. estoble, Fr. éteule, &c.), unless *stup-* and *stip-* are original byforms. (On *mitulus* and *mytilus,* see Brambach, *Hülfsbüchl.* s. v., cf. Gk. Μυτιλήνη and Μιτυλήνη, Lat. *Ŭtĭca* and Greek Ἰτύκη.)

§ 32. Diphthongs. We have no reason to doubt that Latin *au, ae* were in the classical period, and for some time after, diphthongal sounds. None of the grammarians who discuss these diphthongs suggests that they were anything else. But in various dialects of Italy *au* had been early reduced to a single sound *o, ae* to a single sound *e,* a dialectal or 'rustic' pronunciation which shows signs of its presence in the speech of everyday life. The Romance languages indicate that in Vulgar Latin *ae* had become hardly distinguishable from an open E-sound; and the reiterated warnings of grammarians, from the fourth cent. A.D. onwards, against the confusion of words like *aequus* and *equus* tell the same story. Welsh praidd (Latin *praeda*, for *prae-héda or *prae-hida, from *prehendo*, *prae-hendo*) must have been borrowed before this decay set in; but Varro's use of *ae*, instead of *ē*, to express the sound of Greek η (probably open *e*), in *scaena*, seems to show that the process of development had at least begun before the Imperial Age. On the other hand, *au* has been preserved intact by several of the Romance languages; and in the others (e.g. Italian and French), where it has developed to *o* (Ital. cosa, poco, &c., with open *o*; Fr. chose), this development can be proved to be post-Roman. In Latin loanwords in Welsh we have sometimes *au*, e.g. aur (Lat. *aurum*), sometimes close *o*. The pronunciation of these diphthongs must have been a combination of the simple sounds of which they are composed; *au*, an *a* rapidly followed by a *u* (or *o*), something like German *au*; *ae*, an *a* rapidly followed by an *e*, something like Welsh *ae*; but how modified from century to century, it is impossible to say. In (originally) unaccented syllables in compounds, *au* was reduced to *ū* (through *eu*?), e.g. *dēfrūdo*, from *fraudo* (see ch. iii. § 18) (cf. Ital. udire, from Lat. *audire*); *ae*, or rather the earlier *ai*, to *ī* (through *ei*?), e.g. *distīsum*, from *taedeo* (ibid.); but in later Latin the reduction was seldom carried out (ch. iii. § 23). The interjection *au*, only used by women, seems to have been a cry expressing wonder or indignation, e.g. Ter. *Adelph.* 336 au, au, mi homo, sanusne es? while the diphthong *ae* occurs in several exclamations, such as *vae* (the Lettish wai), *hahae* and *hahahae*, &c. (Cf. *baubari* to bark.)

Ae had been in early times *ai*; and this old spelling was often used by lovers of antiquity in the Imperial period, though the pronunciation was of course *ae*, and not *ai*. A curious feature of Vulgar Latin, reflected in Romance, was the substitution of *a* for *au* in syllables before the accent, when the next syllable contained the vowel *u*, e.g. *Agustus*, found on Inscriptions for *Augustus*. (Ital. agosto.) The same tendency is shown in the Sardinian dialect of Italian, where Lat. *laurus* is laru, &c., and in our 'laughter' *au* has an *a*-sound.

§ 33.]   PRONUNCIATION. DIPHTHONGS.   39

Oi, a diphthong used in early times, had been reduced first to *oe*, then to a simple sound *ū* (through some *ö*-sound probably) before the classical period. What was the exact sound of the later diphthong *oe*, which we find in words like *coetus* (from *co(m)-itus*), is difficult to determine; and the small number of words which possessed this diphthong makes it impossible to ascertain its treatment in Romance. We have already seen (§ 28) that it is occasionally found as an expression of Greek *ū*, e.g. *goerus* (beside *gȳrus*), *coloephia* (beside *cōlȳphia*). The interjection *oiei* was a cry of pain. Thus in Plautus, *Mil.* 1406, when the soldier is being thrashed, he shouts: oiei, satis sum verberatus; and in Terence, *Phorm.* 663, the miserly father, hearing of the large sum demanded by the parasite, cries out, as if he had received a blow : oiei, nimium est.

Eu is another diphthong, which arose at a later period through fortuitous combination, e.g. *nĕuter*, a trisyllable (Consentius p. 389. 28 K.) (from *nĕ* and *ŭter*, with the accent on the *nĕ*, § 149), *seu* (so *neu, ceu,* ch. x. § 16 and 11) (by reduction of *sī-ve, sei-ve,* ch. x. § 4); while I.-Eur. *eu* was, like I.-Eur. *ou*, in the Italic languages. *ou*, a diphthong found in early Latin, but reduced to *ū* (as I.-Eur. *ei* to *ī*) by the second cent. B.C. (ch. iv. § 26). Latin *eu* of the Interjection *heu* (cf. Greek φεῦ) must have been pronounced like *e* followed rapidly by *u* (or *o*); for a fifth century grammarian (Agroecius 122. 11–16 K.) dwells on the distinction between *eo*, *eho*, and *heu*. Greek ευ seems to have been usually pronounced as a disyllable in Latin. *Ui*, which can hardly claim to rank as a Latin diphthong, is seen in the interjection *hui*, where it may express the sound of a whistle, our 'whew!' and in the Dative *cui*, which does not seem to have much differed in pronunciation from the Nominative *quī*.

§ 33. **Grammarians' account of diphthongs.** Nigidius (first cent. B.C.), *ap. Gell.* xix. 14. 6 a et o semper principes sunt, i et u semper subditae, e et subit et praeit; praeit in 'Euripo,' subit in 'Aemilio'; Ter. Scaurus (second cent. A. D.) vii. 16. 5 K. a igitur littera praeposita est . . . e litter(ae) . . . et apud antiquos i littera pro ea scribebatur, . . ut 'pictai vestis,' et 'aulai medio' . . . sed magis in illis e novissima sonat (cf. Quint. i. 7. 18); Marius Victorinus (fourth cent. A. D.) vi. 32. 4–6 K. duae inter se vocales jugatae ac sub unius vocis enuntiatione prolatae syllabam faciunt natura longam, quam Graeci diphthongon vocant, veluti geminae vocis unum sonum, ut ae, oe, au; cf. Ter. Maur. vi. 338. 418-427 K. and 365. 1326-1334; [Probus] *de ult.*

syll. iv. 219. 25 K. ; Servius, *in Don.* iv. 423. 30 K. ; Mallius Theodorus vi. 586.
25-26 K. ; Bede vii. 229. 20-25 K.

§ 34. Ter. Maurus on au. Terentianus Maurus makes a distinction between Latin *ău* and *āu*, while Latin *eu*, he says, is like Greek ευ always *ĕu*. *Ău*, as in 'aut ăgĕ,' 'aut ŭbi,' 'Aurunci' of Virgil, he compares to Homer's αυέρυσαν (presumably ἀϝέρυσαν) and ἀτάρ for αὐτάρ, in contrast to the (accented) *āu* of *aurum, auspices,* Greek αὖριον :—

> 'aut age' inquit ille vates, saepe dixit 'aut ubi'
> dixit 'Aurunci,' quod aeque barbarum est producere:
> pes ubique lege constat, prima cum correpta sit,
> consonans et una plenum non queat tempus dare
>
> . . . .
>
> αυέρυσαν inquit poeta sic et αὐτάρ corripit.

If this means anything, which is doubtful, it ought to mean that in '*aut age*, '*aut ubi*' the diphthong had a more reduced sound than the *au* of *aurum*, a reduction which was similar to that seen in pretonic *au* followed by a syllable with *u, Aruncus* like *Agustus* (Cf. ARVNCEIO, *C. I. L.* vi. 13416 ; *Arunci* in Virgil MSS., &c. ; Ribbeck, *Ind.* p. 388.)

§ 35. au in Romance. Had *au* been an open O-sound in Vulg. Lat. it would have been merged in Latin *ŏ*, has *ae* as been merged in *ĕ*. But that the *o* of Ital. poco, Fr. chose, is a late development we see from the forms of the words, which would otherwise have been *pogo, *cose (Meyer-Lübke, *Rom. Gram.* i. p. 235). We may similarly infer the diphthongal character of *au, ae*, at the time of the Empire, from the frequently-repeated statement of the grammarians that after a diphthong it was impossible to pronounce a double consonant, e. g. *paulum* (not *paullum*), *Paulus* (usually spelt *Paullus*, but not so pronounced), while after a long vowel double *l* was common, e. g. *stēlla, Pōlla, vīllum* (Diminutive of *vīnum*) (see § 127).

§ 36. u for accented au. The change of *au* to *ū* in the (originally) unaccented syllable is in conformity with the rule in *dēfrūdo*, the spelling recommended for Plautus and Terence on the strength of the MSS. by Ritschl (*Parerga*, i. 540) (see also Georges s.v.). But we find also *sed frude* in the Lex Repetundarum (123-122 B. C.) (*C. I. L.* i. 198, § 64) (but *sed fraude*, § 69), where there seems no reason for supposing the syllable to have been unaccented [Another instance of the confusion of *au* and *ū* in this word is the spelling *fraustra*, often found in MSS. of Virgil (see Ribbeck, *Index* s.v.), which also exhibit *frude* for *fraude* in *A*. iv. 675, as the MSS. of Lucretius have *frudem* ii. 187, *frudi* vi. 186 (see Lachm. p. 85)]. Similarly the *u* for unaccented *au* which appears regularly in the compounds of *claudo*, seems to have called into life a byform of the simple verb, *cludo*, in the first cent. A. D. (Georges, *Lex. Lat. Wortf.* s.v. *claudo*, and p. 750), which remains in the Italian *chiudo*. (For *cludam*, lame, in Plaut. *Pseud.* 659, read with the palimpsest *claudam*.)

§ 37. o and au. *o* for *au* is a feature of the Umbrian language (e. g. *ote*, Lat. *aut*) and other dialects, and was preserved in 'rustic' Latin, and even in the Latin of the streets of Rome. Festus tells us of a millionaire who was nicknamed *Orata* (i. e. *aurāta*, goldfish), because he wore two gold ear-rings [Festus 202. 13 Th. orata, genus piscis, appellatur a colore auri quod rustici 'orum' dicebant, ut auriculas 'oriculas,' itaque Sergium quoque quendam praedivitem ... Oratam dicunt esse appellatum, &c. (For *oricula*, cf. App. Probi 198. 11 auris non 'oricla.' *Oricla* occurs as a cognomen on inscriptions, *C. I. L.* xii. 5686, no. 652.)] Cicero's rival Clodius, was the first of the gens to change the name *Claudius* to the plebeian form *Clodius*, no doubt with the view of conciliating the mob. Cicero himself in his letters often uses the more homely forms with *o*, e. g. *loreolam* (*Att.* v. 20. 4), *pollulum* (*Fam.* xii. 12. 2 ; *oricula* (*Quint. Fr.* ii. 13. 4), like *oricilla*, Catull. xxv. 2 (see *A. L. L.* vi. 84), while *plodo* is quoted from his ' De Gloria' by Diomede (p. 382. 26 K.), and in Plautus we seem to find assonance of *aurum* with *ornamentum*, *ornatus*, of *auspicium* with *omen*, of *auribus* with *oculus* (*Bursian's Jahresbericht*, 1881, p. 33). So too Priscian (i. 52, p. 39 H.) says : (au) transit in o productam more antiquo, ut 'lotus' pro lautus, ' plostrum ' pro plaustrum, ' cotes ' pro cautes : sicut etiam pro o, au, ut 'austrum' pro ostrum, ' ausculum' pro osculum, frequentissime hoc faciebant antiqui. This usage of *au* for *o* [cf. Paul. Fest. 21 (apparently referring to a passage of Plautus) ausculari dicebant antiqui pro osculari] is found in Plautus, not merely in *aurichalcum* (Greek ὀρείχαλκος), where it is due to confusion with *aurum*, but also in *auscŭlātur* (*Bacch.* 897, &c.). *Aula* (or *aulla* as in the palimpsest) of Plautus became *olla*, as *Paulla*, *Paula* became *Pŏlla*. It is perhaps confined to derivatives of *ōs* (see Georges s. vv. *oreae*, *ostium*, *osculum*, *osculor*), which seems to have had two parallel stems in early Latin, *aus-* and *ōs-* (cf. *jĕcur* and *jŏcur*); so this gives no evidence on the pronunciation of Lat. *ō*. In the Lex Metalli Vipascensis of the first cent. A. D. (*Eph. Epigr.* iii. p. 180) we have *scauria* for the Greek σκωρία, which the Romance languages show us to have been *scōria* in Vulgar Latin. Rustic or dialectal *o* for *au* is found in the name *M. Lornti* (=*M. Laurenti*), on a jar in the old Esquiline cemetery (c. 200 B. C.) (*Ann. Inst.* 1880, p. 260), while on plebeian inscriptions we have such forms as *Oli* (for *Auli*) on the tombstone of a praeco (*Eph. Epigr.* iv. p. 297), *Olipor* (*C. I. L.* xi. 1973), &c. In Greek inscriptions we have 'Ωλος from the time of Augustus, but always Παυλλος (though often Πωλλα and Πολλα, like Lat. *Pŏlla*). (See Eckinger, p. 13.) In *cauda* (Lith. kůdas) the original vowel may be *ō*, and the spelling *au* be due to the similarity of sound between *ō* and *au*. (See *K. Z.* xxviii. 157 for this and other doubtful instances.) [For other examples of *au-o*, see Schuchardt, *Vok.* ii. p. 301 sqq., and Georges, *Lex. Wortf.* s. vv. *caupo*, *auspicor* (Diom. 383. 10 K. Claudius octavo Historiarum ' Flacco ospicatur'), *caulis*, *cauliculus*, *caurus*, *raudus* (also *rudus*), *pausea*, *lauretum*, *plaudo*, *claudus*, *claustrum*, *sorix* (cf. Mar. Vict. 26. 7 K. sorix vel saurix, *C. G. L.* v. 242. 33), *codex*.] (See Diomedes, pp. 382-3 K., Probus Inst. 118-9 K.) Suetonius (*Vesp.* viii. 22) tells us an anecdote of the homely Vespasian : Mestrium Florum consularem, admonitus ab eo plaustra potius quam plostra dicenda, postero die ' Flaurum' salutavit [cf. the glosses : plostrum dicimus magis quam 'plaustrum' (*C. G. L.* v. 93. 13), and : ' odit' audit (ibid. 89. 7 and 125. 26).]

§ 38. a for au. (Schuchardt, *Vok.* ii. p. 305 sqq.) *Agustus* for *Augustus*, e. g. *C. I. L.* ix. 1365 (411 A. D.) (cf. Greek 'Αγουσταλιος, *Mitt. Inst.* xiii. p. 236 *n.* 5 ; Eckinger, p. 12). The Romance name of the month points to Vulg. Lat.' *Agustus*, e. g. Ital. agosto, Span. agosto, Fr. août, and shows that the *a* was not merely a conventional symbol for *o*. *Asculto* was the Vulg. Lat. form of *ausculto* (cf. Caper 108. 6 ausculta non ' asculta '), as we see from the Romance forms, e. g. Ital. ascoltare, Span. ascuchar ; *agurium of *augurium* (Raet. far agur, to consider, Ital. sciagurato, from *exaguratus, unlucky,

Span. janro). *Cladius* often occurs for *Claudius* on inscriptions (e. g. *C. I. L.* ii. 4638, of 275 A.D.) (cf. Greek Φαστος, *C. I. A.* iii. 10, of 209-210 A.D.; *Bull.* viii. p. 247, of 11 A.D., from Eumenia). For similar spellings in Glossaries (e. g. 'agustae' sanctae ; *fastus* for *faustus*, &c.), see Löwe, *Prodr.* p. 421. In MSS. of Virgil, &c., we find *Arunci* for *Aurunci* (Ribbeck, *Ind.* p. 388, cf. *Arunceio, C. I. L.* vi. 13416) ; and modern Italian place-names like Metaro, Pesaro show a similar change.

§ 39. Greek transcriptions of au. In Greek inscriptions we find usually αυ for Latin *au* ; but also αο, e. g. Φαοστινι, *C. I. L.* ix. 6229 and 6230 ; Φαοστινες 6209 (the form Παολος does not occur till the fourth or fifth cent. A. D.) ; also αου, e. g. Παουλλινα, *C. I. G.* 6665 ; Αουλου (2656 b *add.*) (see Eckinger, p. 13).

§ 40. ae for au. *Ae* is found now and then on inscriptions for *au*, e. g. *maeso*(*leum*), *C. I. L.* i. Fast. min. ix of 1 A.D.; *Paelinus*, &c.

§ 41. e for ae. (Brambach, *Orthogr.* p. 205 ; Schuchardt, *Vok.* i. p. 224 sqq.) *E* for *ae* (*ai*) is a feature of the Umbrian language, e. g. *pre* (Lat. *prae*), and is found on Latin inscriptions in the Umbrian territory, e. g. *Cesula, C. I. L.* i. 168 (Pisaurum), and elsewhere (see Sittl, *Lok. Verschied.* p. 4). It was a feature too of rustic Latin, as we see from Varro, *L. L.* vii. 96 rustici pappum 'Mesium,' non Maesium ; v. 97 in Latio rure 'edus' ; qui in urbe, ut in multis, a addito aedus ; and from Lucilius' ridicule of a praetor who called himself *Cecilius* instead of *Caecilius* (ix. 10 M. Cecilius pretor ne rusticus fiat. Cf. Diom. 452. 17 K.). The same variation of *e* and *ae* found its way into ordinary pronunciation in the case of country-terms, e. g. *faenisicia* and *fenisicia*, the hay-harvest. The Romance forms point to *sēpes*, not *saepes* ; *sēptum*, not *saeptum* (e. g. Port. sebe, Span. seto) (Gröber, *A. L. L.* v. 465). From Varro's remark that *scaena* (and *scaeptrum* ?) represented the pronunciation of Greek σκηνή, σκῆπτρον at his time, we should infer that this *ae* had a sound approaching to long open *e*, for Greek η probably still had at this period the open sound (Varro, *L. L.* vii. 96 obscaenum dictum ab scaena ; eam ut Graeci Accius scribit 'scena.' In pluribus verbis a ante e alii ponunt, alii non, ut quod partim dicunt 'scaeptrum,' partim 'sceptrum,' alii Plauti 'Faeneratricem,' alii 'Feneratricem' ; sic 'faenisicia' ac 'fenisicia'). This spelling of the title of a play of Plautus, *Feneratrix*, for *Faenĕrātrix*, the Usuress, agrees with another remark of Varro that *fenus*, not *faenus*, was the pronunciation of Old Latin, used by Cato and others (Non. 54 M. ; Varro lib. iii de sermone Latino : 'faenus autem dictum a fetu, et quasi fetura quadam pecuniae. Nam et Catonem et ceteros antiquiores sine a littera 'fenus' pronuntiasse contendit, ut fetus et fecunditas). How thoroughly *ae* (through *œe* ?) became identified with the long sound of open *e* at a later time, we see from the remark of a fifth century grammarian, that *ĕquus*, when the first syllable, through being accented, was unduly lengthened in pronunciation, became *aequus* (Pompeius 285. 6 K. plerumque male pronuntiamus, et facimus vitium ut brevis syllaba longo tractu sonet ... si (quis) velit dicere 'aequus' pro eo quod est equus). (Cf. *prehendo*, with shortening of *prae* before a vowel, as *dĕamo* of *dĕ*, and Marius Victorinus' use of -*aeus* to express the disyllabic pronunciation of Gk. -ευς (67 K.).) Another grammarian of the same century gives a caution against the confusion of *vae* and *vĕ* (Agroecius 114. 21 K.), of *quaeritur* and *quĕritur* (id. 116. 18 K.) ; while he speaks of the first syllable of

§§ 39-43.] PRONUNCIATION. DIPHTHONGS. 43

praemium, prĕtium, prĕcor, as if they were distinguished in writing only, not in pronunciation (id. 115 K. praemium cum diphthongo scribendum ; pretium, precor sine diphthongo. Veteres enim majoris rei sermones cum diphthongo, et quadam dignitate scribi voluerunt). Even in the fourth cent. Servius, in a note on Virgil, *Aen.* i. 344 :—

huic conjux Sychaeus erat, ditissimus agri
Phoenicum, et magno miserae dilectus amore,

thinks it necessary to point out that *miserae* is the Adjective, not the Adverb *miserē*. The 'Orthographies' of Bede and Alcuin (the latter served as a text-book for Carlovingian scribes of MSS.) abound in similar distinctions (e. g. *quaeritur* and *queritur*, Alcuin 308. 16 K.; Bede 287. 8 K.; *quaestus* and *questus*, Alcuin 308. 17 K.; *saevit* and *sevit*, Alcuin 310. 5 K.; Bede 289. 30 K.; *caelo* and *celo*, Alcuin 299. 6 K. ; Bede 268. 27 K.), some of which may have been taken from earlier grammarians [cf. Charisius (fourth cent.), p. 98 K. on the spelling *erumna* for *aerumna* ; Marius Victorinus (fourth cent.), p. 25 K. on the spelling *cesaries* for *caesaries*]. Philargyrius, the Virgil Scholiast, on *Ecl.* iii. 39, defends the *ae* of *haedera* (for *hĕdĕra*) by connecting the word with *haereo* (cf. Paul. Fest. 71. 26 Th. hedera dicta, quod haereat, sive quod edita petat, vel quia id, cui adhaeserit, edit.). With all this it is no wonder that it is often difficult to decide whether the proper spelling of a word is with *ae* or *e*. [For the rival claims of *e* and *ae* in some words, see Georges, *Lex. Wortf.* s. vv. *meles, nenia, gleba, maena, muraena, paelex, feles, cetra, ne* (the Interjection), *gaesum*.]

On Greek inscriptions we find ε for Latin *ae* from the middle of the second cent. A.D., e. g. Κεκιλιος, but never η. (Eckinger, p. 78.) Instances of Latin *ae* for Greek η in inscriptions and MSS. are given by Schuchardt, *Vok.* i. p. 227 sqq., a very frequent case being that Genitive ending of female names in *-aes* (Greek -ης) from the last century of the Republic, e. g. *Laudicaes* (C. I. L. i. 1212), which is discussed in ch. vi. § 18.

§ 42. ai for ae. The old spelling *ai* is found on Imperial inscriptions, especially in the reign of the grammarian-emperor Claudius (e. g. C. I. L. vi. 353, of 51 A.D., *Caisare*); but we have the express testimony of Terentius Scaurus (second cent.) (16. 7 K. sed magis in illis e novissima sonat), not to speak of Quintilian (first cent.) (i. 7. 18 cujus secundam nunc e litteram ponimus), that the second element, as pronounced, was *e*, not *i*. The change of the earlier *ai* to the classical form of the diphthong, *ae*, took place in the second cent. B.C. (e.g. *aedem*, beside *aiquom, tabelai, datai*, &c., on the S. C. Bacch. of 186 B.C., C. I. L. i. 196). The spelling *aei*, found once or twice towards the end of the second cent. B.C., e. g. *conquaeisivei, Caeicilius, Caeician[us]*, may mark the transition (see ch. iv. § 29). In *ain* for *aisne, aibat* (disyll.) the diphthong must have had the sound of O. Lat. *ai*.

§ 43. Greek ει. Before a consonant Greek ει is always ī in Latin, e. g. *Atrīdes*. Before a vowel it is *ē* till the first cent. A.D., then *ī*. Thus *Alexandrēa, Darēus*, &c., are the earlier spellings ; *Alexandrīa, Darīus* the later. (See Brambach, *Hülfsbüchlein*, p. 4.) The *-ē-, -ī-* was often shortened (cf. § 143); e. g. *balnĕum* (Gk. βαλανεῖον) (cf. Prisc. i. p. 71 H. and p. 73 H. on *Alphĕus, Hectorĕus*, &c.). The Greek diphthong which probably passed into the *ī*-sound about 100 B.C. is a common expression of Latin ī, e. g. Ἀντωνεῖνος, but of Latin *ĭ* only in hiatus, e. g. ἀτρειον (for *atrium*), Πουπλειος (for *Publius*) (see

Eckinger, p. 42). Latin *ei* in words like *Pompeius* is in Greek ηι; but from the first century A. D. we find also ει, e. g. Πονπειος (Eckinger, p. 81).

§ 44. oe and e. Alcuin and Bede give almost as many rules for the distinction of *oe* and *e*, as for the distinction of *ae* and *e* [e. g. *cepit* and *coepit*, *coepta* and *incepta*, Alcuin vii. 299. 18 K. ; Bede vii. 269. 14 K. ; *fedus* (quod est deformis) and *foedus*, Alcuin vii. 301–302. 2 K. ; Bede vii. 273. 4 K. ; cf. Orthogr. Bern. 293. 9 K. ; *pene, penes*, and *poena*, Alcuin vii. 306. 35 K. ; Bede vii. 286. 1 K.], some of which may come from earlier grammarians. [For variations in spelling between *oe, e, ae* see Schuchardt, *Vok.* ii. p. 288 sqq., and consult Georges and Brambach s. vv. *cena, caenum, faeteo* (cf. Span. hiede), *amoenus, fenus, maereo, paene, proelium, caelebs, caelum, caecus, oboedio, foedus, fecundus, obscenus, pomoerium, femina, fetus,* &c.] Greek φ is in classical Latin *o*, e. g. *melodia*, but earlier *oe*, e. g. *comoeds* (cf. *Thraex* and *Thrax*, Blass, p. 43).

§ 45. oe in Romance. *pēna for *poena* is indicated by the Romance forms (e. g. Ital. pena, Span. pena, Fr. peine), and probably *fēdus for *foedus*, foul (e. g. Span. hedo, feo). *Cēna* (e. g. Ital. cena, Span. cena) is thought to have been the correct spelling (cf. Osc. kersna-), though the spelling with *oe* (due to confusion with Greek κοινός, as *coelum*, for *caelum*, confused with κοῖλος) is very old (COEN- on a Praenestine cista. *Mél. Arch.* 1890, p. 303).

§ 46. Greek ευ. Marius Victorinus vi. 66–67 K. consimili ratione quaeritur, Orpheus in metro, ut

> non me carminibus vincat nec Thracius Orpheus,

utrum trisyllabum an disyllabum sit, an idem nomen duplici enuntiatione promatur, aut sine a littera, ut Peleus Pentheus, aut cum a, ut ita declinetur Orphaeus, ut Aristaeus. visum est tamen hoc posse discerni, ut illa sine a littera graeca sit enuntiatio, haec latina, quae per diphthongon effertur. The proper spelling is *euhoe, Euhius, euhan*, not *evoe, Evius, evan* (see Brambach, *Hülfsbüchlein* s. vv.). For a corruption of Greek ευ in vulgar pronunciation, see App. Probi 199. 6 hermeneumata non 'erminomata.' On an old mirror of Praeneste we have *Taseos* (Tasei, Gen.) for Θασεύς (*Eph. Epigr.* i. 23).

§ 47. ui of cui. Quint. i. 7. 27 illud nunc melius, quod 'cui' tribus quas posui litteris enotamus, in quo pueris nobis ad pinguem sane sonum qu et oi utebantur, tantum ut ab illo 'qui' distingueretur. Ter. Scaur. 28. 1 K. c autem in dativo ponimus, ut sit differentia cui et qui, id est dativi [et vocativi] singularis et nominativi et vocativi pluralis. Annaeus Cornutus ap. Cassiod. 149. 8 K. 'qui' syllaba per q u i scribitur ; si dividitur, ut sit cui et huic, per c.

§ 48. J, V. That Latin *j* and *v* had some sound like our *y, w*, and not like our *j, v*, there can be no doubt whatever. We see this from the close relation that exists between *i* and *j*, *u* and *v* in different forms of the same word in Latin, e. g. *jam* and *nunciam* (3 syll.), *tenuis* and *tenvia* (3 syll.), as well as from the express testimony of grammarians. The signs *j* and *v*, which suggest to us a difference between the sound of these letters and of the corresponding vowels, are, as we saw (ch. i. § 7), of quite a late date. In the Roman period *jus* and *vos* were written with *i* and *u*, *ius*, *uos*, exactly like *pius* and *tuos* (ch. i. § 1). The only question is whether *j* and *v* were actual consonants (*y*, *w*) or half-vowels (*i̯*, *u̯*). Our *y*, for example, in 'you' is a spirant consonant, but is often in pronunciation weakened into a half-vowel (Sweet, *Handb.* p. 37). The distinction is so slight a one that it seems impossible to determine the exact pronunciation of *j* and *v* in a dead language like Latin; and probably the pronunciation varied at different times; but we certainly have one or two clear testimonies to the consonantal character of these sounds. Thus a fifth (?) century grammarian remarks on the difficulty experienced by the Greeks of his day (as by the Greeks of our own time) in pronouncing this *y*-sound in such a word as *jus*. They make the word, he says, almost a disyllable (Consentius v. 394 K.). And the same writer in another passage mentions a corresponding mispronunciation of the *w*-sound in *veni* (v. 395. 15 K. u quoque litteram aliqui pinguius ecferunt, ut, cum dicunt 'veni,' putes trisyllabum incipere). And much earlier, in the first cent. A. D., we have a distinction drawn between *v* of *valente*, *primitivo*, &c., and the *u* of *quis*. The former is said to sound 'cum aliqua aspiratione' (Velius Longus vii. 58. 17 K.), much as Varro, the contemporary of Cicero, says that *v-* had a strong thick sound (crassum et quasi validum) in *vafer*, *velum*, *vinum*, *vomis*, *vulnus*, &c. (*L. L.* iii. fr. p. 148 Wilm.). That this consonantal character of *j* and *v* intensified and developed itself as the centuries went on, we see from the Romance languages, e.g. Italian, where Latin *v* has become our *v-*, Latin *j* our *j*-sound (e.g. vostro, Lat. *voster*, giurare, Lat. *jūrāre*); and it is possible that the further back we go in the history of the Latin language the less consonantal was the sound of *j* and *v*[1]. But there is no evidence of this, unless we count as such the scansion *ăbicio* in Plautus and Terence, where the *j* appears to be so entirely sunk in the following *i* (*e*), as not to make the first syllable long by position,

---

[1] I.-Eur. swĕ- became Latin sŏ-, e.g. *soror* (through *svo-* ?), but not I.-Eur. wĕ-, e.g. *vetus*, which may indicate that the *v* of *sve-* was more consonantal than ordinary *v*.

whereas in *ăbicio* of the classical poets the first syllable is so lengthened (*A. L. L.* iv. 560) (but see ch. iii. § 25). This merging of *j* in a following *i* has been compared with the merging of the *u* of *qu*, which Velius Longus tells us was more vocalic than the *v* of *valente*, &c., in a following *u*, e. g. *cum* (earlier *quom*) for *quum, locuntur* (earlier *loquontur*) for *loquuntur* (cf. § 93). A similar unconsonantal character for *v* in early Latin has been inferred from the reduction of *īvi* to *ī* in such Plautine forms as *oblīscor* for *oblīviscor, dīnus* for *dīvīnus*; but in the absence of express testimony, such as we have for the consonantal character of *j* and *v* at a later time, it is impossible to decide positively so minute a point. An untrained ear can hardly distinguish between the spirants *y*, *w*, and the half-vowels *i̯*, *u̯*, nor yet between the various nuances of the *w*-sound, such as our *wh*, e. g. 'which,' the unvoiced *w*, differing from the voiced *w* of 'witch' as *p* from *b*, *t* from *d*, *c* from *g*, or such as in French 'oui,' the consonant of the vowel of French 'sou,' while our *w* is the consonant of the vowel of English 'full,' 'put' (Sweet, *Handbk.* p. 42). So much we can say, that the pronunciation of *j* and *v* certainly became more and more removed from the half-vowels in the centuries of the Empire; and it is natural to infer a movement in the same direction in the Republican period. But when exactly *j* and *v* ceased to be half-vowels and became consonants, or how far their character varied according to their position in the word it is impossible to determine with precision.

The same tendency to syncopate a short unaccented syllable that produced *calda* out of *călĭda* affected the vowels *i*, *u* when they preceded other vowels. The word *lārua* is a trisyllable in Plautus; it has become a dissyllable in classical Latin, just as *lărĭdum* of Plautus became *lārdum*. The only forms known to Plautus are *mĭluos, rĕlĭcuos, grātĭis*, which in classical Latin are *milvos, reliquos* (by the middle of the first cent. A.D. *relicus*), *gratīs*. In the first cent. A.D. *tĕnuis* wavered between a dissyllable and a trisyllable (Caesellius ap. Cassiod. vii. 205 K.).

This reduction of the vowel *i* after *t*, *c* led, as we shall see (§§ 90, 94), to the assibilation of these consonants. *Titius* became *Tityus and then something like *Titsus (cf. our 'orchard' for 'ort-yard'), as we learn from the remark of a fifth cent.

grammarian, quoted below: si dicas 'Titius' (i) pinguius sonat et perdit sonum suum et accipit sibilum.

As to the pronunciation of words like *Maia, Pompeius, ejus*, where the diphthong is followed by a vowel, we have very clear information from the grammarians that the *i*-sound was shared both by the first and the second syllable, Mai-ja or Mai-ya, not Ma-ja, Ma-ya. To express this sound Cicero proposed to write *Maiia, Aiiax* with two *i*'s (Velius Longus vii. 54. 16 K.; Quint. i. 4. 11); and on inscriptions we find spellings like MAIIOREM (*C. I. L.* ii. 1964, col. iii. 10) (see ch. i. § 7), where the long form of I may express the consonantal or half-vocalic sound *j*, as in coniivnx (*C. I. L.* vii. 8, &c.) (ch. i. § 1). Whether it was this already existing practice of writing long I for *j*, which made Claudius abstain from proposing a new letter for *j*, when he introduced the inverted F-sign for *v*, or whether he followed the Greek alphabet which had a sign for *w* (the digamma), but none for *y*, we cannot say. Possibly the reason is to be found in the more rapid development of the *w*-sound (Latin *v*) than of the *y*-sound (Latin *j*).

V and *b* (which had by this time become between vowels the bilabial spirant) were, as early as the third cent. A. D., hardly distinguishable, as is seen from the frequent warnings given by the grammarians against confusion of *labat* and *lavat* (Probi Appendix 199. 22 K.), *libido* and *livido* (ib. 201. 4 K.), &c., &c. Indeed one grammatical treatise (of the fifth century) is devoted to this very subject: Adamantii sive Martyrii *de B vocali et V vocali.* It was summarized by Cassiodorus for the book on Orthography which he compiled for the use of Benedictine copyists of MSS. (Keil, *Grammatici Latini*, vol. vii).

At some time before the fifth cent. A.D., when precisely we cannot say, initial *v*, and possibly *v* in other positions too, seems to have passed from the bilabial spirant (Spanish *b*) to the labio-dental spirant (our *v*). After *l, r* it assumed in time the sound of the voiced mute *b*.

§ 49. **Testimony of grammarians.** Quintilian i. 4. 10, 11, after saying that a letter is wanting to the Latin alphabet to express the sound of *v* in *servus, vulgus*, the Aeolic digamma, goes on to speak of the consonantal (*pro consonantibus*) character of the vowels *i, u*, e. g. *iam* but *etiam, uos* but *tuos*. Of *conjicit* he says, *littera i sibi insidit*, and so with *u* in *vulgus, servus*. In another passage

(i. 7. 26) he tells us that *seruos* was the spelling of his teachers, *seruus* that of his own time, but that neither spelling quite expressed the sound, so that the emperor Claudius had good reason to introduce a new letter like the Aeolic digamma (cf. xii. 10. 29). The usual expression of the grammarians for *j* and *v* is '(i, u) transeunt in consonantium potestatem' (e. g. Mar. Victorin. vi. 5. 18 K. ; Donat. iv. 367. 12 K. ; Charisius i. 8. 1 : cf. Diom. i. 422. 14 K. ; Ter. Maur. vi. 341. 536 K.). Later they talk of the 'pinguis sonus' as opposed to the 'exilis' or 'tenuis' (vocalic), the first to use this term being Servius (fourth cent.) (iv. 422. 1 K.), e. g. Pompeius (fifth cent.) (v. 103 K. 'vanus' quando dico pinguior sonus est. numquid dicis u a nus? ergo vides quia, si ponantur solae, tenuem sonum habent, si jungantur ad alias litteras, pingues sonant. similiter et i sic patitur. 'itur,' ecce tenuius sonat; si dicas 'Titius,' pinguius sonat et perdit sonum suum et accipit sibilum). Finally Priscian (sixth cent.) speaks of the 'diversus sonus' of *j* and *v* from *i* and *u*, and questions the soundness of Censorinus' (third cent.) contrary opinion (i. p. 13 H. non sunt in eisdem, meo judicio, elementis accipiendae : quamvis et Censorino, doctissimo artis grammaticae, idem placuit) (cf. Nigidius ap. Gell. xix. 14. 6). In another passage Priscian talks of *v* and *b* as quite similar in sound (i. 18. 10 H.), where he says that *caelebs* should be written *caelevs, the word being derived from *caelum* and *vita*, and meaning literally *caelestium vitam ducens* (!), were it not that *v* is never allowed to stand before a consonant. He goes on to say that *b* had this sound in very early Latin, because Quintilian quotes *Belena* for *Hĕlĕna* (Ϝελένα) (cf. Serv. in Don. 422. 2 K., and *C. I. L.* i. 1501) from early literature. This remark is interesting as showing how early MS. corruptions showed themselves. When we turn to the passage in Quintilian (i. 4. 15), we find that he is discussing the use of *b* for Greek π and φ in early Latin. His examples are *Burrus* (for Πυρρός), *Bruges* (for Φρύγες) and *balaena* (for φάλλαινα). The whole passage is taken from Verrius Flaccus, who used these same examples. In our MSS. of Quintilian there is the corruption *Belena* for *balaena*, a corruption which must have also existed in the MS. used by Priscian, and which led him to make this mistake (*Fleck. Jahrb.* 1889, p. 394). We notice that Consentius (fifth cent. ?) happens to use *pinguis* in precisely the opposite sense when he speaks of that mispronunciation of *veni* which made the word almost like a trisyllable (v. 395. 15 K.), unless indeed he is referring to the bilabial (*w*) as opposed to the labiodental spirant sound (*v*) (see below). Other barbarisms which he mentions as 'in usu cotidie loquentium' are *so-lu-it* for disyllabic *solvit*, *uam* for *uvam*, *induruit* (a trisyllable) (v. 392. 35 K.).

§ 50. *j* and *v* in early Latin. Priscian (i. p. 17. 3 K.) is certainly wrong in explaining the *sine invidia* of Terence (*Andr.* 66) by the vocalic character of *v* (see ch. iii. § 34) ; Accius' *augŭra* (*Trag.* 624 R.) : pró certo arbitrábor sortis, óracla, aditus, aúgura, may be a byform, and not a case of suppression of *i* (*y*); *progenie mi genui* on a hexameter line of a Scipio epitaph of c. 130 B.C. (*C. I. L.* i. 38) is perhaps a graver's error for *progeniem genui* ; the use of -*i*, not -*ii*, in the Gen. Sing. of IO-stems in the older writers has nothing to do with the sound of *j* (see ch. vi. § 20), nor have the Plautine forms *ain* (always), *aibat* (occasional) (see ch. viii. § 35) ; *peiĕro*, where the *r* of the preposition has been dropped, owing to the consonantal nature of the *i*, seems to be a later spelling than *periero* (see Georges, *Lex. Wortf.* s. v.) ; and the true account of *puleium* fleabane (also *pulegium*, see Georges) is a matter of doubt (see ch. iv. § 116).

§§ 50—52.]   PRONUNCIATION. J, V.   49

Between $\bar{\imath}$ and another i, v disappears at a very early time, e. g. *obliscor*, *dinus* in Plautus (see *Rhein. Mus.* xxxv. 627); and Plautus' trisyllabic *avonculus* (*aunculus* or *aonculus*) seems to be a suppression of pretonic v like the later *Noembris* for *Novembris* (see below). The vocalic nature of v in *cave* (pronounced with $\breve{e}$, ch. iii. § 44) is seen from Cicero's story (*Div.* ii. 84) of the confusion of *Cauneas* (sc. *ficus vendo*) with *cave ne eas*, as well as from the spelling *causis* for *cave sis* in Juvenal ix. 120; of v in *ave* (pronounced with -$\breve{e}$, Quint. i. 6. 21) from Phaedrus' fable (*App.* 21) of the man who mistook the caw of a crow for this word (*famila* for *familia* on an inscr. of Ameria in Umbria, *C. I. L.* xi. 4488, may be a dialectal variety, like the Oscan *famelo* 'familia' of Bantia, Zv. *I.I.I.* 231). Our w is similarly suppressed in 'Ha(w)arden,' 'Main(w)aring,' &c.

§ 51. in late Latin and Romance. With Latin j (our y) were merged in Vulgar Latin g before e, i, and d before i followed by a vowel (see below), for these three Latin sounds are indistinguishable in the Romance languages. Spellings therefore on late inscriptions like *Diuliali* (Rossi 1118, of 568 A. D.), *Madias* (Rossi 172), *Giove* (*I. R. N.* 695), *Gianuaria* (Fabr. x. 632, Interamna, of 503 A. D.) do not indicate that j had passed from the y-sound (see *A. L. L.* i. 220), but that -*diu*-, -*dia*-, *gio*-, *gia*- were pronounced like -*yu*, -*ya*, *yo*-, &c. The occasional spelling with Lat. z, Greek ζ, e.g. *Zanuario* (*C. I. L.* x. 2466), ζουλεια (*I. I. S.* 826. 22, Naples), κοζους (Lat. *co(n)jux*, *C. I. L.* x. 719, Surrentum) is probably nothing but an attempt to indicate the spirant sound of j (our y) as opposed to the vocalic sound of i; for Lat. z, Greek ζ had at this time the soft or voiced s-sound of our verb 'to use,' and not our j-sound, nor the sound of -*dz*- in 'adze' (see § 120). (For other examples see Schuchardt, *Vok.* i. pp. 66 sqq.) This Vulgar Latin y-sound of triple origin is y in Spanish (in most situations), in Sardinian, and (by Greek influence ?) in South Italian, but in ordinary Italian (except when pretonic, e.g. rione from Lat. *regiōnem*, ajuta, pronounced ayuta, from Lat. *adjūtat*) it has become the sound of our j; while in French (in most situations) it has assumed the sound which we write s in 'pleasure,' z in 'azure.' Thus Latin *jugum* is Span. yugo, Ital. giogo, Fr. joug; Lat. *majus* is Span. mayo, Sicilian mayu, Ital. maggio; Vulg. Lat. *Jenuarius* is Sicil. yennaru, Ital. gennajo, Fr. janvier. In loanwords in Welsh Latin j has the y-sound, e. g. Ionawr (Lat. *Jānuārius*), dydd Iau (Lat. *dies Jovis*). In Greek inscriptions, besides the usual ι, e. g. 'Ιουλιος, Ποντπειος, we have sometimes η and ει, e. g. 'Ηουλιος, Ειουλιος, Γαειος and Γαηος (see Eckinger, p. 80).

The barred d of the Pelignian dialect (Petie*d*u, ui*d*adu, Uib*d*u, af*d*ed in the same inscription, Zvetaieff, *Inscr. Ital. Inf.* 13) expresses some sound into which consonantal $i(y)$ and di in hiatus had developed (Latin *Pettiedia*, *viam-do*, *Vibidia*, *abiit*) (*Rhein. Mus.* xliii. 348; *Class. Rev.* vii. 104), and seems to be a dialectal anticipation of the coincidence of di in hiatus and j in Vulgar and late Latin. After a short accented vowel y suffered some similar change in Teutonic, witness Goth. iddja I went, from the root EI to go.

§ 52. v confused with b in late Latin and Romance. From the beginning of the second century A. D. we begin to find b and v interchanged on inscriptions (see Schuchardt, *Vok.* i. 131 and iii. 67; Brambach, *Orth.* p. 238), and by the third century the confusion is complete. The b-symbol is, as is natural, used for the v-sound more frequently than the vowel symbol (capital V, uncial U, see i. 7) for b. Latin b had probably by this time become, when between

E

vowels, a spirant (see § 78), so that the tendency is to restrict V, U to the vowel- (*u*), B to the spirant-sounds (*b, v*). (For examples of the interchange see the Indices to the *Corpus*.) In Greek inscriptions ου is the earliest spelling for Lat. *v*, and continues to be the usual spelling throughout the Imperial period, e.g. ἀρουαλις Mon. Ancyr., Οὐεσπασιανος (never Βεσπ-), οὐετεράνος and οὐετρανος, &c. But we find β occasionally even in the first cent. A. D., the earliest examples being Φλαβιος, Λειβιος (the usual spelling), Σιλβανος, Βαλεριος. This use of β may have been stimulated by the preference of a single to a double symbol. Λειβιος is more pleasing to the eye than Λειουιος; and in this way we may explain why Latin ου is more often οβ than οου. (It is often ου, e. g. Νουιος) (see Eckinger, pp. 82 sqq.) Little light however is thrown on the pronunciation of Latin *v* by this Greek use of β; for in the first place, the pronunciation of β itself in the Imperial age is uncertain (Blass supposes it to have become a spirant, as in modern Greek, in the second cent. A. D. *Aussprache d. Griech.*² p. 91), and in the second, the use of β followed in all probability the use of *b* in the Latin spelling. (Thus on the Edict of Diocletian *vulva* is spelt *bulba* in the Latin inscription, βουλβη in the Greek.) We sometimes find ου and β on the same inscription, e.g. Νερουα and Νερβα (second cent.), Φλαουιανος and Φλαβιανος on an inscr. of Cyrene, 117-125 A. D. (see Eckinger). The remarks however of the Grammarians point, as we have seen, to *v* having retained its connexion with the vowel *u* till a later time in correct pronunciation; and the same thing is indicated by the loss of intervocalic *v* in *paimentum*, &c., for *pavimentum* (see below). At what time the bilabial spirant *v* (our *w*) became the labiodental spirant *v* (our *v*) is not easy to say. It would be rash to conclude from spellings like *convivium, convivio* (where the *m* of *com* is changed to *n*) on the Lex Municipalis of Julius Caesar (*C. I. L.* i. 206), and still more from *invitei, inviteis* (where the *n* of *in* is retained) on the Sententia Minuciorum of 117 B. C. (i. 199), that the change had taken place in the Republican period; for as early as 189 B. C. we have *inpeirator* (Wilm. 2837), and in the Sen. Cons. de Bacchanalibus of 186 B. C. *conpromesise* (i. 196), clear instances of *n* before an undoubted bilabial. The facts certainly point to *com-, im-* being the oldest spellings before *v-* (and *f-*, see § 64), e.g. *comvovise* (and *coventionid*) i. 196; *comvalem, confluont* (but also *conflouont*) i. 199; and the *im uita* of the Palimpsest of Plautus (*Merc.* 471), *comuiuas* (*Men.* 224), may rest upon old tradition; but the substitution of -*n* for -*m* of a preposition before a consonant in a compound is no certain evidence for the nature of the consonant (see § 65). More weight may be attached to Cicero's deliberate preference of the spelling *com* before *v*, mentioned by Marius Victorinus (fourth cent. A. D.) (18. 14 K.) : item consonantes inter se, sed proprie sunt cognatae, quae simili figuratione oris dicuntur, ut est b, f, m, p, quibus Cicero adicit u, non eam quae accipitur pro vocali, sed eam quae consonantis obtinet vicem, et anteposita vocali fit, ut aliae quoque consonantes. quotiens igitur praepositionem sequetur vox cujus prima syllaba incipit a supradictis litteris, id est b, f, m, p, v, quae vox conjuncta praepositioni significationem ejus confundat, vos quoque praepositionis litteram mutate, ut est 'combibit,' 'comburit,' 'comfert,' 'comfundit,' 'commemorat,' 'comminuit,' 'comparat,' 'compellit,' 'comvalescit,' 'convocat,' non 'conbibit,' 'conburit,' et similia. sic etiam praepositio juncta vocibus quae incipiunt a supradictis litteris n commutat in m, ut 'imbibit,' 'imbuit,' 'imfert,' 'imficit,' 'immemor,' 'immitis,' 'impius,' 'impotens.' The ordinary rule that *com-, im-* are used before *p, b,*

§ 52.] PRONUNCIATION. J,V. 51

m is quoted by Priscian (i. p. 31. 2 H.) from Pliny, Papirian, and Probus (cf. Papir. ap. Cassiod. 162. 6 K.; Prob. 150. 6 K.) with no mention either of *f* (which Mar. Vict. must have taken from some older grammarian), or of *v*. It is true that Cicero's spelling, *comuocat*, &c., might equally well be taken as a proof of the more vocalic nature of *v* in his time; for before a vowel *com* is often the form in use, e. g. *cŏmĕdo*, *cŏmĭtor*, &c. [Caesellius Vindex (end of first cent. A.D.) (ap. Cassiod. 206. 17 K.) recommends *com-* before a vowel, *con-* before a consonant or *v*: tunc pro m littera n litterae sonum decentius efferemus]. But the Latin and Teutonic loanwords give a similar indication of a change in the pronunciation of *v* (at any rate of initial *v*), during the period of the Western Empire. The early Latin loanwords in Teutonic languages show invariably *w* for Latin *v-*, e. g. Goth. wīns, our 'wine,' 'wall,' '-wick' (Latin *vinum*, *vallum*, *vicus*). But Teutonic loanwords in Italian &c., which date from the Gothic occupation in the fifth cent. A.D., show *gu-* for Gothic *w-* (e. g. guarire from Gothic warjan; guisa, our ' -wise '), an indication that the initial *w-* sound had passed out of use in Latin. An examination of the Romance languages does indeed suggest that the change from the bilabial to the labiodental spirant was not completed in the Vulgar Latin of all the provinces; but on the other hand the close connexion of the *w-* and the *v-*sounds, and the frequent passage of a language from either sound to the other, weaken the force of the evidence. In Vulgar Latin intervocalic *b* had been merged in *v*. This *v*, of double origin, has the labiodental sound in Italian and French; but is bilabial in Spain, and (possibly through Greek influence) in South Italy. Spanish and South Italian also merge initial *b* and *v*. Thus, while initial and intervocalic *b* of Latin *bibo* receive a different treatment in Italian bevere, they have the same spirant sound in Spanish beber, Sicilian viviri, Calabrian vivere. The identification of Latin *v* and intervocalic *b* in all the Romance languages, and therefore in Vulgar Latin, shows that it was in this position, in the middle of a word between vowels, that *b* first became a spirant sound (see below). Confusions of spelling between *b* and *v* are usually of this sort, e. g. *Dānŭvius*, the spelling of the classical period, later *Danubius* (see Georges, *Lex. Wortf.* s. v., and for other examples, s. vv. *abellana*, *gabata*, *viduvium*, *Suebi*, *sebum*, *Vesuvius*, *sevir*). That the development also of *v* differed according to its position in a word is a natural inference, and is confirmed by the evidence. Initial accented *v* would, owing to the stress with which a consonant was pronounced in this position, develop its consonantal character more rapidly than intervocalic *v*, especially than pretonic intervocalic *v* (see below). A good instance of a confusion of spelling due to this is the word *vĕnēfĭcus*, which so often assumed the form *beneficus*, that it produced in late Latin a new word for a sorcerer, *maleficus* (*A.L.L.* i. 79) (cf. Probi App. 200. 9 K. inter beneficum et veneficum hoc interest, quod beneficum bene facientem significat, veneficum autem veneni datorem esse demonstrat). *Vătillum* is the correct spelling, not *bătillum* (Nettleship, *Contributions to Lat. Lexic.* s. v.).

After *r* and *l* the same thing seems to have happened; cf. late Lat. *albeus* (Agrim. 82. 24), *arba* (75. 19), Vulg. Lat. *corbus*, *curbus* (Fr. corbeau, courbe, &c.). Pliny's example of preconsonantal *l* is the word *silva* (§ 99); and the classical spelling of the Perfect of *ferveo*, where *rv* is followed by *u* is *ferbui* not *fervui* (*feruui*) (cf. Georges, *Lex. Wortf.* s. vv. *vulva*, *ervum*, *gilvus*; Probi App. 198. 7 alveus non 'albeus.' *Albeus* occurs often on inscrr., e. g. *C.I.L.* x. 1.

E 2

1695, 1696, 4752, 6850, Eph. Epigr. iii. 48). The only (?) early example of *rb, lb* becoming *rv, lv* is *acervissimam* (*I. N.* 1951, of 155 A. D.), a misspelling due to confusion of two similar words *acerbus* and *acervus*, and not to be taken as evidence of a change of the sound *rb* to the sound *rv*. But *rb, lb* for *rv, lv* is common on inscrr., e.g. *coserba, Helbius, salbus, serbat, serbus, balbis* (see index to *C.I.L.* xiv). Assimilation also often played a part in the development of *v* and *b*; e.g. *vervex* is in Vulg. Lat. *berbix (Fr. brebis, Ital. berbice) ; *vervactum* is *barbactum (Span. barbecho, Sard. barvatu, Port. barbeito), and the only change of *rb* to *rv* that is common to all the Romance languages, viz. *morvus* for *morbus*, seems to show the influence of the initial *m* (Span. muermo, Port. mormo, Prov. vorma, Fr. morve, Sicil. morvu. See *A. L. L.* iv. 121). *Primilegium* for *prīvīlēgium* (Caper, III. 2 K.) is due to confusion with *primus*. We have *f* for *v* in the spellings *judicafid* (*C.I.L.* vi. 6592), *Mafortio* (le Blant, *I.G.* 612 A, of 527 A.D. from Narbonne).

§ 53. **Intervocalic v dropped.** Between vowels *v* seems to have retained a vocalic character much longer. It was dropped before *u* of the Nom. Sing., thus *dīvus* (older *deiv-*) became **deius, deus, Gnaevus* became *Gnaeus*, &c. (ch. iv. § 70), but was usually restored from the other cases, e.g. *rīvus* from *rīvo*, &c., but Vulg. Lat. had *rius*, &c. (Ital. rio, Prov. rius, O.Fr. riu) ; between similar vowels it is very prone to disappear, e. g. *ĭ-ĭ, sīs,* for *sī vīs, obliscor, dīnus* (Plaut.), just as in Mod. Tuscan between *e-e*, bee for beve ; late spellings like *noicius,* for *novicius, Noe(m)bris* for *Novembris,* &c., are very frequent, especially when *v* stands before the accent. (For examples see Schuchardt, *Vok.* ii. pp. 471 sqq., e. g. *Flaus C.I.L.* i. 277, viii. 9422, *ao E. E.* v. 777; cf. the remarks of grammarians like Probus, *Inst.* 113. 17 K. hoc ovum et non hoc 'oum'; Probi App. 198 5. K. flavus non 'flaus'; ib. 199. 2 K. rivus non 'rius'; ib. 198. 8 K. favilla non 'failla'; ib. 199. 2 K. pavor non 'paor'; ib. 197. 28 avus non 'aus'; similarly on Greek inscriptions Νοεμβριος is the usual form (as early as 73 B.C. in S. C. of Oropus) ; cf. 'Οκταϊος (time of Augustus); 'Αϊανος (*C.I.I.* 4750); Σεηρος, &c. (Eckinger, p. 92) (see also Georges, *Lex. Wortf.* s. vv. *longao, boa, boo,* Ribbeck, *Index,* p. 448 for spellings in Virgil MSS. like *fluius, exuiae, iuenis,* beside which we find *fluventa, bovum, fluvidus, fluvitantem, ingruvit, tenuvia*).

§ 54. **Postconsonantal v dropped.** Vulg. Lat. *v* (in classical Latin the vowel *u*) is also dropped after consonants not only before *u* (for examples see Schuchardt, *Vok.* ii. pp. 464 sqq.), e. g. *mortus* for *mortuus, cardus* for *carduus* (cf. *cardelis* Petron 46. 4) (Ital. morto, cardo ; Span. muerto, cardo ; Fr. mort, chardon from **cardo, -ōnis*), just as *-quu-* became *-cu-* in the beginning of the first cent. A. D. e. g. *ecus, locuntur, locutus* (see § 93), but also when pretonic in words like *Jān(u)ārius, Febr(u)ārius, batt(u)ĕre, cons(u)ĕre, contin(u)ari* (see Georges and Brambach s. vv. and for *contin(u)ari, A. L. L.* viii. 129, 136. Examples of this spelling in Inscriptions and MSS. have been collected by Schuchardt, *Vok.* ii. pp. 467 sqq. Compare the Romance forms, e. g. Ital. gennajo, febbrajo, battére, cucire, &c.) (see ch. iii. § 15). In the App. Probi we have : 199. 12 Februarius non 'Febrarius'; 197. 23 vacua non 'vaqua,' vacui non 'vaqui' (cf. *Febrarius* in various Latin inscriptions, such as *C. I. L.* ix. 3160; xiv. 58. 2795). *Pituīta* must have had in ordinary speech the trisyllabic pronunciation which Horace gives it (*Epp.* i. 1. 108 nisi cum pituita molesta est), and not the quadrisyllabic of Catullus (xxiii. 17 mucusque et mala pituita nasi). For Aelius Stilo's derivation of the word was 'quia petit vitam' (ap. Quint. i. 6.

37), and the Vulgar Latin form was *pipīta or *pippīta (Ital. pipita, Span. pepita, Fr. pépie; cf. Mid. Engl. pippe, Swiss pfiffis). On the other hand *suāvis* seems to have been a trisyllable in Vulg. Lat. (as in Sedulius, e. g. i. 274, and later poets), e. g. Ital. soave, O.Fr. so-éf, Prov. soáu. Servius (ad *Aen.* i. 357) tells us that many persons in his day considered *suādet* to be a trisyllable.

§ 55. **ai, ei before a vowel.** Velius Longus says that Cicero wrote *Maiia*, &c., because he thought these words should be written as they were pronounced (*auditu emensus scriptionem*); so *coïicit* might be written *coiiicit* to express the sound of the first syllable *coi* and the second and third syllables *iicit* (Vel. Long. vii. 54. 16 K.): in plerisque Cicero videtur auditu emensus scriptionem, qui et 'Aiiacem' et 'Maiiam' per duo i scribenda existimavit: quidam unum esse animadvertunt, siquidem potest et per unum i enuntiari, ut scriptum est. unde illud quod pressius et plenius sonet per duo i scribi oportere existimat, sic et 'Troiiam,' et siqua talia sunt. inde crescit ista geminatio, et incipit per tria i scribi ' coiiicit,' ut prima syllaba sit coi, sequentes duae iicit. . . at qui Troiam et Maiam per unum i scribunt, negant onerandam pluribus litteris scriptionem, cum sonus ipse sufficiat. hanc enim naturam esse quarundam litterarum, ut morentur et enuntiatione sonum detineant, quod accidit et in eo quod dicimus ' hoc est' [pronounced 'hoccest' p. 54. 12], cum ipsa vastitas litterae in enuntiatione pinguescat. atque ipsa natura i litterae est ut interjecta vocalibus latinis enuntietur, dum et prior illam adserit et sequens sibi vindicat. So Priscian (x. 1. 494) says that *aio* was spelt *aiio* in former times, and is still pronounced 'ayyo' (*i loco consonantis habet duplicis*). Our ordinary pronunciation *Trō-ja*, *ē-jus* is wrong. The first vowel of the diphthong retained its natural quantity, *ējero*, *Gāius*, but *ĕjus*, *ăio*, *măjor* (see *Arch. Glott. Ital.* x), as we see from Romance forms like Ital. peggio (with open *e*) for Latin *pējor*, and from the remark of Terentianus Maurus (p. 343 K.), that in *Troja*, *Maia*, *pejor*, *jejunium* the vowel preceding *j* is short in each of these words, though the syllable is long. Similarly *ejŭlo*, to utter the cry *ei* (Plaut. *Aul.* 796 ei mihi!.. Cur eiulas?) must have been pronounced ei-i̯ulo. In unaccented syllables *j*, *i̯* seem to have been dropped after a short vowel in Latin, e. g. the Adj. suffix *-eus* for *-eyos* (*Riv. Filolog.* 1891 p. 18) (ch. v.). Spellings like *aiio* are sometimes found in MSS. of classical authors, e. g. *aio* in the archetype of Hor. *Epp.* i. 15. 45 was written *aiio*, whence the corruption *alio* in several MSS (*Class. Rev.* v. 296); *eiius* in the Ambrosian Palimpsest of Plautus, *Most.* 981 &c.; *piiaculum* (in the Vetus Codex *pilaculum*) *Truc.* 223.

§ 56. **H.** Latin *h*, the representative of Indo-European GH (e. g. *hostis*, our 'guest') must in prehistoric times have had some sound like German *ch* in 'ach,' Scotch *ch* in 'loch,' but by the literary period had been reduced to the mere spiritus fortis, our *h*. We have no reason to doubt that the sound was dropped in Vulgar Latin as early as the middle of the third cent. B. C., for we have not a trace of initial or medial *h* in any of the Romance languages, not even the oldest; and one of the earliest tasks of grammarians at Rome was to draw up rules for the correct use of initial *h*, their usual practice being to appeal to the Sabine dialect where I.-Eur. *gh*- had become *f* (e. g. *fostis*), as *gh* in our 'enough' (ch. iv. § 121). The Greek aspirated consonants θ, χ, φ (t-h, k-h, p-h, as in 'an*t-h*eap,' 'in*k-h*orn,' 'u*p-h*ill') were expressed by the simple tenues *t, c, p* in the Latin of the Republic, until at the time of Cicero it was felt necessary to express them more accurately by *th, ch, ph* (ch. i. § 11); and this pronunciation was carefully followed in polite circles. The struggle to attain the new shibboleth of fashion led to ludicrous misapplications of the *h*-sound by the uneducated classes, which have been satirized by Catullus in his famous epigram on Arrius (84):—

'Chommoda' dicebat siquando commoda vellet
dicere et insidias Arrius 'hinsidias';

and the dropping of *h* seems to have been even in the time of St. Augustine an unpardonable breach of manners. (On *rh, rrh* for Greek ῥ-, -ῥῥ- see ch. i. § 11.)

Between vowels the omission of *h* was sanctioned by current usage in a number of words such as *nēmo* (for *ne-hemo), *dēbeo* (*dehibeo*), *praebeo* (*praehibeo*), *praeda* (for *prae-heda, *praehida). By the first cent. *prendo* and *nīl* had established themselves in pronunciation, also *deprendo*, through *reprehensus* was heard as well as *reprensus*.

In the Umbrian language the length of a vowel was often indicated by writing it before and after an *h*, e. g. *comohota* (Lat. *commōta*); and it has been suggested that this usage may have been adopted in Latin in a few words like *vehemens*, just as the Oscan habit of doubling a vowel to express its length (e. g. trístaamentud, Latin *testāmento* abl.) was adopted by Accius (ch. i. § 9). *Vehemens*, according to this theory, is derived from *vē* and *mens*, like *vēsanus* from *vē* and *sanus* (*Etym. Lat.* p. 113). We have NAHARTIS (*C. I. L.* xi. 4213, time of Augustus), as well as NART(is) (ib. 4201, 240 A.D.), &c., in Latin inscriptions from the Umbrian territory, and Cicero (*Orat.* xlv. 153) speaks of the name *Āla* (*Ahala*) as representing *Axilla* (but cf. Diom. p. 424, Dositheus, p. 382 K.). We find *h* put to the same use in modern German, through analogy of words like stahel 'steel' (with *h* for I.-Eur. *k*; cf. O. Pruss. stakla) which became stāl.

§ 57.] PRONUNCIATION. H. 55

§ 57. **Testimony of grammarians**: Quint. i. 5. 19 quamquam per adspirationem, sive adicitur vitiose sive detrahitur, apud nos potest quaeri, an in scripto sit vitium, si h littera est, non nota. cujus quidem ratio mutata cum temporibus est saepius. parcissime ea veteres usi etiam in vocalibus, cum 'aedos ircosque' dicebant. diu deinde servatum, ne consonantibus adspirarent, ut in 'Graccis' et 'triumpis.' erupit brevi tempore nimius usus, ut 'choronae chenturiones praechones' adhuc quibusdam inscriptionibus maneant, qua de re Catulli nobile epigramma est. inde durat ad nos usque 'vehementer' et 'comprehendere' et 'mihi': nam 'mehe' quoque pro 'me' [*leg.* mi?] apud antiquos tragoediarum praecipue scriptores in veteribus libris invenimus. Similarly Gellius ii. 3. 1-4: h litteram sive illam spiritum magis quam litteram dici oportet, inserebant eam veteres nostri plerisque vocibus verborum firmandis roborandisque, ut sonus earum esset viridior vegetiorque; atque id videntur fecisse studio et exemplo linguae Atticae. satis notum est, Atticos ἰχθύν et ἵ pronomen et multa itidem alia, contra morem gentium Graeciae ceterarum, inspirantis primae litterae dixisse. sic 'lachrumas,' sic 'sepulchrum,' sic 'ahenum,' sic 'vehemens,' sic 'incohare,' sic 'helluari,' sic 'halucinari,' sic 'honera,' sic 'honustum' dixerunt. In his enim verbis omnibus litterae seu spiritus istius nulla ratio visa est, nisi ut firmitas et vigor vocis, quasi quibusdam nervis additis, intenderetur. Then he goes on to tell of a bookhunting friend of his who had bought for twenty gold 'sigillarii' a MS. of the second Aeneid, 'mirandae vetustatis,' which was reputed to have belonged to Virgil himself. In v. 469 telis et luce coruscus aena, the last word had been corrected to *ahena*, just as *aheni*, not *aeni*, was the reading of the 'optimi libri' in *Georg.* i. 296. This account of *h* as (like the Greek spiritus asper), a mere 'nota adspirationis,' not properly called a 'littera' is a commonplace of the grammarians, e. g. Mar. Victor. vi. 5. 27 K.; ib. vi. 3; Charisius i. 265. 20 K.; Priscian i. 47, &c. The only contradiction is the absurd remark of Pompeius (v. 117. 14 K.), that in Virgil's line (*Aen.* ix. 610) terga fatigamus hasta, the *h* causes length by position, a remark often repeated by the later writers on metre and followed in practice by the Christian poets.

Terentianus Maurus in his description of the sound of *h* discusses its claims to stand in the alphabet (vi. 331. 213) (Cf. Quint. i. 4. 9):

> nulli dubium est faucibus emicet quod ipsis
> h littera, sive est nota, quae spiret anhelum.
> quin hanc etiam grammatici volunt vacare,
> quia non adicit litterulis novum sonorem,
> sed graecula quaedam scholicae nitela vocis
> vocalibus apte sedet ante posta cunctis,
> 'hastas' 'hederas' cum loquor 'Hister' 'hospes' 'hujus.'

Marius Victorinus says (vi. 34. 7 K.) profundo spiritu, anhelis faucibus, exploso ore fundetur; and Martianus Capella (iii. 261) H contractis [conrasis *Eyss.*] paululum faucibus ventus exhalat. Cf. Priscian i. 24; Alcuin vii. 303. 18 K.

Rules for the use and omission of initial *h* are very frequent in the grammarians. Nigidius (first cent. B.C.) emphasized the importance of correctness in the use of this letter: rusticus fit sermo si adspires perperam, a dictum quoted by Gellius (xiii. 6. 3), who explains that by 'rusticism' Nigidius meant what grammarians of a later date called *barbarismus*. Velius Longus quotes Varro's argument for the pronunciation *hărēna*, viz. that the Sabine form of the word is *fasena*. Similarly *haedus* is supported by *faedus*, *hircus* by *fircus* (Vel. Long. vii. 69. 4–10 K.). Quite a number of dialectal forms have been preserved for us through the grammarians' practice of using dialectal *f* as a criterion for Latin *h*, e. g. *fordeum* (with *fasena*, *firci*, *faedi*) (Vel. Long. vii. 81 K.) : the doubtful *fariolus* (Ter. Scaur. 11 K.) (with *faedus*, *fordeum*, and p. 13 *fircus*) : Faliscan *haba* (id. 13 K.) : *fibra* (= *herba*) (Nigidius ap. 'Serv.' ad *Georg.* i. 120) : *forda bos*, a cow in calf, *Fordicidia* (Paul. Fest. 59 ; 73 Th. *folus*, *fostis*, *fostia* (id. 59) : *horctus*, good (id. 73) : *hanulum*, a shrine (id. 73) : *fuma* (= *humus*), *Haunii* (= *Faunii*) (glosses ap. Löwe, *Prodr.* 426) ; and a large number of etymologies were made on the strength of this relation between *f* and *h*, such as *Formiae* 'velut Hormiae' from Greek ὅρμος (Paul Fest. 59) : *horreum* from *far* (id. 73) : *firmus* from Greek ἕρμα (id. 64). So Servius (ad *Aen.* vii. 695) : Faliscos Halesus condidit. hi autem, inmutato h in f, Falisci dicti sunt, sicut febris dicitur quae ante 'hebris' dicebatur, Formiae quae 'Hormiae' fuerunt, ἀπὸ τῆς ὁρμῆς : nam posteritas in multis nominibus f pro h posuit. These dialectal words are often loosely called 'old Latin' : *haba*, for example, which Terentius Scaurus expressly declares to have been a Faliscan word (13 K.), is referred by Velius Longus (69 K.) to the 'antiqui' ; and Quintilian (i. 4. 13), amongst other genuine instances of old Latin, such as *Valesii*, *Fusii*, *mertare*, says : quin 'fordeum' 'faedosque' [dicebant], pro adspiratione f ut simili littera utentes. There is however no reason to believe that in Latin itself these forms were used, though they may have been heard in the country districts about Rome, where dialectal influence often strongly asserted itself. At other times grammarians defend the use or omission of *h* by more or less ingenious etymologies, e. g. Servius in Don. iv. 444. 28, 29 K. dicta est enim [harena] quod harida sit terra ; Charisius i. 103. 21, 22 K. harena dicitur quod haereat, et arena quod areat ; gratius tamen cum adspiratione sonat. Velius Longus (vii. 68. 18, 19 K.) defends *ălĭca* : cum ab alendo possit alica dici, et aliculam existimentis dictam, quod alas nobis injecta contineat, and *ortus* : quod ibi herbae oriantur. Charisius says of this word *ălĭca* that Verrius Flaccus approved of the form without *h*, whereas a line of Lucilius ran : nemo est halicarius posterior te (i. 96. 9 K.). Caper's dictum is : alica non halica (vii. 107. 12 K.). Another doubtful case was the salutation *ăve*. Quintilian (i. 6. 21) tells us that though the proper form was *ăvē*, the verb being *avēre* and not *havēre*, yet no one, except a precisian, thought of saying anything else than *havĕ* : multum enim litteratus, qui sine adspiratione et producta secunda syllaba salutarit ('avere' est enim), . . . recta est haec via : quis negat ? sed adjacet alia et mollior et magis trita, &c. (For examples of uncertainty in the use of *h*-, see Georges and Brambach, s. vv. *Hiberus, harena, haurio, exaurio, harundo, haruspex, hebenus, hedera, helluor, Henna, heia, eiulo, Hilotae, Aedui, alica, allec, halucinor, Hadria, Halaesa, Halicarnassus, Hamilcar, Hammon, Hannibal, Hanno, elleborum, ercisco, erctum, erus, Hadrumetum, haedus, hamus, hariolus, hibiscum, hinnuleus, hircus, hostia, holus, holitor, onustus, umeo, umerus, ulcus, Hister, Hirpini, onero, Ilerda, Illyria.*) Cf. Probi App. 199. 17 K. adhuc non 'aduc' (*aduc* in *C. I. L.* v. 6244).

The right employment of *h* is a leading subject in Alcuin's handbook of Orthography (vii. 300. 27 K. ; 303. 11, 13 and 19 ; 306. 2) ; and St. Augustine (*Confess.* i. 18) playfully remarks that the dropping of an *h* was generally regarded as a more heinous sin than an offence against the law of

Christian charity : si contra disciplinam grammaticam sine adspiratione primae syllabae 'ominem' dixerit, displiceat magis hominibus, quam si contra tua praecepta hominem oderit, quum sit ' homo.'

§ 58. h between vowels. Quintilian (ix. 4. 59) says that *deprendere*, not *deprehendere*, was the form in use in his time. Gellius (second cent.) (ii. 3) speaks of *ahenum* (cf. *aheneam*, Comm. Lud. Saec. A 60, &c.), *vehemens*, *incohare* (along with *lachrumae*, *sepulchrum*, *helluari*, *halucinari*, *honera* and *honustus*) as old-fashioned forms now obsolete. A fourth century grammarian, called Probus, says that *trăho* retains the *h* in spelling merely to indicate that the *a* and *o* are pronounced separately, the word being spoken ' trao ' (IV. 185. 5 K.). On the other hand in the second century Terentius Scaurus while declaring that *prendo*, never *prehendo*, was the form in use, says that *věho* 'sine dubio aspiratur,' and speaks of *vemens* and *vehemens*, *reprensus*, and *reprehensus* as optional (vii. 19. 14 K.) [cf. Velius Longus (second cent.), vii. 68. 15 K., who gives *vemens* and *reprendo* as the usage of the 'elegantiores,' *prendo* as universal, and Annaeus Cornutus (first cent.), the friend of Persius, who mentions *prendo*, *vemens*, *nil* as the pronunciation of his day (ap. Cassiodor. vii. 153. 7 K.) (see also Alcuin vii. 311. 26, 27 K. ; Papirian vii. 159. 18-21 K.; Eutyches vii. 200. 8 K.; Caper vii 98. 12 K.)]. (For examples of confusion in spelling, see Georges and Brambach s. vv. *cohors*, *incoho*, *aeneus*, *Ahenobarbus*, *Dahae*, *Phraates*, *coerceo*, *euhan*, *prooemium*, *periodus*. For Greek compounds with aspirate initial of second member following a consonant, see *exedra*, *exodus*, *synodus*, *Panhormus*, &c. On the interjections *aha*, *ehem* cf. Richter in Studemund's *Studien*, i. ii.)

§ 59. h in Old Latin. H was dropped earliest between vowels (e.g. *nēmo*); and the disuse of initial *h* would no doubt begin with words which were preceded in the sentence by a word ending in a vowel. Teutonic loanwords with *h-* in Romance lost their *h* rapidly in Italian, Spanish, and Portuguese, but retained it for some time in French, which in the Middle Ages abounded in consonantal terminations. This was doubtless the principle of elision of a final vowel before initial *h* in Latin poetry, whether the vowel was actually final, or was followed by the vague nasal ' after-sound,' *m* (see §§ 153, 61). There is no reason to suppose that initial *h* was in Early Roman poetry more resistive of elision, than in the classical period. The Plautine *flagitiŭm hŏminis* formed really a single word (ch. iii. § 12), and the hiatus is to be compared to hiatus in compounds like *circŭit* from *circum it*. The weak nature of early *h* is seen in compounds like *cohonesto* (*co-* before a vowel as in *coeo*, *coorior*, &c.) which in Accius, *Trag.* 445 R. appears as *cōnesto* (see § 149). *Nihil* is always a monosyllable in Plautus apparently. But the dropping of initial *h* on the older inscriptions is hardly known. (See Sittl. *Lok. Verschied.* p. 39.)

§ 60. Greek aspirates in Latin. The Greek aspirates lost their aspiration in loanwords used by the early writers, e.g. Plautus, as we gather from the MSS. (see the statistics given in *Fleck. Jahrb.* 1891, p. 658 *n.*), from puns like those on *Chrysalus* (*Crusalus*) and *crucisalus*, on *Charinus* (*Carinus*) and *careo* :— *Pseud.* 736, non Charinus mihi quidemst sed copia, on *Thales* and *talentum Capt.* 274, and from the statements of later grammarians (cf. the pun on *excalciaverat* 'cum adspiratione secundae syllabae' (robbed of one's money, χαλκός), and *excalceaverat*, i. e. taken off one's boots, *calcei*) in Porphyr. ad Hor. *S.* i. 8. 39).

Quintilian for example (i. 5. 20) says: diu deinde servatum ne consonantibus [veteres] adspirarent, ut in 'Graccis' et in 'triumpis.' There are not wanting in Plautus indications that the vulgar Greek pronunciation of χ as *k-kh* (see Blass, p. 86) influenced some loanwords in popular use so as to lengthen (by position) the previous vowel. *Acc(h)eruns, Acc(h)il(l)es,* like *bracc(h)ium* seem to be required by the metre (Baier, *Philologische Abhandlungen zu Hertz.* 1888). Similarly the word *trīcae*, whose origin has been traced to S. Italy, where the word was applied to hair-shackles put on the legs of fowls to prevent their straying, seems to be nothing but the Greek τρίχες in a Latinized form (*trīcae* and *triccae, like *brāchium* and *bracchium*, &c.). The proverb '*ăpinae trīcaeque*,' used of trifles (Mart. xiv. 1. 7):—

sunt apinae tricaeque et siquid vilius istis,

has likewise been referred to S. Italy, where ἀφάναι (Latinized *apinae*), 'the unseen realms,' was in popular story the name of an imaginary country of bliss, like Aristophanes' 'Cloud-cuckoo-land' (Ribbeck, *Leipziger Studien*, 1887). The Vulg. Latin *muttus*, a word, from which Fr. *mot* is derived (*mūtus*, Non. 9. 16 M.?) seems to be similarly Greek μῦθος (*muttus* for *mūtus*), as *trīcae* for *triccae; also *strŭppus* a rope is Gk. στρόφος (Festus, 452. 21 Th., says that at Tusculum the word had the sense of a wreath, and that a Faliscan 'Garland-festival' was called *Struppearia*; the Romance forms point to *strŏppus*, a form found in this passage of Festus). Gk. φ was in early Latin transcription *p*, e.g. *Pilipus* on a denarius of the time of the Gracchi (*C.I.L.* i. 354), though sometimes (like Gk. π in *Burrus*, Πυρρός) *b*, e.g. *Brŭges* for Φρύγες, *balaena* for φάλλαινα (Quint. 1. 4. 15, from Verrius Flaccus) (see § 49). F was not regularly used till the middle of the fourth cent. A.D. (see ch. i. § 11). Blass, *Griech. Aussprache*[2], p. 85, dates the change of Greek φ from the *p-h* to the *f*-sound at about 400 A.D.; and the language of Diomede (fourth cent.) seems to imply that the difference between Lat. *f* and Gk. φ was in his time very slight (423. 28 K. 'et hoc scire debemus quod f littera tum scribitur, cum latina dictio scribitur, ut 'felix,' nam si peregrina fuerit, p et h scribimus, ut 'Phoebus,' 'Phaeton'). The difference between the two sounds in Cicero's time is seen from Quintilian's story of Cicero ridiculing a Greek witness who could not pronounce the first letter of Fundanius (Quint. i. 4. 14). Φ is however, as is natural, the Greek transcription of Latin *f* (Eckinger, p. 97); e.g. Φονδανιος is the Greek transcription of this very name on an inscription of 81 B.C. (*Bull.* ix. p. 457, from Lagina in Caria). The old spelling persisted in a few words like *tūs* (Gk. θύος), &c. (see ch. i. § 11). A curious interchange of *s* and *th* is occasionally seen in the Notae Tironianae, e.g. *agatho* for *agāso*, *Apollopisius* for *Pythius* (Schmitz, *Beitr.* 109). With the introduction however of Greek grammatical studies at Rome a more exact transcription came into fashion (see ch. i. § 11), and it is to this tendency that we must refer the aspiration of some consonants even in Latin words about this time, not merely in words which were supposed to be borrowed from Greek, e.g. *pulcher* (ch. i. § 11) (referred to πολύχρους, Ter. Scaur. vii. 20. 4-8), and *sĕpulchrum* (*sē* and *pulcher*! Charis. i. 73 17; cf. *C.I.L.* i. 1007 heic est sepulcrum hau pulcrum pulcrai feminae), *lachrȳma* (to Gk. δάκρυμα), &c., but to others which could hardly be so misunderstood, e.g. *praecho*, *lurcho*. In the *Orator* xlviii. 160, Cicero tells us that he was forced in spite of his convictions to yield so far to popular usage as to pronounce *pulcher*, *Cethēgus*, *triumphus*, *Karthāgo*, though he still adhered to *Orcivius, Mãto, Õto, Caepio, sĕpulcrum, cŏrōna, lacrĭma* : quin ego ipse, cum scirem ita majores locutos esse, ut nusquam nisi in vocali aspiratione uterentur, loquebar sic, ut 'pulcros,' 'Cetegos,' 'triumpos,' 'Kartaginem' dicerem. aliquando idque sero convicio aurium cum extorta mihi veritas esset, usum loquendi populo concessi, scientiam mihi reservavi. 'Orcivios' tamen et 'Matones,' 'Otones,' 'Caepiones,' 'sepulcra,' 'coronas,' 'lacrimas,' dicimus, quia per aurium judicium licet. Similarly Quintilian, in a passage already mentioned (1. 5. 20), says : diu deinde servatum, ne consonantibus [veteres] adspirarent, ut in 'Graccis' et in 'triumpis.' erupit brevi tempore nimius usus, ut 'choronae,' 'chenturiones,' 'praechones,' adhuc quibusdam in inscriptionibus maneant. qua de re Catulli nobile epigramma est. In the second cent. A.D. *pulcher* was the current pronunciation (Ter. Scaur. vii. 20. 4–8 K.; Vel. Long. vii. 69. 13–17 K.), also *Carthāgo, Gracchus, Ŏtho, Bocchus* ; unaspirated were *cīlo, coclea, cocleāre* (Vel. Long. l. c.). In the fourth cent. *Orcus, Vulcānus, cŏrōna, ancŏra, sĕpulcrum* (Mar. Victorinus vi. 21. 20 K.; Serv. ad *Georg*. iii. 223, but for *ancora* cf. Serv. ad *Aen*. vi. 4), but *Gracchus* (Charis. i. 82. 11 K.), *pulcher* (Serv. l. c.) were the forms in use. *Pulcher* held its ground most persistently in spite of the rule, first apparently stated by Varro (Charis. i. 73. 17 K.), and often repeated by the Grammarians (Ter. Scaur. vii. 20. 4–8; Probus Cath. iv. 10. 19 K.; Ter. Maur. vi. 332. 219-221 K.; Mar. Vict. vi. 34. 5–6 K.; cf. Vel. Long. vii. 69. 13–17 K.) that no consonant should be aspirated in a native Latin word. On the other hand *thūs* (Gk. θύος), *chŏrōna* (from Gk. χορός, *Etym. Lat.* p. 23), with *lurcho, sĕpulchrum, Orchus*, &c., were only adopted by imitators of the Ciceronian age (Probus Cath. iv. 10. 19 K., Serv. ad *Aen*. vi. 4 ; Mar. Victor. vi. 21. 20 K. ; cf. Ter. Scaur. vii. 14 K.). Of *cŏrōna* Festus (26 Th.), quoting probably from Verrius Flaccus (time of Augustus), says : corona cum videatur a choro dici, caret tamen aspiratione. For examples of these varieties of spelling on inscriptions, see Brandis, *De consonantium aspiratione apud Romanos* (in Curtius, *Studien*, ii. 1869). Consentius (v. 392. 19, 27) censures the mispronunciations *Tracia, Trachia, Chartago*. For φθ we have *pth* in *pthoibus* in the Comm. Lud. Saec. The use of *rh* for Gk. initial ρ- was not approved by Varro (*L.L.* iii. fr. 58, p. 182 Wilm.) (see ch i. § 11). [For examples of this confusion of spelling, see Georges and Brambach, s.vv. *ancora, arca, tropaeum, baccar, Cethegus, Gracchus, murra, Orcus, Otho, pulcher, Regium, rhombus, talasio, letum, simulacrum, charta, Bosporus* (*Bosphorus* not till third or fourth cent. A.D.), *chlamys, chorda, clatri, cochlea, concha, cothurnus, cyathus, lurco, lumpa, schema, schola, sepulcrum, raeda, Raetia, Ramnes, Rhodope, Rhodus, rhūs, Riphaeus, romphaea, theatrum, Viriathus, triumphus, racana, ciniphes* (κνῖπες), *triclinium* (Abl. Plur. *trichilinis, C.I.L.* ix. 4971 ; xiv. 375, 17). On the spellings *Calphurnius* and *Calfurnius*, see Schuch. *Vok*. i. p. 18, and for the confusion of *ph, p, f*, see ibid. on the spelling *phidelis*, and Georges on *phaseolus, sifo, sulfur*. Late Latin *culfus* (see *A. L. L.* vii. 443) is the precursor of the Romance forms of Gk. κόλπος (Ital. Span. golfo, &c.). In the Probi App. we have (199. 7 K.) strofa non 'stropa' ; (199. 17) amfora non 'ampora' ; (197. 19) porphyreticum marmor, non 'purpureticum marmur,' and perhaps (199. 8) zizifus [zizibus MS.] non 'zizupus.'

The Romance forms show that Vulgar Latin retained the old equivalence of the Latin tenues to the Greek aspirates ; e. g. Gk. κόλαφος is Ital. colpo, O.Fr. colp, Fr. coup ; χαλᾶν is Ital. calare ; θάλλος is Ital. tallo, Span. tallo, Fr. talle. [Cf. the cautions given in Prob. Appendix against *stropa, ampora* (see above).]

So that misspellings like *ch* for *c*, *th* for *t*, *ph* for *p* on plebeian inscriptions cannot have implied a different pronunciation. The aspirated forms were to the uneducated Romans mere equivalents of the tenues. *Ch*, the equivalent of *c*, was in Italian utilized to distinguish the guttural from the palatalized sound, e.g. chi (Lat. *qui*), chiave (Lat. *clāvis*) (see Schuch. *Vok.* i. p. 74). Similarly *h* is written, but not pronounced, in Italian to distinguish a few synonyms like ho (Lat. *hăbeo*), and o (Lat. *aut*), &c.

§ 61. **M, N.** The pronunciation of the nasals varied according to their position. At the beginning of a word or a syllable *m* and *n* had their normal sound. What this was for *m* there can be little doubt. M, the lip-nasal, has in all Romance languages at the beginning of a word the same sound, that namely of our *m*. The N-sounds on the other hand vary considerably. There is 'dental *n*,' as Sweet calls it, the point-nasal, with many varieties according as the tongue touches the teeth (the true 'dental' *n* as in French, Italian, &c.), or the gums a little behind the teeth, as in English, and so on. There is 'palatal' *n*, Sweet's front-nasal, as in Fr. Boulogne, vigne, Italian ogni, Spanish señor, cañon (something like our 'vineyard'). There is 'velar' or 'guttural' *n*, Sweet's back-nasal, of English 'sing,' German singen. And *n* (like *m*), may be unvoiced, as in Icelandic knı́f, hnut, a sound common in England 200 years ago in words beginning with kn like 'know,' 'knife,' which have now lost all trace of the initial *k*. Voiceless *m* is heard in the interjection 'hm!' Normal Latin *n* was not the true 'dental' (as Italian *n* is) according to the Latin phoneticians. The tongue touched not the teeth but the palate; what precise part of the palate, we are not told (Nigidius ap. Gell. xix. 14. 7). Before a guttural, *n* was 'velar' or 'guttural' *n*, like Greek γ in ἄγγελος, ἀγκάλη, a sound called the Agma by Greek phoneticians and by their Latin imitators (Nigidius l. c.; Priscian i. 39; Mart. Vict. vi. 19. 11 K.), to express which Accius proposed to follow the Greeks and write *g*, e. g. *aggŭlus, aggens, agguīla, iggĕrunt*. At the end of a syllable, before a consonant, Latin *m, n* had again a parallel in Greek, and accordingly have received attention at the hands of the Latin grammarians. The sound is described as 'something that is neither *m* nor *n*,' as in Greek σάμβυξ (Mar. Vict. vi. 16. 4 K.), a description that would apply to the sound of *n* in our own 'unpractical,' 'unmerciful' in careless utterance, as well as to the preposition in Ital. impero, intacco. There was however one sound of Latin *m* which had no parallel in Greek; and here the Latin grammarians do not give us so much information as we could wish. The curious usage of Latin poetry, by which a word ending with -*m* elides its final syllable before an initial vowel or *h*, just as though it ended with a vowel, has nothing like it in Greek. Quintilian (ix. 4. 40) tells us that final *m* before an initial vowel was hardly pronounced, and had a sound not represented in the alphabet: neque enim eximitur, sed obscuratur, et tantum in hoc aliqua inter duas vocales velut nota est, ne ipsae coeant. Cato, he adds, wrote 'dicae' 'faciae' for *dīcam, făciam* (cf. Quint. i. 7. 23; Paul. Fest. 20. 6 and 51. 10), although this spelling was often changed by ignorant persons: quae in veteribus libris reperta mutare imperiti solent, et dum librariorum insectari volunt inscientiam, suam confitentur. And according to Velius Longus (80. 20 K.), Verrius Flaccus, in the time of Augustus, proposed a new letter, the first half of the ordinary letter M, to express final *m* before an initial vowel: ut appareret exprimi non debere. Priscian (i. p. 29. 15 H.) says: m obscurum in extremitate dictionum sonat, ut 'templum'; apertum in principio, ut 'magnus'; mediocre in mediis, ut 'umbra.' What the exact sound of -*m* was, is not easy to determine. From Latin poetry we see that a word ending in -*m*, e.g. *fīnem*, is, when the next word begins with a vowel, treated like a word ending in a vowel, e.g. *fīne*. In both cases the final syllable suffers what is called 'elision,' *fīn(em) onerat* and *fīn(e) onerat* (see § 153). Final -*m* therefore lacks the weight of an ordinary consonant, the power to prevent two vowels from coalescing, and in this respect is on a par with initial *h*-. Before e.g. *honorat* the final syllable of *fīne, fīnem* suffers 'elision' in exactly the same way as before *onerat*. But are we to say that in *fīnem* the *em* became a nasal vowel, an *e* spoken 'through the nose,' or in stricter terms, spoken with the passage into the nose not covered by the uvula? In this case *em* would have a sound like that of our exclamation 'eh!', spoken with something of a nasal twang; and to give this sound to the Latin interjection *hem* (expressing surprise, sorrow, indignation, &c., e.g. Ter. *Andr.* 435: quid Davos narrat? . . .

nilne hem? Nil prorsus), would not be unnatural. Or should we say that *e* had its ordinary sound, and that this sound was followed by some reduced form of *m*, probably some adumbration of unvoiced or whispered *m*, at any rate something of as slight a consonantal character as *h*? A very probable account is that *-m* was reduced through the lips not being closed to pronounce it. If instead of closing the lips, all that were done were to drop the uvula, a nasal sound would be given to the following initial vowel, so that *finem onerat* would be pronounced *finewonerat* with a nasalized *o* (Gröber, *Commentationes Woelfflinianae*, pp. 171 sqq.). When the next word began with a consonant, final *m* seems to have had more weight in ordinary Latin, if not in Vulgar Latin, for it never fails to make its vowel long by 'position' in poetry of all periods, whereas final *s* in the earlier poetry usually does so fail. Plautus, for example, could not end an iambic line with *nullum fert*, though he does with *nullus fert* (which we often write *nullu' fert*). But that it had not the definite *m*-character of initial *m*, that *m* of *viam continet* did not sound like *m* of *mira continet* we see from the remark of a first century grammarian, that in the phrase *etiam nunc*, although *m* was written, something else (like *etiannunc*), was pronounced (Vel. Longus vii. 78. 19 K. cum dico 'etiam nunc,' quamvis per m scribam, nescioquomodo tamen exprimere non possum). How far this differed from that sound of the nasal before a consonant in the middle of the word, which is described as 'something that is neither *m* nor *n*,' it is difficult to say. Compounds with prepositions at any rate, like *co(n)necto, comprimit, continet* seem quite on a level with *etiam nunc* (or *etiamnunc*?). In both these cases Latin *m* is treated like Greek *ν* in συγκαλέω, συντείνω, συμβάλλω, and the spellings found on inscriptions ἐγ κύκλῳ, ἐμ Πρυτανείῳ, τὴγ γυναῖκα, τὴμ βουλήν, which has led in the Rhodian dialect of the present day to a complete assimilation of the nasal to the consonant, e. g. *τιχ χάρι* (τὴν χάριν) (G. Meyer, *Griechische Grammatik*,[2] § 274). As close a parallel is offered by Sanscrit final *m* which is described as 'a nasal of a servile character always to be assimilated to a following consonant of whatever nature that may be' (Whitney, *Sanscrit Grammar*, § 71). This Sanscrit *-m* before initial *y*, *v* becomes 'a nasal semivowel, the counterpart of each respectively.' If

§ 61.]   PRONUNCIATION. NASALS.   63

the same happened in Latin, if *coniunctus, coniux* were pronounced *coiiunctus, coiiux*, with the first *i* nasalized, and *conuentio* were *couuentio with the first *u* nasalized, it would explain why it is that, in spelling, the nasal is often omitted, *coventionid* (*C. I. L.* i. 196), *coiugi* (id. 1064) (cf. Sweet *Primer*, p. 104).

Final *n* had not this weak sound. Priscian tells us (1. p. 30) n quoque plenior in primis sonat et in ultimis partibus syllabarum, ut 'nomen,' 'stamen': exilior in mediis ut 'amnis,' 'damnum.' In the Umbrian language however it seems to have been on the same footing as Latin final *m*, for it is sometimes omitted, e. g. *nome* (Lat. *nomen*), and sometimes written *m*, e. g. numem. Both in Umbrian and Oscan final *m* shows the same character as in Latin, e. g. Umbr. ku and kum (Lat. *cum*), Osc. vía and víam (Lat. *viam*), *con preivatud* (Lat. *cum privato*) and *cum atrud* ; and in both languages a nasal is often omitted before a consonant in the middle of a word, e. g. Umbr. iveka and *ivenga* (Lat. *juvenca*), uzo- and onso- (Lat. *humero-*); Osc. aragetud (Lat. *argento*) and *praesentid* (Lat. *praesenti*): Umbr. apentu and ampentu (Lat. *impendito*); Osc. Λαπονις (Lat. *Lamponius*). This omission occurs on Latin inscriptions too, e. g. DECEBRIS (*C.I.L.* i. 930), MERETI (iii. 2702, &c.), but was a tendency not allowed to develop, as we see from the fact that in Romance *n* and *m* are always retained, e.g. Ital. Dicembre, Span. Diciembre, Fr. Décembre. The Plautine scansion of *nempe* in such a line as *Cas.* 599 :—

quin tú suspendis té ? Nempe tu te díxeras,

has often been quoted as an instance of such a suppression of the nasal (*něpe*) in ordinary speech. But the true scansion is *nemp(e)* with the same syncope of final -*ĕ* as in *tun* and *tune*, *ac* (for *atc) and *atque*, *nec* and *neque*. A nasal is only dropped before certain consonants in Latin according to fixed laws and never without doubling the consonant or lengthening the vowel (Skutsch, *Forschungen*, i. § 2). Before *s*, for example, this was the case; so *mensa* was pronounced *mēsa*, with the ordinary close sound of the long vowel, to judge from the Romance forms, e.g. Ital. mesa (with close *e*); in *consŭles* the *n*, though written, was not sounded (Quint. i. 7. 28, 29). Whether this *e*, *o* were at any period of the language nasal vowels we are not told. In O. Engl. n was dropped before th (of 'thin,' &c.), s, f with nasalization and lengthening of the preceding vowel, e. g. mūþ, 'mouth' (Germ. Mund), gōs, 'goose.' (Germ. Gans), fīf, 'five' (Germ. fünf).

Another internal group that calls for notice is *mn*. In most Romance languages this has become *nn*, e. g. Ital. danno (Lat. *damnum*), donna (Lat. *domna* and *domina*), colonna (Lat. *columna*), but in French the *n* has yielded to the *m*, e. g. dame (Lat. *damnum* and *dŏm(i)na*) (colonne is a bookword). That in the Latin pronunciation the *n* had here a weak sound seems to follow from Priscian's remark (i. p. 30): n exilior in mediis [sonat] ut 'amnis,' 'damnum' (where the syllable begins with *m*, *a-mnis*, *da-mnum*, while in *ĕtiamnunc* the syllable begins with *n*), as well as from Quintilian's many centuries earlier (i. 7. 28, 29): quid quae scribuntur aliter quam enuntiantur? ... 'columnam' et 'consules' exempta n littera legimus. *gn* likewise takes different paths in the Romance languages. Usually it becomes a palatal *n*-sound, e. g. Ital. legno (Lat. *lignum*), Span. leño, but in Sardinian *nn*, e. g. linna. There is no evidence to show that the *g* in this position in Latin took the velar guttural sound ŋ; and probably the pronunciation was merely ordinary *g* followed by *n*. *nct* was pronounced at least in Vulg. Latin *nt* (probably not with velar *n*), with suppression of the *c*, e. g. *quīntus* (Ital. quinto, with close *i*) (see § 144). *nd* shows a tendency to *nn* (as in Oscan and Umbrian) in forms like Plautus' *dispennite, distennite*; but this assimilation was not carried out in literary or Vulgar Latin (e. g. Ital. risponde, Lat. *respondet*).

M, *v* are 'liquids' (ὑγραί) in Greek, because they readily combine (like λ, ρ) in one syllable with a preceding mute. But in Latin, though this was the case with *l*, *r*, it was not with *m*, *n*. Greek loanwords in Latin which presented this combination, tended to be pronounced with a parasitic vowel, e. g. *Těcŭmessa* for Greek Τέκμησσα: and this is the form in which they appeared in the earlier literature. At the end of the Republic, when it was considered a requisite of polite speech to express with greater exactness the Greek sound of these loanwords, this spelling was generally abandoned; though even in the literary language it persisted in some forms, such as *mĭna*

(Greek μνᾶ), and in Vulgar Latin, as the Romance languages testify, it never was given up (e.g. cĭcĭnus, Ital. cecero, for κύκνος) (see § 154).

§ 62. **Phonetic descriptions of normal m, n.** Ter. Maur. vi. 332. 235 :
at tertia [sc. littera m] clauso quasi mugit intus ore ;
quartae [n] sonitus figitur usque sub palato,
quo spiritus anceps coeat naris et oris.

Mar. Vict. vi. 34. 12, 13 K. m impressis invicem labiis mugitum quendam intra oris specum attractis naribus dabit ; n vero sub convexo palati lingua inhaerente gemino naris et oris spiritu explicabitur. Martianus Capella (iii. 261), M labris imprimitur ; N lingua dentibus appulsa collidit. Priscian i. 29, 30 H. m obscurum in extremitate dictionum sonat ut 'templum,' apertum in principio ut 'magnus,' mediocre in mediis ut 'umbra.' . . . n quoque plenior in primis sonat et in ultimis partibus syllabarum ut 'nomen,' 'stamen,' exilior in mediis ut 'amnis,' 'damnum.' Nigidius (ap. Gell. xix. 14. 7), speaking of the Agma, says : si ea littera [n] esset, lingua palatum tangeret. Ter. Scaurus mentions the exertion necessary to produce the labial *m* (as also *b*, *p*), vii. 14. 3 K. non sine labore conjuncto ore.

§ 63. **The Agma.** Nigidius (*l. c.*), in Augustus' time, speaks of the *n* in words like *anguis, increpat, ingenuus* as a sound 'between *n* and *g*,' a spurious *n* (*adulterinum*), in which the tongue does not touch the palate, as in normal *n*. Varro (ap. Priscian i. p. 30) says it is a sound common to Greek and Latin, written *g* in Greek, and by the poet Accius in Latin, e. g. *aggulus, agceps* (cf. Mar. Vict. vi. 19. 11). Marius Victorinus (fourth cent.), vi. 16. 4. K., declares that this was the sound of the nasal before *qu* in *nunquam, numquam, quanquam, quamquam*, which is a sound between *n* and *g*, though, he says, it is usually spoken of by grammarians as if it were the sound between *m* and *n* of Greek σάμβυξ. Spellings on late inscriptions like NUNCQVAM (*C.I.L.* v. 154) NVNC-QVAM (iv. 1837), VNCQVAM (x. 8192) may indicate this pronunciation, though in IVNCXI (viii. 8692), &c., CX may be merely the common symbol for *X* as in VCXOR (ii. 3330), a spelling which has led to the corruption *voxor* in MSS. of Plautus (*Class. Rev.* v. 293).

§ 64. **m, n before consonant.** Marius Victorinus, speaking of *nunquam, numquam*, &c. (vi. 16. 4 K.) says : clari in studiis viri, qui aliquid de orthographia scripserunt, omnes fere aiunt inter m et n litteras mediam vocem, quae non abhorreat ab utraque littera, sed neutram proprie exprimat, tam nobis deesse quam Graecis : nam cum illi σάμβυξ scribant, nec m exprimere nec n. sed haec ambiguitas in his fortasse vocabulis sit, ut in 'Ampelo,' 'Lycambe.' nam in nostris supra dictis non est. The word σάμβυξ, apparently the stock example of Greek phoneticians for this 'sound which is neither *m* nor *n*,' is an unfortunate instance. It is not a native Greek word, but a loanword from another language, and in its original form seems not to have had a nasal [Aramaic sabb'kā (Daniel iii. 5), Greek σαμβύκη]. [Is the word connected with the Latin *sambūcus*, elderwood, where we have a similar variety of spelling between *sambūcus* and *sābucus* (*sab-* in Romance)? On Lat. *labrusca*, in Vulg. Lat. *lambrusca* (a MS. reading in Virg. *Ecl.* v. 7), Ital. lambrusca, Fr. lambruche, Span. lambrusca, see below.] We might be inclined from this to believe that the Greek phoneticians were speaking of a sound that is not a native Greek sound, were it not for spellings on Greek inscriptions like ποντπῆς, 'Ολυνπίῳ, Cret. ἀνφόταρος, &c. This Greek sound was appealed to by Latin grammarians to explain varieties of spelling like *eorumdem* and *eorundem*, *quamtus* and *quantus*, where *m* was required by the etymology, true or false (*eorum*, *quam*) (Cornutus ap. Cassiod. vii. 152. 3`, but *n* by the pronunciation, and even, as we have seen, to explain *numquam* and *nunquam*, *tamquam* and *tanquam*, &c. Here again a doubt suggests itself whether the reference of this sound 'between *m* and *n*' to the Latin language is not based on mere varieties of spelling which were not varieties of pronunciation; but an appeal to the inscriptions tends to remove it. SENTEMTIAM (*C. I. L.* i. 206), DECENBER (ii. 4587, &c.) (see Indices to *C. I. L.*) can most easily be explained on the supposition that this sound really existed in Latin, unless indeed they are due to the general confusion between *mt* and *nt*, *nb* and *mb* caused by the co-existence of etymological and phonetic spellings like *comtĕro* and *contĕro*, *inbūtus* and *imbūtus*. (The spelling *sentemtiam* is that of the Lex Julia Municipalis and may be due to some orthographical theory of Julius Caesar; for on the same inscription we have *damdum*, *damdam*, *faciumdei*, *tuemdam*, *tuemdarum*, *quamta*, *quamtum*, *tamtae*, *tamtam*.) The spelling of these verbs compounded with the prepositions *in*, *cum* (*com*) is frequently discussed by the grammarians (see the passages collected by Seelmann, p. 279) (cf. *jandūdum* for *jamdūdum* in Virgil MSS., Ribbeck, *Index* s. v.). To the ordinary consonants before which *n* becomes *m*, viz. *b*, *p*, *m* (cited by Priscian, i. p. 31. 2 H., from the elder Pliny), Marius Victorinus (fourth cent.) adds *f* (probably from some earlier grammarian`, and on Cicero's authority *v*, e. g. *comfert*, *comvocat*. Whether the change in the fashion of spelling compounds of *com*, *in* with verbs beginning with *f*, *v*, is a proof that these spirants passed from a bilabial to a labiodental pronunciation is discussed in § 52. It is possible that the nasal was not sounded before *f*, *v* or only slightly sounded (as before *h*, or a vowel initial), so that the variation of *m*, *n* in the spelling would not indicate a change in pronunciation (cf. the suppression of Latin *n* before *f*, *v* in Provencal: see below). The form *co-* often appears on inscriptions before *j*, *v* in compounds as before a vowel or *h* (*coŏrior*, *coeo*, *cohortor*, *cohaereo*, but also *comest*, and in the older spelling *comauditum*, &c.). Before *v* only on early inscriptions, e. g. COVENVMIS (*C. I. L.* i. 532), COVENTIONID (i. 196); before *j* also on later, e. g. COICITO (*C. I. L.* ii. 1964, col. ii. 51), COIVGI (*C. I. L.* i. 1064, 1413, vi. 2516, &c.) (see Indices to *C. I. L.*). The nasal is also often dropped in simple words before mutes, *m* before Labials, e. g. *Novebris*, *n* before Dentals and Gutturals, e. g. *eudem*, *provicia* (*Mon. Ancyr.*) (see Schuchardt, *Vok.* i. p. 105). Greek inscriptions treat the Latin nasals in the same way, e. g. Νοεβρ., Ποπωνιος, on the one hand; Νοενβριος, Πονπωνιος, on the other (Eckinger, pp. 109 sqq.). Occasionally a nasal is wrongly inserted in plebeian and late inscriptions, *m* before Labials, *n* before Dentals and Gutturals, e. g. *semptem*, *singnifer*. (Examples from inscriptions and MSS. are given by Schuchardt, *Vok.* i. p. 113 sqq.) (*Co* may be an original byform of *com* in *cōgo*, &c.; see ch. ix. § 22.)

In Romance, however, there is no trace of any variety of sound in these cases. The classical spelling is invariably reproduced, e. g. Ital. immobile (Lat. *immōbĭlis*`, tanto (Lat. *tantus*); and this fact strengthens the doubt expressed above regarding the existence of this 'sound between *m* and *n*' in Latin. Vulg. Lat. **rendo* (Ital. rendo, with open *e*, Span. rendir, Fr. rendre, &c.) follows the analogy of *prendo*; and *lambrusca*, just quoted, for *labrusca*, should probably be explained in the same way. But the dropping of the nasal in such a form as *infatibus*, quoted (perhaps from some older grammarian) as a 'barbarismus' by Julian, Bishop of Toledo (end of seventh cent.) (*Exc. in Don.* v. 324. 9 K.) is not reflected in the Romance forms (Ital. infante, Span. infante, Fr. enfant, &c.). Before *s*, where we know that in Latin the nasal was dropped in pronunciation with lengthening of the preceding vowel, e. g. *mensa*, the pronounced form, *mēsa*, is the form reflected in the Romance languages, e. g. Ital. mesa, with close *e*. Before *f*, the same thing seems to have happened in Latin, but almost the only instances of Latin words with *nf* in Romance are compounds with the preposition or particle *in*, e. g. *infans*. These show *n*, except in Provençal, where *n* is dropped, e. g. effas, eferns, efranher (Lat. *infringere*), efern, afra (Lat. *infra*), cofes, cofondre [as *n* before *v* in evers, eveja (Lat. *invidia*), covens (Lat. *conventus*), covertir]; but this *n* of Vulgar Latin may be due to what is called 'Recomposition' (see ch. iii. § 18).

§ 65. **Final m.** In the only other Indo-European language which has not changed final -*m* into *n* we are confronted with a curiously similar difficulty to that in Latin. The native grammarians of India, who at an early time devoted themselves to a minute and exhaustive analysis of the phonetics and accidence of Sanscrit, the sacred language of India, have left conflicting accounts of the sound of *m* at the end of a word. Some hold that in a word like Sanscr. tam (Greek τόν), the sound was that of a nasalized (*anunāsika*) vowel; others teach the 'intervention after the vowel of a distinct nasal element called the *anusvāra*, or after-tone' (Whitney, *Sanscrit Grammar*[2], § 71). The Romance languages do not help us to decide whether one or any of these processes took place in Latin, for they offer no indication that in Vulgar Latin *finem* differed at all from *fine*. The only cases where Latin final *m* is preserved are a few monosyllables; and in these *m* has been changed to *n* (*rem*, French rien, *quem*, Span. quien). The Latin nasals in the middle of a word have passed into nasal vowels in countries under Celtic influence, viz. France and North Italy, and also in Portugal, where Latin *n* between vowels has passed into a nasal vowel, e. g. Romão, Lat. *Rōmānus*, mão, Lat. *mănus*, lãa (contracted to lã), Lat. *lāna*. The Portuguese suppression of intervocalic *n* is not a complete parallel to the Latin usage; for it is in the middle of a word that the nasal is so treated, and *m* is never suppressed like *n*, e. g. fumo, Lat. *fūmus*, fama, Lat. *fāma*. The *n* is described as having first nasalized the previous vowel, *mano (with nasal *a*), and then having been dropped (Meyer-Lübke, *Rom. Gram.* i. p. 314). Nor is the suppression of intervocalic *m* in Irish in such a word as fearail, manly. This word is a compound of fear, man (cf. Lat. *vĭr*), and amhail, like (cf. Lat. *sĭmĭlis*). Between two vowels in Irish *m* passed into a *v*-sound; and this *v* often combines with a preceding vowel into a nasal diphthong like German *au* nasalized. In an unaccented syllable, as in feáramhail, this diphthong is so far reduced, as to allow the last two syllables to coalesce into one. In Latin, *m* never had this tendency to become *v*; and so the elision in such a phrase as *feram illud* cannot be explained by the Irish reduction of fearamhail to fearail. A better parallel to the latter would be the reduction of *comuentio, couentio* to *contio*. (But see ch. ix. § 22). (On Port. tam with *m* sounded like nasal *w*, see Sweet *Phil. Soc.* xvii. 203.)

Final -*m* is omitted very frequently on the oldest inscriptions till 130 B.C., or thereabouts, and again on late plebeian inscriptions (see § 137). Still there is no evidence that -*m* was more easily dropped in early Latin poetry than in the classical age. Indeed Priscian (i. p. 30 K.) speaking of final -*m* says : vetustissimi tamen non semper eam subtrahebant, and quotes a hexameter of Ennius (*A*. 354 M.) ending with *milia militum octo* (cf. Enn. *A*. 322 M. beginning *dum quidem unus*); but this remark need not drive us to the opposite extreme, of believing that -*m* was more sounded in early than in classical times. To the Roman ear at all periods a syllable ending in -*m* seems to have been the equivalent in hiatus of a syllable ending in a long vowel. This appears to be the rule in Saturnian versification (see *Amer. Jour. Phil.* xiv. 309); and Plautus, with the older poets, Horace, with the classical poets, allow prosodical hiatus in the one case as much as in the other. Lucilius, for example, scans as a short syllable without eliding, *quam* (i. 32 M. irritata canes quăm homo quam planius dicat. He is speaking of the letter *r*), exactly as he shortens *quo* (xxx. 24 M. quid seruas quŏ eam, quid agam? quid id attinet ad te?). Horace's *nŭm adest* is on a par with his *si mĕ amas*; and the prosodical hiatus quoted from Ennius by Priscian may be equated with the instance quoted by Cicero (*Or*. xlv. 152) from the same poet *Scipiŏ inuicte* (*A*. 345 M.). Nor was this a mere usage of poetry. The same thing is seen in compounds, such as *cŏmest*, *cŏire* (the spelling with *com* probably was the older usage before a vowel. cf. *comauditum*, and *comangustatum*, Paul. Fest. 46 Th. : *comegit* Gl. Plac. xiv. 39 G.; on *cōgo*, see above), which have the first syllable short, like *praeire*, *praeeunt*. The compound of *circum* and *it* is a trisyllable *circŭit*; of *antĕ* and *it* a dissyllable, *anteit*. (On *flagitium-hóminis* in Plautus, see above, § 59.) But the disregard of -*m* in metre before an initial consonant (except under the law of Breves Breviantes, like Plautus' almost invariable *ĕnim*)[1] is unknown until late plebeian verse, e. g. *umbră(m) levem* (along with *talĕs amici*) on the epitaph of a praeco (*C. I. L.* vi. 1951), *moriente(m) viderent* (vi. 7578), &c. Even in the careless hexameters of the dedicatory inscription of Mummius (i. 542; of 146 B. C.), which contain *facilia* occupying the place of a dactyl, *pacĕ* need not represent *pacem* (as in i. 1290 : *pacem petit*), but may be the Abl. (as in Plaut. *Rud.* 698 : *tua pace*) :

<blockquote>
tua pace rogans te
cogendei dissoluendei tu ut facilia faxseis.
</blockquote>

The dropping of final -*m* in vulgar pronunciation is attested by the remarks in Probi App. (198. 27) triclinium non 'triclinu'; (199. 14) passim non 'passi' ... numquam non 'numqua' ... pridem non 'pride,' olim non 'oli'; (199. 17) idem non 'ide,' and by the spellings on late and plebeian inscriptions (see § 137). Consentius (fifth cent.?), p. 394 K., alludes under the name of 'Mytacismus' to a practice of joining -*m* to the initial vowel of the next word : sicut plerumque passim loquuntur 'dixeram illis.' Similarly Pompeius (fifth cent.), p. 287. 7 K., quotes from Melissus (second cent.) the rule for the correct pronunciation of a phrase like *hominem amicum* as a mean between the two extremes, 'homine mamicum' and 'homine amicum.' Velius Longus (54. K.) says : cum dicitur 'illum ego' et 'omnium optimum,' 'illum' et 'omnium' aeque m terminat, nec tamen in enuntiatione apparet ; with Quintilian (ix. 4. 39), quoted above, cf. Diom. 453. 9 K.; Serv. *in Don.* 445. 14 K.

---

[1] Cf. Enn. *A*. 287 non enim rumores ponebat ante salutem (with *non enim* in all MSS.).

Before *n* the pronunciation alluded to by Velius Longus is found expressed in writing, in MSS. of Virgil (see Ribbeck, *Index*, p. 430); so '*etiannunc*' on the Herc. Papyri (*Class. Rev.* iv. 443).

Tanne for *tamne* is quoted by Festus (p. 542 Th.) from Afranius : tanne arcula tua plena est aranearum ? Cf. Quint. viii. 3. 45 on the sound of *cum* before a word beginning with *n*- (cf. Cic. *Orat.* xlv. 154 ; *Fam.* ix. 22. 2). Final -*n* of the preposition *in* is sometimes changed to -*m* before an initial labial consonant (see Ribbeck, *Ind.* p. 433 for instances in Virgil MSS. like *im burim, im flammam, im mare, im puppibus*). So *forsam* and *forsitam* in MSS. (see Ribbeck, *Ind.* p. 420, and Georges, *Lex. Wortf.*, and for other examples of the confusion of -*m* and -*n*, Schuchardt, *Vok.* i. pp. 117 sqq.).

§ 66. ns. (See § 144.) In Greek inscriptions we find *n* dropped before *s* in Latin words frequently, at all dates and in all localities. The nasal is usually dropped in the terminations -*ans* and -*ens*, also in -*ensis*, e. g. Κλημης, καστρησια. But Latin *census* and its derivatives usually retain *n*, e. g. κῆνσος, Κηνσωρινος (*Mon. Anc.*), also the combination -*nst*- (Eckinger, pp. 114, 115). [For the variation of *s* with *ns* in Latin spelling, see Georges, *Lex. Wortf.* s. vv. *centies, decies, Consentia* (modern Cosenza), *pinso, mensis, mensor,* &c. Cf. Probi App. 198. 9 ansa non 'asa' ; 198. 2 Capsesis non 'Capsessis.'] The pronunciation of *ns* as *s*, with lengthening of the preceding vowel, led to the use of *ns* for *s* after a long vowel, e. g. *thensaurus* for *thesaurus* [see Georges s.v. Other examples, e. g. *occansio* (cf. *Rhein. Mus.* xvi. 160), in Schuchardt, *Vok.* i. p. 112]. The Appendix Probi gives cautions against the use of 'occansio' for *occasio* (198. 21 K.), of 'Herculens' for *Hercules* (197. 25 K.). Velius Longus (p. 79. 1 K.) says that Cicero 'libenter dicebat *foresia, Megalesia, hortesia,* and Papirian (ap. Cassiod. 160. 14 K.) says that *tosus, tusus, prasus* were the older spellings, but that the rule of his time was to retain *n* in the P.P.P., not in Adjectives, e. g. *formosus* (cf. Probi App. 198. 14 K. formosus non 'formunsus'; Caper 95. 18 K. : Ter. Scaur. 21. 10 K. ; we have *formonsae, C. I. L.* vi. 2738); in the P.P.P. the *n* seems to have been restored from the other part of the verb. Charisius (58. 17 K.) says : mensam sine n littera dictam Varro ait quod media poneretur ; sed auctores cum n littera protulerunt, Vergilius saepe, &c. (cf. Varro *L. L.* v. 118). On *quotiens* (the better spelling) and on *vicensumus*, &c., see Georges, *Lex. Wortf.* s. vv., and Brambach, *Lat. Orth.* p. 269.

§ 67. nx. Of the spellings *conjux* and *conjunx* (statistics in Georges, s.v.), Velius Longus (first cent. A. D.) says (p. 78 K.) that the spelling without *n* is due to the analogy of the other cases. *conjugis, conjugi,* &c. In actual pronunciation, he declares, the *n* is heard ; for 'subtracta n littera, et difficilius enuntiabitur et asperius auribus accidet.' The comparison of other I.-Eur. languages, e. g. Greek σύ-ζυξ, Sanscr. sam-yuj-, shows that the form without *n* must have been the original form of the Nom. too, and that the *n* has been introduced by the analogy of *jungo* (cf. Ter. Scaur. p. 20. 10 K.).

§ 68. mn. In the fifth cent. Pompeius (p. 283. 11 K.) mentions as a barbarism *columa* (cf. the Diminutive *cŏlŭmella*) for *cŏlumna*, which looks very like the pronunciation mentioned by Quintilian as normal in his day (columnam exempta n legimus). This *colum(n)a* seems to have become **culoma*, as *cŏlŭber* became *colober*, by assimilation of unaccented *u* to accented *o* (see ch. iii. § 33), whence *colomna* (Probi App. 197. 25) with open accented *o*, the origin of the Romance words for pillar, as **colóbra* (open *o*) of the Romance words for snake.

But the analogy of *cŏlŭmen* may have had something to do with the pronunciation *colum(n)a* (cf. *scămellum* and *scamnum*. See Georges s. v.). *Sollennis* is explained as a byform of *sollemnis* (from **amno-*, around, Osc. amno-), due to a supposed connexion with *annus* (*Etym. Lat.* p. 97). (On confusions of *mn* and *nn*, *n*, see Schuchardt, *Vok.* i. p. 147, and Georges, *Lex. Wortf.* s. vv. *antenna*, *Portunus*, *lamna*.) The insertion of *p* between *m* and *n* occurs in late plebeian spellings like *calumpnia*, *dampnum*, *sollempnis* (see Schuchardt, *Vok.* i. p. 149, and Georges, s. v. *damnum*). On *mpt* see below. *Hiemps* (cf. *consumpsi*, &c.), is the regular spelling of the Codex Mediceus of Virgil, and is accepted by Ribbeck; though this form is condemned by the grammarians, e. g. Caesellius ap. Cassiod. 161. 17 K.; Ter. Scaur. 21. 6 and 27. 3 K.; Alcuin 303. 8 K.

§ 69. gn. Spellings on inscriptions like *ingnominiae* (*C. I. L.* i. 206, 45 B. C.), *congnato* (x. 1220) seem to be mere etymological spellings like *inpello*, &c. *Singnifer*, on a soldier's grave (*C. I. L.* vi. 3637), has been explained above in § 64 (cf. § 144). Nor are we entitled to conclude that *g* passed into a nasal sound before *m* from spellings like *subtēmen* and *subtegmen*, *exāmen*, and perhaps *exagmen* (*Class. Rev.* 1891, p. 294) (see ch. iv. § 116). (For instances of the spelling of *gn-*, consult Georges and Brambach s.vv. *coniveo*, *conitor*, *dinosco*, *cognosco*, *navus*, *natus*, *narus*, *aprugnus*, and see Schuchardt, *Vok.* i. p. 115. On *cōnitor*, &c., but *cognosco*, &c., see ch. iv. § 119.)

§ 70. nct. The suppression of the guttural in *quintus* is something like the dropping of *-g* of 'going' in the mispronunciation 'goin' to.' *Quinctus* is the spelling of the Republic, *Quintus* of the Empire, according to Brambach. So on Greek inscriptions of the beginning of the second cent. B. C. Κοίγκτος, but also Κοιντος (Eckinger p. 122). For the byforms *nanctus* and *nactus* (see Brambach) we have a parallel in *sactus* (reflected in Welsh *saith*) beside *sanctus*, while Vulgar *santus* (see Georges) is Welsh *sant*. The *-ct-* is not a development of *-nct-* but a byform (see ch. viii. § 10).

§ 71. nd. In all S. and Central Italy *nd* has followed the course taken in Umbrian and Oscan and become *nn*; and similarly Latin *mb* is *mm*. In ordinary Italian, Latin *nd* has become *nn* (*n*) in the pretonic syllable, as is shown by *ne* for Lat. *inde*, *manucare* for Lat. *mandūcāre*. Similarly we have *mm* for *mb* in *amendue* beside *ambidue* (Lat. *ambo duo*), the same assimilation as we have in English, e. g. 'lamb' (*nn* for *nd* is seen in 'Lunnon town' for 'London town,' &c.). (For Latin confusions of *nd* and *nn*, see Schuchardt, *Vok.* i. p. 146, e. g. *Secunnus*, and consult Georges s. v. *grundio*). *Nt* competes with *mpt* in *lanterna* (better *laterna*) apparently from Greek λαμπτήρ, and *tempto* (not *tento*), *Pomptīnus* (not *Pontinus*), *pĕdĕtentim*, &c. (see Georges and Brambach). Thus *vŏluntas* and *vŏluptas* are sometimes confused in MSS. through the intermediary form *volumptas* (Schuchardt, *Vok.* i. 5). But *emptum*, *rĕdemptum*, *consumptum* are the established spellings, though Marius Victorinus (21. 12 K.) demands on etymological grounds *emtum*, *redemtum*, *consumtum*, as also *redemsi*, *consumsi*, &c. (ch. iv. § 76).

§ 72. Parasitic vowel in Greek loanwords. The Early Latin instances have been discussed by Ritschl, *Opusc.* ii. 469 sqq., who on the strength of MSS. spelling, and the requirements of prosody, restored to Plautus such forms as *drăchŭma*, *tĕchĭna*, *Alcŭmēna*, *Alcŭmeus*, *Cŭcinus*, *gŭmĭnăsium*, *Prŏcina*. Marius

Victorinus (8. 6 K.) tells us that the form *Tecmessa* was first used by Julius Caesar Vopiscus (an older contemporary of Cicero) in the title of his tragedy of that name, and was so pronounced, at his orders, by the actors : juxta autem non ponebant cm : inde nec Alcmenam dicebant nec Tecmessam, sed 'Alcumenam'; inde 'Alcumeo' et 'Alcumena' tragoediae, donec Julius Caesar, qui Vopiscus et Strabo et Sesquiculus dictus est, primus 'Tecmessam' inscripsit illam, et in scena pronuntiari jussit (cf. Prisc. i. p. 29 H. [u] saepe interponitur inter cl vel cm in Graecis nominibus, ut Ἡρακλῆς 'Hercules,' Ἀσκληπιός 'Aesculapius,' et antiqui Ἀλκμήνη 'Alcumena,' Ἀλκμαίων 'Alcumaeon'). Similarly the Sardinian mouflon was called in Latin *mūsĭmo* (a name applied to a much-prized breed of diminutive horses; cf. Lucilius vi. 15 M. praedium emit, qui vendit equum musimonem), but in Gk. μούσμων (Strabo). (On the parasitic vowel between a mute and *l* in Latin words, like *pĕrĭc(u)lum*, see ch. iii. § 13.) The difference of Greek and Latin in this respect is seen in the fact that Δεκμος is the earliest and most usual form of the name *Dĕcĭmus*, older *Decumus*, on Gk. inscriptions, just as awkward combinations with *l*, e. g. Λεντλος, Ἀρβουσκλα, Μασκλος, Πατερκλος, Πουρκλα (Lat. *Porcula*) are commoner on Greek inscriptions than on Latin (Eckinger, pp. 47, 75). The parasitic vowel is really the visible expression of a 'voice-glide' (Sweet, *Handb.* p. 84), as in Germ. Knie pronounced 'kᵉnie'; cf. Fr. canif from Low Germ. knif. (For examples on inscriptions, e. g. *Himinis*, *C. I. L.* i. 982, see Seelmann, p. 251, and cf. below § 154.)

§ 73. **Tenues and Mediae.** In pronouncing *p, t, c* the vocal organs are in the same position as in pronouncing *b, d, g*, but the breath comes through the open glottis, as the space between the two vocal chords which stretch across the larynx is called. With *b, d, g* we close the glottis, by drawing these vocal chords together, and produce what phoneticians call 'voice.' *B, d, g* are now therefore usually termed 'voiced' mutes as opposed to *p, t, c*, the unvoiced or 'breath'-mutes. An older designation was tenues and mediae. In some languages what are called tenues and mediae do not really differ by the absence and presence of 'voice,' but merely by energy and weakness of articulation. In one German-Swiss dialect, for example, German *k* and *g* are really the same consonant pronounced strongly and pronounced weakly. For such languages the terms 'fortes' and 'lenes' are more suitable than 'breath-mutes' and 'voice-mutes.' In investigating the sound of the Latin mutes we have accordingly to consider whether the tenues differed from the mediae in being uttered with the glottis open, or merely in being articulated with greater energy. Another point to be taken into consideration is that mutes, especially voiceless mutes, have in many languages a 'breath-glide,' what we roughly call *h*, after them. In Danish every initial *t* is pronounced with this *h* following; and the same peculiarity in Irish-English is well known. That Latin *p, t, c* were not so pronounced we can infer from the fact that for the more exact expression of the Greek aspirates, *ph, th, ch* were brought into use in the last century of the Republic, which shows that *p, t, c* had not, at least at that period, the sound of φ, θ, χ (like our 'up*h*ill,' 'an*t*heap,' 'ink*h*orn'). The other question, whether the Latin tenues and mediae are more properly distinguished as breath- and voice-mutes, or as fortes and lenes, is more difficult to settle. The Latin phoneticians, who, as we have seen (p. 28), are not very safe guides on any point of Latin pronunciation, are especially at fault here; for neither they nor their Greek masters seem to have carried their analysis of sounds as far as the phoneticians of India, who had at an early time discovered the distinction between unvoiced (*aghōśa*) and voiced (*ghōśavant*) consonants, and its dependence on the opening (*vivāra*) or closure (*saṁvāra*) of the glottis. The Latin phoneticians talk of *p* and *b*, of *t* and *d*, of *c* and *g* as entirely different types of sounds, produced by different positions of the vocal organs. Seelmann professes to find in their descriptions evidence that *p, t, c* had a more energetic articulation than *b, d, g*. This is certainly true of their account of *c* and *g*; but it is doubtful how far it is true of the others, and even if it were, how much authority should be allowed to these descriptions. A better reason for believing that the Latin tenues were pronounced with more energy of articulation than the mediae has been found in the fact that the Greek tenues, which must have lacked this energy, are often represented in Latin as mediae, e. g. Greek κωβιός, Lat. *gōbius*. This is, as is natural, especially the case in the initial accented syllable, which seems in Latin to have been uttered with a strong stress. It must be added, however, that an examination of the instances shows that they are almost wholly confined to Greek κ, especially when preceding certain sounds; and that the same tendency is shown by Latin *c* to be weakened in the same position to *g*, e. g. Vulgar Latin **gavia* for *căvea* (Ital. gabbia).

On the other hand, when we consider the Latin loanwords in Welsh and the Teutonic languages, we are led to believe that this energy of articulation was not the only thing which distinguished the tenues from the mediae in Latin. Had it been, we should probably have found the two classes of mute confused in their Welsh and Teutonic forms. But this is not the case; cf. Welsh poc, Lat. *pācem*; Welsh bendith, Lat. *běn(ě)dictio*; Lat. *cŏquīna*, *cocina* is our 'kitchen,' Lat. *gemma* our ·gem.'

And in Italian of the present day *p, t, c* are unvoiced, *b, d, g* voiced. So we have grounds for believing the Latin tenues to have been unvoiced, the Latin mediae to have been voiced; and the guttural mutes, if not all three classes, to have been also distinguishable as fortes and lenes.

In native Latin words the tenues and mediae are not confused to any great extent. The same tendency that turned I.-Eur. *d* into *t* before *r* in *atro-*, &c. (ch. iv. § 113) is seen in the old spellings mentioned by Quintilian (i. 4. 16) *Alexanter* and *Cassantra* (cf. *C.I.L.* i. 59, ALIXENTROM; 1501, ALIXENTE(r) CASENTER(a), both inscriptions from Praeneste, and in Ital. Otranto for Greek Ὑδροῦς -οῦντος, Lat. *Hydruntum*). In very early times the single letter *c* (Greek γ) was used for the *c*-sound and for the *g*-sound; but, as we saw before, the two sounds must have been throughout this period distinguished in pronunciation, though not in spelling. It is perhaps only at the end of a word that we find a real variation between tenuis and media. Final syllables were pronounced as weakly in Latin as initial syllables were pronounced strongly; and we might expect to find the tenuis fortis at the end of a word replaced by the media lenis.

This is apparently the explanation of the Roman preference of the spelling *ab, ob, sub* to *ap* (as in *ap-erio*), *op* (as in *op-erio*, Oscan *op*), **s-up*; though in actual utterance these words were no doubt sounded with *-p* when followed by a word beginning with a tenuis, e.g. *ab templo, ob templum* (like *obtĭneo*, pronounced *op-tineo*). The spelling was not so established in the case of similar subordinate or proclitic words ending in a dental, e.g. *at*, often written *ad*; but the change on plebeian and late inscriptions of final *-t* of verbs to *-d*, e.g. *reliquid*, is probably due to this weakening. On the other hand, a final is often reduced to a whispered sound in languages, and a voiced consonant, if whispered, sounds more like an unvoiced.

In the Romance languages the Latin tenues and mediae, when

initial, and when the initial syllable, to which they belong, has the accent, retain their identity with wonderful persistence, e.g. Ital. puro (Lat. *pūrus*), bene (Lat. *bĕnĕ*), tale (Lat. *tālis*), duro (Lat. *dŭrus*); but in the middle of a word, and when in the unaccented syllable (though not after the Latin diphthong *au*, e.g. Span. poco), the tendency is almost universal to turn the tenuis into a media, the media into a spirant. In one language, however, Roumanian, the tenuis is usually preserved, e.g. mică (Lat. *mīca*), lăptucă (Lat. *lactūca*), muta (Lat. *mūtāre*), and in Italian the reduction of the tenuis is of limited extent, e.g. amico (Lat. *ămīcus*, Span. amigo), uopo (Lat. *ŏpus*, Span. huebos), vite (Lat. *vītis*, Span. vide), fuoco (Lat. *fŏcus*, Span. fuego), &c., though before *a* we have the media in miga (Lat. *mīca*), strada (Lat. *strata*), lattuga (Lat. *lactūca*), &c., and when the vowel following has the accent, e.g. siguro (Lat. *sēcūrus*), mudare (Lat. *mūtāre*). Misspellings on plebeian inscriptions like *Amada* (le Blant, *I. G.* 576 a), *iradam* (Or. 2541, of 142 A. D.), *Segundae* (Mur. 2076. 10) are precursors of these changes. That they obtruded themselves into the recognized Latin pronunciation is more than doubtful. One tendency indeed of the Romance languages, to turn *pr, tr, cr* into *br, dr, gr*, e.g. Span. padre (Lat. *păter*), sobra (Lat. *sŭpra*), magro (Lat. *măcer*), lagrima (Lat. *lăcrĭma*, cf. *C. I. L.* ix. 648 LAGREMAS), is directly contrary to that treatment of *d* before *r* in early Latin (*ātro-* for **ādro-*, &c.), which we have just mentioned. In Italian *tr* remains after any vowel except *a*, e.g. vetro (Lat. *vĭtrum*, Span. vedro), but padre (Lat. *păter*), and *pr* is retained when it follows the accented vowel, e.g. sopra (Lat. *sŭpra*), capra (Lat. *căpra*), but cavriuolo (Lat. *capreolus*), obbrobrio (Lat. *opprobrium*; cf. Or. Henz. 6086 ii).

(For the phonetic descriptions of the Latin tenues and mediae by Roman grammarians see §§ 79, 86, 92.)

§ 74. **Greek tenues in loanwords.** The most frequent instance of the change of a Gk. tenuis to a Lat. media, is the change of Gk. κ to Lat. *g*, especially before the vowels *a, o, u*. Thus *gummi* for κόμμι, *gōbius* for κωβιός, *gŭbernāre* for κυβερνᾶν, Săguntum for Ζάκυνθος, &c., have always, or usually, *g* in Lat. (see Georges, *Lex. Wortf.* s.vv.). The spelling varies in *conger* and *gonger*, *gŏrȳtus* and *corytus*, *cammărus* and *gammarus* (see Georges). Ter. Scaurus (xiv. 9, 10) says that some pronounced *gaunăce*, some *caunace*; so *gamellus* and

§§ 74, 75.]　　　PRONUNCIATION. MUTES.　　　75

cămellus [cf. Probi App. 198. 9 calathus non 'galatus'; Gloss. ap. Mai, *Cl. Auct.* vi. 578 corax per c non per g; and see Georges and Brambach s. vv. *Caieta* (now Gaëta), *Agrigentum, grabatum*]. In the modern Milanese dialect, the French cabriolet has similarly become gabriolé. Before *n, c* became *g* in Latin (ch. iv. § 116), so that the spellings *cygnus, Gnōsus, Gnĭdus* are only natural (see Georges and Brambach). Of the final -*ca* of *ămurca* (Gk. ἀμόργη), Servius (ad *G.* i. 194) says that it was written with *c*, but pronounced with *g*. (A similar interchange of -*ca, -ga*, is seen in *leuga* and *leuca, raca*, and *raga*, &c.) For Gk. π we find Latin *b* in the initial accented syllable before the vowel *u* in the word *buxus*, and in the Old Latin name of King Pyrrhus, *Burrus* (the form used by Ennius in his Annals, according to Cicero *Or.* xlviii. 160 Burrum semper Ennius, numquam Pyrrhum; ipsius antiqui declarant libri; cf. Quint. i. 4. 15, and Ter. Scaur. 14 K., who adds *Byrria* as the equivalent of Gk. Πυρρίας). The form *burrus* was retained in rustic and colloquial Latin; *burra* was a name for a cow, *burrus* for a red-faced man, as we learn from Paul. Fest. (p. 22. 32 Th. burrum dicebant antiqui quod nunc dicimus rufum; unde rustici 'burram' appellant buculam, quae rostrum habet rufum. pari modo rubens cibo ac potione ex prandio 'burrus' appellatur), who also mentions *burranica potio*; lacte mixtum sapa, a rufo colore (p. 26. 19 Th.), and *burranicum*; genus vasis (p. 26. 7). Quintilian (i. 5. 13) quotes Cicero's phrase *Canopitarum exercitum* with the remark, ipsi Canobon dicunt. (On Latin *Cănōpus*, Gk. Κάνωβος see Brambach s. v.) In Probi Append. (199. 5 K.) we have, plasta non 'blasta.' Gk. βατάνιον for πατάνιον is quoted by Hesychius as belonging to the Sicilian dialect (πατάνια .. ποτήρια. τινὲς δὲ διὰ τοῦ β βατάνια λέγουσιν, and βατάνια· τὰ λοπάδια. ἡ δὲ λέξις Σικελική). So *carpătĭnae crĕpĭdae* of Catull. xcviii: 4 are in Gk. καρβάτιναι and καρπάτιναι. Old Lat. *Telis* for Θετίς (*C. I. L.* xiv. 4102, on a Praenestine mirror) (cf. Varro, *L. L.* vii. 87 lymphata dicta a lympha; *lympha* a Nympha, ut quod apud Graecos Θετίς, apud Ennium : Thelis illi mater, and *R. R.* iii. 9. 19 antiqui ut Thetim 'Thelim' dicebant, sic Medicam 'Melicam' vocabant) perhaps implies an intermediary form with *d* for Gk. τ. The relation of *cotonea*, the origin of the Romance words for quince (Ital. cotogna, Fr. coing) to Gk. κυδωνία is not clear (cf. Macrob. vii. 6. 13 mala cydonia quae cotonia Cato vocat; Pliny, *N. H.* xv. 10). In Vulg. Lat. we find additional examples of *g* for Gk. κ, such as *grupta (Ital. grotto), *garofulum (from καρυόφυλλον), *gontus : not to mention *gattus for (Teutonic?) *cattus*, and probably *gamba*. Of spellings on Gk. inscriptions may be instanced καλικων for *călĭgarum*, σαραγαρον (from *serrācum*), σγαλη all on the Edict of Diocletian; also Γαντιος for *Cantius*, and Κανδιτος for *Candĭdus* (Eckinger, pp. 98, 100, 102). The same interchange of tenues and mediae is seen in Gk., e. g. τήκω and τήγανον, especially in loanwords, e. g. τάπης, ταπίς and δάπις, Ἀμπρακιώτης and Ἀμβρακιώτης : in dialects we have, e. g. κλάγος· γάλα, Κρῆτες, Hesych., and in later Vulg. Gk. τ often becomes δ between two vowels. It is thus often possible that the Roman word represents a Greek byform. [Other examples of the variety in Latin loanwords are *carbăsus*, Gk. κάρπασος, *crŭmīna*, Gk. γρῡμέα a bag, *galbănum*, Gk. χαλβάνη, *spēlunca*, Gk. σπήλυγγα, not to mention *incitega*, Gk. ἐγγυθήκη. Cf. also *lătĭces* with Gk. λάταγες, *plăga* with Gk. πλάξ. On *citrus* (also *cedrus*), and Gk. κέδρος, see ch. iv. § 113. Both *Creisita* and *Crisida* occur on old Praenestine cistae for 'Chryseis' (*C. I. L.* xiv. 4109; i. 1501)].

§ 75. **Confusion of mediae and tenues in Latin words.** A large number of seeming instances are not due to any Latin, or even Italic, law of sound, but are survivals of that interchange of media and tenuis, which shows itself occasionally in I.-Eur. roots, e. g. *sūcus* and *sūgo*. Many are dialectal variations; for in parts of Italy the tenuis was used where the Latin form had the media and vice versa, just as in modern Italian the Neapolitan dialect has *t* corresponding to the *d* of lapidi (Lat. *lăpĭdes*), &c.; the Roman dialect affects grosta, gautela, &c., with *g-* for *c-*. Thus Quint. i. 5. 12 tells us that a certain Tinca of Placentia used 'precula' for *pergŭla* (see K. Z. xxx. 345). Of the misspellings of this kind in inscriptions and MSS. (collected by Schuchardt, *Vok.* i. pp. 124 sqq.), not a few are due to the similar appearance of the letters G, C, B, P. But there is a residuum of undoubted instances of variation between the tenuis and the media, at least for *c* and *g*. For *p* and *b* we have the (dialectal?) word *ropio*, a red mullet, given as nickname to Pompey, who had a florid complexion (Mar. Sacerd. 462 K. quotes a lampoon, perhaps a Fescennine line sung by soldiers at his triumph, quém non púdet ét rúbet, non est hómŏ sed rópio). The word, which should probably be read in Catull. xxxvii. 10 (see Sacerd. l. c.), is evidently connected with *robus* and *rufus*, for Sacerdos adds, ropio autem est minium aut piscis robeus aut penis [cf. Ter. Scaur. 14 K. on the doubtful examples of *Palatium* and 'Balatium' (by analogy of *balo*); *Publicola* and O. Lat. *Poplicola* (by analogy of *populus*); *propom* on early coins for *probum, C. I. L.* i. 19; *aduocapit* in the Carmen Arvale]. For *t* and *d*, probably not *petiolus*, 'a little foot' (?) (Afranius ap. Non. 160 M. atque ádeo nolo núdo petiolo ésse plus [*MSS.* es pus], for this is better explained as *peciolo-* (Ital. picciuolo, O. Fr. peçuel, &c.). But the most examples are of *g* for *c*, as we found to be the case with Greek loanwords; and this perhaps throws some light on the early use in the Latin alphabet of the Greek Gamma-symbol as the symbol for Latin *c* as well as for *g*. In Vulgar Latin *-cit-* and *-cer-* in the proparoxytone syllable seem to have become *-git-, -ger-*, e. g. **plagitum, *fager*, to judge from the Romance forms (see *Arch. Glottol.* ix. 104). (Is *dĭgĭtus* a similar transformation of *dicitus? Dicitus* is censured in Probi App. 198. 10, and occurs in MSS. See Schuchardt, *Vok.* ii. 413); initial *cra-* may have become *gra*, e. g. Ital. grasso, Span. graso, Fr. gras from Latin *crassus*; Ital. grata, Span. grada from Lat. *crātis* (Meyer Lübke, *Rom. Gram.* i. p. 353); Lat. *gavia* for *cavea* is reflected in Ital. gabbia, Span. gavia, Prov. gabia; so **gonflāre* in Ital. gonfiare, &c. [For other examples of *g-c*, see Georges and Brambach s. vv. *vicesimus, viceni, triceni, tricies, nongenti, cremia, neglego, graculus, gurgulio*, &c.; on the change of *d* before *r* to *t*, e. g. *ătrōx* for **adrox* (cf. *ŏdium*), see ch. iv. § 113, of *c* before *n* to *g*, e. g. *dignus*, see ch. iv. § 119; *bibo* (I.-Eur. *pibo) is due to the Latin tendency to assimilate adjacent syllables (ch.iv. § 163); cf. also Quint. i. 6. 30 nonnumquam etiam barbara ab emendatis conatur discernere, ut cum Triquetram dici Siciliam an 'Triquedram,' meridiem an 'medidiem' oporteat, quaeritur.]

§ 76. Mediae and Tenues at end of word. Quintilian, who includes among the points of inferiority of Latin to Greek the use of *-b, -d* at the end of syllables (xii. 10. 32 quid quod syllabae nostrae in b litteram et d innituntur adeo aspere, ut plerique, non antiquissimorum quidem, sed tamen veterum, mollire temptaverint, non solum 'aversa' pro 'abversis' dicendo, sed et in praepositione b litterae absonam et ipsam f [s *edd.*] subiciendo), mentions (i. 7. 5) with disapproval the practice of distinguishing *ad*, the preposition, from *at*, the conjunction. The right use of *-t* and *-d* in words like *ăt* and *ăd, sĕd, quit* (from *queo*), and *quĭd* (from *quis*), *quŏt* and *quŏd*, &c., is a subject of frequent remark in the grammarians, e. g. Ter. Scaurus (12. 8 K.) approves *sed* on the ground that the old form was *sedum* [cf. ib. 11. 8 K. ; Vel. Long. 69–70 K. ; Probi App. 202, 37 K. ; Cassiod. 212. 5 K. ; Alcuin 308. 8 K., and (on *haut* and *haud*) 303. 3 K. ; on *caput* and *apud* Bede 264. 35 K., &c.]. Charisius (229 K.) quotes *ad* for *at* from a speech of Licinius Calvus ; and Vel. Long. 70 K. says that *sed* in *sed enim* 'd litteram sonat.' Instances of the confusion or suppression of final -*d* and -*t* in inscriptions and MSS. have been collected by Schuchardt, *Vok.* i. pp. 118 sqq. and Seelmann, pp. 366 sqq. They include, beside the cases just mentioned, the use of -*d* for -*t*, or the suppression of -*t*, in verbal forms, like *rogad*, *C. I. L.* iv. 2388 (but on O. Lat. *feced*, &c., for *fēcit*, &c., see ch. viii. § 69), *peria* (for *pĕreat*) iv. 1173 ; also the loss of -*t* in the combination -*nt*, *fecerun* vi. 3251, just as -*t* is lost in the combination -*ct*, *lac* from *lact* from older *lacte*, an I-stem). The preposition is spelt *at* in the Lex Col. Jul. Genetivae Urbanorum of 44 B.C., except when the next word begins with *d*-, e. g. at it judicium atsint, i. 2. 13 ; ateo .. ad decuriones, iii. 8. 7 (*Eph. Epigr.* ii. p. 122), but always *ad* (even in *adtributionem*, &c.), beside *aput* in the Lex Julia Municipalis of 45 B C. (*C. I. L.* i. 206). This uncertainty of usage has been taken as evidence of the final dental having been uttered faintly, or having been a sound intermediate between *d* and *t*, like the final dental of German, written *dt*, in Stadt, &c. The instances, however, mentioned by grammarians are all words which would be closely joined in utterance with a following word, *quid tibi ?*, *quid dicis*, *ad templum*, *ad deos*, &c. ; so that it is most natural to believe, as was suggested of the confusion between -*m* and -*n*, that the sounds adapted themselves to the initial of the following word. *Quid tibi* would be pronounced as *quit tibi*, and *ad templum* as *at templum* (like *at-tineo*, &c.). The spellings *quid tibi*, *ad templum* would be historical (like *ad-tineo*), not phonetic. The weakness of final *d* is better shown by its suppression after a long vowel. Thus the Abl. Sg. ceased to be pronounced with -*d* about the end of the third cent. B. C. (see § 137), though *d* remained till later in the monosyllables *med*, *ted*, while *haud* was retained before words beginning with vowels (Ritschl, *Opusc.* ii. 591, &c., v. 352) ; and the affection of -*t* by the spellings on plebeian and late inscriptions of verb-forms like *reliquid*, &c. In Vulgar Latin -*t* cannot have been dropped till after the conquest of Gaul (*A. L. L.* i. 212).

P is not found at the end of any Latin word, if we except *volup*, for *vŏlŭpe*, the Neuter of an adj. **volupis* ; but it is common in Oscan, e. g. op (Lat. *ob*), íp 'there.'. (On the spellings *optineo*, *obtineo*, &c., see § 80). On the other hand final *g* never appears in Latin, though we have *c* in *ac* (for *atqu*[*e*]), *nec* (for *nĕqu*[*e*]), *lac* (for *lact*[*e*]), *illīc* for *illī-c*[*e*], &c. ; but *nec* is written *neg*- invariably in *negotium*, and usually in *neglego* (see Georges, s.v.). (Cf. ch. x. § 18.)

§ 77. **Mediae and tenues in the Dialects.** There is a good deal of interchange of tenues and mediae in Umbrian and Oscan (e. g. Osc. deketasiúí and degetasiús), which has led some to the theory that the Umbro-Oscan mediae were not voiced (Conway, *Amer. Journ. Phil.* xi. 306), while others refer the variation to the defects of the Umbrian and Oscan alphabets, which being derived from the Etruscan had not originally the means of distinguishing fully the tenues from the mediae (the Umbrian alphabet, for example, uses the *t*-sign for both *t* and *d*, the *k*-sign for both *k* and *g*, &c., see von Planta, *Gramm. Osk.-Umbr. Dial.* i. p. 547). In a Falisco-Latin inscr. (Zvet. *I. I. I.* 72) we have *gondecorant*, *gonlegium*, beside *communia*.

§ 78. **B, P.** Latin *b, p* were labial mutes, apparently with the same sound as *b, p* in Ital., e.g. bene (Lat. *bĕnĕ*), pino (Lat. *pīnus*), and English *b, p*, Between vowels *b* became in course of time a labial spirant, and by the third cent. A. D. became identified with Latin *v* (*w*) (see § 52). In Spanish, *b* has a *w*-sound, which differs from our *w*, in that the back of the tongue is not raised, nor the cheeks narrowed. It is the same as the *w* of South German wie, wein.

B was often written, though *p* was pronounced, before *s, t*, in such words as *urbs, obtĭneo*. It was a frequent subject of discussion among Latin grammarians whether these words should not be spelt with *p*, so that the spelling might agree with the pronunciation. The *b* was defended in *urbs*, &c., on the ground that it would be unreasonable to spell a nominative case with *p* and the other cases with *b, urbis, urbi*, &c., and in *obtineo*, &c., because the form of the preposition when alone, and often in composition, had the *b, ob, obdūco*, &c. The *-b* of the preposition similarly assimilated itself in pronunciation to *m* in compounds like *submitto, summitto*. In *ŏmitto* all traces of this *b* have disappeared (see ch. iii.).

Latin *b* represents an I.-Eur. aspirate in words like *rŭber*, stem *rubro-*, I.-Eur. **rudh-ro*, Greek ἐ-ρυθρός. In these cases *f* in various parts of Italy corresponded to Latin *b*, e.g. Umbrian rufro-. This dialectal *f* for *b* is seen in forms like *sīfĭlus*, beside genuine Latin *sibĭlus*, forms which do not prove anything about the pronunciation of Latin *b*, but are merely corresponding words to the Latin, which have come from some dialect or other. A good many of these dialectal *f*-forms have found their way into the Romance languages.

§ 79. **Phonetic descriptions of b, p.** To the usual phoneticians, Ter. Maur. vi. 331. 186–193 K.:

> b littera vel p quasi syllabae videntur
> junguntque sonos de gemina sede profectos :
> nam muta jubet portio comprimi labella,
> vocalis at intus locus exitum ministrat.
> compressio porro est in utraque dissonora ;
> nam prima per oras etiam labella figit,
> velut intus agatur sonus ; ast altera contra
> pellit sonitum de mediis foras labellis ;

Mar. Vict. vi. 33. 15 K. (whose *b* seems to be the *p* of Ter. Maur.) b et p litterae conjunctione vocalium quasi syllabae (nam muta portio penitus latet: neque enim labiis hiscere ullumve meatum vocis exprimere nisus valet, nisi vocales exitum dederint atque ora reserarint) dispari inter se oris officio exprimuntur, nam prima exploso e mediis labiis sono, sequens compresso ore velut introrsum attracto vocis ictu explicatur; Martianus Capella iii. 261 B labris per spiritus impetum reclusis edicimus . . P labris spiritus [spiritu *Eyss.*] erumpit; we may add the remark of Terentius Scaurus vii. 14. 3 K. b cum p et m consentit, quoniam origo earum non sine labore conjuncto ore respondet.

80. bs, bt. Latin *bs* had the sound of Greek ψ (Vel. Long. vii. 61 K.), and was one of the sounds for which the Emperor Claudius proposed a new letter, on the ground that a separate sign for *cs* (*x*) justified a separate sign for *ps*. The general opinion however pronounced this new letter unnecessary. Some even went so far as to question the necessity of *x* (Quint. i. 4. 9 nostrarum ultima [*sc.* x], qua tam carere potuimus, quam psi non quaerimus). The spelling *abs* is defended on the strength of *ab* by Velius Longus (vii. 61 K.), who also tells us that some authorities always spelt *opstitit, absorpsi, urps, nupsi, pleps* (id. vii. 64 and 73-4 K.) (cf. Mar. Vict. vi. 21. 10 K. Ter. Scaur. vii. 14. 7; 21. 8 K.). It was Varro who laid down the rule that nouns with -*p*- in the Genitive should have -*ps* in the Nominative, nouns with -*b*- should have -*bs*, e. g. *Pelops, Pĕlŏpis*, but *plebs, plēbis, urbs, urbis* (Ter. Scaur. vii. 27. 11 K.; cf. Varro, *L. L.* x. 56). [So in the Appendix Probi: (198. 4 K. and 199. 4) celebs non 'celeps'; (199. 3) plebs non 'pleps'; (199. 11) labsus non 'lapsus.'] That *obtinuit* was pronounced *optinuit*, we are told by Quintilian (i. 7 7): secundam enim b litteram ratio poscit, aures magis audiunt p. The spellings *ps, pt* are common enough in MSS. and inscriptions (see Indices to *C. I. L.*) [cf. *Obscus, Opscus* and *Opicus*, old forms of *Oscus* (as *supscribo, subscribo* of *suscribo*), Fest. 212 and 234 Th.; and see Georges, *Lex. Wortf.*, s. v. *cambsi, campsi*]. Curtius Valerianus (ap. Cassiod. 157 K.) says *ps* belong to the same, *bs* to different syllables. In the Lex Col. Jul. Genetivae Urbanorum of 44 B. C. *op-* is used in *opsaepire, optemperare, opturare, optinere*, but always *ab-*, never *ap-* (*Eph. Epigr.* ii. pp. 122 and 221). *Absinthium* (vulgar *absentium*), *absida* late Lat. for *apsis* follow the analogy of *abs*.

§ 81. ps, pt. In Romance the sounds of Latin *pt* and *ps* have been retained in Roumanian, but in other languages have passed into *tt, ss*, e. g. Ital. sette (Lat. *septem*), cassa (Lat. *capsa*), esso (Lat. *ipsĕ*), medesimo (Vulg. Lat. *met ipsimus, O. Fr. medesme, Fr. même). *Isse* for *ipse* found its way into colloquial Latin (see Georges, *Lex. Wortf.* s. v.), though, if the story mentioned, but discredited, by Suetonius (*Aug.* 88), be true, the use of *issi* (or *ixi*?)[1] for *ipsi* by a 'legatus consularis' led to his being cashiered by Augustus as 'rudis et indoctus.' Cf. *sussĭlio* for *supsilio, subsilio*; and for some examples of *ss* for *ps* in MSS. and late plebeian inscriptions, see Schuchardt, *Vok.* i. 148; for *tt, t* for *pt*, ib. i. 143, and see Georges s. vv. *scratta, septimus*. The lap-dog, the subject of one of Martial's prettiest epigrams (i. 109) was called *Issa* (i. e. *ipsa* in the sense of *domina*), 'M'lady.' Its master had made a painting of it : in qua tam similem videbis Issam, Ut sit tam similis sibi nec ipsa.

---

[1] Plautus puns on *opsecro* and *mox seco, Mil.* 1406.

§ 82. bm, mb. *Ommentans* was the spelling in a line of Livius Andronicus' translation of the Odyssey (ap. Fest. 218. 14 Th. *aut in Pylum deuenies aut ibi ommentans*. Cf. Gl. Plac. ommentat : expectat). *Amněgo* occurs on inscriptions (*C. I. L.* vi. 14672) ; *amnuo* in Glosses (Löwe, *Prodromus*, p. 421). (On *āmitto, submitto*, pronounced *summitto*, &c., see Brambach, *Hülfsb.*³ pp. 16-18. On *mb* becoming dialectally *mm*, see § 71.)

§ 83. b and dialectal f. *Alfius* was the dialectal, *Albius* the Latin form of the name. The two forms are found, for example, on Interamna inscriptions (*Albius, C. I. L.* xi. 4240, *Alfia*, 4242). So with other proper names like *Orbĭlius* and *Orfīlius*. *Sifĭlus*, a mispronunciation of *sĭbĭlus*, censured in the Appendix Probi (199. 3 K.; cf. Non. 531. 2), was a dialectal variety ; similarly *scrŏfa* a sow has been connected with *scrŏbis*. In glosses we find *crefrare* with *cribrare, bufus* with *būbo* (Löwe, *Prodr.* p. 421), and in modern Italian sufilare (cf. Fr. siffler) beside sibilare (Lat. *sibilare*), tafano (Lat. *tăbānus*), &c. (other examples in *Arch. Glott. Ital.* x. 1).

§ 84. b and m. B became *m* in Latin before *m, n* (cf. *summitto, amnego*, above). But *glŏmus* and *glŏbus* (cf. Probi App. 198. 8 globus non 'glomus') are two different stems, *globus, -i* and *glomus, -eris* (see *Rom. Forsch.* vii. 217).

§ 85. D, T. We have clear evidence that Latin *n*, the dental nasal, was, like our *n*, not a pure dental (see § 61). The dental mutes, *d* the voiced dental, *t* the unvoiced, cannot then have been pure dentals either. The Latin phoneticians speak of Latin *d* and *t* as differing in more respects than the mere presence or absence of what is technically called 'voice'; though the suspicion under which they stand of being unduly influenced by their Greek authorities makes them uncertain guides. In Italian, *t*, e. g. tu (Lat. *tū*), *d*, e. g. dono (Lat. *dōno*) are both pure dentals, differing like any other unvoiced and voiced mute. But there is on Italian soil a curious sound, a cacuminal *d*, exemplified by Sicilian cavaḍḍu (Lat. *căballus*), on which see Meyer-Lübke, *Ital. Gram.* § 264.

Both *l* and *r* are sounds closely related to *d*, the position of the tongue, &c., being very similar in the formation of all three sounds. In *d* there is a complete closure of the mouth passage; in *l* the middle of the passage is closed, but the sides are left open ; in *r* there is an opening in front at the tip of the tongue. Through neglect of the side closure *d* has passed into *l* in words like *lăcrŭma* (older *dacruma*) (see ch. iv. § 111); through neglect of the front closure it passed into *r* in Old Latin in words like *arfuise* (later *adfuisse*) on the Senatus Consultum de Bacchanalibus (*C. I. L.* i. 196, of 186 B.C.) before the bilabial spirants *f* and *v* (see ch. iv. § 112). A fifth (?) century grammarian speaks of the mispronunciation *peres* for *pĕdēs* as one specially affected by the poorer classes at Rome in his time (Consentius v. 392. 15 K.); and the same change of sound is still found in dialects of Italy. In Naples, for example, pere is the word used for 'foot' to this very day. Before *r*, *d* seems to have been changed to *t*, e. g. *āter*, stem *ātro-* for **ādro* (see ch. iv. § 113), a tendency seen in spellings like *Alexanter, Cassantra*, which Quintilian tells us he had noticed on old inscriptions at Rome (i. 4. 16), and which is found on Praenestine cistae (see § 73). Of *dr, dl*, &c. we are told 'nullo modo sonare d littera potest' (Cassiod. 151 K.; 207 K.). Before *l, t* could not be pronounced, but passed into the sound of *c*, just as the phrase 'at least' often takes with us the sound 'a cleast.' The I.-Eur. suffix *-tlo* had on this account become *-clo* in Latin words like *pĕrīclum* (ch. v. § 25); and when at a late period the Latin suffix *-tulus* became contracted by the syncope of the penult, it was changed to *-clus, vĕtŭlus*, for example, becoming *veclus* (Ital. vecchio). Another change of *d*, namely its tendency to be assimilated by a preceding *n* in words like *distenno* for *distendo* is discussed in § 71, and its assimilation in compounds like *adtĭneo*, pronounced *attineo, adsum*, pronounced *assum*, in ch. iv. § 160. The most important changes of *d, t*, however, are those which these letters experienced when they were followed by *i* before another vowel. The same syncope that reduced *vetulus* to *veclus, călĭda* to *calda*, made 'Tityus' out of *Tĭtius*, 'hodye' out of *hŏdie*. Through this combination of *y* with a preceding consonant in unaccented syllables, a new series of sounds, unknown in Latin, has arisen in Romance. Latin *sīmia* has become French singe (through **simya*), Latin *apium* Fr. ache (**apyum*), Lat. *răbies* Fr. rage (**rabyes*), Lat. *cambiare* Fr. changer (**cambyare*). *Dy*, as we saw before (§ 51), became identified with *gi, ge*, and Latin *j* (our *y*), and has assumed in Italian the sound of our *j*, e.g. Ital. giorno from Lat. *diurnus*; while *ty* has developed in Italian into the sound of *ts*, a sound reduced in French to an *s*-sound, in Spanish to a sound like our *th* in 'thin' (written in Spanish *z*), e.g. Ital. piazza, Fr. place, Span. plaza, all from Latin *plătea, *platya*. The grammarians of the later Empire have fortunately left us a good many remarks on the palatalization of *t*, so that we can trace pretty clearly the course of its development in Latin. It seems from their accounts to have begun in the fourth cent. A.D., and to have been fairly established by the fifth; and this is confirmed by other evidence, such as the fact that in the Latin loanwords in Welsh (borrowed during the Roman occupation of Britain which ceased in the fifth cent.), *ty* has not become an *s*-sound. About the same time *cy* became assibilated; and so confusions of -*ci*- and -*ti*- before a vowel are common in late inscriptions and in MSS.

§ 86. **Phonetic descriptions of d, t.** Terentianus Maurus makes the back of the tongue come into play in the formation of *d*, which would make Latin *d* to have been what phoneticians call 'dorsal' *d* (from Lat. *dorsum*, the back), like the *d* of Central and S. Germany. Seelmann understands *t, l, r*, and *n* also to have been dorsal sounds. Ter. Maur. vi. 331. 199-203 K. :

> at portio dentes quotiens suprema linguae
> pulsaverit imos modiceque curva summos,
> tunc d sonitum perficit explicatque vocem ;
> t, qua superis dentibus intima est origo,
> summa satis est ad sonitum ferire lingua.

Similarly Marius Victorinus speaks of the two sounds as having marked difference in their formation (vi. 33. 24 K.): d autem et t, quibus, ut ita dixerim, vocis vicinitas quaedam est, linguae sublatione ac positione distinguuntur. nam cum summos atque imos conjunctim dentes suprema sui parte pulsaverit, d litteram exprimit. quotiens autem sublimata partem, qua superis dentibus est origo contigerit, t sonore vocis explicabit. They represent the formation of *t*, in conformity with what we have already learned about *n*, as the contact of the tongue with the alveolars, or gums of the upper teeth, whereas in uttering *d* both the lower and the upper teeth are touched by the tongue, which is so bent down as to touch the lower teeth with its tip, and the upper with its blade. Martianus Capella (iii. 261) : D appulsu linguae circa superiores dentes innascitur. . . T appulsu linguae dentibusque impulsis extunditur [extruditur *Eyss.*, extuditur *MSS.*].

§ 87. **d and l.** In some Italian dialects *d* in the Latin suffix -*ĭdus* becomes *l* if the stem ends in a labial. Thus Lat. *tĕpĭdus* is in the Neapolitan dialect *tiepolo*. Some examples of *l* for *d* in MSS. and late inscriptions are collected by Schuchardt, *Vok.* i. 142.

§ 88. **d and r.** In the Abruzzi (the ancient country of Oscan and Sabellian tribes) we find *đ* (English *th* in 'there') and *r* for Latin *d*, e. g. *đicere* and *ricere* (Lat. *dīcere*), *đa* and *ra* (Lat. *dat*). The close connexion of *đ* with *r*, as phases of *d*, we see from Spanish, where in the literary language *d* has assumed the *đ*-sound in words like 'Madrid,' while in the Andalusian dialect this *đ* has sometimes developed into *r*, e. g. soleares, sometimes been dropped e. g. naa, for *nada. Final *đ* is weakly pronounced in Spanish, and often dropped ; and the same is true of the Galician dialect of Portuguese, e. g. bondá (Lat.

bŏnĭtātem). In Provençal too Latin *d* became *đ* and was dropped when final. All this throws light on the Umbrian treatment of I.-Eur. *d*, which in the middle of a word is expressed by a peculiar sign in the Umbrian alphabet (conventionally written *đ* or *ř*), a sign rendered in Latin characters by *rs*, e. g. kapiđe, *capirse* (Lat. *căpĭdi*, Dat. of *capis*, a bowl), and which seems to interchange with *r*, e. g. tertu and teđtu (Lat. *dăto*, or rather *dĕdato), but which at the end of a word is often dropped, e. g. asam-a and asam-ađ (Lat. *ad āram*, or rather *aram ad*), always when a long vowel precedes, e. g. pihaclu (Lat. *piācŭlo*, older *piācŏlŏd*, Abl.). Not unlike is the Latin treatment of *d*, with the occasional change to *r* on the one hand, and the loss of final *d* after a long vowel [e. g. *piacolō(d)*, but *quŏd*] on the other. In Italian *d* is always dropped in words like fe (Lat. *fĭdēs*), and in the other Romance languages *d* between any two vowels is liable to the same thing; e. g. Latin *mĕdulla* is in Spanish meollo, in French moelle, though in Italian it is midolla; Italian preda (Lat. *praeda*) is in Sardinian prea, &c.

§ 89. tl. *Veclus* for *vĕtŭlus*, *viclus* for *vĭtŭlus*, *capiclum* for *căpĭtŭlum*, were mispronunciations in vulgar speech (Probi App. p. 197. 20 and 198. 34 K.). *Stlis* the old form of *lis* (Quint. i. 4. 16) is spelled *sclis* on inscriptions (e. g. *C. I. L.* x. 211 and 1249). Caper censures the use of *sclataris* for *stlātāris*, a pirate ship, *marculus* for *martŭlus*, a priest of Mars (vii. 107. 1; 105. 21 K.). (For examples of *cl* for *tl* in MSS. and late inscriptions see Schuchardt, *Vok.* i. 160.)

§ 90. **Assibilation of ty, dy.** In the fourth cent. we have an indication that *ti, di* before a vowel were in process of change. Servius (*in Don.* iv. 445. 8–12 K.) tells us that they often pass into a *sibilus* (which need not imply an *s*-sound) when in the middle of a word, though often they retain a pronunciation in accord with their spelling (etiam sic positae sicut dicuntur ita etiam sonandae sunt, ut 'dies' 'tiaras'). The same grammarian, in a note on Virgil, *Georg.* ii. 126, remarks that the Greek word *Mĕdĭa* must be pronounced in Greek fashion *sine sibilo*, that is to say without that consonantal *y*-sound which Latin *mĕdius*, *media* had in the time of Servius, that 'pinguis sonus' of *i* which the grammarians, as we saw before (§ 14), declared to be particularly alien to Greek pronunciation. In the early part of the fifth cent. Papirian (MS. 'Papirius') is more explicit. The letters *ti* before a vowel, in words like *Tatius*, *ōtia*, *justĭtia*, have, he says, a sound as if *z* (i. e. Greek ζ, which had at this time the soft or voiced *s*-sound) were inserted between them (ap. Cassiodor. vii. 216. 8 K.): 'justitia' cum scribitur, tertia syllaba sic sonat quasi constet ex tribus litteris t, z, i. This, he points out, is the case only when *ti* is followed by a vowel, and not always even then, not, for example, in Genitives like *otii* nor when *s* precedes *ti*, e. g. *justius, castius*. In the same century Pompeius censures as a fault the very pronunciation allowed in the preceding century by Servius, whereby *ti, di* were pronounced as spelled. He lays down the rule (v. 286. 10 K.): quotienscumque post ti vel di syllabam sequitur vocalis, illud ti vel di in sibilum vertendum est . . . ergo si volueris dicere ti vel di, noli, quem ad modum scribitur, sic proferre, sed sibilo profer. He goes on to say that this pronunciation is not found with initial *ti, di*; nor with the combination *sti*; for here 'ipsa syllaba a litteris accepit sibilum,' a remark which shows pretty clearly that Pompeius understands by *sibilus* an *s*-sound, cf. v. 104. 6 K. si dicas 'Titius,' pinguius sonat [i] et perdit sonum suum et accipit sibilum. A grammarian of the fifth cent.(?),

Consentius (395. 3), describes the new sound of *ti* in *ĕtiam* as 'breaking something off the middle syllable' (de media syllaba infringant). He, like Pompeius, declares the old pronunciation to be a 'vitium,' and tells us that the Greeks in their anxiety to correct this fault were apt to go to the extreme of giving the new sound to *ti* even when not followed by a vowel, e. g. in *optĭmus* (mediam syllabam ita sonent quasi post t, z graecum ammisceant). Finally Isidore in the seventh cent. tells us (*Orig.* i. 26. 28) that *justitia* 'sonum z litterae exprimit,' and (xx. 9. 4) that the Italians of his time pronounced *hŏdie* as ozie. The spellings on inscriptions confirm this account of the grammarians, though, as was to be expected, the assibilation shows itself on plebeian inscriptions even earlier than the fourth cent., e. g. *Crescentsian(us)* (Gruter, p. 127, vii. 1, of 140 A. D.), and even in the case of accented *ti, di*; Isidore's statement about the pronunciation of *hodie* (now oggi) is perhaps supported by ozE (*C. I. L.* viii. 8424): z (=zes, for *dies*) (*C. I. L.* v. 1667), &c., this *z* being pronounced like our *z* in 'amaze.' But *dy*- first passed through the stage of *y*, unlike *ty*- (see ch. iv. § 62), and this *z* may be merely an attempt to express the *y*-sound. Seelmann, p. 323, gives a list of these spellings. Some may be dialectal, for in Oscan we have on the Bantia tablet (*Zv.* 231) *Bansa*- (Lat. *Bantia*), *zicolo*- (Lat. *diēcula*) (pronounce *z* as above); and in Etruria the assibilation of *ty* seems also to have been known (see Sittl, *Lok. Verschiedenheiten*, p. 11); *Marsus* (cf. *Martses* Abl. Pl. on a Marsic inscr.) was the native name for *Martius*. The rationale of the change of sound is easy. While forming the *t*-sound the tongue unconsciously adapted itself to the position for the *y*-sound, so that the interval between the two letters was bridged over by a glide-sound which the Latin grammarians compare to Greek ζ, like the connecting *p* in the group *mpt*, from original *mt*, in words like *emptus*. (For a full account of the process see *K. Z.* xxix. 1 sqq., especially p. 48. On the interchange of *ti*- and *ci*-, see § 94.)

§ 91. K, C, G, QU, GU. What we call Guttural Consonants are more properly divided into (1) Gutturals proper, or Velar Gutturals, or simply 'Velars,' formed by the back of the convex surface of the tongue against the soft palate or velum, and (2) Palatals, formed by the middle of the convex surface of the tongue against the hard palate; and these two classes, which are also called back gutturals and front gutturals, might be still further subdivided according as the sound is made more to the back, or more to the front of the mouth. The Velars and Palatals may be found side by side in a language. German *ch*, for example, with a broad vowel like *o, a*, is a velar, e.g. 'ach,' but with a narrow vowel like *i*, in such a word as 'ich,' it is a palatal, being spoken more in the front of the mouth, so that it often sounds like English *sh*. Italian *ch* of chi, chiesa, is spoken more in the front of the mouth than *c* of casa, and the same is true of Engl. *k* of 'key' compared with *c* of 'caw.' The distinct lines of development which the Latin gutturals, *c* (*k*), *g*, took before broad and before narrow vowels, makes it possible, or even probable, that in Latin, as in Italian, *c* in *centum* had a more palatal sound than *c* in *cantus*, *contus*, &c., although this distinction is not mentioned by any of the Roman grammarians. The only guttural of which they give us a clear account is *qu*, in which the *u*-element seems to have been more of a vowel than Latin *v* (our *w*). A first century grammarian (Vel. Long. vii. 58. 17 K.) makes the difference to consist in the latter being sounded 'cum aliqua aspiratione,' i.e. as a consonantal spirant, not as a half-vowel, like *u* of *quis*, and in the fourth century *u* of *quŏniam*, *quĭdem* is said to be ' nec vocalis nec consonans ' (Donat. iv. 367. 16 K.). Priscian (seventh cent.) says the same of the *u* of *sanguis*, *lingua* (i. 37), so that Latin *qu*, *gu* must have had a sóund very like their sound in Italian quattro, &c. The palatalization of *c*, *g* before a narrow vowel is found in all Romance languages, with the exception of a dialect in the island of Sardinia. It was also a feature of the Umbrian language, so that we should expect it to have appeared early in Vulgar Latin at least. But all the evidence points to as late a period as the sixth and seventh centuries A.D. as the time when the change of sound took place. No grammarian hints at a difference of sound in *c*, *g* before a broad and before a narrow vowel, although the assibilation of *ti* before a vowel is mentioned again and again. Greek transcriptions of Latin words with *c* invariably reproduce it by κ, in cases like ΚΗΝΣΟΝ for *censum*, ΚΡΗΣΚΗΝΣ for *crescens*; Latin loanwords in Welsh (first to fifth centuries) show that Latin *c* was hard in all positions, e.g. Welsh cwyr (Lat. *cēra*), ciwdawd (Lat. *cīvĭtātem*), and similarly German Keller (Lat. *cellārium*), Kiste (Lat. *cista*); it is not till the seventh century that spellings like *paze* for *pace* (Muratori, 1915. 3) assert themselves on inscriptions. At an earlier period, it is true, *ci* (*cy*) before a vowel in unaccented syllables, and *ti* (*ty*) in the same position, had been confused, so that *ci* was written *ti* in words like *sōlātium*, and expressed like genuine *ti* a sibilant sound. But this proves nothing for *c* in words like *centum*, *cĭtra*. *G* before *e*, *i* became (like *dy*) the *y*-sound, and is in the Romance languages indistinguishable from Latin *j* (our *y*) (see § 51). The group *ct* has become *tt* in Italian, e.g. Ottobre, Lat. *Octōbris*, and had assumed the sound in late Latin, to judge from spellings on inscriptions like *lattuca* in the Edict of Diocletian, *Otobris* (Rossi 288, of 380 A. D.) and *autor*.

§ 92. Phonetic descriptions of the Gutturals. Ter. Maur. vi. 331. 194-205 K. :
utrumque latus dentibus applicare linguam
c pressius urget : dein hinc et hinc remittit,
quo vocis adhaerens sonus explicetur ore.
g porro retrorsum coit et sonum prioris
obtusius ipsi prope sufficit palato.
. . . k perspicuum est littera quod vacare possit
et q similis ; namque eadem vis in utraque est.

Mar. Vict. vi. 33. 20 K. c etiam et g, ut supra scriptae, sono proximae oris molimine nisuque dissentiunt. nam c reducta introrsum lingua hinc atque hinc molares urgens haerentem intra os sonum vocis excludit : g vim prioris pari linguae habitu palato suggerens lenius reddit . . . [q, k] quarum utramque exprimi faucibus, alteram distento, alteram producto rictu manifestum est. Mart. Cap. iii. 261 ; G spiritus [facit] cum palato . . . K faucibus palatoque formatur . . . Q appulsu palati ore restricto. Ter. Scaur. vii. 14. 1 K. x littera cognata est cum c et g, quod lingua sublata paulum hae dicuntur. Bede (228. 21), in criticizing Donatus' remark, quoted above, on the pronunciation of *u* in *qu*, explains him to mean that ' tam leviter tum effertur ut vix sentiri queat.' Pompeius (v. 104. 25 K.) calls the *u* a 'pars litterae praecedentis.' Priscian (i. 6) seems to speak of it as the 'contractus sonus' of normal *u;* but the passage is corrupt and the meaning uncertain. The statement of the phoneticians that Latin *c* was uttered with more energy of articulation than *g*, is confirmed by certain phenomena of the language, as has been shown in § 73.

§ 93. qu, gu. In Oscan and Umbrian, where I.-Eur. *qu* had become *p*, Latin *qu* is expressed in loanwords by *kv* (Osc. kvaísstur, Umbr. kvestretie [Lat. *quaestūrae*]). In Faliscan the *qu*-sound is written cv (*cu* or *cv*) e. g. *cuando*. Greek transcriptions have normally κου-, e. g. Κουάδρατος : but κοι- is the earliest expression of *qui*-, e. g. Κοίνκτιος (*C. I. G.* ii. 770, of 196-4 B. C., see Eckinger, p. 120 sqq.). In the Augustan age when *o* before a final consonant was weakened to *u* even after *v*, *u* (ch. iv. § 20), *qu*, *gu* became before this *u* reduced to *c*, *g*, which points to their being more like *cu*, *gu* than *cw*, *gw*, *relicus* from *reliquos* (in the time of Plautus *rĕlĭcuos*, of four syllables), *lŏcuntur*, *sĕcuntur*, *extingunt*. The grammarians of the first cent. A. D. were puzzled by the want of correspondence between Nom. Sing. *ĕcus*, Nom. Pl. *equi*, and reconstituted the Nom. Sing. as *equus* (in the time of Trajan) (Vel. Long. 59. 3 K. auribus quidem sufficiebat ut equus per unum u scriberetur, ratio tamen duo exigit) ; *guu* in *extinguunt*, &c., followed somewhat later. In the fifth cent. we find *co* definitely ousting *quŏ*, and *go*, *guŏ*, though *quŏ* seems to have been pronounced *cŏ* as early as the beginning of the second cent. B. C. (see ch. iv. § 137). Grammarians find great difficulty in deciding which verbs should be written with *-guo* and which with *-go*. The rule they usually follow is to write *-go* when the Perfect has *-xi*, *ungo*, *tingo* (see Bersu *Die Gutturalen*). (A Vulg. Lat. **laceus* for *lăqueus* is the original of Romance words for 'noose' like Ital. laccio, Fr. lacs; cf. Probi App. 197. 27 K. exequiae non 'execiae'; Cassiod. 158. 15 K. on 'reliciae'). The spelling of the Pronoun *qui* in its various forms was also matter of discussion as early as the time of Quintilian. He tells us (i. 7. 27) that in his younger days the Dative Singular used to be written *quoi* to distinguish it from the Nom. *qui*, but that the fashion had since come in of spelling it *cui* : illud nunc melius, quod ' cui ' tribus quam posui litteris enotamus, in quo pueris nobis ad pinguem sane sonum qu et oi utebantur, tantum ut ab illo 'qui' distingueretur. Annaeus Cornutus, Persius' teacher, tells us that at a much earlier period Lucilius laid down the rule that *qu* should be used when a vowel followed in the same syllable, otherwise *cu*, and this rule he himself accepts. His comments on it seem to show that there was not much difference in the sound. 'Some,' he goes on to say, ' think we should spell as we pronounce, but I do not go so far as that' (ego non omnia auribus dederim). Then he adds, 'qui' syllaba per q u i scribitur ; si dividitur, ut sit cui ut huic, per c (ap. Cassiod. 149. 1 K.). So Ter. Scaurus (first cent.), 27. 18 K. quis quidem per 'cuis' scribunt, quoniam supervacuam esse q litteram putant. sed nos cum illa u litteram, si quando tertia ab ea vocalis ponitur, consentire jam demonstravimus. c autem in dativo ponimus, ut sit differentia cui et qui. Velius Longus (first cent.) (75. 10 K.) thinks it necessary to point out the distinction between *ăquam* Noun and *ăcuam* Verb. Another tendency that appears in late Latin is to make a short vowel before *qu* long by position, as indeed any consonant followed by *u* (*w*), e. g. Ital. Gennaio with double *n* from **Jenuarius; aqua* is scanned with the first syllable long by the Christian poets, and appears in Ital. as acqua (cf. Probi App. 198. 18 K. aqua non ' acqua '). A sixth cent. grammarian ventures to give this quantity to the word in a line of Lucretius, vi. 868 quae calidum faciunt aquae tactum atque vaporem, where, however, the MSS. read *laticis*. Lachmann proposed to read *aqŭae* of three syllables, but was not able to prove that this form (like Horace's *silŭae*) existed in Old Latin (see Schrœder in Studemund, *Studien*, ii. 20). In Plautus and the older dramatists, where the short syllable of a word like *păti*, *lŏci* has a shortening influence on the following long syllable, so that the words may be occasionally scanned *păti*, *lŏci* (see ch. iii. § 42). a short vowel before *qu* seems hardly to have had this shortening power, e. g. rarely (if ever) *lŏqui*. So to the ear of Plautus *qu* almost made a preceding vowel long by position, unless we say that *loqui*, &c., sounded to Plautus something like a trisyllable. At any rate *qu* can hardly have had merely the ' rounded ' *k*-sound of Russian.

§ 94. c, g before narrow vowels. That *c*, *g* remained hard before *e*, *i*, &c. (when a vowel did not follow), down to the sixth and seventh centuries A. D. we have a superabundance of proof. For the earlier period we may point to the fact that in Umbrian, where *c* (*k*) before a narrow vowel became a sibilant, expressed by a peculiar sign in the native alphabet, the Latin *c* was not used for this sound in inscriptions (from the time of the Gracchi) written in Latin characters, but a modification of *s*, namely *s* with a stroke like a grave accent above it, e. g. *dešen* (Lat. *dĕcem*), *šesna* (Lat. *cēna*). That Plautus (who by the way was an Umbrian) makes a play on the words *Sōsia* and *sŏcius*, proves nothing (*Amph.* 383) :

Ámphitruonis te ésse aiebas Sósiam.—Peccáueram :
nam ' Ámphitruonis sócium' dudum me ésse volui dícere.

88   THE LATIN LANGUAGE.   [Chap. II.

He makes a play on *arcem* and *arcam* in *Bacch.* 943 : atque híc equos non in árcem verum in árcam faciet ímpetum.

At Cicero's time the spelling *pulcher, Gracchi* with *ch* for supposed Greek χ is evidence that in declension of nouns and adjectives (*acer, acris,* &c.) the *c* did not change to a sibilant when it came to stand before an *e* or an *i*, as it does in Italian (amico with hard *c*, amici with sibilant *c*).   Varro (ap. Prisc. i. 39) quotes *agceps* (another spelling of *anceps*) as one of the words where the Agma-sound (the *ng* of 'thing') was found in Latin before *c* (therefore presumably hard *c*). In the first cent. A. D. Plutarch and Strabo render Latin *c* before a narrow vowel by Greek κ, Κικέρων, &c. None of the grammarians of the Empire hint at a variety of pronunciation for *c*, *g*, not even Priscian in the sixth cent. ; and all through this period we have Greek κ for Latin·*c* in all positions (on documents of the sixth cent. δεκιμ, δωνατρικι, &c.), and on Latin inscriptions an interchange of *c*, *k*, *q* (e. g. *pake, C. I. L.* x. 7173 : *cesquet* for *quiescit*, viii. 1091) (see Seelmann, pp. 342 sqq.). This interchange is not regulated by any principle. We do not find *k* used for 'hard *c*,' *c* for 'soft *c*' &c., as would have been the case had there been a real difference of pronunciation. All the examples quoted for interchange of *c* before a narrow vowel (not in hiatus) with a sibilant earlier than the sixth cent. in S. Italy, the seventh cent. in Gaul, are illusory (see G. Paris in *Acad. Inscr.* 1893, *Comptes Rendus*, xxi. p. 81).

The evidence that Latin *c* was what we call hard *c* before *e*, *i* down to a late period is thus overwhelmingly strong. But while holding to this fact we may make two concessions. First, that *c* before *e*, *i* was probably more of a palatal (like Italian *ch* in chiesa) than a velar (like Italian *c* in casa). This palatal character was more and more developed in the Romance languages till *c* became a sibilant. Since however this assibilation is not known in the Sardinian dialect of Logudoru, it may be that at the time of the occupation of Sardinia (c. 250 B. C.) Latin *c* had still a velar character before narrow as before broad vowels. Second, that *ci* (*ce*) before a vowel underwent the same process of assibilation, as *ti* before a vowel did in the fifth cent. A. D., although interchange of spelling between prevocalic *ci* and *ti* before that time means merely that *cy, ty* were confused, as *cl, tl* were confused (cf. Quint. i. 11. 6), not that both *cy* and *ty* expressed a sibilant sound. (For instances of the confusion see Schuchardt, *Vok.* i. pp. 154 sq., and consult Georges and Brambach s. vv. *Mucius, mundities, negotium, otium, nuntius, Porcius, propitius, provincia, spatium, Sulpicius, indutiae, infitiae, condicio, contio, convicium, dicio, fetialis, solacium, suspicio, uncia,* &c. The earliest examples date from the second cent. A. D.) On Greek inscriptions Latin *ci* and *ti* are similarly confused, the earliest example being 'Αρουκιανος ('Αθην. iv. p. 104) of 131 A. D. In a Pisidian inscription (*Journ. Hell. Stud.* iv. p. 26), of 225 A. D., with Μαρσιανος, the σ (written C) is no doubt merely a confusion with the Latin letter *c*.

G before *e*, *i* may have been a palatal, rather than a velar, even earlier than *c* ; for in Sardinian hard *g* is not preserved as hard *c* is in this position. At what precise period it was developed to *y* we do not know. The Appendix Probi mentions as a mispronunciation 'calcosteis,' for *calcostĕgis*, though this may be a case of that spirant pronunciation of Greek γ, like Tarentine ὀλίος for ὀλίγος, Boeotian ἰών for ἐγώ. In the Romance languages it is treated exactly like Latin *j* (*y*), e. g. Ital. genero, Span. yerno (Lat. *gĕner*), like Ital. giace, Span. yace (Lat. *jacet*). It is dropped between two vowels in spellings like *vinti* for *viginti* (*C. I. L.* viii. 8573), the precursor of Ital. venti, &c. ; so *trienta*, (xii. 5399), &c. (*A.L.L.* vii. 69. See the list in Schuchardt, *Vok.* ii. 461). Vulg. Lat. **mais* is seen in Fr. mais, Ital. mai, &c. But this dropping of intervocalic *g* is found also before other vowels in late inscriptions and MSS., e. g. *frualitas* for *frugalitas* (see Schuchardt's list, *Vok.* i. 129), as in Vulg. Lat. *eo* (Ital. io, &c.) for *ego*, just as in Italian and other Romance languages, every intervocalic *g* when pretonic is dropped, e. g. Ital. reale from Lat. *regalis*. So *g* in this position may have become a spirant (like *g* of German Tage), just as intervocalic *b* became a *w*-sound in the third cent. (§ 78).

§ 95. ct, tt. For examples see Schuchardt, *Vok.* i. 134; *Rhein. Mus.* xlv. p. 493, and consult Georges and Brambach s. vv. *cottana, coturnix, setius* (?), *vettonica, pittacium, brattea, salapitta, virecta.* So *nictio*, to 'give tongue,' of a dog who has picked up the scent, is spelled *nittio* in the lemma of Festus (p. 188. l. 16 Th.), where he quotes the spirited line of Ennius, *Ann.* 374 M. :

nare sagaci
Sensit ; voce sua nictit ululatque ibi acuta.

Autor, with *autoritas*, is censured in the Appendix Probi (198. 30 K.), and is found on late inscriptions (*C. I. L.* viii. 1423 ; cf. xii. 2058, of 491 A. D.). For *nct*, which became *nt* by loss of the guttural, see § 70. So *mulcta* became *multa* (Georges s. v.).

gm or at least Greek γμ seem to have tended, like *lm*, to the sound *um*. In Vulg. Lat. *sagma* was **sauma* (Prov. sauma, Fr. somme), Isid. *Orig.* xx. 16. 5 sagma quae corrupte vulgo 'sauma' dicitur (*v. l.* salma ; cf. Span. salma, Ital. salma and soma). Cf. Probi App. 198. 11 pegma non ' peuma.' (For other examples, see Schuchardt, *Vok.* ii. p. 499.) For *gn*, see § 144.

§ 96. L,R. The liquids *l, r* are, as we have seen (§ 85), closely connected with the voiced dental mute *d*. The tongue has a similar position with each of the three sounds; but while with *d* the mouth passage is completely closed by pressure of the point of the tongue against the front, and of the edges of the tongue against the sides of the mouth, with *l* the sides are left open, and with *r* the front. The connexion of the three sounds in Latin is seen, as was before remarked, in the interchange of *d* with *l* in *lingua*, older *dingua*, &c., of *d* with *r* in *arfuisse* for *adfuisse*, &c., and, as we may now add, of *r* with *l* in words like *caerŭleus* for **caeluleus*, not to mention occasional occurrences of the dental nasal for *r* or *l*, like Vulgar Latin *menetris* for *mĕrĕtrix, cuntellum* for *cultellum*.

The grammarians give us a good deal of information about the pronunciation of *l* in different parts of the word. It had a 'pinguis sonus,' or 'plenus sonus,' in two cases, (1) when it ended a word, or syllable followed by another consonant, e.g. *sōl, silva, albus*; (2) in combinations like *fl, cl*, e. g. *flāvus, clārus*.

In contrast with this 'pinguis sonus' it has what is called an 'exilis' (or 'tenuis') 'sonus' (presumably its normal sound) in other two cases, viz. (1) at the beginning of a word, e.g. *lectus, lāna, lŭpus*, and especially (2) when it ends one syllable and begins the next, e.g. *il-lĕ, Mĕtel-lus, al-lia* [pronounced with two *l*'s as in our 'mill-lade,' 'hotel-landlord' (see § 127)]. When we examine the development of Latin *l* in the Romance languages we find the explanation of this distinction. In Italian, for example, Latin *l*, when initial, or when repeated, has the normal *l*-sound, e.g. lana, valle (Lat. *vallis*), pelle (Lat. *pellis*), but after a consonant *l* has become an *ly*-sound, now reduced to *i* (the half-vowel), e.g. chiaro (Lat. *clārus*), pieno (Lat. *plēnus*), fiume (Lat. *flūmen*). At the end of a syllable before a consonant, it has in most Romance languages been reduced to a *u*-sound, e.g. Fr. autre, Prov. autre, Span. otro (Lat. *alter*), and so in parts of Italy, e.g. Sicil. autru, while in other parts it is represented by an *i*-sound, e.g. aitro in the Florentine dialect. All this points to *l* in *clārus*, &c., and *l* in *alter*, &c., having been pronounced with what phoneticians call an 'off-glide' and an 'on-glide' c*l*arus, a*l*ter, which glides have been more and more developed in the Romance languages, till they reduced, or even completely extinguished, the *l*-sound. In Sardinian, which reflects the oldest type of Vulgar Latin, *l* remains unaffected after a consonant to a large extent, e.g. klaru, plenu, flumen, so that this affection of *l* may not have been begun in Vulgar Latin till about 200 B.C.

With regard to *r*, we should expect from the analogy of the Romance languages that Latin *r* was trilled (i.e. formed with the tip of the tongue vibrating), like the German and Scotch *r*, not like English *r* in 'red.' This is confirmed by the Roman name for *r*, 'littera canina,' the growling letter, Pers. i. 109 (Latin *hirrio* must have expressed the sound better than English 'growl'), and by Lucilius' description of it as like the growl of a lazy dog, or as he puts it, like 'what care I?' in dogs' language (ix. 29, 30 M.):

> r non multum abest hoc cacosyntheton atque canina
> si lingua dico 'nihil ad me.'

This rough sound of Latin *r* explains the reluctance of the Romans to begin two successive syllables with a consonant followed by *r*, a reluctance seen in forms like *praestīgiae* for *praestrigiae*, *incrēbui* for *increbrui*, and in spellings on inscriptions like *propius* for *prŏprius*. Before *s*, *r* was assimilated, e.g. *rūssus*, *rūsus* for *rūrsus*, as we see from Plautus' pun on *Persa* and *pessum* (*Pers.* 740 Persa me pessum dedit). It was assimilated too before *l*, e.g. *perlĭcio*, pronounced, and often spelled, *pellicio*. Metathesis of *r* (and *l*) was as common in bad Latin as in bad English, as *interpertor* (? *interpĕtror*) for *interpretor*, *coacla* for *cloāca* testify, and other mispronunciations censured by the grammarians. *Dr* became *tr* in Latin, e.g. *ătrox* (cf. *ŏdium*) (ch. iv. § 113). Neither *r* nor *l* remained unaffected by the palatalizing influence of *y*, that later sound of *ĭ* in words like *Jānuārius*, *făcio*, *hŏdie*, which worked so great a transformation of the language in the later period of Roman history. The palatalization of *r* led to its disappearance in Italian, e.g. Gennajo (Vulg. Lat. **Jen(u)aryus*), a process exemplified in earlier times by the form *peiuro* for *periŭro*, while *ly* has become the *l* mouillée, written *gl* in figlia, miglia (cf. our 'million'), bigliardo (our 'billiards'), and in some dialects, e.g. the patois of Rome and the neighbourhood, has sunk to *y*. Some spellings on late Latin inscriptions seem to be precursors of these changes of *ry*, *ly*. (On Umbrian *l*-, see ch. iv. § 85.)

§ 97. **Phonetic descriptions of l.** Ter. Maur. vi. 332. 230–234 K.:

> adversa palati supera premendo parte
> obstansque sono quem ciet ipsa lingua nitens
> validum penitus nescio quid sonare cogit,
> quo littera ad aures veniat secunda nostras,
> ex ordine fulgens cui dat locum synopsis ;

Mar. Vict. vi. 34. 10 K.: sequetur l quae validum nescioquid partem palati, qua primordia dentibus superis est, lingua trudente, diducto ore personabit; Mart. Cap. iii. 261 l lingua palatoque dulcescit.

§ 98. **of r.** Ter. Maur. vi. 332. 238, 239 K.:

> vibrat tremulis ictibus aridum sonorem
> has quae sequitur littera ;

Mar. Vict. vi. 34. 15 K. sequetur r quae vibrato †vocis palatum linguae fastigio fragorem tremulis ictibus reddit ; Mart. Cap. iii. 261 R spiritum lingua crispante corraditur. Ter. Scaurus (13. 10 K.) mentions the connexion of *r* and *l* with *d* : item l et d et r et s [inter se mutuis vicibus funguntur], cujus rei maximum argumentum est, quod balbi, qui r exprimere non possunt, aut l dicunt aut s, nec minus quod capra per diminutionem capella dicitur et frater fratellus.

§ 99. The grammarians on the pronunciation of l. The earliest taccount (ap. Prisc. i. p. 29 H.) is that of Pliny the Elder, who gives *l* three varieties of sound: (1) *exilis* : quando geminatur secundo loco posita ut 'ille' 'Metellus'; (2) *plenus* : quando finit nomina vel syllabas et quando aliquam habet ante se in eadem syllaba consonantem ut 'sol' 'silva' 'flavus' 'clarus'; (3) *medius*, in other positions: ut 'lectus' 'lectum.' Similarly in the fifth(?) cent. Consentius (v. 394 K.) makes only two divisions (1) *pinguis* : cum vel b sequitur, ut in 'albo,' vel c ut in 'pulchro,' vel f ut in 'adelfis,' vel g ut in 'alga,' vel m ut in 'pulmone.' vel p ut in 'scalpro' (2) *exilis* : ubicumque ab ea verbum incipit, ut in 'lepore' 'lana' 'lupo,' vel ubi in eodem verbo et prior syllaba in hac finitur, et sequens ab ea incipit, ut 'il-le' et 'Al-lia.' Not so clear is his account of the two mispronunciations to which *ille* was liable. The Greeks, he says, pronounce 'ille mihi dixit' *subtilius* as if *ille* had only one *l*; others pronounce 'ille meum comitatus est iter,' or 'illum ego per flammas eripui' *pinguius*, 'ut aliquid illic soni etiam consonantis ammiscere videantur.' Possibly this means that the Greeks made the double *l* into one as we do in pronouncing Italian (see § 127), and that others (e. g. Spaniards) gave it the *ly*-sound that it now has in Spain, e. g. villa (Ital. villa), which is pronounced like Italian viglia. Diomede (i. 453. 3 K.) remarks on the fault of pronouncing *l* in *lūcem* or *almam* 'nimium plene.' Servius *in Don.* iv. 445. 12-13 K. calls it a 'labdacismus' (mispronunciation of *l*) to make a single *l*, e. g. *Lūcius*, too 'tenuis,' or a double *l*, e. g. *Mĕtellus*, too 'pinguis.' Pompeius (v. 286-287 K.) makes the same remark, and explains it thus: debemus dicere 'largus' ut pingue sonet ; et si dicas 'lex,' non 'lex,' vitiosa sunt per labdacismum. item in gemino l, si volueris pinguius sonare, si dicamus 'Metellus' 'Catullus,' in his etiam agnoscimus gentium vitia; labdacismis scatent Afri, raro est ut aliquis dicat l : per geminum l sic locuntur Romani, omnes Latini sic locuntur : 'Catullus' 'Metellus.' His explanation would doubtless be intelligible to his auditors when accompanied by his oral examples of the different sounds ; to us, who have to infer these, it is not so clear. All that seems certain is that initial *l* had some distinction of sound from the *l* of *Mĕtellus*, *Cătullus*, &c., but whether this distinction consisted merely in the more emphatic articulation which every initial consonant received in Latin or in some other modification, such as the slight on-glide, which initial *l* has in the Gaelic language, and which makes a word like long, a ship (Lat. *longa* sc. *navis*), sound almost like 'along,' it is impossible to say (cf. § 117 ; ch. iv. § 149). The sound of the initial is described as 'pinguis,' in comparison with the *l* of *Metellus*, but as 'exilis' in comparison with the *l* of *clārus, alter,* &c. (See also Isid. *Orig.* i. 31. 8). In O. Engl. also there were three different kinds of *l*, (1) deep gutteral *l*, as in 'chalk,' (2) ordinary *l*, as in 'field,' (3) palatal *l*, as in 'whi(l)ch' (Paul's *Grundr.* i. p. 860). The fact that *e* could become *o* before *l*, but not before *ll*, in Latin (ch. iv. § 10) suggests that normal Latin *l* was deeper, or less palatal, than *ll*.

§ 100. of r. Varro (*L. L.* iii. fr. p. 146 Wilm.) mentions the rough sound ('asperum') of *crux, ācre, vĕpres* (also *crura*), beside *vŏluptas, mel, lēna*.

§ 101. Interchange of r and l. On the confusion of *flāgro* and *frăgro*, and the misspelling of both as *fraglo*, see *A. L. L.* iv. 8. In Probi App. 201. 19 the distinction between the two words is carefully pointed out (cf. ib. 198. 9 flagellum non 'fragellum') (Ital. fragello). Pliny gave the rule for the employment of the suffixes -*lis* and -*ris*, that -*lis* should be used when the stem contained an *r*, -*ris* when it contained an *l*, e. g. *augŭrāle*, *mŏlāre* (ap. Charis. 135. 13; cf. Prisc. i. p. 132 H.). So too the I.-Eur. suffix -*tlo*-, Latin -*clo*-, became -*cro*- after a stem with *l*, e. g. *lavacrum*, *fulcrum*, *simulacrum*. The same tendency to dissimilation is seen in Vulgar Latin forms like *veltrahus*, beside *vertrăgus* (see Georges s. v., and cf. Prov. veltres, O. Fr. viautre), and *pelegrinus* (*C.I.L.* iii. 4222, &c.), from which come the Romance words, Ital. pellegrino, Fr. pèlerin, our 'pilgrim,' &c.; in the mispronunciations *telebra* (see Georges s. v.), censured in Probi App. 198. 21 K.; in the spellings of MSS. and late Latin inscriptions, collected by Schuchardt, *Vok.* i. 136 sqq. (cf. *meletrix*, Non. 202. 13; 318. 6); in spellings on Greek inscriptions like Βαρβιλλεια, Βαρβιλλος, beside Βαλβιλλεια and Βαλβιλλος, Φεβλαριος, Μελκουριανος, &c. (see Eckinger, p. 107); in Romance forms like Ital. albero (from Lat. *arbor*), reclutare (our 'recruit'), Mercoledì (from *Mercŭrii dies*), urlare (from *ŭlŭlare*), which show that the same process is going on in modern, as in ancient, times on Italian soil. The town *Cagliari* in Sardinia was in Latin called *Carales* plur. or *Caralis* sing.; but we find byforms *Calaris* and *Cararis*. From *Crustumeria*, or *Crustumium*, we have the adjective-forms *Crustŭmĭnus* and *Clustuminus* (Greek Κροστομεινα and Κλουστουμεινα, Eckinger, p. 107).

§ 102. **Parasitic Vowel with l, r.** The sounds *l*, *r* were called 'liquidae' by Latin phoneticians, λ, μ, ν, ρ, ὑγραί by Greek), because they united easily with a preceding consonant. Cf. Mar. Vict. vi. 20 eaedem autem 'liquidae' dicuntur, quando hae solae [he includes *m*, *n*] inter consonantem et vocalem immissae non asperum sonum faciunt, ut 'clamor' 'Tmolus' 'Cnosus' [*MSS.* consul] 'Africa.' But in Latin, especially after the time of Plautus, there was a tendency to facilitate the pronunciation of a mute followed by *l*, particularly when post-tonic by the insertion of a vowel, written on early inscriptions *o*, later *u*. Thus *pō-clum*, which is formed with the I.-Eur. suffix -*tlo*- (ch. v. § 25), became *po-colom*, *po-culum*. These forms with the parasitic vowel underwent at a later time the same process of syncope that reduced *călĭda* to calda, *Tĭtius* to *Tityus*, *porcŭlus* (from the stem *porco*- with the suffix -*lo*-) to *porclus*, and so resumed their earlier appearance *poclum*, &c. Traces are not wanting of the same parasitic vowel-sound showing itself between a consonant and *r*. The development in Romance of a word like *patrem*, suggests that it must in Vulgar Latin have sounded almost like a trisyllable, **pat^erem* (Meyer-Lübke, *Rom. Gram.* i. p. 251); and the same is indicated perhaps by Varro's derivation of *Gracchus*, or, as he spelt it, *Graccus* (quasi **Geraccus*), from *gero*, 'quod mater ejus duodecim mensibus utero eum gestaverit' (ap. Charis. 82. 7 K.), certainly by spellings on inscriptions like *Terebuni* for *Trĕbōn*- (*Eph. Epigr.* i. 116), though a good many of these may be dialectal. For this parasitic vowel was a marked feature of the Oscan language, and its kindred dialects, e. g. Oscan aragetud (Lat. *argento* Abl.), Pelignian Alafis (Lat. *Albius*). Bede cannot be right in explaining spondaic hexameters, like

  illi continuo statuunt ter dena argenti,

as ending really with a dactyl and spondee, the last two words being pronounced 'denarigenti'; for it is not the case that all, or most, spondaic lines end in a word in which *r* is combined with a consonant. But his description of the sound is interesting, though of course he is not to be regarded as an authority on Latin pronunciation, except when he is quoting from some older grammarian. He says (p. 250. 11 K.), after instancing some spondaic hexameters ending with *argenti, incrēmenta* (!), *respergebat, interfectae, intercepto,* neque enim in quinta regione versus heroici spondeum ponere moris erat, sed ita tamen versus hujus modi scandere voluisse reor, ut addita in sono vocali, quam non scribebant, dactylus potius quam spondeus existeret, verbi gratia, 'intericepto' 'inceremaenta' 'interefectae' 'resperigebat' et per synalipham 'denarigenti.' quod ideo magis r littera quam ceterae consonantes patitur, quia quae durius naturaliter sonat durior efficitur, cum ab aliis consonantibus excipitur; atque ideo sonus ei vocalis apponitur, cujus temperamento ejus levigetur asperitas; and he goes on to say that this use of a parasitic vowel between *r* and a consonant was much affected by monks, when chanting the responses at divine service. At the same time it is possible that the existence of this parasitic vowel may explain another feature of Latin poetry, namely the optional treatment of a short vowel before a mute followed by *r* as long by position. Plautus, who, as we have seen, avoided the parasitic vowel with *l*, as alien to the conversational Latin of his time, also refuses to allow the first syllable of a word like *pătri, ăgri* to be scanned long, though (see ch. iii. § 42) such a syllable is not so short as the first syllable of *păti, ăgi,* &c., for it cannot exercise a shortening influence (by the law of Breves Breviantes) on the following syllable. Plautus scans *pătĭ, ăgĭ,* but only *pătrī, ăgrī.* In the same way he always scans *vehĭclum* (the invariable form), *cubĭclum* (though this last word is an exception to the rule in being usually quadrisyllabic, *cubiculum*), and never *vehĭclum, cubĭclum.* And this is the usage in all the dramatic poetry of the Republic. But Ennius in his Epic, Lucilius in his Satires, allow themselves such scansions as *nīgrum, lātrat, fībras, trīclini*; and this suggests that in poetry, where the words were sounded with more deliberation than the rapid conversational utterance of the drama allowed, the presence of this parasitic vowel was felt to add another unit of time, another 'mora' to these syllables, so that they might on occasion be treated as long. Lucilius' scansion *trīclini (Inc.* 145 M.), for example, reminds us of the form used by Varro, *tricilinium (R. R.* iii. 13. 2. So the MSS.), and the forms found on inscriptions *trichilinis (C. I. L.* ix. 4971; xiv. 375, 17, &c.), should perhaps be replaced by the quadrisyllabic form. In the time of Servius the accent rested on the second syllable of *maniplus,* so that the word was regarded in ordinary conversation, either as being almost a quadrisyllable, or as having a penult equivalent to a long syllable (Serv. ad *Aen.* xi. 463 maniplis: in hoc sermone ut secunda a fine habeat accentum usus obtinuit); and the Vulgar Latin shifting of the accent from the first to the second syllable of words like *tenebrae,* &c. (see ch. iii. § 11), is no doubt to be justified in the same way; though in Servius' time it was not allowed in correct pronunciation (Serv. ad *Aen.* i. 384 peragro: 'per-' habet accentum . . . muta enim et liquida, quotiens ponuntur, metrum juvant, non accentum). This explanation of the optional scansion *pătri, făbrum* competes with another (§ 142), according to which the consonant before the *r* was doubled in pronunciation, as it is in modern Italian fabbro, &c. (beside fabro), just as a consonant was doubled in later Latin before consonantal *u (w)* in *acqua* (Ital. acqua), and before consonantal *i (y),* the development of *l,* in Ital. occhio (Vulg. Lat. *oc(u)lus*), &c. It is quite possible that the shifting of the accent to the second syllable of words like *tenéb'rae,* may have had the effect of strengthening the sound of the mute. The doubling of the consonant in the

§ 103.] PRONUNCIATION. LIQUIDS. 95

proparoxytone syllable is a feature of Italian, e.g. femmina, collera, legittimo (§ 131).

The parasitic vowel between a mute and *l* is generally wanting on Greek inscriptions, perhaps because the Greeks were more conversant with combinations like γλ, τλ, &c. than the Romans, e.g. Λεντλος, Βιγλεντια (Lat. *Vigilantia*), and the syncopated forms of *-ulus* (as in *porcu-lus*, &c.) are usual in the instances quoted by Eckinger (p. 75), 'Αρβουσκλα, Μασκλος, Πατερκλος, Πουρκλα, though it must be added that they mostly date from a time when Syncope had taken a strong hold of the Latin language itself. The Appendix Probi condemns several of these syncopated words (as he condemns *calda*, &c.), including with them some whose vowel in the classical spelling is not original but parasitic: *speclum, masclus, veclus, viclus* (for *vitulus*), *vernaclus, articlus, baclus, juglus, oclus, tabla, stablum, tribla, vaplo, capiclum.* He also mentions *mascel, figel*, which may be South Italian, for the Oscan equivalent of *famulus* was *famel* (Paul. Fest. 62. 1 Th.). The early date of the parasitic vowel with *l* is seen in the old Latin form *piacolom*, quoted by Mar. Vict. p. 12 K., and *pocolom*, the usual spelling on the Praenestine vases (*C.I.L.* i. 43 sqq.). Plautus seems to regard the use of these lengthened forms as a licence, only to be resorted to in cases of metrical necessity; for they are found, especially when a long vowel precedes the syllable with *l*, only at the end of a line or hemistich, e.g. *Capt.* 740,

períclum vitae meaé tuo stat perículo (see ch. iii. § 13).

(For the parasitic vowel in Greek loanwords with *m, n* preceded by a consonant, see § 154.) *Calicare*, from *calx*, lime (Paul. Fest. 33. 8 Th. calicata aedificia, calce polita; ib. 41. 21 calicatis, calce politis; ib. 53. 16 decalicatum, calce litum; Gl. Cyrill. κονίω, decalico, calce albo; *C.I.L.* i. 1166 basilicam calecandam), apparently the normal spelling, and to be read probably in the Placidus Glossary (60. 19 G.), (where the MSS. have decalcatis, de calce albatis), is not a case of parasitic vowel between *l* and a following consonant (like Gk. Καλιπορνιος), (Dittenb. *Syll.* 240 of 138 B.C.), and (on the edict of Diocletian) καλικιος. It merely retains the Greek loanword χάλιξ in its dissyllabic form, instead of syncopating it to its usual form in Latin, *calx*. (For examples of the parasitic vowel in misspellings on inscriptions, see Seelmann, p. 251.)

§ 103. **Avoidance of two r's.** (See *A. L. L.* iv. 1 sqq.) The changes of *r* to *l* in Vulg. Lat. *pĕlĕgrīnus*, &c., and the doubtful cases of *n* for *r*, e.g. low Latin *menetrix*, may be considered as examples of this avoidance. The use of *gnāritior* for *gnārior* (not before Augustine), *fĕrōcior*, for **ferior, măgis vērus* beside *verior, magis mīris mŏdis* (Plaut. *Mil.* 539) for *mirioribus modis, dĕcentior* for *dĕcōrior* in Quintilian and Tacitus, *sanctior* for *săcrior*, all exhibit the same tendency. Pompeius (283. 13 K.) mentions *mamor* as a mispronunciation of *marmor*; and the form *Mamers, Mamertini* beside *Marmar* of the Carmen Saliare, also *Fabaris*, the Latin name of the Sabine river *Farfarus*, perhaps show the same dropping of *r* in the reduplication-syllable. So too the form *porrīgo* was preferred to **prorigo*. On *praestīgiae*, from *praestringo*, to dazzle, *crēbresco* and its compounds (*rŭbesco*, is like *pūtesco*, from a stem without *r*), see Georges, *Lex. Wortf.* s. vv. On inscriptions, *de propio* (Ital. propio and proprio) for *de prŏprio* occurs (*Not. Scav.* 1890, p. 170), *propietas* (*C.I.L.* ix. 2827 of 19 A.D.), &c. (see Schuchardt, i. p. 21, for other instances). Vulg. Lat. **trono*, to thunder, for *tŏno*

(Ital. tronare and tonare, Span. O. Port. Prov. tronar), has inserted *r* for onomatopoeic effect; *frustrum* (Probus 199. 3 K. frŭstum non 'frustrum'), found, with *crustrum* and *pristris*, in MSS. of Virgil (see Ribbeck's *Index*) and *aplustrum* (*aplustre*) for Greek ἄφλαστον: *crētārias* (Caper. 108. 13 K. cetariae tabernae, quae nunc 'cretariae' non recte dicuntur) by false analogy (see Schuchardt, i. 21 for other examples: and cf. Fr. trésor from Lat. *thēsaurus*, beside Ital. tesoro; Span. estrella from Lat. *stēlla* beside Ital. stella and (dial.) strella. In Italian we find the same tendency; e.g. Federico, Certosa (Fr. Chartreuse), arato (Lat. *ărātrum*), frate (Lat. *frātrem*), deretano (Vulg. Lat. *deretranus from *retro*), &c.; gomitolo, a ball of thread, from Lat. *glŏmus*, shows the same suppression of one of two *l*'s.

§ 104. rs. Velius Longus 79. 4 says: sic et dossum per duo s quam per r dorsum quidam ut lenius enuntiaverunt, ac tota littera r sublata est in eo quod est rusum et retrosum. Cf. Probi App. 198. 29 persica non 'pessica' (a peach). [For other examples, see Georges, *Lex. Wortf.* s. vv. *controversia* (and other compounds of *-versus*, e. g. *prosa*), *Marspiter, Sassina, Thyrsagetes, assa*, &c.] In the Sententia Minuciorum of 117 B.C. (*C.I.L.* i. 199) we have *controvorsieis, controvosias, suso vorsum, sursuorsum*, and *sursumuorsum, deorsum* and *dorsum* side by side. Since double consonants are usually written single on this inscription (*posidebunt, posedeit*, &c., beside *possiderent*) *controuosias* probably represents the pronunciation *controuossias*. (On these spellings in Plautine MSS., see Ritschl, *Prolegg.* p. civ.)

§ 105. r-n. *Menetris*, a byform of *mĕrĕtrix* (see *A. L. L.* iii. 539 and cf. Probi App. 198. 28 K. meretrix non 'menetris') may have been influenced by *mănēre* or Greek μένω (cf. Non. 423. 11 M. menetrices a manendo dictae sunt). Nor is *cancer* a clear case of 'Dissimilation' for *carcer (Greek καρκ-ίνος), seeing that a nasal in the reduplication-syllable is not unknown in other I.-Eur. languages, e. g. Greek γογ-γύλλω, τον-θορύζω, O. Ind. cañ-curyate, cf. *gin-grire*. In the Gaelic language *n* when following *c, g* becomes *r*, such a word as *cnu*, a nut, being pronounced *cru* (with nasal *u*). Some see this change in *grōma*, a land-measuring instrument, which they consider to be the Greek γνώμων. But other instances are wanting; and *gn-* in Latin became *n*, not *gr*, e. g. *nosco, nātus*. (Cf. Probi App. 197. 32 pancarpus non 'parcarpus') (see ch. iv. § 80).

§ 106. l-n. *Nuscitiosus*, 'qui plus videret vesperi quam meridie' (Fest. 180. 21 Th.), and *nusciosus*, 'qui plus vespere videt' (Löwe, *Prodromus*, p. 17), are byforms of *luscitiosus* and *lusciosus*, which may be due to the analogy of *nox*. *Leptis*, 'filia fratris' (ib. p. 340) seems to be a byform of *neptis*. The Diminutive of *colus*, a spindle, was in Vulg. Lat. **conuc(u)la* (Ital. conocchia, Fr. quenouille). A more certain example of *n* for *l* is the mispronunciation censured in Probi App. 197. 24 K. cultellum non 'cuntellum' (see below) (see also Seelmann, p. 327; Schuchardt, *Vok.* i. p. 143). When Latin *n* follows *n* in successive syllables we find *l-n* in Ital. veleno and veneno (O. Fr. velin) from Latin *vĕnēnum*, Bologna from *Bŏnōnia*, Palestrina from *Praeneste, Praenestinus*, calonaco and canonico (cf. Ital. gonfalone, a banner, Fr. gonfalon, Span. confalon, O. Fr. gonfanon, Prov. gonfanons from O. H. Germ. grand-fano).

§ 107. l before consonant. For the *u*-affection of *l* before a consonant, see some instances collected by Schuchardt, *Vok.* ii. p. 493 sqq., e. g. *cauculus* for *calculus* in MSS. (cf. Georges). In the Edict of Diocletian (301 A.D.) we have

§§ 104–111.]   PRONUNCIATION.   LIQUIDS.   97

καυκουλατορι for *calcŭlātōri*. The letters L and I are so similar that spellings like SAITEM (le Blant. *I. G.* i.) may be nothing but a graver's error. On the other hand the Umbrian form of the Latin *Volsiēnus* was certainly *Voisienus*; and in *C. I. L.* xi. 5389 and 5390 (= i. 1412) we have epitaphs of a father in Umbrian, and a son in Latin, with the father's name *Voisieno*- and the son's *Volsieno*-. In Probi Appendix 197. 24 K. the mispronunciation *cuntellum* for *cultellum* is mentioned. This treatment of *l* before a consonant is found in Central Italy (Latium, Sabina, la Marche, and Umbria) in modern Italian, e.g. untimo for ultimo in a fourteenth cent. text (see *Wien. Stud.* xiv. 315 *n.*). Cf. *muntu* from Pompeii (*C. I. L.* iv. 1593).

§ 108. rl. Velius Longus 65. 11 K. per vero praepositio omnibus integra praeponitur, nisi cum incidit in l litteram, adfinem consonantem, quam elegantioris sermonis viri geminare malunt quam r litteram exprimere, ut cum 'pellabor' malunt dicere quam perlabor. nec aliter apud Lucilium legitur

in praeposito per,
'pelliciendo,' hoc est inducendo, geminato l (Lucil. ix. 32 M.);

'pellicere' malunt quam perlicere, unde et apud Virgilium non aliter legimus 'pellacis Ulixi' (see ch. iv. § 160). In the Probi Appendix 198. 14 K. we have : supellex non 'superlex,' with the (marginal?) note utrumque dicitur. (On the late spelling *superlex*, see Georges, *Lex. Wortf.* s. v.) The only example of *rl* in the Indices of the *Corpus* is *perlegere* (vol. i).

§ 109. r before consonants. R is sometimes dropped before a consonant on Greek inscrr., e. g. Κοατα (Lat. *Quarta*) (*C. I. G.* add. 43151), Σατωνιλος (*Brit. Mus.* ii. 341, from Cos); and in Latin plebeian inscrr., we have misspellings like *Fotunate* (*C. I. L.* vi. 2236) for *Fortūnātae* (sometimes *Fórt-*, i. e. *Fort-* with close *o*, see § 145). [Cf. the rude Faliscan inscr. Zvetaieff, *Inscr. Ital. Inf.* 63 with *Maci Acacelini* (as *Votilia* for *Voltilia*) for the usual *Marci Acarcelini* of n° 62, &c.] But it would be unsafe to rely on these as evidence that Latin *r* ever became the mere voice-glide which English *r* always becomes when not followed by a vowel, e. g. in 'here,' 'hark' as opposed to 'herein,' 'harass.'

§ 110. final r. All final consonants were, as we have seen, weakly pronounced in Latin. Some instances of the omission of *-r* in spellings of inscriptions and MSS. have been collected by Schuchardt, *Vok.* ii. p. 390.

111. Metathesis. Quint. i. 5. 13 'Trasumennum' pro Tarsumenno, multi auctores; i. 5. 12 duos in uno nomine faciebat barbarismos Tinga Placentinus, si reprehendenti Hortensio credimus, 'preculam' pro pergula dicens. Examples from Plautus are *Phyrgio*, *Aul.* 508, *corcotarii*, *Aul.* 521. Consentius (392. 23 K.) censures *perlum* for *prelum*, *reilquum* for *reliquum*, *interpertor* for *interpretor*, *coacla* for *cloaca*, *displicina* (a schoolboy's joke surely) for *disciplina*: Diomedes (452. 30 K.), *leriquiae* for *reliquiae*, *lerigio* for *religio* (and *tanpister* for *tantisper*) ; Julian, *in Don.* v. p. 324. 18 K. *intrepella* for *interpella* ; Probi Appendix has (199. 12 K.) glatri [*leg.* clatri?] non 'cracli.' This late Latin *cracli* (cf. Probi App. 195. 23 K.) comes from **cratli* as *veclus* (ib. 197. 20) from **vetlus* for *vetulus*. *Clustrum* for *crustlum* is found on inscriptions of the Empire (e. g. *clustrum et mulsum*, *Not. Scav.* 1877, p. 246 of second cent. A.D., cf. κλουστροπλακοῦς, Athen. xiv. p. 647 c, d). *Colurnus* is the adjective from *corulus*. (On the confusion of *fragro, flagro* and the form *fraglo*, see *A. L. L.* iv. 8.) In Italian nothing is

H

commoner than this Metathesis with *r*. Thus in S. Italy crapa is used for capra (Lat. *căpra*), which reminds us of the statement of Paul. Fest. that the old Latin word for *capra* was *crepa* (33. 36 Th. caprae dictae, quod omne virgultum carpant, sive a crepitu crurum. Unde et 'crepas' eas prisci dixerunt. The Luperci, who wore goatskins and ran about striking people with goatskin thongs, were called *crĕpi*, ib. 39. 34 K. crepos, id est lupercos, dicebant a crepitu pellicularum, quem faciunt verberantes); so interpetre for interprete (should we read *interpetror* in Consentius 392. 23 K.?); and preta for petra is used in various parts of Italy; formento is Lat. *frŭmentum*, farnetico Lat. *phrĕnēticus*, &c., &c. For *l* we have padule, a marsh (Lat. *pălūdem*); falliva beside favilla, fiaba, a fable, for Lat. *fabla*, *fābŭla*. Paduan requilia for reliquia (should we read *requilum* in Consentius 392. 23 K.?) is in Venetian leriquia (cf. *leriquias* of Diomedes 452. 30 K.); in many parts of Italy, grolia is used for gloria. [For some instances of Metathesis in late inscriptions and in MSS. spellings, see Schuchardt, *Vok*. i. p. 29 on *Prancatius* for *Pancratius*, *padules* for *paludes* (cf. Ital. padule), and Seelmann, p. 330 on *Procobera* for *Porcobera*, &c.; and for examples in Latin byforms, see Georges, *Lex. Wortf.* s. vv. *pristis*, *crocodilus*, *Trasumenus*, *trapezita*, and Wölfflin, *A. L. L.* viii. 279 on *accerso* and *arcesso*.] The Latin *Prōserpĭna* (*C. I. L.* i. 57 PROSEPNAI dat. case) for Greek Περσεφόνη (Pelignian *Perseponas* gen. case) may be due to the analogy of *prōserpo*; but Vulg. Lat. **alenare* for *ănhēlare* (Ital. alenare, Fr. haleiner), **plopus* for *poplus*, *pōpŭlus*, poplar-tree (Ital. pioppo, Roum. plop, Catal. clop) are clear cases of metathesis of *l*.

§ 112. ly. For misspellings on late inscriptions and in MSS. like *fius* for *filius*, see Schuchardt, *Vok.* ii. pp. 486 sqq. Some of them may be due to the confusion of the L and I (see above). Ital. giglio, a lily, seems to come from a form **lyīlyum*.

§ 113. ry. Servius ad *Aen.* ii. 195 approves *pejuro* for the Verb, but *perjurus* for the Adjective : in verbo r non habet : nam pejuro dicimus, corrupta natura praepositionis : quae res facit errorem, ut aliqui male dicant 'pejurus' ut pejuro.

§ 114. F. The Latin phoneticians cannot be suspected of any influence from Greek sources in their account of *f*, a sound unknown to the Greek alphabet; so their description may be taken as a true account of the pronunciation of *f* at their time, or possibly even at an earlier, the date, namely, of the treatise on Latin phonetics from which they seem to have borrowed. That time was probably the Augustan age. Their words leave no doubt whatever that *f* was a labiodental spirant, as it is in Italian and most languages, formed by the upper teeth pressed against the lower lip, not a bilabial spirant, formed by the upper and lower lips pressed against each other:

> imum superis dentibus adprimens labellum
> spiramine leni (Terentianus Maurus, second cent. A. D.).

The *spiramen lene* was more a feature of the normal *f*-sound when a vowel followed, than in combinations with consonants like *fr, fl*, as we learn from Quintilian, who, when discussing the more musical nature of the Greek language than the Latin, speaks of Latin *f*, especially in words like *frangit* (to a less extent when followed by a vowel), as rough and harsh compared with the softer sounds of Greek. This more vehement articulation of *f* before a consonant explains the different treatment of the Latin spirant in Spanish, in words like haba (Lat. *făba*), humo (Lat. *fūmus*), but fraga (Lat. *frāgum*, *fraga). Quintilian's account does not mention the labiodental character of the sound (xii. 10. 29 paene non humana voce vel omnino non voce potius inter discrimina dentium efflanda est), but is quite consistent with it. It is, in fact, very like the account given by phoneticians of our *f*, as 'formed with a strong hiss, by pressing the lower lip firmly against the upper teeth, and thus driving the breath between the teeth' (Sweet, *Handb.* p. 41).

But it is highly probable that Latin *f* was at some time bilabial, as it is to this day in Spanish, where *v* (*b*) is bilabial too. Bilabial *f* naturally tends to become labiodental, because by bringing the teeth into play it is possible to give a stronger and more distinct sound than can be produced by the lips alone. The voiced bilabial spirant *v* has, as we saw before (§ 48), become labiodental *v* in Italian and other Romance languages. And we have some evidence of *f* being still bilabial in the last centuries of the Republic from spellings like *im fronte* (*C. I. L.* i. 1104), not to speak of *comfluont* beside *conflouont* on the Sententia Minuciorum of 117 B.C. (*C. I. L.* i. 199), and possibly from the fact that *ad*, in composition with a word beginning with *f* (or *v, b*, &c.) became in Republican Latin *ar*, e.g. *arfuise* on the S. C. de Bacchanalibus of 186 B.C. (*C. I. L.* i. 196). Another passage of Quintilian tells us of the difficulty felt by Greeks in pronouncing this thoroughly Roman letter (i. 4. 14 Graeci adspirare f ut φ solent). He illustrates it by the story of Cicero's ridicule of a Greek witness who could not pronounce the first letter of *Fundānius*. By the fifth cent. A.D., however, the Greek aspirate had become a spirant, differing from Latin *f* only in being bilabial.

§ 115. **Descriptions of the sound of f.** Quintilian (xii. 10. 29) : nam illa, quae est sexta nostrarum, paene non humana voce, vel omnino non voce potius, inter discrimina dentium efflanda est : quae, etiam cum vocalem proximo accipit, quassa quodammodo, utique quotiens aliquam consonantem frangit, ut in hoc ipso 'frangit,' multo fit horridior ; Terent. Maur. 332. 227 K. :

> imum superis dentibus adprimens labellum,
> spiramine leni, velut hirta Graia [i. e. φ, p-h] vites,
> hanc ore sonabis, modo quae locata prima est ;

Marius Victorin. 34. 9 K. f litteram imum labium superis imprimentes dentibus, reflexa ad palati fastigium lingua, leni spiramine proferemus; Mart. Cap. iii. 261 F dentes [faciunt] labrum inferius deprimentes. In the sixth cent. A. D., Priscian mentions as the only difference between Latin ƒ and Greek φ, that the former was not pronounced *fixis labris* (i. p. 11. 27 H. hoc tamen scire debemus, quod non fixis labris est pronuntianda f, quomodo p et h ; atque hoc solum interest) [Blass, *Griech. Aussprache* ², p. 85 dates the change of Greek φ (written in Latin ph, or as Priscian puts it 'p et h'), from the aspirate to the spirant sound at about 400 A. D.]. Two centuries earlier than Priscian, the difference between Latin ƒ and Greek φ seems to have been very slight, for Diomedes (fourth cent. A. D.), from whom, or from whose original authority, Priscian may be quoting, says (423. 28 K.) : et hoc scire debemus quod f littera tum scribitur, cum Latina dictio scribitur, ut 'felix.' nam si peregrina fuerit, p et h scribimus, ut 'Phoebus,' 'Phaeton.' *F* is the normal equivalent of Greek φ in Greek loanwords from the middle or end of the fourth century onwards, e. g. *strofa*, Greek στροφή (see ch. i. § 11).

The remark of Priscian (i. p. 35. 17 H.) that F, the Aeolic digamma, used to have the sound of consonantal v (w), probably refers to a fashion of some early grammarians of writing 'Fotum,' 'Firgo,' &c., alluded to by Cornutus ap. Cassiodor. 148. 8 K. and by Donatus ad Ter. *Andr.* i. 2. 2 (see ch. i. § 7).

§ 116. **mf.** Mar. Victorinus (18. 14 K.) : item consonantes inter se [invicem sibi succedunt], sed proprie sunt cognatae, quae simili figuratione oris dicuntur, ut est b, f, [s], m, p, quibus Cicero adicit v, non eam quae accipitur pro vocali, sed eam quae consonantis obtinet vicem, et anteposita vocali fit ut aliae quoque consonantes. quotiens igitur praepositionem sequetur vox cujus prima syllaba incipit a supradictis litteris, id est b, f, [s], m, p, v, quae vox conjuncta praepositioni significationem ejus confundat, vos quoque praepositionis litteram mutate, ut est 'combibit' 'comburit' 'comfert' 'comfundit' 'commemorat' 'comminuit' 'comparat' 'compellit' 'comvalescit' 'comvocat' non 'conbibit' 'conburit' et similia. sic etiam praepositio juncta vocibus quae incipiunt a supradictis litteris n commutat in m, ut 'imbibit' 'imbuit' 'imfert' 'imficit' 'immemor' 'immitis' 'impius' 'impotens.' He must be quoting from some grammarian of the Republic in his rule about ƒ; for the usual teaching of the grammarians of the Empire is that the consonants before which *m* is used are b, p, m ; and Priscian, i. p. 31. 2 H. quotes as early an authority as the elder Pliny to this effect (cf. Prisc. i. p. 29. 18 H. 'am' praepositio f vel c vel q sequentibus in n mutat m : 'anfractus' 'ancisus' 'anquiro'). But the spelling with *m* before ƒ (and *v*) was undoubtedly an old usage, of which such MS. spellings as *comferre*, *Poen.* 1048, *comfragosas*, *Men.* 591 in the Plautus Palimpsest, *im flammam*, *Aen.* xii. 214, *comfieri*, *Aen.* iv. 116 in Virgil MSS. may be relics. On the other hand since *inpĕrātor* is found both in early and later times beside *imperator*, and since the nasal may have been in pronunciation dropped before *f* (cf. *cofisse, covenere* in Virgil MSS., Ribbeck, *Ind.* p. 393), the evidence of these early spellings is not conclusive.

§ 117. **S, X, Z.** In the noun 'use' and the verb 'to use' the letter *s* has two different sounds, which we often call 'hard *s*' and 'soft *s*.' Hard *s* is more scientifically termed 'unvoiced,' soft 'voiced' *s*, the two sounds differing exactly as the unvoiced and voiced mutes, *p* and *b*, *t* and *d*, *c* and *g*. The Latin *s* in a word like *urbs* was hard or unvoiced *s*, we know from the frequently repeated statements of the grammarians, that the spelling *urps* expressed the pronunciation; while the spelling with *b* was justified only by the analogy of other cases, *urbis, urbi, urbem*, &c. (see § 80); and *p* in *sumpsi, hiemps* tells the same tale. Initial *s*, whether in the accented or unaccented syllable, may also be put down as unvoiced *s*, since the Romance languages agree in giving it this sound (e.g. Ital. sì, Fr. si, Span. sì for Lat. *si*; Ital. sudare, Fr. suer, Span. sudare for Lat. *sudare*), and similarly when *s* is the initial of the second member of a compound, in words like Ital. risalire, Fr. résilier, Span. resalir from Lat. *rĕsĭlire*, later *resalire*. None of the Latin grammarians ever suggest that Latin *s* had anything but one and the same sound; and their silence is evidence of some weight that the soft or unvoiced variety of *s* was unknown in Latin. This voiced *s*-sound seems to have been the sound of Greek ζ in and after the Macedonian period (cf. ζμάραγδος for σμάραγδος, Ζμύρνα for Σμύρνα), which explains why Oscan voiced *s*, which corresponds to Umbrian and Latin *r*, is in those inscriptions which are written in Latin characters, expressed by *z*, e. g. *eizac* (Umbr. erak), *eizazunc egmazum* (in Lat. *earum rerum*) on the Bantia Tablet c. 130 B.C. Between vowels *s* had at an early time in Latin (c. 350 B.C. according to Cicero, *Fam.* ix. 21. 2) become *r*, as it did in Umbrian; and this earlier *s* may very well have had in this position the voiced sound (ch. iv. § 146). Intervocalic *s* in the classical and Imperial period is only found as a rule where there had been formerly some consonant combined with *s*, e.g. *formōsus* earlier *formonsus, causa* earlier *caussa, ūsus* earlier *ussus* (see ch. iv. § 148). In such words *s* has become voiced in many Romance languages, e. g. Fr. épouse (Lat. *sponsa*), but only in those in which every Latin unvoiced consonant becomes voiced in this position. In Italian intervocalic *s* is unvoiced, except in the few cases where Latin unvoiced mutes also become voiced, e.g. sposare, like mudare (§ 73). There is hardly any evidence, therefore, that *s* in classical Latin was in any circumstances pronounced like our *s* in 'to use'; and the opinion, a widely spread one, that the change of spelling from *caussa* to *causa*, &c., indicated a change from hard to soft *s* is utterly wrong.

The pronunciation of double -*ss*- is discussed in § 131. Here we need only mention the curious practice that grew up in the later Empire of prefixing *i* to initial *st*, *sp*, *sc*, seen in spellings on inscriptions like *istatuam* (Orelli 1120, of 375 A.D), *ispose* (i.e. *sponsae* C.I.L. viii. 3485), and in Romance forms like Fr. épouse. These last show that this spelling does not indicate an *sh*-sound of *s* before a mute like German stehen (pronounced 'shtehen'), but that there was an actual *i*-sound before the *s*-sound, an *i*-sound which developed from a vowel-glide, due to beginning the word before the vocal-organs were properly in position for the initial consonant. These 'initial on-glides,' as phoneticians would term them, are a feature of Romance languages (cf. Greek ἐρυθρός), but not of Teutonic. We have already seen that there is some indication of initial *l* having had an 'on-glide' in Latin (§ 99); and spellings on inscriptions suggest the same for other initial consonants. Can this have been the 'circa s litteram deliciae' which elocution teachers had to correct in their pupils (Quint. i. 11. 6), just as singers are taught nowadays to avoid the 'breathy' gradual beginning of an initial vowel?

X had, as the grammarians repeatedly tell us, the sound of *c* followed by the sound of *s*. The *c* (as the *c* of *ct*, § 95), tended to be dropped after a consonant, whence the spelling *mers* in Plautus for *merx*; and in careless pronunciation *x* in any position tended to *ss* (so *ct* became *tt*, § 95), as we see from forms like *cossim* for *coxim*, used in the farces of Pomponius (ap. Non. 40 M.). There are traces, too, of the substitution of *sc* for *cs*, e.g. *ascella* is the Late-Latin form of *axilla*. In Italian we have *ss* [as in ancient Pelignian, e.g. *usur* (Lat. *uxōres*), and other dialects], for example, sasso (Lat. *saxum*), but before a consonant (as probably in Vulgar Latin), *s*, e.g. destro (Lat. *dexter*) (as in ancient Umbrian *destra*, &c.). Latin loanwords in Welsh indicate *cs*, e.g. O.W. Saes for Latin *Saxo*, croes for Latin *crŭx*, but *s* before a consonant, e.g. estron (Lat. *extrāneus*), estynn (Lat. *extendo*).

Z of Old Latin had perhaps the soft or voiced sound of *s*, which passed into the *r*-sound about the time of Appius Claudius, the famous censor, when *z* was discarded from the alphabet (see ch. i. § 5). Greek ζ differed from it in causing length by 'position.'

Final -*s* after a short vowel was weakly pronounced at all periods of the Latin language, and in the early poetry often did not constitute 'position' before an initial consonant, though by Cicero's time it was regarded as an essential of correct pronunciation to give *s* at the end of a word its full sound.

§ 118. Phonetic descriptions of s, x : Ter. Maur. vi. 332. 239-243 K. :

> mox duae supremae
> vicina quidem sibila dentibus repressis
> miscere videntur : tamen ictus ut priori
> et promptus in ore est, agiturque pone dentes,
> sic levis et unum ciet auribus susurrum.

Mar. Vict. vi. 34. 16 K. dehinc duae supremae, s et x, jure jungentur. nam vicino inter se sonore attracto sibilant rictu, ita tamen, si prioris ictus pone dentes excitatus ad medium lenis agitetur. Mart. Cap. iii. 261 S sibilum facit dentibus verberatis. . . . X quicquid C atque S formavit exsibilat. Cledonius, v. 28. 1 K. s . . . sibilus magis est quam consonans.

§ 119. **Latin s in Romance.** Initial *s*- becomes our *sh* (cf. Ital. scimmia) in Venice and some other parts (similarly intervocalic *s* becomes the voiced form of this sound, as in our 'pleasure'), and was possibly voiced *s* in ancient Italic dialects (e. g. Faliscan *Zexto-* for *Sextus* (?)). On a late inscription of Tibur we have ZABINA (*C. I. L.* vi. 12236). Intervocalic -*s*- between the accented and unaccented vowels is unvoiced in Spanish (where however all sibilants are unvoiced), Roumanian and Italian, e. g. Italian mese (Latin *mēnsis*) [MHZEΣ on a Naples' inscription (*C. I. L.* x. 719), if it represent actual pronunciation, must have been a dialectal variety]. Italian sposa (with voiced *s* and open *o*) is influenced by sposare (Latin *spo(n)sare*), where the *o* and the *s* precede the accent; the voiced *s* of rosa is anomalous, but may represent Greek ζ ; or rosa may be a bookword and not a direct descendant of the Latin, for its French and Spanish forms too are irregular (Gröber's *Grundr.* p. 522). It is voiced in the other Romance languages, in which also (as in Spanish) unvoiced mutes between vowels become voiced, e. g. Fr. épouse (Lat. *spo(n)sa*), chose (Lat. *causa*) with voiced *s*, like O.Fr. ruede (Lat. *rŏta*, Span. ruede), vide (Lat. *vīta*, Span. vida). It is voiced also in North Italian. Intervocalic -*s*-

before the accented vowel is voiced in Italian, e. g. sposare (Latin *spo(n)sare*), precisely as any Latin unvoiced mute becomes voiced in this position ; e. g. mudare (Latin *mūtare*), pagare (Lat. *pācare*). So does any *s* which by Syncope, &c. has come to stand before a voiced consonant, e. g. sdegno (Vulg. Lat. *disdigno*), while in Spanish it has developed to *d̄, r* (though written *s*), e. g· desden.

§ 120. **Greek ζ, Latin z.** The letter *z*, the Greek letter ζ, was, as we saw (ch. i. § 1), brought into use at Rome in the transcription of Greek words (and of those only) about the close of the Republic. Previously to that time *ss* had been used, e. g. *massa* (Greek μᾶζα), which at the beginning of a word was *s*, e. g. *Setus* (*C. I. L.* i. 1047, 1299, Greek Ζῆθος) (Plautus makes this *s-* alliterate with ordinary *s-*, e. g. sonam sustuli *Merc.* 925, solve sonam *Truc.* 954), and, if we are to believe the grammarians, *d*, e. g. *Medentius* for *Mezentius*. [But *Septidonium* a mispronunciation of *Septizonium*, a building at Rome (Probi App. 197. 23), seems to be a popular etymology from *donum*.] (Prisc. i. 49 y et z in graecis tantummodo ponuntur dictionibus, quamvis in multis veteres haec quoque mutasse inveniantur, et pro *v* u, pro ζ vero ... s vel ss vel d posuisse, ut ... 'Saguntum,' 'massa' pro Ζάκυνθος, μᾶζα, ... 'Sethus' pro Ζῆθος dicentes, et 'Medentius' pro Mezentius.) Blass, in his book on Greek Pronunciation, gives the history of the Greek sound as follows. The combination *zd* in words like ὄζος (Germ. Ast), ἵζω (Lat. *sīdo* for **sisdo*), Ἀθήναζε (Ἀθήνας-δε) was expressed by the letter ζ (the Semitic letter Sain, a symbol in the Semitic alphabet of voiced *s*), as the combination *ks* by ξ (the Semitic Samech). This was the original use of ζ. It came to be applied to the combination *dz* (from *dy*), e. g. πεζός (for πεδyός), ζάπλουτος (for διάπλουτος) ; and at this period came the transference of the Greek alphabet to Italy, with the result that in the Italic alphabets, Umbrian, Oscan, &c., the *z*-symbol had the sound of *dz* or *ts*. In course of time *dz* came round to the sound of *zd*, so that πεζός and ἵζω had now the same sound of ζ. This *zd*-sound further developed into the sound of *zz*, or *z*, apparently in the Macedonian period ; and so we find the town Gaza, whose Semitic name has voiced *s* or Sain, written in Greek characters Γάζα. This then was the sound which the Romans had to express in Greek loanwords, voiced *s*, not the earlier sound *zd*. Voiced *s*, as we have found reason to believe, was a sound unknown in Latin words since 350 B. C., which explains Quintilian's remark (xii. 10. 28 ; cf. Maxim. Victorinus, vi. 196. 3 K.) about the beauty of the sound of ζ, and its absence from the Latin alphabet. To express it, double or single *s* (the unvoiced *s*-symbol) was used by the early Republican writers and occasionally by later authors (e. g. *saplutus*, Petron. 37, for ζάπλουτος), perhaps even *d* (with the sound of *th* in 'this'?), until a later age felt the necessity of employing, for the sake of exactness, the Greek letter itself, as they did also in the case of Greek *v*, φ, χ, θ. The history of ζ is a common point of discussion among Greek grammarians who remark on its origin from the combinations σδ and δσ, and their remarks are repeated by their Latin imitators, but need not be taken to imply that ζ had at the time of the Empire any other sound than that of voiced *s* (Mar. Vict. vi. 6. 6 K.: Maxim. Vict. vi. 196. 3 K. : Audacis exc. vii. 327 K.). Thus Velius Longus (vii. 50. 9 K.), in criticizing the remark of Verrius Flaccus : 'sciant z litteram per sd scribi ab iis qui putant illam ex s et d constare,' states positively that ζ had not the sound of a double letter, unlike ψ and ξ : denique siquis secundum naturam vult excutere hanc litteram, inveniet duplicem non esse, si modo illam aure sinceriore exploraverit... et plane siquid supervenerit, me dicente sonum hujus litterae, invenies eundem tenorem, a quo coeperit. The interchange of *dy* and *z* on late inscriptions, e. g. *baptidiata*, Rossi i. 805, of 459 A. D., and in spellings like *zabulus* for *diăbŏlus* (see Georges, *Lex. Wortf.* s.v.) implies merely that the spirant *y*-sound which *dy* had come to take in Latin (§ 51, cf. *Madia* for *Maia*) was felt to resemble the sibilant sound of voiced *s*. *Z* has however the *ts*-sound in alphabets derived from Latin, e. g. O. Engl. Bezabe 'Bathsheba.'

§ 121. **Old Roman z**, found in the Carmen Saliare (Velius Longus, vii. 51. 5 K.), and according to tradition discarded through the influence of Appius Claudius, one would naturally suppose to have had the same sound as that of *z* in the Umbrian, Oscan, and other Italic alphabets, viz. *dz* or *ts*[1]; so that Claudius might, like Papirius, Ruga, and other traditional reformers of spelling, have exemplified the new orthography in his own family-name by writing *Claudius* for an earlier *Clauzus*. This would harmonize well with the fantastic remark of Martianus Capella, that Claudius objected to the letter because it gave the teeth the appearance of a death's-head (iii. 261 Z vero idcirco Appius Claudius detestatur, quod dentes mortui, dum exprimitur, imitatur), which happily describes the appearance of the mouth in uttering the *dz*-sound of our 'adze.' But this description will also suit for the voiced *s*-sound; and the contemporary change of intervocalic *s* (voiced *s*) to *r*, exemplified in the new spelling of *Papisius* as *Păpīrius*, as well as the use of *z* for voiced *s* on a very early coin of Cosa, suggests that this rather was the sound of early Roman *z* (see ch. i. § 5 ¹, though the matter is uncertain.

§ 122. **Old Roman s (z), later r.** The change of intervocalic *s* to *r* is a common one in various languages, and is generally taken to imply that the *s* first became voiced *s*, then passed into *r* (cf. Span. desden, see above). That Old Roman *s* of *Fūsius*, &c. took this course is indicated by the fact that the Oscan sibilant, corresponding to Latin and Umbrian *r*, is in the inscriptions in Latin characters written *z*, and not *s*.

§ 123. **Prosthetic vowel with st, &c.** For instances of the prosthetic vowel in MSS. and late inscriptions, see the list given by Schuchardt in *Vok.* ii. pp. 338 sqq., who refers the earliest traces of its use to the second cent. A. D. It is written *i* or *e*, e.g. *istudium*, *estudium*, sometimes *hi*-, *he*-, e.g. *histudiis* (often misread in MSS. as *hisstudiis*), rarely *y*, *ae*, and is often confused with the prepositions *in*, *ex*. Thus *iscribere*, *escribere* may represent either *scrībĕre* or *inscribere* or *exscribere*. In late Latin where *ab* is used before an initial vowel, *ā* before an initial consonant, we find *ab* normally before an initial *sp*-, *sc*-, *st*-, even though the prosthetic vowel is not expressed in writing (*A. L. L.* iii. 149). Along with the dropping of this prosthetic vowel, and the restoration of the original form *scribere*, &c., went the dropping of the initial *i*-, *e*- of *i(n)scribere*, *e(x)scribere*, so that we get spellings like *splorator* for *explōrātor* (Cagnat, *Ann. Epigr.* 1889, no. 55), *Spania* for *Hispānia* (see Schuchardt's list, *Vok.* ii. pp. 365 sqq.). In Italian, a language in which almost every word ends in a vowel, the prosthetic vowel has been dropped, e.g. studio, and with it the genuine

---

[1] Initial Z, however, in Umbro-Osc. may have been a variety of s, e. g. Umbr. zeřef 'sedens' (von Planta, i. p. 71).

initial vowels of words like Lat. *história, Hispania, instrūmentum,* Ital. storia, Spagna, stromento or strumento. But after words like con, in, non (all ending in a consonant), both vowels are restored in pronunciation, so that the spelling con estudio, non estoria represents the actual sound. These forms studio and estudio (istudio), storia and estoria (istoria) are what are called 'doublets,' the one being used after a final vowel, the other after a (rare) final consonant; and that is, no doubt, the explanation of these double forms *splorator, esplorator,* &c. on late inscriptions. In French, where consonant endings were far more preserved than in Italian, the prosthetic vowel remains, e.g. étude, écrire. It is before *st-, sc-, sp-,* &c., for the most part, that the prosthetic vowel asserted itself sufficiently to require expression in spelling; but its presence before other consonantal initials may be inferred from occasional spellings like *ilocus, ireddere, imerito* (misread in MSS. as *immerito*), &c. (see the list of examples in Schuchardt, *Vok.* ii. pp. 360 sqq.; some in MSS. are merely misreadings of critical signs). In Italian, where, as we have said, almost every word ends in a vowel, we could hardly expect this Latin prosthetic vowel to show signs of itself. Indeed the tendency is rather for a genuine initial vowel to be suppressed under the influence of a preceding final vowel. Thus la apecchia, the bee (Lat. *ăpĭcŭla*) has become la pecchia, Lat. *ecclēsia* has become chiesa, *inimīcus,* nemico, and so on. Whether the same Procope is the explanation of the mispronunciation *rabo* for *arrăbo,* which Plautus puts into the mouth of the slave in the Truculentus, for the sake of poking fun at the Praenestines, it is impossible to say:

      STR. tene tibi
rabonem habeto ...
 AST. Perii, 'rabonem.' quam esse dicam hanc beluam?
 Quin tu arrabonem dicis?
      STR. 'a' facio lucri,
 Ut Praenestinis 'conea' est ciconia.

We do not find mention of the prosthetic vowel by Latin grammarians till quite late times, which shows that however far it had developed in Vulgar Latin, it did not threaten to encroach on the speech of the educated classes. Thus Isidore (seventh cent.) derives *escarus* (i.e. *scarus*) from *esca* (*Orig.* xii. 6. 30 escarus dictus eo, quod escam solus ruminare perhibetur), and *iscurra* (i.e. *scurra*), somewhat comically, from the same word (ib. x. 152 [under I not E] iscurra vocatur, quia causa escae quempiam consectetur; cf. ib. xx. 4. 9 discus antea 'iscus' vocabatur a specie scuti). He warns his readers against the mispronunciations *yspissa, yscena, ystimulus,* (4. 509, App. 3. 40. Ar. spissa, scena, stimulus et cetera similia y carent). Similar warnings are given in the Glosses ap. Mai, *Cl. Auct.* against *iscena, iscandalum, iscapha, iscribtura* (vi. 580), and directions to write 'per solam s' *sceda* (vii. 578 b), *stimulus, spissa,* and *splendor* (vi. 581). (Theophilus non 'izofilus,' Probi App. 198. 1, should perhaps read 'T. non ziofilus,' and in 199. 10, stabilitus non 'istabilitus,' is a mere conjecture.) It is not found in the early Latin loanwords in Teutonic, e.g. O. H. Germ. scriban (Lat. *scribo*), or Celtic languages, e.g. O. Ir. scol, Bret. skol (Lat. *sc(h)ola*). But Welsh, which has the same tendency as late Latin to use a prosthetic vowel (written *y,* pronounced like *u* of our 'but'), before initial *s* followed by a consonant has subsequently added this *y-* to these Latin loanwards, e.g. ysgol, ysgrifo, as it has done to other words of a similar form, e.g. ysgub, a sheaf. That Procope had shown itself in Vulgar Latin we see from the Romance forms, Ital. bottega, Span. botica, Fr. boutique, which point to Vulg. Lat. *poteca for ăpŏthēca, and Ital. morchia, Span. morga from Vulg. Lat. *murca for ămurca, both Greek words. (On ste for istĕ, see ch. vii. § 17.)

A further result of the confusion of a word like scrībo with a compound, exscribo, inscribo, was that some words beginning with sc-, sp-, st-, &c. were regarded as compounds with the prepositions ex, in, and were deprived of their initial s. This, at any rate, seems to be the explanation of forms like Vulg. Lat. *pasmus for spasmus (Span. pasmo, Port. pasmo, and the French verb pâmer, to swoon) (see the list of examples in Schuchardt, Vok. ii. pp. 354 sqq.). Another result possibly was that such a form as sponere for exponere being regarded as the equivalent of ponere, the letter s- might occasionally be prefixed at random to words beginning in c-, t-, p-, &c., e.g. spictus for pictus (Schuchardt, l.c., mentions a few doubtful examples; but includes cases where the s- was original, e.g. O. Lat. strītavus, later trītavus. See ch. iv. § 146.)

§ 124. s before a consonant. I.-Eur. s before m, n, &c. was dropped in Latin or rather assimilated (iv. 159), e.g. prīmus (Pelignian Prismu for Lat. Prima), cōmis (on the very ancient Dvenos inscription cosmis), dūmus older dummus (cf. Dusmus). So tra(n)s became tra- before j, d, and optionally before m, p, according to Velius Longus, 66. 9 K., e.g. transtulit, but trajecit, trāduxit transmisit or trāmisit, transposuit or trāposuit. Spellings on late plebeian inscriptions and in MSS., such as prebeteri for presbyteri (Rossi, i. 731, of 445 A.D.), have been collected by Schuchardt, Vok. ii. pp. 355 sq. But though s is suppressed in this position in some Romance languages, notably in French, e.g. château (Ital. castello, Span. castillo) from Lat. castellum; blâmer (Ital. biasmare, Catal. blasmar, Prov. blasmar) from Vulg. Lat. *blas(i)mare for blasphēmare, this suppression is by no means universal, and was unknown in French itself at an earlier stage, e.g. blasmer; so that these spellings cannot convince us that Latin s in the middle of a word had at all the same weak sound that it had at the end of a word. (Schuchardt's examples of the assimilation of c or t to s, with ss for sc and st, e.g. Crissana, Vok. i. pp. 145 sq., are perhaps better explained as cases of palatalization of c, t.)

A vowel before st, &c. is not shortened under the influence of a preceding short syllable in Plautine versification any more readily than a vowel before any other consonant group, e.g. volŭptátem, beside potĕstátem, minĭstérium. (See ch. iii. § 34.)

§ 125. x. On the spellings cs, cx, xs, &c. see ch. i. § 4, and for the interchange of x with ss and (with consonant) s, see Georges and Brambach s. vv. mixtus, Ulixes, sesoenti, Esquiliae, Xerxes, Sestius, &c. Schuchardt, Vok. ii. p. 351, and i. 133, gives some instances of es- for ex- before c, t, p in late Latin inscriptions and in MSS. (Cf. Placidus' Glossary, 67. 18 G. exspes, sine spe . . . ' espes' vero sine x nihil est), and of -ss-, -s- for -x-, e.g. vissit for vixit, Alesander for Alexander. Vissit for vixit is common on late Christian inscriptions (e.g. C. I. L. x. 4546), but the earliest instance of ss for x is probably on an epitaph of a cavalry soldier at Cologne, which cannot be later than Nero's reign [ve]ssillo (A. L. L. viii. 589.) On mers for merx (mer(c)s, like pars for par(t)s) in MSS. of Plautus, see Ritschl, Opusc. ii. p. 656. Caper 98. 10 K. allows both cals and calx : cals dicendum, ubi materia est, per s ; at cum pedis est, calx per x. In late Latin final -s and -x are often interchanged. Thus x is written for the final s (originally ss) of *mīles, ăries, pŏples, lŏcŭples*. All these are forms censured in the Appendix Probi (197. 28 K. ; 198. 29 ; 199. 4, 5) ; and on inscriptions we have *milex, milix, pregnax*, &c. (see Seelmann, p. 353). The similarity of the sound of this -s with -x may be inferred from Probus, *Inst.* 126. 36 K. quaeritur qua de causa miles per s et non per x litteram scribatur, &c. Similarly *obstetrix* was made *opstitris* (Probi App. 198. 34 K., cf. 198. 28 meretrix non 'menetris') ; and on inscriptions we have coɴɪvs and coɪvs (Greek ΚΟΖΟΥΟ, *C. I. L.* x. 719), *subornatris*, &c. (see Seelmann, p. 353). The *felatris* (iv. 1388 and 2292) on inscriptions of Pompeii reminds us of -s, -ss for x, cs, on Oscan inscriptions of the same town, e. g. meddíss (for *meddĭcĕs Nom. Pl.) Zv. *I. I. I.* 140 (cf. Osc. Santia for Ξανθίας).

§ 126. **Final s.** (See Havet on 'l'S latin caduc' in *Études dédiées à G. Paris*. 1891 ; he shows that it is the rule, and not the exception, that -s does not constitute 'position' in the older poetry ; cf. Plautine endings of lines like *estis vos*). Cicero (*Orator*, xlviii. 161) : quin etiam quod jam subrusticum videtur, olim autem politius, eorum verborum, quorum eaedem erant postremae duae litterae, quae sunt in 'optimus,' postremam litteram detrahebant, nisi vocalis insequebatur ; ita non erat ea offensio in versibus, quam nunc fugiunt poetae novi ; ita enim loquebamur :

qui est omnibu' princeps,
non ' omnibus princeps,' et
uita illa dignu' locoque,

non dignus. quod si indocta consuetudo tam est artifex suauitatis, quid ab ipsa tandem arte et doctrina postulari putamus ? ; Quint. ix. 4. 38 quae fuit causa et Servio, ut dixit, subtrahendae s litterae, quotiens ultima esset aliaque consonante susciperetur, quod reprehendit Luranius, Messala defendit. nam neque Lucilium putat uti eadem ultima, cum dicit 'Aeserninus fuit' et 'dignus locoque,' et Cicero in Oratore plures antiquorum tradit sic locutos. (On the dropping of -s on inscrr. see § 137.)

§ 127. **Double Consonants.** No point of Latin pronunciation is more certain than that a double consonant in such a word as *bucca* was really pronounced as a double, and not as a single consonant, with 'the first syllable ending in one *c,* and the second syllable beginning with another *c,*' as the Latin grammarians put it, or in more scientific language, with a new force-impulse beginning in the second half of the consonant. The word would be uttered, not, as we are accustomed to pronounce it, with one *c*-sound, but with the double *c*-sound of our 'bookcase.' The statements of the grammarians are so clear on this matter as to leave no room for doubt; and even without their help, we might have inferred the Latin usage from the evidence of the Romance languages. For although it is only the Italian which has entirely preserved to this day the double pronunciation (e.g. Ital. boc-ca, but Span. boca, Fr. bouche), there are traces in the others of its previous existence. Latin *ss* is hard *s*, where Latin *s* has become soft, or voiced *s*. Latin *rr*, *nn*, *ll* have developed into different sounds in Spanish from Latin *r*, *n*, *l*; and in French a Latin vowel before a double consonant has been differently treated from one before a single consonant: *tālis* becomes tel, but *vallis*, val; *mănus* becomes main, but *annus*, an. The only thing open to question is whether the spelling with two consonants did not sometimes indicate a lengthened rather than a doubled consonant, a consonant on which the voice dwelt for a time, without dividing it between two syllables. This distinction between a long and a double consonant is more clearly marked in the case of a mute (e.g. long *c* and double *c*), than of a liquid, nasal, or sibilant (e.g. long *l* and double *l*, long *n* and double *n*, long *s* and double *s*). The greater force and abruptness of the mute as compared with the liquid would make the syllable-division in *bucca* more readily caught by the ear than in *mille*.

This lengthened pronunciation may have been given to *m*, &c., in *āmitto* for *ammitto* (cf. *ammissam* in the Medicean MS. of Virgil, *A*. ii. 741); and it was probably a stage in the development of words like *milia* older *millia*, *causa* older *caussa*, *casus* older *cassus*.

From the statements of the grammarians, and from the spelling of Inscriptions and the oldest MSS., we see that the orthography, and presumably the pronunciation, of the Empire did not allow *ss* after a diphthong, nor (with possible exceptions) after a long vowel, nor yet *ll* between a long *i* and another *i*. The *caussa*, *cāssus*, *glōssa*, *mīssi*, *mīllia* of an earlier time were reduced to *causa*, *cāsus*, *glōsa*, *mīsi*, *mīlia*, and show in Italian to-day the single letter in spelling and pronunciation (cosa, chiosa, misi, &c.). Seelmann's explanation is that the length of the diphthong would detract from the length of the consonant in *cau-ssa*, and make it no longer than a single consonant *causa*, while in *milia* the similarity of the articulation of *ī* and *l* was the reason why the vowel organs passed so quickly over the intervening *l*-position back to the *i*-position, as to prevent the voice from dwelling for the due period of time on the *l* itself. However that may be, we can at least be positive that the spelling *ss* did not, as Corssen suggests, merely indicate the hard or unvoiced quality of the *s*-sound (e.g. Engl. 'ass' with hard *s*, 'as' with soft *s*).

The practice of writing the consonants double was not adopted, as we saw (ch. i. § 8), until the time of Ennius. But there is no evidence, apart from this fact, to show that the pronunciation of *bucca, penna,* &c., in earlier times was not the same as the later pronunciation (like our 'bookcase,' 'penknife'). Plautus may have written these words with a single letter; still he always treats the first syllable as long by position; so that it would be as rash to infer that the older spelling was anything more than a mere usage of orthography, as to regard the temporary use of the sicilicus in the Augustan age (ch. i. § 8), e.g. *osa (C.I.L.* x. 3743), as an indication that the consonant had at that time a lengthened rather than a doubled pronunciation.

§ 128. **Testimony of the grammarians.** The grammarians' rule is 'Write two consonants, when two consonants are pronounced': ubi duarum consonantum sonus percutiet aures, Mar. Victorinus vi. 9-10 K.; who quotes *sab-batis, sac-cis, ef-fert, ef-fugit, fal-lit, gal-lus, val-lus, macel-lum, nul-lus, pal-lium Pal-las, an-num, Cin-nam, ap-paratum, lap-pam, Ar-runtium, bar-rum, cur-rit, fer-rum, as-siduum, Cas-sium, fes-sum, At-tius, Vet-tius,* and adds: nam ut color oculorum judicio, sapor palati, odor narium dinoscitur, ita sonus aurium arbitrio subjectus est. Similarly Papirian (ap. Cassiodor. vii. 162. 10 K.) says: sono internoscemus, quoting *ac-cedo, at-tuli, as-siduus, ap-pareo, an-nuo, al-ligo.* So Vel. Longus vii. 61-62 K.: *ac-cipio, ac-currere, ag-gerat,* Pliny (ap. Priscian, i. p. 29. 8): *il-le,* Metel-*lus.* They speak also of one syllable ending with the consonant, and the next syllable beginning with the same consonant (prior syllaba in hac finitur, et sequens ab ea incipit, Consentius, v. 394. 35 K., who quotes *il-le, Al-lia*). Similarly Priscian, i. p. 45. 5 of *il-le,* p. 46. 8 of *Sab-burra, sab-bata, gib-bus, gib-berosus, gib-ber, ob-ba,* . . . *sub-bibo,* p. 47. 5 of *vacca* (MSS. *bacca), buc-ca, soc-cus, ec-quis, quic-quam,* p. 47. 9 of *abad-dir, abad-dier, ad-do, red-do, red-duco* (' quod etiam reduco dicitur ',) p. 48. 5 of *of-ficio, suf-ficio, af-fectus, ef-ficio, dif-ficilis, dif-fundo,* p. 49. 29 of *lip-pus, ap-paret,* p. 50. 25 of *mit-to, Cot-ta, at-tinet.* Velius Longus' remarks on the pronunciation of *reduco* and *reddo* must be understood in the same way (vii. 66. 3 K.).

§ 129. **Reduction of ll to l, ss to s, after a diphthong or long vowel.** Some grammarians ascribe this reduction to a diphthong, others to any long vowel. Quintilian (i. 7. 20-21) tells us that *caussae, cassus, divissiones* was the spelling of Cicero's time, and that the double *s* was found in autograph MSS. both of Cicero and of Virgil, and adds that in still earlier times (i. e. before the introduction of double letters), *jussi* was spelt with a single *s.* Velius Longus (vii. 79. 20 K.) censures the proposal of Nisus (first cent. A.D.) to write *comese, consuese,* and his argument 'quia juxta productam vocalem geminata consonans progredi non soleat,' and declares positively that 'geminari consonantes productis vocalibus junctas usus ostendit,' quoting

§§ 128, 129.] PRONUNCIATION. DOUBLE CONSONANTS. 111

as examples *errasse, saltasse, abisse, calcasse*. He inclines however to the spelling *paulum* on the ground that *paullum* 'repetito eodem elemento [*sc.* l] . . . enuntiari nullo modo potest,' and declares the true rule to be that the presence of a diphthong, not of any long vowel, forbids the doubling of a consonant (cf. Prisc. i. p. 109. 22 H.). Still he contrasts *dossum* (for *dŏrsum*), with *rūsum, retrōsum*; and in another passage (72. 11 K.) he approves of the spelling and pronunciation *accūsātor*, as of *cōmisātor*. Annaeus Cornutus (ap. Cassiodor. 149. 12-15 K.), speaking apparently of the old spelling *caussa*, says: in qua enuntiatione quomodo duarum consonantium sonus exaudiatur, non invenio. Terentius Scaurus (21 22 K.) declares that neither *s* nor *r* are doubled, unless the preceding vowel is short; when it is long,. the syllable ends with the vowel, and the consonant begins the next syllable, e. g. *plau-sus, lū-sus*. The spelling *caussa* he makes etymological (due to *cavissa*), not phonetic: apparet 'causam' geminatum s non recipere, quoniam neque in fine praecedentis alterum potest poni, neque a gemino sequens incipere. The remarks of Velius Longus (72. 19 K. s vero geminata vocis sonum exasperat), and of Marius Victorinus (viii. 5 6 K. iidem [*sc.* antiqui] voces quae pressiore sono eduntur,.'ausus,' 'causa,' 'fusus,' 'odiosus,' per duo s scribebant 'aussus'), must be regarded in the light of the previously quoted statements; though the latter may imply that the sound of an -*s*-, which represented a former -*ss*- was not quite the same as the sound of ordinary *s*. That this was probably the case with final -*s* (e. g. *miles* for *miless) we shall see below (§ 133). Elsewhere Terentius Scaurus defends the spelling *paullum* on etymological grounds, comparing *pullum, pusillum* (20. 15 K.); and Annaeus Cornutus (first cent. A.D., ap. Cassiodor. 149. 19 K.) speaks of some grammarians who wrote *mallo* (the older spelling, as we shall see) for *mālo*, because they connected the word with Greek μᾶλλον. Another reason apparently alleged for this spelling *mallo, nollo*, was the analogy of the Infinitive *malle, nolle*, to judge from Papirian's dictum ap. Cassiodor. 159. 1 K.: malo per unum l, quod est magis volo; malle per duo l, quod est magis velle; nolo per unum l, est enim non volo, nolle per duo l, quod est non velle (cf. Probi App. 201. 33 K. inter velit et vellit hoc interest quod, &c.) (cf. *vellint, C. I. L.* v. 2090; vii. 80; *nollis*, vii. 140). A further instance of the influence of an etymological theory on spelling is furnished by Alcuin (310. 32 K.), who defends the spelling *solemnis* by referring the word to *sōleo*. But if we overlook spellings warped by etymological theories, and here and there a traditional spelling retained, we may lay down the rule that *l* after a diphthong, and *s* after a long vowel or diphthong, were not written, or pronounced double in the period of the Empire, so that it is unlikely, for example, that *cessi* (though from *cēdo*), *jussi* [though the spelling *jous*- occurs on old inscriptions (see *C. I. L.* i¹. Index p. 583), and cf. *jūssus* (along with *Anniùs!*), vi. 77], *ussi* (though from *ūro*; cf. *A. L. L.* ii. 607), had a long vowel in the Imperial age. (*Cēssi, ūssi*, according to Priscian, i. p. 466. 6, 7 H.) The use of *ll* after a long vowel, but not after a diphthong, shows that the diphthongs still retained their diphthongal sound.

The statements of the grammarians about the older spelling are borne out by a reference to the Republican inscriptions. On the Lex Rubria of 49 B. C. we have *promeisserit, remeisserit, repromeisserit*, and on other inscriptions *caussa, accussasse, missit, paullum, millia, milliarium* (see the Index to *C. I. L.* vol. i¹. pp. 601-2); on the Comm. Lud. Saec. both *caussa* and *causa*, but always *quaeso*; on the Mon. Anc. *millia, clausum* and *claussum, caussa, caesae, occasio*.

Paullus is the usual form even on later inscriptions, also *Pollio* and *Polio* (see Georges, *Lex. Wortf.* s.vv.; cf. *Pŏlla* with apex on *o*, *C.I.L.* xi. 4572, &c.). *Aulla*, the oldest spelling, preserved in the Ambrosian MS. of Plautus (see below), similarly became *aula* and *olla* (see Georges); *crisso* (with *ī*, cf. *crĭspus*) became *criso* (ib.); *glossa* and *glossema* became *glosa*, *glosema* (Löwe, *Prodromus*, pp. 1 sqq.); *nassiterna* is the old spelling of this old word, like *nassum* (later *nāsus*) (see Georges). Thus *abscīsio* (from *caedo*), and *abscissio* (from *scindo*) were not distinguished in spelling till Tiberius' reign.

In the best and oldest MSS. of Republican writers, and (archaistic) writers of the Augustan age, such as Plautus and Virgil, we have a good many spellings with *ll*, *ss*, where the later orthography used the single letter. Thus in Virgil MSS. we have examples of the old spelling, with double *s*, of the Perfect and Perf. Part. Pass. of verbs like *edo* (*adessus*, *ambessus*, *exessus*, *obessus*, *peressus*, *semessus*, i.e. *adēssus*, &c.), *video* (*provissa*, &c.; also the verb *invisso*), *audeo* (*aussa*), and other verbs in *-do*, *-deo*; *haereo* (*haessit*) and *haurio* (*haussere*, *hausserat*): *mitto* (*missi*, *missere*); we have *-nss-* and *-ss-* for later *-ns-*, *-s-* in *conprenssa* and *compressa*, *emenssi*, &c., *lapidossa*, *undossi*, &c.; similarly *caussa*, *incusso*, &c.; and in foreign words *cassia* (Gk. κασσία, a misspelling of κάσία), *Crinisso* (*A.* v. 38), *gessa* (*A.* viii. 662), *Passiphae*, *Rhessus*; though some of these last may be a wrong spelling (e.g. *gessa* should be *gaesa*, for O.Ir. gae, O.H. Germ. gaizon- point to *gaiso-*, with *g* for I.-Eur. *gh-*, cf. Sanscr. hĕšas). And in the Ambrosian Palimpsest of Plautus we have *essum*, *essurire*, *essitabunt*, *exscīssus* (*Most.* 826), *ussus*, *ussura*, *incusses*, *uisso*, *ueisse*, *dimissero*, *quaesso*, *caussa*, *-ossus* (*laboriossi*, *odiossae*, *negotiossam*, *radiossus*); also *nassum*, *uassa*, and even *sesse* (perhaps rightly, for *sēd-sē(d)*), *Merc.* 249, *Stich.* 365, and *noss*, *Stich.* 536; and in Greek words *paussam*, *Alcēssimarche*, and (perversely) *bāssilice*, *Poen.* 577 (cf. *bassim*, *C.I.L.* i. 1181). For *ll* we have in Virgil MSS. some words where *s*, *x*, &c. have been dropped before *l* with lengthening of the vowel, or rather have been assimilated, like *quallus*, *G.* ii. 241 (cf. *quăsillus*), *anhellitus* and *anhellus*, *tellum*, *vellum*, along with some of doubtful origin; *collum*, a strainer, *G.* ii. 242 (probably first *cavillum*, then *caulum* or *collum*, then *cōlum*, like *Paullus*, *Paulus*, *Pollio* and *Polio*), *illex*, *A.* vi. 180, *mallim*, *G.* iii. 69 and *A.* iv. 108, *paullatim*, *millia*, *opillio*; as well as *-ella*, *-ellus* in *loquella*, *querella* (the normal spelling), *Philomella*, *fasellus*. (On *olli* Dat., *ōlim* Adv., see ch. vii.) And in the Plautus Palimpsest, *aulla*, a jar (later *aula* and *olla*), *millia*, *paullum* (see Ribbeck's *Index*, and the Index to Studemund's Apograph of the Codex Ambrosianus). In the Palatine MSS. of Plautus we have also *nollo* (see Goetz, preface to the *Stichus*, p. xiv).

Of these, we know that *millia*, &c., where long *ī* precedes and *i* follows the double *l*, became *milia*, &c. in the Imperial age. Pompeius (185. 16 K.) quotes the rule of the elder Pliny : Plinius Secundus in libris dubii sermonis ita expressit, 'mille non debemus aliter dicere nisi per geminum l, in numero plurali unum l ponere debemus et dicere milia' (cf. ibid. 172. 13 K.). *Mīlia*, *vīlicus* are the normal spellings on inscriptions, beside *mīlle*, *vīlla*, from the reign of Tiberius; but in earlier inscriptions (excepting in very early ones where no consonant is written double) we have *ll*. In the Monumentum Ancyranum, that valuable evidence of the orthography of the Augustan age, we have *millia*, *milliens*. (On *stilicidium* from *stīlla*, Diminutive of *stīra*, *stīria*, see Lachmann ad *Lucr.* i. 313.) In other circumstances double *ll* was retained after a long vowel, e.g. *villa*, *stēlla*, which show the long vowel and double *l*, or its traces, in the Romance languages, e.g. Ital. villa, stella (with close *e*), as in the Welsh loanword ystwyll, Epiphany. So *mīlle, rāllum, stīlla, vīllum* (Dim. of *vīnum*), *trūlla, corōlla* (Dim. of *corōna*), *ūllus* (from *ūnus*), *nūllus*, &c. (Priscian i. p. 109. 21 H. attests *vīllum*, and *ūllus*; and on inscrr. we have *ūlla* C.I.L. ii. 1473; *ūlli*, vi. 10230; *nūllum*, x. 4787; *villānī*, ix. 348, &c.) But in a group of words, as before remarked, we have *ll* in the older, *l* in the Imperial spelling, viz. words where there has been what is called 'compensatory lengthening,' e.g. *quālus* for **quas-lus* (cf. *quăsillus*), *vēlum* for *vex-lum* (cf. *vexillum*). Of these words Cicero says (Orat. xlv. 153), quin etiam verba saepe contrahuntur non usus causa, sed aurium; quo modo enim vester 'Axilla' Ala factus est nisi fuga litterae vastioris? quam litteram etiam e 'maxillis' et 'taxillis' et 'paxillo' et 'vexillo' et 'pauxillo' consuetudo elegans Latini sermonis evellit.

That the suppression of the *s*-sound was in the earlier period expressed by doubling the letter, we may infer from these spellings in Virgil MSS. and *aulla* (for *aux-la*, cf. *auxilla*) in the Palimpsest of Plautus. The change to the single *l* seems to have been made after the reign of Augustus, simultaneously with the adoption of *l* for *ll* in *paulum, milia*, &c., of *s* for *ss* in *causa, fusus*, &c., and, as we shall see, of *m* for *mm* in a similar case of 'compensatory lengthening,' *dumus* from **dus-mus*. *Anhellus*, if for **anhenslus* from stem **an-anslo-*, must have had long *e*. Thus *lŏquella* for **loques-la*, *quĕrella* for **queres-la* may have been the older forms, which were banished for a time, and were restored in later Latin. (For statistics, see Brambach, *Orth.* p. 259.) *Mallo, nollo* are attacked by the grammarians of the Empire, along with *millia, caussa, fussus*, &c., and represent with these the older fashion of spelling and pronunciation. Diomedes (p. 386. 13 K.) blames those 'qui geminant l litteram et enuntiant' in these two verbs. (Does Velius Longus allude to the verb in p. 80. 5 K., where he says: quis autem nescit 'malum' una l littera scriptam multum distare a 'mallo' eodem elemento geminato?) How far other consonants were doubled after a long vowel is discussed below.

§ 130. **Confusion of single and double letter in Latin.** In the misspellings of inscriptions and MSS. we find a double written for a single consonant, especially in the case of (1) mute before *r*, e.g. *frattre* (*C. I. L.* viii. 111), *suppra* and *suppremus* in Virgil MSS. (Ribbeck, *Ind.*); (2) before consonantal *u* (*w*), e.g. *tennuis* in Virgil MSS., *strennuior* in MSS. of Lucil. xvi. 19 M. (cf. Probi App. 198. 18 K. aqua non 'acqua'); (3) *s* before mute, e.g. *disscente* (*C. I. L.* iv. 1278). We find the same doubling of a consonant in the first two cases in Italian in fabbro, acqua, &c. (see below); and in classical Latin we have perhaps traces of them in the normal spellings, *quattuor, battuo*. The third type of misspelling probably reflects the attraction of *s* to the first syllable (see § 139). The opposite error, of writing a single consonant for a double, appears especially (1) after a long vowel, e.g. *nula*, *Eph. Epigr.* iv. no. 557 (Consentius warns against mispronunciations like *mile, vila*, 392. 7 K.); (2) in syllables before the accent, usually in words compounded with prepositions, where the final consonant of the preposition has been assimilated to the initial of the verb or noun, e.g. *acepi, comunis*, but also in other cases, such as Diminutives, e.g. *sacellus* (see Georges, *Lex. Wortf.* s.v.). There are in the classical language a few traces of the reduction of a long syllable to a short in the pretonic syllable, possibly in Diminutives like *ŏfella* (from *offa*), *măm̄illa* (from *mamma*) (cf. Ital. vanello), but certainly in prepositional compounds. Thus *ommitto* from *ob* and *mitto* has become *ŏmitto* (Priscian i. p. 46. 18 H. omitto dicimus pro 'ommitto'); in *reddūco* the preposition was changed, perhaps by the analogy of other compounds, to *re*, but not in *reddo*, where it is accented (unless the true explanation here is that *reddo* represents *re-dido with a reduplicated form of the verb found in Umbro-Oscan, ch. viii. § 9). (Velius Longus 66. 3 interdum haec d littera geminatur, quotiens ab eadem littera sequens vox incipit; nec tamen semper, siquidem 'reddere' dicimus geminata d, . . . unde adnotanda imperitia eorum qui sic 'redducere' geminata d littera volunt enuntiare, quasi 'reddere,' tamquam necesse sit totiens eam duplicem esse, quotiens sequens vox ab eadem littera incipit.) The versification of Plautus shows us that after a short syllable the preposition in the pretonic syllable of a compound was especially liable to be so slurred in pronunciation, that it might optionally be scanned as a short syllable, e. g. *quid ăccépit?* (see ch. iii. § 34). How far the weakness incident to the first syllable of *accepit* after a short syllable adhered to it in other circumstances, and tended to reduce the *acc-* to the sound of *ac-*, it is difficult to say. We have *ore cŏrupto* in Lucil. ix. 1. M., expressly attested by Consentius (400. 8 K.); and there seems no reason for setting aside the reading of the MSS. in Lucr. vi. 1135 an caelum nobis ultro natura cŏrumptum Deferat, a reading confirmed by Isidore, *Nat. Rer.* 39. The usual practice, where the preposition is assimilated, is to write a double letter in some cases, e.g. *corruptus, ommentans* (Liv. Andron.); in others to write a single letter and lengthen the vowel, e. g. *āmitto*. It is not always easy to draw a hard and fast line between these two practices. A scansion like Plautus' *quid ămittis* suggests that the second word was pronounced rather *ammittis* (cf. *ammissam* in Virgil MSS., Ribbeck, *Ind.*) than *āmittis*; for Plautus does not shorten the first syllable of the compound in *quid insanis*, &c., where we know the *i* to have been a long vowel before the group *ns* (see ch. iii. § 34). The *a* of *amittis* could then hardly be on precisely the same footing as a vowel long by nature. *Adm-*, though written *amm-* was not written *ām-*. (*Amentum*, beside *ammentum* and *admentum*, is probably not non-existent. See Nettleship, *Contributions* s. v.) Again, Gellius says of the preposition *com*, compounded with *ligo*, and *necto* (ii. 17. 8) coligatus et conexus producte dicitur. (*Com* before *n-* is always *cŏn-* in the best spelling, e.g. *cŏnubium*, but not before *gn*, e.g. *cognatus*, unless *gn* has previously become *n*, e. g. *cōnitor*.) The late spelling *oportunus* (see Georges) may be due to the analogy of *ŏportet*; but on Greek inscriptions we often have ω, instead of the usual ο, in compounds with *com*, the assimilated *m* being sometimes omitted, e. g. Κωμοδος, sometimes expressed, e. g. κωρρεκτωρ (Eckinger pp. 51-2). It is therefore an open question how far these late spellings, such as *corigia* in the Edict of Diocletian, indicate a real reduction of the double consonant to a single, *cŏrigia*, or a transference to the vowel of the extra length of the consonant, *cōrigia*. Greek spellings of Latin words are very uncertain guides; for Consentius mentions as a fault of the Greeks their inability to pronounce the double consonant in words like *jussit, ille,* 395. 13 K. s litteram Graeci exiliter ecferunt adeo, ut cum dicunt 'jussit,' per unum s dicere existimes ; 394. 25 K. ubi enim [Graeci] dicunt 'ille mihi dixit,' sic sonant duae ll primae syllabae, quasi per unum l sermo ipse consistat[1]; and on Greek inscriptions we find double confused with single, single with double consonant in Latin words to a very great extent, especially *l* and *ll*, but not

---

[1] In Martial ii. 60 *puer Hylle* has assonance with *puerīle*.

§ 130.] PRONUNCIATION. DOUBLE CONSONANTS. 115

often *s* and *ss* (see Eckinger). Similarly in Latin inscriptions we find Greek words misspelt in this particular, e. g. *tesera, eclesia* (so in Vulg. Lat. ; cf. Ital. chiesa, &c.), *bassilica* (e.g. *C.I.L.* iv. 1779), &c. So Probi App. (199. 9 K.) censures 'bassilica' ; (198. 11) 'cammera' (cf. Sicil. Neap. cammara); (198. 17) 'dracco' ; (198. 27) 'fassiolus.' (In each case the vowel is *a*, the quality of which was the same, whether short or long.) On a Republican inscription (*C. I. L.* i. 1181) we have *bassim*, and in the Palimpsest of Plautus *bassilice*. The Plautine form of the name 'Ιλλυρία is *Hillüria*. In other foreign words we have a like confusion, e. g. *Brĭtanni* and (later) *Brittanni* (see Georges s.v.), as we have a confusion in the quantity of the vowel of *Batăvi*, &c. Very often a wrong etymology, or wrong association, is the cause of a misspelling ; e. g. *pellex*, a late spelling of *paelex* (see Georges), was due to connexion with *pellicio* ; and the established spelling *accĭpiter* for *acŭpeter* [probably with *ă*, weak grade of *ŏ* of Greek ὠκυ-πέτης (epithet of hawk in Hesiod, *Op.* 210), Sanscr. āçupátvan-, ch. iv. § 54] to connexion with *accĭpio* ; cf. the vulgar form *acceptor* (Caper 107. 8 K. accipiter non 'acceptor') used by Lucilius (*inc.* 123 M.) exta acceptoris et unguis. The misspelling *cŏminus* for *comminus* (see Georges) is due to the analogy of *ēminus*; and the analogy of Diminutive terminations *-ellus, -illus, -ullus* is generally believed to be responsible for the later spellings *camellus, anguilla, cucullus*, &c. The corrupt form *cămellus* instead of *camēlus* (Greek κάμηλος) is indicated by the spelling in the Itala (see Rönsch, *Itala*, p. 460), and in the Edict of Diocletian (11. 6, &c.), as by the Italian cammello (with open *e*), Span. camello, Fr. chameau (cf. *phasellus* for *phasēlus* in Virgil MSS.) ; *anguila*, the spelling of good MSS. of Latin authors, is reflected by Span. anguila (*A. L. L.* viii. 442); on *cucūlus* and *cucullus*, see Brambach, *Hülfsbüchlein*, s. v. The same explanation is generally given of *-ella* for *-ēla* of *loquela, querela, suadela, tutela, medela*, &c. (on which see Brambach, *Orthographie*, p. 258 sq.). The grammarians approve of the single *l* in these words (Ter. Scaur. 11. 1 K. on *querela* ; Mar. Vict. 17. 9 K. on *loquela, querela, suadela, tutela*, also *camelus* ; Caper 96. 6 K. on *querela, loquela*) ; but by the time of Papirian, the latter part of the fourth cent. A. D., *querella* was the usual spelling (see Papir. ap. Cassiod. 159. 4 K. Cf. Bede 287. 6 K. ; Alcuin 299. 6 K.; Quaest. Gram. Cod. Bern. 83. *Suppl.* 175. 7 K.). At the same time we have seen that *querella* (for *queres-la*), *loquella*, &c. were probably the older spellings, and stand beside *quallus* for *quas-lus* in Virgil MSS., so that their use in Vulgar Latin may be really a case of adherence to the older form, just as we find vulgar spellings like *ussus, vissus, messor, fressus, allium* (on these see Georges), and Vulg. Lat. **vessica*, attested by Ital. vescica, &c. (cf. Capsesis non 'Capsessis,' Probi App. 198. 2). *Pĭlla* was in late Latin **pĭlla, pillula* (see Georges s.v. *pilula*, and cf. the Romance forms). *Pōno*, for *pŏ-s(ĭ)no*, a compound with the preposition *po*, for **apo*, a by-form of *ab*, was treated in vulgar speech as if **por-s(ĭ)no*, a compound with *por-*. Hence the double *s* (for *rs*, as *dossum* from *dorsum*) in *possitus* (quasi 'por-situs'), *possui* on plebeian inscriptions (e. g. *possuit, C. I. L.* v. 5623 ; vii. 47. 137. 246 ; *dipossitus*, Rossi, i. 103, of 348 A. D.). In the Appendix Probi 202. 12 K. one is warned against the confusion of *sera*, a bolt, with *serra*, a saw, a confusion seen in Ital. serrare, Span. cerrar (cf. 201. 33 on *velit* and *vellit*). Other misspellings depend merely on the substitution of a single consonant with long vowel for a double consonant with short vowel, and vice versa, e. g. Probi App. 199. 4 K. garrulus, non 'garulus' (probably *gārulus*) ; 198. 21 K. caligo, non 'calligo.' This substitution was allowed, as we have seen, in prepositional compounds, like *āmitto*, to which we may add *stipendium* for *stĭp[i]pendium* (*stupendiorum*, C.I.L. vi. 2496, 2787, 2795; *stependiorum* 3069, of 221 A.D. point to *ĭ* in vulgar pronunciation), *tricae* (see § 60) for **tricc[h]ae* (cf. Ital. treccare, beside Neapolitan tricare). It appears to be consistently carried out in a group of words, *cūpa* (cf. Sanscr. *kū́pas*) and *cŭppa*, *stūpa* and *stŭppa* (Greek στύπη and στύππη), *mūcus* and *mŭccus*, *pūpa* (cf. PVVPAE, C.I.L. x. 4315; PÝPIVS, PÝPIA, vi. 6021) and *pŭppa*, *gūtus* and *gŭttus*, *mūtus* (Greek μῦθος, see *Class. Rev.* v. 10) and *mŭttus*, **būtis* (Greek βοῦτις) and **bŭttis* (cf. Ital. botte, bottiglia). The forms with short vowel and double consonant seem to be those of late Latin and Romance (e.g. *cuppa*, Ulp. Dig. xxxiii. 6, 3 § 1 and xxxiii. 7, 8 M.; Augustine, *Conf.* ix. 8. 18; Not. Tir. 156: *puppa*, Acron, in Hor. S. i. 5. 65; Ital. coppa, Span. copa, &c., while *cūpa* is reflected in Ital. cupola, Span. cuba and in the Welsh cib), so that the variety in form has arisen through the consonant being allowed to assert itself before the articulation of the vowel had been completed, and thus to take away from the vowel some of its force. [Similarly Middle High German muoter (I.-Eur. **māter*), with long vowel and single consonant has become n modern German mütter.] *Strēna* seems in the same way to have become *strĕnna* at the end of the Republican period; for *strēna* is indicated by Span. estrena, &c., *strĕnna* by Ital. strenna (with open *e*), Fr. étrenne, though the byform *strenua* (see Georges) may indicate confusion with *strēnuus*, later *strennuus* (see above). In Italian the same thing is very common, e.g. venni for vēni, leggi for lēgi, brutto for brūto; and this may be the explanation of the puzzling form tutto for Latin *tōtus* (see Körting, *Lat.-Roman. Wörterb.* s.v.; and cf. Consent. 392. 1 K. 'tottum' pro toto, 'cottidie' pro cotidie), as of Latin *Juppiter* (the usual spelling, see Georges) for *Jūpiter*[1] (ch. vi. § 32). *Sūcus* however retains this form in Vulgar Latin, and similarly *brāca*; while both classical and Vulgar Latin show *bāca* (see Georges, and cf. Ital. bag-ola, Fr. baie), which, if the ordinary derivation be correct (see *Etyma Latina* s.v.), should be bacca for **bat-ca*. Latin *ciccus* seems to have been in Vulg. Latin **cīcus*, to judge from Ital. cica, cigolo, &c.

Scribes of Irish nationality were specially liable to miswrite a double for a single consonant in a Latin word; for in the orthography of their own language the double letter often indicated merely that the consonant had not degenerated into a spirant. Thus a repeated substitution of double for single consonants in a Latin MS. is frequently an indication that the MS. has been written in an Irish monastery (see Zimmer, *Glossae Hibernicae*, proll. xi). Again the confusion of single with double consonants in inscriptions may often be due to local influence. Thus the Greeks, as we have seen, had a difficulty in pronouncing the Latin double consonants; the Oscan dialect often shows a double letter, where a single is etymologically correct, especially before a *y*-sound, e.g. Vitelliú (Lat. *Italia*), before a *w*-sound, e.g. dekkvíarim (cf. Lat. *decem*), before an *r*, e.g. alttreí (Lat. *alteri*), and similarly *ss* before *t*, e.g. kvaisstur (Lat. *quaestor*), which remind us of Latin misspellings like *acqua*, *frattre*, *disscente*; in the Umbrian inscriptions a double consonant is never found in those written in the native alphabet, and very seldom (sometimes perversely, e.g. *ennom*, cf. Lat. *ĕnim*; *avvei*, cf. Lat. *ăvis*) in those written in Latin characters.

---

[1] *Juppiter, quippe* (ch. ix. § 7), *ipsippe* (ch. vii. § 20) suggest that this doubling of *p* was a usage in the literary language.

§ 130.]   PRONUNCIATION. DOUBLE CONSONANTS.   117

But in spite of all these facts, it still remains true that there is usually a sufficient consensus between inscriptions and the best MSS. to enable us to decide with certainty on the single, or on the double letter, as the classical spelling of the word, a spelling with which the Romance forms, as well as the loanwords in Celtic and Teutonic languages, show a remarkable agreement. The classical form generally agrees with the form postulated by the etymology of the word, though there are some exceptions, e.g. *băca* (see above) instead of *bacca*, *damma* (but in the proper name, *Dāma*; see Georges) instead of *dāma*. This implies that a sharp line was drawn in Latin between the single and double consonant[1] (e.g. *mūlus* and *mŭllus*), a fact which should make us suspicious of etymologies which ignore this distinction, such as the identification of *annus*, a year (with *ă*, Terent. Maurus v. 1239), cf. *perennis*), with *ānulus*, a ring. For examples of this kind of uncertainty in Latin spellings, see Georges, *Lex. Wortf.* and Brambach, *Hülfsbüchlein* s.vv. *lammina* and *lamina* (syncopated *lamna*), *văcillo* and *vaccillo*, *māmilla* rarely *mammilla*, *buccella* and *būcella*, *disicio* and *dissicio* (cf. *porricio*), *cotidie* and *cottidie* (see *Etyma Latina* s.v.), *mutonium* and *muttonium*, *muttio* and *mutio*, *glutto* and *gluto*, *murgiso* and *murgisso*, *mantisa* and *mantissa*, *favisae* and *favissae*, *favisor* and *favissor*, *comissor* and *comisor*, *Masinissa* and *Massinissa*, *phaseolus* and *passeolus*, *Tissaphernes* and *Tisaphernes*, *Porsenna* and *Porsĕna* [cf. Pompeius, p. 284 K., who also censures (a suppositious ?) *Catilinna*], *meddix* and *medix* (Oscan meddís *Nom.*, medíkeís, *Gen.*), *Apuleius* and *Appuleius* (but *Apulia* better than *App-*), *Marcomani* and (later) *Marcomanni*. (*Pānus* and *pannus* may be different words. See *Berl. Phil. Woch.* 1887, p. 214.) The double consonant is declared by them to be the better spelling of *bracchium* (with *cch* for χ of Gk. βράχιον : see § 60), *littera* [cf. Romance, e.g. Fr. lettre, and Welsh llythyr. In the Lex Repet. (*C. I. L.* i. 198) of 123-122 B.C., once LEITERAS, but the spelling of a single for a double consonant is usual on this inscription, and *ei* is used for *ĭ* in *seine*], *futtilis*, *caccăbus*, *cŭlleus*, *trŭlleum*, *cuppes*, *cuppēdo* (for *cūp-*), *lollīgo* (Fritsche, ad Hor. S. i. 4. 100), *fello* (for *fē-lo*), *helluor*, *sollers*, *sollemnis*, *sollĭcĭto*, *pappare* (Plaut. *Epid.* Goetz, pref. p. xxx), *cippus*, *lippus*, *căperro* (see Nettleship in *Class. Rev.* 1892, p. 168), *Messalla* (cf. *Hispāllus* with *ll* on *C.I.L.* i. 39), *Sallustius*, *barrītus*, *Arruns*, *Arrētium* (now Arezzo), *allēc*, *Allecto*, *Allīfae*, *Sardănăpallus*, *ballaena* (Gk. φαλλ- rather than φαλ-), *ballista*, *Sallentini*, *cŏvinnus*, *pĕtorrītum*, *Trăsŭmennus*, *Appennīnus* (and *Ap-*), *nummus*, *immo*, *bissextum* ; the single of *balbutio*, *litus* (so Vulg. Lat., e.g. Ital. lito and lido), *bucina*, *alucinor*, *besalis*, *belua*, *sărio*, *muriola* (cf. Paul. Fest. 125. 13 Th. *murrina*, genus potionis, quae Graece dicitur nectar. Hanc mulieres vocabant muriolam), *Erinys*, *Apulia*, *Sufes*, *tăpete*, *Larisa*, *sarisa*, *Gnosus*, *Parnasus*, *talasio*, *pedisequus*, *ilico* ; the double consonant appears to be the older spelling, the single the later in *mantellum* (Plaut.) and *mantēle*, *stēllio* and *stelio*, *pĭlleus* (so, for example, in MSS. of Martial ; see Friedländer's edition, i. p. 117), and *pīleus* (*pĭll-* in Romance, *K.Z.* xxxiii. 308), *marsuppium* and *marsūpium*, *Marpessos* and *Marpēsius*, and possibly the legal *parret* and *păret* (Fest. 292. 25 Th., parret, quod est in formulis, debuit et producta priore syllaba pronuntiari et non gemino r scribi, ut fieret 'paret,' quod est invenitur, ut comparet, apparet). The spelling *paricida* for *parricida* belongs to a period before the doubling of

---

[1] Plautus, however, puns on *mittis* and *mitis* in *Mil.* 1424, when the soldier is getting a thrashing:

Vérberon etiam, án iam mittis ?
Mítis sum equidem fústibus.

consonants was practised. Of Greek loanwords we have O. Lat. *creterra* (Gk. κρητήρ), perhaps *grammosus* (from Gk. γλήμη) in Caecil. *Comm.* 268 R. (but *gramae* Plaut. *Curc.* 318, Büch. *Rh. Mus.* xxxv. 72), *grabattus* (Gk. κράβατος), &c. *A. L. L.* viii. 367)[1]. (See also Ellis *Catullus* p. 338 on *Varus* and *Varro.*)

§ 131. **Double consonants in Italian.** These are not known in the dialects of Umbria and of North Italy; and their use varies a good deal in different parts. They form one of the greatest difficulties to English learners; for a double consonant is unknown in our language, except in compound words like ' bookcase,' 'penknife'; as they proved a stumbling-block in old times to Greeks (cf. §§ 99 and 117 on the Greek mispronunciation of *ll*, *ss*). Double consonants have replaced Latin single consonants before *y*, e. g. occhio (Lat. ŏc(*u*)*lus*), vendemmia (Lat. *vindēmia*); before the *w*-sound of Latin *ăqua* (Ital. acqua); before *r*, e. g. fabbro (Lat. *făber*). (Compare the doubling of a consonant in these positions in Oscan orthography, and similar misspellings in late Latin inscriptions.) Doubling is very common under the accent of a paroxytone word, e. g. femmina (Lat. *fĕmĭna*), legittimo (Lat. *lēgĭtĭmus*), and on the first syllable, when it has a secondary accent, e. g. pellegrino, tollerare (cf. late Latin *suppellectĭlis*, see Georges). Forms like allodola (Lat. *alauda*), commedia (Lat. *cōmoedia*) seem to be due to the analogy of words compounded with prepositions, like Latin *allūdo*, *commŏdus* (cf. Osc. Appelluneís ' Apollinis'?).

§ 132. **Double consonant (not l, s) after long vowel.** We know that the *e* of *fressus*, for *frensus*, later *fresus*, was long; but we cannot tell whether the true explanation of the change from *dummetum* to *dūmētum* (see Georges) is to make it similarly a reduction of a double to a single consonant after a long vowel, or merely a substitution of a vowel length (*ūm*) for consonant length (*ŭmm*), like *āmissam* for *ammissam* (in MSS. of Virg. *A.* ii. 741), as the *-amm-* of *flammen*, a blast, in Virg. MSS. (see Ribbeck) seems to represent the usual *-ām-* of *flā-men*. A spelling like *ruppes* for *rūpes* in Virgil. MSS. (see Ribbeck) suggests rather the alternation of *cŭppa* with *cūpa*, *pŭppa* with *pūpa* (see above); and the quantity of the vowel before the double consonant of *lammĭna* (see Georges), *vaccinnia* (see Ribbeck, *Index*) is quite uncertain. Clear cases of a long vowel before *nn* are *mercennarius* (the correct spelling, according to Brambach, *Hülfsbüchl*. s. v., later *mercenarius*), *tinnire* (for *ī* and *nn* are attested by Port. tinir, Sard. tinnire), and perhaps *hinnuleus* (also *innuleus*, *inuleus*, see Georges) (cf. Agroecius 115. 14 K. hinnuleus, ut *i* acutum sit, quia nomen a sono vocis accipit), and *Vinnius* (also *Vinius*; see *C. I. L.* vi. 28978 sqq. Long *i* is indicated for *Vinnia*, 28986); but before other double consonants they are difficult to establish. NÁRREM on the carefully written inscription of the Emperor Claudius (48 A. D.) at Lyons (Allmer et Dissard vol. i. p. 70ª; Boissieu p. 136) may be due to the analogy of *gnārus*, *nārus*, which made the spelling *naro* (proposed by Varro, if we are to believe Papirian

---

[1] Sometimes the interchange of single and double consonant is I-Eur. In pet-names we often find a double consonant : e. g. Gk. νάννα beside O. Ind. naná; Lat. *mammas atque tătas* (ch. v. § 81) beside Gk. ἄττα, O. Ind. attā;

Lat. *Acca Larentia*, Gk. 'Ακκώ (a name of Demeter), O. Ind. akkā; Gk. Ξεννώ, &c. The double consonant of *Eppius*, *Seppius*, &c. has been so explained, though others refer it to a dialectal doubling before *y* like Osc. Vitelliú.

§§ 131-134.] PRONUNCIATION. FINAL CONSONANTS. 119

ap. Cassiodor. 159. 8; cf. Varro. *L.L.* vi. 51) approved by some grammarians (e.g. Velius Longus 80. 9 K.), though never accepted in popular usage (see Georges) (cf. *vārus* and *Varro*). (On **trippa*, the original of Ital. trippa, our 'tripe,' &c., see Körting's *Lexicon* s.v.) A certain instance of the reduction of *tt* to *t* after a diphthong is the late form *autor* (censured, with *autoritas*, in Probi Appendix 198. 30 K., and found on late inscriptions, e.g. *C.I.L.* viii. 1423; cf. xii. 2058, of 491 A.D.), where the *t* represents *tt* for original *ct* (see § 95). Ital. freddo, Fr. froid point to **friddus*, from *frigdus*, a vulgar form of *frigidus* (Probi App. 198. 3 frigida non 'frigda'); O. Span. frido to **frīdus* or **friddus*.

§ 133. **Final double consonant.** A final double consonant was not allowed in Latin orthography, but was written single, e.g. *mīles* for **miless*, from **milit-s*. But that it differed in pronunciation from an ordinary final single consonant, we may infer from the forms censured in the Appendix Probi, where -*x* is wrongly substituted for this -*s* (originally -*ss*) (197. 28 K. miles non 'milex'; 198. 29 aries non 'ariex'; 199. 4-5 poples non 'poplex,' locuples non 'locuplex'), forms which are found on inscriptions (e.g. *milex*, *C.I.L.* vi. 37, 2457, 2549, &c.). We may infer also that there was a change in its pronunciation in course of time; for in Plautus *miles* has the last syllable long (*Aul.* 528), while in Ennius, Lucilius, &c., its last syllable is short (*Ann.* 277 M.; so *milĕs*, Lucil. xi. 8 M.), though never shortened before an initial consonant like ordinary -*ŭs,-ĭs*. Plautus also scans *ter* for **terr* (cf. *terruncius*, the true spelling; see *Rhein. Mus.* xlvi. p. 236) from **ters*, **tris* (Greek τρίς), as a long syllable (*Bacch.* 1127), as he scans *es* (2 Sg. Pres. Ind. of *sum*), *prōdes*, &c. like **ess*, **prodess* (contrast *cŏr*, Lucil. xv. 9 M.; *prodĕs*, id. *inc.* 128). A relic of this usage remains in the scansion of *hoc* for **hocc* from **hod-(c)e* as a long syllable by the classical poets; and the remarks of the grammarians on this scansion explain the reason of the change and uncertainty in the quantity of these final syllables. Thus Velius Longus (54. 6 K.), commenting on Virgil's 'hoc erat, alma parens' says: ergo scribendum per duo c, 'hoc-c-erat alma parens,' aut confitendum quaedam aliter scribi, aliter enuntiari; Pompeius (119. 13): item c littera aliquando pro duabus consonantibus est... ut... 'hoc erat alma parens': 'hoc,' collide c, ut sit pro duabus consonantibus. in illo alio exemplo brevis est, 'solus hic inflexit sensus': sic lubrice et leniter currit. (Velius Longus also fails to make this proper distinction between *hocc* for **hod-c* and *hi-c*.) They show us that in pronunciation **hocc* (and presumably **corr*, **ess*) were actually sounded with double consonant when the next word began with a vowel, at least if the accent fell on them, while before a consonant initial, and probably when unaccented, the double consonant would be reduced to a single, *hoc fuit* but *hocc erat*. The unaccented nature of the Substantive Verb **ess*, and of the final syllable of **miless, prodess*, &c. explains their speedy reduction in Latin prosody (see ch. iii).

§ 134. **Final consonants.** A final consonant is always more liable to weakening than an initial, because of the general tendency of languages to pronounce with diminishing stress. It is especially so in English after a long vowel. Thus in the word 'cat' the *t* is uttered with less force than the *c*, while the same final after a long vowel, as in 'cart,' is still weaker. It is a rule of our language that a final consonant is always short after a long vowel, as we may see, if we contrast a word like 'heel' with a word like 'hill.' The weakness of Latin final consonants has been already mentioned. Final -*d* was dropped in pronunciation after a long vowel about the end of the third cent. B.C.; final *s* does not constitute position before an initial consonant in that species of poetry which most closely imitated ordinary pronunciation, Dramatic Poetry; final -*m* offers but slight resistance to the elision of the vowel which precedes it; the tenues fortes seem to have been replaced when final in pronunciation by the mediae lenes, e.g. *ab*, *sub*, *relīquid*, &c. (cf. *negōtium*?) (see § 73).

In considering the pronunciation of final consonants it is necessary to regard not isolated words, but words as they stand in the sentence. The accent of a word, when standing alone, is something different from its accentuation in the sentence; e.g. Greek πρός, but πρὸς πόλιν ἦλθε. And the same is true of its pronunciation. The Greek orthography indicates the first distinction, but rarely the second; though we find it to some extent on inscriptions τημ πολιν, ἐγ δικης, &c., especially in Cretan inscriptions (see ch. iii. § 41). But in writing Sanscrit the principles of 'Sandhi' (i. e. putting together, synthesis), to use the native term, were carefully followed by the grammarians of India. The neuter Demonstrative, for example, tad (Lat. *is-tŭd*) had its final *d* changed according to the following initial consonant in tat tapas, that heat (Lat. *is-tud *tepus*), tal lihati (Lat. *is-tud lingit*), tan nahyati (Lat. *is-tud nectit*), &c. There was something like this in Latin. Traces of it appear occasionally in inscriptions and MSS., e.g. *im burim* in MSS. of Virgil, *G.* i. 170; and we have 'doublets' like *neque, atque* before vowels, *nec, ac* before consonants; but for the most part it is not indicated in spelling.

Final consonants lingered longest in monosyllables, especially accented monosyllables, and before being entirely discarded in spelling, passed through the 'doublet' stage; that is to say, they were retained in pronunciation in certain positions in the sentence, before an initial vowel usually, and dropped in others; e.g. *hau scio* but *haud habeo*, just as the *r*-sound is found in English only before an initial vowel following without any pause, e.g. 'here he is.' The same process went on in the Romance languages, of which French was the most retentive of final consonants till comparatively modern times; though now, for example, final -*t*, -*s*, -*r* exist only in pre-vocalic 'doublets,' e.g. vient-il ? with *t* sounded, but il vien(t). An English example of 'Sandhi' is the different vowel-sound of the article 'the' before a vowel and before a consonant, and an example of the abandonment of one 'doublet' and the exclusive use of another is the preposition 'with,' which now ends only in the *th*-sound of thin, but which in early modern English had in certain collocations the *th*-sound of 'this.' Both 'doublet' forms remain in 'my' and 'mine,' 'one' and 'a,' 'an,' 'naught' and 'not,' &c.

The treatment of final vowels in Latin is most naturally considered in connexion with the changes produced by the accent; for they are affected much in the same way as the vowels in post-tonic syllables (see ch. iii. § 40).

§ 135. 'Sandhi' in Latin :—Verrius Flaccus proposed a new symbol for final *m*, when the next word in the sentence began with a vowel, a symbol like the half of the ordinary letter M ; while Cato the Elder wrote *dicae* for *dicam*, *faciae* for *faciam* (see § 61). The tendency of final -*m*, -*n* to adapt themselves to a following consonant-initial, is seen in spellings on inscriptions, like *im balneum*, *C.I.L.* iv. 2410, *imbello*, iii. 4835, *im pace*, viii. 10542 (for examples see Indices to *C. I. L.*) and in MS. spellings like *im mare*, *im medio*, *im pace*, *im puppim* in Virgil MSS. (see Ribbeck, *Ind.* p. 433), *im praeda*, *im uita* in the Plautus Palimpsest (see Ind. to Studemund's Apograph.). Caper (106. 17 K.) says : in Siciliam dicendum, non 'is Siciliam,' κατὰ τὸ ν, non κατὰ τὸ σ, quia nunquam sine n pronuntiatur (*leg.* insicia . . non 'is.'?). We have *etiannunc* in the Herculanean papyri (*Class. Rev.* iv. 443), and *etiannum*, *jandudum*, &c. in MSS. of Virgil (see Ribbeck), spellings which agree with the statement of Velius Longus (78. 19 K. cum dico ' etiam nunc,' ' quamvis per m scribam, nescio quomodo tamen exprimere non possum), and Cicero's remarks on the sound of *cum* followed by *n-* (*Or.* xlv. 154 ; *Fam.* ix. 22. 2 ; cf. Quint. viii. 3. 45 ; Diom. 450. 34 K. ; Pompeius 293. 17 K. ; Prisc. i. 372. 8 and 594. 21 H. &c.). *Est* was curtailed in writing, as in pronunciation, like our 'is,' in ' it 's,' ' he 's,' &c., *audiendust*, *audiendast*, *audiendumst*, &c., a spelling recommended by Mar. Victorinus (22. 14 K.), and found in MSS., e. g. in Virgil MSS. *acerbist*, *locutast*, *ventumst*, *amantemst*, *cupidost*, *suprast*, &c. (see Ribbeck's *Index*, p. 419), in the Plautus Palimpsest *copiast*, *aegrest*, *homost*, *olimst*, *palamst*, *meliust*, &c., and similarly with *es*, *iratas*, *dignus*, *iturus* (generally printed by editors *irata's*, &c. ; once with *es* Imperat., viz. *molestus, Most.* 955) (see Studemund's *Index*, p. 505). One may perhaps see the beginnings of the suppression of final consonants in the tendency of pronunciation mentioned by Consentius (fifth cent. ? A. D.) (395. 7 K.), the tendency to detach a final consonant from its word, and join it to a following initial, ' si cludit ' for *sic ludit*, 'si(c) custodit' for *sic custodit* : item litteram c quidam in quibusdam dictionibus non latine ecferunt, sed ita crasse, ut non discernas, quid dicant : ut puta siquis dicat ' sic ludit,' ita hoc loquitur, ut putes eum in secunda parte orationis cludere dixisse, non ludere ; et item si contra dicat illud, contrarium putabis. alii contra ita subtiliter hoc ecferunt, ut cum duo c habeant, quasi uno c utrumque explicent, ut dicunt multi ' sic custodit.' [Cf. his remarks (394. 7 K.) on the pronunciation ' dixera millis ' for *dixeram illis*.]

§ 136. **Latin 'Doublets.'** By pretonic Syncope (see ch. iii. § 13) *ac* (for *atc), *nec, neu, seu*, replaced *atque, neque, neve, sive* before a word beginning with a consonant. In Dramatic poetry the final *-ĕ* is always suppressed, in similar circumstances, of *nempe*, and often of *unde, inde, quippe, ille*, and perhaps *iste*. Similarly *proin, dein* seem to have developed from *proinde, deinde*, when a consonantal initial followed. Final *-d*, after it had been dropped after a long vowel in the pronunciation of most words, remained in monosyllables like *haud, med, ted* ; *haud* being the form used before a vowel, *hau* before a consonant (Caper. 96. 4 K. 'hau dolo' [*leg.* haud uolo?] per d recte scribitur, etenim d inter duas vocales esse debet. quod si consonans sequitur, d addi non debet, ut 'hauscio'; Mar. Vict. 15. 21 K. So in Plautus, Ritschl *Opusc.* ii. 591 *n.* and v. 352) ; the same probably being true of *med, ted*. (On *qui(n)e, quandoc* and *quandoque*, see ch. x. § 15, ch. ix. § 10.) Preposition 'doublets' *ā, ăb, abs* ; *ē, ec, ex*, &c., on which see ch. ix. §§ 12 and 29.

§ 137. **Dropping of final consonant in Latin.** It was a rule of Latin, pointed out by Julius Caesar, in criticizing Varro's spelling *lact*, that no word could end in two mutes (Pompeius 199 K.; Caper 95 K. On *lacte, lact, lac*, see Georges, *Lex. Wortf.* s.v.). Nor was a double consonant allowed to end a word. Plautus gives to *miles, es*, &c. the scansion of *miless* (for *milit-s), *ess*, &c. (see ch. viii. § 2) ; but almost the only trace (a doubtful one) of spelling with *-ss* is *noss* in the Ambrosian Palimpsest in *Stich.* 536; though Velius Longus (54. 6 K.), commenting on Virgil's ' hoc erat, alma parens,' half proposes to write *hoccerat* : ergo scribendum per duo c, ' hoccerat alma parens' aut confitendum quaedam aliter scribi, aliter enuntiari (cf. Pompeius 119. 13 K. ; Prisc. ii. p. 6. 1 H. So *hoccine* for *hocce-ne, *hod-ce-ne, Prisc. i. p. 592. 22 H.). *Mel* (for *mell, *meld), *cor* (for *corr, *cord), *ter* (for *terr*, cf. *terr-uncius*, *ters, *tris) are short in Ovid, &c., though long (neither *mĕl* nor *mēl* are found) in Plautus ; but the difference between *-s* (from original *-ss*) and ordinary *-s* is shown even at a late period by spellings like *milex, praegnax* (see § 125).

Final *-d* after a long vowel is written throughout the S. C. de Bacchanalibus of 186 B.C. (*C. I. L.* i. 196, *sententiad, exstrad, facilumed*, &c.), though it is not found in the decree of Aemilius Paulus Macedonicus of 189 B.C. (*ib.* ii. 5041, *in turri Lascutana, ea tempestate*), and probably does not appear in Plautus, excepting in the Pronouns (Abl. and Acc.) *med, ted, sed*. Even these Pronoun forms are out of use by Terence's time. The retention of *haud* along with *hau* shows the course which this final *d* must have taken. Before vowels it would remain pronounced until the preconsonantal form had driven the full form from the field (so in post-Augustan poetry we find *nec* more and more supplanting *neque*) ; before consonants it would probably be first assimilated, e.g. *haud ligo*, pronounced *haulligo*, like *alligo*, *haud scio*, pronounced *hausscio* like *a(s)scisco*, then dropped. After a short vowel, it is often written *-t* on late inscriptions (and indeed from the end of the Republican period), but is not dropped (see Seelmann's list, p. 366).

Final -*m* is dropped in early inscriptions before a consonant or a vowel-initial with equal frequency, in the earliest inscriptions more after *o* of the Gen. Plur. (perhaps not yet shortened before -*m*), than after *o* of the Acc. Sg. Masc. and Nom. Acc. Sg. Neut. On the older Scipio epitaphs it is usually dropped, e. g. *oino* (Acc. Sg.), *duonoro* (Gen. Pl.) (*C. I. L.* i. 32). But from c. 130 it is regularly retained in spelling [as also on State inscriptions like the S. C. Bacch. of 186 B. C., the (restored) Columna Rostrata, &c.], until the plebeian inscriptions of a later date (see § 65). On these it is not merely dropped but also is written -*n*, as final -*n* is occasionally written -*m* (see Seelmann's lists, p. 364). It never fails, as final -*s* may fail, to constitute 'position' before an initial consonant in early poetry; though the frequency of the scansion *enim* before a consonant in Plautus (where the final syllable is shortened by the law of Breves Breviantes) suggests that this represents the usual pronunciation of the word. Final *m* before an initial vowel seems to have been equally adapted with a final long vowel or diphthong for what is called 'Prosodical Hiatus,' i. e. for being scanned as a short syllable, instead of being elided. Ennius, for example, ends a line with *millia militūm octo*, as he begins another with *Scipiŏ invicte*. (Cf. *circu(m)ire, septu(m)ennis, septu(m)- aginta*, but *septumus*, &c.) (On the treatment of -*m* in poetry, see § 65; and on its weak pronunciation in ordinary speech, § 61.) The course it took is perhaps indicated by Consentius (394. 7 K.), who says that the common way of pronouncing a phrase like 'dixeram illis' was to detach the -*m* from the first word, and join it to the initial of the second. (Cf. Pompeius 287. 7 K.) (see §. 61.)

Final -*s* is dropped on early inscriptions especially in the Nom. Sing. of IO-stems, written -*io*, or -*i* (see Index to *C. I. L.* i[1]. p. 602). That both *io* and -*i* represent the same sound -*ĭ(s)* (ch. vi. § 2) is quite possible. (Cf. *Cornelio* on one Scipio epitaph, *C. I. L.* i. 31, c. 250 B. C., *Corneli* on another, i. 35, c. 160 B. C.) But as a rule -*s* is dropped only after a short vowel, except in the dialect of Pisaurum, e. g. *matrona(s)* (*ib.* i. 167 sqq.), and is more often retained than dropped.

Cicero speaks of its failure to prevent elision of a preceding ĭ in the phrase *vas' argenteis*; and some have thought that it is occasionally elided before an initial vowel in Plautus, e. g. *com(is) incommodus*, *Bacch.* 401, *amatu(s) es* written in the MSS. *amatus*. But all the instances admit of other explanations; *amatu's* is rather a case of prodelision, like our ' it 's ' for ' it is ' (the length of the *u* is due to the double *s* with which *es* ended in Plautus' time, ch. viii. § 2); *plur(is) existumo* of Plaut. *Pers.* 353 may easily be a mistake for *plure*, which Charisius tell us was used in O. Lat., and so on. Whether *aequănĭmĭtas* implies a pronunciation *aequ(us) animus* is doubtful; it seems rather to come from the Compound (ch. v. § 80) *aequ-animus* (cf. the gloss ' Animus aequus ' duae partes orationis; 'animaequus' ipse homo, *C. G. L.* v. 266. 11–12). (On final *s* not constituting 'position' before an initial consonant in the older poetry, see § 126.) The Latin loanwords in Teutonic seem to have still possessed -*us* (e. g. Goth. sakkus, a U-stem, Germ. kurz, from Lat. *saccus, curtus*), but to have lost the final consonant of -*um* (*Zeitschr. Roman. Philologie*, xvii. 559).

Final -*t* is often written -*d* on late inscriptions, e. g. *reliquid, fecid* (see Seelmann's list, p. 366), which probably indicates change to the media lenis in pronunciation. It is dropped with great frequency in the graffiti of Pompeii, e. g. *valia, ama* (see Index to *C. I. L.* iv.).

Final -*nt* loses the dental, and is written -*n*, or -*m*, on late inscriptions, e. g. *fecerun* (see the Indices to the *Corpus*), though, no doubt, the -*t* was heard before an initial vowel, like the -*t* of Fr. vient in vient-il ? *Dedro* (*C. I. L.* i. 177 Matre Matuta dono dedro matrona 'Matri Matutae donum déderunt matronae') is a form belonging to the dialect of Pisaurum in Picenum. The dropping of final consonants (-*m*, -*d*, -*r*, -*f*; -*t*, -*n*, -*s*) in this order of frequency is a feature of Umbrian (see von Planta i. 568).

§ 138. **Dropping of final consonants in Romance.** Lat. final consonants are better preserved in monosyllables than in other words. *Ĕt* is in Italian e, before vowels ed ; in O. Fr. and Prov. e and ed ; in Span. y and e ; *aut* is in Italian o, od ; Fr. ou, Span. o ; *ăd* in Ital., Prov. and O. Fr. is a before consonants, ad before vowels, &c. -*M* remains in the monosyllables, Fr. rien (Lat. *rem*), Span. quien (Lat. *quem*), &c. ; -*l* in a monosyllable like *mel*, Fr. miel, Span. miel, Ital. miele ; -*r* in the monosyllable *cor*, Fr. cueur, O. Span. cuer, Ital. cuore ; -*n* remains in *non* (Ital. no and non). In longer words, -*m* is dropped, e. g. Ital. dieci from Lat. *dĕcem*, amava from Lat. *ămābam* ; -*t* is retained in Fr., e. g. O. Fr. aimet, but Ital. ama, Span. ama. In Sardinian the form used 'in pausa' (at the end of a sentence, &c.) is amat, before a vowel amad, e. g. amad issu, before a consonant ama, e. g. ama su padre ; -*l* and -*r* are lost in Italian, e. g. frate, tribuna, insieme (cf. Span. ensieme, but Fr. ensemble) ; -*s* is lost in Ital. (though in monosyllables it leaves an *i*, e. g. noi, crai, which is absorbed in a preceding *e*, e. g. tre), but it is retained in Fr. and Span., e. g. Ital. tempo, Fr. temps from Lat. *tempus*, and from Lat. *cantas, lĕgis*, Fr. chantes, lis, Span cantas, lees ; -*d* is lost in Ital. chè, Span. que from Lat. *quid*, but remains in O. Fr. qued ; -*c* has disappeared in Ital. di (Lat. *dic*), si (Lat. *sic*) ; -*nt* is -*n* in Ital., Span. e. g. Ital. aman-o, Span. aman, but remains in Fr., e. g. aiment ; -*x* remains in Fr. six, Span. seis, but not in Ital. sei. It thus appears that French has been far more retentive of final consonants than Italian or Spanish. In the Sardinian dialect of Italian (Sardinia was the earliest province, and its dialect is a descendant of the earliest stage of Vulgar Latin), all final consonants remain, except -*m*, e. g. tempus, amas, amat, ses, amant, nomen, but adapt themselves to the following initial, e. g. est bennidu (pronounced 'es b-') (see Meyer-Lübke *Ital. Gramm.* p. 156). But in standard Italian there are still traces of these lost final consonants of monosyllables, e. g. ebbene for e bene (Lat. *et bĕnè*), ovvero for o vero (Lat. *aut vērō*), dimmi for di mi (Lat. *dīc mĭhi*), checcosa for chè cosa (Lat. *quid causa*), where the double consonant is due' to the final having assimilated itself to the following initial, as Latin *ā* arose from a collocation like *ab-bŏnis*, *am-me (for *ab me*), *ap-patre (for *ab pătre*). In French we see 'Sandhi' carried to far greater lengths than Italian, where almost every word ends in a vowel. Before an initial vowel, French -*s*, -*t*, -*r* are heard in pronunciation, and a nasal vowel resolves itself into an oral vowel followed by *n*. And, more curious still, -*l* of words closely joined to a following word beginning with a consonant suffers the same change as *l* before a consonant in the middle of a word and becomes *u* ; e. g. du père, au père, beau, like autre, &c. In S. Spain -*s* becomes *h*, or is dropped, e. g. 'Cađi(h)' (Storm. *Engl. Phil.*[2] i. p. 71).

§ 139. **Syllable - Division.** The Romance languages show a remarkable agreement in their division of the word into syllables, their principle of division being to make the syllable end with a vowel, and begin with a consonant, or combination of consonants. Any combination of consonants, that is pronounceable at the beginning of a word is made to begin the syllable, with the one occasional exception of combinations beginning with *s*, where the *s* is in some languages allowed to end the preceding syllable. An Italian says o-bli-quo, te-cni-co, e-ni-gma, a-tle-ta, no-stro, be-ne, a pronunciation which often offers considerable difficulty to Englishmen, who would, for example, more naturally pronounce the last word as ben-e, like 'any.' A Spaniard says ha-blar, bu-llir, but nues-tro, attaching the *s* to the first syllable. The Roman division of syllables was that of the Romance languages, not of the English, as is proved to certainty by the very precise and unmistakable statements of the grammarians on the subject. Their rule is 'Never let a syllable end in a consonant if the consonant can possibly be pronounced at the beginning of the next syllable'; and they give examples like *pŏte-stas, no-ster, a-mnis, ma-gno, a-gmen.* The same method is followed in those inscriptions which indicate the syllables by dots, e.g. *C. I. L.* vi. 77 T·AN·NI·VS·HE·DY·PNVS, 11682 VI·XIT·AN·NIS, as well as by contractions, where the initial letters of the syllables are used, like M̄G (*magnus*), ŌMB (*omnibus*), P̄P (*propter*); though on inscriptions we often find *s* taken with the preceding syllable in words like CAE·LES·TI (vi. 77), SES·TV·LE·IVS (ix. 4028), with which we may compare misspellings like *disscente* (vide § 130). Occasionally a grammarian urges the advisability of regarding the etymological formation of compounds like *abs-tēmius, ob-līviscor*; but such remarks only show that the natural pronunciation of these words was *ab-stemius, o-bliviscor*, just as we in natural utterance disregard the formation of phrases like 'at all,' 'at home,' and pronounce 'a-tall,' 'a-tome.'

§ 140. **Testimony of grammarians.** Servius, *in Don.* iv. 427. 20 K., states the rule as follows : quotienscumque quaerimus, quae consonantes in scribendo sibi cohaereant vel cui syllabae imputentur, utrum priori an sequenti, similitudo aliorum nominum hunc solvit errorem. ut puta 'aspice' ... intelligimus ... s et p ... consonantes sequenti tantummodo dare nos debere, eo quod invenitur sermo qui a duabus istis consonantibus inchoetur, ut ' spica.' similiter 'amnis': debemus m et n sequenti syllabae dare in scribendo, quoniam invenitur sermo qui ab his consonantibus inchoetur, ut

'Mnestheus,' 'attulit': non possumus duo t sequenti syllabae dare, quia nullus sermo invenitur, qui a duabus t consonantibus inchoetur, et hoc in ceteris consonantibus observabimus. plane scire debemus, conexiones quod dico consonantium non eas quae latinis syllabis congruunt, sed etiam quae graecis, excepta scilicet ea syllaba quae constat de b et d, quae in latinum sermonen numquam ita transit, ut cohaereat, ut est βδέλλα. quando enim scribimus 'abditur,' non possumus a in una syllaba ponere et b et d in sequenti. He thus testifies to *a-spice, a-mnis, at-tulit, ab-ditur*. Similarly Caesellius (ap. Cassiod. vii. 205. 1 K.) to *pote-stas, no-ster, ca-pto, plo-strum, lu-strant, capi-strum, clau-strum, ra-strum, campe-stre, a-stla* (for *astula*), *pe-stlum* (for *pestulum*), *car-po, dor-sum, Por-cius, Pa-ris, la-pis, tu-tus, sol-vo, ner-vus, vol-vo, lar-va, pul-vis, te-nu-is,* but dissyllabic *ten-vis, be-lu-a* and *bel-va, ma-lu-a* and *mal-va* ; Terentianus Maurus (vi. 351, v. 879 K.) to *o-mnis, a-mnis,* and (v. 904 K.) *ma-gnus, di-gnus, a-gnus, si-gna, pu-gna* (v. 941 K.), *fa-xo, a-xis, ne-xus, u-xor, no-xia* ; Marius Victorinus (vi. 29. 20 K.) to *a-mnis, ar-ma, a-xis* (cf. Charisius, i. 11. 19 K. ; Dositheus vii. 387. 4 K.) ; Caper (vii. 96. 9 K.) to *no-strum, ve-strum, maje-stas*; Dositheus (vii. 385. 5 K.) to *a-gmine, ma-gno* ; Priscian (i. p. 42 H.) to *a-bdomen, My-gdonides, Abo-dlas, A-tlas, Ae-tna, i-pse, nu-psi, scri-psi, scri-ptum, dra-chma, a-gmen, vi-ctrix, sce-ptrum,* thus admitting, unlike Servius, *bd* into the list of pronounceable combinations, and (p. 50 H.) *pa-scua, lu-scus, Co-smus, pro-spera, te-stis,* &c. Bede and Alcuin insist on copyists of MSS. breaking up words at the end of a line according to these rules, *ma-gnus, pro-pter, colu-mna,* &c. Etymological division is recommended by Quintilian (i. 7. 9) with the instances *haru-spex, abs-temius* (quia ex abstinentia temeti composita vox est) ; by Caesellius (ap. Cassiodor. vii. 206. 1 K.), *ob-liviscor,* and (205. 18 K.), *di-spicio. abs-tulit, trans-tulit, abs-condit*) ; by Alcuin (vii. 306. 4 K.), *ob-stipui, ob-sum, ob-strepo, obs-olevit* (cf. Cassiodor. vii. 204. 19 K.). Priscian similarly says (i. p. 45 H.) si antecedens syllaba terminat in consonantem, necesse est etiam sequentem a consonante incipere, ut 'ar-tus' 'il-le' ' ar-duus,' nisi sit compositum, ut 'ab-eo' ' ad-eo' ' per-eo,' but adds that Herodian in his treatise on Orthography declared it to be 'rationabilius sonoriusque' to follow the ordinary syllable-division in the case of Compounds too ; and in another passage (i. p. 42) he hesitates between *a-bnuo* and *ab-nuo*. Terentius Scaurus (vii. 12. 1 K.) censures 'nes-cio' for *ne-scio*, a mispronunciation which shows the tendency already mentioned (§ 139) to detach *s* from a following consonant or consonant group, or perhaps rather to divide it between the two syllables, 'nes-scio.'

The law of Breves Breviantes in Plautine prosody, it may be mentioned, takes no account of syllable-division. Shortening is allowed (after a short syllable) of a pretonic syllable long by position in words like *gŭbĕrnābunt, căvillātor, vŏlŭntātis,* where the consonant group is divided between two syllables neither more nor less readily than in words like *ĕgĕstāti, vĕnŭstāti,* where the consonant group is confined to one syllable.

§ **141. Quantity.** The quantity and the quality of a vowel are two different things. We are apt to distinguish in our minds a long and a short vowel (say *ĕ* and *ē*) by quality, not by quantity, thinking of *ĕ* as an open E-sound, of *ē* as a close E-sound, whereas the terms 'long' and 'short' should be applied only to the amount of time taken in pronouncing the vowel, so that there is, properly speaking, a long and a short open E and a long and a short close E. It is true that difference in quantity and in quality often go together; thus Latin ĕ was, like our ĕ, open E, Latin ē was close E, though the long sound of open E was also known in Latin, and was written *ae* (§ 6). The Romance languages, which have lost all other distinction of the Latin long and short vowels, distinguish them according to quality (e.g. Lat. *bĕllus* is Ital. bello with open E, Lat. *stēlla* is Ital. stella with close E), though this distinction of quality does not always correspond to distinction of quantity (e.g. the ĭ of Lat. *video* and the ē of Lat. *credo* are similarly represented in Fr. vois, crois) (§ 6). Consonants, too, may differ in their quantity like vowels. For example, English final consonants are long after short, short after long vowels, e.g. 'hill,' 'heel.'

We may distinguish at least three degrees of quantity or length,—long, short, and half-long,—an example of the last being the vowel of our 'note,' while 'node' and German 'Noth' have a long vowel. Latin half-longs may be detected by the metrical scansion of a syllable as either long or short, e.g. in Plautus' time the final syllables of *ămat, tĕnet, ăbit, dŏlor* (ch. iii. § 40)[1].

The marked distinction between a long and a short vowel in Latin made it possible for the Romans to imitate the quantitative metre of the Greeks. Their own native metre, the Saturnian, which is represented in literature by the 'Odyssea' of Livius Andronicus and the 'Bellum Poenicum' of Naevius, but which was banished from the domain of poetry by Ennius, was,

---

[1] A poetical scansion may of course be traditional. Thus Martial (iii. 95. 1) has *havē*, although Quintilian (i. 6. 21) tells us that in the ordinary pronunciation of his time the final vowel was short. Nor is variation in the scansion of proper names proof of half-long quantity; it is rather to be referred to ignorance or carelessness. The first syllable of *Fīdenae*, for example, was certainly long, the vowel being written with *ei*, or with the tall form of *i* (to indicate the long sound) on inscriptions, and being usually so scanned by poets; but Virgil (*A*. vi. 773) has urbemque Fīdenam. Scansions like *Ītalia* (an imitation of a Greek prosodical usage) are mere metrical licences, and prove nothing about actual pronunciation ('Italiam'... extra carmen non deprendas. Quint. i. 5. 18).

like the metre of the Teutonic and other I.-Eur. stocks, accentual, not quantitative[1]. But the Romance languages do not possess this distinction. We are in the habit of calling an accented vowel, such as the second vowel of the Italian word 'Toscana,' long; but in reality it is pronounced with no more length than the unaccented vowels of the same word. One of the chief differences of such a language as Italian from Teutonic languages is the equal length which it assigns to each vowel, even a final unaccented vowel. Contrast, for instance, the final *e* of Ital. notte with that of Germ. Gabe, or the final *i* of Tivoli in the Italian and in the usual English pronunciation of the word. Almost the only really long syllables in Italian are syllables long 'by position,' e.g. the first syllables of 'tanto,' 'tempo,' which, as we shall see (ch. iii. § 4), have in fact a circumflex accentuation, 'tânto,' 'têmpo.' Similarly the Spanish accent does not impair the quantity as the English accent does; and in French the usual quantity of every vowel is the half-long, e.g. jeune. (See Storm on Romance Quantity in the *Phonet. Stud.* 1888.) All this points to a period of 'Vulgar Latin' when all vowels were equally short or half-long, and when the only predominance of one vowel over another would be that conferred by the stress of accentuation. And we detect traces of this process of 'levelling' in the evident uncertainty of the grammarians of the fourth and fifth centuries A.D. about the quantities of words for which they have not one of the classical poets to appeal to [2], and above all in the errors in scansion of those

---

[1] The Saturnian line had three accents (main or secondary, ch. iii. § 7) in the first hemistich (one always on the first syllable of the line), and two in the second, and like Romance poetry reckoned (with permissible variations) a definite number of syllables to the line, seven to the first hemistich, six to the second. Its two chief types were:

A-type—

x́x(,) x́x, x́x́x ‖ x́xx, x́x́x
dábunt málum Metélli Naéuio poétae,

B-type (less usual)—

x́x(,) x́x, x́xx ‖ x́xxx, x́x
prím(a) incédit Céreris Prosérpina púer,

a variety of the second hemistich of the A-type being ‖ xxx́x, x́x adlocútus súmmi, and of the B-type ‖ xx́x, x́x fuísse uírum. (See *Amer. Journ. Phil.* vol. xiv.)

[2] The passages quoted from the grammarians by Seelmann, p. 75, are not conclusive; e.g. Ter. Scaurus' distinction of *facilis* Sg. from *facileis* Pl. is a matter of orthography, not of pronunciation, and is suggested by Lucilius' proposed distinction of the symbols *i* and *ei* (see ch. i. § 9).

§ 142.]   PRONUNCIATION. VOWEL-QUANTITY.   129

Christian poets who imitate the quantitative verse of the Augustan poets. Grammarians often censure mispronunciations due to the overmastering of quantity by accent, e.g. *Cēres* (Mar. Sacerd. 451. 13 K.), *pīcĕs* (Consent. 392. 18 K.), *pīper* and *ŏrator* (*ib.* 392. 3, 11 quod vitium Afrorum speciale est); they frequently caution against the confusion of *equus* (with accented short open *e*) and *aequus* (with accented long open *e*) (Pompeius, 285. 8 K., &c.). Cf. the haphazard use of the apex and tall I on late inscriptions (ch. i. § 1). For a discussion of the influence of accentuation on the quantity of the Latin vowels (e.g. late Lat. *ĭdŏlum* for εἴδωλον), see ch. iii. § 1; for variations like *păciscor* and *pācem*, (I.-Eur. *păk-* and *pāk-*), see ch. iv. § 51.

§ 142. 'Position.' In Latin poetry a syllable is scanned long, even though it have a short vowel, if the vowel precedes any consonant-group requiring a certain period of time for pronunciation. A long syllable of this kind is said to be long by 'position' (*positio*, e.g. Quint. ix. 4. 86; i. 5. 28); and the way in which a Roman apprehended this length by 'position' may be seen from a passage of a fifth cent. grammarian (Pompeius, 112. 26 K.): ut puta si dicas ' et,' unum semis habet. e vocalis est brevis, unum habet tempus. t consonans est, et omnis consonans dimidium habet tempus: ecce ' et ' unum semis habet tempus. adhuc non est nec longa nec brevis; plus tamen habet a brevi, minus quidem habet a longa. adde ad ' et ' s, etiam fit longa. quare? e brevis unum tempus habet, t dimidium tempus habet, s dimidium tempus habet : ecce duo tempora sunt, fecerunt duo tempora longam syllabam. With a naturally long vowel there would be really extra-length, but there is no account taken in Roman poetry of the different length of, say, the second syllables of *calesco* (with *ē*) and *modestus* (with *ĕ*), both being treated as long syllables. Plautus, however, seems not to shorten by the Brevis Brevians Law (ch. iii. § 42) a syllable with naturally long vowel, scanning *quĭs ĭncēdit?* but not *quĭs ĭnsĭstit? quĭs ĭnfērtur?* (before *s-*, *f-* the vowel of *in* was long, § 144).

Consonant groups which admitted of more rapid pronunciation were not necessarily scanned long, viz. groups composed of a mute and a liquid (*r, l*). Thus in Virgil *agrum* (with *ă*) may

K

be scanned with the first syllable long or short as the poet chooses. Plautus and the older dramatists, who follow more the actual pronunciation of everyday life, never scan such a syllable long, though in other than dramatic poetry this scansion is found; e.g. Ennius in his epic has *nigrum* (*Ann.* 187 M.), *sacruficare* (*ib.* 233), &c., with first syllable long, whence we may infer that in rapid unconventional utterance such a syllable was short, but in measured ceremonious speech the longer dwelling of the voice on the mute and liquid justified a long scansion. That such a syllable differed from an ordinary short syllable is seen in the avoidance by the dramatists of the shortening of a vowel after a mute and a liquid by the Brevis Brevians Law; e.g. Plautus scans *ăbĭ* readily, but avoids a scansion like *ăgrĭ*. The same pronunciation of a mute with *r* seems to have prevailed in Imperial times, to judge by Servius' note on Virg. *A.* i. 384 Libyae deserta peragro] 'per' habet accentum; nam 'a' longa quidem est, sed non solida positione; muta enim et liquida quotiens ponuntur, metrum juvant, non accentum (cf. Quint. i. 5. 28; ix. 4. 86), but not of a mute with *l* in the word *maniplis*, according to the same authority (Serv. ad *A.* xi. 463 in hoc sermone, ut secunda a fine habeat accentum usus obtinuit). The establishment of the pronunciation *maníplus* with long second syllable (but short *ĭ*) has been plausibly referred to the longer form *manípulus* (on the presence and absence of the parasitic or svarabhaktic vowel in Latin between a mute and *l*, see § 102); but it may be objected that Plautus scans *poplus* with first syllable short, as well as trisyllabic *pŏpulus*; and makes the suffix *tlo-* (ch. v. § 25) one syllable, with preceding vowel scanned short, in *vĕhĭclum*, though (normally) two syllables in *cŭbĭcŭlum*. In the Romance languages the accent has been shifted to all penultimate vowels followed by a mute with *r*, e.g. Ital. allegro (with accent on second syllable) from Lat. *álacris* (Vulg. Lat. **alecro-*) (see ch. iii. § 11), which shows that in Vulgar Latin the combination of a mute with *r* came universally to constitute length by position. This, too, has been explained by the supposition of a parasitic vowel, **alécᵉro-*, like the occasional spelling *arbiterium* (in poetry, however, *arbitrium* is invariably scanned with short second syllable), but may also be referred to the practice which we see most clearly in Italian of lengthening a mute before *r*, e.g. fabbro (Lat. *făbro-*), febbre (Lat. *fĕbris*), and Ital. occhio from Lat. *ŏculus* (Vulg. Lat. *oclus*, **occlus*?), suggests a similar account of the Imperial Latin pronunciation of *maniplus*. We see the same doubling in English 'fodder' (from 'food'), 'bitter' (from 'bite'), 'apple.' Gröber ascribes this consonant lengthening (*Comm. Woelffl.* p. 171) to what is called the 'legato,' as opposed to the 'staccato' pronunciation; that is to say, *fabro- was pronounced with linking of the two syllables fa- and bro-, not with that marked break of one syllable from another that we see in Ital. be-ne (§ 139). The same 'legato' pronunciation of the two syllables of a word like *factum, omnis* (but cf. § 139), he makes the scientific explanation of the scansion of the first syllable as long (similarly with *fac tumulum*, &c.), and by the tendency to attach an *s* in a group like *st, sc, sp* to the preceding syllable (seen in misspellings like *disscente*, § 130), he explains the scansion *esto, nescio*, &c., with first syllable long. On the other hand, when a word ended in a vowel and the next began with *st, sc, sp*, the 'legato' pronunciation did not equally assert itself, so that Lucretius allows a scansion like *liberă sponte* (v. 79) and the like, though Virgil does not[1]. The Italian pronunciation of festa, pescare, aspro, &c., lengthens the *s*, similarly the *l* in alto, the *r* in morte, the *n* in mondo, the *m* in campo, and so on.

In early Latin poetry final *-s* as a rule does not before an initial consonant constitute length by position, a fact due to the weak pronunciation of *-s* at that period (§ 126). Similarly initial *h-*, both in early and classical poetry, has not the weight of an ordinary consonant. But final *-m* always has this weight (§ 65).

§ 143. **Shortening of long vowel before another vowel.** In the word *pius* the *i* was originally long (cf. Osc. Piíhioí 'Pio' Dat. Sg.), and the scansion *pīa* (MSS. *diu, dia*) has been ascribed to Ennius in his Epic (ap. Cic. *Rep.* i. 41. 64:

    pectora pia tenet desiderium, simul inter
    sese sic memorant: O Romule, Romule die),

---

[1] In *A.* xi. 308—
    spem siquam adscitis Aetolum
    habuistis in armis
ponite. spes sibi quisque, &c.,
a pause in the sentence intervenes
between the two words.

though Plautus in his homelier dramatic poetry recognizes only *pĭus*. The shortening of the *i* is due to the difficulty found by the Romans in maintaining the long quantity of a vowel before another vowel. The same is true of diphthongs; we find, for instance, the compound of *prae* and **hendo* assuming the form *prĕ-hendo* (and even *prendo*, § 58). The amount of length assigned to a long vowel or diphthong in such a position would differ at different periods, and even in the pronunciation of the same period. Plautus is no doubt using the colloquial pronunciation of his own day when he scans *Chĭus* (Adj.) (*Poen.* 699; *Curc.* 78); whereas *unĭus* was not in vogue at Quintilian's time (extra carmen non deprendas, sed nec in carmine vitia ducenda sunt, Quint. i. 5. 18), and Servius (ad Virg. *A.* i. 451) says that *audĭit*, and not *audīit*, *lenĭit* and not *lenīit*, was the ordinary pronunciation, the forms with the short penult being a usage of poetry. Here the retention of long *i* in Servius' pronunciation may be ascribed to the presence of the forms with *v*, *audīvit*, *lenīvit*, and similarly we find in Ter. *Phorm.* 573 *audīeras*. The *fūi* of Ennius, e.g. *Ann.* 431 M.:

nos sumus Romani qui fuimus ante Rudini,

is sometimes used (especially at the end of a line, i.e. through metrical necessity) by Plautus, who makes similar use of *fīeri*, *fīerem*. (On Ennius' *adnŭit* Perf. &c. see ch. viii. § 50; we have FVVEIT, *C.I.L.* i. 1051.)

The same shortening must have appeared in the pronunciation of the sentence, when a word ending in a long vowel or diphthong preceded a word beginning with a vowel, so that the 'prosodical hiatus' of Latin poetry, e.g. Plaut. tŭ amas, Enn. Scipiŏ inuicte (cf. Ennĭ imaginis), Virg. quĭ amant, &c, was a native Latin usage and not an imitation of Greek versification[1]. Final long vowels would, therefore, have a short variety or 'doublet,' which occurred as often as a vowel-initial followed, and this fact, coupled with the tendency of the accent to weaken a long final, especially in iambic words (ch. iii. § 40), explains the early shortening of final *ā*, e.g. *terră*, and the later shortening of final -*ō*, e.g. *ponŏ* in Imperial Latin (ch. iii. § 45).

---

[1] It seems to be the rule in Saturnian metre (*Amer. Journ. Phil.* xiv. 310).

§ 144.]   PRONUNCIATION. VOWEL-QUANTITY.   133

On inscriptions we not unfrequently find a short *i* before another vowel in the middle of a word written with the tall form of the letter, the usual sign of *ī* (ch. i. § 1), e.g. dIe, with prIvsqvam (*C. I. L.* vi. 10239); and in the Romance languages the *i* of *dies* is represented by the usual representative of Latin *ī*, e.g. Ital. di, Prov. dia, Fr. di, Span. dia. This at first sight seems to be in direct opposition to the usual law of shortening a long vowel before another vowel. But it is unlikely that a short vowel was lengthened in this position; all that the Romance forms and the spelling with tall *I* need imply is that the *i* had the quality (not necessarily the quantity) of long *ī*, in other words, had the close and not the open sound (§ 14). This is certainly the explanation of Romance *pio, with close *i* (Ital. pio, &c.), and of the pIvs of inscriptions, e.g. *C. I. L.* vi. 1058, for we have seen reason to believe that a long *ī* shortened in Latin retained the quality of long *i*, *audĭt*, &c., of the classical and later period being pronounced with the close, not the open *i*-sound (§ 14). But the *i* of *dies* must have been originally short (ch. iv. § 63). (The examples from Romance are discussed in *K. Z.* xxx. 337; additional examples of tall I in *dies*, *pius* on inscriptions are given in Christiansen, *De apicibus et I longis*, p. 32.) (Cf. the sound of Engl. ' the ' before a vowel.)

§ 144. **Change in quantity of vowel before certain consonant-groups.** The quantity of a vowel which stands before a group of consonants or a double consonant in Latin is not so easily determined as the quantity of a vowel followed by a single consonant. In a word like *inēlūctăbĭlĕ* the scansion of the word by the Latin poets will fix the quantity of the vowel of every syllable except the third. The *u* of the third syllable is long by ' position,' as it is called, because it stands before the consonants *ct*, but we cannot tell from a line like—

venit summa dies et ineluctabile tempus,

whether it is also long by nature or not. To ascertain the natural quantity of these vowels which are long by position [1], we can refer to two main sources of information; first, the

---

[1] For a list of them, see Marx, *Hülfsbüchlein*[2], Berlin, 1889 (a book to be used with caution).

inscriptions which denote a long *a, e, o, u* by an apex, a mark like the symbol of the acute accent (and from c. 130 B.C. by doubling the vowel), a long *i* by the tall form of that letter; second, the Romance languages which, as we have seen, distinguish a long from a short *e, i, o, u*, when, as seems usually to have been the case, the long and the short vowel differed in Vulgar Latin in quality as well as in quantity. Neither of these sources are wholly satisfactory. The apex and tall *i* seem to be often used at haphazard, especially on inscriptions later than 150 A.D., and the latter has other uses than to express long *ī*, such as for initial *i*, consonantal *i* (our *y*), and so on [1]. The Romance languages, and the Teutonic and Celtic loanwords, often indicate a quantity different from that which can be inferred for a word in Classical Latin, a very natural thing if we consider how much the pronunciation of a vowel is liable to be influenced by the consonant-group next which it stands, and by the analogy of other words of a similar form. Some help is occasionally afforded by the statements of grammarians on the quantity of this or that vowel, though even they sometimes show by their hesitation that the pronunciation of such vowels was in their time not always definitely established. Aulus Gellius (second cent. A.D.), for example, discusses the proper quantity of *e* in *quiesco* (vii. 15), and decides for *ē* on the analogy of *calēsco, nitēsco, stupēsco* and other Inceptives, as well as of the noun *quiēs* (cf. *quiēsco C. I. L.* vi. 25531), though he adds that a friend of his, an educated man, invariably pronounced the word with short *e, quiĕsco*. In another passage (ix. 6) he recommends the pronunciation *āctito*, against a common pronunciation of his time, *ăctito*, which was defended by the analogy of the short vowel of the simple verb *ăgo*. The grammarians of a later date, when the distinction between long and short quantity was beginning to disappear, are still more at a loss about those quantities for which they have not the authority of the classical poets to fall back upon. It is difficult to believe Priscian (ix. 28) (sixth cent.) when he posits a naturally long penult for all perfects with *e*,

---

[1] See Christiansen, *De apicibus et I longis inscriptionum latinarum*, 1889 (a Kiel dissertation).

e.g. *illēxi*, and for no others, e.g. *dŭxi*, nor yet when he makes the *a* of *mansi* long by position only (ix. 27). Greek transcriptions, too, are often dangerous guides; for the quality of Greek ε and η, ο and ω, differed, as we have seen (§ 32, § 21), from that of Latin *ĕ*, *ē*, *ŏ*, *ō*, the Greek short vowels being, at least in the Attic period, close and the long vowels open, while the Latin short vowels had the open, the long the close sound. Greek ου is no indication of the long *ū* of Latin, but merely of the *u*-sound of Latin *ŭ*, as opposed to the *ü*-sound of Greek *v*. Greek ει, however, almost always indicates Latin *ī* (see Eckinger).

Etymology indeed will often help us. Thus we can infer a long vowel in the first syllable of *luctus*, grief (the *u* is marked long on inscriptions), from the analogy of *lūgeo*; though we should never have guessed that *hēsternus*, unlike *hĕri*, had a long vowel, if we had not been informed of the fact by a Latin grammarian (Mar. Victorin. vi. 15. 15 K. 'hesternum' producte dici debet: nemo enim est, qui latine modo sciat loqui, qui aliter quam producta syllaba 'hesternum' dixerit). The metrical treatment of words by the early dramatists may also be appealed to, if it be granted that a vowel long by nature is seldom or never shortened by the influence of a preceding short syllable, in words like *vŏlŭptátem*, or phrases like *quĭd ĭgnóras* (see ch. iii. § 34). With all these aids it is possible to gain a good deal of information about the quantity of vowels long by 'position' in Latin, quite enough to prove the irrationableness of our usual method of pronunciation which ignores all distinction of quantity in their case [1], though hardly enough to settle satisfactorily the question with which this paragraph proposes to deal, namely the extent to which the influence of one consonant-group tended to shorten a vowel naturally long, of another to lengthen a vowel naturally short. To ascertain the limits of our knowledge and of our ignorance on this subject it will be necessary to make a more minute examination of the several words involved than is generally wanted.

---

[1] Our ordinary pronunciation of Latin makes no distinction, for example, between *illĕx*, 'alluring,' and *illēx*, 'lawless.' We pronounce both 'illĕx'!

In one case at least we seem to have safe ground under our feet. Cicero (*Orator*, xlviii. § 159), tells us that *in-* and *con-* lengthened their vowel when compounded with a word beginning with *s* or *f*: quid vero hoc elegantius, quod non fit natura sed quodam instituto, 'indoctus' dicimus brevi prima littera, 'insanus' producta, 'inhumanus' brevi, 'infelix' longa. et, ne multis, quibus in verbis eae primae litterae sunt, quae in 'sapiente' atque 'felice,' producte dicitur, in ceteris omnibus breviter. itemque 'cŏmposuit' 'cōnsuevit' 'cŏncrepuit' 'cōnfecit': consule veritatem, reprehendet; refer ad aures, probabunt. That this rule should be extended to all vowels before *ns*, (*nf*), we see from such statements of grammarians as that Present Participles in *-ens*, *-ans* had in the Nominative a long vowel (Probus iv. 245. 13 K.; Pompeius, v. 113. 23 K.), while the original shortness of this *e* is indicated by the Romance languages for the other cases (e.g. Ital. -ente with open *e* in the penult); that *e* was long in the termination of Numeral Adverbs in *-iens*, *-ies* (Probus iv. 247. 9. K.) (cf. O. Ind. kíyănt, &c.), and in the Nominative Singular of *dēns, gēns, mēns*, &c., (Bede vii. 230. 15 K.), while *ĕ* in the other cases of these nouns is indicated by the Romance forms (e.g. Ital. dente, gente, with open *e*, Span. diente, miente). Probus, however, seems to inculcate *insŏns, insŏntis* as opposed to *fōns, fōntis* (iv. 6. 12 and 28. 26 K.: cf. Prisc. vii. 39). Inscriptions, too, show the apex in words like CLÉMÉNS (*C. I. L.* ii. 4550), PRÓCÉDÉNS (vi. 1527 *d* 28), and a host of other examples with *ns* (see a list of them in Christiansen, *De apicibus*, &c. p. 41); while Greek inscriptions have -ηνς, e.g. Προυδηνς (Eckinger, p. 115). Finally Romance forms like Ital. teso (with close *e*) from Latin *tĕ(n)sus*, the participle of tendo (with open *e*) from Latin *tĕndo*, not only indicate a long vowel before *ns* in Latin, but also seem to show that this long *e* had the same quality as the usual Latin *ē* (close *e*), and was not a mere protraction of the open *e*-sound of short *e*[1]. Quintilian

---

[1] The spellings *t(h)ensaurus* for θησαυρός, *Scaptensula* for Σκαπτὴ ὕλη or Σκαπτησύλη, *Chersonensus* for Χερσόνησος (see Georges) do not then offer *-ens-* as the equivalent of Gk. -ησ- (with long open E, § 41), but are to be compared with the misspelling censured in Probi App. 198. 21 K., *occansio* for *occasio* (see § 66). Long open E was written *ae* (§ 41).

§ 144.] PRONUNCIATION. VOWEL-QUANTITY. 137

(i. 7. 29) tells us that in the word *consules* the nasal was not sounded, a fact possibly expressed by the usual abbreviation of the word on inscriptions, cós. The dropping of the nasal is also indicated by spellings like *novies* beside *noviens*, and by the Romance forms, e.g. Ital. teso (Lat. *tē(n)sus*), and Celtic and Teutonic loanwords, e.g. Welsh dwys (Lat. *dē(n)sus*), O.H.G. îsila (Lat. *ī(n)sula*, cf. Diom. i. 409. 3 K.; Serv. *in Don*. iv. 442. 30 K.) (cf. IFEROS, *C.I.L.* vi. 19873).

The grammarians who repeat the rule of Cicero with regard to *in-* and *con-* (Gellius, ii. 17; Probus, iv. 149. 33 K. and 253. 22; Diomedes, i. 433. 15 K.; Serv. ad *Aen*. i. 187; Max. Vict. vi. 204. 16 K.; Audacis exc. vii. 354. 21 K.), often add the remark that the rule was not strictly followed in the pronunciation of their time. Thus Diomedes (i. 409. 3 K.) says of *in-* and *con-* before *s, f,* 'plerumque producuntur' (cf. Cledonius, v. 76. 9 K.); and Servius (*in Don*. iv. 442. 28 K.) intimates that the rule was often violated in practice, plerumque enim non observantes in barbarismos incurrimus. This probably indicates a tendency of later Latin to give *in-* and *con-* in these compounds the same short vowel-sound that they had in other compounds like *ĭncedo, cŏncedo,* and in the simple forms *ĭn, cŭm*; and this will explain why it is, that on all but the earliest inscriptions of the Empire, the instances of apexed vowels before *ns* are not so frequent in these compounds, as in other words (see the lists given by Christiansen), and also why, both on inscriptions and in Romance forms, instances of a long vowel before *nf* are rare[1]. For the combination *nf* hardly occurs except in the case of verbs beginning with *f* compounded with *in-* and *con-*. The word *consul* was perhaps not regarded as a compound; for the *o* is marked with the apex on inscriptions with great persistency. In Welsh, too, the Old Welsh form cusil points to a Latin *cō(n)silium* (cf. Diom. i. 409. 3 K.: Serv. *in Don*. iv. 442. 30 K.). But, for compounds, which were realized in popular usage to be compounds, the pronunciation of Cicero's time must have gone

---

[1] The tall *I* of INFERI (*C.I.L.* vi. 7579), quoted by Christiansen and Seelmann, is no certain indication of long *i*. Every initial *i* of this inscription has the tall form, e.g. ITA, IMPETRA. It is always difficult to be sure whether INS-, INF- on inscriptions indicate long *i*, or merely initial *i*.

more and more out of fashion under the Empire. Its prevalence in the time of Plautus may be inferred from the fact that Plautus is averse to *ins-*, *inf-* being shortened by the influence of a preceding short syllable (see § 142). In Umbro-Oscan we see lengthening of a vowel before *ns*, *nf* in Osc. keenzstur, 'censor,' (with long open E, § 6), Umbr. aanfehtaf, 'infectas.'

The remark of Priscian (ii. 63), that the terminations *-gnus*, *-gna*, *-gnum* are always preceded by a long vowel, has been extended by Marx and others into a rule that the combination *-gn-* always lengthened a preceding vowel. Of Priscian's examples (*rēgnum, stāgnum, benīgnus, malīgnus, abiēgnus, privīgnus, Paelīgnus*), *abiēgnus, rēgnum, stāgnum* had probably originally a long vowel (cf. *abiēs, rēgem, stāre*); *privīgnus* gets a certain amount of confirmation from the spelling PRĪVĪGNO on a soldier's epitaph (*C. I. L.* vi. 3541); but *benīgnus, malīgnus* receive none from Romance forms like Ital. benigno, maligno, which are probably 'bookwords,' acquired by recent borrowing from Latin, not naturally transmitted by continuous usage from Roman times.

The Romance forms (e.g. Ital. degno, Span. des-den, 'disdain'; possibly 'bookwords,' *A. L. L.* viii. 324), point to Vulg. Lat. *dĭgnus*; but the word has the tall *I* in *C.I.L.* vi. 6314 DIGNE, and elsewhere. They point also to *sĭgnum* (cf. *sĭgillum*), (Ital. segno, Span. seña, &c.); but on inscriptions we have sIGNUM (*C. I. L.* vi. 10234, a carefully written inscription of 153 A. D., and elsewhere), sIGNIFICABO (vi. 16664). The grammarian Diomedes (fourth cent.), speaking of the rhythmic arrangement of some of Cicero's clauses (i. 470. 9 K.), seems to speak of *dignitas* as an anapaest, just as he calls *jŭstam* a trochee; and if this be the right construction of his words, it suggests that he pronounced *dĭgnĭtās*. Welsh swyn, a charm, Old Irish sén, blessing, sénaim, to bless, to sain, Old High German sëgan, charm against evil, blessing, are all from a late Latin *signum* in its Christian sense of 'the sign of the cross'; and their form indicates a form *segnum*, with close *e*, a development of an earlier *sĭgnum*, not *sīgnum* (cf. § 14). The Romance forms indicate, too, a short vowel in *lignum, pignus, pugnus*, and show us that if the lengthening of a vowel before *gn* was a tendency of Latin pronunciation at all, it was not one so marked, and so persistent, as the lengthening before *ns*. [For further discussion of this question, see *Bezz. Beitr.* xvi. 189 sqq.; *Mém. Soc. Ling.* vi. 34 note; *K. Z.* xxx. 337, where it is suggested that the change in the vowel was one of quantity merely, not of quality, so that *dignus, signum,* would have the long open *i*-sound. Before *gn*, by a phonetic law of Latin, *ĕ* became *i* (ch. iv. § 8)]. The spelling PĪGMEN(tum) on an African inscription (*C. I. L.* viii. 1344) is not evidence enough for a lengthening of the vowel before *gm*; nor is the exact relation clear between *subtegmen* and *subtēmen, exagmen* (?) and *exāmen* (*Class. Rev.* vol. v. p. 294 : *Etym. Lat.* p. 126) (see ch. iv. § 116).

In the Perfect Participle Passive and kindred formations of verbs whose Present ends in *-go*, preceded by a short syllable, e.g. *lĕgo, ăgo,* we find a long vowel. Thus *lēctor, lēctum, āctum, līctor* (from a third-conjugation form **ligere?*) are attested by Aul. Gellius (xii. 3 and ix. 6), *lēcto* by Porphyrio (ad Hor. *S.* i. 6. 122), while on inscriptions we have *lēctor* (*C. I. L.* vi. 9447, the epitaph of a grammaticus, and so presumably correct in spelling ; vi. 27140), *adlēctō*, xiv. 376 (second cent. A.D.), &c., *āctīs* (vi. 1527 *d* 59, B.C. 8–2), &c., *infrāctā* (ix. 60, c. 100 A.D.) (while *ă* for *frango* is proved by *effringo, confringo* (*ĭ* from *ĕ*)), *rēcte*[1] (xii. 2494, beginning of first cent. A.D.), *tēctor* (vi. 5205), and the like (see Christiansen, p. 47, and cf. λητκτος, προτηκτο[ρος] on Gk. inscrr., *K. Z.* xxxiii. 402.). The long vowel is also found in the Perfect (properly S.-Aorist, see ch. viii. § 39) of these verbs, *rēxi, tēxi* (Prisc. ix. 28, who adds *illēxi*[2]), *rēxit* (*C. I. L.* v. 875, 105 A.D.), *tēxit* (x. 1793) (see Christiansen, p. 49). Whether it is due to the consonant-groups *g* and *t*, *g* and *s*, or is a lengthening peculiar to the Perfect and kindred forms of the verb (see ch. viii. § 39), it is difficult to say, but the latter supposition is certainly the more probable. The single instance on inscriptions of a form that is not Verbal, viz. *māx(imo)* (vi. 2080, the Acts of the Arval Brotherhood, c. 120 A.D.) is not sufficient

---

[1] So that there was complete assonance between *rēx* and *rēctē* in the children's verse :

réx eris, si récte facies ; sí non facies, nón eris,

alluded to by Hor. (*Epp.* i. 1. 59) rex eris aiunt Si recte facies.

[2] Plautus puns on *illectus*, the Verbal Noun from *illicio*, and *lectus* (from *lego*), a bed, *Bacch.* 55.

evidence for the former. Diomedes (431. 17 K.) says the *i* of *nix* is short. A similar difficulty presents itself in connexion with the parallel formations from Verbs ending in -*ngo*. Gellius (ix. 6) attests *ūnctus* beside *ŭngo*; and on inscriptions we have *sejūnctum* (*C. I. L.* vi. 1527 *e* 38, B.C. 8–2), &c., *dēfūnctis* (v. 1326), &c., *conjūnxit* (xii. 4333, time of Antonines), *extīnctos* (vi. 25617, A.D. 10), *cīnctus* (x. 4104) (see Christiansen, pp. 44 sqq.). Here the spelling *sānctus* (cf. Osc. saahtúm, Umbr. sahata), frequent on inscriptions, seems to show that the lengthening occurs before original *nc* (*sacer* [1]), as well as before *nc* from original *ng*; but the few instances of non-verbal forms, viz. *conjūnx* (vi. 6592, 6593), the numeral *quīnctus*, frequent on inscriptions (Christiansen, p. 46) (cf. *quīnque, quīni*), are again insufficient evidence to separate the lengthening from the ordinary lengthening of the Latin Perfect. The absence of the nasal in *nactus* (beside *nanctus*), *fictus* (but *finctus* Ter. *Eun.* 104), plebeian *defuctus* (ii. 4173), and *sactissimae* (vi. 15511; v. 6580) (cf. Welsh saith beside sant, § 70), is explained in ch. viii. § 10. In *quīntus* it is the guttural that disappears. All the Romance forms point to *quīntus* (cf. Greek Κονεωτος and Κοεωτος, though the earliest forms are Κοιγκτιος and Κοιντος: see Eckinger, pp. 122 sqq.), but declare for the short vowel in *pŭnctus, ŭnctus, cĭnctus, tĭnctus, cĭnxi, fĭnxi*.

In the absence of express testimony, such as we have for *ns*, *nf*, it is impossible to be sure that the combination of *g* with a consonant, like *n, m, t, s*, whether preceded or not by a nasal, had a lengthening effect on a preceding vowel; though there certainly are a good many apparent indications of this. It is equally impossible to decide whether the supposed influence exerted on the vowel may have been a change of quality merely, and not of quantity, just as the combination *ngu* had the effect of changing an *o* to a *u*, e.g. *unguis* for *onguis (ch. iv. § 20).

145. r with consonant. Spellings on inscriptions like *Fŏrtun(a)*, *Fŏrtunata* (*C. I. L.* vi. 7527) (cf. *Fotunate* vi. 2236) suggest that the *o*, which was certainly originally short (Lat. *ŏr* for I.-Eur. *r̥*, see ch. iv. § 92), has been lengthened by the influence of the following *rt*. If this be so, it could only have been a local pronunciation, or at least one that never gained a secure footing in the

---

[1] A fresh complication arises from the fact that beside *săcro-*, we have a stem *săcri-* (*săcres*, Plautus), pointing to a root *săc-* beside *săc-*.

§§ 145–147.]   PRONUNCIATION.   VOWEL-QUANTITY.   141

language; for the Romance languages testify abundantly to short vowels in words like *porcus*, *cornu*, *certus*, &c. Marius Sacerdos (vi. 451. 5 K.) quotes *pērnix* as a barbarism; and Pompeius (v. 126. 5) censures the mispronunciation *ărma*. So that the initial *o* of *ŏrno*, if long, as attested by inscriptions, [e.g. *ōrnav(it)* *C.I.L.* x. 6104 (time of Augustus), *ōrnare* xii. 4333 (time of Antonines; (for other instances on inscriptions, see Christiansen, p. 53], and by Celtic loanwords (e.g. Welsh addurn, 'ornament,' addurno, 'to ornament,' Lat. *adōrno*) must have been originally long and cannot owe its length to the influence of the following *rn*. (Similarly *fŏrma*, *ŏrdo*, *ŏrca*.) But it is more likely that the *o* was not really long, but merely had the quality of long Latin *ō*, in other words was close *o*. Plautus seems to scan *ŏrn-* after a short syllable; though the instances are so few as to leave a slight doubt (*Trin.* 840 might possibly be *novo cum ōrnatu*, *Aul.* 721 *eo ōrnatus*). There are not wanting indications that *r* with a nasal tended to modify the quality of a vowel, e.g. *fornus* and *furnus*, *formica* and *furmica*, *turnus* (Greek τόρνος), just as in Italian to-day (though not in the Toscana) close *e* becomes open before *r* with a consonant, e.g. verde, erpice (Meyer-Lübke, *Ital. Gram.* § 54). How far this may explain the discrepancy between the *fĭrmus* of inscriptions (Christiansen, p. 53), and the Vulg. Lat. *fĭrmus*, postulated by Romance forms like Ital. fermo, and the Welsh loanword fferf, it is difficult to say. Arvum with short *a* expressly attested by Audacis exc. p. 328. 8 K., originally the neuter of the adjective *ărvus*, e.g. Plaut. *Truc.* 149 non aruos hic sed pascuos ager est, appears with long *a* in an inscription of Tiberius' time (*ārvāli*, *C.I.L.* vi. 913). (For other cases of long vowel before *r* with consonant on inscriptions, see Christiansen, pp. 51 sqq.) [*Ārma*, attested by Serv. *in Don.* 426. 11 and 36 K. Prisc. *Acc.* 521. 15, Audacis exc. 328. 6, is proved by *inermis*, for *ā* is not weakened to *e* (ch. iii.); *ărx* Pomp. 130. 7 is proved by *coerceo*.]

§ 146. s with consonant. The short vowel before *sp*, *sc*, *st*, &c., attested by the Romance languages for words like *vĕsper*, *pĭscis*, *crĭsta*, is quite strong enough evidence to disprove the theory that an originally short vowel was lengthened before these combinations, and to show that the long vowel indicated by inscriptions for *pāstor*, *prīscus*, *trīstis*, *jūstus*, &c. (see Christiansen, pp. 54 sqq.) must have been originally long. Diomedes (p. 431, 31; 432, 16.) attests *fenĕstra*, *ăsper*; Quintilian (ix. 4. 85) *agrĕstis*, Audax (359. 15 K.) *campĕstris*, &c. *Hĕsternus* (Mar. Victorin. vi. 15. 15 K.) beside *hĕri* is puzzling; also the discrepancy between *crŭstum* of *C.I.L.* i. 1199 and Vulg. Lat. *crŭsta* indicated by the Romance forms, e.g. Ital. crosta. Festus (86. 8 Th.) distinguishes *lŭstra*, wallowing-places, from *lūstra*, purifications.

§ 147. n with single consonant. *Vēndo* (Ital. vendo with close *e*), *fŏntem* (Probus 6. 12 K.; but Romance **fŏnt-* by analogy of other *nt*-stems), *prĭnceps* (Ital. principe, &c.) are enough to disprove the theory that this combination shortened a preceding long vowel. There are, however, points of difficulty. Servius (*in Don.* 426. 34 K.) attests *prīnceps*; Diomedes 433. 18 *cŏntio* (by anal. of *cŏm-*?) (for *coventio*, and so originally *cōntio*, or perhaps **cŭntio*; French nonce, annoncer points to a Latin form *nŭntius* (for *noventius*, and so originally *nūntius*, Mar. Victorin. vi. 12. 18 K.); Romance words for 'eleven,' like Span. once, Fr. onze, point to a Vulg. Lat. *ŭndecim* (properly *ūndecim*, from *ūnus* and *decem*) (*sinciput* is usually explained as **sĕm(i)-caput*). There are some indications that the quality of a vowel was liable to change before this combination. Thus -*ond*- appears as -*und*- in *frundes*, a form ascribed to Ennius (see *K. Z.*

xxx. 336); *unguis* seems to be for *onguis (ch. iv. § 20). The remark of a late grammarian (Anon. Bern. *Suppl.* 111 H.), that *hirundo, arundo* have *ŭ*, is a mistake based on a misunderstanding of Priscian i. p. 123. 7 H.

§ 148. l with consonant. Vulg. Lat. *remŭlcum* (Ital. rimorchio, Span. remolque, Fr. remorque), properly *remŭlcum* (from Greek ῥυμουλκέω) is not evidence sufficient to justify us in supposing that this combination had the effect of shortening a preceding long vowel. *Ŭltra*, the form attested by the Romance languages, was in all probability also the classical form; in Varro, *L. L.* v. 50 read ULS, miswritten in the Archetype *uis*, as in v. 83, and then changed by scribes to *ouis*: *ultrā*, not *ūltra*, is the true reading of the Claudius Tablet at Lyons, col. 1. l. 40 (Allmer et Dissard, *Inscriptions antiques, Musée de Lyon*, vol. i. pp. 70 sqq.). The influence of this combination, however, in changing the quality of a vowel is seen in *culmen* beside *cŏlŭmen*, *vult* beside *vŏlo*, &c. (see ch. iv. § 20).

The shortening of a long vowel before certain single final consonants, -*r*, -*t*, &c. is, like the shortening and change of final vowels, dependent on the Accent, and so is discussed in the next chapter. (On the Assimilation of Consonants, e. g. *summitto* for *submitto*, see ch. iv. § 159.)

§ 149. Crasis of vowels, Synizesis, &c. Two neighbouring vowels in the middle of a word became a Diphthong if the second was *i* or *u*, e.g. *coetus* for *co-itus* (used literally in Plaut. *Amph.* 657 primo coetu uicimus), suffered Crasis if they were suitable vowels, e.g. *cōmo* from *co-emo* (cf. Engl. 'doff' for do-off, 'don' for do-on), while if the first was *i* or *u* (or in certain cases *e* or *o*) Synizesis was a common result, e.g. *larva* from *lārua* (a trisyllable in Plautus). Compounds of a Preposition ending in a vowel, and a Verb, &c., beginning with a vowel or *h*, show vowel-contraction more regularly in the early dramatists than in the Augustan poets, e.g. *coercē* (a dissyllable) Pacuv., *cōnestat* (for *cohonestat*) Accius, whether it be that these contracted forms are a relic of the earlier accentuation of the first syllable of every word, *cóerce*, and the uncontracted the result of the shifting of the accent, *cö-érce*, or that the contracted belong to the conversational language of everyday life, the uncontracted to the artificial diction of the higher poetry. Possibly a trisyllabic *coerce* is a 're-composition' like *ē-nĕco* beside older *enico* (with weakening of unaccented vowel), or *adcurro* beside *accurro* (with assimilation of consonants) (see ch. iv. § 159). Synizesis went hand in hand with Syncope [*lārua* became *larva* at the same time that *lāridum* became *lardum* (see ch. iii.)], and asserted itself more and more under the Empire; e.g. *quetus* (*quyētus) for *quiētus* is a common spelling on late inscriptions (cf. Ital. cheto, Span.

quedo, Prov. quetz). The palatalization of a consonant under the influence of a following *i* (become *y*) before a vowel has played a great part in the Romance languages, e.g. Fr. bras from *bracchium*, *braccyum (see § 48). A final vowel before an initial vowel suffered elision (see the next section), and the same thing may have happened to the *e* of *ne-* in *neutiquam*, &c., which is scanned with the first syllable short (or should we pronounce *nyŭtiquam*, *nyullus*, *nyusquam*?), while *nĕuter*, in which the accent by the Penultima law fell on the *ne-*, was pronounced as a trisyllable.

§ 150. **Vowel-contraction in compounds in the early dramatists.** *Coerce* (dissyll.) is found in Pacuvius, *Trag.* 47 R. :

gradere átque atrocem cóerce confidéntiam

(cf. l. 345); and in Plautus *deartuare* (*Capt.* 640, 672), *deasciare* (*Mil.* 884); *deosculari* (*Cas.* 136, 453, 454, 467) are quadrisyllables. But *dehortari* (four syllables) stands in contrast to *hortari* in *Poen.* 674—

neque vós hortari néque dehortarí decet.

(Ennius, *Ann.* 401 has the same verb in Tmesis : de me hortatur.) The phrase *coemptionalis senex*, used of old, and therefore valueless, slaves who were bought not singly but in numbers (from *coemere*, to buy in a lump) is irreverently applied to his master by the cunning slave in the *Bacchides*, 976—

nunc Príamo nostro si ést quis emptor, coémptionalém senem
uendam ego,

where the word *coemptionalem* is scanned with five syllables, as *cohonestat* appears in the form *conestat* in a line of Accius (*Trag.* 445 R.)—

pró se quisque cúm corona clárum conestát caput. (MSS. *conectat, constat*.)

Of the compounds of *hăbeo*, *dēbeo* always has the contracted form in Plautus ; *cohibeo* may in all cases scan as *cōbeo*, and *prohibeo* as *prōbeo* ; *praebeo* is sometimes spelt *praehibeo* in the MSS., but the scansion may always be trisyllabic, and must be so in *Merc.* 1023 ; and the same holds true of all the older poets. In Terence we find only *prendo* and *reprendo*, not *prehendo* (unless possibly *Andr.* 353), nor *reprehendo* (from *prae* and *hendo). (For other instances, see Klotz, *Altröm. Metrik*, p. 139.) In the classical literature the full forms of these verbs are generally restored [but e. g. *cōgo* from *co-ago, *cōgito* from *co-agito (ch. viii. § 31), *dēbeo*, *praebeo*, &c.], though Derivative words often retain the shorter form, e. g. *cōpula* from *co-apula, from *ăpere*, to fasten ; *praeda* for *prae-heda (cf. *prehendo*) ; *praemium* from *prae-emo (cf. *exĭmius* from *ex-ĕmo*), &c. (see ch. v. § 4).

Coepi Perf., with its O. Lat. Present *coepio*, comes from an old verb *ăpere* (cf. *ăpiscor*) meaning 'to fasten' (Paul. Fest. 14. 2. Th. comprehendere antiqui vinculo 'apere' dicebant), derivatives of which are *aptus*, *aptare*, as well as *cōpula* just mentioned. In the Perfect we should expect *cŏēpi* like *cŏēgi* from *cōgo* (*co-ago*), and this scansion is occasionally found, as in this hexameter line (usually referred to Ennius' *Annals*) (536 M.)—

rex ambas intra fossam retinere coepit

(cf. Lucr. iv. 619). Like dissyllabic *coepi* (the usual scansion both in the early and in the classical poetry) is Terence's trisyll. *coemisse* (*Ad.* 225).

§ 151. **Synizesis in Late and Vulgar Latin.** For a list of spellings from late inscriptions and from MSS. like *quesco* (for *quiesco*), *Febrarius* (Ital. Febbrajo, Span. Febrero, &c.), see Schuchardt, *Vok.* ii. pp. 444 sqq., and cf. Georges, *Lex. Wortf.* s. vv. *virđ(i)arium, sesqu(i)alter, vac(u)efacio, ventr(i)osus, sem(i)ermis, sem(i)- ustus, sem(i)uncia, vitr(e)arius, alv(e)arium.* All these show suppression of *ŭ* (*w*), *ĭ* (*y*) before an accented vowel, long by nature or by position. Similarly Lat. *coactus* has become Ital. quatto, Prov. quait, Span. cacho, through Vulg. Lat. *quattus (from *cwactus), Lat. *coāgulum*, Ital. quaglio, Span. cuajo, and so on. Forms with Synizesis occasionally appear in the Latin Poets (classical as well as ante-classical), e. g. *praemjatores*, Naevius, *Com.* 17 R., *injurjatum*, Lucilius ii. 9. M., *malvisti*, id. *Inc.* fr. ix M., *genva*,' *tenvia*, *arjete* (with the first syllables of these three words scanned long by position) (see Luc. Müller, *De Re Metrica*, pp. 249 sqq.). (On 'scyo' or 'scïŏ,' see Charisius, p. 16. 9 K.)

§ 152. **Other examples of vowel-contraction.** *Nīl* from *nihil* (always monosyllabic in Plautus) ; *nēmo* from *ne-hemo ; dissyllabic *deinde, proinde* (according to the grammarians these were accented on the first syllable ; see next chapter, and cf. the Plautine scansion *perĭnde*, Stich. 520) ; *cōmburo* for *co-amb-uro ; *bīmus* for *bi-himus, ' of two winters ' (cf. Engl. ' twinter,' meaning a two-year old beast) from *hiems* : *cōpia* and O. Lat. *cōpi-* Adj. for *co-opia, **co-ŏpis-* (cf. *in-ŏpi-*) ; *antehac* (see § 58 for other examples of the loss of intervocalic *h* with contraction). The loss of intervocalic *w, y* led to contraction in words like *dītior* for *dīvitior*, *dīnus* a form of *dīvīnus*, *stō* for *stāyō (Umbr. stahu, ch. viii. § 2) (but *e* and *o* do not coalesce in *mŏneo, pleo,* &c., nor *a* and accented *ē* in *ăhēnus*) ; on these see ch. iv. §§ 66 and 70. So did the loss of intervocalic *m* in *cōgo* for *cŏmăgo, &c., (unless *co* was a by-form of *com*, ch. ix. § 22). The tendency to contraction of vowels appears at all stages of the history of Latin, and asserted itself in colloquial Latin even more than in the literary language. (For a fuller list of examples see Stolz in Müller's *Handbuch*, ii². p. 275). (On the merging of *i* in a following *i*, *u* in a following *u*, see § 48.)

§ 153. **Elision.** Elision of a final vowel, or vowel preceding final -*m*, before the initial vowel (or *h* with vowel) of a following word is a feature of Latin poetry. That it was also practised in speaking we see from passages like Cicero, *Orator*, xliv. § 150; xlv. § 152; Quint. ix. 4. 33 ; xi. 3. 33-34 ; Seneca, *Epp.* 40 [cf. Cicero's story of Crassus mistaking *Cauneas* (sc. ficus vendo) for *cave ne eas* ; *Div.* ii. 40]. Marius Sacerdos (448. 6 K.) says that in reading a line like Virgil's *monstrum horrendum*, &c., the final -*um* of *monstrum* was entirely suppressed, but this does not quite agree with the statement of Probus (ap. Gell. xiii. 21. 6) that *turrim* had a more melodious sound than *turrem* in the line *turrim in praecipiti stantem*, &c. In the Saturnian Poetry a final syllable ending in -*m* seems to have been not elided but left in

§§ 151–154.] PRONUNCIATION. PARASITIC VOWELS. 145

prosodical hiatus (see § 65), like the *-um* of *circum* in the compounds *circŭ(m)ago*, *circŭ(m)eo*, or of *sublatum*, &c., in the forms *sublatuiri*, &c. (ch. viii. § 87), and the same treatment is found occasionally in the older poets, e.g. Ennius (*Ann.* 354 M.) (quoted by Prisician i. p. 30 H.) millia militŭm octo, and even in the Augustan poets with monosyllables, e.g. nŭm abest Hor.; a final long vowel was also shortened, not elided, like any long vowel before another vowel in the middle of a Latin word, e.g. *prĕ-hendo*, *illĭus*, and so in the older poets frequently, occasionally in Augustan poetry, e.g. quĭ amant, Virg., Esquilinaĕ alites, Hor. (see § 143). This must be a native usage, and not an imitation of Greek poetry. Cicero's remarks on this subject may be quóted (*Orat.* xlv. 152): nobis, ne si cupiamus quidem distrahere voces conceditur: indicant orationes illae ipsae horridulae Catonis, indicant omnes poetae praeter eos, qui, ut versum facerent, saepe hiabant, ut Naevius:

> uos, qui accolitis Histrum fluuium atque algidam,

et ibidem:

> quam numquam uobis Grai atque barbari;

at Ennius semel:

> Scipio inuicte;

et quidem nos:

> hoc motu radiantis Etesiae in uada ponti:

hoc idem nostri saepius non tulissent, quod Graeci laudare etiam solent. How far they indicate a change in actual pronunciation or in the mere technique of verse-making is doubtful (cf. ch. iii. § 41).

§ 154. **Parasitic vowels** (cf. §§ 72, 102, and ch. iii. § 13). When two adjoining consonants are not easily pronounced together a vowel is often inserted to facilitate pronunciation. This is called Anaptyxis. The inserted or 'parasitic' vowel (sometimes styled in the terminology of the Sanscrit grammarians 'svarabhaktic' vowel, from Sansc. svara-bhakti-'partial vowel') is often seen in the older Latin loanwords from Greek, when the Greek word contained a combination of consonants which was not easily pronounced by Roman lips. A Roman did not begin a word

L

with the letters *mn-*, as the Greeks often did, so the Greek μνᾶ took in Latin the form *mĭna*, just as in French the Low German knif became canif; similarly we find in Plautus *tĕchina* (e.g. *Poen.* 817), *drăchŭma* and the like. Marius Victorinus (8. 6 K.) says that the un-Latin character of the combination *cm* produced the forms *Alcŭmeo*, *Alcŭmēna* (so on an old Praenestine mirror, *C. I. L.* xiv. 4102), *Tĕcŭmessa*, and adds that the tragedian Juliŭs Caesar Vopiscus (an older contemporary of Cicero) was the first to conform the third word to the Greek Τέκμησσα, writing the title of his tragedy *Tecmessa*, and ordering the actors to pronounce the name in this way on the stage (cf. Prisc. i. 29. 5 H.). (For a list of Greek words so treated, see Ritschl, *Opusc.* ii. pp. 469-523.) The same thing is found in native Latin words. The suffix *tlo-* (ch. v. § 25), for example, which indicates the instrument with which an action is performed, or the place of its performance, is in Lat. *-culo-*, as well as *-clo-*, e.g. *vĕhĭcŭlum*, 'that by which one is carried' (in Plautus always *vĕhĭclum*), *cŭbĭcŭlum*, 'the place where one lies down.' In Plautus the *-clo-* form is the more usual, especially after a long vowel; e.g. *pĕrīcŭlum* is a quadrisyllable only at the end of a line (i.e. through metrical necessity) in his plays, so that in his time the parasitic vowel between *c* and *l* had not quite asserted its claim to rank as a separate syllable (see § 102), though between consonants of less affinity, e.g. *b* and *l* in the ending *-bŭlum*, it is normal; he uses both *pŏpulus* and *pŏplus* (the latter only at the end of a line) (cf. *pilumnoe poploe*, quoted from the Carmen Saliare by Festus, 244. 24 Th., a phrase for the javelin-bearing Romans). On the oldest inscriptions we have *poplo-* (e.g. *poplus*, *C.I.L.* ii. 5041, of 189 B.C.; *poplom* on the (restored) Columna Rostrata, *pro poplo Ariminesi*, *Not. Scav.* 1887, p. 120); *piaclum* (*C. I. L.* xi. 4766) may be like *cedre* 'caedere' due to Umbrian influence; but *pocolom* on the early Praenestine vases (*C. I. L.* i. 43 sqq.), *tabola* (i. 197, 198), &c. (Marius Victorinus, if we can trust the reading, quotes from the 'libri antiqui foederum et regum' *piacolom* with *populoi Romanoi*.) At a later time the spelling *-cul-* established itself so firmly in the language that it became impossible to discriminate an original *co-lo*, e.g. *cor-cu-lum* (formed with the diminutive suffixes *ko-* and *lo-*, ch. v.), *por-*

§ 154.]   PRONUNCIATION. PARASITIC VOWELS.   147

culus for **porco-lo-*, from an original -*clo-*; and still later the wave of Syncope which swept over the language reduced all these forms to the same type, *porclus*, *stablum*, *cubiclum*, &c. (see ch. iii. § 13).

Anaptyxis played a great part in the Oscan language, and its kindred dialect, the Pelignian. We have in Oscan aragetud for Lat. *argento* (Abl.), Helevis for Lat. *Helvius*, teremenniú for '*terminia' (Lat. *termĭni*), with liquid preceding; and with liquid following, patereí (Lat. *pătri*), Sadiriis (Lat. *Satrius*), in Pelignian sacaracirix (Lat. *săcrātrīces*), pristafalacirix (Lat. *praestăbŭlātrīces*), and so on. The inserted vowel takes the quality of the vowel in the syllable containing the liquid, e.g. aragetud for *ar-getud, patereí for *pa-treí (so Lat. *stăbŭlum* for *stă-blum, *stăbĭlis* for *sta-blis). The long preceding syllable is the reason of its absence in Osc. maatreís (Lat. *mātris*) (cf. O. H. G. hlūtres beside fŏgales and Plautus' preference of *perīclum*, &c.). It is not found in the initial syllable, so that *Terebonio* (*C. I. L.* i. 190), if a dialectal form, does not belong to the Oscan dialect (cf. *Terebuni*, *Eph. Epigr.* i. 116; Ital. calabrone from Lat *crabro*, a 'hornet'[1]). Accentuation often seems to influence its presence or absence in Latin; for example, Plautus has usually *mănŭplāris* (once at least *manipularis*), as in classical Latin *discĭpulus* stands beside *disciplina*. But the cross-working of Anaptyxis and Syncope, and the difficulty of ascertaining in which words a suffix has been directly added to a stem ending in a consonant, and in which there was originally an intervening vowel (ch. v. § 21) has hitherto prevented the drawing up of exact rules for its use in the language. [A full list of Latin examples will be found in Stolz, *Lat. Gram.* (in Müller's *Handb. Klass. Alterthumswissenchaft*) p. 277 (2nd ed.) (see also above, § 102)].

---

[1] Varro's derivation of the name *Gracchus*, 'a gerendo' (*Lib. Gramm.* p. 184, Wilm.), suggests a pronunciation like *G*ᵉ*racchus*.

CHAPTER III.

ACCENTUATION [1].

§ 1. **Nature of the Latin Accent.** Was the Latin accent one of pitch or stress? Did the accented syllable in a Latin word differ from the other syllables in being uttered at a higher note than they were, or with a greater force? The two things are obviously quite distinct. For a syllable to be sounded at a high or low note is one thing, with energy or with gentleness is another, just as a musical note may be sounded strongly or gently (forte or piano), a thing quite different from its being a note high or low on the musical scale. Most languages do indeed combine in a greater or less degree pitch-accent with stress-accent. The accented syllable, if pronounced with more energy than the unaccented, is generally at the same time pronounced at a slightly higher (or lower) pitch. But, for all that, it is usually possible to say decidedly of one language : this language has a stress-accent; of another : this language has a pitch-accent. Our own language for example is clearly a language of stress-accent. It distinguishes its accented syllables by giving them greater energy of articulation than the unaccented; and it shows the usual characteristics of a language with stress-accentuation, namely, a slurring or Syncope of short syllables immediately following the accented syllable (e. g. ' méd(i)cine'; cf. dám(o)sel,' 'fánt(a)sy' and 'fancy,') and an obscuring or reduction of unaccented vowels (e. g. 'father,' where the *e* has the sound of the

---

[1] Seelmann, *Aussprache des Latein*, Heilbronn, 1885, is the chief exponent of the stress-theory; Weil et Benloew, *Théorie générale de l'Ac-centuation Latine*, Paris, 1855, of the pitch-theory. For sentence-accentuation, see the *Class. Rev.* v. pp. 373, 402.

'obscure' vowel of the word 'but'; 'savage,' 'minute,' 'orange'). In a long word, say the adjective 'characteristical,' we might number each syllable according to the amount of force with which it is uttered, the strongest (with the main accent) being the fourth syllable of the word, the next strongest (with the secondary accent) the first. The weakest syllables are, as is usually the case with stress-accentuation, those following immediately on the most strongly accented, thus 'chărăctĕrĭstĭcăl.' In the Romance languages the accent is, like ours, an accent of stress, but this stress is much weaker than ours, corresponding to our secondary stress rather than to our main accent. This is notably the case in French, where the stress is weaker than it is, for example, in Italian. But the Romance languages show the same tendency to syncope of short unaccented syllables, and to the reduction of unaccented vowels, as our language does, though in a much less marked degree (e. g. Italian gridare from Latin quĭrītare, balsimo from Latin balsămum). Pitch-accentuation is seen in English more in the accentuation of the sentence than of single words. A question like 'Are you ready?' differs by its rising tone from a statement of fact like 'He is ready.' In some languages however, such as Swedish, Lithuanian, Servian, these tone-distinctions are cleary marked in single words, a word of the same spelling as another being often distinguished from it by the tone alone. In English we have no example of this, unless it be such a word as 'rather,' which by a difference of tone can imply two different meanings, in answer to a question like 'Is it raining?' If we are asked, 'Is it raining?' and reply 'Rather,' the word, if we give it one tone, will imply 'slightly,' 'not much,' with another tone will convey the notion of 'heavily,' 'violently.' But in the main the distinctions of tone are unknown in our language; and it is this that makes it difficult for us to understand the nature of a language which uses entirely or predominantly a pitch-accentuation, such as in ancient times the Greek language, and of living languages, Chinese. In the case of a dead language, we have two means of ascertaining whether its accent was one of pitch or of stress. We have the phenomena of the language itself on the one hand, and we have the statements of native grammarians, if they are trustworthy, on the other. Both these means of evidence point to the pitch-character of the ancient Greek accent. The words of the language do not show that Syncope and Reduction of unaccented vowels, which we have seen to be characteristic effects of a stress-accent. The Greek grammarians' accounts of the accent of their own language point in the same direction. Modern Greek has, however, a stress-accentuation, so that the Greek accent must have changed its nature in the course of time, though at what precise period the change took place it is difficult to say. No doubt the nature of the accent differed more or less in different parts of Greece; and the accent in one dialect may have allowed stress to predominate over tone at an earlier period than in another (in the N. Greek dialects, for example, as in the N. Greek dialects of modern times; see Hatzidakis, *K. Z.* xxx. 388). The accent is taken into account in Greek metre in the verse of Babrius, a contemporary probably of Augustus, and author of a verse translation of Aesop's fables.

When we turn our attention to Latin, we are confronted with the difficulty that, while the Latin grammarians often speak of their accent in terms properly applicable only to a pitch-accent, all the features of their language point to its having been a stress-accent. The reduction of the unaccented vowel (e. g. *ăbĭgo*, &c., but Greek ἀπάγω, &c.), the Syncope of syllables following the accent (e. g. *objŭrgo* from *objūrĭgo*, *caldus* from *călĭdus*), all indicate unmistakably the presence of a stress-accent. And the difference of its accentuation from Greek, though not a single grammarian definitely informs us of this difference, comes out clearly in the treatment of Greek loan-words, especially in the language of the less educated Romans. Greek Σοφία (with short ι) became *Sofīa*, a stress-accent replacing the pitch-accent with the result of lengthening the accented vowel; Greek εἴδωλον became *ĭdŏlum*. Instances like these show that the Romans had much the same difficulty as we have, in pronouncing Greek words with a short accented paenultima, or with an accented antepaenultima and long penult. The difficulty would not be so great for a Roman as for us, if his stress-accent, like that of his modern descendant, the Italian, was not so strong as ours; nor would it be so much felt at an earlier period, when the distinctions of quantity were more vividly marked (see ch. ii. § 141) than in the later Empire. The Hungarian language, where the sense of quantity is equally vivid, accentuates the first syllable of every word without detracting from the quantity of vowels in the following syllables. No doubt too the nature of the stress-accent would differ in various parts of Italy in ancient times, as it does to-day (see Meyer-Lübke, *Ital. Gram.* § 122, p. 71). In Praeneste, if we are to believe such indications as the spelling MGOLNIA for the name *Magolnia* on inscriptions, and perhaps the form *conea* for *ciconia*, 'a stork,' Syncope was carried to greater lengths than in Latin, and the stress of the accent must have been stronger (see § 14 below). But that the Latin language of all periods, at which we have definite knowledge of it, was a language of stress-accentuation, is proved by all the evidence at our disposal, and disproved by nothing except the silence of the grammarians. The same tendency to Syncope, which before the literary period produced *undecim* out of *$\bar{u}n\breve{o}$děcim*, is seen working in the Early Literary time in words like *objurigo* (Plaut.), *objurgo* (Plaut. and Ter.), and in the Augustan age in *calidus* and *caldus* (the form preferred by the Emperor Augustus, Quint. i. 6. 19), while *virdis* for *vĭrĭdis* asserted itself still later, and the same tendency, as we have seen, still shows itself in modern Italian. And hand in hand with Syncope goes the reduction and change of unaccented vowels. How then are we to explain the absence of comment on the part of the grammarians? We must, I think, take three things into consideration. First, that the study of Accentuation, and all the terminology used, came to the Romans from Greece. It was Tyrannio who in the first cent. B.C. brought this new lore to Rome, including among his earliest pupils possibly Varro and certainly Cicero's friend Atticus. Cicero, in a letter which has been preserved (*ad Att.* xii. 6. 2), banters his friend on his enthusiasm for so trivial a subject (te istam tam tenuem θεωρίαν tam valde admiratum esse gaudeo . . . sed quaeso quid ex ista acuta et gravi refertur ad τέλος?), and in his own treatise, the 'Orator,' published at this time, makes mention of the wonderful 'law of nature' which prescribes that the accent shall never be further from the end of a word than the third syllable (*Or.* xviii.

58). The word *accentus* itself was nothing but the Greek word προσῳδία in a Latin dress; and not only the terms employed, but the description of the phenomena of accentuation are taken directly from Greek authorities.

In the second place, the contrast between their accent and the Greek would not be felt so markedly by Roman grammarians as it would by us, whose accent has so much stronger a stress than the Latin, or modern Italian, a consideration which makes it less surprising that they did not remark on the essential difference between the two systems of accentuation. And thirdly, the Greek accent itself had probably at the time of these grammarians already entered that process of change which ended in the stress-accentuation of modern Greek. The Greek writers on accentuation would no doubt go on using the terminology of the earlier phoneticians, without perceiving that their terms and descriptions were no longer so applicable to the actual phenomena as they had once been; and if the Greek contemporary theorists on accent misused the terminology in this way, a Roman imitator might be excused for carrying the misuse a little further, in applying the same terminology to Latin accentuation. Indeed, the writers on Latin Grammar were seldom Roman by birth; they were usually Greeks, and would have the same difficulties in describing the Latin accent as a Frenchman in describing the strong stress-accent of English. These considerations may explain how it is that only a few statements of the writers on Latin Grammar are rid of the terms 'high' and 'low' (instead of 'strong' and 'weak') accent, such as the remark of a fifth-century grammarian, that the accented syllable in a Latin word is the syllable which would be heard at a distance, when the others were inaudible (quoted in § 2). We may then believe the Latin accent to have been in the main an accent of stress, like that of modern Italian, though like it (and the accent of the Romance languages generally), the stress-accent may have been accompanied by a higher tone than the tone of the unstressed syllables.

The discredit, which we have found it necessary to attach to the language the grammarians use in describing the nature of accentuation, makes us hesitate about accepting their distinction, evidently borrowed from the Greek, of three kinds of accent,—grave, acute, and circumflex. They postulate a circumflex for those syllables with naturally long vowels which would have one in Greek, namely, long paenultimas followed by a short final syllable, e.g. *Rômă* but *Rômāe*. The quantity of the final syllable is the chief factor in Greek accentuation, but not in Latin, where the quantity of the paenultima takes its place, so that one would not expect the accent of the first syllable of *Romă* to differ from that of *Romāe*. Other circumflex words are, according to the grammarians, long monosyllables like *rês, flôs, môs*, and final long syllables of words whose last vowel has been dropped by Apocope or Syncope, e.g. *illîc* from **illíce, nostrás* from *nostrātis*. In modern Italian these apocopated words have a strong acute accent on the final syllable, e.g. bontà, città, virtù, for *bonitatem, civitatem, virtutem*, but in Spanish a word like amó (Latin *ămāvĭt*, Vulg. Lat. *amaut) has a tone-circumflex in the last syllable, the voice rising first and then falling slightly. There is hardly evidence enough to enable us to test this theory of a circumflex in Latin, nor to show, supposing such an accent did exist, whether it was a tone-circumflex, formed of a rising and falling tone, like Spanish amó or our 'Oh!' when used sarcastically, or a stress-' circumflex,' formed by two impulses of the voice, something like our diphthongal pronunciation of a long vowel, e.g. 'foe,' 'two.' In modern Italian a paenultima long by position has a very long pronunciation, and we might write a circumflex accent over the first syllable of words like tanto (pronounce 'tânto'), tempo (pronounce 'têmpo'), while the different treatment of a Latin penultimate from a Latin antepenultimate vowel in words like popolo (Lat. *pŏpulus*), uopo (Lat. *ŏpus*), suggest the possibility of a Latin *Rôma*, &c. as distinct from *Rómulus*, &c.

On the whole, then, we may say that a circumflex accent may have existed in Latin in words like *flôs, illíc*, and even in *Rôma* (though the grammarians' distinction of *Rôma, Rómae* is doubtful), but that certainty on this matter is not to be had. The Latin accent was an accent of stress, a stress which was not so strong as ours, and which may have been accompanied, as in Romance, by a high tone.

§ 2. **Testimony of the grammarians.** (1) On the Nature of the Latin Accent. The remarks of the Latin grammarians on accentuation have been collected by Schoell, *De Accentu linguae Latinae* (in the *Acta Soc. Philolog. Lipsiensis*, vol. vi. 1876). They include remarks not only on accentuation, but on proper pronunciation generally; for *accentus* is often defined as 'vitio carens vocis artificiosa pronuntiatio' (*ib.* p. 78). Here are one or two of the more important descriptions of the Latin accent. Varro, who probably learnt the theory of accentuation from Tyrannio (Schoell, *ib.* p. 6), speaks of the *altitudo* of a word as opposed to its *longitudo* (i. e. the quantity of the syllable). By *altitudo* he means its accentuation, cum pars verbi aut in grave deprimitur aut sublimatur in acutum (ap. Serg. *de Acc.* p. 525. 28 K.) (cf. *ib.* p. 533. 4 cum verbum enuntietur aliqua in eo syllaba necesse est summum illud vocis fastigium possideat). His imitator, Martianus Capella (fourth and fifth cent. A.D.)(iii. p. 65. 19 Eyss.), prettily describes accentuation as 'anima vocis et seminarium musices,' adding, quod omnis modulatio ex fastigiis vocum gravitateque componitur; and Nigidius, a contemporary of Varro (ap. Gell. xiii. 26. 1–3 H.), describes the accentuation *Váleri* by the words summo tono est prima, deinde gradatim descendunt (cf. Audac. exc. 7. 357. 14–358. 1 K.). On the other hand Pompeius (fifth century A.D.) (5. 126-7 K.) uses language suitable to stress-accentuation (*plus sonat*), when he says, illa syllaba, quae accentum habet, plus sonat, quasi ipsa habet majorem potestatem, and goes on to use the illustration of the accented syllable of the word *optimus* being the only syllable heard at a distance, finge tibi quasi vocem clamantis ad longe aliquem positum, ut puta finge tibi aliquem illo loco contra stare et clama ad ipsum. cum coeperis clamare, naturalis ratio exigit ut unam syllabam plus dicas a reliquis illius verbi; et quam videris plus sonare a ceteris, ipsa habet accentum. 'optimus,' quae plus sonat? illa quae prior est. numquid hic sonat 'ti' et 'mus' quemadmodum 'op'? Ergo necesse est, ut illa syllaba habeat accentum, quae plus sonat a reliquis, quando clamorem fingimus. [The same language is used by Servius (fourth cent.), *in Don.* iv. 426. 10–20 K.]. Some would explain this difference of language by supposing the Latin accent in the time of Varro to have been more of a pitch-accent than it was in the time of Pompeius, while others try to make out that it is those grammarians who were themselves Greeks, or who follow implicitly Greek authorities, who speak of 'high' and 'low' accent, while the native grammarians of a more independent turn of mind use the more correct terms, 'strong' and 'weak.' I cannot see much ground for discriminating between the accent of Varro's time and of a later age. The same processes of syncope and vowel-reduction are at work at both periods and the cause of these processes must have been the same stress-accentuation. But there may well have been a change in the Greek accentuation which became more and more apparent in each successive century.

(2) **On the circumflex accent.** Servius (*in Don.* 426. 10 K.) distinguishes the acute accent of *árma* from the circumflex of *Mûsa*, acutus dicitur accentus quotiens cursim syllabam proferimus, ut 'árma'; circumflexus vero, quotiens tractim, ut 'Mûsa' (cf. Pompeius, 126. 4 K. non possumus dicere 'árma,' non possumus dicere 'Músa'; Cledonius, p. 31. 30 K. 'árma' excusso sono dicendum est, while 'Rôma' is pronounced *tractim*). Similarly Priscian (i. p. 7. 11 H.) speaks of three different sounds of *ā*, with the acute, the grave, and the circumflex accent, as in *hámis, hámorum, hâmus,* or *árae, árarum, âra,*

and Vitruvius, in a passage borrowed apparently from Aristoxenus, says of the words *sol, lux, flos, vox*, nec unde incipit nec ubi desinit [*sc.* vox] intelligitur, sed quod [*v. l.* nec quae] ex acuta facta est gravis, ex gravi acuta. (*Archit.* v. 4. 2).

§ 3. **Accentuation of Greek loanwords.** (See the passages quoted by Schoell, pp. 201 sqq.) An educated Roman would of course pronounce a Greek word correctly with the same quantity and accentuation that the Greeks themselves gave to it. The grammarians of the Empire prescribe the Greek accentuation for such Greek words in a Latin author as retained their Greek form and declension. Thus in Virg. *Georg.* i. 59 Eliadum palmas Epiros equarum; Servius, in his note on the passage, says that the word *Epiros*, since it has its Greek form, must be pronounced with the accent on the first syllable, *Épiros*, unlike the Latinized form *Epírus*: sane 'Epiros' graece profertur, unde etiam 'E' habet accentum; nam si latinum esset, 'Epirus,' 'pi' haberet, quia longa est. But Greek loanwords which became naturalized at Rome were adapted to the Latin accentuation and declension. This was specially the case in the Republican period, according to Quintilian (i. 5. 60), who tells us that Julius Caesar followed the old habit of using *Calypsōnem*, a form which Quintilian himself does not approve, though he accepts *Castōrem, Olýmpus, tyránnus*. In the plays of Plautus, who uses the language of the educated society of his day, Greek words appear as a rule in a Latinized form with a Latin accent, but in some words of use among the common people the Greek accent is retained with the effect of altering the quantity. Thus the gold coin known as a 'Philip,' Greek Φίλιππος, is always *Philĭppus* with the second syllable shortened after an accented short syllable. The shortening of the second syllable, long by position not by nature, is, like the reduction of the vowel in *Tarentum* (Greek Τάραντα, Accus., now Táranto), an indication that the Roman accent in early times, as well as late, produced an effect on the word that the Greek accent did not produce, an effect always traceable to a stress-accentuation. But whether a naturally long vowel was at this period ever shortened by the accent in a Greek loanword is doubtful. *Ancŏra* (Greek ἄγκῦρα), with *o* instead of *u*, is not a certain example, and still less the hypothetical *cunĭla* (Greek κονίλη, not κόνῑλα) in Plaut. *Trin.* 935 (*Journ. Phil.* xxi. 205). It was frequently done at a later age when the long and short quantity had more approximated to each other (see ch. ii. § 141), e. g. *bŭtīrum* (Greek βούτῡρον), *blăsfēmus* (Greek βλάσφημος), *ĭdŏlum* (Greek εἴδωλον), *ĕrĕmus* (Greek ἔρημος beside ἐρῆμος), *selīnum* (Greek σέλῑνον), our 'celery.' In all these popular words which passed into the Romance languages (Ital. ermo, sedano, &c.) the rule seems to be that the Greek accent was always retained, even at the cost of the quantity, except in oxytone words, which followed rather the Latin accentuation, e. g. *tapĭnus* (Greek ταπεινός) [see Meyer-Lübke, *Gram. Rom. Sprach.* i. p. 34, and cf. *Anecd. Helv.* 177. 4 H. on 'abȳssus' (ἄβυσσος): paenultima positione longa sed acuitur antepaenultima. So *abȳssus* Paulinus of Nola (19. 651; 35. 228); Cyprian, *Gall. gen.* 288 P.]. This inability of the Romans to reproduce the Greek accentuation of a final syllable is a subject of frequent remark in the grammarians. A Greek writer of the sixth cent. (Olympiodorus in Aristot. *Meteor.* p. 27) makes the curious remark that the Roman paroxytone pronunciation of words like Γραικοί, &c., was due to their haughtiness (διὰ τὸν κόμπον), and had earned for them the epithet of the 'overweening' Romans (ὅθεν ὑπερηνορέοντες ἐκλήθησαν ὑπὸ τῶν ποιητῶν). I have heard a Frenchman ascribe the English mispronunciation of words like 'Français' to the same cause.

§ 4. **Romance Accentuation.** The clearness with which each part of the word is pronounced in Italian and Spanish always strikes an English traveller. Every syllable has due effect given to it. There is nothing like the swallowing of parts of words, that is seen in our own and in other Teutonic languages. The unaccented vowel in Italian notte, Spanish noche, is clearer and more definite than in German Gabe; but on the other hand there is less difference in quantity between a long and a short vowel, the accented long vowel in the word 'Toscana,' for example, being hardly, if at all, longer than the unaccented vowels of the word. The accent is one of stress, but is accompanied by a high tone, the drop of the voice in a Spanish word like mano (Lat. *manus*), being about one-fifth, though máno, sometimes in emphatic utterance the word is pronounced with a lengthening of final vowel and a slight rise of the voice on the second, the unaccented, syllable, [music: mánō]. The French accent must have at one time been of very powerful stress, so great is the reduction which French vowels and syllables have undergone, but it is now much weaker than in any other Romance language, so weak that it is usually difficult to say on which syllable the accent rests. The difference of pitch, say between the two syllables of the word 'jamais!' is often very considerable, especially in excited utterance, [music: ja-mais!] or [music: ja-mais!] (see Storm in *Phon. Stud.* 1888).

§ 5. **The Earlier Law of Accentuation.** The Indo-European accentuation, which we can generally ascertain from the Sanscrit and Greek (e.g. Sansc. pitá, Greek πατήρ, father), has not left in Latin the traces which it has left in the Teutonic languages. According to a law discovered by Verner, and known as 'Verner's Law,' a Teutonic spirant, developed from an Indo-European unvoiced mute, remained unvoiced when the immediately preceding vowel bore the accent in the Indo-European, but became voiced when that vowel did not. The Indo-European verb *wértō, to turn or become (Sanscr. vártāmi, Lat. vĕrto), is in Goth, vaírþa (our 'worth' in 'Woe worth the day!') with the unvoiced-spirant sound (our *th* in 'thin'); while Gothic fadar (Engl. 'father') had the voiced-spirant sound of our *th* in 'then.' By the same law Indo-European *s* appears in Teutonic words as unvoiced or voiced under the same conditions, e.g. unvoiced in Old High Germ. *mūs*, our 'mouse' from Indo-Eur. *mūs (Sanscr. múš, Gk. μῦς, Lat. *mūs*), where the immediately preceding vowel had the accent, voiced in Goth. áiza-, our 'ore' from Indo-Eur. *áyos (Sanscr. áyas, Lat. *aes*), where the Indo-European accent fell on another vowel. (On the change of voiced *s* to *r* in Latin, see ch. iv. § 148). The Lithuanian accentuation, too, often enables us, when we compare it with the Greek, to determine in what cases the Indo-European accent was 'circumflex,' and in what cases 'acute,' e.g. circumflex in Gen. Sg. of Ā-stems (Greek τιμῆς, Lith. rañkōs), acute in Nom. Sg. of the same stems (Greek τιμή, Lith. rankà from *ranká) (see Hirt's articles in *Indogerm. Forsch.* i. &c.).

We have, however, in Latin, as Corssen proved, traces of an

older accentuation than the system which prevailed in the classical period, which show us that at some early time the Indo-European accent-law had been replaced by a new law, namely, that the accent should fall on the first syllable of every word. A change of the same kind seems to have taken place in the Teutonic languages (see Paul's *Grundriss Germ. Philol.* i. p. 339), and probably also in Celtic (Thurneysen in *Revue celtique*, vol. vi); and in some languages of the present day, such as Lettish, this uniform accentuation of the first syllable prevails. The traces it has left in Latin are these:—

(1) Syncope of the second syllable of a word when that syllable was short, e.g. *undecim*, which under the ordinary Latin accentuation must have been *unódecim, a compound of *ūnus* and *dĕcem* (see § 13).

(2) Reduction of vowels, which would by the accentuation of the classical period bear the accent, e.g. *infringo* from *in* and *frango*; *concīdo* from *cum* and *caedo*; *triennium* from *tri-* (*tres*) and *annus*; which point unmistakably to an earlier *cóncaido, *triánniom, &c. (see § 18). At what precise period the change, no doubt a gradual one, from this earlier system to the Pænultima Law of Cicero's time began and completed itself, it is difficult to ascertain. But there is some evidence that it was still incomplete in one particular in the period of the Early Drama, for the metrical treatment of words like *facilius, mulierem* (‿‿‿⌣), in the plays of Plautus and Terence, indicate that the pronunciation of such words in their time laid the accent on the first, and not on the second syllable. A line in which the metrical ictus falls on the second syllable occurs very rarely in their plays (*Philologus*, li. 364 sqq.). At the same time the incidence of the metrical ictus in all other types of words points to the prevalence of the Paenultima Law for all words, except these quadrisyllables with the first three syllables short. But though we cannot fix the time when Latin words passed from the old to the new accentuation, when, for example, *sápientia* became *sapiéntia*, *témpestatibus* became *tempestátibus*, we can guess, partly from the analogy of other languages, partly from the inherent probabilities of the case, what the nature of that change was. A long word like *săpientia, tempestatĭbus* must have had at all periods a secondary

as well as a main accent; it could hardly be pronounced otherwise, as we can see from our own pronunciation of such words as 'chàracterístical' (with secondary accent on first, main accent on fourth syllable). So that *sápientia* would be more accurately written *sápièntia*. The change from the old accentuation to the new would be, in reality, nothing but a usurpation by the secondary accent of the prominence of the main accent; *sápièntia* would become *sàpiéntia*, *témpestàtibus* would become *tèmpestátibus*. *Dīmĭdius*, unless it takes its *-mi-* by analogy of *dimidiatus*, &c. (which is unlikely), must have been accentuated on the first syllable about 250 B.C., for the change of unaccented *ĕ* to *ĭ* is not found on the oldest inscriptions (§ 22).

The Umbro-Oscan dialects seem to have passed through the same stages as Latin. Traces of the first stage, the accentuation of the first syllable, are e.g. Osc. Maakdiis, Vezkeí, 'Vetusco' (with syncope of the second syllable), of the second stage (the Paenultima Law), Osc. teremenniu, '*terminia,' with doubling of consonant before the *y*-sound and after the accented vowel (see von Planta, *Gramm. Osk.-Umbr. Dial.* i. p. 589).

§ 6. **Traces of I.-Eur. accentuation in Latin.** The occasional appearance of *ă* for I.-Eur. *ĕ* in Latin has been explained by the I.-Eur. accentuation by Wharton (*Etyma Latina*, p. 119), who thinks that *ĕ* (and *ŏ*) became *ă* when they preceded the syllable which bore the I.-Eur. accent, e.g. *magnus* from **meg-nós*, Gk. μέγας). For other theories of the kind, see Bugge in *Bezz. Beitr.* xiv. 60. 67. 70; Froehde, *ib.* xvi. 182. 191. 215; Stolz in *Wien. Stud.* viii. 149; Conway, *Verner's Law in Italy*, &c. (on a trace of the I.-Eur. accent in Umbro-Oscan, von Planta, i. p. 491).

§ 7. **Secondary and main accent.** The Saturnian verse recognizes this secondary accent, if we are right in regarding it as accentual and not quantitative verse, with three accents in the first hemistich and two in the second (see ch. ii. § 141),

    e. g. dábunt málum Metélli ‖ Naéuio poétae.

For a five-syllabled word always counts for two accents in Saturnian verse,

    e. g. mágna sàpiéntia ‖ multásque uirtútes,
    e. g. dédet Tèmpestátibus ‖ aíde méretod,
    e. g. òneráriae onústae ‖ stábant in flústris;

and a four-syllabled word (at any rate of the forms - ⌣ - ⌣ and ⌣ - ⌣ ⌣) does the same at the beginning of the line,

    e. g. immolábat áuream ‖ uíctimam púlchram,
    e. g. sùpérbiter contémptim ‖ cónterit legiónes,
    e. g. Còrnélius Lúcius ‖ Scípio Barbátus.

A Latin secondary accent in long words such as *àrmatūra* is indicated by the Romance forms, which treat the vowel of the first syllable in the same way as they treat accented *a*. Italian Fiorentino beside Firenze may point to the secondary accent having been stronger in the first syllable of Lat. *Flōrentīnus* than of Lat. *Flōrentia* (cf. Ital. tollerare, scellerato, &c., with doubling of the consonant which follows the vowel with secondary accent) (see Meyer-Lübke, *Gram. Rom. Sprach.*, i. p. 501). There are some indications (e. g. Alliteration) that the first syllable was even in the classical period pronounced with a certain amount of stress.

§ 8. **The Paenultima Law.** The law of accentuation which prevailed in the classical and subsequent periods is that known as the 'Paenultima Law,' a very simple one, namely, that the accent falls on the antepenultimate syllable, if the paenultima be short, on the paenultima itself, if long, e.g. *décŏres, decóres*. The earliest notice of Latin accentuation, the remark of Cicero (*Or.* xviii. 58) mentioned above (§ 1), speaks of it as a law of nature that the accent should never go further back in a word than the third syllable from the end. We have seen reason to believe that at an earlier period this 'law of nature' was broken in the case of four-syllabled words, like *făcĭlĭus*, beginning with three short syllables. These were at the time of Plautus accented on the fourth syllable from the end, *fácilius*, &c. But in all other words the evidence to be obtained from the versification of Plautus, and such processes of language as syncope and reduction of unaccented vowels, points to the operation of the Paenultima Law in the earliest literary period.

The Latin grammarians agree in pointing out the difference between the Greek and Roman systems of accentuation, and the greater simplicity of the Roman, which (like the Aeolic, and unlike the Attic, &c.) never lets the accent fall on the last syllable of a word; though they are strangely silent on the difference, which one would have thought would have been quite as striking, between the pitch-accent of the Greek, and the stress-accent of their own language. They posit for Latin the three kinds of accent used by the Greeks, the acute, the circumflex, and the grave, understanding by the last term rather the absence of accent than any particular form of accent, and assigning the circumflex, as we have seen, to vowels long by nature in the penultimate syllable of words whose final syllable is short, and in monosyllabic words. Thus the name *Cĕthēgŭs*, with a naturally long paenultima and a short final, takes the circumflex on the paenultima, *Cethêgus*, and the grave accent on the antepaenultima, *Cèthêgus*; the name *Cătullus*, with a naturally short vowel in the paenultima, takes the acute accent instead of the circumflex, *Catúllus*, with the grave on the antepaenultima, as before, *Càtúllus*.

Monosyllables like *lux, spes, flos, sol, mons, mos, fons, lis*, whose vowel is naturally long, have the circumflex, *lûx, spês*, &c., while *ars, pars, pix, nix, fax*, with vowel naturally short and lengthened only by 'position,' take the acute accent, *árs, párs*, &c. Apocopated words like *illīc, nostrās* retain their old circumflex accent, *illîc(e), nostrâ(ti)s*.

A compound word, or word-group, like *rēspūblĭca, jūsjūrandum, mălĕsanus, intĕreālŏcī*, has only one accent, *respública, malesánus, intereáloci*, &c., though, if resolved into two independent words, each takes its separate accent, *résque pública, mále sánus, intérea lóci*. Thus *Argīlētum*, which the etymological fancy of the Romans explained as *Argi letum*, 'the death of Argus,' is mentioned as a unique example of a word combining all three accents, the acute on the first, the grave on the second, and the circumflex on the third syllable, *Árgìlêtum*. (On these word-groups, see below, § 12.)

The secondary accent, which, as we have seen (§ 7), must have existed in longer words like *àrbŏrétum, tèmpĕrátus, ìntĕmĕrátus, exìstĭmátus*, is ignored by the Roman grammarians, unless we are so to understand the *media prosodia*, mentioned by Varro, in imitation of the μέση προσῳδία of Greek Accentual Theorists, an accent which he describes as something between the grave (i.e. entire absence of accent) and the acute accent. The secondary accent shows traces of itself in Italian in the doubling of the consonant in words like pellegrino (Lat. *pĕrĕgrīnus*), scellerato (Lat. *scĕlĕrātus*), tollerare (Lat. *tolerare*), &c. (see above, § 7).

The simplicity of the Latin accentuation made it unnecessary to indicate by written signs the accent with which a word was to be pronounced. The mark of the Greek acute accent, a line sloping up from left to right, and placed above the vowel of the syllable, was used in Latin inscriptions to indicate a long vowel, and was called the 'apex' (see ch. i. § 1). It was employed especially where two words of similar spelling differed in quantity alone, e.g. *mălus* and *mālus* (Quint. i. 7. 2), and has remained with a quantitative use in several alphabets derived from the Latin, e.g. the Irish alphabet.

§ 9. Testimony of the grammarians. Quintilian's remarks on Latin pronunciation are generally so free from Greek bias, that his account of the Paenultima Law is worth quoting in full (i. 5. 29-31) : difficilior apud Graecos observatio est [*sc.* legis sermonis], quia plura illis loquendi genera, quas διαλέκτους vocant et quod alias vitiosum, interim alias rectum est ; apud nos vero brevissima ratio. namque in omni voce acuta intra numerum trium syllabarum continetur, sive eae sunt in verbo solae, sive ultimae, et in iis aut proxima extremae, aut ab ea tertia. Trium porro de quibus loquor, media longa aut acuta aut flexa erit, eodem loco brevis utique gravem habebit sonum ideoque positam ante se, id est ab ultima tertiam, acuet. Est autem in omni voce utique acuta, sed nunquam plus una, nec unquam ultima, ideoque in disyllabis prior ; praeterea nunquam in eadem flexa et acuta : itaque neutra cludet vocem Latinam. Ea vero quae sunt syllabae unius, erunt acuta aut flexa, ne sit aliqua vox sine acuta. In another passage (xii. 10. 33) he praises the variety of the Greek accent in contrast to the monotonous accent of the Romans, who never give the acute or the circumflex to the last syllable of a word, so that every word has its last syllable, sometimes both its last syllable and its paenultima, grave (i. e. unaccented) ; and adds that Roman poets like to give a charm to their lines by the use of Greek names pronounced with the Greek accent. (For other similar statements of the Paenultima Law, see the passages quoted by Schoell pp. 100 sqq.: e. g. Diomedes 431. 6 K. ; Donatus 371. 2 K. ; Servius *in Don.* 426. 15 K. &c.) Examples are *sól, dós, Càtúllus, Cèthégus* (Sergius, *De Acc.* p. 483. 11 K.) *indoctíssimus* (Pomp. 127. 15 K.), *Caélius, Sallústius, Curiátius, caélum, Cicero, Galénus, Galéni, Camílli* (Mart. Cap. iii. p. 65. 22 Eyss.), *Románus, Hispánus* ('Priscian,' *De Acc.* p. 520. 17 K.), *áb, mél, fél, árs, párs, pix, nix, fáx, lúx, spés, flós, sól, móns, môs, fóns, lis* (Diom. 431. 15 K.), *núx, rês* (Don. 371. 8 K.), *néc, nóx* (Serv. *in Don.* 426. 27 K.), *rôs* (Serg. *De Acc.* 524. 21 K.), *aés, ét, qué* (Pomp. 128. 15 K.), *déus, citus, dátur, árat, póntus, cóhors, lúna, Rôma* (Diom. 431. 18 K.), *hóra, léges, sálus, hómo* (Dositheus 378. 1 K.), *mêta, Crêta, nepos, bónus, málus* (Don. 371. 11 K.), *marínus, Crispínus, amícus, Sabínus, Quirínus, lectíca, Metéllus, Marcéllus, látebrae, ténebrae, Fidénae, Athénae, Thébae, Cúmae, tabéllae, fenéstrae, Sérgius, Mállius, áscia, fúscina, Július, Claúdius, Románi, legáti, praetóres, praedónes* (Diom. 431. 23 K.), &c.

Of compound words and word-groups with one accent (like our ' són-in-law,' ' man-of-wár,' ' pockethándkerchief,') we have examples such as *malesánus, intereáloci* (Don. 371. 22 K. ; Diom. 433. 30 K. ; Pomp. 130. 18 K. ; Cledonius 33. 12 K.). *Argilétum* (Prisc. ii. p. 113. 10 H. ; but with all three accents, Mart. Cap. iii. p. 68. 15 Eyss.), *propediem* [Don. ad Ter. *Ad.* v. 5. 7 (888)], *respublica, jusjurandum* (Prisc. i. p. 177. 10 H. ; i. p. 180. 12 H.), *jurisperitus, legislator, praefectusurbis* and *praefectusurbi, tribunusplebis, tribunusplebi, mentecaptus, orbisterrae, orbisterrarum, paterfamilias, paterfamiliarum, armipotens, armorumpotens, magistermilitum, asecretis, acalculis, aresponsis, abactis* (Prisc. i. p. 183. 5 H.), *istiusmodi, hujusmodi, cujusmodi* (Prisc. i. p. 440. 2 H.). Of *hujuscémodi,* &c., Priscian (i. p. 205. 16 H.) says that some regard them as two separate words, but the accent, resting as it does on the last syllable of the pronoun, shows that they are compounds. He distinguishes the separate accentuation of *decimus et septimus*, &c. from the single accent of *septimus-decimus*, &c. (*de Fig. Num.* xxi. p. 413. 11 K.).

§ 10. **Exceptions to the Paenultima Law.** The rule of Latin Accentuation, that final syllables are always unaccented, is, according to the grammarians, violated, or apparently violated, by certain classes of words. They are words which have dropped or contracted their last syllable, so that the accent, which in the uncurtailed form fell on the paenultima, remains in the curtailed form on the same syllable, which has now become the ultima. Under this category come :—

(1) Nouns, or rather Adjectives, in *-as*, Gen. *-atis*, indicating the country of one's birth, e. g. *cujás, nostrás, Arpinás*, with *primás, optimás* (Caper ap. Prisc. i. p. 128. 23 H.). These words, which in Early Latin (e. g. Plautus) have the full form *cujātis, nostrātis*, when at a later time they became contracted, retained their old accentuation; and so *nostrás*, 'a countryman of ours,' was distinguished by its accent from *nostras*, Acc. Pl. Fem. of the Possessive Pronoun (Priscian i. p. 454. 11 K.).

(2) Some Verbal Forms; *addĭc, addŭc*, &c., *fumát* (for *fūmāvĭt*), *audít* (for *audīvĭt*), and the like (Servius ad *Aen.* iii. 3). Another remark of Servius (ad *Aen.* i. 451), and other grammarians, throws some light on the last example. They tell us that *audĭit* and not *audĭit*, *lenĭit* and not *lenĭit*, was the ordinary pronunciation, the forms with the short penult being an artificial usage of poetry, much as in English the word 'wind' is allowed a different pronunciation in poetry from its ordinary one. From *-ĭit* to *-ĭt* is so short a step that it is difficult to justify a disbelief of the grammarians' statements about *audít*. The third Sing. Perf. Act. in Romance languages (e. g. Span. amó, Latin *ămāvĭt*, Ital. dormì, Latin *dormīvĭt*) points to Vulgar Latin forms in accented *-aut, -ĭt* (cf. *-aut* on graffiti of Pompeii, *C. I. L.* iv. 1391, 2048).

(3) Words ending in *-c* (the Enclitic *-cĕ*), whose last syllable is long by nature or by position, e. g. *adhúc, posthác, antehác, istíc, illíc, istúc, illúc, istinc, illinc, istác, illác, istóc, illóc* (Caper ap. Prisc. i. p. 130. 2 H.). Vulgar Latin accentuation of the final vowel of *illíc, illác*, &c. is indicated by the Romance adverbs, e. g. Ital. lì, là, Span. allí, allá.

(4) Words ending in *-n* (the Enclitic *-nĕ*), whose last syllable is long by nature or by position, e. g. *tantón, Pyrrhín* (Servius ad *Aen.* x. 668, &c.). This rule cannot however have been absolute, for forms like *vidĕn ut* in Old Latin Poetry, and even in Augustan poets (Virg. *Aen.* vi. 779; Tib. ii. 1. 25) show that when the final vowel of the particle was elided, the verb might retain the ordinary accentuation, *viden*, like *vides*. Servius (fourth cent.) tell us that *vidĕn* was the usage of his time (ad *Aen.* vi. 779 viden ut geminae stant vertice cristae] 'den' naturaliter longa est, brevem eam posuit, secutus Ennium : et adeo ejus est inmutata natura, ut jam ubique brevis inveniatur), and Plautus seems, when *-quĕ, -nĕ* is elided, to let the metrical ictus fall normally on the syllable which would have the accent in the absence of the particle, e. g. *prósp<u>ĕ</u>rēqu(e), surrúptasqu(e)* (*Amer. Journ. Phil.* xiv. 313).

An accent originally on the antepaenultima remains in the curtailed form on the paenultima, according to the grammarians, in contracted vocatives and genitives of IO-stems, e. g. *Vergíli, Valéri, tugúri* (Serv. ad *Aen.* i. 451 ; Prisc. i. p. 301. 21 H.). Gellius (second cent. A. D.) tells us that Nigidius Figulus (first cent. B. C.) wished to distinguish *Váleri* Voc. from *Valéri* Gen., but adds that in his own time such an accentuation as *Váleri* Voc. would sound very strange : siquis nunc Valerium appellans in casu vocandi secundum id praeceptum Nigidii acuerit primum, non aberit quin rideatur (*N. A.* xiii. 26).

Lastly, Interjections are excluded by the grammarians from the ordinary rule. They are said to have no ' certi accentus,' whatever that may mean ; and the statement of a late grammarian (Audacis exc. 361. 11 K. that *papaé* and *attát* (also *ehem*, MSS. *hoehem*?) were accented on the last syllable, is confirmed, in the case of at least the former, by the incidence of the metrical ictus in Plautus (always *papaé*, never *pápae*). The Greek εὖγε appears in Plautus' dramas with the last syllable lengthened[1] (cf. the MSS. spelling *eugae*), and the phrase *eugae-eugae* always has the metrical ictus *eugae-eúgae*.

Greek words, as was mentioned before (§ 3), when they were used by a Latin author with their Greek form and declension, retained also their Greek accent, e. g. *Epīros* in Virg. *Georg.* i. 59 (Serv. *ad loc.*).

§ 11. **Vulgar-Latin Accentuation.** The Latin accentuation is retained with wonderful tenacity by the Romance languages. Where they agree in deviating from the classical Latin accent, the accentuation which they reproduce is that of Vulgar Latin. There are four important cases of deviation :—

(1) First of all, in words ending in *-iĕrem, -iŏlum*, e. g. *mŭliĕrem, fīliŏlum*, the accent in Vulgar Latin was shifted from the *i* to the *e* and *o, muliérem, filiólum*. The precept of an unknown grammarian (Anecd. Helv. p. ciii. K.) sanctions this usage (mulierem in antepenultimo nemo debet acuere, sed in penultim potius), and in Christian poets of the third and fourth centuries we find scansions like insuper et Salomon, eadem muliĕre creatus, Drac. *Satisf.* 161 ; cf. Ital. figliuolo, Span. hijuelo, Fr. filleul. Nouns in *-iēs*, Gen. *-iētis* followed a somewhat different course. Their Nominative became *-ēs*, and this form was extended to the other cases, e. g. PARETES (*C. I. L.* vi. 3714), Acc. Sg. *parētem is attested by the Latin loanword in Welsh, parwyd, and by the Romance forms, e.g. Ital. parete (with close *e*), Span. paréd, &c., while *muliérem is the original of Ital. mogliére (with open *e* in the penult).

(2) Again the occurrence of a mute with the liquid *r* at the beginning of the last syllable seems to have attracted the accent to the penult. Thus Vulg. Lat. *tenébrae is attested by Span. tinieblas, and other Romance forms. We cannot be wrong in connecting this with the practice of Latin poets of treating a short syllable before a mute with *r* as a long syllable, when it suits their convenience (see ch. ii. § 142).

Servius (fourth cent.) (ad *Aen.* i. 384) seems to say that the accent was not in his time attracted to the penult in correct pronunciation ; for he remarks with regard to *peragro* in this line of Virgil ; ' per ' habet accentum . . . muta enim et liquida quotiens ponuntur metrum juvant, non accentum (cf. Diom. 431. 28 K.).

(3) In Compound Verbs the accent seems to have shifted to the stem-vowel of the verb in Vulgar or Late Latin, e. g. *recipit* is indicated by Ital. riceve, Fr. reçoit ; *renégat* by Ital. riniega, O. Fr. renie. With this we may connect the tendency in the spelling of post-classical inscriptions, and of our earliest MSS. to restore the vowels in compound verbs to their undecayed form, e. g. *consacro, compremo* (§ 18).

---

[1] Like our ' bravo ! ' 'hillo ! ' often pronounced with the voice dwelling on the final vowel.

§§ 11, 12.] ACCENTUATION OF SENTENCE. 165

(4) Lastly, the Romance forms of the Numerals give indications that the Vulgar Latin accentuation was *viginti, quadrāginta,* &c. (see Meyer-Lübke, *Gram. Rom. Sprach.* i. p. 494). *Triginta* is one of the barbarisms 'quae in usu cotidie loquentium animadvertere possumus,' enumerated by a fifth-century (?) grammarian (Consentius p. 392. 4 K.). On a fifth-cent. inscr. (vid. *A. L. L.* v. 106) we have *quarranta* for *quadrāgintā* (Ital. quaránta), and an epitaph in hexameters has *vinti* for *vīgintī* (Ital. venti) [Wilm. 569 (cf. *C. I. L.* viii. 8573):

et menses septem diebus cum vinti duobus].

§ 12. **Accentuation of the Sentence.** Hitherto we have been considering only the accentuation of words by themselves. But there is also such a thing as the accentuation of the sentence; and the accent which a word would bear, if uttered separately, may be different from the accent assigned to it when standing with other words in a sentence. The Greek preposition πρός, for example, had, if mentioned by itself, an acute accent. But in the sentence its accent was obscured by the accent of the noun which it governed, e.g. πρὸς πόλιν, and this by the Greek system was expressed by replacing its acute by a grave accent. So that the Greek system of marking the accents recognized both the word-accent and the sentence-accent.

By the Indo-European sentence-accentuation the verb in a main sentence was treated as a subordinate word, and apparently occupied the position proper to enclitic words, namely, the second place in the sentence, while in dependent clauses it received the accent like any other word, and stood at the end of the clause, an arrangement which has been, curiously enough, preserved in German to the present day (see Wackernagel in *Indog. Forsch.* i. pp. 333 sqq.). Indefinite pronouns were enclitic or subordinate words, while interrogatives were accented (cf. Greek ἀνήρ τις and τίς ἀνήρ;). Other enclitics were the copula *q^{u}e (Greek τε, Lat. quĕ), the personal pronouns (unless specially emphasized), &c.

We can determine with a fair amount of accuracy the accentuation of the Latin sentence, partly by the help of the remarks of Latin grammarians, partly from observing the phonetic changes of Latin words in the Romance languages, where an accented word or syllable is not subject to the same laws of development as an unaccented, partly from the analogy of other languages, and to a large extent from the versification of the early dramatists. For Plautus and Terence leave, as a rule, the subordinate words of the sentence, the words, in fact, which we omit in writing telegrams, in the theses of the line, where no metrical ictus falls on them:

e. g. Plaut. *Trin.* 21 [rogat] ut líceat possidére hanc nomen fábulam,

where *ut* and *hanc*, words which might be omitted without obscuring the meaning, are relegated to the theses of the first and fourth feet. The Latin grammarians, with their usual adherence to Greek terminology, speak of the 'attraction' of the accent by enclitics or subordinate words. But this statement of the facts is corrected by Quintilian (i. 5. 25, 26), who shows that a subordinate relative, like *qualis* in the sentence, talis est qualis Cicero fuit, or a subordinate preposition, like *circum* in Virg. *Aen.* iv. 254 quae circum litora, circum Piscosos scopulos, &c., is really in Latin united with the following word into a word-group, which takes the ordinary accent of a single word: cum dico 'circum litora,' tamquam unum enuntio dissimulata distinctione, itaque tamquam in una voce una est acuta. The Latin pronunciation would thus be *qualis-Cícero, circum-lítŏra.* Priscian (i. p. 183 H.) objects similarly to a statement of Hellenizing grammarians, that *quĭs*, the indefinite pronoun, in *sīquis*, *numquis*, &c., is an enclitic like τις in εἴτις, and prefers to call *siquis* a compound or word-group with the natural accent of a single word. With this correction, the rules of the Latin grammarians about enclitics and subordinate words are in the main probable enough in themselves, and are confirmed by the evidence of the Romance languages, and the early dramatists' versification, though some of their distinctions between the accentuation of words of the same spelling, such as *né*, 'verily,' *né*, prohibitive, *ne* 'lest'; *ádeo*, the verb, and *adéo*, the adverb; *út*, 'how,' *ut*, 'in order that'; *érgo*, 'therefore,' *ergó*, 'on account of,' require additional evidence before we can accept them.

§ 12*a*. **Latin Sentence-Enclitics.** Among Latin Sentence-Enclitics we may class:—

(1) Enclitic Particles like *quĕ* (I.-Eur. *q͡ʷĕ, O. Ind. ca, Gk. τε, all unaccented), *vĕ* [I. Eur. *wĕ, O. Ind. vā (unacccented), Gk. *ϝε in ἤ-ὲ from *ἦ-ϝε], and so on. Their enclitic nature is shown by their being always joined in writing with the preceding word, e. g. *atque*, *sīve*. In the rapid utterance of ordinary con-

§ 12ᵃ.] ACCENTUATION OF SENTENCE. 167

versation these words often lost their final vowel, and so appear also in the forms *ac* (for **atq*), *seu*, &c. (see § 35).

(2) The various parts of the substantive verb. The mode in which *es*, *est* are written in the best MSS. of Plautus, for example, *amatus* (*amatu's*), *amatust*, *amatumst* for *amatus es*, *amata est*, *amatum est* (cf. *ventumst*, &c. in Virgil MSS., Ribbeck, p. 419), shows that they were treated as mere appendages of the past participle passive. For the unaccented nature of ĕ*rat*, ĕ*rit*, &c. we have proof, if proof be needed, in Romance forms like Ital. era and Span. era (Lat. *erat*), O. Fr. ert (Lat. *erit*), for an accented ĕ would have taken another form, such as Ital. *iera, Span. *yera (cf. Ital. niega, Lat. *nĕgat*). It need hardly be said that the extent to which these words, and indeed all 'Sentence-Enclitics,' were suppressed, would depend on the caprice of the speaker, on the nuance of thought, on the style of composition, &c. No hard and fast rule can be laid down about them, just as no rule could be made for the use of "'s' for 'is,' ''re' for 'are' in English. A sentence, for example, of Cicero, ending with the words *lĭcĭtum est*, is quoted by a grammarian as an instance of a sentence ending with a monosyllable (Mar. Sacerd. 493. 14 K.).

(3) The personal and possessive pronouns, when unemphatic. In the Romance languages two distinct series have been developed for the personal pronouns : (*a*) the enclitic, e. g. Ital. mi, ti ; Fr. me, te : (*b*) the accented, e. g. Ital. me, te ; Fr. moi, toi. Similarly a Vulgar-Latin possessive **mus*, **mum*, **ma*, beside the regular *meus*, *meum*, *mea*, is indicated by French mon, ma, and Vulgar-Italian ma-donna, padre-mo, &c., which resemble O. Lat. *sis* for *suis*, &c. (see ch. vii. § 11), in such a line as Ennius, *Ann.* 151 M., postquam lumina sis oculis bonus Ancus reliquit. It is true that Priscian (ii. p. 141. 15 H.) expressly says that there is no distinction in Latin corresponding to the Greek distinction between εἶδέν με and εἶδεν ἐμέ, οὐκ ἐκεῖνον, apud nos autem pronomina eadem et discretiva sunt ut 'vidit me' vel, 'vidit me, illum autem non'; but he seems to refer rather to the identity of the written form of the emphatic and unemphatic pronoun, than to that of their intonation in discourse. In Plautus and Terence the ictus always falls on the preposition in phrases like *in me, ád me, intér se*, unless the pronoun is emphatic (or elided), just as in Greek we have πρός με, πρός σε, &c., or as in English we lay the stress on ' for,' ' with ' in ' for me,' ' with him,' &c. In O. Irish this tendency of pronunciation reduced the pronouns to mere suffixes, e. g. for-m, 'on me,' for-t, 'on thee,' &c. (but cf. Censorin. ap. Prisc. ii. p. 51. 11 H.).

(4) The demonstrative pronouns, when unemphatic. The Romance forms point to (*il*)*lum pătrem*, (*il*)*la māter*, &c. as the origin of the definite article in all the Romance languages, while *ille pater* seems to have been pronounced sometimes *il*(*le*) *pater*, e. g. Ital. il padre, Span. el padre, Prov. el paire, sometimes (*il*)*le pater*, e. g. Fr. le père. Similarly (*i*)*ste*, indicated by Ital. stasera, 'this evening,' is actually found in old MSS. (see Neue, *Formenlehre*³ ii. pp. 402 sq. ; on *sta* in the Itala, see Georges, *Lex. Wortf. s. v.*), and *isté* is mentioned as a barbarism by a third-century grammarian (Mar. Sac. p. 451. 10 K.).

(5) The relative and indefinite pronouns, while the interrogative and exclamatory were accented, e. g. *tális est quális Cicero fuit*, but *quális fuit Cicero !* The grammarians often distinguish between the accentuation of *quis, quális, quantus, quŏt, quŏtus, cujus, ŭbi, unde*, &c. when used interrogatively, and when they are merely relative or indefinite pronouns (e. g. Prisc. i. p. 61. 5 H., interrogativum est quod cum interrogatione profertur, ut *quis, quális, quántus,*

quót, quótus, cum suos servant accentus. Infinitum est interrogativorum contrarium, ut *quis, qualis, quantus, quot, quotus,* cum in lectione gravi accentu pronunciantur, cf. ii. p. 127. 2 H. *Partit.* p. 501. 14 H. So for *qui* interrog. and rel. *ib.* ii. p. 9. 20 H. ; *cujus,* interrog. and rel. *ib.* ii. p. 179. 3 H. ; *quo, ubi, unde, qua, ib.* ii. p. 132. 3 H. ; ii. p. 83. 11 H. 'qua' quando relativum est gravatur; *quando,* Charis. p. 111. 27 K. ; Prisc. ii. p. 82. 24 H. ; *quorsum, ib.* ii. p. 83. 11 H. &c.). Their usual expression for the subordination of the relative and indefinite forms of these words is that they 'have the grave accent' (gravi accentu pronuntiantur, gravantur), though sometimes they use language more applicable to Greek (e. g. ποῖος interrog., ποιός rel.), and say that 'they take the acute accent on the last syllable'; and Charisius (p. 111. 27 H.) gives an actual Latin example of this accentuation of the last syllable in the sentence quandó tot stragis acervos Vidimus. Quintilian, as we saw, corrects this statement of the case, and shows that the true account for the Latin language is to say that the relative is joined with the noun or important word beside it, this word-group taking the accent of any ordinary word. The line from Virgil would thus be really pronounced *quandó-tot stragis acervos,* &c., so that the accentuation of the final syllable of *quando* is due to the accident that it stands next to a monosyllabic word. The relative would have no accent in a sentence like quem testem te adducturum dixeras, for it would be joined with the noun into a word-group, *quem-téstem,* with the accent on the first syllable of the noun. When in a line of poetry the relative followed the noun, as in Plautus (*Amph.* 919) Testém quem dudum te ádducturum díxeras, the accentuation would presumably be by the same reasoning *testém-quem;* and this presumption seems to be confirmed by the versification of the dramatists.

(6) Prepositions, while adverbs, are accented. Thus we should say *sūpra hábitat,* but *supra moénia est; ánte vénit,* but *ante Caésarem vénit.* This distinction is often inculcated by the grammarians ; e. g. Palaemon (first cent. A. D.) (ap. Charis. p. 189. 10 K. = Diom. p. 407. 19 K.) insists on the different accentuation of *infra, supra, extra, intra, ultra, citra, circa, juxta, contra, subtus, coram, ante, post, prope, usque, super,* when adverbs, and when prepositions ; cf. Charis. p. 231. 24 K. ; Audax, p. 353. 22 K. ; Probus, *Inst.* p. 149. 27 K. ; Mart. Cap. iii. p. 67. 21 Eyss.; Prisc. ii. p. 28. 24 H. ; ii. p. 30. 25 H. ; ii. p. 33. 1 H. ; ii. p. 42. 7 H. ; ii. p. 45. 25 H. ; ii. p. 51. 11 H. &c.). Priscian (ii. p. 27. 4 H.) says that Latin prepositions, like Greek, had, by themselves the acute accent on the last syllable (*supér, ὑπέρ*), but in the sentence lost this accent ; (accentum habent praepositiones acutum in fine, tam apud Graecos quam apud nos, qui tamen cum aliis legendo, in gravem convertitur) (cf. Don. p. 391. 11 K.) ; and Quintilian, as before mentioned, says that what really happened in Latin was that the preposition was fused with its noun into a word-group, which was then accented like any ordinary word, e. g. *circum-litora* (accented like *circumsistite, circumlitio*). Indeed the words are often written together in old MSS. and inscriptions; cf. Mar. Vict. 23. 12 K. and Indices to *C. I. L.* (so Umbr. preveres 'ante portas'). This suggests that in collocations like *in via, per dolum, in manus* the preposition itself may have received the accent of the word-group, unless it were desirable for some special reason to give prominence to the noun. This view is supported by some word-groups, which established themselves in Latin usage, such as *obviam, sēdŭlo (sē, sinē dolo), commĭnus, dēnŭo (dē nŏvo), admŏdum, affătim* (but cf. Gell. vi. 7), as well as by the versification of the dramatists, which also points to *in-rem,*

in-spem, in-jūs, &c. (cf. *quamobrem.*) A preposition placed after its noun received an accent, as in Greek, according to the grammarians (e. g. Prisc. ii. p. 27. 4 H. cum praepostere ponuntur, monosyllabae acuto, disyllabae paenultimo acuto proferuntur) ; but remained unaccented in phrases like *virtutem propter imperatoris* or *justitia in legum,* where the preposition is followed by a genitive dependent on the noun (Censorinus ap. Prisc. ii. p. 33. 20 H.).

(7) That conjunctions, like prepositions, had a different pronunciation according as they came first or second in the sentence is asserted by Priscian (ii. p. 24. 21 H.) praepositae gravantur omnibus syllabis, postpositae acuuntur in principio. He refers expressly to *ĭgĭtur, quŏniam, saltem,* so that he would have us pronounce, e. g. *igitur Cicero vēnit,* but *vēnit igitur Cicero*. That the monosyllabic conjunctions *ĕt, sĕd,* and the like, were enclitic words in the sentence, may be proved, if proof be wanted, from the versification of the early dramatists, in whose lines these conjunctions are relegated as a rule to the theses, and do not receive the metrical ictus, and also from the Romance languages, where the Latin monosyllabic conjunctions have suffered the same phonetic changes as the unaccented syllables of Latin words. *Et,* for example, if the word had been accented, would have become **iet,* or some similar form, instead of Ital. e, Fr. et, Span. y.

(8) Auxiliary verbs in Latin must, like those in other languages, have been enclitic, or rather, according to the Latin practice, must have been joined with their verb into a word-group, e. g. *volo-scire, coctum-dabo, missum-facit, cave-fácias.* In Plautus *volo-scire* is always scanned *volŏ-scīre,* never *volŏ-scire* ; and the metrical ictus in his verses of phrases like *factum-volo, faciás-volo, missám-face, cavĕ-pársis, cavĕ-fáxis* supports our rule. Cicero's story about Crassus at his departure for Parthia mistaking the cry of a fig-seller, *Cauneas ! Cauneas !* (sc. *ficus vendo*) for *căve nē eas* (*Div.* ii. 40. 84) seems to show that in ordinary talk this verbal phrase was treated as a word-complex with a single accent *cau(e)-n(e)-eas.* Similarly a verbal phrase like *ŏpĕram-dăre, fidem-dăre, dōnŏ-dăre* would probably have ordinarily only one accent, just as we throw the stress on the noun 'noise' and not on the verb 'make' in the phrase 'to make a noise.' The dramatists let the metrical ictus fall on these phrases thus : *fidém-ḍans, operám-dat, operám-dabam, donó-data.* The reduction of other unemphatic verbs to mere members of a compound word is indicated by the traditional way of writing *quōlĭbet, quamvīs, quantumvīs,* and the like. *Sīs,* 'if you please,' from *sī vīs* (cf. *sultis,* Plur.), is an enclitic appendage of the imperative, e. g. *prŏpĕrā-sis* as much as *dum* in *excŭtĕ-dum, aspicĕ-dum.* (Plautus gives to these phrases the ictus *properá-sis, excútedum, aspicedum,* &c.)

(9) Some nouns too of subordinate meaning must have become members of word-groups. In English 'thing,' 'kind,' 'state,' 'part' are used in this way without stress, in such sentences as 'something (nothing) of that kind,' 'some parts of England.' That *mŏdus, rēs* were so used in Latin we see from the traditional spelling *quŏmŏdo ? quārē ?* So *dies* in *propediem* (Don. ad Ter. *Ad.* 888), *quotidie, postridie.* Gellius (x. 24) says that in the time of Cicero and the earlier period, the phrase *diequinte* or *diequinti* was in vogue, ' pro adverbio copulate dictum, secunda in eo syllaba correpta,' and we may guess that *dies* formed a compound with *triginta* (*viginti*) from the fact that these two numerals are perhaps never found in Plautus and Terence with the ictus on the last syllable, except when *dies* (or *minae*) follows, e. g. *Men.* 951

át ego te pendéntem fodiam stímulis trigintá dies,

where the last two words seem to make a compound noun, like our 'fortnight,' 'twelvemonth.' *Lŏcus* too might be subordinated in a phrase like *intĕreā loci* (Don. ad Ter. *Eun.* 255), *ŭbi loci*, &c. The versification of the early dramatists, and the compound words in Romance suggest as similar wordgroups phrases like *vaé-mĭhi*, *vaé-miseró-mĭhi*, *bene-rém-gĕrit*, *male-rém-gĕrit* (with metrical ictus normally on these accented syllables in Plautus), *ad-illam-hôram* (Ital. allora, Fr. alors), *ad-mentem-habêre* (Prov. amentaver, O. Fr. amentevoir), *avis-strūthio* (Fr. autruche, Span. avestruz), *avis-tárda* (Ital. ottarda, Fr. outarde, Port. abetarda), *foris-făcĕre* (O. Ital. forfare, Fr. forfaire), *male-hăbĭtus* (O. Sp. malato, Prov. malapte, Fr. malade), &c., (cf. Engl. 'goodbye' for 'God be wi' ye').

§ 13. **Syncope.** The syncope or suppression of an unaccented vowel is a common feature of languages which have a stress-accent, and is carried to the greatest length by the language whose stress-accent is most powerful. The Celtic languages had a stronger stress-accent than Latin, and so we find in Old Irish some words borrowed from Latin (which the Romans had themselves borrowed from the Greeks), reduced by syncope to a much greater extent than they were in Latin, e.g. felsub, Latin *phĭlŏsŏphus*, apstal, Latin *ăpostŏlus*. And in countries under Celtic influence, such as France or the northern parts of Italy (e.g. in the Romagna dmeng for *dŏmĭnĭca*, Sunday), Latin words have been curtailed much more than in other parts of the Romance-speaking world. In ancient Italy, too, we see syncope more developed in some districts than in others, e.g. Mgolnia for Magolnia on a Praenestine inscription (*C.I.L.* i. 118), though it is not always easy to say when such forms are merely graphic, and indicate the use not of a contracted pronunciation, but only of a contracted system of writing. The conditions under which vowel-syncope was carried out differed at different periods. In Latin a vowel between *n* and *m* was not syncopated, because the consonant-group *nm* was difficult to pronounce, e.g. *ănĭma* not *anma. But in the Romance languages syncope has been pushed a stage further, e.g. Prov. anma, alma, arma, Old Fr. anme, alme, arme, Fr. âme, Span. alma, Sicil. arma, Ital. alma (in poetry), the unmanageable group *nm* being often changed to *rm*, just as original *nm* in Latin *can-men from *căno*, *gen-men from *gĕno, gigno* became *rm* in *carmen, germen* (ch. iv. § 78). Similarly *pertĭca*, which resisted syncope in Latin, in Italian (pertica), and in other languages, has succumbed in French (perche, our 'perch') and Provençal (perga). *Frīgĭdus* appears in all the

Romance languages in a syncopated shape (Ital. freddo, Fr. froid, &c.) (ch. ii. § 132). *Vĭrĭdis*, too, was in Vulg. Lat. *vĭrdis* (Ital. verde, Span. verde, Fr. vert), and *călĭdus* appears early as *caldus*. Analogy also may often prevent syncope, or, after words have been syncopated, may restore them to their original form. Thus *porgo*, for example, was restored to *porrĭgo* by the analogy of the perfect *porrexi*; and the analogy of other adjectives in *-ĭdus* where this termination was preceded by some uncombinable consonant, e.g. *frigidus*, may account for the existence of unsyncopated adjectives like *calidus*; for the consonants in *calidus*, *l* and *d*, are of a kind that would be easily combined. A Nom. Sing. like *hortus*, if syncopated to **horts*, **hors*, would soon be restored to its old form by analogy of the other cases *horti, horto*, &c. In the compound *cohors* we do indeed find this monosyllabic form; and one might be tempted to think that the syncope of *hortus* to **hors* had led to the word becoming an I-stem for an O-stem, **hors, *hortis*, from *hortus, horti*. But the I-stem of *cohors* is more easily accounted for by the Latin predilection for I-stem compounds of O-stem nouns, e.g. *exanimis, unanimis* from *ănĭmus* (ch. v. § 34.). It is doubtful whether any clear case of a change of stem through syncope of the final syllable of a Nom. Sg. is to be found in Latin.

It appears, then, that vowels resisted syncope when they stood between consonants which did not easily combine, and that the analogy of unsyncopated forms might prevent or efface syncope in whole classes of words. With these exceptions, it seems to have been the law of Early Latin that *ĕ, ĭ* in the syllable after the accent always suffered syncope, unless they were long by 'position.' This *ĕ, ĭ* might be original *ĕ, ĭ*, or the reduced (posttonic) form of original *ă, ŏ* (§ 18). The Early Latin accent fell, as we have seen above (§ 5), on the first syllable of each word, so that every *ĕ, ĭ* in a second syllable not long by position must have suffered syncope.

The syllable *-rĭ-*, preceded by a consonant, followed laws of its own. It appears in the posttonic syllable as *ĕr*, e.g. *păternus* for **patrĭ-nus*. Similarly *-lĭ-* appears in the posttonic syllable as *ŭl (ŏl)* in *făcultas*, &c. (see ch. iv. § 13). The syllable *-vĭ-* also stands apart from others owing to the vowel-nature of its con-

sonant, which facilitated syncope. Thus we have syncope of
a vowel preceded by *v* even in a syllable long by position, e. g.
aunculus (Plautus), the ordinary conversational form of *ăvoncŭlus*
(cf. *anculus*, *C. I. L.* viii. 3936, ix. 998); or rather the semivocalic
w has dropped out between the two vowels. Similarly *dītior*
for *dīvĭtior*, *děorsum* (dissyllabic *deorsum* in Plaut.) for *dēvorsum*,
and the like, are different from the ordinary cases of syncope.

The tendency to syncope continued to assert itself at all
periods of the language. Words which resisted it at an earlier
period often, as we have seen, succumbed at a later. The new
law of accentuation, the Paenultima Law (§ 8), brought with it
the possibility of a new variety, namely, suppression of the
syllable preceding the accent. Pretonic syncope is a feature of
Indo-European, where indeed it was much commoner than post-
tonic syncope, but it could play no part in Latin so long as the
accent remained invariably on the first syllable. It is often
difficult to say whether a case of syncope is pretonic or post-
tonic. In words like *ārdēre*, *ārdōrem*, for example, we say
that the syncope of *ĭ* of **ărĭdēre*, **ărĭdōrem* is due to the new
accent on the penult; **arĭdére*, **aridórem*, but it might possibly
be referred to the influence of the old accent on the first syllable,
*áridere, **áridorem*. Words like *artēna* (Greek ἀρύταινα), *perstrōma*
(Greek περίστρωμα) Lucil. (i. 41 M. and Löwe, *Prodr.* p. 347),
both borrowed no doubt after the old accent law had ceased to
operate, are clearer cases of pretonic syncope. So are enclitic or
subordinate words which drop final *ĕ* before an initial consonant,
e. g. *nempe, proinde, deinde*, which before a consonant often took
the forms **nemp* (so scanned by Plautus and Terence, ch. x. § 7),
proin, dein, as *atque, nĕque* became *ac* (for **atq, atc*), *nec*. So
benfĭcium, malfĭcium, calfăcio, &c. And the influence of the
following accent, rather than the mere addition of extra syllables,
seems to be the real factor in the syncope in the literary period
of such words as *frigdária* (Lucil. viii. 12 M.) beside *frígĭdus*,
caldárius beside *cálĭdus, portórium* beside *pórtĭtor, postrídie* beside
pósteri, altrínsĕcus beside *álteri*. The weakening effect on an
unaccented syllable of a following accent is shown by Plautine
scansions like *sĕnĕctútem, vŏlŭntátem, pŏtĕstátem, perĭstróma*, where
an additional weakening element is supplied by the short syllable

§ 13.]   ACCENTUATION. SYNCOPE.   173

preceding. These scansions must reflect the pronunciation of these words in ordinary conversation. Similarly *calē-fácere* became *calĕ-fácere* and *cal-fácere*, and *mĭnĭstérium* passed into *minstérium* or *mistérium* (cf. Plaut. *Pseud.* 772), the consonant-group *st* being specially adapted to combination with a preceding liquid or nasal (cf. *per(i)stroma* above). The unaccented -*vĭ*- of *ăvĭdus*, which resisted syncope in the simple adjective-form, succumbs to the influence of the following accent in the lengthened derivative **avidḗre, audḗre*, to have a mind for, to dare [e. g. *si audes* (Plaut.), if you please, in the classical period *sōdes*].

Arid- of *ăridus* becomes *ard*- in *ardḗre, ardṓrem*, and by their analogy sometimes appears in the simple adjective (*ardus*, Lucil. xxvii. 40 M.). Similarly *aet*- for *aevĭt*- in *aetās* may have come into use first in the lengthened cases *aetā́tis, aetā́ti, aetā́tem*, or in derivatives like *aetérnus*, though here the syncopated form of the trisyllable established itself in ordinary usage, unlike *ardus*. Forms like *caldárius* may have had some influence in introducing *caldus* into the colloquial usage (it hardly came into the literary) of the Augustan period. Quintilian (i. 6. 19) tells us that Augustus stigmatized as a piece of affectation the use of *calidus* for *caldus* (non quia id non sit latinum, sed quia sit odiosum, et, ut ipse Graeco verbo significavit, περίεργον), and yet in the Appendix Probi we find *calda* under the same condemnation as *frigda, virdis* (198. 3 K.).

Post-tonic syncope, under the new accent law, seems, during the Republic and Early Empire, to occur only when the accented vowel is long [1], e. g. *júrgo* (in Plautus still *júrigo*), *usūrpo* for **usūripo, -ās* for (Plautine) -*átis* in *nostrás, Arpinás, summás*, &c., though we find it in the period of the Early Literature after a shortened vowel in words of four or more syllables where three short syllables followed each other before the final syllable, e. g. *bălĭnĕum* [so Plaut. and Ter., and *balineator, Rud.*, 527 (A.)], a spelling which did not yield for some time to later *balneum* [*balinearium, C.I.L.* i. 1166 (c. 130 B. C.); Caper (first cent. A. D.)(108. 7 K.) prefers *balneum*; cf. Gloss. Plac. 9. 29, and see Georges, *Lex. Wortf.* s. v.;

---

[1] Syncope after a long vowel is due to the tendency to make a long vowel extra long.

balineum occurs frequently on the Lex Metalli Vipascensis of the first century A.D. (*Eph. Epigr.* iii. p. 166)], *ŏpĭtŭmus* [the spelling OPITVMA of an archaizing inscription, *C. I. L.* i. 1016 (=vi. 1958) of the late Republic or early Empire shows that this form had not been so long obsolete as to be forgotten, though as early as the Scipio Epitaph, *C. I. L.* i. 32, c. 200 B.C., we have OPTVMO, 'optimum']. These words, as we saw above (§ 5), had in the time of Plautus and Terence the accent on the first syllable, *bălĭnĕum* producing *balneum*, *ŏpitumus optumus. Similarly *ŏpĭfĭcīna*, *ŏpificína* (Plaut. *Mil.* 880), produced *officina*, *puĕrĭtĭa* (with the ictus *puéritia* in all the instances, not many, of its occurrence in the early dramatists) produced the *puertia* of Horace [*C.* i. 36. 8 actae non alio rege puertiae; Charisius (fourth century A.D.) still recognized *pueritia* as the correct form, 266. 7 K.]. But forms like *caldus, virdis, domnus* belong to colloquial or to Vulgar Latin, and were not as a rule established in the language till the later Empire, though *valde*, older *vălĭde*, Plaut. *Pseud.* 364, and a few other words, were current at a much earlier time. The same wave of syncope that reduced *viridis, dŏmĭnus*, &c., to dissyllabic form attacked *u, i* in hiatus (cf. ch. ii. § 48). As early as the latter half of the first century A.D. *tĕnuis* varied between a dissyllable and a trisyllable (Caesellius ap. Cassiod. vii. 205. 16 K.); *cardus* (for *carduus*) (ch. ii. § 54), *mortus* (for *mortuus*), &c., are the precursors of the Romance forms (Ital., Span. cardo, Ital. morto, Span. muerto, Fr. mort); while the similar reduction of *i* (*e*), led to that palatalization of consonants which has so transformed the whole appearance of the Romance languages, e. g. Ital. piazza, Span. plaza, Fr. place from Vulg. Lat. *platya, Lat. *plătĕa*, &c. (see ch. ii. § 48).

Forms like *saeclum* beside *saeculum* are not to be classed with forms like *jurgo* beside *jurigo*, for *saeclum* is the older form, while in *saeculum* a vowel has been inserted between the *c* and the *l* to facilitate pronunciation, a vowel which is generally called a 'parasitic' vowel, or, in the terminology of the Sanscrit grammarians, a 'svarabhaktic' vowel (from Sanscr. svarabhakti-, 'partial vowel'); see chap. ii. § 154. The termination *-cŭlus, -cŭlum* in Latin sometimes represents the I.-Eur. suffix *-tlo*, which indicates the instrument with which an action is performed, or the place of its performance, sometimes the suffix *-colo*, a compound of two I.-Eur. diminutive suffixes, *-co* and *-lo*. To the first class belong words like *vĕhĭculum*, 'that by which one is carried'; *pōculum*, 'that out of which one drinks'; *cŭbĭculum*, 'the place where one lies down'; *pĕrīculum* from **perior, perītus, experior*: *ōrāculum* from *orare*. To the second, diminutives like *corculum, uxorcula, sucula*. These two classes of terminations are not distinguished by us in our ordinary practice of writing Latin; they show, however, in the hands of Plautus a notable difference of metrical treatment. For in his verses the first suffix appears normally as one syllable, *-clus, -clum*, reflecting without doubt the current pronunciation of his time; the second as two syllables, *-culus, -culum*. Thus Plautus has always *vĕhĭclum*, with that monosyllabic form of the suffix which we find invariably when by dissimilation the *cl* is changed into *cr*, e. g. *ambŭlācrum*, 'a place for walking in,' for **ambulaclum*, while diminutives like *aurĭcula, pulvisculus* retain the dissyllabic suffix in his plays as persistently as *ăgrĭcŏla, incŏla*, or any other compound of the verb *cŏlo*. So do nouns formed by the addition of the suffix *-lo* to *-co*-stems, in distinction to those formed by its addition to *-c*-stems, e. g. *porcu-lus, cĕlōc-la*, 'a yacht.' Probably not a single instance occurs in his verses of *-col-* reduced to *-cl-* by syncope, even after a long vowel, e. g. never **corclum* from *cor-cu-lum*, **porclus* from *porcu-lus* (*Class. Rev.* vi. 87). (But *privicloes*, 'priviculis,' Carm. Sal., ch. vi. § 49.)

Forms with the parasitic or svarabhaktic vowel, with *-colo*- for *-clo*-, are indeed not infrequent with him. *Cubiculum*, for instance, always or almost always, appears as a quadrisyllable. But he uses these expanded forms as a rule (especially when a long vowel precedes), only at the end of a line or half-line; that is to say he regards the equivalence of the parasitic vowel to an actual short syllable as a licence only to be resorted to in cases of metrical necessity. For example, *periclum* is the normal form of the word, while *periculum* occurs only at the end of a line or hemistich. *Capt.* 740 is a good example of this distinction:

periclum vitae meae tuo stat periculo;

and it is only at the end of a line that the phrase *nullumst peri-*

clum (e. g. *Pseud.* 1076) becomes *nullum periculumst* (e. g. *Capt.* 91). *Poculum*, too, shows this full form usually in a similar position, while *saeclum* is never allowed trisyllabic scansion at all. The Romance languages show that a later wave of syncope not only reduced *saec(u)lum*, &c. to their original form *saeclum*, but also words like *porculus* to *porclus*, e. g. Ital. cerchio, (Lat. *circ(u)lus*), teschio (Lat. *test(u)la*), spillo (Lat. *spīn(u)la*). (Cf. *oclus*, *C. I. L.* x. 7756, &c., *crustlum*, xi. 3303, of 18 A.D., *Proclaes*, xv. 1157, of 123 A.D., *Vitlus*, viii. 9432, &c., Λεντλος, &c. on Greek inscriptions, Eckinger, pp. 73-5, *Masclus* (Gk. Μασκλος, &c.); so in Probi App. 197. 20-22 K. speculum non 'speclum,' masculus non 'masclus,' vetulus non 'veclus,' vitulus non 'viclus,' vernaculus non 'vernaclus,' articulus non 'articlus,' baculus non 'baclus,' angulus non 'anglus,' jugulus non 'juglus,' and 198. 18 oculus non 'oclus,' 198. 23 tabula non 'tabla,' 198. 27 stabulum non 'stablum,' 198. 34 capitulum non 'capiclum,' 199. 9 tribula non 'tribla,' 199. 14 vapulo non 'vaplo' (MS. baplo); and see George's *Lex. Wortf.* s. vv. *coag(u)lo*, *aedic(u)la*, *assec(u)la*, *bub(u)lus*, *conch(u)la*, *Vist(u)la*, *cop(u)la*, *cop(u)lo*, *cubic(u)lum*, *vit(u)lus*, *discip(u)lina*, *extemp(u)lo*; *fib(u)la*, *fig(u)linus*, *laterc(u)lus*, *Herc(u)le*, *jug(u)lans*, *manic(u)la*, *ment(u)la*, *masc(u)lus*, *orac(u)lum*, *poc(u)lum*, *peric(u)lum*, *pedic(u)lus*, *saec(u)lum*, *scrup(u)lus*, *sextula* (*sescla*), *surc(u)lus*, *spec(u)lum*, *sub(u)la*, *temp(u)lum*, *trich(i)la*, *vinc(u)lum*, *vet(u)lus*, *vernac(u)lus*, *Asc(u)lum*, *Vist(u)la*, &c.; cf. Schuch. *Vok.* ii. 402 sqq.). Fr. roule, &c. from unsyncopated *rŏtŭla* points to a re-formed diminutive; so in Roumanian, e.g. teule or tiule (Lat. *tēgŭla*) (Taverney in *Études* ... *G. Paris*, p. 267). (See also § 21.)

Another case of syllable-suppression which differs from ordinary syncope is that of words like *arcubii* ('qui excubabant in arce,' Paul. Fest. 19. 10 Th.) for *arcĭ-cŭbii*, where the proximity of two almost identical syllables *cĭ* and *cŭ* has caused or facilitated the dropping of the former. [Similarly *sēmĭmŏdius* and *semodius*, *dēbĭlĭtare* for *debilitātāre*, *fastīdium* for *fastĭtīdium*, *īdōlatria* for *īdōlŏla*-, *limitrophus* for *limitotro*-, *Restūtus* for *Restĭtūtus* (*A. L. L.* viii. 368), &c., as in Greek ἀμ(φι)φορεύς, ψη(φο)φορία, λει(πο)πυρία, &c.].

And a large number of words, like *dixem* (beside *dixissem*), *audissem* (beside *audīvissem*), *audī-trix* (beside *auditor*), *gi-gno* (beside *gĕn-us*), are often wrongly included with genuine cases of Latin syncope like *lardum, jurgo*. In some of these there is either no syncope at all (so some explain *dixem* for **dic-sem*, like *es-sem*; but see ch. viii. § 3), or, if there is, it took place in the I.-Eur. period, e.g. I.-Eur. **ĝĭ-ĝnō* (ch. iv. § 51), *-trī-* (*ib.*); others, e.g. *dixem*, if a reduction of *dixissem* (ch. viii. § 3), are rather to be explained like *ar(ci)cubii* above; *audissem*, if a reduction of *audivissem* (ch. viii. § 3), like *sīs* for *sī vīs*.

§ 14. Syncope in the Praenestine Dialect of Latin. On the Latin inscriptions found at Praeneste there are a large number of omissions of vowels, e.g. *Dcumius* (for *Dĕcŭmius*), *C.I.L.* i. 1133, *Gminia* (for *Gĕmĭnia*), *Eph. Epigr.* i. 72, *Diesptr* (for *Diēspĭter*), *C.I.L.* i. 1500; *Ptronio* (for *Pĕtrōnio*), *Eph. Epigr.* i. 92; a full list in Sittl, *Lokal. Verschied. Lat. Sprache*, p. 22. This tallies so remarkably with a reference by Plautus to a peculiar pronunciation of the Praenestines, *conea* for *cĭcōnia*, 'a stork,' that it is likely that these spellings represent the actual sound of the words. In the *Truculentus* of Plautus the surly, taciturn slave Truculentus, whose mispronunciations are more than once a subject of jest (cf. line 683), turns the word *arrăbo*, 'a prepayment,' 'earnest-money,' into *rabo*, 'a raver' (cf. *rabere*, 'to rave,' *rabula*, 'a bawling pettifogging lawyer'); and on being taken to task, says that he has pocketed a part of his *arrabo* as the Praenestines do with *ciconia* (line 690):

'ar' facio lucri,
ut Praenestinis 'conea' est ciconia.

(Cf. *misisia* for Ital. *amicizia* in the modern Parmese dialect; Ital. *nemico* for Lat. *inĭmīcus*, &c.) The omitted vowel is *e* or *i*, once *a* (*Mgolnia*, *C.I.L.* i. 118) (besides *Acmemeno* for *Ăgămemno*, on an old Praenestine cista, *Eph. Epigr.* i. 19), and the omission is easily explained by the influence of the accent in words like *Diésp(i)t(e)r*, *P(e)trónio*, and, if we admit that the antepaenultima was accented in these words in the Praenestine dialect at this period, in *D(e)cumius*, *G(e)minia* (cf. *Cem(i)na*, *C.I.L.* i. 99). But an accented vowel is omitted in *Trtia* (for *Tertia*), *Eph.* i. 108, *Pol(i)dia*, *Eph.* i. 95, and even a long accented vowel in *Atlia* (for *Ātīlia*), *Eph.* i. 33.

A grammarian of the second cent. A.D. (Terentius Scaurus, pp. 14, 15 K.) tells us of a practice of an earlier date of substituting a letter for the name of the letter. The name of *c* was '*ce*,' of *d* was '*de*,' of *k* was '*ka*'; and so *cra* was written for *cĕra*, *kra* for *kara* (*cāra*). His example for *d* is almost exactly our first example of the Praenestine contraction, viz. *Dcimus* for *Decimus*. These words of Terentius Scaurus suggest that spellings like *Albsi* for *Albēsi*, *Albensi* on an inscription of Alba Fucentia, a town not far removed from the Praenestine district (Zvetaieff, *Inscr. Ital. Inf.* 46), *lubs mereto* (for *lubēs, lubens merito*) on an inscription found near Avezzano, in the same neighbourhood (*C.I.L.* i. 183), are indications of a syllabic system of writing in partial use in this region of Italy (ch. i. § 13), and leave us in doubt about the real nature of Praenestine pronunciation.

§ 15. **Syncope under the Old Accent Law.** (1) The preposition *ambi-* (Gk. ἀμφί) loses its second syllable in compounds like *ánculus*, 'a servant,' for **ámbi-cŏlus* (Gk. ἀμφί-πολος, Sanscr. abhi-caras), an old Latin word from which came *anculare*, 'to serve' (Paul. Fest. 15. 7 Th.) and *ancilla*; *ancĭpes* (Plaut. Rud. 1158), later *anceps* (from *ambi-* and *căput*); *am-plector*, &c. The same shortening may have caused that confusion of the old preposition *indo* (*endo*) (ch. ix. § 27) with the preposition *in* (*en*) (*ĭnd(o)grĕdior*, &c. becoming by syncope identical with *ingredior*) which led to the disuse of *indo* and the adoption of *in* in its place. Thus *indaudio* (Plaut.) was completely ousted by *inaudio* in the time of Terence, and in the classical period compounds with *indo* are only found as archaisms in poets, e. g. *indŭpĕrātor* Juv.

(2) The second syllable of the first member of a compound is syncopated in *hospes* for **hostĭ-pes*, *princeps* for **prīmĭ-ceps* (cf. *primi-gĕnia*, an epithet of the goddess Fortuna, unsyncopated because *m* and *g* do not easily combine); *forceps* for *formĭ-ceps* (from *formus*, 'hot,' connected with Gk. θερμός. Paul. Fest. 59. 18 gives us this etymology, forcipes dicuntur, quod his forma, id est calida, capiuntur; cf. Vel. Long. 71. 15 K.); *quindecim* from *quīnquĕ* and *dĕcem*; *undecim* from *ūnus* and *decem*; *universus* is a re-formation from an older syncopated form which we find on the Decree of the Senate against the Bacchanalian orgies, an inscription of the time of Plautus (186 B. C.) (though Plautus himself uses the four-syllabled *universus*) (*C. I. L.* i. 196. 19 homines plous V oinuorsei uirei atque mulieres sacra ne quisquam fecise uelet) (this may be a mistake for **oinuuorsei*, like *sursuorsum* on the Sentent. Minuc. l. 15); *vindēmia* for **vīnĭ-dēmia*; *Marpor* (*C. I. L.* i. 1076) for *Marcĭ-por*, &c.

(3) The first syllable of a verb compounded with a preposition is suppressed in *pergo* for **per-rĭgo* (cf. *perrexi, perrectum*); *porgo*, the old form of *porrĭgo*, **por-rĕgo* (cf. Fest. 274. 15 Th. antiqui etiam ' porgam ' dixerunt pro porrigam), e. g. *exporgere lumbos*, 'to stretch one's legs,' Plaut. *Pseud*. prol. 1, cf. *Epid*. 733; the word, sanctioned by the usage of Virgil (*A.* viii. 274 pocula porgite dextris), appears now and then in the Silver Age poets (Val. Flacc. ii. 656; Stat. *Theb.* viii. 755, &c.), but the classical form is *porrigo*; *surgo* for *surrĭgo*, **sub-rĕgo*; a deponent perf. participle *sortus* for **surctus*, formed on the analogy of the syncopated pres. ind., was often used by Livius Andronicus (Paul. Fest. 423. 1 Th.); beside *surrŭpui* (classical *surrĭpui*) we have the syncopated form *surpui* in Plautus (e. g. *Capt.* 760), and even a perf. part. pass. formed after its type, *surptus* (*Rud.* 1105). Lucretius also uses the contracted form of the present (ii. 314 motus quoque surpere debent), and Horace (*S.* ii. 3. 283 unum me surpite morti; cf. *C.* iv. 13. 20 quae me surpuerat mihi); *pono* for **pŏ-sĭno* (the preposition is *pŏ*-a byform of **ăpŏ*, *ăb*), *postus*, *depostus*, *compostus*, very common for *pŏ-sĭtus*, &c.; like *postus* is *prae-stŏ*, earlier *prae-stŭ* (Cassiod. 157. 22 K.), ready, at hand, for **prae-sĭtu*; *cette* for **cedite*, **cĕ-dăte*, where the particle *cĕ*, 'here,' 'hither,' is prefixed to the verb, as in Oscan ce-bnust, ' huc venerit ' (Zvetaieff, *Inscr. Ital. Inf.* 231. 20). These syncopated forms were probably far more frequent in the early period, than at a later time, when the same tendency to recomposition which produced *con-sacro* out of *consecro*, *ad-sum* out of *assum* (ch. iv. § 160) restored *por-rigo*, *sur-ripui*, &c. The older forms might remain undisturbed in derivatives whose connexion with the verb was unnoticed, e. g. *refriva faba* (*referiva*, Plin. xviii. 119), the bean brought back by the farmer from the field for luck (in Fest. 380. 17 Th. we are told that the word was also associated with *refrīgo*, 'to roast,' 'parch '); *aprīcus, Aprīlis* may be similar

§ 15.]   ACCENTUATION. SYNCOPE.   179

traces of an *ap-(e)rio* (cf. *ŏp-ĕrio*), unless the syncope in all three words was pretonic syncope under the Paenultima Law of Accentuation, *ref(e)rīva*, *ap(e)rĭcus*, *Ap(e)rĭlis*. Verbs beginning with a vowel unite it into one sound with the final vowel of the preposition, though to what period of the language this crasis should in each case be referred is uncertain, for it might be caused by a following as well as by a preceding accent. Crasis was the rule in such compounds in the early period, to judge from the usage of the older poets. *Coerce*, for example, is dissyllabic in Pacuvius (*Trag.* 47 R.),

gradere átque atrocem coerce confidéntiam (see ch. ii. § 150).

(4) The first syllable of a reduplicated perfect of a compound verb is dropped in *reppĕri*, *rettŭli*, *reccĭdi*, &c., where the double consonant seems to preserve a trace of the syncope (see ch. viii. § 44). The syncope would in these perfects be facilitated by the Latin tendency to drop one of two neighbouring syllables of like sound (see on *arcubii* for *arcĭ-cŭbii*, above § 13); and it is natural to suppose that the perfects without reduplication, like *ex-scĭdi* (O. Lat. *scĭcĭdi*), *con-curri* (and *con-cŭcurri*, older **con-cĕcurri*), &c., originated in this way (ch. viii. § 44), just as in modern Greek βιβάζω has become βάζω in compounds like διαβάζω, ἐμβάζω, &c. Another syncopated verb-form is *cante* (2 Plur. Imperat. of *căno*), quoted from the Carmen Saliare by Varro (*L. L.* vii. 27). But as a rule all traces of syncope in the declension of the verb have been obliterated, the full forms (e. g. *cănĭte*) having been restored through the influence of forms where the consonants were not adapted for combination (e. g. *sistĭte*), or where the syllable in question did not immediately follow the (early) accent (e. g. *cóncinĭte*), as well as from the analogy of other conjugations, e. g. *amā-te*, *monē-te*, *audī-te*. In Umbrian and Oscan these imperatives are syncopated, e. g. Umbr. sistu (Lat. *sistito*), Osc. *actud* (Lat. *ăgito*). The same is true of derivative adjectives, e. g. in *-ĭdus*, *hūmidus*, *frīgidus*, *călidus*, *sŏlidus*, *rĭgidus*, *āridus*, &c. (but *nūdus* for **novidus* from a root *nogw-*, Sanscr. nag-nas, our 'naked,' is syncopated ; on *ŭdus* see below), in *-ĭcus*, e. g. *ūnicus*, *civicus*, *mĕdicus*, but the nouns *Plancus*, *lurco*, 'a glutton' (from *lŭra*, 'the mouth of a sack,' according to Paul. Fest. 86. 23 Th. lura, os cullei, vel etiam utris ; unde lurcones capacis gulae homines), *juncus*, &c. are syncopated (see below on *raucus*). Similarly *vivĭdus* is saved from syncope by the influence of other adjectives in *-ĭdus*, while the noun *vīta* for **vīvĭta* (Lith. gywatà) is not. The Umbrian adj. in -co-, *tōtco-* (Latin *pūblicus*) from *tōta-*, **touta-*, 'the community,' 'people,' shows the contraction which Latin adjectives of this formation escape (cf. Osc. *toutico-*).

(5) Diminutives in *-lo-*, on the other hand, extended the syncope from dissyllabic to other forms, e. g. *ūllus* from **ūno-lus*, *vīllum* from **vīno-lum*, Ter. *Adelph.* 786, and from their analogy, *cŏrōlla* for **corōnula*, *persōlla* for **persōnula*, *ampulla* from *amp(h)ŏra* (Greek ἀμφορᾶ, Acc. of ἀμφορεύς), &c.

(6) Greek words borrowed at an early period probably owe their syncope to the early accent, e. g. *Hercŭles* (Greek Ἡρακλῆς), *Pollūces* (the early form of *Pollūx*), Plaut. *Bacch.* 894 (Greek Πολυδεύκης), *calx* (Greek χάλιξ, with ă) ; cf. Praenestine *Acmemeno* (above, § 14).

(7) Other examples are *alter* from *ălĭter* ; *postulo* from **poscĭ-tŭlo* ; *ulna* from **ulĭna* (Greek ὠλένη) ; original *-ln-* becomes *-ll-* in Latin, e. g. *collis* from **colnis* (Lith. káḷnas, Greek κολωνός) ; *propter* from **prŏpĭ-tĕr*.

(8) For the syllable *-rĭ-*, examples are : *săcerdōs* from **sacrŏ-dōs*, **sácrĭ-dōs*,

from săcer and root dō, 'to give'; ăcerbus for *ăcrĭ-dho-, with the same termination (belonging to root dhē, 'to make') which becomes -dus when not preceded by r, e. g. frĭgĭdus, călĭdus (see ch. iv. § 114); săcellum for *sacer-lum, *sacrŏ-lom, săcrĭ-lum, &c. Nouns like ăger (Greek ἀγρός), căper (Greek κάπρος), and adjectives like ācer show this treatment of the unaccented final syllable of the Nom. case, whereas hortus, &c. are saved from syncope by the analogy of other cases, horti, horto, hortum, &c., and of other Nominatives, whose final syllable did not immediately follow the (early) accent, like ănĭmus, aŭtŭmnus. In the Italian dialects we find this -er- in similar positions, e. g. Osc. Aderla- from *Adrola- (Lat. Atella), Abella- probably from *Abrola- (Lat. *Apella), Umbr. ager, pacer, 'propitious,' from pācri-, often spelt -r-, e. g. Sabine Atrno- (Lat. Aternus), Osc. Tantrnnaiúm (Gen. Pl.) (ch. iv. § 92). In Latin we seem to have -er- for -ri, in the accented syllable too, e. g. ter (Greek τρίς), in Plautus (e. g. Bacch. 1127) scanned as a long syllable, and so pronounced terr (cf. terruncius, the right spelling; see Bücheler in Rhein. Mus. xlvi. 236), from *ters. The substitution of ĕr for rĭ would then be due rather to metathesis (cf. N. Ital. fardor, &c. for fredor, &c., Meyer-Lübke, Rom. Gramm. i. p. 291, and see above, ch. ii. § 111). Ter would however be unaccented in phrases like ter-mille (cf. terdeciens written as one word on Mon. Anc. i. 29). On ter, see ch. vi. § 61, on er for rĭ ch. iv. § 13.

(9) For the syllable -vĭ-, e. g. autumo for ăvĭ-tŭmo (Greek οἴω for ὀϝ-ιω); claudo *clāvĭ-do, from clāvis; cūria for *cŏvĭria (cf. Volscian covehriu, Zv. Inscr. Ital. Inf. 47); gaudeo for *gāvĭdeo, part. gāvīsus (Greek γηθέω for γᾰϝε-θέω); naufragus for *nāvĭ-frăgus¹; nūper, cf. adj. nuperum Acc. Sg., Plaut. Capt. 718 recéns captum hominem núperum nouícium), for *nŏvĭ-pĕrus from nŏvus and păro; praeco for *prae-vĭco from prae and vŏco; praedes, earlier praevĭdes (praevides Plur., praes Sing. on the Lex Agraria of Sp. Thorius, 111 B.C., C.I.L. i. 200, but only praedes on the older Lex Repetundarum, 123–2 B.C., i. 198), from prae and vas, perhaps suffered syncope after the new accent law, as did ūdus (as early as Lucil. inc. 172 M.), in Plautus only ūvĭdus; raucus for rāvĭcus from rāvis, 'hoarseness'; vīta for *vīvĭta (see above); auceps for *ăvĭ-ceps; Opiter, a name given to a child 'who had a grandfather for a father,' cujus pater avo vivo mortuus est (Paul. Fest. 207. 15 Th.), Plur. Opiteres (Löwe, Prodr. p. 396), seems to be colloquial Latin for *Aupater for *ăvĭ-păter from ăvus and păter. The form māvŏlo is found (with mălo) in Plautus, but in the classical period only mālo.

The syllable -vĭ-, -vĕ- is syncopated, even when long by 'position,' in auspex for *ăvĭ-spex; nūntius, older nŏventius [the older form occurs in a prophecy of the famous Marcius, published 213 B.C. (ap. Fest. 164. 28 Th.) quamvis noventium duonum negumate, 'quamvis bonum nuntium negate']; nundinae for *nŏven-dinae from novem and dĭn- a bystem of dies (Sanscr. dínam, O. Slav. dĭnĭ). And -v- is dropped even before a long vowel when a vowel of the same quality precedes, e. g. lābrum, earlier lăvābrum, Lucr. vi. 799. (Marius Victorinus, ix. 20 K. quotes lavābrum for lābrum among other instances of Old Latin forms such as hacetenus for hāctĕnus, hocedie for hŏdĭē, semol for sĭmŭl); lātrina for lăvātrina, the old word for a bath, supplanted by the Greek loanwords bal(i)neum (βαλᾰνεῖον) (cf. Non. 212. 7 M. lātrina ... est lavatrina, quod nunc balneum dicitur), as balneum itself was succeeded by lavācrum: dīvīnus was early contracted to dīnus (Leo in Rhein. Mus. xxxviii. 2), e. g. reidinai and

---

¹ Or for *nău-fragus, which became năŭ-fragus (ch. iv. § 45), and so with claudo, gaudeo (?).

§ 16.] ACCENTUATION. SYNCOPE. 181

res deina on an old inscription (*C.I.L.* xi. 4766), so *obliscor* for *obliviscor* in the early dramatists (see Georges, *Lex. Wortf.* s. v.), and in universal usage, *sīs*, for *sī vīs*, from which a plural *sultis* was formed. (On loss of intervocalic *-v-* see ch. ii. § 53 and ch. iv. § 70.

This liability of every short second syllable to syncope under the Early Accent Law makes it dangerous to infer from Latin forms the presence or absence of a short vowel in the corresponding Indo-European forms, e. g. to infer from the distinction between Lat. *ŭltrā, cĭtrā, infrā, sŭprā, extrā, contrā* on the one hand, and *ŭltĕrior, cĭtĕrior, infĕrior, sŭpĕrior, extĕrior* on the other, that the original stem-suffix was *-tr-*, *-r-* in these adverbs and *-ter-*, *-er-* in these adjectives. Priscian (ii. p. 30. 1 H.) tells us that the older forms were *supera, infera, extera,* &c. quaedam etiam syncopam passa sunt, ut 'supra' pro 'supera,' et 'infra' pro 'infera,' et 'extra' pro 'extera,' nam antiqui trisyllaba ea proferebant, ut Cicero in Arato :

> Torvus Draco serpit supter superaque retorquens
> Sese,

tenuit tamen, ut disyllaba magis ea proferantur (cf. ii. p. 55. 23 H.). *Sŭpĕra* is found in an elegiac epitaph, of the time of the poet Accius (to judge from its use of a double letter to indicate a long vowel), *C. I. L.* i. 1011 Ree fuit ee vero plus superaque parens, and on another inscription, with the same indication of date (cf. Ritschl, *P. L. M.* p. 46) (*-ee-* for *ē* in *seedes*) we have *infera*, i. 1166 quae infera scripta sont, but on the earlier S. C. de Bacch. (i. 196 of 186 B. C.) we have *suprad* and *exstrad*, so that *supera* (which is used also by Lucretius) may be a form that is not genuinely antique. On the spelling *arbiterium* for *arbitrium*, see Georges, *Lex. Wortf.* s. v., and cf. *magistero-* *C. I. L.* i. 73, *ma*[*gi*]*steratus, Eph. Epigr.* ii. 298 ; on *dextĕra* and *dextra*, see Brambach, *Lat. Orth.* ; on *sinistera* for *sinistra* (e. g. Ter. *Eun.* 835), on *Tĭbĕris* and *Tĭbris*, see Georges, *Lex. Wortf.* s. vv., and for other examples of syncopated byforms, s. vv. *sol*(*i*)*dus,* *Vir*(*i*)*domarus, frig*(*i*)*dus, ful*(*i*)*ca, Temese* (Gk.) and *Tempsa* (Lat.) ; but *audac-ter*, later *audācī-ter, prīvī-gnus* beside *privi-genus* (cf. Paul. Fest. 225. 2 Th. 'oenigenos' unigenitos), *teg-men* beside *tĕgĭ-men,* &c. admit of other explanations. (On the use of a Parasitic Vowel with r see ch. ii. § 102.)

Syncope is carried even further in Umbro-Oscan than in Latin, but in Umbrian the Perf. Part. Pass. is not syncopated, while the 3 Sg. Imper. is (but not *-net-*, e. g. kanetu, 'let him sing') ; thus sektu is Imper., seçetu is P. P. P. (see von Planta, i. p. 214). Contrast Osc. *toutico-* with Umbr. *totco-*, 'publicus,' Osc. minstro- with Lat. ministro-, Osc. Vezkú- with Lat. *Vetusco-*.

§ 16. **Syncope of Final Syllable.** In Oscan and Umbrian, as in Gothic, *ĕ, ŏ, ĭ*, but not *ŭ* (?), in a final syllable are syncopated, e. g. Osc. húrz, Lat. *hortus*, Bantins, Lat. *Bantīnus,* túvtíks for *touticos from touta-, 'community,' 'people,' Umbr. emps, Lat. *emptus,* pihaz, Lat. *piātus*, all with syncope of *-ŏs* ; Osc. μεδδειξ for *med-dik-ĕs Nom. Pl. of *meddix,* the title of the Oscan chief magistrate, censtur for *censtor-ĕs, Lat. *censōrēs,* with syncope of *-ĕs* of Nom. Pl. (see ch. vi. § 40). Umbr. pacer for *pāc-ri-s, 'propitious,' with syncope of -rĭs. In Latin we have this syncope, unless it should rather be called metathesis (§ 15. 8), in Nom. Sg. of *-ro-*, and *ri-* stems, e. g. *ăger* for *ag-ro-s, in-tĕg-er for *en-tag-ro-s, ācer* for *ac-ri-s, vŏlŭcer,* &c., but perhaps in no others. *Quattuor* might be for *quetuor-ĕs,* Masc. (Doric Gk. τέτορες, Sanscr. catváras), but may also be the Neuter form (Sanscr. catvắri) (see ch. vi. § 63). The contraction of -*ātis* to -*ās* in the Nom. Sg. of adjectives or nouns denoting the place of one's birth, e.g. *Arpinas*, *Casilas (Umbr. Casilós), is later than Plautus, who always uses the full form -*ātis* : while *Campans* (Masc. not Neut.) in his cruel sneer at the conquered Campanians, *Trin.* 545 :

Campans genus
Multo Surorum iam antidit patientia,

seems intended to mimic an Oscan *Campans for *Campānus*, like Osc. *Bantins* for *Bantīnus*. Like *Arpīnātis*, later *Arpinas*, are *Samnītis*, later *Samnis*, *Laurentis*, later *Laurens*, *Tīburtis*, later *Tiburs*, &c. (Prisc. i. p. 134 H.). Nominatives Sg. of *i*-stems like *sors* (in Plaut. *Cas.* 380 *sortis*), *quiēs* (if an I-stem like O. Pers. šiyātiš, Av. šyẹ̄itiš) may have dropped *i* in their final syllable, not by syncope, but by analogy of consonant-stems ; cf. *nubs* used by Liv. Andr. for *nūbēs* (Serv. ad *Aen.* x. 636), *plebs* and *plēbēs* (for other examples, see Ritschl. *Opusc.* ii. 652). Or these may be instances of parallel stem-formations, like *penu-*, *peno-*, *penos-* of *pĕnus*, Gen. *penūs*, *penum*, Gen. *peni*, *penus*, Gen. *penŏris*. So *viŏlens* and *viŏlentus*, *fluens* and *fluentum*, &c., *epulonus* (Paul. Fest. 55, 15 Th. ' epolonos' dicebant antiqui, quos nunc epulones dicimus), and *ĕpŭlo*, *centurionus* and *centŭrio*, *curionus*, *decurionus* and *cŭrio*, *decŭrio* (Paul. Fest. 34. 36 Th. ' centurionus' antea, qui nunc centurio, et 'curionus' et 'decurionus' dicebantur), *infans*, once used by Accius (*Trag.* 189 R. infans facinus) in the sense of *infandus*. Compounds like *in-dex*, *iŭ*(*s*)-*dex*, *vin-dex* differ from *causĭ-dĭcus*, *iurĭ-dĭcus*, *fātĭ-dĭcus* in being formed directly from the weak verb-stem *dĭc-*, like Sanscr. ā-diś-. So *conjux* (cf. Sanscr. sạyuj-, Gk. ἄζυξ) beside *bĭjŭgis* and *bĭjŭgus*, *bĭgae*, &c. So *for*(*m*)*ceps*, *au-ceps*, *prin-ceps* beside *urbĭ-căpus* (Plaut.), *hosti-capas* (Paul. Fest. 73. 10 Th. ' hosticapas' hostium captor) ; *ŏpĭ-fex*, *artĭ-fex*, *carnĭ̆-fex* beside *mūnĭ-fĭcus*, *magnĭ-fĭcus* ; *rēm-ex* beside *prōd-ĭgus*. *Man-suēs* (Acc. mansuem and mansuētem) beside *man-suētus*, *in-quiēs* beside *in-quiētus* are like Gk. ἀδμής and ἀδμῆτος, ἀκμής and ἄκμητος. *Praeceps*, *anceps* from *prae-*, *ambi-* and *căput*, in Plautus *praecĭpes* (*Rud.* 671), *ancĭpes* (*Rud.* 1158) (cf. *procapis*, Paul. Fest. 281. 22 Th. ' procapis' progenies, quae ab uno capite procedit ; and *concapit* (?) of the XII Tables ap. Fest. 556. 27 Th. tignum iunctum aedibus uineaue et concapit ne soluito) were afterwards assimilated to compounds of *căpio*, e.g. *prin-ceps* (cf. Prisc. i. p. 280. 15 H. antiqui tamen 'ancipes' et 'praecipes' et 'bicipes' proferebant in nominativo ... idem tamen vetustissimi etiam ' praecipis' genetivum ... secundum analogiam nominativi protulerunt). Old Latin *Pollūcēs* (Plaut. *Bacch.* 894, cf. Gk. Πολυδεύκης) was shortened to *Pollūx*, probably by analogy of *lūx*, Gen. *lūcis*. Priscian (i. p. 282. 12 H.) tells us that the old forms of *concors*, *discors*, &c. were *concordis*, *discordis* (cf. i. 354. 13 H.) (cf. late Lat. *orbs*, e.g. Ven. Fort. ix. 3. 14 ; orbis non ' orbs' Probi App. 198. 8 K.).

O-stem adjectives often have their Nom. Sg. shortened through their tendency, especially when compound (ch. v. § 34), to become I-stems. Thus *hĭlărus* (Gk. ἱλαρός, one of those loanwords from Greek to express subtle nuances of feeling, for which the Romans had no word of their own, like our loanwords from French, such as 'triste') became, after the time of Plautus, *hilaris* (ch. v. § 34) ; *fortis* was perhaps originally *forctus* (Paul. Fest. 73. 9 Th. ' forctum' pro bono dicebant), though as early as the XII Tables we find *forctes* for loyal allies, (ap. Fest, 524. 15 Th., in XII cautum est, ut idem iuris esset 'Sanatibus' quod

§ 17.] ACCENTUATION. SYNCOPE. 183

'Forctibus,' id est bonis, et qui numquam defecerant a Populo Romano ; cf. Paul. Fest. 59. 26 'forctes,' frugi et bonus, sive validus, where Paulus may have put the Nom. Pl. *forctes* by mistake for the Nom. Sg. *forctis*); *săcro-* and *săcri-* are parallel stems in O. Latin (*săcres porci*, 'pigs for sacrifice,' Plaut. *Men.* 289, *Rud.* 1208, cf. Fest. 464. 7 Th.), and similarly *māno-* and *māni-,* 'good,' though in classical Latin the only survival of this group was *im-mānis* 'bad,' 'hurtful,' and the *di Mānes*. In the Carmen Saliare occurred the phrase *Cerus mānus*, explained by Paul. Fest. 87. 29 Th. ás *creator bonus*, and at Lanuvium the old word *mānis* was in use even in the time of Macrobius (fourth cent. A.D.) (Macr. i. 3. 13 nam et Lanuini 'mane' pro bono dicunt; sicut apud nos quoque contrarium est 'immane'). Varro (*L. L.* vi. 4) connects with O. Latin *mānus*, 'good' the adverb *māne*, 'early,' and in support of his etymology mentions a curious Greek custom of uttering the words φῶς ἀγαθόν as a good omen when a light was brought into the room, diei principium 'mane,' quod tum manat dies ab oriente, nisi potius quod bonum antiqui dicebant 'manum,' ad cujusmodi religionem Graeci quoque, cum lumen affertur, solent dicere φῶς ἀγαθόν (see ch. vi. § 38). The O-stem *hortus* became in the compound **co-horto-* an I-stem **co-hortis,* which (like *sors*, &c. above) changed its Nom. Sg. to *co-hors*. Even the Perf. Part. Pass. *sānātus* appears in the form *sanati-* in the expression quoted from the XII Tables by Festus 524. 10 Th. for the repentant allies, who had first revolted and then returned to their allegiance, 'Sanates' dicti sunt, qui supra infraque Romam habitaverunt. quod nomen his fuit, quia, cum defecissent a Romanis, brevi post redierunt in amicitiam quasi sanata mente. And the Old Latin legal phrase *dare damnas esto, tantum damnas esto* (Cato ap. Gell. vi. 3. 37 ; Quint. vii. 9. 12, &c.) may be a case of substitution, for the usual O-stem *damnāto-,* of an I-stem *damnati-,* which has taken a cons.-stem Nom. Sg. *damnas*, like *aetas, tempestas*.

IO-stems had at all periods a tendency to pass into I-stems. The older adj. termination *-ārius* (frequent in Plautus, vid. Lorenz ad *Pseud.* 952, e. g. *singularius, virginarius*) may have been often replaced by *-āris* in MSS. of Plautus (ch. v. § 4). Cf. Caper 112. 2 K. vates olim 'vatios' dicebant ; so *Verres* and *Verrius*. In Vulg. Lat. *-ius* (*-eus*) became *-is* in *actuaris, abstemis, sobris, caerulis, consanguinis*, &c. (Löwe, *Prodr.* p. 420), thus repeating the early confusion between *-io-* and *-i-* in the declension of names like *Caecīlius*, Acc. *Caecīlium, Caecīlis*, Acc. *Caecīlim* (see ch. vi. § 5). But none of these are clear cases of the change of stem of a Latin word owing to the syncope of its final syllable in the Nom. Sg. Perhaps the most likely instance is *Lucipor*, from *Lūcius* and *puer* (stem *pŭĕro-*), of which the Plur. is given by Pliny, *H. N.* xxxiii. 26 as *Lucipores* (cf. Dat. Sg. *Naepori* on an inscription of the end of the Republican period, *C. I. L.* i. 1539 *e*), but even this might be otherwise explained. The weakening of final vowels in Latin (see below) gives an à priori probability to the syncope of final short syllables like *-ĭs, -ŏs, -ĕs* as in Oscan and Umbrian, but it has not yet been satisfactorily proved that syncope did actually occur in any syllables except those immediately preceding or following the accent. (Schuchardt, *Vok.* ii. 394 sqq. has collected a number of instances on late plebeian inscriptions of the omission of a short vowel of the final syllable, e. g. *fect* for *fĕcit*.)

§ 17. Syncope under the Paenultima Accent Law. (1) Pretonic. Compounds of *jăcio* like *căle-facio*, which shortened their *ĕ* by the law of Brevis Brevians (see below), took the further step of suppressing the vowel altogether before the accent of the next syllable, *cal-fácere, cal-fáctus*. Quintilian (i. 6. 21) tells us that in his time the full form *calĕfacere* was never used in ordinary talk. *Olfacere*, not *olefacere*, is the regular form. Ritschl proposed to help the metre occasionally in Plautus by reading *benfĭcium, malfĭcium* for *bĕnĕfĭcium, mălĕfĭcium, benfacta, malfacta* (e. g. *Trin.* 185) for *benefacta, malefacta* of the MSS. He supported his proposal by the old spelling BENVENTOD on a coin of Beneventum (*C. I. L.* i. 19), c. 250 B.C. On later inscriptions spellings like BENMERENTI are frequent, also MALDICTVm (see Ritschl, *Opusc.* ii. 716). So firmly established was the syncopated form of compounds of *facio* like *olfacio* that even *ārĕfacio*, whose *ĕ* could not be shortened by ordinary phonetic change, since it is preceded by a long syllable, seems after their analogy to have been made a quadrisyllable by Cato, for the MSS. of the *Res Rustica* agree wonderfully in presenting the word in this form (c. 69 ; 125 ; 157. 12). To pretonic syncope we must refer the currency of the forms *discĭplīna, fīglīna* beside *discipulus, fīgulus*, and on later inscriptions *vetranus* (cf. *C.I.L.* iii. Ind. p. 1159 for *vĕtĕrānus*, &c. (on Greek inscriptions almost always οὐετρανος or βετρανος). Festus 466. 16 Th. tells us that *scēna*, an old word for the priest's knife (used by Liv. Andr. *Com.* 2 R. corruit quasi ictus scena) had a byform *sacēna*; and another obsolete term *sculna*, discussed by Gell. xx. 11, a synonym of *sĕquester*, was explained by a grammarian, who compiled a sort of 'Slang Dictionary' (Lavinius 'De Verbis Sordidis') as a contraction of *seculna*. Vulg. Lat. *māt(ū)tīnus* (Ital. mattino, &c.) may be explained either as a case of the suppression of one of two similiar neighbouring syllables, like *Res(ti)tūtus* above (§ 13, p. 176) or of pretonic syncope, such as is seen in Ital. cervello (Lat. *cĕrĕbellum*), vergogna (Lat. *vĕrĕcundia*), bontà (Lat. *bŏnĭtāt-*), gridare (Lat. *quīrītare*), dritto (Lat. *dīrectus*), &c. Procope is common in Italian, owing to the frequency of final vowels, e. g. vescovo (Lat. *ĕpiscŏpus*), nemico (Lat. *ĭnimīcus*), cagione (Lat. *occāsion-*), &c. Synizesis of the pretonic short vowel is seen in Vulg. Lat. *qu(i)ētus*, *dyurnus* (Ital. giorno); *coactus* became *quattus* (Ital. quatto), &c. (cf. Georges, *Lex. Wortf.* on *Num(i)torius*, *Lug(u)dunum*).

(2) Post-tonic. A good example of syncope after a long accented syllable under the new Accent-law is the word *barca* (our 'barque'), a word which seems to have been introduced at the time of the naval displays given by Caesar for the amusement of the people, and which is clearly a contraction of *bārĭca* from the Egyptian *bāris* (Prop. iii. 11. 44) (see *Rhein. Mus.* xlii. 583). Another is *lamna* (Hor. *C.* ii. 2. 2 inimice lamnae), in Vulg. Lat. *lanna* (Arnob. ii. 41), the older form of which was *lammĭna* (e. g. Plaut. *Asin.* 549). And we have many words which appear in Plautus in their full form, but in later writers are reduced by syncope, such as *obiŭrigo*, by Terence's time always *obiŭrgo*, nouns or adjectives in *-ātis* denoting the country of one's birth, &c., e. g. *infīmatis* (*Stich.* 493). The same shortening tendency attacked *u*, *i* in hiatus, e. g. *lārua* is a trisyllable in Plautus, a dissyllable later, so *grātŭis*, later *grātīs*, while it has left traces of itself in spellings on old inscriptions like *iugra* (for *jūgĕra*) on the Lex Agraria of Sp. Thorius, 111 B. C. (*C. I. L.* i. 200. 14, 25), not to mention others which may be dialectal, such as PROSEPNAI (Dative) on a very old mirror of Cosa (*C. I. L.* i. 57. -AI, not -AIS, is what is written; see *Rhein. Mus.* xlii. 486), and CEDRE for *caedere* on an early inscription of Spoletium in Umbria (*C. I. L.* xi. 4766). *Ardus* for *āridus* appears occasionally, e. g. Plaut. *Aul.* 297; *Pers.* 266; Lucil. 27. 40 M., and on an inscription copied in the Empire from an original of 105 B. C. (*C. I. L.* i. 577. 2. 21 =

§ 18.]   ACCENTUATION. VOWEL-WEAKENING.   185

x. 1781), which also contains *uda* (2. 18) for *ūvida* (but *āridus*, Plaut. *Rud.* 574, 726, 764, &c.); so *Raude* for *Ravide*, Catull. xl. 1 ; *aspris* for *aspĕris*, Virg. *Aen.* ii. 379 (cf. *asprĭtūdo*, *asprētum*, *asprēdo*, and other derivatives, as well as Ital. aspro), *aspriter*, Sueius ap. Non. 513 M. Syncope after a short accented syllable is seen in *soldus*, used even in the Lex Municipalis of Julius Caesar, 45 B. C. (*C. I. L.* i. 206. 114, 115), and admitted by Horace into his Satires (*S.* ii. 5. 65 metuentis reddere soldum, and *S.* i. 2. 113), in *possum* for *pŏtĕ-sum* (ch. viii. § 97), and in *ferme*, for *fĕrĭme*, Superl. of *fĕrē*, if the corruption *fert me* of the Palatine MSS. in Plaut. *Trin.* 319 be evidence of the spelling *ferime* in Plautus' time. Plautus has never the form *culmen*, which appears to be a form proper to the oblique cases, so that the declension was : Nom. *cŏlŭmen*, Gen. *cŏl(u)mĭnis* (cf. Georges, *Lex. Wortf.* on *later(i)culus*, and possibly *fer(i)culum*). In Vulgar Latin we have slave-names like *Marpor* (*C. I. L.* i. 1076), *Naepori* (Dat. Sg.) (i. 1539 *e*), of which full forms like *Quintipor*, *Marcipor*, *Gaipor*, are given by Festus (340. 17 Th.), *mattus* for *mădĭtus*, 'drunk' (Petron.), *virdis* (cf. Probi App. 199. 9 viridis non 'virdis'); on *vir(i)desco*, *vir(i)darium*, see Georges, *Lex. Wortf.* s. vv. ; *dictus* for *dĭgĭtus* (see Georges); *fridam* for *frĭgĭdam* on an inscription of Pompeii (*C. I. L.* iv. 1291) (cf. Probi App. 198. 3 K. calida non 'calda'; frigida non 'frigda'; *infrigdo* for *infrĭgĭdo*, Oribas. fragm. Bern. iv. 34. p. 1. 6 and 10 Hag.); cf. *frigdor* (see Georges, *Lex. Wortf.* s. v.); *calda* is read in Cato, *R. R.* vi. 1 and 75, Varro, *R. R.* i. 13, &c., and the proper name *Cald(us)* is found on coins as early as 109 B. C. (*C. I. L.* i. 382); on *domnus* for *dŏmĭnus*, see Georges s. v., and cf. the proper name *Domnus*, *Domna*, Gk. Δομνος (*C. I. G.* i. 6505, end of second cent. A. D.), and Vulg.-Lat. *nit(i)dus*, *horr(i)dus*, *rig(i)dus*, *col(a)phus*, &c. are indicated by the Romance forms, e. g. Ital. netto, ordo (but with close initial o), reddo, colpo, &c. (For a list of syncopated forms in late inscriptions and MSS., see Schuchardt, *Vok.* ii. pp. 394 sqq.)

§ 18. **Change of Unaccented Vowels.** In a language with a stress-accent the unaccented vowels are liable to be obscured. We see this in our own language, where the unaccented vowels in words like 'father,' 'sister,' have become what we call *par excellence* 'the obscure vowel,' the vowel-sound of *u* in 'but.' We notice too a difference in this respect between Italian pronunciation and our own; for an Italian pronounces the vowels of the unaccented syllables more clearly, and does not slur them to the same extent as we do. But in Italian also the same tendency to weaken an unaccented vowel is present, though not in so marked a degree. The unaccented vowel often fails to preserve its individuality, and is open to influence from a neighbouring consonant, *r*, for example, changing a preceding short vowel to *e*, *l* changing one to *o*. Thus Latin *arbor*, or rather its oblique case-form *arbŏrem*, &c. has become in Italian albero ; Latin *dēbĭlis* has become debole. And in the pretonic syllable of signore (Lat. *sĕniōrem*), midolla (Lat. *mĕdulla*), the unaccented vowel has become *i*. Exactly the same thing happened in Latin. In the last chapter we saw that a short vowel in the syllable following the accented syllable remained unsyncopated only when its syllable was long by position, or when some other cause prevented syncope. But though unsyncopated, it did not remain unaffected. Its quality was changed. In a syllable long by position we see a short unaccented vowel becoming *e*, e.g. *remex*, from *rēmus* and *ăgo*, in other syllables *i*, e.g. *remigis*, *jŭrigo* (Plaut.), later *jŭrgo*. Under the influence of a following labial consonant or *l* it assumes a *u-* or *ü*-sound (see ch. ii. § 16), e.g. *occŭpo, in-cĭpio*, from *căpio*; a following *r* makes it *e*, e.g. *pĕpĕri*, from *păriο*. Some vowels retained their individuality better than others. Short *o* in compounds of verbs like *voco, rogo*, &c. remains unchanged, e.g. *convoco, invoco, irrogo, arrogo*; short *u* in *tu-tudi*, &c.

Final syllables too cannot have been so liable to affection as others, or the difference between Nominatives Singular of different stems, such as *cĭnis, ŏpus* (Old Lat. *opos*), *mănus*, &c. could not have been so well maintained. Perhaps they were saved by the analogy of trisyllables, and longer words, where the final syllable was not in the weakest of all positions, viz. immediately following the accent.

Even diphthongs were changed, their first element being affected, *ai* becoming *ī* (through *ei), *au* becoming *ū* (through *eu), just as single *a* was originally weakened to *e* (see below). Thus the compound of *ob* and *caedo* became, under the influence of the early accent, *occīdo*, of *ob* and *claudo, occlūdo*. But long vowels were more resistive of change, e.g. *invādo*, from *vādo*, *irrēpo*, from *rēpo*.

The regularity with which these changes of short vowels and diphthongs are carried out in the second syllables of Latin words is a strong proof of the fact discovered by Corssen, that the Latin accent at some early time rested invariably on the first syllable; for it is the syllable immediately following the accented syllable, which in a language with stress-accent is most liable to be affected. A syllable with a secondary accent, like the paenultima of **párri-caìda-* (under the old accent law) would not be liable, just as in the Romance languages the vowel of the first syllable of words like classical Latin *àrmatúra*, &c. shows the same treatment as the vowel of the syllable with the main accent (cf. Ital. Fiorentino from *Flòrentínus*, like fiore from *flórem*, but Firenze from *Floréntia*). It might, however, change its vowel after the analogy of kindred words where the same vowel followed immediately on the accent, e.g. **óc-caido*, and so we get the Old Latin form *paricídas* (Paul. Fest. 278. 10 Th.). On the other hand the analogy of the simple word with accented root-vowel would often save the vowel of the compound from being changed, e.g. *vades et subvades*, XII Tab., where the *a* of *vades* is not weakened as it is in *praevides* (*C. I. L.* i. 200), later *praedes*. And at any period in the language the sense of the relation of a compound to a simple word might lead to the restoration of the vowel in the compound to its accented quality, e.g. **prŏvĭcare* might become *provŏcare*, though the noun *praeco* (for **prae-vico*) was left unchanged; *ĕnĭco* might become *e-neco*; *consecro*, *con-sacro*. This restoration of compounds to their unweakened form, 'Recomposition' as it is sometimes called, is a feature of the late Republican and the Imperial period, and possibly had some connexion with the grammatical studies imported from Greece towards the close of the Republic, and prosecuted with great zest for many centuries.

In the period of the earlier literature the change of unaccented vowels is more the rule than it is later, e.g. always *enico* in Plautus, &c., in spite of the old practice of separating the preposition from its verb by tmesis, *ob vos sacro*, for *obsecro vos*, *sub vos placo*, for *supplico vos*.

Analogy, however, was at work in all periods, and exerted its influence now in one way, now in another. The analogy of the Nominative preserved from change the vowel in the oblique cases of *arborem*, *fulguris*, &c., at least in the literary lauguage (cf. Ital. albero; *fulgerator*, Gruter. *Inscr.* xxi. 3); the analogy of the Oblique Cases, *integri*, *integro*, &c. has substituted *e* for *i* in the Nominative *integer*. Compounds, too, which were made for the occasion, or were rarely used, like O. Lat. *hosti-capas*, hostium captor (Paul. Fest. 73. 10 Th.), *urbi-capus* (Plaut.), would escape the change which befel a word established in use, like *prin-ceps*, *muni-ceps*. But with these exceptions the change of short vowels of the second syllable is very regular in Latin, though the oldest inscription extant, *Manios med fefaked Numasioi*, on a brooch perhaps of the sixth cent. B. C. found at Praeneste, is suggestive of an epoch when this law was not in operation.

The exact rules of change seem to be these. The older representative of *i*, the modification of a short vowel in an ordinary short unaccented syllable was *e* (Gk. ε); while the older representative of *ŭ*, the modification of an unaccented short vowel before a labial or *l*, was *o* (Gk. o). *E* was replaced by *i*, *o* by *u* about 230 B.C. Up to that time the process of change might be so described. An unaccented short vowel was changed before a labial *l* to *o*, in all other circumstances to *e*. Thus on old Praenestine jewelcases, &c. we find spellings like *Belolai* (*C.I.L.* i. 44) for *Bellulae*, *Salutes* (i. 49) for *Sălūtis*, *Aecetiai* for *Aequitiae* (al. *Angitiae*), (i. 43); and these older spellings often persist to a much later period. The MSS. of Plautus, for example, preserve traces of *abegit* for *abigit*, *Capt.* 814; *exsolatum* for *exulatum* in *Merc.* 593 (B), *Most.* 597 (A), &c., and the Lex Repetundarum of 121 B.C. (*C.I.L.* i. 198) has, with the conservativeness of legal orthography, forms like *detolerit*, *oppedeis* side by side with *detulerit*, *ediderit*, &c. *E* was especially long retained after the vowel *i*, e.g. *ēbrietas*, *părietem*. And after consonantal *i* (*y*) we find *conieciant* on the Lex Repetundarum, *proiecitad* (for *projicito*) on the Titulus Lucerinus (*Eph. Epigr.* ii. 298); while the spelling *inieciatis*, Plaut. *Truc.* 298 has led to the corruption *illeciatis* in the Ambrosian Palimpsest (so in Lucretius MSS. *traiĕcĕre*, iii. 513. For other examples, see Lachmann ad Lucr. ii. 951); *o* was similarly retained after *i*, *e*, e.g. *fīliolus*, *Pŭteoli*, lit. 'little wells,' and after vocalic or consonantal *u* (*u*, *w*), e.g. *paruolus*. (See ch. iv. § 70.)

The *iĕ* of compounds of *jacio*, &c. became *ĭ*, e.g. *conicio*, through loss of accent (ch. iv. § 51), and similarly *uĕ* of compounds of *quatio*, &c. became *ŭ*, e.g. *concutio*. This older *e* remained in short syllables before *r*, e.g. *peperi*. Also in syllables long by position, except where the first of the two consonants was a labial or *l*; and even into these it found its way in time with the exception of the combination of *l* with another consonant (not *ll*), e.g. *con′emno*, older *condumno* (both forms are found on the Lex Bantina of 130 B.C., *C.I.L.* i. 197); *surreptum* (*surruptum* Plaut.), but always *insulto, insulsus, inculco* (ch. iv. § 10). The *o*, proper to syllables whether short or long by position in which the vowel was followed by a labial or *l*, became *u*, which might pass into the *ü*-sound (ch. ii. § 16), written at first *u*, later *i*. The spelling of MSS. of Plautus, *testumonium*, &c. became in time *testimonium*, &c. In Superlatives *i* for earlier *u* was adopted for State Inscriptions through the influence of Julius Caesar (Quint. i. 7. 21; Varro ap. Cassiod. p. 150. 11 K.), so on the Lex Julia Municipalis of 45 B.C. (*C.I.L.* i. 206) *maximam* and *maxumam*, though we find it occasionally used long before his time, e.g. *proxsimum* (i. 1291, an inscription which Ritschl dates 'not after 130 B.C.'). *I* came in earliest probably in syllables which were followed by a syllable with *i* in hiatus, e.g. *recipio* (*recipit* on a Scipio epitaph of c. 180 B.C., i. 33).

The same vowel appears in *confringo, infringo*, &c. in accordance with the phonetic law of Latin which gives us *i* for *e* in the accented syllables of words like *tingo* (Gk. τέγγω), ch. iv. § 11.

The succession of *o, u, i* in words like *maxomos, maxumus, maximus* is also seen in the parasitic or 'Svarabhaktic' vowel (ch. ii. § 154) of *pōculum* (Plaut. *poclum*), &c. The earliest spelling is *o*, e.g. on the Praenestine vases of third cent. B.C. *belolai pocolom* (*C. I. L.* i. 44), *Salutes pocolom* (i. 49), *Aisclapi pococolom* (for *pocolom*), (*Eph. Epigr.* i. 5). The classical Latin spelling is *u, poculum, stăbulum,* &c. The *i* in I-stem Adjectives, &c., e.g. *stabilis, ăgilis, făcilis,* where *i* follows in the next syllable, is in O. Lat. *e*, e.g. *fameliai* (*C. I. L.* i. 166), on Greek inscriptions Καικελιος, &c.

An *o* which had escaped the reduction to *e* became at the end of the third cent. B.C. *u*, e.g. *ŏpus*, earlier *opos* (*ib.* i. 52), *Lūcius*, earlier *Luciom* (*ib.* i. 32) (cf. ch. iv. § 17); *industrius* (older *endostruo-*, if we may believe Paul. Fest. 75. 28 Th.); *-unt* in 3 Pl. for older *-ont*, e. g. *praedopiont* of Carm. Sal. (Fest. 244. 13 Th. MS. *-oti-*) in the sense of *praeoptant*. A *u* became *ü, i*, e.g. *sătura, satira*.

The weakening of the diphthong *ai* (later *ae*) to *ī* was frequently abandoned in the late Republican and Imperial time, a number of forms which exhibit this weakening, e.g. *consīptum, obsīptum,* from *saepio,* being recognized as Old Latin forms. The same weakening may have occurred when *ai* stood in hiatus, but here by the Latin law of shortening a long vowel in hiatus (ch. ii. § 143), *ī* sank further to *ĭ*, e.g. *Bŏvianum* for *Boviānum* (Oscan Búvaianúd Abl.), *Mărius* (cf. Oscan Maraiio-). Similarly unaccented *au* in hiatus sank to *ŭ* in *ēluo, eluācrum* (Cato) from *lăvere* (Old Lat.), *lavācrum*. (For other examples, see Parodi in *Stud. Ital.* i. 385.) (For reduction of final vowels, see § 37.)

Greek loanwords in Latin show the same changes of the post-tonic vowels, though a vowel may be retained unchanged in words which were borrowed after the operation of the law affecting that particular vowel, or which never became part and parcel of the common language. The change is seen in *bălineum* (Plaut. &c.), classical *balneum* (βαλανεῖον), *trŭtina* (τρυτάνη), *tălentum* (τάλαντον), *phălerae* (φάλαρα), &c., but not in *plătanus* (πλάτανος), *barbarus* (βάρβαρος), &c. Vulgar Latin *cĭtera* (κιθάρα), Probi App. 197. 26 K.), Ital. cetera and cetra, but Span. guitarra from *citára* (κιθάρα) (as from κάμμαρος Ital. gambero, but Span. gambaro), carry out the vowel-reduction which was omitted in the classical forms of these words. The analogy too of native words may often have interfered with the normal development of these unaccented vowels; the *ŏ* of *ancŏra* (ἄγκυρα) and the *e* of *plăcenta* (πλακοῦντα, Acc. Sg.), for example, may have arisen in this way, just as πρόθυρον became *protulum* (Löwe, *Prodr.* p. 376) by the analogy of diminutives, or Περσεφόνη, *Prōserpina* (*Prosepnai*, Dative, on an old mirror of Cosa, *C.I.L.* i. 57) by the analogy of *prōserpo*.

Under the early law of accentuation, when the accent fell on the first syllable of every word, pretonic change could take place only in proclitic or subordinate words like prepositions preceding their nouns. Whether *Menerua* of early inscriptions (e.g. *C.I.L.* i. 191 *Meneruai*; cf. Quint. i. 4. 17), a quadrisyllable in Plautus (ch. iv. § 148), became *Mĭnerva* through loss of accent in the first syllable or by analogy of *mĭnor* is uncertain. But the pretonic change of *au* to *u* in Ital. udire (Lat. *audire*), uccello (Vulg. Lat. **aucellus* from *ăvis*), and of *ae* to *i* in Ital. cimento (Lat. *caementum*), cisello, our 'chisel' (Lat. *caesellum*), may have already occurred in Vulgar Latin. The pretonic syllable is often assimilated to the accented, e.g. *momordi* for earlier *memordi*, and the same tendency in the post-tonic syllable

§ 19.]   ACCENTUATION. VOWEL-WEAKENING.   191

is seen in mispronunciations like *tonotru* (Probi Append. 198. 32 K.), preventing reduction in *ălăcer, hĕbĕtem,* &c.

A long vowel in an unaccented syllable was not shortened (except in the final syllable, see §§ 40-50 infr.) until a late period, when the length of all long syllables had been reduced to something not far removed from a short syllable (see ch. ii. § 141).

But a syllable long by position, when preceded by a short syllable and followed immediately by the accented syllable, was so reduced as to be often scanned as a short syllable by the early dramatists, e.g. *volŭptatem, senĕctutem* (Plaut. Ter.).

In Oscan and Umbrian, though syncope is of frequent occurrence, the quality of an unsyncopated unaccented vowel is retained in the spelling. The name, for instance, of the Latin poet, Propertius, who was a native of Umbria, is in Umbrian form Propartio-, not Propertio- (Vois. Ner. Propartie on an Umbrian inscription, *C.I.L.* xi. 5389, would be in Latin *Vols. Propertii, Neronis f.*; cf. xi. 5518 sqq.).

§ 19. **Other Examples. I. Syllables long by position.** Anteclassical *exercirent* from *sarcio,* Ter. *Heaut.* 143 (*e* in all the MSS.; cf. Paul. Fest. 57. 12 Th. *exercirent* : sarcirent) ; *ommentans,* from *manto,* Frequentative of *măneo,* quoted by Fest. (218. 14 Th.) from Livius Andronicus (cf. Gl. Plac. *ommentat* : expectat, &c.); *inpetritum* : inpetratum (Paul. Fest. 77. 3 Th.); *inermat* : armis spoliati (id. 78. 28 Th.); *inlĕx* : inductor, ab iniliciendo (id. 80. 29 Th., with quotation of Plaut. *Asin.* 221) from O. Lat. *lăcio* (id. 83. 36 Th., *lacit* : inducit in fraudem. Inde est 'allicere' et 'lacessere'; inde 'lactat,' 'illectat,' 'oblectat,' 'delectat.' Cf. 83. 14 Th. *lacit* : decipiendo inducit. 'Lax' etenim fraus est); *procestria* (id. 282. 6 Th.), apparently from *castra,* seems to be the word equated with Gk. προάστεια in the 'Philoxenus' and 'Cyrillus' Glossaries ; *compectus* is in Plautus the Participle of the compound of *păciscor, compăctus* (ch. ii. § 144) of *compingo.* We have *e* before a labial with a consonant in *incepsit,* the old 'Perf. Subj.' of *incipio* (Paul. Fest. 76. 23 Th.); *peremne* dicitur auspicari, qui amnem, aut aquam, quae ex sacro oritur, auspicato transit (Fest. 316. 32 Th.) ; *indeptare* : consequi (Paul. Fest. 75. 27 Th.). The gloss *indepisci* : adsequi, adipisci, on the same page, l. 31 (cf. Gloss. Plac.) is perhaps given more correctly in the 'Philoxenus' Glossary, *indepti* : ἀνύσαντες ; *praeceptat* : saepe praecipit Carm. Sal. (Fest. 244. 10 Th.) ; *inebrae* aves : quae in auguriis aliquid fieri prohibent (id. 78. 7 Th.). But *enubro* : inhibenti (id. 54. 7 Th.). Cf. the questionable spellings in the 'Philoxenus' Glossary, *eniber, enibra, enibrum* (for *enub-* ?). On the Falisco-Latin inscription of the Faliscan 'collegium cocorum' in Sardinia (Zv. *I. I. I.* 72), an inscription with bad spelling and worse metre, we have *aciptum* for *acceptum* in the first line : Gonlegium quod est aciptum aetatei agedai.

Classical examples are *gĕnetrix* beside *genitus* ; *obstetrix* beside *stator, constituo* ; (but *prōdĭtrix,* &c., influenced by *prōdĭtor*) ; *fulgĕtrum* (all these Neuters in -*trum* and Fems. in -*tra* have *ĕ*, except a few with *ā*, e. g. *verĕtrum, mulcĕtra, arātrum*. But *tonĭtru* : see *A. L. L.* i. 111); *id-ent-idem* from *ante*; *expers* from *pars*; *pĕrennis* from *annus*, and *imberbis* from *barba*, with the usual I-stem of Compound Adjectives; *incestus* from *castus*; *forceps* from *formus*, 'warm,' and *căpio*; *compesco* from **păc-sco* (cf. *păciscor*). So in Reduplicated Perfects, e. g. *peperci* from *parco*; *fefelli* from *fallo*. And in Final Syllables like *mīles* for **milets*, **milit-s* (in Plaut. the last syllable of such words is long by position, ch. ii. § 137); *cornicen* for **cornicens*, **cornu-can-s*. An original *o* becomes *e*(*i*) in *trīginta* for **trigenta* (Gk. τριάκοντα) (on *i* for *e* before *nt*, cf. ch. ii. § 147), *ille* from unaccented *olle* (ch. vii. § 13), and perhaps *pĕren-die* (cf. Osc. perum) (on -*undo*- and -*endo* in the Gerund, -*unt*- and -*ent*- in the Pres. Part., see chap. viii.). An original *u* becomes *e* in *con-sternari* (cf. Gk. πτύρομαι, O. H. G. stornem); an original *i* perhaps in O. Lat. *magester* Quint. i. 4. 17). Other examples of the variation of weakened and unweakened forms are : *comperco* and *comparco, contrecto* and *contracto, aspergo* and *aspargo, āmando* and *amendo, dispertio* better than *dispartio, bĭpartītus* and *bipertitus, quinquepertitus* and *quinquepartitus, retracto* better than *retrecto, conspergo* and *conspargo, căliandrum* and *caliendrum, attrecto* and *attracto* (so perhaps *Sarepta* and *Sarapta*), on which see Georges, *Lex. Wortf.* s. vv.; cf. *abarcet* Paul. Fest. 11. 36, *abercet* id. 19. 26 Th. On Greek inscriptions we have πρινκίψ, μανκίψ, βιξιλλαριος, ούιτρανος, &c., from the end of the first cent. A.D. ; see Eckinger; *prae-fiscĭnī* is usually derived from *fascinum*, but neither *exintero* beside *exentero*, nor *bĭpinnis* beside *bipennis* are certain cases of the change of *e* to *i*, nor yet Antistius beside *Antestius* (§ 39). (On *i* for *e* in *infringo, triginta*, see ch. iv. § 11.)

§ 20. II. **Short Syllables (1) in -r.** The compound of *lēx* and *rumpo* has in Plautus the spelling *legerŭpa* (e. g. *Pers.* 68, corrupted to *lege rumpam*), cf. *vīverādix*, Cato, *R. R.* xxxiii. 3), though at a later time the usual 'Composition-Vowel' *i* was used, e. g. *pinnirăpus*, Juvenal (see *Rev. Phil.* 1892, p. 109); from *paro* come *aequipero, impero, pauper*, but *ŏpĭ-parus*; *jūnĭperus* (and *junipirus*) (see Brambach, *Lat. Orth.* p. 142), derived by Verrius Flaccus from *jŭvĕnis* and *pĭrus* (' Serv.' ad *Ecl.* vii. 53); *sŏcer, soceri* may be the direct development of *swĕkŭros*, Gk. ἐκυρός, Skt. śvāśuras, but see § 15, *K. Z.* xxxii. 564); *cineris, cineri*, but *cinis, cinisculus* (cf. Georges, *Lex. Wortf.* s. vv. *Sīlerus, mataris, Samiramis*, and for plebeian spellings like *Caeserem*, see Schuchardt, *Vok.* i. 195, ii. 214). [The late spelling *facinerosus* is capable of being explained, like *temperi* Adv. beside *tempori* Dat., by the variation of the suffix -*os*- and -*es*- in the Declension of these Neuter stems (ch. v. § 71); cf. *pignera* for *pignora* (see Georges)].

§ 21. (2) in -l or Labial. Anteclassical: *consoluerunt* and *cosoleretur* on the S. C. de Bacchanalibus of 186 B. C. (*C. I. L.* i. 196. But *consuluere* i. 185 beside *consoltu* i. 186 on two old inscriptions of Venusia); the MSS. of Plautus show *exsolatum*, *Merc.* 593 (B), *exolatum, Most.* 597 (A), &c. (see Brix ad *Trin.* 535); *consol* on two inscriptions of 211 B. C. (i. 530-1) on another of 200 B. C. (*Not. Scav.* 1887, p. 195), and so normally till the third Punic War, even in one of 71 B. C., *consolibus* beside *consulibus* (*C. I. L.* i. 204); *exsoles* is the Old Latin form (Cornutus ap. Cassiod. p. 152. 7 K.; Caesellius ap. eund. p. 204. 2 K.), while Velius Longus says, 'consol' scribebatur per *o*, cum legeretur per *u* (p. 49. 14 K.); *incolomis* is the spelling of the best MSS. (B, C) in Plaut. *Truc.* 168 (cf. *colomnas C. I. L.* i. 1307). *O* remains in the classical period in *vīnolentus* (perhaps by analogy of *vīnō lentus*), *somnolentus*, and *sanguinolentus*. For the Superlative suffix we have the oldest spelling *o* in the proper name *Maxomo* in an inscription in the Faliscan dialect (Zv. *I. I. I.* 60 Maxomo Iuneo he cu*pat*, 'Maximus Junius hic cubat') (cf. Gk. Δεκο[μος *C.I.A.* iii. 61. A (3). 18, end of first cent. A. D. (?); *maxumus*, &c., as was said above (§ 18), is the usual spelling on inscriptions till the time of Julius Caesar, though *maximus*, &c. is occasionally found much earlier. The spelling of Plautus has *u* in words like *magnufice, Pseud.* 702 (A.); *pultufagis, Most.* 828 (A.); *sociufraude, Pseud.* 362 (A.); *sacruficem, Pseud.* 327 (both A, the Ambrosian Palimpsest, and the Palatine family of MSS.); *carnufex*, &c. (see Index to Studemund's Apograph of A, p. 522). So *Oinumama* for *Unimamma*, an Amazon, on an old Praenestine cista (*C.I.L.* i. 1501); *testumonium* on the Lex Bantina of 133-118 B.C. (i. 197); *Cornuficia* on an inscription (i. 1087), which Ritschl dates 'not long after Caesar' (cf. Gk. Κορνοφικιος, e.g. *C.I.G.* 6948), *tubulustrium* (Varro), but *aedificandam* 108 B.C. (*C.I.L.* i. 565 and *Eph. Epigr.* viii. 460), *opiparum* on the old Falisco-Latin inscription with *aciptum* (Zv. *I.I.I.* 72), *vadimonium* and *aedificium* on the Lex Agraria of 111 B.C. (*C.I.L.* i. 200); *testimonium* on the Lex Repetundarum of 121 B.C. (i. 198), &c. *Mănufestus* is the anteclass., *manifestus* the classical spelling (Georges, *Lex. Wortf.* s.v.). [For other examples see Georges s.vv. *Hadrumetum, quadrupes, septu(m)ennis, septu(m)aginta, crassupes* (Gk. Κρασσοπης, *Bull.* vi. p. 280, of the Republican period), *manupretium, maritumus, incolumis, coluber, marsuppium, monumentum, cornupeta, aurufex, existumo, lacruma mucculentus, recupero, ustulo, acupenser, sterculinum, intubus, sescuplex, victuma, pontufex*]. The influence of a following syllable with *i* (especially in hiatus) is shown in *fămilia* (O. Lat. *famelia*, § 18) beside *famulus*; *subrimii haedi*, from *rumis*, mamma (Paul. Fest. 369. 8 Th.) beside *subrumari* (Fest. 442. 32 Th.); *moinicipieis* beside *mancup(um)* on the Lex Agraria of 111 B.C. (*C.I.L.* i. 200); *manibieis, Eph. Epigr.* i. p. 215 (but *manubies, ib.* viii. 476, on a Capua inscription c. 135 B.C.); *surripias* is the spelling of both families of MSS. of Plautus in *Pseud.* 876, *surripere* in *Pseud.* 290, 675, *surripitur* in *Mil.* 602, but with *u* in the next syllable *surrupui, surrupuisse* seem to be the Plautine forms (also *surruptus*); we have *recipit* on a Scipio Epitaph of c. 180 B.C. (*C.I.L.* i. 33), *accipito* and *concilium* on i. 197 of 133-118 B.C., *accipito, conciliatum, conciliaboleis* on i. 198 of 123-122 B.C.; *acipiant* on i. 199 of 117 B.C.; only the *i*-form is quoted of *inipitus* : implicatus vel inretitus (Gl. Plac.), from root *ap-* (cf. *aptus*). [For *inipite* : inpetum facite (Paul. Fest. 78. 5 Th.), see below]. In Gk. inscriptions Σεπτουμιος is very rare; we find almost always Σεπτιμιος. (See also Georges on *Lanivium*).

Classical: *u* remains in *contubernium* (but *adtibernalis*, Paul. Fest. 9. 9 Th.) from *taberna*; *nuncupo, occupo* from *capio, occulo*, &c., and was retained in the spelling of Dat. and Abl. Plur. of some U-stems to distinguish them from similar I- or Cons.-stems, e.g. *artubus*, but according to the second-cent. grammarian in the spelling only (Ter. Scaur. p. 25. 11 K. nemo autem tam insulse per *u* ' artubus ' dixerit) (*trebibos* on an old inscription in the British Museum, *Eph. Epigr.* ii. 299); *dissupo* is the anteclassical, *dissipo* the classical spelling (Georges, *Lex. Wortf.* s.v.); so *victuma* and *victima* (*ib.* s.v.); *monumentum* and *monimentum* were both used, e.g. *monimentu* (*C.I.L.* i. 1258, 'not after 130 B.C.' Ritschl), while *monementum* and *monomentum* are incorrect spellings (Georg. s.v.). *Dŏcumentum*, &c. but *spěcimen*, &c. by Assimilation.

The Parasitic Vowel. Anteclassical : *piacolom*, the old spelling according to Mar. Victorinus (p. 11. 14 K. ut apparet ex libris antiquis foederum et legum, qui etiamsi frequenti transcriptione aliquid mutarunt, tamen retinent antiquitatem... pro 'piaculum' ibi 'piacolom'), is on a law of 58 B.C. (*C.I.L.* i. 603), *piacul-* (*piaclum* on the Spoletium inscription, xi. 4766), but the ancient o remains in Plautine spellings like *aemolos*, Acc. Pl., *Pseud.* 196 (A.); *epolonos* dicebant antiqui quos nunc epulones dicimus (Paul. Fest. 55. 15 Th.); *agolum*: pastorale baculum, quo pecudes aguntur (Paul. Fest. 21. 37 Th.); *Tuscolana*, C. I. L. i. 1200; *tabolam* on S. C. Bacch. of 186 B. C. (i. 196); *taboleis, popolum* (beside *popul(o)*) on Lex Bantina of 133-118 B. C. (i. 197); *singolos, taboleis* (and *tabula*), *conciliaboleis* on the Lex Repetundarum of 123-122 B. C. (i. 198); *singolos* (but *vinculeis*) on the Sententia Minuciorum of 117 B. C. (i. 199); *tabolam, singolis* on i. 208, an inscription referred by Ritschl to about the time of the Lex Agraria (i. 200, which however has only *tabula, tableis, singula, trientabule(is)*),viz. 111 B. C.; *angolaria* (but *opercula*), on the (restored) Lex Parieti Faciendo of 105 B. C. (i. 577), so that the old spelling does not seem to have died out till the end of the second cent. B. C. (On Greek inscriptions we have Λεντολος (first cent. B. C.), Λεντελος (c. 140 B. C.), Λεντυλος (first cent. A. D.), but usually Λεντλος (cf. ch. ii. § 102); the Gk. loanword *drachma* is in the earlier writers *drac(h)uma*; for spellings like *vigulum, vigulo, vigelia, titelus, sibelo, sepulivit*, see Georges.)

§ 22. **in other short syllables.** Anteclassical: *accĕdo* (for *accĭdo*) is preserved by the MSS. in Enn. *Trag.* 77. 206 R.; Lucr. ii. 1025, v. 609 and elsewhere (see Ribbeck, *Prolegom. Verg.* p. 416); so *timedus* in Naev. *Com.* 35 R.; *acetare* dicebant, quod nunc dicimus agere (Paul. Fest. 17. 30 Th.). Similarly *e* is retained without weakening in spellings of the oldest MSS. of Plautus like *detenet*, *Pers.* 505, *contenuum*, *Stich.* 214, *contenuo* 623, &c. (so the corruption *ad te alienent*, *Pers.* 497, points to *attenent* not *attinent*); in the MSS. of *Poen.* 266 *proseda* (cf. Paul. Fest. 282. 16 Th. prosedas meretrices Plautus appellat), *optenui* on a Scipio Epitaph of c. 130 B. C. (C. I. L. i. 38); *conregione* in the augur's formula (Varro, L. L. vii. 8; Paul. 46. 24 Th.); *promeneruat*, promonet, Carm. Sal. (Fest. 244. 12 Th.); cf. *mereto(d)* on a Scipio Epitaph of c. 215 B. C. (C. I. L. i. 32) (but *meritod* i. 190, 'early part of the sixth cent. A. U. C.'), and even on a recent inscription (i. 1012). This *e* in Old Latin spellings often appears for I.-Eur. *i* in syllables unaccented under the Old or the Paenultima Law, e. g. *aidiles* Nom. Sg. on a Scipio Epitaph of c. 250 B. C. (i. 31); *Fabrecio* (i. 106); *Tempestatebus* on a Scipio Epitaph of c. 215 B. C. (i. 32); *Lepareses* for *Liparenses* (Gk. Λιπάραι), (quoted probably from Ennius by Paul. Fest. 87. 6 Th.), and Greek inscriptions often retain the older orthography, e. g. κομετιον (usually), Καικελιος (till c. 50 B. C., then Καικιλιος), Καπετωλιον (usually, Καπιτ- not till first cent. A. D.), Λεπεδος (in Rep., but Λεπιδος in Empire), Δομετιος and Δομιτιος. But the weakening to *i* is old, as is seen from *dimidius*, which must have changed *e* to *i* at a time when the accent rested on the first syllable; *confice* on an old Praenestine cista of third cent. B. C. (*Mél. Arch.* 1890, p. 303); *subigit* and *opsides* on a Scipio Epitaph of c. 200 B. C. (i. 30); *habitarent* oppidum, *possidere* on the Decree of L. Aemilius Paulus, 189 B. C. (ii. 5041); *obstinet*, dicebant antiqui, quod nunc est ostendit, ut in veteribus carminibus, &c. (Fest. 228. 6 Th.); *prospices*, prospice, Carm. Sal. (Fest. 244. 13 Th.); *ēnico* is the old spelling, later *eneco* (Georges, *Lex. Wortf.* s. v.); *prosicium*, quod praesecatum projicitur (Paul. Fest. 282. 13 Th., cf. *prosiciae*, Gl. Philox.); *exsicas* from *ex* and *seco*, Plaut. *Rud.* 122; *obigitat* antiqui dicebant pro ante agitat (Fest. 214. 2 Th.); *jūrigo*, later *jūrgo* (cf. *jūrgium*); *gallicinium* from *cano*, by analogy of which was formed *conticinium* (cf. Gl. Plac. p. 58. 24 G. *conticinio* : tempore noctis post galli cantum quando cecinit et conticuit) (see Goetz, praef. in Plaut. *Asin.* xxv). Classical: *Juppiter* from *pater*; *sistite* (cf. Gk. ἵστατε); *compitum*, explained by Varro, 'ubi viae competunt' (L. L. 6. 25) (cf. *propitius*); *dīmico* from *maco*

§§ 22, 23.] ACCENTUATION. VOWEL-WEAKENING. 195

(cf. *macto*) ; of the rare weakening of *o* we have examples in Compounds like *hŏmicīda, armiger*, &c. for the Composition-Vowel, which is ŏ in other languages, is *ĭ* in Latin (see ch. v. § 83) ; *inquilīnus* beside *incola*? Of *ŭ*, examples are *cornicen* (Gk. κορνοκλάριος, κορνουκλάριος and κορνικλάριος) ; *sŭpercilium* (cf. Gk. κύλα, Plur.); both *inclutus* (*incluto* in all the MSS. of Plaut. *Pers.* 251) and *inclitus* are attested spellings ; (cf. *arbita*, not *arbuta*, in the MSS. of Lucretius, v. 941 and 965). For other examples of *e-i*, see Georges, *Lex. Wortf.*, s. vv. *eligo, compitum, tremebundus, caeremonia, fenisicium, cervesia, ploxenum, subsicivus, quatenus, internecio, protinus, seneca, querimonia, intellegentia, neglego, interimo*, also for late and plebeian spellings like *segitis, patena, tredecem, decim*. (On late *adjecentia* see Schuchardt, *Vok.* i. 193.) The change of *e* to *i* in syllables long by position is claimed for *praefiscini gĕnista*, &c. (on these see ch. ii. § 12), certainly with right in *infringo*, &c. (see ch. iv. § 11), before a consonant-group like *ng* (so *tingo* for *tengo*, Gk. τέγγω). Assimilation saves the vowel in *segetem, teretem*, &c.

§ 23. (3) Diphthongs, ai, ae. Anteclassical : *distisum* et *pertisum* dicebant, quod nunc ' distaesum ' et ' pertaesum ' (Paul. Fest. 51. 25 Th., cf. 271. 2 Th.). Festus, 372. 7 Th. tells us that Scipio Africanus Minor was twitted for his use of *pertisus* by Lucilius :

    Quo facetior videare, et scire plus quam caeteri
    'Pertisum' hominem, non pertaesum, dices.

Lucilius was right, for compounds with intensive *per* are Separable Compounds like *bene-facio, sat-ago* (see below); *pertaesum* is the spelling on the Claudius tablet at Lyons ; *consiptus* was used by Ennius, according to Paul. Fest. 43. 37 Th. (cf. 45. 15), and an example is quoted by Non. 183. 14 M. s. v. *venor*: teneor consipta, undique uenor (Enn. *Trag.* 254 R.) ; *adsipere* et *praesipere* dicebant antiqui, sicut nos quoque modo dicimus ab aequo 'iniquum,' ab quaerendo 'inquirere' (Paul. Fest. 16. 9 Th.) ; *obsipiam*, quoted from Caecilius by Diomedes (p. 383. 10 K. quod vulgo ' obsepio ' dicimus veteres ' obsipio ' dixerunt. Caecilius, &c.) (*Com.* 65 R.) ; *praecidaneam* porcam dicebant, quam immolare erant soliti antequam novam frugem praeciderent (Paul. Fest. 273. 5 Th.). (Gellius, iv. 6 discusses this word and its cognate *succidaneae*, which, he says, was sometimes mispronounced in his time *succidaneae*: succidaneae nominatae, littera i scilicet tractim pronuntiata; audio enim quosdam eam litteram in hac voce corripere) ; *occisit* is quoted from the Laws of Numa by Festus (194. 21 Th.) ; so *decidito* in XII Tab., *inceideretis* on S. C. Bacch. of 186 B. C. (*C. L I.* i. 196, 27). But *exquaere* is quoted by Priscian (i. p. 38 H.) from Plaut. *Aul.* 800, and the MSS. of Plautus often show this spelling of the word (see Ritschl, *Opusc.* iv. p. 141) (so *defaecato, Aul.* 79, but *deficatam, Most.* 158 are the likely spellings) ; *conquaeri, conquaesiuerit, exaestumaverit* occur on the Lex Repetundarum of 123–122 B. C. (*C. I. L.* i. 198), while on the Edictum Popillianum of 132 B. C. (i. 551) we have the curious spelling *conquaeisiuei* [cf. i. 547, an inscription of 141 or 116 B. C., with *Caeicilius* (and *consulto*), while a similar inscription, i. 548, has the older spelling *Caicilius* (and *consolto*, § 26)]. Later, the retention of *ae* became the rule, e. g. *opsaeptum* on the Lex Col. Jul. Urbanorum of 44 B. C. (*Eph. Epigr.* ii. p. 105) ; *lapicaedinis* on the Lex Metalli Vipascensis of the first cent. A. D. (*Eph. Epigr.* iii. p. 166) ; we have usually *fabri subaediani* on inscriptions (*C. I. L.* x. 6699. 5 ; vi. 9559. 8, &c.), or *subediani* (vi. 9558. 7 ; viii. 10523. 5) (of which last, *subidiani* on ii. 2211. 7, seems to be a misspelling). The weakened forms are used in the classical period in the compounds of *quaero*, in *existimo* (cf. Mar. Victor.

p. 22. 6 K. quid enim facietis in his quae, velitis nolitis, et scribenda sunt et legenda ut scripta sunt, ut exempli gratia 'existimo' non 'exaestimo'), in *fastidium* for **fasti-tidium* (§ 13, p. 176), &c.

au; *offucare* aquam : in fauces obsorbendam dare (Paul. Fest. 223. 8 Th.) ; *defrudo* seems to be the spelling of Plautus and Terence (Ritschl, *Parerg. Plaut.* p. 540) ; *accuso, incuso,* &c. from *causa* are classical forms. The *ū* of the compounds of *claudo* was in time adopted in the simple verb too, *cludo* by analogy of *recludo,* &c. (of Ital. chiudo) (see Seelmann in *Gött. Gel. Anz.* Aug. 15, 1890) (cf. *sed frude* § 64, beside *sed fraude* § 69, on the Lex Repetundarum, *C. I. L.* i. 198). The *ō* of *explodo,* &c. is not due to the loss of accent, but is a by-form of *au* found in the simple verb. (Diom. p. 382. 26 K. plaudo frequens est, apud veteres plodo ; then after quoting the form *ploderent* from Cicero, he adds, secundum eam consuetudinem qua 'au' syllaba cum 'o' littera commercium habet, ut cum dicimus 'claustra' et 'clostra,' item 'caudam' et 'codam' et similia), just as *oe* (older *oi*) and *ū* are byforms, e. g. *commūnis, immūnis,* COMOINEM in S. C. Bacch. (*C. I. L.* i. 196), *immoenis* (Plaut.). *Oboedio* from *audio* is difficult to explain. (See also Georges, *Lex. Wortf.* s. vv. *dissaeptum, exquiro, existimo,* and Brambach, *Orth.* on *pertaesus, lapicidinae.*)

§ 24. (4) Diphthongs in Hiatus. (On these see also ch. iv.) The *u*-diphthong is retained in *ăb-avus, ăt-avus, trĭt-avus* (O. Lat. *strit-avus*) but becomes *ŭ* in *ēluo* beside *lavo, eruum (ervum)* from *eregʷ- (Gk. ἐρέβινθος), dēnuo* for *de novo,* &c. The Greek'Αχαι(ϝ)οί became Lat. *Achīvi* (through **Acheiv-*); Gk. ἔλαι(ϝ)ον, *olīvo-,* older *oleivo-,* which became when *-om* was weakened to *-um* **olei(v)um* Nom., **oleivi* Gen. &c. (see ch. ii. § 53), whence *oleum* (for *ey* before a vowel loses *y,* e. g. *eo,* 'I go,' for **ĕyō,* ch. iv. § 63), and *olīvum, olei* and *olīvi,* &c. (like *dei(v)us, deivi,*whence *deus* and *dīvus, dei* and *dīvi,* ch. iv. § 70) ; Gk. ῥομφαία, a Thracian claymore, became *rumpia* (Enn. *Ann.* xiv. fr. 8 M. ; Liv. xxxi. 39. 11). In *cloāca* for *clovaca,* the *v* has been dropped, as usual, before the accented vowel (ch. ii. § 53), while *nŏcīvus* and *nocuus* are different formations (ch. v. § 7).

§ 25. (5) je and ve. On *ĭ, ŭ* as a weak or unaccented form of *yĕ, wĕ* in Indo-European see ch. iv. § 51. Whether the *ĭ* of *ăbicio,* &c. should be explained as a similar Latin weakening, or as a modification of *-jĭ-,* is an open question. The *ŭ* of *concutio* may also be compared with the use of Greek κυ for Lat. *-quĭ-* (especially unaccented), e. g. Greek 'Ακύλας for Lat. *Aquila,* Greek Κυρεινος for Lat. *Quirīnus,* see ch. ii. § 28. Cf. *ancunulentae* 'unclean,' (Paul. Fest. 8. 29 Th.), and *inquinare* ; *bīgae* is the reduction of *bi-jugae* (see Georges, *Lex. Wortf.* s. v. *bijugus*), *quadrīgae* of *quadri-jugae* ; *abicio* has the first syllable short in the old dramatic poets (cf. ch. ii. § 48, p. 45).

§ 26. (6) Later change of o to u, u to ü, i. In syllables long by position this is the usual development of original *o,* for cases like *trī-gintā* with *e(i)* for unaccented *o* (cf. Greek τριάκοντα) are rare, e. g. *vĕtustus* from I.-Eur. *wetos (Greek ἔτος, 'a year') and similar derivative TO-stems from Neuter S-stems, *fĕrundus* and similar Gerundial DO-stems from third Conjugation Verbs, *vŏluntas* and the like formations [that *fūnestus, ferendus, ferentarius* (cf. Osc. Herentat-, the Oscan Venus), &c. show a weakening of *o* to *e,* and not rather a bystem *funes-, ferend-, ferent-* cannot be proved ; cf. ch. viii. §§ 89, 94, and see above, § 20 ; cf. *lugubris (-os)* and *funebris (-es)*]. Similarly in final syllables long by position we have *-unt* in 3 Pl. of Verbs for O. Lat. *-ont,* e. g. *nequinont* (Liv. Andron.), *cosentiont* (Scipio Epitaph) (ch. viii. § 73). The change of *o* to *u*

§§ 24-27.] ACCENTUATION. VOWEL-WEAKENING. 197

in unaccented syllables is further discussed in ch. iv. § 20. *Dŭpundius* (and *dupondius*; see Georges, *Lex. Wortf.* s. v.), *promuntŭrium*, are not good examples, for before *nd*, *nt* we find even accented *o* becoming a *u*-sound, e. g. O. Lat. *frundes*, *Acheruntem* (ch. ii. § 22). For examples of the change in syllables not long by position, see Georges, *Lex. Wortf.* s. vv. *formidolosus, adulescens, lemures, fulgurio, bajulus, lautumiae,* and cf. Brambach, *Orth.* on the misspellings *pulenta, amulum, Aequiculi* and Georges on *subules, eburis* Gen., *rigura* Plur., *vinulentus, sanguinulentus, somnulentus, tripudo.* But *cŏralium* (Greek κωρ-) and *curalium* (Greek κουρ-) are not examples, nor *mamphur* (leg. *mamfar*) the 'thong' round a turner's wheel (Paul. Fest. 101. 1 Th.) (see Meyer-Lübke, *Comm. Schweizer-Sidler*, p. 24), and O. Lat. *colina* is a doubtful form. Examples of *u-i* are *inclutus*, later *inclitus, dēfrutum* and *defritum* (see Georges), *arbutum* and *arbitum* (Lucr.), *sătura* and *satira*.

§ 27. (7) Greek words with Vowel-change. *a. Aleria* (Αλαλία in Herodotus), a town in Corsica (cf. the Scipio Epitaph, c. 215 B.C. *C.I.L.* i. 32 hec cepit Corsica Aleriaque urbe); *tessera* (τέσσαρα); *Agrigentum* ('Ακράγαντα Acc.), now Girgenti ; *Tarentum* (Τάραντα Acc.), now Táranto or Taránto ; *Alixentrom* ('Αλέξανδρον) on a Praenestine cista of third cent. B.C. (i. 59), and on another (i. 1501) *Alixente(r)* ('Αλέξανδρος), *Casenter(a)* (Κασσάνδρα), *Ateleta* ('Αταλάντη); *Hecuba,* O. Lat. *Hecoba* (Quint. i. 4. 16) ('Εκάβη) ; *camera* (καμάρα), also *camara*, (the spelling approved by Verrius Flaccus, Charis. 58. 23 K.), which was specially used in the sense of a decked boat (see Georges, *Lex. Wortf.* s. v.); *Camerīna* and *Camarīna* (Καμάρινα), *crāpula* (κραιπάλη) (see Meyer, *Rom. Gram.* i. pp. 32, 36); *machina* (μηχανή, μαχανά) ; *Catina* (Κατάνη); *scutula* (σκυτάλη); *strangulo* (στραγγαλάω).

ε. *catapulta* (καταπέλτης) ; *scopulus* (σκόπελος) ; *tarpessita* Plaut. (τραπεζίτης) ; *pharetra* (φαρέτρα); *Acheruns* Plaut. ('Αχέρων) ; *enocilis* (Löwe, *Prodr.* p. 376) (ἔγχελυς).

ι. *dapsilis* (δαψιλής) ; *cupressus* (κυπάρισσος).

ο. *amurca* (ἀμόργη) ; *cothurnus* (κόθορνος); *epistula* (ἐπιστολή) ; also epistola (see Georges, *Lex. Wortf.* s. v.) ; *paenula* (φαινόλης) ; *tribulus* (τρίβολος) ; *Patricoles* (Πάτροκλος), the old form, used by Ennius (*Trag.* 314 R. ; a line of Livius Andronicus is quoted by Gellius, vi. 7. 11, with this name in the form *Patroclus*, without any divergence in the MSS.) ; *lautumiae*. *Avernus*, popularly connected with *ἄορνος*, and late Lat. *averta* (Greek ἀορτή) admit of other explanations. (See Solmsen, *Stud. Lat. Lautgesch.* p. 23). On the spelling *numisma* (Gk. νόμισμα) see Keller ad Hor. *Epp.* ii. 1. 234, and on late Lat. *zabulus* for *diabolus,* Georges, *Lex. Wortf.* s. v.

υ. *arytaena,* but *artaena* (*artena*) in Lucilius (ἀρύταινα) ; *incitega* (ἐγγυθήκη) (Paul. Fest. 76. 3 Th. incitega : machinula, in qua constituebatur in convivio vini amphora, de qua subinde deferrentur vina) ; *mattea,* 'mincemeat' (Varro, *L. L.* v. 112) (ματτύη). (The word appears in a curious military term *mattiobarbulus*, used by Vegetius for a leaden bullet, or a soldier armed with these, apparently for ματτυο-πάρβολος, lit. 'mincemeat-scattering.' See *A. L. L.* v. 135) ; *serpillum*, (if from Greek ἔρπυλλος), with *s* by analogy of *serpo*.

αι, αυ. *Achivi* ('Αχαιοί) ; *olivum* and *oleum* (ἔλαιον) ; *oliva* and *olea* (ἐλαία) ; *Centurum,* Centaurum (Gl. Plac. p. 54. 7 G.) (Κένταυρον).

Parasitic Vowel. 'Ηρακλῆς is on Praenestine cistae and mirrors *Hercle* ... (*C.I.L.* xiv. 4105), *Hercles* (? *Fercles*) (*C.I.L.* i. 1500), *Hercele* Acc. (i. 56), and on old Praenestine inscriptions (xiv. 2891-2) *Hercole* Dat. On a Roman inscription of 217 B.C. (i. 1503) *Herculei* Dat. So *Hercolei* (i. 1175), *Hercoli* (i. 815), but *Herculis* Gen. on an inscr. of 146 B.C. (i. 541), classical *Hercules, mehercle* (cf. Prisc. i. p. 27. 13 H. Romanorum vetustissimi in multis dictionibus loco ejus (u) o posuisse inveniuntur... 'Hercolem' pro 'Herculem'); 'Ασκληπιός is *Aiscolapio* Dat. on an old inscr. (*Ann. Epigr.* 1890, no. 85, but *Aisclapi*, *Eph. Epigr.* i. 5), classical *Aesculapius*; 'Αλκμήνη is in Plautus *Alcumena*; on *techina*, &c., *musimo*, see ch. ii. § 72.

§ 28. (8) Vowel unchanged. i. in Latin words. Anteclassical: *incantassit* and *excantassit* of XII Tab. (ap. Plin. xxviii. 18), but 'occentassint' antiqui dicebant, quod nunc convicium fecerint (Fest. 196. 12 Th.); *ancaesa*, dicta sunt ab antiquis vasa, quae caelata appellamus (Paul. Fest. 15. 10 Th.), but Prisc. i. p. 29. 20 H. cites as instances of *am-*, 'anfractus,' 'ancisus,' 'anquiro,' and Varro, *L.L.* vii. 43 explains 'ancilia': quod ea arma ab utraque parte, ut Thracum, incisa ; *perfacul* antiqui, et per se ' facul' dicebant, quod nunc facile diximus (Fest. 266. 20 Th.) is normal, for compounds with *per-* 'very' seem not to change the vowel, e. g. *persalsus* (beside *insulsus*), *persapiens* (beside *insipiens*) : *perfacilis* (beside *difficilis*), being what are called 'Separable' Compounds, cf. *per pol saepe peccas*, Plaut. *Cas.* 370, *per ŏpus est*, Ter. *Andr.* 265 (so that Lucilius was right in his objection to *pertisum*, see above); *procapis* progenies: quae ab uno capite procedit (Paul. Fest. 281. 22 Th.); *concapit* tignum XII Tab. (ap. Fest. 556. 27 Th. tignum iunctum aedibus uineaue et concapit ne soluito); *resparsum* vinum (Paul. Fest. 353. 6 Th.); *concapsit*, conprehenderit (*C. G. L.* v. 182. 22). *occanuere* (3 Pl. Pft.) is quoted from Sallust's *Histories* by Priscian, i. p. 529. 5 K.

Classical : *rĕdarguo*, but 'rederguo,' was used by Scipio Africanus Minor (Fest. 372. 7 Th. *redarguisse* per e litteram Scipio Africanus Pauli filius dicitur enuntiasse, ut idem etiam 'pertisum'); *ălacris*, but Vulg. Lat. *alecer* (so in a glossary in MS. Vind. 482) (Ital. allegro, &c.); *augurātus*, *augur* were formerly 'augeratus,' 'auger' according to Priscian, i. p. 27. 17 H.; *impetus*, but 'inipite,' inpetum facite (Paul. Fest. 78. 5 Th., apparently a corruption for 'impite,' impetum fac), 'compitum'; *undecim*, *duodecim* weaken the *e* of the final syllable but not of the paenultima ; *incola*, but O. Lat 'inquilīnus' (ch. vi. § 10); *inaequālis*, but 'iniquus,' &c. *U* remains in *tŭtudi* (see ch. viii. § 39), *pĕcudem*, *contumax*, &c. (See also Georges, *Lex. Wortf.* s. vv. *instauro*, *conquaestor*, *comparo*, *sepelio*, &c.)

§ 29. ii. in Greek loanwords: *amygdala* (ἀμυγδάλη) (but Vulg. *amiddula*, Probi Appendix 198. 26 K.), *artemo* Lucil. (ἀρτέμων); *astraba*, the title of a play ascribed to Plautus (ἀστράβη) ; *ballaena* or *balena*, Plaut. &c. (φάλλαινα) ; *balanus*, Plaut. &c. (βάλανος) ; *barathrum*, Plaut. &c. (βάραθρον); *calamus*, Plaut. &c. (κάλαμος), apparently Vulg. Lat. **calmus* (Ital. calmo and calamo, Fr. chaume); *cantharus*, Plaut. &c. (κάνθαρος); *cinaedus*, Plaut. &c. (κίναιδος) ; *cottabus*, Plaut. &c. (κότταβος); *cymbalum*, Lucr. &c. (κύμβαλον); *daedalus*, Enn. &c. (δαίδαλος); *drapeta*, Plaut. (δραπέτης); *gaunacum*, Varro (καννάκη); *gausape*, Lucil. &c. (γαυσάπης, γαύσαπος); *Hecata*, Plaut. &c. ('Εκάτη); *hilarus*, Plaut. &c., later *hilaris* (ἱλαρός); *Hiluria*, Plaut., later *Illyria* ('Ιλλυρία); *lapathus*, Lucil. (λάπαθος); *machaera*, Plaut. &c. (μάχαιρα) ; *malacus*, Naev., Plaut. &c. (μάλακος) ; *margarita*, Varro, &c. (μαργαρίτης) ; *metallum*, Varro, &c. (μέταλλον) ; *murena*, Plaut. &c. (μύραινα); *narcissus* (νάρκισσος) ; *obrussa*, 'touchstone,' Cic. (ὀβρύζη, ὄβρυζον); *onager* (ὄναγρος) ; *palaestra*, Plaut. &c. (παλαίστρα); *petasus*, Plaut. &c. (πέτασος); *phalanga*, Varro, &c.; *pittacium* (πιττάκιον); *ptisana*, Varro, &c. (πτισάνη) ; *raphanus*, Cato, &c. (ῥάφανος) ; *sesamum*, Plaut. (σήσαμον), but *sesuma*, Plaut.

§§ 28–31.] ACCENTUATION. VOWEL-WEAKENING. 199

Poen. 326, sesima (see Georges s. v.) ; stomachus, stomachor, Ter. &c. (στόμαχος) ; Tartarus, Tartarīnus, Enn. &c. (Τάρταρος), sometimes mispronounced 'Tarterus' (Consent. 392. 17 K.) ; thalamus (θάλαμος) ; thesaurus, t(h)ensaurus, Plaut. &c. (θησαυρός) ; tropaeum, Accius, &c. (τρόπαιον) ; tympanum, Plaut. &c. (τύμπανον) ; tyrannus, Plaut. &c. (τύραννος) ; paedagogus, Plaut. &c. (παιδαγωγός).

§ 30. (9) Long vowels. None of the examples adduced to prove that long unaccented vowels were sometimes changed are conclusive : dēlīro from līra, 'a furrow,' root leis- (O. Sl. lěha, Lith. lýsė, 'a garden-bed, 'O. H. G. wagan-leisa, &c.), is the correct form, while delēro, as Varro (ap. Vel. Long. 73. 2 K.) pointed out, is due to confusion with Greek ληρεῖν. Dēlīnio (so spelt in all the MSS. apparently of Plaut. Stich. 457), beside delenio, subtūlis (but protēlum, &c.), suspīcio, convīcium, all with i in the following syllable, show the change to which even accented ē is liable, e. g. Plīnius (ch. iv. § 7). Occidamus, attributed to Plautus, as an example of ob in composition, by the MSS. of Festus (196. 10 Th. occidamus Plautus ponit pro contra cedamus, cum plurimae aliae praepositiones familiariores huic verbo sint ; cf. Paul. 197. 1 Th.) is clearly a corruption for occēdāmus. For not only does Placidus' Glossary of Plautus (p. 89. 4 G.) give occedere : occurrere vel obviam cedere, but the MSS. (the Palatine family) of Plautus read in the passage referred to by Festus, viz. Pseud. 250, Accedamus hac obviam, where the corruption accedamus points to an original occedamus. Consiva, an epithet of the goddess Ops (Fest. 210. 26 Th., Varro, L. L. vi. 21) has been connected with consĕro, consēvi. The examples of unchanged ē are numerous, such as the compounds of cēdo, rēpo, cēlo, crēdo, crētus, spēro, irrētio from rēte, &c. For the change of ā to ē through want of accent (for a similar change through influence of palatal j (y) in Vulg. Lat. Jēnuarius, &c., see ch. ii. § 3) the examples usually adduced are anhēlus (cf. hālo), and subtēl (cf. tālus). But anhēlus (spelt anellus in MSS. of Virgil ; see Ribbeck's Index) has probably come from *an-ĕnslos, the a of hālo, from *ănslo (root an augmented by s), having been changed to e while its quantity was still short. The word subtel quoted by Priscian (i. p. 147. 9 H.) as an instance of -ĕl, and explained as τὸ κοῖλον τοῦ ποδός (what does he mean by hostis hostilis, subtel subtilis, i. p. 131. 21 H. ?) may similarly be due to a change of the short vowel in the original form *sub-tax-lus (cf. taxillus) (or from tellus ?). None of the Compounds of clāmo, fāma, fātus, clārus, pāreo, pāx, plāco, prāvus, rādo, vādo, gnārus, grātus, lābor, māno, nātus, gnāvus, &c. ever change the vowel. Profestus is a compound of fēstus (cf. fēriae for *fēsiae), not of fastus, fās (cf. nefastus). Nor do ō, ū change ; witness the Compounds of plōro, dōno, flōs, &c. Praestōlor and praestŭlor come, the one from praestō, the other from praestū (§ 15. 3). Pejĕro and ējĕro (cf. conierat, coniurat, C. G. L. iv. 322. 33) have not yet been thoroughly explained.

§ 31. (10) Recomposition and Analogy. In Vulgar Latin, as was mentioned before (§ 11), the accent seems to have rested on the first syllable of the verb in Compound Verbs, e. g. renégat, Ital. riniega, O. Fr. renie ; dimórat, Ital. dimora (with close o), Fr. demeure. The vowel of the simple verb usually appears unchanged in the Compound, e. g. reddédit, Ital. rendiede, O. Fr. rendiet. From the inscriptions of the Empire and the remarks of grammarians we see that the same 'etymological' treatment of Compound Verbs was a feature of Imperial Latin. On the Latin Papyri of Herculaneum (first cent. A. D.) the preposition of a Compound Verb, &c. is usually retained in its simple form and not assimilated to the initial of the verb, or noun, e. g.

ad-siduo, ad-fini (Class. Rev. iv. 443), by a similar 're-composition'; and Velius Longus (p. 62. 16 K.) mentions *adluo, adlŏquor, adlābor* as the forms in use at his time, though Assimilation was the custom with other verbs, e. g. *alligo* (see ch. iv. § 159). The same grammarian, in another passage, while he approves of the pronunciation *commendo*, adds that the popular pronunciation was *commando* (73. 10 K. quamvis 'commendo' dicamus, tamen 'commando' in consuetudine est.) (So *amendo* and *amando*. See Georges, *Lex.Wortf.* s. v.). And his remark on the word *comprimo* shows the tendency of his time (first cent. A.D.) to follow in these Compound Verbs the Analogy of the Simple Verb, or of the Perfect Participle Passive (76. 9 K. 'comprimo' quoque per i malo scribi, quamvis 'compressus' dicatur). (Cf. Mar. Vict. 10. 6 K. sacratum autem in compositione 'consecratum' facit per s et e, non per s et a, sic et castus facit 'incestum' non 'incastum'; Caper 110. 7 K. 'insipiens' non 'insapiens'; Diom. 378. 30 K. ; Prisc. i. p. 437. 25 H.) The analogy of the Perf. Part. Pass. (or was it Assimilation ?) brought *e* instead of *i* into the second syllable of *perpeti, depecisci,* &c., while the analogy of the simple verb is seen in spellings on Imperial inscriptions like *consacravit (C. I. L.* vi. 3716, of 182 A. D.), *consacravi* on the Mon. Ancyr. ii. 30 ; iv. 25) (for other examples see Seelmann, *Ausspr.* p. 60). Often the two forms, the old with changed vowel and the new popular form, are retained side by side, and are used by the grammarians to express different shades of meaning. Thus Velius Longus (75. 6 K.) differentiates *aspergo* the Verb, from *aspargo* the Noun ; Caper (100. 5 K.) *protinus* the Adverb of time, from *protenus* the local Adverb. The *i* of the Oblique Cases of *levir*, **laevir,* ' brother-in-law' (cf. Greek δαήρ, I.-Eur. *daiwer-) and indeed of the Nom. Sg. too, is due to the analogy of *vir* (cf. Non. 557. 6 M. levir dicitur frater mariti, quasi laevus vir) ; of the inferior spelling *gĕnitrix*, for *genetrix* (see Georges, *Lex. Wortf.* s. v.) to the analogy of *genitor*. Sometimes the Analogy of the Compound affects the Simple Verb, when the Compound is more frequently in use than the other. The Analogy of *conspicio, aspicio, despicio,* &c. changed the spelling of the little used simple verb from *specio* (e. g. Varr. *L. L.* vi. 82, Plaut. *Cas.* 516) to *spicio* ; *complico, explico,* &c. have effected the change of **pleco* (Gk. πλέκτω) to *plico*. (For other ex. of ' Re-composition,' see Seelmann, *Ausspr.* p. 60, and Georges, *Lex.Wortf.* s.vv. *dispando, infacetus, praecanto, infarcio, peremo, indamnis* beside *indemnis* ; see also above, § 28).

§ 32. (11) **Pretonic.** *Miniscitur* pro reminiscitur antiquitus dicebatur (Paul. Fest. 88. 12 Th.) (or by Analogy of Compound ?) ; the Preposition *en* of O. Lat. became *in* from its position before the accented syllable in phrases like *in-aéde esse, in-témplum ire,* &c. Caper (p. 93. 3 K.) corrects the mispronunciation *pinaria* cella for 'penaria,' and (p. 106. 4 K.) *pulenta* for 'polenta,' and (p. 100. 23 K.), *pidato* for 'pedatu' in the phrase 'primo pedatu'; Probi Append. 198. 5 K. *sinatus (C. I. L.* i. 206, l. 135; viii. 10525, &c.). We may similarly explain the *u* of *Ulixes*, from Ὀλυσσεύς, the 'Aeolic' form of Ὀδυσσεύς (Quint. i. 4. 16, who also quotes the spelling *Pulixena* for *Polyxena*) ; cf. Ἰουβῖνος on a Gk. inscription of Syracuse, *I. I. S.* 125 ; Βουλουμνιος on a Cyzicus inscription of the Republican period, *Mitth.* vi. 124. (See also Georges, *Lex. Wortf.* for the spellings *rutundus, lulligo, ciminum, Sigambri, Lundinium,* &c.) In Italian the influence of the following labial is shown in somiglia (Lat.*similiat*), domanda (Lat. *demandat*), dovere (Lat. *debere*), of a following *r* in smeraldo (Lat. *smaragdus*). But examples in Republican Latin of the weakening of initial syllables are doubtful (cf. § 7).

§§ 32–34.] ACCENTUATION. VOWEL-WEAKENING. 201

§ 33. (12) **Assimilation, Dissimilation, and False Analogy.** In Italian the unaccented vowel is often assimilated to the vowel of the neighbouring syllable. Thus Latin *aequālis* has become uguale ; cronaca (Lat. *chronica*) owes its penultimate *a* to Assimilation. The same tendency is seen in Vulgar Latin **aramen* for *aerāmen* (Span. arambre, Port. arame, Prov. aram, &c.), **salvaticus* for *silvātĭcus* (Fr. sauvage, our 'savage,' Span. salvaje), &c., and in classical Latin in Perfects like *momordi, poposci, cucurri*, of which the older forms were *memordi, peposci, cecurri* (Gell. vi. 9). So strong is the tendency in Latin to assimilate completely an initial syllable which has some resemblance to a following syllable that we find this Assimilation even in the accented syllable of Perfects like *pupŭgi*, older *pepugi* (Gell. *ib.*) [*cecini* reflects the older spelling **ce-cen-ei*, but when the Stem-syllable had originally *i*, we have *i* in the Reduplication-syllable, e. g. *di-dĭc-i* (see ch. viii. § 22) from **dic-sco*]. (On the Assimilation of Syllables in Latin, see ch. iv. § 163). Mispronunciations of this kind censured in the Appendix Probi (197–9 K.) are : *toloneum, tonotru, passar, ansar, parantalia, butumen*, and on late inscriptions we have misspellings like *monomentum* (*C. I. L.* vi. 2888, 11131, 24481, xiv. 416 and 523 and 864 ; *Bull. Comm. Rom.* 1880, p. 137, 1887, p. 43), *optomo* (*C. I. L.* ii. 4291) (cf. *oppodum* as early as the Lex Agraria of 111 B. C., i. 200. 81), *passar* (*I. R. N.* 7160 ; *C. I. L.* vi. 2698), *ansare* (v. 7906), *pataris* (vi. 2060. 12, the Act. Arval. of 81 A. D.), *carcares* (vi. 2065, 2066, 2067, the Act. Arval. of 87–90 A. D.), *cubuc(u)larius* (*C. I. L.* vi. 6262, 8766), *figilinae* (xv. praef. p. 8). See also Georges, *Lex. Wortf.* on the spellings *lucuna, lucusta, tŭburis, Berenice, carcar, passar* [e. g. Itala (Ash.) *Lev.* xi. 5, (Taur.) *Matth.* x. 29 and 31, (Cantabr.) *Luc.* xi. 150], *Ptolomais, Dolobella, tugurium*, and cf. Romance forms like Span. pajaro, Ital. passaretta (from Vulg. Lat. *passar*). The opposite tendency, viz. Dissimilation, perhaps appears in Vulgar Latin in a word like *vīcīnus*, where the first *ī* (close *i*) has been changed to open *i* (Span. vecino, Prov. vezins, &c.). To the false analogy of *lăcus* has been referred the *a* of Vulg. Lat. **lacusta* (Roum. lăcustă), while forms like Prov. langosta, O. Fr. langoste point to an original l'angusta (*illa angusta*). The tendency of plant-, bird-, and beast-names to be changed by all sorts of false analogies is well seen in the dialectal Italian descendants of Lat. *vespertilio*, 'a bat' (Tosc. pipistrello, and vipistrello Caserta sportiglione, Pisa pilistrello, Parma pálpástrel, &c.). (For exx. of vowel retained by Assimilation, see §§ 22, 29).

§ 34. (13) **Shortening of Syllables long by Position.** In the dramatists of the Republic a syllable long by nature or by position is occasionally scanned as a short syllable when a short syllable precedes, a law of Prosody which is usually called the Law of Breves Breviantes. Of final syllables, syllables whether long by nature or by 'position' are shortened by this law especially in iambic words like *căvĕ, pŭtă, fĕrŭnt, lĕgŭnt*, the liability of a final unaccented syllable to be shortened being increased by the precedence of a short accented syllable (see next section). Putting final syllables aside for the present, the usual case of syllable-shortening is in a word of four or more syllables, where a syllable long by position is preceded by a short syllable, and followed by the accented syllable. Thus *volŭptatis, volŭptatem, volŭptarius*, &c. are common scansions in the early dramatists, and *volŭntatis, juvĕntutis, gubĕrnare* and *gubĕrnator, egĕstatis, venŭstatis, supĕllectilis* come next in order of frequency. The normal scansion of all these second syllables is that of Classical poetry; but the position of the syllable between a short syllable on the one hand and the accented syllable on the other, made it especially liable to be slurred in pronunciation, so that the dramatic poets, who followed more closely the pronunciation of everyday life than others, felt themselves at liberty, when exigencies of metre demanded, to treat it as a short syllable. In the word *ministerium* this pronunciation was carried so far as to syncopate the second syllable, *minsterium, misterium* (Ital. mestiero, Fr. métier, Chaucer's 'mistery,' ed. Morris, iii. 348); and this form seems to occur as early as Plautus, *Pseud.* 772 :

paruis magnisque misteriis praefulcior,

where the MSS. offer *miseriis*. Less frequently we find the preposition shortened in a Compound when preceded by a short monosyllable (or elided dissyllable), e. g. *Capt.* 83 *in ŏcculto, Most.* 896 *tibi ŏptemperem*, phrases which may be considered as word-groups *in-occúlto, tib(i)-optémperem*, and so fall under the same category as the polysyllables *voluptatis, voluptarius* just mentioned, but also, e. g. *Trin.* 318 *quid ĕxprobras*? *Capt.* 70 *quia ĭnuocatus*, where the accent does not fall on the syllable immediately following the preposition. The tendency of a preposition in a Compound to be weakened (ch. ii. § 130) (cf. *ŏ-mitto* for *om-mitto, *obmitto; *rĕ-cido, rĕ-latus, rĕ-duco*, earlier *reccido, rellatus, redduco*, but see ch. ix. § 49), is here increased by the precedence of a short syllable ; or perhaps the truer explanation is that the Preposition was regarded as separable from the other member of the Compound, and *quid ĕx-, qui(a) ĭn-* show the same shortening as in the final syllable of iambic words. Similarly in Greek and other loanwords a syllable long by position may be shortened when the preceding short syllable has the accent, as in Plautus always *Philĭppus* (Φίλιππος) in the sense of a 'Philip,' a gold coin, and in the Christian poets *abўssus* (ἄβυσσος) (Paul. Nol. 19. 651 ; 35. 228 ; Cypr. Gall. *Gen.* 288 P.). In Vulgar and Late Latin we have syllables long by nature shortened in this way, e. g. *erĕmus* (ἔρημος) in the Christian poets (e. g. Prud. *Psych.* 372 ; *Cath.* v. 89), whence the Romance forms, Ital. erèmo and ermo, O. Fr. erme, Span. yermo, &c. ; *merĕbatur*, a mispronunciation censured by Consentius 393. 23 K. (also *ŏrator* 392. 11 K.) ; *verĕcundus* in the Christian poets (e. g. Fort. vii. 6. 10) (cf. *vericundus C. I. L.* x. 1870), whence the Romance syncopated forms of *ver(e)cundia*, Ital. vergogna, Fr. vergogne, Span. verguenza, &c. ; but the instances which can be quoted from the early dramatists are so few and so uncertain as not to warrant us in ascribing this pronunciation to an earlier time (see *Journ. Phil.* xxi. 198 ; xxii. 1). In Ter. *Phorm.* 902 *an uerĕbamini*, some MSS. have *an ueremini*; and *Clutĕmestra* or *Clutaĕmestra* (Κλυται-μήστρα, a better spelling than Κλυταιμνήστρα), in Livius Andronicus, *Trag.* 11 R., may be a case of false analogy, like *orichalcum* (ὀρείχαλκος), which is in Plautus *aurichalcum*, by confusion with *aurum*, and owes its short *i* to this earlier form (cf. aquaeductus non 'aquiductus' Prob. App. 197. 26 K., like terrae motus non 'terrimotium' ib. 198. 32). *Ancŏra* (ἄγκυρα), where the shortened vowel follows a syllable which is not short but long by position, seems, with its *o* for *u* before *r*, not to be a direct development of the Greek word. The early dramatists do not shorten by the law of Breves Breviantes the prepositions *in, con* in Compounds when the letter following the preposition is *s* or *f* (see *Journ. Phil.* ll. cc.) ; and we know from Cicero (*Or.* xlviii. § 159) that the *i, o* were long in these cases. *Calĕfacio*, &c. (in Quintilian's time apparently *calfacio*, i. 6. 21), are really separable compounds, *cale facio* (cf. *facit ārē*, Lucr. vi. 962), so that the *e* is properly regarded as a final vowel; and the same is true of *diĕquinte* (cf. Gell. x. 24. 1).

§ 35.] ACCENTUATION. REDUCTION OF FINAL SYLL. 203

§ 35. **Change and Shortening of Vowel in Unaccented Final Syllable.** The final syllable in Latin requires a separate treatment, for besides the want of accent, there are other weakening influences to which a final syllable is always liable. Phoneticians tell us (Sweet, *Primer*, § 105) that 'the general tendency of language is to pronounce with diminishing force,' so that in English, for example, the *c* of 'cat' is pronounced with more force than the *t*, and the final consonants of 'obliged' are 'whispered'; and in Portuguese the final *o* of a word like campo (Lat. *campus*) is similarly uttered with what is known as 'whisper,' not with 'voice.' When a vowel actually ended a word, it would also be liable to elision, more or less complete, before a word which began with a vowel or the letter *h*.

I. LOSS OR SYNCOPE OF SHORT VOWEL. i. *Final vowel.* The weakness of a final short vowel in Latin is seen in Plautine versification. Plautus (according to Langen, in *Philologus*, xlvi. p. 419) shows a preference to elide a final short vowel rather than allow it to constitute by itself a thesis, so that endings of iambic lines like *expectare vis*, where the final *ĕ* of *expectare* forms the thesis of the last iambus, are not common. The weakness of final *ĕ* in particular, the vowel to which, as we shall see, every short final vowel was changed, is shown still more by its occasional suppression in words like *quippe, unde, inde*, and perhaps *ille, iste*, before an initial consonant in Plautus and the early dramatists. *Nempe* is always scanned *nemp* in this position by Plautus and Terence, while *proinde, deinde*, have developed the byforms *proin* and *dein*, and *nĕque, atque*, the monosyllables *nec, ac* (for *atc). All these are words which would naturally be closely joined in utterance with a following word, so that we may compare the Italian suppression of *-e, -o*, after *n, l, r* in word-groups, such as of the final vowel of bello, buono, signore, &c., in phrases like bel tempo, buon giorno, signor padre, tal cosa, &c. Similarly the subordinate or auxiliary verbs *făcio, dīco, dūco*, lose their *-e* in the 2 Sg. Imper. *fac, dic, duc* (see ch. viii. § 28). The same loss of *-ĕ*, whether due to syncope in a word-group, or to elision before an initial vowel, or to both causes, has produced *-l* from *-le*, *-r* from *-re*, in forms like *bacchānal* for earlier *bacchanāle, *calcar* for *calcāre (Neut. of *calcaris*, for *calcare ferrum*, 'the iron attached to the heel'), &c., and has reduced the particles *-ce*, *-ne*, to *-c*, *-n*, in *hic, hunc, viden, audin*, &c. The loss of final *-um* in *nĭhil* for *nihilum*, *sĕd* for *sedum* (Ter. Scaur. 12. 8 K.), &c., can have been due to elision, but not to syncope (see ch. x. § 18).

ii. *In final syllable.* The syncope of a short vowel in a final syllable ending in a consonant has been already discussed in § 16. We there saw that this syncope, a prominent feature of the Oscan and Umbrian languages, e.g. Osc. húrz (Lat. *hortus*), Umbr. *emps* (Lat. *emptus*), is difficult to establish with certainty for Latin, since *vĭŏlens* beside *violentus, mansuēs* beside *mansuētus, rēmex* beside *prōdĭgus*, &c., may be instances of parallel stem-formations like *pĕnu-, peno-, penos-*, of *penus*, Gen. *penūs, penum*, Gen. *peni, penus*, Gen. *penŏris*; and even stronger examples, such as *Arpīnas*, older *Arpinātis, praeceps*, older *praecĭpes*, may have arisen otherwise than by syncope.

§ 36. **Loss of -e.** For other examples in Plautus such as *Pseud.* 239 *mitt(e) mé sis*, and for a list of instances of *quipp(e), nemp(e)*, &c. see Skutsch, *Forsch.* i. Plautus' use of *-ne* and *-n* seems to depend, not on whether the initial of the following word is a vowel or a consonant, but on whether the preceding syllable is short or long (Schrader, *De part.* '*ne*' . . . *apud Plautum*) (for Terence's use of *-ne, -n*, see Dziatzko ad *Phorm.* 210 Anh.) ; while he employs the forms *hisce, illisce*, &c. before an initial vowel, *hi, illi*, before an initial consonant (Studemund in Fleckeisen's *Jahrb.* 1876, p. 73). Parallel forms like *atque*, and *ac* (for **atc*), Ital. *tale* and *tal*, which have arisen from the same original form according to its position in the sentence, are called 'doublets.' (German 'Satzdoubletten') (ch. ii. § 136.) The Latin *măgis* has thus become in Italian mai, when used independently as an Adverb ; but ma, with loss of the final vowel, when used as a Conjunction, and so joined to a following word. In Oscan, avt, in the sense of Latin *autem* or *at*, and avti, in the sense of Lat. *aut*, may be similar doublets. The syncopated form of the I.-Eur. preposition **ăpŏ* (Greek ἄπο, Sanscr. ápa) has become universal in Latin, e. g. *ap-ĕrio, ab-dūco* (cf. *sub*, Greek ὑπο), almost the only trace of the final vowel being *po-situs, pōno* for **po-s(i)no* ; I.-Eur. **pĕrĭ* (Greek πέρι, Sanscr. pári) is Lat. *per-* in *permagnus, persaepe*, &c. ; I.-Eur. **ĕtĭ* (Greek ἔτι, Sanscr. áti) is Lat. *et* (Umbr. et) ; I.-Eur. **ŏpĭ* (Greek ὄπι-σθεν) is Lat. *ob* (Oscan *op*) ; I.-Eur. **ambhĭ* (Greek ἀμφί) is Lat. *amb-ustus, an-cīsus*), whether the Syncope of these words took place in the Latin period (*ab* from **ape*, earlier **apo*), or at a much more remote period (cf. Goth. af, English 'of,' 'off'). *Neu, seu, ceu*, which are not used in Latin poets before a vowel, are cases of Syncope in the Latin period o *sīve* &c. ; also *quin* (see ch. x. § 16) for *quī-ne* [cf. Ter. *Andr.* 334, if *nĕ*) :

efficite qui detúr tibi ;
égo id agam mihi quí ne detur) ;

sin for *si-ne* ; *quot, tot* (cf. *tŏtĭ-dem*, Sanscr. káti, táti). (On *fer* and *vel*, see ch. viii.

§§ 36, 37.] ACCENTUATION. REDUCTION OF FINAL SYLL. 205

§ 58, and on *em*, originally **eme*, the Imper. of *ĕmo*, 'to take,' ch. x. § 19). As late as the time of Terence we find *abduce* used before a vowel, *abduc* before a consonant, while *face* is the form employed at the end of a line (Engelbrecht, *Studia Terentiana*, p. 63); but in the classical period, owing to the prevalent use of these imperatives *dic*, *duc*, *fac*, in word-groups, i. e. in close connection with a following word, the syncopated 'doublet' has ousted the other form, just as in post-Augustan poetry we find *nec* more and more supplanting *neque*, and usurping the position before vowel- as well as before consonant-initials. Other Imperatives occasionally appear without final -*ĕ*, e. g. *inger mi* Catull. xxvii. 2 (see ch. viii. § 58). So with -*ĕ* of the Infinitive. *Biber dari* is quoted by Charisius (124. 1 K.) from Fannius (cf. Caper 108. 10 K. bibere non 'biber'); and a plausible etymology of *instar*, a word first used in Cic. *Verr.* ii. 5. § 44, and literally meaning 'weight' (cf. Cic. *Off.* iii. 3. 11 ut omnia ex altera parte collocata vix minimi momenti instar habeant), makes it the Infinitive, used, like *biber*, as a Substantive, of *insto*, 'to be of equal weight,' 'to show equipoise of the balance,' like Swiss-German 'die Stimmen stehen ein,' 'the votes are equal.' (Wölfflin in *A. L. L.* ii. 581.) *Bustar* or *bostar*, glossed by βουστάσιον in the 'Cyrillus' and 'Philoxenus' Glossaries, may be for -*stare*, as *instar* for *instare*. We find -*al*, -*ar* for -*ale*, -*are* in trisyllabic or longer Nouns like *animal*, but from *sedŭle*, &c. we do not find **sedil*, &c., nor from *ūle*, &c. *ul*, though *subtĕl* (τὸ κοῖλον τοῦ ποδός, Prisc. i. p. 147. 11 H.) is said to stand for **subtĕle*, Neut. of **subtĕlis* from *tālus*. *Sirempse*, an old legal word, found in the phrase *sirempse lex esto*, 'let the same law apply,' e. g. Plaut. *Amph.* prol. 73:

sirempse legem iussit esse Iuppiter,

is found without the final -*e* in the Tabula Bantina of 133-118 B. C. (*C. I. L.* i. 197. 13 siremps lexs esto), and other early laws. *Lacte*, the Plautine form (though *lac* is the reading of the MSS. in *Amph.* 601, perhaps a corruption of *lact*) is *lact* in Varro, *L. L.* v. 104 (*lacte* Cato ap. Char. 102. 9 K.), and in classical Latin *lac* (cf. Charisius, 102. 4 K. lactis nominativum alii volunt lac, alii lact, alii lacte 'e' postrema). *Vŏlŭp*, 'pleasurably,' seems to be for **volupe*, Adverbial Neut. of an Adj. **volupis*; and Ritschl (*Opusc.* ii. 450) would analyze the *volupest* of Plautus, *Mil.* 277, &c. into *volupe est*, a form which the phrase seems actually to bear in late Latin writers, like Arnobius, Prudentius and others (see Georges, *Lex. Wortf.* s. v.). We have similarly *facul* for *făcĭlĕ*, e. g. Lucilius vi. 3 M. nobilitate facul propellere iniquos, and *difficul* for *difficile* (see Nonius, p. 111. 21 M. ; Paul. Fest. 61. 32 Th. ; Fest. 266. 20 Th. 'perfacul' antiqui et per se facul dicebant, quod nunc facile dicimus). The O. Lat. Adverb *poste* (e. g. Enn. *A.* 244 M. poste recumbite, uestraque pectora pellite tonsis) is in classical Latin *post* ; *ante* does not appear without the final -*e* in Latin, but we have in Oscan ant, as well as púst, *post*, Umbr. *post*. The suppression of a final short vowel was a common feature of Oscan and Umbrian, e. g. Oscan nep, Umbrian *nep* (Lat. *neque*), &c. (See also ch. x. §§ 9 and 12, on *ut* and *ŭtĭ-nam*, *dōnec* and *donĭque*, and cf. Georges, *Lex Wortf.* s. vv. *altar(e)*, *animal(e)*, *autumnal(e)*, *boletar(e)*, *cervical(e)*, *cochlear(e)*, *laquear(e)*, *pulvinar(e)*, *virginal(e)*, *lucar*, *specular*, *toral*, *torcular*, *vectigal*, &c. Quint. i. 6. 17 speaks of *tribunale* as out of use in his time).

§ 37. **II. Change of Vowel.** i. *Short Vowel*. We have already seen (§ 18) that, in the syllable immediately following the early accent, every short vowel was changed to *ĕ*, unless diverted by a following labial to *ŏ*. It is probable that short final vowels took the same course, and were one and all changed to *ĕ*. This *ĕ* might be dropped (§ 36) or retained, but did not become *ĭ*, as unaccented *ĕ* in the middle of a word did (§ 18), so that *ĕ* is preeminently the final vowel of the Latin language. A final *ĭ* becomes *ĕ* in *măre* for *mari, *ănĭmāle* (later *animal*) for *animali, &c., while in the middle of the word it remains, e.g. *maria*, *animalia*. Similarly final -*ĕ*, when, by the addition of a particle, it ceases to be a final vowel, becomes *ĭ*, e.g. *bĕnifĭcus* beside *bene*, *quippini* beside *quippe*, *sicine* beside *sic(e)*, *hoccine* beside *hoc-ce* from *hod-ce (ch. vii. § 16).

ii. *Diphthong*. A diphthong in the final syllable was treated like a diphthong in the posttonic syllable. As we have *ei*, class. *ī*, for posttonic *ai* in *inceido* (S. C. Bacch.), class. *incīdo* from O. Lat. *caido*, class. *caedo*, so we find final *ei*, class. *ī* representing I.-Eur. ai (or *ai*? ch. viii. § 66) in the I Sing. of the Perfect Active, &c., e.g. *tŭtŭd-ī* (older -*ei*). And while an example of the weakening of *oi* to *ei*, *ī* in the posttonic syllable is difficult to find (§ 18), it is regular when final, e. g. *foideratei* (S. C. Bacch.), class. *foederati*, from an original ending -*oi*. On the treatment of the final long diphthongs -āi, -ēi, &c., see ch. iv. §§ 45 sqq.

iii. *Long Vowel*. In the post-tonic syllable, as we saw (§ 30), a long vowel was not changed through the influence of the preceding accent. Nor was it changed in quality in the final syllable, though its quantity suffered. Long final *a* became -*ă* in *terră*, *arvă*, &c., but did not pass into another vowel, such as *ē*. The shortening of long final vowels is discussed below (§ 40).

§ 38. **Change of final short vowel to ĕ.** An example of *ĕ*- for an original -*ŏ* is the ending of the 2 Sg. Imperat. Pass. and Depon., e. g. *sequere* for *sequesŏ (Gk. ἕπε(σ)ο, ch. viii. § 77), of -*ĕ* for -*ŭ*, perhaps *sat* from an older **sat(ŭ)*, if this was a *u*-stem *satu- (cf. *satu-r*) (but see ch. ix. § 4). An -*ŏ* which has escaped this weakening (e. g. *endo*, on which see ch. ix. § 27) became -*ŭ* (as in the posttonic syllable, § 26), e. g. *indŭ*. (On *noenŭ*, a byform of *noenum*, see ch. x. § 18).

§ 39. **Alternation of final e with internal i.** Other examples are *istic*, *illic* from *iste*, *ille*, increased by -*ce* ; *isticine*, *illicine*, further increased by -*ne* ; *hicine*, *nuncine*, *tuncine* ; *tutin*, for *tute* with *ne*, is the spelling of the MSS. in Plaut. *Mil.* 290 ; *undique* from *unde*, *indidem* from *inde*; *ante* is *anti-* in compounds like *antici-*

pare, antistes, antistita, antigerio (O. Lat. for *valde*), and *antisto* (a better spelling than *antesto*: see Georges, *Lex. Wortf.* s. v.); *facilin* for *facile* with *ne*, *servirin* for *servire* with *ne*, is the spelling of the MSS. in Plaut. *Men.* 928 and 795; *benivolus, benificus, malivolus, malificus* (beside *benevolus, malevolus*, &c., a spelling much discussed by the grammarians, e. g. Vel. Long. 76–77 K.; Alcuin 298. 14 K.; Probus, 119. 2 K. See Brambach, *Lat. Orth.* and Georges, *Lex. Wortf.* s. vv.) (For additional examples see Ritschl, *Opusc.* ii. 556).

§ 40. III. **Shortening of Long Syllable.** i. *Final long vowel or diphthong.* A long vowel or diphthong in the middle of a Latin word may be shortened in hiatus, e. g. *pĭus* (cf. Oscan piíhio-), *balnĕum* (βαλανεῖον), *dĕamo, prĕhendo* (see ch. ii. § 143). The same thing happened apparently to a final long vowel or diphthong when the next word began with a vowel or *h*, so that scansions like Plautus, *Aul.* 463 *mĕĭ honóris, Asin.* 706 *dĕ hórdeo* (cf. class. *mĕhercle*), Ennius, *Ann.* 45 M. *Scipĭŏ inuicte*, need not have been imitations of Greek poetry, but rather expressed the actual Latin pronunciation. How far the shortening proper to this position may have attached itself to the vowel, even when a consonant initial followed, is not easy to say. From the earliest period of Latin literature we find a tendency to shorten every final long vowel. Some offer more resistance than others; -*ī* and -*ū* than -*ā* and -*ō*. The final *ā* of Nom. Sg. of A-stems and of Nom. Acc. Pl. of Neuter O-stems seems never to occur even in the earliest poetry in any but a shortened form, while in the Oscan and Umbrian dialects it has been reduced to some sound which is written *o*, and which is treated by Lucilius as a short vowel (Lucil. *inc.* 106 M.), if we may trust the quotation by Festus (426. 7 Th.) Lucilius: 'uasa quoque omnino dirimit non sollo dupundi,' id est, non tota). Final *ō* of verbs and nouns is, on the other hand, always long in the earlier poetry, except when the precedence of a short vowel, especially an accented short vowel, allows it to be scanned as a short syllable, e. g. *legŏ, modŏ*, less frequently *pellegŏ, dicitŏ*. But by the time of grammarians like Charisius and Diomedes (fourth century A.D.), this -*o* was universally shortened in pronunciation, so that a fifth-century grammarian (Pompeius, p. 232 K.), cannot explain Virgilian scansions like *cantō*, except on the theory that they are imitations of the Greek -ω of ποιῶ, &c.! The course of development taken by -*ŏ* in the literary period, viz. its shortening first in iambic words like *legŏ*, then in cretic words like *pellegŏ*, finally in all words, e. g. *cantŏ*, we may suppose to have been taken in the pre-literary age by final *-ā*. From *feră*, &c. the shortening would spread to *efferă*, &c., and would in time be extended over every Nom. Sg. Fem. of Ā-stems and Nom. Acc. Pl. Neut. of O-stems. That the shortening was mainly the work of analogy we see from *trīgintā, quadrāgintā,* &c., which, though really Neuters Plural, were regarded as mere numerals and so escaped the shortening which was enforced on every Neuter Plural Noun. But it must have been aided, partly by the inherent weakness of every final syllable, partly by the shortening of a final long vowel in pronunciation when the next word began with a vowel. The former presence of a final consonant does not seem to have made much difference. Ovid scans *estŏ* (earlier *estōd*) as he scans *Sulmŏ*; and Plautus allows the shortening by the Brevis Brevians law of *datŏ, dicitŏ, probĕ, maxumĕ, manŭ* and other Ablatives (earlier *datōd*, &c.).

ii. *Long vowel followed by consonant.* The quantity of a vowel in a final syllable is often influenced by a following consonant. In English the long vowel-sound of 'node' becomes a half-long sound before the dental tenuis, 'note.' Similarly in Latin a long vowel tended to be shortened by a following final *t, r,* &c. Under the shortening influence of a preceding short accented syllable, the final syllable (with naturally long vowel) is readily shortened by Plautus in words like *tenet, amat,* and, to a less extent, *soror, moror,* but seldom in words like *tenes, amas, moras* (for the statistics, see Leppermann, *De correptione,* &c. p. 78); and in classical poetry every originally long vowel is scanned as a short vowel before final *-t, -r,* &c., but not before final *-s*. Final *-l* also shortens a preceding long vowel; thus *bacchānāl* (for *bacchanāle*) became, when the accent shifted to the second syllable, *bacchanăl*, as *calcār* (for *calcāre*) became, under similar circumstances, *calcăr*. And, though we cannot trace the effect of final *-m* in poetry, seeing that a syllable so ending is elided before an initial vowel, we are told by Priscian that it had the same power of shortening a long vowel (even in monosyllables), e. g. *spĕm, rĕm, diĕm, meridiĕm* (Prisc. i. 23. 13; 366. 21 H.).

iii. *Final syllable long by position.* In Plautus *legŭnt, dixerŭnt* are admitted as well as *legŏ, dixerŏ*. But in the hexameters of Ennius, Lucilius, &c., these shortenings of final syllables long by position are avoided, as they were in the poetry of the classical period. They were apparently regarded as vulgarisms, much as the change of final *-ng* to *-n* is with us.

§ 41. **Final long vowel in Hiatus.** In Greek poetry (dactylic, anapaestic, &c.) besides the shortening of final diphthongs like αι, οι before an initial vowel (a scansion due to the consonantal character of ι, ἄνδρα μοι ἔννεπε being pronounced ἄνδρα μογέννεπε, G. Meyer, *Griech. Gram.*² § 154), we sometimes find shortening of final ā, ω, η in similar circumstances. This shortening seems to have reflected the ordinary pronunciation, as we can see from inscriptions in the Cretan dialect, a dialect in which the nuances of sound taken by a word in its various positions in the sentence were more regularly expressed in the orthography than in other dialects. On the Tablet of Gortyn, for example, μή is written με when the next word begins with a vowel (*K. Z.* xxxiii. 133) In the native metre of the Romans, the Saturnian, a final long vowel or diphthong (or syllable in *-m*), seems similarly to be left in Prosodical Hiatus, i. e. shortened, not wholly elided, before an initial vowel or *h-* (see ch. ii. § 143); and this Prosodical Hiatus, as well as Hiatus proper, such as the non-elision of a final short vowel, is much more common in Plautus than in Terence, as it was in Naevius, according to Cic. *Or.* xlv. § 152, than in Ennius. Plautus employs it in dialogue metres with (1) (accented ?) monosyllables preceding a short initial syllable, e.g. *quŏ eam*? (2) iambic words with verse ictus on the first syllable, e.g. *meī honoris*; (3) monosyllables following a short final syllable which has the verse ictus, e. g. *omniă quaĕ isti dedi*; (4) iambic words or word-endings, when the final syllable has the verse ictus and the following initial syllable is short and has the natural accent, e. g. *virī habitat, una operā ebur, obsequī animo*. In Anapaestic Metres also with (5) Cretic words, and in other cases. (For a list of examples, see Klotz, *Altröm. Metrik*, p. 119. They include not merely instances of dissimilar vowels, but also of similar, e. g. *i-i* in *ĕrī imágine, Pseud.* 1202). Terence, and apparently Lucilius, restrict it to the first of these cases; but Virgil has not only examples like *quī amant* (*Ecl.* viii. 108), but also like *vale valē inquit* (*Ecl.* iii. 79), and *sub Iliŏ alto* (*A.* v. 261). Virgil thus employs it (1) to prevent the entire suppression by elision of a monosyllable (accented ?), ending in a long vowel or *-m*; (2) in cases where a long final vowel would be shortened by the law of Breves Breviantes in the dramatists. That a vowel shortened in Hiatus was not so long as an ordinary short vowel, we may infer not only from the fact that it is normally elided, but also from the disinclination shown by Plautus to allow a vowel so shortened to constitute by itself the thesis of a metrical foot. It is allowed to go with another short syllable to form a resolved thesis, e. g. *quŏ ĕám*, but is never allowed to dispense with the proximity of another short syllable, except in a few phrases which may be considered as word-groups or compound words, e. g. *dē hórdeo, Asin.* 706, which might be written *de-hordeo* like *dĕhortari, Poen.* 674. The difference in this respect between Plautine and Saturnian versification (see ch. ii. § 143) need not imply a change in the pronunciation of these final long vowels in Hiatus; but may be due merely to the different character of the verse. The Saturnian poetry was of a more solemn and dignified tone than the conversational verse of the dramatists, and would naturally be uttered with a greater pause between the words. Imitation of the Greek dactylic and anapaestic prosody is inconceivable in the Saturnian poetry, and unlikely in the trochaic and iambic verse of Plautus; so that we can hardly be wrong in supposing this Prosodical Hiatus to reflect the ordinary pronunciation in Latin, as it did in Greek.

§ 42. **Breves Breviantes.** The syllables most affected by this law are those ending in a long vowel in words which were in ordinary talk closely joined with a following word. Forms like *mihĭ, tibĭ, sibĭ, modŏ, citŏ,* &c. have forced their way even into classical poetry; and in Plautus we find this shortening chiefly in verb-forms, which go closely with a following word, e. g. *volŏ-scire, abĭ-rus, cavĕ-dicas*, while the examples of nouns are mostly confined to adverbial forms, e. g. *domĭ-restat, domŏ-prodit,* or subordinate words like *homŏ* (see statistics in Leppermann, *De correptione*, p. 78). Ennius in his Epic restricts this usage to words ending in a vowel, and subsequent Hexameter poets follow him, e. g. *putŏ* but not *legŭnt, dixerŏ* (Hor. *S.* i. 4. 104) but not *dixerŭnt.* That this shortening was not a mere metrical licence, but reflected the actual pronunciation, we see from Quintilian's remark (i. 6. 21) that *havĕ*, not *avĕ*, was the normal form in his time, as well as from Phaedrus' fable of the man who mistook this word for the caw of a crow (*App.* 21), and Cicero's story (*Div.* ii. 40) of Crassus mistaking a figseller's cry, *Cauneas* (*sc.* ficus vendo), for *cave ne eas.* The spelling *causis* for *cave sis* in Juvenal ix. 120 points to the same thing; and Servius (ad *Aen.* vi. 780) says that *vidĕn* was the pronunciation of his day. (Should we read *rogăn* for *rogăs* in Pers. v. 134?) Plautus in his dialogue metres allows the scansion of a cretic word as a dactyl in the first foot only of the line or hemistich; Terence not at all; but Horace in his *Satires* and *Epistles* has *Polliŏ, dixerŏ, mentiŏ,* &c. ; *commodă* Catull. x. 26 is probably Neut. Plur. (see Owen ad loc.). (On the operation of the Breves Breviantes Law in Plautus, see *Journ. Phil.* xxi. 198 and xxii. 1.) Plautus requires that the preceding short syllable shall be perfectly short; he does not allow a short vowel preceding a mute and liquid to act as a Brevis Brevians, e. g. not *pătrĭ* like *pătĭ*, nor even a short vowel preceding *qu*, except under particular circumstances. But in classical poetry we find *putrĕfacta, liquĕfiunt,* &c.

§ 43. **Shortening of final -ā.** We have *-ā* in Greek words in the early poets (Enn. *A.* 567 M. *agoeā longa repletur* is very uncertain; cf. Gk. ἀγυιά), just as we have in later poetry, e. g. Stat. *Theb.* vi. 515 *Nemeā* (cf. Prisc. i. p. 202. 16 H.). But the instances quoted of *-ā* in Nom. Sg. of Ā-stems or Nom. Acc. Pl. of O-stems seem to be illusory. They are really cases of (1) metrical lengthening, e. g. Enn. *A.* 149 M. *et densis aquilā pinnis obnixa volabat*, a lengthening of a short syllable before the penthemimeral Caesura, like the lengthenings before the hephthemimeral in *A.* 85 M. *sic expectabat populūs atque ora tenebat*, Virg. *A.* iii. 464 *dona dehinc auro graviā sectoque elephanto*, where we have an originally short syllable (e. g. *populŭs*, I.-Eur. *-ŏs*) lengthened, by a metrical licence borrowed from Greek poetry, before the two chief caesuras of the hexameter; (2) syllaba anceps, e. g. Plaut. *Mil.* 1226 *namque édepol uix fuit cópiă* | *adeúndi atque impetrándi* (at the end of the first hemistich of an Iambic Septenarius, like *-ŭs* in *Truc.* 149 *non áruos hic sed páscuŏs* | *ager ést : si aratiónes*); Plaut. *Rud.* 1086 TR. *Ét crepundiá* (*ă*). GR. *Quid, si ea sunt aúrea?* TR. *Quid istúc tua?* (at change of speaker,

§§ 42-44.] ACCENTUATION. FINAL SYLLABLES. 211

like -ŭ of Voc. Sg., I-Eur. -ĕ, in *Pers.* 482 TO. Quíd agis ? DO. Credo. TO. Únde agis te, *Dórdalĕ*. DO. Credó tibi). Or they are cases of wrong scansion, e. g. *Trin.* 251 nox datur : ducitur familia tota (where the metre is Anapaestic with *familiă*, not Cretic with *fámiliă*), *Mil.* 1314 Quíd uis ? Quin tu iúbes ecferri ómnia quae isti dedi [where we should scan ómniá quaĕ istí, not ómniá qu(ae), istí], or of wrong reading, e. g. *Asin.* 762 Ne epístula quidem úlla sit in aédibus (where we might insert *usquam* before *ulla*, as in *Rud.* 529, and scan *epistulă*, not *epistulā*). A few apparent instances of *-ā* in Plautus have not yet been explained, viz. *Bacch.* 1128 ; *Epid.* 498 ; *Men.* 974 *a*. (For a list of examples in Plautus, see C. F. Müller, *Plaut. Prosodie*, p. 1 ; in Ennius, see Reichardt in *Fleck. Jahrb.* 1889, p. 777.) In the Saturnian fragments there is no reason for scanning *-ā* in Nom. Sg. or Neut. Pl. (see ch. ii § 141). Final *-ā* for *-ād* is long in Early Latin, as in Classical poetry, e. g. Abl. *mensā*, *erā*, Adv. *extrā*, *suprā* (*exstrad*, *suprad* on S. C. Bacch. of 186 B. c., *C. I. L.* i. 196), so that Early Latin *contră*, *frustră* (e. g. Plaut. *Rud.* 1255 ne tu frustră sis, at the end of an Iambic line ; Naev. *praet.* 6 R. contră redhostis, at the beginning of the second hemistich of a Trochaic Septenarius ; Enn. ap. Varr. *L. L.* vii. 12 quis pater aut cognatu' uolet nos contrā tueri ?) cannot have been originally **contrād*, **frustrād*. But it may be shortened by the influence of a preceding short syllable, like any other long vowel, e. g. *venustissumă*, *Poen.* 1177, *gratiă*, *Stich.* 327, *rustică*, *Pers.* 169. Similarly with *-ā* of Imperatives of the first Conjugation. We have in the dramatists *amă*, *pută* beside *amā*, *pută*, and so even e. g. Persius iv. 9. hoc *pută* non justum est. But this shortening was not extended by analogy to all Imperatives in *-ā*. We never find **plantă* for *plantā*, **mandă* for *mandā* in Early or in Classical poetry. This is perhaps due to the influence of the other Persons of the imperative *plantāto*, *plantāte*, while for nouns like *mensa* the length of the final *-a* would not be impressed on the memory by other cases like *mensae*, *mensam*, &c. The *-ā* of Numerals like *quadraginta*, &c. is not scanned as a short syllable till late times, e. g. *C. I. L.* vi. 28047 (= Meyer, *Anth.* 1326) *quadragintă* per annos ; vi. 29426 (= Mey. 1389) *septvagintă*, when Abl. *-ā* is similarly treated, e. g. *C. I. L.* xiv. 3723 hic situs Amphion ereptus *primā* juventa (see ch. ii. § 141).

§ 44. **Shortening of final -ē.** Final *-ē* of the Imperatives of the second Conjugation is scanned short by Plautus under the same conditions as final *-ā* of first Conjugation Imperatives, e. g. *monĕ* and *monē*, *cavĕ* (almost always short). That this scansion corresponded with the pronunciation we see from the remark of Quintilian (i. 6. 21) that *havĕ*, not *avē*, was the universal pronunciation in his time (multum enim litteratus, qui sine adspiratione et producta secunda syllaba salutarit—'avére' est enim—et 'calefacere' dixerit potius quam quod dicimus, et ' conservavisse,' his adiciat ' face ' et ' dice ' et similia. recta est haec via : quis negat ? sed adjacet et mollior et magis trita) (cf. § 42). This shortening was not extended to Imperatives with long penult, e. g. *splendē*, never**splendĕ*. Similarly the *-ē* of *calē*, *frigē*, &c. in the compounds *calefacio*, *frigefacio* is in all Latin poetry scanned short only when the first syllable is short, *călĕfacio* (but never **frĭgĕfacio*), which in Quintilian's time was apparently pronounced *calfacio* (Quint. i. 6. 21 quoted above ; for this spelling see Georges, *Lex. Wortf.* s. v.). Cato's *arfacit*, so spelt in MSS. of the *Res Rustica* 69 ; 125 ; 157. 12, seems to follow the analogy of *calfacit*. These Compounds were Separable Compounds (cf. *facit are* for *arefacit*, Lucr. vi. 962), so that their *-ē* is properly regarded as final *-ē*. This *-ē* already

P 2

shortened to some extent under the influence of the preceding accented short syllable in *călĕ*, *mădĕ*, &c., is in the Compounds *cale-fácio*, *made-fácio* (cf. Prisc. i. p. 402. 10 H.) subjected to the additional weakening influence of a following accented syllable, and so is scanned by the dramatists invariably as a short syllable, although other writers sometimes make it long, e. g. Enn. *Ann.* 573 M. *patēfecit* ; Catull. lxiv. 360 *tepēfaciet* beside *tepĕfacsit* of lxviii. 29 (see Ritschl, *Opusc.* ii. p. 618). A short vowel before a mute and liquid (and to some extent before *qu*) (see ch. ii. § 93) was not so short as a short vowel before a single consonant, and was not so capable of acting as a Brevis Brevians in the dramatists' versification. Hence Ritschl was wrong in scanning *pŭtrĕ-facit*, Plaut. *Most.* 112, though Ovid has *putrĕfactus*, *liquĕfiunt*. Similarly in the compound of *dies* and *quintus*, &c. the *ē* of the second syllable, properly regarded as a final *-ē*, was shortened in the Republican forms *diĕquinte*, &c. (Gell. x. 24. 1 'die quarto' et 'die quinto' . . . ab eruditis nunc quoque dici audio, et qui aliter dicit pro rudi atque indocto despicitur. Sed Marci Tullii aetas ac supra eam non, opinor, ita dixerunt ; 'diequinte' enim et 'diequinti' pro adverbio copulate dictum est, secundā in eo syllaba correpta. Divus etiam Augustus, linguae Latinae non nescius, munditiarumque patris sui in sermonibus sectator, in epistulis plurifariam significatione ista dierum non aliter usus est.) Final *-ē* in the Abl. of the fifth Declension is treated by Plautus exactly as final *-ā* of first-Declension Ablatives, that is to say, it is occasionally scanned short when preceded by a short, especially an accented short, syllable, but not otherwise, e. g. *diĕ*, *fidĕ*. This shortening was not extended to Ablatives with long penult. So with Adverbs in *-ē* (originally *-ēd*, e. g. *facilumed* on S. C. Bacch. of 186 B.C., *C.I.L.* i. 196). Plautus scans *prŏbĕ*, *maxŭmĕ*, though an instance of the shortening of this *-e* is wanting in Terence.

§ 45. **Shortening of final *-ō*.** In Plautus and the other dramatists final *-ō* is shortened under exactly the same conditions as final *-ē*, that is to say, only under the influence of a Brevis Brevians, e. g. *vŏlŏ*, which normally has this scansion when joined closely as an auxiliary verb with an infinitive, *vŏlŏ-scire*, &c. This shortening of *-ō* in some iambic and cretic words had so established itself in pronunciation that even the later Republican and Augustan poets admit scansions of iambic words like *homŏ* (Lucr. vi. 652), *volŏ* (Catull. vi. 16), *dabŏ* (Catull. xiii. 11), *vetŏ* (Hor. *S.* i. 1. 104), and even of cretic words like *Pollio* (Hor. *S.* i. 10. 42, 85 ; and even in the *Odes*, ii. 1. 14), *mentiŏ* (Hor. *S.* i. 4. 93), *dixerŏ* (Hor. *S.* i. 4. 104), *quomodŏ* (Hor. *S.* i. 9. 43). The shortening of final *-ō*, like that of final *-ā*, and unlike that of final *-ē*, rapidly extended itself to all instances, even when a long syllable preceded. In Ovid we have *ergŏ* (*Her.* v. 59, and elsewhere), *estŏ*, *Trist.* iv. 3. 72, *Sulmŏ*, *Nasŏ*, &c. ; and even Cicero uses *Vettŏ*, if his epigram is rightly quoted by Quint. (viii. 6. 73) fundum *Vettŏ* vocat, quem possit mittere funda, &c. (On *endŏ*, see ch. ix. § 27.) But *-ō* of the Dat. and Abl. is not shortened till very late times. The fourth-century grammarians speak of the final *-o* of Nouns (Nom. Sing.), Verbs (1 Pers. Sing. Pres. Ind.), Adverbs and Conjunctions, as universally shortened in the pronunciation of their time, except in monosyllables and foreign words. [Charis. p. 16. 5 K. etiam illud magna cura videndum est quod veteres omnia vel verba vel nomina quae o littera finiuntur, item adverbia vel conjunctiones producta extrema syllaba proferebant, adeo ut Vergilius quoque idem servaverit, in aliis autem refugerit vetustatis horrorem, et carmen

§§ 45-49.] ACCENTUATION. FINAL SYLLABLES. 213

contra morem veterum levigaverit . . . paulatim autem usus invertit, ut in sermone nostro 'scribo' 'dico' et item talibus, ubi o non solum correpta ponitur, sed etiam ridiculus sit qui eam produxerit . . . sane monosyllaba fere quaecumque sunt verba πρωτότυπα o littera finita tam versu quam etiam prosa similiter productam habent : necesse non corripi, ut 'sto' 'do.' quibus si conferatur 'dico' 'curro' 'disco' item producta o littera, dijudicari poterit quam sit aliud absurdum, aliud per euphoniam gratum; cf. p. 63. 17 K. nullum autem nomen o producta finitur nisi peregrinum, veluti 'Ino' 'Sappho' 'Dido' (cf. Diom. p. 435. 22 K.; 'Prob.' *de ult. syll.* p. 220. 15 K.); Mar. Victorinus (p. 28. 23 K.) distinguishes the Verbs *monstrŏ, ostentŏ*, &c. from *monstrō, ostentō*, the Dat. and Abl. cases of the Nouns *monstrum, ostentum*. Servius (ad A. iv. 291) attests *quandŏ*. Priscian (i. p. 409. 16 H.) excuses *vigilandŏ* of Juv. iii. 232, &c. on the ground that it is part of a verb (: nos in 'do' utimur terminatione, quae similis est dativo vel ablativo nominis, nisi quod verbum hoc existimantes quidam etiam corripiunt o finalem ejus.]

§ 46. Shortening of final -ĭ. The shortening of -ĭ by the Brevis Brevians Law is common in Plautus in Imperatives like *abĭ, redĭ,* and Perfects like *dedĭ*; while in nouns we have *domĭ* (very frequent), *erĭ, virĭ, senĭ,* &c., with the Ablatives *avĭ sinistra, Pseud.* 762, *parĭ fortuna, Bacch.* 1108 (cf. Ter. *levĭ sententia, Hec.* 312).

§ 47. Shortening of final -ŭ. By the Brevis Brevians Law we have *manŭ* in Plaut. *Trin.* 288, but owing to the few words with short paenultima ending in -ū, the examples are not frequent. Terence has always *diŭ,* never *diŭ*, but Plautus has *diŭ* (or *djū*?) very frequently.

§ 48. Shortening of final diphthong. A final diphthong is almost never shortened by the Brevis Brevians Law in Plautus (e. g. novaĕ nuptae, *Cas.* 118), and never in Terence. This is rather to be referred to the infrequency of words so ending (Noms. Plur. and Dats. Sing. in *-ae*), than to be quoted as a proof of the difference in sound between a diphthong and a long vowel.

49. Shortening of long vowel before final Consonant. -l. In Plautus we have still the long quantity, e. g. *Aul.* 413 aperitur Bacchanāl : adest, but in Classical poetry *-ăl*, e. g. *tribūnăl*, Ovid (cf. Mar. Victorinus *de Finalibus* p. 231. 11. K.). *Subtel* (apparently for **subtēle*, Neut. of **subtēlis*, a Compound of *sub* and *tālus*) (but see § 30), is quoted as an instance of *-ĕl* by Priscian, i. p. 147. 11 H., and explained as τὸ κοῖλον τοῦ ποδός.

-m. Whether the different treatment of -*m* after *o* of the Gen. Plur. and *o* of the Acc. Sg. Masc. and Nom. Acc. Sg. Neut. of O-stems on the earliest inscriptions (e. g. *C. I. L.* i. 16 *Suesano probom*, 'Suessanorum probum') is a proof that a long vowel was at the end of the third cent. B. C. not yet shortened before final -*m* is uncertain (see ch. ii. § 137). If Lat. -*m* sounded like -*w* owing to the lips not being closed in pronouncing it (ch. ii. § 61), the shortening *spēm* may be compared with *nĕu* (ch. ii. § 34). Osc. paam 'quam' Acc. Sg. Fem., Umbr. *pracatarum* Gen. Pl. Fem. (with *u* the equivalent of Lat. ō) indicate a retention of the long quantity in Umbro-Oscan.

-r. (1) Nouns like *calcar(e)*. The final syllable was without doubt long in Plautus, though there is no certain evidence of its quantity, or of its loss of final *-e*. . It is short in Classical poetry, e. g. *exemplăr*, Hor. (but *exemplāre*, Lucr. ii. 124), though the grammarians recognize that it ought to be long by the analogy of the other cases -āris, -āri, &c. (Charis. exc. p. 541. 2 K. : Mar. Victorin. de Fin. p. 232. 9 K., and similarly of -al p. 231. 10 K.).

(2) Nouns and Adjectives like sŏror, maeror, minor, major, have the long quantity invariably in Plautus, unless in cases of shortening by the Brevis Brevians Law, e. g. sorŏr, Poen. 364 ; amŏr, Cist. i. 1. 69, and probably always patĕr. Iambic nouns often retain the old Nominative ending -os, e. g. odos, Pseud. 841 ; honos, Trin. 697. Ennius in his Annals has -ŏr. Whether he ever (A. 455 M. sūdŏr) uses -ŏr is doubtful ; but Lucilius has normally -ŏr (e. g. strīdŏr, inc. 90 M.), and the two probable examples of -ōr in Lucilius, (dŏlōr v. 55 M. ; pŭdōr xxx. 70 M.) are perhaps metrical lengthenings before the chief Caesuras, like Virgil's lăbŏr (G. iii. 118), dŏmĭtŏr (A. xii. 550), &c. There is a lack of decisive instances in the plays of Terence (see Boemer, De correptione, p. 25).

(3) Verbs like mŏror, ūtor Ind., morer, utar Subj., in Plautus always have a long final, unless shortened by the Brevis Brevians Law, e. g. Rud. 1248 níl morōr ullúm lucrum ; Aul. 232 utār ; Bacch. 153 nil mórŏr. By Lucilius' time it is invariably short, e. g. fruniscŏr xviii. 3 M. ; oblīnăr xxx. 25 M. In the Comedies of Terence the evidence is defective (e. g. sĕquăr, Andr. 819). In Tibullus, i. 10. 13 trăhōr is of course a case of metrical lengthening before the penthemimeral Caesura. Oscan patír 'pater,' keenzstur 'censor' apparently retain the long vowel.

-t. The shortening of a long vowel before final -t was perhaps slightly earlier than before final -r. It is indeed not found in Plautus, except where the Brevis Brevians Law interposes (and here the shortening is much more frequent than with -r), e. g. cubăt, Amph. 290 ; timĕt, Amph. 295 ; vĕnĭt, Aul. 226 ; arăt, Asin. 874 ; solĕt, Merc. 696 ; aĭt, Cas. 693 ; but in Ennius' hexameters, though the long quantity is usual, we find shortening occasionally even after a long syllable, e. g. mandebăt, A. 138 M. (but ponebāt, A. 288) ; splendĕt, Sat. 14 (but jubĕt, A. 465) ; potessĕt, A. 235 (but essĕt, A. 81). In Lucilius the short quantity is normal, though we have crissavĭt ix. 70 M. But Terence, to judge from the slender evidence at our disposal, seems to follow rather the usage of Ennius' hexameter poems, for we have more long scansions, e. g. stetĭt, Phorm. prol. 9 ; augeăt, Adelph. prol. 25, &c. beside audirĕt, Adelph. 453. On a Scipio epitaph of c. 130 B.C. written in elegiac metre (C. I. L. i. 38) we have nobilitauĭt, though the spelling -eit in the Perfect is found much later (e. g. probaueit beside coerauit, in C. I. L. i. 600, of 62 B. c.) (see ch. viii. § 70). Ovid repeatedly lengthens the -it of interiit, abiit, rediit, &c. and of petiit (see Munro ad Lucr. iii. 1042). On attăt in the Dramatists see § 10. p. 164.

Before final -s the long quantity persisted to classical times. It is occasionally shortened by the Brevis Brevians Law in Plautus, e. g. Mil. 325 sunt manŭs ; Aul. 187 habĕs ; and the same is true of the plays of Terence (e. g. bonĭs, Eun. prol. 8), which however do not offer any example of a verbal form in -s being shortened (potĕs, adĕs are for *potĕss, *adĕss, not *potĕs, *adĕs). But this shortening is very rare in both dramatists, and not at all so frequent as the shortening by the same Brevis Brevians Law before -t, -r (see the statistics in Leppermann, De correptione . . . apud Plautum, and in Boemer, De correptione . . . Terentiana). Horace's pălŭs aptaque remis (A. P. 65) is a unique scansion in Augustan poetry (cf. vidĕn, rogăn § 42). Ennius has in his Annals (l. 102 M.) virginĕs (cf. Plaut. Pers. 845) before a consonant initial (see below).

§ 50. Shortening of Final Syllable long by position. Abĕst in Lucilius

(ix. 29 M.), which seems to be the right reading, stands perhaps alone as an instance in non-dramatic poetry of the shortening by the Brevis Brevians Law of a final syllable long by position. Horace allows *dixĕrŏ*, but not e. g. *dixerŭnt*. Ennius' *virgĭnĕs* in *Ann*. 102 M. :

uirgines nam sibi quisque domi Romanus habet sas,

shows shortening of a final syllable long both by nature (*-ĕs* for *-ens*, ch. vi. § 2), and by position. In the dramatists the shortening by the Brevis Brevians Law of final syllables long both by nature and by position, or by position only, is freely allowed in the case of dissyllables in the dialogue metres (e. g. Nil pótĕst (?) suprá, Ter. ; ex Graécis bónïs Latínas fecit nón bonas, Ter.), in the case of trisyllables, &c. only (as a rule) in Anapaestic and other lyric metres (e. g. vénerănt húc, Plaut. ; odio énicăs míseram, Plaut. ; qui hic líberăs vírgĭnĕs mércatúr, Plaut.).

Final syllables which had originally a double consonant are long in Plautus, e. g. *miles* for **miless*, *Aul.* 528 milés inpransus ástat, aes censét dari, though they may, of course, be shortened by the influence of a Brevis Brevians, e. g. *potĕs*, *Stich*. 325. But after Plautus' time they appear to be short syllables. Ennius has not only *ĕquĕs* (*Ann*. 484. 249 M.), but also *mīlĕs* (*Ann*. 277) ; Terence has always *adĕs*, *potĕs* ; Lucilius has *milĕs* (xi. 8 M.), *prŏdĕs* (*inc*. 128 M.) ; Lucretius (iii. 721) *exŏs*, and so on. But final -*s* for -*ss* never fails before an initial consonant to make 'position' in Early Latin versification as original -*s* usually fails ; *milĕs vult* could not end an Iambic Senarius like *occidistïs me*, Plaut. *Bacch*. 313. Perhaps the reduction of the final double consonant was proper to a position before an initial consonant, so that the actual pronunciation would be originally, e. g. *miless impransus*, *miles pransus* (see below § 51, on *hoc*(c)).

§ 51. **Shortening of Monosyllables.** The connexion of all these cases of shortening with the absence of accent is seen from the fact that monosyllabic words are as a rule not shortened, unless they are subordinate or enclitic words. Thus a long vowel is shortened before final -*r*, -*l*, in Classical poetry in unaccented syllables, e. g. *candŏr*, *majŏr*, *fundŏr*, *calcăr*, *trĭbūnăl*, but not in the monosyllables *fūr*, *sōl*, where the natural length of the vowel is retained. The monosyllable *cor*, however, which represents **cord*, with vowel naturally short, but long by position, is scanned short in classical poetry, though it is long in Plautus, *Poen*. 388 :

húius cŏr, huiús studium, huius sáuium, mastígia,

the pronunciation of his time having probably been *cord huius*, *cord ardet*, when the next word began with a vowel, but *cor calet* (like *cor(d)culum*, ch. iv. § 157), when the next word began with a consonant. Similarly the more or less subordinate word *ter*, older *terr (cf. terr-uncius) for *tĕrs (I.-Eur. *trĭs, ch. vi. § 61), is a long syllable before an initial vowel in Plautus, Bacch. 1127 (a bacchiac line):

<blockquote>rerín tēr in ánno posse hás tonsitári,</blockquote>

while in subsequent poetry the 'doublet' used before an initial consonant, e.g. ter(r) durus, like hor(r)deum (from *horsdeum, ch. iv. § 158), established itself before initial vowels too. Hoc Neut. for hocc (*hŏd-ce, ch. vii. § 16; cf. hocci-ne) retained its antevocalic 'doublet' form in classical poetry, e.g. Virg. (A. ii. 664):

<blockquote>hōc erat, alma parens, &c.,</blockquote>

and Velius Longus, commenting on this line, tells us that the actual pronunciation of his time was 'hocc erat' (54. 6 K. ergo scribendum per duo c, 'hoc-c-erat alma parens,' aut confitendum quaedam aliter scribi, aliter pronuntiari). Plautus uses the proper 'doublet' of all these monosyllables which have a vowel naturally short followed by a consonant that represents two consonants; thus he invariably makes es, 'thou art' (I.-Eur. *es-s(i), ch. viii. § 2), a long syllable before a word beginning with a vowel (unless under the operation of the Brevis Brevians Law, just as we find hŏc in a line like Men. 522 quid hŏc ést negoti?). But in Terence es is a short syllable, and so in Lucilius (e.g. iv. 4 M.) (On the reduction of a final double consonant, see ch. ii. § 133).

The shortening of sī in sĭ-quidem, and (in the older poetry only) of tū, tē, mē, &c. before quidem (e.g. tŭquidem, Lucil. xiv. 26 M., Plaut. Epid. 99), is due to accentuation, and should be understood in connexion with the rule that antepenultimate syllables could not be circumflexed in Latin (ch. iii. § 2, p.153), and with the modern Italian practice of diphthongizing a paroxytone vowel, e.g. buono (Lat. bŏnus), but not a proparoxytone, e.g. popolo (Lat. pŏpŭlus). The shortening of English sheep, know in shep-herd, shepherdess, know-ledge, is similarly due to accentual conditions, and of Welsh brawd, 'a brother,' in brod-yr, 'brothers,' &c.

§ 52. **Loss of Final Syllable with -m.** This could hardly take place except in the case of words closely joined in ordinary talk with a following word [e.g. noen(um) est, noen(um) habet, nihil(um) est, nihil(um) habet, would be the 'doublet' forms

§ 52.]   ACCENTUATION. FINAL SYLLABLES.   217

before initial vowels, *noenum dat, nihilum dat*, the ante-consonantal doublets], so that the theory which explains adverbs in -*ter*, e.g. *breviter*, as Accusatives Sing. Neut. of adjectives with the ' comparative ' suffix -*tero* (ch. v. § 18), for *breviter(um)*, &c., is unlikely to be correct (see ch. ix. § 2). The Preposition *circum*, when compounded with a verb beginning with a vowel, has its final syllable not entirely elided but left in prosodical hiatus, e.g. *circŭ(m)it* (a trisyllable); (cf. *sublatuiri* for *sublatum iri*, ch. viii. § 89), and it is possible that *non,ni(hi)l*, should not be referred to *noen(um)*, *nihil(um)*, but should receive another explanation, such as *non* for *noe-ne* (on *noenŭ*, see ch. x. § 18), *nihil* for *ni-hile, Neut. of I-stem (cf. *imbellis* and *imbellus*, *subtĕl* from *sub-tēle, Neut. of an I-stem compound of *tālus* (?), and see § 49). But *vĕnire* seems to represent *venum ire*, though *pessum ire* did not become *pessire. The grammarians defend the spelling *sed* against *set* by a reference to an older *sedum* (Charisius, 112. 5 K.; Mar. Vict. 10. 13 K.) (see ch. x. § 5). (On *donec* and O. Lat. *donicum*, see ch. x. § 12).

By comparing the various Romance words for, let us say, 'horse,' Ital. cavallo, Span. caballo, Port. cavallo, Prov. cavals, Fr. cheval, Roum. cal, &c., it is possible to conjecture the form of the Latin prototype from which they all have descended, *caballus*. In the same way we can guess at the early form, what is called the 'Indo-European' form, underlying any cognate group of words in the various Indo-European languages; e.g. Lat. *māter*, Dor. Gk. μάτηρ, O. Ind. mātár-, O. Ir. māthir, O. Slav. mater-, Arm. mair, O. Eng. mōdor, point to something like *mātēr as their prototype. We may similarly trace back inflexions to an 'Indo-European' form, and may out of these conjectured words and inflexions construct an 'Indo-European' alphabet.

In the last two chapters we have discussed the pronunciation and accentuation of Latin, and the phonetic changes of the language produced under the influence of the accent, or due to peculiarities (often local and temporal merely) of pronunciation. In the next chapter we shall compare Latin with the other languages of the Indo-European family; we shall investigate the form in which the various sounds of our imaginary 'Indo-European' alphabet appear on Latin soil, and how that form differs from the forms assumed in the various languages of Asia and Europe, which are classed under the name 'Indo-European.' These languages are: (1) the Aryan, including i. Indian, ii. Iranian (Zend, Persian, &c.); (2) the Armenian; (3) the Greek; (4) the Albanian; (5) the Italic, including i. Latin, ii. the Umbro-Oscan dialects; (6) the Celtic, including i. Gaulish, ii. Goidelic (Irish, Gaelic of Scotland, &c.), iii. Brythonic (Welsh, Breton, &c.); (7) the Balto-Slavic, including i. Baltic (Lithuanian, &c.), ii. Slavonic; (8) the Teutonic, including i. Gothic, ii. Scandinavian, iii. W. Teutonic (German, English, &c.), (see Introduction to Brugmann's *Comparative Grammar*).

CHAPTER IV.

THE LATIN REPRESENTATIVES OF THE INDO-EUROPEAN SOUNDS.

Ā, Ă.

§ 1. Ā. I.-Eur. ā is Latin ā. Thus in the declension of A-stems we have Latin *fămĭliās* (the old genitive preserved in legal language, *păter familias*), *terrāī* (later *terrāi, terrae*), *praedā* (O. Lat. *praidād*), *fīliārum, fīliābus* (another legal form, required for distinction from *filiis*, Dat. Abl. Plur. of *filius*); the word for 'mother,' I.-Eur. *māter- (O. Ind. mātár-, Arm. mair, Dor. Gk. μᾱ́τηρ, O. Ir. māthir, O. Slav. mati, with o as the equivalent of I.-Eur. ā in Lithuanian and in the Teutonic languages, Lith. motė̃, 'wife,' O. Eng. mōdor, O. H. Germ. muoter, now Mutter, with short vowel and double consonant instead of long vowel and single consonant) is in Latin *māter*.

I.-Eur. ā, Lat. *ā*, is often found in developments from simple roots like ĝĕn-, 'to beget,' e.g. Lat. *gnātus*, later *nātus*, beside *indĭ-gĕna, gĕn-us* : tel-, 'to carry,' Lat. *lātus* for **tlātus*, P.P.P. of *tollo*; stel- (O. Slav. stelją, 'I spread'), Lat. *lātus*, wide, earlier *stlātus, stlāta*, sc. *nāvis*, whence the adj. *stlātarius*, or with -*ătt*- for earlier -*āt*- (ch. ii. § 127), *stlatta, stlattarius* (Paul. Fest. 455. 1 Th. stlatta, genus navigii, latum magis quam altum, et a latitudine sic appellatum, sub ea consuetudine, qua 'stlocum' pro locum, et 'stlitem' pro litem dicebant; Gl. Philox. stlata: πειρατικοῦ σκάφους εἶδος : Juv. vii. 134 stlattaria purpura); ster- (Lat. *sterno*), Lat. *strā-tus, strā-men*; ĝer-, 'to rub,' 'wear away,' 'make old' (Gk. γέρων), Lat. *grā-num*; keld-, 'to strike' (Lat. *per-cello*), Lat. *clādes*; *k*ert-, 'to bind,' 'weave together' (O. Ind. cṛtáti, 'he binds,' kṛṇátti, 'he spins'), Lat. *crātes*; *k*er-

(Gk. κέρας, horn), Lat. *crābro* for **crās-ro* (§ 152), a hornet. The *lā, rā, nā* has been variously explained in some or all of these instances, as (1) long sonant or syllabic l, r, n (§§ 81, 92), (so Brugmann, *Grundr.*[1] i. §§ 253, 306), so that, for example, Lat. *grānum* would represent I.-Eur. *ĝr̄no-, while Goth. kaurn, Eng. corn, represent I.-Eur. *ĝr̥no- (cf. Lat. *rād-īx*, I.-Eur. *wr̄d-, but Goth. vaurts, Eng. wort, I.-Eur, *wr̥d-): (2) due to the fusion of an *e*-sound with an *a*-sound in a grade of a dissyllabic root of the form ĝena-, &c., so that e.g. Lat. *gnātus* would come from ĝena-, the root ĝen- with the addition of an *a*-sound, while Gk. (Att. and Dor.) -γνητος would come from ĝene-, the root ĝen- with the addition of an *e*-sound (so Bechtel, *Hauptprobleme*, p. 203); the **crās-* of Lat. *crābro* for **crās-ro* will thus be a grade of I.-Eur. *ḱeras- (Greek κέρας-): (3) a secondary root, formed by the addition of a stem-suffix ā to the weak grade of the simple root (see Brugmann, *Morph. Unt.* i. p. 1; Persson, *Wurzelerweiterung*, p. 91), so that e.g. Lat. *gnārus* would show a root formed from ĝn-, the weak grade of the root ĝen-, 'to know,' by the addition of the suffix ā, as *gnōtus, gnōsco* would show a root similarly formed from ĝn- by the addition of the suffix ō; Lat. *lātus*, 'carried,' for **tlātus*, will thus be like Dor. Gk. ἔ-τλᾱ-ν from root tel-, 'to carry,' ἔ-πτᾱ-ν from root pet-, 'to fly.'

Latin *ā* is often *ă* lengthened by 'compensation' (§ 162), e.g. *quālus* for **quăs-lus* (cf. *quăsillus*); *hālo* for **ăns-lo*, from the root an-, 'to breathe,' with the addition of s, ans-, 'to be fragrant' (O. Sl. ạchati, 'to be fragrant'), with compound *ăn-hēlo* from **an-enslo*, with change of *ă* to *ĕ* before the vowel became lengthened by 'compensation' (ch. iv. § 162). The older spelling was with *ll* (cf. *quallus, anhellus,* and *anhellitus* in Virgil MSS.), so that the *ā* is due to the shifting of the long quantity from the consonant to the vowel. In *octāvus* from *octō* we seem to have before *v* an *ā* developed from an *ō*, just as in *căvus* we have *ăv* for *ŏv* (§ 19).

Unaccented *ā* remains unchanged, e.g. *immānis*, from an old word, *mānus*, good; but when final, or when preceding final *m, t, r, l,* it was, like other long vowels, shortened in course of time. When final, perhaps only in iambic words, originally (ch. iii. § 43), *fĕră*, noun, *pŭtă*, imper.; but this shortening was extended to all Noms. Sing. of Ā-stems and Noms. Accs. Plur. Neut. (see ch. vi. §§ 3 and 45). Thus in the declension of Ā-stems, the 'First Declension,' final -*a* of the Nom. Sg. is even in the earliest poetry a short vowel; the Acc. Sg. has -*ăm*; the final syllable of the 3 Sg. Pres. Subj. Act., e. g. *mittat*, and Pass. *mittar* was shortened in the second cent. B.C.; -*al* (older -*āle*) was also shortened (see ch. iii. § 49). In Umbro-Oscan I.-Eur. ā was likewise retained (von Planta, i. p. 77), e. g. Osc. maatreís, Umbr. *matrer* 'matris'; Osc. fratrúm 'fratrum,' Umbr. frater 'fratres.' But final -ā became an O-sound, written in Oscan ú (in Lat. alph. *o*, in Gk. alph. ο), in Umbr. u (in Lat. alph. *o*) and a, e. g. Osc. *molto*, Umbr. mutu and muta, 'multa' ('a fine'), Osc. víú 'via.' It is scanned (in the Neut. Pl. of an O-stem) as a short syllable by Lucilius (*sollŏ*, Lucil. *inc.* 106 M.; cf. ch. ii. § 1), so that I.-Eur. final -ā may have been modified at a very early period in the Italic languages (Latin as well as Umbro-Osc.), and the Latin shortening may not have been confined originally to iambic words (but see ch. iii. § 43).

§ 2. **Latin ā for I.-Eur. ā.** Other examples are (1) in suffixes, &c. : I.-Eur. ā of the Subjunctive, Lat. *ferāmus, ferātis*, &c. ; I.-Eur. noun-suffix -tāt- (e. g. O. Ind. dēvá-tāt-, 'divinity,' Dor. Gk. νεό-τᾱτ-), Lat. *nŏvĭtāt-, vŏluptāt-* ; I.-Eur. adjective-suffix -āko- [e. g. Ir. buadhach, 'victorious' (from buaid, 'victory'; cf. Boudicca, wrongly called by us Boadicea), Gaulish Teuto-bōdiācī, Bĕn-ācus, Lith. saldókas, 'sweetish,' O. Sl. novakŭ ; cf. Gk. νέᾱξ], Lat. *mĕrācus, vĕrāc-*; (2) in individual words : I.-Eur. *bhrātor-, 'brother' (O. Ind. bhrátar, Gk. φράτωρ, the member of a φρατρία, O. Ir. bráthir, W. brawd, Goth. brōþar, O. Eng. brōþor, Lith. broter-ĕli-s), Lat. *frāter* ; I.-Eur. *bhāgo-, 'beech-tree' (Dor. Gk. φᾱγός, O. Engl. bōc-trēow, 'beech tree,' bōc, 'a book,' lit. the runes scratched on a piece of beech-wood), Lat. *fāgus* ; I.-Eur. *swādu-, 'sweet' (O. Ind. svādú-, Dor. Gk. ἁδύς, O. Sax. swōti), Lat. *suāvis* for *suādvis* ; similarly Lat. *clāvis* (Dor. Gk. κλᾱ(ϝ)ίς), *nāvem* Acc. (O. Ind. náv-am, Hom. Gk. νῆ(ϝ)-α, O. Ir. nau), *fāri, fāma, fābula* (Dor. Gk. φᾱ-μί, O. Sl. ba-jati, 'to converse'), *vātes* (O. Ir. fáith, the *i* being due to 'Infection,' that is, to the influence of an *i*, which was suppressed in pronunciation in a following syllable, from stem fāti-, I.-Eur. *wāti-).

§ 3. **Ă.** I.-Eur. ă is Latin *ă*. Thus I.-Eur. *ăĝō, 'I drive' (O. Ind. ájāmi, Gk. ἄγω, Ir. agaim, O. Isl. aka inf.), is in Latin *ăgo* ; its derivative, I.-Eur. *ăĝros, 'a field' (O. Ind. ájra-s, Gk. ἀγρός, Goth. akrs, Engl. acre), is in Latin *ăger*, stem *ăgro-*.

I.-Eur. ă varies with ā, and similarly Latin *ă* with *ā*, in this root ăĝ-, 'to drive' (Lat. *amb-āges*, Sanscr. ājí-, 'a race, contest,' Ir. āg, 'a contest'), and in others, some of which are enumerated in § 56. The P. P. P. of *stō*, from root stā-, 'to stand,' is *stătus* (Gk.

στατός), with ă for the weak grade of ā. Latin ă (probably Eur. ă) is also the vowel of a weak grade of ō, e.g. in a root like dō-, 'to give' (Gk. δά-νος, δῶ-ρον), Latin dă-tus beside dō-num. Like Lat. dă-tus from root dō- is Lat. să-tus from root sē-, 'to sow'; and this ă seems to be an Eur. ă, a weak grade of ē, e.g. in root ked- (Gr. ἐκεκήδει and κεκάδοντο, Lat. cēdo). This I.-Eur. vowel, found in a weak grade of roots with ā, ō, ē, whether it was in each case ă, or in some or all cases was an indeterminate vowel (written ə by Brugmann), appears in Latin as ă, stătus, dătus, sătus, but in O. Ind. we have ĭ in sthitás, á-di-ta 3 Sg. Aor., -dhitas P. P. P. of dhā- (I.-Eur. dhē-), 'to place.' The same O. Ind. ĭ is seen in words like I.-Eur. *pəter-, O. Ind. pitár-, where in the other languages we have ă, Gk. πατήρ, O. Ir. athir, Goth. fadar, O. Engl. fæder, as ă in Latin *pater*, probably a derivative from the root pā-, 'to protect,' with this weak-grade vowel. In other words, like Latin *păteo*, ă seems to vary with ĕ (Gk. πετάννυμι); and in Latin we have a few instances of ă, where other languages, or kindred Latin forms, offer ĕ, *frango fragĭlis* (Goth. brikan, Engl. break), *flagro* (Gk. φλέγω), *gradus* (Goth. griþs), *aper* (O. Engl. eofor, Germ. Eber). They are mostly cases of ă with a liquid or nasal, and so admit of the explanation that they are a form of the sonant or syllabic l, r, m, n (so Osthoff, *Morph. Unt.* vol. v. pref.), while *aper* has been explained as 'a contamination' of I.-Eur. *kapro- (Gk. κάπρος) and I.-Eur. *epro; they have also been explained by the theory that I.-Eur. ĕ and ŏ when pretonic became ă in Latin (Wharton, *Etyma Latina*, p. 128). The more or less complete fusion of I.-Eur. ă and ŏ in other languages makes it impossible to be sure that this use of *a* in words connected with ĕ-roots is not a peculiarity of Latin, or rather of the Italic languages generally (cf. Osc. patensíns, Umb. abro-), depending, it may be, on the pronunciation of Latin or Italic *a* (see ch. ii. § 1). For Latin ă for ŏ, under influence of *v*, e.g. *căvus*, older *covus*, see § 19, and for *ar, al, an*, from sonant r, l, n, §§ 81, 92.

Unaccented Latin ă in the posttonic syllable became at first ĕ, except before *l* and labials, where it became ŏ. This ĕ became, perhaps about the end of the third century B.C., ĭ in syllables not long by position (except when it preceded *r*), and before *ng*;

while this *o* became *u* or the *ü*-sound, which in most cases passed into *ĭ* at the close of the Republican period. Thus the compound of *ab* and *cado* became *accēdo* (so spelt by Ennius), then *accĭdo*; from *in* and *arma* we have the compound *inermis*; from *sub* and *rapio* first *surropio* probably, then *surrŭpio* (Plaut.), then *surrĭpio*; from *ex* and *frango*, *effringo* (see ch. iii. § 18). Final Latin *ă* probably became *ĕ*, and might be dropped (see ch. iii. § 37).

In Umbro-Oscan I.-Eur. *ă* remains, as in Latin, e.g. Umbr. *ager*, 'a field,' Osc. *actud* 'agito' third Sg Imperat., also I.-Eur. *a*, e.g. Osc. patereí 'patri,' Umbr. Iupater 'Juppiter' (von Planta, i. p. 75).

§ 4. I.-Eur. ă. The I.-Eur. preposition *ăpŏ (O. Ind. ápa, Gk. ἀπο, Goth. af, Germ. ab, Engl. of) is Latin *ăp-* of *ap-ĕrio*, usually written *ăb*, with suppression of the final vowel ; but the form *pŏ-* of *po-sĭtus*, from *pōno* for *pŏ-sĭno*, shows suppression of the initial vowel ; *ăd (O. Ir. ad, Goth. at, Engl. at) is Latin *ăd*. The I.-Eur. pronoun *ălyo-, 'other' [Gk. ἄλλος, O. Ir. aile, Gaul. Allo-broges, 'those of another country'(Schol. Juven. viii. 234), (as opposed to *Combroges, 'native,' whence Welsh Cymry), W. all-, Goth. aljis, Engl. el-se] is Latin *ălius*. Similarly *mădeo* (Gk. μαδάω) ; *sălio* (Gk. ἅλλομαι) ; *sălix* (Ir. sail, a C-stem, Bret. haleg-en, O. H. Germ. salahā, O. Engl. sealh, Engl. sallow) (but see §§ 92-94) ; *dăcrŭma*, later *lacruma* and *lacrima* (Gk. δάκρυ, O. Ir. dēr, W. dagr, Goth. tagr, O. Eng. tēar, Germ. Zähre) ; *ango*, *angor*, *angustus* (O. Ind. ạ́has, 'need,' Gk. ἄγχω, Ir. t-achtaim, W. t-agu, Lith. anksztas, 'narrow,' O. Sl. ązŭkŭ, Goth. aggvus, Germ. enge) ; *arceo* (Gk. ἀρκέω, Arm. argel, 'hindrance') ; *măcer*, 'thin' (Gk. μακρός, long, Av. masah-, 'size,' O. H. Germ. magar, 'thin') ; *albus* (Gk. ἀλφός, white leprosy) ; *ănĭmus*, *ănĭma*, 'soul' (O. Ir. anim, anman Gen., 'soul,' Gk. ἄνεμος, wind, from root an-, 'to breathe') ; *căno* (O. Ir. canim, W. canu, Goth. hana, 'a cock,' Engl. hen) ; *ălo* (Ir. alaim, W. alu, Goth. ala, 'I grow up,' Gk. ἄν-αλτος, insatiate) ; *ăqua* (Goth. ahva); *scăbo* (Gk. σκάπτω, Lith. skabù, 'I cut,' Goth. skaba, 'I shave,' O. Engl. scafe, Engl. shave) ; *ăro* (Arm. araur, 'a plough,' Gk. ἀρόω, O. Ir. arathar, 'a plough,' W. ar, 'tilth,' Lith. ariù, 'I plough,' O. Sl. orją, Goth. arja, Engl. to ear) ; *sal-* (Arm. αλ, Gk. ἅλς, O. Ir. salann, W. halen, O. Sl. soli̇̈, Goth. salt, Engl. salt).

I.-Eur. ă or ɵ (see § 51).

ă—ŏ (see § 55) e. g. *atrox* and *odium*, *acer-bus* and *ocris*.

ă—ĕ (see § 61) e. g. *aser* blood (Gk. ἔαρ), *sacena* a priest's knife (cf. *seco*).

Ē, Ĕ.

§ 5. Ē. I.-Eur. ē is Latin *ē*. Thus the optative-suffix, I.-Eur. -jē- (-ĭyē-) (O. Ind. syās, siyás, Gk. εἴης for *ἔσιης) is *-iē-* of O. Lat. *siēs*. From the root plē-, 'to fill' (O. Ind. prā-tá- Part., 'full,' Arm. li, Gk. πλή-ρης, O. Ir. līn, 'number,' O. Isl. fleire, 'more') comes Latin *plē-nus*, *im-plē-tus*, *plērī-que*, O. Lat. *ex-plē-nunt*; from sē-, 'to throw, throw seed' (Gk. ἵημι for *σι-ση-μι, ἧ-μα for *sē-mn, O. Ir. síl, 'seed,' W. hīl, Goth. mana-sēþs, 'mankind,' Engl. seed, Lith. sėju, 'I sow,' O. Sl. sěją, sě-mę, 'seed') Latin sē-vī, sē-men. This I.-Eur. ē is often found in developments from simple roots with ĕ, as, for instance, plē-, from the simple root pĕl-, 'to fill' (Goth. filu, 'much,' O. Ir. il), or psē- (O. Ind. psā-, 'to devour,' Gk. ψῆν, to rub) from the simple root bhĕs-, (O. Ind. bhas-, 'to devour'), the ē being either due to the fusion of ĕ with an e-sound, in a grade of a dissyllabic root (thus plē- would be a grade of pele-), or a stem-suffix added to the weak grade of the simple root (thus psē- is ps-, the weak grade of bhes-, with the addition of the suffix ē). The same doubt we found to exist about roots with ā, like ĝnā- (Lat. *gnā-tus*) from ĝena- or ĝn-ā- (§ 1). Occasionally ē became ī in Latin through the influence of an *i* (*y*) followed by a vowel in the next syllable, e.g. *fīlius* for *fēlius*. Latin ē is often ĕ, lengthened by 'compensation,' e.g. *ănhēlus* for *an-ĕnslo* from *an-ănslo-* (cf. *hālo*), written in the older orthography (in Virgil MSS.) *anhellus*, a spelling which indicates the lengthening of the *e* to have been a transference of the long quantity from the consonant to the vowel. Sometimes Latin ē is due to the fusion of two vowels, e.g. *prēndo* from *prehendo*, *trēs* from *trĕyĕs* (ch. vi. § 61).

In the unaccented syllable, Latin ē remained unchanged, e.g. *concēdo*, *accēdo* (see ch. iii. § 30). But when final, it was shortened in iambic words in course of time, so that while Plautus scans *căvĕ* and occasionally *căvē*, the ordinary pronunciation in Cicero's time was *căvĕ* only. When preceding final *m*, it was shortened like other long vowels; hence the first Pers. Sg. of the optative would be *siĕm* in Latin, unlike Gk. εἴην for *ἐ(σ)ιην*; and before final -*t*, -*r*, -*l* it became (like *ā*, &c.) a short vowel in the second century B.C. (For this shortening, see ch. iii. § 40.)

In Oscan I.-Eur ē is í (the symbol also of I.-Eur. ĭ, § 13), íí (Lat. alph. *i*), e.g. lígatúís 'legatis,' *ligud* 'lege'; in Umbr. e, sometimes i, e.g. *plener* 'plenis,' habetu and *habitu* 'habeto' (von Planta, i. p. 89).

§ 6. **Lat. ē for I.-Eur. ē.** Other examples are: I.-Eur. dhē-, 'to suck,' 'suckle' (O. Ind. dhā-, dhā-rú-, 'suckling,' dhā-trī, 'nurse,' Arm. diem, 'I suck,

§§ 6–8.] REPRESENTATIVES OF I.-EUR. SOUNDS. Ē, Ĕ. 225

Gk. θῆσθαι, θῆ-λυς, θη-λή, O. Ir. dith, 'he sucked,' dīnu, Pres.-Part., 'a lamb,' Goth. daddja, 'I suckle,' O. H. Germ. tāu, Lith. dė-lė̃, 'a leech,' pirm-dė̃lė̃, 'young mother,' O. Sl. dĕ-tę̌, 'infant'), Latin fē-mina, fello (vulgar form of fēlo), fī-lius for *fēlius; I.-Eur. nē-, 'to sew, spin' (Gk. νῆν, νή-θω, νῆ-μα, νῆ-τρον, Goth. nē-þla, 'needle,' O. H. Germ. nādela, nāen, Germ. nāhen), Lat. nē-re, nē-tus, nē-men; I.-Eur. *sēmi-, 'half' (O. Ind. sāmi-, Gk. ἡμι-, O. H. Germ. sāmi-, O. Engl. sām-, Engl. sand-blind), Lat. sēmi-. Similarly Lat. rēs (O. Ind. rá-s, 'property'); Lat. vērus (O. Ir. fīr, W. gwir, Goth. tuz-vērjan, 'to doubt,' O. Sl. věra, 'belief'); Lat. rē-ri (Goth. rēdan, 'to advise,' O. Engl. rǣdan, Engl. rede, Germ. rathen); Lat. spēs (Lith. spėti, 'to have leisure,' O. Sl. spěti, 'to advance,' Goth. spēdiza, 'later,' Germ. spät). This I.-Eur. ē is often a 'doublet' of ēi (see § 47); rē-, for example, of Lat. rēs, O. Ind. rá-s, is a byform of rēi-, rēy- (O. Ind. rāy-ás Gen.), and some refer the fī- of Lat. fīlius to an I.-Eur. dhī-, a grade of a root dhēi-, dhēy, 'to suckle.' That the Romans of Plautus' day regarded filius as a cognate of fēlo (fello) appears from a line preserved only in the Ambrosian MS., Pseud. 422 iam ille felat filius, and in Umbrian the word seems to have had the sense of 'suckling,' e. g. sif filiu trif, tref sif feliuf, 'tres sues lactentes' Acc., as well as that of 'son,' e. g. fel. for felis, 'filius' on an Umbrian epitaph. (Büch. Umbr. p. 174.) (On Praenestine file(i)a, a nurse (?), see A.L.L. ii. 482).

§ 7. ī for ē. Delīnio, a byform of delēnio; Plīnius (dialectal?) apparently from plēnus; convīcium from root wēqᴴ-, 'to speak' (?); suspīcio from root spĕk-, 'to look,' all seem to be examples of this change of ē to ī, produced by a y-sound in the next syllable. Fīlius is spelt felius on an inscription (C. I. L. xiv. 1011), and seems in Umbrian to have the ē-sound, spelt e or i. On the spellings Cornilius, Aurilius, which prove the affinity of Latin ē with an i-sound before a syllable with y, see ch. ii. § 11 [Aurilius occurs on an inscr. of 200 B.C. (C. I. L. xiv. 4268, with eisdim)]; and on the spelling stilio, for stēllio, a newt, see Georges, Lex Wortf. s. v. (Parodi in Stud. Ital. i. 385 gives other exx., and adds tīlia, &c.)

§ 8. E. I.-Eur. ĕ is Latin ĕ: for example, in the present stem, e.g. of the root bhĕr-, I.-Eur. *bhĕrō, first Pers. Sg. (O. Ind. bhárāmi, Arm. berem, Gk. φέρω, O. Ir. berim, W. ad-feru Inf., Goth. baira, Engl. I bear, O. Sl. berą), Lat. fĕro; in the Neuter ES-stem, e.g. of root ĝĕn-, I.-Eur. *ĝĕnos, Nom. Sg. (O. Ind. jánas, Gk. γένος, O. Ir. gein), Lat. gĕnus; in the numeral 'ten,' I.-Eur. *dĕkm̥ (O. Ind. dáśa, Gk. δέκα, O. Ir. deich, W. deg, Goth. taihun, O. H. G. zehan, Lith. dēszimt, O. Sl. desętĭ), Lat. dĕcem.

Latin em, en may represent I.-Eur. m̥, n̥, the sonant or syllabic nasal, e.g. I.-Eur. *km̥tom (or *k̂ᵉmtom), O. Ind. śatám, Gk. ἑ-κατόν, O. Ir. cēt, W. cant, Goth. hund, Lith. szim̃tas, O. Sl. sŭto), Lat. centum (see § 81). I.-Eur. ĕw became ŏv in Latin, which in the unaccented syllable passed into u, e.g. nŏvus (Gk. νέος) and dē-nuo), and similarly I.-Eur. wĕ became ŏ, e.g. sŏror for I.-Eur. swĕsor-, in certain circumstances (see below), and I.-Eur. el became ŏl (ŭl) except before e, i or in the group ell, e.g. vŏlo, but vĕlim, velle. Latin ĕ became i before ng, e.g. tingo (Gk. τέγγω),

Q

before *gn*, e. g. *dignus* from *decet* (? see § 119), just as in the Teutonic languages ĕ has become ĭ before a nasal and a consonant, e. g. Engl. 'wind.' It became *i* also in open unaccented syllables, except when final, or when preceding *r*, but passed into a *u*-sound before *l* or a labial. Thus the compound of *nĕco* was *ē-nĭco* (later spelt *eneco*), the ordinal of *dĕcem* was *dĕcŭmus*, class. *decimus* (ch. iii. § 18). Latin *ĕ* sometimes represents ei (ĕy) before a vowel, e. g. *ĕo* from the I.-Eur. root ei-, 'to go,' on which see § 63. Final Latin *ĕ* may represent any I.-Eur. short vowel, as may also *e* in unaccented syllables before *r* or a consonant-group, e. g. *pĕ-pĕr-i* from *părio, an-ceps* from *căput* (see ch. iii. § 18). Final *-ĕ* was often dropped, e. g. *nĕc* for *nĕquĕ*, *exemplăr*, older *exemplāre*, as *ĕ* (and *ĭ*) in the middle of a word might be suppressed by syncope, e. g. *surgo* for *sub-rĕgo* (see ch. iii. § 13). On the substitution of *-ĕr-* for *-rĭ-* in *ter*, older *terr* (cf. *terr-uncius*) for **ters*, I.-Eur. **trĭs*, &c., see ch. iii. § 15. 8. I.-Eur. *ĕ* remains in Umbro-Oscan, though before some consonants it appears as *ĭ*, e. g. Osc. estud 'esto,' Umbr. fertu 'ferto.' The change to *ŏ* before l is apparently unknown. (For particulars, see von Planta, i. p. 83.)

§ 9. **Latin ĕ for I.-Eur. ĕ.** I.-Eur. -ĕ in the Voc. Sg. of O-stems (O. Ind. vŕka, Gk. λύκε, Lith. vilkè, O. Sl. vlŭče) is Latin *-ĕ* of *lupĕ*, &c., as in the Imperative 2 Sg. Act., e. g. *ăĝĕ (O. Ind. ája, Gk. ἄγε) Lat. *ăgĕ*, dropped in *dīc, dūc, făc* (ch. iii. § 36); the conjunction 'and,' I.-Eur. *qʷĕ (O. Ind. ca, Gk. τε) is Latin *quĕ*, with *-ĕ* dropped in *nĕc* for *nĕquĕ*, &c. ; the first personal pronoun (O. Ind. ahám, Arm. es, Gk. ἐγώ, Goth. ik, O. Eng. ic, Lith. àsz, O. Sl. azŭ) is in Latin *ĕgo*. Other examples are Lat. *nĕbŭla* (Gk. νεφέλη, O. Ir. nēl from *neblo-, W. nifwl, O. H. Germ. nebul, Germ. Nebel); Lat. *sĕquor* (O. Ind. sác-, Gk. ἕπομαι, O. Ir. sechur, Lith. sekù); Lat. *ĕt* (Gk. ἔτι); Lat. *mĕdius* (O. Ind. mádhya-, Gk. μέσσος, μέσος, Goth. midjis, O. Ir. medōn, 'the middle,' O. Sl. mežda; Lat. *ĕquus* (O. Ind. áśva-, O. Ir. ech, Gaul. Epo-rēdia, W. ebol, 'a colt,' Goth. aihva-tundi, 'a bush,' lit. 'horse-tooth,' O. Engl. eoh, Lith. aszvà 'a mare'); Lat. *vĕho* (O. Ind. vah-, Pamphyl. Gk. ϝέχω, Ir. fēn from *wegno-, 'a waggon,' Goth. ga-viga, 'I move,' Germ. be-wege, Lith. vežù, O. Sl. vezą).

§ 10. **ŏ for ĕ with w and l.** I.-Eur. *nĕwṇ (O. Ind. náva, Gk. ἐννέα for *ἐν-νεϝα, Ir. nōi, W. naw, Goth. niun) is in Latin *nŏvem*; I.-Eur. *nĕwo- (O. Ind. náva, Gk. νέος, O. Ir. nūe from *nowio-, Gaul. Novio-dūnum, W. newydd) is Lat. *nŏvus, Novius*, while in the unaccented syllable we see *ŭ* for I.-Eur. ew in *dēnŭo*. (For other examples of this *u*, see ch. iii. § 24.) The change of *ĕ* to *ŏ* before *w*, which is shared by the Celtic languages (e. g. Gaul. Noviodunum, O. Ir. nūe for *nowio-, W. newydd from *nawydd for *nowio- from I.-Eur. *nĕwio-, cf. Gk. νειός, Goth. niujis; O.-Ir. nōi, W. naw from I.-Eur. *newṇ), and by the Balto-Slavic (e. g. Lith. tãvas for I.-Eur. *tĕwo-, Gk. τε(ϝ)ός; O. Sl. novŭ for I.-Eur. *nĕwo-, Gk. νέ(ϝ)ος), does not affect the *ev* (Latin *ev*, but not I.-Eur. -ew-) of words like *lĕvis* (Gk. ἐ-λαχύς), *sĕvērus*, apparently from root sĕĝh-, brĕvis (Gk. βραχύς), so that the law of change must have ceased to operate before these words assumed in Latin this form. It is like the change of the diphthong eu to ou in the Italic, Celtic, and Balto-Slavic languages, e. g. O. Lat. *douco* for I.-Eur. *deuḱō (Goth. tiuha) (see § 35). I.-Eur. swĕ- appears as sŏ- in Latin, e. g. I.-Eur. *swĕsor- (O. Ind. svásar-, Gk. ἔορ-ες, O. Ir. siur, and after a vowel fiur, W. chwaer, Goth. svistar, Lith. sesŭ, O. Sl. sestra) is in Latin *sŏror*; I.-Eur. *swĕḱuro- (O. Ind. śváśura-, Gk. ϝεκυρός, W. chwegrwn, O. H. Germ. swehur, Germ. Schwäher, Lith. szeszuras, O. Sl. svekrŭ) is Lat. *sŏcer*; I.-Eur. *swĕpno- (O. Ind. svápna-, O. Scand. svefn, O. Engl. swefen) is Lat. *sŏmnus* for *sŏpnus*; cf. *sŏpor*. I.-Eur. ḱwĕ is said to appear as cŏ- in Latin in *combr-ētum*, a bulrush (Lith. szveñdrai Plur.) from a stem ḱwĕndhro-, though this may stand for *quombr-ētum with the O-grade of stem (see § 137); *fŏrem* seems to represent dissyllabic *fwĕrem. But ĕ of dwĕ- remains, e. g. *bellum*, older *duellum*, *bĕnĕ* (cf. older *Duenos*). *Quĕ* from I.-Eur. qᵘĕ, kwĕ, &c. remains, and does not become co, e. g. *-quĕ* (I.-Eur. qᵘĕ), *quĕror* from kw-ĕs- (cf. Gk. κωκύω), though *quo* became *co* in course of time, e. g. *cŏlo*, the O. Lat. form of which was *quolo*, as in the old inscription of the Faliscan 'collegium cocorum,' written in rude Saturnians, and with equally rude spelling (Zvetaieff, *Inscr. Ital. Inf.* 72 a):

> gonlegium quod est aciptum aetatei aged[ai],
> opiparum ad ueitam quolundam festosque dies,
> quei soueis astutieis opidque Uolgani
> gondecorant saipisume comuiuia loidosque,
> ququei huc dederunt inperatoribus summeis (i. e. Jupiter, Juno
>   and Minerva)
> utei sesed lubentes beneiouent optantis,

where also *coqui* is written *ququei* (so *qolunt* for *colunt* in the Plautus Palimpsest in *Pseud.* 822). The compound *inquilīnus*, with -*quil*- for *quŏl*- in the unaccented syllable, was formed before the change from *quo* to *co*, and being a legal term kept its old spelling, unlike *incŏla*, (but see p. 229). That *quŏ* had come to sound like *cŏ* as early as the beginning of the second cent. B. C., we may infer from the spelling *in oquoltod*, for *in occulto*, on the S. C. de Bacchanalibus (C. I. L. i. 196) of 186 B. C.; for *occŭlo* must be connected with *cēlo*, which has not the qᵘ- guttural (cf. Ir. cĕlim, W. cĕlu with the ĕ-grade of the same root). The analogy of *quam*, *quem*, &c. would preserve the spelling *quom* till a late date, though the word was probably pronounced *com, for the preposition, I.-Eur. *ḱŏm or *kŏm, is usually spelt *quom* till the time of the Gracchi (Bersu, *Gutturale*, p. 42); and similarly *loquontur*, &c. would be written after the fashion of *lŏquantur*, *loquentur*, with *quo*; so that it is not until the fifth cent. A. D. that every *quŏ* has assumed the spelling *co*, e. g. *cot*, *cōrum*, *coque* (the conjunction), *condam* (the adverb), *locor* (Bersu, p. 90). The form *quotidie* is censured by Quintilian (i. 7. 6 frigidiora his alia ut . . . 'quotidie,' non cotidie, ut sit quot diebus: verum haec jam etiam inter ipsas ineptias evanuerunt), by Velius Longus (79. 16 K. illos vitiose et dicere et scribere [qui potius] per 'quo' 'quotidie' dicunt quam per 'co' cotidie, cum et dicatur melius et scribatur. non enim est a quoto die 'quotidie' dictum, sed a continenti die cotidie tractum), and by Marius Victorinus [13. 21 K. nam concussus quamvis a quatio habeat originem, et cocus a coquendo (*v. l.* quoquendo), et cotidie a quoto die, et incola ab inquilino, attamen per c quam per qu scribuntur]. *Cottidie* and *cotidie* are the spellings of the best MSS., and are found on inscriptions (see Georges, *Lex. Wortf.* s. v.), though no doubt the older spelling would have *quo-*.

Lat. *vo-* became *ve-* (see Solmsen, *Stud. Lat. Lautg.* p. 1) in the middle of the second cent. B. C. Quintilian tells us that Scipio Africanus (Minor) was credited by tradition with this change of orthography (i. 7. 25 quid dicam 'vortices' et 'vorsus,' ceteraque in eundem modum, quae primus Scipio Africanus in e litteram secundam vertisse dicitur?). (On these spellings in inscriptions, see Brambach, *Orth.* p. 101.) The MSS. of Plautus show the older spellings *vorto, vorsus,* and compounds, *voster, voto* (I.-Eur. g^u-), *-vorro*; and *invorto, divorsi, vortex* are found even in the MSS. of Augustan poets, like Virgil. The grammarians of the Empire sometimes advised the retention of these forms for the sake of distinctions, e. g. Caper, 99. 11 K. vortex fluminis est, vertex capitis; 97. 15 vorsus paginae dicetur, versus participium est a verbo vertor. One of the *o-*forms indeed, *vŏster*, was retained to the last (perhaps by analogy of *vōs*, or of *nŏster*) in Vulgar Latin (cf. Roumanian vostru, Ital. vostro, Fr. vôtre), as *o* was retained in classical *vŏco* (by analogy of *vōx* ?), *vŏmo, vŏro* (I.-Eur. g^u-). *O* was retained before single *l* and *l* before another consonant, e. g. *volo*, to wish, *volo*, to fly, *vola*, hollow of hand, *volvo, volnus*, later *vulnus*, &c., and before *v*, e. g. *voveo*; though Cassiodorus, a doubtful authority, makes *convollere* the old spelling of *convellere* (149. 17 K.). *Vŏlăterrae* for Etruscan Velaθri, *Vŏlumnius* for Etruscan Velimna cannot be quoted to prove that Latin *vĕ-* was ever pronounced *vŏ-*. They exemplify the phonetic law that *ĕl* became *ŏl* in Latin (see below). There is no evidence that *vĕho* was ever *voho*, or *Vĕnus *Vonus*, or *vĕntus *vontus*, or *vĕru *voru*, &c. The old spelling *vorto* (I.-Eur. *wĕrtō, Goth. wairþa) probably belongs to a period when *vo-* had come to take the sound of *ve-* and was occasionally used as a symbol of this sound (ch. viii. § 8); it has also been referred to the analogy of the P. P. P. *vorsus* (I.-Eur. *wṛt-to-), where Lat. *or* represents I.-Eur. *ṛ*.

Oi may similarly have become *ei* after *v*, so that *vidi* may represent an I.-Eur. *woidai (O. Sl. vĕdĕ; cf. Gk. οἶδα, ch. viii. § 39); but the appearance of *ĕ* beside *ŏ* in Latin in words like *amplector*, O. Lat. *amploctor* (Prisc. i. p. 25. 15 H.; cf. below ch. viii. § 33) is better referred to the same 'variation' (Ablaut) as that seen in *tego* beside *toga, procus* beside *precor,* &c., on which see § 51.

El is found in the group *ell*, e. g. *velle, vellem* (that *ll* had a more 'exilis' sound than *l*, in technical language was 'front-modified,' is attested by the grammarians, ch. ii. § 96), and before *e, i (y)*; but in other circumstances it seems that the character of Latin *l* so asserted itself as to change *e* to *o*, e. g. *volo*, though there are a few exceptions to the rule, and not very many instances[1]. Thus the Greek ἐλαί(ϝ)ā, when adopted by the Romans (in the period of the Tarquins, Plin. *Nat. Hist.* xv. 1), became *olaiva*, then *oleiva* (§ 27), *oliva*. A following *e-* or *i-*vowel prevents the change, e. g. *vĕlim, mĕlior*. The older type of declension *hŏlus, *hŏleris* (from *heleses*) has left traces of itself in *holus, holeris* and O. Lat. *helus* (Paul. Fest. 71. 13 Th. 'helus' et 'helusa' antiqui

---

[1] Pliny contrasts the *l* of *lectus, lectum* with the 'exilis' *l*-sound of *Metellus*, so that we cannot suppose Latin *l* to have been pronounced exactly as Russian or Gaelic l, viz. a 'deep' *l* before *a, o, u,* a 'palatal' *l* before *e, i*.

§ 11.]   REPRESENTATIVES OF I.-EUR. SOUNDS. Ē, Ĕ.   229

dicebant, quod nunc holus et holera ; cf. the gloss 'helitores' hortolani Löwe, *Prodr.* p. 339), but *scŏlus* has not survived beside *scĕleris*. Before a consonant *el* became *ol* (*ul* § 17) (on the pronunciation of *l* before a cons., see ch. ii. § 96), e. g. *vult*, older *volt*. (On *gelu, helvus, sĕmel, celsus,* and for other instances of the change to *ol*, see Osthoff, *Dunkles u. helles 'l' im Lat.*). *Inquilīnus* may thus represent an older *enquĕlino-, incŏla* an older *enquolā-,* both from an early q^uĕl-.

§ 11. I for (accented) e. Other examples are : before *ng*, Lat. *lingua*, older *dingua* from I.-Eur. dṇgh^u- (O. Ir. tenge, W. tafod, Goth. tuggō) ; Lat. *inguen* from I.-Eur. ṇg^u- (Gk. ἀδήν) ; Lat. *stringo*, I bind, draw tight (O. Ir. srengim, 'I draw'); Lat. *septingenti, confringo, attingo,* &c. for *septengenti, *confrengo, *attengo,* &c. ; before *gn, ignis* from I.-Eur. *ṇgni- (O. Ind. agní-, Lith. ugnìs, O. Sl. ognĭ) ; *Ignatius,* a late spelling of *Egnatius* (see Schuchardt, *Vok.* i. 334) ; *ilignus* and *iligneus* from *ilex*, but *abiĕgnus* (with *ĕ*, according to Priscian, i. p. 82. 8 H.) from *ăbies* ; the old religious term for a sheep, brought with its two lambs to the sacrifice, is given by Paul. Fest. as *ambegna* (4. 7 Th. ' ambegni ' bos et vervex appellabantur, cum ad eorum utraque latera agni in sacrificium ducebantur), but in Glossaries as *ambigna* (Mai, vi. p. 506 b. 'ambignae,' oves ex utraque parte agnos habentes ; and ' ambignae,' oves quas Junoni offerebant, quia geminos parerent), while the MSS. of Varro give *ambiegna*, which may indicate a correction of *ambegna* to *ambigna* (*L. L.* vii. 31 ' ambiegna ' bos apud augures, quam circum aliae hostiae constituuntur). We have *sim-* for *sem-* (I.-Eur. sm̩-, Gk. ἁ-πλόος, &c.), in *simplus, simplex, simpludiarea funera* (quibus adhibentur duntaxat ludi corbitoresque, Fest. 498. 24 Th.) as well as *singuli, sincerus, sincinia* (cantio solitaria, Paul. Fest. 500. 23 Th.) and in *sĭmul,* older *semul* (see Georges, *Lex. Wortf.* s. v.), *sĭmĭlis, sĭmītū*, but *e* does not become *i* before *mpl* of *templum*, nor before *nc* in *jŭvencus*, and Umbrian sumel, Gk. ὁμαλός, &c. suggest that the *sim-* of *similis* and its cognates is I.-Eur. som-, and has the *ŭ*-sound of *sŭmus*, written also *sĭmus, lŭbet* later *lĭbet* (see ch. ii. § 16) ; *sincĭput* is derived from *sēmicaput* by Velius Longus (78. 18 K.), &c. On the quantity and quality of the vowel *i* before *gn* in *dignus*, &c., see ch. ii. § 144. The I.-Eur. word for 'five' *pĕnq^uĕ (O. Ind. páñca, Arm. hing, Gk. πέντε, O. Ir. cōic, Gaul. πεμπέδουλα, cinqfoil, O. W. pimp, Goth. fimf, Lith. penkì, O. Sl. pętĭ) is in Latin *quīnque* [with long *i* indicated both by inscriptions and by the Romance forms, a quantity which has been referred to the influence of *quīn(c)tus* (*K. Z.* xxx. 501) (see ch. ii. § 144)]. In rustic and dialectal Latin *ĕ* before *rc* became *i*, e. g. *Mircurios, Mirquriös* (*C.I.L.* i. 1500 and 59, both from Praeneste), *stircus* (*C. I. L.* ix. 782, from Luceria, in Apulia on the borders of Samnium), *commircium*, mentioned as an older form by Velius Longus (77. 12 K. ' mium ' et ' commircium ' quoque per i antiquis relinquamus, apud quos aeque et ' Mircurius ' per i dicebatur, quod mirandarum rerum esset inventor, ut Varro dicit. nostris jam auribus placet per e, ut et Mercurius et commercia dicantur). The *i* of country-terms like *hirsutus, hirtus,* &c. (apparently from root *ghers-*, 'to be rough,' whence Lat. *horreo, hordeum,* &c.) may be explained by this dialectal pronunciation of *stircus* for *stercus*, &c. (cf. Osc. amiricatud 'immercato'). In other positions than before *rc*, &c. the 'rustic' pronunciation seems to have substituted *e* for *i* (ut iota litteram tollas et e plenissimum dicas, Cic. *de Orat.* iii. 12. 46) (cf. above, ch. ii. § 17). To this confusion is perhaps due the uncertainty in the spelling of country-terms like *fīlix* or *fĕlix*, a fern (the latter approved by Caper, p. 106. 1 K. ; see Georges s. v.), *fīber* and *fĕber*, a beaver, from I.-Eur. bhĕbhr- (see Georges) ; but the byforms *pinna* and *penna, vigeo* and *vegeo, villus*

M. and *vellus* N. have not yet been satisfactorily explained. *Levir*, a brother-in-law, a word only found in late Latin writers, and so misspelt with *ĕ* for *ae* (see § 28), from I.-Eur. *daiwer- (Gk. δαήρ, Lith. dēverìs) takes *i* by anal. of *vir*. (On other byforms due to the late Latin identification of *ĭ* with *ē*, and to the change of *ĕ* to *ĭ* in unaccented syllables, see ch. ii. § 6).

Ī, Ĭ.

§ 12. **Ī.** I.-Eur. ī has been faithfully retained by the various languages in almost all circumstances, and is in Latin *ī*, though often written in O. Lat. *ei*, after the I.-Eur. ei-diphthong had come to take the sound of *ī* (ch. i. § 9). The diphthong ει in Greek developed to the same sound (thus ἔτεισα, the proper spelling, became ἔτῑσα), so that in Greek also ει was in course of time often written for ῑ, e. g. πολείτης, and Ulfilas adopted this symbol *ei* for the long *i*-sound of Gothic. For examples of I.-Eur. ī we may take the adjective-suffix in -īno- (O. Ind. nav-ína-, 'new,' Gk. ἀγχιστ-ῖνος, often with names of animals, e. g. κορακ-ῖνος, δελφακ-ίνη, χοιρ-ίνη, Goth. gulþ-eins, O. H. G. guld-īn, Engl. gold-en, Goth. sv-ein, O. Engl. sw-īn, Engl. swine, O. Sl. mater-inŭ, 'motherly,' sv-inŭ), in Latin *su-īnus*, *dīv-īnus*, &c.; the optative-suffix ī (varying with yē, ch. viii. § 55) (O. Ind. dviṣī-máhi, Gk. εἰδεῖμεν from εἰδε(σ)-ῑ-μεν, Goth. vil-ei-ma) in Lat. *s-ī-mus*; the adjective *gʰīwo-*, 'alive,' (O. Ind. jīvá-, Lith. gývas, O. Sl. živŭ, O. Ir. biu, W. byw) in Lat. *vīvus*, in old spelling *veivos*; Lat. *vīs* (Gk. ἴς, ῑ-φι); Lat. *vīrus* (Gk. ἰός for *Fῑσος), Lat. *vītex* (Gk. ἰτέα and εἰτέα, Eng. withy, Lith. výtis). I.-Eur. ī is usually a grade of an ei-root, and it is often difficult to say whether Lat. *ī* represents the ī-grade or the ei-grade.

After *ĭ*, Latin *ī* appears as *ē* in *lăni-ēna* for *lani-īna*, &c. (cf. *tonstr-īna*), as we have *ĕ* in *sŏcĭĕtas*, *anxĭĕtas*, but *ĭ* in *castĭtas*, *nŏvĭtas*, &c. (see ch. v. § 83). Latin *ī* represents I.-Eur. ei in *dīco* (O. Lat. *deico*, Gk. δείκ-νῡ-μι), *ad-dīco*, &c., *fīdo* (Gk. πείθω for *φειθω), *con-fīdo*, &c. (see ch. viii. § 6), and has come from *ĭ* lengthened by compensation in words like *nīdus* for *nisdo-* (*nizdo-) (Arm. nist, 'situation,' Engl. nest). In the unaccented syllable it may represent older *ei* (Latin *ei*, not I.-Eur. ei), viz. an I-diphthong whose first element has been weakened; as in *con-cido*, older *con-ceido*, from *caedo*, older *caido*, and in the final syllable of Perfects like *tŭ-tŭd-ī* (older -*ei*) (O. Ind. tu-tud-é), which have the

§§ 12, 13.] REPRESENTATIVES OF I.-EUR. SOUNDS. ī, ĭ. 231

I.-Eur. ī Sg. Perf. Middle ending -ai (-ai) (ch. viii. § 66); oi in the final syllable of Noms. Plur. of O-stems like *populi* (oldest Lat. *poploe*, then *populei*, ch. vi. § 40). *Vīdī*, older *veidei*, from I.-Eur. *woidai (O. Sl. vědě) shows *vei-*, a development of an older *voi-*, as *versus* (I.-Eur. *wr̥t-to-) shows *ver-*, a development of an older *vor-* (§ 10). On the use of *ē* for Lat. *ī* (perhaps properly only I.-Eur. ei) in rustic Latin, e. g. *speca*, *vella*, see ch. ii. § 17, and cf. below, § 32; on *ī* for *ē* in *filius*, § 7. I.-Eur. ī remains in Umbro-Osc. and is written in the Oscan alphabet ií or i (in Lat. alph. *i*), in Umbr. i (in Lat. alph. *i* and *ei*), e. g. Osc. liímitú[m 'līmitum,' Umbr. si, *sir*, *sei*, 'sit' (see von Planta, i. p. 102).

§ 13. ĭ. I.-Eur. Ĭ is Latin ĭ, sometimes written in Old Latin *e* (e. g. *Tempestatebus* on a Scipio epitaph), after unaccented *ĕ* had come to take the *ĭ*-sound (see also ch. iii. § 18). The I.-Eur. pronoun *ĭ- (O. Ind. i-d-ám Neut., Goth. is Masc., ita Neut., Engl. it) is Lat. *ĭs* M., *ĭd* N.; the pronoun *k̑ĭ-, 'this' (Goth hi-mma Dat., hi-drē Adv., Engl. him, hither, Lith. szìs, O. S. sĭ) appears in Latin *cĭs*, *cĭtra*; the interrogative and indefinite pronoun *qʷĭ- (O. Ind. ci-d, Gk. τί(δ), O. Sl. čĭ-to) is Latin *quĭs* M., *quĭd* N. (cf. Umbr. pis); from the root mĭn-, 'to lessen,' from the primary root mei- (O. Ind. minómi, Gk. μινύ-θω, Goth. mins Adv., O. Sl. mĭnjijĭ Adj.) we have Lat. *mĭnuo*, *mĭnor*.

I.-Eur. Ĭ is generally the weak grade of the diphthong ei (as mĭn- from mei-, 'to lessen'), and so in Latin, e. g. *in-dĭco* beside *dīco* (older *deico*), *fĭdes* (cf. Gk. ἔ-πιθ-ον) beside *fīdo*, older *feido* (cf. Gk. πείθω for *φειθω). For ĭ varying with ī, e. g. I.-Eur. *wĭro, 'a man,' see § 58. Latin ĭ may represent any short vowel in an unaccented syllable, not long by position, e. g. *concĭno* for *con-cano*, *dĭlĭgo* for *dilego*, *inquĭlīnus* for *inquolinus*, *quidlĭbet* for *quidlubet* (whence *libet* for *lubet*, ch. ii. § 16). In an unaccented syllable long by position ĭ became ĕ, e. g. *indĕx* beside *indĭco*, *jūdĕx* beside *jūdĭco* (cf. *jūri-dĭcus*), *cŏmes*, properly *comĕss*, Gen. *com-ĭt-is*, and in an open unaccented syllable before *r*, e. g. *cĭn-er-is* from *cinis*, and also when final, e. g. *marĕ* but *maria*, *mari-tĭmus*; *lĕvĕ*, Neut. of *levis* (contrast Gk. ἴδρι, Neut. of ἴδρις), *rurĕ*, Loc. of *rūs*, in which case it may be dropped, e. g. *ănĭmăl* for *animāle*, Neut. of *animālis*. Latin -rĭ- in the unaccented syllable, when preceded by a consonant, became ĕr, e.g. ăcerbus for *acrĭ-bus from *acrŭ-dho- (Lith. asztrùs, O. Sl. ostrŭ), incertus for *incrĭtus (Gk. ἄ-κριτος); and apparently this may occur in the accented syllable too, e.g. ter, properly tĕrs (cf. terr-uncius) for *tĕrs from *trĭs (Gk. τρίς), testis for *trĭ-stis (cf. Oscan trístaamentud, in Lat. testāmentō Abl.) (but see ch. iii. § 15. 8). Similarly for -lĭ-, when, through syncope, the l has to play the part of a vowel (sonant or syllabic l), as is seen in our 'able,' and more clearly in French able, we find ŭl (older ŏl) in Latin, e.g. făcultas for *facl(ĭ)tas beside facilitas, sĭmultas for *siml(ĭ)tas beside sĭmĭlĭtas.

After i we find ĕ not ĭ in sŏcietas, anxietas, &c., beside prŏbĭtas, castĭtas, &c. (cf. Engl. yĕ- for yĭ- in 'yet,' 'yes'), as we find lănīena beside tonstrīna (§ 12). In Oscan I.-Eur. ĭ is í (in Lat. alph. i, in Gr. ει); in Umbr. it is i (Lat. alph. i), but in O. Umbr. often e; e.g. Osc. pís, Umbr. pis 'quis.' (von Planta, i. p. 96).

§ 14. **Other examples of Lat. ĭ for I.-Eur. ĭ.** The -ĭs- of the I.-Eur. Superlative suffix ĭs-to- (O. Ind. svấd-iṣṭha-, Gk. ἥδιστος, Goth. sut-ista, 'sweetest') appears in Latin măg-ĭs-ter (in O. Lat. written magester according to Quintilian, i. 4. 17 quid? non e quoque i loco fuit? ' Menerua ' et ' leber ' et ' magester ' et ' Diove Victore,' non Diovi Victori), mĭn-ĭs-ter. The weak grade of an ei-root is seen in I.-Eur. trĭ- from root trei-, 'three' (O. Ind. trĭ-ṣú Loc., Gk. τρι-σί, Goth. þri-m Dat., Lith. tri-sè Loc., O. Sl. trĭ-chŭ) and Latin trĭ-bus, though in ter, terni, &c. there is the usual change of -rĭ- to -er-; Lat. piscis (Goth. fisks), while O. Ir. iasg from *peisco-shows the ei-grade; Lat. vĭdeo (O. Ind. vid-má, 1 Pl., Hom. Gk. Fίδ-μεν, W. gwedd, 'aspect,' Goth. vit-um, 1 Pl., Engl. wit, Germ. wissen) from root weid-, 'to see, know,' with Perfect-stem woid- (Gk. οἶδα); Lat. fĭd-i, fĭndo (O. Ind. bhid-), ' to split,' Goth. bitum, 1 Pl. Pret., Engl. bit, Germ. bissen), from root bheid- (Goth. beitan, Engl. to bite, Germ. beissen).

ĭ **in the unaccented syllable.** See ch. iii. § 18 for other instances.

§ 15. **iĕ, not iĭ.** Other examples are pietas, sătietas, ēbrietas and other derivatives in -tat- from io-adjective stems, ărietis, ăbietis, &c., văriego, &c. beside lēvĭgo, &c., hietare, and the eárlier spellings conieciant, proiecitad, inieciatis, traiĕcere, &c. (see ch. iii. § 18, p. 188).

Ō, Ŏ.

§ 16. **Ō.** I.-Eur. ō is Latin ō. Thus the I.-Eur. root pō-, 'to drink' (O. Ind. pā-, pā́-na-, Noun, Gk. πέ-πω-κα, ἄμ-πω-τις, the ebb, Aeol. πώ-νω, Lith. pú-ta) is Latin pō- of pō-to, pō-tus, pō-culum; dō-, 'to give' (O. Ind. dá-na- and dá-ti-, 'a gift,' Arm. tur, Gk. δῶ-ρον and δωτίνη, Lith. dů-tis, O. Sl. da-rŭ, dan-ŭ, P.P.P.; in Celtic, the I.-Eur. word for 'gift' has taken the sense of 'an accomplishment,' O. Ir. dān, W. dawn) is in Latin dō-num, dō-s. On the other hand, I.-Eur. ō is often a grade of ĕ or ē (e.g. Gk. πωτάομαι from root πετ-, κλώψ, a thief, from κλέπτω, θωμός from τίθημι) (see §§ 51, 53). A root like ĝnō- (Gk. γνωτός, Lat. nōtus, older ᵹnōtus, gnōsco) beside ĝen-, admits of being explained either as an addition of the suffix -ō- to the weak grade ĝn-, or as a grade of a dissyllabic root ĝeno-, so that gnōtus from ĝeno- would be like ᵹnārus from ĝena-, &c. (§ 1).

Latin ō sometimes represents an ŏ lengthened by 'compensation,' e.g. pōno from *pŏ-s(i)no (cf. pŏ-sĭtus); sometimes it is due to crasis, e.g. cōpula for *co-apula, cōmburo for co-amb-uro (see ch. ii. § 149); sometimes it is the 'rustic' development of Latin ou, which in standard Latin became ū, e.g. rōbus for *rūbus (cf. rūbidus) from I.-Eur. reudh- (Goth. rauþs) (see § 41); sometimes it is the 'rustic' form of au, e.g. plōstrum, a byform of plaustrum, from plaudo (ch. ii. § 37). But ō is also found to vary with au in Latin, when both are sprung from an original ōu, e.g. ōsculum, ausculum (ib.).

In unaccented syllables ō remained unaltered, e.g. con-dōno and co-gnōsco, but final -ō became shortened in course of time (see ch. iii. § 45). Octāvus from octō (I.-Eur. *oktō, *oktōu) appears to show āv for ōw, as cavus shows ăv for ŏw (§ 19). Fūr, cūr (O. Lat. quōr) seem to represent an I.-Eur. *bhōr (Gk. φώρ, p. 254), *qᵘō-r (Lith. kur̃, 'where,' for *kŭr, ch. x. § 10), and nōn to stand for *nūn, a development of noen(um) (ch. x. § 18).

I.-Eur. ō is in Osc. u, uu (in Lat. alph. u), but the endings -ōs, -ōD appear in Osc. as -ús, -úd (with ú, the symbol of I.-Eur. ŏ); e.g. d]uunated 'dōnavit,' dunum 'dōnum,' Abellanús 'Abellani' Nom. Plur., Búvaianúd 'Boviano' Abl. Sg. In Umbr. it is usually o (in Lat. alph., for the native alphabet writes u for both the U-sound and the O-sound, ch. i. § 1), but -ōR appears as -ur, e.g. nome 'nōmen,' postro 'retrō,' arsferture 'adfertōri' (see von Planta, i. p. 116).

§ 17. **Ŏ.** I.-Eur. ŏ is Latin (accented) ŏ, e.g. I.-Eur. *ŏk̑tō, 'eight' (O. Ind. aṣṭá, Arm. ut', Gk. ὀκτώ, O. Ir. ocht, W. wyth, Goth. ahtau, O. Engl. eahta, Lith. asztůnì, O. Sl. osmĭ), Lat. ŏctō; I.-Eur. *pŏti-, 'master' (O. Ind. páti-, Gk. πόσις, Goth. brūþ-faþs, 'bridegroom,' O. Engl. fadian, 'to arrange,' Lith. pàts, vẽsz-patis, 'lord'), Lat. pŏtis, potior.

I.-Eur. ŏw seems to have become ăv in the beginning of the second century B.C., e.g. căvus, older covus (Gk. κόοι, cavities, Hesych., κοῖλος for *κοϜιλος). Latin vŏ- became vĕ- in the middle of the second century B.C. in versus, older vorsus, &c. (§ 10); but vŏco was the older form of văco, as we see from Plautus' pun in Cas. 527:

fác habeant linguám tuae aedes. Quíd ita? Quom ueniám, uocent.

Latin -ŏv- may represent I.-Eur. -ĕw-, as in nŏvem, nŏvus (see § 10); Latin sŏ-, I.-Eur. swĕ-, as in sŏror, sŏcer, somnus (see § 10); Latin ŏl, ŏr, the I.-Eur. sonant or syllabic l, r, as in fors, cor (see § 92). In the accented, as well as the unaccented syllable, Latin ŏ became u, before l with a consonant (not ll), before m with a labial, before ngu, e.g. vult (volt) from volo, lumbus, unguis. Before certain other consonant-groups it tended to the close o- or to the u-sound (see ch. ii. § 22). In the unaccented syllable, Latin ŏ offered more resistance than, for example, Latin ă, to the rule that a short vowel became ĕ, then ĭ, in open syllables; e.g. adnŏto, arrŏgo have not changed their vowel like adĭgo (from ăgo). In syllables long by position, ŏ became ŭ about the end of the third century B.C.; and any ŏ which had escaped weakening to ĕ, ĭ took the same course (see ch. iii. § 18). The terminations -os, -om became -us, -um towards the end of the third century B.C. [Luciom, filios, on one Scipio epitaph (C.I.L. i. 32), Lucius, prognatus on another (ib. i. 30), -us, -um invariably in the S.C. Bacch. of 186 B.C., (ib. i. 196), and on the decree of L. Aem. Paulus Macedonicus of 189 B.C. (ib. ii. 5041)]. But after v, u, qu, gu we find the spelling -os, -om down to the end of the Republic. There are similar traces in Osc. of unaccented ŏ becoming ŭ, e.g. dolom and dolum (von Planta, i. p. 111). Final ŏ became ĕ, like final ă, ĭ, &c., e.g. sĕquĕre imper. for I.-Eur. *seq^{u}eso (Gk. ἕπεο) (see ch viii. § 77).

§ 18. Latin ō for I.-Eur. ŏ. Other examples: from the I.-Eur. root ŏq^u-, 'to see' (varying with ŏq^u-) (O. Ind. ákṣi-, 'the eye,' Arm. akn, Gk. ὄμμα, ὄψομαι, Lith. akìs, O. Sl. oko) comes Lat. oculus; the I.-Eur. preposition *prŏ, 'forth' (O. Ind. prá, Gk. πρό, O. Ir. ro, used like the Augment to indicate past time, e.g. ro chan 'I sang' from canim 'I sing,' O. Bret. ro-, Goth. fra-, Lith. pra-, O. Sl. pro-) is Lat. prŏ- of prŏ-ficiscor, &c.; another preposition, I.-Eur. *kom 'with' (Gk. κοινός from *κομ-yos, O. Ir. com-, Osc. com) is Lat. com, which when unaccented, or when preceding b, p, gu, &c., became cum, its usual form in classical Latin; I.-Eur. *nokti-, 'night' (O. Ind. nákti-, Gk. νύξ, O. Ir. in-nocht, 'to-night,' W. henoeth, nos, Goth. nahts, O. Engl. neaht, niht, Lith. naktìs, O. Sl. noštǐ) is

§§ 18-20.] REPRESENTATIVES OF I.-EUR. SOUNDS Ō, Ŏ. 235

Lat. nŏx, nŏctis Gen. ; I.-Eur. root od-, 'to smell' (varying with ōd-) Gk. ὀδμή, ὄζω, Arm. hot) appears in Lat. ŏd-or, oleo for *od-eo (§ 111).

§ 19. Lat. ă for I.-Eur. ŏ, under influence of v. Other examples are Lat. căveo for *cŏveo (Gk. κο(ϝ)έω, to perceive, ἀ-κούω), Lat. autŭmo for *ăvi-tumo from *ŏvi-tumo (Gk. ὀίω), Lat. lăvo for *lŏvo (Gk. λούω). Lat. făvilla for *fŏvilla from I.-Eur. root dheghᵫ-, 'to burn' (O. Ind. dah-, Gk. τέφ-ρα, ashes, Lith. degù, 'I burn'). The example previously quoted, Lat. căvus for covus, enables us to assign a date to this change of I.-Eur. ow, Lat. ov to av. The Spanish and Portuguese words (Span. cueva, Port. cova) show that covo-, not cavo-, was the Vulgar Latin stem at the time when Spain was made a province. The country-term coum, (cohum), the hollow in the plough, used by Ennius of the innermost part of the heavenly sphere, retained the o, as did ovis (Gk. ὄ(ϝ)ις), though whether the avi- of aububulcus 'pastor ovium' (Löwe, Prodr. p. 348), avillus 'agnus recentis partus' (Paul. Fest. 10. 32 Th.) is better referred to this root or to agᵫ- the root of agnus (Gk. ἀμνός for *ἄβνος) is not clear. (Varro, L. L. v. 135 explains coum as 'sub jugo medio cavum, quod bura extrema addita oppilatur,' and adds 'vocatur coum a covo'; cf. Paul. Fest. 28. 1 Th. ; Isid. Nat. Rer. 12 cous (v. l. chous) est quo caelum continetur, unde Ennius,

vix solum complere coum (MSS. choum, cous) terroribus caeli.

Partes ejus sunt, cous (v. l. chous), axis, clima, cardines, convexa, poli, hemisphaeria ; Diomedes (365. 17 K.) says that Verrius Flaccus spelt incoho, not inchoo, for he derived the word from cohum, the Old Latin word for mundus). We have already found that I.-Eur. ŏw became ŏv in Latin (e. g. Lat. novus for I.-Eur. *newos), and that probably at a very early date, seeing that the change is shared by other Italic languages (e. g. Osc. Núvellum). If then it be the case that I.-Eur. ow became av in Latin in the third or second cent. B. C. we must suppose that Latin ov from I.-Eur. ew had a different sound from Latin ov from I.-Eur. ow ; for the former ov does not undergo change to av (e. g. novus, not *navus; novem, not *navem). Latin ov from I.-Eur. oghᵫ shares the change to av, e. g. făvilla from I.-Eur. dhŏghᵫ-, the o-grade of the root dhĕghᵫ-. 'to burn' ; but nūdus for *nov(e)dus from I.-Eur. *nogᵫ-, 'naked,' shows that the change of ov to av was later than the syncope of ĕ in the post-tonic syllable.

Lat. vŏco (Plaut. Cas. 527) for văco (Umbr. vaçeto- P. P. P., vakaze, for *vakaz se, Lat. vacatio sit ?), is probably nothing but an indication of the o-sound assumed by a when preceded by v (see ch. ii. § 4). This o-sound in *vŏcĭtus, the Vulg. Lat. word for 'empty,' must have persisted till late times, for Italian voto, as well as O. Fr. voit, reflect this form.

§ 20. ŭ for ŏ. (1) in close syllables, unaccented (according to the early Accent-law) : vĕtŭstus for *vetŏs-to- (Gk. (ϝ)ἔτος), and other derivatives from Neuters in -os (class. Lat. -us), such as angustus, vĕnustus, ŏnustus ; hŏmŭllus for *homŏllus from *homŏn-lo-, and other lo- Diminutives from ŏn-stems, like lĕnullus, whereas Diminutives from on- have -ōll-, e. g. persōlla, cŏrōlla ; so also Diminutives in -co-lo- from on-stems, like hŏmŭnculus, latrunculus ; ălŭmnus (cf. Gk. τρεφ-όμενος) and similar formations, Vertumnus, Autumnus, cŏlumna, &c.

(2) before l with consonant (not ll) : cŭlmen (contrasted with cŏlŭmen); stultus (contrasted with stŏlĭdus) ; pulvis (contrasted with pollen) ; fulvus (contrasted with solvo for *soluŏ). In Old Latin we have o, e. g. on inscriptions, Folvius (C. I. L. vi. 1307, of 187 B. C. ; Eph. Epigr. viii. 476, c. 135 B. C. ; C.I.L. i. 554 and

555, both of 130-129 B. C. &c.) *Polc*[*er*] (*ib.* i 552 of 132-131 B. C.). Priscian (i. p. 27. 33 H.) tells us that *colpa* was the O. Lat. form of *culpa*; and in the lines of Ennius about Servius Tullius (*Ann.* 337 M.) the corrupt reading of the MSS. *optimus* for *ultimus*, probably indicates the spelling *oltimus* (cf. Osc. últiümam) :

mortalem summum Fortuna repente
reddidit, ut summo regno famul oltimus esset.

On the spellings *volva* and *vulva*, Fem. of adj. *volvus from *volvo*, see Georges, *Lex. Wortf.* s. v. *Vulnus* is the pronunciation of Varro (*L. L.* iii. fr., p. 148 Wilm. vafer, velum, vinum, vomis, vulnus, where he gives examples of initial *v* followed by the various vowels of the alphabet). This *ol* may be I.-Eur. ĕl, e. g. *volt, vult* (§ 10).

(3) before *m* with labial : *umbo* for *ombo, like *umbīlĭcus* for *omb- (Gk. ὀμφαλός); the Greek (Thracian ?) ῥομφαία is *rumpĭa* in Ennius (A. xiv. fr. 8 M.) and Livy (xxxi. 39. 11). Perhaps also before *ms*, e. g. *ŭmĕrus* from *omso*- (O. Ind. ásạ-, Arm. us, Goth. ams, Umbr. *onso*-).

(4) before *ngu*: *unguo, unguen, unguentum* for *ongu- (O. Ind. añj-, 'to anoint'); *ungula*, like *unguis* (Gk. ὄνυξ) ; but *longus*, where the *g* is not velar (*gu*), retains the *o* (we find however *lun*[*gum*] beside *lon*[*gum*] in neighbouring inscrr., *C. I. L.* i. 1073). We have also *uncus* for *oncus (Gk. ὄγκος), (but *sesconciam C. I. L.* i. 1430, in a Cremona inscription), &c. On the occasional use of *u* for *o*, often for Greek *o*, before other consonant-groups, e. g. *turnus* beside *tornus*, from Greek τόρνος, O. Lat. *frundes* (see ch. ii. § 22). Some isolated cases of *ŭ* for accented *ŏ* have various explanations ; *hŭmus*, for *homus (cf. Gk. χθών), may take its *u* from the analogy of *hūmeo*, for the word (not common in the oldest writers ; *humi*, for example, not occurring till Terence, *Andr.* 726) seems to have been first used in the sense of moist ground, clay, e. g. Laevius ap. Prisc. i. p. 269. 7 H. humum humidum pedibus fodit ; Varr. *Men.* 531 B. in pavimento non audes facere laconam†, at in humu calceos facis elixos ; Enn. *Trag.* 396 R. cubitis pinsibant humum ; Pac. *Trag.* 351 R. tractate per aspera saxa et humum ; cf. Gracch. *Trag.* 3 mersit sequentis humidum plantas (MS. plantis) humum ; Priscian's 'old Latin *huminem*' (i. p. 27. 1 H.) may be an etymological spelling to suit a derivation from *humus*, like the spelling *colina*, adapted to the derivation from *colo* (Varro ap. Non. 55. 20 M.) ; 'Serv.' ad *Aen.* iii. 134) ; *fŭlĭca*, if for *fŏlĭca, either follows the analogy of *fūlīgo*, or shows the vowel of *fulca*, the form used by Furius Antias ap. Gell. xviii. 11. l. 4.

(5) in syllables unaccented under the later Accent-law : the 3 Plur. suffix -*ont* became -*unt* at the end of the third cent. B. C., though the old spelling was sometimes retained even later. On old inscriptions we have e. g. *dederont* (*C. I. L.* i. 181, from Picenum), *cosentiont* on a Scipio epitaph (i. 32) (so on the restored Columna Rostrata, *exfociont*, i. 195). Festus (244. 13 Th.) quotes *praed-opiont* (MS. *praedotiont*), in the sense of *praeoptant*, from the Carmen Saliare, and *nequinont*, an old 3 Pl. form of *nequeo*, from the *Odyssea* of Livius Andronicus (ap. Fest. 162. 24 Th. ; cf. Paul. Fest. 163. 14 Th.) :

pártim érrant, nequínont Graéciam redíre ;

the Nom. Sg. termination of Neuter ES-stems is -*os* on an old inscription, *opos* (*C. I. L.* i. 52, probably from Orvieto) (cf. *Uenos* on old mirrors, i. 57 and 58) ; the Acc. Sg. termination of O-stems is -*om* in the older period, e. g. *donom*, the Nom. Sg. is -*os* (see Index to *C. I. L.* i.), and this spelling remained after *u, v*,

e. g. *equos, arvom*, till the time of Quintilian, though the pronunciation may have been the *ŭ*-sound (see § 70). (On this reduction of *ŏ* to *ŭ* in unaccented syllables, see ch. iii. §§ 18, 26; another example is the verb *sum*, for **som*, with *u* for *o*, because of its usual unaccented character.) In late Latin, when *ŭ* and *ō* had come to have nearly, or altogether, the same sound, *o* is often written for *ŭ*, so that the older spelling seems to be revived (see ch. ii. § 29).

Ū, Ŭ.

§ 21. **Ū.** I.-Eur. ū is Latin *ū*, I.-Eur. **dhūmo-*, 'smoke,' from root dheu-, 'to move violently' (O. Ind. dhūmá-, Gk. θῡμός, passion, Lith. dúmai Pl., O. Sl. dymŭ), Lat. *fūmus*; I.-Eur. **mūs-*, 'a mouse' (O. Ind. mū́ṣ-, Gk. μῦς, Q. Engl. mūs, O. Sl. myšĭ), Lat. *mūs*. It is generally a grade of a eu-root as ī of an ei-root (§ 12). Latin *ū*, older *ou*, may represent also I.-Eur. eu or ou, e.g. *dūco*, older *douco* (see §§ 35, 41), Latin *ū*, older *oi*, *oe*, I.-Eur. oi, e.g. *cūra* (§ 38), and sometimes has arisen from *ŭ* by 'compensation,' e.g. *dūmus*, older *dŭsmo-* (Paul. Fest. 47. 20 Th.), a spelling retained in the proper name *Dusmius*; *dūmetum* for *dusm-*, in Virgil MSS. spelt *dummetum*, shows that *-ūm-* is equivalent to *-ŭmm-*. In the unaccented syllable *ū* may represent *au*, e.g. *dēfrūdo* from *fraudo*, *inclūdo* from *claudo* (ch. iii. § 18). On *fūr*, *cūr* for **fōr*, *quōr*, see § 16. I.-Eur. ū is in Umbr. and perhaps in some other dialects *i̭*, e.g. Umbr. *frif* 'fruges' Acc. Pl. (see von Planta, i. 129).

§ 22. Other examples of Lat. ū, I.-Eur. ū. Lat. *frūnisci* (Goth. brūkjan, 'to use,' Germ. brauchen, O. Engl. brūcan, Engl. to brook); *jūs*, broth (O. Ind. yūṣa-, Gk. ζύ-μη for *ζύσ-μη, leaven, Lith. júszė); *sūtus* (O. Ind. syūtá-, Gk. νεο-κάττυτος); *so-lūtus* (Hom. βουλῡτόν-δε).

§ 23. **Ŭ.** I.-Eur. ŭ, Lat *ŭ*, appears often in the weak grade of an eu-root, e.g. I.-Eur. **yŭgo-*, 'a yoke,' weak grade of yeug-, 'to join' (O. Ind. yŭgá-, Gk. ζυγόν, Goth. jŭk, O. Sl. igo for jŭgo), Lat. *jŭgum*; I.-Eur. lŭk-, weak grade of leuk-, 'to shine' (O. Ind. rŭc-, Gk. ἀμφι-λύκη, twilight), Lat. *lŭcerna*. I.-Eur. ŭ (Lat. *ŭ*) is also the weak grade of a wĕ-root, e.g. I.-Eur. **pĕruti*, 'last year' (Gk. πέρυσι), from **wetes-, 'year,' and similarly in the unaccented syllable Latin *ŭ* often appears for *uĕ*, e.g. *concutio* for **conquetio* from *quătio* (see ch. iii. § 25). Lat. *u* often represents I.-Eur. (and older Latin) ŏ; for an ŏ passed at the end of the third cent. B.C. into the sound *ŭ*, when in the unaccented syllable (unless saved by a preceding *v*, *u*), e.g. *donum* from earlier *donom*, but *equom* till the time of Quintilian; and even in the accented syllable *ŏ* came to assume a *u*-sound before certain consonant-groups, e.g. *culpa*, older *colpa*, *Fulvius*, older *Folvius* (see § 20). (On *equom*, *divom*, &c., see §§ 70, 135).

Lat. *ŭ* offered more resistance than *ă* to the usual transition of a short vowel in the open unaccented syllable to *ĭ* (earlier *ĕ*, and always before *r*), e.g. *sŏcer* (Gk. ἑκυρός) (ch. iii. § 18). Before *l* and labials it passed in open unaccented syllables (especially when the next syllable contained an *i* in hiatus) into the *ü*-sound, which ultimately was written and pronounced *ĭ*, e.g. *mănubiae, manibiae, manibus, dissupo, dissipo*. That it ever had the *ü*-sound, the sound of Greek *υ*, in the accented syllable of native Latin words is doubtful. [On (quid)lubet and (quid)libet, &c. see ch. ii. § 16]. Before a vowel in the unaccented syllable Latin *u* may represent I.-Eur. ew, ow, Lat. *ov*, e.g. *dēnuo* for *dē novo*, *ēluo* for *ē-lavo* (I.-Eur. *lŏwō) (ch. iii. § 24); before *l* and labials any short vowel, e.g. *occupo* from *cap-*, to take (ch. iii. § 18), and before any consonant-group Latin *ŏ*, e.g. *hŏmullus* for *homŏn-lo-* (see § 20). Final *-ŭ*, like other short vowels, normally became *ĕ*, and might be elided (ch. iii. §§ 37, 38).

A close relation exists in Latin, as in I.-Eur., between *ŭ* and *w*, vocalic and consonantal u. After *l* and *r* the vowel *ŭ* became a consonant in the second cent. B.C. in Latin, e.g. *lārva* (*lārua*, Plaut.), *arvum* (*ăruos*, *-a*, *-om* Plaut.), *mīlvus* (*mīluos*, Plaut.), *pelvis*, &c. (see ch. iii. § 48). For Latin *ŭ* (earlier *ŏ*), the parasitic, or svarabhaktic vowel, in *oculus* from *ŏc-lo-*, *speculum* from *spĕc-lo-*, *ōraculum* from *orā-clo-*, see ch. ii. § 154.

I.-Eur. *ŭ* is Umbro-Osc. u, e.g. Umbr. *subra* 'supra,' though sometimes we find *o* written in Umbr. [i.e. in the Lat. alph., for the native alphabet did not distinguish the O- and the U-sound (see ch. i. § 1)]. In Oscan we find iu after t, d, n (s?), e.g. tiurrí 'turrim,' Diumpaís 'Lumpis' ('to the Nymphs'), Niumsieís 'Numerii' Gen. Sg., an affection of u which resembles Boeot. τιούχα (Att. τύχη), or Engl. 'pure,' &c. (pronounced pi̯u-), (see von Planta, i. p. 122).

§ 24. **Lat. ŭ for I.-Eur. ŭ.** I.-Eur. -ŭ- in the U-stem suffix is Latin *ŭ* of *fructŭs, mănŭs*, &c.; the I.-Eur. preposition *ŭpŏ (O. Ind. úpa, Gk. ὕπο, O. Ir. fo for *wo, with p dropped between vowels, and u turned into w, Goth. uf,

§§ 24-26.] REPRESENTATIVES OF I.-EUR. DIPHTHONGS. 239

Engl. of-ten) is Latin *s-ub* (see ch. ix. § 52); the preposition *ŭpĕr, *upĕrĭ (O. Ind. upári, Gk. ὑπείρ, ὕπερ, O. Ir. for, from *wer, with suppression of p, Goth. ufar, Engl. over, o'er) is Latin *s-uper* (see ch. ix. § 53); I.-Eur. *snŭso-, 'daughter-in-law' (O. Ind. snušá-, Arm. nu, Gr. νυ(σ)ός, O. Engl. snoru, Germ. Schnur, O. Sl. snŭcha), is Lat. *nŭrus*; I.-Eur. *k̑lŭto-, 'famous,' from k̑leu-, 'to hear' (O. Ind. śrutá-, Gr. κλυτός, O. Ir. cloth, Gaul. Cluto-ida, O. H. Germ. Hlud-olf, Hlot-hari, from hari, 'army,' whence Lothair, &c.), is Lat. *in-clŭtus*, later *in-clŭtus*; I.-Eur. *rŭdhro-, 'red,' from the root reudh-, 'to be red' (O. Ind. rudhirá-, Gk. ἐρυθρός, O. Sl. rŭdrŭ) is Lat. *rŭber* ; Lat. *mŭsca* (the Romance forms prove *ŭ*), Gk. μυῖα for *μυσγα, Lith. musẽ ; Lat. *jŭvenis* (O. Ind. yúvan-), *jŭvencus* from I.-Eur. *yŭwn̥k̑o- (O. Ind. yuvašá-, Gk. Ὑάκ-ινθος, O. Ir. ōac, Welsh ieuanc, Gaul. Jovincillus, Goth. juggs for *juvunga-, O. Engl. geong) ; Lat. *fŭga* (Gk. φυγή) from root bheug-, 'to flee' (Gk. φεύγω) ; Lat. *urgeo* from urg-, the weak grade of the root werg-, 'to confine, press' (Gk. ἐ-(ϝ)έργω, Lat. *vergo*.)

§ 25. **Latin ŭ and Latin ŏ.** We have seen that Latin ŏ became *ŭ* when unaccented, and even in the accented syllable before certain consonant-groups, and that in late Latin *ŭ* and *ō* came to have the same sound and were often exchanged in spelling (see § 17 and ch. ii. § 29). Some doubtful cases may be discussed here. As *turbo* and *turba* (Gk. τύρβη, στυρβάζω) come from I.-Eur. turb-, from tŭr-, the weak grade of twĕr-, 'to twirl,' so I.-Eur. qᵘr̥-, ghᵘr̥-, the weak grades of qᵘĕr-, ghᵘĕr-, seem to appear in Latin as *cur-, fur*, e. g. *furnus*, an oven, from I.-Eur. ghᵘr̥no- (O. Sl. grŭnŭ, 'a kettle'), but *formus*, warm, from I.-Eur. ghᵘormo- (O. H. G. warm, Engl. warm). Whether Nonius, who derives *furnus* from *formus*, has any justification in spelling the word *fornus* (531. 24 M.) is uncertain ; but *fornax* has *o*, and Plautus *Epid*. 119 puns on *furno* (so the MSS.), and *foro*. *Curro* may then stand for *qᵘr̥so- from the root qᵘer- (cf. Lat. *querquĕrus*) ; *curtus* cannot be the same as Gk. καρτός, from the root *ker-* of Gk. κείρω, but must stand for *qᵘrto-, from a root qᵘer- ; *corpus* must represent *qᵘorpes-, not *qᵘrpes- (cf. O. Ind. kŕp-) ; *ursus* may be a loanword (Lucanian, according to Varro, *L. L.* v. 100), or may owe its *u* to a velar guttural -rqᵘ- ; *ŭrceus* cannot be connected with *ōrca* ; the spelling *forcillis* in MSS. of Catullus (cv. 2) must be late, if the word is connected with Hesychius' φουρκορ, φυρκος, which point to *u* (Cyprian φορκες = χάρακες shows dialectal *o* for *v*) ; *urbs* (cf. Mars. *en urbid* ' in urbe') cannot be connected with *orbs*, so that there is no etymological appropriateness in the play on these words which is often found in the later poets (e. g. Rutil. i. 66).

§ 26. **The Diphthongs.** In its treatment of the diphthongs *ai, au, ei*, [(1) I.-Eur. ei and in Latin also, (2) I.-Eur. ai (oi ?) in the post-tonic syllable, (3) I.-Eur. ai, oi in the final syllable], *oi, ou*, [(1) I.-Eur. eu, (2) I.-Eur. ou], Latin stands halfway between Oscan an Umbrian. In Oscan they are all retained intact, except that the *i*-element has sunk to an *e*-sound[1]. In Umbrian they are all reduced to simple sounds, e.g. Umbr.

---

[1] Perhaps both in Oscan and Latin the second element of ai, &c. was a sound between open i and e, just as in German and English.

dēvo-, Osc. deívo-, 'god'; Umbrian tōro-, Osc. ταυρο-, bull; Umbr. *tōto*, Osc. τωFτο, people, community [I.-Eur. *teutā-, Goth. þiuda, whence some derive 'Teuton,' O. Ir. tuath, Gaul. Teuto-bōdiāci, W. tud (in Gaelic tuath is used for 'the country-people,' 'the tenantry'), Lith. tauta], (see von Planta, i. p. 137). In the Latin of Cicero's time *ae* (from *ai*) and *au* are the only survivors; and even they tend in rustic or colloquial speech to single sounds, *ē*, *ō*, e.g. *pretor*, *plostrum*. Diphthongs whose two elements had affinity of sound, such as ei, ou, are naturally the first to be simplified; ei, for example, both in Greek and in the Teutonic languages, passed early into a long *ī*-sound. The oldest Latin inscriptions offer with great fidelity *ei* for I.-Eur. ei, as also for the *ei* to which I.-Eur. ai, oi, when unaccented, were reduced. Thus on the S. C. de Bacchanalibus of 186 B.C. (*C.I.L.* i. 196) we have *deicerent* (I.-Eur. ei), *inceideretis* (I.-Eur. post-tonic ai), *foideratei* (I.-Eur. final -oi). But this diphthong soon became identical in pronunciation with the long *i*-vowel, so that spelling-reformers like Accius and Lucilius used *i* and *ei* for this long *i*-sound without sufficient regard to the past history of the sound (see ch. i. § 9), and the practice grew up of using *ei* to indicate the long vowel-sound, *i* to indicate the short. *Ou* is also sometimes used for Latin *ū* (I.-Eur. oi), e.g. *couraverunt* (*C.I.L.* i. 1419, from Picenum), though not at all to the same extent as *ei* for *ī*. *Ou* seems to have been reduced to a simple sound at the end of the third century B.C. *Ai* became *ae* a little later. Towards the end of the second cent. B.C. we find the spelling *ae* established in use, with an occasional resort at the transition period to a spelling *aei*; but the original spelling (not pronunciation) was again brought into fashion in the reign of Claudius and is found occasionally on epitaphs even of the late Empire. On the diphthongal sound of *ae* (Germ. Kaiser is evidence of this sound in Lat. *Caesar*), *au*, see ch. ii. § 32.

Oi passed (through *oe*) into *ū* at the beginning of the second cent. B.C., though *oi*, and afterwards *oe*, were long retained on official inscriptions in phrases like *faciundum coiraverunt* (*coeraverunt*), e.g. *C.I.L.* i. 567 (Capua) of 106 B.C.: *murum et pluteum faciund. coeravere*, where the spelling *murum* (older *moerum*, *moirom*) shows that the pronunciation was *ū*, not *oe*, and in some words of the official or legal style like *poena, foedus*.

The long diphthongs are not common in I.-Eur., so that we have hardly sufficient material from which to discover their history in Latin. In the Veda, the oldest literature of India, we see a tendency to use final -*ā* (I.-Eur. -ō) before a consonant initial, final -*āu* (I.-Eur. -ōu) before a vowel initial (e.g. dēvā́ and dēvāu in Dual of devá-, I.-Eur. *deivo-, 'god'); and the development of ēi and ōu in roots and suffixes in the various I.-Eur. languages suggests that doublets of this sort, ēi and ē, ōu and ō, already existed in the case of these two diphthongs of kindred elements in what is called 'the Indo-European period.' Long diphthongs, composed of sounds not so nearly allied as ē and i, ō and u, may have taken on Latin soil a different course of development, according as they were final or not. When final, the second element may have been suppressed (probably after passing through the doublet-stage), just as in later times a short final vowel has been suppressed after a long syllable in words like *exemplār(e)*, *nēv(e)*. When followed by a consonant the long element must have been shortened, by the rule that any long vowel is shortened before y, w, n, m, l, r, &c. followed by a consonant, so that āi (āy) would pass to the ordinary diphthong-sound *ai*, āu (āw) to *au*, ēu to *eu*, ōi to *oi*; just as we have *vĕntus* from *wēnt- (root wē-, 'to blow,' Gk. ἄημι) (see below, § 45).

§ 27. **AI.** I.-Eur. ai is Lat. *ae* (older *ai*), e.g. the I.-Eur. root aiwĕ-, 'time, life' (Gk. αἰών, ἀεί for *αἰϝε(σ)ι, with Ion. Att. ᾱ for αιϝ-, as in ἐλάᾱ for *ἐλαιϝᾱ, O. Ir. ais, aes, Goth. aivs, O. Engl. ǣ), appears in Latin *aevum*; I.-Eur. aidh-, 'to burn,' (O. Ind. édhas-, 'firewood,' Gk. αἴθω, O. Ir. aid, aed, 'fire,' O. H. G. eit, 'pyre,' O. Engl. ād), in Latin *aedes*, lit. 'where the fire is kept up,' *aestus*. In the last root I.-Eur. ai is the weak grade of ayĕ, thus aidh- of ayĕdh- (aye- is seen in I.-Eur. *ayes-, 'metal, gleaming metal'), and in the first of āi (§ 45) (cf. O. Ind. ā́yu-). In the unaccented syllable *ae* became *ī*, e.g. *inquīro*, *occīdo* from *quaero*, *caedo* (see ch. iii. § 18), or rather *ai* became *ei*, then *ī*, e.g. *inceideretis* on the S. C. de Bacch.; and in the final syllable, e.g. *tŭtŭdī* (O. Ind. tutudé) with the 1 Sg. Perf. Middle ending -ai or -*ai* (ch. viii. § 76). On rustic and colloquial *e* for *ae*, and on the late Latin confusion of *ae, e, oe* (that is, *oe* which had been restored, § 38), see ch. ii. §§ 41, 44. A spurious diphthong *ai* is found in the verb *aio* (for **ahio*, § 116), *ain* (for **aisne*), *aibat* (dissyllabic),&c.

§ 28. I.-Eur. ai, Lat. ae (ai). Lat. *caedo* from I.-Eur. root skaidh- (Goth. skaidan, O. Engl. scādan, Engl. water-shed, Lith. skĕ́džiu, 'I separate'); Lat. *scaevus* (Gk. σκαι(ϝ)ός); Lat. *laevus* (Gk. λαι(ϝ)ός, O. Sl. lĕvŭ); Lat. *caecus* from I.-Eur. **kaiko-*, 'blind' (O. Ir. caech, with another sense, 'empty,' cf. Gael. caoch-ag, 'a nut without a kernel,' Goth. haihs; in Gk. κοικύλλω, 'to gape about,' the *ai* has become *oi*, through the assimilating influence of the accented *v*); Lat. *haereo* from I.-Eur. root ghais- (Lith. gaīszti, 'to tarry'; Goth. us-gaisjan, 'to frighten,' lit. 'cause to hesitate,' Engl. gaze); Lat. *haedus* (Goth. gaits, Engl. goat); Lat. *lēvir* from I.-Eur. **daiwer-*, O. Ind. dēvár-, Arm. taigr, Gk. δāήρ, O. H. G. zeihhur, O. Eng. tācor, Lith. dēverìs, O. Sl. dĕverï) is a late Latin spelling for *laevir*, the *i* being due to the analogy of *vir*.

§ 29. AI, AE on Inscriptions. We have *ae* on the S. C. Bacch. (*C.I.L.* i. 196) of 186 B. C. in *aedem* (along with *aiquom, tabelai, datai*, &c.); *Aemilius* on three inscriptions of 187 B. C. (i. 535-7), but *Aimilius* (*C. I. L.* ii. 5041) of 189 B. C.; *aetate* on a Scipio epitaph of c. 130 B. C. (i. 34), (along with *quairatis*); *quaestor, quaero, praetor* are established spellings in the Lex Bantina of 133-118 B. C. (i. 197), the Lex Repetundarum of 123-122 B. C. (i. 198), &c. The spelling *aei*, which we find once or twice towards the end of the second cent. B. C., *conquaeisivei* (in the post-tonic syllable under the older Accent Law) (i. 551, of 132 B. C.), *Caeicilius* (i. 547 b., 'of 141 or 116 B. C.,' Momms., and i. 1487, from Majorca), *Caeician[us]* [i. 378, on a coin with an alphabet A-X, so older than the introduction of Y, Z (ch. i. § 2)], *Caeidia* (ix. 3087, from Sulmo), seems to mark the transition stage. Often *ai* and *ae* are found side by side, e. g. *praitores aere Martio emeru* (i. 1148, from Cora); *aetatei* and *saip[is]ume* on the dedicatory inscription of the Faliscan 'collegium cocorum' (Zvet. *I. I. I.* 72 a). The spelling *Caisar*, &c. is frequent on inscriptions of Claudius' reign, when antiquarian lore was in fashion (e. g. *C. I. L.* vi. 353), and we find on epitaphs of the late Empire *Valeriai* (Rossi, i. 113, of 352 A.D.), *quai* and *filiai* (Rossi, i. 410, of 393 A.D.), &c. *E* is not regularly exchanged with *ae* till the fourth cent. A. D. on inscriptions (Seelmann, *Ausspr. Lat.* p. 225), but in dialectal inscrr. it is of course much earlier, e. g. *cedre* for *caedere* on an old inscr. of the Umbrian territory (*C. I. L.* xi. 4766), and in plebeian from the first cent. A. D. (Hammer, *Loc. Verbr.* p. 11). The use of *ai, ae* for *ā* is a feature of inscriptions of the Etruscan country (see *Mem. Ist. Lombard.* 1892), e. g. *Painsscos* on a Praenestine mirror (*C. I. L.* xiv. 4098) [cf. *Saeturni* on a Praenestine vase (i. 48), and perhaps Lat. *Aesculāpius* for Ἀσκλᾱπιός]; we have *ei* in *queistores* (i. 183, Marsic).

§ 30. AU. I.-Eur. au is Latin *au*, which in the unaccented syllable became *ŭ* (see ch. iii. § 18), and in the accented syllable was in dialectal Latin *ō* (e. g. Plautus' Umbrian name was *Plotus* 'splay-foot,' Paul. Fest. 305. 7 Th.). Thus the I.-Eur. root aug-, indicating 'growth' or 'strength,' a weak grade of the root aweg- of Gk. ἀ(ϝ)έξω (O. Ind. ójas-, Goth. aukan, 'to multiply,' Engl.

eke vb., Lith. áugu, 'I grow,' Gk. αὔξω, αὐξάνω) appears in Latin *aug-eo, augus-tus*; the I.-Eur. particle *au [Gk. αὖ, αὖ-τε, αὖ-τις, Goth. au-k, 'also' (with -k like Gr. γε), O. Engl. ēac, Eng. eke advb.], in Latin *au-t* (Osc. avti, Umbr. *ote*), *au-tem* (Osc. avt). This I.-Eur. *au is perhaps similarly the weak grade of *a-we, (see ch. x. § 4). Lat. *au* represents the weak grade of an I.-Eur. ōu-root in *ausculum* (Plaut.) beside *ōs* from I.-Eur. *ōus (cf. *cătus* beside *cōs*, § 54).

§ 31. Other examples. Lat. *paucus* (Goth. favai Pl., Engl. few) ; Lat. *auröra* for *ausōsa* (Gk. αὔριον for *αὔσριον, ἄγχ-αυρος νύξ Apoll. Rhod., 'nearing the dawn,' Lith. ausz-rà, O. Scand. austr, O. H. G. ōstar, Engl. east) from I.-Eur. aus-, a weak grade of ăwĕs-, 'to gleam' (cf. Gk. ἠώς for *ἀϝως), whence *auso-, 'gold' (Lat. *aurum*, Lith. áuksas); Lat. *auris* for *ausis, aus-culto* (O. Ir. au, a Neuter S-stem, Goth. ausō, an N-stem, Lith. ausìs) from I.-Eur. *aus-, a weak grade of *ăwĕs- [cf. Gk. αἴω (ᾄω), I perceive ; but οὖς is a Greek development of the high grade *ōus ; cf. O. Ind. āvís, 'openly']. Lat. *au-*, away, as in *au-fero, au-fugio* (Pruss. au- of au-mū-sna-n Acc., 'washing off' ; O. Sl. u- of u-myti, 'to wash off') from I.-Eur. *au, a weak grade of *awe (*awo ?) (O. Ind. áva, 'away,' ava-bhṛ-, 'aufero'). It is often difficult to distinguish this Lat. *au*, representing I.-Eur. au (a reduction of I.-Eur. ăwĕ) from Lat. *au*, a reduction of Lat. *ăvĕ, ăvĭ,* e. g. *audeo* from *avidus*. (Other examples in ch. iii. § 16. 9.) On the occasional appearance of *ū* for *au* in the accented syllable, e. g. *sed fraude* 'sine fraude' in the Lex Repetundarum, post-class. *cludo*, and on the plebeian and dialectal reduction of *au* to *ō*, e. g. *plostrum, Clodius*, see ch. ii. §§ 36-37.

§ 32. EI. I.-Eur. ei was in Old Latin *ei*; but this diphthong became identical with the sound of long *i*, so that in inscriptions from the latter part of the second century B.C. the symbol *ei* is used not only for I.-Eur. ei, but also for I.-Eur. ī, and some spelling reformers proposed to reserve the letter I for short *i*, and the diphthong-symbol EI for long *i* (see ch. i. § 9). In Oscan, however, the diphthong is preserved. In Latin it is used in the interjection *hei, ei*, from which comes the verb *ejŭlo*. Instances of I.-Eur. ei, Latin *ei* or *i*, are: I.-Eur. deik-, 'to show, say' (Gk. δείκ-νῡμι, Goth. ga-teiha, 'I declare'), Lat. *dīco*, O. Lat. *deico*, Osc. *deicum* Inf.; I.-Eur. bheidh-, 'to believe, trust' (Gr. πείθομαι), Lat. *fīdo*, O. Lat. *feido*. Before a vowel *ei, ej* became *e* in Latin, e. g. *eo* from I.-Eur. ei-, 'to go,' both in the accented (§ 63), and in the unaccented syllable (ch. iii. § 24). O. Lat. *ei*, class. *ī*, may represent other I-diphthongs in the final or unaccented syllables, e. g. in *tŭtŭdī* Perf. (O. Ind. tutudé), I.-Eur. -ai or -ai (ch. viii. § 76); in *pŏpŭlī* Nom. Pl. (oldest Lat. *poploe*),

R 2

244   THE LATIN LANGUAGE.   [Chap. IV.

I.-Eur. -oi; in *con-cīdo* from *caedo*, older *caido*, I.-Eur. ai. The older spelling of all these words shows *-ei, tutudei, pop(u)lei, conceido*, sometimes *e*, e.g. *ploirume* 'plurimi,' Nom. Pl., on a Scipio epitaph (*C. I. L.* i. 32). Greek ει before a vowel was written *ē*, e.g. *Alexandrēa, Dārēus* (shortened to *ĕ*, e.g. *balnĕum*), later *ī*, e.g. *Alexandrīa* (shortened to *ĭ*) (cf. ch. ii. § 143).

§ 33. Other examples of I.-Eur. ei. I.-Eur. *ei-ti, 3 Sg. Pres. Ind. of ei-, 'to go' (O. Ind. éti, Gk. εἶσι, Lith. eĩti, eĩt), Lat. *it* (with *ī* in Old Latin, but class. *ĭ*, a shortening produced in the course of the second cent. B.C. by the influence of the final *-t*, ch. iii. § 49); I.-Eur. *deiwo-, 'god' (O. Ind. dĕvá-, Lith. dĕvas, Ir. día, Gaul. Δειονονα, W. dwy-fol, 'divine,' O. Engl. Tīwes-dæg, 'Tuesday'; but Gk. δῖος is for *διϝιος, like O. Ind. divyá-), Lat. *dīvus*, on the Dvenos inscription *deiuo-*. When *ŏ* of the final syllable was weakened to *ŭ, deivos* became **deius* (for **deivus*, the *v* being absorbed by the following *u*, § 70), *deivom* became **deium*, which passed into *de(y)us, de(y)um* as **ei-um*, Acc. M. of *is*, into *e(y)-um*, **ei-o* 1 Sg. into *e(y)o*, so that the word would be declined *deus, deivei, deivō, deum*, &c.; from this variation arose the 'doublets' *dīvus, divi, divo, divum*, &c., and *deus, dei, deo, deum*, &c. (cf. *C. I. L.* i. 632 sei deo sei deivae); some grammarians of Varro's time proposed to restrict *dīvus* to the sense of a mortal made a god (so later *divus Augustus*), but Varro contested the accuracy of this usage, showing that in old times *divus* was the word for any god (Varro, *L. L.* iv. fr., p. 150 Wilm.; cf. Serv. ad *Aen.* xii. 139 diva deam, &c.). *Reus* (cf. *rīvālis*, older *reiv-*), *seu* (cf. *sīvĕ*, older *seive*) are to be similarly explained, though some prefer to suppose that the prior stages of all three words were **dĕus, *rĕus, *sĕu* (like *Alexandrēa, Darēus*, &c.), and quote *lēvis* as an example of the passage of *ei* before *v* into *e* (cf. Gk. λεῖ(ϝ)ος) (von Planta, *Osk.-Umbr. Dial.* i. p. 145). *Neu, ceu* are most naturally explained as shortenings from **nēu* (cf. *nēve*), **cēu* (cf. Gk. κῇ, Lat. *cē-teri*, *B. B.* xv. 313), though they also admit of being referred to **nei-u* (from O. Lat. *nei, ni*, used in the sense of class. *nē*), and from a Locative, either Demonstr. **cei* (ch. vii. § 15) or Relative *quei, qui* (ch. vii. § 23)., On *meio* see ch. viii. § 6, *ejus* ch. vii. § 13, *peior* below § 116.

§ 34. EI and I in Inscriptions, &c. On the S. C. de Bacchanalibus of 186 B.C. (*C. I. L.* i. 196) we have *deicerent* (I.-Eur. ei), *inceideretis* (I.-Eur. post-tonic ai), *foideratei* (I.-Eur. final -oi). But we have *ei* employed merely to indicate long *i* in *audeire* of the Lex Repetundarum of 123-122 B.C. (i. 198); *ameicitiam* of the Lex Agraria of 111 B.C. (i. 200); *ameicorum, vēneire* (i. 203, of 78 B.C.); *erceiscunda deividunda* and *feient* of the Lex Rubria of 49 B.C. (i. 205); *esureis* on a leaden bullet used at the siege of Perusia with the cruel message carved on it, *esureis et me celas* (i. 692); *veivos* (i. 1256), &c.; and this seems to be the function of *ei* in the Plautine text represented by the Codex Ambrosianus (see Index to Studemund's Apograph, p. 504). Even as early as the end of the third cent. B.C. we have *opeinod deuincam ted* on a Praenestine mirror with a representation of a gaming-table (*Rendic. Accad. Lincei*, v. p. 253, 1889). The transition stage from *ei* to *i* is perhaps marked by the spelling *e* in *ploirume* (Nom. Pl.) on a Scipio epitaph of the end of the third cent. B.C. (*C. I. L.* i. 32), *conpromesise* on the S. C.

Bacch. of 186 B. C. (i. 196; cf. *ameiserunt*, i. 204), though this spelling is often nothing but a dialectal variety, e. g. *uecos* (Lat. *vei-*, *vīcus*) on an inscription from the Marsic territory (i. 183) (cf. Umbr. devo-, 'god,' Lat. *dīvo-*). Now and then we find *ei* written for a short vowel, as in *inpeirator* on the inscription of Aem. Paulus Macedonicus, from Spain (*C. I. L.* ii. 5041, of 189 B. C.), *leiteras* (see ch. ii. § 130), and *seine* on the Lex Repetundarum (i. 198); so in the Ambrosian Palimpsest of Plautus, *ibeis*, *Cas.* 92; *curabeis*, *Merc.* 526. And *ei* appears occasionally even for the *ē*-sound, as in *pleib-*, in an old inscription found between Rome and Ostia (*Eph. Epigr.* i. 3), in *leigibus* on a Praenestine cippus of erratic orthography (*pro sed sueq* for *pro se suisque*, &c.) (*C. I. L.* xiv. 2892), and in *decreivit* on the Spanish inscription of 189 B.C., just mentioned (*C. I. L.* ii. 5041) (see ch. ii. § 11). The Dative forms in *-e* on old inscriptions (e. g. *C. I. L.* i. 1110 Iunone Seispitei Matri) are best explained as graphical varieties of the Dat. in *-ei*, class. *-ī* (see ch. vi. § 28), and similarly the 3 Sg. Perf. Act. forms in *-ed*, *-et*, e. g. *fefaced* on the Praenestine fibula, *dedet* (beside *cepit*) on a Scipio epitaph (*C. I. L.* i. 32), as graphical varieties of *-eit* (e.g. *probaveit* beside *coeravit*, i. 600) (see ch. viii. § 70). The Plautine spelling must have been *mendīco-*, *eira* to judge from the remarks in *Rud.* 1305 that *mendicus* has 'one letter more' than *medicus*, and in *Truc.* 262 that *comprime sis eiram* becomes *comprime sis eram* by 'taking away a single letter.' (Cf. Early Greek E for EI).

§ 35. **EU.** This diphthong has been merged in *ou* in most languages; but Greek, with ευ and ου, and Gothic, with iu and au, will serve as criteria. We find *eu* in Latin in the interjections *heu* (cf. Gk. φεῦ), *eheu*, *heus*; the pronoun *neuter* [a trisyllable (ch. ii. § 32), from *nĕ* and *uter*, with accent on the *ne*, whereas in *neutiquam*, pronounced *nŭtiquam* (or *nyŭtiquam*, ch. ii. § 149), *ne* being unaccented, was elided]; the conjunction *neu*, a byform of *nēvĕ*, *seu*, a byform of *sīve* (older *seive*), *ceu* from **cē-ve* or **cei-ve* (§ 33). (On the pronunciation of *eu* in these words and in Latinized Greek words, like *Orpheus*, see ch. ii. §§ 32, 46.) *Eu* is assigned to the Carmen Saliare on the strength of the quotations *Leucesie* (Ter. Scaur. 28. 11 K.), and *cozeulodorieso* of Varro, *L. L.* vii. 26 (perhaps *O Zeu*, &c., ch. ii. § 5), but whether rightly or not is a matter of doubt. (See *Rhein. Mus.* xxxiv. 1 on Latin *eu*.)

Examples of I.-Eur. eu, Latin *ū* (O. Lat. *ou*) are: Lat. *dūcere* (Goth. tiuhan, O. Engl. tēon, Germ. ziehen); Lat. *jūgeribus* Abl. Pl. from **jūgus* (Gk. ζεῦγος); Lat. *ūro* (Gk. εὕω for **εὔhω*). The Greek Πολυδεύκης is in O. Lat. **Pollouces*, written in the orthography of the early Praenestine inscriptions *Poloces* (*C. I. L.* i. 55), and *Polouces* (xiv. 4094), then *Polluces* (so the MSS. in Plaut. *Bacch.* 894; cf. Varro, *L. L.* v. 73 in latinis litteris veteribus nomen quod est, inscribitur ut Πολυδεύκης, 'Polluces,' non ut nunc, Pollux).

Before a vowel *eu (ev)* from I.-Eur. ew similarly became *ov* in the accented syllable, e. g. *nŏvus* from I.-Eur. *něwo- (see § 10), and in the unaccented was reduced to *u*, e. g. *dēnŭō* (see ch. iii. § 24, and for other examples Solmsen, *Stud. Lat. Lautg.* p. 128); in *cloāca*, &c. *v* has been dropped before the accent (ch. ii. § 53), leaving *o*.

§ 36. Other examples of I.-Eur. eu. *Jūpiter*, in the usual Latin spelling *Jŭppiter* (ch. ii. § 130), may have been originally a vocative like Gk. Ζεῦ πάτερ. (Can the fragment of the Carmen Saliare quoted above from Varro have *O Zeu* with *Z* for the sound *dy-*, as in Oscan inscriptions written in Roman characters we find *zicolo-* as the Diminutive of the word for 'day,' like Latin *diēcŭla* ?).

§ 37. OU, U in Inscriptions. The diphthong was reduced very early to a simple sound, as is natural where the two elements of the diphthong have so close affinity as *o* and *u*. We have *ū* for *ou* (I.-Eur. eu) in the name *Lucius* in two of the oldest Scipio epitaphs (*C. I. L.* i. 32 *Luciom* ; i. 30 *Lucius* with *Loucanam*, and *abdoucit*), not later than 200 B. C. ; *deducundae*, 181 B. C. (i. 538) ; *Lucius* in a dedicatory inscription of the consul Mummius, 146 B. C. (i. 542) ; *luuci* and *iurarint* (with *iouranto, ioudicetur, ioudex*, &c.) in the Lex Bantina of 133-118 B. C. (i. 197) ; *iurato, iudicibus, duco* (with *ioudicium, ioudicatio, ious*) on the Lex Repetundarum of 123-122 B. C. (i. 198), while the spelling with *ou* is entirely discarded in the Lex Cornelia of 81 B. C. (i. 202, with *iuus, iure*, &c.). Now and then *ou* occurs for a short vowel, e. g. *ioubeatis* (beside *iousiset*) in the S. C. Bacch. (i. 196) (but see ch. viii. § 29), *proboum* on old coins (i. 16), *Laoumeda* on an old Praenestine vase (xiv. 4108, or *Lad-* ?), possibly to represent the transition-sound between *ŏ* and *ŭ*, or in imitation of the Greek orthography, in which *ov* represented the u-sound, *v* the ü-sound. *Ou* is sometimes used for *ū* (I.-Eur. oi), e. g. *couraverunt* (i. 1419, from Picenum), *plourume* (with *Cloul*[ī] for *Cloelius*, i. 1297, from near Amiternum), though not at all to the same extent as *ei* for *ī*. (On *ou* for I.-Eur. ou, see § 41.) The spelling *o* for *ou* (I.-Eur. eu) is dialectal, e. g. *Poloces* and *Losna* on a Praenestine mirror (i. 55) (cf. Umbr. toro- for Latin *tauro-*, bull). On Latin inscriptions *o* occurs for I.-Eur. ou, and for the new *ou*-diphthong, which arose by syncope in words like *nov(e)ntius, cov(e)ntio*, but not for I.-Eur. eu or ū. The spellings *poblico-*, *puplo-*, &c. (see index to *C. I. L.* i.), are due to confusion of the two radically different words *pūbes* and *pŏp(u)lus*.

§ 38. OI. I.-Eur. oi was *oi* till the second century, then came to be written *oe*, and finally passed into the sound *ū*, though *oe* was still written in some words which belonged to legal or official diction, e.g. *foedus*, a treaty, *poena* (but *punio*), *Poenus*, *moenia* (but *munio*), *ŏboedio*, in the poetic words *foedus*, foul, *ămoenus*, and in the family name *Cloelius*. Thus I.-Eur. *oino-, 'one' (cf. *oiwo-, Gk. οἶος, 'alone') (Gk. οἴνη, the ace, O. Ir. oen, W. un, Goth. ains, O. Engl. ān, Engl. one, an, a, Pruss. ains, Lith. vénas, O. Sl. inŭ; in Greek the numeral-root used was I.-Eur. sem- of Lat. *sĕmel*, &c., εἷς for *sem-s, μία for *σμια, ἕν for *sem), Lat. *ūnus*, older *oenus, oino-*. I.-Eur. oi is a grade of an ei-root, often seen in the Perfect Tense or in a derivative noun, e.g. woid- in the Perfect of weid-, 'to know' (Gk. οἶδα and πέποιθα from πείθω, I.-Eur. bheidh-, Lat. *fīdo, feido*), *qʰoinā-, 'an assessment, fine,' from qʰei-,' 'to value, care for' (Gk. ποινή, from τείω, often written τίω, borrowed by the Romans, *poena*, Zend. kaęnā-, O. Sl. cěna, the k and c in these two examples indicating oi not ei) and similarly in Latin, e.g. *foedus*, a treaty, from *feido*, *fīdo*, just as ŏ appears in the similar grade of ĕ-roots, in *pondus* from *pendo*. After initial v- Latin oi became ei, as ŏ became ĕ in *vorsus, versus*, &c. (§ 10), e.g. *vīdi* in older spelling *veidei*, from I.-Eur. *woidai (-ai), Perf. Mid. (O. Sl. vědě; cf. Gk. οἶδα, Goth. wait, O. Engl. wāt, Engl. wot).

In the unaccented syllable oi became ei, class. ī in the nautical term *anquīna*, a truss, a loanword from the Greek (ἀγκοίνη), perhaps adapted to Latin nouns in *-īna* (Non. 536. 5 M. anquinae vincla quibus antennae tenentur), but in most cases was as resistive of weakening as o (ch. iii. § 18), e. g. *sē-curus* from *cura*, older *coira, impunis* (*impoene* Cato *frag.* p. 37. 21 Jord.) from *poena* (cf. *punio*); in the final syllable *ei, ī* is regular, e.g. Nom. Pl. *populi*, earlier *pop(u)lei*, from a still earlier *poploe*. (Fest. 244. 24 Th. quotes from the Carmen Saliare *pilumnoe poploe*, a designation of the Romans 'velut pilis uti assueti.') A spurious diphthong *oi, oe*, class. *ū*, has arisen through composition in *coepi* (older *cöepi*), *coetus* for *co-itus*, and through loss of v before the accent in *Julius*, older *Iuilio-* from **Io(v)illius* (§ 43) (cf. *Cloelius*, older *Cluilius*, from the root *klew-, 'to be heard, famous'). On *cui* from *quoi*, see ch. vii. § 25, and on *nōn* from *noen(um)*, ch. x. § 18.

§ 39. **Other examples of I.-Eur. oi.** Lat. *mūnus*, Pl. *mūnera*, *mūne*, Pl. *moenia, mūnia, mūnicīpium, com-mūnis, im-mūnis*, O. Lat. *moini-cipio-, comoinem* (*C. I. L.* i. 196, of 186 B. C.) (Goth. ga-mains, Germ. ge-mein, 'common,' Lith. maĩnas, 'exchange,' O. Ir. moini, maini, 'gifts'), and from the same root *mūto*, to exchange, *mūtuus*, lent (Sicil. Gk. μοῖτος, requital, Goth. maiþms, 'a gift,' Lett. meetōt, 'to exchange'); Lat. *ūtor*, O. Lat. *oit-ile* (*C. I. L.* i. 201. 9), *oeti* (i. 603. 6. 8), &c. (cf. Mart. Cap. iii. 236 'oisus' etiam dicitur; sic enim veteres usum dixere) seem to show, like Gk. οἶτος, fate, 'portion,' the o-grade of a root eit-, seen perhaps in Osc. eítiuvā-, 'money,' for *eitu-; *cūnae* shows the o-grade of the root k̂ei-, 'to lie' (Gk. κεῖ-μαι; cf. κοίτη).

§ 40. **OI, OE, U on Inscriptions.** *Oi* is reduced to *ū* in a Scipio epitaph of the beginning of the second cent. B. C. (*C. I. L.* i. 33) with *utier*; so *usura* in one of Mummius' tithe-dedications to Hercules (i. 542) of 146 B. C.; *muru* Acc. on a Capua inscription of c. 135 B. C. (*Eph. Epigr.* viii. 476) ; *procurandae* (with *oinā* and *moinicipieis*) on the Lex Agraria of 111 B. C. (*C. I. L.* i. 200). But the spelling *oi*, and after it the spelling *oe*, long continued to be used, especially in such phrases as *faciundum coiraverunt* (*coeraverunt*) in magisterial inscriptions (e. g. i. 566, of 106 B. C. *coiravere* and *loid*[*os*] ; i. 600, of 62 B. C. *coeravit* ; i. 617, of 51 B. C. *coeraver.*) ; and Cicero in the laws which he draws up for his ideal state seems to think that the official style demands the spelling *oe* (e. g. *ploeres, Legg.* iii. 3. 6 ; *oenus, ib.* iii. 3. 9 ; *coerari* and *oesus, ib.* iii. 4. 10), though in the Lex Julia Municipalis of 45 B. C. (*C. I. L.* i. 206) we have regularly *curo, utor, municipium* (once *foidere*), and similarly on the Lex Rubria of 49 B. C. (i. 205), *ludus* (not *loedus*), the form used in the Comm. Lud. Saec. and the Mon. Anc., both of Augustus' reign, though Virgil MSS. often show *moerus* for *murus* (see Ribbeck's *Index*). The traditional nature of this spelling, even in the second cent. B. C., is seen from the occurrence of spellings like *murus* side by side with *coeraverunt*, &c., e. g. i. 567, of 106 B. C., *murum . . . coeravere . . . loedos*; i. 568, of 104 B. C., *murum . . . coiraver-* ; *Eph. Epigr.* viii. 460, of 108 B. C., *murum . . . coiraverunt*. Examples from the older literature are, *oenigenos* 'unigenitos' Paul. Fest. 225. 2 Th. ; *oenus* Plaut. *Truc.* 104 (B.) ; *proilio Men.* 186 (P.) ; *moenis*, obliging, quoted by Nonius 23. 9 M. from Pacuvius ; *moerus* Accius *Trag.* 347 R. ; *moenio* in the Ambrosian Palimpsest of Plautus (see Index to Studemund's Apograph); 'loebesum' et 'loebertatem' antiqui dicebant liberum et libertatem Paul. Fest. 86. 30 Th. (*Loebasius* is given as the Sabine name for Liber by Serv. ad *Georg.* i. 7 quamvis Sabini Cererem Pandam appellent, Liberum Loebasium ; cf. Gl. Plac. 80. 22 G.). This *oe* seems to have represented to the Romans a long *ü*-sound, the sound, in fact, of Greek $\bar{v}$; and the earlier instances of *u* for I.-Eur. oi probably indicate this sound. Plautus (*Bacch.* 129) puns on *Lydus* (Gk. Λῡδός) and *ludus* :

non ómnis aetas, Lýde, ludo cónuenit ;

and *oe* is often used to express Gk. $\bar{v}$, e. g. *goerus, coloephia* (ch. ii. § 28).

§ 41. OU. I.-Eur. ou before a vowel (ow) became, as we saw (§ 19), first *ov* in Latin, then in the second century B. C. *av*, which in the unaccented syll. fell to *u*, e. g. *ēluo* (ch. iii. § 24). For I.-Eur. ou before a consonant we find sometimes *ō*, sometimes *ū*. Occasionally both these spellings occur for the same word. Thus I.-Eur. **roudho-*, 'red' (Goth. rauþs), is Latin *rōbus, rōb-īgo* [the form *rubigo* (with *ū* like *rufus*, or with *ŭ* like *ruber*?) is rejected in the Probi Appendix, 199. 5 K. ; cf. the gloss robigo non 'rubigo' *C. G. L.* v. 144. 32, and see ch. ii. § 24], and *rūfus*, the last being shown by its *f*, instead of *d* or *b* (§ 114), to be dialectal. *Rŭbĭ-dus* comes from a verb in *-eo* (cf. *hūmĭdus* from *hŭmeo*, *călĭdus* from *căleo*, &c.), **rŭbeo*, with I.-Eur. eu of Gk. ἐρεύθω, while the ordinary form of the verb, *rŭbeo*, shows, like *rŭber* (Gk. ἐρυθρός), the ŭ of the weak grade of the root, I.-Eur. rŭdh-. The same variety of spelling is seen in a word indicating unshaped metal, &c., *rōdus* and *rūdus*, though the normal spelling is perhaps *raudus* (see Georges, *Lex. Wortf.* s. v.), the weak grade of this stem (perhaps connected with the stem of *rōbus*, *rŭfus*) being apparently seen in *rŭdis*, which means rough, literally, e. g. *aes rude*, or rough, metaphorically, e. g. *arte rudis*, in Ovid's criticism of Ennius : Ennius ingenio maximus, arte rudis. [Varro, *L. L.* v. 163 deinde (porta) Rauduscula, quod aerata fuit. Aes 'raudus' dictum : ex eo veteribus in mancipiis scriptum 'raudusculo libram ferito'; Festus 356. 4 Th. rodus, vel raudus significat rem rudem et imperfectam, nam saxum quoque raudus appellant poetae, ut Accius ... hinc manibus rapere roudus (so the MS.) saxeum ; Paul. Fest. 377. 1 Th. Rodusculana porta appellata, quod rudis et impolita sit relicta, vel quia raudo, id est aere, fuerit vincta]. This variety of spelling suggests that I.-Eur. ou became in Latin an *au*-sound, which was sometimes written, like Lat. *au* from I.-Eur. au (§ 30), as *ō*, sometimes, like Lat. *ou* from I.-Eur. eu (§ 35), as *ū*; though, owing to the scarcity of reliable instances, it is impossible to determine how far these spellings corresponded to the pronunciation of the diphthong at various periods, or how far they were influenced by the analogy of other grades of the same root. For the higher grade with I.-Eur. ōu, ō would have in Latin *ō* (§ 50), and the weak grade of an eu-root with I.-Eur. ŭ would have in Latin *ŭ* (§ 23), while a *ū*-grade (I.-Eur. ū, Lat. *ū*) was also not unknown (§ 51). The Latin diphthong corresponding to I.-Eur. eu had thus a different sound from the representative of I.-Eur. ou. An *ou*-diphthong arose in Latin also from I.-Eur. -og(h)ṷ-, for the velar g(h)ṷ took in Roman lips the sound of *v* (*u*). Thus I.-Eur. *nŏgṷĕdo- became in Latin *novedo-*, *noudo-*, whence *nūdus*, an example which suggests that the *ou* from I.-Eur. og(h)ṷ had the same sound as the *ou* from I.-Eur. eu, and was developed in the same way to long *u*. Also by syncope in words like O. Lat. *noventius* (as in the prophecy of Cn. Marcius : quamuis nouentium duonum negumate, ap. Fest. 164. 28 Th.) with Lat. *ŏv*, I.-Eur. ĕw, O. Lat. *novendīnae*, from *nŏvem* (I.-Eur. *nĕwn̥) and *dĭn*-, a stem for 'day,' seen in O. Sl. dĭnĭ, 'a day,' O. Ind. dína-, &c. For this spurious *ou* we have first *ō*, later *ū*.

§ 42. **Other examples of I.-Eur. ou.** From the root neud-, 'to use, enjoy' (Goth. niutan, 'to enjoy') comes the Latin *nūtrio*, *nūtrix* (in Old Latin *notrix*,

Quint. i. 4. 16), perhaps showing the o-grade, I.-Eur. noud- (Goth. nauþs, O. Engl. nēad, Engl. need, Germ. Noth. Cf. Latin *usus est*, there is need) ; Lat. *clūnis* seems to represent I.-Eur. k̑loun- (O. Scand. hlaunn, 'haunch,' but Gk. κλόνις), though the word occurs so seldom in the older writers that we cannot say whether *claunis, *clōnis were earlier spellings ; Lat. *lūcus* is I.-Eur. *louko- (O.H.G. lōh, 'copse, brushwood,' the -loo of Water-loo, O. Engl. lēah, Engl. lea), properly an open space in a wood, like the German Lichtung (cf. *collūcare*, to make a clearing in a wood), showing the o-grade of the I.-Eur. root leuk- of Lat. *lūceo*, &c., so that the old etymology ' lucus a non lucendo' had a grain of truth after all. The O. Lat. spelling shows -*ou*-, e. g. in *hoce loucarid* on the inscription of Luceria (*C. I. L.* ix. 782) ; *honce loucom . . . quod louci siet* on the inscription of Spoletium (*C. I. L.* xi. 4766) ; the Perfect Part. Pass. of *lăvo*, to wash, I.-Eur. lŏw- (Gk. λούω) is *lautus*, later *lōtus* (see Georges, *Lex. Wortf.* s.v.); the Dat. (Abl.) Plur. of *bōs, bŏvis* (I.-Eur. *gʱŏu-s, *gʱŏw-es) is *bōbus* and *bŭbus* ; formed from the same stem *bou-* after the fashion of *instar* (ch. iii. § 36), comes the word spelt *bustar* in the Glossary of Philoxenus, and *bostar* in the Glossary of Cyrillus, and stated in both glossaries to be the equivalent of the Greek βουστάσιον, a word which must have belonged to the older period only, for Spanish and Portuguese alone preserve it [Span. bostar, Port. bostal, indicating a Latin original *bōstar* ; *bustar*, a place for burning a dead body, (Charisius 38. 19 K.), is a quite different word, connected with *bŭstum*] ; Lat. *ūber* appears to show the ū-grade of the root, like O. Ind. úḋhar, O. Engl. ūder, Lith. ūdrŭti, ' to give milk,' but the ou-grade of Gk. οὖθαρ, Gen. -ατος for -ṇtos, meaning (1) udder, (2) fertility of soil, may appear in the (dialectal) name of a river in Latium, *Ūfens* (modern Uffente) [cf. the Apulian river, *Aufidus* (modern Ofanto)], from which comes the name of one of the Roman tribes *Ūfentina*, in Old Latin *Oufentina* (see Index to *C.I.L.* i.), also *Vofentina*, and *Ofentina* (*C.I.I.* xi. 5702), in Greek inscriptions 'Ωφ-, Οὐωφ- (Eckinger, p. 44).

§ 43. ū for older ovĭ, ovĕ. By the composition of *com-, co-* with *vir* we get the word **covĭriă* (cf. Volsc. covehriā-), which became by syncope **cou(ĭ)ria*, *cūria-*. The name *Jūlius* (written *Iuilio* on a lamp found in one of the oldest graves in the Esquiline burying-place, *Ann. Inst.* 1880, p. 260) seems to come from an earlier **Jovillio-*, from a word found in Oscan in the form diuvilā-, later iúvilā-, meaning apparently a gift presented yearly by a corporation or clan to its tutelary god. Here the older spelling *Iuil-* suggests that the *ū* represents not *ov(i)* but *o(v)i*, the *v* having been suppressed before the accent (see ch. ii. § 53). *Jullus* is the original form of the substantival name, of which *Julius* is an adjectival derivative. The trisyllabic *Iulus* is an invention of Virgil's (*Herm.* xxiv. 155). Similarly *Cluilius*, the older form of *Cloelius* (written on an old inscription *Cloul[is]*, *C. I. L.* i. 1297), shows its derivation from the name *Cluvius*, a name evidently connected with the root k̑leu-, ' to be famous ' (Gk. κλέϝ-ος) [compare the gloss *cluvior*: nobilior, Löwe, *Prodr.* p. 364 ; Paul. Fest. 39. 2 Th. refers the word to *Clonius*: Cloelia familia a Clonio Aeneae comite, est appellata. The family name retained, as often happens, the older spelling with *oe, Cloelius*, not *Clūlius*]. Similarly O. Lat. *coventio* (*couentionid* on the S. C. Bacch. of 186 B. C., *C. I. L.* i. 196), lost its *v* before the accent, and the two vowels *o* and *e* were fused into *ō* ; *contio* (but see ch. ii. § 147, and below on *nuntius*).

§ 44. The spurious diphthong ou. *Nontio*, the older spelling (*denontiari* on

§§ 43-45.] REPRESENTATIVES OF I.-EUR. SOUNDS. ĀI, &C. 251

the Lex Bantina of 133-118 B. C., *C. I. L.* i. 197; *pronontiato* on the Lex Repetundarum of 123-122 B. C., i. 198; *nontiata* on the Epistula ad Tiburtes of c. 100 B. C., i. 201; *pronontiato* and *pronontiatum* on fragments of old Laws, i. 207 and 208) became *nuntio* at the close of the Republican period (*renuntio* is the spelling throughout the Lex Julia Municipalis of 45 B. C., i. 206; so *nuntiationem* on the Lex Rubria of 49 B. C., i. 205), though Cicero in his Laws (ii. 21) uses *nontius*. Marius Victorinus (12. 18 K.) says the old spelling had *ou*. For *nundinae* the oldest spelling is with *ou*, *noundinum* on the S. C. Bacch. of 186 B. C. (*C. I. L.* i. 196, then with *o*, *nondinum* on the Lex Bantina) (i. 197).

§ 45. ĀI. The I.-Eur. root, referred to in § 27, as aiwĕ-, 'time, life,' is perhaps more correctly āiwĕ- (cf. O. Ind. áyu-, 'life'), with the diphthong originally long, but shortened in Latin *aevum*, according to the rule that a long diphthong (including combinations with a nasal or liquid as second element) shortened in Latin its first element when a consonant followed. Final I.-Eur. -āi, the ending of the Dat. Sg. of Ā-stems, shows traces in Latin of 'doublet' forms, (1) *ā* (with suppression of the second element, by a similar syncope as produced *exemplar* from *exemplāre*), a form which seems to occur on a few old inscriptions, e. g. *Iunonei Loucina* (*C. I. L.* i. 189), *Iunone Loucina Tuscolana sacra* (i. 1200); (2) *-ai* (one syllable), class. *-ae* (presumably *ăe*; cf. Osc. -aí, Umbr. -e, Rustic and Late Latin *e*, ch. ii. § 41) (with a shortening of the first element, which properly took place only before a consonant). Similar doublets -*ō* and -*oi* seem to show themselves for I.-Eur. -ōi in O-stem Datives [(1) class. *ĕquō*, *dŏmĭnō*, (2) O. Lat. *populoi Romanoi, Numasioi*; cf. Osc. -úí, Umbr. -e], though in O-stems the first (not the second doublet as in the Ā-stems) established itself in the classical usage. (On these Datives, see ch. vi. § 23.) In Greek this I.-Eur. -āi became -ᾳ, e. g. χώρᾳ, later -ᾱ, but in dialects also -αι (presumably ᾰι), while this I.-Eur. ōi became -ῳ, e. g. ἵππῳ, later -ω, in dialects -οι.

Shortening of long 'diphthong' before consonant. It seems to have been a law very widely spread through the I.-Eur. languages that a long vowel became shortened before any y (in i-diphthongs), w (in u-diphthongs), m, n, r, or l, when this was followed by a consonant. Thus I.-Eur. *wēnt- from the root wē-, 'to blow' (Gk. ἄ-ημι) has become in Gk. ἀ-έντ-, in Goth. vinds, our 'wind,' as in Latin *vĕntus* (Span. viento); the I.-Eur. word for the heel or the ham (O. Ind. párṣṇi-) is in Gk. πτέρνα, in Goth. fairzna, and in Latin *pĕrna* (Span. pierna) [curiously enough Mar. Sacerdos (vi. 451. 5 K.) cites a derivative of this word, *pernix*, swift (lit. 'strong in the ham,' and properly used of horses and other animals, *A. L. L.* viii. 453) as an illustration of a short

252   THE LATIN LANGUAGE.   [Chap. IV.

e, the long pronunciation of which is a barbarism : barbarismus . . . fit . . . si dicas pernix et 'per' producas, quae correpta est] ; the Dat. (Abl. Loc. Instr.) Plur. Suffix of O-stems, I.-Eur. -ōis has become in Greek -*οις*, as in Latin -*eis*, -*īs* (ch. vi. § 48) ; *lĕntus* is a cognate of *lēnis*. (Cf. Engl. 'kept,' 'wept' from 'keep,' 'weep').

§ 46. ĀU. The I.-Eur. long diphthong āu is seen in the stem nāu-, 'ship' (O. Ind. nāús, nāvás, Gen.; Hom. Gk. νηῦς, νηός Gen., Arm. nav, O. Ir. nau, naue or nōe, Gen., W. noe, 'a dish,' like our 'butter-boat,' O. Scand. nōr), which is in Latin an *i*-stem *nāvis*, like *clāvis* (Gk. κλη(ϝ)ίς). The -*au*- of *nau-frăgium*, *nau-stĭbulum* 'vas alvei simile' (Fest. 172. 23 Th.), *claudo* shortens the first element owing to the fact that a consonant follows (see above, § 45). [That *claudo* had the same *au*, as the equivalent of I.-Eur. au (e. g. *fraus*), we see from its sinking to *ŭ* in the unaccented syllable, e. g. *exclŭdere*, like *defrŭdare*.] For Latin *āv* from I.-Eur. ōw, e. g. *octāvus*, and perhaps *flāvus* (beside *flōrus*, Gk. χλωρός), see § 50. *Gāius* (a trisyllable till late Latin, *Harvard Studies*, 1891) is the class. form of older *Gāvius* (Osc. Gaaviis), with suppression of intervocalic *v* (§ 70), a name apparently derived from the root of *gaudeo*, *gāvisus sum* (Gk. γηθέω for *γᾱϝεθεω) (cf. *Raius* and *Rāvius*) On the curious remark of Terentianus Maurus about the pronunciation of Lat. *au*, see ch. ii. § 34.

§ 47. ĒI. I.-Eur. ēi appears e. g. in *rēi-, 'property' (O. Ind. rā́s, Gen. rāyás), Lat. *rēs*, Gen. *rēī* for *rēyī*, a root in which the diphthong had apparently in the 'Indo-European period' the doublets ēi (ēy) and ē. The Loc. Sing. ending of Ē-stems shows the second of these doublets in Latin, e. g. *diē crastini*, *postrĭdiē*, &c.

§ 48. ĒU. The I.-Eur. Nom. *dyēus, 'the sky,' shows the long diphthong ēu (O. Ind. dyāús, Acc. dívam and dyā́m, diyā́m; Gk. Ζεύς for *Ζηυς, Lat. *diēs* like Acc. *diem*; on *Jŏvis*, &c., from the stem dyĕw-, see ch. vi. § 9). A final *ēu*-diphthong arose in Latin by the suppression of the final -*ĕ* of *nĕve*, and produced the form *neu*; *ceu* is probably to be referred to an older *cē-ve (ch. x. § 11). The Loc. Sg. ending of U-stems, if this was I.-Eur. -ēu, appears in *noctū*, where the *ŭ* represents an earlier ·*ĕu* with shortening of the first element of -ēu (see § 26), so that I.-Eur. *dyēus should be Lat. *diūs (*nŭ-dius-tertius?*).

§ 49. ŌI. An example of final -ōi has been already mentioned, the ending of the Dat. Sg. of O-stems. This in Latin shows the doublets, (1) -ō, the classical ending, e. g. *equō, dŏmĭnō*, (2) -*oi* (presumably -*ŏi*), an ending found in very old inscriptions, e. g. *Numasioi* (Osc. -úí, Umbr. -e) (ch. vi. § 26).

§ 50. ŌU. I.-Eur. ōu- is seen in the numeral *ŏktōu, a dual in form, with the sense apparently of 'two sets of four' (O. Ind. aṣṭā́u, aṣṭā́, Gk. ὀκτώ, Goth. ahtau, O. Engl. eahta, Lith. asztù-nì), in Latin *octō*. Duals in the Veda show generally -āu (I.-Eur. -ōu) before an initial vowel, -ā (I.-Eur. -ō) before an initial consonant, e. g. dēvā́u and dēvā́, 'twin-gods;' and it is probable that these doublets existed even in what is called the I.-Eur. period, so that the -ō of Latin *octo* (cf. *ambo, duo*) will represent an I.-Eur. -ō, and not -ōu. As I.-Eur. ŏw became ăv in Latin (§ 19), so I.-Eur. ōw is said to have become ā́v in the corresponding ordinal number, *octāvus* for *octōvus* (Gk. ὄγδο(F)ος). The long diphthong seems to have occurred in the I.-Eur. declension of the word for 'ox,' stem *g^{n}ŏu- (O. Ind. gāús, Loc. gā́vi, Acc. gā́m, Nom. Pl. gā́vas, &c., Arm. kov, Gk. βοῦς, Dor. βῶς, according to the grammarians, O. Ir. bou, bō, W. bu, buw, O. Engl. cū, Lett. gûws); but the Latin *bōs* is a doubtful example, for its *b-* instead of the normal *v-* (§ 139) suggests that it is a dialectal (or rustic) form like *ŏvis* for **avis* (I.-Eur. *ŏwi-, § 19), and not a genuine Latin development.

§ 51. Variation (Ablaut) of Vowels. A root like pet- of Gk. πέτεσθαι, to fly, O. Ind. pátati, ' he flies,' appears in the form pt- in Gk. πτέσθαι, O. Ind. á-pa-pta-t, 'he flew,' the shorter form being a syncopated form of the other, due to loss of accent. Similarly the root ei-, 'to go' (Gk. εἶ-σι, 3 Sg., Lith. eĩ-ti, Lat. *it*, older *ei-t*, ch. viii. § 2), loses the *ĕ* of the diphthong in the P. P. P. *ĭ-tó- (O. Ind. -ĭtá-, Gk. -ιτος, Lat. -*itus*), where the accent falls on the suffix; and eu becomes ŭ, through loss of accent, in I.-Eur. *bhŭgā́, 'flight' (Gk. φυγή, Lat. *fŭga*) from *bheúgō, ' I flee' (Gk. φεύγω); while en, em, er, el, similarly reduced, appear before a vowel as n, m, r, l, e.g. Gk. γί-γν-ομαι, Lat. *gi-gn-o*, beside Gk. γέν-ος, Lat. *gĕn-us*, but before a consonant assumed in Greek the forms α, ρα, λα, e.g. φατός from φεν-, to kill, I.-Eur. gh^{u}en-, δρακών (O. Ind. dr̥sánt-) from δερκ-, to glance, I.-Eur. derk-, in Latin en, em, or, ol, e.g. *ten-tus* (O. Ind. ta-tá-, Gk. τα-τός) from ten-, 'to stretch,' *fors* (O. Ind. bhr̥-tí-, O. Ir. brith, Goth. gabaurþs) from bher-, 'to bear' (see §§ 81, 92). We may call these reduced forms pt-, bhŭg-, bhr̥-, &c., the 'weak grade' of the roots, and pet-, bheug-, bher- the normal or Ĕ-grade. We find these roots also with their ĕ replaced by ŏ in such words as Gk. γέ-γον-α Pft., οἶτος, a Derivative Noun from the root ei-, 'to go,' γόνος from the root ĝen-, φόνος from gh^{u}en-; and ĝon-, oi-, gh^{u}on- may be called the Ŏ-grade of these roots. There are also occasionally forms with ē, ō, e.g. Gk. πωτάομαι from pet-, 'to fly.' This variation, or gradation, called by the Germans 'Ablaut,' of I.-Eur. vowels has not yet been thoroughly explained or systematized; the relation for example of ū, ī to the ordinary weak grade ŭ, ĭ in words like I.-Eur. *k̑lū-tó- (O. H. G. hlūt, 'loud,' Zend. srū-ta) beside I.-Eur. *k̑lŭ-tó- (O. Ind. śrŭ-tá-, Gk. κλῠ-τός) is not quite clear, nor yet that of the Ē- and Ō-forms to the Ĕ- and Ŏ-forms, e.g. Gk. πωτάομαι beside ποτέομαι. They are generally called 'lengthenings' of the weak grade (of diphthongal roots), of the Ĕ-grade and of the Ŏ-grade, and are by German philologists classed under the term 'Dehnstufe' ('lengthened grade'). [On these see Streitberg in *Indog. Forsch.* iii. 306, who explains them as produced by syncope of a following short vowel in *bhōr (Gk. φώρ) for *bhŏr(o)s, &c., *rēks- (Lat. *rēx-ī*) for *rĕĝ-ĕs-, &c]. Nor have the grades of other than E-roots been properly equated to grades like pĕt-, pt-, pŏt-; the variation of the root dō-, 'to give,' for example, which has ō in Gk. δί-δω-μι, Lat. *dō-num*, but a short vowel in Gk. δο-τός, Lat. *dă-tus*, of the root sē-, 'to throw,' or 'to throw seed,' with ē in Gk. ἵ-η-μι for *σι-ση-μι, Lat. *sē-men*, but with a short vowel in Gk. ἑ-τός, Lat. *să-tus*, of the root stā-, 'to stand,' with ā in Gk. ἵ-στημι for *σι-στᾱ-μι, Lat. *stā-re*, but with a short vowel in Gk. στᾰ-τός, Lat. *stă-tus*; similarly the variation of ă and ā, e.g. in the I.-Eur. root meaning 'to drive,' ăĝ- in O. Ind. ăjā-mi, Gk. ἄγω, Ir. agaim, Lat. *ăgo*, āĝ- in O. Ind. ājí-, 'a contest,' O. Ir. āg, 'a contest,' Lat. *amb-āges*; and the variation of ŏ and ō, e.g. in Lat. *fŏdio* beside *fōdi*, Gk. ὀδ-μή beside εὐ-ώδης; not to mention the variation of ă and ŏ in Lat. *scăbo* beside *scŏbis*, *ăcies* (Gk. ἄκρος, Hom. ἄκρις, a hill-top) beside O. Lat. *ŏcris*, a rugged hill (Gk. ὄκρις, a point), from the root ak̑-, ok̑-, 'sharp.'

§ 51.] REPRESENTATIVES OF I.-EUR. VOWEL-GRADES. 255

Examples of this variation of vowels in Latin are I. in E-roots: (a) Weak grade in (1) Derivative Nouns with Ā-suffix, O-suffix, TI-suffix, &c. (ch. v. §§ 2, 42), e.g. fŭga (Gk. φυγ-ή) from the root bheug-, 'to flee,' jŭg-um (O. Ind. yŭg-ám, Gk. ζŭγ-όν) from the root yeug-, 'to join'), fors (O. Ind. bhṛ-tí-), mens (O. Ind. ma-tí-), mors (O. Ind. mṛ-ti); (2) in P. P. P. with TO-suffix, e.g. dŭc-tus from dūco for *deuco, ŭs-tus (A.L.L. ii. 607) from ūro for *euso (Gk. εὕω for *εὔhω), per-culsus for *kld-to- (cf. clādes); (3) in Reduplicated Present-stem, e.g. gi-gn-o from the root ĝen-, sīdo for *si-sd-o from the root sed-; (4) in Nasalized Present-stems, e.g. jŭ-n-g-o from the root yeug-, lĭ-n-quo from the root leiqⁿ- (Gk. λείπω), fĭ-n-d-o from the root bheid- (Goth. beita, 'I bite'); (5) in some Present-stems with the YO-suffix, e.g. fŭg-io from the root bheug-.

(b) Normal or E-grade in (1) Neuter ES-stems, e.g. gen-us from the root ĝen- (Gk. γέν-ος), decus from the root dek̂-, nemus from the root nem-; (2) Present-stems formed with the Thematic Vowel, e.g. veho from the root weĝh- (O. Ind. vah-, Lith. vežù, O. Sl. vezą), sequor from the root seqᴿ- (O. Ind. sac-, Gk. ἕπομαι, O. Ir. sechur), fīdo, O. Lat. feido, from the root bheidh- (Gk. πείθω for *φειθω), dīco, O. Lat. deico, from the root deik̂- (Gk. δείκνυμι), dūco, O. Lat. douco for *deuco (§ 35), from the root deuk- (Goth. tiuha), ūro for *euso from the root eus- (Gk. εὕω for *εὔhω), pluo, O. Lat. plovo for *plewo, from the root pleu- (Gk. πλέ(F)ω). (On the u of pluo see ch. viii. § 6.)

(c) O-grade in (1) Derivative Nouns with Ā-suffix, O-suffix, &c., e.g. procus from the root prek̂-, 'to ask' (Lat. precor), domus (Gk. δόμος) from the root dem-, 'to build' (Gk. δέμω), toga from the root (s)teg-, 'to cover, thatch' (Gk. στέγω, Lat. tego); (2) Causative Verbs, e.g. moneo, lit. 'cause to remember,' from the root men- (Lat. me-min-i), torreo, lit. 'cause to dry up,' from the root ters- (Gk. τέρσομαι).

II. in E-suffixes. (1) Nouns of the Second Declension with Voc. Sg. in -ĕ, e.g. eque, Nom. Acc., &c. in -os, -om, e.g. equos, equom; (2) N-stems, R-stems, S-stems, &c., e.g. temp-ŭs (O. Lat. temp-ŏs), temp-ŏr-is for *temp-ŏs-es Gen., temp-ĕr-i Adv., aug-us-tus for *aug-ŏs-to-, auxĭlium for *aug-s-ilio-, plēb-ēs, dĕc-or (O. Lat. dec-ōs); nō-mĕn, car-n-is, rătī-ōn-i. In the I.-Eur. declension of these stems the suffix may have shown in the Nom. Sg. ē when accented, ō when unaccented, e. g. Gk. δο-τήρ, δώ-τωρ, in the other 'strong' cases ĕ when accented, ŏ when unaccented, e. g. Gk. πα-τέρ-α, φρά-τορ-α, and in the 'weak' cases the weak grade, e. g. Gk. πα-τρ-ός, πα-τρά-σι (O. Ind. pi-tṛ́-ṣu), but the divergences of the suffix-form have been to a great extent removed in the various I.-Eur. languages, e. g. Gk. μητέρος as well as μητρός, πατέρων instead of πατρῶν. The alternation of strong and weak stems in Declension, depending on the accentuation of the stem or the suffix, has left its mark in the divergent form of words like Gk. πούς, ποδός (cf. Lat. trĭ-pŏd-are) and Lat. pes, pĕd-is (cf. Gk. πέζα, τρά-πεζα, lit. 'four-footed,' πεζός, &c., for *ped-ya-, *ped-yo-), Lat. pecten and Gk. κτείς for *πκτενς, &c.

The combination yĕ, wĕ was treated somewhat similarly to ei, eu, being reduced by the loss of accent to ĭ, ŭ, e. g. Gk. ὕπ-νος for *sŭp-nos (O. Sl. sŭnŭ) from the root swep (O. Engl. swefn, 'a dream'), Gk. πέρυσι, last year, for πέρυτι (O. Ind. par-ut) from the root wet- (Gk. (F)έτος, a year, Lat. vĕtus). This root wet- seems to have lost by procope an initial ă, and the reduced form of ăwĕt- appears in Gk. ἐνι-αυτ-ός, just as the reduced form of ăwĕg- (Gr. ἀ(F)έξω) in the aug- of Lat. aug-eo, Gk. αὔξω, O. Ind. ójas-, 'strength,' while ŭg- the reduced form of wĕg- (with procope of initial ă) appears in O. Ind. ukṣ-, 'to grow strong,' Gk. ὑγιής for *ὐγιής, &c. And as we sometimes find ī, ū beside ĭ, ŭ the weak grades of ei, eu, so we find the same long vowels in forms of yĕ- and wĕ-roots, e. g. k̑ū- (O. Ind. śū́na-, 'want, emptiness') from the root k̑wĕ- (Gk. κ(F)ενός, empty). On the variation of ĭ with yĕ (ĭye) in I.-Eur. YO-stems, see ch. v. § 4, of ī with yē in the I.-Eur. Athematic Optative (O. Lat. siēs and sīmus, &c.), see ch. viii. § 55. Latin con-cŭt-io for *con-quĕt-io from quătio, ab-ĭc-io (with the first syllable short in the older poetry), for *ab-yĕc-io from jăcio, shows that the Latin language had the same tendency as the I.-Eur. to reduce unaccented yĕ to ĭ, wĕ to ŭ, and in many cases it is impossible to say whether the reduction belongs to the 'Indo-European' period or is a Latin development.

III. in other roots. I.-Eur. ē (Lat. ē) varies with Lat. ă in Lat. sē-men (Gk. ἧ-μα, a casting) and să-tus (Gk. ἐ-τός) from the

§ 51.] REPRESENTATIVES OF I.-EUR. VOWEL-GRADES. 257

root sē-, *fēc-i* (Gk. ἔ-θηκ-α) and *făc-io*, an extension of the root dhē- (Gk. τί-θη-μι); I.-Eur. ō (Lat. *ŏ*) varies with Lat. *ă* in Lat. *dŏ-num* (Gk. δῶρον), and *dă-tus* (Gk. δοτός, δόσις) from the root dō-, *cōs* (O. Ind. śā-, 'to sharpen') and *cătus*, which in O. Lat. meant 'sharp,' 'shrill' from the root kō-; I.-Eur. ā (Lat. *ă*) varies with Latin *ă* in Lat. *fā-ma* (Gk. φή-μη) and *făt-eor* (ch. viii. § 32) (Gk. φătós), *stā-re* (Gk. ἵστημι for *σι-στᾱ-μι) and *stă-tus* (Gk. στᾰ-τός). In all these cases the Latin weak-grade vowel is *ă*, while in Greek we have ε for Ē-roots, o for Ō-roots, ă for Ā-roots, but in Sanscrit ĭ for all roots (e. g. hĭ-tá- from root DHĒ-, dĭ-ti- from root DŌ, sthĭ-tá- from root STĀ-), just as we have Lat. *ă* of *pater*, which is also *ă* in Greek and other languages (Gk. πατήρ, O. Ir. athir, Goth. fadar) represented by Sanscrit ĭ (pĭtár-). We find even in Greek occasionally *ă* in the weak form of Ē-, Ō-roots (e. g. κεκᾰδοντο beside ἐκεκήδει, δᾰνος beside δῶρον), so that we are perhaps justified in supposing a short *a*-sound (*ă*) to have been the form of the weak grade of ē, ō, as well as of ā, in European languages (see § 3).

The Latin tendency to weaken every unaccented vowel has greatly obscured the traces of the I.-Eur. variation of vowels; *prosperus*, for example, has *spă-* (cf. O. Ind. sphĭrá-, 'wealthy') the weak grade of *spē-* of *spēs*, *spēro* (O. Ind. sphā-, O. Sl. spē-ti), with *ă* weakened before *r* in the unaccented syllable to *ĕ*, and *crēditus* (O. Ind. śrád-dhĭta-) has the same vowel weakened to *ĭ*.

Words like *frăngo* (*ă* is shown by *con-fringo* for *con-frengo*, &c.), with the weak grade *frăg-* in the Nasalized Present-stem of the I.-Eur. root bhreg- (Goth. brikan, 'to break'), *grădus*, *grădior*, with a weak form *grăd-* from the I.-Eur. root ghredh-, 'to step' (Goth. griþs, 'a step'), suggest that in Latin (as perhaps in other languages, *M. U. v. pref.*) *ră*, *mă*, &c. were the weak grades of rĕ, lĕ, mĕ, nĕ, although we have seen Lat. *ŏr, ŏl, ĕm, ĕn* to be the weak grades of ĕr, ĕl, ĕm, ĕn where the liquid or nasal follows the ĕ. But we occasionally find in Latin (and perhaps in the other Italic languages) *ă* in forms of Ē-roots where ĕ is not preceded by a liquid or nasal, e. g. *pateo* (Osc. pate-) from the root pet- (Gk. πετάννυμι); its relation to the obscure or indeterminate vowel (like the Hebrew sh^eva), written *ă*, ə, ^e, &c., is not clear (see §§ 3, 83, 94).

As an I.-Eur. *ă* is the weak grade of ō, so *ău* may be the weak

s

grade of ōu; the Plautine *aus-culum*, for example, may then exhibit the weak grade of the stem *ōus- (O. Ind. ás-, Lat. ōs-). It may also be the weak grade of ēu (*Caurus* or *Cōrus*, Lith. sziáurė, beside O. Sl. sĕverŭ, is quoted as an example), and of āu; and similarly ăi of ōi, ēi, āi. It is also possible that as ă varies with ŏ, so ai may vary with oi (e. g. Lat. *aemidus* and Gk. οἰδάω), and au with ou (e. g. Gk. καυλός, a stalk, and κοῖλος for *κοϜιλος, hollow); and some explain in this way Latin forms like *lăvo* beside Gk. λούω (on which see § 19).

§ 52. I.-Eur. and Lat. ĕ and ŏ. Lat. *procus* (Lith. praszýti, O. Sl. prositi) from I.-Eur. root prek̂- (Lith. perszù and Lat. *preces, precor*); Lat. *noceo*, the Causative of I.-Eur. nek̂- (O. Ind. naś-, Gk. νέκυς, Lat. *nex*, &c.); Lat. *pondo*, in weight (used with ellipse of *libra*, e. g. centum pondo es, 'you weigh a hundred pounds'), the Abl. of an O-stem **pondus, -i*, beside *pondus, -eris*, from *pendo*, to weigh; Lat. *domus*, an O-stem in Plautus and the writers before Sulla, I.-Eur. *domo- (O. Ind. dáma-, Gk. δόμος) from I.-Eur. root dem-, 'to build' (Gk. δέμω, δέμας, form, Goth. tim-r-jan, 'to build,' Engl. tim-ber, Germ. Zim-mer; Goth. ga-timan, 'to be suitable, conformable,' Germ. ziemen); Latin *rŏta, rŏtundus* (O. Ir. roth, 'a wheel,' W. rhod, O. H. G. rad, Lith. rãtas) from I.-Eur. root reth-, 'to run' (O. Ir. rethim, W. rhedu Inf., Lith. ritù, 'I roll'); Latin *ŏrbus*, I.-Eur. *ŏrbho- (Arm. orb, Gk. ὀρφανός, ὀρφο-βόται, O. Ir. orbe, from stem *orbio-, 'an inheritance,' Goth. arbi) from I.-Eur. root erbh- (O. Ir. erbim, 'I entrust, bequeath'); *cūnae* from **coinae* (cf. Gk. κοίτη) from k̂ei- 'to lie' (Gk. κεῖμαι).

§ 53. ē and ō. This ō is best seen in the Noun Suffixes -ōn-, -ōr- which vary with -ĕn-, -ĕr- and -ĕn-, -ĕr-, as well as with -ŏn-, -ŏr-, e. g. Lat. *hŏmō* Nom., *hominis* for **homĕnis* Gen., Lat. *dător, datōris* beside Gk. δώτωρ, δώτορος and δοτήρ, δοτῆρος (see ch. v. § 57); in Greek it is seen also in the Perf. of verbs with ē, e. g. τέθωκται from θήγω, ἀφέωκα from ἀφίημι, &c. The root of Lat. *flōs, Flōra* is bhlō- (Ir. bláth, Goth. blō-ma, Engl. bloom; O. Engl. blōs-tm, Engl. blossom; O. Engl. blō-wan, Engl. to blow, of flowers), which is connected with the root bhlē- of Lat. *flēmina*, congestion of blood (Goth. uf-blēsan, Germ. auf-blasen), just as the root plē-, 'to be full' (Latin *plēnus*, Gk. πλήρης; Lat. *plēbes*, Gk. πλῆθος) seems to be connected with the root plō- of Ir. lār, Engl. floor, &c.; but these are rather to be explained like ĝnō- and ĝnā- of Lat. *gnōtus*, and *gnārus* (§ 1).

§ 54. ō-ă, ē-ă. From root lēd-, 'to leave, to let' (Goth. lētan, O. Engl. lǣtan, Engl. let), with ō-grade in Goth. lai-lōt Perf., we have in the weak grade Lat. *lăssus* (Goth. lats, Germ. lass); Lat. *catus*, which Varro makes the equivalent of *ăcūtus*, used in Old Latin and in the Sabine dialect of sounds, i. e. sharp, shrill (*L. L.* vii. 46 apud Ennium :

iam cata signa fere sonitum dare voce parabant.

Cata acuta ; hoc enim verbo dicunt Sabini : quare :

catus Aelius Sextus

non, ut aiunt, sapiens, sed acutus) is in O. Ind. śitá-, 'sharp,' from śā-, 'to

§§ 52–56.] REPRESENTATIVES OF I.-EUR. VOWEL-GRADES. 259

sharpen,' and is connected with Lat. *cōs*, a whetstone (like *dōs* from root dō-). Similarly we have *ră-tus* beside *rē-ri*, *făc-io* beside *fĕc-i* (ch. viii. § 41), and from I.-Eur. ŏk-, 'swift' (connected with ak-, 'sharp'?) (O. Ind. āśú-, Gk. ὠκύς, Lat. *ōcior*) *acupedium* (presumably with *ă*), equated in the Philoxenus and Cyrillus Glossaries to ὀξυποδία (cf. Gl. Plac. p. 7. 40 G.; the *acupedius* of Paul. Fest. 7. 19 Th. is a mistake, see *Class. Rev.* v. p. 9); *accĭpĭter* (*ăcc*- Ter. Maur. 1267) is probably a corruption of *ăcu-peter (cf. O. Ind. āśu-pátvan- for *ŏku-, 'swift-flying,' and Gk. ὠκυ-πέτης, the epithet of a hawk in Hesiod, *Op.* 210), due to a popular etymology from *accipio*; the form *acceptor*, the original of O. Span. acetore, is used by Lucilius (*inc.* 123 M.) exta acceptoris et unguis, but is censured by the grammarian Caper (p. 107. 8 K. accipiter non 'acceptor'); *ămārus* shows the root *ăm-* (O. Ind. am-lá-, ' sour'), which is usually regarded as the weak form of ōm-, ' raw ' (O. Ind. āmá-, Gk. ὠμός).

§ 55. **ă–ŏ.** Examples of this interchange are Lat. *atrox* for *adrox* (Arm. ateam, 'I hate') and *odium*; *scabo*, to scrape (Gk. σκάπτω, to dig) and *scobis*, sawdust ; *acuo, acus, acies, acer-bus* (Gk. ἄκρος, Hom. ἄκρις, a hill-top) and *ocris* (Gk. ὄκρις, a point, ὀκριόεις, an epithet of unhewn stone in Homer), an Old Latin word for a rugged hill. [Fest. 196. 17 Th. ocrem antiqui, ut Ateius Philologus in libro Glossematorum refert, montem confragosum vocabant, ut apud Livium :

sed qui sunt hi, qui ascendunt altum ocrim ?

... unde fortasse etiam ocreae sint dictae inaequaliter tuberatae ; in Umbrian, and Marrucinian the stem *ocri-* (Nom. Sg. *ocar*, in Umbrian) seems to bear the sense of citadel]; *ancus*, an Old Latin word for a person with a crook-elbow (Paul. Fest. 15. 3 Th. ancus appellatur, qui aduncum bracchium habet, et exporrigi non potest), which went out of use c. 200 B.C., to judge from the fact that the word survives only in Portuguese anco, ' the elbow ' (Gk. ἀγκών and ἀγκάλη, O. Ir. ēcath, 'a hook,' from root ank-), and *uncus*, a hook, *reduncum* bracchium, *aduncus* unguis (Gk. ὄγκος, a hook); *doceo* and Gk. διδάσκω for *δι-δακ-σκω. We have Oscan a, Latin o in *tongere*, a word used by Ennius, declared by Aelius Stilo to be equivalent to *noscere*, and to be still employed in the Praenestine dialect (Paul. Fest. 539. 5 Th. tongere nosse est, nam Praenestini ' tongitionem ' dicunt notionem. Ennius : alii rhetorica tongent. Cf. Fest. 538. 9 Th. [tongere Aelius Sti]lo ait noscere esse), appearing in Oscan in the noun tangion- with the sense of *sententia*, e. g. senateís tanginúd, ' senatus sententia,' the cognate of our word 'think,' probably from a root teng-. [Cf. the (dialectal ?) variation of names like *Blossius, Blassius ; Fabius, Fobius.*]

§ 56. **ā and ă.** I. Eur. pāĝ-, ' to fasten ' (cf. pãk-) (Sanscr. páśa-, 'cord,' Dor. Gk. πάγνυμι and ἐπάγην, Mid. High. Germ. vuoge, ' deftness in fastening,' &c., Mod. Germ. Fuge, and Goth. fagrs, 'suitable),' Lat. *păngo* (with *ă*; cf. *com-pingo*), *pepĭgi* (from *pe-păg-i) and *com-pāges, păciscor* and *pāc-em* Acc. ; I.-Eur. swād-, 'to make pleasant ' (O. Ind. svádati and svādatē, Dor. Gk. ἅδομαι and Hom. Gk. εὔαδον, ἅδον Aor.), Lat. *suādeo* ; I.-Eur. *nãs-, ' the nose,' probably Nom. nās(s), Gen. năs-os (O. Ind. nās- and năs-, Lith. nósis and O. Sl. nosŭ), O. Lat. *nāssum*, class. Lat. *nāsus* (ch. ii. § 129), *nāris*; similarly Lat. *sāgio, sāgus* and *sāgax* (Dor. Gk. ἁγέομαι, Ir. saigim, 'I seek,' Goth. sōkja, Germ. suche, O. Engl. sēce). The Latin words *sāgio* and *sāgax* were used of hounds on the track,

S 2

whence *praesāgio*, to 'scent out' the future (Cic. *Div.* i. 65: cf. Ennius, *A.* 375 M. nare sagaci Sensit; voce sua nictit ululatque ibi acuta); *săga* was applied to an old match-maker, like Gyllis in the first Idyll of Herondas (Non. 22. 34 M. sagae mulieres dicuntur femina*rum* ad libidinem virorum indagatrices; cf. Lucil. vii. 6 M. saga et bona conciliatrix). So Latin *ācer*, stem *ācri*-, and *ăcuo* (Gk. ἄκρος, Lith. asztrù-s, &c., show I.-Eur. ă); Lat. *ācri*- beside Gk. ἄκρο- reminds us of Latin *sācri*- (*sācres porci*, pigs for sacrifice, Plaut.) beside *săcro*-.

§ 57. ĕ and ē. I.-Eur. ĕ́d-, 'to eat' (O. Ind. ad-, 'to eat' and ādyà-, 'eatable,' Gk. ἔδομαι and ἐδηδώς, Goth. itan and ētum, Lith. ė́d-ęs Part., O. Sl. jad-ŭ), Lat. *ĕdo* and *ēdi* Perf.; Lat. *lĕx*, *lĕg-is* and *lēgo*, &c.; I.-Eur. rĕ̆g- 'to stretch, rule' (O. Ind. ráji-, 'a row,' ráj-, 'a king,' O. Ir. rĭgim, 'I stretch,' rī, 'a king'), Lat. *rĕgo*, I rule, *rēg*-, a king. This lengthening appears chiefly in Preterites, e. g. O. Sl. nĕsŭ, 'I carried' (beside nĕsą, 'I carry),' Goth. sētum, 'we sat' (beside sĭtam, 'we sit'), O. Ir. ro mīdar, 'I judged' (beside mĭdiur, 'I judge, think,' from the root mĕd- of Gk. μέδομαι), and in the nouns derived from Verb-stems like *lēx*, *rēx*. The occurrence of the long vowel in some Present-forms like Lith. ė́d-mi, 'I eat,' is probably due to the use of a Perfect-stem as a Present (like Gk. ἀνώγω Pres. from ἄνωγα Perf.).

§ 58. ĭ and ī. I.-Eur. *wĭro-, 'a man' (O. Ind. vīrá-, Lith. výras have ī; O. Ir. fer from *wĭro-, Goth. vair from *wĭro-, O. H. G. wer, Germ. Wer-wolf, Engl. were-wolf and Lat. *vĭr* have ĭ); I.-Eur. *gu̯ī́ro-, 'lively' (O. Ind. jīrá-, Lat. *vīreo*). But most examples of Latin *ĭ-ī* are really cases of ĭ-ei, e. g. *fīdes* and *ĭdo*, older *feido* (see § 13).

§ 59. ŏ and ō. The I.-Eur. root ŏ̆qu̯-, 'to see' (Gk. ὄψομαι and ὤψ) appears in Lat. *ŏc-ulus*; the root ŏ̆d-, 'to smell' (Gk. ὀδμή, Arm. hot, and Gk. δυσ-ώδης, Lith. ūdziu) in Lat. *ŏdor*; nŏ̆gu̯-, 'naked' (O. Ind. nagná-, Ir. nocht, Goth. naqaþs, and Lith. nŭgas), in Lat. *nūdus* for *nŏv(i)dus*; ŏ̆len-, 'the elbow' (Gk. ὠλένη, Goth. aleina, 'a cubit,' 'ell,' O. Ir. uile, uilenn Gen., W. elin, O. Engl. eln, Engl. ell, el-bow) is Lat. *ulna* for *ŏl(i)na*. As with ē (varying with ĕ) we find ō (varying with ŏ) in the Perfect-stem, in nouns derived from Verb-stems, &c., e. g. Gk. ὀπ-ωπ-α, ὤψ.

§ 60. ŭ and ū. I.-Eur. *nŭ̆, 'now,' from the root neu- of *newo-, 'new' (O. Ind. nŭ, Adv. and Particle, nūnám, Gk. νῠ, νῦν, O. Ir. nŏ and nŭ, a Verbal Part. often used with the Present Tense, e.g. no chanim, 'I am singing,' Goth. nŭ, O. Engl. nŭ, Germ. nun and sometimes nu, Lith. nù-gi, O. Sl. ny-nĕ), Lat. *nu-dius tertius* the day before yesterday, lit. 'now the third day,' *-num* in *etiam-num*, &c. (Gk. τοί-νυν), *nŭn-c*; I.-Eur. lŭ̆- from the root leu-, 'to loose' [Gk. βουλῡτόν-δε, about the time of loosing the oxen from the plough, towards midday (*Class. Rev.* ii. 260; Schulze, *Quaest. Ep.* p. 321), and λῠτός], Lat. *so-lūtus*; I.-Eur. sŭ̆-, 'a sow' (O. Ind. sū-kará-, Gk. ὗς, O. Engl. sū), Lat. *sūs* and *sŭ-cerdae*, 'stercus suillum' (Fest. 432. 8 Th.; cf. Paul. Fest. 433. 2 Th.; Non. 175. 14 M.) (W. hw-ch, Goth. sw-ein, O. Engl. sw-īn); I.-Eur. tŭ̆, the accented and the unaccented form of the 2nd Personal Pronoun (Gk. τύ-ν-η and σύ, &c.), Lat. *tū* (on *tŭ-quidem*, see ch. iii. § 51); I.-Eur. pŭ̆-, 'to rot' (Gk. πύθω, Goth. fūls ist, 'he stinketh,' O. Engl. fūl, Engl. foul, Lith. púti; Gk. πύος for *πῦσος), Lat. *pŭteo* and *pŭter*; I.-Eur. *kŭ̆ti-, 'skin' (Gk. ἐγ-κυτί and O. Engl. hȳd, Engl. hide, O.H.G. hūt, Germ. Haut), Lat. *cŭtis*. But usually the alternation of *ū* with *ŭ* in Latin is the alternation of I.-Eur. eu, ou with ŭ, e. g. *dūco* and *dŭx*, *fūgi* and

§§ 57-62.] REPRESENTATIVES OF I.-EUR. VOWEL-GRADES. 261

fŭgio (see § 23). The ū-grade of eu-roots and the ī-grade of ei-roots are frequent before certain suffixes, especially the TO-suffix (ch. v. § 28), e. g. I.-Eur. **lū-to-* (Lat. *so-lūtus*, Hom. βου-λῡτόν-δε), though the ŭ-grade and ĭ-grade are most common in the P. P. P., e. g. Gk. λῠ-τός (*ib.*) (cf. *defrŭtum*, must boiled down, Plaut. *Pseud.* 741, Mar. Vict. 24. 15 K. in defruto apicem secundae syllabae imponere debetis, nam a defervendo et decoquendo fit tale; but *defrŭtum* Virg. *G.* iv. 269). [See Osthoff's list of forms with ī, ū in *Morph. Unters.* vol. iv., such as Lat. *fŭ-mus* (I.-Eur. *dhū-mo-, O. Ind. dhū-má-), *sūtus* (Gk. νεο-κάττῡτος, O. Ind. syū-tá-), *pŭ-rus*, &c.]

§ 61. ĕ and ă. Cognate with O. Ind. asán-, Lettish asins, 'blood,' is an O. Lat. word *aser*, blood, with a derivative *aseratum, a mixture of wine and blood (Paul. Fest. 12. 19 Th. assaratum apud antiquos dicebatur genus quoddam potionis ex vino et sanguine temperatum, quod Latini prisci sanguinem 'assyr' vocarent; Gl. Philox. 23. 56 G. aser : *alμa*) which appears with an *e*-sound in Greek (ἔαρ in the Cretan dialect, μέλαν εἶαρ Callimachus). Another Old Latin word *sacena*, a priest's knife or axe, whose byform *scēna* recalls the Irish word for a knife, scian (stem scēnā-) (Fest. 466. 16 Th. scena ab aliis; a quibusdam 'sacena' appellatur, dolabra pontificalis; id. 488. 33 Th. scenam genus [fuisse ferri] manifestum est, sed utrum securis an dolabra sit, ambigitur. quam Cincius in libro qui est de verbis priscis, dolabram ait esse pontificiam. Livius in Lydio :

corruit quasi ictus scéna, haut multó secus)

may be, like another word for a priest's knife, *secespita* (Fest. 522. 4 Th.; Paul. Fest. 523. 3 Th. dicta autem est secespita a secando ; 'Serv.' ad *Aen.* iv. 262) derived from *seco*, to cut. O. H. Germ. sahs, O. Engl. seax Neut., 'a knife,' suggest connexion with Lat. *saxum*. Lat. *aries*, Gk. ἔρι-φος, is in Lithuanian éras, 'a lamb,' with ē, and has in Umbrian some *e*-sound, erietu Acc., so that it has been suggested that Lat. *ă*, Gk. ε (but see § 51 on κεκάδοντο with *ă* from root κηδ-), may be weak grades of an ē-root; and the same explanation might be given of *aser* and *sacena*. In several cases of Lat. *ă*, Gk. ε we have a Gk. byform with ι, e. g. Lat. *pateo*, *pando*, Gk. πετάννυμι and πίτνημι ; Lat. *quattuor* (Osc. *petora*, Umbr. *petur*-), Dor. Gk. τέτορες, Aeol. πέσυρες and Hom. πίσυρες ; Lat. *lapis*, Gk. λέπας, and in Hesych λίψ . . . πέτρα. Other examples are : Lat. *gradior*, and *gressus* (O. Sl. gredą, 'I come,' O. Ir. ingrennim, 'I pursue,' from root grend-, Goth. griþs, 'a step') ; Lat. *magnus* (cf. *măgis*, *măjor*, ch. ii. § 55), Gk. μέγας (Goth. mikils, Arm. mec) ; Lat. *nancis-cor*, *nactus*, Gk. ἐ-νεγκεῖν (Lith. nèszti, 'to carry,' O. Sl. nesti, O. Ir. conicim, 'I am able') ; Lat. *labium*, *labrum* (by analogy of *lambo* ?), O. Engl. lippa from root leb- (?) ; Lat. *glacies* and *gelu*; Lat. *alnus*, Lith. elksnis, O. Sl. jelīcha, O. H. G. elira and erila, Germ. Erle). *Farcio* (cf. *frequens*) shows *ăr* (cf. *confer(c)tus*), perhaps by metathesis (like Gk. φαρκτός beside φρακτός) (but see § 92).

§ 62. ōu-ău. Another example of **ăus-*, the weak grade of the I.-Eur. stem **ōus-*, 'mouth,' is *aureae*, whence, by composition with *ăgo*, *aurīga* (Paul. Fest. 6. 27 Th. 'aureax': auriga, 'aureas' enim dicebant frenum, quod ad aures equorum religabatur; 'orias' quo ora cohercebantur, with an absurd reference to *auris*, ear), a byform of *ōreae* (Fest. 202. 23 Th. 'oreae': freni quod ori inseruntur . . . *Nae*vius in Hariolo :

depránd¡ autem leóni si obdas óreas,

like our proverb 'to beard a lion'); *austium (C. I. L.* i. 1463) (O. Pruss. austin, 'mouth,' O. Ind. ṓṣṭha-, 'lip'), a byform of *ōstium* (Lith. ŭstà; 'mouth of river,' Lett. ōsta, 'harbour'). (Schmidt, *Pluralb.* p. 221.)

Y, W.

§ 63. Y. I.-Eur. initial y is represented in Greek sometimes by the rough breathing, e.g. Ὑάκ-ινθος, from I.-Eur. *yŭwn̥k-, sometimes by ζ, e.g. ζυγόν (I.-Eur. *yŭgo-), the same letter as we find used for an initial *y-* or *yy-*sound which has developed from an original dy-, e.g. Ζεύς (I.-Eur. *Dyĕu-). But in Latin both these kinds of I.-Eur. y are represented by *j*, as we write the letter, but, as the Romans wrote it, *i*, e.g. *jŭvenc-us, jŭgum*. The question whether this *j* was pronounced like a consonantal spirant (*y*), or like the half-vowel *i̯*, is discussed in ch. ii. § 48. In the middle of a word it is often difficult to say whether the original form of the sound, the 'Indo-European form,' as we call it, is more correctly expressed by the spirant y, or by the vowel i (or iy, i̯i, əy, &c.). This would no doubt often depend upon the preceding consonant or consonant-group. The I.-Eur. word for 'middle,' for example, we write *mĕdhyo- (cf. O. Ind. mádhya-, Gk. μέσ(σ)ος, Goth. midjis, O. Sl. mežda, 'the middle'); the word for 'paternal,' *patrio- or *patriyo- (*patrii̯o-, *patrəyo-) (cf. O. Ind. pítriya-, Gk. πάτριος). In Latin, this suffix -yo-, -io- appears as *-io-, mĕdius, pătrius*, though a word like *sŏcius* gives us a clue that *-yo-* may often have been the original form. For in this word the *qu* of the root seqᵘ-, 'to follow, accompany' (Lat. *sequor*), has become *c* in the derivative with this suffix, and with the o-grade of the root; and this would not have happened unless qᵘ (Lat. *qu*) had preceded a consonant (§ 116) (cf. Gk. ἀ-οσσητήρ from *ὀσσο- for *soqᵘyo-); so that the word originally *socyo-* has become in time a trisyllable, **socio-*.

At a later period, owing to that wave of Syncope which, as we saw, passed over Late and Vulgar Latin, this Adjective-ending *-ius*, and similar dissyllabic endings, were reduced to single syllables, the *i* (now become *y*) merging itself in the preceding consonant and giving it a palatal character, e.g. *Titius* became **Tityus*, and then something like **Titsus*; the *i* 'lost itself in a sibilant sound,' as a fifth-century grammarian puts it (perdit sonum suum et accipit sibilum; see ch. ii. § 90; also § 151).

It is this palatalization of a consonant before an *i*, reduced to *y*, which has made many Romance words, especially French, so unlike their Latin originals, e.g. Fr. bras from Lat. *bracchium*, through *braccy-; nièce from *neptia*, through *netty-; ache from *ăpium*, through *apy-; rage from *răbies, rabia*, through *raby-; singe from *sīmia*, through *simy- (see ch. iii. § 13). The history of the suffix -yo- in Latin is very like that of the suffix -lo-. After a consonant both developed a parasitic vowel; **soc-yo-* became **soc-iyo-*, *socius*, as **oc-lo-* (from root oqu-) became **oc-olo-*, *oculus*; and this vowel was in both cases absorbed by syncope at a later period, *soc-yus, *oclus (whence the Romance forms, e.g. Ital. occhio). Between vowels *y* was dropped in Latin, e.g. I.-Eur. *eyā-, the Fem. of the Demonstrative (Goth. ija Acc.) is Latin ea (so in Umbro-Osc., Umbr. *eo, ea*, Osc. íú, *io*; von Planta, i. p. 175). Causative Verbs, which ended in I.-Eur. in -eyō (e.g. O. Ind. mānáyā-mi from root man-, the I.-Eur. root men-; Gk. φοβέω from root φεβ-), end in Latin in -eō, e.g. *mŏneo*, I remind, 'cause to remember,' from root men- of *mĕmĭni* for *me-men-i, I remember. On the weakening of -yĕ- to ĭ in I.-Eur. and in Latin (e.g. *ab-icio*), see § 51, p. 256.

The intervocalic *j* (*y*) which we find in *major, aio*, &c. (pronounced ' măyyor,' ' ăyyo,' ch. ii. § 55), has arisen through suppression (or assimilation) of *h* (for I.-Eur. ĝh) before *y*. In the first syllable *y* is not found after any consonant in Latin, except *d*, and that only in the older period, e.g. O. Lat. *Diovem*, classical *Jŏvem* (from dyĕu-, O. Ind. Dyāús, Gk. Ζεύς, while Lat. *diēs* shows a bystem *diĕu-, O. Ind. Diyāús), though how far this *j* (*y*) of *Jovem* (for *yy*-, I.-Eur. dy-, Gk. ζ-) differed at any time in pronunciation from the *j* of *jŭvenis* (I.-Eur. y-: Gk. '-) and from the *j* of *jugum* (I.-Eur. y-, Gk. ζ-), we cannot say. All these have developed to the same sound in the Romance languages, e.g. Ital. Giove, giovane, giogo (with the sound of our j or -dge in 'judge').

The Oscan orthography shows both ii and i for intervocalic i (y), though the paucity of the remains of the language makes it impossible to determine how far this was arbitrary or reflected the actual pronunciation, e.g. diíviiaí *' dīviae,' mefiaí 'mediae'; heriiad is 3 Sg. Pres. Subj. of the verb and heriam Acc. Sg. of the noun derived from her-, 'to wish' (I.-Eur. ĜHER-). The presence of the *y*-sound is indicated by the doubling of a preceding consonant after the accented vowel, e.g. medikkiaí 'meddiciae' Dat. Sg., Σταττιηις 'Statii' Gen. Sg., *Pettio*-, &c. In the Oscan dialect of Bantia this *y*-sound is merged in the preceding consonant, e.g. *Bansae* 'Bantiae,' *allo* 'alia' (see von Planta, i. p. 165). [Cf. Pel. *đ* (ch. ii. § 51), written *s* in Musesa.]

§ 64. I.-Eur. initial y. I.-Eur. *yŭwn̥ko- (O. Ind. yuvaśá-, Gk. 'Τάκ-ινθοs, O. Ir. ōac, Welsh ieuanc, Gaul. Jovincillus, Goth. juggs for *juvunga-, O. Engl. geong), Lat. *jŭvencus*, with its cognates *jŭvĕnis* (O. Ind. yúvan-), *jŭventa* (Goth. junda, Engl. youth), &c.; I.-Eur. *yŭgo-, (O. Ind. yugám, Gk. ζυγόν, Goth. juk, Engl. yoke, O. Sl. igo for *yĭgo, *yŭgo), Lat. *jŭgum*, from the root yeug-, 'to join' (O. Ind. yuj-, Gk. ζεύγνυμι, Lith. jùngiu, 'I yoke'), Lat. *jungo*; I.-Eur. *yūs- (O. Ind. yūṣa-, Gk. ζύ-μη for *ζύσ-μη, leaven, Lith. júszė), Lat. *jūs*, broth, while Lat. *jūs*, law, older *jous*, is I.-Eur. *yeus- (O. Ind. yós, 'welfare'); I.-Eur. yă-, 'to go,' formed by adding the suffix ā to i-, the weak grade of the root ei-, 'to go' (O. Ind. yă-, 'to go,' Lith. jóti, 'to ride,' O. Sl. jad) appears in Lat. *jā-nua*, a door, *Jānuarius*. (On the tendency to give Latin *a* after initial *j* the open *e*-sound, whence Vulg. Lat. **Jenuarius*, see ch. ii. § 1.) Similarly Lat. *jŏcus* with I.-Eur. yŏ- (cf. Lith. jŭkas, 'ridicule,' with I.-Eur. yō-, *B. B.* xviii. 255) (cf. § 59 above). On *riēn* (Plaut.; cf. *liēn*) and *rēn*, see Prisc. i. 149. 7 H. On Vulg. Lat. *qu(i)ētus*, ch. ii. § 151, and cf. ch. iii. § 11 on *par(i)ēs*.

§ 65. I.-Eur. y preceded by a consonant. (1) In the first syllable:— This y has been dropped in the Latin derivatives from I.-Eur. roots like syū-, 'to sew' (O. Ind. syū-, Gk. κα-σσύω, a compound with κατ(ά), Goth. siujan, O. Engl. seowian, Lith. siúti, O. Sl. šiti), Lat. *suo*; *ĝhyĕs-, 'yesterday' (O. Ind. hyás, Gk. χθές; cf. Goth. gistra-dagis), Lat. *hĕri*, with Adj *hĕster-nus*; though it is possible that there were sometimes I.-Eur. byforms without y (cf. O. Ind. sū-tra-, 'thread,' also used, in the sense of 'clue,' for ritual and grammatical text-books, the Sûtras). So Lat. *spuo* (Gk. πτύω, Lith. spiáuju, O. Sl. pljują, &c.). There is a similar doubt about dy-. It may have lost the dental at a very early period, for we have *Ioves* ('*Jovios*'?) on the ancient Dvenos inscription, and it is not possible to prove that the form *Diovem* had gone out of use by the time that the form *Jŏvem* came in (cf. *Diouem, C. I. L.* i. 57, *Iouei*, i. 56, both on old Praenestine mirrors). *Diovem* may quite well have come from a byform *dĭyĕw-, as O. Lat. *siēs* from *siyēs (O. Ind. siyás), a byform of *syēs, (O. Ind. syás) and have been discarded in course of time for the other 'doublet' *dyĕw- *Jovem*.

(2) In other syllables:—Y after a consonant in other syllables than the first became vocalic in Latin. Thus after p we find y becoming τ in Greek in verbs formed with the suffix -yo- (-iyo-), e.g. τύπ-τω for *τυπ-yω, χαλεπ-τω for *χαλεπ-yω; but in Latin these verbs appear with -*pio*, e.g. *căpio*, *săpio*; after n we find y producing epenthesis in Greek, e.g. βαίνω for *gʷm̥-yō, root gʷem-, but not in Latin, e.g. *vĕnio*. But -ĝhy-, as has been mentioned, became *hy*,

§§ 64–68.] REPRESENTATIVES OF I.-EUR. SOUNDS. Y, W. 265

then *y* or rather *yy*, e. g. *ăio*, pronounced *ayyo*, and often written *aiio* (ch. i. § 7), from ăgh-, 'to say.'

§ 66. I.-Eur. y between vowels. The Nom. Pl. of I-stems shows I.-Eur. -ĕyĕs, e. g. I.-Eur. *treyes from the stem tri-, 'three' (O. Ind. tráyas), *ĝhosteyes from the stem ĝhosti-, 'a stranger' (O. Sl. gostije), in Latin *-ēs* for *-*e-es*, e. g. *trēs*, *hostēs*. In the words *ăhēnus*, *ahēneus* the letter *h* indicates the hiatus caused by the dropping of y of I.-Eur. *äyĕs-, 'metal,' *ayes-no-, 'made of metal' (O. Ind. áyas-), like *h* in the Umbrian *stahu* for *stā-yo, 'I stand' (Lat. *sto*). Like Lat. *stō* for *stā-yo (Lith. pa-stó-ju), are *fleo* for *flē-yo (O. Sl. blĕ-ją), *neo* for *nē-yo, &c., where the similar vowels *a* and *o* are blended into one sound, but the dissimilar, *e* and *o*, remain in hiatus. Similarly Lat. *formo* for *formā-yo, from *forma* (stem *formā-), and other 1st Conj. verbs from 1st Decl. nouns, like Gk. τιμῶ, for τιμά-ω, *τιμάyω, from τιμή, Dor. τιμά (stem τιμā-).

§ 67. Latin j. Any *j* which has been developed by the phonetic changes of the language is treated in much the same way as I.-Eur. y. Thus the group *sj-* (*sy-*) has been produced by the union under one accent of the two words *si audes*. The *j* (*y*) is dropped, like I.-Eur. y in *suo*, in the form *sōdes*, a form which seems to have come into use in the period between Plautus and Terence. For Plautus has the full *si audes*, e. g. *Poen.* 757 mitte ád me, si audes, hódie Adelphasiúm tuam, but Terence the shortened form, e. g. *Andr.* 85 dic, sodes. Internal *j* (*y*) after a consonant becomes vocalic in *nunc-iam* (3 syll. Plaut.), and between two vowels disappears in *bīgae* for *bi-jigae* from *bi-* and *jugum*. On *abjĕcio*, *abjĭcio*, *abĭcio* see ch. iii. § 18, ch. ii. § 48, ch. i. § 7.

§ 68. W. I.-Eur. initial w is represented in Latin by the sound which we write *v*, and which the Romans wrote *u*. (On the spelling and on the pronunciation of the letter, see ch. ii. § 48), e. g. I.-Eur. *weĝhō, 'I carry' (O. Ind. váhā-mi, Gk. (ϝ)όχος, Pamph. ϝέχω, O. Ir. fēn for *fegn, 'a waggon,' W. gwain, Goth. ga-viga, Germ. be-wege), Lat. *vĕhō*. The suffix wo- after a consonant was perhaps, like the suffix yo- (§ 63), vocalic in early Latin, e.g. *furvus* for early *fusuos (§ 148 ; cf. *fus-cus*), *Minerua*, a quadrisyllable in Plautus (*Bacch.* 893); though like Syncope, like that which reduced *Titius*, &c. to *Tityus*, reduced *ăruum*, *lărua*, *mīluus* (all trisyllabic in Plautus) to *arvum*, *larva*, *milvus*. Between vowels *v* remains, e. g. *ăvis*, *ŏvis*; but in the unaccented syllable we find *u* for *ăv*, *ĕv*, *ŏv*, e. g. *dēnuo* for *de novo* (see ch. iii. § 24), and before the accent *v* is often dropped, e. g. *seorsum* (and *sorsum*) for *sēvorsum*, especially between similar vowels, e. g. O. Lat. *dī(v)īnus*, *lă(v)ābrum* (see ch. ii. § 53). After a consonant in the initial syllable, w is dropped in *pius* for *pw-īyo- (?) from the same root as *pūrus*, but remains (like y) after d, e. g. O. Lat. *duonus*, *Duenos*, *duellum*; though at the beginning of the literary period this *dv-* passed into *b-*, e. g. *bŏnus*, *bĕnĕ*, *bellum*. Side by side with dissyllabic *duonus*, *duellum* we find trisyllabic *duonus, duellum,* just as in I.-Eur. we have duw- and dw- in the words for 'two' (O. Ind. duvá, and dvá, Gk. δύω and *δ(F)ίς, Lat. *duo* and *bĭs*), 'dog' (O. Ind. šuván- and šván-, Gk. κύων and Lith. szŭ). And side by side with I.-Eur. *twoi, the Locative case of the 2nd Pers. Pron. Sg. we have the unaccented form *toi (O. Ind. tvé and tē, Gk. σοί and τοι), so that it is often difficult to say when the I.-Eur. form has dropped w, when it has w, and when it has uw (əw), and to determine when the w has been dropped in the 'I.-Eur. period' and when in the 'Latin period.' An ĕ has been turned into ŏ through the influence of a preceding w in the group swĕ-, e.g. *sŏror* (I.-Eur. *swĕsor-); *sŏcer* (I.-Eur. *swĕkŭro-), &c. (see § 10). Before a consonant (l, r) I.-Eur. w is dropped in Latin, e.g. *rādix* for *wrād- (cf. Goth. vaurts, Engl. wort). On the weakening of unaccented wĕ to ŭ in I.-Eur., e.g. *pĕrŭt(i) (O. Ind. parut, Gk. πέρυσι) from the root wĕt- (Gk. Ϝέτος, a year, Lat. *vĕtus*), and in Latin, e.g. *con-cŭtio* for *-quetio,* see § 51, and on *ferbui* for *fervui*, ch. ii. § 52.

Latin *v* often represents I.-Eur. g^u, gh^u (see §§ 139, 143), both initial, e.g. *vĕnio* for *g^umyō from the root g^nem- (Gk. βαίνω, O. Ind. gam-, Goth. qima, Engl. come), and between vowels, e.g. *nĭv-em* Acc. for *nigh^{u}m (Gk. νίφα Acc., W. nyf) from the root sneigh^u- (e. g. O. Ir. snechta, Goth. snaivs, Lith. snaigýti, 'to snow,' O. Sl. snĕgŭ, 'snow').

In Umbro-Osc. there are separate symbols in the native alphabets for the consonantal and for the vocalic U-sound (written in our transcription v and u respectively). The rules for the use of uv and v in Umbr. have not yet been determined; we have arvia and (once) aruvia, vatuva (never *vatva), &c. (see von Planta, i. p. 180).

§ 69. I.-Eur. initial w. The I.-Eur. root weid-, 'to know, to see' (O. Ind. véda, Arm. gitem, Gk. Ϝοῖδα, O. Ir. fiadaim, Goth vait, O. Engl. wāt, Engl. wot, O. Sl. vidĕti, 'to see,' vĕdĕti, 'to know') appears in Lat. *video* ; the I.-Eur. *weiḱ- (O. Ind. víś-, vēśá-, Gk. οἶκος, Goth. veihs, O. Sl. vïsĭ), in Latin *vīcus* ; the conjunction *wĕ, 'or' (O. Ind. vā, Gk. ἠ-(Ϝ)έ), Lat. *-vĕ* ; the root wert-, 'to turn' (O. Ind. vart-, Goth. vairþa, Engl. 'woe *worth* the day,' W. gwerthyd, 'a spindle,' Lith. vartaũ, O. Sl. vratiti Inf.) in Lat. *verto*. Similarly Lat. *vieo, vītis* (O. Ind. vi-, Lith. výti, O. Sl. viti, Ir. fëith, 'woodbine,' W. gwydd-fid) ; Lat. *vellus*, with *ll* for ln (§ 78), (Goth. vulla, Engl. wool, Lith. vìlnos, O. Sl. vlŭna) ; Lat. *vērus* (O. Ir. fīr, W. gwir, Goth. tuz-vērjan, 'to doubt,' O. Engl. wǣr, 'true,' Germ. wahr; cf. Lith. vĕrà, 'faith,' O. Sl. vĕra) ; Lat. *vespa* (O. Engl. wæsp and

§§ 69–71.] REPRESENTATIVES OF I.-EUR. SOUNDS. Y, W. 267

wæps, O. Sl. vosa); Lat. *vīrus* (O. Ind. vīṣā-, Gk. *ῖós* for ϝίσος); Lat. *vŏmo* (O. Ind. vam-, Gk. ἐμέω for *ϝεμ-, Lith. vemiù).

§ 70. I.-Eur. w (and Latin v) between vowels. I.-Eur. *gu̯īwo-, 'alive' [O. Ind. jīvá-, W. byw, O. Ir. biu, Goth. qius, O. Engl. cwicu- (with -c- developed before u), Engl. quick, Lith. gývas, O. Sl. živŭ] is Lat. *vīvus*; I.-Eur. *nĕwo-, 'new' (O. Ind. náva-, Gk. νέ(ϝ)ος, O. Sl. novŭ) is Lat. *nŏvus*; I.-Eur. *nĕwṇ, 'nine' (O. Ind. náva, Gk. ἐν-νέα, O. Ir. nōi, W. naw, Goth. niun) is Lat. *nŏvem*; I.-Eur. *yŭwṇko-, (O. Ind. yuvaśá-, Gk. Ὑάκ-ινθος, Gaul. Jovinc-illus, W. ieuanc) is Lat. *jŭvencus*. Similarly Lat. *clāvis* (Gk. κλη(ϝ)ίς); Lat. *lēvir*, better *laevir*, brother-in-law (O. Ind. dēvár-, Arm. taigr, Gk. δᾱήρ from *δαιϝερ-) ; Lat. *aevum* (Gk. αἰ(ϝ)ών, Goth. aivs, O. Engl. ǣ) ; Lat. *laevus* (Gk. λαι(ϝ)ός).

The question of the change of the ending *-vos* to *-vus* and *-us* is a difficult one. The most natural explanation of the change of *deivos* to *deus* (the form in ordinary use as early as Plautus) is that given in § 33 (through *de(i)us*), which takes for granted that *-vos* became *-vus* when *-os* became *-us* (§ 17) [cf. *Flaus* on a coin of 200–150 B.C (*C. I. L.* i. 277), *Gnaeus*, *boum*, *coum* and *cohum* (§ 19)], and seems to conflict with the fact that the spelling *-vo-* (with *-quo-*, *-guo-*) is retained to the end of the Republic. But it is by no means clear that the spelling *vo* did not represent the sound *vu*, the spelling *vo* being preferred to *vv*, because this last might be confused with the sound *ū* (ch. i. § 9) or *uv*. Velius Longus (first cent. A.D.) expressly asserts this (58. 4 K.) : a plerisque superiorum 'primitivus' et 'adoptivus' et 'nominativus' per v et o scripta sunt, scilicet quia sciebant vocales inter se ita confundi non posse ut unam syllabam [non] faciant, apparetque eos hoc genus nominum aliter scripsisse, aliter enuntiasse. Nam cum per o scriberent, per u tamen enuntiabant. The tendency to re-insert the *v* from other cases and cognate words, *divo*, *divos*, *diva*, &c., would interfere from time to time with the natural development of the sound. (Cf. § 67 on *abjecio*, *abjicio* and *abicio*.) On Republican inscrr. we find v in IVENTA (*C. I. L.* i. 1202), &c., where vv (*uv*) is the orthography of the Augustan age, but that this always represents the pronunciation (as in *Pācu(v)ius* also written *Pāquius*; *Vēsu(v)ius*, cf. Galen x. 364) is unlikely. [For examples of the spellings vo, vv, v (*vo, vu, uv, u*), and for a fuller discussion of the treatment of intervocalic *v* in Latin, see Solmsen, *Stud. Lautg.* sect. iii.]

The process of Syncope affected at various periods intervocalic *v* in different ways. Under the early Accent Law *ăvi-spex* was reduced to *auspex* (cf. *au-ceps*), *vīvĭta* (Lith. gywatà ; cf. Gk. βιοτή) to *vīta*, &c.; under the Paenultima Law *ăvidēre* became *audere*, &c.; in the period of the Early Literature *aevĭtas* became *aetas*, *ūvĭdus* became *ūdus*, *praevides* became *praedes*, &c.; while four-syllabled words with the first, second, and third syllables short, which were in the second cent. B.C. still accented on the first syllable (ch. iii. § 8), may have suffered syncope within the literary period or at a much earlier time, e. g. *Aulius* from *Auilios* (*C. I. L.* i. 83, Praeneste). (On the loss of *-v-* through Syncope see ch. iii. § 16. 9.)

§ 71. I.-Eur. w after a consonant. (1) In the first syllable :—Latin *sērius* (Goth. svērs, 'honourable'; Germ. schwer, 'heavy') is from the root swer-, 'to weigh' (Lith. sveŕti) ; for Latin *si* we have in Oscan svaí, in Umbr. sve ; Latin *sīdus* is connected with Lith. svidéti, 'to shine'; Lat. *suf-fīo*, to fumigate, with Gk. θύω, from I.-Eur. *dhw-iyō. But swā- is Lat. *suā-* in *suavis* (a trisyllable in Vulg. Lat., cf. Ital. soave ; Servius ad *Aen.* i. 357 says that many persons in his day made *suădet* a trisyllable). Lat. *dĭs-*, apart, asunder, seems to be I.-Eur. *dĭs-, a byform of *dwĭs (Lat. bĭs, O. Lat. duis), as I.-Eur. *toi (unaccented) was a byform of *twoi (accented), though some regard Lat. dis as the direct descendant of I.-Eur. *dwis, and O. Lat. duis (class. bis) as the descendant of I.-Eur. *dŭwis. Sāvium, a kiss, seems to represent s(u)āvium. On sos, &c. for suos, &c., see ch. vii. § 12.

(2) In other syllables :—Internal -dw- becomes -v- in suavis for *suad-vis ; *derviosus, later derbiosus (see ch. ii. § 52), for *der-dwi-oso- (O. Ind. dardū- ; cf. Engl. tetter). Vĭduus does not show I.-Eur. -dhw-, but -dhĕw-, for it represents I.-Eur. *wĭdhĕwo- (O. Ind. vidháva-, Gk. ἠ-(ϝ)ίθε(ϝ)ος, O. Sl. vĭdova, 'widow.') Postconsonantal u, later v, is in Vulgar and Late Latin dropped before the accent in Jan(v)arius, Febr(v)arius, batt(v)ére, cons(v)ére, quatt(v)ordecim, contin(v)ari, whence Ital. Gennajo, Febbrajo, quattordici, &c. (see ch. ii. § 54), like v between vowels before the accent (see above). The suffix -uo- remains dissyllabic in the classical form of words like mortuus (O. Sl. mrĭtvŭ). So quattuor (O. Ind. catváras, Lith. ketverì, O. Sl. četvero) ; tĕnuis (O. Ind. tanvī F.), gĕnua (Zend. zanva, Lesb. Gk. γόννα for *γονϝα), though tenvia, genva are found in classical poetry, and in the first cent. A. D. tenuis is declared to have wavered between a dissyllable and a trisyllable (Caesellius ap. Cassiod. vii. 205 K.). Late-Lat. mortvus, &c. (ch. ii. § 48) became mortus, &c. (Ital. morto), as rĭvus, &c., rius.

dw-, duw-. Duellius (Duill- ?), consul of 260 B. C., was the first to change his name to Bellius (Cic. Orat. lv. 153 ; cf. Quint. i. 4. 15) ; duonus seems to be a trisyllable in the Saturnian fragments (cf. ch. ii. § 141 n), viz. C. I. L. i. 32: dùonóro óptumo fuíse uíro, and Naevius(?) ap. Fest. 532. 22 Th.: símul dúona eórum pórtant ad náuis, duellum to be a disyllable (Aem. Lepidus' inscr. ap. Caes. Bass. 265. 25 K. : duéllo mágno diriméndo, régibus subigéndis), as it always is in Plautus (e. g. Amph. 189 ; extíncto duello máxumo), whereas Ennius has (A. 168 M.) : pars occidit illa duellis, a scansion imitated by later poets. (On O. Lat. duis, dui- for bis, bi- see ch. vi. § 59 ; on du- in glosses, see Löwe, Prodr. p. 363, and add Duellona, C. G. L. ii. 56. 34.)

§ 72. I.-Eur. w before a consonant. Lat. līquo, līquor stand for *vlĭq- (O. Ir. fliuch, ' wet ') ; Lat. rĕpens may be a Pres. Part. of I.-Eur. wrĕp- (Gk. ῥέπω, to fall ; cf. Lith. virpĕti, 'to tremble') (but see ch. viii. § 18).

§ 73. M, N. In Sanscrit various kinds of nasals are distinguished in writing. The palatal n (made palatal by the preceding j) of yajñá-, ' worship ' (Gk. ἁγνός, holy) is written differently from the cerebral n (made cerebral by the preceding r) of mṛṇā́mi, ' I crush, annihilate ' (Gk. μάρναμαι Mid.). And in Greek, owing to the fact that γ before ν of γίγνομαι, &c. had come to take the sound of the Agma (see ch. ii. § 63), *γιɜνομαι (cf. Dor. γίνομαι), γ was used to express the guttural nasal, e. g. ἄγκυρα, ἐγγύς, though in inscriptions we often find ἄνκυρα, ἐνγύς. But in Latin we have only the symbols m, n (see ch. ii. § 63, and on their pronunciation, ch. ii. § 61). Before a consonant, though sometimes omitted on inscriptions, they were not dropped in correct speech. Lĭgŭla, spoon (cf. O. Ir. liag, W. llwy), is not the same word as *lingŭla*, strap; **něpe* in Plautus should be corrected to *nemp(e)*. (For other instances, see Skutsch, *Forsch.* i. § 2.) **M.** I.-Eur. m is Latin *m*, whether initial, e.g. I.-Eur. **māter-* (O. Ind. mātár-, Arm. mair, Dor. Gk. μάτηρ, O. Ind. māthir, O. H. G. muoter, O. Engl. mōdor, Lith. motė̃, 'wife,' O. Sl. mati), Lat. *māter*, or internal, e.g. from I.-Eur. root wem- (O. Ind. vám-, Gk. (ϝ)ἐμέω, Lith. vemaĩ, Pl.), Lat. *vŏmo*; I.-Eur. *termen- (O. Ind. tárman-, Gk. τέρμων), Lat. *termō, termĭnus*; I.-Eur. rump-, 'to break' (O. Ind. lumpámi), Lat. *rumpo*, or final, e.g. I.-Eur. -m of the Acc. Sg., as in I.-Eur. *tŏm (O. Ind. tám, Gk. τόν, Goth. þan-a, Lith. tą̃, O. Sl. tŭ), O. Lat. *is-tom*, class. Lat. *is-tum*. Before *y (i), t, s, d, c* we find *n* in *quŏniam* (for *quom jam*, and originally used in a temporal sense 'when now,' 'now that,' ch. x. § 13), *quan-sei, C. I. L.* i. 200. 27 (on *quăsi*, see ch. x. § 11), *altrin-sĕcus, centum* from I.-Eur. *ḳm̥tom (Lith. szim̃tas), *septen-triōnes* (lit. 'the seven oxen,' according to Aelius Stilo and Varro, who regarded the *-trio* not as a mere termination, but as a rustic word for an ox, Gell. ii. 21), *septen-dĕcim, nunc* (from *num*, now, which survives in *etiamnum* in a temporal sense, but usually has the interrogative sense of 'now,' as in our 'now is this the case?', 'now is that true?', where 'now' has something of the dubitative significance of Lat. *num), princeps* for **prīm(i)-ceps*; though a traditional spelling is often used, e.g. *numcŭbi, quamtus*, O. Lat. *quamde*, than, &c. (see ch. ii. § 61). A *p* is inserted to facilitate the pronunciation of these groups in *sumptus, sumpsi* for *sumtus, sumsi, exemplum* for **exemlum*, &c. I.-Eur. mr is Latin *br* in *hībernus* from **hibrĭno-* (§ 13), (Gk. χειμερινός), but initial mr probably became in Latin *fr*. On the loss of final *-um* by elision in *sed* from older *sedum, nihil* from *nihilum*, &c., see ch. iii. § 52.

Latin *m* represents an original *n* before a labial, &c., e.g. *impello* for *inpello*, an original labial before *n*, e.g. *scamnum* from the root skabh-, 'to support,' with Diminutive *scabellum*. It is sometimes lost in a consonant-group, e.g. *forceps* for **form(i)-ceps*, from *formus*, warm.

I.-Eur. m is Umbro-Osc. m, e.g. Umbr. *matrer*, Osc. maatreís 'matris.' Final -m is usually dropped in Umbrian (see von Planta, i. pp. 301, 570).

§ 74. I.-Eur. m; other examples. I.-Eur. *mĕdhyo- (O. Ind. mádhya-, Gk. μέσ(σ)ος, Ir. medōn, 'the middle,' Goth. midjis, O. Sl. mežda, 'the middle') is Lat. mĕdius ; I.-Eur. root men-, 'to think' (O. Ind. man-, mánman-, 'thought,' O. Ir. men-me, 'thought,' O. H. G. minna, 'remembrance,' Lith. menù, 'I remember') appears in Lat. mĕmĭni for *me-men-i, mens, &c. Similarly Lat. mē (O. Ind. mắm, Gk. με, Ir. mi, Goth. mi-k) ; Lat. sēmi- (O. Ind. sāmi-, Gk. ἡμι-) ; Lat. hŏmo (Goth. guma, Engl. groom, bride-groom) ; Lat. cum, com-, with (O. Ir. com-); Lat. mors, mortis (O. Ind. mṛti-, Lith. mirtìs, O. Sl. sŭ-mrĭtĭ ; cf. Goth. maurþr, 'murder'); Lat. fūmus (O. Ind. dhūmá-, Lith. dúmai, Pl., O. Sl. dymü).

§ 75. n for m. Lat. con-tra from com ; quon-dam from quom ; vēnun-do, class. vēndo, from vēno-, sale (cf. Gk. ὦνος), lit. 'to put or make sale,' like vēnum eo, class. vēneo, lit. 'to go to sale' (cf. pessum do, to ruin, and pessum eo, to be ruined). On the spellings damdum, damdam (C. I. L. i. 206. 17. 49,) &c. see ch. ii. § 64.

§ 76. I.-Eur. ms. In Lat. tĕnĕbrae (Plur., like O. Ind. támạsi, Russ. sumerki) from the I.-Eur. root tem- (Lith. témti, 'to grow dark', Ir. tem, 'dark,' temel, 'darkness') the n seems to be due to the influence of s, for O. Ind. támisrā, O. H. G. dinstar, Germ. finster, show that *temĕsrā- or *temsrā- was the old form of the stem in Latin. The m remains in tĕmĕre Loc., 'in the dark' (ch. ix. § 5) (cf. O. Ind. támas- from I.-Eur. *tĕmes-, 'darkness,' and Germ. Dämmerung). Another example of I.-Eur. -ms- (mes-?) is Lat. ŭmĕrus (Umbr. onso-, O. Ind. ạ́sa-, Arm. us, Gk. ὦμος, Goth. ams), and perhaps Lat. nŭmĕrus, Numerius (cf. Numisius, O. Lat. Numasio-,Oscan Niumsio-) ; and another example of -msr- is Lat. membrum for *mems-ro- (cf. Goth. mimz, 'flesh,' O. Sl. męso ; also Gk. μηρός for μησρο-, the thigh, O. Ind. mạsá-, 'flesh,' Arm. mis.) The fewness and the contrariety of these instances make it difficult to decide how I.-Eur. -ms- was treated in Latin. Latin -ms- became ns, e. g. con-sentio, con-silio, &c., from com-, where the m might be regarded as the final letter of a separate word, but mps, e. g. sumpsi, dempsi, where the m could not be so regarded. (On the spellings sumpsi, sumsi, &c., hiems, hiemps, see Brambach, Lat. Orth. p. 248 ; the Roman grammarians approve of sumpsi, &c., but not of hiemps.)

§ 77. I.-Eur. mr, ml are equally difficult to trace in Latin. They are represented by βρ, βλ in Greek when initial, e. g. βροτός, βλώσκω, βλίττω (from μέλι), by μβρ, μβλ when medial, e. g. ἄμβροτος, μέμβλωκα. In Irish we find initial mr- to be an early spelling, which was changed later to br-, e. g. mraich, 'malt,' later braich, from a stem *mrăci-, and similarly ml-, later bl-, e.g. mlicht, blicht, 'milk.' The Latin fraces, olivelees, seems to be the same as this Irish word mraich, in which case fr- will be the Latin equivalent of I.-Eur. mr- (for other examples, see Osthoff, Morph. Unters. v. 85), and the b of hibernus, tūber, a swelling, a truffle (from tumeo, to swell), will be like the b of ruber, &c. (§ 114), for which f is found in other dialects, e. g. Umbr. rufro-. [Ital. tartufo, 'truffle,' lit. 'earth-mushroom,' from terra and tŭber, a name borrowed by the Germans in the eighteenth cent. for the potato, Kartoffel, shows that the dialectal form of tūber had f (ch. ii. § 83)]. The long vowel in hībernus, tūber might then be explained like the long i of infero, infringo, &c., (ch. ii. § 144), and the original forms would be *himfrino-, tŭmfro-. On the other hand the analogy of other languages and the connexion of m and b in

Latin would make us expect to find Latin *br* as the equivalent of I.-Eur. initial mr-. A further difficulty is caused by *gĕner*, a word which it is hard to dissociate from Gk. γαμβρός, with *n(e)r* for -mr-. I.-Eur. medial -ml- appears in *exemplum* for *ex-em-lo-*, lit. 'something taken out,' with a euphonic *p* inserted, while a vowel seems to have intervened between m and l in *trĕmulus, tŭmulus*, &c. (ch. v. § 21).

§ 78. **N.** I.-Eur. n is in Latin *n*, whether (1) initial, e.g. I.-Eur. *nĕwo-, *newio-, 'new' (O. Ind. náva-, návya-, Arm. nor, Gk. νέος, O. Ir. nūe, Gaul. Novios, W. newydd from *noviyo-, Goth. niujis, O. Engl. nēowe, Lith. naũjas, O. Sl. novŭ), Lat. *nŏvus, Nŏvius*, or (2) internal; e.g. the I.-Eur. root sĕn-, 'old' (O. Ind. sána-, Arm. hin, Gk. ἔνη καὶ νέα, O. Ir. sen, W. hen, Goth. sineigs, sinista Superl., Lith. sēnas) appears in Lat. *sĕnex, senior*, the root angh-, 'to choke' (O. Ind. ą́has-, 'need,' Arm. anjuk, 'narrow,' Gk. ἄγχω, O. Ir. cum-ung, 'narrow,' Goth. aggvus, 'narrow,' Engl. anger, Lith. añksztas, 'narrow,' O. Sl. ązŭkŭ) in Lat. *ango, angor, angustus*, or (3) final; e.g. the I.-Eur. preposition *ĕn (Gk. ἐν, O. Ir. in, Goth. in, Lith. į̃) Lat. *ĭn*, O. Lat. *en*. Before a labial we find *m*, e.g. *impello, immūto*. But nm seems to have become in Latin *rm*, if *carmen* stands for *can-men*, *germen* for *gen-men*, just as the *nm* which arose at a later time from the syncope of *i* in *ănĭma* has become in some Romance languages *rm* (e.g. Prov. anma, alma, and arma, O. Fr. anme, alme, and arme, Catal. arma and alma, Sicil. arma, Milanese armella). Before *l* it was assimilated, e.g. *cŏrōlla* for *corōn-la, hŏmŭllus* for *homŏn-lus, illĭgo, illex, malluviae*, water for washing the hands, from *man-luviae* (so before *r* in *irritus*, &c.), and also after *l*, e.g. *collis* for *col-ni-s* (Lith. kálnas; cf. Gk. κολωνός), *vellus* (Lith. vìlna, O. Sl. vlŭna), as in Greek we have λλ for λν in ἐλλός, a fawn (Lith. élnis, O. Sl. jelenĭ), &c. In *ulna*, &c. a vowel originally came between *l* and *n* (cf. Gk. ὠλένη). On the pronunciation of *ns* as *ss*, or *s*, with lengthening of the preceding vowel, e.g. *vicessimus* and *vicēsimus* from *vīcensimus*, see ch. ii. § 64. So with *nf* (*ib.*).

I.-Eur. n is in Umbro-Osc. n, e.g. Umbr. *nerus*, Dat. Pl., Osc. *nerum*, Gen. Pl., from the same root as Gk. ἀνήρ (cf. *Nĕro*). Before mutes and spirants we find n often dropped, especially in O. Umbr., e.g. iveka 'juvencas' (N. Umbr. *ivenga*), but in Umbr. of all periods before s, e.g. aseriatu and *aseriato, anseriato*; in Oscan before a mute in an unaccented final syllable, e.g. -et for

272   THE LATIN LANGUAGE.   [Chap. IV.

-ent 3rd Plur., íak in Acc. Sg. for íank (Lat. *eam*, with the particle
-ce, ch. vii. § 15) (see von Planta, i. p. 301).

§ 79. I.-Eur. n; other examples. I.-Eur. *nĕwn̥, 'nine' (O. Ind. náva, Gk.
ἐν-νέα, O. Ir. nōi, W. naw, Goth. niun, O. Engl. nigon, Lith. dewynì, O. Sl.
devęti̇́ with d- by analogy of the words for ten, just as Vulg. Engl. 'thruppence' takes its *u* from 'tuppence,' 'twopence.') Lat. *nŏvem* [for *noven* (§ 81) :
a similar substitution of *-m* for *-n* has been found in Subj. *feram*, (O. Ind.
bharāṇi)]; I.-Eur. *nō, *nōu, 'we' (O. Ind. nāu, Gk. νώ, O. Sl. na ; cf. O. Ir. ni),
Lat. *nō-s*; I.-Eur. *nās-, 'the nose' (O. Ind. nā́sā Du., Lith. nósis; cf. O. Engl.
nosu), Lat. *nāris* for *nās-is ; I.-Eur. *nāu-, 'ship' (O. Ind. nḁ̄ú-, Arm. nav,
Gk. ναῦς, O. Ir. nau, W. noe, 'a dish, vessel'), Lat. *nāvis*; I.-Eur. *nĕpot-,
'grandson' (O. Ind. nápāt-, M. Ir. niae, niath Gen., W. nai), Lat. *nĕpōs*, Gen.
nepōtis; I.-Eur. sneigh⁴-, 'to snow' (Zend. snaežaiti, Gk. νίφα Acc., ἀγάννιφοςfor
*ἀγα-σνιφος, O. Ir. snecht, W. nyf, Goth. snaivs, Lith. snaīgo, Vb., O. Sl. sněgŭ),
Lat. *nix, ninguit* ; I.-Eur. *ĝnō-to-, 'known' (O. Ind. jñātá-, Gk. γνωτός, O. Ir.
gnáth, 'accustomed'), Lat. *nōtus*, O. Lat. *gnōtus* ; the I.-Eur. root bhendh-,
'to bind' (O. Ind. bándhana-, 'binding,' bándhu-, 'a relation,' Gk. πενθερός,
stepfather, πεῖσμα, a rope, for *πενθ-σμα, Goth. bindan, 'to bind') survives in the
religious term, *of-fendices*, the knots with which the priest's apex was tied on,
an old word wrongly connected by some Roman antiquarians with *offendo*
[Festus 244. 2 Th. offendices ait esse Titius nodos, quibus apex retineatur et
remittatur. At Veranius coriola existimat, quae sint in loris apicis, quibus
apex retineatur et remittatur, quae ab offendendo dicantur. nam quom ad
mentum perventum sit, offendit mentum. Paulus Diaconus, the epitomator
of Festus, has been misled by the corruption *offendimentum* for *offendit mentum*
(Paul. 245. 1 Th.) : offendices dicebant ligaturae nodos, quibus apex retinebatur. Id cum pervenisset ad mentum, dicebatur ' offendimentum ;' whence
the 'ghost-word' *offendimentum* has come into our Latin dictionaries ; cf.
C. G. L. iv. 132. 3 offendix nodus proprius quo apex flaminum rětinetur (MS.
restinguitur) et remittitur]; I.-Eur. *ĝhans-, 'a goose' (O. Ind. haṣá-, Lith.
žąsìs, O. Engl. gōs ; cf. Gk. χήν : in Irish the word means a swan, gēis from
stem *gēsi-, originally *ghansi-), Lat. *anser*, properly *hanser*.

The instances of a nasal (*n* or *m*) being dropped before a consonant in Latin
without 'compensation' are illusory : *lĭgŭla*, a spoon, from *lingo*, to lick, is
a different word from *lĭngŭla*, a strap, lit. 'a little tongue,' though the two
were sometimes confused , as we learn from Martial's lines on a silver spoon
(xiv. 120):

quamvis me ligulam dicant equitesque patresque,
dicor ab indoctis 'lingula' grammaticis,

(see Friedländer ad loc.) ; *lanterna* (from Gk. λαμπτήρ) is the correct spelling
(see Georges, *Lex. Wortf.* s.v.), *laterna* being probably a corruption due to
a fanciful connexion of the word with *lātus* ; *tympănum* is Gk. τύπανον, tympanum, Gk. τύμπανον, &c.

§ 80. nm. How far the theory that *canmen* became *carmen* is supported
by the comparison of *cancer* with O. Ind. karkara-, 'hard,' Gk. καρκίνος, and of
crĕpus-culum with Gk. κνέφας is doubtful. For the change of *r* to *n* in the first
of these examples is due to Dissimilation, like the change of *l* to *r* in the first
syllable of *caeruleus* (§ 84), and the second example, if correct, would exhibit

the same change of initial cn- to cr- for facility of pronunciation, as is seen in dialects of Gaelic, e.g. cnu, 'a nut' (pronounced cru with nasalized vowel), cnoc, 'a hill' (pronounced similarly cr- ; in Manx, cronk), gnath (I -Eur. *ĝnōto-) (pronounced grā with nasalized ā). In Latin, however, I.-Eur. cn- and gn- seem to have become n- (§ 119), so that *crepus-culum, creper*, 'dark,' if they represent an earlier cn-, must be dialectal. Varro makes them Sabine words (*L. L.* vi. 5 secundum hoc dicitur 'crepusculum' a crepero. id vocabulum sumpserunt a Sabinis, unde veniunt 'Crepusci' nominati Amiterno, qui eo tempore erant nati, ut 'Lucii' prima luce in Reatino ; 'crepusculum' significat dubium ; ab eo res dictae dubiae 'creperae,' quod crepusculum dies etiam nunc sit an jam nox multis dubium). The Probi Appendix censures the pronunciation 'parcarpus' instead of *pancarpus* (Gk. πίγ-καρπος) (197. 32 K.; the reading is doubtful, and 'prancarpus' has been proposed).

The evidence for the change of n to r in *carmen, germen* (cf. § 91 on n for r) is thus not very strong, and a good deal may be said for the view which refers *germen* to *ges-i-men* (from *gĕro* for *geso*, cf. *ges-si, ges-tum*) and *gemma* to *gen-ma*. *Carmen* may be connected with O. Ind. kārú-, 'a singer,' or with *cāro* (in Lat. a portion of meat, flesh, but in Osc. any portion, e.g. *maimas carneis senateis tanginud* 'maximae partis senatus sententia '), as O. Ir. drecht means (1) part, portion, (2) song. (O. Ind. śás-man- Neut., 'praise,' a word which occurs only once in the Rig Veda, comes from the O. Ind. root śas-, 'to praise,' which is usually connected with Lat. *censeo*). In Compounds with *in, con-*, &c. -*nm*- became mm, e.g. *im-mitto, com-mitto*, so that *gemma* seems a natural development of *gen-ma*.

The connexion of n with l seen in Provençal alma for Lat. *an(i)ma*, &c. receives an equally doubtful support from the mispronunciation censured in the Probi Appendix (197. 24 K.) 'cuntellum' for *cultellum*, and in the curious form of the word *neptis* mentioned in glossaries, 'leptis' (Löwe, *Prodr.* p. 340) ; *nuscicio* explained as 'caecitudo nocturna' [Fest. 180. 23 Th.; cf. *nusciciosus, ib., nusciosus* in glossaries (Löwe, *Prodr.* p. 17 'qui plus vespere videt ')] seems to be a popular adaptation of *luscitio* (-*cio* ?) (Paul. Fest. 86. 21 Th.), derived from *luscus*, to the word *nox*. *Conucella*, the Diminutive of *cŏlus* (*C. G. L.* iii. 322. 9) (cf. Ital. conocchia, 'a distaff,' from Lat. *conucula*, Fr. quenouille, &c.), may be influenced by *cōnus*. N appears as l in dialectal Greek, e.g. λάρναξ for νάρναξ. (*K. Z.* xxxiii. 226.) On the affinity of the n-, l-, and r-sounds, see ch. ii. §§ 61, 96, 105, 106. (Cf. Germ. Himmel, Goth. himins, Engl. heaven ?).

§ 81. **The M- and N-Sonants.** For the sounds to which ĕm, ĕn (mĕ, nĕ) are reduced in the unaccented syllable of such a word as I.-Eur. *tn̥tó- (O. Ind. tatá-, Gk. τατός, Lat. *tentus*) from the root ten-, 'to stretch,' some write, m̥, n̥, others əm, ən (mə, nə), the ə indicating an obscure vowel sound, or else ᵉm, ᵉn (mᵉ, nᵉ). In Latin these sounds became ĕm, ĕn, e.g. dĕcĕm (Gk. δέκα, Goth. taihun), *tentus*, the ĕ being subject to all the changes of ĕ for I.-Eur. ĕ (e.g. *incertus*, Gk. ἄκριτος, *undĕcim, decumus, decimus*, &c.) ; in Greek they became a before a consonant [but αμ, αν before vocalic i (y)] ; in Teutonic um, un, and so on ; so that it is only

T

by reference to another I.-Eur. language that we can tell whether Lat. *ĕm, ĕn* are I.-Eur. ĕm, ĕn, or I.-Eur. m̥, n̥. We occasionally find *mă, nă* in Latin words from roots in mĕ, nĕ, which are probably to be explained similarly by the weakening influence of the accent, e. g. *nactus* from the root nek̑-, nenk̑-, 'to obtain' (O. Ind. naś-, Gk. ἐ-νεγκ-εῖν, Mid. Ir. co-emnacar, 'potui,' Lith. nèszti, ' to carry,' O. Sl. nesti). (See Osthoff, *Morph. Unt.* v. Pref., and cf. above, § 61.) Whether Gk. *vā*, Lat. *nā* of Gk. νῆσσα (Lat. *ănas*) for *vāt-ya, a duck, Lat. *gnātus*, and Lat. *an*, O. Ind. ā of Lat. *antae*, O. Ind. jātá-, ' born,' are rightly called the long sonant nasals from roots like g̑en-, &c. is a point which has not yet been settled (see § 1). I.-Eur. initial m̥, n̥ have been also referred to a weakening of an original initial am-, an-, e. g. *m̥bhi beside *ambhi (Gk. ἀμφι), like *po beside *apo (Gk. ἀπο) (ch. ix. § 12).

I.-Eur. m̥, n̥ are in Umbro-Osc. treated as in Latin, e.g. Umbr. *desen-* 'decem,' *ivenga* 'juvencas,' Osc. trístaamentud 'testamento' Abl. Sg. Why an- should appear for Lat. *in- (en-)*, in Umbr. antakres 'integris,' Osc. *amprufid* 'improbe,' Umbro-Osc. anter 'inter,' is not quite clear (see von Planta, i. p. 315).

§ 82. **Other examples of the Nasal Sonants.** I.-Eur. -mn̥ of the Nom. Sg. Neut. of men-stems (e. g. Gk. ἦμα) is Lat. *-men*, e. g. *sēmen*; the weak form of the root ten-, 'to stretch,' appears also in I.-Eur. *tenú-, 'thin' (O. Ind. tanú- ; cf. Gk. τανυ-, stretched, of τανύ-γλωσσος, τανύ-πτερος, τανύ-πεπλος), Lat. *tenuis* from the Fem. form (O. Ind. tanvī) (ch. v. § 47); I.-Eur. *k̑m̥tóm, 'hundred' (O. Ind. r̥atám, Gk. ἐ-κατόν, O. Ir. cēt, W. cant, Goth. hund, Engl. hund-red, lit. ' 100-number,' Lith. szimtas, O. Sl. sŭto) is Lat. *centum*; I.-Eur. *gu̯m̥ti-, the Verbal Noun from the root gu̯em-, 'to go' (O. Ind. gáti-, Gk. βάσις, Goth. ga-qumþs, 'assembly,' Germ. Her-kunft, &c.), Lat. *in-venti-o*; I.-Eur. *sm̥-, the weak grade of the root sem-, ' one ' (O. Ind. sa-kr̥t, ' once,' Gk. ἅ-παξ, ἁ-πλόος), Lat. *simplex*; I.-Eur. *m̥n̥tó-, mn̥ti-, the P. P. P. and Verbal Noun of men-, ' to think' (O. Ind. matá-, matí- Gk. αὐτό-ματος, O. Ir. dēr-met, 'forgetting,' Goth. ga-munds, ' remembrance,' O. Engl. gemynd, Engl. mind, Lith. miñtas, O. Sl. mętŭ, pa-mętĭ, 'memory') appear in Lat. *com-mentus, mens*, Gen. *mentis*. Similarly Lat. *ensis* (O. Ind. así-); Lat. *ingens*, lit. 'unknown,' 'uncouth ' (O. Eng. un-cūð) from the root g̑en-, 'to know '; Lat. *jŭvencus* (see § 64) ; Lat. *lingua*, older *dingua* (Goth. tuggō, O. Engl. tunge.) (On *nŏvem* for *noven, see § 79.) The late retention of the m-, n-sounds (as of the l-, r-sounds, § 92) has been inferred from *patrĕm* (beside *patris*), *nōmĕn* (not *-in*) (but see p. 186).

§ 83. **Other examples of am, an, mā, nā.** Lat. *gnārus* from root g̑en-, ' to know' (O.Ind.jānā́mi); *antae*, pillars at door of a temple (O. Ind. ā́tā-, Arm. dr-and) ; Lat. *janitrices*, sisters-in-law (O. Ind. yātar-, cf. Gk. εἰνάτερες, O. Sl. jętry). Lat. *ămāre* is explained by some as derived from *ĕmo*, 'I take,' with a reduction of the *ĕm-*, as *dīcāre* shows reduction of the *deic-* of *dīco* (O. Lat. *deico*). (Cf. § 94 on *al, ar,* and § 3 on *pāteo* (Gk. πετ-), *ăper.*

§ 84. **L, R.** These two sounds are often interchanged in Latin by 'Dissimilation' of *l-l,* e.g. *caerŭleus* from *caelum, pŏpŭlā-ris* and *austrā-lis* (ch. ii. § 101). The same thing is found in other languages, e.g. O. H. G. turtula-tūbā, our 'turtle-dove' from Lat. *turtur* (Gk. κεφαλαργία and κεφαλαλγία) and perhaps occurred in what is called the I.-Eur. period, e.g. I.-Eur. g^{u}er-g^{u}el- in the reduplicated root (Lat. *gur-gul-io,* O. H. G. querechela, Lith. gargalŭju). On the parasitic vowel often found between a consonant and *l* (*r*), see ch. ii. § 103, and on the avoidance of *r-r,* e.g. *praest*(*r*)*īgiae* (like Gk. δρύ-φακτος for δρύ-φρακτος) *ib.*

§ 85. **L.** I.-Eur. l is Lat. *l,* e.g. the I.-Eur. root leiq^u, 'to leave' (O. Ind. ric-, Arm. lk'anem, Gk. λείπω, O. Ir. lēcim, Goth. leihvan, 'to lend,' O. Engl. lēon, Lith. lëkù, 'I leave,' O. Sl. otŭ-lěkŭ, 'remainder') appears in Latin *linquo,* Pft. *līqui*; the root k̑lei-, 'to lean' (O. Ind. śri-, Gk. κλῑ́νω, O. Ir. cloen, 'awry,' Goth. hlains, 'a hill,' Lith. szłaítas, szlȩ̃ti, 'to lean'), appears in Lat. *clīvus, ac-clīnis*; suffixal -lo, -lā, as in derivatives from the root dhē-, 'to suck' (O. Ind. dhārú-, Arm. dal, 'beestings,' Gk. θηλή, θῆλυς, O. Ir. děl, 'teat,' Gael. deal, 'leech,' O. H. G. tila, 'teat,' Lith. dėlė, 'leech'), in Lat. *fellare* for *fē-lare,* &c. (ch. ii. § 130).

We find *ll* in Latin for original ld, e.g. *per-cello* (cf. Gk. κλαδαρός, brittle, Lat. *clādes*), ln, e.g. *collis* (Lith. kálnas ; cf. Gk. κολωνός) (*ulna* had I.-Eur. -lěn- ; cf. Gk. ὠλένη), ls, e.g. *collum,* O. Lat. *collus* (O. Engl. heals, Germ. Hals M.), *velle* for *vel-se (cf. *es-se*), rl, e.g. *stēlla* for **stěr-la, ăgěllus* for **ager-lus.* So dl in compound verbs, e.g. *allĭgo* for *ad-ligo.* But usually a parasitic vowel was inserted to facilitate pronunciation, when *l* was preceded by a consonant, e.g. *piāculum* for *pia-clum* (see ch. ii. § 154).

I.-Eur. d became *l* in the Sabine dialect (see *I. F.* ii. 157), and this form was sanctioned in a few words in Latin, e.g. *lingua,* older *dingua,* from I.-Eur. **dṇgh^{u}ā-* (Goth. tuggō) (§ 111). On *făcul,* &c. for **faclī, fac*(*i*)*lě,* &c., see § 13 ; on *leptis,* a byform of *neptis,* ch. ii. § 106; on the change of *ě* to *ŏ* (*ŭ*) before Latin *l* [except before *l* followed by *e, i* (*y*) or before the group *ll*], § 10, and on the various pronunciations of Latin *l* when alone, when double, and when preceding a consonant, ch. ii. § 96.

I.-Eur. l is Oscan l, e. g. lígatúís 'lēgātis.' Similarly we have Umbr. *plener* 'plenis,' veltu 'vulto' Imperat.; but initial l does not occur in the Eugubine Tables, the chief record of the language, and it is not impossible that at the beginning of a word I.-Eur. l is Umbrian v in words like *vapef* (Lat. *lăpĭdes*? Acc. Pl.), Vuvçis (Lat. *Lūcius*? cf. Osc. Luvkis), vutu (Lat. *lăvĭto*?); between vowels l became (like d) ř (*rs*) in kařetu, *carsitu* 'let him call' (Gk. καλέω, Lat. *cālāre*), fameřias 'familiae,' &c.; before t it was dropped in muta 'multa' ('a fine,' Osc. múlta-), &c., while the Umbrian name *Voisieno-* (Lat. *Volsiēno-*)[1] suggests that it became i before s (see von Planta, i. p. 285).

§ 86. I.-Eur. l; other examples. The I.-Eur. root leuk-, 'to shine' (O. Ind. ruc-, Gk. λευκύς, O. Ir. lōche, lōchet Gen., 'lightning,' Gaul. Leucetios, W. lluched, Goth. liuhath, O. Engl. lęoht, O. Sl. luči̇̆) appears in Lat. *lūx, lūceo, lŭcerna*; the root ĝhel-, 'green, yellow' (O. Ind. hári-, Gk. χλωρός, χλόη, O. Ir. gel, 'white,' O. H. G. gelo, O. Engl. geolo, 'yellow,' Lith. žélti, 'to grow green,' O. Sl. zelije, 'vegetables,' zelenŭ, 'green'), in Lat. *helvus, hĕlus*, and *hŏlus*. Similarly Lat. *sal* (Arm. aλ, Gk. ἅλς, O. Ir. salann, W. halen, Goth. salt, O. Sl. solǐ, Lith. salunka, 'salt-box'); Lat. *flōs* (O. Ir. blăth, 'bloom,' W. blodau, 'flowers,' Goth. blōma, O. H. G. bluomo); Lat. *clūnis* (O. Ind. śróni-, W. clun, O. Scand. hlaunn, Lith. szĩaunìs); Lat. *plēnus, plērī-que, plētus* (O. Ind. prātá-, Arm. li, Gk. πλήρης, O. Ir. līnaim, 'I fill,' līn, 'a number,' Lith. pìlnas, 'full,' O. Sl. plŭnŭ); Lat. *in-clŭtus* (O. Ind. śrutá-, 'heard,' Gk. κλυτός, in Hom. 'heard, loud,' e.g. ὄνομα κλυτόν, λιμὴν κλυτός, O. Ir. cloth, 'famous'; cf. O. Engl. hlūd, 'loud').

§ 87. R. I.-Eur. r is Lat. *r*. Thus the I.-Eur. *rēĝ-, 'a king' (O. Ind. ráj-an-, O. Ir. rī, rīg Gen., W. rhi, Gaul. Catu-rīges, lit. 'kings in fight') is Lat. *rēx*, stem *rēg-*; I.-Eur. *bhĕrō, 'I carry' (O. Ind. bhárā-mi, Arm. berem, Gk. φέρω, O. Ir. berim, W. ad-feru Inf., Goth. baira, O. Engl. bere, O. Sl. berą) is Lat. *fĕrō*; I.-Eur. wert-, 'to turn' (O. Ind. vr̥t-, Goth. vairþan, Engl. worth, in 'woe worth the day,' Lith. veřsti and vartýti, O. Sl. vratiti) is Lat. *vĕrtere*; I.-Eur. *kăpro- (Gk. κάπρος, boar, O. Engl. hæfer, 'goat') is Lat. *căper*, stem *căpro-*, I.-Eur. rs before a vowel became *rr* in Latin, e. g. *torreo* for *torseo* (O. Ind. tr̥ṣ-, Goth. þaursjan, 'to thirst'; cf. Gk. τέρσομαι). But r was assimilated to a following s in pronunciation, e. g. *Persa* pronounced *Pessa* (see ch. ii. § 96),

---

[1] On inscrr. of Asisium the Umbr. Voisiener Gen. Sing. (*C. I. L.* xi. 5389 = Bücheler, *Umbrica* Inscr. Min. i., p. 172) corresponds to Lat. *Volsienus* (xi. 5390 = i. 1412). The Volsienus of no. 5390 seems to be the son of the Volsienus of no. 5389.

and I.-Eur. rs before a consonant became *ss*, e.g. *tostus* for
*tosstus, *torstus from *torreo*. R was also assimilated to *l* in
Latin, e.g. *stella, ăgĕllus* for *stĕrla, *agĕrlus. The Campanian
town of which the Latin name was *Ātella* has on its coins *Aderl*,
so that its Oscan name must have been *Aderlo, a name apparently meaning 'the little black town.' On the metathesis by
which *rĭ* became *ĕr*, e.g. *ter, terr-* (*ters) for *trĭs, see § 13.
Sometimes the cacophony of a repetition of *r* (§ 84) seems to be
avoided by using *n* for one *r*, e.g. *cancer* for **carc-* (Gk. καρκ-ίνος;
cf. O. Ind. kar-kar-a-, 'hard') (but see ch. ii. § 105). On *carmen*,
possibly for *can-men, see § 78, and on *r* for *d* before *f, v, g*, e.g.
arfuerunt, arvorsum, arger, § 112. Between vowels I.-Eur. s became
r in Latin, e.g. *gĕnĕris* from the stem ĝĕnĕs- [cf. Gk. γένε(σ)ος], on
which see § 148). I.-Eur. r is Umbro-Osc. r, e.g. Umbr. rehte
'recte,' Osc. Regatureí *'Regātori' (see von Planta, i. p. 285).
In Umbrian, as in Latin, intervocalic s became r, but not in
Oscan (cf. infr. § 146).

§ 88. I.-Eur. r; other examples. Lat. *rŏta* (O. Ind. rátha-, 'chariot,' O. Ir. roth, 'wheel,' Gaulo-Lat. petor-rĭtum, 'a four-wheeled vehicle,' O. H. G. rad, 'wheel,' Lith. rătas); Lat. *porcus* (Gk. πόρκος, O. Ir. orc, O. H. G. farh, Engl. farrow, Lith. paršzas, O. Sl. prasę); Lat. *vir* (O. Ir. fěr, Goth. vair; cf. O. Ind. vīrá-, Lith. výras); Lat. *inter* (O. Ind. antár, O. Ir. eter); Lat. *serpo* (O. Ind. sṛp-, Gk. ἕρπω); Lat. *rūber* (O. Ind. rudhirá-, Gk. ἐ-ρυθρός, O. Sl. rŭdrŭ; cf. O. Ir. ruad, Goth. rauþs); Lat. *rumpo*, (O. Ind. rup- and lup-, O. Engl. berēofan, 'to bereave,' Lith. rūpéti, 'to trouble'); Lat. *prŏ-* (O. Ind. prá, Gk. πρό, O. Ir. ro, used like the augment to indicate a past tense, e.g. ro alt, 'he nourished,' ro char, 'he loved,' O. Bret. ro, Lith. pra-, O. Sl. pro-).

§ 89. ss for rs before consonant. Other examples are: Lat. *testāmentum* for **tesst-, *terst-* from **trĭst-* (Osc. tristaamentud Abl. Sg.) ; *cēna* for *cesna, *cessna from *cersna (Osc. kersna-, Umbr. šesna-). The spelling *coena*, due to the analogy of Gk. κοινός, is very old. It appears on an early Praenestine cista of the third cent. B. C. with the representation of a kitchen where cooking operations are going on. One servant is saying *feri porod* (= *feri porro*); another replies *cofeci* (= *confeci*); a third orders *made mirecie* (= *made mi regie* or *made mire, cie*); a fourth *misc sane* (= *misce sane*); a fifth says *asom fero* (= *assum fero*); a sixth *confice piscim*. The title is *coenalia* or *coena pia* (see *Mél. Arch.* 1890, p. 303). Similarly Lat. *fastīgium* for **farst-* (O. Ind. bhr̥ṣṭí-, 'a point'); *posco* for *porcsco (O. Ind. pr̥chámi, O. H. G. forscōn, Germ. forschen).

§ 90. rr for rs before vowel. Other examples: Lat. *farreus* (Umbr. farsio- and fasio-; cf. O. Sl. brašĭno, 'food'); *garrio* (Lith. garšas, 'noise'); *horreo* (O. Ind. hr̥ṣ-); *porrum* (Gk. πράσον); *terreo* [O. Ind. tras-, Gk. τρέ(σ)ω, Umbr. *tursitu tremitu*]; *verres* (Lith. veršzis, 'calf'; cf. O. Ind. vr̥ṣṇi-, 'ram'); *verrūca*, 'a rising-ground' in O. Lat. (Lith. virszùs; cf. O. Ind. várṣman-); *Maspiter*, a byform of *Marspĭter* ; *Tuscus* (Umbr. Tursco- and Tusco-). Lat. *fers* has probably re-appended -s to an older **fer*, **ferr* for **fer-s* [so *ul-s* has appended -s a second time to **ul*, **ull* for **ol-s* (ch. ix. § 56).] In Umbrian inscriptions written in the Latin alphabet, the Umbrian đ-sound (see ch. ii. § 88) is written *rs*, e. g. *capirse* (in the native alph. kapiře), (Lat. *capidi*), Dat. Sing. of *căpĭd-*, a bowl.

§ 91. n for r. Lat. *crĕpuscŭlum*, if it has *cr-* for *cn-* (compare Gk. κνέφας), with that change of *cn-* to *cr-* which we find in some languages, e. g. Gael. cnu (pronounced cru with nasal vowel), Bret. kraoun, 'a nut,' must be like our 'gloaming,' a dialectal word : Varro (*L. L.* vi. 5) makes it Sabine (see § 80). On the spellings *menetris* for *meretrix*, &c., see ch. ii. § 105.

§ 92. **The L- and R-Sonants.** For the sounds to which ĕl, ĕr (lĕ, rĕ) are reduced in the unaccented syllable of such a word as I.-Eur. **dr̥tó-*, **dr̥ti* (O. Ind. dŕ̥ti-, Gk. δρατός and δαρτός, δάρσις, Lith. nu-dirtas, Goth. ga-taurþs) from the root der-, 'to flay,' some write ḷ, r̥, others əl, ər (lə, rə), the ə indicating an obscure vowel sound (also ᵉr, ᵉl, &c.). In Latin these sounds became ŏl, ŏr, e. g. *mors*, Gen. *mortis* (O. Ind. mr̥ti-, Goth. maurþr, O. H. G. mord, Lith. mirtìs, O. Sl. sŭ-mr̆tĭ), *fors*, stem **forti-* (O. Ind. bhr̥tí-, O. Ir. brith, Goth. ga-baurþs, 'birth,' O. Engl. gebyrd, ' fate '), the *o* being subject to all the changes of ŏ for I.-Eur. ŏ (e. g. *pulsus*, Gk. παλτός from the root pel-), while before a vowel we seem to find ăl, ăr in *sălix* (O. Ir. sail ; cf. Gk. ἑλίκη with E-grade), *căro* (Umbr. karu,' a portion ' ; cf. Gk. κείρω) ; in Greek they became ἄρ (ρᾰ, e. g. πατράσι), ἄλ (λᾰ), in Teutonic ŭr, ŭl ; in Slavonic ĭr, ĭl, and so on ; so that it is only by reference to another I.-Eur. language that we can tell whether Lat. ŏl, ŏr are I.-Eur. ŏl, ŏr, or I.-Eur. ḷ, r̥. (Lat. ŏl may also be I.-Eur. ĕl, § 10.) We occasionally find lă, ră in Latin words from roots in lĕ, rĕ, which are probably to be explained similarly by the weakening influence of the accent, e. g. *frăngo, frăgĭlis* from the root bhre*g*-, ' to break ' (Goth. brĭkan, O. Engl. brĕcan) (see Osthoff, *Morph. Unt.* v. Pref., and above § 3). Whether Gk. ρω, ρᾱ, Lat. *rā*, of Gk. στρωτός, πέπρωται, κρᾶτός, Lat. *strātus, clādes*, and Gk. ορ (αρ), Lat. *ar* of Gk. στόρνυμι, Lat. *pars, părtior, quārtus*, are rightly called the long-sonant vowels from roots ster-, per-, &c. is a point which has not yet been settled (see § 1). There are some indications that vocalic l and r were sounds not unknown to the Italic languages down to a fairly late period, e. g. Marrucinian *pacrsi* ' pacer (pacris) sit,' ' may she be propitious ' (Zv. *I. I. I.* 8) (cf.

Umbr. *pacer*, Lat. *acer, acris* Fem.), Sabine *Atrno* (Zv. 10), Osc. Tantrnnaiúm Gen. Pl., though how far these are merely graphic is hard to decide (cf. ch. iii. § 14); corresponding to Gk. ἀγρός we have in Lat. *ager*, in Umbr. *ager*, and so on (see ch. vi. § 4). On Lat. *ter*(*r*) for *trĭs, *facul* for *fac*(*i*)*lĭ*, see § 13. I.-Eur. ḷ, ṛ receive the same treatment in Umbro-Osc. as in Latin, e. g. Umbr. *orto*- (Lat. *ortus*), Osc. *molto* (Lat. *multa*, a fine) (see vonPlanta, i. p. 314).

§ 93. **Other examples of the liquid Sonants.** I.-Eur. *pṛk̑-sk̑ŏ (O. Ind. pṛchā́mi, pṛchā-, 'enquiry,' Arm. harçanem, harç, O. H. G. forscōn, forsca) Lat. *posco* for *porc-sco ; I.-Eur. *k̑ṛd-. (O. Ind. hṛ́d, Gk. καρδία and κραδίη, O. Ir. cride, Lith. szirdìs, O. Sl. srĭdĭce), Lat. *cor* for *cord ; I.-Eur. *pṛk̑ā-, 'the ridge of a furrow' (W. rhych F., O. Engl. furh F.), Lat. *porca* (Varro, *R. R.* i. 29. 3 qua aratrum vomere lacunam striam fecit, 'sulcus' vocatur. quod est inter duos sulcos elata terra dicitur ' porca' ; Paul. Fest. 77. 1 Th. explains the name *Imporcitor* as ' qui porcas in agro facit arando,' the name of a deity invoked by the flamen in the sacrifice to Tellus and Ceres, with a number of other agricultural divinities : Vervactor, Reparator, Imporcitor, Insitor, Obarator, Occator, Saritor, Subruncinator, Messor, Convector, Conditor, Promitor, whose names are given by Fabius Pictor ap. Serv. ad Virg. *G.* i. 21. The word *porca* occurs also in a line of Accius ap. Non. 61. 19 M. bene proscissas cossigerare ordine porcas) ; I.-Eur. k̑ṛn- (Gk. κάρνος Hesych., Goth. haurn), Lat. *cornu* (cf. Lat. *cornus*, cornel, Gk. κράνος, κράνον) ; I.-Eur. *pṛso- (Gk. πράσον), Lat. *porrum* for *porsum. Certain examples of I.-Eur. ḷ in Latin are not numerous. *Ulmus* may stand for *ḷmo- (Ir. lem, Russ. ilemü) ; or for *elmo- (O. Engl. elm); or for *olmo- (O. Scand. almr) ; *mulctus*, milked, for *ml̑kto- (Lith. mìłsztas, O. Ir. mlicht or blicht, ' milk ') ; *oc-cultus* for *-kḷto- from the root *k*el-, ' to hide ' ; cf. *sepultus* from *sĕpĕlio*.

§ 94. **Other examples of al, ar, lā, rā.** Lat. *palma*, palm of hand (O. Ir. lām F. ; cf. Gk. παλάμη) ; *scalpo* (cf. *sculpo*) ; *clādes* (cf. Gk. κλαδαρός, *perculsus*, from the root *k*eld- of *per-cello*) ; *clāmo* (cf. *calo, cǎlendae*) ; *flāvus* (cf. *fulvus*, O. Lat. *Folvius*) ; *lātus*, carried (cf. *tollo*) ; *lātus*, wide, earlier *stlātus*, from the root stel-, ' to extend ' (O. Sl. steljǫ) ; *ardea* (cf. Gk. ἐ-ρωδιός) ; *armus* (O. Ind. īrmás, Goth. arms, O. Sl. ramę ; cf. Pruss. irmo) ; *carpo* from the root kerp-, ' to cut ' (Lith. kerpù) (cf. Gk. καρπός, Engl. harvest) ; *fastīgium* for *farst- (cf. O. Ind. bhṛṣṭí-, ' point,' O. Engl. byrst, ' bristle '), or *frast- (see ch viii. § 18, on *farcio* for *fracio) ; *crābro* for *crā-sro (cf. Lith. szirszů, O. Sl. srŭšenĭ) ; *crātis* and *cartilāgo* (cf. Gk. κάρταλος, basket, O. H. G. hurt, Engl. hurdle) ; *fraxĭnus* and *farnus* (O. Ind. bhūrja-, ' a birch-tree ') from the root bherǵ-, (O. Engl. beorc, Lith. béržas, O. Sl. brěza) ; *grānum* (O. Ind. jīrṇá-, ' worn out' ; cf. Goth. kaurn, ' corn,' Lith. žȧrnis, ' pea,' O. Sl. zrŭno, ' a grain ') ; *grātus* (O. Ind. gūrtá-, ' welcome') ; *rādīx* for *vrā- (cf. Goth. vaurts, Engl. wort); *strāmen* (Gk. στρῶμα) from *sterno* ; *lāna* for *vlāna (O. Ind. ū́rṇā, Gk. οὖλος for **f*oλνος). On Lat. *ăl, ăr* for ǝl, ǝr before a vowel, see *M. S. L.* viii. 279, Osthoff, *Dunkles u. helles l*, p. 52, (*palea, parens, varix*, &c.), and cf. § 3 on *pǎteo* (Gk. πετ-), &c.

§ 95. **Tenues, Mediae, and Aspirates.** In Sanscrit we have four varieties of each class of mutes or stopped consonants,

(1) tenues, or unvoiced, (2) mediae, or voiced, (3) tenues aspiratae, or tenues followed by *h* (like our *th* in 'ant-hill'), (4) mediae aspiratae, or mediae followed by *h* (like our *dh* in 'sandhill'). But these varieties are not kept distinct in other I.-Eur. languages. In Greek tenues aspiratae take the place of the Sanscrit mediae aspiratae (e.g. θῡμός, O. Ind. dhūmás); in the Celtic and Slavonic families the mediae and mediae aspiratae of Sanscrit are merged in mediae (e.g. Lith. dŭ-ti, 'to give,' O. Ind. dā-, O. Ir. dān, 'a gift, an accomplishment'; Lith. dėlė̃ 'a leech,' O. Ind. dhā-, 'to suck,' O. Ir. děl, 'teat'). The tenues aspiratae of Sanscrit are especially difficult to trace in the other languages; nor is it always easy to say whether they are due to some phonetic law peculiar to Sanscrit, or represent I.-Eur. tenues aspiratae. In the O. Ind. root sthā-, ' to stand,' where the dental tenuis is found in all other languages (Gk. ἵστημι, Lat. *sto*, &c.), it seems probable that the I.-Eur. form of the root was stā-, whereas in O. Ind. nakhá-, ' a nail, claw,' for which we have an aspirate in Gk. ὄνυχ- the tenuis aspirata may be original. Tenues aspiratae have been with more or less probability conjectured for such words as I.-Eur. *k̂onkho-, ' a shell ' (O. Ind. śaṇkhá-, Gk. κόγχος, Lat. *congius*, a quart) ; I.-Eur. skhi(n)d-, ' to split ' (O. Ind. chid-, Gk. σχίζω, σχινδαλμός, a splinter, Lat. *scindo*, O. H. G. scintan, Germ. schinden); the suffix of the 2 Sg. Pft. Ind. (O. Ind. vét-tha, Gk. οἶσ-θα, Lat. *vīd-is-ti*, Goth. las-t, &c.); and the same hypothesis has been used to explain the anomalous correspondence of Latin *h*- and Goth. h- in the verb, ' to have,' Lat. *hăbet*, Goth. habaiþ (I.-Eur. khabhē- ?), &c.

These I.-Eur. tenues, mediae, and aspiratae were liable to change their character under the influence of an adjoining consonant. A media became a tenuis before an unvoiced consonant, e.g. I.-Eur. *yukto-, P. P. P. from the root yeug-, 'to join' (O. Ind. yuktá-, Lat. *junctus*). A tenuis similarly became a media before a voiced consonant, [cf. I.-Eur. *si-zd-o, the reduplicated form of the root sed-, ' to sit ' (Lat. *sīdo*)]. A media aspirata before *t* or *s* is in Latin and other languages treated like a tenuis, e. g. *vectus, vexi* (*vecsi*), from Lat. *věho* (I.-Eur. root weĝh-), but whether this was the case in what is called 'the Indo-European period' is not certain. More plausible is the theory that t before t or th, and perhaps d before d, dh, produced already at this period some sibilant sound; for a trace of this appears in every branch of the I.-Eur. family, e. g. from the root sed-, with the P. P. P. suffix -to-, we have Zend ni-šasta-, Lat. -*sessus*, Lith. sėstas, O. Scand. sess) (for other examples in Latin, see § 108). The occasional confusion, too, which we find between tenues and mediae (e. g. Gk. σκαπάνη beside Lat. *scabo*), mediae and aspiratae (e.g. Gk. στέμβω beside ἀστεμφής; O. Ind. ahám beside Gk. ἐγώ, Lat. *ĕgo*, &c.) may in many instances date from the same early time.

In Umbrian a tenuis becomes a media before r in *subra* 'supra,' *podruhpei* 'utroque,' regularly after n, e. g. *ivenga* 'juvencas,' *ander* 'inter' (Osc. anter) (von Planta, i. p. 547); and we have both in Oscan and Umbrian many instances of a tenuis appearing for a media, which are by some explained as miswritings, due to the earlier use of the tenuis-symbol only in the native alphabets (derived from Etruscan, ch. i. § 1), but are by others considered as a proof that the Italic mediae were not voiced (ch. ii. § 77). (For instances, see von Planta, i. p. 555.)

§ 96. **Media or aspirata assimilated to unvoiced consonant in Latin.** Other examples are *cet-te* for *cĕ-dăte, the plural of *cĕdŏ*, give, lit. 'give here' (ch. vii. § 15), *hoc(c)* for *hod-ce (ch. vii. § 16); *topper* for *tod-per (ch. ix. § 7); *ac-tus* from *ăgo*; *scriptus* from *scrībo*; *vec-tus* from *veho*, &c. On spellings like *optenui* (Scip. Ep.), *apscede*, *urps*, see ch. ii. § 80.

§ 97. **Tenuis assimilated to voiced consonant in Latin.** On *ob-duco* beside *op-tenui*, see ch. ii. § 73. I.-Eur. d becomes *t* before *r* (unvoiced?) in Latin, e. g. *ātrox*, from ad-, a byform of the root od- of *ŏdium* (§ 113).

Interchange of tenuis and media in Latin. (See ch. ii. §§ 73-77.)

Interchange of media and aspirata in Latin. On *g* occasionally appearing for I.-Eur. *gh*, see § 116.

P, B, BH, PH.

§ 98. **P.** I.-Eur. p is Lat. *p*, e. g. I.-Eur. *pĕku- N. (O. Ind. páśu, Goth. faihu, Germ. Vieh, Engl. fee), Lat. *pĕcu*, I.-Eur. *sĕptm̥ (O. Ind. saptá, Arm. evt'n, Gk. ἑπτά, O. Ir. secht, W. saith, Goth. sibun; cf. Lith. septyní). *P* becomes *m* before *n*, e. g. *somnus* for *sop-nus; it is assimilated before labials, e. g. *summus* for *supmus, *suffio* for *supfio.

282   THE LATIN LANGUAGE.   [Chap. IV.

The Labial Tenuis receives a similar treatment in Umbro-Oscan, e.g. Umbr. patre, Osc. pateref 'patri'; but pt is in Osc. ft, in Umbr. ht, e.g. Osc. *scrifto-*, Umbr. *screihto-* 'scripto' (see von Planta, i. p. 424).

§ 99. Other examples of I.-Eur. p. I.-Eur. *păter-, (O. Ind. pitár-, Arm. hair, Gk. πατήρ, O. Ir. athir, Goth. fadar) Lat. *păter* ; O.-Eur. *pro (O. Ind. prá, Gk. πρό, O. Ir. ro, O. Bret. ro, Lith. pra-, O. Sl. pro-), Lat. *prŏ-* ; I.-Eur. *serpō (O. Ind. sárpā-mi, Gk. ἕρπω\, Lat. *serpo* ; I.-Eur. root speḱ- (O. Ind. spaš-, O. H. G. spehōn, Engl. spy), Lat. *au-spex, con-spĭcio* ; from I.-Eur. root preḱ- (O. Ind. praš-ná-, 'a request,' Goth. fraihnan, Germ. fragen ; Lith. praszýti, O. Sl. prositi) come Lat. *prĕcor*, and *prŏcus* ; I.-Eur. *nĕpot- (O. Ind. nápāt-, M. Ir. niae, niath Gen., O. H. G. nefo), Lat. *nĕpōs* ; I.-Eur. root paḱ-, pāĝ- (O. Ind. páša-, 'string,' Dor. Gk. πάγνυμι, Goth. fāhan, 'to catch,' Germ. Fuge) Lat. *pāx, păgina* ; I.-Eur. *ḱăpro- (Gk. κάπρος, O. Engl. hæfer, 'goat'), Lat. *căper*.

§ 100. B. I.-Eur. b is Lat. *b*, e.g. I.-Eur. *pĭbō, 'I drink' (O. Ind. píbāmi, O. Ir. ibim), Lat. *bĭbo* for **pibo* (§ 163). Lat. *b*, whether from I.-Eur. b or bh, becomes *m* before *n*, e.g. *scamnum* beside *scabellum*. Latin *b* may represent I.-Eur. -bh-, e.g. *scrībo* (cf. Gk. σκαρῑφάομαι, scratch) (§ 103), -dh-, e.g. *rŭber* (Gk. ἐρυθρός (§ 114), m before r, e.g. *hībernus* (Gk. χειμερινός) (§ 77), s before r, e.g. *cĕreb-rum* for **cerĕs-rum* (§ 152), dw-, e.g. *bis* for **dwĭs* (Gk. δίς) (§ 68). On the confusion of *b* and *v* in late spellings, see ch. ii. § 52, and on the substitution of *-b* for *-p* in *sub, ab*, ch. ii. § 73.

§ 101. Other examples of I.-Eur. b. Lat. *balbus* (O. Ind. balbalā-, Gk. βάρβαρος) ; Lat. *lambo* (O. H. G. laffan, O. Sl. lobŭzŭ ; cf. Gk. λάπτω) ; Lat. *lūbrĭcus* (Goth. sliupan, 'to slip') ; Lat. *lăbium* (O. H. G. lefs, O. Engl. lippa).

§ 102. mn for bn. *amnis* from abh- (O. Ind. ámbhas-, 'water,' Ir. abann, 'river'). On the spellings *amnuere* in glosses, see Löwe, *Prodr.* p. 421 ; cf. *amnegaverit* (*C.I.L.* vi. 14672). Similarly bm of **glŭb-ma* (root gleubh-, Gk. γλύφω) became *mm*, and was reduced to *m* (ch. ii. § 127), *glūma*.

§ 103. BH. I.-Eur. bh when initial became Latin *f*, when medial *b*, e.g. I.-Eur. root *bher-, 'to carry' (O. Ind. bhar-, Arm. berem, Gk. φέρω, O. Ir. berim, W. ad-feru Inf., Goth. baira, Engl. I bear, O. Sl. berą) is Lat. *fĕro* ; I.-Eur. *orbho- (Arm. orb, Gk. ὀρφανός, O. Ir. orbe, 'inheritance,' Goth. arbi, Germ. Erbe, 'heir'), Lat. *orbus* ; I.-Eur. root bheu- (O. Ind. bhū-, Gk. φύω, O. Ir. buith, Lith. bú-ti, O. Sl. by-ti), Lat. *fui, fŭtūrus* ; I.-Eur. *bhrātor- (O. Ind. bhrátar-, Gk. φράτωρ, O. Ir. brāthir, W.

brawd, Goth. brōþar, Lith. broter-ēlis, O. Sl. bratrŭ), Lat. *frāter*.
A good example of the different treatment of initial and medial
bh in Latin is the word for a beaver, I.-Eur. *bhĕbhru- (O. H. G.
bibar, Lith. bĕbrus, O. Sl. bebrŭ ; O. Ind. babhrú-, 'brown'),
Lat. *fĭber*. On *mn* for *bn* (with *b* from I.-Eur. b or bh),
e.g. *scamnum* from skabh- 'to support,' with Dim. *scabellum*
(*-illum*) (also *scamillum* Ter. Scaur. 14. 6 K.), see § 102, and on
dialectal *f* for *b* (e.g. *Alfius*, a byform of *Albius*), see ch. ii.
§ 83. I.-Eur. bh is Umbro-Osc. f, whether initial or internal,
e.g. Umbr.-Osc. fust ' erit,' Umbr. *alfo-*, Osc. Alafaternum ' albo-.'
On Faliscan *haba* for Lat. *făba*, see § 121, ch. ii. § 57.

§ 104. I.-Eur bh ; other examples. Lat. *nĕbŭla* (Gk. νεφέλη, O. Ir. nēl for
*neblo-, O. H. G. nebul, Germ. Nebel), Lat. *făteor, făma* (Gk. φημί) ; Lat.
sorbeo (Gk. ῥοφέω, Arm. arb-enam, Lith. srebiù) ; Lat. *umbo, umbĭlĭcus* (O. Ind.
nābhi-, nābhīla-, Gk. ὀμφαλός, O. Ir. imbliu, O. H. G. naba, nabolo, Pruss.
nabis, Lett. naba); Lat. *flōs* (O. Ir. blāth, ' bloom,' Goth. blōma); Lat. *albus* (Gk.
ἀλφός, white leprosy) ; Lat. *ambĭ*- (O. Ind. abhí, Gk. ἀμφί, O. Ir. imme for
imbe, Gaulish *Ambi-gatus*' O. Engl. ymb, Engl. ember-days, from O. Engl.
ymb-ryne 'running round, circuit,' Germ. um for umb) ; Lat. *ambō* (O. Ind.
u-bhá-, Gk. ἄμφω, Goth. bai, baj-ōþs, Engl. b-oth, Lith. abù, O. Sl. oba); Lat.
findo from I.-Eur. root bheid- (O. Ind. bhid-, Goth. beita, Engl. I bite); Lat.
fāgus (Dor. Gk. φᾱγός, O. Engl. bōc). *Barba* for *farba* (I.-Eur. bhardh-, O. Sl.
brada, Lith. barzdà, Engl. beard) is due to assimilation (see § 163).

T, D, DH, TH.

§ 105. T. I.-Eur. t is Lat. *t*; e.g. the I.-Eur. root ten-, ' to
stretch' (O. Ind. tan-, Gk. τείνω, O. Ir. tennaim, Goth. uf-þanja,
Germ. dehnen ; O. Ind. tanú-, ' thin,' Gk. τανύ-πτερος, O. Ir. tana,
W. teneu, O. H. G. dunni, O. Engl. þynne, Lith. dial. tenvas, O. Sl.
tĭnĭkŭ) appears in Latin *ten-do, tĕnuis* ; I.-Eur. *wert-, ' to turn '
(O. Ind. vártatē 3 Sg., Goth. vairþan, Germ. werden, Lith. veřszti,
vartýti, O. Sl. vratiti, W. gwerthyd, ' spindle') is Lat. *vertĕre*.
Before *l* it is dropped when initial, e.g. *lātus* for *tlātus*, P. P. P. of
fĕro, tŭli, but becomes *c* when medial ; thus the suffix -tlo-,
which indicates the instrument with which an action is performed, or the place of its performance, appears in Latin as
-clo-, e.g. *vĕhiclum* or *vehĭcŭlum*, 'that by which one is carried' ;
poclum or *pōcŭlum*, ' that out of which one drinks,' *cŭbiclum* or
cubĭcŭlum, ' the place where one lies down,' &c., by the same
change as is seen in later Latin *veclus* for *vĕt(ŭ)lus*, in the

English mispronunciation 'acleast' for ' at least,' in Mod. Gk. σεῦκλο from Gk. σεῦτλον, &c. Before c it is assimilated, e.g. *ac* for *acc from *atc, *atqu*(*e*), while *tt* became *ss*, after a consonant *s*, e.g. *passus* for *pattus from *patior*, *salsus* for *salttus from *sallo*, *saldo, *versus* from *verto*, &c. Final -nt seems to have become *-ns* in the Umbro-Oscan languages, for the 3 Plur. Act. ending of Secondary Tenses (I.-Eur. -nt) appears in them as -ns, e.g. Osc. fufans 'erant' quasi 'fubant' (ch. viii. § 73). The same may hold of Latin, for *quŏtiens*, *tŏtiens* suggest the O. Ind. suffix -yant of ki-yant, ' how large,' &c. (See *A. L. L.* v. 575). Latin *t* represents an original d before *r*, e.g. *ătrox* beside *ŏdium* (see § 113). On the loss of *t* in consonant-groups, e. g. *nox* for *noc(*t*)*s*, *vermĭna* for *ver(*t*)*mina*, see § 157, and on *nn* for tn, e. g. *annus*, § 161. In Umbro-Osc. I.-Eur. t remains, e. g. Umbr. tota-, Osc. τωfτο, a community, but tl became (as in Latin) kl, e. g. Umbr. pihaklu, Osc. sakaraklúm (cf. Pelignian sacaracirix ' sacratrices,' pristafalacirix ' praestabulatrices ').

§ 106. **Other examples of I.-Eur. t.** I.-Eur. *k̑m̥tom (O. Ind. śatám, Gk. ἑ-κατόν, O. Ir. cēt, W. cant, Goth. hund, Lith. szìmtas, O. Sl. sŭto) is Lat. *centum*; I.-Eur. *ŏk̑tō(u) (O. Ind. aṣṭā́, Arm. ut', Gk. ὀκτώ, O. Ir. ŏcht, W. wyth, Goth. ahtau, O. Engl. eahta, Lith. asztů-nì, O. Sl. os(t)-mi), Lat. *ŏctō*; I.-Eur. *māter- (O. Ind. mātár-, Arm. mair, Dor. Gk. μά̄τηρ, O. Ir. māthir, O. Engl. mōdor, O. Sl. mater-, Lith. moterà, ' woman '), Lat. *māter*; I.-Eur. *wĕtos, 'a year' (O. Ind. vats-á-, ' calf,' lit. 'yearling,' Gk. (ϝ)έτος, O. Sl. vetŭchŭ, ' old'), Lat. *vĕtus-tus*, *vĕtus*; I.-Eur. *ĕs-ti (O. Ind. ásti, Gk. ἐστι, Goth. ist), Lat. *est*; I.-Eur. root steig-, ' to pierce' (O. Ind. tij-, tigmá-, 'sharp,' Gk. στίζω, στιγμή, Goth. stiks, ' point of time,' Germ. Stich), Lat. *instigo*; the ' Comparative' Suffix -tĕro- (O. Ind. katará-, Gk. πότερος, O. Ir. -ther, Goth. hvaþar, Engl. whether, Lith. katràs, O. Sl. kotory-jï) is in Lat. -*tĕro-*, e. g. *ŭter*.

§ 107. **I.-Eur. tl.** Lat. *lŏquor* is I.-Eur. tloqu-. (O. Ir. atluchur for ad-tluchur in the phrase atluchur bude, ' I thank,' 'ad-loquor gratias '). On the spellings *stlis*, *sclis*, *slis* for class. *lis*, see § 150.

§ 108. **I.-Eur. tt.** Verbs whose stem ends in a dental show *ss* (after a diphthong, &c. reduced to *s*, ch. ii. § 127) in their P. P. P., formed with the suffix -to (e. g. *fissus* from *findo*, *ausus* from *audeo*, *fīsus* from *fīdo*, &c. (see § 155 and ch. v. § 28). So in formations with the suffix -*tŭmo-*, e. g. *vicensumus* for **vicent-tumo-* (ch. v. § 14), Adjectives in -*ōsus* (ch. v. § 65), &c.
The combination *tt* in Latin appears where a vowel has been dropped by syncope, e. g. *cette* for *cĕ-dăte 2 Plur. Imper., *egret*(*t*)*us*, *adgret*(*t*)*us* (§ 109).

§ 109. **D.** Of I.-Eur. d, Lat. *d* examples are : I.-Eur. *dĕk̑m̥, 'ten' (O. Ind. dáśa, Arm. tasn, Gk. δέκα, O. Ir. deich, W. deg, Goth. taihun, O. H. G. zehan, Lith. dĕszimt, dĕszimtis, O. Sl. desętĭ), Lat. *dĕcem*; I.-Eur. root weid-, 'to see, know' (O. Ind. véda, Arm. git-em, Gk. οἶδα, O. Ir. ad-fiadaim, 'I narrate,' Goth. vait, Engl. wot, O. Sl. věděti Inf.), Lat. *vĭdeo, vīdi*. In the Sabine dialect d became l (*I. F.* ii. 157); and we find the spelling *l* sanctioned in a few Latin words at the beginning of the literary period, e.g. *lăcrĭma*, older *dacrima, dacruma* (Gk. δάκρυ, Welsh dagr, Goth. tagr), (Paul. Fest. 48. 15 Th. 'dacrimas' pro lacrimas Livius saepe posuit). *D* became *r* before *g* in *mergo, mergus* (O. Ind. madgú-, 'a waterfowl'), &c., and before *v* and *f*, though the old forms *arger, arvorsus, arfuerunt*, had their *d* restored from *ad* at the beginning of the second cent. B.C. Initial dw- became *b*, e.g. *bellum* (older *duellum*, always a dissyllable in Plautus), *bĭs* for *dwĭs (Gk. δίς), (see § 68), and initial dy- became *j*- (*y*), e.g. *Jŏvis*, O. Lat. *Diovis* (see § 63), but internal -dw- leaves *v* in *suāvis* (§ 71). D is assimilated to a following *m* in *rāmentum* from *rādo, caementum* from *caedo, c* in O. Lat. *reccĭdo, hoc* for **hod-ce, l* in *rellĭgio, pelluviae*, water for washing the feet, *grallae*, stilts, from *grădior*, but assimilates a preceding *l* in *percello* for **-celdo* (cf. *clādes*), &c. (see ch. viii. § 33), *sallo* for **saldo* (Goth. salta). It became *t* before *r*, e.g. *ătrox* (cf. *ŏdium*), and before *t*, this *tt* becoming *ss* (see § 108), e.g. *egressus, adgressus*. The forms *egrettus, adgrettus* (Paul. Fest. 55. 3 Th. quotes *egretus, adgretus*, apparently from some early writer, earlier than the practice of writing the double consonant) seem to stand for**egred(i)to-,adgred(i)to-*(§ 108).

I.-Eur. d remains in Umbro-Osc., e.g. Umbr. devo-, Osc. deívo- 'divus,' but between vowels became in Umbrian a sound (ď? ch. ii. § 88) which is expressed in the native alphabet by a sign conventionally written by us ř and in the Latin alphabet by *rs*, e.g. teřa, *dersa* 'det' (quasi *dědat) (Pel. dida; cf. Osc. didest). For nd we have in Umbro-Osc. nn as in -nno- the Gerundive ending, e.g. Umbr. pihano- 'piandus,' Osc. úpsanno- 'operandus.'

§ 110. **Other instances of I.-Eur. d, Lat. d.** I.-Eur. root deik-, 'to point' (O. Ind. diś-, Gk. δείκνυμι, Goth. ga-teihan, ' to proclaim '), Latin *dīcere, indĭcare*; I.-Eur. root dĕks-, 'right hand ' (O. Ind. dákṣiṇa-, Gk. δεξιός, δεξιτερός, O. Ir. dess, Gaul. Dexsiva, W. deheu, Goth. taihsva, Lith. deszinĕ̃, O. Sl. desĭnŭ), Lat. *dexter*; I.-Eur. root sed-, 'to sit' (O. Ind. sad-, Gk. ἕδος, O. Ir. sudim, sadaim, W. seddu Inf., Goth. sita, O. Sl. sedlo,'saddle '), Lat. *sĕdeo*. Similarly Lat. *scindo*

(O. Ind. chind-, Gk. σχινδ-αλμός, a splinter) ; Lat. dīvus (O. Ind. dēvá-, Lith. dĕvas) ; Lat. pes, Gen. pĕdis (O. Ind. pád-, Gk. πούς, ποδός Gen., πέζα, Goth. fōtus, Lith. pédà, 'footprint') ; Lat. suādeo (O. Ind. svādú-, 'sweet,' Gk. ἡδύς, Goth. suts) ; Lat. ĕdo (O. Ind. ad-, Arm. ut-em, Gk. ἔδω, Goth. ita, Lith. ĕdu, O. Sl. jadǐ, ' food ').

§ 111. Lat. 1 for d. *Lautia*, which usually occurs in an alliterative formula,e.g. Liv. xxx. 17. 14 aedes liberae, loca, lautia legatis decreta; xxviii. 39. 19 locus inde lautiaque legatis praeberi jussa) was in Old Latin *dautia*, a form quoted from Livius Andronicus by Paul. Fest. 48. 16 Th. 'dautia' (Livius saepe posuit', quae lautia dicimus, et dantur legatis hospitii gratia ; *lingua*, for I.-Eur. *dṇghᵘ̯ā- or *dṇĝhwā- ₁Goth. tuggō ; cf. O. Ir. tenge) was in Old Latin *dingua* [nos nunc . . . linguam per l potius quam per d (scribamus), Mar. Vict. 9. 17 K.; communionem enim habuit littera (l cum d) apud antiquos, ut 'dinguam' et linguam, et 'dacrimis' et lacrimis, et 'Kapitodium' et Kapitolium, id. 26. 1 K.). (Was *Aquilonia* the Oscan Akudunnia-, now Cedogna ? cf. O. Umbr. akeđunia-.) Pompey, according to Mar. Vict. 8. 15 K., affected the old spelling and pronunciation *kadamitas* for *călămĭtas* (perhaps from the same root as Oscan *cadeis amnud*, ' with intent to injure,' ' out of malice,' Gk. κεκαδῆσαι, explained by Hesychius as βλάψαι, κακῶσαι, στερῆσαι) ; the *di Novensiles* appear on an old inscription from Picenum as DEIV. NOVESEDE (*C.I.L.* i. 178) (cf. the Marsic *esos novesede*, Zv. *I.I.I.* 39). In many or all of these words the preference of the byform with *l* can be explained by false analogy ; in *lingua* by the analogy of *lingo* (cf. O. Ir. ligur, ' the tongue,' Arm. lezu, Lith. lëžuvis) ; in *calamitas* by the analogy of *calamus* ; in *lautia* by the analogy of *lavo*, &c. Similarly O. Lat. *dēlĭcare* with the sense of *indĭcare* (e. g. Plaut. *Mil.* 844) may owe its *l* to the influence of *dēlĭquare*, to clarify. Perhaps Lat. *lympha*, a Graecized form (cf. Gen. Pl. *lymphon*, Varro, *Sat. Men.* 50 B.) of *dumpa*, (Osc. Diumpa-), with Lat. *Ulysses*, does not exhibit a Latin change of d to *l*, but a change which had already been made in Greek ; for Quintilian, i. 4. 16, quotes dialectal Gk. 'Ολυσσεύς ; and on Gk. vases (see Kretschmer, *Gr. Vas.* p. 146) we have 'Ολυσευς (*C.I.G.* 7697), frequently 'Ολυτευς (*C.I.G.* 7383, 7699, 8185, 8208), while Varro, *L.L.* vii. 87, quotes λυμφόληπτος (cf. O. Lat. *Thelis* for Θέτις, Varro, *L.L.* vii. 87). The exact relation of *sĭmĭla*, *similāgo*, fine wheaten flour (cf. Germ. Semmel), to Gk. σεμίʳαλις is doubtful, as also that of *casila* (Paul. Fest. 33. 22 Th.; for *cassilla ?*) to *cassis*, *cassida* (an Etruscan word according to Isidore, *Orig.* xviii. 14. 1). The form *reluvium* mentioned by Festus (370. 17 Th. rediviam quidam, alii ' reluvium ' appellant, cum circa unguis cutis se resolvit, quia luere est solvere) never ousted the form *redivia*. It does not appear to have been a phonetic variety of *redivia*, but rather a separate word, perhaps a grammarian's coinage, derived from *luo*, as *redivia*, *red-uvia* was derived from *ŏvo of *ind-uo, ex-uo, exŭviae. Some of the forms with *l* mentioned above, e. g. *calamitas*, 'injury to crops,' may similarly have been different words from the d-forms. [So *consĭlium*, &c. beside *praesidium*, &c. ; cf. Mar. Vict. 9. 18 K. praesidium per d potius (scribamus) quam per l ; *considium* Plaut. *Cas.* 966 (see below on *solium*)]. Some appear to be dialectal ; e. g. *lepesta* or *lepista* [Greek δεπεστα (but cf. λεπαστή), according to Varro, *L. L.* v. 123] was Sabine (Varro, *l. c.*), and perhaps *Novensiles* (id. v. 74) (cf. Paul. Fest. 77. 7 Th. 'inpelimenta' inpedimenta dicebant) ; so probably *lărix* for **darix* (O. Ir. dair for *darix, ' an oak '), and possibly *laurus* for **daurus* (O. Ir. daur for *darus, ' an oak ') ; *Melica* (gallina) for *Mēdica* (Varro, *R.R.* iii. 9. 19) (cf.

§ 111.] REPRESENTATIVES OF I.-EUR. SOUNDS. T, D, DH. 287

Paul. Fest. 89. 27 Th.); and the few modern Italian words which show this change of *d* to *l* may be dialectal too, e.g. cicala from Lat. *cĭcāda*, ellera from Lat. *hĕdĕra*, trespolo from Lat. *trēs* and *pĕdes*, as tiepolo is a dialectal variety of tepido (Lat. *tĕpĭdus*) (cf. the *Dĭgentia*, now Licenza, in the Sabine district). It is possible, but unlikely, that Lat. *pūblĭcus* (Umbr. pupďiko-), *Pūblius* from *pūbes*, a name whose spelling was often altered after *Poplicola* and other names derived from *pŏpŭlus* (cf. Umbr. Puplecio-), may stand for **pūbdĭ-* and exhibit that change of *d* to *l* after a labial which is seen in these Italian forms tiepolo and trespolo (cf. the byform *impĕlīmenta*). The town-name *Telēsia* shows d on Oscan coins with Tedis (Zv. *I. I. I.* 262). Other examples of *l* for *d* are *levir*, better *laevir*, a brother-in-law for **daever* (O. Ind. dēvár-, Gk. δαήρ for **δαιϝηρ*, Lith. dēveris, O. Sl. děverï), which Nonius (557. 6 M.) explains : quasi laevus vir ; *ōleo*, which stands in puzzling contrast to *ŏdor* from the root od-, ' to smell ' (Arm. hot, Gk. ὀδμή, Lith. ŭdžiu) (*odefacit* of Paul. Fest. 193. 21 Th. 'odefacit' dicebant pro olfacit, may be a grammarian's coinage). But the other instances usually quoted are doubtful : *ūlīgo* may come from **ūvīlis* as well as from *ūvĭdus* ; *sōlium* and O. Lat. *sŏlum* (e. g. Enn. *Ann.* 93 M. scamna solumque) may be from a root swel- (Gk. σέλμα, Lith, sŭlas, ' a bench '), and not represent **sodium* (O. Ir. suide) from the root sed-, as *sŏlum*, the ground, the sole of the foot (cf. *solea*, a slipper) stands for **swolo-*, (O. Ir. fol, ' the base, foundation ') ; *mālus* might be from **maz-lo-*, as Engl. mast is from **maz-do-*. The interchange of *d* and *l* in *lacruma*, *lingua*, &c. was well known to the native Latin grammarians, and was often appealed to by them to support theoretical etymologies of words with *l*. Thus they explained *sella* (really for **sed-la* ; Lacon. Gk. ἐλλά ; cf. Goth. sitls, Engl. a settle, O. Sl. sedlo, ' a saddle ') by this interchange (Mar. Vict. 26. 3 K.) ; similarly *ancĭlia* from *ambe-cido* (Varro, *L. L.* vii. 43) ; *sēlĭquastra* from *sĕdeo* (Fest. 508. 10 Th.) ; *mĕdĭtor* from μελετάω (Serv. ad *Ecl.* i. 2); *dēlĭcatus* from *dēdĭcatus* [Paul. Fest. 49. 17 Th. ; who quotes a (suppositious) *delicare*, 51. 35 Th. 'delicare' ponebant pro dedicare ; cf. Gl. Plac. 16. 11 G. delicare: deferre, quod et ' dedicare ' dicebant pro commercio litterarum]. This *delicare* for *dedicare* is either an etymological coinage to explain *delicatus*, or the Old Latin *delicare*, to explain, inform, which was mentioned above. Modern etymologists have adopted a similar course to explain some difficult words like *mŭlier*, *mīles*, *sĭlicernium*, *lūdus* (for other examples, see Wharton : *On Latin Consonant Laws*, in the *Phil. Soc. Trans.* 1889 ; and Conway, *Indogerm. Forsch.* ii. 157). But the evidence rather points to this *l*-like pronunciation of *d* having asserted itself at the beginning of the literary period, but not having gained admission into the literary language, except in the case of a few words where the *l* was supported by analogy or other causes. (Latin *baliolus*, from *bădius*, is a 'ghost-word,' the true reading in Plaut. *Poen.* 1301 is *baiiolus*, the old spelling of *bajulus*).

Whether an original l is ever represented by *d* in Latin is doubtful. The mispronunciation *alipes* for *ădĭpes* (Prob. App. 199. 3 K.) was probably influenced by the Gk. ἄλειφα, but is no argument that the Greek and Latin words are connected ; the O. Lat. *sedda* for *sella*, quoted by Ter. Scaur. 13. 14 K., seems to be a grammarian's coinage to illustrate the etymology from *sĕdeo*, though it might possibly be the same dialectal *sedda*, with a peculiar form of *d*, which is still heard in S. Italy and Sardinia, where every Italian *ll* is replaced by this *dd*-sound (see ch. ii. § 85). (On *medipontus* and *melipontus*, see Keil on Cato *R. R.* iii. 5.)

§ 112. Lat. r for d. Priscian (i. p. 35. 2 H.) tells us that the 'antiquissimi' used *arvenae, arventores, arvocati, arfines, arvolare, arfari*, also *arger*; and other grammarians mention *arventum* (Mar. Vict. 9. 17 K.), *arvorsus, arvorsarius* Vel. Long. 71. 22 K.), *arveniet* (Gl. Plac.), *arferia* (Paul. Fest. 8. 32 Th.; Gloss. ap. Löwe Prodr. p. 13 vas vinarium quo vinum ad aras ferebant; cf. *adferial*, Gl. Cyr.). In Cato we find *arveho* (e. g. *R. R.* 135. 7; 138); and on inscriptions *arfuerunt, arfuise* and *arvorsum* (*C. I. L.* i. 196) in the S. C. de Bacchanalibus of 186 B. C., *arvorsario* beside *advorsarium* (i. 198), in the Lex Repetundarum of 123–2 B. C., *arvorsu* (ix. 782).. *Apur* (Mar. Vict. 9. 17 K.), *apor* (Paul. Fest. 19. 34 Th.), the old form of *apud*, was probably a 'doublet' used before a word beginning with *g, v, f* (cf. *apur finem* in an old inscription from the Marsic territory, Zv. *I. I. I.* 45); but *quirquir* in the augur's formula for marking out a *templum* (Varro, *L. L.* vii. 8) is a doubtful example; and *arduuitur* (Legg. XII Tabb. 10. 7 Br.), *ar me* Lucil. ix. 30 M. unlikely readings. The affinity of the sounds is seen in the (dialectal) mispronunciation 'in usu cotidie loquentium' (Consent. 392. 15 K.) *peres* for *pĕdes* (cf. *arcenire* Diom. 452. 29 K.); and *r* (or else đ, the *th*-sound of our 'this,' 'then') takes the place of Italian *d* in the dialects of S. Italy and Sicily, e. g. dicère and ricere for Ital. dicere in the Abruzzi; Neapolitan rurece for Ital. dodici, and (like Consentius' *peres*) pere for Ital. piede, &c. *Arger* persisted in Vulgar Latin (Ital. argine, 'a dam,' Span. arcen, 'a parapet.') *Arbĭter*, from the root gu̯et- of Lat. *vĕto* (O. Scand. at-kvaeđa, 'a decision') seems to be dialectal (O. Umbr. ađputrati, in Lat. '*arbitratu*') (cf. *mŏnērŭla*, the form used by Plautus, classical *mŏnēdŭla* with the termination of *acrēdula, ficēdula, querquēdula, nītēdula, alcēdo*; and the glosses *maredus* for *mădĭdus*, *solerare* for *sŏlĭdare, marcerat* for *marcĭdat* (Löwe, Prodr. 352; Opusc. 142). The change of *d* to *r* in O. Lat. *arfuerunt* (preserved in the formula SCR. ARF. scribendo *arfuerunt*), &c. was often mentioned by the native grammarians, who regarded a reference of any *r* to an original *d* as a legitimate device in framing etymologies. Thus Velius Longus (71.23 K.) derives *aurĭcŭla* from *audio*, and *mĕrīdies* (older *merĭdie* Adv.) from *mĕdius* and *dies*. This explanation of *meridies* is probably right, the *r* being due to dissimilation (cf. Cic. *Orat.* xlvii. 157 jam videtur nescire dulcius. ipsum meridiem cur non 'medidiem'; Varro, *L. L.* vi. 4, says that *medidies* was the old form, and that he had seen it on a Praenestine sundial: meridies ab eo quod medius dies. d antiqui, non r, in hoc dicebant, ut Praeneste incisum in solario vidi), though a good deal may be said for the derivation from *merus* (cf. mero meridie, Petr. 37. p. 25. 1 B.), and the Praenestine D seen by Varro may have been merely an old form of the letter R, as LADINOD, LADINEI on all coins (c. 250 B. C.) of Larinum (modern Larino) (*C. I. L.* i. 24) may show the Oscan D, the symbol of *r*, as R was of *d*. Isidore (*Orig.* xii. 7. 69) similarly explains *mĕrŭla*: merula antiquitus 'medula' vocabatur, eo quod moduletur; and Varro (*L. L.* v. 110) derives *perna* 'a pede.'

Modern etymologists explain in the same way *glārea* (Gk. χλῆδος), possibly a dialectal form, *sĭmītur* (ch. ix. § 8) beside *simitu*, and other words of doubtful origin (see Wharton, *Latin Consonant Laws*, in *Phil. Soc. Trans.* 1889, on *căreo, plōro*, &c.). But the available evidence hardly allows us to ascribe any *r* to an original *d* in a Latin word except before *g, v, f. Cādūceus*, a loanword from Gk κηρύκιον (Dor. κᾱρ-) may owe its *d* to a fanciful connexion of the word with *cădūcus*. In Umbrian ar- is found for the Preposition ad in compounds perhaps only before f-, v-, e. g. arveitu 'advehito,' *arfertur* (and *arṣfertur*) 'adfertor' (von Planta, i. p. 408). (On Lat. *arcesso* and other doubtful exx. of *ar-* for *ad-*, see Schoell, *xii Tabb.*, p. 81.)

§§ 112–115.] REPRESENTATIVES OF I.-EUR. SOUNDS. T, D, DH. 289

§ 113. tr for dr. Lat. *citrus* was the old form of Gk. κέδρος, for Naevius has *citrosa vestis*, while *cedrus* is not found till Virgil; *Cassantra* and *Alexanter* were the old forms of Κασσάνδρα, 'Αλέξανδρος, according to Quint. i. 4. 16 [we find *Alixentrom* (C. I. L. i. 50), *Alixente*(*r*), *Casenter*(*a*) (i. 1501), on old inscriptions from Praeneste]. So Gk. Ὑδροῦς, -οῦντος, Lat. *Hydruntum*, is modern Otranto, Lat. *nūtrio* is for *noud-rio (§ 42) (Lith. naudà, 'use,' Goth. niutan, 'to enjoy,' Germ. geniessen) ; *taeter* for **taed-ro-* (cf. *taedet*) ; so *ŭter*, Gen. *ŭtris* (Gk. ὑδρία) ; *lŭtra*, an otter, may be a malformation of *ŭtra (O. Ind. udrá-, Lith. údra, Engl. otter). The group *dr* is not found in Latin, except in *quadru-*, *quadra*, &c. (but cf. *triquetrus*). The name *Drūsus* (cf. Gloss ap. Löwe, *Prodr.* p. 398 drusus: patiens, rigidus, contumax) is declared by Suetonus (*Tib.* iii.) to be a Gaulish name : Drusus, hostium duce Drauso comminus trucidato, sibi posterisque cognomen invenit ; *andruare* and *drua* (Paul. Fest. 7. 15 Th.) are very doubtful spellings of *antruare* (*antroare*) and *trua* (*ib.* l. 17).

§ 114. DH. I.-Eur. dh became *f* in Latin, which in proximity to *r* became *b* ; but in the middle of a word between vowels *d* is found; e.g. I.-Eur. **dhūmo-* (O. Ind. dhūmá-, Gk. θυμός, Lith. dúmai Pl., O. Sl. dymŭ), Lat. *fūmus*; I.-Eur. rŭdhro- (Gk. ἐ-ρυθρός, O. Sl. rŭdrŭ ; cf. O. Ind. rudhirá-), Lat. *rŭber*, stem *rubro-*; I.-Eur. root bheidh- (Gk. πείθω for *φείθω), Lat. *fīdo*. This *f*, *b*, *d* may have all three developed from an older *đ*-sound, the sound of our *th* in 'this,' 'that,' 'then;' but whether Sicilian λίτρα (for Lat. *lībra*) is a survival of the *đ*-stage is uncertain. The change of *đr* to *fr*, *br* may be compared with the change of *sr* to *fr*, *br* in *tenebrae* for *tenes-rae, &c. (§ 152).

I.-Eur. dh is in Umbro-Osc. f, whether initial or internal, e.g. Umbr. façia, Osc. fakiiad 'faciat,' Umbr. rufra 'rubra,' Osc. mefiaí 'mediae' (von Planta, i. p. 451). This f for Lat. (internal) *d*, *b* is found in some dialectal words, e.g. *crefrare* for *cribrare*, like dialectal f for Lat. (internal) *b* from I.-Eur. bh (see ch. ii. § 83).

§ 115. Other examples of I.-Eur. dh. (1) Initial: I.-Eur. root dhē-, dhēk-, 'to place, do' (Gk. ἔ-θη-ν, ἔ-θηκ-α, Arm. d-nem, 'I place,' Goth. ga-dē-þs, Engl. deed, Lith. dĕ-ti, O. Sl. dĕ-ti, 'to lay'), Lat. *făc-io*, but with *ah* medial, *condo* (*făc-* shows the weak grade of dhēk-); I.-Eur. root dhē-, dhēy-, 'to suck,' (O. Ind. dháyāmi, Arm. diem, Gk. θῆσθαι, O. Ir. dīth 3 Sg. Pret., Goth. daddjan, 'to suckle,' O. Sl. dĕtę, 'an infant'), Lat. *fēlo*, usually spelt *fello*, *fīlius* (§ 7). Similarly Lat. *forum* (Lith. dvāras, 'court,' O. Sl. dvorŭ) ; Lat. *fŏveo*, *făvīlla* from the I.-Eur. root dheghu-, 'to burn' (O. Ind. dah-, Lith. degù, Gk. τέφρα for *θέφρα, ashes) [the original meaning of *foveo* was 'to warm' (see the dictionaries, and cf. Paul. Fest. 60. 15 Th. a fovendo, id est calefaciendo); hence *fŏculum*, a fire-pan, e. g. Plaut. *Capt.* 847 foveri foculis ferventibus].

(2) Medial: from I.-Eur. root reudh-, 'to be red' (O. Ind. rőhita-, 'red,' lōhá-,

U

'metal,' Gk. ἔ-ρευθω, O. Ir. ruad,' red,' 'strong,' Gaul. Roudos, W. rhudd, Goth. rauþs, 'red,' O. H. G. rost, 'rust,' O. Sl. rŭdĕti, 'to blush,' ruda, 'metal,' rŭžda, 'rust') come Lat. raudus, rōdus and rūdus, unshaped metal, rŭdis, unshaped, and with b, besides rŭber mentioned above, rŭbeo, rōbus, rōbur, rōbigo, while rūfus with f, is dialectal; from I.-Eur. root bhendh-, 'to bind' (O. Ind. bándhana-, Gk. πεῖσμα for *πενθσμα, πενθερός, Goth. bindan), Lat. offendix (§ 79) with d, while Lat. lumbus shows b for dh (or dhw?) (O. Sl. lędvija, O. Engl. lenden), and b appears for dh of the suffix dhlo- (see ch. v. § 26), in trī-bulum, stăbulum, &c. as -bro- for I.-Eur. dhro- in crī-brum, vertĕ-bra, &c.; I.-Eur. *mĕdhyo- (O. Ind. mádhya-, Gk. μέσ(σ)ος, Goth. midjis), Lat. mĕdius; I.-Eur. root aidh-, 'to burn' (O. Ind. édha-, 'firewood,' Gk. αἴθω, O. Ir. aid, 'fire,' O. Engl. ād, 'pyre),' Lat. aedes, house, lit. 'hearth.' Similarly Lat. vĭdua (O. Ind. vidhávā, O. Ir. fedb, Goth. viduvō, O. Sl. vĭdova); fĭdēlia (Gk. πίθος); grădus (Goth. griþs); vădes (Goth. vadi, Germ. Wette, Lith. vadŭti, 'to redeem'); ūber (O. Ind. ūdhar, Gk. οὖθαρ, O. Engl. ūder); combrētum, a bulrush (cf. Lith. szveñdrai Pl.); barba for *farba (§ 104) (Engl. beard, O. Sl. brăda, Lith. barz-dà); arbos (O. Ind. ardh-, 'to grow, thrive'); glăber (O. H. G. glat, 'smooth,' Engl. glad, Lith. glodùs, 'smooth,' O. Sl. gladŭkŭ); verbum (Goth. vaurd, Neut., Lĭth. vařdas, 'a name').

§ 116. **The Gutturals.** There are three series of Gutturals, viz. (1) Palatals (in some languages Sibilants, e.g. O. Ind. śatám, Lith. szim̃tas, O. Sl. sŭto, 'hundred' corresponding to Lat. centum); (2) Velars, better called Gutturals proper (Gutturals in all languages, e.g. the onomatopoetic name of the cuckoo, O. Ind. kóka-, Gk. κόκκυξ, Lat. cucūlus; cf. Lith. kukŭti, 'to cry cuckoo'); (3) Velars with Labialisation, i.e. followed by a w-sound (in some languages Labials, e.g. Hom. Gk. πίσυρες, W. pedwar, Osc. petora, 'four,' corresponding to Lat. quattuor). They are most conveniently written, (1) k̑, ĝ, &c., (2) k, g, &c., (3) q^u, g^u, &c., while the symbols k, g, &c. may be reserved for Gutturals whose exact nature is doubtful. So far as Latin is concerned, we might write (1) and (2) as k, g, &c., and (3) as kw, gw, &c.. for the same letter c represents the k̑ of centum and the k of carpo (O. Ind. kr̥p-), nor does the k̑w of equus, &c. (O. Ind. áśva-) present a different appearance from the q^u of quattuor, sequor (O. Ind. sac-). I.-Eur. k̑ and k became Lat. c (k), ĝ and g Lat. g, ĝh and gh became a guttural spirant, which was written g with a consonant, elsewhere h; I.-Eur. q^u is Lat. qu (which we might write kv, kw), g^u is Latin gu, gv (gw), which became g before a consonant, but lost its g when initial just as dj- (dy-) when initial became j- (y-), or as Teut. gw from I.-Eur. gh^u became w in 'warm,' 'snow,' &c. It lost its g also when medial between vowels. I.-Eur. gh^u became a guttural spirant followed by a w- sound, which was written with a consonant *gu* or *g*, but elsewhere became *hw*, this *hw* developing at the beginning of a word into *f* [just as the Greek *hw*-sound from I.-Eur. initial sw- seems to have developed into some *f*-sound (ch. i. § 3)], but in the middle of a word into *v* (*w*). (For examples see below.) The I.-Eur. Gutturals offer considerable difficulty. It is not only that we find occasionally the confusion, found with every species of Mute, between Tenuis and Media (ch. ii. § 75), Media and Aspirate, &c.; e.g. the guttural Media seems to replace the Aspirate in Lat. *lĭgurrio* (cf. *lingo*), from the root leiĝh-, 'to lick' (Gk. λείχω), Lat. *adagio, prōdĭgium*, from the root aĝh-, 'to say' (O. Ind. ah-), Lat. *fĭgūra* (cf. *fingo*) from the root dheiĝh-, 'to mould,' (O. Ind. dih-, ' to smear,') just as we find the labial Media replacing the Aspirate in Gk. στέμβω beside ἀστεμφής. We find also apparent confusion of one series of Gutturals with another; thus in Greek (and perhaps in other languages) the proximity of the vowel *u* seems to change a Guttural of the third into a Guttural of the second series, e.g. γυνή[1] (Boeot. βανά, O. Ir. ban), λύκος (dial. Lat. *lŭpus*); and very often the want of a cognate word in a language which treats one series differently from another, prevents us from ascertaining to which series a Guttural properly belongs, e.g. whether the *c* of *collum* is a palatal or a true guttural. We are also confronted with an apparently I.-Eur. dialectal change of q^u to p, perhaps made in order to avoid that similarity between two successive syllables which was so sought after in Latin (§ 163). Thus the I.-Eur. word for 'five' may have been *q̑ĕnq^{u}ĕ in one dialect (O. Ind. pánca, Gk. πέντε, &c.), *q^{u}ĕnq^{u}ĕ in another (Lat. *quinque*, O. Ir. cōic); the root meaning 'to cook,' peq^u- (O. Ind. pac-, Gk. πέσσω), q^{u}eq^u- (W. pobi, with *p*- from I.-Eur. q^u, Lat. *cŏquus*), and even q^{u}ep- (Lith. kepù. What of Gk. ἀρτο-κόπος?). The same explanation has been suggested for the q^u of Lat. *quercus* beside the p- of O. Engl. furh, Engl. fir, and for the p- of Goth. fidvōr, Engl. four, beside the q^u of other languages, e.g. Lat. *quattuor*.

A Latin Guttural, to whatever series it belongs, combines with a following *s* into *x*, e.g. *vexi* from *vĕho* (I.-Eur. ĝh), before *t* becomes the group *ct*, e.g. *vectus, actus*, which in late Latin

---

[1] So *w* is dropped before the *u*-sound in Engl. 'two.'

came to be pronounced *tt* (Ital. atto), before *n*, *m* becomes the group *gn*, *gm*, e.g. *ilignus* from *ilex*, or the loanword *cygnus* from κύκνος. Initial *gn-* became *n-* at the beginning of the second cent. B.C., e.g. *nātus*. But *lūna* does not stand for *lucna, but for *lucsna (Zend raoxšna-, 'shining,' Pruss. lauxnos, 'stars'), as we see from the old form on a Praenestine mirror, *Losna* (*C. I. L.* i. 55), just as *vēlum*, a sail, stands for *vex-lum (O. Sl. veslo, 'a rudder'), as we see from the Diminutive form *vexillum*, so that Gk. λύχνος has been declared to represent *λυκsνος (*M. S. L.* vii. 91). Another instance of Greek χν appearing in Latin as *n* with long vowel is the (loanword?) *arānea* (Gk. ἀράχνη). *Exāmen* beside *agmen*, *amb-āges* (on *exagmen* see *Class. Rev.* v. 294), *contāmino* beside *contāgium*; [contrast *propagmen* (Enn. *Ann.* 587 M.) beside *propāgo*, and cf. *subtēmen* from *texo* beside *subtegmen*, e.g. Virg. *Aen.* iii. 483], have been variously explained by hypotheses that have as yet failed to establish themselves, such as (1) that the Guttural is assimilated (like *d* in *caementum* from *caedo*) after a long vowel, *exāg-men becoming *exāmmen, *exāmen*, while *ăg-men* remains *agmen*; (2) that the Guttural is assimilated in the unaccented syllable (under the earlier Accent Law), whence *éxāmen* but *ágmen*; (3) that the unassimilated forms had originally a connecting vowel, e.g. *ăg(ĭ)men* (cf. *jugumentum*, a joining, Cato, *R. R.* xiv. 1 and 4). Another theory, that these forms add an *s* to the final Guttural of the root, *exāmen* for *ex-ax-men from **ags-men-* (cf. *ax-la, *ax-is*), connects the forms with a known law of Latin phonetics, and is preferable on that account.

The cognates of *major*, *aio* show *g* in Latin, e.g. *magnus*, *măgis*, *adagio*, *prōdĭgium*, but the guttural Aspirate in other I.-Eur. languages (O. Ind. mah-, ah-); so it is better to refer them to the ordinary law that Latin *h* may be dropped between vowels, than to posit a new law that the guttural Media was dropped before *y*. *Major* will thus come from an older *măhior (cf. O. Ind. máhīyas-); *pūlēium*, fleabane, apparently from *pūlex*, a flea, may be dialectal, like Umbr. *muieto* P. P. P., with i for palatalized g, beside *mugatu* Imperat.; *brĕvis* (Gk. βραχύς) will represent an older trisyllable *brehuis*, and *lĕvis* (Gk. ἐλαχύς: what of ἐλαφρός?) an older *lehuis, while *pinguis* (Gk. παχύς),

§§ 117-119.] REPRESENTATIVES OF I.-EUR. GUTTURALS. 293

where the Aspirate is preceded by the consonant *n*, will represent an older trisyllabic form **pinguïs* (see § 127).

Aspirate Tenues, which are difficult to trace (see § 95), have been found in *unguis* (cf. O. Ind. nakhá-, Gk. ὄνυχ-, O. Ir. inge, Lith. nãgas, O. Engl. nægel) (see *B. B.* xvii. 133), *congius* (O. Ind. śaṅkhá-, 'a shell,' Gk. κόγχη, Lett. sence). On dat. *cl* for I.-Eur. -tl-, e.g. *pōc(u)lum* see § 105; on *cc* for *tc*, e.g. *ac* for **atc*, *atque*, *hoc* for **hod-c(e)*, § 109; on the mispronunciations *ss, sc* for *x*, e.g. *coxim, ascella*, ch. ii. § 117.

In Umbrian the combination kt, when due to Syncope, seems to be differently developed according as the k represents on the one hand an I.-Eur. q^u or on the other an I.-Eur. k̂ (or k); in the former case it becomes kt, e.g. fiktu (Lat. *fīgito* for *fivito*, ch. viii. § 7), in the latter, i̯t, e.g. *deitu* (Lat. *dīcito*). In Osc. both are kt, e. g. fruktatiuf 'fru(v)itationes,' *factud* 'facito,' while I.-Eur. q^ut (not due to Syncope) is Umbro-Osc. kt, and I.-Eur. k̂t, kt (not due to Syncope) is Umbro-Osc. ht (for examples see Buck, *Vocalismus Osk. Sprache*, p. 145).

§ 117. x for Guttural with s. *Vexi* from *vĕho* (I.-Eur. root weĝh-, 'to carry'); *panxi* (cf. Gk. πήγνυμι); *finxi* from *fingo* (I.-Eur. dheiĝh-); *nix* for **(s)nighᵘs*; *coxi* from *cŏquo*; *līxa, prō-lixus, ē-lixus* from *līquor* for **vliquor* (O. Ir. fliuch, 'wet,' W. gwlyb). Before most consonants *x* became *s*, e. g. *sescĕni* for **sex-ceni*, (as after *r* in *mers* for *merx, sparsi, tersi*, &c., § 158), but not before *t* in *dexter, dextra, sextus*, &c. (but *lustro*, to illuminate, *illustris*, &c. from **lucs-tr-*; on *Sestius, mistus*, see ch. ii. § 125), while before *m, n, l* it was (like *s* for I.-Eur. s, e. g. *quālus* for **quas-lus*, cf. *quāsillus*, § 151) dropped with 'Compensation,' e. g. *pālus* for **pax-lus* (Dim. *paxillus*); *āla*, wing, shoulder, for **ax-la* (Dim. *axilla*), like *axis*, an axle, from the root aĝ- of *ăgo* (O. H. G. ahsala, 'shoulder,' W. echel, 'an axle,' Engl. axle); *tēlum*, for **tex-lum*, from *texo*, to shape (O. H. G. dehsala, 'an axe,' O. Sl. tesla); *tēla*, for **tex-la*, from *.texo*, to weave (Ter. *Heaut.* 285 texentem telam); *tālus*, for **tax-lus* (Dim. *taxillus*); *sēni* for **sex-ni*; *aula*, Dim. *auxilla*.

§ 118. ct for Guttural with t. *Vectus*, with *vectis*, a lever, from *vĕho* (ĝh); *panctum* and *pactum* from *pango* (ĝ?); *fictum* from *fingo* (ĝh); *luctus*, grief, from *lūgeo* (ĝ); *coctum* from *cŏquo* (qᵘ); *nicto*, to wink; cf. *co-nīveo* (ghᵘ). After a consonant *c* was dropped in course of time (§ 157), e. g. *fortis*, in O. Lat. *forctis* [in the XII Tables *forctes* was the name given to the loyal neighbours of Rome, *sanates* to those who had swerved from their loyalty, but had returned to it, Fest. 524. 15 Th.; cf. Paul. Fest. 59. 26 'forctes' (*leg.* 'forctis') frugi et bonus, sive validus]; *quintus*, in the older spelling *quinctus*, the older form being long retained in the names *Quinctilius, Quinctius, Quinctilis*, &c. (see Georges, *Lex. Wortf.* s. v.). On Vulg. and Late-Lat. *tt* for *ct*, e. g. *brattea*, see ch. ii. § 95, and cf. *Rhein. Mus.* xlv. p. 493.

§ 119. gn, gm for cn, cm. Like *ilignus* from *ilex* are *larignus* from *lărix, salignus* from *sălix*; similarly *segmentum* from *sĕco*; *dignus*, usually explained as **dec-nus* from *děcet*, but better as **dic-nus* (O. Scand. tiginn, 'high-born,' tign, 'rank') a P. P. P. NO-stem from the root deik̑- of *dīcere*, *indĭcare*, &c. *Aprunus* is a late spelling of *aprugnus*; *aprinus* is an entirely different formation (see Georges, *Lex. Wortf.* s. v.). After a consonant the Guttural is dropped, e. g. *quernus* for **querc-nus* from *quercus*; *farnus* for **farg-nus*, a byform of *fraxĭnus*, though not in Compounds with *ad*, &c., e. g. *agnosco*. When the consonant is a Nasal, it seems to combine with the following Nasal, e. g. *quīni* for **quinc-ni*, so that *contāmino* might stand for **con-tang-mino* as well as for **con-tags-mino*. Compounds with *in*, *con* show different spellings; *in-* with *gnosco* gives *ĭgnosco*, *con-* with *gnosco* both *cognosco* and *cōnosco*, as *con-* with *necto* gives *cōnecto*, &c. (cf. ch. ii. § 130).

Initial Latin *gn* became at the beginning of the second cent. B. C. *n* (as in Engl. 'gnat'), e. g. *nōsco*, older *gnōsco* (ĝn-), *nātus*, older *gnatus* (ĝn-) (*gnatare* παιδοποιῆσαι, *C. G. L.* ii. 35. 10), *nixus*, older *gnixus* (k̑n-; cf. O. H. G. hnīgan, Germ. neigen), *nārus*, older *gnarus* (*gnaritur* γνωρίζεται, *C. G. L.* ii. 35. 12), *nāvus*, older *gnavus*, *Naevius* (cf Gk. Ναιος on the Mon. Anc.) beside *Gnaeus* (cf. *Gnaivod*, Abl., on a Scipio epitaph, *C. I. L.* i. 30). For instances of the older forms, see Georges, *Lex. Wortf.* s. vv., and Löwe, *Prodr.* 354: e.g. *gnoscier* on the S. C. Bacch. of 186 B. C., *C.I.L.* i. 196. 27, but *nationum*, *noverit* (beside *gnatus* Part.) on the Lex Repetundarum of 123–122 B. C., i. 198; *natus* Part. on the Sent. Minuciorum of 117 B. C., i. 199. Plautus and Terence use, as a rule, *natus* for the Participle, *gnatus* for the Substantive; the *g* of these forms appears in the compounds *agnosco*, *agnatus*, *ignarus*, *ignavus*, &c., and strangely also in *agnomen*, *cognomen*; for *nōmen* (so in S. C. Bacch.) was not originally **gnomen* (cf. O. Ind. nā́ma-, and for the various forms of the root, see B. B. xvii. 132). On *crĕpusculum* and Gk. κνέφας, see § 80.

§ 120. **Lat. h dropped between vowels.** *Bimus* for **bi-himus*, lit. 'two winters old,' like Engl. twinter, a two-year old beast (cf. χίμαρος, goat, lit. 'a winter old,' Scotch gimmer, a yearling lamb); *nīl* (so always in Plautus), for *nĭhĭl*, *nĭhīlum* from *nĕ* and *hīlum* (cf. Enn. *A.* 8 M. nec dispendi facit hilum; Lucil. xiv. 11 M. hilo non sectius vivas; Lucr. iii. 830 nil igitur mors est ad nos neque pertinet hilum), *hīlum* being explained as 'quod grano fabae adhaeret' (Paul. Fest. 72. 10 Th.); *praebeo* for *praehĭbeo*; *cors* for *cŏhors*. On the *h* of *ăhĕnus* (*aenus*) for **ăyĕs-no-*, and on the question whether *h* was used in *vehemens*, &c. to indicate a long vowel (as in Umbrian, e. g. comohota 'commōta'), see ch. ii. § 56.

§ 121. **Dialectal f for h.** In Spanish, Latin *f* has become *h*, e. g. hablar, 'to speak' (Lat. *fābulari*, O. Lat. *fabulare*), and an interchange of *h* and *f* shows traces of itself in the dialects of Italy. We find the form *fasena* for *hăsēna* ascribed to the Sabine dialect by the grammarians (Vel. Long. 69. 8 K.), along with *fircus* (cf. the name of a citizen of Reate mentioned by Varro, *Fircellius*) and *fedus*. Similar forms roughly classed by the grammarians as 'Old Latin' we may believe to have been dialectal, e. g. *fordeum* for *hordeum*, *folus* for *hŏlus*, *fostis* for *hostis*, *fostia* for *hostia*, &c., though some of them may be mere coinages to strengthen the argument for the spelling with *h-* (see Quint. i. 4. 14; Ter. Scaur. pp. 11, 13 K.; Vel. Long. p. 81 K.; Paul. Fest. 59. 21 Th. &c.). A Faliscan inscription has foied for *hodie* (*Not. Scav.* 1887, pp. 262, 307): foied uino pipafo kra karefo 'hodie vinum bibam, cras carebo,' but a Sabine inscription has *hiretum*, apparently from the root ĝher- (?gher-) (Osc. heriiad, Gk. χαίρω, &c.), and Ter. Scaurus (13. 9 K.) quotes *haba* (Lat. *faba*, O. Sl. bobu,

I.-Eur. bh-) as Faliscan. (See von Planta, i. p. 442 ; Löwe, *Prodr.* p. 426 ; and on the interchange of f and h in Etruscan inscriptions, Pauli, *Altitalische Forschungen*, iii. p. 114). Lat. *fel* has been explained as a dialectal form for **hel* (cf. Gk. χόλος), and *fovea* for **hovea* (Gk. χειά) (cf. the gloss 'fuma' terra, C. G. L. v. 296. 50).

§ 122. **The Palatal Gutturals: K̂, Ĝ, ĜH, K̂H.** These were in Latin, as in Greek, Celtic, and Teutonic, guttural sounds, while in the Asiatic languages and Slavonic they were sibilants. K̂. I.-Eur. k̂, Lat. *c*, is seen in I.-Eur.*k̂m̥tom,'hundred'(O. Ind. śatám, Gk. ἐ-κατόν, O. Ir. cēt,W. cant, Goth. hund, Lith. szimtas), Lat. *centum* ; *swĕk̂ŭro-,' step-father' (O. Ind. śváśura-, Arm. skesur F., Gk. ἑκυρός, O. Corn. hwigeren, hweger F., Goth. svaihra, Germ. Schwäher, Lith. szeszuras), Lat. *sŏcer* ; *ŏk̂tō(u), ' eight' (O. Ind. aṣṭáu, aṣṭā́, Gk. ὀκτώ, O. Ir. ocht, W. wyth, Goth. ahtau, O. Engl. eahta, Lith. asztŭnì, O. Sl. osmĭ), Lat. *ŏctō*. I.-Eur. k̂w was merged in *qu*, the representative of I.-Eur. q^u ; thus I.-Eur. *ĕk̂wo-, ' horse' (O. Ind. áśva- ; cf. Lith. aszvà, ' mare,' &c.) is Lat. *ĕquus*.

I.-Eur. k̂ is Umbro-Osc. k, e.g. Umbr. kletram Acc., ' a litter' (Gk. κλίνω, &c.), Kluviier, Osc. Kluvatiium from the root k̂leu- (Lat. *clueo*, Gk. κλέος, &c.), (von Planta, i. p. 326). In Umbrian k (whether from I.-Eur. k̂ or k) was palatalized before e, i, and was written in the native alphabet by a sign which we conventionally express by ç, in the Latin alphabet by *ś* (sometimes *s*), e. g. çersnatur, *śesna* (Lat. *cēna*, Osc. kersna-) (*ib*. p. 359).

§ 123. Other examples of I.-Eur. k̂. From I.-Eur. root weik̂-, ' to enter' (O. Ind. viś-, vĕśá- M., ' a tent,' Gk. ϝοῖκος, Alb. vis M., ' a place,' Goth. veihs, ' a village,' Lith. vĕszĕti, ' to be lodged,' O. Sl. vĭsĭ, ' a farm '), Lat. *vīcus* ; I.-Eur. *yŭwn̥k̂o- (O. Ind. yuvaśá-, Gk. Ὑάκ-ινθος, O. Ir. ōac, W. ieuanc, Goth. juggs), Lat. *jŭvencus* ; I.-Eur. *k̂r̥d-, ' heart' (O. Ind. śrad-dhā́-, ' confidence,' Arm. sirt, Gk. καρδία, O. Ir. cride, Goth. hairtō, Lith. szirdìs, O. Sl. srĭdĭce), Lat. *cor, crēdo* ; I.-Eur. root k̂leu-, ' to hear' (O. Ind. śru-, Gk. κλύω, O.-Ir. cloor, cluinim, W. clywed Inf., Goth. hliu-ma, 'hearing,' O. Sl. sluti, ' to be famous '), Lat. *clueo* ; I.-Eur. *pŏrk̂o- (Gk. πόρκος, O. Ir. orc, O. Engl. fearh, Engl. farrow, Lith. pařszas, O. Sl. prasẹ̆), Lat. *porcus* ; I.-Eur. k̂i-, a Demonstrative Pronoun-stem (Arm. -s, Gk. -κι, Alb. si-, O. Ir. cē, Goth. hi-mma, Lith. szis, O. Sl. sĭ), Lat. *cĭs, cĭter, citra* ; I.-Eur. k̂lei-, ' to lean' (O. Ind. śri-, Gk. κλίνω, O. Ir. cloen, 'awry,' Goth. hlains, ' a hill,' Lith. szłaítas), Lat. *ac-clīnis, clīvus* ; I.-Eur. *dĕk̂m̥, ' ten' (O. Ind. dáśa, Arm. tasn, Gk. δέκα, O. Ir. deich, W. deg, Goth. taihun, Lith. dĕszimt, O. Sl. desẹtĭ), Lat. *dĕcem* ; I.-Eur. root deik̂-, ' to point, say ' (O. Ind. diś-, Gk. δείκνυμι, Goth. gateihan, ' to proclaim),' Lat. *dīcere, indīcare* ; I.-Eur. root prek̂-, ' to ask ' (O. Ind. praś-ná-, ' a question,' O. Ir. imm-chom-arcim, ' I ask,' O. W. di-erchim, Goth. fraih-na, Germ. frage, Lith. praszaŭ, O. Sl. prošą), Lat. prĕcor. Similarly Lat. crābro for *crāsro (cf. Lith. szirszů, O. Sl. srŭšenĭ, Engl. hornet); ăcus, ācer, &c. from the root aḱ-, 'to be sharp' (O. Ind. aśrí-, 'edge,' Arm. aseλn, 'a needle,' Lith. asztrùs, 'sharp,' O. Sl. ostrŭ, &c.); cĕrĕbrum for *cerĕs-rum (cf. O. Ind. śiras-, N., 'head,' Gk. κάρᾱ, &c.).

§ 124. I.-Eur. k̑w. Lat. combretum, bulrush, from the stem k̑wĕndhr-, seen in Lith. szveñdrai Pl., has been compared to sŏror for *swĕsor- (§ 68); but it more probably shows the O-grade of the stem, *quombr-etum (cf. O. Scand. hvönn 'angelica'), with reduction of quo- to co- as in cŏlo for older quolo (cf. § 137).

§ 125. Ĝ. Of I.-Eur. ĝ, Lat. g, we have examples in the I.-Eur. roots ĝen-, ĝnō-,' to know, learn' (O. Ind. jā-ná-mi, jñātá-, Arm. can-eay Aor., Gk. γι-γνώ-σκω, γνωτός, O. Ir. gnāth, 'accustomed,' W. gnawd, O. Engl. cnāwan, Engl. to know, Lith. žin-óti, O. Sl. zna-ti), Lat. gnō-sco, gnō-tus; melĝ-,' to milk' (O. Ind. mṛj-, 'to wipe off,' Gk. ἀμέλγω, O. Ir. bligim, O. Engl. melce, Lith. méłžu, O. Sl. mlŭzą), Lat. mulgeo.

I.-Eur. ĝw would be indistinguishable in Latin from I.-Eur. gṷ; thus ūvĭdus (cf. Gk. ὑγρός), if connected with the root weĝ-, ' to be strong' (cf. Gk. ὑγιής), shows v between vowels for ĝw.

In Umbro-Osc. I.-Eur. ĝ is g, e. g. Umbr. ager 'ager,' Osc. aragetud 'argento' Abl. (von Planta, i. p. 329). In Umbrian g, whether I.-Eur. ĝ or g, suffers before e, i palatalization, and is written i, e. g. muieto, P. P. P. of a verb whose Imperat. 3 sg. is mugatu (von Planta, i. p. 372).

§ 126. Other examples of I.-Eur. ĝ. I.-Eur. ĝeus-, ' to taste' (O. Ind. juṣ̄-, Gk. γεύω for *γεύσω, O. Ir. to-gu, 'I choose,' Goth. kiusa), Lat. gŭstus; I.-Eur. reĝ-, 'to stretch, rule' (O. Ind. ṛj-, rā́j- or rā́j-an-, 'king,' ὀ-ρέγω, O. Ir. rigim, rīg Gen., Gaul. Catu-rīges, W. rhi, Goth. uf-rakja, Lith. rā̆žau), Lat. rĕgo, rēgis Gen.; I.-Eur. ĝen-, 'to beget' (O. Ind. jan-, jánas-, Arm. cin, Gk. γίγνομαι, γένος, O. Ir. gĕnar Pft., gein, W. geni, genid, Goth. kuni, 'race,' Engl. kin), Lat. gi-gn-o, gĕnus. Similarly Lat. argentum (Zend erᵉzata-, Arm. arcat'; cf. O. Ind. árjuna-, 'white,' Gk. ἀργής); Lat. glos (Gk. γάλοως, O. Sl. zlŭva); Lat. ăgo (O. Ind. aj-, Arm. acem, Gk. ἄγω, O. Ir. ag-, O. Scand. aka), Lat. grānum (O. Ind. jīrṇá-, 'crushed,' Goth. kaurn, Lith. žirnis, 'a pea,' O. Sl. zrĭno); Lat. gĕnu (O. Ind. jā́nu, Arm. cunr, Gk. γόνυ, Goth. kniu N., O. Engl. cnēo N.); Lat. vĕgeo, vĕgĕtus (O. Ind. vaj-, 'to be strong,' Zend vaz-, Gk. ὑγιής, Engl. I wake, Germ. wacker); Lat. gĕlu (O. Sl. žlĕdica) (on ĕl instead of ŏl, see § 10).

§ 127. ĜH. I.-Eur. ĝh is in Latin h, but g before or after a consonant, e. g. I.-Eur. *ĝhŏrto- (Gk. χόρτος, O. Ir. gort, Lith. žaŕdis), Lat. hortus; I.-Eur. root weĝh- (O. Ind. vah-, Gk. ὄχος, Goth. ga-viga, Germ. be-wege, Engl. waggon, Lith. wežù,

§§ 124–129.] REPRESENTATIVES OF I.-EUR. SOUNDS. K,G,GH. 297

O. Sl. vezą), Lat. *věho*; I.-Eur. root angh- (O. Ind. áhas-,'need,' Arm. anjuk,' narrow,' Gk. ἄγχω, O. Ir. cum-ung,'narrow,' Goth. aggvus, O. Engl. ange, Germ. eng, O. Sl. ązŭkŭ), Lat. *ango, angor, angustus*; Lat. *grando* (O. Ind. hrādúni-). A good example of the rule for *g* and *h* is *mingo* beside *mejo* for *meiho, from the root meigh- (O. Ind. mih-, Lith. mįzaũ, Gk. ὀ-μῐχέω).
I.-Eur. ĝhw was in Latin merged in I.-Eur. gh^u, e.g. I.-Eur. *ĝhwēr-,' a wild animal' (Gk. θήρ, Thess. φείρ, Lith. žvėrìs, O. Sl. zvěrĭ), with which is connected Lat. *fĕrus*, Fem. *fĕra*, a wild animal. (But Engl. deer, Germ. Thier, Goth. dius point to some I.-Eur. original like *dheusó-, cf. Lat. *fŭro* for *fuso*?).
I.-Eur. ĝh is in Umbro-Osc. h, as in Latin, e.g. Umbr. *hondra*, Osc. huntro- from the root of Lat. *hŭmus* (von Planta, i. p. 436). On h for f in Sabine *fasena* 'harena,' &c., see above § 121.

§ 128. **Other examples of I.-Eur. ĝh**. Lat. *hiems* (O. Ind. himá-, Arm. jiun, Gk. χιών, χειμών, O. Ir. gam, O. W. gaem, Lith. žėmà, O. Sl. zima) ; Lat. *hŭmus* (O. Ind. jmá- F., Gk. χαμαί, Lith. žĕmė̇, O. Sl. zemlja) ; Lat. *hŏlus*, older *helus, helvus* (§ 10) (O. Ind. hári-, 'yellow,' O.Ir. gel,'white,'O. Engl. geolo, Engl. yellow, Lith. želù, ' I grow green,' O. Sl. zelije, 'vegetables'); Lat. *lingo* (O. Ind. lih-, Arm. lizum, Gk. λείχω, Goth. bi-laigō, Lith. lëžiù, O. Sl. ližą̨) ; Lat. (*h*)*anser* (O. Ind. hasá-, Gk. χήν, O. Ir. gēis, 'a swan,' Engl. goose, Lith. žąsìs) ; Lat. *fingo* (O. Ind. dih-,'to smear,' dēhí,'a wall,' Arm. dizem, Gk. τεῖχος, O. Ir. dengaim, 'I fasten,' Goth. deigan, 'I mould,' daigs, 'dough,' Germ. Teig) ; Lat. *hiare* (O. H. G. gīēn, Engl. to yawn, Lith. -žióti, O. Sl. zijati).

§ 129. **The Gutturals Proper: K, G, GH, KH.** These appear as Gutturals in all the I.-Eur. languages. The fact that the I.-Eur. onomatopoetic name for the cuckoo shows this form of Guttural (O. Ind. kóka-, Gk. κόκκυξ, Lat. *cucūlus*, O. Ir. cuach, W. cog; cf. Lith. kukŭti,' to cry cuckoo') indicates what sort of Guttural it was.

K. I.-Eur. k is Lat. *c*, e. g. I.-Eur. root kert-, 'to plait'(O. Ind. cṛt-, káṭa-, ' mat,' Gk. κάρταλος, basket, Goth. haurds F., ' door,' Engl. hurdle), Lat. *crātes, cartilāgo*; I.-Eur. kerp-, ' to cut, reap ' (O. Ind. kṛpāṇa-,' a sword,' Gk. καρπός, fruit, Engl. harvest, Lith. kerpù, ' I cut '), Lat. *carpō* (on *ar*, see § 3).

In Umbro-Osc. I.-Eur. k remains as in Latin, e. g. Umbr. kanetu 'canito' (von Planta, i. p. 327), though in Umbrian k suffers palatalization before e, i (see above § 122).

§ 130. I.-Eur. k; other examples. Lat. *cruor, crūdus* (O. Ind. kraviṣ- N., 'raw meat,' Gk. κρέας, O. Ir. crū, 'gore,' W. crau, Lith. kraũjas, O. Sl. krŭvĭ, O. Engl. hrēaw, 'raw'); Lat. *collis* (Goth. hallus M., Lith. kálnas; cf. Gk. κολωνός); Lat. *clāvis, clāvus* (Gk. κληίς, O. Ir. clō M., 'a nail,' Germ. schliessen, O. Sl. ključi, 'a hook, a key'); Lat. *ancus, uncus* (O. Ind. aŋká-, Gk. ἀγκών, ὄγκος, O. Ir. ēcath); Lat. *căpio* (Arm. kap, 'a fetter,' Gk. κάπη, O. Engl. hæft, 'captive,' Lett. kampu, 'I seize'); Lat. *coxa* (O. Ind. kákṣa-, O. Ir. coss, 'the foot,' W. coes, 'the leg,' M. H. G. hahse, 'bend of knee, hough'); Lat. *cūpa* (O. Ind. kúpa-, 'a pit,' Gk. κύπη); Lat. *sĕco* (O. Scand. sigđr, 'a sickle,' O. Engl. sage, 'a saw,' O. Sl. sěką, 'I cut'), O. Lat. *clepo* (Gk. κλέπτω, Goth. hlifa, Engl. shop-lifter, Pruss. au-klipts, 'hidden'); Lat. *vinco* (O. Ir. fichim, 'I fight,' Goth. veiha, Engl. wight, Lith. vĕkà, 'strength,' ap-veikiù, 'I compel'); Lat. *scando* (O. Ind. skándā-mi, 'I spring,' Gk. σκανδάληθρον, a springe, O. Ir. ro-sescaind, 'he sprang').

§ 131. G. Of I.-Eur. g, Lat. *g*, examples are : I.-Eur. root gar-, 'to shout' (O. Ind. gṛ-, Gk. γηρύω, O. Ir. gāir, 'a shout,' W. gawr, O. H. G. chirru, 'I shout,' Lith. garˇsas, 'noise'), Lat. *garrio*; I.-Eur. *yŭgo-, 'a yoke' (O. Ind. yugá-, Gk. ζυγόν, Goth. juk, O. Sl. igo), Lat. *jŭgum*.

I.-Eur. g is g also in Umbro-Osc. (von Planta, i. p. 330); but an Umbrian g, as we have seen, is palatalized (written i) before the vowels i, e, &c. (§ 125).

§ 132. Other examples of I.-Eur. g. Lat. *grūs* (Arm. křunk, Gk. γέρανος, Gaul. Tri-garanus, W. garan, O. Engl. cran, Lith. gérvė, O. Sl. žeravĭ); Lat. *tĕgo* (O. Ind. sthágā-mi, Gk. στέγω, στέγος, and τέγος, O. Ir. teg, O. W. tig, Engl. thatch, Germ. Dach, Lith. stógas) ; Lat. *augeo* (O. Ind. ójas-, 'strength,' Gk. αὐξάνω, O. Ir. ōg, 'entire,' Goth. auka, 'I multiply,' Engl. eke, Lith. áugu, 'I grow'), O. Lat. *ē-rūgo*, of which *e-ructo* is the Iterative form (Paul. Fest. 58. 30 Th.), used by Ennius, *Ann*. 593 M. :

contempsit fontes quibus ex erugit aquae uis,

comes from the I.-Eur. root reug- (Gk. ἐρεύγομαι, Lith. rúgiu, O. Sl. rygaję).

§ 133. GH. I.-Eur. gh, like I.-Eur. ĝh, became *h* in Latin, except before or after a consonant, when it became *g*. Examples are : I.-Eur. *ghŏsti- (Goth. gasts, Engl. guest, O. Sl. gostĭ), Lat. *hostis, hos(tĭ)pes* (O. Lat. *hostis*, 'stranger,' Varro *L. L.* v. 3); I.-Eur. root ghred- (O. Ir. ingrennim, 'I pursue,' Goth. griþs, 'a step,' O. Sl. gręda, 'I come'), Lat. *grădior* (on *a*, see § 3), *gradus*.

In Umbro-Osc. also I.-Eur. gh is h (von Planta, i. p. 438). On f for h in some dialects, such as the Sabine, see above, § 121.

§ 134. I.-Eur. gh : other examples. Lat. *prĕ-hendo* (Gk. χανδάνω, Alb. ģeń, 'I find,' ģendem, 'I am found,' Goth. bi-gita, Engl. I get); Lat. *hordeum* (Arm. gari, Germ. Gerste); Lat. *haereo* (Goth. us-gaisja, 'I frighten,' Engl. gaze, Lith. gaisztù, 'I tarry').

§ 135. **Velar Gutturals with Labialisation.** These appear as Gutturals in some languages, and as Labials in others, and show this divergence even on Italian soil, e. g. Umbr., Osc. pis, Lat. *quis*. (On the Italic treatment of the Gutturals of this series, see von Planta, i. pp. 331 sqq.). **Q^u. I.-Eur.** q^u is Lat. *qu* (but *qoi* for classical *qui* on the Dvenos inscription). Before *u* we find *c*, e. g. *sĕcūtus* from *sequor*, a change which may have been very ancient (see § 116). Before *o* this *qu*, though often retained in writing, seems to have come to sound like *c*; hence *quŏquo-*, a cook, was written *coquo-* as well as *quoquo-*, and on the other hand the Preposition *cum*, older *cŏm* [for k͡om or kom (Osc. kúm, Umbr. -kum)], was written *quom* till the time of the Gracchi, and the P. P. P. of *occŭlo*, from a root k͡el- or kel- (W. celu), appears with the spelling *oquoltod* on the S. C. de Bacch. of 186 B.C. (*C. I. L.* i. 196). When in the eighth cent. A. U. C. *o* before a final consonant, came to be universally changed in spelling (see § 20) to *u*, we find the spelling *quo* (*guo*) replaced by *cu* (*gu*), so that *ĕquos* became *ecus* (Gen. *equi*), *quoquos* or *coquos* became *cocus* (Gen. *coqui*). The grammarians of the first cent. A. D. were puzzled by the want of analogy between *ecus* Nom., and *equi* Gen., &c., and reconstituted the Nom. as *equus*, &c. Instances of I.-Eur. q^u in Latin are: I.-Eur. root seq^u (O. Ind. sac-, Gk. ἕπομαι, O. Ir. sechur, Lith. sekù), Lat. *sequor*; I.-Eur. root leiq^u- (O. Ind. ric-, Arm. e-lik', 'he left,' Gk. λείπω, O. Ir. lēcim, Goth. leihva, 'I lend,' Germ. leihe, Lith. lëkù), Lat. *linquo*; I.-Eur. *q^{u}i- (O. Ind. -cid Neut., Gk. τί for *τιδ, O. Sl. čĭ-to 'what?'), Lat. *quĭd* Indef.; I.-Eur. *q^{u}ĕ (O. Ind. ca, Gk. τε, O. Ir. -ch, W. -p, Goth. -h), Latin -*quĕ*. Before a consonant this *qu* became *c*, e. g. *sŏcius*, older *socyo-* from the *o*-grade of the root seq^u, with the adjectival suffix -yo- (O. Ind. sācya-, Gk. ἀ-οσσ-ητήρ, with σσ for κy); *ŏcŭlus*, older *oclo-* from the root oq^u-, 'to see' (Gk. ὄσσε, with σσ for κy, ὄμμα for *ὄπ-μα, Lith. akìs, O. Sl. oko) with the suffix -lo.

I.-Eur. q^{u}w has been postulated for the initial *u* (*v*) of *ŭbi* (Osc. puf, Umbr. pufe), *ŭt*, *ŭti* (cf. Osc. puz, Umbr. puze) (with *cu* in the middle of a word, e. g. *sī-cŭbi*), *văpor* (Lith. kvãpas), *in-vītus* and *in-vīto* (Pruss. quāits, 'will'; Lith. kvëcziù, 'I invite'), &c. (see *K. Z.* xxxii. 405).

In Umbro-Osc. I.-Eur. q̯ is p. (On the date of the change, see von Planta, i. p. 331). Latin pŏpina, lŭpus, &c. are dialectal, just as Pontius and Pompeius are the dialectal names corresponding to Lat. Quintius, and Petreius to Lat. Quartius. (A full list of examples in von Planta, l. c.).

§ 136. I.-Eur. q̯, Lat. qu : other examples. Lat. quattuor (O. Ind. catvā́ras, Arm. čork', Ion. Gk. τέσσερες, Aeol. Gk. πέσυρες, O. Ir. cethir, W. pedwar, Gaulo-Lat. petor-ritum, Lith. keturì, O. Sl. četyrije) ; Lat. quīnque (O. Ind. páñca, Arm. hing, Gk. πέντε, O. Ir. cōic, W. pump, Lith. penkì) ; Lat. quī, quam, &c. (O. Ind. ká-, Gk. πόθεν, πῇ, O. Ir. cia, W. pwy, Goth. hvas, hvē, Lith. kàs, O. Sl. kŭ-to).

§ 137. c for qu. (1) Before u ; arcus (Goth. arhv-azna, ' an arrow,' O. Engl. earh), beside arquĭtĕnens, arquĭtes, the old word for săgittārii (Paul. Fest. 15. 32 Th.) ; the change to -cu- appears to be Italic and not merely Latin, if Umbr. arślata- (cf. Paul. Fest. 12. 15 'arculata' dicebantur circuli, qui ex farina in sacrificiis fiebant) comes from arcus ; from quinque come quincunx, quincuplex ; from sesque comes sescuplus (but cf. Löwe, Prodr. p. 403).

(2) Before a consonant : Lat. něc for něquě, ac from *atc for atque, with Syncope of -ĕ before an initial consonant (ch. iii. § 36) ; torcŭlus from torqueo; cŏcŭlum from cŏquo. On ct for q̯-t, x for q̯-s, see § 116.

(3) Before o : cŏlo (older quolo: we have qolunt in the Ambrosian Palimpsest of Plautus, Pseud. 822, and quolundam on the inscription of the Faliscan 'collegium coquorum,' which also has ququei for coqui, Zv. I. I. I. 72) beside inquĭlīnus ; cŏlus, a distaff (Gk. πόλος, an axle). The fact that quo (I.-Eur. q̯o or k̑wo) had come to be pronounced like co (I.-Eur. k̑o or ko) explains why qu seems not to offer the same resistance to the Brevis Brevians law in the Early Poets when it precedes o, as when it precedes other vowels, e. g. coquŏ but only loquī (ch. iii. § 42). But the indiscriminate spelling of every quo as co is not found till the fifth cent. A. D., e. g. cot, corum, condam, locor (see Bersu, die Gutturalen, p. 90) and the analogy of the other cases and persons kept quo as the spelling in the Nom. Sg. of equos, &c., and the 3rd Pl., sequontur, &c., until the o, hitherto preserved in spelling by the preceding u, became in the eighth cent. A. U. C. u (ch. iii. § 17), when ecus, secuntur were adopted as the proper spelling. In words where the analogy of other forms played no part (e. g. sesconciam, C. I. L. i. 1430) the spelling co is found much earlier. Similarly the first syllable of the stem coquo- shows co earlier than the second syllable ; we have qu- however in the older period (e. g. in all the MSS. of Plaut. Pseud. 382 ; cf. ququei on the inscription of the Faliscan 'collegium coquorum,' Zv. I. I. I. 72). Puns are unsafe evidence of pronunciation ; but the punning reply may be quoted of Cicero to the cook's son who asked for his vote : ego 'quoque' tibi favebo (Quint. vi. 3. 47). The spelling equus, &c. was instituted by Velius Longus in Trajan's time. (On this transition of orthography -quo-, -cu-, -quu-, see Bersu, die Gutturalen, who quotes a large number of instances of these spellings, as also of the use in the time of the Gracchi of q for c before u, e. g. oqupare, pequnia, &c., and has collected those passages of the grammarians which bear on the subject. A list of the instances of the spelling quom for cum in the MSS. of Plautus is given by Probst, Gebrauch von 'ut' bei Terenz, p. 178 n.) I.-Eur. quĕ did not, as is often stated, become quŏ, cŏ in Latin (as

it did in Celtic, e. g. Ir. cōic, W. pump, but Lat. *quinque*); and though -wĕ- after other initial consonants appears as ŏ in Latin *sŏcer* (swĕk̑-), *sŏror* (swĕs-), &c., it probably did not after a palatal ; for the evidence points to k̑w, ĝw, &c. having been merged in qᵘ, gᵘ in Latin. *Combrētum*, bulrush, may show the O-grade of the stem k̑wendhr- of Lith. szveñdrai Pl. (cf. O. Scand. hvönn ' angelica ').

§ 138. Lat. qu of other origin. We have already seen that I.-Eur. k̑w became *qu* in Latin, e. g. I.-Eur. *ĕk̑wo-, ' horse ' (O. Ind. áśva-, cf. Lith. asžvà, ' mare '), Lat. *ĕquus*. The guttural of *lăcus* (Gk. λάκκος, 'a tank,' O. Ir. loch), *lacūnar*, is not I.-Eur. qᵘ, but when followed by a consonantal *u* we find *qu* in *ăquear*. The occasional spelling *sterquilīnium* (see Georges, *Lex. Wortf.* s. v.) may be like that usage of Late Latin orthography, whereby *qui* is written for Greek κυ, e. g. *quinicus, helquisticon, liquiritia* (see ch. ii. § 28), the *ui* being meant to express the *ü*-sound of Greek υ, or possibly the *qu* being meant to indicate the hard unpalatalized guttural. In Italian, Latin *qu* before *e, i* has this hard sound (written ch), e. g. chi, che, retaining the labial affection (the following *w*-sound) before *a*, e. g. quale (see ch. ii. § 91), though in cinque, ' five,' where two Latin labialized velars stood in successive syllables, the first seems to have lost its labialization in Vulgar Latin.

§ 139. Ǥu. I.-Eur. gᵘ is in Latin *v*, but after a consonant *gu*, and before a consonant *g*. Thus I.-Eur. *gᵘīwo-, ' alive ' (O. Ind. jīvá-, O. Ir. biu, Lith. gývas) is Lat. *vīvus*; I.-Eur. root ongᵘ-, ' to anoint ' (O. Ind. anj-, O. H. G. ancho, ' butter ' ; cf. O. Ir. imb, ' butter,' W. ymen-yn) is Lat. *unguo* ; Lat. *gravis* is cognate with O. Ind. gurú-, Gk. βαρύς, Goth. kaurus. Before *u* I.-Eur. gᵘ was replaced by *g* in Latin, a change probably of a very early date, e. g. *gurges* (Gk. ὑπό-βρυχα, ὑπο-βρύχιος), though the *u* may be often regarded as a weak form of the wĕ of *gwĕ* (see § 51). Before *o*, Latin *gu* (*gv*) seems to have come in time to sound like Latin *g*, as *quo* came to sound like *co* (§ 137). After *o* in terminations had come to be written *u*, even when preceded by *v*, *u*, we find spellings like *distingunt, extingunt*, for which *distinguunt, extinguunt*, &c. were afterwards restored by the analogy of the other persons, *distinguimus*, &c. The grammarians of the Empire have difficulty in determining the proper spelling of verbs in *-guo* and *-go*, and generally follow the rule of writing *-go* when the Perfect ended in *-xi*, e. g. *extingo, ungo*.

§ 140. I.-Eur. gᵘ, Lat. v: other examples. Lat. *vĕnio* (O. Ind. gam-, gach-, Arm. e-kn,' he came,' Gk. βαίνω, βάσκω, Goth. qima, Engl. I come, Germ. komme; Lat. *vŏro* (O. Ind. gr̥-, Arm. ker, ' food,' Gk. βορά, βιβρώσκω, Lith. geriù, ' I drink,' O. Sl. žĭrą, ' I swallow '); Lat.*vĕru* (O. Ir. bir N., a U-stem, W. ber) ; Lat. *nūdus* for *novedo- (Goth. naqaþs ; cf. O. Ind. nag-ná-, Lith. nŭgas, O. Sl. nagŭ).

An intervocalic *gw* of later origin is similarly treated in *māvŏlo* (*mavvolo) from **mag(e)-volo*.

§ 141. Dialectal b. In Umbro-Osc. I.-Eur. gʱ is b, e. g. Umbr. *benust*, Osc. *ce-bnust* from the root of Lat. *vĕnio*. So Lat. *bōs*, &c. seem to be dialectal or rustic (see von Planta, i. p. 335).

§ 142. g for I.-Eur. gʱ. (1) Before consonant: Lat. *agnus* (Gk. ἀμνός for *ἀβνός, O. Sl. jagnę) (on *ăvillus*, see § 19); Lat. *migro* (Gk. ἀ-μείβω, O. Sl. miglivŭ, 'mobile'); Lat. *glans* (Gk. βάλανος, Arm. kaλin, Lith. gìlė, O. Sl. želądĭ).
(2) Before *u*. (On the spellings *distingunt*, &c., see Bersu, *die Gutturalen*).
(3) Before *o*. (On the spellings *distingo*, &c., see Bersu, *die Gutturalen*). Similarly *gu* from I.-Eur. ghʱ is written *g* before *o* in *ningo*.

§ 143. GHʱ. I.-Eur. ghʱ is Latin *f*, when initial, but between vowels *v*, after a consonant *gu* (before *u* reduced to *g*), and before a consonant *g*. Thus Lat. *formus* (O. Ind. gharmá-, 'heat,' Arm. ĵerm, Gk. θερμός, Engl. warm for *gwarm, Pruss. gorme, 'heat'); *nivem* Acc., O. Lat. *nīvit* [Gk. νίφα, νίφει (νει-); cf. Zend snaežaiti, Goth. snaivs, 'snow,' Lith. snaigýti Inf., O. Sl. sněgŭ, 'snow,' W. nyf]; *ninguit* (Lith. sniñga) from the root sneighʱ-, 'to snow.'

I.-Eur. ghʱ is f in Umbro-Osc. whether initial or intervocalic, &c. (see von Planta, i. p. 447, for examples).

§ 144. I.-Eur. ghʱ in Latin: other examples. Lat. *cō-nīveo* from the root kneighʱ- (Goth. hneivan, Germ. neigen); *tergus* (Gk. στέρφος, τέρφος); Lat. *fŏveo*, the original meaning of which is 'to warm' (e. g. Plaut. *Capt.* 847; foueri foculis feruentibus) from the root dheghʱ-, 'to burn' (Lith. degù), and from the same root, Lat. *făvilla* (Gk. τέφρα for *θέφρα).

§ 145. The Sibilants: S, Z. In Sanscrit, besides the ś (I.-Eur. k̂), which corresponds to a guttural in Greek, Latin, &c. (e. g. O. Ind. śatám, Gk. ἑ-κατόν, Lat. *centum*) we have s (I.-Eur. s) which corresponds to s in other languages (e. g. O. Ind. saptá, Lat. *septem*, O. Ir. secht, Goth. sibun, Lith. septynì), and ṣ (like our *sh*) which appears after *i*- and *u*-, *r*- and *k*-sounds, e. g. uṣṭa-, Lat. *ūstus*. Sanscrit kṣ is the equivalent of Greek κτ in r̥kṣa-, Gk. ἄρκτος, &c., of Greek ξ in ákṣa-, Gk. ἄξων, &c., and even of Greek χθ in kṣām-, Gk. χθών. The exact number and nature of the I.-Eur. sibilants have not yet been determined, but we can at least discriminate an unvoiced and a voiced sibilant, which we may call S and Z (cf. Engl. 'use'

§ 146. S, Z. Latin *s* was, as we have seen (ch. ii. § 117), unvoiced or hard. The voiced or soft sibilant, for which the symbol Z may have been used in early times (ch. i. § 5) passed in the fourth cent. B. C. into *r* between vowels (cf. Engl. 'forlorn,' Mid. Engl. forloren, beside 'lost'). Before a consonant the voiced sibilant was dropped with lengthening of the preceding vowel, e. g. I.-Eur. *nĭzdo (O. Ind. nīḍá-, Arm. nist, 'situation,' O. Ir. net M., 'a nest,' Engl. nest), Lat. *nīdus*. An initial sibilant was often dropped in I.-Eur.; thus we have a root teg-, 'to cover, roof' (Lat. *tĕgo*, Gk. τέγος, O. Ir. teg,' house,' Engl. thatch), as well as a root steg- (O. Ind. sthag-, Gk. στέγω), the roots without initial s- being perhaps those used after words ending in -s (cf. ταιστέγαις for ταῖς στέγαις on the Gortyn inscr., δύστηνος for *δυσ-στηνος, &c.); and it is not always easy to say whether Latin words, which lack an initial sibilant that is found in cognate words of other languages, have lost it through the phonetic laws peculiar to Latin, or represent an I.-Eur. 'doublet.' *Lātus*, broad, from the I.-Eur. root stel-,'to extend'(O. Sl. steljǫ), appears in Old Latin in the form *stlātus*, *stlātaria* or *stlattaria navis* (ch. ii. § 130); and we have *stlo-cus*, *stlis* (*slis*) as the old forms of *lŏcus*, *līs*, just as in Greek σμικρός, &c. are the older forms of μικρός, &c. An initial sibilant is not found in Latin before *m*, e. g. *mordeo* from the root smerd- (Gk. σμερδαλέος, O. H. G. smerzan, 'to feel pain,' Engl. to smart), before *n*, e. g. *nŭrus* from I.-Eur. *snŭso- (O. Ind. snuṣā, Arm. nu, Gk. νυ(σ)ός, O. H. G. snur), before *l*, e. g. *lăbo* for *slabo (O. H. G. slaf, 'loose,' Lith. slăbnas, 'weak'). Before *r* in the middle of a word a sibilant becomes *b*, e. g. *sobrīnus* for *swesrinus (Lith. seserynai, Pl.), from I.-Eur. *swĕsor-, 'a sister,' probably from an earlier *f* (§ 114); whether it becomes *f* at the beginning of a word, e. g. *frīgus* (Gk. ῥῖγος), or is dropped, e. g. *repo* for *srepo (cf. *serpo*), or becomes *str-*, e. g. *stringo* (O. Ir. srengim, 'to draw'), is uncertain. After *r* and *l* it is assimilated, e. g. *verres* for *verses (Lith. veršzis; cf. O. Ind. vŕ̥ṣa-), *collum*, O. Lat. *collus*, for *colso- (O. Engl. heals, Germ. Hals). Initial ps-, ks- appear to have become *s-,

e. g. *săbŭlum*, sand (Gk. ψάμμος for *ψαφ-μος), *dis-sŭpo* (O. Ind. kṣip-, ' to throw ').

Latin *s* often represents an original dental sound, e. g. *adgressus* formed from the stem of *adgrĕdior* with the participial termination *-to-*. This change was probably very old, so that the form *adgrettus* (written in the earlier orthography *adgretus*), quoted from Ennius by Paul. Fest. 5. 6 Th., probably represents **ad*-gred(i)tus* (like *cette* for **cĕ-dĭte*, § 108). A double *ss* (generally arisen from *tt, ts*; cf. our ' gossip ' for god-sip) was after a diphthong or long vowel (see ch. ii. § 129) reduced in the Early Empire to single *s*, e. g. *fūsus*, older *fūssus*, *ūsus*, older *ūssus*. In *sescēni*, from *sex*, the second *s* represents an original *x* (i. e. *c-s*) (see § 158); and *x* reduced to *s* is first assimilated, then dropped with lengthening of the vowel, in words like *tēlum*, older *tellum*, for **teslum*, **texlum* (§ 117). On initial *s-* for *sy-*, e. g. *suo*, see § 65; for *sw-*, e. g. *sūdor*, § 71. On *ns*, see ch. ii. § 66, on I.-Eur. ms, above, § 76.

In Umbro-Oscan I.-Eur. s remains when initial, e. g. Umbr. *sent*, Osc. set ' sunt,' but when intervocalic became first voiced *s* (written in Oscan in the native alphabet s, in the Lat. alph. *z*, e. g. Fluusaí ' Florae,' *egmazum* ' rerum '), which in Umbr. passed into r, e. g. kuratu ' curato ' (Pel. coisatens ' curaverunt '). I.-Eur. ss became tt if the Perfect ending -atted 3 Sg., -attens 3 Pl. (e. g. Osc. prúfatted ' probavit,' prúfattens ' probaverunt ') is rightly compared with the Lat. Future in *-sso*, e. g. *amasso* (ch. viii. § 3); sr probably became fr (Lat. *br*) (cf. mod. Neapolitan Uttrafe for Ital. Ottobre,' October'); sn, sm, sl remain, e. g. Umbr. snata P. P. P. (Lat. *nare*), Osc. Slabiis ' Labius ' (cf. Lat. *Stlaborius*); rs appears in Osc. sometimes as r with ' compensatory ' lengthening, e. g. teerúm ' terram,' sometimes as rr, e. g. Kerrí, in Umbrian sometimes as rs (s), e. g. *tursitu*, tusetu (cf. Lat. *terreo*), sometimes as rf, e. g. Çerfu-; ns in the middle of a word became nts, e. g. Umbr. menzne ' mense'; when final it is in Osc. -ss, in Umbr. -f, e. g. Osc. víass ' vias,' Umbr. turuf ' tauros'; final -nts is in Umbr. (and Osc. ?) -f, e. g. Umbr. zeřef ' sedens.' (On the treatment of I.-Eur. s in Umbro-Oscan, see von Planta, i. p. 472.)

§§ 147, 148.] REPRESENTATIVES OF I.-EUR. SOUNDS. S, Z. 305

§ 147. I.-Eur. s, Latin s : other examples. I.-Eur. *sĕno-, 'old' (O. Ind. sána-, Arm. hin, Gk. ἕνη καὶ νέα, 'the old and new day,' i. e. the last day of the month, O. Ir. sen, W. hen, Goth. sinista Superl., Lith. sĕnas), Lat. sĕn-ior, sĕn-ex, Gen. senis; I.-Eur. root wes-, 'to clothe' (O. Ind. vas-, vástra-, N., 'clothing,' Arm. z-gest, Gk. ἐσ-θής, Goth. vasjan, vasti F.), Lat. ves-tis; I.-Eur. *aks(i)-, 'axle' (O. Ind. ákṣa-, Gk. ἄξων, O. H. G. ahsa, Lith. aszìs, O. Sl. osĭ), Lat. axis; I.-Eur. *pŏtis Nom. Sg. (O. Ind. pátis, 'master,' Gk. πόσις), Lat. pŏtis.

§ 148. Lat. r for intervocalic sibilant. Intervocalic s became h in Greek, e. g. εὕω for εὕhω (I.-Eur. *eusō), and was dropped, e. g. γένεος, γένους Gen. (I.-Eur. *ĝĕnĕs-ŏs), but in Latin it appears as r, e. g. ūro, gĕnĕris, having probably passed through the stage of voiced s (z), a stage at which the sibilant remained in Oscan, e. g. ezum 'esse,' while it suffered rhotacism in Umbrian, as in Latin, e. g. erom. The grammarians often quote Old Latin forms with intervocalic s, e.g. lases, Valesii, Fusii (Quint. i. 4. 13; cf. Ter. Scaur. 13. 13 K. Fusius, asa, lases); dasi, arbosem, robosem, helusa 'holera,' loebesum 'liberum' (Paul. Fest. 48. 19; 11. 20; 71. 12; 86. 30 Th.); r pro s littera saepe antiqui posuerunt, ut maiosibus, meliosibus, lasibus, fesiis (id. 359. 1 Th.); pignosa (id. 260. 11 Th.) (for other passages see Müller ad Paul. Fest. p. 15), and often refer similar forms to the Sabine dialect (e. g. Paul Fest. 6. 36 Th. aurum . . . alii a Sabinis translatum putant, quod illi 'ausum' dicebant; id. 18. 3 Th. Aureliam familiam ex Sabinis oriundam a Sole dictam putant, quod ei publice a populo Romano datus sit locus, in quo sacra faceret Soli, qui ex hoc 'Auseli' dicebantur, ut 'Valesii,' 'Papisii' pro eo quod est Valerii, Papirii ; Varro, ap. Vel. Long. 69. 8 K. (cf. L. L. vii. 27) gave fasena as Sabine for Lat. harena. Varro (L. L. vii. 26) quotes examples of this older spelling from the Carmen Saliare ; Livy speaking of Sp. Furius Fusus, the consul of 464 B. C., says that some of his authorities spelt the name Fusio- (iii. 4. 1 Furios 'Fusios' scripsere quidam) ; on the inscription with the Carmen Arvale (C. I. L. i. 28) we have Lases 'Lares': enos, Lases, iuuate ; in the most ancient piece of Latin preserved for us, the Praenestine fibula, Numasioi ' Numerio' (xiv. 4123 Manios med fefaked Numasioi), and in the Dvenos inscr. Toitesiai 'Tuteriae.' But words of the literary period with intervocalic s are either (1) dialectal, e. g. ămāsius, a gallant (Sabine ?, see Nettleship, Contributions, s. v.), or (2) foreign loanwords, e. g. gaesum (Gaulish ; cf. gaesati, Gaulish mercenaries, C. G. L. v. 71. 23, O. Ir. gai) (so ăsīnus, lāser, rŏsa, sĭser, &c.), or (3) had originally ss, whether derived from I.-Eur. tt, e. g. caesus for *caet-tus from caedo, from ns (I.-Eur. ntt, &c.), e.g. vīcēsimus older vicensumus (ch. ii. § 66), formōsus, older formonsus (ib.), from I.-Eur. ss, e. g. quaeso, older quaes-so, a different word from quaero (ch. viii. § 33), nāsus, older nassum, or from some other consonant-group. This older ss was after a long vowel or diphthong written s after the close of the Republic, but Quintilian tells us that caussae, cassus, divissiones, &c. was the spelling of Cicero and Virgil (i. 7. 20 quid quod Ciceronis temporibus paulumque infra, fere quotiens s littera media vocalium longarum vel subjecta longis esset, geminabatur? ut 'caussae, cassus, divissiones': quomodo et ipsum et Vergilium quoque scripsisse manus eorum docent), and this spelling is by no means uncommon in the MSS. of Plautus, Virgil, &c. (see ch. ii. § 129). After a short vowel ss remained, e. g. fĭssus. Quăsillus, pŭsillus (cf. pūsus) are said to show the same reduction in the pretonic syllable as ŏfella (beside offa), māmilla (beside mamma) (ch. ii. § 130) ; rather the Dim. quasillus was formed from *quas-los

X

after Rhotacism had ceased to operate; *miser* (on the spelling *myser* see ch. ii. § 16, p. 29) has been explained as a loanword from the Greek (μυσαρός), like other adjectives expressive of nuances of feeling, e. g. *hĭlăris* older *hĭlarus* (Gk. ἱλαρός). An initial *s* is not rhotacized when it comes after the final vowel of a preposition, &c., in a compound, e. g. *pŏ-sĭtus* from *po-*, a byform of *ab* (I.-Eur. *ăpŏ) and the P. P. P. of *sĭno*, but the final *s* of a preposition, &c., in a compound is rhotacized before an initial vowel, e. g. *dir-imo* from *dĭs-* and *ĕmo*, *diribeo* from *dis-* and *hăbeo*. *Furvus* points to an earlier trisyllabic *fus-uo-* (cf. *arvum* from trisyllabic *aruum*, § 68), a byformation of *fus-cus*, and *Mĭnerva* to *Menes-uā* (the word is a quadrisyllable in Plaut. *Bacch*. 893, Attius, *Trag*. 127 R.), but before consonantal *v* we have *s* dropped with 'Compensation' in *dī-vello, dī-vendo,* &c. Other examples of forms with *r* beside forms with *s* are *maereo* (*maestus*), *gĕro* (*ges-si, ges-tum*), *haurio* (*haus-(s)i, haus-tum*), *quaero* (*quaes-tus*; but *quaes(s)ivi, quaes(s)ītum* come from *quaes(s)o,* ch. viii. § 33), *Etrūria* (*Etrusci*), *auris* (*aus-culto*), *nāres* (*nās-(s)um*), and oblique cases of S-stems, e. g. *fūneris* (*funes-tus*), *ŏneris* (*onus-tus*), *verberis* (*subverbustam* Plaut. ap. Fest. 444. 15 Th.), *hŏnōris* (*honestus*) ; by analogy of these oblique cases *r* has found its way into the Nominative of *honor* (older *honos*), *arbor* (older *arbos*; cf. *arbustum* and *arbŏrētum*), *ŏdor* (older *odos*), &c. (ch. vi. § 7). (For a fuller list of examples of the Latin and Umbro-Oscan treatment of I.-Eur. intervocalic *s*, see Conway, *Verner's Law in Italy*). The change of intervocalic *s* to *r* is a common occurrence in language. English *r* corresponds to Gothic *z* in words like 'ore' (Goth. aiz-, I.-Eur. *ayes-, Lat. *aes, aeris* Gen.), and in Polish a word like może, 'can,' has a trilled sound of the voiced sibilant that is hardly to be distinguished from *r* (see *B. B.* xv. pp. 270 sqq.).

§ 149. **Initial Sibilant before Consonant**: (1) before unvoiced consonant : I.-Eur. root stā-, 'to stand' (O. Ind. sthā-, Gk. στάσις, Goth. staþs, O. Sl. stati Inf.), Lat. *stāre, stătio* ; I.-Eur. root sper-, 'to strike with the feet' (O.Ind. sphur-, Gk. σπαίρω, Engl. spurn, Lith. spiriù), Lat. *sperno* ; I.-Eur. root skand-, 'to spring' (O. Ind. skand-, Gk. σκανδάληθρον, a springe, O. Ir. ro se-scaind, 'he sprang'), Lat. *scando*. Similarly we have str-, e. g. in Lat. *strātus, strāmen* (cf. Gk. στρωτός, στρωμά), spr- in *sprētus*, scr- in *scrŏbis*, a ditch (Lett. skrabt, 'to scrape'), while stl- of O. Lat. *stlātus, stlātaria* (*stlatt.*) *navis* has become class. Lat. *l-* of *lātus*, broad.

(2) Before voiced consonant: I.-Eur. root sneigh^u-, 'to snow' (Zend snaẹžaiti, Gk. νείφει, ἀγά-ννιφος for *ἀγα-σνιφος, O. Ir. snechta, W. nyf, Goth. snaivs, Lith. snẽgas, O. Sl. snĕgŭ) Lat. *nĭvem* Acc.; I.-Eur. root snā- (O. Ind. snā-, 'to bathe,' Gk. νήχω, I swim, O. Ir. snāim), Lat. *nāre* ; I.-Eur. root slēg- (Gk. λαγγάζω, to slacken, λήγω, to cease, O. Ir. lac, 'weak,' W. llag, O. H. G. slach, Engl. slack), Lat. *langueo* ; I.-Eur. root sleub- (Goth. sliupan, Engl. to slip), Lat. *lūbricus* ; I.-Eur. root smerd- (Lith. smirdẽti, 'to stink'), Lat. *merda*; Gk. (σ)μῑκρός, Lat. *mīca*. If we may infer from the treatment of an internal sibilant before a voiced consonant, e. g. *nīdus* for *nizdo-, it would seem that the initial sibilant was first assimilated, *nnix* for *snix (cf. Gk. φιλο-μμειδής for *φιλο-σμειδης) then dropped, *nix*.

(3) Before *r*. The use of *t* for I.-Eur. *d* with *r* in Latin, e. g. *āter*, stem *ātro-* for *ādro-*, suggests that Latin *r* was not voiced, so that it is better to consider separately the treatment of an initial sibilant before *r*. The instances are unfortunately few and uncertain. Lat. *frĭgus* goes naturally with Gk. ῥῑ́γος, but it has also been connected with Gk. φρίσσω, while Lat. *rigor, rĭgidus* has been assigned to ῥῑ́γος ; Lat. *frāga*, strawberries, has been referred by some to

§§ 149–151.] REPRESENTATIVES OF I -EUR. SOUNDS. S, Z. 307

Gk. ῥάξ, a grape, by others to *fragro*, and certainly Lat. *răcēmus* goes more naturally with ῥάξ than *frāga*. Whether Greek ῥῖγος, ῥάξ originally began with σ or ϝ is a moot point. Lat. *rēpo* goes naturally with *serpo*, but Lith. rėplióti, Zend rap-, ' to go,' suggest an I.-Eur. 'doublet' without the initial sibilant. The I.-Eur. root sreu-, ' to flow ' (O. Ind. sru-, Gk ῥέ(ϝ)ω, Lith. sraviù, Ir. sruaim, ' a stream,' O. H. G. stroum), has been sought in the Latin words *rūmen*, (*ficus*) *Rūmĭna*, *Rumon*, the old name of the Tiber (Serv. ad *Aen.* viii. 63. 90) and in the name *Rōma* itself; Lat. *rătis* has been connected with *sĕro*, Lat. *rŭbus* with Germ. Ge-strüpp, and so on (for other examples see Osthoff, *M. U.* v. 62). On the other hand Latin forms with initial *r* which have in other languages a sibilant before the r, may come from an I.-Eur. 'doublet' which lacked the sibilant, as *tĕgo* comes from I.-Eur. teg-, a byform of the root steg-, ' to cover,' roof. Another possibility is that *str-* may be the Latin equivalent, as in our ' stream,' &c. It is not always easy to decide where Lat. *str-* and str-, sr-, in other languages, represent an original str- or an original sr- ; and similarly O. Lat. *stl-*, of *stlŏcus*, *stlīs* and *slis* may have been originally sl- and not *stl-*.

§ 150. O. Lat. stl, sl, scl. Quintilian (i. 4. 16) quotes *stlocus* and *stlites* as O. Lat. forms. The old form *stlis* was retained in the legal phrase *decemviri stlitibus judicandis* in Cicero's time (Cic. *Or.* xlvi. 156); on the Lex Repetundarum of 123–122 B.C (*C. I. L.* i. 198) we have once *slis* but usually *lis*, and SL. IVDIK on a Scipio epitaph of c. 130 B.C. (i. 38), *sclitib*... (x. 1249); cf. *stloc*[*us*] (v. 7381). *Stlembus*, slow, is quoted from Lucilius (Paul. Fest. 455. 4 Th.); *scloppus* (v. l. *stloppus*), is used by Persius (v. 13) to indicate the sound of slapping the cheek when distended (cf. Ital. schioppo) :

nec scloppo tumidas intendis rumpere buccas.

In dialectal names these combinations are preserved, e. g. *Stlaccius* (*C. I. L.* vi. 26863, &c.) (cf. Lat. *lacca*, a swelling on the leg?), *Stlaborius* (Wilm. 1913, Pompeii) (cf. Lat. *lăbor* ?), Oscan Slabio-. In Latin the *t* of *stl-* (or *c*, for *tl* became *cl*, § 105) would be dropped, as it is in the name *Foslius* (cf. *Fostulus, Faustulus*), *C. I. L.* i². p. 130) (cf. *for(c)tis*, § 157), leaving *sl-*, which would become **ll-* (see above), then *l-*.

§ 151. Sibilant before voiced consonant in middle of word. Lat. *audio* for **aus-dio*, from **aus*, a byform of *auris* ; Lat. *pēdo* from I.-Eur. pezd- (M. H. G. fist, Pruss. peisda, ' podex ') with o-grade of root in *pōdex* for **posd-ex* ; Lat. *sīdo* for **si-sdo* from the weak grade of the root sed-, ' to sit,' with *i*-reduplication (ch. viii. § 9); Lat. *sūdus* for **sus-dus* from the root saus-, ' to dry ' (O. Ind. śuṣ-, Gk. αὖος, Lith. saũsas, Engl. sear) ; Lat. *mālus* for **mas-lus* or for **mas-dus* (§ 111) (Engl. mast) ; Lat. *dūmus* (O. Lat. dusmus), *dūmetum, dummetum* in the earlier spelling, e. g. in Virgil MSS. (see Ribbeck's Index) for **dusmetum* (cf. O. Ir. doss, ' a bush ') (the dialectal name *Dusmia* is found on inscriptions, *Eph. Epigr.* viii. 128. 820, both from Teate Marruc). Lat. *cōmis* (*cosmis* on the Dvenos inscr.) ; Lat. *prīmus* for **prismus* (cf. *priscus, pristinus*, Pelign. prismo-); Lat. *pōmērium* for **pos(t)moerium* (Varro, *L. L.* v. 143 ; cf. Paul. Fest. 327. 13 Th.) ; Lat. *prēlum* for **pres-lum* (cf. *pres-si* : a Latin **preso* must have existed beside *premo*, as Gk. τρέ(σ)ω beside τρέμω); Lat. *quālus* for **quas-lus* (cf. *quăsillus* ; Lith. kắszius, O. Sl. košĭ') ; Lat. *cānus* for **casnus* (cf. *cascus*, Osc. casnar, an old man) ; Lat. *fānum* for **făsnum* (cf. Osc. fíisna-, Umbr. fesna-, from stem **fēsnā- ; on *ă-ē*, see § 54) ; Lat. *fēs-tus, fĕriae* from *fĕs-iae*, Osc. fíisía-); Lat.

X 2

pōne for *pos(t)-ne; Lat. pōno for *po-s(i)no, a compound of pŏ-, a byform of ab, ap- of aperio (cf. O. Ind. ápa, Gk. ἄπο), and sĭno [cf. the P. P. P po-sĭtus, and Pft. Ind. originally po-sīvi, then by false analogy of pos-ĭtus, posui (ch. viii. § 39)]; aēnus, ahēnus for *ayes-no-, Umbr. ahesno-), and so with many stems in -ēno-, -ĭno-, -ēlo-, &c. In some of these examples the sibilant is a development from an earlier group of sounds, e.g. from st in pōmērium, pōne, from s(ĭ) in pōno; similarly from (1) cs, x in lūna, written Losna on an old Praenestine mirror (C. I. L. i. 55), for *lux-na (Zend raoxšna-, 'shining,' Pruss. lauxnos, 'stars'); sēni, sēmenstris (cf. ses-ceni) for *sexni, *sex-menstris; tēla from texo, &c. (other examples in § 162`; (2) ns in (h)ālo for *anslo (O. Sl. achati, 'to be fragrant'); pīlum from pinso. The older spelling showed a double consonant in these cases. Thus vēlatura, the carrying trade, for *vex-latura, from veho, was probably spelt vellatura by Varro in a passage (R. R. i. 2. 14) where he connects the word with vella, the rustic form of villa; a sibilant which came at a later time to stand before a voiced consonant was similarly treated, e. g. dīvello for dis-vello, dīmota for dismota (S. C. Bacch. C. I. L. i. 196), dīmitte ('dismitte' non dicas, Caper, 97. 7 K.), dī-numero, dī-luo. In the same way the form ē arose from ex in collocations like ē-vello, ē-moveo, ē-mitto, ē-numero, ē-luo (see ch. ix. § 29); vidēn for vidēs-ne was shortened to vidēn (ch. iii. § 42). Cămillus (Camelio on old Praenestine epitaphs, C. I. L. i. 74; 1501 a) was derived by the Romans from a Greek (or Etruscan?) κάσμιλος, meaning a servant of the gods (see Varro, L. L. vii. 34; Macr. iii. 8. 5: Paul. Fest. 44. 33 Th.; cf. Virg. Aen. xi. 542). Varro refers Cămena to an earlier Casmena, which he connects with carmen (L. L. vii. 26). How Casmillus and Casmena (if the word ever existed in this form) failed to become *Cămillus, *Cămena is not clear. The group rsd became rd (through *rrd, for rs becomes rr), e. g. hordeum (cf. O. H. G. gerstā, Germ. Gerste); turdus (Lith. strāzdas, O. Ir. truit, Engl. throstle). The I.-Eur. prototype of custos (Goth. huzd, Engl. hoard), hasta (Goth. gazds, 'a sting,' Germ. Gerte, Engl. yard, O. Ir. gat) may have had sth-, not -zdh-.

Quăsillus from *quas-los (class. quālus) shows that sl remained later than the change of intervocalic s to r (§ 148). Dusmus Adj. occurs in Liv. Andronicus (end of third cent. B.C.) (Trag. 39 R.) dusmo in loco. Plautus' viden for videsne, ain for aisne, &c. show that the law was operative in his time.

§ 152. **Sibilant before r in middle of word.** Lat. cĕrĕbrum for *cerĕsrum (O. Ind. śiras-, 'the head'); Lat. crābro for *crāsro (Lith. szirszů, O. Sl. sršeni); fībra for fīsra (cf. fīlum for *fīslum, Lith. gýsla, 'a sinew'); Lat. tĕnĕbrae for *tenĕsrae (O. Ind. támisrā, from támas-, 'darkness,' Germ. Dämmerung); fūnĕbris for *funĕs-ris.

§ 153. **Assimilation of sibilant to preceding r, l.** Lat. farreus for *farseus (Umbr. farsio-, cf. O. Sl. brašĭno, 'food'; Goth. barizeins, 'made of barley'); Lat. torreo for *torseo (O. Ind. tṛṣ-, Gk. τέρσομαι); Lat. ferre for *fer-se; Lat. velle for *velse; Lat. erro for *erso (Goth. airzjan, 'to mislead,' Germ. irren); Lat. garrio for *garsio (Lith. gaŕsas, 'noise'); Lat. porrum from I.-Eur. *prso- (Gk. πράσον); Lat. terruncius for *ters-, older *trĭs- (Gk. τρίς). This rr from rs was when final reduced to r, e. g. ter (scanned as long by position in Plautus) (ch. ii. § 133), far, Gen. farris. Before t the s kept its place, and the r was dropped, e. g. testāmentum for *tersta- from older *trĭsta- (Osc. tristaamento-); tostus for *torstus.

An s (ss), arisen out of an earlier ts, &c. was not assimilated, e. g. versus for *verttus, rursus and reversus for *reverttus, ars beside far. Latin rs was

§§ 152–157.] REPRESENTATIVES OF I.-EUR. CONS.-GROUPS. 309

pronounced like *ss*, as we see from the pun in Plautus, *Pers.* 740 Persa me pessum dedit, and often came to be written *ss*, and after a long vowel, *s*; hence *russus* and *rusus*, *introsum*, *prosa*, &c. (see ch. ii. § 129).

§ 154. **Assimilation of preceding dental to the sibilant.** Lat. *suāsi* for **suāssi* from *suādeo*; *concŭssi* from *concŭtio*, &c.; *pŏssum* for **pŏt(e)sum*. Similarly in the final syllable, *hospes* for **hospets*, *mīles* for **milets*; this -*es* is short in classical poetry, but probably long by position in Plautus (ch. ii. § 133).

§ 155. **Lat. ss for tt.** Before *r* we find *st* for *tt*, e. g. *pĕdestris* for **pedet-tris* from *pedes*, Gen. *peditis*, *assestrix* Fem. of *assessor*, and perhaps at the end of a word, e. g. *est*, 3 Sg. Pres. of *ĕdo*. But in other cases *tt* became *ss*, e. g. *ūsus*, older *ŭssus*, from *utor* (older *oitor*, *oetor*) for **ut-tus*, *ūsio* for **ut-tio*, **oit-tio* (Osc. oíttiuf 'usio,' beside Pel. oisa 'usa' is best explained as ***oit(i)tions); so *făssus* from *fāteor*, *sĕssus* from *sĕdeo*, *morsus* from *mordeo*, *perculsus* from *per-cello*, **per-celdo*, &c., all formed by adding the participial TO-suffix (see ch. v. § 27) to the root of the verb. In the second cent. B. C. some verbs whose root ended in a guttural followed the analogy of these verbs, owing to the similarity of their Perfect Indicative Active, e. g. *spargo*, *sparsi* made *sparsus*, as *ardeo*, *arsi* made *arsus*; *tergo*, *tersi* made *tersus*, as *mordeo*, *morsi* made *morsus*. But in the period of the older literature these false forms in -*sus* had not established themselves; Paul. Fest. quotes *mertat* for *mersat* (57. 16 Th.; cf. 89. 26); Quintilian (i. 4. 14) says: 'mertare' atque 'pultare' dicebant; and Nonius (179. 4 M.) quotes from Varro *tertus* for *tersus*, and from Accius *mertare* for *mersare*. *Exfuti*, explained by Paul. Fest. 57. 16 Th. as *exfusi* (cf. *con-fūto*, *futtilis*, *fūtilis*) has been referred to **fūtus*, P. P. P. of a verb **fuo*, to shake (O. Ind. dhū-); if it comes from *fundo* it must represent an older **fud(i)tus*, a byform of **fud-tus* as *al(i)tus* of *al-tus*; so *mattus*, drunk (the Romance forms attest tt) for **mad(i)tus*, like *adgrettus* (§ 109). *Estis*, *este*, &c. from *edo*, to eat, must be due to the analogy of *ămā-tis*, *ama-te*, &c.; so *com-estus* beside *comessus*. *Fĕrunto*, &c. for **feront-tŏd* (ch. viii. § 57), *vehementer*, if for **vehement-ter* (ch. ix. § 2) retain *t* in the same way.

§ 156. **Other groups with a sibilant.** When a sibilant came between two labials or gutturals, the first was dropped, e. g. *asporto* for **abs-porto*, *dĭsco* for **dĭc-sco* (cf. *di-dic-i*), *sescēni* for **sex-ceni*, **secs-ceni*. Similarly *pst* becomes *st* in *ostendo* (but O. Lat. *obstĭnet*) beside *obstrūdo*, *obstĭno*.

As *rs* became *rr*, and *ls* became *ll*, so *rs*, *ls* before a consonant become *r*, *l*, e. g. *hordeum* for **horsdeum*, *ainus* for **alsnus* (Lith. elksnis), *perna*, the ham, from I.-Eur. **pērsnā-, 'the heel' (Gk. πτέρνα, Goth. fairzna, O. Engl. fyrsn, Germ. Ferse; cf. O. Ind. pā́rṣṇi-), but an unvoiced consonant preserves the *s* at the expense of the *r*, *l*, e. g. *tostus* for **torstus*, *posco* for **porsco* (O. H. G. forscōn, Germ. forschen), properly for **pr̥ksko* from the root preḱ- of *precor*, &c. (On these groups see the next paragraph.)

§ 157. **Loss of Consonant in Group.** It is convenient here to bring together the various examples of the loss of consonants, when they occur between two other consonants, or in some unpronounceable combination (cf. Engl. 'hal(f)penny,' 'Satur(n)-day,' 'be(t)st,' 'cas(t)le,' 'go(d)spel'). It is not always possible to decide whether the consonant was already ejected in what we call the ' Indo-European period,' e. g. mĭsk-,' to mix ' (Lat. *misceo*, O. Ir. mescaim, W. mysgu Inf., O. H. G. miscu), for *mĭk-sk-, from the root meĭk-, ' to mix ' (O. Ind. miś-rá-, ' mixed,' Lith. sumìszti, ' to get mixed '), with the addition of the Inceptive suffix (ch. viii. § 21), or whether its ejection is due to the phonetic laws of Latin, e. g. *lūna* (on an early Praenestine mirror *Losna*) for *lu(c)sna* (Zend raoxšna-, ' shining,' Pruss. lauxnos, ' stars ').

A consonant between two others is dropped in such groups as : (1) l(c)t, l(c)s, r(c)t, r(c)s, r(t)c, s(c)t, s(t)l, s(c)l, c(t)s, r(t)s or r(d)s, e. g. *ultus* for *ulctus*, *mulsi* for *mulcsi*, *fortis*, O. Lat. *forctis* (§ 118), *tortus* for *torctus*, *torsi* for *torcsi*, *corculum* for *cort-culum* from *cor(d)*, *pastum* for *pasctum*, O. Lat. *slis*, class. *lis* for *stlis (sclis)* (§ 150), *nox* for *nocts*, *ars* for *arts*, *arsi* for *ardsi*.

(2) r(g)n, r(g)m, r(d)n, r(d)m, r(b)m, e. g. *urna* for *urgna* (cf. *urceus*), *tormentum* for *torgmentum*, from *torqueo*, *orno* for *ordno* (cf. *ordĭno*), *vermina*, gripes (Gk. στρόφος, Paul. Fest. 571. 12 Th.) for *verdmina* from *verto*, *sarmentum* for *sarbmentum* from *sarpo*.

The first consonant is dropped in groups like :

(3) (t)sc, (c)sc, (p)sp, (p)st, (p)sc, (s)ps, (n)gn, (r)st, (r)sc, e. g. *esca* for *etsca* from *ĕdo*, *disco* for *dicsco* (§ 156) (cf. *dĭ-dĭc-i*), *asporto* for *apsporto* from *abs* (ch. ix. § 12) and *porto*, *ostendo* for *opstendo* from *obs* and *tendo* (but *obstĭnātus*, O. Lat. *obstinet*, &c.), Oscus, older *Opscus (Obscus)* (see Fest. 212. 24 and 234. 29 Th.), *ipse* for *ispse*, *ignis* for *engnis* (I.-Eur. *ṇgni-, O. Ind. agní-, Lith. ugnìs, O. Sl. ognĭ. See *M. S. L.* viii. 236), *fastĭgium* for *farstigium* (cf. O. Ind. bhṛṣṭí-, ' a point,' Engl. bristle), *Tuscus* (Umbr. *Tursco-* and *Tusco-*).

(4) (c)sn or (g)sn, (c)sl or (g)sl, (c)sm or (g)sm, e. g. *lūna* for *lusna* (Praen. *Losna*) for *lucsna*, *tēlum* for *teslum* for *tecslum*, *āla* for *asla* for *agsla*, *subtēmen* for *subtesmen* for *subtecsmen*.

The group *nct* is preserved in *junctus*, *defunctus*, anteclass. *quinctus*, but drops the *c* in class. *quintus*, late Lat. *defuntus* (*C. I. L.* iii. 2137), *santus* (v. 8136), *nantus* (iii. 1635. 4), &c. (see ch. ii. §§ 70, 95), and cf. *conctione* miswritten for *contione* on the Lex Repetundarum, i. 198. 18). The group *ncs* remains, e. g. *planxi, lanx*.

§ 158. **Other examples.** On the forms *cals* for *cal(c)s*, *calx*, and *mers* for *mer(c)s*, *merx*, see ch. ii. § 125; they are like *farsi* for *farcsi*, *fulsi* for *fulcsi*, *mulsi* for *mulcsi*. Like *for(c)tis* is *fertum*, O. Lat. *ferctum*, a sacrificial cake, from a lost verb *fergo, to bake (cf. O. Ir. bairgen 'bread'); also *fartus* from *farcio*, O. Lat. *tertus* (§ 155) from *tergo*, *sartus* from *sarcio*. Cf. *fulmentum* for *fulcmentum*, *quernus*, for *quercnus*. The *b* of *ambe*, around, is dropped in *am-termini*, *am-caesa*, *am-sĕgĕtes*, &c. (see ch. ix. § 16), and the loss of the *d* in *indu-* in similar circumstances probably led to its being ousted by *in*, e.g. *imperator*, *ingredi* (O. Lat. *induperator*, *indugredi*, ch. iii. § 15). The sibilant is dropped in *hordeum* for *horsdeum* (O. H. G. gersta), *turdus* for *tursdus* (Engl. throstle; cf. Lith. strāzdas), *perna* (Goth. fairzna, 'the heel'; O. Ind. pārṣni-), *alnus* (cf. Lith. elksnis for *elsnis) (see § 156); also in *inquam*, *coinquo* if these stand for *ind-squam*, *co-ind-squo*, but remains in *exta* if this stands for *encsta* (Lith. ĭnkstas, 'kidney'). Like *asporto*, &c. are *suscipio* for *sups-cipio*, *astŭlit* (Charis. 237. 2 K.) for *apstulit* (*abstulit*). *Posco* represents *por-sco* (O. H. G. forscōn, Germ. forschen), I.-Eur. pr̥(k̑)-sko- like *mĭ(k̑)-sko-. The group *nst* remains in *monstrum*, &c. but becomes *st* between vowels, e.g. *mostellum*. Like *fastīgium* is *testāmentum* for *terstamentum* (Osc. tristaamentud Abl.).

The weakening of a root often produces an unpleasing consonant-group which has to be changed and often becomes unrecognizable. Thus the I.-Eur. weak-grade of dek̑- (of the numeral 'ten,' I.-Eur. *dĕk̑m) appears in the word for hundred as dk̑-, which is changed to k̑- (I.-Eur. *km̥tom for *dk̑m̥tom, ch. vi. § 76; Lat. *centum* beside *dĕcem*); the weak-grade of the root ĝen-, 'to be born,' appears in Lat. *gnātus*, which in class. Lat. lost its initial g (§ 119). Similarly *tlātus* from the root tel- of *tollo*, &c., became *lātus*, 'carried' (§ 105), and *stlātūs*, from the root stel- of O. Sl. steljǫ, 'I extend,' was reduced to the same form *lātus*, 'extended, broad' (§ 146). Other initial consonant-groups avoided in Latin are *dr-*, *cn-*, *dl-*, *sm-*, *wl-*, *wr-*, &c. (see this chapter passim).

§ 159. **Assimilation of Consonants.** The loss of a consonant in a group is often really due to assimilation. Thus the loss of *s* in *hordeum* for *horsdeum* can hardly be separated from the assimilation of *s* to *r* in the group *rs*, e.g. *horreo* for *horseo*. In the case of Assimilation, as of Ecthlipsis, it is often difficult to say whether the Assimilation already existed in 'the I.-Eur. period' or not. Assimilation plays a great part in the compounding of Prepositions with verbs, e.g. *accurrere* for *ad-currere*, O. Lat. *ommentans* for *ob-mentans*, *pellĕge* (Plaut.) for *perlege*, *al-lĭgare* for *ad-ligare* (the assimilated form had so established itself by the time of Pliny that he treats it as a simple verb and re-compounds it with *ad*, *ad-alligare*), but the unmodified forms of the preposition were often restored in spelling at least (thus Servius ad *Aen.* i. 616 says that *applicat* was the spelling formerly in vogue, *adplicat* the spelling of his own day), a restoration which went hand in hand with the restoration of the unweakened form of the vowel in verbs like *ē-neco* (older *enico*), *intel-lego*, &c. (see ch. iii. § 31). Examples of Assimilation are:

pc, e.g. *oc-caeco, suc-curro*; **pf**, e.g. *of-fĭcīna* (O. Lat. *ŏpĭ-ficĭna*), *suf-fĭcio*; **bg**, e.g. *og-gĕro, sug-gero*; **bm**, e.g. *ommentans* (quoted from Liv. Andron. from Festus 218. 14 Th., and explained by *obmănens*, 'waiting'; cf. *C. G. L.* v. 37. 3 *ommentat*: expectat), *summitto, āmitto* (for *ammitto*, ch. ii. § 127) (but *ŏmitto*), *glūma* for *glūb-ma* from *glūbo*. *B* is assimilated to *r* in Prepositional Compounds like *surripio*, and before *n* becomes *m* in *scamnum* (cf. *scabellum*), *amnegaverit* (*C. I. L.* vi. 14672), &c. (§ 102), though in Prepositional Compounds the spelling with *b* is usually retained, e.g. *ab-nĕgo*; **cf** (rather **c(s)f**, § 157), e.g. *effĕro* from *ex-fero*; **tc**, e.g. *ac-curro, hoc* for **hod-ce*; **tf**, e.g. *affero*; **dg**, e.g. *ag-gero*; **dl**, e.g. *al-luo, pel-luviae*, water for washing the feet, *lăpillus* for **lapid-lus*; **dm**, e.g. *rāmentum* from *rādo*; **dn**, e.g. *an-nuo, mercēnnarius* from *mercēd-*; **tp**, e.g. *ap-pāreo*; **tq**, e.g. *quicquam*; **dr** (**tr**), e.g. *ar-rīdeo*; **ds** (**ts**), e.g. *as-sĭdeo*; **ln**, e.g. *collis* (Lith. káĭnas), but *ulna* had originally a short vowel between *l* and *n* (Gk. ὠλένη); **ld**, e.g. *per-cello* (cf. *clādes*), but *valdē* from *vălĭde*, *calda* from *călĭda*; **ls**, e.g. *collum*, O. Lat. *collus* (Goth. hals Masc.), *velle* for **vel-se* (cf. *es-se*); *m* and *n* are assimilated in Compounds of the Prepositions *com-, in,* and the Negative Prefix *in-*, e.g. *col-laudo, il-lābor, illaudabilis, cor-ruo, ir-ruo, ir-rĭtus, con-necto* or *cōnecto, im-mitto, im-mĕmor,* and similarly the final *-m* of *ĕtiam, tam,* &c. was often written *n* (ch. ii. § 65) before an initial *n*, e.g. *etian-num tan-ne* (ch. ii. § 135); **nl** (as in Engl. 'eleven,' Mid. Engl. enleven), e.g. *cŏrolla* for **corōn-la, hŏmullus* for **homŏn-lus*; **rl**, e.g. *Ātella* (Osc. Aderl-), *ăgellus* for **agerlus* (cf. supellex non 'superlex,' Probi App. 198. 14 K.); **rs**, e.g. *torreo* for **torseo* (cf. Gk. τέρσομαι), *ferre* for **fer-se* (cf. *es-se*). On the Assimilation of *s* to a following voiced consonant, and the consequent lengthening of the preceding vowel by 'Compensation,' e.g. *quālus* (older *quallus*) for **quăs-lus* (cf. *quăsillus*), see § 151, on a like treatment of *n* before *s* or *f, ib.*, and on the Assimilation of Mediae to Tenues (e.g. *scriptus* for **scribtus*), *cĕt-te* for **cĕd(i)te*), Tenues to Mediae, e.g. *ab-duco* from *ap-* (I.-Eur. **ăpŏ*), see § 95. In dialectal Latin *nd* became *nn* as in Osc. úpsanno- ' operando-,' whence *dispennĭte* and *distennĭte* (Plaut.) (see ch. ii. § 71); on the pronunciation *ss* for *rs* (cf. *russus* for *rursus*), see ch. ii. § 104.

§ 160.] REPRESENTATIVES OF I.-EUR. CONS.-GROUPS. 313

§ 160. Assimilation in Preposition compounded with Verb. The passages of the Roman grammarians dealing with this subject are enumerated by Brambach, *Lat. Orth.* pp. 294 sqq. Lucilius declared it to be immaterial whether one wrote *d* or *c* in *adcurrere, accurrere* (ix. 25 M.) :

'adcurrere' scribas
dne an c, non est quod quaeras eque labores,

but seems (though the reading is doubtful) to have insisted on the necessity of distinguishing *ad-bitere* (from *ad* and *baeto*) and *ab-bitere* (from *ab* and *baeto*) (ix. 27 M.) :

'abbitere' multum·est
d siet an b ;

(*absimilis* seems to have been discarded in Latin for *dissimilis*, through fear of confusion with *adsimilis*) ; he pronounces in favour of *pellicio* (ix. 32 M.) :

in praeposito per
'pelliciendo,' hoc est inducendo, geminato l.

Similarly Priscian (i. 50. 7 H.) quotes *pellege, pellucet* from Plautus.
The MSS. of Plautus and Terence show great prevalence of Assimilation ; Plautus puns on *adsum* and *assum*, *Poen.* 279 :

Mílphio, heus ubi tu és ? Assum apud te eccum. Át ego elixus sís uolo,

where however the MSS. read *adsum*, and Stilo (end of second cent. B. C.) derived *as-siduus* 'ab asse dando' (Cic. *Top.* ii. 10). It is quite a mistake to suppose the unassimilated forms to be the older, and the assimilated the more recent (see Dorsch in the *Prager philol. Studien*, 1887). In the Herculanean papyri the preposition is generally not assimilated, e. g. 'adsiduo,' 'inridens,' 'inlita,' 'adfini,' but 'imminet,' 'imperiis' (*Class. Rev.* iv. 442). The byform *ā* of *ab* originated in an assimilated form, e. g. before *f-* in the verb *ā-fluo*, to be abundant (cf. *ab-undo*), often confused in MSS. with *af-fluo*, to flow to (see Nettleship, *Contributions*, s. v. *affluo*), and before *m-*, *v-*, e. g. *ā-mitto*, *ā-vello*, the forms *ammitto*, &c. being avoided apparently through fear of confusion with compounds of *ad* ; in classical spelling *ad* is assimilated usually before *c-*, e. g. *ac-cĭpio* (sometimes before *q-*, e. g. *ac-quīro*), before *g-*, e.g. *aggrĕdior* and *ad-gredior*, before *l-*, e. g. *allīgare* but *adluere*, *adlŏqui* (Velius Longus, p. 61 K.), before *p-*. e. g. *ap-pōno*, rarely *ad-pono*, before *r-*, e. g. *arrĭpio* and *ad-ripio*, before *s*, e. g. *as-sideo* and *ad-sideo*, *ad-sum*, before *t-*, e. g. *at-trĭbuo* ; *com-* is assimilated before *l-*, e. g. *col-lēgium*, *col-lŏco* and *con-loco*, before *r-*, e. g. *cor-rigo*, and becomes *con-* before *c-*, *d-*, *f-*, *g-*, *j-*, *n-*, *q-*, *s-*, *t-*, *v-*; on *ex* see ch. ix. §29 ; *in-* is assimilated before *m-*, e. g. *im-mitto* (becoming *im-* also before *b-*, *p-*), occasionally before *r-*, e. g. *ir-ruo* and *in-ruo*, not so often before *l-*, e. g. *in-lūdo* and *il-ludo* ; *ob-* is assimilated before *c-*, e.g. *oc-curro*, before *f-*, e. g. *of-fendo*, before *g-*, e. g. *og-gĕro*, before *p-*, e. g. *op-pĕrior*, and occasionally before *m-*, e. g. *ob-mănĕo*, O. Lat. *om-mentare* ; *per-* is assimilated before *l-*, e. g. *pel-lĭcio*, *pel-lĕgo* and *per-lego* ; *sub* is assimilated before *c-*, e. g. *suc-curro* before *f-*, e. g. *suf-fĕro*, before *g-*, e. g. *sug-gĕro*, before *p-*, e. g. *sup-pōno*, and optionally before *m-*, e. g. *sum-mitto* and *sub-mitto*, and *r-*, e. g. *sur-rĭpui* (contracted *surpui*) and *sub-ripui* ; *trans-* often becomes *trā-* before *j-*, *d-*, *l-*, *m-*, *n-*, e. g. *trā-do* (*trans-dere* attested by Donatus for Terence, *Phorm.* 2, where all our MSS. have *tradere*) ; before *j-* we find *co-* in *coicio*, &c., *pe-* in *pejĕrare*, a later spelling of *perjerare* (see Georges, *Lex. Wortf.* s. v.) (cf. *peiiuri* Plaut. *Truc.* 612 (B)) (cf. Ital. Gennajo for Lat., *Jānuarius*). (See Brambach, *Lat. Orth.* pp. 296 sqq. on the Assimilation of Prepositions on Inscriptions, and the Indices to *C.I.L.*)

§ 161. Other examples of Assimilation. If Festus (252. 7 Th.) is right in saying that both *petna* and *pesna* were O. Lat. words for 'a wing,' we must suppose *penna* to be the development of the former, while the latter (from **petsnā-*) would become **pēna* (cf. *luna* for **lucsna*); *annus* is most naturally derived from **at-no-* (Goth. aþn Neut., 'a year'). The assimilation of *c* to a following *t* was a feature of dialectal (e.g. *blatta* for **blacta*, Lett. blakts, 'a bug') and Late Latin (see ch. ii. § 95). Like *glūma* from *glūbo* is *rumentum* (glossed by 'abruptio' Paul. Fest. 369. 12 Th.) from *rumpo*; like *rāmentum* from *rādo* is *caementum* from *caedo*. (On the reduction of *mm* after a long vowel or diphthong to *m*, e.g. **caemmentum* to *caementum*, see ch. ii. § 127). For *dp* we have O. Lat. *topper* (see ch. ix. § 7) for **tod-per* (on *quippe, quippiam*, see ch. x. § 7). *Idcirco* is sometimes spelt *iccirco* (see Brambach, *Hülfsbüchlein*, s. v.). Whether *nm* became *mm*, e.g. *gemma*, or *rm*, e.g. *germen*, is discussed in § 80, and whether *exāmen* represents **exăgmen* or **ex-ags-men* in § 116. In the Probi App. (198. 26 K.) we have: amygdala non 'amiddula'; the *gd* of *frig(i)dus* (*frigda* Probi App. 198. 3 K.) became *dd* (cf. *fridam, C.I.L.* iv. 291; Ital. freddo, &c.).

§ 162. Lengthening by Compensation. Closely connected with the Assimilation of Consonants is what is called the 'Compensatory' Lengthening of Vowels, where the assimilated consonant lends itself rather to increase the length of the preceding vowel, so that the loss of the consonant is, as it were, compensated by the additional quantity of the vowel. (English examples are 'lady,' 'maid,' 'rain,' 'thane.') *Quālus*, for **quăs-lus* (cf. *quăs-illus*, § 148), is in the older spelling *quallus*, *ănhēlus* for **anhenslus* is *anhellus, vēlum* for **vexlum* (cf. *vexillum*) is *vellum, aula*, a pot (later *olla*), for **auxla* (cf. *auxilla*) is *aulla*, &c.; the Adjective ending *-ōsus* for **o-went-to-* (ch. v. § 65) is in the older spelling *-onssus, -ossus* (see Brambach, *Orth.* p. 268, and the Indices to Ribbeck's Virgil and Studemund's Apograph of the Ambrosian Palimpsest of Plautus); *dūmetum* for **dusmetum* is in Virgil MSS. *dummetum*, as *dīminuo* is in Plautus MSS. *dimminuo* [cf. *dirrumpo, Bacch.* 441 (C D), but *disr-* (B)], and so on. (On the spellings with double consonant in the MSS. of Plautus, Virgil, &c., see ch. ii. §§ 127–133, where the question is discussed how far a long vowel with a single consonant might be substituted for a short vowel with a double consonant in Latin. On the lengthening of a vowel before *ns*, see ch. ii. § 144, and for additional examples of the loss of *s, x* with 'compensatory' lengthening, § 151 above.)

§ 163. **Assimilation of Syllables.** The change of the older Perfect-forms *cĕcurri, mĕmordi, pĕposci, pĕpŭgi*, &c. to *cŭcurri, mŏmordi, pŏposci, pŭpugi*, &c. (see ch. viii. § 43) shows the partiality of Latin for the complete assimilation of two neighbouring syllables. The I.-Eur. dissimilation of $*q^uenq^ue$, 'five,' to $*penq^ue$ (§ 116) (O. Ind. páñca, Lith. penkì, &c.) is not seen in Lat. *quinque; quercus* (for **querquus*), *querquētum* may be another example, for O. Engl. furh, our 'fir,' points to I.-Eur. $*perq^u$- (cf. *bĭbo* from I.-Eur. pib-, O. Ind. píbāmi, O. Ir. ibim). The same similarity of initial and following syllable, whether an original similarity preserved in Latin or first produced by the Latin partiality for a repetition of the same sound, is seen in words like *cincinnus*, a curl (Gk. κίκιννος), *quisquiliae*, shreds (Gk. κοσκυλμάτια), *barba* for **farba* (Engl. beard, O. Sl. brada), *querquĕra*, ague, *murmur* (Gk. μορμύρω), *ŭpŭpa* (Gk. ἔποψ), *furfur, tintinno, cŭcŭmis, turtur*, &c. But in Vulgar Latin we find *qu* becoming *c* when a following syllable has *qu*, e. g. *cinque* for *quinque, cesquo* for *quiesco* (Bersu, *die Gutturalen*, p. 98).

CHAPTER V.

FORMATION OF NOUN AND ADJECTIVE STEMS.

§ 1. I. **STEM-SUFFIXES**. We have seen how the several sounds of the Latin language were written (ch. i.), and pronounced (ch. ii.), and what original or 'Indo-European' sounds they represent (ch. iv.). We have now to see how Latin words were formed, and how the Latin process of formation was related to the 'Indo-European.'

For the forming of words we find sounds combined into roots, and these developed into stems; thus the sounds t, e, and g, are combined into the root teg-, ' to cover' (Lat. *tĕg-o, teg-men, tectus* for *teg-tus, *tŏg-a* with O-grade of root), which is further developed into the stems tŏgā- (Lat. Nom. Sg. *togă*, earlier *togā, Gen. Pl. *togā-rum*, &c.), tegmen- (Lat. Nom. Sg. *tegmen*, Gen. *tegmĭnis*, earlier *tegmen-es, &c.) by the addition to the root of the stem-suffixes -ā-, -men-. It is these stem-suffixes, used in the making of Nouns and Adjectives, which will be the subject of this section.

§ 2. **Suffixes ending in -ŏ, -ā** (Nouns and Adjectives of the First and Second Declension). **-Ŏ-, -Ā-.** -Ŏ-, which should rather be called the ĕ-ŏ-suffix, since it alternates with ĕ (e.g. I.-Eur. Voc. Sg. of Masc. o-stems ended in -ĕ, *ĕk̑wĕ, ' O horse,' Gk. ἵππε, Lat. *equĕ*, &c.), is associated with the Masc. and Neut. Gender. -Ā-, which should rather be called the ă-suffix, since it alternates with ă (e.g. I.-Eur. Voc. Sg. of Fem. ā-stems ended in -ă, *ĕk̑wă, ' O mare '; cf. Hom. Gk. νύμφă), is associated with the Fem. Gender. Hence the ŏ- and ā-suffixes were used in Adjectives, e.g. I.-Eur. něwo-, Masc. and Neut., *newā-, Fem. (Gk. νέ(F)ος, νέ(F)ον, νέ(F)ᾱ, Lat. *nŏvos, novom, nova*, &c.). Special circumstances have however produced a few instances of Fem. o-stems and Masc. ā-stems. Thus Lat. *fāgus*, Gk. φηγός are Fem., being names of trees; and Lat. *agricola*, when it passed from its original abstract sense of 'field-tillage' into the concrete sense of a 'field-tiller,' became Masc. (cf. Gk. *νεανιᾱ-, youth, νεανίᾱς, a youth). (See ch. vi. § 1.)

Of the many uses of the ŏ-suffix, two may be selected for particular notice: (1) in Abstract Nouns (Nomina Actionis), these having the accent on the root, e.g. I.-Eur. *ĝóno-, 'production' (O. Ind. jánam, Gk. γόνος), from root ĝen-, 'to produce'; (2) in Nomina Agentis, these having the accent on the suffix, e.g. I.-Eur. *tŏró-, 'a piercer' (Gk. τορός), from root ter-, 'to pierce'; I.-Eur. *prŏk̑o-, 'an asker' (Lat. *prŏcus*, a suitor), from root prek̑-, 'to ask.' The root in all these examples shows the o-grade (ch. iv. § 51).

The ā-suffix is similarly used in Abstract Nouns (Nomina Actionis), e.g. I.-Eur. *bhŭgā, 'the action of fleeing' (Gk. φυγή, Lat. *fŭga*), from the weak grade of the root bheug-, 'to flee.'

How far these simple suffixes -ŏ- and -ā- have been combined with others to form the large number of suffixes which end in the letter ŏ, or the letter ā, e.g. -io-, -iā-, -to-, -tā-, -tuo-, -tuā-, -tro-, -trā, &c. need not be discussed here. In Latin we find them more used in the older stages of the language, while fuller suffixes seem to be required in the classical period; thus *pervĭcus* (from the root weik-, 'to fight,' Lat. *vinco*) is O. Lat. for *per-vicāx*, and *squālus*, Enn., became *squālĭdus*. The Verbal Noun used as Infinitive by the Umbro-Samnite nations was probably a Neuter ŏ-stem, e.g. Osc. *ezum*, Umbr. *erom* from root ĕs-, 'to be,' Lat. *esse*; Osc. *deicum* corresponds to Lat. *dīcere*, Osc. *moltaum* to Lat. *multare*); and at all periods of Latin we see a tendency to make rough-and-ready coinages of words with the help of these simple suffixes, e.g. *Carna*, from *căr(o)n-, flesh, the goddess of the vital organs, to whom a temple was dedicated by Junius Brutus in 510 B.C., *Carda* (or *Cardea*), from *cardon-, a hinge, the goddess of hinges, *nola*, 'a say-no' from *nōlo*, in Caelius' punning description of Clodia (Quint. viii. 6. 53).

§ 3. **Latin ŏ- and ā-suffixes; other examples.** Lat. *uncus* from **oncos* (O. Ind. aṅkás, Gk. ὄγκος) from the root ank-, ' to bend ' ; Lat. *dŏlus* (Gk. δόλος), perhaps the O-grade of a root del- ; Lat. *jŭgum* (O. Ind. yugám, Gk. ζυγόν, Goth. juk Neut., O. Sl. igo Neut.) from the root yeug-, ' to join ' ; Lat. *plāga* (Gk. πληγή) from the root plāg-, ' to beat ' ; *con-vīva* from *vīvo*, to enjoy oneself (e.g. Catull. v. 1 ; Plaut. *Pers.* 30 uiues mecum ; so *vita* Plaut. *Trin.* 477 ; cf. Non. 14. 16 M. sicuti qui nunc est in summa laetitia, ' vivere' eum dicimus); *parcus* from *parco* ; with lengthened root *col-lēga* (cf. *tĕg-ŭla*, *rĕg-ŭla*, and *cĕlāre*, if from **tĕga*, **rĕga*, **cĕla*, Verbal Nouns from the roots tĕg-, rĕg-, kĕl- ; cf. § 23). Of early forms, and occasional coinages, may be mentioned : *condus* and *prōmus* from *condo*, *promo*, e.g. Plaut. *Pseud.* 608 condus promus sum, procurator peni ; *trăha*, a harrow, for which Virgil substituted (invented ?) the form *trahea* (cf. the note of Servius on *G.* i. 164 traheaeque : Epenthesin fecit causa metri, ut 'navita.' traha autem vehiculum est a trahendo dictum ; nam non habet rotas), from *traho*, like *sĕra*, the bolt of a door, from *sero*, to join ; from *aio* was formed *Aius Locutius*, the god to whom a temple was dedicated in gratitude for the supernatural warning against the attack of the Gauls, 390 B.C. ; from *pando*, *Panda*, the goddess of opening, after whom was named the *Pandāna porta* (Varro, *L. L.* v. 42), the Oscan name of the goddess being Patana-. Nonius quotes *pervĭcus*, stubborn, persistent, from Accius (*Trag.* 158 R.) :

sed péruico Aiax ánimo atque aduorsábili,

derived from *pervinco*, to be stubborn, persistent, as we may see from the assonance of Ennius (*Trag.* 408 R.) :

peruínce pertináci peruicácia ;

coa and *nola*, from *coeo* and *nolo* are quoted from Caelius by Quintilian (viii. 6. 53): quadrantariam Clytemestram, et in triclinio coam, in cubiculo nolam ; so perhaps *confeta sus*, for *sus cum fētu*, explained by Paul. Fest. (40. 28 Th.) : quae cum omni fetu adhibebatur ad sacrificium ; *Domi-duca*, *Prō-nūba* (an epithet of Juno), *Juga* (another epithet of Juno), *Lua*, *Vica Pota*, *noctĭ-lūca*, *sanguĭ-sūga*. *Scrība* was the early word for ' a poet' (Fest. 492. 19 Th.).

§ 4. **-IŎ-, -IĀ- (-YŎ-, -YĀ-).** It is difficult to distinguish in Latin the I.-Eur. suffixes (1) -yŏ-, -yā-, (2) -ĭyŏ-, -ĭyā- (by some written -əyo-, -əyā-), for as we have seen (ch. iv. § 65), y after a consonant in the middle of a word became vocalic *i* in Latin, so that Lat. *mĕdius* from I.-Eur. **mĕdh-yo-* (O. Ind. mádhya-, Gk. μέ(σ)σος) is, unlike the O. Ind. and Greek forms of the word, a trisyllable. The weak grade of I.-Eur. -yŏ-, -ĭyŏ- (or -yĕ-, -ĭyĕ-, § 2) seems to have been -ĭ-, -ī- ; e. g. Goth. brūks, ' useful,' for **brūkĭs*, I.-Eur. **bhrūg^u-ī-*, **bhrūg^uyŏ-* (-yĕ-), from the root bhreug^u-, ' to use, enjoy ' (Lat. *fruor*); Goth. hairdeis, ' a herd, shepherd,' for **hairdīs*; and this opened the way to a confusion of io- stems with i-stems. Another byform seems to have been -īyŏ-, -īyā-, e. g. O. Ind. tṛt-íya-, ' third,'

Hom. Gk. προθυμ-ίη, a form which would in Latin shorten the ī before the following vowel, and become identical with I.-Eur.-ĭyo-. These IO- suffixes have three chief uses in I.-Eur.: (1) to form Verbal Adjectives, especially Gerundives, the Neuter and Fem. being often employed as Verbal Nouns, e.g. I.-Eur. *sŏq^u-yo-, 'requiring help or company' (Lat. *sŏcius*; cf. O. Ind. sáciya-, Gk. ἀ-οσσητήρ from *ὁσσο-) from the root sĕq^u-, 'to accompany' (O. Ind. sac-, Gk. ἕπομαι, Lat. *sĕquor*). Similarly Latin *exĭmius* in the sense of *eximendus* (e.g. Ter. *Hec.* 66 utin eximium neminem habeam? 'am I to make no exception?'); Lat. *stŭdium* from *studeo*, Lat. *exŭviae* from *exuo*; *plŭvia* from *pluo*; (2) as a secondary suffix of Adjectives, the Neuter and Fem. being often used as Abstract Nouns; often too in Compound Adjectives; e.g. I.-Eur. *pătrĭyo-* (O. Ind. pítriya-, Gk. πάτριος, Lat. *patrius*) from the noun *păter-* (I.-Eur. pitár-, Gk. πατήρ, Lat. *păter*); Lat. *somnium* (O. Ind. svápnyam, O. Sl. sŭnĭje, sŭnije) from *somnus*, stem *somno-* (O. Ind. svápnas, O. Sl. sŭnŭ); Lat. *falsi-jŭrius* from *falsus* and *jus*, *discordia* from *discors*; (3) in Adjectives which have a sense of comparison or distinction, indicating a special locality, direction, &c., e.g. I.-Eur. *mĕdhyo-* (O. Ind. mádhya-, Gk. μέ(σ)σος, Lat. *mĕdius*); I.-Eur. *ălyo-* (Arm. ail, Gk. ἄλλος, Lat. *ălius*, Goth. aljis); Gk. δεξιός has this suffix, while Lat. *dexter* (Gk. δεξιτερός) has the -tero- suffix, which has the same force (§ 16). So in some Ordinal Numbers, e.g. Lat. *tertius* (cf. O. Ind. trtíya-, Goth. þridja, O. Sl. tretĭjĭ, ch. vi. § 61).

A notable use of this suffix in the Italic languages is in the formation of Proper Names. While in all, or most, of the other I.-Eur. languages Compounds were used for Proper Names, the son taking a Compound slightly varied from the father's (e.g. Gk. Δινο-κράτης, son of Δινο-κλῆς, Teut. Walt-bert, son of Wald-ram), the Italic stocks employed simple stems with this IO- suffix, e.g. Lat. *Lūcius, Stătius*, &c., which correspond to some contracted or 'pet'-names in the other I.-Eur. nations, e.g. Gaul. Toutius, a familiar shortened form of Toutio-rix, Gk. Ζευξίας, for the more ceremonious Ζεύξ-ιππος, &c., Λεῦκις beside Λεύκ-ιππος, &c. (see Fick, *Personennamen*).

The Oscan inscriptions enable us to distinguish two varieties of this suffix in Patronymics (or family names), which cannot so easily be distinguished in Latin: (1) -yo-, in Patronymics derived from praenomina (what we call 'Christian names') in -o, e.g. Osc. Úhtavis, Lat. *Octāvius*, the patronymic derived from Lat. *Octavus*; Osc. Statis from a praenomen *Stato-. The Oscan suffix is in native characters written -is (i.e. -īs), in Latin characters -*is*, in Gk. -ις: (2) -ĭyo-, in Patronymics derived from praenomina in -yo-, e.g. Statiis, a patronymic from the praenomen Statis (stem *Statyo-). This suffix is in Oscan characters -iis, in Latin characters -*ies*, in Gk. -ιες. To these we may add a third variety, -īyo-, apparently the unshortened form of -ĭyo-. This is used in ceremonious language on inscriptions bearing the names of magistrates, &c., and is written -iís, Gk. -ειες, e.g. Viínikiís, Ἀϝδειες, both quaestors. How far Latin spellings like *Clodeius*, *Publeius*, *Vareius*, if they are genuine Latin forms and not dialectal, may be distinguished from the normal forms *Clodĭus*, *Publĭus*, *Varĭus* is hard to determine. The diphthong *ei* in O. Latin may, as we have seen, represent the weakening of an original -ai- (-oi-) in the unaccented syllable, e.g. *occeido*, as well as an original -ei-, e.g. *deico*; it may also be a graphic expression of the long simple vowel *ī*, for this -*ei*- came to be pronounced, and in time spelt, in the same way as *ī*; and before another vowel *ī* would be shortened to *ĭ*. Thus Osc. Bovaiano- was in Latin *Bovĭanum* through *Bovĭanum from *Boveianom*; Osc. Púmpaiians is Lat. *Pompeianus*; Osc. Maraio-, Falisc. Mareio-, is Lat. *Marĭus* (cf. Umbr. pernaio-, 'in front,' postraio-, 'behind,' in Lat. *antīcus*, *postīcus*). Analogous to the Oscan -īyo- as opposed to -ĭyo- is perhaps the Latin use of the full ending -*ius*, as opposed to the shorter -*is* or -*i* (with -*ī*- like Osc. -īs?), in names of magistrates; for example, on the S. C. de Bacchanalibus (*C. I. L.* i. 196) the consuls' names are *Marcius* and *Postumius*, but the names of the clerks who 'scribendo arfuerunt' are *Claudi*, *Valeri*, *Minuci*.

As the IO-suffix is often added as a secondary suffix to Verb-stems (e.g. *pinsio* and *pinso*, ch. viii. § 15), so it is added to Nouns. O-stems either drop their final vowel before it, e.g. *somn-ium*, or show -ĕyo- which became -ĕo- (ch. iv. § 66), e.g. *aureus*. (On rustic -*eo*- for -*io*-, see ch. ii. § 10). This ending

§ 4.]   NOUN AND ADJECTIVE STEMS. -IŎ-, -IĀ-.   321

was often assigned to other stems, e.g. *flammeus* (Ā-stem), *corneus* (U-stem), *vīteus* (I-stem), to denote material. The TER-stems augmented by -io- produce in Latin a numerous class of Neuter Nouns indicating the place or instrument of an action, with the ending -*tōrio*- corresponding to Greek -τηριο-, e.g. *audī-torium*, 'the place of hearing,' *deversorium* for *devert-torium, 'a lodging-place,' *scalp-torium*, 'an instrument for scratching' (Martial xiv. 83). (Cf. Gk. βουλευ-τήριον, ἐργασ-τήριον, both indicating place, καυσ-τήριον, 'instrument for burning,' κρι-τήριον, 'means of deciding'). (On Fem. -*toria* in Late Lat. see Rönsch, *Collectanea*, p. 197.) Similarly we have -*mōnium*, -*mōnia* from MEN-stems, e.g. *ălĭmonia* and *ălĭmonium* (cf. *ălĭmentum*), *flāmonium* (on the spelling, see Nettleship, *Contributions*, s.v.) from *flamen*, an ending extended to *tristĭ-monia, sanctĭ-monia*, &c. The Adj. ending -*ārius* (from *āsios*, ch. iv. § 160) was to some extent supplanted by -*āris* in later Latin (ch. iii. § 16), though the popular speech retained the older forms (e.g. *vīnarius*), forms which should perhaps be restored to various lines of Plautus (see Langen, *Beiträge*, p. 324; e.g. *militariis*, *Pseud*. 1049). The same may be true of -*ālius* and -*ālis*, &c., e.g. *mănualium*: ἐγχειρίδιον (Gl. Cyrill.), *ŏvīlium* (*ib*.) A common ending of Abstract Nouns is -*ĭtia* (often -*ities*), e.g. *laetitia* from *laetus*, like *mīlĭtia* from *miles* (see also YĒ-stems, § 51), -*ĭtium*, e.g. *servitium*, *flāgitium*, *lānitium*. From N-stems we have, e.g. *cŏlōnia*, in O. Lat., 'a dwelling-place' (Plaut. *Aul*. 576 : ut conmutet coloniam).

-ārio- and -āri-, -ālio- and -āli-. Caper (p. 103. 9 K.) approves the old form *vinarius* :

Vasa istaec vinaria sunt, vinaria cella :
Vulgus adhuc retinet de prisca verba loquella ;

and similarly *atramentarium* (p. 108. 3 K.) ; but Probi Appendix (p. 198. 7 K.) primipilaris, non 'primipilarius.' (For other examples of -*arius*, -*alius*, see Rönsch, *Collectanea*, pp. 196, 208 ; Neue ii[3]. p. 158.)

Other examples of IO-stem Compounds. From *jūs* and *ăgo* was formed *jūr(i)-gium*; so *lītigium* ; from *dīco*, *jūdĭcium*, *indĭcium* ; from *eo*, *cŏmĭtium*, *exĭtium*, *inĭtium* (cf. § 77) ; similarly *praemium* from *ĕmo*, *incendium*, *suspĭrium*, *discĭdium*, *connūbium*, *subsĭdium*, *aedi-fĭcium*, *lecti-sternium*, *stīlli-cĭdium*, *obsĕquium* [wrongly declared (Cicero ap. Quint. viii. 3. 35 ; but cf. *Lael*. xxiv. 89) to be a coinage of Terence, for it is used by Plautus (*Bacch*. 1082) and Naevius (Don. ad Ter. *Andr*. i. 1. 40)] and *exsĕquiae*, *excŭbiae*, *suppĕtiae*, *vindēmia* from *vīnum* and *dĕmo*, *incūria* from *cūra*, &c.

Y

§ 5. -UŎ-, -UĀ-. Here again the two I.-Eur. forms of the suffix, (1) -wŏ-, -wā-, (2)- ŭwŏ-, -ŭwā-, (or -əwo-, &c.) are difficult to distinguish in Latin, where w after a consonant in the middle of a word became vocalic *u* at first, though it might afterwards become a consonant by the process of Syncope described in ch. iii. § 13, e. g. *furvus*, which must have been trisyllabic, *fusuos* (cf. *fus-cus*), at the time when *s* between vowels became *r* in Latin. An original -ăwŏ-, -ĕwŏ-, -ŏwŏ- would also become -ŭŏ-, and in time -vŏ- in Latin (ch. iii. § 24, p. 174), so that the exact origin of the Latin suffix -ŭo-, -vŏ- is often doubtful. Another element of confusion is that the weak grade of the I.-Eur. suffixes -wŏ-, -ŭwŏ- (-wĕ-, -ŭwĕ-, see § 2) was ŭ, which opened the way to these stems coalescing with ŭ-stems.

The UO-suffix is much used in Latin and in Teutonic in adjectives denoting colour, e. g. Lat. *helvus* (O. H. G. gelo, Engl. yellow, from **ĝhĕl-wo-), furvus, flāvus, rāvus*, &c. Greek Verbal Adjectives in -τεος for **-τεϝος, with Gerundive force, e. g. διωκτέος, requiring to be pursued, capable of being pursued (cf. O. Ind. kártva-, kártuva-, 'requiring to be done'), are in Latin represented by formations in *-uus*, e. g. *caeduus, excĭpuus, praecĭpuus, conspĭcuus*, while another class of Verbal Adjectives, denoting state or condition, end in *-tīvus*, e. g. *nātīvus, captīvus, vōtīvus*. These Adjectives in *-tīvus* seem to be derived from Verbal Nouns with a TIO-suffix or a TI-suffix (cf. *furtīvus* from **furti-*, a stem seen in Adv. *furtim*, ch. ix. § 4; *sēmentīvus* from *sementis*, Late Lat. *sementium*, Rönsch, *Collect*. p. 209), though some have tried to connect them with Sanskrit Gerundives in -tavyà-, e. g. O. Ind. kartavyà-, 'requiring to be done.' (See Thurneysen, *Verba auf -io*, p. 41; von Planta, *Gramm. Osk.-Umbr.* i. p. 169), while Verbal Adjectives of the same sense in *-īvus*, e. g. *rĕcĭdīvus* [cf. *cadivus* (morbus), 'the falling sickness,' in Gaulish Latin, e. g. Marc. Emp. xx. 93], *sub-sĕcīvus*, O. Lat. *vocīvos* from *vocare* (classical *văcare*), may come from Verbal Nouns with an IO-suffix. The forms *dē-cĭduus, văcuus* are not phonetic developments of these, but follow the analogy of Gerundive Adjectives like *caeduus, excipuus*, &c.

§ 6. I.-Eur. Stems in -wŏ-. I.-Eur. *gṇī-wŏ-, 'alive, lively' (O. Ind. jīvá-, O. Ir. biu, W. byw, Goth. qius, Lith. gývas, O. Sl. živŭ), Lat. *vīvus*; I.-Eur.

*laiwo-, 'left' (Gk. λαι(F)όs, O. Sl. lĕvŭ), Lat. *laevus*, probably connected with Engl. slow, from Teut. *slaiwa-. Similarly Lat. *calvus* (O. Ind. kulva-) ; Lat. *scaevus* (Gk. σκαι(F)όs) ; Lat. *clīvus* (Goth. hlaiv Neut. 'tomb,' O. Engl. hlāw, hlǣw, 'hill,' esp. 'grave-hill,' Sc. law) from the root k̑lei-, 'to lean, slope.' The thematic vowel is inserted in I.-Eur.*wĭdh-ĕ-wo-, 'unmarried, widowed' [O. Ind. vidháva-, Gk. ἠ-ίθεοs ; cf. Goth. viduvō (n-stem), O. Sl. vĭdova, 'a widow,' O. Ir. fedb, W. gweddw]. Lat. *vĭduus*, from the root weidh-, 'to separate,' of Lat. *dī-vĭdo*, &c.

§ 7. **Latin Verbal Adjectives in -uus, -īvus, -tīvus.** *Relĭcuus* (rather *relicuos*) is a word of four syllables in Plautus, and indeed in all the Republican literature, though it afterwards became *reliquos* and finally *relicus* ; similarly *dēlicuus*, &c. (see Bersu, *die Gutturalen*, p. 59). This ending *-uus* (*-uos*), indicating state or condition, is seen in *contĭnuus*, *ingĕnuus*, *assĭduus* (whence the Adverb *assĭduo*, for the sake of a pun with which Plautus coins the form *accŭbuo*, *Truc.* 422), *exĭguus*, *ambĭguus* [though we find other Compounds like *prōdĭgus* from *ăgo* (*prodigivus* in the Comm. Lud. Saec.), *indĭgus* from *ĕgeo* with the O-suffix] ; from first conj. verbs we have *ăruus*, *irrĭguus* (*irrĭgīvus* Cato), *văcuus* (*vocīvus* Plaut.) ; from *ineo* we have *Inuus*. Derivative IO-stems from these are e.g. *reliquiae*, *deliquium*. Examples of Adjectives, &c. in *-uus*, derived from nouns, are : *annuus* from *annus* (O-stem), *Mĭnerva* for *menes-uā* (cf. O. Ind. manas-vín-, 'intelligent') from *menes-, 'intelligence' (O. Ind. mánas-, Gk. μένεσ-), a quadrisyllable in Plautus (ch. iv. § 148), *strēnuus* (cf. Gk. στρῆνοs, health, Engl. stern, Pruss. sturnawiskan, 'earnest'), *patruus* from *păter* (R-stem). Another example of a Gerundive Verbal Adjective in *-uus* is *pascuus*, fit for pasture, intended for pasture, with which Plautus contrasts *ăruus*, fit for ploughing (*Truc.* 149) :

non aruos hic, sed pascuos ager est ;

(cf. Cic. *de Rep.* v. 2. 3 agri arvi et arbusti et pascui), whence *arvum*, with O. Lat. *aruae* Plur., a field for ploughing. Of Nouns and Adjectives in *-īvus*, *-īva*, which some would make Derivative IO-stems of Adjectives in *-uus* (*recidīvus* from *reciduus* ; but cf. *deliquium*, *reliquiae* from *delicuus*, *relicuus*), examples are : *internĕcivus* (cf. *internecio* and *internecium*) from *nĕcare*, *subsĭcivus* [cf. *i(n)sicium*, *fēni-sicium*] from *sĕcare*. (*Subsicivus* denotes what remains over and above a division of land, &c., hence *subsicivus ager*, spare land, *subsicivum tempus*, spare time, whence the proverb *subsicivis operis*, Cic. *de Orat.* ii. 89. 364). Another word often confused with this last, viz. *succisivus*, from *succīdo*, shows the more usual mode of derivation, from a Verbal Noun TI- or TIO-stem (cf. *succīsio*), like *passivus*, *fŭgĭtivus*. *Lĭxivus*, whence the derivative IO-stem *lĭxivius*, comes from *lixius*, derived from *lĭxa*, water, lye, *lĭxare (Ital. lessare), to boil, words connected with the root wleiq%2 of Lat. *liquor*, O. Ir. fliuch, 'wet' (see *Class. Rev.* v. 10). The O. Lat. word *sonivius* (Paul. Fest. 409. 6 Th. 'sonivio,' sonanti) used in the augur's phrase *sonivium tripudium* (Serv. ad *A*. iii. 90 ; cf. Fest. 422. 19 Th.), will, if the second syllable is long, be similarly related to *sŏnare*, as *lixivus* to *lĭxare*, *subsicivus* to *subsicare*, &c. [*Nŏcivus*, Plin. Phaedr., &c. from *nŏceo*, I.-Eur. *nŏkéyō (ch. viii. § 23), has been compared to O. Sl. chodī-vŭ, 'wandering,' from chodī-ti, 'to go,' ljubī-vŭ, 'loving,' from ljubī-ti, 'to love'].

The I.-Eur. suffixes -twŏ-, -twā-, or -tŭwŏ-, -tŭwā-, closely connected with the Verbal Noun suffix -tu- (§ 47), are frequent in O. Ind. and Slav. (e.g.

O. Ind. kár-tuva-, kár-tva-, 'requiring to be dòne,' kár-tva-m, 'a task'; cf. Gk. -τε(F)os of διωκ-τέος, &c.), but hardly appear in Latin ; e. g. *mor-tuus* (O. Sl. mrĭ--tvŭ) ; *Fā-tuus* another name of Faunus, the god of prophecy, derived from *fā-ri* (but *fătuus*, foolish, with short *a*, means literally 'gaping,' from *fătiscor*, &c.). In *mūtuus* the t belongs to the Verb-stem (cf. Lett. meetōt, 'to exchange,' Goth. maiþms, 'a gift ').

§ 8. **-NŎ-, -NĀ-.** The I.-Eur. suffix -nŏ-, Fem. -nā-, seems to vary with the higher grades -ĕnŏ-, -ĕnā-, and -ŏnŏ-, -ŏnā- ; sometimes a vowel-sound seems to precede the nasal, representing some such variation as -ənŏ-, -ənā- (ch. iv. § 81). Its chief use is in the formation of Verbal Adjectives, usually with the force of a Perfect Participle Passive ; thus in Sanscrit a certain number of Verbs have P. P. P. in -ná-, the others in -tá- (I.-Eur. -to-, § 27), and likewise in Teutonic and Balto-Slavic, e. g. O. Ind. pūrṇá-, ' filled,' O. Engl. bunden, ' bound,' O. Sl. danŭ, ' given.' In Latin, as in Greek, the P. P. P. suffix is -to-, but traces of a similar use of -no- are found in words like *plēnus*, full (cf. *implētus*) ; while of Verbal Nouns formed with this suffix we have, e. g. *dōnum* (O. Ind. dána- N., O. Ir. dān), *somnus* from the root swep-, ' to sleep ' (O. Ind. svápna- M., Arm. k'un, O. Ir. suan, O. Engl. swefen, Lith. sãpnas ; cf. Gk. ὕπνος, O. Sl. sŭnŭ). An N-stem which passes into the O-declension shows this suffix; thus *rĕgnum* (ch. ii. § 144) may be from stem *rēgen- (cf. O. Ind. rāján-, 'rule'). The suffix is preceded by s in *lūna* for *luxna (cf. *losna* on an old Praenestine mirror, *C. I. L.* i. 55) (Zend raoxšna-, ' shining,' Pruss. lauxnos Pl., ' stars '). In Greek we find some Adjectives of Time in -ῐνος, derived from a Locative Case ending in ῐ, e.g. χειμερι-νός (Lat. *hībernus* for *himrĭ-no-*, ch. iv. § 77), ἐαρι-νός (Lat. *vernus*), ἑσπερι-νός (cf. Lat. *vesperna*), &c. Adjectives in -*ĭnus* in Latin like *făgĭnus, juncĭnus* show an I.-Eur. suffix -ĭnŏ-, denoting material or origin, e. g. Gk. φήγ-ῐνος, made of beech-wood, βύβλῐνος, made of papyrus, &c. In Latin, owing to the weakening of vowels in unaccented syllables, -*ĭnus* may represent an older -ănŏ-, -ĕnŏ-, -ŏnŏ-, &c., as well as -ĭnŏ- ; and, owing to the syncope of such vowels, -*nus* may represent the same formations. It is however often possible to distinguish between original -no- and original -ĭno-, &c.; thus *pōpulnus*, made of poplar-wood, must have had originally a vowel between the *l* and the *n*, for original *ln* becomes *ll* in Latin (e. g. *collis* for

§ 8.]   NOUN AND ADJECTIVE STEMS. -NŎ-, -NĀ-.   325

*colnis; cf. Lith. káłnas; see ch. iv. § 78). The suffix -ῑνος in Greek, denoting species, occurs frequently with names of animals, e. g. δελφακ-ίνη from δέλφαξ, κορακ-ῖνος from κόραξ; and similarly in Latin we have bŏvīnus, ĕquīnus, suīnus (Goth. sv-ein, Engl. swine, O. Sl. sv-inŭ), fibrīnus (O. H. G. bibir-īn; cf. Zend bawraęniš, Lith. bebr-ìnis), &c., the feminine often being employed with ellipse of căro, as vĭtŭlina, veal, suina, pork, &c. Latin -īnus is often due to the addition of the NO-suffix to IO-stems, e. g. Lătīnus from Latium (though, when the suffix -īno-, and not -no-, is added, we have -iēnus, e. g. ălienus from alius, lăniena from lanius, with the same dissimilation of the i- and e-vowels, as in pietas instead of *piitas, mĕdietas instead of *mediitas, &c., Engl. ' yet,' ' yes,' for 'yit,' ' yis '), or to I-stems, e. g. mărīnus from mare, piscina from piscis, omninō from omnis. It is often seen in the transference of an ION-stem into the Ŏ- or Ā-declension (cf. § 55 on ĕpŭlōnus beside epulo), e. g. in names of gods like Jugatinus, ' qui conjuges jungit,' from jŭgātio, Potina, the goddess worshipped when a child first took milk (Non. 108. 17 M.), from pōtio, &c. Lat. -īno may also represent an earlier -aino-, &c., for ai in the unaccented syllable, became ei, which passed into ī, but Osc. deiv-ino-, &c. proves an original -īno- for dīvīnus, &c. The suffix -tīnus of diu-tinus, cras-tinus, pris-tinus, &c., corresponding to the O. Ind. suffix -tna-, -tana- used to form Adjectives from Adverbs of Time, e. g. divā-tana- and divā-tána-, 'daily,' nū-tna-, nū-tana-, ' of the present time,' pra-tná-, ' former,' &c., may be connected with O. Ir. tan, ' time,' and so be more strictly the second element of a compound than a mere suffix, just as -gnus in privi-gnus, bignae, twins (Paul. Fest. 24. 25 Th.), represents the root ĝen-, of gĕnus, gigno, &c. The -gnus of īlignus, sălignus, lărignus on the other hand shows the suffix -no-, the g being the development before n (ch. iv. § 119) of the final c of the stems ilĭc-is, salĭc-is, larĭc-is, and was by their analogy extended to other tree-adjectives like abiegnus from ăbiēs, Gen. abiĕt-is [ferrūgĭnus (cf. aurīgĭneus, fūlīgineus) adds the O-suffix to the stem of ferrūgĭn-is]. Similarly -ānus, the ending of Adjectives formed with the NO-suffix from Ā-stems, e. g. silvānus, arcānus, is extended to Adjectives from other stems, e. g. urbānus. By the addition of this NO-suffix to Nomina Agentis in -or we get

-*urnus*, e.g. *tăcĭturnus* (and -*urnius*, e.g. *Plausurnius*) ; while ES-stems give -*ēnus* ; e.g. *ahēnus*, Umbr. ahesno- from *aes*, I.-Eur. *ayes- ; *vĕnēnum*, lit. ' philtre,' ' love-potion,' for **vĕnĕs-no-* (cf. *Vĕnus*); *ĕgēnus* (cf. *ĕges-tas*), &c. ; we have -*ūna* from a U-stem in *lăcūna*. A common use of the NO-suffix in Latin is to form Distributive Numerals, e.g. *quăterni, bīni, trīni, terni* (see ch. vi. §§ 59, 61, 63).

§ 9. I.-Eur. NO-suffix. I.-Eur. *oi-no-, 'one' [Gk. οἴνη, the ace on dice, (though οἶος, Cypr. οἶϝος, alone, has the WO-suffix, like Zend aēva-, ōiva-), O. Ir. oen, W. un, Goth. ains, Lith. vénas, O. Sl. inŭ), Lat. *ūnus*. Similarly Lat. *cānus* for **caisnus* (cf. *cascus*), Osc. *casnar*, an old man ; Lat. *urna* for **urcna* (cf. *urceus*) ; Lat. *quernus* for **quercnus* ; Lat. *agnus* (Gk. ἀμνός for *ἀβ-νος, O. Ir. uan, W. oen ; cf. O. Sl. jagnę) ; Lat. *grānum* from root ger-, 'to rub down, wear out' (O. Ind. jīrṇá-, ' rubbed down,' Goth. kaurn, ' corn,' O. Sl. zrĭno).

§ 10. Latin -nus. Other examples are *păter-nus, māter-nus*, from R-stems ; *alter-nus, infer-nus, exter-nus ; prōnus* from the preposition *pro*, as Osc. amno-, 'a circuit,' from the preposition am- (Lat. *ambi*-), Osc. com(o)no-, Umbr. kumno-, corresponding to the Latin *cŏmĭtium*, from the preposition com ; *mātĕrinus* from *materiēs* (-*ĭn*- probably) ; from U-stems *trĭbūnus*, (cf. *pĕcūnia*). The suffix -ĕno-, -ŏno- appears in O. Lat. *Duenos, bĕne* (cf. *bĕnignus, bellus* for **ben-lus*), O. Lat. *duonus, bŏnus* from the same root as O. Ind. dúvas-, ' honour.' From *sarcio* we have *sarcĭna*, from *pango* (*compāges*), *pāgĭna*, from *ango, angĭna*, from *sto, destina*, a prop (cf. *destĭnāre*, like *lancĭnāre*, &c., ch. viii. § 10).

§ 11. Latin -īnus. From Ā-stems, names of animals, we have *ăquĭlinus, formīcinus, noctuinus, mustēlinus, cŏlumbinus, vĭpĕrinus*, &c., and from names of persons, *Agrippina, Jŭgurthinus, Messālina, Sĭbyllinus*, &c. Other examples are : from O-stems, *dīv-inus, vīcinus* ; from an R-stem, *sobr-inus* (for **sosr-inus* from *sŏror*, I.-Eur *swĕsor-*) ; from U-stems, *gĕnuinus dens*, from **genus*, the jaw (Gk. γένυς), *veruina* from *vĕru* ; from Verbs in -*io, offĭcina, fŏdina*. (For a list of Nouns in -*ina*, see Rönsch, *Collectanea*, p. 199).

§ 12. Latin -ānus. (See *A. L. L.* i. 177.) From town-names of the first declension we have *Rōmanus, Căpuanus*, &c. Names of persons in -*ānus* are usually derived from place-names, and often preserve the names of lost towns ; e.g. *Apscillanus* points to a town **Apscilla* (*Eph. Epigr.* ii. pp. 25-92). Derivative Adjectives from the fem. of ordinal numbers show -*ānus*, e.g. *undĕcĭmani* from *undecima*, sc. *lĕgio, cohors*. So *decimanus* from *decima*, sc. *pars*, the tenth part, tithe, e.g. *ager decimanus*, land paying tithes, an adjective which somehow acquired the sense of large, huge, e.g. *decumana scuta, decumanus fluctus, decumana ova*, all quoted by Paul. Fest. (3. 31 ; 50. 27 Th.), *decimanus acipenser*, Lucil. iv. 6 M. The same ending appears in some names of gods which are derived from Verbs of the first conjugation, e.g. *Levana* from *lĕvāre*, to lift, the goddess who protected the newly-born child when first lifted from the ground, *Tutana* from *tūtāri, Praestana* from *praestāre*, &c. The ending -*iānus*, properly affixed to iā-stems, e.g. *Octāvianus* from *Octāvia*, sc. *gens* (the cognomen of a person who had passed by adoption from the gens Octavia to another

§§ 9–13.] NOUN AND ADJECTIVE STEMS. -MĔNŎ-, -MĔNĀ-. 327

gens), was much affected with N-stems, e.g. *Cicerōnianus*, *Pīsōnianus*, which seem to have pleased the Roman ear more than *Ciceron-anus*, *Pison-anus*, and was in time extended to other Proper Name-stems, e.g. *Caesăriānus* (but *Caesarīnus* in Cicero, &c.). The ending *-ītānus*, e.g. *Abdērītanus*, was produced by adding the Roman termination to the Greek *-ίτης*, e.g. 'Aβδηρίτης; so *Neāpŏlītanus*, *Pănormītanus*, &c. The ending *-īcānus* often denotes a resident alien as opposed to a native, e.g. *Africanus*, an Africander, opposed to *Afer*, *Gallicanus*, to *Gallus*. (Varro, *L. L.* i. 32. 2: legumina Gallicani quidam 'legarica' appellant.)

The Romance languages point to a great extension of the *-ānus* endings in Vulgar and Late Latin, e.g. Fr. certain from *certānus*, moyen from *mediānus*.

§ 13. -MĔNŎ-, -MĔNĀ-. Other grades of this suffix were -mŏnŏ-, -mŏnā-, and -mnŏ-, -mnā-, &c. In Latin -mĕno- and -mŏno- would both become *-mĭno-* or (by Syncope) *-mno-* (cf. *lamna*, earlier *lammina*). The suffix was used in the Middle or Passive Participles of Thematic Tenses of the I.-Eur. Verb (e.g. O. Ind. bhára-māṇa-, Gk. φερό-μενος); and although the Pres. Part. Passive was lost in Latin, traces of this formation remain in the 2 Pl. Pres. Ind., e.g. *lĕgĭmini* for *legimini estis* (while *legimini*, 2 Pl. Pres. Imper., may equally stand for the Inf., Gk. λεγέμεναι, used in Imperatival sense; see ch. viii. § 81), *ălumnus*, ὁ τρεφόμενος (sometimes a nurse, as in the *Ciris*, 441: communis alumna omnibus, of the earth), *fē-mina* from the root dhē(y)-, ' to give suck,' *Vertumnus*, the god of the changing seasons, from *verto*, *Volumnus*, the deity who guarded new-born children, from *vŏlo*, **calumnus* (cf. *călŭmnia*) from *calu-or*, *calvor*, to deceive. Analogous, but irregular, formations seem to be O. Lat. *pilumnoe poploe*, from *pīlum*, a javelin, used of the Romans in the Carmen Saliare (Fest. 244. 24 Th.), like classical *pilāni*, and the names of deities, *Pilumnus*, from *pīlum*, a pestle, *Vitumnus*, ' per quem vivescat infans,' from *vīta*, &c. We find -mo- (from an earlier -mno- ?) in Umbro-Oscan Imperative forms like Umbr. *persnihimu* ' supplicato,' Osc. *censamur* ' censetor '; cf. Lat. *praefāminō*, *antestāminō* (see ch. viii. § 60). Sometimes the suffix is used in the transference of a MEN- or MON-stem into the ŏ- or ā-declension, e.g. *cŏlumna*, beside *cŏlŭmen* (cf. *columella* for **columen-la*), *terminus*, beside *termen* and *termo* (quoted by Festus, 550. 22 Th., from Ennius, e.g. *A.* 591 M.: qua redditus termo est).

The ending *-mnus* in Latin often arises from the addition of the suffix -no- to a stem ending in a labial consonant, e.g. *som-*

nus for **sopnus* (cf. *sŏpor*), *damnum* (cf. Gk. δαπάνη), *scamnum* (cf. *scabellum*), &c.

§ 14 -MŎ-, -MĀ-. This suffix was used to form Adjectives (e.g. Gk. φύξιμος from φύξις, λύσιμος from λύσις) and Nouns, especially Masculine nouns, but sometimes Fem. (e.g. Gk. Abstracts in -μός like λῑ-μός, λοι-μός). Examples are I.-Eur. *dhūmós (O. Ind. dhūmás, Gk. θῡμός, Lith. dúmai Pl., O. Sl. dymŭ), Lat. *fūmus*, from the root dheu- ; I.-Eur. *gh^{u}ormós, *gh^{u}ermos (O. Ind. gharmás, ' warmth,' Arm. ǰerm, ' warm,' Gk. θερμός, Engl. warm), Lat. *formus*, from the root gh^{u}er-.

It was also used to form Superlatives (with Comparative in -ĕro-, ch. vi. § 52), e.g. Lat. *summus* for **s-up-mo*, with Comp. *s-ŭpero-* (O. Ind. upamá-, with Comp. úpara-; cf. O. Engl. yf(e)m-est). In Latin *pulcerrimus* for **pulcersimus*, **pulcrĭsimus*, it is affixed to the Comparative suffix -is- of *măgĭs*, &c. The more usual Superlative suffix however was -temo- (-t°mo-) (with ' Comparative ' in -tĕro-, ch. vi. § 52), e.g. Lat. *in-timus*, with ' Comp.' *intero-* (O. Ind. án-tama-, with ' Comp.' án-tara-). (On the Lat. Superlative see ch. vi. § 54.) But originally this suffix, like the Comparative -tero- (ch. vi. § 52), had the sense rather of likeness (O. Ind. gó-tama-, lit. ' like an ox '), or position (Lat. *mărĭtimus*, older *mari-tumus*, lit. ' placed by the sea '). The Ordinal Numeral ending *-mus* of *dĕcĭmus*, &c. may owe its *m* to the final of the Cardinal Numeral stem ; but -t°mo- appears in *vīcēsimus*, &c. (ch. vi § 74).

§ 15. Other Examples : (1) of the Noun- or Adjective-suffix. Lat. *ănimus* (Gk. ἄνε-μος) ; Lat. *fāma* (Gk. φή-μη) ; Lat. *pal-ma* (Gk. παλά-μη, O. Ir. lă-m Fem., O. Engl. fol-m Fem.) ; Lat. *culmus* (Gk. κάλα-μος, O. Engl. healm, Lett. sal-ms, O. Sl. sla-ma Fem.) ; Lat. *dūmus*, O. Lat. *dusmus* Adj. (Liv. Andr. dusmo in loco) (cf. O. Ir. doss, ' a bush ') ; Lat. *līmus* (O. H. G. līm, Engl. lime).

(2) Of the Superlative suffix, (*a*) alone : Lat. *mĭnĭmus*, *brūma* from *brĕvis* for *breghu-* (cf. Gk. βραχύς) ; Lat. *infĭmus* beside *infĕrus*. (*b*) With *-is-* : *cĕlerrimus*, *făcillimus*, *sĭmillimus*, &c.. The suffix -temo- (-t°mo-) has its original sense in *fīnī-timus*, *lēgĭ-timus*, *aedĭ-tumus*, a temple attendant, which was changed in Varro's time to *aedi-tuus*, through a false reference of the word to *tueor* (Varro R. R. i. 2. 1) ab aeditimo, ut dicere didicimus a patribus nortris, ut corrigimur a recentibus urbanis, ab ' aedituo '; cf. Gell. xii. 10). *Ultimus* (Osc. últiumo-) is Superl. of *ulterior*, *cĭtimus* of *citerior*, &c.

§ 16. -RŎ-, -RĀ-. This suffix in its various forms was used to form Adjectives and Concrete Nouns, e.g. I.-Eur. *rŭdhró-, 'red,' from the root reudh- (O. Ind. rudh-irá-, Gk. ἐ-ρυθρός, O. Sl. rŭdrŭ; cf. O. Scan. rōđra Fem., 'blood'), Lat. *rŭber*; I.-Eur. *ăĝro-*, 'a field,' from the root aĝ-, ' to drive ' (O. Ind. ájra-, Gk. ἀγρός, Goth. akrs), Lat. *ăger*. In Latin the ending *-rŏs* (and *-rĭs*, § 40) became *-er*, as is seen in these two examples [cf. ch. iii. § 15 (8)]. The suffixes -ĕrŏ- and -tĕrŏ-, which in Latin might through Syncope lose the *ĕ* and appear as *-ro-*, *-tro-* have been already mentioned as Comparative Suffixes, corresponding to Superlatives in -mo- (-m̥mo-), -tm̥mo- (-tᵉmo-). Their original sense however was rather that of likeness, of equal than of greater degree, e. g. O. Ind. vatsa-tará-, lit. 'like a calf' (cf. Lat. *mātertera*), and similarly O. Ind. -tama in gó-tama-, lit. 'like an ox,' &c.; and in O. Ir. the suffix -tero- retains this sense, e. g. demnithir, 'equally certain' (not 'more certain'), from demin, 'certain,' while in O. Ind. and Greek it has developed into a regular Comparative suffix (but cf. Hom. θηλύτερος, ἀγρότερος). Latin nouns like *fīliaster, matraster, patraster* have this suffix with a prefixed *-as-* (see Ascoli, *Suppl. Arch. Glott.* i), while in *măg-is-ter, mĭn-is-ter*, the Comparative sense belongs to the suffix *-is-*, not to the suffix *-ter*; *cĭter, exter*, &c. are not Comparatives; *ci-ter-ior, ex-ter-ior*, &c. are. (On the Latin Comparative, see ch. vi. § 53). Latin Adverbs in *-ĭter* have probably this suffix, e. g. *brĕviter* (see ch. ix. § 2); though some have explained *-iter* as the noun *ĭter*, a way, so that *brev-iter* would correspond to the German adverb kurz-weg. It is used in Possessive Pronouns in Latin, e. g. *vester*, as in Gk., e. g. ὑμέτερος, and in various pronominal and locative Adjectives, with the sense of 'like,' 'in the direction of,' e. g. *al-ter, ĭ-terum, sŭp-erus*, to which Adverbs with -(t)ro- correspond, e. g. *intrō* (ch. iii. § 15). This suffix -tero-, in Lat. -tero- or -tro-, must be distinguished from the I.-Eur. suffix TRO-, which was used to form Neuter nouns indicating an instrument, &c., e. g. *ărā-trum*, 'an instrument for ploughing,' a plough, and from the Latin suffix -cro- which represents the stem *cĕro-*, making, from the root ker-, 'to make' (cf. Lat. *Cerus, creare*, &c.), e.g. *lūdĭ-cer*, or stands by assimilation for -clo- (I.-Eur. -tlo-) when an *l* precedes, e. g. *involū-crum* for *involu-clum (ch. ii. § 101). This -clo- (I.-Eur. -tlo-) is a suffix closely associated with -tro-, forming Neuter Nouns which indicate a tool or instrument. Another suffix, -dhro-, is used in the same way, though in Latin it affects also the Feminine gender, *-bra* for *-frā, *-dhrā (ch. iv. § 114), e. g. *tĕrĕbra*, a gimlet, borer, from *tero*, to bore; *crībrum*, a sieve, from *cerno*, to sift. Latin *-ōrus*, of *honōrus, dĕcōrus, cănōrus, ŏdōrus*, &c. stands for *-ōso-* (§ 74); we have *-ĕrus* in e. g. *sĕvĕrus, prōcĕrus*.

§ 17. **Other examples of the RO-suffix.** Lat. *pro-sper*, stem *pro-spĕro-* for **pro-spăro-*, with the weak grade (ch. iv. § 51) of the root of *spēs* (O. Ind. sphirá-, O. Sl. sporŭ); Lat. *vĭr* (O. Ir. fer, Goth. vair, Engl. wer-wolf; cf. O. Ind. vīrá-, Lith. výras); Lat. *tĕnĕbrae* for **temes-rae* (O. Ind. tamis-ram, támis-rā, O. H. G. dinstar); Lat. *căper* (Gk. κάπ-ρος, O. Engl. hæfer); Lat. *măcer* (Gk. μακ-ρός); Lat. *plē-rus, gnā-rus, in-tĕger, glăber* for **gladhro-* (cf. O. Sl. gladŭkŭ, 'smooth'), *cĕrĕbrum* for **ceres-rum* (cf. O. Ind. śíras-, 'head'), *mātū-rus* (cf. *pēnūria*). (On Fut. Part. in *-tūrus*, see ch. viii. § 86.)

§ 18. **Examples of I.-Eur. -tĕro- and -ĕro- in Latin:** (1) attached to Nouns. Adjectives formed with this suffix from Nouns seem to have passed into i-stems in Latin (cf. § 34); they have often a locative sense and correspond to Adjectives in *-tĭmus* like *mărĭtimus, fīnĭtimus* : e. g. *camp-ĕs-ter, silv-es-ter*, &c. which take *-es-* by the Analogy of Neuter ES-stems (cf. Gk. ὀρέσ-τερος, &c.); *ĕques-ter* for **equit-tri-*, *pĕdester* for **pedit-tri-* ; *pălūster* for **palūd-tri-, tellūs-ter*. The ending *-aster* of Nouns or Adjectives, especially in Vulgar or colloquial Latin (cf. Ital. giovinastro, poetastro), derived from Nouns or Adjectives, implies likeness, and is often used contemptuously in the sense of 'a poor imitation of,' e. g. *pĕdĭtaster*, of which Plautus uses the Diminutive in the sense of 'tagrag and bob-tail soldiery' in *Mil.* 54 :

at péditastelli quía erant, siui uíuerent,

Antōniaster (Cic. *fragm. orat. pro Vareno*, 10); *ŏleaster*, wild olive, and similarly *ăpiastrum*, wild parsley, &c.; *fīliaster*, a stepson, *mātrastra*, a stepmother, *pătraster*, a stepfather; *surdaster*, with other Adjectives indicating bodily defects, such as *calvaster, claudaster*, and the diminutive *rāvastellus* from *rāvus*, grey (v. l. *grāvastellus*; cf. Gk. γραῦς?) in Plaut. *Epid.* 620. Derivative Adjectives show *-ast(r)īnus*, e. g. *mĕdiastinus* and *mediastrinus, oleastinus, fīliastinus*. (On these formations in *-aster*, see A. L. L. i. 390.)

(2) Attached to Prepositions, &c. : Lat. *sŭpero-* (O. Ind. úpara-, Gk. ὕπερος, O. Engl. ufer-ra with *-ra* for Goth. *-iza*), *sŭp-er* and *sub-ter*; Lat. *inter-ior* (O. Ind. ántara-, Gk. ἔντερον, the entrails, O. Sl. jętro Neut., 'the liver'); Lat. *exter* (O. Ir. echtar), *postero-, postrī-diē, contrā, praeter* (ch. ix. § 2). Other locative words are *cĭ-ter* (Goth. hi-drē, 'hither'), *dex-ter* (Gk. δεξι-τερός), *sĭn-is-ter*.

(3) Forming Pronouns: Lat. *ŭ-ter*, Osc. potoro- (cf. O. Ind. katará-, Gk. πότερος, Goth. hvaþar, Lith. katràs); *ĭterum*, for another time, again, from *itero-*, other (O. Ind. ítara-, 'other'). The suffix often expresses that a pair of persons or things is spoken of, e. g. *al-ter*, the other (of a pair), but *ălius*, another (of many). The Possessives 'our,' 'your' take *-tero-* in Latin, *nos-ter, ves-ter*, and Greek ἡμέ-τερος, ὑμέ-τερος, but *-ero-* in Teutonic, e. g. Goth. unsar, Germ. unser.

§ 19. **I-Eur. -tro-.** Lat. *ărā-trum* (cf. Gk. ἄρο-τρον, Arm. arōr, Ir. arathar, W. arad(r) from *aro* (*arātus*); *spectrum* from *spĕcio* (*spectus*); *rŭtrum* from *ruo* (*rŭtus*); *vĕrĕtrum* from *vereor* (*verĭtus*) (so *fulgetrum* from *fulgeo* ; cf. *tŏnĭtru* from *tono*, *tonĭtus* A. L. L. i. 111); *mulctrum*, a milkpail, from *mulgeo* (*mulctus*) ; *rōstrum* from *rōdo*. We find -stro- in Lat. *căpistrum*, a halter, from *căpio* (or for **capittrum* from *căput*?), *monstrum* from *mŏneo* (cf. O. H. G. gal-star Neut., 'a song,' from galan, 'to sing'), &c. The Dim. of *monstrum* is *mostellum* (ch. iv. § 158).

§ 20. I.-Eur. d-hro-. The Greek and O. Ir. cognates of Lat. *tĕrĕbra* show the suffix -tro- (Gk. τέρετρον, O. Ir. tarathar Neut.); so O. Ir. criathar, 'a sieve,' for *kreitron (cf. Lat. *palpĕbra* and *palpĕtra*). Other examples of Lat. -*bra* are *dōlā-bra*, from *dolāre*, whence the name (originally a nickname) *Dōlābella*, *lătĕ-bra*, lit. 'a place for hiding,' from *lateo*, *vertĕ-bra* from *vertĕrc*, *pel-lĕcĕ-bra* from *lacio*, to allure (cf. κήλη-θρον from κηλέω). Examples of Lat. -*brum* are *flā-brum* from *flāre*, O. Lat. *polubrum* (quod Graeci χέρνιβον, nos trullum vocamus, Non. 544. 20 M.) from *pŏ-luo* in the sense of *ab-luo* (cf. ch. ix. § 12), *dēlūbrum*, *ventĭlā-brum* from *ventĭlā-re*. (On the possibility of referring all these forms to the suffix -dhlo-, see § 26). Latin -*bro*-, -*brā*- also represent an original -s-ro-, -s-rā- (ch. iv. § 152), e. g. *tĕnĕbrae* (O. Ind. támisrā-) from **temis*, **temus* darkness (cf. *tĕmĕre*), *cĕrĕbrum* (cf. O. Ind. śíras-, 'the head'); and some would explain *terebra*, &c. as *teres-rā, from the Verbal Noun-stem teresseen in Inf. *terere* (§ 71).

§ 21. -LŎ-, -LĀ-. This suffix in its various forms was used for Nomina Agentis (Nouns and Adjectives), and often came to denote an instrument, while as a secondary suffix it was specially used to form Diminutives. Thus Engl. shovel, literally 'an instrument with which one shoves,' meant originally 'the shover'; Engl. throstle, is a Diminutive. Latin examples are *lĕgŭlus*, a picker, from *lego*, *pendŭlus*, hanging, from *pendo*, *pendeo*, *vincŭlum*, a bond, 'an instrument for binding,' from *vincio*, *mensŭla*, a little table, from *mensa*. In Latin, since every short vowel in a syllable which had not the accent under the early Accent Law (ch. iii. § 5) became before *l* the short *u*-vowel, it is impossible to distinguish -ĕlo- (e.g. Gk. νεφέλη, Lat. *nĕbŭla*), from -ŭlo- (e.g. Gk. παχυλός, O. Ind. bahulá-), &c. Further, owing to the tendency to insert a short *u*-vowel between a consonant and *l* to facilitate pronunciation (ch. ii. § 102), it is not always possible to decide whether the original suffix was -lo- or -ĕlo-, -ŭlo-, &c., though in words like *exemplum*, &c. (as contrasted with words like *trĕmulus*, &c.) it is clear that no vowel intervened between the final consonant of the root and the LO-suffix. The wave of Syncope which passed over the Latin language reduced all these formations in Late and Vulgar Latin to -*lus*, -*la*-, -*lum* (e.g. *aurĭ-cŏ-la*, formed by adding the

Diminutive Suffix -*la* to the Diminutive Suffix -*co*- (§ 31), in classical Latin *auricula*, became *auricla*, *ōricla*, whence Ital. orecchia and orecchio, Fr. oreille, &c. (ch. iii. § 13). From these formations with the two Diminutive Suffixes -*co*- and -*lo*- we must distinguish Neuter nouns formed by the suffix -*tlo*-, denoting the instrument with which an action is performed, or the place of its performance. This took in Latin the form -*clum*, or with parasitic vowel -*culum*, e.g. *vĕhĭ-clum* (*vĕhĭculum*), 'that by which one is carried,' *pō-clum* (*pōculum*), 'that out of which one drinks,' *cŭbĭ-clum* (*cŭbĭculum*), 'the place where one lies down'; and we have seen (ch. ii. § 154) that Plautus generally makes this suffix monosyllabic, and the Diminutive -*co-lo*- dissyllabic, e.g. *vĕhĭclum*, *pĕrīclum*, but *corcŭlum*, *uxorcŭla*. The suffix -dhlo- (in Latin -*bŭlum*) had much the same function as -tlo-, e.g. *stăbulum*, 'a place for standing.' The presence of an *l* in the stem of the word causes a dissimilation of -*clum* to -*crum*, -*blum* to -*brum* in *ambŭlā-crum*, 'a place for walking,' &c. (ch. iv. § 84). Beside Neuters in -*bŭlum* we have Passive Adjectives in -*bĭlis*, with much the same sense as the Passive Adjectives in -*lis*, e.g. *ăgĭ-bilis*, that can or ought to be driven, from *ăgo*, like *ăgĭlis*, 'that can easily be driven,' nimble.

§ 22. **Adjectives formed by the LO-suffix.** Other examples of Adjectives expressing the action of a Verb are Lat. *bĭbŭlus* from *bĭbo*, *crēdŭlus* from *crēdo*, *trĕmŭlus* from *trĕmo*, *garrŭlus* from *garrio*, *ēmĭnŭlus* from *ēmĭneo*, *pătulus* from *păteo*. With a passive sense they become I-stems in Latin, and indicate capacity, suitability, &c., e. g. *ăgilis* (O. Ind. ajirá-), 'easily driven,' nimble, from *ago*, to drive, *dŏcilis* from *dŏceo*, *frăgilis* from *frango*, *bĭbĭlis* from *bibo*. This -*li*- suffix is often added with the same sense to P. P. P. stems, e. g. *coctĭlis* from *coctus*, *fissĭlis* from *fissus*, *flexĭlis* from *flexus*.

In Adjectives derived from Nouns, &c., we find -*li*-, e.g. *hŭmĭlis* (Gk. χθαμαλός) from *hŭmus*, *herbĭlis* from *herba*, *sĭmĭlis* (Gk. ὁμαλός) (on these see § 40). Active Verbal Adjectives in -*lo*- are used in O. Sl. in the periphrastic perfect tense, e. g. zna-lŭ jesmi, 'I have known,' lit. 'I am acquainted,' from znati, 'to know.'

§ 23. **Nouns denoting the Agent or the Instrument,** e. g. Lat. *fĭgŭlus*, a potter, from *fingo* ; *tēgŭla* from *tĕgo*; *rēgŭla* from *rĕgo* (unless these are Diminutives of **tĕga*, **rēga* ; cf. *col-lēga* ; cf. § 3) ; *căpŭlus* from *căpio* ; *spĕcŭla*, a place of outlook, and *spĕculum*, a looking-glass, from *spĕcio*, to look ; *torcŭlum* (with Adj. *torculus*), a wine-press (later *torcular*), from *torqueo* ; *cingŭlum* and *cingŭlus*, a girdle, from *cingo* ; *jăcŭlum*, (1) a javelin, (2) a throw-net (*rete iaculum*, Plaut. *Truc.* 35), and *jaculus*, a kind of snake, from *jăcio* ; *sella* for **sed-la* (Lac. Gk. ἑλλά) from *sĕdeo* ; *grallae* from *grădior* : *pīlum* for **pinslum*, a pestle, from *pinso*.

§§ 22-25.] NOUN AND ADJECTIVE STEMS. -LŎ-, -LĀ-. 333

Often we have the terminations -slo-, -slā-, e. g. -ālum for *ans-lum, from ans- (cf. O. Sl. ach-ati, ' to be fragrant '), a byform of the root an-, ' to breathe'; pālus for *pax-lus (cf. Diminutive paxillus), from pango ; vēlum, a sail, for *vexlum (cf. vexillum), from vēho (cf. O. Sl. veslo, 'a rudder'). Nouns in -ēla may be derived from Neuter es-stems (e g. quĕrēla for *queres-la, sĕquēla for *seques-la) or may have had originally ē (e. g. çi-cindēla, a glow-worm, from candeo, candē-re, like Gk. μιμηλός from μιμέομαι). These nouns in -ēla were in Late and Vulgar Latin confused with Diminutives and became querĕlla, sequĕlla, &c. (see ch. ii. § 130), just as camēlus became camĕllus, çucūlus became cucullus, anguīla (A. L. L. viii. 442) became anguilla. We have -rum for -lum by dissimilation of l in scalp-rum from scalpo, &c.

§ 24. **Diminutives.** Lat. cistula; auxilla from aula (olla) for *aux-la; porculus (Germ. Ferkel) ; servolus ; fīliolus ; līneola ; lactucula from lactūca ; lŏquāc-ulus ; misellus (occasionally misĕrulus) ; Ātella (Osc. Aderlā-) ; asellus from ăsĭnus ; gemellus from gĕmĭni ; lapillus from lăpĭd-. Sometimes this termination is added a second time, e. g. cistella from cistula ; ollula from olla ; porcellus from porculus ; asellulus from asellus ; gemellulus from gemellus. Sometimes it is added to the Diminutive suffix- co-, e. g. ollĭ-cu-la, servĭ-cu-lus, cor-cu-lum, lĕgiun-cu-la, cănĭ-cu-la (cf. febrī-culōsus, mĕtū-culōsus), ăpĭ-cu-la, vallē-cu-la, diē-cu-la, corpus-cu-lum, artĭ-cu-lus. The Diminutive retains the Gender of the simple Noun, unlike Greek Diminutives in -ιον, which are Neuter (A. L. L. iv. 169). This suffix -cŭlus gives to Adjectives the sense of 'somewhat,' e. g. mĕlius-culus, 'somewhat better,' and other Comparatives like plus-culus, majus-culus, &c. ; also grandĭ-cu'us, dulcĭ-culus, lĕvĭ-culus, &c. With the Diminutive suffix -lo-, familiar or pet names are often formed in I.-Eur. languages, e. g. Gk. Θρασύ-λος, the familiar form of Θρασύ-μαχος, Goth. Vulfi-la. The gradual weakening of the diminutive force of these suffixes, which is to some extent accountable for the doubling of the suffix in puellula, cistella, &c. (cf. anellus from ānulus, Dim. of ānus, a large ring, e. g. Plaut. Men. 85 anum lima praeterunt) is seen in words like ancilla (Fem. of servus), which had ceased to be a Diminutive as early as the time of Plautus. Adulescentulus always differs from ădŭlescens in Plautus, but in Terence is hardly distinguishable. Diminutives were a feature of Vulgar Latin, as we see from the forms censured in the Probi Appendix : juvencus non 'juvenclus' (197. 29 K.) ; catulus non 'catellus' (198. 2), auris non 'oricla' (198. 11 ; cf. Ital. orecchio, Fr. oreille) ; fax non ' facla ' (198. 23) ; neptis non 'nepticla,' anus non 'anucla' (199. 1) ; mergus non 'mergulus' (199. 7). The ending -ĕllus, as we have seen, may denote a Diminutive of a LO-Diminutive, e.g. ānellus (on -ell-, see ch. iv. § 10), Dim. of ānulus, or the Diminutive of a Noun with a RO-suffix, e.g. ăgellus from ăgro- for *agrŏ-lo- (ch. iii. § 15. 8), or of a Noun with ĕ in the penult, e.g. fĕmella from fĕmina (earlier -mena). Similarly we have -illus for -ĭd-lus in lapillus, -ēlla for -ēn-la in catēlla, -ĭllum for -ĭn-lum in vĭllum, -ŭllus (older -ŏllus) for -ŏn-lus in hŏmullus, -ŏlla for -ŏn-la in corōlla, -ŭllus for -ŭn-lus in ūllus, -āllus for -ān-lus in Hispāllus, &c. (cf. nĭtēdula and nĭtēlla).

§ 25. **Neuters formed with the Suffix -tlo-.** Lat. discernĭculum (' acus quae capillos mulierum ante frontem dividit : dictum a discernendo,' Non. 35. 29 M.) ; piāclum (piāculum), 'a means of appeasing the gods,' a victim, then 'a sin for which the gods must be appeased,' from piāre ; rĕceptāculum from receptāre ; pavicula, a mallet, from păvīre ; sediculum from sĕdeo ('sediculum' sedile, Paul. Fest. 500. 9 Th.); ŏperculum from operio (opertus); sĕpulcrum, from sĕpĕlio (sepultus). We have -crum by dissimilation of l-l in lăvā-crum, 'a place for bathing,' from lavāre; invŏlūcrum from involvo, &c.

§ 26. The suffix -dhlo-.

Lat. lătĭbulum, 'a place for hiding,' from lateo; vēnābulum, 'an instrument for hunting,' a hunting-spear, from venāri; vectābulum (quod nunc vehiculum dicitur, Non. 54. 26 M.); concĭlĭābulum (locus ubi in concilium convenitur, Paul. Fest. 27. 9 Th.); cf. făbula, sūbula. We may have -brum by dissimilation of l-l in lăvābrum; and it is possible that some, or all, of the examples of Lat. -brum (I.-Eur. -dhro-), quoted in § 20, had originally -blo- and not -bro-, e. g. po-lubrum. Just as I-stem adjectives with a Passive sense like ăgĭlis, 'easily driven,' are connected with Neuter Instrumentals in -lo- like ăgŭlum ('agolum,' pastorale baculum, quo pecudes aguntur, Paul. Fest. 21. 37 Th.), so we have Passive I-stem Adjectives connected with the suffix -dhlo-, e. g. amā-bĭlis, horrĭ-bĭlis, flē-bĭlis, vŏlū-bĭlis, mō-bĭlis, intellĭgĭ-bĭlis, &c. (cf. Umbr. façefele 'facibile'), sometimes derived from the P. P. P. stem, e. g. persuāsĭ-bĭlis, flexĭ-bĭlis, sensĭ-bĭlis, and sometimes showing -bris (-ber) for -bĭlis, when an l precedes, e. g. ălēbris (and ălĭbĭlis), anclābris. For a list of Adjs. in -bĭlis in early authors (e. g. nōbĭlis, known, Plaut. Pseud. 1112 neque illis nobilis fui; cf. Pacuv. Trag. 221 R.), see Hanssen in Philol. xlvii. 274, who denies that they ever have a transitive sense, e. g. incogitabĭlis, 'thoughtless,' Plaut.

§ 27. -TŎ-, -TĀ-.

This I.-Eur. suffix was used to form (1) Verbal Adjectives, which in Latin and some other languages have the function of perfect participles passive, e. g. gĕnĭ-tus from the root ĝen-, while with the negative particle prefixed they may express incapacity, e. g. I.-Eur. *ņmŗto-, 'incapable of being killed,' immortal (O. Ind. amŕta-, Gk. ἄμβροτος); (2) Ordinal Numbers, and when added to the Comparative suffix -is- (§ 76), Superlatives; e. g. I.-Eur. *sĕksto- (O. Ind. šaš-thá-, Gk. ἕκ-τος, Goth. saihs-ta, an N-stem), Lat. sextus; I.-Eur. *ōk-is-to- (O. Ind. āś-iṣṭha-, Gk. ὤκιστος). In Latin this formation of Superlatives is not found, but another, e. g. ōcissĭmus (ch. vi. § 54). Abstract Nouns in -tā- are found beside Verbal Adjectives in -to-, e. g. Gk. γενετή, birth, Goth. junda 'juventa'[1], which occasionally pass into a concrete sense and become Masculine. e. g. γενέτης, ἱππότης (cf. Lat. ĕques from an earlier Abstract Fem. *equita?), though the suffix in Latin was ousted by -tās, -tūdo, &c. (§ 67). I.-Eur. -to- is often seen added to the MEN-

---

[1] Lat. jŭventa seems to be a formation on the analogy of sĕnecta (sc. aetas), for juventūs is the form used by the oldest writers, both in the sense of 'period of youth' and 'a number of young men.' (Fleck. Jahrb. Suppl. 1891.) We have aetate iuenta on an inscription (C. I. L. i. 1202).

§§ 26–28.] NOUN AND ADJECTIVE STEMS. -TŎ-, -TĀ-. 335

suffix (§ 54) in neuter nouns, e.g. Lat. *cognō-men-tum* beside *cogno-men*, such forms being apparently the Neuter of Participles or Verbal Adjectives, formed not from verbs but from nouns, e.g. **cogno-mentus* beside *cogno-mĭnātus*, like *scĕlestus* beside *scelĕrātus* (cf. Engl. compounds like 'bare-footed,' 'black-headed,' where the participial suffix is added to the nouns 'foot,' 'head'). The forms with *-mentum* are, as a rule, those used by prose writers, the forms with *-men* being relegated to poetry. With *-mentum*, Plur. *-menta* has been compared Gk. Plur. -ματα, e.g. στρώματα (Lat. *strāmenta*), κασσύματα (cf. Lat. *assūmenta*).

§ 28. **Participles in -tus.** The weak grade of the root is used with I.-Eur. verbal adjectives in -to-, and the suffix is accented, e.g. I.-Eur. **klŭ-tó-, 'heard, heard of, famous,' from the root k̑leu-, 'to hear,' [O. Ind. śrutá-, Gk. κλῠτός, which perhaps retains the old sense of 'heard,' 'loud' in such Homeric phrases as κλυτὰ μῆλα, O. Ir. cloth, from *clŭto-, O. H. G. Hlot-hari (from O. H. G. hari, Germ. Heer), the name Lothair, corresponding to Greek Κλυτό-στρατος; cf. Zend srūta-, O. Eng. hlūd, 'loud'], Lat. *in-clŭtus*; though with the noun we often find the high-grade and the accent on the root, e.g. Gk. κοίτη from κεῖμαι, οἶτος from εἶμι, &c. In Latin *-sus* replaced *-tus* when the verbal stem ended *d* or *t* (ch. iv. § 155), e.g. *salsus* from *sallo* for **saldo*; occasionally the P. P. P. took *-sus* when the Perfect Ind. had *-si*, e.g. *tersus* from *tergeo* (Perf. Indic. *tersi*), though the older spelling appears in the earlier literature, e.g. *tertus* (Varro) (see ch. viii. § 92; ch. iv. § 155).

Examples of Latin participles in *-tus* are *strātus* (from the root ster-, O. Ind. stṛta-, Gk. στρωτός, O. Sl. -strĭtŭ); *mulctus* from the root melĝ- (Lith. mìlsztas); *com-mentus* from the root men- (O. Ind. matá-, Gk. αὐτό-ματος, Goth. munds, Lith. miñtas, O. Sl. mętŭ); Lat. *gnātus* from the root ĝen-, **ĝnā- (O. Ind. jātá-, Goth. -kunds); Lat. *sūtus* for *syūto- (O. Ind. syūtá-, Gk. νεο-κάττῡτος, Lith. siútas, O. Sl. šitŭ; Lat. *gnōtus* (O. Ind. jñātá-, Gk. γνωτός, O. Ir. gnāth); Lat. *junctus* (cf. O. Ind. yŭktá-, Gk. ζευκτός). The different treatment of the stem vowel before the suffix is exemplified by *ămātus*, *dŏmĭtus* from first conj. Verbs; *viētus*, *vĕgētus*, *exercĭtus* (but *ar(c)tus*), *mŏnĭtus* (but *Monēta*), *mulctus* from second conj.; *ălĭtus* and *altus*, *cultus*, *factus* (but *făcētus*) from third conj.; *fīnītus* and *ŏpertus* from fourth conj. (On these Verb-stems see ch. viii.); *aegrō-tus*, *argū-tus*, *inclŭ-tus*, *cĭtus* and *cĭtus*. Words like *pīlāti*, 'armed with the *pilum*,' *barbātus* (O. Sl. bradatŭ), *aurītus*, *cinctūtus*, do not of course imply the existence of verbs, **pīlare*, **barbare*, **aurire*, &c. Of similar formations from Noun- or Adjective-stems examples are: Lat. *lībertus* beside *lībĕratus*; *ŏnustus* beside *ŏnĕratus*; *sĕnectus* from *senex*; and the words indicating a place planted with trees, &c., e.g. *arbus-tum*, *sălic-tum*, the Neuters of *arbustus*, 'provided with trees' (arbustus sive silvestris, Columella), &c. (*Arbŏrētum* is a quasi-participle from **arboreo*, *arboresco*, like *ăcētum* from *acesco*; so *nŭc-ētum*, *pīn-etum*, *īlĭc-etum*. The *-cētum* of *ilicetum*, &c. and the *-ctum* of *salictum*, &c. were extended by false analogy, e.g. *būcetum*, *virectum*). For a list of Adjectives in *-estus*, *-ustus*, *-ūtus* with this sense of 'provided with,' see Rönsch, *Collect.* p. 217, and cf. Plaut. *Capt.* 392: qui me honore honestiorem semper fecit et facit). Latin participles in -to- have often become nouns, e.g. *tectum*, *lēgatus*, *rĕpulsa*, *sĕnecta*, or Adjectives (ch. viii. § 92), e.g. *sanctus*, *lātus*, broad (for **stlātus*, from the root stel-, ' to extend,' O. Sl. stelją).

§ 29. Abstract Nouns in -ta (-sa). The Fem. of the Participles *rĕpulsus*, *dĕprensus*, &c. is used in an abstract sense: *repulsa*, 'defeat at an election,' *deprensa*, 'genus militaris animadversionis, castigatione major, ignominia minor' (Paul. Fest. 50. 30 Th.). These Abstracts must be distinguished from Concretes like *torta* (sc. *plăcenta*), a roll, *expensa* (sc. *pĕcūnia*), a sum expended (for a fuller list, see Rönsch, *Collect.* p. 195). The Fem. Abstract **equita*, ' horsemanship,' seems to have been made a Masc. Concrete in O. Lat. with the sense also of ' a horse'; thus Ennius (*A*. 249 M.), describing a charge of cavalry and elephants, says :

> denique ui magna quadrupes eques atque elephanti
> proiciunt sese,

a usage imitated by Virgil (*G*. iii. 116):

> equitem docuere sub armis
> insultare solo et gressus glomerare superbos,

and commented on by Aulus Gellius (xviii. 5 ; cf. Non. 106. 24 M.).

§ 30. Neuters in -mentum. Other examples are *augmentum* beside *augmen* (poet.) : *fundāmentum* beside *fundamen* (poet.) ; *intĕgŭmentum* beside *tegumen*, *tĕgĭmen*, *tegmen* ; *cognōmentum* beside *cognomen* ; *termentum* and *trīmentum* beside *tĕrĭmen* ; *argūmentum*, from *arguo*, ' a making clear,' a proof, then 'the subject of a story, picture, &c.,' e.g. Virg. *A*. vii. 791 argumentum ingens ; Prop. iii. 9. 13 : argumenta magis sunt Mentoris addita formae ; *vestīmentum*, from *vestio* ; *caementum* for **caed-mentum* (ch. iv. § 161) from *caedo* ; *jugmentum* (et paries, *C. I. L.* vi. 24710), and *jugumentum* (Cato) ; *jūmentum* from *juvo*, according to Augustine, *Quaest. in Heptat.* iii. 2 and v. 38 ; *mōmentum* beside *mōmen* (poet.) from *mŏveo*. *Nūmen*, *crīmen*, *culmen* (cf. *cŏlŭmen*), &c. have no byforms in -*mentum* ; *implēmentum*, *incrēmentum*, *mŏnŭmentum*, &c. have no byforms in -*men*.

§ 31. -KŎ-, -KĀ-. I.-Eur. -*ko*-, the -y of Engl. 'stony,' 'angry,' &c., is rarely -k̑o- (with palatal k), e.g. I.-Eur. **yŭwn̑ko*- (O. Ind. yuvaśá-, O. Ir. ōac, W. ieuanc, Goth. juggs), Lat. *jŭvencus*, but usually -ko- or -q^{u}o-. It is used as a primary suffix, e.g. *cascus* (cf. *cānus* for **casnus*, Osc. *casnar*) *fuscus* (cf. *furvus* for **fusuus*), but mainly as a secondary suffix employed in the formation of Adjectives from Adverbs, e. g. *antīcus* (of place), *antīquus* (of time) from *ante* (cf. O. Ind. antĭká-), Nouns, e. g. *bellĭcus*, *cīvĭcus*, and Adjectives, e. g. O. Ind. nágnaka-, 'naked,' beside nagná-, having often a diminutive significance, which is in Latin denoted by -*cŭlus* (§ 24), the addition to -*co*- of the other diminutive suffix -lo- (§ 21), e.g. *nigrĭculus* beside *nĭger, ŏvicula* (O. Sl. ovĭca), [*albĭcare* and *nigrĭcare* are Verbs with the Diminutive KO-suffix (ch. viii. § 33 (7)], (cf. *hŏmun-c-io* and *homun-cu-lus, sĕnĕca*, Non. 17. 18 M., *senecio* and *senĭculus*), as in Gk. by -ισκο- of παιδίσκος, &c. We also find it preceded by ĭ, e. g. εἰρων-ικός, Lat. *histriōn-icus* (without the vowel we should have had *histriuncus), often *-tĭco-*, e. g. *rus-ticus, herbā-ticus, errā-ticus* after the analogy of Participle-stems in -to- (§ 28); by ī, e. g. Goth. mahteigs, 'mighty,' Lat. *ămīcus, pŭdīcus* (ī not *ei* is attested for *mendīcus* by Plaut. *Rud.* 1305; see ch. iv. § 34); by ā, e. g. *mĕrācus*. Adjectives in -āko- had the sense of English adjectives in -ish, e. g. Lith. saldókas, ' sweetish,' and came in some languages to acquire the force of Comparatives, e. g. Lett. saldáks, ' sweeter,' W. glanach, ' fairer.'

In Latin the -ko- and -qᴴo- suffixes seem often to have been confused, e. g. *antīcus* and *antīquus, tesca* or *tesqua*, lit. ' dry places,' for **tersc-*, from the root ters-, ' to dry ' (cf. *torreo*, Gk. τέρσομαι), and, as in Greek, &c. there are often byforms of the Consonantal declension, e. g. *bĭbāx*, &c. beside *merācus, fēlīx*, &c. beside *pudīcus*, &c., like Greek ἧλιξ and ἡλίκος, μεῖραξ (O. Ind. maryaká-). For *-ĭcus* we have *-ĭcius* in *aedīlĭ-cius, trĭbūnĭcius, patrĭcius, adventīcius, commendātīcius*, &c.; for *-ācus* we have *-āceus* in *herbāceus, gallīnāceus, ărundĭnāceus*, &c.

§ 32. **Adjectives with the KŎ-suffix.** From the adverbs *rĕ-* and *prŏ-* we have *rĕcĭ-prŏcus*, while *prŏcul* adds the lo- (li-) suffix to *procus (O. Sl. prokŭ) (*Rhein. Mus.* xliii. 402); *postīcus* is the opposite of *antīcus*; *prīs-cus* (cf. *primus* for *pris-mus). From the numeral *ūnus* we have *unīcus* (Goth. ainahs, O. Sl. inokŭ; cf. O. Ind. dvīka-, Gk. δισσός for *δϝίκιος). From nouns: *patrīcus* (cf. *patrīcius*); *hostīcus*, used in Plautus like *hostīlis* (hostica manus, *Capt.* 246 ; hostilis manus, *Capt.* 311) ; *cīvicus* (beside *cīvīlis*). (Cf. Porph. ad Hor. *C.* ii. 1. 1 adtende autem non 'civile' sed 'civicum' dixisse antiqua figura. illi enim ' civica ' et ' hostica,' deinde ' civilia ' et ' hostilia ' dicebant. denominationes autem hae fere liberae sunt apud doctos). Other noticeable forms are *cădūcus, mandūcus* (cf. *fĭdūc-ia* from *fĭdūcus, and *pannūcia*) ; *lingŭlāca, verbēnāca ; hiulcus, pĕtulcus* from *hiare* and *petere* with the (diminutive ?) LO-suffix. [For a list of Nouns in *-ūca*, e. g. *verruca*, a wart, in O. Lat. a hill (Cato ap. Gell. iii. 7. 6 ; Quint. viii. 3. 48 and viii. 6. 14), from the root wers- of Lith. virszùs, ' the top,' O. Ind. várṣman, ' a height,' see Stolz, *Beiträge*, p. 6, who points out the connexion of this ending with the ending *-ūgo*, e. g. *Verrugo*, a Volscian town in Latium.] A gloss has: manubrium, quod rustici 'manicum' dicunt (*C. G. L.* v. 115. 17); (*manĭco-* in Romance, e. g. Ital. manico, Span. mango, Fr. manche) ; Paul. Fest. quotes *olentica* ' mali odoris loca ' (223. 4 Th.).

§ 33. **Adjectives in -ĭcius.** Denominatives (i. e. derivatives from Nouns or Adjectives) have -ĭ-, e. g. *patrĭcius* from *păter*, *natalĭcius* from *nātālis*; Derivatives from P. P. P. in -to (Vb. Nouns in -tio-, -ti-) have -ĭ-, e.g. *dedĭticius* from *dēdĭtus*, *insĭticius* (cf. *insĭtīvus*) (also *nŏvĭcius*). (For a full list, see *A. L. L.*v. 415.)

§ 34. **Suffixes ending in ĭ (Nouns and Adjectives of third Declension).** -Ĭ-. In the declension of these stems ĭ varies with ei and oi (see ch. vi.). The Ĭ-stems are often confused with IO-stems (§ 4), with Ī-stems (§ 51), and with YĒ-stems (§ 51). Examples of the primary suffix -ĭ- are Lat. *anguis* (Lith. angìs, O. Sl. ąžĭ, Arm. auj), and another I.-Eur. word for a snake, *ĕĝhi- (O. Ind. áhi-, Zend aži-, Arm. iž, Gk ἔχις).

Neuter Ĭ-stems in I.-Eur. (like Neuter R-stems, &c., see § 56) seem occasionally to show a heteroclite declension, a nasal replacing the vowel in oblique cases, e. g. O. Ind. ákṣi, akṣṇás Gen., ' the eye,' ásthi, asthnás Gen., ' a bone,' which may have led to a confusion of I- and N-stems in such words as I.-Eur.*aksi-, ' an axle' (Lat. *axis*, Lith. aszìs, O. Sl. osĭ; but Gk. ἄξων). As a secondary suffix -i- is used in many languages to give an adjectival sense, especially in the formation of Compound Adjectives from Nouns, e. g. Lat. *exsomnis* from *somnus*, O. Ir. *essamin* for *exomni-, from omun (*omno-), ' fear,' though we often find in the early Latin literature the O-stem, e. g. *ĭnermus*, class. *inermis* (so Gaulish *Exobnus, Exomnus* for O. Ir. essamin).

In Latin the I-declension has been greatly extended; thus consonantal stems of the third declension often take the Ĭ-stem case-suffixes, e.g. *pĕd-ĭ-bus*, *fĕrent-ium*, &c.; and a stem-suffix ending in ŏ or ŭ passes readily, if it be an adjective, into an I-stem, e. g. *sĭmĭlis* (Gk. ὁμαλός), *hŭmĭlis* (Gk. χθαμαλός), *nāvis* (I.-Eur.*nāu-, O. Ind. nāús, Gk. ναῦς), *brĕvis* (cf. Gk. βραχύς), *lĕvis* (cf. O. Ind. raghus, Gk. ἐ-λαχύς, Lith. lengurìs). The Greek loanword *hĭlărus* (ἱλαρός) is also *hilaris* by the time of Terence.

§ 35. Other examples of I-stems. Lat. *ensis* (O. Ind. así-); Lat. *trŭdis* from *trūdo* (root treud-, Goth. us-þriutan, ' to trouble,' Engl. thrust, threat, O. Sl. trudŭ, ' toil '); Lat. *rŭdis*, unworked, rude, originally of metal, from the root reudh-, ' to be red ' (cf. *raudus*, unworked metal, ch. iv. § 41); *jŭgis*, continual, from *jungo*; Lat. *scŏbis* from *scăbo*; Lat. *măre* (O. Ir. muir Neut., for *mori, O. H. G. meri Neut., Germ. Meer Neut., Engl. mere).

§ 36. Adjective I-stems from O-stems. Other examples are: O. Lat. *sublīmus*, e.g. Enn. *Trag.* 2 R. deum sublimas subices, Lucr. i. 340 sublimaque caeli (see Munro's note); O. Lat. *stĕrĭlus*, e.g. Lucr. ii. 845 sonitu sterila (cf. Paul. Fest. 463. 1 Th. ' sterilam' sterilem). Greek αὐστηρός had the same tendency to the I-declension in Latin as Greek ἱλαρός, for Caper gives

§§ 34–40.] NOUN AND ADJECTIVE STEMS. -I-, -RI-, -LI-. 339

a caution against the form *austeris* (p. 108. 4 K.). Nonius (494. 26 M.) quotes *prōnis* from Varro (*Men.* 391 B.). On O. Lat. *forctus*, see ch. viii. § 92. The Noun *torris* from the root *ters-* (Gk. τέρσομαι; cf. Lat. *torreo* for *torseo*, ch. viii. § 23) was in O. Lat. *torrus* (Non. 15. 22 M.; Serv. ad *Aen.* xii. 298 'hic torris'... ita nunc dicimus : nam illud Ennii et Pacuvii penitus de usu recessit ut 'hic torrus, hujus torri' dicamus), but is rather to be explained as an Ē-stem become an I-stem (like *sordes*, § 51). The form *torres* F., a burning, read by Lachmann in Lucretius iii. 917 (MSS. *torret*) is doubtful (*A. L. L.* viii. 587). On *hīlarus* beside *hilaris*, see Neue, ii³. p. 149.

§ 37. -NI-. This suffix, varying with -ĕni-, -ŏni-, &c. is more common in those languages which have extended the use of the P. P. P. in -no- (§ 8) than in Latin. Examples are : Lat. *ignis* (cf. O. Ind. agnī́-, Lith. ugnìs F., O. Sl. ognĭ M.), Lat. *clūnis* (O. Ind. śróṇi-, O. Scand. hlaunn, Lith. szlaunìs). Adjectives in *-nis* may have been originally NO-stems (§ 36), e. g. *immānis* from O. Lat. *mānus*, good (with a bystem in -ni-, *Mānes*, lit. 'the good deities'); cf. *Janis*, a byform of *Janus*, in Carm. Sal. (Tert. *Apol.* 10).

§ 38. Other examples of Latin -nis. Lat. *amnis* for **ab-nis* (cf. O. Ir. abann), Lat. *crīnis* for **crisnis* (cf. Lat. *crista*), *pānis* for **pasnis* (cf. Lat. *pastillus* .

§ 39. -MI- is a still rarer suffix than -ni-. An example is Lat. *vermis* (O. H. G. wurm), a word the relation of which to I.-Eur. *qᵘr̥mi- (O. Ind. kŕ̥mi-, O. Ir. cruim, W. pryf, Lith. kirmis) is not quite clear. Latin Adjectives in *-mis* like *ĭnermis*, *sublīmis* were originally -MO-stems (cf. § 36); thus Nonius 489. 7 M. gives some examples of *sublimus* from the older literature (cf. Georges, *Lex. Wortf.* s. v.).

§ 40. -RI-, -LI-. These are not nearly so common I.-Eur. suffixes as -ro-, -lo-, e. g. O. Lat. *ŏcris*, a hill (in Umbrian, &c. used of the citadel) (Gk. ὄκρις, a point, ἄκρις, a hill; cf. O. Ind. áśri-, but also Gk. ἄκρος), Lat. *tālis, quālis* (O. Sl. tolĭ Adv., kolĭ Adv.; cf. Gk. τηλί-κος, πηλί-κος); but -li- is fairly frequent in the Slavonic languages, where the P. P. P. in -lo- is much in vogue. In Latin, Adjective -RO- and -LO- stems often show -*ris*, -*lis*, e. g. O. Lat. *sācres*, used of animals for sacrifice (e. g. Plaut. *Rud.* 1208 súnt domi agni et pórci sācres) beside *săcer* (cf. *Mānes* beside O. Lat. *mānus*, good), *sĭmĭlis* (Gk. ὁμαλός), *hŭmĭlis* (Gk. χθαμαλός). And the use of -li- and -ri- for Adjectives derived from Nouns is very widely extended in Latin, far more widely

Z 2

than in any other I.-Eur. language, e.g. *vītālis* from *vīta*, *ālāris* for *alalis(?) from *āla*, so that the Greek Adj. δαψιλής, when borrowed by Latin, assumed the form *dapsĭlis*. Dialectal examples are Osc. luisarifs, ' *lusaribus,' Sab. Flusare ' Florali,' while Osc. Fiuusasiais ' Florariis ' has -āsio- (Lat. -ārio-, § 4).

§ 41. Other examples of Latin ˘-li-, -ri-. *ŭter*, a skin, for *ŭd-ri-, beside *ŭtĕrus* (O. Lat. *uterum*) ; *ācer*, sharp (cf. Gk. ἄκρος). Verbal Adjectives in *-lis* are, as we have seen (§ 22), byforms with Passive sense of Active Verbal Adjectives in *-lus*, e. g. *ăgĭlis*, ' easily driven,' *bĭbĭlis*, ' easily drunk' (beside *bĭbŭlus*, ' easily drinking,' inclined to drink), *dŏcĭlis* (like *dŏcĭbĭlis*) ; sometimes formed from the Perf. Part. Pass., e.g. *fictĭlis*, *fissĭlis*, *flexĭlis* (and *flexĭbĭlis*), *hāmātĭlis et saxātĭlis* (Plaut. *Rud.* 299), *missĭlis*. The ending *-ĭlis* of *aedĭlis* has I.-Eur. ī, not ei, to judge from old inscriptions, e. g. *C. I. L.* i. 61 *aidilis* (cf. *ib.* 31). This *-ĭlis* (proper to I- and IO-stems) as well as *-ālis* (proper to Ā-stems) is often extended by analogy ; e.g. *ănūlis* (for *anūlis) by analogy of *sĕnūlis* ; *vernūlis* is from *verna*, *vernālis* from *ver* ; from *libra*, a pound, we have *librīlis* and *librālis* ; from *scurra*, *scurrīlis* ; from *manu* not *manūlis, but *manuālis* (so *dorsuālis* from *dorso-*). Examples of *-ēlis* are *fĭdēlis* from *fĭdē-*, *crūdēlis* (cf. *fămē-lĭcus*, *contŭmē-lia*) as well as *patruēlis* and *matruēlis*. Like *trĭbūlis* (from *trĭbu-*), *ĭdūlis* (from *ĭdu-*), is *ĕdūlis*. From O-stems we have *puĕrĭlis*, *virīlis*, *hĕrīlis*, *servīlis*, &c. ; *annālis*, *fātālis*, &c. ; from Cons.-stems *căpĭt-ālis*, *virgĭn-ālis*, *hospĭt-ālis*, *jŭvĕnālis* and *jŭvĕnīlis*, &c.

§ 42. -TI-. As -to- was the I.-Eur. suffix of Verbal Adjectives, especially of the Perfect Participle Passive, so -ti- was the suffix of Verbal Nouns (Nomina Actionis), e. g. Gk. πιστός and πίστις. These nouns were of the feminine gender, had the weak form of the root, and are accented sometimes on the suffix, and sometimes on the root, e. g. O. Ind. matí- and máti- for I.-Eur. *mn̥-ti- (Lat. *mens*) from the root men-, ' to think.' In Latin, as in Celtic, we find this suffix enlarged by an EN-suffix, e. g. Lat. *mentio*, Acc. *mentiōnem*, O. Ir. -mitiu-, -mitin Acc., and this compound suffix, which in Latin supplanted almost entirely the older -ti-, appears also in other languages, e. g. Goth. raþjō (Lat. *rătio*), Gk. δωτίνη (cf. Lat. *dătio*, Acc. *dationem*). The supplanting may be accounted for, wholly or partly, by the change which the phonetic laws of the Latin language would produce in the TI-suffix, a change which would often make the suffix unrecognizable. From the root men-, the Verbal Noun **mn̥ti*- became *mens* in Latin and from the root bher-, the Noun **bhr̥ti*- became *fors*, while from *mĕto* we have *messis* for *met-tis, from the root wes-, *vestis*, from *sătiăre*, *sătiās*, &c., forms whose common formation has been obscured past recognition. A similar

§§ 41–44.]   NOUN AND ADJECTIVE STEMS. -TI-.   341

explanation has been offered for the fact that in Teutonic also the same suffix -ti- ceased to be a living suffix, namely that under the working of the Teutonic phonetic laws it would assume the various forms -þi, -di, -ti, -si, &c. The older suffix remains in Adverbs like *raptim, furtim,* &c. (see ch. ix. § 4). Occasionally the feminine abstract passed into a concrete noun and might change its gender. Thus Lat. *hostis* (Goth. gasts, ' a guest,' O. Sl. gostĭ) may have been originally abstract, just as Lat. *agrĭcŏla*, a field-tiller, meant originally 'field-tillage' (§ 2).

The secondary suffix -tāti- (or -tāt-), used to form feminine Abstract Nouns, derived from Adjectives and Nouns, and the similar suffix -tūti- (or -tūt-) exhibit this suffix -ti- added to the suffixes -tā- and -tu-, e.g. Lat. *jŭventās* beside *jŭventa* (see § 27). The suffix -tāti- (-tāt-) is found in O. Ind., Greek, and Latin, while -tūti- (-tūt-) is found in Latin, Celtic, and Teutonic, e.g. Lat. *nŏvĭtās* (Gk. νεότης), Lat. *ūnĭtās* (O. Ir. oentu), Lat. *jŭventūs* (O. Ir. ōitiu). In Latin, in addition to -tūti- (-tūt-), which is much less in use than -tāti- (-tāt-), we find a form augmented by an N-suffix, -*tūdo*, Gen. -*tūdinis*, e.g. *servĭtūdo* beside *servĭtūs*, *hĭlărĭtudo* (so in Plaut., not *hilaritas*), *beātĭtudo*, which (with *beatitas*) was a coinage of Cicero (Quint. viii. 3. 32).

§ 43. **Other examples of the suffix -ti- in Latin.** Latin *vectis*, a lever (cf. *vectio*), from *věho*; Lat. *vĭtis* from the root wei-, ' to plait, weave' ; Lat. *messis* (cf. *messio*) from *měto*; Lat. *fors* (O. Ind. bhṛtí-, O. Ir. brith, Goth. ga-baurþs, O. H. G. giburt, O. Engl. gebyrd, ' fate ') from *fĕro* ; Lat. *mens* (O. Ind. matí- and máti-, Goth. gamunds, ana-minds, Lith. at-mintìs, O. Sl. pamętĭ) from the root men-, ' to think ' (cf. *mentio*) ; Lat. *gens*, from *gigno* (cf. *nātio* for **gnatio*) ; Lat. *mors* (O. Ind. mṛti-, O. Lith. mirtìs, O. Sl. sŭ-mrĭtĭ) from *mŏrior*; Lat. *dōs* (O. Ind. dáti-, Lith. dûtis, O. Sl. datĭ) from root dō- (cf. *dătio*, Gk. δωτίνη) ; so Lat. *cōs* beside *cătus* (ch. iv. § 54) ; Lat. *ars* (O. Ind. ṛtí- means ' attack ') ; Lat. *pars* (cf. *portio*) ; Lat. *grātes* beside *grātus* ; Lat. *quiēs* beside *quiētus* (*inquies* for *inquietus* is due to the tendency to turn Compound Adjectives into I-stems) ; Lat. *vestis* from the root wes-, ' to clothe,' meant originally, like our word ' clothing,' the act of arraying oneself, then the raiment itself.

§ 44. **Examples of Lat. -tiōn-.** Lat. *vīsio* (cf. O. Ind. vitti-, O. Sl. -vistĭ and věstĭ) from the root weid-, 'to see, know' ; Lat. -*ventio* (cf. O. Ind. gáti-, Gk. βάσις, O. H. G. cunft, Lith. -gimtìs) from the root gu̯em-, ' to come' ; Lat. *sătio* (cf. Gk. ἄν-εσις, Goth. -sēþs, ' seed,' Lith. sēti) from the root sē-, ' to throw, throw seed ' ; Lat. *con-dĭtio* for **con-dătio* (cf. O. Ind. -hiti-, Gk. θέσις, Goth. -dēþs, ' a deed,' O. Sl. -dĕtĭ) from the root dhē-, ' to put, place '; Lat. *ăd-eptio* for **ad-ăptio* (cf. O. Ind. ápti-) beside *aptus* ; Lat. *ex-plētio* (cf. O. Ind. prāti-, Gk. πλῆσις), beside *ex-plētus* ; Lat. *nōtio* for **gnōtio* (cf. O. Ind. -jñāti-, ' the act of knowing,' jñātí-, 'an acquaintance,' Gk. γνῶσις, O. H. G. ur-chnāt, O. Sl. po-znatĭ, Goth. ga-kunþs, ga-kunds, Germ. Kunst, O. Sl. zętĭ, 'son-in-law') beside (g)nōtus; Lat. *dictio* (cf. O. Ind. diṣṭi-, Gk. δεῖξις, O. H. G. -ziht) from the root deik̑-; Lat. *stātio* (cf. O. Ind. sthíti-, Gk. στάσις, O. H. G. stat, O. Sl. -statĭ) from *stāre*; Lat. *in-tentio* (cf. O. Ind. tati-, Gk. τάσις) from the root ten-, 'to stretch'; Lat. *junctio* (cf. O. Ind. yukti-, Gk. ζεῦξις, Lith. jùnkti) from *jungo*.

§ 45. **Adjectival -ti- for -to- in Latin.** The same tendency to turn O-stem Adjectives into I-stems, which we have seen in *sĭmĭlis* (Gk. ὁμαλός), *hŭmĭlis* (Gk. χθαμαλός), appears in an adjective like *fortis*, in O. Lat. *forctus* (Paul. Fest. 73. 9 Th. horctum et forctum pro bono dicebant), originally a P. P. P. from the root dherĝh-, ' to establish' (O. Ind. dṛḍhá-, 'stablished, firm'). The older spelling *forctis* occurs in the clause of the XII Tables quoted by Festus (524. 15 Th.), which provided: ut idem juris esset Sanatibus quod Forctibus, the Sanates being allies who had revolted but had returned to their allegiance, 'quasi sanata mente,' the Forctes being those who had never broken faith [cf. Paul. Fest. 59. 26 Th. forctis (MSS. forctes), frugi et bonus, sive validus]. The word *Sanates* shows a similar transference to the I-declension of the P. P. P. of *sānare*, and throws light on the termination, *-ās* O. Lat. *-ātis* (see ch. iii. § 16), which indicates the country or the party to which one belongs, e. g. *optĭmates, infĭmatis* (Plaut. Stich. 493), *Arpīnates*.

§ 46. **Other examples of Lat. -tāt(i)-, -tūt(i)-, -tūdin-.** The tendency of the I-stems to encroach on the Consonant-stems in Latin (mentioned above, § 34) makes it difficult to decide when -tāt-, -tūt-, and when -tāti-, -tūti- were the suffixes used, e. g. Gen. Pl. *cīvĭtatum* and *cīvitatium*. In O. Ind. -tāt- (e. g. sarvátāt-, 'completeness') is rarer than -tāti- (e. g. sarvátāti-), while in Greek only -tāt- is found. Other Latin examples of -tās (see *A. L. L.* viii. 321) are *scaevĭtas* (Gk. σκαιότης), *commūnĭtas* (Goth. gamaindūþs), *bŏnĭtas* from *bŏnus*, *lībertas* from *līber*, *cīvĭtas* from *cīvis*, *ūbertas* from *ūber*, *făcultas* and *făcĭlĭtas* from *făcĭlis*, *vŏluptas* from *vŏlŭp(e)*, *tempestas* from *tempus* (cf. *tempĕri*), *vŏluntas* from *vŏlens*. Examples of -tūs: *sĕnectus* from *sĕnex*, *virtus* from *vir*; O. Lat. *tempestus* (Varro *L. L.* vii. 51 libri augurum pro tempestate 'tempestutem' dicunt supremum augurii tempus). Examples of -tūdo: *altĭtudo* from *altus*, *lātĭtudo* from *lātus*, *sollĭcĭtudo* from *sollĭcĭtus*.

§ 47. **Suffixes ending in -ŭ (Nouns of fourth Decl.).** -Ŭ-. In the declension of these stems ŭ varies with eu and ou (see ch. vi.). I.-Eur. Adjectives in -u- usually show the weak form of the root, and are accented on the suffix, e. g. *pḷtú-*, ' broad' (O. Ind. pṛthú-, Gk. πλατύς, Gaul. litu-). They formed their Nom. Sing. Fem. in -wī, e. g. *swādu-*, 'sweet,' with Nom. Sg. Masc. *swādús (O. Ind. svādús, Gk. ἡδύς), Nom. Sg. Fem. *swādwí (O. Ind. svādví). In Latin these Adjectives, aided by the analogy of the Fem., have followed the tendency of O-stem Adjectives, and have passed into the I-declension (as in Teutonic *tᵉnu- 'thin' became þunni- by influence of the fem. *tᵉnwí); thus *suāvis* for **suādvis*, *tĕnuis* (O. Ind. tanú-, Gk. τανύ-γλωσσος,

O. Sl. tĭnŭ-kŭ), lĕvis (cf. O. Ind. raghú-, Gk. ἐ-λαχύς, O. Sl. lĭgŭ-kŭ), brĕvis (Gk. βραχύς), grăvis (O. Ind. gurú-, Gk. βαρύς, Goth. kaurus). Of nouns with the U-suffix examples are I.-Eur. *pĕk̑u- (O. Ind. paśú- M., Goth. faihu N., 'property,' O. H. G. fihu, O. Engl. feoh, Germ. Vieh, Engl. fee), Lat. *pĕcu* and *pecus*; Lat. *lăcus* (O. Ir. loch, a Neuter U-stem); with the rarer NU-suffix, Lat. *cornu* and *cornus, mănus, pīnus*. The -ru- of Gk. δάκρυ is augmented by the suffix -mā- in Lat. *dacrŭma, lacrŭma*. The Romance languages show us that U-stems had come in Vulg. Lat. to be merged in the O-declension; and even as early as Plautus Noun-stems in -u retained little of a distinctive declension in ordinary speech.

-TU-. As we have seen -ti- used to form feminine Verbal Nouns (Nomina Actionis), connected with the P. P. P. in -to-, similarly -tu- was used for masc. nouns of the same kind, sometimes with accent on the root (strong grade), sometimes with weak grade of root and the root unaccented, e. g. O. Ind. étum but ĭtvá, from the I.-Eur. root ei-, ' to go.' The Latin first Supine is the Accusative of a TU-stem, used with a verb of motion, e. g. *vīsum it* (cf. O. Ind. vēttum ēti, O. Sl. vidĕtŭ idetĭ), and the second Supine is another case (ch. viii. § 88) of a similar stem. Occasionally these Abstract Verbal Nouns become concrete, e. g. Lat. *măgistrātus*, a magistrate. In Greek (they are mostly confined to the Ionic dialect) they are feminine, e.g. ἀρτύς, a fitting, a connexion (Lat. *artus*, M., a limb) (cf. O. Lat. *metus* F.).

§ 48. Other examples of U-stems in Latin. Lat. *gĕnu* (cf. O. Ind. jánu, N. Gk. γόνυ N., Goth. kniu N.); *vĕru* (O. Ir. bir, a Neut. u-Stem, W. ber).

§ 49. Interchange of U- with O-stems. This interchange is found also in Umbro-Osc. Thus Osc. senateís shows the same Gen. Sg. suffix as an O-stem (e.g. sakarakleís 'sacraculi'), Umbr. maronato 'magistratu,' the O-stem Abl. In Plautus the U-stems appear mostly in the Nom. Acc. Abl. Sg., and so are hardly to be distinguished from O-stems; the Dat. Sg. is usually in *-ui* (ch. vi. § 27), but the Gen. Sg. is normally in *-i* (ch. vi. § 21); in the Plural instances are comparatively seldom and almost only in the Nom. Acc. and Abl.; the only certain instance of a Gen. Pl. is *mille passum*. On the S. C. Bacch. of 186 B.C. we have Gen. Sg. *senatuos*, but at the end of the same century *senati* (C. I. L. i. 199, 200, 547), and Quintilian (i. 6. 27) states that it is impossible to say whether *sĕnāti* or *sĕnātus* is the Genitive form. *Nura* for *nŭrus*, *socra* for *socrus*, forms censured in the Probi Appendix (198. 34 and 199. 1 K.) occur on late inscriptions (*nura, C. I. L.* viii. 2604. 4293, &c.; *nurua*, v. 2452; *socra*, ii. 530, 2936; iii. 655; viii. 2906, 3994; xiv. 526, &c.; *socera*, iii. 3895, vii. 229, &c.) and *nŏra, sŏcĕra* or *socra* are the prototypes of Ital. nuora,

344   THE LATIN LANGUAGE.   [Chap. V.

suocera, Span. nuera, suegra, &c. On Greek inscriptions the only fourth Decl. Nouns found are *īdus, trĭbus*, and the forms used are Nom. Pl. εἴδοι (ἴδοι), Gen. Pl. εἰδῶν (second cent. B.C., but later εἴδων) Abl. Sg. τρίβου (see Eckinger, p. 134). *Dŏmus* is declined only according to the second Decl. in Plautus and till Sulla (see Langen, *Anal. Plaut.* ii. p. 5). Quintilian (i. 6. 5) mentions it as a word about whose declension there might be doubt. We find in the older writers *humu* (Varro, *Men.* 422, 531 B.; the gender of *hŭmus* is Masc. in O. Lat., see Georges, *Lex. Wortf.* s. v.), *lectus* (fourth Decl., Georges s. v.), *sŏnus* (fourth Decl., Georges s. v.), and in a quotation from a Law of Numa (ap. Fest. 212. 17 M.) occurs the form *Jānui* Dat. Sg. : Janui Quirino agnum marem caedito. Priscian, discussing the interchange of second and fourth Decl. forms (i. p. 256 H.), mentions the variants *fastos* and *fastus* in Hor. *C.* iii. 17. 4, *cĭbus* Gen. Sg. (doubtful), *arci* Gen. Sg. (Cic. *Deor. Nat.* iii. 20. 51 ; *arcus* is Fem. in O. Lat.), as well as the parallel forms *spĕcus* and *specum, pĕnus* and *penum, fīco* and *ficu*, &c. For statistics of the O- and U-declension of such words see Neue, i², pp. 509 sqq. Names of trees like *laurus, fagus*, &c. show this uncertainty (Varro *L. L.* ix. 80 alii dicunt cupressus, alii cupressi, item de ficis platanis et plerisque arborĭbus), an uncertainty perhaps due to the rarity of fem. O-stems (e. g. *fāgus*, Gk. φηγός F.) in I.-Eur. (see ch. vi. § 1. p. 369).

§ 50. **Other examples of -tu-stems.** Lat. *ēsus* from *edo* (O. Ind. áttu-, Lith. ēstū, O. Sl. jastŭ); Lat. *vitus*, the felly of a wheel (Gk. ἴτυς F.); Lat. *actus*, (1) a driving, (2) a road for driving (Paul. Fest. 13. 17 Th. iter inter vicinos quattuor pedum latum), (3) the space over which something is driven, a measure of land, like our 'plough-gate,' (Plin. xviii. 9 in quo boves agerentur cum aratro uno impetu justo); Lat. *fētus*, a brood (cf. Gk. τροφή, e. g. Soph. *O. T.* 1); O. Lat. *metus* F., e. g. Enn. *A.* 526 M. nec metus ulla tenet.

§ 51. **The Suffixes -YĒ- (Nouns of fifth Decl.) and -Ī-. The Stems in -Ē.** As the feminines of O-stems were formed with the suffix -ā- (§ 2), so the feminines of other stems appear with the suffix -yē-, e. g. Lat. *tempĕriēs* from the ES-stem *tempus*, or -ī-, e. g. O. Ind. dātrī́, fem. of dātár- (in Latin with c added, e.g. dătrī-x, stem dătrīc-; cf. Gk. αὐλητρῐδ- with added dental and short i), or -yā-, e. g. Lat. *temperia* (cf. Gk. ἀλήθεια for *ἀληθεσ-yă, δότειρα for * δοτερ-yă). How far these differences are due to a variation of -yē- with -ī-, as in the Optative, e. g. Lat. *siēs, sītis* (ch. viii. § 55), or to a confusion of Ī-stems (thus O. Ind. naptī́-, Lat. *neptis*, may be an Ī-stem corresponding to the Ū-stem, O. Ind. śvaśrū́-, Lat. *socrus*, O. Sl. svekry), has not yet been satisfactorily determined. It is possible that the ē-vowel of Latin and the Balto-Slavic languages (e. g. Lith. žem-ė- for *žem-jē-, 'land,' O. Sl. zēm(l)-ja- for *zem(l)jē-, whence the name Nova Zembla, connected with Lat. *hŭmus* and Gk. χθών) may be a modification

§§ 50, 51.] NOUN AND ADJECTIVE STEMS. -YĒ-, -Ī-. 345

of an original ā under the influence of the preceding y-sound (cf. Vulg. Lat. *Jenuarius* for *Jānuarius*, ch. ii. § 3), so that O. Lat. *heriem* Acc., a word occurring in the liturgical formula *heriem Junonis* (Gell. xiii. 23. 2), will exactly correspond to Osc. heriam [on an execration-tablet, Zvet. *I. I. I.* 129. 1; the i (not ii) of the Oscan word probably indicates a y-sound (ch. iv. § 63)]. Verbal Nouns with -yē- are a feature of Latin, e. g. *pro-gĕnies, răbies, scăbies, pernĭcies*, and *permĭties* [in *făcies, spĕcies* the *i* (*y*) appears also in the Pres. stem].

Other examples of these suffixes are: of U-stems, O. Ind. svādvī́, Gk. ἡδεῖα for *σƑᾱδεƑyᾰ (cf. Lat. *suāvis* M. and F., § 47), fem. of I.-Eur. *swādu-; of N-stems, O. Ind. yūnī, fem. of yúvan-, ' young' (the Plautine *iuuenix, Mil.* 304 points to Lat. *jūnix* being rather a contraction of a stem *yŭwenī- than a direct development of the stem yūnī-), O. Ind. rājñī (mod. Ranee), fem. of rājan-, ' a king'; of NT-stems, O. Ind. bhárantī, fem. of the Pres. Part. bhárant- (Gk. φέρουσα for *φεροντyᾰ ; cf. Lat. *praesentia*, &c.).

Other fifth Decl. stems are suffixless, e.g. *rē-s* (O. Ind. rā́-s, rāy-ás Gen. from the root rēi- (ch. iv. § 47) [1]; *diēs* from a stem d(i)yēw- (O. Ind. dyāús Nom. Sg.), a byform of d(i)yĕw-, ' sky, day' (ch. iv. § 48). Some seem to have the same Verbal Ē-suffix as is seen in verbs like *călē-facio, candē-facio* [ch. viii. § 33 (9)], e. g. *făm-ē-s* (cf. Gk. ἐ-χάν-η-ν from χαίνω for *χαμγω), which is really a fifth Decl. noun like *fĭd-ē-s* (cf. Gk. ἐ-πίθ-η-ν). Another noun declined according to the fifth Decl. is *sordēs*, Abl. *sordē*, Lucr. vi. 1271, Gen. Pl. *sordērum*, Plaut. *Poen.* 314 (cf. *sordeo*). So from *ŏleo, to grow, *prōles* for *pro-ŏles, sub-ŏles, ind-ŏles* (cf. *ol(e)-facio* from *ŏleo*, to smell); from *luo lues*, from *struo strues* from *ruo rues* ['rues' ruina, *C. G. L.* iv. 281. 5; cf. *lue rue*, ' luem ruem' (?) on the Carmen Arvale]. Against the association of *lābes* with *lăbe-facio* is the different quantity of the root-vowel. A long vowel is seen also in *mōles* (*mōles-tus*), *sēdes* (*sĕdeo*), *amb-āges* (*ăgo*),

---

[1] *spēs* may be of similar formation (cf. O. Ind. sphāyatē, ' he extends himself, increases '); it is used by Plautus only in Nom. Acc. Abl. Sg. and in Nom. Acc. Pl. (*spes*). But Ennius treats it as an S-stem in *Ann.* 448 M.: spero, si speres quicquam prodesse potis sunt (cf. 119 M.). With the variants *spēs* and *spērēs*, compare *vīs* (Nom. Pl.) and *vires*.

contāges (*tăngo*), *propāges* and *compāges* (*păngo*), *rūpes* (*rŭmpo*). The cognates *mŏles-tus*, Gk. ἔδος, νέφος have suggested the reference of *mōlēs*, *sēdēs*, *nūbēs* (though the *ū* is difficult to explain) to ES-stems (§ 71), with the same -ēs that we see in Gk. ἀληθής from λῆθος, Dor. λᾶθος (cf. ἔλᾰθον). But perhaps a better explation of *sēdēs* is to regard it as a Plural of an I-stem *sēdis*, used as a Singular (cf. O. Ind. váyas, ' a bird,' properly ' birds,' and for the long vowel Gk. μῆνις, &c.); for a good many of these nouns in -ēs were more used in the Plural than the Singular, e. g. *ambāgēs* (O. Ind. ājí-, ' contest,' Ir. āg, ' contest '), *aedes*, *vepres*, and byforms of the Nom. Sg. occur with -*is*, e. g. *nubis*, Plaut. *Merc.* 880 (cf. *nubs*, Liv. Andr.), *saeps*, Cic. (cf. *prae-saepe* Neut.), *vātis* (cf. O. Ir. fāith for *wāti-), *vĕhis*, *clādis*, *aedis* (*C. I. L.* i. 206. 30), *caedis*, *molis*, *sedis*. Many of them belong to poetical diction; e. g. neither Plautus nor Terence use *sedes* (the usual word for a seat being *sŏlium* or *sella*), *rupes*, *tābes*, *caedes*, &c.; and they must have been liable on that account to confusion of Number. A certain amount again of Nouns in -*ēs* are fem.[1] names of animals, e. g. *cănēs* (F., beside *cănĭs* M., in O. Lat.), *fēlēs*, *mēlēs*, *vulpēs* (cf. *vulpēcula*), *pălumbēs*. The last two, perhaps all, are dialectal, so that this -*ēs* may be the dialectal expression of -eis, a byform of the Nom. Sg. suffix of I-stems. *Plēbēs* has been called an ES-stem like πλῆθος, but it is more persistently declined after the fifth Decl. (cf. *plebeius*), than any of the others, whose Abl. is often the only Singular case found in use (e. g. *ambage*, *vepre*, Ovid, &c.); *pūbēs* (cf. *pūber-tas*, *im-pūbĕr-es* Nom. Pl.) has a better claim, although the Abl. *pubē*, Plaut. *Pseud.* 126, would have to be explained as due to a false analogy of the Nom. Sg., such as has produced *requiē* Abl., *requiem* Acc. from *requiēs*, -*ētis*.

The declension of a good many of these Nouns with Nom. Sg. in -*ēs* wavers between the third and fifth Decl. Plautus makes the Gen. Pl. of *sordēs sordērum* (*Poen.* 314), like *rērum*, but we find *sordium* in late Lat. Cicero (*Top.* vii. 30) says that *specierum*, *speciebus* are impossible forms (nolim enim, ne si Latine quidem

---

[1] Priscian (i. pp. 168. 15, 169, 9, and 321. 19 H.) seems to think that *adip-* F. implies a Nom. Sg. *adipēs*.

§§ 52, 53.] NOUN AND ADJECTIVE STEMS. -YĒ-, -Ĭ-. 347

dici possit, 'specierum' et 'speciebus' dicere), and so prefers *forma* to *species* as a translation of the Greek εἶδος. Yet *specierum* and *speciebus* are common in late authors, e. g. Apuleius, and Priscian (i. 367. 23 H.) quotes *facierum* from a speech of Cato. Quintilian (i. 6. 26) expresses the doubt felt about the declension of *progenies* and *spes*: quid progenies genetivo singulari, quid plurali spes faciet? (For statistics of fifth Decl. forms, see Neue, i². pp. 370 sqq.) And the use of *-iēs* itself in the Nom. Sing. seems to have been a matter of gradual extension. Plautus has *făcies, permĭties, mātĕries* (but *materiam* on the Sententia Minuciorum of 117 B. C., *C. I. L.* i. 199), *segnĭties, vastĭties*, and possibly *caesăries, inlŭvies, intempĕries, răbies* (but *effĭgia*, &c.), to which Terence adds *mollĭties*, Lucretius *nōtĭties, spurcĭties*, &c. These yē-forms are generally confined to the Nom. Acc. Sg., while in other cases yā-forms are preferred, e. g. *intemperiae* Nom. Pl., *materiae* Dat. Sg., *luxŭriae* Dat. Sg., *mollitiis* Abl. Pl., in Abl. Sg. *barbăriā, Poen.* 598, *mollitiā, Vidul.* 35. Still Plautus adheres to the fifth Decl. type for *facies* (Nom. Gen. Acc. Abl. Sg.), and apparently *ăcies* (Acc. Abl. Sg.), *permities* (Nom. Acc. Abl. Sg.), *species* (Acc. Abl. Sg.), though he does not use these words in the Plural. Pliny (ap. Charis. p. 118. 15 K.) allowed *plānĭties, luxuries, mollities*, but not *ămīcities* (*amicitiem*, Lucr. v. 1019), 'because the Plural is *amicitiae*,' while Charisius (p. 57. 3 K.) confines *cānĭties* to poetry, and makes *canitia* the proper proseform. (For fuller statistics, see Neue.) The *-tiē*-stems are found also in Umbr., e. g. uhtretie 'auctoritate,' kvestretie, 'in the quaestorship.'

§ 52. Other examples of Latin Fems. in -ĭ, -ĭc, &c. Latin *cornīx* (cf. Gk. κορώνη); *gĕnĕtrīx* (O. Lat. jánitrī, Gk. γενέτειρα); from *mĕreor* comes *mĕrĕtrīx*, but from *mĕdeor* the name of the deity *Mĕditrīna*, whose festival, the Meditrinalia, is mentioned by Varro (*L. L.* vi. 21) and Paul. Fest. (88. 36 Th.) in connexion with the curious Roman custom of hallowing the first taste of new wine with the words: novum vetus vinum bibo; novo veteri morbo medeor; *cănīcula* (cf. O. Ind. śunī́); *clāvis, -im* Acc., *-ī* Abl. (cf. Gk. κληΐς, stem κληῑ-δ-).

§ 53. -yē- and -ī-. *Acisculus*, a small pickaxe (there was a Roman familyname Valerius Acisculus), has been referred (with supposed ĭ) to *ăcies* (*Rhein. Mus.* 1891, p. 236); the Probi Appendix (p. 198. 12 K.) censures a large number of forms in *-is* beside forms in *-es*, e. g. *vatis* beside *vates*, and among them *facis* for *facies* (cf. *facitergium* Isid. beside *facietergium* Greg. Tur.).

§ **54. Suffixes ending in -n (Nouns of third Decl.).
-EN-, -YEN-, -WEN-, -MEN-.** Beside I.-Eur. Masc. stems in -o- (-e-), -yo- (-ye-), -wo- (-we-) (§§ 2, 4, 5), we find masc. stems in -en- (-on-), -yen- (-yon-), -wen- (-won-). The relation between the two seems to be that the O-stem is the Adjective, but becomes an N-stem when a Substantive, e.g. Lat. *multĭ-bĭbus* Adj., but *bĭbō* Subst. An adjective which is restricted to denote one individual, in other words which becomes definite from indefinite, takes this suffix, e.g. Lat. *rūfus*, red, but *Rūfō*, 'the Red' (cf. Gk. στραβός and Στράβων); and this process, which has been more consistently carried out in the Teutonic languages than in any other, is still seen in the German 'weak declension' of the Adjective, e. g. rothe Nom. Pl. indef. (strong decl.), die rothen Nom. Pl. def. (weak decl.) (Goth. raudai and þai raudans). This early connexion between O- and N-stems explains why an N-stem in a Compound is often replaced by an O-stem, e.g. Gk. ἀκμό-θετον, stithy, compounded of ἄκμων and τίθημι, and why an N-stem in one language often corresponds to an O-stem in another, e.g. Gk. αἰ(F)ών to Lat. *aevom* (also explained as *aiwŏn), Goth. ga-juk-a (N-stem) to Lat. *con-jŭg-us* (O-stem), or in the same language, e. g. Lat. *lănio* to Lat. *lănius*, *incŭbo* to *incŭbus*. In the declension of these Masc. N-stems, n varies with en, on, ēn, ōn, &c., yen also with ĭn, and wen also with ŭn. They are sometimes transferred by the addition of -o- or -ā- into the O- and Ā-declension, e. g. Lat. *ĕpŭlōnus* beside *ĕpŭlō*, *termĭnus* beside *termō* (§ 13). Neuters in -n are connected with neuters in -r, &c., the n apparently being proper to the Oblique Cases, e. g. Lat. *femur*, Gen. *feminis* (§ 56). They are therefore better considered in the paragraph which deals with the R-suffix § (56).

Neuters in -men are Verbal Nouns (Nomina Actionis), and are used in various languages as Infinitives (like -sen-, e.g. O. Ind. nĕšāṇi from nī-), e. g. O. Ind. vid-mán-ē, Hom. Gk. ἴδμεν-αι (perhaps Lat. 2 Pl. Imper. Pass., e. g. *lĕgĭmini*, is a similar Infinitive form with Imperative sense ; see ch. viii. § 81). They have usually the E-grade of root, e. g. *teg-men*, but the Latin law of Syncope seldom allows us to decide when there was a connecting vowel, when an s preceded, &c. (cf. *regimen*, *integumen-tum*,

§§ 54–56.] NOUN AND ADJECTIVE STEMS. -N-, -R-. 349

jugmen-tum and *jugumen-tum*, *augmen-tum*, *sūmen* from *sūgo*, and see ch. iv. § 116 on *agmen* and *exāmen*). Their byforms with *-mentum* in Latin, e. g. *ălĭmentum*, have been mentioned in § 30, and the extension of MEN-stems by the YO-, YĀ- suffixes, e. g. *alimōnia, alimonium,* in § 4.

Fem. Verbal Abstracts in -yen-, -tyen- (-tien-) in Lat., Celt., Teut., e. g. Lat. *ūsū-căpio, captio* have become fem. by the analogy of other abstract nouns. They sometimes appear as Ā-stems with the ending -*īna*, -*tīna*, e. g. *Potina*, the goddess worshipped when a child first drank (Non. 108. 15 M.) from *pōtio, Statina*, 'statuendi infantis,' *offĭcina* (*ŏpĭ-fĭcina* Plaut.), *răpina, ruina* (cf. § 8).

§ 55. **Masc. en-stems in Latin.** Lat. *liēn*, Gen. *liēnis* shows *-ēn*, and *pectĕn*, Gen. *pectĭnis* (Gk. κτείς for *πκτενς?*) shows *-ĕn*, but the usual form is *-ō* in the Nom. Sg., *-ōn-* or *-ĭn-* (with *ĭ* for older *ŏ* or *ĕ*) in the oblique cases, e. g. *ĕdō*, Gen. *edōnis* from the verbal root ed-, 'to eat,' *hŏmō*, Gen. *hŏmĭnis* from the nounstem *humo-*, the ground. The Fem. *căro*, Gen. *carnis*, is exceptional in reducing the stem-suffix in the oblique cases to *n*. In Umbr.-Osc. the word has the same declension and gender, but retains the older sense of 'a part,' a 'share,' e. g. Osc. *maimas carneis senateis tanginud*, which would be in Latin, 'maximae partis senatūs sententiā'; and originally the word seems to have been a Verbal Abstract (Nomen Actionis), 'the act of cutting or dividing,' whence the feminine gender. (On the variation of gender in *cardo, margo, cŭpīdo, grando, ŭlīgo, farrāgo*, see Neue, i². p. 654; Abstracts in *-go*, like *ŏrīgo*, are fem., and Nouns indicating defects or ailments like *ferrūgo, aerūgo, cālīgo, prūrīgo*).

Nouns in *-ō*, *-ōnis* Gen., used of persons, belong as a rule to plebeian or colloquial Latin and express contempt, e. g. *āleo, bĭbo, Căpĭto, Nāso*; in the earliest period they are derived only from Adjectives, e. g. *străbo*, but later from Nouns and Verbs, e. g. *commīlĭto* from *mīles, lănio* from *lănius, erro* from *errare, sătŭrio* from *sătŭrire*. The more respectful formation was in *-ōnus*, e. g. *patronus* (but πατρων always on Greek inscriptions, as early as 150 B. C., Eckinger, p. 135); Paul. Fest. quotes O. Lat. *epolonus* for *ĕpŭlo* (55. 15 Th.), *centŭrionus, cŭrionus* and *dĕcŭrionus* (34. 36 Th.); so Dor. Gk. Λᾱτώ became *Lātona*. (On these nicknames, &c. in *-ō*, *-ōnis*, see Fisch, *Lat. Nomina Pers. auf -o, -onis,* 1890.)

§ 56. **Suffixes ending in -r (Nouns of third Decl.).**
-R-. I.-Eur. Neuters in -r (-r̥) seem to have substituted n for r in the oblique cases, e. g. Lat. *fĕmur*, Gen. *fĕmĭnis*, O. Ind. údhar, ' the udder,' údhnas Gen., which has led to confusions of R- and N-stems, e. g. Lat. *jĕcur*, but O. Ind. yakán-, and to such curious declensions in Latin as *ĭt-ĭn-ĕr-ĭs, jĕc-ĭn-ŏr-ĭs*, and *joc-in-er-is*, &c.

§ 57. **Neuter R-stems.** Many of these are names for parts of the body, e. g. *fĕmur, jĕcur, ūber* (*Amer. Journ. Phil.* xii. 1). On O. Lat. *aser*, blood (O. Ind. ásr̥-k Nom., asn-ás Gen.) and on other Neut. R.-stems, see ch. vi. § 15.

§ 58. -ER- and -TER-. As the Comparative suffix is sometimes -ero-, sometimes -tero- (§ 16), so we find -er and -ter as the suffix for forming words of relationship, and masculine Nomina Agentis [with fem. in -(t)rī, -(t)ria, &c., § 51]. This -(t)er- varies with -(t)or-, -(t)ēr-, -(t)ōr-, -(t)r-, &c., e. g. Gk. πατήρ, Acc. πατέρα, and φράτωρ, Acc. φράτορα, Gk. δοτήρ beside δώτωρ, βοτήρ beside βώτωρ, &c. The Nomina Agentis in Latin show -tōr-, e. g. *actor*, Gen. *actōris* (Gk. ἄκτωρ, -ορος and ἐπ-ακτήρ, -ῆρος). Abstracts in *-or*, *-ōris* Gen., often connected with Verbs in *-eo* and Adjectives in *-ĭdus* (e. g. *călor*, beside *caleo*, *calidus*), are not R-stems but S-stems, and had in O. Lat. *-ōs* in the Nom. Sg., e. g. *calos*, though in the classical period the *r*, into which intervocalic s in the oblique cases had passed by the phonetic law of Latin (ch. iv. § 148), forced its way into the Nom. Sing. also (see ch. vi. § 7).

§ 59. Nouns of relationship. Lat. *păter* [O. Ind. pĭtár-, Arm. hair, Gk. πατήρ, O. Ir. athir, Goth. (rare) fadar]; Lat. *māter* [O. Ind. mātár-, Arm. mair, Gk. μήτηρ, O. Ir. māthir, O. Engl. mōdor (in Goth. aiþei, 'mother,' atta, 'father') O. Sl. mater-]; Lat. *frāter* (O. Ind. bhrátar-, Arm. eλbair, Gk. φράτωρ and φράτηρ, a clansman, O. Ir. brāthir, ' a brother,' W. brawd(r), Goth. brōþar ; cf. O. Sl. bratrŭ); Lat. *sŏror* (O. Ind. svásar-, Arm. k'oir, O. Ir. siur and fiur, Lith. sesů̃; cf. Goth. svistar, O. Sl. svestra); Lat. *lĕvir* better *laevir*, for *laever* by Anal. of *vir* (I.-Eur. *daiwer-, O. Ind. dēvár-, Arm. taigr with g for w, Gk. δᾱήρ for *δαιϝηρ, O. Engl. tācor, O. H. G. zeihhur; cf. Lith. dēver-ìs, O. Sl. dĕver-ĭ).

§ 60. Latin Nomina Agentis. Lat. *praetor* for *prae-ĭtor (O. Ind. pura-ētár-, ' he who goes before,' 'a guide'); *junctor* (O. Ind. yōktár-, Gk. ζευκτήρ) (cf. *junctus*); *con-dĭtor* for *con-dător from the root dhē-, 'to put, place' (O. Ind. dhātár- and dhátar-, Gk. θετήρ) (cf. *condĭtus*); *pōtor* (O. Ind. pātár- and pátar-, Gk. ποτήρ) (cf. *pōtus*); *gĕnĭtor* (O. Ind. janitár-, Gk. γενετήρ and γενέτωρ) (cf. *gĕnĭtus*) with Fem. *gĕnĕtrīx* (O. Ind. jánitrī, Gk. γενέτειρά) (on ĕ see ch. iii. § 19); *textor* (O. Ind. táštar-, ' carpenter') (cf. *textus*) ; *ēsor* (O. Ind. attár-, Gk. ὠμηστήρ) (cf. *ēsus*).

§ 61. Suffixes ending in -t (Nouns and Adjectives of third Decl.). -T-. Latin stems in -*t* are probably of various origins. A compound like *com-es* (stem *cŏm-ĭt-) from *cum* and *ire*, which has the sense of a Participle Active, ' going along with,' reminds us of the use of this suffix in O. Ind. with verbal roots ending in vowels, &c., when these roots form the second part of a compound, e. g. O. Ind. viśva-jít-, 'all-conquering,' from ji-, ' to conquer.' To this category belong Latin *t*-stems like *anti-stes* from the root stā-, ' to stand,' *săcer-dōs* from the root dō-, ' to give.' On the other hand adjectives of passive meaning like *man-suēs*, Gen. *mansuētis*, ' accustomed to the hand,' tame (beside *mansuētus*), *in-gens*, Gen. *ingentis*, ' not known,' huge (cf. Engl. uncouth), may be for *mansuetis, *ingentis with that transference of the Adjective to an I-stem which we have seen in O. Lat. *Sanates*, beside *sanati*, *forctis* (class. *fortis*) beside *forctus* (§ 45). It has further been suggested (§ 29) that nouns like *ĕques*, Gen. *equĭtis*, may be connected with Greek formations like ἱππότης, the fem. Abstract *equita, horsemanship, becoming masc. *eques*, a horseman, just as *antistita* fem. is related to *antistes* masc.

Again Feminine *t*-stems like *tĕges*, Gen. *tegĕtis*, a mat, lit. ' a covering,' *sĕges*, Gen. *segĕtis*, a crop, lit. ' a sowing' (W. hau for *sog-, ' to sow '), *merges*, a sheaf, lit. ' a dipping ' (if *merga*, a pitchfork, be rightly explained by Paul. Fest. 89. 13 Th.: quia ... messores eas in fruges demergunt, ut elevare possint manipulos), or ' a plucking ' (cf. Gk. ἀ-μέργω), may have been originally Fem. TI-stems (Nomina Actionis), like *messis* for *met-tis, ' a reaping,' harvest (§ 42), and may show that confusion of the TI- and the T-suffix which is shown by words formed with -tūt(i)-, -tāt(i)-, (§ 46), and bystems like Gk. νυκτ-, Lat. *nocti-*. But Greek nouns like κέλης, -ητος, a horse, lit. ' runner,' from the root kel-, ' to run, go quickly ' (O. Ind. car-; cf. Lat. *celer*), and adjectives like ἀργῆτ- and ἀργέτ-, bright, from the root arĝ-, ' to shine ' (O. Ind. arj-; cf. Lat. *argentum*), rather point to by-forms in -t, beside the usual Pres. Part. stems in -nt, just as Greek compounds like ἀγνώς,-ῶτος, (1) unknowing, (2) unknown, beside ἄγνωτος and ἄγνωστος, προβλής, -ῆτος, a headland, beside προβλητος, thrown forth, suggest that Latin *mansuēs*, &c. may be quite separate forms from *mansuētus*, &c., and not sprung from *mansuētis, still less produced by Syncope of the last syllable of *mansuetus* (cf. ch. iii. § 16).

§ 62. **Other examples of Lat. T-stems.** Lat. *tĕres*, Gen. *terĕtis*, from *tero* ; *hĕbes*, Gen. *hebĕtis* ; *āles*, Gen. *alĭtis*, with the sense of *alātus* ; *tŭdes* (cf. *tŭdĭtare*), an old word for a hammer (Fest. 530. 30 Th. ; Paul. Fest. 531. 12. Th.), from *tundo*, is a rather doubtful form ; and the origin of I.-Eur. *nĕpot- (O. Ind. nápāt-, M. Ir. niae, Gen. niath, W. nai ; cf. Hom. Gk. νέποδες), Lat. *nĕpōs*, with its cognate *nĕptī (O. Ind. naptí-, Goth. ni(f)þjis, 'kinsman,' O. Sl. ne(p)tiji-, ' nephew,' &c.), Lat. *neptis* is not clear. The termination *-es* was much in vogue in the earlier period, e. g. *caelés, -ĭtis, circes, -ĭtis*. From it were formed Abstract Nouns in *-ĭtia, -ĭties*, &c. (see §§ 4, 51) (cf. *axĭtiōsi*, Paul. Fest. 2. 34 Th. : a. factiosi dicebantur, cum plures una quid agerent facerentque, from *axites* id. 3. 1 Th. a. mulieres sive viri dicebantur una agentes. The adj. *axĭtiōsus* is quoted by Varro, L. L. vii. 66 from the *Astraba* of Plautus :

áxitiosae annónam caram e uili concinnánt uiris).

§ 63. -NT-. The suffix -ent-, -ont-, -nt-, &c. plays an important part in the I.-Eur. languages, being used in the formation of all Active Participles, except the Perfect (ch. viii. § 89). In the thematic conjugation we have -ont- in all the cases in Greek (φέροντ-ος, φέρουσι for *φεροντσι, &c.) and other languages; and O. Lat. forms like *flexuntes* (?), as well as the classical *éuntes* where *e* precedes, have been quoted as proof that Lat. *ferent-is*, *ferent-em*, &c. represent an older *feront-, with change of the short vowel before double consonant in the syllable unaccented under the early Accent-law (ch. iii. § 5) into *ĕ* (but see ch. viii. § 90). These Participles have often become adjectives and nouns, e.g. Engl friend (Goth. frijōnds, lit. 'loving'), fiend (Goth. fijands, lit. 'hating,' Germ. Feind), Gk. ἄρχων, Lat. *rudens*, sometimes with transference to the O-declension, e. g. Lat. *vĕntus* (Goth. vinds) beside the Participle, O. Ind. vánt-, Gk. ἀείς for *ἀϜεντς.

§ 64. Other examples of Lat. -ent. Lat. *ăgens* (O. Ind. ájant-, Gk. ἄγων); *fĕrens* (O. Ind. bhárant-, Gk. φέρων, Goth. bairands, .O. Sl. bery); *rudens* (O. Ind. rudánt-), (1) 'roaring,' (2) ' a rope' ; *vĕhens* (O. Ind. váhant-, Goth. gavigands, Lith. vežąs, O. Sl. vezy) ; *bĕnĕvŏlens* is often a Noun (cf. *bĕnĕmĕrens*) in the Comedians, and is closely connected with the Adjective *benevolus*, so that *benevolentior* and *benevolenter* have taken the place of the Comparative and Adverb of the latter, as *magnificentior, magnificentissimus* supply a Comparative and Superlative to *magnificus*. Other Nouns are *părens* (beside the verb *părio*), *serpens, ădŭlescens* ; other Adjectives, *ēlŏquens, săpiens, innŏcens*. The addition of the ya-suffix, which forms the fem. of these participles in Greek (e. g. φέρουσα for *φεροντγᾰ) forms Abstract derivatives in Latin. e. g. *benivolentia, praesentia, eloquentia* (all of these first used by Terence), *confidentia, mălĭvŏlentia, pătientia, săpientia, pollentia*, &c. (all used by Plautus), *sententia* (beside the verb *sentio*). On the rare ending *-entium*, e. g. *silentium*, see Rönsch, *Collect*. p. 208. *Fluentum* and *cruentus* probably originated in Neut. Pl. *fluenta, cruenta* (cf. *silenta loca* Laev.), a formation like Gk. φέροντα, &c. The ending *-lentus* of *ŏpŭlentus* (beside *opulens*), *vĭŏlentus* (and *violens*), *trŭcŭlentus, escŭlentus, vīrŭlentus,* &c. comes from an Adj.-stem in *-lo* (*-li* § 21) ; cf. *grăcĭlentus* (the *o* of *vīnŏlentus, somnŏlentus* has been explained by 'popular etymology' from *vīnō lentus, somnō lentus* ; see ch. iii. § 21).

§ 65. -WENT-. This suffix, like our '-ful,' added to Noun-

§§ 63-67.] NOUN AND ADJECTIVE STEMS. -WENT-, -D-. 353

stems to form Adjectives, with the sense 'possessed of,' 'abounding in,' and occasionally 'resembling,' e. g. O. Ind. agni-vánt-, 'provided with fire,' χαρίεις for *χαριϝεντς, possessed of grace, graceful, στονόεις (Corcyr. στονοϝεσαν, Acc. Sg. Fem.), woeful, is in Latin augmented by the TO-suffix, e. g. *dŏlōsus* (Gk. δολόεις) for *dolo-venssus from *dolo-went-to- or *dolo-wn̥t-to-, *nĭvōsus* (Gk. νιφόεις). In O. Ind. it was often added to the P. P. P. TO-stem, e. g. kr̥ta-vant- from kr̥tá-, P. P. P. of kr̥-, 'to do,' and came to be used in the sense of a Perfect Indicative (with omission of the Substantive Verb), e.g. sa tad kr̥tavān, 'he has done this.'

§ 66. Other examples of Lat. -ōsus. Lat. *vīrosus* (cf. O. Ind. vīṣá-vant-); *vinosus* (cf. Gk. οἰνόεις), (1) full of wine, (2) like wine; *cădăvĕrosus*, like a dead body. From U-stems, *-uosus*, e. g. *aestuosus* (but *fastōsus*, and from the stem *mont-*, *montuōsus*), but from I-stems *-osus*, e. g. *piscosus* (Virgil's rendering of Homer's ἰχθυόεις), (but *bīliosus*). *Incūriosus* (from *incūria*) produced *cūriosus* (instead of **cūrōsus*); *călămĭtōsus* stands for **calamitātosus* (ch. iii. § 13, p. 176). On the change of *-ovenssus* to *-ōsus* (cf. *retrōrsum*, *retrōsum* from *retrōversum*, &c.), see ch. ii. § 53. The older spelling is *-onssus*, *-ossus* (see Brambach, *Orth.* p. 268, and the *Indices* to Ribbeck's Virgil and to Studemund's Apograph of the Ambrosian Palimpsest of Plautus). Gellius (ix. 12) comments on the Active and Passive sense of these Adjectives: ut 'formidulosus' dici potest et qui formidat et qui formidatur, ut 'invidiosus' et qui invidet et cui invidetur, ut 'suspiciosus' et qui suspicatur et qui suspectus est, ut 'ambitiosus' et qui ambit et qui ambitur, ut item 'gratiosus' et qui adhibet gratias et qui admittit, ut 'laboriosus' et qui laborat et qui labori est, &c.

§ 67. **Suffixes ending in -d (Nouns of third Declension).** D-suffixes are not frequent enough in the I.-Eur. languages to enable us to determine the formation of Latin *d*-stems like *lăpis* (cf. Gk. λέπας ?), *mercēs*, *hērēs*, nor to trace the passage of original D-stems into other stems. The -αδ- of Gk. χοιράς, a reef, 'like a hog's back,' πελειάς, a wild dove, has been declared to be the first part of the Latin *-astro-* (for *-ad-tro-) of *poētaster*, 'like a poet,' *ŏleaster*, 'a wild olive,' &c. Lat. *-ēdŭla* occurs in names of birds, &c., e.g. *fīcēdula* (and *ficēlla*?), a beccafico, *acrēdula*, *querquēdula*, *nītēdula* and *nītēlla* (cf. *alcēdo*); Lat. *-ēdo* in names of ailments like *frīgēdo*, *rŭbēdo*, *grăvēdo* (and *gravĭdo*) resembles the -ηδών of Gk. ἀχθηδών, χαιρηδών. Lat. *-dus* of Adjectives beside Verbs in *-eo* and Abstract Nouns in *-or*, e. g. *pallĭdus* (beside *palleo* and *pallor*), *splendĭdus* (beside *splendeo* and

A a

splendor), *squālĭdus* (O. Lat. *squalus*) (beside *squāleo* and *squalor*), has been referred to the root dō-, ' to give ' (cf. O. Ind. jala-das, lit. 'giving moisture,' like Lat. *imbrĭ-dus*, artha-das, ' giving benefit,' but see ch. iii. § 15. (8)); and the termination of Gerundives like *laudandus*, &c. has been similarly explained (**laudamdus*, ' praise-giving ') with the Acc. Sg. of a Verbal Noun as the first part (cf. *vin-dex*) of the compound (see ch. viii. § 94), as well as Verbal Adjectives in *-bundus*, e. g. *errābundus, pŭdĭbundus, fŭrĭbundus, gĕmĕbundus, mŏrĭbundus, lascīvibundus* (*-ib-* probably) and *-cundus*, e. g. *jūcundus, rŭbĭcundus, vĕrēcundus, fēcundus, īrācundus, fācundus*. (On these also, see ch. viii. § 94.) The termination *-tŭdo*, Gen. *-tŭdĭnis*, has been called the amplification of the stem *-tūt-* by an N-stem, *tūt-n- producing *tūd-n- (but see ch. iv. § 161), but it may also be derived from a tu-stem, as *rŭbēdo* from an ē-stem.

§ 68. **Other examples.** Lat. *pĕcus, -ŭdis* beside *pecus, -ŏris* ; Lat. *cassis*, an Etruscan word, according to Isidore (*Orig*. xviii. 14. 1), with transference to the Ā-declension in the byform *cassida*.

§ 69. **Suffixes ending in a Guttural (Nouns and Adjectives of third Declension).** These also are infrequent in I.-Eur. languages, and often have, as we have seen (§ 31), byforms with added -o-, e. g. Gk. ἀλώπηξ (O. Ind. lōpāśá-), Gk. μεῖραξ (O. Ind. maryaká-), Gk. νέαξ (O. Sl. novakŭ), Lat. *sĕnex* (O. Ind. sanaká-, cf. Goth. sineigs; perhaps with the Diminutive suffix -ko-, so that Lat. *senex* may be for **sĕnĕcis*, ' oldish,' with that transference to the I-declension so frequent in Adjectives; cf. *seni-* from I.-Eur. **sĕno-*, O. Ind. sána-, Gk. ἔνος, O. Ir. sen, Lith. sēnas, &c.). Latin Adjectives in *-āx* express tendency or character, e. g. *bĭbāx, dĭcāx, răpāx, pervĭcāx* (O. Lat. *pervicus*) ; of adjectives in *-ix* we have *fēlix* from **fēla*, Gk. θηλή, the breast, *pernix* (properly of horses, &c. *A. L. L.* viii. 453) from *perna*; *-trix* is the fem. ending (O. Ind -trī, Gk. -τρyă) of Masc. Nomina Agentis in -tor, e. g. *gĕnĕtrix* (O. Ind. jánitrī, Gk. γενέτειρα, § 51); *-ōx* appears in the derivatives from Adjectives, *fĕrōx* (from *fĕrus*), *sollōx* (from *sollus*), *ătrōx* (from **ătro-*; cf. *ŏdium*), and in *vēlōx, cĕlōx*, which suggest connexion with *ōcior*. We have O-stem Adjectives with *-ācus*, e. g. *mĕrācus*, and *-īcus*, e. g. *mendīcus, ămīcus* (§ 31), and Ā-stem Nouns with *-īca*, e. g.

lectīca, and *-ūca*, e.g. *lactūca* (§ 32). The Latin termination *-īgo*, in names of ailments, e.g. *vertīgo*, *dēpĕtīgo*, *impĕtīgo*, *cālīgo*, may be due to the addition of an N-suffix to Adjectives in *-īx*, *vertīc-n-, *calīc-n-, &c., and the somewhat similar *-ūgo* of *ferrūgo* (cf. *rōbīgo*), *aerūgo*, *lānūgo*, and in names of plants, e.g. *mollūgo* (*-īgo*), *aspĕrūgo* may similarly represent *-ūc-n-*, the *c* becoming *g* before *n* by the phonetic law of Latin (ch. iv. § 119).

§ 70. **Other examples.** Lat. *pūlĕx*, *-ĭcis*, a flea, but *pulegium*, fleabane; Lat. *lătĕx*, Pl. *latĭces* (but Gk. λάταγες; cf. Gk. ὄρτυγ- but O. Ind. vartaka-); Lat. *vertĕx* from *verto*; Lat. *vervĕx*, a wether; Lat. *nătrix*, *-ĭcis*, a watersnake (O. Ir. nathir, nathrach Gen.).

Words like *aureax* (a. auriga, Paul. Fest. 6. 27 Th.), *aurĭfex*, &c. do not show the Guttural suffix, but are Compounds of *ago*, *facio* (§ 78).

The number of words ending with *-x* that indicate parts of the body is noticeable, e.g. *calx*, *faux*, *coxendix*, *cervix* (or rather *cervīces* Plur., for the Sing. was a poetical usage; cf. Varro, *L. L.* viii. 14 and Quint. viii. 3. 35), *mātrix*, *pantex*, *pōdex*, also bodily marks, e.g. *varix*, *vĭbix*, *famex*, &c.; bird-names in *-ix* are, e.g. *cornix*, *coturnix*, *spinturnix*. Adjectives in *-āx* from second Conj. Verbs are *audax*, *tĕnax* (cf. *rĕtīnāculum*), *mordax*, &c.; from IO-Verbs *căpax*, *efficax*, *perspĭcax*. With *fallax* cf. *falla*, O. Lat. for *fallācia*; with *dĭcax* cf. *dīcā-re* beside *dīcĕre*; with *căpax*, *oc-cŭpā-re*.

§ 71. **Suffixes ending in -s (Nouns and Adjectives of third Declension). -ES-.** The suffix -es-, varying with -os-, -s-, &c. was used to form Neuter Abstract Nouns, with E-grade of root and accent on the root, e.g. I.-Eur. *ĝénos Nom. Sg., *ĝenes- in Oblique Cases, from the root ĝen- (O. Ind. jánas, Gk. γένος Nom., γένε(σ)-ος Gen.), Lat. *gĕnŭs* Nom., *genĕr-is* for *genes-es Gen. These Neuter-stems became adjectives by transferring the accent to the suffix and substituting -ēs for -ŏs in Nom. Sg. Masc., -ĕs in Nom. Sg. Neut., e.g. Gk. εὐ-γενής Masc., -νές Neut. Beside them we find occasionally Masc. or Fem. Nouns with -ōs in Nom. Sg., a formation which came into great favour in Latin, e.g. *tĕnor* Masc. for *tenōs, beside *tenus* Neut. (Gk. τένος, a string), from the root ten-, 'to stretch'; *tĕpor* Masc. for *tepōs (cf. O. Ind. tápas Neut. for *tépos), from the root tep-, 'to be warm.' A case of these Neuters is used as the Infinitive in various languages, e.g. Lat. *vīvĕre* Loc., O. Ind. jīvásē Dat., 'to live' (see ch. viii. § 83).

§ 72. **Neuter ES-stems in Latin.** The original declension with -os Nom., -es- in Oblique Cases and Derivatives, is sometimes departed from, e.g. *tempus*,

356   THE LATIN LANGUAGE.   [Chap. V.

-ŏris (but cf. tempĕri, tempes-tīvus); ŏnus, ŏnustus (but cf. oneris, onerare); Velius Longus (p. 73. 1 K.) calls attention to the discrepancy between faenoris and faeneratorem, făcĭnoris and facinerosus. We have the O-grade of the root, e. g. in mŏdes-tus (by analogy of the O-stem mŏdus) from *modes-¹, from the root med- (but Umbr. mers for *med(o)s Neut., the right, the due, is normal), foedus [also fīdus, i. e. *feidos, to judge from Varro L. L. v. 86 per hos (Fetiales) etiamnunc fit foedus quod 'fidus' Ennius scribit dictum; cf. Paul. Fest. 64. 3 Th. fidusta a fide denominata, ea quae maximae fidei erant] from the root bheidh-, pondus by analogy of pondo- (Abl. pondō) from pendo. Mĭnerva was in earlier times *Menes-ua (§ 7), a derivative of the Neut. stem *ménes- (O. Ind. mánas-, Gk. μένος), from the root men-. From other than E-roots we have, e. g. ŏpus (O. Ind. ápas and ápas, 'work,' especially 'a religious performance'). The ending -nus is seen in făcĭnus (cf. Gk. δά-νος), &c. The -r of rōbur (O. Lat. robus, see Georges, Lex. Wortf. s. v.) may be due to the Masc. byform robor (cf. O. Lat. robosem Acc., quoted by Paul. Fest. 11. 20 Th.); cf. călor Neut. (Plaut. Merc. 860). The weak grade of the suffix, -s-, is seen in the derivative O-stem O. Ind. vats-á- for *wetso-, 'a calf,' lit. 'a yearling,' from *wetos, 'a year' (Gk. ϝέτος), &c. Other examples are Vĕnus (originally Neuter and meaning 'glamour,' like O. Ind. vánas-; cf. vĕnēnum for *venes-num, properly 'a philtre'); tergus (Gk. στέρφος and τέρφος).

§ 73. **Adjective ES-stems.** Of the transference of a Neut. S-stem into an Adjective a good example is Lat. vĕtus, which is nothing but I.-Eur. *wĕtos (Gk. ϝέτος, a year) used in apposition as a predicate (cf. Hom. Gk. πῖαρ, Lat. ūber, &c.). The ordinary way of making an Adjective from a Neuter S-stem was by adding the suffix -to- (§ 27), e. g. vĕtustus, to which however, owing to the cacophony of the two similar syllables, vetus was preferred in the Positive and veterrimus in the Superlative, though vetustior was the Comparative in vogue (cf. Varro, L. L. vi. 59 a vetere vetustius ac veterrimum), ŏnŭs-tus, scĕlĕs-tus, fūnĕstus, jūs-tus. Perhaps another way was to add the suffix -o-, e. g. O. Lat. scĕlĕrus, and perhaps fūnĕrus (beside fūnereus) (see Fleck. Jahrb. 1891, p. 676; both forms are doubtful) (cf. dĕcōrus from dĕcor, § 74). The veter used by Ennius (Ann. 16 M. cum ueter occubuit Priamus sub Marte Pelasgo) and Accius (Trag. 481 R.) may be of this formation, or of the third Decl. like pūber (beside pubēs Adj.) and the Compounds dēgĕner, bĭcorpor, &c.

§ 74. **Masc. (and Fem.) ES-stems.** The usual termination is -or Nom., -ōris Gen. (older -ōs, -ōsis), e. g. dĕcor (beside decus; with Adj. decōrus, O. Lat. decōrem Accus.; cf. indecōrem beside indecōrum); angor (O. Ind. áhas Neut.; with Adj. angustus); hŏnor (with Adj. honestus); arbor F. (with Adj. *arbustus, cf. arbustum, § 28); paedora is Vulg. Lat. for paedores (C. G. L. iv. 270. 4 'paedora' aurium sordes). The -s remains in flōs [like Flōra F. beside flōs M. is aurōra beside I.-Eur. *ausōs (Gk. ἠώς F.)]; while some have found -ēs in the Fem. nouns sēdēs, beside I.-Eur. *sĕdŏs (O. Ind. sádas, Gk. ἕδος), plēbēs (Gk. πλῆθος), and perhaps aedēs beside aedis (see Georges, Lex. Wortf. s. v.) (O. Ind. édhas, Gk. αἶθος) (but see § 51). These Masc. Nouns in -or are widely used as Verbal Abstracts, connected with Verbs in -eo and Adjectives in -ĭdus, e. g. pallor (palleo, pallidus), timor (timeo, timidus) (see § 67; and for a list of examples

---

¹ Plaut. Curc. 200 immodestis tuis modereris moribus.

§§ 73–77.] NOUN AND ADJECTIVE STEMS. -YES-. 357

A. L. L. viii. 313). The Verb in *-eo* is not found with *fluor, fluidus, cruor, crūdus* (cf. O. Ind. kraviṣ-, 'raw flesh,' Gk. κρέας); the Adj. in *-ĭdus* is not found with *fāvor (făveo)*, a coinage of Cicero's time (Quint. viii. 3. 34).

§ 75. Other S-stems. Lat. *cĕrĕbrum* for **ceresrum* points to an S-stem like O. Ind. śíras-, 'the head,' Gk. κέρας, a horn; Lat. *tĕnĕbrae* for **tenesrae* (cf. O. Ind. támis-rā beside támas, 'darkness'; cf. Lat. *tĕmĕre*, lit. 'in the dark'); Lat. *cĭnis* M., sometimes F., resembles Gk. κόνις F. in its termination; Lat. *fār, farris* Gen. for **fars, *farsis* has a derivative *fărīna* for **farisna*, Fem. of an Adj. **farisnus* (cf. Goth. bariz-eins, 'made of barley').

§ 76. -YES-. This suffix, used to form Comparatives (cf. the 'Comparative' use of -yo-, § 4), appears in Latin as *-ior* Nom. M., F., *-iōris* Gen., *-ius* Nom. N. (older *-iōs, -iōsis, -iŏs*), e. g. *suāvior, suāviōris, suāvius*. The variations of the suffix are not easy to determine amid the variety of forms in the various languages (e. g. O. Ind. svā́d-īyas-, with Nom. svā́d-īyān, Gk. ἡδίων, Acc. ἡδίω for **ἡδιοσα*, Goth. sutiza for **sut-izen-, Lith. sald-ēs-nis, &c.), but it is certain that the weak grade -ĭs- was prefixed to the suffix -tŏ- (-thŏ-?) to form Superlatives in various languages (O. Ind. svā́d-iṣṭha-, Gk. ἥδιστος, Goth. sutists), though in Latin this formation was ousted by *-issimus* (cf. however *măgis, magis-ter*, &c.). These suffixes were originally affixed to the root without the suffix of the Positive stem (so Lat. *ōc-ior*, O. Ind. ā́ś-īyas-. Gk. ὠκ-ίων from a Positive stem **ōku-), but we have also in Latin, e. g. *tĕnu-ior, suāvior* for **suadv-ior, aspĕr-ior*, &c.

For other details of the formation of Comparatives and Superlatives in Latin, see ch. vi. section 2.

§ 77. Suffixless Forms. Nouns formed directly from the root, without any suffix except those of the cases, are especially frequent as the second element of a Compound, and take in this position the function of a Nomen Agentis, e. g. Lat. *au-spex*, 'seer of birds,' from the root spek-, 'to see,' *parti-ceps*, 'taking a share.' They are also found independently, e. g. O. Ind. spáś-, 'a spy,' often with a high grade of vowel, e. g. Gk. σκώψ, an owl (cf. ch. iii. § 51, p. 254), both from the same root spek̑- (sk̑ep-). The passage of such forms into the vowel declension is a very near one, so that we find bystems with and without a suffix in the same language, e. g. Lat. *auspex* beside *exti-spĭcus* (a late form of *exti-spex*), or in different languages, e. g. O. Ind. naú-, Gk. ναῦς beside Lat. *nāv-i-s*, O. Ind. úd-añc- beside Gk. ποδ-απ-ό-ς, Lat. *prŏp-inqu-o-s*. The Latin Inf. Pass., e. g. *ăgī*, seems to be a case of a suffixless Verbal Noun (cf. O. Ind. nir-ájē, dŕ̥śḗ, Inf. of dr̥ś-, 'to look'), just as the Inf. Act., e. g. *ăgĕrĕ*, seems to ,be the Locative case of a Verbal Stem in -es- (see ch. viii. § 83).

§ 78. Suffixless stems at end of Compounds in Latin. From *jungo*, *con-jux* (cf. O. Ind. sa̱-yuj-, Gk. σύ-ζυξ) and *con-junx* (O. Ind. yúnj- beside yúj-) ; from *făcio, artĭfex, carnĭfex, ŏpĭfex*, &c. ; from *căpio, manceps, auceps, forceps* for **formi-ceps, prīnceps*, &c. ; from *dico, jūdex, vindex* ; from *sĕdeo, dēses, rĕses* ; from *căno, cornĭcen, fĭdĭcen* ; from *ăgo, rēmex, aureax*, &c. Beside these we have often O-stems, &c., e. g. *jūrĭ-dĭcus* beside *jū-dex, prōd-ĭgus* beside *rĕm-ex*, O. Lat. *hosti-capas* (hostium˘ captor, Paul. Fest. 73. 10 Th.), *urbĭ-căpe* Voc. (Plaut. *Mil.* 1055) beside *auceps*, &c. The presence of suffixless stems in the second part of Compounds in other I.-Eur. languages forbids us to regard the third Decl. forms as due to Latin syncope of the O-suffix in the Nom. Case, **avi-cap(o)s*, &c. (see ch. iii. § 16). But in some adjectives original O-stems may have become I-stems (cf. § 34), and the Nominative form may be due to syncope or to the analogy of consonant-stems (just as *pars* Nom. for *parti-s, with Gen. *partis*, is due to syncope or to the analogy of *rēx* Nom. with Gen. *rēg-is*, &c.), e. g. *praecox* beside *praecŏquis* and *praecoquus, cohors* for *cohortis from *hortus*. The Feminines add *a*, e. g. *exti-spĭc-a, fĭdĭ-cĭn-a*.

§ 79. Latin Independent suffixless stems. Lat. *rēx* (O. Ind. ráj-, O. Ir. ríg Gen.) from the root reĝ-, of *rĕgo* ; *lēx* from *lĕgo* ; *pēs* Nom., *pĕd-is* Gen. (cf. O. Ind. pad-, pád-am Acc., Dor. Gk. πούς Nom., ποδ-ός Gen., &c.); *fur* for *fŏr (ch. iv. § 16) (Gk. φώρ) from the root bher- ; *rēs* (O. Ind. rás) ; *hiems* (Zend zyå, Gk. χιών) ; *ōs*, the mouth (O. Ind. ās-) ; *mūs* (O. Ind. mūṣ́-, Gk. μῦς, O. H. G. mūs) ; *dĭc-is* Gen., in the phrase *dicis causa*, for form's sake (O. Ind. díś-, 'direction') from the root deik-, of *dīco* ; *nĭx* (Gk. νίφ-α Acc.); *sal* (Gk. ἅλς) ; *sūs, sŭbus* Dat. Pl. (Gk. ὗς, O. H. G. sū) ; *dŭx* from *dūco* ; *prĕc-es* Plur. from root prek̂-, 'to ask'; *vŏx* (O. Ind. vāć- F.) beside *vŏco*. (On the long vowel, see ch. iv. § 51, p. 254.)

§ 80. II. COMPOSITION. Compounds are seldom resolvable into two intact words like Gk. Διόσ-κουροι, ἀρηί-φατος, slain in battle, Lat. *sĕnātūs-consultum, patres-fămĭliārum, jūris-jūrandi, res-publĭca*, O. Engl. Tīwes-dæg, 'Tuesday.' Sometimes, as in reduplicated words, one element is reduced almost beyond recognition, either the second element (in 'broken' or curtailed Reduplication), e. g. Lat. *bal-b-us* (cf. O. Ind. bal-balā-karōmi), *gur-g-es*, a whirlpool (cf. O. Ind. gár-gara-), or more usually the first, e. g. *ci-cindē-la*, a glow-worm, while Lat. *gur-gŭl-io*, the throat, *quer-quĕr-us, mur-mur*, &c. give equal prominence to both elements. But generally the full stem without the case suffixes

§§ 78-80.] NOUN AND ADJECTIVE STEMS. COMPOUNDS. 359

is used in the first part of the Compound, e.g. *patrĭ-cīda* (contrasted with *patres-familiarum*), *jūrĭ-dĭcus* (contrasted with *jurisjurandi*). The treatment of these stems which begin the Compound is the special subject of this section.

Owing to the weakening of unaccented vowels in Latin, every vowel in the final syllable of such a stem was liable to change under the early accentuation of the first syllable of each word (ch. iii. § 5). It is therefore often necessary to call in the aid of other I.-Eur. languages before one can determine the original vowel in a Latin Compound, e.g. *ālĭ-ger* from *āla* may be shown to have been originally **alŏ-ger* by Greek ὑλο-τόμος, &c. from ὕλη (§ 82), though, so far as the Latin form goes, it might equally well have been **ală-ger*, **alĕ-ger*, &c., while in *forceps* for **formi-ceps* the vowel has been suppressed altogether by Syncope (ch. iii. § 13), in *arcŭbii* for *arci-cubii* by Dissimilation (*ib.* p. 176). Ŏ is the I.-Eur. 'Composition-Vowel' *par excellence*. Not only does it appear in O-stems, but it is often added to Consonant-stems, and sometimes takes the place of the -ā of Ā-stems. In Latin post-tonic ŏ (like ă and other short vowels) became, as was shown in ch. iii. § 18, ŭ before labials (later ĭ), and ĭ before other single consonants (except *r*), so that ĭ is the 'Composition-Vowel' of Latin as ŏ of I.-Eur. (cf. *Unŏmammia* Plaut., *Oinu-mama* on a Praenestine inscription, *ūnĭmamma*, an Amazon).

The second part of a Compound is often scarcely to be distinguished from a suffix. Thus the second part of *imbrĭ-dus* (cf. O. Ind. jala-da-, lit. 'moisture-giving,' § 67) is often called the 'suffix' *do-*; and the form taken by the final vowel of the stem before a suffix is often determined by the same laws as before the second element of a Compound (cf. *făbā-ginus* with *fabā-ceus*, *fabā-tus*, *fabā-rius*, *fabā-lis*; *imbrĭ-dus* with *imbrĭ-cus*). For these laws with suffixes, laws often disturbed by the influence of analogy, e.g. *ănīlis* (from *anu-*) for **anŭlis* by analogy of *sĕnīlis* (from *seni-*), see the preceding section.

Composition does not play so great a part in Latin as in Greek (cf. Liv. xxvii. 11. 4 quos 'androgynos' vulgus, ut pleraque, faciliore ad duplicanda verba Graeco sermone, appellat). The early dramatists and other imitators of Greek poetry incurred the censure of Quintilian for their attempts to reproduce Greek compounds like κυρταύχην in Latin (Quint. i. 5. 70 sed res tota magis Graecos decet, nobis minus succedit: nec id fieri natura puto, sed alienis favemus, ideoque cum κυρταύχενα mirati simus, 'incurvicervicum' vix a risu defendimus, alluding to Pacuvius' line:

Nérei repándirostrum incuruiceruicúm pecus);

and Virgil uses a periphrasis like (Averna) *sonantia silvis* (*A.* iii. 442) where an earlier poet might have employed a compound like *silvĭsŏnus* (cf. *silvĭfrăgus*, used by Lucretius, who however complains that the 'patrii sermonis egestas' prevented him from reproducing the Greek compound ὁμοιομέρεια, i. 832). The compound Proper Names of other I.-Eur. languages are, as we have seen (§ 4), replaced in Latin (and Umbro-Oscan) by Adjective IO-stems, such as *Lūcius* [on the compound *Opiter*, see ch. iii. § 16 (9)]. The Latin language does not therefore give the same occasion as the Greek for a study of the I.-Eur. types of Compounds, or the various irregularities which disturbed the normal course of Composition; and a brief account of these types and irregularities will suffice.

I.-Eur. Compounds, Nouns and Adjectives, are sometimes classified according to the scheme of the Sanscrit grammarians [Dvandva or Collectives, Bahuvrîhi or Possessives, Tatpurusha or Determinatives (including Karmadhâraya formed of Adj. and Noun, and Dvigu formed of Numeral and Noun), Avyayîbhâva or Adverbial Compounds], sometimes by the more rational criterion of the change or retention of the meaning of the second element (thus the Possessive *longĭ-mănus*, 'possessing long hands,' 'long-handed,' changes its second element from a Noun to an Adjective, while the Determinative *perennĭ-servus*, 'a constant slave,' retains the Noun-meaning of *servus*), these two main classes being subdivided according to the nature of the first element [a Noun or Adj. stem as in *longi-manus*, a Particle as in *in-certus*, *vē-sānus*, a Preposition as in *con-servus*, a Noun or Adj. Case as in *vin-dex*, *lēgislator*, *jurisdictio* (contrast *jūrĭ-dĭcus*), the last being, as we have seen, rather Word-groups than Compounds; cf. *parcē-prōmus* Plaut., *bĕnĕ-vŏlus*, *paen-insŭla* (contrast

§ 80.]   NOUN AND ADJECTIVE STEMS. COMPOUNDS.   361

lĕvĭ-densis, sollĭ-cĭtus)], &c. Of Possessive Compounds (Sanscr. Bahuvrîhi) examples are *anguĭ-pes*, 'possessing a foot which is a snake,' 'snake-footed'[1]; *pŭdōrĭ-cŏlor*, 'possessing the colour of shame,' 'shame-coloured,' *sicc-ŏcŭlus*, 'possessing dry eyes,' 'dry-eyed.' Of Determinatives with first element consisting of (1) a governed Noun (Sanscr. Tatpurusha): *vītĭ-sător*, 'planter of the vine,' *artĭ-fex*, *ăquĭ-lex*; (2) Adjective qualifying a Noun (Sanscr. Karmadhâraya): O. Lat. *albŏ-gălērus*, the white cap of the Flamen Dialis, *suāvĭ-sāviātio* Plaut., *vīvĕ-rādix* Cato, *lātĭ-clāvus* (the Adj. contrary to rule follows the Noun in Pliny's *equifer*, a wild horse; cf. *ovĭfer*, a wild sheep); (3) Numeral, *trĭ-nummus*. (For other examples of Numeral Compounds, see ch. vi. sect. iii.) Coordinate Compounds (Sanscr. Dvandva, e.g. agnidhūmau, 'fire and smoke') are not found in Latin, except in Derivatives, e.g. *su-ŏvĭ-taurīlia* (but not *su-ovi-taurus*), a sacrifice of a swine, a sheep, and a bull, *stru-fer(c)tarii*, those who offered 'struem et fertum.' Scaliger's rule that a Noun is never compounded with a Verb was a law of I.-Eur. Noun-compounds, and is not broken in good Latin, though Tertullian coins *vinci-pes* by false analogy of *nudi-pes*, whose first element he conceives as a verb, 'qui pedes nudat' (*de Pall.* 5 quem enim non expediat in algore et ardore rigere nudipedem quam in calceo vincipedem?), and *Verti-cordia* was a name under which Venus was worshipped. As we have seen in the chapter on the Latin Accent (ch. iii.), the line is often hard to draw between a Word-group (united under a single accent) and a Compound, e.g. *affatim* (from *ad fatim*), *denuo* (from *de novo*), *Juppiter* (from *Jū-pater*, Voc., ch. vi. § 32). From the group *per noctem* has been formed the Compound Adj. *pernox*, much as *mērī-die* [a single word like O. Lat. *diequinte* or *diequinti*, ch. iii. § 12[a] (9)], which is only found in this form in the earlier writers, gave rise to the Compound Noun *meridies*; from *Sacra Via* we have the derivative *Sacravienses*, from *quarta dĕcĭma* (sc. *legio*) the derivative *quartadecimāni* (cf our 'get-at-able,' &c. formed from the

---

[1] These Possessives were originally used in Apposition, e.g. *angui-pes*, 'Snake-foot.' Hence in Greek -os is retained in the Fem. of Compounds like ῥοδο-δάκτυλος ('Ηώς), 'Rose-finger.'

phrase 'to get at'). *Holusatrum* differs from a word-group by the fact that the first element remains undeclined in *holusatri* Gen., &c. (§ 85); *vin-dex*, by the fact that *-dex* (*-dix*) is not used as a separate word, though the first element shows the Noun in its proper Case (for a similar explanation of *laudan-dus*, &c., see ch. viii. § 95). Similarly the Case instead of the Stem appears in the first element of *centum-pĕda* (cf. Gk. ἑκατόμ-πεδος), beside *centĭ-peda* (but see ch. vi. § 76), while the reverse is seen in the forms *multĭ-mŏdis* (for *multis modis*), *omnĭ-modis* (for *omnĭbus modis*), which are used by Plautus. Plautus is especially fond of whimsical compounds coined on the Greek type, and often half-Greek, half-Latin, e. g. *Pers.* 702–5:

Uaníloquidorus Uírginesuendónides
Nugíepiloquides Árgentumextenebrónides
Tedígniloquides Núm*mos*expalpónides
Quodsémelarripides Númquameripides : óm tibi.

Căvaedium may stand for *cav(um) aedium*, *domnaedium* Accus. for *dŏmĭn(um) aedium*, as *ănĭmadverto* for *anim(um) adverto* (ch. iii. § 52) (*ănĭmaequĭtas* has similarly been referred to *anim(i) aequitas*); Lucr. uses *ordia prima* for *primordia*; and *summopere*, *magnŏpere*, &c. represent *summo opere*, *magno opere*, and the like. Greek compounds like ἀριστό-χειρ (with a Superlative as first element), αὐτό-χειρ (with a Pronoun) are alien to the spirit of the Latin language.

These Noun and Adjective Compounds sometimes retain the stem of their second element unchanged, e. g. *sicc-ŏcŭlus*, sometimes add a suffix (on *ŏpĭfĭcus*, &c. beside *ŏpĭfex*, &c., see § 77). Compound O-stem Adjectives, as we have seen (§ 34), tended to become I-stems, e. g. O. Lat. *ĭnermus*, class. *inermis*; and Compound Nouns (and Adjectives) affected the IO-suffix, e. g. *lātĭclāvium* beside *lātĭclāvus* (so the Vulgar Compound formed from the Word-group *terrae mōtus* assumed the form *terrimotium*, Prob. App. 198. 32 K.). Often the selection of a suffix for a Compound is determined by the usage in Derivatives from the simple word, e. g. *transmărīnus* from *trans mare*, like *marinus* from *mare*, *dŭbingĕniōsus* from *dubius* and *ingenium*, like *ingeniosus* from *ingenium*, *simplūdiārius* (cf. *ludiarius*).

Compound Verbs have normally as their first element a Preposition (see ch. ix.). Whether the Negative Particle *in* might be used, e.g. *ig-nosco*, 'not to notice,' to overlook or pardon, is doubtful (see ch. x. § 18; cf. *ne-scio, ne-queo,* &c.). But Compounds like *aedĭfĭcare* from *aedes* and *facio* are really Derivatives from Compound Adjectives or Nouns, *aedificus* or *aedifex*; so that Scaliger's law (see above) is not violated (cf. Gk. οἰκοδομέω, &c. from οἰκοδόμος); so *nāvĭgare* from **navigus, ŏpĭtŭlari* from **opitulus* (like *philosophari* from *philosophus*). (On these Deriv. Verbs, see ch. viii. §§ 21, 33.) *Bĕnĕfăcio, mălĕfacio*, &c. are really word-groups, and so are *călĕfacio, arefacio*, &c. (cf. *facit āre* Lucr.). *Crēdo* comes from an I.-Eur. word-group (O. Ind. śrád dadhāmi, 'I set the heart to,' see ch. viii. § 27). Compound Adverbs like *dērĕpentĕ, dēsŭbĭtō* are discussed in ch. ix., and also Compound Prepositions like Vulg. Lat. *ăbante* (Fr. avant). (For a fuller treatment of Latin Compounds than can be permitted within the limits of this book, see Skutsch, *Nom. Lat. Comp.*).

§ 81. **Reduplicated Nouns and Adjectives in Latin.** Lat. *gur-g-es*, whirlpool, *gur-gŭl-io*, throat (O. Ind. gár-gar-a-, 'whirlpool,' Gk. γαρ-γαρ-εών, uvula, γέρ-γερ-ος, throat, O. H. G. quer-chal-a and quer-ch-a, Germ. Gurgel); *bal-b-us* (O. Ind. bal-bal-ā-karōmi, 'I stammer,' Gk. βάρ-βαρ-o-s); *quer-quĕr-u-s*, cold, shivering (frigidus cum tremore, Paul. Fest. 343. 5 Th., who quotes from Lucilius febris *querquera*, the ague) (cf. Hom. Gk. καρκαίρω), has reduplicated form like other words for trembling, shivering, such as Germ. zittere from **ti-trō-mi; *can-cer* (cf. O. Ind. kar-kaṭ-a-, Gk. καρ-κίν-ο-s); *mur-mur* (O. Ind. mar-mar-a-, Gk. μορ-μύρ-ω, Lith. mùr-m-iu); *ta-ta*, like *mamma*, children's words mentioned in Martial's witty epigram (i. 100):

'mammas' atque 'tatas' habet Afra; sed ipsa tatarum
dici et mammarum maxima mamma potest,

and found on children's epitaphs, e.g. *C.I.L.* vi. 25808 destituisti, Vitilla mea, miseram mammam tuam (cf. ch. ii. p. 118 *n*), *qui-squĭl-iae*, shreds of leather, &c. (Gk. κο-σκυλ-μάτια) (Caec. *Com.* 251 R. quisquilias uolantis, uenti spolia); *fīber* (the I.-Eur. name was *bhe-bhr-u-, O. Ind. ba-bhr-ú-, 'brown,' O. H. G. bi-bar, 'a beaver,' Lith. bĕ-br-u-s, O. Sl. be-br-ŭ). Reduplication is common in onomatopoetic words, e.g. *cŭ-cūlus* (cf. Gr. κόκκυξ, Lith. ku-kŭ́-ti, 'to cry cuckoo,' &c.), *ŭp-ŭp-a* (cf. Gk. ἔπ-οψ), *ŭl-ŭl-a* (cf. O. Ind. ul-ul-í-, Gk. ὀλ-ολ-ῡγή), *tur-tur*. The Latin tendency is to assimilate the first to the subsequent syllable, e.g. *cin-cin-nus* (Gk. κί-κιν-νος) (cf. *mŏ-mord-i* for earlier *mĕ-mord-i*, &c., see ch. iv. § 163). Often a reduplicated Noun is a derivative from a reduplicated Verb-form, e.g. *ci-cindē-la* from **cĭ-cinde-o*, a reduplicated form of *candeo*, like Gk. δι-δαχ-ή from δι-δάσκω, κε-κράγ-μός from κέ-κράγ-α. (On these reduplicated Verb-forms, see ch. viii. § 9.)

§ 82. **Ā-stems** show sometimes ā, but usually ŏ in I.-Eur. compounds,

(e. g. Gk. νικη-φόρος and Νικό-μαχος, O. Ind. urvarā-jít- and ukhă-chíd-, Lith. sziksznó-sparnis and gaĭvă-raisztis, Gaul. Teutŏ-bōdiăci, Goth. airþă-kunds), so that Lat. ĭ of *tŭbi-cen, āli-ger,* &c. must have been originally o. The long a is probably seen in *fābā-ginus, ŏleā-ginus*, as before suffixes like *Rōmā-nus, ālā-ris*. Stems in -iā seem to show a similar divergence of forms, *tŭbĭ-cen* with ĭ for iŏ (§ 4), and before a suffix *viā-tĭcus*.

§ 83. O-stems appear with -ŏ in Gk. ἱππό-δαμος, Gaul. Dēvo-gnāta, Eporēdia, Teut. Austro-valdus, &c., so that Lat. ĭ of *belli-ger, magni-fĭcus*, earlier ŭ before a labial, e. g. *magnu-ficus*, is probably a weakening in the unaccented syllable of original ŏ. O. Lat. spellings (mostly before a labial), like *Ūnomammia* (Plaut. *Curc.* 445 ; cf. *Oinu-mama*, an Amazon, on an old Praenestine cista, *C. I. L.* i. 1501), *sescento-plāgus* (Plaut. *Capt.* 726), *albo-gălĕrus* (Paul. Fest. 8. 6 Th.), *Ăhĕno-barbus* may thus be genuine relics of the oldest spelling, though late compounds like *mālo-grānātum* must be imitations of the Greek. Before a vowel this -ŏ is elided in Latin (as in Greek, &c., e. g. ἱππ-αγωγός), e. g. *magn-ănimus, aequ-ănimitas*, forms like *multi-angŭlus* being late. Lat. -IO-stems show -iĕ- for -iĭ- by Dissimilation (ch. iv. § 13) before a suffix in *sŏcie-tas, anxietas*, &c., but -ī- in *Lucūlius*, &c. (cf. *hostī-lis* from the I-stem *hosti-*). Like *sescentoplāgus*, &c. is O. Lat. *sŏcio-fraudus* or *sociu-fraudus* in Plaut. *Pseud.* 362. (The Palatine MSS. have o, the Ambrosian Palimpsest u.) Latin ro-stems show -ĕr- by rule [ch. iii. § 15. (8)], e. g. *sacer-dōs*, but sometimes -rĭ-, e. g. *sacri-fex*, after the law by which -rĭ- became -ĕr- had been forgotten.

§ 84. I-stems had ĭ in I.-Eur. compounds (e. g. O. Ind. tri-pád-, Gk. τρίπους, Gaul. *tri-garanus*, O. Engl. þri-fête, Lith. tri-kójis, O. Sl. tri-ząbŭ), and so Lat. *tri-ennium, trĭ-gĕminus*, though by rule -rĭ- [at least unaccented -rĭ-, ch. iii. § 15. (8)], became -ĕr- in Latin, e. g. *ter-geminus*, and before a labial ĭ was by the older spelling properly ŭ, e. g. *ācrŭfŏlios* Cato (*R. R.* xxxi. 1), as before r it was ŏ, e. g. *lĕgĕrŭpa* Plaut. Before a vowel this ĭ (now become y) might be dropped, e. g. *fūn-ambulus* (coined by Messalla to express Gk. σχοινοβάτης, Porph. ad Hor. *S.* i. 10. 28), from **funy-ambulus, sēm-ermis* for **semyermis*.

§ 85. U-stems had originally ŭ (e. g. O. Ind. svādu-rātí-, Gk. ἡδυ-(ϝ)επής, Gaul. Catu-rīges ; O. H. G. Hadu-mar, Lith. virszù-kalnis), so that the older spelling *mănŭ-festus* preserves the earliest form (class. *mănĭ-festus*). From diphthongal U-stems we have *nau-frăgus* (see ch. iv. § 46), *bū-caeda* beside *bŏvĭcīdium*, *bu-star* and *bo-star*, an ox-stall (ch. iv. § 42), *jū-glans* (Gk. Διὸς βάλανος) (Macr. iii. 18. 3). *Dies-pitris* (*C. L. L.* xi. 3259), *Dies-pitri* Arnob. ii. 70 (cf. *Dies-pitrem*, Macrob. i. 15. 14 'ut diei patrem') may be a case of the declension only of the second part of a word-group, like *holus-atri* for *holeris atri* (§ 80), or pronouns like *alter-uter, alter-utrius* Gen. (ch. vii. § 29). On *Juppiter*, see ch. vi. § 32.

§ 86. N-stems show, as we have seen (§ 54), their close connexion with O-stems, by substituting -ŏ for -n whether in the first half of a compound, e. g. Gk. ἀκμό-θετον, stithy, from ἄκμων, Lat. *hŏmĭ-cīda*, from *homo* (cf. Goth. guma-kunds, 'of male sex'), or in the second, e. g. Gk. ὅμαιμος beside ὁμαίμων. We find also n̥ in Gk. ὀνομά-κλυτος, so that the en of Lat. *nomen-clātor*, &c. was originally n̥; also the 'Composition vowel' -ŏ- added to the stem, e. g. Gk. φρεν-ο-βλαβής, Lat. *ĭmāgĭn-ĭ-fer*.

§§ 83-90.] NOUN AND ADJECTIVE STEMS. COMPOUNDS. 365

§ 87. R-stems, like N-stems, take the weak grade of the stem suffix before a consonant, ṛ (e. g. O. Ind. pitṛ-śrávaṇa-, Gk. τετρά-γυος, Goth. brōþru-lubō), before a vowel, r (e. g. O. Ind. pitr-artham, Gk. πατρ-ωνύμιος), and often add the 'Composition vowel' ŏ (e. g. Gk. πατρο-φόνος). Since Latin -ŏr- (for I.-Eur. ṛ), -ri- (for I.-Eur. -rŏ-) would generally become in the unaccented syllable -ĕr-, it is not easy to decide on the origin of -ĕr- in each case. For patrĭ-cīda, patrĭ-cus, &c. we should expect *patercida, *patercus; cf. acertas on the Aes Italicense. (C. I. L. ii. 6278, l. 36, of 176-180 A.D.)

§ 88. Dental and Guttural Stems. The frequent interchange of consonantal with I-stems in Latin (§ 34), suggests that the -ĭ- of dent-i-frangĭbŭlus, pĕd-i-sĕquus, rĕg-i-fŭgium, may have been original ĭ. It may also have been the ŏ, which is often used as 'Composition vowel,' with these stems, in other languages [e. g. Gk. δρακοντ-ό-μαλλος, νιφ-ό-βολος, Gaul. Carant-o-magus, Cinget-o-rīx (lit. 'king of warriors'; cf. O. Ir. cing, 'a warrior,' from cingim, 'I march')]. Before r we should have ĕ, e. g. lĕgĕrŭpa (Plaut.), and before a labial ŭ (ŏ) in the older spelling (see ch. iii. § 18).

§ 89. S-stems. The S-stems, like other consonant-stems in Latin, often show ĭ, e. g. mŭr-ĭ-cīdus, jūr-ĭ-dīcus, whether the ĭ of I-stems or the 'Composition vowel' ŏ it is not easy to decide. But we find also the normal stem, e. g. mūs-cĭpŭla (cf. Gk. μῦσ-φόνος). The ES-stems took -ĕs- in I.-Eur. compounds [e. g. Gk. σακεσ-φόρος (the poetical form), Goth. sigis-laun], and so before suffixes in Latin tempes-tīvus, hŏnes-tus, &c., though -ŭs-, by Analogy of the Nom. Sing., is found in ŏnus-tus, &c. In Latin compounds the stem suffix is either displaced by ĭ [the ŏ of Gk. ἐπο-ποιός (the prose form), ἀληθό-μαντις, &c. O. Sl. čudo-točĭnŭ], e. g. foedĭ-frăgus, or augmented by it, e. g. foedĕr-ĭ-fragus, hŏnŏr-ĭ-fĭcus (cf. O. Sl. čudes-o-točĭnŭ, Goth. aiz-a-smiþa).

§ 90. Stem-suffixes and Composition in Romance. The Latin suffixes have for the most part remained productive in Romance (e. g. Ital. cannonata with the TO-suffix), though their meaning has sometimes undergone a change. Thus -ino-, which has ousted -e(y)o-, the suffix denoting material (§ 4), e. g. Fr. ferrin, ivoirin, has acquired in Italian and Portuguese a Diminutive sense, e. g. Ital. tavolino, Port. filhinho; -āceo- has taken the sense of large size or inferior quality, e.g. Ital. corpaccio, acquaccia. And new suffixes have been gained from other languages, such as -issa (from the Greek), a fem. suffix used especially in titles, e.g. Ital. duchessa, Fr. duchesse; -itto- with Diminutive sense, e. g. Ital. biglietto, Fr. amourette; -ia (from the Greek), denoting Abstracts, e. g. Ital. villania, Span. villanía, cortesía, and so on. (For a full account of the Romance suffixes, see Meyer-Lübke, Rom. Gram. ii. pp. 448 sqq.) Of Composition these varieties are noteworthy: Word-groups like Fr. pourboire; Bahuvrīhi Compounds like Fr. rouge-gorge; Dvandva Compounds like Ital. acqui-vento, 'wind and rain'; Verb with Noun (violating Scaliger's rule), e. g. Fr. garde-robe, Ital. guarda-boschi, becca-fico, lit. 'peck-fig,' with the Verb apparently in the 2 Sg. Imperat. (see Meyer-Lübke, ib. pp. 577 sqq.).

CHAPTER VI.

DECLENSION OF NOUNS AND ADJECTIVES.

COMPARISON OF ADJECTIVES. NUMERALS.

§ 1. I. **DECLENSION OF NOUNS AND ADJECTIVES.**
The I.-Eur. Noun had three Genders, Masc., Fem., and Neut., three Numbers, Sing., Dual, and Plur., and at least eight Cases, Nom., Gen., Dat., Acc., Voc. (if the Voc. may be called a Case), Abl., Instrumental, and Locative (the Dat., Abl., Instr., Loc. are not always easy to discriminate in the Plural). The three Genders are retained in Latin, but of the Numbers the Dual has disappeared, though traces of it remain in the Numeral forms *duō* (§ 59), *octō* (lit. 'two sets of four'?), and in the Pronoun form *ambō* (ch. vii. § 29)[1]. (On *vī-gintī*, see § 74.) Of the Cases the Voc. hardly survives except in O-stems (§ 31), and the Instr. has left only doubtful traces of itself in some Adverb forms (§ 36); the Locative became by the operation of the phonetic laws of the language indistinguishable in Ā-stems from the Gen. Sg., while in O-stems it seems to have ousted the Genitive (§ 17), and in Cons.-stems the Ablative (§ 33).

The I.-Eur. Cases were indicated sometimes by the addition of suffixes, e. g. -s for Nom. Sg. Masc., -m for Acc. Sg., sometimes by modification of the stem, e. g. *pătēr* Nom. Sg. of stem *pătĕr-*, 'a father,' sometimes by both, e. g. *patr-ŏs, *patr-ōm Gen. Sg., Pl. of the same stem. This modification (called by the Germans

---

[1] With the gradual loss of these peculiar suffixes (in Plautus *ambos* has begun to oust *ambō* Acc., and in Late Latin *ambis* ousts *ambōbus*) we may compare our plural 'shoes,' with disuse of the older suffix of 'shoon,' a suffix still retained in 'oxen,' &c. The Dual is rapidly disappearing at the present time in the Prussian dialect of Lithuanian, though in the other dialects it is better preserved.

§ 1.]   DECLENSION OF NOUNS, ETC.   367

'Abstufung') of the stem is due to the different accentuation of the different cases; and the I.-Eur. cases have been divided into (1) 'Strong' Cases, viz. the Nom., Voc. M. and F. of all Numbers, and the Acc. M. and F. of the Sing. and Dual, along with the Loc. Sing.; (2) 'Weak' Cases, where the accentuation of the suffix weakened the stem, e.g. *patr-ós (Gk. πατρ-ós). This alternation of unweakened and weakened stem is a feature of the Sanscrit declension, but has been effaced in most other languages by the natural tendency to make one Case like another in everything but the suffix (cf. Hom. Gk. πατέρος on the analogy of πατέρα), Lat. *patr-em* on the analogy of *patr-is*), and often the only trace left of it is the existence of varieties of the same stem; e. g. the varieties *pŏlen-* (Lat. *pŏlen-ta*) and *poll-* for **poln-* (Lat. *poll-en*) may be due to a former declension with the stem *polen-* in the strong, and the stem *poln-* in the weak cases. [The variations *homĕn-*, e.g. *hŏmĭnis*, *hemōn-*, e.g. O. Lat. *hĕmōnem* (Paul. Fest. 71. 18 Th.), and *homō(n)-* have been similarly explained.] The appropriation of different stems to different cases leads to what is called Heteroclite declension; thus *ĭtĕr-* is the stem appropriated to the Nom. Sing., *ĭtĭnĕr-* the stem appropriated to the other cases in Latin [so *sĕnĕc-* (ch. v. § 69) Nom. Sg., but *sĕn(i)-* in the other cases, *sŭpelleg-*, for *super-leg-*, a suffixless stem (ch. v. § 77) in the Nom. Sg., *supellectĭli-* for *super-lectĭli-* (an Adjectival LI-stem, ch. v. § 40) in the oblique cases]. Lat. *fĕmŭr* Nom., *fĕmĭnis* Gen., &c. retain a very ancient type of heteroclite declension of Neuter Nouns, in which the consonant R was the mark of the Nom., Acc., the consonant N of the Gen., Dat., &c. (see ch. v. § 56). In discussing the declension of the Latin Noun it will be better to put aside the conventional division made by the native grammarians, and to class nouns rather according to the final letter of their stems as Ā-stems, Ŏ-stems, &c. The heterogeneous composition of the fifth declension (*rēs* stem *rēi-*, *fĭdēs* stem *fĭd-ē-*, *tristĭtĭēs* stem *tristĭtĭā-* (?)) has been already pointed out (ch. v. § 51); also the close connexion of Consonant and I-stems (ch. v. § 34; cf. below, § 46, on *cīvĭtātium*, *fĕrentium*, *audācium*, &c.), and the absorption of the U- into the O-declension (ch. v. § 49). O-stems had, as we saw (ch. v. § 34), a tendency, when used as Adjectives, to become I-stems, e.g. *ĭnermis*, O. Lat. *inermus*, from the stem *armo-*; and in Vulg. Lat. we find a similar confusion of I-stem Adjs. with O-stems, e.g. tristis non 'tristus,' Prob. App. 198. 3 K. (cf. *trista* N., Rossi, i. 842, of 472 A. D., Ital. tristo).

In the Romance languages the Latin Declensions have been 'levelled' to a much greater extent than the Latin Conjugations, owing to the fact that the distinction of the Cases came to be expressed rather by Prepositions than by Case-suffixes. The sign of the Genitive was the Preposition *de*, of the Dative *ad*, and so on; and these Prepositions ceased to retain their classical construction [as early as the first cent. A. D. we have on a Pompeian graffito (*C. I. L.* iv. 275) Saturninus cum discentes]. Thus the Cases have been reduced in most languages to one, though O. Fr. and O. Prov. retain the distinction of the Nom. and Acc. (e.g. O. Fr. chars Nom., char Acc. of Lat. *cārus*; suer Nom., serour Acc. of Lat. *sŏror*), and in Roumanian we see the Dat. Fem. in roase Dat. (Lat. *rŏsae*) beside roasă Nom. (Lat. *rŏsa*), &c. More important was the distinction of Singular and Plural; and so the two Numbers are always distinguished, except (in pronunciation) in French, though a Latin Plural has often become a Romance Singular, e. g. *ligna*, Ital. legna, *biblia*, Ital. bibbia. The fourth Declension has been merged in the second, a process which shows itself very strongly even in the conversational Latin of Plautus (ch. v. § 49), the fifth in the third or first; and forms like Span. polvo (Vulg. Lat. *pulvus for *pulvis*), Ital. serpe (Vulg. Lat. *serpi-* for *serpens*) illustrate how the 'levelling' influence of Analogy gradually removed the distinctions of declension. (For particulars of the Romance declension, see Meyer-Lübke, *Gram. Rom. Sprach.* ii. pp. 1 sqq.).

As regards Gender, the laws according to which one Noun was Masculine, another Feminine, and a third Neuter in I.-Eur. have not yet been determined. The Neuter Gender seems to have been restricted to things without life. Thus while names of trees were masc. (in O. Ind., e. g. bhūrjas, 'a birch') or fem. (in Greek and Latin, e. g. φηγός, *fāgus*, 'a beech'), names of fruits were Neuter (e. g. O. Ind. āmrám, 'mango-fruit,' beside āmrás, 'mango-tree,' Lat. *mālum* beside *mālus*) (see Delbrück in Brugmann's *Grundriss*, iii. ch. i.); the difference between the gender of names of rivers in O. Ind. (fem.) and in Gk. and Lat. (masc.)

may be due to the different gender of the word for 'river' in these languages (O. Ind. nadí F., Gk. ποταμός M.), just as the names of the months, winds, &c. in Latin are really Adjectives agreeing with *mensis, ventus* (e. g. *Jānuārius, Februārius, Martius; Auster, Caurus, Făvōnius*). But the proneness of nouns to take a new gender by analogy of a noun which had a similar termination, or a kindred meaning, or with which they were often joined in speech[1], makes it impossible to trace the original gender of each and every noun. The feminine gender seems to have been associated with Abstract Nouns, e. g. Lat. *optio*, 'choice.' But if an Abstract Noun came to be used as a Concrete, it might change its gender; and so *optio* in the sense of 'a centurion's assistant' was masculine. Similarly *agrĭcŏla*, lit. 'field-tillage,' became masc. in the sense of 'a field-tiller'; and this is probably the reason why Ā-stems, which were associated with the feminine gender in I.-Eur., are often masc. in the various I.-Eur. languages (ch. v. § 2). O-stems were similarly associated with the masculine (with Nom. Sg. in -ŏs) and the neuter gender (Nom., Acc. Sg. in -ŏm); but we have feminine O-stems in the various languages, e. g. Gk. ὁδός, κέλευθος, λίθος, ψῆφος, and names of trees like φηγός, &c. In Latin (as we have seen, ch. iv. § 49) we seem to detect a tendency of these feminine O-stems to pass into the fourth declension. Thus *fāgus* is treated like a U-stem (fourth Declension) in the *Culex*; l. 139 : umbrosae-que patent fagus (cf. Varro ap. Charis. p. 130. 5 K.); and the declension of *dŏmus* (an O-stem in the earlier literature, ch. v. § 49 ; cf. Gk. δόμος[2]), *cŏlus* (Gk. πόλος), *nŭrus* (Gk. νυός for *νυσός) has been so explained.

The confusion of masculine and neuter O-stems may be illustrated by the words *collum*, which in Plautus is *collus* (I.-Eur. *k*olso-, Germ. Hals M.), and *ŭtĕrus*, which in Plautus is *uterum* (cf. O. Ind. udáram). (Other exx. in Neue, i². p. 529.) (On *lŏcus, loca* Plur., &c., see § 45.) In Late and Vulgar Latin the masculine seems to oust the neuter in these stems, as we see from

---

[1] Thus the fem. gender of *diēs* has been ascribed to the analogy of *nox*.

[2] O. Slav. domŭ is a U-stem, but in Slavonic the O- and U-declensions have been mixed up, as in Latin.

the precepts of the grammarians [e. g. Caper (first cent.) censures *pratus* 105. 6 K., *solius* 94. 19 K., and expresses himself forcibly about *cereber* 103. 6 K.: hoc cerebrum est nam 'cereber' qui dicunt sine cerebro vivunt], and from the 'sermo plebeius' of Petronius (e. g. *fatus*, 42, p. 28. 13 B.). On plebeian epitaphs we find *collegius* (e. g. *C. I. L.* xi. 4579. 4749), *monimentus* (e. g. *ib.* vi. 19319), and especially *fatus* in the stock-epitaph of the lower classes (like our 'Affliction sore long time he bore'):

noli dolere mater eventum meum.
properavit aetas : hoc voluit fatus mihi.

(On the disuse of the Neuter in later Latin, see Appel, *De genere neutro intereunte in lingua Latina*, Erlangen, 1883).

In the Romance languages the Neuter has disappeared, though it has influenced the formation of the Plural. Thus O. Prov. pratz points to *pratus* for *prātum*, but Ital. tempora Plur. (tempo Sg.), braccia Plur. (braccio Sg.), retain the Neut. Plur. formation *tempora, bracchia*. (On change of gender see Meyer-Lübke, ii. 416.)

The Adjective Declension took advantage of the connexion of O-stems with the masculine and neuter, and of Ā-stems with the feminine gender, e. g. I.-Eur. *nĕwŏs M., *nĕwā F., *nĕwŏm N. (Lat. *nŏvus, -a, -um*) (see ch. v. § 2). Consonant-stems formed their feminine with the Ī-suffix, e. g. I.-Eur. *nĕptī F. beside nĕpot- M. (Lat. *neptis* beside *nĕpōs*.) (On the Ī-suffix, see ch. v. § 51, and on other feminine formative suffixes, as in Lat. *gall-īna* beside *gallus, rēg-īna* beside *rēx*, consult the same chapter.) The Greek extension to the Feminine of the masculine suffix -ος in Compound Adjectives, which were originally Nouns in Apposition, is not found in Latin, e. g. ῥοδοδάκτυλος Ἠώς, lit. 'Dawn Rose-finger' (ch. v. § 80), though we have in O. Lat. *lupus femina, agnus femina*, &c. (e. g. Ennius, *A.* 59 M., in the story of the nursing of Romulus and Remus, has:

indotuetur ibi lupus femina).

But a usage peculiar to Latin is the extension to the Neuter of the S-suffix of the Masc. and Fem., not merely in Present Participles like *fĕrens*, where *ferens* Neut. may represent an older *ferent* (ch. iv. § 105), and in *vĕtus*, which was probably originally

§ 2.] DECLENSION OF NOUNS, ETC. NOM. SING. 371

a noun (Gk. Fέτος, § 55), but also in Adjectives like *audāx* (facinus audax, Plaut.), *dīves* (dives opus, Ovid). It is to be compared with the extension of Derivatives in *-trīx* (properly feminine, e.g. victrices lauros, Virg.) to Neuters, e.g. victricia arma, Virg., though *victrix* Sing. is not used with a Neuter Noun till Late Latin (see Neue, ii[3]. p. 40; and cf. below, § 16). The distinction in RI-stems[1] between the Nom. Sg. Masc. in *-er*, and the Nom. Sg. Fem. in *-ris* is not always found in the earlier authors (e.g. Ennius has *somnus acris*, *A.* 400 M., and *acer hiemps*, *A.* 471 M., and Virgil himself has *alacris* Masc., *A.* vi. 685), and is not rigorously enforced even in classical Latin, e.g. *mediocris* Masc., *illustris* Masc. (see Neue, ii[3]. p. 15). (On the Romance declension of Adjectives, e.g. Ital. buono M., buona F., Span. bueno M., buena F., O. Fr. bon, bone, &c., see Meyer-Lübke, *Rom. Gram.* ii. p. 75.) (On the Pronominal declension of certain Adjectives in I.-Eur., see ch. vii. § 29.)

§ **2. Nom. Sing. I. Masc., Fem.** Ā-stems took -ā in I.-Eur. (e.g. O. Ind. áśvā, 'a mare,' Gk. χώρᾱ). By the time of the oldest Latin poetry this ā has in every Nom. of an Ā-stem been shortened to ă, a shortening which may have begun in dissyllables with short first syllable, e.g. *hera*, where the working of the Law of Breves Breviantes would shorten the final syllable, *hĕră* like *căvĕ*, *hăvĕ* (ch. iii. § 40); though an early reduction of this -ā, as well as of the -ā of Nom. Pl. Neut. of O-stems (§ 45), on Italian soil is indicated by the fact that in Oscan both have been replaced by an *o*-sound (in Oscan alph. ú, in Lat. *o*, in Gk. o), and in Umbrian are written sometimes -a, sometimes -o (in Umbr. alph. -u), e.g. Osc. vío 'via,' Umbr. mutu and muta 'mulcta' (see ch. ii. § 1)[2]. O. Lat. *hosticapas* (hostium captor, Paul. Fest. 73. 10 Th.), *paricidas* quoted from the Laws of Numa (Paul. Fest. 278. 10 siqui hominem liberum dolo sciens morti duit, paricidas esto) may be analogous to the Greek usage of

---

[1] Many were originally RO-stems (ch. v. § 40; cf. O. Lat. *hĭlărus*). They are often RO-stems in Late and Vulgar Latin, e.g. Vulg. Lat. *ălĕcer*, Ital. allegro; cf. Ital. campestro, &c.

[2] For the Umbro-Oscan forms of these and the other case-suffixes, see *Class. Rev.* ii. pp. 129, 202, 273.

adding -s to a fem. Abstract ā-stem when used as a masc. Concrete, e. g. *νεανίᾱs*, a youth, from *νεανίᾱ, youth, though the usual practice in Latin is to retain the ordinary Nom. form, e. g. *agrĭ-cŏla*, a field-tiller, originally ' field-tillage.'

YA-stems, the fem. of consonant-stems, &c. (ch. v. § 51), which in O. Ind. take -ī, e. g. bháranti, Pres. Part of bhṛ-, 'to carry,' naptí, Fem. of nápāt-, 'grandson,' in Greek -*ιă*, e. g. *φέρουσα* for *φεροντyă, show in Latin -*ia*, e. g. *prae-sentia*, possibly also -*ĭs*, e. g. *ferentĭs which became *ferens*, *neptĭs* (older Lat. -*īs*?). Beside -*ia* (first Decl.) we find -*iēs* (fifth Decl.), e. g. *mātĕr-ies* beside *materia*. The exact relation between O. Ind. -ī, Gk. -*ιă*, Lat. -*ia* and -*iēs* has not yet been determined (see ch. v. § 51).

Ŏ-stems took -os in I.-Eur. (e. g. O. Ind. vṛ́kas, 'a wolf,' Gk. λύκος, Gaul. tarvos, 'a bull'), and in Latin, e. g. *lupus*, *taurus*, older *lupos, *tauros (ch. iv. § 19). In RŎ-stems the final -ros, when preceded by a consonant, was changed by a phonetic process common to Latin with other Italic languages to -*er*, e. g. Lat. *ăger* for *agro-s (Gk. *ἀγρός*), Umbr. *ager*; even when a short vowel precedes, we find, e. g. Lat. *sŏcer* (in Plautus *socĕrus*) for *socŭros, *socĕros (I.-Eur. *swĕkŭros), *vĭr* for *vĭros, *sătur* for *satŭros.

YO-stems, whose suffix in I.-Eur. seems to have varied with i (e. g. Goth. hairdeis, 'a herdsman;' Lith. gaidÿs, 'a cock,' beside svēczias, 'a guest') show in Latin usually -*ius*, but in familiar language also -is, e. g. *Cornēlis* and other proper names.

All other stems took -s in I.-Eur. and in Latin, e. g. *ŏvĭs* (O. Ind. ávi-s, Gk. *ὄ(ϝ)ις*, Lith. avis), *mănŭs* (O. Ind. svādús, 'sweet,' Gk. *ἡδύς*, Lith. sūnùs, 'a son'), *vīs* (Gk. *ἴs*), *sūs* (Gk. *ὗs*), *rēs* (O. Ind. rás), *mīlĕs* for *milets (the last syllable is scanned long by Plautus, *miless, ch. ii. § 133), *mūs* for *mūs-s, *rēx*, &c. S-stems have -ēs (e. g. I.-Eur. *dus-menēs, O. Ind. dur-manās, Gk. *δυσ-μενής*) or -ōs (e. g. I.-Eur. *āusōs, Hom. Gk. *ἠώς*; cf. O. Ind. uṣā́s), and so in Latin, e. g. *pūbēs*, *hŏnōs* M., later *honor*, *tĕnor* M. (beside *tenus* N.). But N-stems, which in I.-Eur. showed (1) -ōn, -ēn, (2) -ō (-ē) [e. g. (1) Gk. *κύων*, *ποιμήν*, (2) O. Ind. śvā́, 'dog,' O. Ir. cū, Lith. szũ], show -*ō* in Latin, e. g. *hŏmō*, *rătiō*, *uirco* 'virgo' on the very ancient Dvenos inscr. I.-Eur. R-stems had similarly (1) -ōr, -ēr, (2) -ō, -ē [e. g. (1) Gk. *μήτηρ*, *δώτωρ*,

§ 3.] DECLENSION OF NOUNS, ETC. NOM. SING. 373

(2) O. Ind. mātā́, dā́tā, Lith. motė̃ and mótė, sesů̃, 'sister'], but display only the first formation in Latin, e. g. *mātĕr, dătŏr, sŏrŏr* (in O. Lat. **matēr, datōr, sorōr*; see ch. iii. § 49). So in Umbrian karu, 'a part' (Lat. *cărō*), with u as equivalent of Lat. *ō*, but in Osc. statíf 'statio,' fruktatiuf ' fruitatio,' úíttiuf ' utitio ' with -f for ns, the ns being perhaps a re-formation just as *carnis* sometimes replaces *caro* in Latin (Prisc. i. p. 208. 19 H.). Umbro-Oscan R-stems form their Nom. like the Latin, e. g. Umbr. *arsfertur*, Osc. *censtur* 'censor' (both with *u*, the equivalent of Lat. *ō*).

§ 3. Nom. Sing. of Ā-stems in Lat. We have seen in ch. iii. § 43 that all supposed instances of *-ā* Nom. Sg. in early poetry are illusory [*aquīlā́*, Enn. *A.* 149 M. is a case of metrical lengthening of a short syllable before the penthemimeral caesura ; *copiā̆*, Plaut. *Mil.* 1226 shows 'syllaba anceps' at the end of the hemistich ; *familia, Trin.* 251 is a proceleusmatic (*fămĭlĭă*). representing an anapaest, and so on]. The only genuine instances are Greek words with *-ā̄*[1], which are long in later poetry too, e. g. *Nemeā́* (Stat. *Theb.* vi. 516). Greek Nominatives in *-as, -ης* were especially in the older literature changed to the ordinary Latin Nom., e. g. *Anchīsă* (Enn. *A.* 19 M.), *Aenea* (Quint. i. 5. 61 ne in a quidem atque s litteras exire temere masculina Graeca nomina recto casu patiebantur, ideoque et apud Caelium legimus 'Pelia cincinnatus' et apud Messalam 'bene fecit Euthia,' et apud Ciceronem 'Hermagora,' ne miremur, quod ab antiquorum plerisque 'Aenea' ut 'Anchisa' sit dictus), and similarly in classical Latin *poētā̆, nautā̆, bibliŏpŏlā̆*, &c. (cf. *Atrīdā̆*, Propert. ii. 14. 1 ; *Marsyă*, Hor. *S.* i. 6. 120 ; and for other instances see Neue, *Formenl.* i². pp. 31 sqq.) ; though they usually in the classical literature retain *-ās, -ēs*. just as Greek Noms. in -η retain *ē*, e. g. *Andrŏmăchē*, or take the Latin suffix, e. g. *ĕpistŭlă*. *Hosticapas*, quoted by Paul. Fest., is a strange form. Compounds of *căpio* usually show *-ceps*, e. g. *mŭnĭ-ceps*, while Plautus has *urbĭ-căpe* Voc. (*Mil.* 1055). *Paricidas* (i. e. *parricidas*, for the double consonant was not written double till Ennius' time, ch. i. § 8) is indeed in the Republican and Classical period an Ā-stem (e. g. *parrīcīda* Voc., Plaut. *Pseud.* 362 ; but adjectively *mūrĭ-cīde homo* Voc., 'you coward,' *Epid.* 333) ; however, if these Masc. Ā-stems originally took *-as* in Latin, they had conformed to the ordinary usage of Fem. Ā-stems as early as the beginning of the second cent. B. C., for Plautus, *Rud.* 652, has *lēgĭrŭpa* (better *legerupa*, ch. iii. § 20) Nom. Sing. with its last syllable elided :

légerupa, inpudéns, inpurus, ínuerecundíssimus,

where *legerupa*, originally 'the act of law-breaking,' a fem. Abstract, then masc. and Concrete, 'a law-breaker,' cannot have been written by Plautus *legerupas* (ch. ii. § 137). The names on Oscan inscriptions (Μαρ)ας (Zv. *I. I. I.*

---

[1] *agoeā* in Enn. *A.* 567 M. : multa foro ponet et agoea longa repletur, is not a certain example. The Greek word seems to have been ἄγυιά, and one MS. reads *ponens ageaque*.

253 from Messana), Maras (*I. F.* ii. p. 437 from Puteoli or Cumae), whence the derivative Osc. Maraio-, Falisc. Mareio-, Lat. *Mărĭus* (ch. v. § 4), and Tanas (Zvet. 102 from Samnium) suggest that Noms. in -ās (for -ăs would probably be syncopated in Oscan) were used in Oscan like Noms. in -ās, -ης in Greek. But they may belong to some un-Italic dialect. Ξανθίας is Osc. Santia (Zvet. 228).

§ 4. RO-stems. The substitution of *-er* for *-ros* is extended even to Gk. loanwords, e. g. *Alexander*, though the usage varied, e. g. *Euandrus* and *Euander* in Virgil (see Neue, *Formenl.* i². p. 77). It is not found in Latin words when a long syllable precedes *-ros*, e. g. *sĕvē-rus, sŭsur-rus, mātū-rus*, nor in these tribrach words *hŭmĕrus, nŭmĕrus, ŭtĕrus*. Plautus has the tribrach stem *sŏcĕro-* (I.-Eur. *swĕkŭro-, O. Ind. śváśura-, Gk. ἑκυρός, Lith. szesziùras) with Nom. *socerus* (*Men.* 957), and Priscian (i. 231. 13 H.) says that *puerus* was used by the older writers, though he is perhaps referring to Voc. *puĕre*, probably the invariable form of the Voc. Sg. of *puer* in Plautus, for *puerus* is not found in any extant literature. It is not however certain that *puer* was originally an O-stem, for the cognate Greek word is πα(ϝ)ίδ-, and the old Saturnian poets used *puer* as fem. as well as masc. (see Charis. 84. 5 K.; Prisc. i. p. 232 H.), e. g. Naevius, *Bell. Pun.* ii. :

príma incédit Céreris Prosérpina púer,

while the curious compound slave-names *Marcipor, Gaipor, Quintipor*, &c. are I-stems, Plur. *Marcipores* (e. g. Plin. xxxiii. 26). *Infĕrus*, with *sŭpĕrus*, is used in Livius Andronicus' translation of the Odyssey (at least in the later dactylic version of it) :

inferus an superus tibi fert deus funera, Ulixes?,

but *infer* and *super* by Cato (*R. R.* cxlix. 1 ubi super inferque uicinus permittet), like *cĭter* (Cato, *Orat.* fr. lxii. p. 65 J.). Of compounds ending in Verbal Adjective in *-rus* we have always *mŏrĭ-gĕrus* (e. g. Plaut. *Capt.* 966), *prŏ-pĕrus*, (*jūnĭ-pĕrus* is by some explained as *jun*(*on*)*i-pirus*, 'Juno's pear,' like *jū-glans*, 'Jove's acorn,' by others is derived from **jūnus*, cf. *jun-cus*, and *părio*), but the normal usage favoured *-ger, -fer*, &c. (for details, see Kühner, *Lat. Gram.* i. pp. 278 sqq.). All this points to *-er* having originally been substituted for *-ros* only when a consonant preceded, e. g. *ăger* for **ag-ros*. After the vowel *i* we find *-ros* curtailed to *-r* in *vĭr* (but *pĭrus* beside *pĭrum*); after the vowel *u*, in *sătŭr* (as early as Plautus; see *A. L. L.* v. 34), although *voltŭrus* (class. *vultur*, *-ŭris* Gen.) is used by Ennius, *A.* 138 M. The tendency to curtail *-rus* to *-r* increased in Vulgar Latin, as we see from the Probi Appendix 197. 30 K. : barbarus non 'barbar,' although the opposite tendency (due to Greek influence of S. Italy?) is also mentioned (*ib.* 198. 26) : teter non 'tetrus,' aper non 'aprus.' In the Umbro-Oscan dialects *-los* was similarly changed to *-el*, e. g. Osc. *famel*, apparently for făm-lo-, 'a dweller' (cf. Osc. faamat, 'he dwells') with the same formation as Lat. *fīgulus*, stem *fĭg-lo-* from *fīgo*, &c. (ch. iv. § 51). But this was not the Latin usage, e. g. *fămŭlus, bĭbŭlus, mascŭlus*, &c. (cf. ch. iv. § 10), though Ennius borrows from his native Oscan the form *famul* in his reference to Servius Tullius (*A.* 336 M.) :

mortalem summum fortuna repente
reddidit, ut summo regno famul oltimus esset,

§§ 4-6.] DECLENSION OF NOUNS, ETC. NOM. SING. 375

in which he is imitated by Lucretius, who echoes the rhythm of this passage (iii. 1035):

Scipiadas, belli fulmen, Carthaginis horror,
ossa dedit terrae proinde ac famul infimus esset.

The S. Italian forms *figel, mascel* found their way into plebeian Latin under the Empire (Prob. App. 197. 28 K. figulus non 'figel,' masculus non 'mascel'); but the usual Vulgar Latin form *masclus* is mentioned in the same treatise (197. 20 K. speculum non 'speclum,' masculus non 'masclus,' vetulus non 'veclus,' vernaculus non 'vernaclus,' articulus non 'articlus,' baculus non 'baclus,' angulus non 'anglus,' jugulus non 'juglus.') (On the curtailment of *-ris* and *-lis*, see ch. iv. § 13; the restriction of *-er* to Masc., *-ris* to Fem. Nom. Sing. is not observed in the older literature; e.g. Ennius has *somnus acris* and *acer hiems*; cf. § 1, p. 371).

§ 5. YO-stems. The -ĭs of the Nom. Sing. of Oscan YO-stems, e.g. Pakis, Lat. *Pācius* (-ĭs would be syncopated in Oscan, e.g. *cevs*, Lat. *cīvis*), is perhaps indicated for Latin by the occasional spellings with *-εις* on Greek inscriptions, e.g. Ἔλεις (Lat. *Aelius*) (*I. I. S.* 928, Ostia, very late), Πετρωνεις (Lat. *Petronius*); the usual Greek transcription, however, is *-ις*. (Neither *-ις* nor *-εις* is found till the beginning of the first century A.D.; see Eckinger, *Orthographie* p. 56). *Alīs* (if we may infer this quantity from *ălĭd*, Lucr. i. 263, &c.) may have its final syllable shortened by the Law of Breves Breviantes, like *cavĕ, havĕ*, &c. (ch. iii. § 42). In the S. C. de Bacchanalibus (*C. I. L.* i. 196) the consuls' names are written in what we may suppose to be the ceremonious form, *Marcius, Postumius*, while the secretaries' names have the *is*-ending, *Claudi, Valeri, Minuci*. Ritschl in a paper entitled 'De declinatione quadam latina reconditiore' (*Opusc.* iv. 446) has collected a large number of these proper names with *-is* or *-i* Nom. (less certainly *-is* Gen., *-i* Dat., *-im* Acc.) from Latin inscrr. The form *alis*, quoted from the older writers (e.g. Catull. lxvi. 28) by the grammarians (see the passages mentioned by Ritschl, *ib.* p. 452), may have been specially used in collocations like *alis alium* (so in the Vulgar Latin of the Itala; cf. *C. I. L.* ii. 2633, of 27 A.D.: eique omnes alis alium ... receperunt), *alis ălĭbi* (e.g. Sallust *fragt.* ap. Charis. p. 159. 31 K.), where the two words formed a single word-group like our 'one another.' This byform of the Nom. (Acc. &c.) must have led to confusion with I-stems, of which we have perhaps a trace in the gradual ousting of the second Decl. suffix *-ārius* by the third Decl. *-āris* (ch. v. § 4), and in the remark of Caper (112. 2 K.) that *vātes* (an I-stem, like O. Ir. fáith for *wāti-, Gaul. οὐάτεις Plur.) was in O. Lat. *vatius*.

§ 6. I-stems. The -ĭs of the Nom. Sing. of I-stems is syncopated in the Umbro-Oscan dialects, e.g. Osc. *cevs* (Lat. *civis*), like the -ōs of the Nom. Sing. of O-stems, e.g. Umbr. *emps* (Lat. *emptus*), *Ikuvins* (Lat. *Iguvinus*), Osc. húrz (Lat. *hortus*), *Bantins* (Lat. *Bantinus*), and the -ĕs of the Nom. Plur. of Consonant-stems, e.g. Osc. μεδδειξ for *med-dik-ĕs Nom. Plur. of *meddix, censtur* for *censtor-ĕs, Lat. *censōrēs*. We have seen (ch. iii. § 16) that it is very difficult to prove a similar treatment of *-ĭs* in Latin; for Noms. like *pars* (for *partis*), Gen. *partis*, may have dropped *i* not by Syncope, but by the Analogy of Cons.-stems like *rēx*, Gen. *rēgis, lēx*, Gen. *lēgis*, &c. Like *-rōs*, however, *-rĭs* was reduced to *-er* in Latin as in Umbro-Oscan, e.g. Lat. *ācer* for *ācris*, Umbr. *pacer* for *pac-*

ris, 'propitious,' connected with Lat. *pāx*. Ennius, who coined *fămŭl* after the type of the Oscan *famel* (§ 4), used *dēbŭl* (Voc. Sing. ?) for *debĭlis* (*A.* 341 M. debil homo), perhaps after Osc. aídil (Lat. *aidīlis*), &c. Nouns with Nom. Sing. in -*l* (*consul, praesul, exul, pŭgil, vĭgil, mūgil*, &c.) are declined as Consonant-stems in Latin (Gen. Plur. *consul-um, pugil-um, vigil-um, mugil-um*) (see Neue, *Formenl.* i². p. 153), though the line between Nouns in -*l* and Adjectives in -*lis*, e.g. *debĭlis*, is, as might be expected, often passed over. Thus Juvenal, (x. 317) has *mugĭlis* (but Mart. Cap. iii. 294 si 'mugilis' esset . . . 'mugilium' faceret.) For *vigil, pugil* we should expect *vigulus, *pugulus, like *bĭbŭlus, fĭgŭlus* (ch.v. § 22), or with adjectival *i* (ch. v. § 34) *vigĭlis, *pugĭlis, although -*ĭlis* has properly a passive sense, e.g. *bĭbĭlis*, 'drinkable, easily drunk,' *ăgĭlis*, 'easily moved,' *hăbĭlis* (whence *dēbĭlis* for *de-hĭbĭlis), 'easily handled' (ch. v. § 41). Beside -*ĭs*, the usual Nom. Sing. of Masc. and Fem. I-stems in Latin, we find occasionally -*ēs*, e.g. *cănēs* F., the O. Lat. form which had been replaced by *canĭs*. by the time of Varro (*L. L.* vii. 32). The -*ēs* of *ambāgēs*, &c., we have seen to be really the -*ēs* of the Nom. Plur. of I-stems, viz. -ëyës (e.g. Lat. *trēs* for *trĕyĕs, O. Ind. tráyas, Cret. Gk. τρέες for *τρεγες, O. Sl. trĭje, &c.) (§ 40) ; it must not be confounded with an early spelling like *aidīles* for *aedīlis* on a Scipio epitaph (*C. I. L.* i. 31, but *aidilis* on another Scipio epitaph, i. 32), where the *e* (pronounced *ĕ*) is merely an expression of the *ĭ*-sound in an unaccented syllable, like the third *e* of *Tempestatebus* for *Tempestātĭbus* (*C. I. L.* i. 32) (see ch. iii. § 22). This use of -*ēs* in the Nom. Sing. of I-stems led to the diversion of other stems, which took -*ēs* in the Nom. Sing., into the I-declension. Thus *plēbēs*, if an ĖS-stem by origin like Gk. περι-πληθής (beside πλῆθος) (ch. v. § 74), should have made its Gen. Sing. *plēbĕris, but was led by the analogy of *canēs*, &c. into taking a Gen. *pleb-is*, as on the other hand the analogy of stems like *rēs*, Gen. *rēī, rĕī* supplied the Gen. *plebēī, plebĕī* ; and the tendency of Vulgar Latin to replace every Nom. Sing. -*es* by the more familiar -*is* was perhaps the cause of the forms *cautis, plebis, vatis, tabis, nubis, subolis, vulpis, palumbis, luis, vepris, fumis, cladis, prolis*, censured in Prob. App. pp. 198-9 K. For the late byform *molis* for *mōles* (an ES-stem, cf. *mŏlĕs-tus*), see Georges, *Lex. Wortf.* s.v., and for other examples, Ritschl, *Opusc.* ii. 654. Beside *plebēs, nubēs, cautes, saepes*, we have *plebs, nubs* (used by Liv. Andronicus, according to Servius ad *A.* x. 636, and frequent in the Itala), *cōs, saeps* ; also *trabs* for older *trăbes* (Varro, *L. L.* vii. 33 sic dictum a quibusdam ut una ' canes,' una ' trabes ' . . . cujus verbi singu-laris casus rectus correptus ac facta trabs.) (On these Noms. in -*ēs*, see ch.`v. § 51.) O. Lat. *sortis* (class. Lat. *sors*) and the like are discussed in ch. iii. § 16 ; *messīs* of Plaut. *Rud.* 763 (AP) is changed by editors to *messĭs*.

§ 7. S-stems. Masc. and Fem. ES-stems, connected with Neuter ES-stems (Nom. -*ŏs*, ch. v. § 71), took -*ōs* M. (class. -*or*), -*ēs* F. in Latin, e.g. *hŏnōs*, class. *honor* (cf. *honĕs-tus*), *plēbēs* (cf. Gk. πλῆθος). As Adjectives (cf. Gk. περι-πληθής beside πλῆθος, ψευδής beside ψεῦδος) they show -*er* in *pūber* (also *pubēs*, -*ĕris* Gen., *impubēs*, -*ĕris* Gen.), *dē-gĕner* ; -*or* in *con-cŏlor, bĭ-corpor* (ch. v. § 73). The -*os* of *honos, lăbos, cŏlos, văpos*, &c. was not quite ousted by -*or* (taken from the oblique cases, *honōris, honōrem*, &c., where *s* came between two vowels, ch. iv. § 148) till the Augustan period (for details, see Neue, *Formenl.* i². p. 167). Sallust, according to Servius ad *A.* i. 253, almost always used the form *labos* ; and -*os* was persistently retained in monosyllables, e.g. *flōs, rōs*.

§ 8. N-stems. We find -*en* in *pecten* M. (Gk. κτείς M. for *πκτενς, Gen.

§§ 7-10.] DECLENSION OF NOUNS, ETC. NOM. SING.   377

κτενός), *flāmen*, and *liēn* (the *ē* is attested by Prisc. i. 149. 7 H., Mart. Cap. iii. 279). *Sanguis* M., which often has its last syllable scanned long by the Latin poets (always *sanguĕn* or *sanguīs* in Lucretius, Munro ad Lucr. i. 853), may represent **sanguins* (ch. ii. § 144), a patchwork of the old Nom. **sanguī*, with the oblique cases **sanguĕn-es* Gen., &c.   (For this declension of some I.-Eur. neuters, e.g. O. Ind. ákṣi Nom., akṣṇás Gen., 'the eye,' see ch. v. § 34.) The scansion *sanguīs* brought with it the treatment of the word as an I-stem, *sanguem* Acc., *sanguis* Gen. &c. (see Georges, *Lex. Wortf.* s. v.).

§ 9. **Diphthong Stems.** I.-Eur. **nāu-s* (O. Ind. nāú-s, Gk. ναῦ-s) is Latin *nāvis* ; I.-Eur. **gʷōús* (O. Ind. gāú-s, Gk. βοῦς) is Lat. *bōs*, but the *b*- points to the form being dialectal; the stem rēy- (O. Ind. rā́s Nom., rāy-ás Gen.) probably formed its I.-Eur. Nom. Sing. as **rē-s*, and so in Lat., *rēs*. I.-Eur. **d(i)yēu-s*, 'the sky, day' (O. Ind. d(i)yāús, Gk. Ζεύς) has in Latin in the sense of 'day' the Nom. *diē-s*, while for the name of the sky-god a compound is used, *Juppĭter* (the correct spelling, ch. ii. § 130. p. 116) for **Jeu-pater*, probably in the Voc. case, unless *Jeu-* be the stem (ch. v. § 85 ; cf. *Jani-patri, C. I. L.* xi. 5374). The grammarians point out the incongruity of a declension like *Juppiter* Nom., *Jŏvis* Gen. ('as absurd as *Phoebus* Nom., *Apollinis* Gen.' Mar. Sacerd. 473. 1 K.), and tell us that in the old liturgical books the word was declined *Juppiter* Nom., *Juppitris* Gen., &c. (Pompeius 172. 25 ; 187. 9 K.), or *Jovis* Nom., *Jovis* Gen., Prisc. i. 229. 10 H.).   We have ιοvos Nom. on an old Praenestine cista (*C. I. L.* xiv. 4105), also [*Die*]*spater* (*Bull.* 1887, p. 232), *Diesptr* (*C. I. L.* i. 1500) ; and in Plautus, &c. *Diespĭter* is not unknown (see Georges, *Lex. Wortf.* s.v. *Juppiter*). *Dies* is like the Accus. *diem*. For the Nom. we should expect **dieus* (Gk. Ζεύς), with *ĕu* from *ēu*, which would become in Latin *diūs* (cf. *nū-dius-tertius* ?).

§ 10. **Nom., Acc. Sing. II. Neut.** Neuter O-stems in I.-Eur. have their Nom. Sing. in -ŏm, the suffix of the Acc. Sg. Masc.; all others use the bare stem, ES-stem Nouns taking however -ŏs, N-stems -n̥, NT-stems -n̥t, &c. So in Latin, e.g. *jŭgum* (older *jŭgom*). (I.-Eur. **yŭgom, O. Ind. yugám, Gk. ζυγόν), *mīte* (older **mītĭ*; see ch. iii. § 37) (cf. O. Ind. śúci, 'pure,' Gk ἴδρι) ; *nōmen* with -*en* for I.-Eur. -n̥ (O. Ind náma; cf. Gk. ὄνομα); *fĕrens* from **ferent* (ch. iv. § 105) with -*ent* for I.-Eur. -n̥t (O. Ind. bhárat), *gĕnus* (older *genŏs*) (I.-Eur. **ĝĕnŏs, Gk. γένος), *cor* for **cord* (O. Ind. hṛ́d ; cf. Gk. κῆρ for **κηρδ). U-stems have in I.-Eur. -ŭ, e.g. **mĕdhŭ,* 'mead,' **swādŭ,* 'sweet' (O. Ind. mádhŭ, svādŭ́, Gk. μέθῠ, ἡδύ); and similarly Latin Neuter Nouns have -u, e. g. *pĕcu, cornu* (U-Stem Adjectives passed into the I-declension in Latin, e. g. *suāve* ; see ch. v. § 47). But there is a doubt with regard to the quantity of the -*u*. Most grammarians declare it to be short, while Priscian (i. 362. 11 H.) controverts their opinion, and proves by quotations from the poets that it is long. (For details, see Neue, *Formenl.* i². p. 345). The existence of byforms like *pecus, cornum,* &c. obscures the question, but there seems to be little doubt that with the Augustan poets *cornū,* &c. was the recognized scansion. The long vowel has not yet been satisfactorily explained (see Brugmann, *Grundr.* ii. § 223 for the various theories, and cf. below, § 45). The Neuter Nom. of consonant-stem adjectives has been assimilated to the Masc. and Fem. form, e. g. *fēlix* for **felīc* (cf. *allēc* N., *allēx* F.), *du-plex* for **dŭ-plĕc* (Umbr. tu-plak) (cf. above, § 1, p. 370).

§ 11. **O-stems.** We find *-um* lost in *nĭhĭl, nĭl,* from *nĭhīlum,* a compound of *nĕ* and *hīlum* (quod grano fabae adhaeret, Paul. Fest. 72. 10 Th.), a loss which seems due to elision before a vowel (ch. iii. § 52). From phrases like *nihīl(um) hoc est* on the one hand, and *nihīlum dicit* on the other, the 'doublets' *nihīl* and *nihīlum* would come into use, and no doubt existed for a long time side by side till the less cumbrous *nihīl, nīl* ousted its rival. Similarly *nōn* for *ne-oenum,* like our 'nought' for 'ne-aught,' *ō* being substituted for *ū* (older *oe*) because of the monosyllabic form or the unaccented character of the Conjunction (but see ch. x. § 18). The Umbro-Oscan neuters have -ŏm, Osc. sakaraklúm 'sacraculum' ('a shrine'), dunum 'dōnum,' Umbr. *esonom,* a sacrifice.

§ 12. **I-stems.** Final *ĕ* is dropped by Syncope (cf. ch. iii. § 36) in Neuters like *facul,* an O. Lat. form of *facile,* e. g. Accius, *Trag.* 460 R.:

érat istuc uiríle, ferre aduórsam fortunám facul,

volup, Neut. of a lost Adj. **volupis,* e. g. Plaut. *Cas.* 784 fácite nostro animó uolup. (On the question whether *volupest* is rightly divided into *volupe est* or into *volup est,* see Georges, *Lex. Wortf.* s. v.). Similarly the old Nom. *lacte,* with the I-stem form (e. g. Plaut. *Bacch.* 19. 1134, *Men.* 1089, *Mil.* 240) became *lact* [Plaut. *Truc.* 903 (?), Varro, *L L.* v. 104], classical *lac* (see Georges s. v.).

§ 13. **U-stems.** The uncertainty of the grammarians of the Empire about the quantity of *-u* of fourth Decl. Neuters may be due to the fact that in later Latin the fourth Decl. was being supplanted by the second Decl. (ch. v. § 49). Priscian elsewhere (i. 161. 26 H., &c.) corrects the extraordinary statement of Charisius (fourth cent.) (22. 15 K.) and others, that the *-u* of *-us* in fourth Decl. Noms. masculine was pronounced long, a quantity indicated neither by poetry nor by the orthography of inscriptions.

§ 14. **S-stems.** The I.-Eur. Nom. Sg. -ŏs of Neut. ES-stems, and -ōs of Masc. ES-stems, remained distinct in Latin, e. g. O. Lat. *opŏs* (*C. I. L.* i. 52), *honōs.* In course of time Neut. -ŏs sank to *-ŭs, ŏpus* (see ch. iv. § 20), Masc. -ōs became by Analogy of the oblique cases (*hŏnōr-is, honōr-em,* &c.) -ōr, then -ŏr, owing to the difficulty of sounding a long vowel before a final -*r* (ch. iii. § 49). There are a few indications of a temporary formation of Neuter Noms. in -*or,* e. g. *calor* (Plaut. *Merc.* 860 nec calor nec frigus metuo), *prior bellum* (Claudius Quadrigarius ap. Prisc. i. p. 347. 7 H.), *bellum Punicum posterior* (Cassius Hemina ap. eund.) (cf. § 53 below). Priscian (*l. c.*), who quotes some instances of Neut. Comparatives in *-or* from the old historians, says : vetustissimi etiam neutrum in or finiebant, et erat eadem terminatio communis trium generum, thus hinting that the justification of this usage was the Analogy of Adjectives of one termination for Masc., Fem., Neut., like *audāx, fēlīx*. And it is possible that a Neuter in *-ŭr* (older *-ŏr* like *rōbur (robor* Acc., Varro, *R. R.* iii. 7. 9) took *-r* for *-s* in the Nom. from the oblique cases *robŏr-is, robŏr-i*, &c., for Cato (*R. R.* xvii. 1) uses the form *robus*, or from an Early Latin Masc. byform [if we may trust Paul. Fest. 11. 20 Th. 'robosem.' pro robore (dicebant antiqui)]. But in spite of these occasional deviations, Latin writers hold with great persistence to the rule that a Neuter ES-stem has a Nom. in *-ŭs* (older *-ŏs*), a Masc. ES-stem in *-ŏr* (older *-ōr, -ōs*), e. g. *tĕnus* N., *tĕnor* M., *dĕcus* N., *dĕcor* M., *frīgus* N., *frīgor* M. The *-us*, not only of Neut. Nouns, but also of Neut. Comparatives, is invariably short in Plautus and the older poetry (Müller, *Plaut. Pros.* p. 55).

§ 15. R-stems. Neuter R-stems show usually *-ŭr* (older *-ŏr*), apparently representing I.-Eur. -r̥, but occasionally *-ĕr*, e.g. *über* (O. Ind. ū́dhar-, Gk. οὖθαρ), in Latin. The obsolete word *aser*, blood (cf. Cret. Gk. ἔαρ, O. Ind. ásr̥-k, asn-ás Gen., Lett. asins), is of doubtful spelling [cf. Paul. Fest. 12. 19 Th. 'assaratum' apud antiquos dicebatur genus quoddam potionis ex vino et sanguine temperatum, quod Latini prisci sanguinem 'assyr' vocarent ; Gl. Philox. asaer (*leg.* -er) : αἷμα].

§ 16. S in Nom. Sg. Neut. of Adjectives. This, if we may believe the MSS., is as old as Plautus, e. g. *facinus audax, Aul.* 460 (so Ter. *Phorm.* 233, &c.), *duplex* (sc. aurum), *Men.* 546, *sagax nasum, Curc.* 110, and occurs in the ancient phrase *quod bonum faustum felix fortunatumque sit*. (For examples, e. g. *dives opus*, Ovid, *pondus iners*, Cic., see Neue, ii³. p. 22). Similar is the extension of the suffix *-trĭc-*, properly fem., to neuter Adjectives, e. g. *victricia arma*, Virg. *A.* iii. 54 (though *victrix* Sg. is not used as neut. till Late Latin). [Does *concapit* of the XII Tables (ap. Fest. 556. 27 Th. tignum iunctum aedibus uineaue et concapit ne soluito) point to an earlier use of the bare stem for the Neuter ?].

§ 17. Gen. Sing. Ā-stems took in I.-Eur. -ās (e. g. Gk. χώρᾱς, Goth. gibōs, Lith. rañkos), and similarly in the Umbro-Oscan languages, e. g. Umbr. tutas, later *totar* ' civitatis,' Osc. *eituas* ' pecuniae,' and in O. Lat., e. g. *escas*, Liv. Andr. But a rival formation, of doubtful origin, which appears in the oldest literature as *āī* (dissyllabic) ultimately established itself in exclusive use in the form *-ae*. In Greek we find Masc. Ā-stems taking the O-stem suffix, e. g. Hom. 'Ατρείδᾱο like Αἰόλοο, and it has been suggested that Lat. *-āī* began in Masc. Nouns such as *agrĭcŏla, advĕna*, &c. (§ 2), and took its *-ī* from the Gen. of the second Decl. Similarly fifth Decl. stems show *-ēī*, later *-ei, -ī*, e. g. *fĭdēī* O. Lat., *fĭdēī* class., *rēī, rĕī*, and *rēī* in the Dramatists, *dii*, Virg. *A.* i. 636, also (like *-ās* from Ā-stems), O. Lat. *faciēs, diēs*.

O-stems, which in Umbro-Oscan show the I-stem suffix, have in Latin, as in Celtic, a long *i*-sound, e.g. Lat. *nātī*, *vĭrī*, Gaul. Ate-gnati, O. Ir. eich for *eci, ' of a horse,' which one would have no difficulty in regarding as the Locative suffix of O-stems, -*ei* (§ 37), were it not that it is written -*i* and not -*ei* in the oldest Latin inscriptions. For IO-stems indeed a Gen. -*ī* would naturally go with a Nom. -*īs* (§ 5); and it is possible that the suffix, or at any rate the spelling of the suffix, has been extended from these over all O-stems.

I-stems have -eis, -ois in various languages (e. g. Goth. anstais for I.-Eur. -ois); and in Umbro-Oscan we have -eis, e.g. Umbr. *ocrer*, of the citadel (Lat. *ŏcris*), a suffix extended to consonant-stems and even to O-stems, e. g. Osc. *carneis*, of a part (Lat. *carn-is*), sakarakleís, 'of a shrine' (Lat. *sacrăcŭli). But in Latin the consonant-stem suffix has enforced itself on the I-stems too, e. g. *partĭs* like *reg-ĭs* (cf. *partus* like *Castorus, C.I.L.* i. 197).

U-stems seem similarly to have had -eus, -ous (e. g. Goth. sunaus, ' of a son,' for I. Eur. -ous), and so in Umbro-Oscan, e. g. Umbr. *trifor* ' tribus,' Osc. *castrovs* ' fundi,' Lat. *mănūs*, all probably with -ous from I. Eur. -eus (ch. iv. § 35). Whether the Gen. form of *dŏmus* affected by Augustus, viz. *domos*, points to the coexistence in Latin of I.-Eur. -ous is uncertain (cf. ch. iv. § 41, on Lat. *ō* for I.-Eur. ou). A common formation, perhaps the usual one in the careless talk of every-day life, in which the fourth Decl. seems to have been greatly merged in the second (ch. v. § 49), was -*ī*, the O-stem genitive. This is the normal genitive in the Dramatists of the Republic; and even Quintilian in the first cent. A. D. declares it impossible to decide whether *senati* or *senatūs* is the proper Gen. of *sĕnātus*. Occasionally the Dramatists have -*uis*, the suffix proper to ū-stems like *sūs, socrūs*, as -*iis, -*īs* to ī-stems like *vīs* (O. Lat. Gen. *vīs*).

Consonant-stems show -ĕs in some languages (e. g. O. Sl. dĭn-e, ' of a day,' with -e from -ĕs), -ŏs in others (e. g. Gk. ποιμέν-ος). Latin -*is*, on old inscriptions -*es*, shows the former suffix, while the -*us* occasionally written on inscriptions seems to be a relic of the latter. To make -*is* a weakening of earlier -*us* (-*os*) is an unlikely theory, seeing that -*us* (-*os*) of the Nom.

Sg. of Neuter ES-stems, &c., e.g. *genus, opus*, was not weakened to *-es, -is*.

The Ā-stem Gen. *-aes* (pronounced *-ēs* with the open E-sound, ch. ii. § 32) is probably a feature of the Italian-Greek patois, for it is practically confined to epitaphs of the uneducated classes (from the last century of the Republic). It is merely an expression in Roman letters of the Greek Genitive-ending -ης (with open E). *Hedoneî* (*C.I.L* xi. 3316 Forum Clodi), may be an example of a Greek name in -η taking a Genitive after the analogy of Latin fifth Decl. stems (or for *Hedonii?*)

§ 18. Ā-stems. (1) In *-ās*. This form is proper to the Saturnian and earliest Epic poetry. Thus *escas, Mŏnētas, Lātōnas* are quoted by Priscian (i. p. 198 H.) from Livius Andronicus, *Terras* and *fortūnas* from Naevius, *vias* from Ennius. (For other passages of the grammarians treating of this Genitive, see Neue, *Formenl.* i². p. 5.) Servius favours the reading *auras* for *aurae* in Virg. *A.* xi. 801, and in his note on the passage mentions that some interpreted *custōdias* as a Gen. Sg. in a passage of Sallust: castella custodias thensaurorum in deditionem acciperentur. A relic of the old usage survived in legal phraseology, so conservative always of old words and ceremonies, in the terms *păter fămĭlĭas, māter familias, fīlius (-a) familias*. But this form is unknown to the conversational language of the Dramatists [*Alcŭmēnas* in the Argument (post Plautine) of the *Amphitruo*, l. 1, is an imitation of the antique], and must have been in their time out of use. (A contrary view is stated in *Studem. Stud.* ii. p. 21.)

(2) In *-āī*, class. *-ae*. Dissyllabic *-āī* is not infrequent in Plautus, and is perhaps found in Terence (*Rhein. Mus.* 1893, p. 305), while in Lucilius it is allowed in hexameters only (e.g. *Tĭrĕsiai*, v. 43 M.), not in the dramatic metres. Lucretius is especially fond of this early form; and it is used occasionally by Cicero, Virgil, and other Epic writers (for instances, see Neue, i². p. 12). To Martial it seems typical of the uncouth early Latin poetry (xi. 90. 5):

> attonitusque legis 'terrai frugiferai,'
> Accius et quicquid Pacuviusque vomunt.

The rarity of the elision of the final *-i* of *-āī*, as of *-ēī* [Plaut. *Bacch.* 307 *Diana(i) Ephesiae*; *Pers.* 409 *pecunia(i) accipiter*, are more or less doubtful instances], may be an indication that the ending had already at the beginning of the second cent. B.C. ceased to be quite two distinct syllables, though it is scanned as a spondee. The change to *-ae* would probably begin by the shortening of the *ā* before the following vowel, so that *āī* (classical *-ae*) would differ from *-āī* in Plautus very much as his pronunciation *Chĭus* (Adj. *pĭus* from *Chīus, pīus* (ch. ii. § 143). Though written *-ai* on early inscriptions (for example on the old Praenestine vases and mirrors) it need not have been pronounced otherwise than the diphthong *ai* of *aidilis*, &c. (ch. iv. § 29), precisely as the archaistic spelling of a later metrical inscription (*C.I.L.* vi. 555) offers as a spondee *ripai*. Another inscription of no early date (i. 1202), seems to show -*aī* with -*i* elided: non aevo exsacto vitai es traditus morti). [For passages of the grammarians referring to this Genitive in -*ai*, see Neue, i². p. 9, e.g. Quint. i. 7. 18 unde 'pictai vestis' et 'aquai' Vergilius amantissimus vetustatis carminibus inseruit. Servius on *A.* vii. 464 says that Virgil ended the line with 'aquae amnis' (*leg.* vis?), which was changed by Tucca and Varius to *aquai*].

A list of 'Greek' genitives in -*aes* from plebeian epitaphs is given by Neue, i². p. 13. On two bricks of the same year (123 A.D.) from the manufactory of Flavia Procula we have (*C. I. L.* xv. i. 1157-8) *Flaviaes Proclaes* and *Flaviae Procule.* [Cf. no. 1425 *Seiaes Isauricae* (123-141 A.D.), but usually *Seiae Isauricae.*]

Some would connect Lat. -*āī*, -*ae* with O. Ind. Gen. -āyās, Dat. -āyāi (used in the Brāhmanas for the Gen.) of Ā-stems, the yo f which forms is of doubtful origin. The derivation of Lat. -*āī* from an earlier *-*ais* is impossible. The supposed ' Prosepnais 'of a Praenestine mirror (*C. I. L.* i. 57) is really *Prosepnai*, and is a Dative, not a Genitive (see *Rhein. Mus.* 1887, p. 486).

§ 19. **Fifth Decl. Stems.** The Genitive of these stems is discussed by Aulus Gellius in the fourteenth chapter of Book ix of the Noctes Atticae. In old copies (aliquot veteribus libris) of the History of Claudius Quadrigarius he found *facies* Gen., sometimes with *facii* added in the margin : meminimus enim in Tiburti bibliotheca invenire nos in eodem Claudii libro scriptum utrumque 'facies' et 'facii.' Sed 'facies' in ordinem (in the text) scriptum fuit, et contra (in the margin) per i geminum ' facii.' He quotes *dies* from Ennius (*Ann.* 433 M.) and from Cicero, *pro Sest.* xii. 28: equites vero daturos illius dies poenas (where our MSS. read *diei*, but where Gellius found *dies* in the older copies : inpensa opera conquisitis veteribus libris plusculis), and mentions a report that in a 'liber idiographus' of Virgil the line (*G.* i. 208) was written :

Libra dies somnique pares ubi fecerit horas[1].

He adds examples of -*ii* (Nom. -*iēs*), -*i* (Nom. -*ēs*) from early literature, *fami* from Cato and Lucilius, *pernicii* from Sisenna and Cicero, *progenii* from Pacuvius, *acii* and *specii* from Matius, *luxurii* from C. Gracchus, and supports the reading *dii* in Virgil, *A.* i. 636 : munera laetitiamque dii (quod inperitiores 'dei' legunt, ab insolentia scilicet vocis istius abhorrentes). Finally he summons the authority of the great Dictator for *die, specie,* &c. : sed C. Caesar in libro de Analogia secundo 'hujus die' et 'hujus specie' dicendum putat, and supports this form from an old MS. of Sallust: ego quoque in Jugurtha Sallustii summae fidei et reverendae vetustatis libro ' die' casu patrio scriptum inveni. (The passage is *Jug.* xcvii. 3, where two of our MSS. have *die*, the rest *diei*.) (For the remarks of other grammarians on this point, see Neue, i². p. 375.) From his account we gather that forms like *diē, speciē*, were grammarians' coinages designed to restore the actual forms *dii̯, specii̯* to the proper e-type of stem. At the same time the tendency to Dissimilation, which in the middle of a word turned *ii* to *iē* in *ăliēnus*, &c., may have been to some extent operative in certain collocations of these words, e. g. *dii-festi, dii-natalis*, &c. [see ch. iii. § 12 *a* (9)]. The spelling *diei, speciei,* &c., in early literature and inscriptions, may often have represented *dii̯, specii̯*, the -*ei* being diphthongal as

---

[1] The form *dies* would, however, produce cacophony with its repetition of -*s* in the Cicero and Virgil passages.

in the old spellings *deico, feido* (ch. iv. § 34). Gellius mentions (*l. c.*) the theory of some grammarians that *die, specie* were Ablative forms used as Genitives, and modern philologists have made them Locatives, like *die crastini*, &c. (§ 37). The rule of the grammarians of the Empire is that in the approved Gen. form, dissyllabic -*ei*, the *e* is short after a consonant, long after a vowel, e. g. *fidĕi, diēi*. In Plautus and Terence we rarely find *rēi* (e. g. Plaut. *Men.* 494), but usually monosyllabic *rêi*, hardly ever the ceremonious form *rēi*, e. g. *Mil.* (prol.) 103 magnái rēī públicai grátia (post-Plautine ?) ; similarly *fidei* is always dissyllabic in Terence and usually in Plautus (but twice *fidēi*) ; *spei* is never a dissyllable. (Seyffert, *Stud. Pl.* p. 25.) (Compare the usage of the dramatists with regard to the Pronoun Dat. Sg. *ēi, ĕi*, and *êi*, ch. vii. § 19.) The normal shortening of *ē* in hiatus (ch. ii. § 143) would be hindered when *i* preceded, e. g. *diei*. Of the elision of the final -*i* of dissyllabic -*ei* examples (more or less doubtful) are : Plaut. *Aul.* 68 Malaé rei euenísse, *Poen.* 479 Quói réi ? Ad fundas uíscus ne adhaerésceret, &c. (Other examples of all these forms of the Gen. of fifth Decl. stems, e. g. *răbiēs* in Lucr. iv. 1083 :

> quodcumque est, rabies unde illaec germina surgunt,

die in Varro, *Ep. ad Fufium* : meridiem die natalis, *fidē* in Hor. *C.* iii. 7. 4 constantis juvenem fide, see in Neue, *l. c.*)

§ 20. **O-stems and IO-stems.** The grammarians tell us that *Vălĕri, Vergíli*, &c. were accented on the second syllable, that is to say they were accented as if they were contractions of *Valerii*, &c. (ch. iii. § 10. 4), though whether this accentuation was due to tradition or to grammarians' rules is open to question. Lucilius' rule for the use of the single symbol *i* for a Singular case, e. g. *pueri* Gen. Sg., and of the double symbol *ei* for a Plural, e. g. *puerei* Nom. Pl. has been mentioned in ch. i. § 9.

The earliest form of the O-stem Gen. Sg. suffix is -*i*, e. g. *Saeturni pocolom C. I. L.* i. 48 ; from the time of Lucilius to the end of the Republic -*ei*, which had come to be an expression of the long *i*-sound (ch. i. § 9) is also found, e. g. *populi Romanei* on the Lex Agraria of 111 B. C. In Faliscan we have -oi in the one instance of the Gen. Sg. of an O-stem, Zextoi ' Sexti ' on a rude inscr. on a tile (Zvet. *I. I. I.* 73) ; IO-stems (with Nom. in -io or -es) have -*i*, e. g. Acarcelini (*ib.* 62), Caui (*ib.* 49) (also -es ?). On the use in the Gen. Sg. of IO-stems of -*i* (the older form) and -*ii* (Propertius, Ovid, &c.), see Neue, *Formenl.* i². pp. 85-94. The passages which he quotes from the grammarians make it clear that -*ii* was a grammarian's restoration[1] on the Analogy of

---

[1] The suggestion of -*ii* seems to have been made as early as Lucilius, who proposed to distinguish in this way the Gen. of *Numerius* from the Gen. of *numerus*. The phrase *servandi numeri* should, he said, mean ' for the purpose of keeping tune' (*inc.* 66 M.):

'seruandi numeri':—numerum ut seruemus modumque.

This use of the Gen. of the Gerundive to indicate purpose (cf. Aegyptum proficiscitur cognoscendae antiquitatis, Tac.) is a genuine Latin construction (see Weisweiler, *Der finale Gen. Gerund.* 1890), and is found in Umbrian, e. g. *esono-* ... *ocrer pihaner* 'sacrificium arcis piandae' (*Tab. Ig.* vi. A. 18), *verfale pufe arsfertur trebeit ocrer peihaner* 'templum (?) ubi flamen versatur arcis piandae ' (*ib.* vi. A. 8).

O-stems, -*i* the actual historical development. Adjective IO-stems have -*ii*, e. g. patrii sermonis, Lucr. [See Neue, ii³. p. 44 ; *fluvii* of Virg. *A.* iii. 702 (Gela fluvii cognomine dicta) has been explained as an Adj.]

§ 21. U-stems. On the S. C. de Bacchanalibus of 186 B. C. (*C. I. L.* i. 196) we have *sĕnātuos*, but in inscriptions of the latter part of the second cent. B.C. *senati* (i. 199, of 117 B. C. ; i. 200, of 111 B. C. ; i. 547, of 141 or 116 B. C.), (cf. *lăci* i. 584, of 82–79 B. C., and see Mommsen's note) ; and in the Comedians and Tragedians -*i* is the usual form (cf. Prisc. i. 257. 18 H.), occasionally -*uis* (dissyll.), e. g. Ter. *Heaut.* 287 eius anuis causa. Gellius (iv. 16. 1) tells us that Varro and Nigidius (first cent. B. C.) approved -*uis*, e. g. *senatuis*, *dŏmuis*, a form which sticklers for Analogy defended by the Dat. Sg. *senatui*, since *patri*, *duci*, *caedi* had as Genitives *patris*, *ducis*, *caedis*. According to Mar. Victorinus (9. 4 K.), Augustus used *domos* for *domus* Gen. (divus Augustus genetivo casu hujus 'domos' meae per o, non ut nos per u litteram scripsit. Cf. Suet. *Aug.* 87). (For other passages of the grammarians dealing with the Genitive of *u*-stems, see Neue, i². p. 352). The -*uos* of *senatuos* must be the ū-stem Gen. with the I.-Eur. Gen. suffix -ŏs (see below), as the -*uis* of *anuis* is the ū-stem Gen. with the I.-Eur. Gen. suffix -ĕs. But the -*ūs* of *senatūs*, *ănūs* can hardly be derived by the ordinary processes of phonetic change from either ; for -*uos*, -*uis* would naturally become -*vŏs* (-*ŭs*), -*vĭs* (*cf. mīluos*, Plaut., *milvos* in class. Lat., *mort(v)ŭs* in Late Lat., ch. iv. § 71).

In Faliscan we have (Zvet. *I. I. I.* 70) : de zenatuo sententiad, where the final -s of zenatuos (Lat. *senatuos*) has been dropped before the following initial s-. Oscan senateís shows the same Gen. suffix as the O-stems.

§ 22. Consonant-stems. The frequency of the Gen. -*us* in S. Italian inscriptions, e. g. *Vĕnĕrus*, *C. I. L.* i. 565 (Capua, 108 B. C.), *Eph. Epigr.* viii. 460 (Capua, 108 B. C.), *C. I. L.* i. 1183 (Casinum), i. 1495 (on a tile, now at Naples), *Cĕrĕrus*, i. 566 (Capua, 106 B. C.), i. 568 (Capua, 104 B. C.), *Hŏnōrus* on the Lex Pariet. Fac. i. 577 (Puteoli, 105 B. C., a copy), may be due to the influence of the Greek Gen. in -*os* [so *rēgus* (with *sŏcĭĕtātis*) on a bilingual Greek and Latin inscr. of 81 B. C., *Not. Scav.* 1887, p. 110], but this Latin suffix cannot have been merely a usage of Italian-Greek patois, like -*aes* in Gen. of Ā-stems. It is found on so early inscriptions as the S. C. de Bacch. (i. 196) with *nōmĭnus*, and the old Praenestine cippus (xiv. 2892) with *Sălūtus*, and on various official inscriptions, e. g. the Epistula ad Tiburtes (i. 201, of c. 100 B. C.) with *Kastorus*, the Lex Agraria of 111 B. C. (i. 200) with *hŏmĭnus*, *praevārĭcātiōnus*, the Lex Bantina (i. 197, of 133–118 B. C.) with *Castorus* and even *partus* (an I-stem), and may be the correct reading in Lucil. ix. 28 M. : foris subteminus panust. (Other examples in Neue, i². p. 191, such as the soldier's message of defiance cut on a glans used at the siege of Perusia : L. Antoni calve, peristi C. Caesarus victoria, *C. I. L.* i. 685).

The Genitive in -*es* on old inscriptions may sometimes be dialectal with -*ēs* for -eis (the I-stem Gen., extended in the Umbro-Oscan languages to Consonant-stems), e. g. Umbr. *matrer*, *nomner* (cf. Osc. maatreís 'matris'), but is more naturally regarded as -*ĕs*, the older spelling of classical -*ĭs* (as early as c. 180 B. C., *flāmĭnis*, *C.I.L.* i. 33) (cf. ch. iii. § 18). Examples are *C. I. L.* i. 49 (Orte) *Salutes pocolom*, i. 187 (Praeneste) *Apolones dederi*, i. 811 (Rome?) [*C*]*ereres*.

On a possible byform -*s*, of the Gen. Sg. suffix, seen in the O. Lat. Adverb *nox*, 'by night' (Gk. νυκτός), see ch. ix. § 3.

§ 23. **Dat. Sing.** The Dat. Sing. of Ā-stems had in I-Eur. the long diphthong -āi (e.g. Gk. χώρᾳ). In Latin and the Umbro-Oscan languages we find the ordinary diphthong -ai (Osc. -aí, Umbr. -e, Lat. -ae, older -ai). Whether in O. Lat. -ā existed beside -ai is not quite certain. If it did, we must suppose -ā and -ai to have been doublets, both sprung from original -āi, just as *atque* and *ac* (for *atc) were doublets, the one representing the sound which *at* with the enclitic *que* took before a word beginning with a vowel, the other its sound before a consonant (ch. ii. § 136; ch. iv. § 45).

O-stems had similarly in I.-Eur. the long diphthong -ōi (e.g. Gk. ἵππῳ). In the most ancient Latin inscriptions we have -*oi* with the quantity of the *o* unascertainable (Umbro-Oscan seem to have had the ordinary diphthong -oi, in Oscan -úí, in Umbrian -e), but in all other inscriptions and in classical Latin, -ō. This -*oi* and -ō are generally regarded as doublets, like -ā and -*ai* of Ā-stems, the long vowel having survived the struggle for existence in the one declension, the diphthong in the other.

As regards Fifth Decl. Stems, we have seen (ch. iv. § 47) that the doublets -ēi (the long diphthong) and -ē probably existed in I.-Eur. times. If Gellius is right in saying that *făcie*, &c. were regarded as the correct forms by the older writers, this may indicate that the latter gained the day in Latin. The alternative Dative which he mentions, *facii*, may then be the Genitive form (*facii* for older *faciēi* from *faciēi*), which was adapted to the dative use on the Analogy of third Decl. datives in -*ī* (just as the classical *faciēi* seems to be a Genitive form), though some prefer to regard it as a relic of the I.-Eur. 'doublet'-suffix ēi-.

I-stems have in Latin -*ī*, older -*ei*, probably (like the Genitive in -*ĭs*, older -*es*, also -*us*, § 22) a loan from Consonant-stems, and so originally -*ai*. The Umbro-Oscan termination was -ei (Osc. -eí, Umbr. -e), as in Consonant-stems.

U-stems have -*uī* in Latin, which is equally traceable to either of the I.-Eur. suffixes, -ĕwai and -wai (e.g. O. Ind. sūnávē, 'to a son,' and śíśv́, 'to a child.' The occasional Latin forms in -*ŭ* are (cf. Umbrian *trifo* 'tribui') really Locatives (§ 37), according to some, Instrumentals (§ 36).

Consonant-stems had -ai (-ai? ch. iv. § 3) in I.-Eur. (e. g. O. Ind.

šún-ē, 'to a dog,' dá-man-ē Inf., Gk. δό-μεν-αι Inf., Lat. *lĕgĭmĭnī* Inf. used as Imper. (?), ch. viii. § 81), in Latin *-ī* from older *-ei* (sometimes written *-e*), the diphthong *-ai* being weakened first to *-ei*, then to *-ī* in the unaccented syllable, as *ai* of *oc-caido* to *ei*, *occeido*, and *ī*, *occīdo* (ch. iii. § 18). In Umbro-Osc. this weakening does not seem to have taken place, so that their *-ei* (Osc. -eí, e.g. medíkeí ' meddíci,' chief magistrate, [A]πελλουνηι; Umbr. -e, e.g. patre, *nomne*) can hardly represent I.-Eur. *-ai*.

§ 24. Ā-stems. Dissyllabic *-āī* is not found in the Dat. of Ā-stems, but only in the Gen. (*terrai frugiferai*, Enn. *A*. 605 M. is, like Virgil's *aulai medio*, with which Charisius couples it, a Genitive, so correct 'dativo' in Char. 19. 1 K.; *uiāī sternendāī*, Lucil. xi. 5 M., even if the reading is right (MSS. *vim sternenda et*), is anything but a certain example (see L. Mueller's note), so that Priscian's remark that the Nom. and Voc. Plur. ending of the first declension did not admit of 'divisio,' as the Gen. and Dat. Sg. did, cannot be quite accurate (Prisc. i. p. 291. 17 H. nominativus et vocativus pluralis primae declinationis similis est genetivo et dativo singulari. Nam in ae diphthongum profertur, ut 'hi' et 'o poetae'; sed in his non potest divisio fieri, sicut in illis). Gellius (xiii. 26. 4) tells us that Nigidius (first cent. B. C.) approved *-ai* (presumably the diphthong) in the Gen., *-ae* in the Dative. (On Lucilius' practice see L. Mueller's note on Lucil. ix. 6.) The *-e* found on some inscriptions is dialectal (cf. Umbr. -e) and rustic, e.g. *Diane* (*C. I. L.* i. 168, Pisaurum), *Fortune* (i. 64, Tusculum), *Uictorie* (i. 183, Marsi). Of the 'Datives in *-a*,' only found on very old inscriptions, most of the apparent examples come from Pisaurum (*C. I. L.* i. 167-180), where *-e* (*Diane* just quoted) was the Dat. suffix of Ā-stems, and may be Genitives in *-ās* with omission of the final *s* (cf. Nom. Pl. *matrona Pisaurese* for *matronas Pisaurenses*, i. 173; so Gen. Sg. *Coira pocolo*, *Eph. Epigr.* i. 6), or else a mere dialectal variety, which would prove nothing for the Latin dative. Others, viz. *Fortuna* (i. 1133, Praeneste); *Fortuna* (*Bull.* 1885, p. 62, Signia); Fortuna Diouo fileia primogenia (xiv. 2863, Praeneste); *Diana* (xiv. 4182 *a* and 4184 *a*, Nemi) are open to similar doubts. The strongest instances are: [*Me*]*nerua dono d* . . . (*Not. Scav.* 1887, p. 179, Rome); *Iunonei Loucina* (*C. I. L.* i. 189, loc. inc.); *Iunone Loucina Tuscolana sacra* and [*Pa*]*le* [*Tusc*]*olana sacra* (i. 1200-1, Capua) [cf. Faliscan Menerua sacru (Zvet. *I. I. I.* 70)].

Examples of *-ai* are *Dianai donum dedit* (*C. I. L.* xiv. 4270, beg. of second cent. B. C.), *Meneruai donom port-* (*C. I. L.* i. 191), [*Iunon*]*e Loucinai* (i. 813). We have *-ai* even on inscrr. of the Emperor Claudius, e.g. *Antoniai Augustai matri* (Orelli 650).

§ 25. Fifth Decl. Stems. Gellius (ix. 14): in casu autem dandi qui purissime locuti sunt non 'faciei,' uti nunc dicitur, sed 'facie' dixerunt. He then quotes two examples of *facie* from Lucilius (vii. 9 and vii. 7 M.), and adds : sunt tamen non pauci, qui utrobique 'facii' legant. In Plautus the treatment of the Dative Sg. of these stems is the same as that of the Genitive (see § 19). In Umbr. ri 'rei' the i may correspond to Lat. *-ē*, as in pru-sikurent 'pronuntiaverint' with the ē-grade of root seen in Lat. *sēdi*, &c. (ch. viii. § 39).

§§ 24-29.] DECLENSION OF NOUNS, ETC. ACC. SING. 387

§ 26. O-stems. The suffix *-oi* (mentioned by Mar. Victorinus 17. 20 K.:
'populoi Romanoi' pro populo Romano solitos priores scribere) is found on
the very ancient Praenestine fibula (*C. I. L.* xiv. 4123): Manios med fefaked
Numasioi (=Manius me fecit Numerio), but *-o* on the Dvenos inscription
(Zvet. *I.I.I.* 285), if the words: die noine med mano statod, be rightly read and
interpreted 'die noni me Mano stato' (cf. Numisio Martio donom dedit meretod, *Not. Scav.* 1890, p. 10; *Lebro* 'Libero' *C. I. L.* i. 174, from Pisaurum. The
Vestine dialect had *-o*, e. g. *Herclo Iouio* (Zvet. *I. I. I.* 11).

§ 27. U-stems. *Senatuei* (*C. I. L.* i. 201, of c. 100 B. C.). Gellius (iv. 16)
informs us that Varro and Nigidius used *senatui, domui, fluctui*, &c. in the
Dative, and *senatuis, domuis, fluctuis* in the Genitive, but gives examples of *-ū*
from Lucilius (iv. 8 M.; *ănu*, iv. 9, cf. vii. 21) and Virgil, and clenches them
with the authority of Caesar: C. etiam Caesar, gravis auctor linguae Latinae,
... in libris Analogicis omnia istiusmodi sine i littera dicenda censet. In
Plautus *-ui* is the usual form, e. g. *quaestui habere, extersui, usui esse*, and with
the force of a second supine, *Bacch.* 62 quia istaec lepida sunt memoratui;
but *-u* is also found, e. g. *Rud.* 294 sunt nobis quaestu et cultu.

§ 28. Consonant-stems. The so-called 'Datives in *-ĕ*' in Latin poets
(cf. Servius ad *A.* x. 653 conjuncta crepidine saxi, *A.* x. 361 haeret pede pes, and
L. Mueller's note on Ennius, *Ann.* 395) are really Locatives or Instrumentals
(see Neue, i². p. 195). The *-e* which we find (along with *-ei*) on old inscriptions
is *-ē*, possibly in some cases (e. g. *C.I.L.* i. 1170, *Ioue*, Marsic), a dialectal form
(cf. Umbr. patre), but certainly in others a mere graphic variety of *-ei*, later
-ī, just as the *e* of *ploirume* on the Scipio epitaph (*C. I. L.* i. 32 honc oino
ploirume cosentiont) represents no different sound from the usual *-ei*, later *-ī*
of the Nom. Pl. of O-stems. Instances of Dat. *-ei* and *-e* are: *Hercolei* (i. 1503,
Rome, 217 B. C.); *Martei* (i. 531, Rome, 211 B. C.); *Hercole* (*Ann. Épigr.* 1890,
no. 84, Rome); *Hercole* (*C. I. L.* xiv. 2891-2, Praeneste). We have the three
spellings of the suffix side by side on a freedman's inscription from the
Roman district (i. 1110): *Iunone Seispitei Matri*, and the two older in i. 638:
[*D*]*iouei Uictore* (Rome, c. 180 B. C.), [Quintilian (i. 4. 17) mentions *Diove Uictore*
as an old form], and in xi. 4766 *Ioue* . . . *Iouei* (Spoletium in Umbria). (For
other instances of these old spellings, see Index to *C. I. L.* i.)

§ 29. Acc. Sing. To form the Acc. Sing. Masc. and Fem.
the suffix -m was added, which in the case of Consonant-stems
took the form -m̥ (e.g. O. Ind. mātár-am, Gk. μητέρ-α, Lat.
matr-em). The Acc. Neut. was the same as the Nom. (§ 10).

Thus Ā-stems had -ām (e. g. O. Ind. áśvām, Gk. χώρᾱν), which
in Latin would become *-ăm* (ch. iii. § 49), *equăm*. The long vowel
is indicated by Osc. paam (Lat. *quam*), the Acc. Sg. Fem. of the
Relative Pronoun, but the usual spelling is e. g. Osc. tovtam, Umbr.
totam, the community. O-stems had -ŏm, in O. Lat. *om*, class.
-um (ch. iv. § 20); IO-stems, *-iom, -ium*, perhaps also in the

c c 2

388   THE LATIN LANGUAGE.   [Chap. VI.

'familiar' declension (§ 5), -im; I-stems, -im, which is found in the older literature and in many examples, *turrim*, &c., in the classical period, though *-em*, the Consonant-stem ending, has usually supplanted it; U-stems, -ŭm; Ī-stems, -īm (also -iyṃ, e. g. O. Ind. dhíyam, 'thought'), which in Latin would become *-ĭm*; Ū-stems, -uwṃ, Lat. *-uem*, e. g. *suem*, also -ūm, Lat. *-ŭm*, e. g. *socrum*. Consonant-stems take in Umbro-Oscan -om, the O-stem Accusative, e. g. Osc. *medicatin-om* (Lat. **meddĭcātiōnem* from *med-dix*, a magistrate). Of Latin ES-stems some are regular, e. g. *dēgĕnĕrem* from **degenes-em*; others follow the analogy of Ē-stems, as in the Gen. and other cases, e. g. *plēbem* (ch. v. § 51).

§ 30. **The endings -im and -em.** We can hardly say that *-ĕm* arose from *-ĭm* by ordinary phonetic change, seeing that final *-im* remains in so many words, e. g. Adverbs in *-im* like *ōlim*, as well as Accusatives like *clāvim*. The change is rather due to that intermixture of I- and Consonant-stems which was the despair of grammarians as early as Varro (*L. L.* viii. 66), and which led to the substitution of *-ĕ* for *-ĭ* in the 'Ablative' (see below, § 33). A list of Accusatives in *-im*, with references to the Latin grammarians who discuss this question, is given by Neue, i². p. 196, to which may be added *piscim* on an old Praenestine cista (*Mél. Arch.* 1890, p. 303), and the instances from the Ambrosian Palimpsest of Plautus given in Studemund's Index, e. g. *imbrim*, *Pseud.* 102. Sometimes the use of *-im* indicates an Ī-stem, e. g. *vim*, sometimes a Greek loanword, e. g. *turrim* (?); it is retained in Accusatives used adverbially, e. g. *partim* (ch. ix. § 4). [*Claudi*, &c. (*C. I. L.* iv. Ind.), if for *Claudi(u)m*, may be dialectal. On Gk. Ἀπφειν for Ἄππιον Nom. Sg. (*I. I. S.* 1411), &c., see Eckinger, *Orth.* p. 56.]

§ 31. **Voc. Sing.** In the Plural and Dual, and in the Neut. Sing., the Nom. form was used also for the Voc. in I.-Eur., and even in the Masc., Fem. Sing. the same thing is often found (e. g. in the Veda, Váyav Índraś ca, 'O Vāyu and Indra'; in Hom., Ζεῦ πάτερ, ... Ἥλιός τε; in Plautus *meus ocellus*, ... *mi anime*). The rule however was that in the Singular the bare stem was used (accented on the first syllable, e. g. O. Ind. pítar, Gk. πάτερ, unlike the Nom., O. Ind. pitá, Gk. πατήρ). Ā-stems had a short A-vowel (Gk. δέσποτα, &c.), O-stems -ĕ (O. Ind. vŕkă, Gk. λύκε, Lat. *lŭpĕ*) and so on. In Latin I-, U- and N-stems substitute the Nom. form for the Voc., e. g. *cīvis*, *mănŭs*, *hŏmo* (contrast Gk. ὄφι, πῆχυ, κύον); and the same was done in R-stems even earlier than the shortening of long vowels before final *-r* in the second cent. B. C. removed the distinction between I.-Eur. -ēr and -ĕr, -ōr and -ŏr, to judge from scansions in

Plautus like *Merc.* 800 Uxór, heus uxor; probably also in S-stems. Final ā was shortened in Nouns of the first declension still earlier, before the literary period (ch. iii. § 43), so that it is impossible to say whether *equă* Voc. is the Nom. form (originally *equā*), or is a special Voc. form. It cannot be the I.-Eur. Vocative, if final I.-Eur. -ă became -ĕ in Latin (ch. iii. § 37), so that I.-Eur. *ekwă would sink to *equĕ*, and would be indistinguishable from the Voc. of O-stems, I.-Eur. *ekwĕ, Voc. of *ekwos. The levelling process to which the other Latin Vocatives have submitted makes it likely that the Nom. was used for the Voc. in the Ā-declension too; and that the Umbrian language, in which a distinction between the Nom. (in -*o*, § 2), and the Voc. (only in -*a*, e. g. Ṡerfia), of Ā-stems is clearly apparent, has retained the I.-Eur. -ă of the Voc. (cf. ch. iii. § 18, p. 191). Latin IO-stems show in the Voc. -*ī*, e. g. *Vălĕri*; but this form is hardly found except in proper names [which, as we saw before, (§ 5), admitted the 'familiar' declension,-*is* Nom., -*im* Acc.(?), &c.], and the word of everyday life, *fīli*, so that the -*ī* need not be a contraction of an older -*ie*, but may be the Voc. byform corresponding to the Nom. byform -*is* (cf. Lith. gaidỹ Voc. from gaidỹs Nom., 'a cock'; see § 5). RO-stems which took -*er* in the Nom. retain this in the Voc. too, though *puĕre*, and not *puer*, seems to be the form always used by Plautus.

§ 32. **Other examples.** *Jū-piter* (better *Juppiter*, ch. ii. § 130, p. 116) corresponds exactly with Gk. Ζεῦ πάτερ, and might be a Vocative used as a Nominative, just as Homer's νεφεληγερέτα Ζεύς, μητίετα Ζεύς, have been explained as obsolete Vocative forms, preserved only in certain liturgies, and treated by the poet as Nominatives through a similar mistake to ours in using 'cherubim' as a Singular. But *Jū-piter* may also be a correctly formed Nominative with the stem *Dyeu-, Lat. *Jov-* (cf. O. Lat. *Jovis* Nom.) as the first part of the Compound (cf. *jū-glans*, ch. v. § 85). The same double explanation is possible for *Dite pater* Voc. (*C. I. L.* i. 818). *Dite* Voc. (*Eph. Epigr.* viii. 529) reminds us of Gk. ὄφι, &c.

The Vocative formation for IO-stems is discussed by Gellius (*Noct. Att.* xiv. 5), who describes a battle royal waged in his presence between two grammarians about the proper Voc. of *egregius*, without satisfactory result (non arbitratus ego operae pretium esse, eadem istaec diutius audire, clamantes compugnantesque illos reliqui). Priscian (i. p. 301. 19 H.) says that the early writers used -*ie* as well as -*i* in the Voc. of proper names : haec tamen eadem etiam in e proferebant antiquissimi, 'O Virgilie,' 'Mercurie' dicentes, though all that he quotes is a couple of instances of *Laertie*, which is a Greek word, and as much an Adjective as a Noun. He adds that the classical form -*ī* must be a contraction of this older *-ie* (as *Arpīnās*, &c., of older *Arpīnātis*, &c.) because Vocs. in *-ī* were accented on the paenultima, e. g. *Valéri* Voc. (like *Valéri* Gen.). Gellius (xiii. 26) tells us that Nigidius Figulus (first cent. B. C.) wished to distinguish *Váleri* Voc. from *Valéri* Gen., but says that in his time both Voc. and Gen. of IO-stems were invariably accented on the paenultima (cf. ch. iii. § 10. 4). (For other passages of the grammarians, see Neue, *Formenl.* i². p. 82.) Priscian elsewhere (i. p. 305. 9 H.) quotes *filie* (apparently the more ceremonious form) from Livius Andronicus:

páter nóster, Satúrni fílie,

but almost the only instance of the Voc. Sg. of a masc. IO-stem to be found in Plautus and the older writers is *voltŭri* (for which some would read *volture*), 'you vulture' (*Capt.* 844). *Publi Corneli* occurs on a Scipio epitaph of c. 180 B.C. (*C. I. L.* i. 33). Adjective IO-stems take at all periods *-ie*, though there is evidently a reluctance on the part of good writers to use these forms (see Neue, *Formenl.* ii². p. 42).

§ 33. **Abl. Sing.** The Ablative suffix, ending in -d, appears to have been used in I.-Eur. only in O-stems, which formed their Abl. Sg. in -ōd and -ēd (the latter suffix being reserved in the Italic languages for Adverbs, ch. ix. § 1), [O. Ind. yugắt, 'from a yoke,' O. Lat. *jugod*, Falisc. rected, class. Lat. *jŭgō*, *rectē*, final *d* being dropped after a long vowel at the close of the third cent. B. C. (ch. ii. § 137)]. In other stems the Genitive ending -ĕs or -ŏs was used (O. Ind. nāvás, 'from a ship,' Hom. Gk. $νη(F)ός$); and in the Greek language this Ablatival use of the Genitive was extended to O-stems too. In the Italic languages on the other hand the Ā-, Ī-, Ŭ- and Ē-stems acquired Ablatives in *-d* on the Analogy of the O-stems; and the Consonant-stems availed themselves in Latin of the I-stem Abl., in Umbro-Oscan of the O-stem Abl. (e. g. O. Lat. *air-īd*, Osc. *ligud*, 'by law'). The Locative Case in -ĕ (possibly Instrumental, § 36) of these Consonant-stems competed with this I-stem Abl. not only in Consonant-stems (e. g. *aerĕ* and *aerī*), but also in I-stems (e. g. *cīvĕ* and *cīvī*), so that Varro declares that *ove* was heard in his time as often as *ovi*, *ave* as *avi*. The confusion of cases was increased by the circumstance that when -*d* of the Abl. was dropped, nothing remained to distinguish Abl. -*ē(d)* of Ē-stems, -*ī(d)* of I-stems, -*ū(d)* of U-stems from Loc. -*ē*, -*ī*, -*ū* (see § 37), so that the *ŏvī*, *ăvī* of Varro's time have as much right to be called Locatives as Ablatives. (On the question whether these forms can have been Instrumentals, see § 36).

The use of -*ĕ* in the 'Abl.' Sg. of I-stems was certainly not so far advanced in the time of Plautus as in the classical period. He uses only *sorti, bīli, cīvi, fusti, nāvi*, &c., not *sortĕ*, &c. Priscian however attests *rete* (presumably *rētĕ*, like *fortĕ, Most.* 694) in *Rud.* 1020, and remarks (i. p. 331. 16 H.): vetustissimi solebant hujuscemodi ablativum etiam in -e proferre. Of Consonant-stems with -*ī* we have, e. g. *părĭĕtī* (MSS. -*e*), *Cas.* 140, *pūmĭcī* (MSS. -*e*), *Pers.* 41, *obĭĕcī*, *Pers.* 203. (For details of the use of -*i* and -*e* forms by the Latin authors, and the rules laid down by the native grammarians, see Neue, i². pp. 212 sqq.). An early example of the Ablatival use of -*e* (presumably -*ĕ*) is the line of the Saturnian Scipio epitaph (*C. I. L.* i. 30, c. 200 B.C.?):

Gnaíuod pátre prognátus fórtis vir sapiénsque.

(Cf. *aire moltaticod* i. 181, Picenum); somewhat later are i. 198 (Lex Repet.) *maiore parte diei*; i. 199 (Sent. Minuc.) *de maiore parte*; i. 603 (Lex Furf.) *mense Flusare* (dial. ? Cf. Sab. mesene Flusare). We have -*ei*, apparently a graphic variety of *ī* (ch. i. § 9), in the Scipio epitaph of c. 130 B.C. (i. 34, along with *aetate*):

ís hic sítus quei núnquam uíctus est uirtútei

(cf. *ab fontei* on the Sent. Minuc., i. 199. 7); -*i* in the Lex Agr. (i. 200. 23 ab eo herediue eius . . . testamento hereditati deditioniue obuenit, and again : curatore herediue), in the Lex Jul. Municip. (i. 206 ubi continenti habitabitur), the Lex Rep. (i. 198. 56 de sanctioni, but also *adessint* for *adessent*). These are clearly the later forms of the older -*īd* of i. 61 *airid*, i. 186 (S. C. Bacch.) *couentionid*, xi. 4766 *bouid*.

§ 34. O. Lat. Abl. with -*d*. Ablatives with -*d* seem to be unknown in Plautus and the earliest Dramatic literature, so that the final dental must have dropped out of the spoken language before the end of the third cent. B. C., though it is found in the Saturnian poetry (e. g. Naevius, *Bell. Pun.* 7 M. nóctu Troíad exíbant cápitibus opértis ; *C. I. L.* i. 30, one of the oldest Saturnian Scipio epitaphs : Gnaíuod pátre (probably -*ĕ*) prognátus fórtis uir sapiénsque (but *Samnio* Abl. on the same epitaph), and is persistently written in the S. C. de Bacchanalibus (i. 196) of 186 B. C. (*sententiad, couentionid, exstrad, suprad, oquoltod, preiuatod, poplicod, facilumed*, &c.). It is as persistently omitted in a nearly contemporary inscription (*C. I. L.* ii. 5041, Spain, of 189 B. C.). [For other examples of Abl. -*d* on inscriptions, and for passages of the Latin grammarians referring to this form, see Neue, i². p. 2, Ritschl, *Neue Excurse*, i., and add *porod* (for class. *porro*) on a Praenestine cista, *Mél. Arch.* 1890, p. 303.] In Oscan the -*d* remains, e. g. trístaamentud 'testamentō,' akrid 'acri,' *egmad* 're ' (cf.

Faliscan sententiad), but in Umbrian it has been dropped as in Latin, e. g. *poplu* 'populo,' *re-per* 'pro re,' *ocri-per*, vea 'viā' (cf. Pelignian oisa 'usā'); similarly with Adverbs in -ēd, e. g. Osc. *amprufid* 'improbe,' Umbr. rehte 'recte;' Cons. stems show the O-stem Abl., e. g. Osc. *ligud* 'lege,' or the Loc. in -ĭ, e. g. Pelign aetate, Umbr. *nomne*.

§ 35. I-stem and Cons.-stem 'Abl.' in -i and -e. There is no evidence of an old Cons.-stem -ēd, later -ē, corresponding to I-stem -īd, later -ī. The *dictatored* (also *navaled*, but *marid*) of the Columna Rostrata (*C. I. L.* i. 195) is probably a mistake, for the inscription is not the actual inscription of 260 B.C., but a copy made in the time of the Empire; and the instances in MSS. of Plautus and the old poets with final -ē may be due to that 'imperitia' on the part of scribes which Priscian (i. p. 345. 1 H.) blames for the change of *civi*, &c. to *cive* in MSS. of Cicero. The reading of the best Palatine MS. (B) in Plaut. *Pseud.* 616 is *militite*, which points to a correction in the archetype of *militī* to *militē* (the Ambrosian Palimpsest seems to have *militi*); and the MSS. often vary between -*i* and -*e*, e. g. Naev. *Bell. Pun.* 14 M. *pietati* (v. l. -*te*), Enn. *A.* 486 M. *montī* (MSS. *montis* and *montè*).

§ 36. Instr. Sing. The Latin grammarians knew nothing of an Instrumental Case.- Quintilian indeed (i. 4. 26) suggests that a seventh case is required in Latin for such a phrase as *hastā percussi*, where *hastā* is not a real Ablative; though of the previous existence of an Instrumental Case in the Latin language he has no conception. But in various I.-Eur. languages we find an Instrumental, and also a Locative Case; Sanscrit, for example, has, in addition to the Abl. devắt, 'from a god,' the Instrumental[1] devéna, 'with a god' (in Vedic also *dēvắ), and the Locative devḗ, 'in a god.' And the suffixes used in these languages to form their Instrumentals and Locatives it is possible to find also in Latin, though the weakening process which attacked every Latin final syllable has made them indistinguishable from other Case suffixes. To form the Instrumental Singular there seem to have been originally two methods used in the Indo-European language : (1) the addition of -ĕ [according to some -ă, which would in Latin become -ĕ (ch. iii. § 37)]; in Cons.-stems this -ĕ is found unchanged, in Ā-stems we have -ā, in O-stems -ō or -ē and so on; (2) the addition of -bhi (e. g. Hom. Gk. ῖ-φι), or -mi (e. g. Lith. sūnu-mì, 'with a son'); and various modifications of these suffixes are found in the different languages. Of Ā-stem

---

[1] The Instrumental, it may be remarked, is the case used after the phrase árthō bhavati (Lat. *opus est*).

Instrumentals with I.-Eur. -ā (and -ām?) (e.g. Gk. λάθρā?) there are no certain examples in Latin, for the Adverbs *suprā, extrā*, &c. are written in the S. C. de Bacchanalibus *suprad, exstrad*, and are therefore Ablatives. Some make O. Lat. *contră* (the invariable scansion in O. Lat. poetry, Skutsch, *Forschungen*, i. p. 3) an Instrumental, with the same shortening of *-ā* as is seen in the Nom. Sing. of Ā-stems, e.g. *terră* (ch. iii. § 43), *contrā*, the classical form being adapted to the type of *suprā, extrā*, &c. But *contră* may be an Acc. Pl. Neut. form, and *frustră* (the O. Lat. quantity, e.g. *ne frustră sis*, Plaut.) need not be an Instrumental either. The Oscan preposition *contrud* (i.e. *contrōd; cf. Lat *contrō-versia*) is an Ablative.

The O-stem suffix -ō would by the second cent. B.C., when *-d* was dropped after a long vowel, be identical with the Abl., so that *modo, cito* (usually with *-ŏ* by the Law of Breves Breviantes, ch. iii. § 42) may be either Instrumentals or Ablatives. *Porro* is shown to be an Abl. by the old spelling *porod*, mentioned above (§ 34). The other O-stem suffix -ē may indeed appear in *běně, mălě*, since the shortening of their final syllable by the Breves Breviantes Law (e.g. Plaut. *dătŏ* for *datōd*) has advanced more rapidly than in the case of *-ēd*; but on the other hand this might be referred to their greater use in everyday life (cf. *havě* but *monē* in Quintilian's time, ch. iii. § 42), and their more frequent occurrence in word-groups, e.g. *bene-rem-geras, male-ficio* (cf. *diěquinte* but *fidē*, ch. iii. § 44). (The scansion *benē, malē* in Plaut. is doubtful.) Superlative Adverbs in *-ē* have lost a final *d*, as is shown by *facilumed* on the S. C, de Bacchanalibus. Similarly *-ē* of Fifth Decl. stems, e.g. *făciē, rē*, may be Instrumental -ē or Ablative -ēd; -ī of I-stems may be Instr. -ī or Abl. -īd; -ū of U-stems may be Instr. -ū or Abl. -ūd; they may also be Locative -ē (e.g. *postrī-die*), -ěyĭ- (Lat. *-ei*, class. *-ī*, e.g. *Neāpŏlī*), -eu- (Lat. *-ū*, e.g. *noctū*) (see § 37). The *-ě* of Consonant-stems, e.g. *patrě*, cannot be an Abl. suffix, but either Instrumental -ě (-ă?), or Locative -ĭ (Lat. *-ě*, e.g. *Tiburě*), used ablatively and instrumentally, as Loc. -ĭ in Gk. Cons.-stems was used to express all the meanings of the Greek Dative case, e.g. πατρ-ί.

It thus appears how difficult it is to establish by certain proof the presence of Instrumental forms in the Latin declension, owing to the lack of a sufficient number of examples from the earlier inscriptions in which Abl. forms have not yet lost their final *d* (e. g. *C. I. L.* xi. 4766 bouid piaclum datod; i. 61 airid [coir]au[it]; i. 181 aire moltaticod; Zvet. *I. I. I.* 72 opidque Uolgani)[1], and Loc. -ī would be distinguished from Instrumental -ĕ (-ă?). Yet the evidence of cognate languages shows that Instrumental case-forms must have been a living part of Latin at some period, however remote; and when we come to examine the formation of Latin Adverbs we shall find that some of them are believed with a fair amount of probability to be Instrumentals. The evidence that we can draw from forms on Oscan inscriptions (they are not very numerous), is all in favour of the supposition that in the declension of the Noun the Instrumental forms had quite dropped out of use. The Oscan language, unlike the Umbrian, does not drop final d; and indubitable Ablative forms with -d are used in all the senses of the Latin 'Ablative,' to express our prepositions 'from,' 'with,' 'by,' &c., e. g. kúmbenniefs tanginud, 'by decree of the assembly,' eítiuvad, 'with money,' úp eísúd sakaraklúd (Lat. *apud id sacellum*). (The doubtful eítie of Zv. *I. I. I.* 89 : súvad eítie upsed (Lat. *sua pecunia operatus est*), requires confirmation before it can be used as evidence that IĒ-stems used an Instr. or Loc. -iē instead of Abl. -iēd. The absence of an Abl. in *-iēd* from the early Latin inscriptions can be explained by the comparative paucity of Fifth Decl. stems.) In the Pelignian dialect, a variety of Oscan, we have in the few inscriptions preserved an 'Ablative Absolute,' oisa aetate (Lat. *usā aetate*, with passive sense of the Deponent, 'his life having been exhausted') (cf. forte, of doubtful meaning, on the same inscription), and an Ablative of uncertain construction, suad(?) aetatu firata fertlid (Lat. *suā aetate . . . fertili*), with apparent dropping of -d before initial f; and this evidence, so far as it goes, points to an Abl. of Cons.-stems in -ud (i. e. -ōd, the O-stem Abl. suffix), beside another case in -e (presumably -ĕ). If however this -e represents an original -ī (cf. Pel. ae for ai, Osc. *Bansae* Loc.) the case will be a Locative, not an Instrumental; and this view is favoured by the fact that other stems have in

---

[1] The (Adverb?) *mĕritō* is spelt *meretod* or *meritod* on the oldest inscriptions.

Oscan a Locative as well as an Ablative Case, e. g. Ā-stems:
víaí mefiaí Loc., beside eítiuvad Abl. (and *eituas* Gen.); O-stems:
Ladinei Loč., beside trístaamentud Abl. (and sakarakleís Gen.).
An isolated example of an Adverb formed apparently by the
Instr. suffix in Osc. is suluh 'omnino' (Zvet. *I. I. I.* 129), though
this stands on a carelessly written inscription, a leaden execration tablet, and is not free from the suspicion of being meant for
sullud, a form which seems to occur (the last letter is unfortunately not quite legible) on another tablet of the same kind (*I. F.*
ii. 435; cf. von Planta, i. pp. 577–80). The conclusion therefore
which the scanty evidence at our disposal entitles us to draw is
that Instrumental formations, though they may be found in some
Latin Adverbs, are not found in the declension of Latin Nouns,
the case-forms which competed with the Latin Ablative (especially in Cons.-stems) being Locatives and not Instrumentals.

§ 37. **Locative Singular.** Locatives in I.-Eur. seem sometimes to have had a final -ĭ (e. g. O. Ind. mūrdhán-i and mūrdhn-í,
'on the head'), sometimes not (e. g. O. Ind. mūrdhán, Gk. δόμεν
Inf., a Loc. as δόμεναι is a Dat.). Of Locatives without -ĭ in
Latin there are only uncertain traces, such as Prepositions like
pĕnĕs (Loc. of *penus*, with -*es* not sunk to -*is*, possibly because
the accent rested on it in collocations like *penés me, penés te*, ch. iii.
§ 12 *a.* 3), and Adverbs like *noctū*. The predominant formation
is with -ĭ. Of these Ĭ-forms, Ā-stem locatives show I.-Eur. -āi
in O. Ind. áśvāy-ām, Lith. rañkoj-e, with Postpositions -ām and -e,
but in Greek the ordinary diphthong -ai (a 'doublet' of āi, ch. iv.
§ 45), e. g. Θηβαι-γενής; and this is also the Italian form (O. Lat.
-*aï*, class. Lat. -*ae*, Osc. -*aí*, Umbr. -e). O-stems took -oi and
-ei (e. g. Gk. οἴκοι and οἴκει). By the phonetic laws of Latin
both these suffixes would become -*ei*, class. -*ī* (ch. iii. § 18); so
the origin of the suffix of *Cŏrinthī*, &c. is, so far as Latin is concerned, doubtful. But in Oscan we have -eí, which must be
I.-Eur. -ei (e. g. múíníkeí tereí, 'on common ground') (Umbr. -e,
e. g. *destre onse*, 'on the right shoulder,' may be -oi or -ei). Fifth
Decl. stems took -ēi, which already in the 'I.-Eur. period' had a
'doublet' -ē. It is this latter form which appears in Latin, e. g.
die in the phrase *postrī-diē, die crastīnī*, &c. (unless *die* has lost

a final *d*; cf. Faliscan foied ' hodie '). I-stems had -ĕyĭ (e. g. Hom. Gk. πτόλει), which in Latin would become -*ei*, class. -*ī*, and would be merged in the Dative (§ 23) [possibly Instrumental (§ 36)] suffixes. U-stems had -ĕwĭ (e. g. Hom. Gk. ἄστει), but Latin U-stem Locatives show -*ū*, the i-less formation, e. g. *noctū*, mentioned above. Ī-stems showed -ĭyĭ, Lat. -ī, as Ū-stems -ŭwĭ, Lat. -*ue*, e. g. *sue*. Consonant-stems had -ĭ (used in Greek as Dative suffix, as well as Locative), which in Latin became -*ĕ*, e. g. *Carthăgĭnĕ*, *rūrĕ*, and Infs. Act. like *ăgere*, *vīverĕ* (contrast O. Ind. jīvás-ē, Lat. *agī*, which are Datives), though by false analogy of O-stems (or I-stems ?) we sometimes find -*ī*, e. g. *rurī*, perhaps introduced to discriminate the locative from the ablative use, e. g. *rurī esse*, from *rurĕ venire*.

§ 38. **Locatives in -ī and -e in Latin.** *Hĕrĭ* is by modern editors written with -*e* when the last vowel has to be scanned short, otherwise with -*i*. The scansion *herĭ* (by the Brevis Brevians Law, ch. iii. § 42) is common enough in the early Dramatists (e. g. Caecil. *Com.* 197 R. herĭ uero, where *heri* has abundant MS. authority), while the spelling *here* is established for passages like Plaut. *Mil.* 59 (quantity of final vowel doubtful), where the Ambrosian Palimpsest has *here* and the Palatine MS. *hercle* (cf. *Pers.* 108). Quintilian (i. 7. 22) says: 'here' nunc e littera terminamus: at veterum comicorum adhuc libris invenio: 'heri ad me uenit,' quod idem in epistulis Augusti, quas sua manu scripsit aut emendavit, deprehenditur.' [On his remark (i. 4. 8), in 'here' neque e plane neque i auditur, see ch. ii. § 16.] The spelling of these forms, especially in the early writers, is often doubtful, and so it is difficult to prove with certainty such a theory as that only *ruri* is used for ' in the country,' and usually *rure* for ' from the country ' in Plautus (Langen, *Beiträge*, p. 308). Charisius (p. 200. 12 K.) attests *heri* for Afranius *Com.* 71 R., *peregri* for Naev. *Com.* 93 R., but *peregre* for Naev. *Com.* 84 R., as *prae-fiscine* for Afranius *Com.* 36 R. The long quantity of the final vowel of *pĕrĕgre* (so both the Ambrosian Palimpsest and the Palatine family) is required by the metre in Plaut. *Truc.* 127, an anapaestic line, and *peregrē* has been explained as the suffixless Locative of an I-stem *peregri-* (ch. v. § 34) with the I.-Eur. ending -ē, a doublet of -ēi (cf. O. Ind. agnā́, Loc. of agni-, 'fire'). *Vespĕrī*, the form always used by the early writers, is naturally referred to the O-Stem *vespero-*. *Tempĕrī* (-*ori*, see Georges, *Lex. Wortf.* s. v.) may be related to *tempore* as *faenŏrī* to *faenorĕ*, *majōrī* to *majorĕ* (§ 33), and so with *rurī* (e. g. Ter. *Phorm.* 363, Plaut. *Cist.* 226), *Carthagini* (e. g. Plaut. *Poen.* 1056 AP), *Accherunti* Plaut., while *māne* (if not an Adverbial Accusative) may show conversely a Cons.-stem ' Ablative ' suffix applied to an I-stem *mani-*, *Manes* Pl. (ch. v. § 37). The close connexion of the Ablative and Locative, already mentioned in § 33, is seen in phrases like *mane sane septimi*, Plaut. *Men.* 1157; *luci claro*, Plaut. *Aul.* 748 (the use of *claro* for *clarā* or *clarae* is due to the fact that *luci* being an Adverb does not have the fem. gender of *lux*). (For fuller details about these Locatives, see Bell on the Latin Locative; Neue, *Formenlehre*, ii³. p. 640, i². p. 242).

§ 39. Ā-stems, &c. O. Lat. *-ai* is never dissyllabic, like *-āī* of the Genitive. In Plautus a common Ā-stem Loc. is *vīcīniae*, as in the phrase *proxumae uiciniae*, 'next door.' We have *Romai* on a very early inscription, *C. I. L.* i. 54: med Romai fecid. *Die quinti* occurs in Cato's account of Maharbal's boast to Hannibal: mitte mecum Romam equitatum; die quinti in Capitolio tibi cena cocta erit (ap. Gell. x. 24. 7).

§ 40. **Nom. Plur. I. Masc., Fem.** The I.-Eur. -ĕs, which appears in Cons.-stems as -ĕs (e.g. O. Ind. mātár-as, Gk. μητέρ-ες), in Ā-stems as -ās, in O-stems as -ōs, and so on, is the suffix in use among the Umbro-Oscan dialects (e.g. Umbr. frater for *fratr-ĕs, Osc. *censtur* for -rĕs, aasas 'arae'), but in Latin is hardly found except in I-stems whose *-ēs* represents I.-Eur. -ĕyĕs (e.g. from the I.-Eur. stem tri-, 'three,' O. Ind. tráyas, Cret. Gk. τρέες for *τρεγες, Att. τρεῖς) Lat. *trēs*. In O-stems this I.-Eur. suffix -ōs is replaced in many of the I.-Eur. languages by -oi, the Nom. Pl. suffix of the Pronominal Declension (e.g. I.-Eur. *toi, O. Ind. tḗ, Hom. Gk. τοί, Lat. *is-tī* from *-tei* from original -toi). Thus in Greek we find -οι (e.g. λύκοι), in Celtic -oi (e.g. Gaul. Tanotaliknoi; O. Ir. fir Nom. Pl., 'men,' points to an original *wiroi, as does Lat. *vĭrī*, while firu Voc. Pl. is either the I.-Eur. Nom. Pl. in -ōs or the Acc. Pl.), Teutonic -ai (used in Adjectives, I.-Eur. -ōs being used in Nouns), Balto-Slav. -ai (e.g. Lith. vilkaĩ, O. Sl. vlŭci, 'wolves'). Similarly in Latin we find *-ī* from *-ei* from still earlier *-oe* or *-oi*, e.g. O. Lat. *poploe* (Carm. Saliare), *poplei*, class. *pŏpŭlī*, which is thus distinguished from Acc. Pl. *populōs* as Nom. Pl. *istī* (originally -toi) from Acc. Pl. *istōs*. The prevalence of this Pronominal oi-suffix among the European languages suggests the possibility that Umbro-Osc. -ōs (e.g. Umbr. *Atiersiur* 'Attiedii,' Osc. *Núvlanús* 'Nolani') may have had at one period a struggle for existence with -oi, and may have owed its acceptance into use to the analogy of Ā-stem Noms. Plur. in -ās. The Latin Ā-stem suffix *-ae*, e.g. *ārae* (O. Lat. *-ai*, never dissyllabic, according to Prisc. i. p. 221 H.), is an example of the contrary change from a prehistoric -ās, of which no traces remain, to a new formation made on the model of the -oi of O-stems. It resembles Greek -ăι (e.g. χῶραι), but must have been originally *-āi*, since the ordinary diphthong *-ăi* would become *-ī* in the unaccented syllable in Latin (cf. *occīdi* for *óc-caido*, ch. iii. § 18). Lat. *iē*-stems with Nom. Pl. *-iēs* may have the I.-Eur. suffix, but U-stems with -*ūs* show the Acc. Pl. suffix, instead of the I.-Eur. Nom. Pl. -*ĕwĕs*, which would be in Latin -*ŭĕs*, -*ŭis*. (This would hardly contract into -*ūs*, as we saw before, § 21). The -*īs* which is occasionally found for -*ēs* in I-stems is also an Acc. Pl. suffix (§ 51); and the Ī-stem Nom. Pl. *vīs* (so in O. Lat., but in class. Lat. *vīr-ēs* for **vīs-ēs*, an S-stem) is probably an Accusative form. The -*ēs* of Cons.-stems, e. g. *matr-ēs*, *censōr-ēs* may either be the I-stem Nom. Pl. ending, since there is so much interchange of Cons.- and I-stems in Latin (§ 30), or the Acc. Pl.; and the same is true of the Ū-stem -*uēs*, e. g. *suēs*.

§ 41. Ā-stems. Ritschl (*Neue Excurse*, i. p. 118) proposed to avoid hiatus in some passages of Plautus by the change of Nom. Pl. -*ae* to -*ās*, reading e. g. *alternas* in *Trin.* 539 :

nam fúlguritae súnt alternae árbores,

where all the MSS., the Palatine family as well as the Ambrosian Palimpsest, read *alternae* (which may be right, the hiatus being palliated by the alliteration, though editors prefer *alternis*, or *alternas*, an Adverb like *álias*, *altĕras*). He quoted in support of this change a line from one of the Atellanae of Pomponius, c. 90 B. C. (*Com.* 141 R.) :

quót laetitias ínsperatas módo mi inrepsere ín sinum,

where *laetitias insperatas* is now usually explained as Acc., governed by *inrepsere*, though it may quite well be a dialectal form, for the Atellanae in imitating the manners of country life may also have imitated its language. Dialectal -*as* Nom. Pl. is found in the old inscriptions of Pisaurum with the *s* dropped (*C. I. L.* i. 173 matrona Pisaurese dono dedrot; 177 dono dedro matrona), along with Gen. Sg. -*ā(s)* [or Dat. Sg. -*ā(i)*, § 24]. In early inscriptions we have -*ai* for class. -*ae*, e. g. *tabelai*, *datai* on the S. C. de Bacch.

§ 42. O-stems. *Pilumnoe poploe* was a phrase used of the Romans in the Carmen Saliare (Fest. 244. 25 Th. velut pilis uti assueti) ; cf. *fescemnoe* (qui depellere fascinum credebantur, Paul. Fest. 61. 10 Th.; should we read *Fesceninoe*, class. *Fescennini* ?). On early inscriptions we have -*ei*, e. g. *foideratei*, *uirei*, *oinuorsei* on the S.C. de Bacch., sometimes written -*e* (cf. ch. iv. § 34), e.g. *ploirume* (*C. I. L.* i. 32). A Nom. Pl. of an IO-stem with -*is* occurs on an inscription of the first cent. A. D. (*C. I. L.* i. 1541 *b*), *filis*. It is impossible to say whether *filei* (i. 1272), *feilei* (i. 1284) (cf. *socei*, i. 1041) is meant for this form (cf. *Clodi* for *Clodis* Nom. Sg.), or is a misspelling of *filiei* (i. 1275) or a contraction of it (like *gratis* for older *gratiis*). O-stems show -*eis*, also written -*es*, -*is*, in some inscriptions of the end of the second or beginning of the first cent. B. C., e. g. *magistreis* (*C. I L.* i. 565, Capua, 108 B. C. : heisce magistreis Uenerus Iouiae muru aedificandum coirauerunt), *lanies* (vi. 168, Rome), *violaries rosaries coronariis* (vi. 169, Rome). (For other examples, see Ritschl, *Opusc.* ii. 646, and add *heisce magistreis*, *Not. Scav.* 1893, p. 164, from Capua, *mustae pieis*, *C. I. L.* iii. Suppl. 12318, from Samothrace.) This form is attested for the pronoun *hic* by Priscian (i. p. 593. 5 H. inveniuntur tamen etiam nominatiuum 'hisce' proferentes antiqui), and is found in the Nom. Pl. Masc. of *hic*, *ille*, *iste* in the Dramatists before a word beginning with a vowel, when the particle -*ce* is added, e. g. Plaut. *Mil.* 374 :

non pőssunt mihi mináciis tuis hísce oculi exfodíri,

(similarly *illisce* and *istisce* are the forms used in Plautus before a word beginning with a vowel, never *illīc, istīc*; Studemund in *Fleck. Jahrb.* 1876, p. 57), though probably never in the Nom. Pl. of O-stem nouns. In the pronouns it seems to be due to the addition of the plural suffix -*s* to the already formed plural in -*ī* (older -*ei*) ; in the Noun O-stems it may have the same origin, though it is not unlikely that the IO-stem formation mentioned above had at least some share in bringing it into use.

Deus has two Nom. Pl. forms, *dei*, a dissyllable (probably the more ceremonious form), and *di*, also written *dii*, a monosyllable. (*Dii* and *dei* are compared to *ii* and *ei* by Prisc. i. p. 298 H.).

§ 43. **Ĭ-stems.** Varro (*L. L.* viii. 66) says that *puppis* and *puppes, restis* and *restes* were rival forms in his time, like Abl. *ŏvi* and *ove, ăvi* and *ave.* On early inscriptions we have usually -*es*, e. g. *aidiles, C. I. L.* i. 187, *Eph. Epigr.* viii. 676, but *ceiveis* on the Lex Repetund. of 123-122 B. C. (*C. I. L.* i. 198. 77), *fineis* and *finis* in the Sent. Minuciorum of 117 B. C. (*ib.* i. 199), and *pelleis* on the Lex Furf. (i. 603) (cf. *coques atriensis* on a Praenestine inscr., i. 1540). (See Neue, i². p. 246.) The O. Lat. Plur. of *vis* was *vis* (Prisc. i. p. 249. 9 H.).

§ 44. **Cons.-stems.** Lat. *quattuor* appears to be a relic of the -*ĕs* formation, for *quattuor-ĕs (§ 63), I.-Eur. *qᵘĕtworĕs (O. Ind. catvā́ras, Dor. Gk. τέτορες, O. Ir. cethir), though some make it represent I.-Eur. *qᵘĕtwōr, supposing this to be a byform of the ordinary Neuter, which would be in Latin *quattuora (Osc. petora or *petoro). Plautine scansions like *cănĕs, turbĭnĕs* (*Trin.* 835) are of course mere examples of the Law of Breves Breviantes, like the Imperatives *căvĕ, pŭtă,* &c. (ch. iii. § 42) (cf. Acc. Pl. *liberăs virginĕs, Pers.* 845) and are no evidence of the use of the suffix -*ĕs*.

§ 45. **Nom., Acc. Plur. II. Neut.** In the Italic, Balto-Slavic, and Teutonic languages all Neuter stems form their Nom. and Acc. Plur. in -ā, while in Greek we have -ă. This ă seems to have been originally peculiar to O-stems, and to be in reality the same as the Nom. Sg. Fem. suffix. Prof. Johannes Schmidt, in his book on the Indo-European formation of Neuter Plurals (*Die Pluralbildungen der Indogermanischen Neutra*, Weimar, 1889) has mustered an array of facts from the various I.-Eur. languages, which point to the Neut. Plur. having been originally a Collective Fem. Sg. like Lat. *f ămĭlia* in the sense of *f ămŭli*, so that, e. g. Lat. *jŭga* originally meant what the Germans would express by 'das Gejöche,' the yoke-material. The use of a Singular Verb with a Neut. Plur. subject in

Greek, O. Ind. (Vedic) and Zend may be explained by this hypothesis, e. g. μῆρα in Hom. *Il.* i. 464 ἐπεὶ κατὰ μῆρ' ἐκάη differs from μηροί of l. 460 μηρούς τ' ἐξέταμον in signifying the mass of meat as opposed to the thighs separately. And the change of Gender in Lat. *caementum* N., *caementa* F., *mendum* N., *menda* F. may be due to the fact that a Collective Sing. Fem. *caementa, menda,* being treated as a Plural (a ' Nom. Plur. Neut.'), developed a new Singular, *caementum, mendum* (Nom. Sing. Neut.). Other illustrations of the connexion between a Collective Sing. Fem. and a Plur. Neut. may be seen in Prof. Schmidt's book, e. g. Lat. *ŏpĕra* Sg. Fem. and *ŏpĕra* Plur. Neut., Hom. Gk. τὰ ἡνία, Att. ἡ ἡνία, with plur. αἱ ἡνίαι. (The Latin examples of change of Gender like *locus* Sg., *loca* Pl. are to be found in Neue, i². p. 540.)

The suffix -ă appears, as we have seen, in the Nom. Plur. of all Neuter-stems in the European languages. But in the oldest Indian and Zend literature we have relics of an earlier state of things, viz. -ā for O-stems, -ī for I-stems (a Latin relic of -ī is *trī-ginta,* lit. ' three tens,' § 74), -ū for U-stems (perhaps the long vowel of Lat. *pĕcu, gĕnu, cornu,* &c. may be due to their having been originally Neut. Plur.; another suggestion is, that *genū, cornū,* &c. were Duals, like I.-Eur. *sūnū, Nom. Dual of the stem *sūnŭ-, ' a son '); while Cons.-stems lengthened the vowel of their final syllable [e. g. Vedic nāmā, ' names,' for *nōmō(n)?; Prof. Schmidt compares Lat. *quattuor* from I.-Eur. *qᵘetwōr, but see § 63]. All these formations Prof. Schmidt identifies with Fem. Sing. Collectives.

Like the -ā of the Nom. Sing. of Ā-stems, Neut. Plur. -ā appears in Latin as -ă in the earliest literature, and in Umbro-Oscan becomes an *o*-sound, Oscan ú, Umbr. u, (a), both written in the Latin alphabet *o,* which is scanned by Lucilius as a short syllable in the Oscan loanword sollo (Lat. *tota* Neut. Pl.) (*inc.* 160 M.):

uasa quoque omnino dirimit, non sollŏ dupundi,

and is written -*a* by Festus in the Oscan numeral *petora,* four (250. 30 Th. petoritum et Gallicum vehiculum esse, et nomen ejus dictum esse existimant a numero quattuor rotarum. alii Osce, quod hi quoque ' petora ' quattuor vocent). In Umbrian

§ 46.] DECLENSION OF NOUNS, ETC. GEN. PLUR. 401

it appears that the Nom. and Acc. Pl. of Neuter-stems were distinguished by the addition to this -*o* of the -*r* (-s) and the -*f*, which are the final letters of the Masc. Nom. and Acc. Plur., though it is possible that this -r and -f were not pronounced, but were used merely as graphic criteria of the two cases, e. g. *tuderor* Nom., *verof* Acc. Whether it is merely accidental, or not, that the ordinary forms in -a, -*o* are found in the Acc. along with forms in -of, but not in the Nom. along with forms in -or, the limited material does not allow us to decide.

With that interchange of the Cons.- with the I-declension mentioned in § 50, we have e. g. *plūria* (cf. *compluria*) and *plura*, forms discussed by Gellius (v. 21), who tells us of a letter written by Sinnius Capito to Pacuvius Labeo to prove the thesis : 'pluria non plura dici debere.' We have -*ia* in the Neut. Plur. of Adjective Stems like *tĕrĕtia, audācia, victrīcia, fĕrentia*, &c. (see Neue, ii³. p. 121), but always *vĕtĕra* from *vetus*, which was originally a Noun (Gk. (ϝ)έτος, a year) (§ 55). In O. Lat. we have *silenta*, for *sīlentia*, quoted by Gellius from Laevius (Gell. xix. 7. 7 ab eo quod est sileo 'silenta loca' dixit et 'pulverulenta' et ' pestilenta') (see ch. v. § 64).

§ 46. **Gen. Plur.** The suffix -ōm is indicated by most of the I.-Eur. languages (e. g. Gk. ἵππων, μητέρ-ων), which would in Latin become in time -*ŏm* (ch. iii. § 49), then -*ŭm* (e. g. *socium* on the S. C. de Bacch.) (cf. Osc. Núvlanúm, Μαμερτινουμ, Λουκανομ, Umbr. *Atiersio*). Ā-stems took in Greek and in the Italic languages -āsōm, e. g. (Hom Gk. θεάων, Att. θεῶν, Lat. *deārum*, Osc. *egmazum* ' rerum,' which was the Gen. Plur. Fem. suffix of Pronouns (e. g. O. Ind. tásām, Hom. Gk. τάων, Lat. *is-tarum*), and after this model a Gen. Pl. of O-stems was formed in Latin with the suffix -*ōrum* (O. Lat. -*orom*), a suffix not found in Umbro-Oscan, which by Cicero's time drove the older -*om*, -*um* off the field. On the same model the Fifth Decl. stems formed their Gen. Pl., e. g. *făciērum*. The use of -*ium* in Gen. Plur. of Adjectives like *fĕrentium, audācium*, and of -*um* in Gen. Pl. *ăpum, vŏlŭcrum, vātum*, &c. (see instances in Neue, i². pp. 258 sqq.; e. g. *cīvĭtātum* and *civitatium*), is due to that confusion of Cons.-stems with I-stems, which played so great a part in the Latin

D d

declension, and which occupied a great deal of the attention of the native grammarians.

§ 47. -um and -orum in O-stems. Cicero's remarks on these suffixes are worth quoting (*Orat.* xlvi. 155): atque etiam a quibusdam sero jam emendatur antiquitas, qui haec reprehendunt ; nam pro deum atque hominum fidem 'deorum' aiunt. Ita credo. Hoc illi nesciebant? an dabat hanc licentiam consuetudo? Itaque idem poeta (Ennius) qui inusitatius contraxerat : Patris mei, meum factum pudet, pro 'meorum factorum,' et : Texitur, exitium examen rapit, pro 'exitiorum,' non dicit 'liberum,' ut plerique loquimur, cum 'cupidos liberum' aut 'in liberum loco' dicimus, sed ut isti volunt: Neque tuum unquam in gremium extollas liberorum ex te genus. Et idem : Namque Aesculapi liberorum. At ille alter (Pacuvius) in Chryse non solum : Ciues, antiqui amici maiorum meum, quod erat usitatum, sed durius etiam : Consilium socii, augurium atque extum interpretes ; idemque pergit: Postquam prodigium horriferum, portentum pauor. Quae non sane sunt in omnibus neutris usitata. Nec enim dixerim tam libenter 'armum judicium,' etsi est apud eundem : Nihilne ad te de iudicio armum accidit ? quam centuriam, ut censoriae tabulae loquuntur, fabrum et procum audeo dicere, non 'fabrorum' et 'procorum.' Planeque 'duorum virorum judicium' aut 'triumvirorum capitalium' aut 'decemvirorum stlitibus judicandis' dico nunquam. Atqui dixit Attius: Uideo sepulcra duo duorum corporum ; idemque : Mulier una duum uirum. Quid verum sit intellego, sed alias ita loquor, ut concessum est, ut hoc vel pro deum dico vel pro deorum, alias, ut necesse est, cum triumvirum, non 'virorum,' cum sestertium, nummum, non 'nummorum,' quod in his consuetudo varia non est. Similarly Varro (*L.L.* viii. 71) : quaerunt, si sit analogia, cur appellant omnes aedem Deum Consentium et non 'Deorum Consentium'? Item quor dicatur mille denarium, non 'mille denariorum'; est enim hoc vocabulum figura ut Vatinius, Manilius, denarius ; debet igitur dici ut Vatiniorum, Maniliorum, denariorum ; et non equum puplicum mille assarium esse, sed mille 'assariorum' ; ab uno enim assario multi assarii, ab eo assariorum. (A list of Genitives Plur. of O-stems in -*um* is given by Neue, i². 103.) *Nostrum* and *vestrum*, Gen. Plur. of *noster*, *vester*, established themselves in class. Lat. as Gen. Pl. of *nos*, *vos* (ch. vii. § 9). Ā-stem Genitives like *agrĭcŏlum* (Lucr. iv. 586) follow the analogy of O-stems, as do *vectīgāliorum*, *anciliorum*, &c., and perhaps *currum*, &c. ; *amphŏrum* and *drachmum* follow the Greek. On the (restored) Columna Rostrata (*C. I. L.* i. 195. 10) we have the Pronoun *olorom* 'illorum'; on a Scipio epitaph of perhaps the end of the third cent. B. C. (i. 32), the Adj. *duonoro* 'bonorum,' but -*o(m)* on the earliest coins, e. g. *C. I. L.* i. 15 *Caleno* (with Νεοπολιτων), i. 16 *Suesano* (with Νεοπολιτων). (See ch. iii. § 49.) In i. 24, of end of third cent. B. C., LADINOD is usually read *Larinor.*, a Gen. Pl.

§ 48. Dat., Abl., Loc., Instr. Plural. These four cases must be considered together ; they are so intermingled in Latin and in other I.-Eur. languages. Latin Ā-stems show -*īs*, older -*eis*, which has come from an earlier -ais (cf. Oscan -aís, Greek -αις), a suffix apparently formed in imitation of the -ois of O-stems.

§§ 47-49.] DECLENSION OF NOUNS, ETC. DAT., ABL. PLUR. 403

This O-stem suffix, in Latin -īs, earlier -eis, and still earlier -oes or -ois (Osc. -úís, -ois) is regarded by some as a Locative, by others as an Instrumental (see Brugmann, *Grundriss*, ii. §§ 357, 380). The suffix -bŭs, O. Lat. -bos, shown by other stems (e.g. cĭvĭ-bus, lēg-ĭ-bus with the i of I-stems, lăcŭ-bus or lăcĭ-bus, sŭ-bus or sŭ-bus), comes from an original -bhŏs. In Umbro-Oscan, as usual, the short vowel of the final syllable is syncopated, e.g. O. Osc. luisari-fs (in Lat. *lūsāribus), Osc. teremn-í-ss (in Lat. termĭnĭbus), lig-i-s (in Lat. lēg-ĭ-bus), Umbr. fratr-u-s, with s for ss and so not changed to r, and preceded by a vowel which may be the I.-Eur. ' Composition Vowel ' o (ch. v. § 80), though this is quite uncertain. This suffix was in O. Lat. employed in the Dat., Abl. Plur. of Ā-stems, e.g. dextrābus (cf. Gaul. Ματρεβο Ναμανσικαβο), but in the classical period this form was retained only in legal language, for the purpose of distinguishing Ā- from O-stems, e.g. *filiis et filiabus*, just as we retain the old Plural suffix in ' oxen ' but have dropped it in ' shoes ' (earlier ' shoon '). Adverbs like ăliās, O. Lat. altĕras, fŏrās may show the I.-Eur. Locative of Ā-stems (Gk. -āσĭ, e.g. θύρᾱσι; O. Ind. -āsŭ, e.g. áśvāsu) (but see ch. ix. § 4).

§ 49. **Ā- and O-stems.** The old form *privicloes* (privis, id est singulis), the Dat., Abl. Plur. of a diminutive of *prīvus*, is quoted from the Carmen Saliare by Festus (244. 21 Th.), and Paul. Fest. 14. 17 Th. has: ab 'oloes ' dicebant pro ab illis, but *-eis*, sometimes written *-es* (ch. iv. § 34), is the spelling of the older inscriptions: e.g. *uieis, leibereis, populeis, aedificieis, agreis, loceis*, on the Lex Agraria of 111 B.C. (*C. I. L.* i. 200); *soueis nuges* on an old epitaph of a mimus (i. 1297):

plouruma que fecit populo soueis gaudia nuges,

which has *ē* for *ei* also in the Nom. Sing. Masc. of the Relative, *que* for *quei* (class. *quī*); *de manubies* (*Eph. Epigr.* viii. 476, Capua, 135 B.C.). We find *-īis* contracted in course of time into *-īs*; thus *grātiis* (always with *-iis*, and similarly *ingratiis*, in Plautus and Terence; cf. *gratiis* in a line of Pomponius, c. 90 B.C., *Com.* 110 R.) became *gratīs* in classical Latin; *provincīs*, &c. beside *judicīīs* (the long *i* being indicated by the tall form of the letter), occur on the Mon. Ancyranum; and of IO-stems we have, e.g. *Januaris* (*C. I. L.* vi. 543, of 115 A.D.), *Junis* (vi. 213, of 131 A.D.). (For other examples, see Neue i². p. 31.) An example of *-ābus* in O. Lat. is quoted by Nonius (493. 16 M.) from Livius Andronicus' translation of the Odyssey: déque mánibus dextrábus. The passages of the grammarians bearing on this form, and details of the use of *deabus, filiabus*, and *libertabus*, the most frequent words of the kind, are given by Neue, i². pp. 22 sqq. We have Masc. *-ōbus* with Fem. *-ābus* in the Duals *duobus, ambobus*, though the rarity of the formation led to the latter being replaced in Vulg. Lat. by *ambis* Masc. and Fem. (Caper 107. 14 K. ambobus, non 'ambis' et ambabus). O-stems sometimes take the I-stem and Consonantal -*ĭbus* in Late and Vulgar Latin, e.g. *C. I. L.* vi. 224 *dibus omnibus deabusque* (197 A. D.); 15267 *amicibus*; 17633 *alumnibus*. Pomponius, the writer of Atellanae, uses *pannibus* (*Com.* 70 R.) for *pannis* in imitation of the rustic mode of speech; and in the Sermo Plebeius of Petronius we have *diibus* (*Sat.* 44. p. 29, 35 B. ita meos fruniscar, ut ego puto omnia illa a diibus fieri). In the O. Lat. inscription (*C. I. L.* i. 814): devas Corniscas sacrum, found in the 'Corniscarum divarum locus trans Tiberim' (Paul. Fest. 45. 16 Th.), the two first words may be Gen. Sing. If Plural, they are Locatives like *alias*. The instances of dialectal and Lat. -os are all doubtful (*Class. Rev.* ii. p. 204).

§ 50. **Other stems.** O. Lat. -*bos* of *trebibos* on a bronze vase in the British Museum (*Eph. Epigr.* ii. 299 Q. Lainio Q. f. praifectos protrebibos fecit), corresponding to class. -*bus*, indicates a short vowel, for -*bōs* would have retained *ŏ* (ch. iii. § 18). The few apparent examples of its being scanned as a long syllable by the Dramatists (collected by C. F. Müller in his *Plaut. Prosodie*, p. 53; add Naev. *Trag.* 57 R.) must be illusory (many of them are cases of syllaba anceps at a pause in the line, e.g. Plaut. *Merc.* 900, *Rud.* 975).

§ 51. **Acc. Plur.** The I.-Eur. suffix was -ns, after a consonant -ṇs. Thus Ā-stems ended in -āns, which became -ās, O-stems in -ŏns, which became -ō^{n}s, I-stems in -ins, R-stems in -rṇs, S-stems in -sṇs, and so on. Latin examples are *viās, lupōs, fratrēs* [with -*ēs* from -*ĕns* (ch. ii. § 64) from I.-Eur. -ṇs], *honōrēs* for -*ōsĕns*. I.-Eur. -ns, -ṇs becomes in Oscan -ss, in Umbr. -f, e.g. Osc. víass ' vias,' feíhúss, walls (cf. Gk. τεῖχος), Umbr. vitlaf 'vĭtulas,' or with loss of -f *vitla, toru* for **toruf* ' tauros,' avef, avif, and *aveif* ' aves.'

I-stems in Latin should show -*īs* (from -*ins*, ch. ii. § 64); and this is the usual form in the best MSS., though we often find -*ēs*, the Nom. Pl. ending or the Cons.-stem ending. Thus *urbis* is attested for Virg. *G.* i. 25 : urbisne invisere, Caesar, &c., but *urbes* for *A.* iii. 106 : centum urbes habitant magnas, *tres* for *A.* x. 350, but *tris* for the following line (Gell. xiii. 21); so on the (restored) Columna Rostrata (*C. I. L.* i. 195) [c]lasesque nauales ... claseis Poenicas ... copias Cartacinienseis ... naueis. (For statistics of the use of -*īs* and -*ēs*, see Neue, i². p. 245.)

§ 52. **II. THE COMPARISON OF ADJECTIVES.** The I.-Eur. suffixes used to form the Comparative and Superlative of Adjectives have been already mentioned in chap. iv. For the Comparative, (1) -yĕs-, with weak grade -is- (e.g. O. Ind. svắd-īyas-, Gk. ἡδίω Acc. for **ἥδιοσα*, Goth. sutiza, Lith. sald-ēs-nis),

Lat. *suāvior*, older **suaviōs, măgis* Adv.; (2) -tĕro- and -ĕro-, the original sense of which was rather that of likeness, of equal, than of greater degree (e. g. O. Ind. vatsa-tará-, lit. 'like a calf,' Lat. *māter-tera*, lit. 'like a mother,' Ir. demnithir, 'equally certain,' from demin, ' certain '); for the Superlative, (1) -is-to- (-is-tho-?), (e. g. O. Ind. áś-ištha-, Gk. ὤκιστος; O. Ind. svád-ištha-, Gk. ἥδ-ιστος, Goth. sut-ists, Engl. sweet-est), apparently composed of the weak Comparative suffix -is- and the TO-suffix (ch. v. § 27); (2) -temo- or -tᵉmo- (-tṃmo-) and -emo- or -ᵉmo- (-ṃmo-)(ch. v. § 14) (e.g. O. Ind. án-tama-, Lat. *in-tĭmus*; O. Ind. upamá-, Lat. *summus* for **sup-mus*). This last Superlative suffix was, like the Comparative -tero-, -ero- (Ascoli, *Suppl. Arch. Glott. Ital.* i. 53), originally a suffix denoting likeness (e.g. O. Ind. gṓ-tama-, lit. 'like an ox ') or position, and it has this force in Latin words like *aedĭ-tumus*, lit. ' living in a temple' (later corrupted to *aedi-tuus*, as if from *tueor*, ' guarding a temple,' Gell. xii. 10; Varro, *R. R.* i. 2. 1); *fĭnĭ-timus, mărĭ-timus*, &c., so that e. g. *cĭ-timus* probably meant originally ' near in position' (cf. *dex-timus*, ' on the right, not ' most on the right '), and is not properly a Superlative. To give Superlative sense, the weak Comparative suffix was added, -is-emo- (-is-ᵉmo-), e. g. *maximus* for **măgis-imus, săcerrimus* for **sacris-imus, făcillimus* for **facĭlis-imus* (on the change of -rĭs-to -ers-, -err-, &c., see ch. iv. § 13). The origin of the usual Latin Superlative ending *-issimus*, older *-issumus*, has been matter of much discussion. One theory makes the I.-Eur. suffix of O. Ind. áś-ištha-, Gk. ὤκ-ιστος -istho-, not -isto-, and explains Lat. *-issimus* as this suffix augmented by -emo- (-mo-). But the change of I.-Eur. sth into Latin *ss* is not satisfactorily proved by Lat. *ossi*-, bone (O. Ind. asthán-, Gk ὀστέον; see ch. iv. § 95), and it seems safer to analyze *-issimus* into the suffixes -isto- and -temo- (on *ss* for (s)tt, see ch. iv. § 108)[1]. The *-is-* of *-issimus*, like the *-is* of *magĭs*, had short *i*, a fact attested not only by grammarians [Mar. Victor., p. 242. 24 K.; Vergilius, p. 189. 17 H. (Suppl.)], but by late spellings like *merentessemo, karessemo*

---

[1] Or *-issimo-*, an ending peculiar, so far as is known, to Latin, may contain the suffix *-is-* twice. The change of **ōcĭs-ume(d)* to *oxime* (**ocsime*) obscured the presence of this suffix, and may have led to a reformation from *ocius* (**ocis*), viz. *ocissime*.

(*C. I. L.* ii. 2997). (The tall form of I in some late inscriptions, e.g. CARISSIMO *C. I. L.* vi 5325, does not prove that the vowel was long; see ch. i. § 9).

The irregular Comparison of simple Adjectives like 'good,' 'bad' (e. g. *bŏnus, mĕlior, optimus*; Gk. ἀγαθός, ἀμείνων; Engl. good, better) is a relic of a very early time when different roots were used to express a Positive, a Comparative, and a Superlative notion,—*bonus* (older *duonus*) from dwen- (cf. O. Ind. dúvas-, 'honour'), *melior, optimus* (*C. I. L.* i. 1016 has *opituma*, an archaism) from the root op- of *opto, ŏpes*, &c. On the Comparison of Adverbs, see ch. ix. § 1.

In the Romance languages Comparison is expressed by the use of the descendants of Lat. *plus* (Ital., French, &c.), *magis* (Span., Port., &c.), e. g. Ital. più ricco, ' richer,' il più ricco, ' the richest,' except in these simple Adjectives like 'good,' 'bad,' which retain their old irregular Comparison, e. g. Ital. migliore and ottimo, ' very good' (il migliore, 'the best'), peggiore and pessimo, ' very bad' (il peggiore, ' the worst'), &c. Ital. -issimo (e. g. ricchissimo, ' very rich,' not ' richest') shows itself by its -is- instead of -es- (for Lat. -*ĭs*-, ch. ii. § 14) to be a late innovation, and no transmission from ancient times. (See Meyer-Lübke, *Rom. Gram.* ii. p. 83.)

§ 53. **The Comparative Suffixes.** The suffix -yes- appears in Latin as -*ior* Nom. Sg., M., F., -*iōris* Gen. Sg., -*ius* Nom. Sg. Neut., of which the older forms were -*iōs*, -*iōses*, -*iŏs*. (On the change of *s* to *r*, see ch. iv. § 148). Varro (*L. L.* vii. 27) quotes from early Latin (from the Carm. Sal.?) *meliosem*, and Paul. Fest. (359. 1 Th.) *maiosibus, meliosibus* (his '*meltom*' *meliorem dicebant*, 87. 25 Th., may be a corruption of a gloss like '*melios*' *melior*; see *Class. Rev.* v. 10 ; so in a Glossary '*meliosa*' *meliora*, Löwe, *Opusc.* p. 170). Priscian (i. p. 347. 2 H.) quotes from the earlier historians Neuter forms like *prior, posterior*; thus from Valerius Antias : hoc senatusconsultum prior factum est; from Cassius Hemina : bellum Punicum posterior ; from Claudius Quadrigarius : prior bellum quod cum his gestum erat ; and : foedus prior Pompeianum (on *calor* Neut. in O. Lat., see § 14) ; though it is conceivable that the actual forms used may have been *priŏs, posteriŏs*, which must have been the predecessors of *priŭs, posteriŭs* (ch. iii. § 18)[1].

The yes-suffix was originally affixed to the root without the suffix of the Positive stem, as in Lat. *ōc-ior*, O. Ind. áś-īyas-, Gk. ὠκ-ίων from a Positive

---

[1] The supposed examples of -*iūs* in Plautus are illusory ; see Müller, *Plaut. Pros.* p. 55.

§§ 53-55.] DECLENSION OF NOUNS, ETC. COMPARISON. 407

stem *ŏku-, but Lat. *suāvior* for *suadv-ior*, *tĕnuior*, *aspĕrior*, &c. start from the Positive stem *swādu-*, &c. On the other hand the suffix -tero-, when added to an Adjective, was affixed to the Positive stem, e. g. ὠκύ-τερος. This -tero- is often added to Prepositions, e. g. *ex-ter*, *cĭ-ter*, *postero-* (similarly -ero- in *sup-ero-*). In Latin it has not Comparative sense unless augmented by the YES-suffix, e. g. *ex-ter-ior*, *ci-ter-ior*, *dex-ter-ior*, *sĭnis-ter-ior* ; *ōcĭter*, &c. being apparently the Latin equivalent of the Gk. ὠκύ-τερο-, &c. (ch. ix. § 1).

§ 54. **The Superlative Suffixes.** The suffix -temo- or -tᵉmo- (-tṃmo-) with -emo- or -ᵉmo (-ṃmo-) is closely associated with Comparative -tero-, -ero-, e. g. *ci-timus* goes with *ci-tero-*, *in-timus* with *in-tero-* (O. Ind. án-tama- with án-tara-), *summus* from *sup-mus* with *sup-ero-*, *infimus* (*ĭmus* seems not to occur in Plautus) with *infero-*. The old augural term *sollistumum tripudium* may combine it with the Comparative -is-. Its original form is difficult to ascertain. The spelling on Republican inscriptions is -*tumus*, -*umus* (ch. iii. § 18). Umbr. *hondomu* suggests an older -tomo-, -omo-, while Osc. últiumam (Lat. *ultimam*) shows an affection of t that is usual before a *u*-sound (cf. Osc. tiurri-, Lat. *turris*). The form without t is seen in *mĭnimus*, *brūma* from *brĕvis* for *breghu-* (Gk. βραχύς), (cf. Osc. maimo- 'maximus'), and apparently attached to a case-form, in *suprē-mus*, *extrē-mus*, *postrē-mus* (cf. *postumus* Virg. *A.* vi. 763), but it is usually combined with the Comparative -ĭs-, e. g. *maximus* for *mag-is-imus* (Falisc. Maxomo-), O. Lat. *oxime* (Paul. Fest. 225. 1 Th.) for *oc-is-ime*, *medioximus* from the stem *medioc-* seen in *mĕdiocris*. This was the formation adopted by Adjective-stems ending in -li-, -ri-, -ro-, e. g. *facĭlis*, *facĭl-limus* for *facli-simus* ; *ācer* (*ācri-*), *acerrimus* for *acri-simus* ; *mĭsero-*, *miser-rimus*[1], &c., though we have *sĕvĕrissimus*, *mātūrissimus* and *maturissime*, but usually *maturrime*, &c. (see Neue, ii³. pp. 187 sqq.). With the last we should probably compare O. Lat. *pūrime* in the phrase *purime tĕtinero*, explained in Paul. Fest. 335. 7 Th. as *purissime tenuero*. Ennius (according to Charisius 83. 22 K.) wrote *equitatus celerissimus*, and *minerrimus* is quoted by Paul. Fest. 88. 11 Th.: 'minerrimus' pro minimo dixerunt.

§ 55. **Some irregular Comparatives and Superlatives.** *Vetustior* appears as the Comparative of *vĕtus*, because *vetustus* with its ill-sounding repetition of the syllable -*tus*- was discarded in the Positive for *vetus*, apparently the I.-Eur. Noun *wĕtos, *wetes- (Gk. ἔτος, a year) ; in the Superlative *veterrimus* and *vetustissimus* (in Livy and later writers) are both found. *Mĭnus*, with -*us* not -*ius*, has been similarly explained to have originated in a Neuter Noun, meaning 'the less quantity,' and to have produced the declension *minor* M., *minor* F., *minus* N.; the Oscan equivalent of *minor* is minstro- (Lat. *minister*), e. g. ampert minstreis aeteis eituas moltas moltaum licitud 'dumtaxat minoris partis pecuniae multas multare liceto' on the Law of Bantia (cf. Umbr. mestro- 'major,' Lat. *măgister*). The coexistence of such forms as *bĕnĕvŏlus* and *benevolens* (ch. viii. § 90) produced a type of Comparison like *magnifĭcus*, *magnificentior*, *magnificentis-simus*; while *frūgī*, which was a Dative Case of a noun [frugi (bonae) sc.

---

[1] It is a mistake to suppose that the scansion *misĕrrimus*, *simĭllimus*, &c. is found in O. Lat. poetry, or that the antepenultimate of -*issimus* is ever shortened (*Class. Rev.* vi. 342).

faciendae aptus; cf. Plaut. *Pseud.* 468 tamen ero frugi bonae; *Poen.* 892 erus si tuos uolt facere frugem) had recourse for its Comparative and Superlative to the Adj. *frūgālis.* The retention of *v* in the Positive with its suppression in the other degrees, causes the anomaly in the Comparison of *dīves,* (but cf. Ter. *Adelph.* 770 dis quidem esses, Demea), *dītior,* *dītissimus* ; *jŭvĕnis, jūnior.* From plē-, a development of the root pel-, ' to fill ' (Lat. *plē-nus, replē-tus, plē-ri-que,* Gk. πλήρης, &c.), were formed Greek πλείων, πλεῖστος ; from plō-, another grade of plē- (ch. iv. § 53), the Latin *plūs* for *plo-is *(ploera* Cic. *Legg.* iii. 3. 6), *plūrimus* for **plois-omo-* (*ploirume* Nom. Pl. Masc. on a Scipio epitaph of the end of the third cent. B. C., *C. I. L.* i. 32 :

> hónc oíno ploírume coséntiont R[ómai]
> dŭŏnóro óptumo fuíse uíro,

' hunc unum plurimi consentiunt Romae bonorum optimum fuisse virum '); the *plous* of the S. C. Bacch. (*C. I. L.* i. 196. 19 and 20) may with its *ou* merely represent the ū-sound which the diphthong oi had by this time assumed (ch. iv. §§ 37, 38), and is hardly sufficient evidence of a formation **plo-us* like *minus*; similarly *plouruma* on the epitaph of a mime (*C. I. L.* i. 1297, in dactylic hexameters :

> plouruma que fecit populo soueis gaudia nuges,

' plurima qui fecit populo suis gaudia nugis ') is a misspelling of *ploeruma* or *plūruma.* The *pleoris* of the Carmen Arvale (*C. I. L.* i. 28), a hymn preserved in a late and wretchedly spelt inscription :

> neve luae rue, Marma, sins incurrere in dleores,
> neve lue rue, Marmar, sins incurrere in pleoris,
> neve lue rue, Marmar, sers incurrere in pleoris,

' neve luem ruem, Marmar, sinas (siveris ?) incurrere in plures,' may be a mistake for *ploeres,* and the *plisima* quoted from the Carmen Saliare by Festus [244. 17 Th. ' plisima ' plurima ; but in Varro's account of the same Carmen (*L. L.* vii. 27) *plusima* is the reading of the MS.] should perhaps be corrected to *ploisuma* (*ploisoma*), though some regard these forms as evidence of Latin derivatives from the root plē-, like Greek πλείων (πλέων) and πλεῖστος. Major is perhaps best referred to an older **mahior* (cf. O. Ind. máhīyas-) with *h* for the Guttural Aspirate, while *magis, maximus* show another form of root with the Guttural Media (ch. iv. § 116), (but cf. Osc. *mais* for **mahis, maimas* for **mahimas,* Umbr. mestru for **mahistro-*) ; the relation however of the Italic forms to Goth. maiza, ' more ' Adj. (I.-Eur. **ma-is*-), O. Ir. māa, mō, O. W. moi, all of which point to a root ending in a long vowel, mā- or mō-, is not perfectly clear.

§ **56. III. NUMERALS.** Of the Latin Cardinal Numbers only 1-3 are inflected, *ūnus -a -um, duō -ae -ō, trēs -ēs -ia,* not 4 (O. Ind. catvā́ras, cátasras, catvā́ri, Gk. τέσσαρες -ες -α), nor 5 (O. Ind. páñca Nom., pañcānā́m Gen., Gk. πέντε, Lesb. πέμπων Gen.). The Numeral Adverbs from 5 upwards end in -iens or -iēs (on the spelling, see Brambach, *Lat. Orth.* p. 269 ; Neue, ii³. p. 335 ; the Mon. Ancyranum has *-iens*), an ending which is also found in *totie(n)s, quotie(n)s*, and which has been connected with the ending of O. Ind. kíyant- (Adj.), ' how great ? ', íyant- (Adj.), ' so great,' probably I.-Eur. -yĕnt. Umbr. nuvis ' novies,' Osc. *pomtis* ' quinquies ' seem to show the same ending, with i as weak grade of yĕ (ch. iv. § 51). [On the change of I.-Eur. -nt to -ns in Lat. and Umbro-Oscan, see ch. iv. § 105; in late Lat. inscriptions we often find *-is* (cf. ch. ii. § 6), e.g. *quinquis*, Rossi, *I. Chr.* i. 508, of 402 A.D., *sexis, ib.* i. 530, of 404 A.D., *decis C.I.L.* xii. 2087, of 559 A.D., also *-es* (cf. *quetus* for *quiĕtus*, ch. ii. § 149), e.g. *quinques*, Rossi, i. 510, of 402 A.D., *deces C. I. L.* xii. 2086, of 558 A.D., *vices* xii. 2187, of 564 A.D.]

Fractions are expressed by divisions of the *as* (= 12 *unciae*), e.g. *uncia*, ' one-twelfth,' *quincunx*, ' five-twelfths,' *septunx*, ' seven-twelfths,' *deunx*, ' eleven-twelfths,' lit. ' minus an ounce.' The I.-Eur. word for ' half,' *sēmĭ- (O. Ind. sāmi-, Gk. ἡμι-, O. Engl. sām-, whence our ' sand-blind '), is in Latin *sēmĭ-*, the declinable form *sēmis*, Gen. *semissis*, &c., being apparently a compound of *sēmi-* and *as* with the *-yĕ-* of *semyĕssis* weakened to *ĭ* (ch. iii. § 18, p. 188); similarly the *-wĕ-* of *centu(m)-essi-*, *dĕcu(m)-essi-* is weakened to *ŭ* in *centussi-, decussi-*. The origin of the *-ns* (for *-nts*) of *triens*, ' one-third,' *sextans*, ' one-sixth,' *quadrans*, ' one-fourth,' *dodrans*, ' three-fourths,' *dextans*, ' five-sixths,' for *dē-sextans*, lit. ' minus one-sixth,' is not clear ; *bessi-* is usually explained as *du-essi-* (on *b-* from *dw-*, see ch. iv. § 71), but it means not ' two asses ' but ' two-thirds of an as '[1]. The Adjective for ' half ' is *dī-midius* from *dis-* and *medius* (ch. iii. § 18). ' One and a half ' is *sesquĭ-*, usually explained as *sēmis-que*, with the same syncope as is seen in *sestertius*, ' two and a half,' for *sēmis-tertius* (cf. Germ. drittehalb).

§ 57. One. I.-Eur. *oi-no- (Gk. οἴνη, an ace, O. Ir. oen, W. un, Goth. ains, Lith. v-énas, O. Sl. i-nŭ ; cf. O. Ind. éka- for *oi-ko-, Cypr. Gk. *oi-Fos*, Att. οἶος, alone, for *oi-wo-), Lat. *ūnus* (-*a* -*um*), O. Lat. *oinos*. Another I.-Eur. word for ' one ' was

---

[1] The Oscan word, often compared with *bessi-*, viz. diasis (Zv. *I.I.I.* 154), has scant claims to existence. All that the inscription shows is . . . iasis.

*sĕm-, which is used in Gk., εἷς for *sem-s, μία for σμ-ια, ἕν for *sem, and in Arm., mi for *sm-i; and in Derivatives and Compounds in all languages, e. g. *sem-, *sm̥- in O. Ind. sa-kŕt, ' once,' Gk. ἅ-παξ, ἁ-πλός, ἁ-πλόος, Lat. *sin-gŭli, simplus, sim-plex, sĕmĕl, sem-pĕr, sincinia* : cantio solitaria, Paul. Fest. 500. 23 Th., *simpludiarea funera* : quibus adhibentur duntaxat ludi, Fest. 498. 24 Th., Goth. simlē,' once.' For the Ordinal was used a derivative from the I.-Eur. root per- (cf. Lat. *prŏ, prae*, &c.; Gk. πέρυσι for πέρ-υτι, ' in the previous year,' O. Ind. par-ut, from pĕr- and the root of *wĕtos, ' a year,' Gk. ἔτος), in Latin *prīs- (cf. *prius*) with the suffix -mo-, *prīmus* for *prīs-mus (Pelign. Prismā-; cf. Lat. *prīs-cus, prīs-tinus*), in O. Ind. a derivative with one Superlative suffix, pra-thamá-, in Teutonic with another, O. H. G. fur-ist (cf. Germ. Fürst), Engl. first.

The Adverb is in Latin *sĕmĕl* from the root sem-, just mentioned, a byform of which furnished the Indefinite Pronoun ' any,' ' some,' in various languages (O. Ind. sama-, Gk. ἁμό-, Goth. sums, Engl. some; *K. Z.* xxxii. 373); the Adjective, *sim-plus* (Gk. ἁ-πλός) or *sim-plex* (from *sem-plax, cf. *du-plex* § 59); the Distributive *sin-gŭli*.

§ 58. Unus. O. Lat. *oinos* appears on the proud epitaph of L. Cornelius Scipio (*C. I. L.* i. 32), written in Saturnian metre :

hónc oíno ploírume coséntiont R[ómai]
dùŏnóro óptumo fuíse uíro,

' hunc unum plurimi consentiunt Romae bonorum optimum fuisse virum'; cf. *oinuorsei* 'universi' on the S. C. de Bacch. (i. 196), and *Oinumama* 'Unimamma' (an Amazon) on an old Praenestine cista (i. 1501), *oinā* Adv. in the Lex Agraria of 111 B.C. (i. 200. 21); *oenus* in Plaut. *Truc.* 103, Cic. *Legg.* iii. 3. 9. But we have *unus* in the Lex Repetundarum of 123-122 B.C. (i. 198). The Neuter, with the Negative particle *nĕ* prefixed, was used as the ordinary Negative, *noenum* (for *ne-oinom), later *nōn* (ch. iv. § 16), like our 'not' and 'nought,' Germ. nicht and Nichts, from Goth. ni waihts (see ch. x. § 18), while to express 'nothing' the Romans used a compound of *ne* and *hīlum* (quod grano fabae adhaeret, Paul. Fest. 72. 10 Th.), *nihīlum*, later *nihĭl, nīl* (ch. iii. § 52). The plural of *unus* is found with Nouns whose Plural is used in a Singular (Collective) sense, e. g. *una castra*, and in the sense of 'only,' 'alone' (cf. Gk. οἶος), e. g. *tres unos passus* Plaut. In the Romance languages the Indefinite Article is formed from Lat. *unus*, as the Definite from Lat. *ille* ; and we see traces of this use in colloquial Latin, e. g. *una adulescentula*, Ter. *Andr.* 118.

§ 59 Two. I.-Eur. *dŭwo- and *dwo- with Dual declension,

*duwō(u) M., *duwai F., *duwoi or *duwei N. (O. Ind. dvāú and dvā́, older duvāú and duvā́ M., dvé, older duvé F., N., Gk. δύω and δύο, also δ(ϝ)ω-, O. Ir. dau and dā M., dī F., W. dau M., dwy F., Goth. tvai M., tvōs F., tva N., Lith. dù M., for *dvǔ, dvì F. for *dvě, O. Sl. dva and dŭva M., dvě and dŭvě F., N.), Latin *duo* M., N., *duae* F., with Dual declension, which however became intermixed with Plural forms, e. g. *duōs* Acc. M. beside *duo*. In Derivatives and Compounds the I.-Eur. stem dwi- appears (O. Ind. dvi-pád-, Gk. δ(ϝ)ί-πους, O. Engl. twi-fēte), Lat. *bĭ-pes*, *bĭ-dens* (O. Lat. *dui-dens*, Paul. Fest. 47. 8 Th., cf. *dui- census* : cum altero, id est cum filio, census, id. 47. 5; *duicensus* . . . δεύτερον ἀπογεγραμμένος Gl. Philox.), while in the Italic languages we have also dŭ- (Lat. *du-plus*, *du-plex*, *du-centi*, Umbr. *du-pursus* ' bipedibus '), apparently the weak grade of an I.-Eur. *dwĕ- (Lat. *du-bius* has the same root; cf. Hom. δοίη, doubt, Germ. Zwei-fel, Zend dvai-dī). For the Ordinal the Romans used *sĕcundus*, lit. ' following,' from *sĕquor*, or *alter*, ' the other of two,' from the same root as *ăl-ius*, ' the other of many ' (O. Ir. aile, W. ail, which have also this sense of ' second '; in O. Engl. ōþer had this numerical sense); for the Adverb I.-Eur. *dwĭs or *dŭwĭs (O. Ind. dvís, Vedic duvís, Gk. δ(ϝ)ίς, M. H. G. zwis, Goth. tvis-, ' apart '; Engl. twis-t), *bĭs* (O. Lat. *duis*, Paul. Fest. 47. 6 Th.; cf. *duidens* ' hostia bidens,' and *duicensus* ' cum altero, id est cum filio census ' quoted above); for the Adjective *dŭ-plus* (Gk. δι-πλός, Umbr. du-plo-) or *dŭ-plex* (Gk. δί-πλαξ; cf. Umbr. tu-plak N.); for the Distributive *bī-ni* from *dwĭz-no- (O. Scand. tvenner) or from *dwī-no- (Lith. dvynù Du., ' twins ').

§ 60. **Duo.** The original quantity of the final vowel of *duo* in Latin is difficult to establish from poetry. We cannot assign much weight to the precept of the grammarians (e. g. Charisius 35. 25 K.) which distinguishes *duō* M. from *duŏ* N., nor to the scansion *duō* in the Christian poets (Neue, ii³. 277; similarly *egō* for *egŏ*). In classical poetry the scansion is invariably *duŏ* (cf. *duŏdēni*), but in the old Republican poets we find *duo* Acc. distinguished from *duos*, not by the quantity of its final syllable, but in being treated as a monosyllable or the equivalent of a long syllable; for example, *duo* Acc. is never allowed to end an iambic line, which points to *dvō rather than to *dŭŏ (A. L. L. iii. 551). The shortening of the final vowel can be easily explained by the Law of Breves Breviantes, which reduced *hăvē* to *hăvě* (ch. iii. § 42); for a similar doubt with reference to the pronunciation of *scio* as *sciō* or *scjō, see

ch. ii. § 151). The Fem. *duae* may retain the old suffix of the Nom. Dual of Ā-stems, -ai (e. g. O. Ind. áśvē for I.-Eur. *ĕkwai, 'two mares'), which would be retained in monosyllabic **dvai* without sinking, as in the unaccented syllable, to -ī (e. g. *occido* from *óc-caido*, ch. iii. § 18). The termination *-ōbus* of *duōbus* M., N. is shared only by the other Dual-form *ambo*, though *-ābus* F. was a common (Dat., Abl. or Instr.) Plural ending of Ā-stems, retained in legal language especially in the words *deabus*, *filiabus*, *libertabus* (§ 48). But the Plural declension encroached more and more on these Dual forms; *dŭōs* Acc. M. competes, as we have seen, in the older literature with *duō*, while *duas* F. is a Plural, as are also the Genitive forms *duorum* M., N. (older *duum*, e. g. *duumvirum* used by Cicero, § 47), *duarum* F. A Nom., Acc. Neuter *dua* appears on inscriptions (e. g. *C. I. L.* v. 1102; other instances in Neue, ii³. p. 277), though it is called a barbarism by Quintilian (i. 5. 15 nam 'dua' et 'tre' diversorum generum sunt barbarismi, at 'duapondo' et 'trepondo' usque ad nostram aetatem ab omnibus dictum est, et recte dici Messala confirmat), which seems to have been supplemented by a Nom. Masc. **duī* in Vulgar Latin, to judge from the Romance forms (e. g. Ital. due, older dui, O. Fr. dui, doi, &c.). In Umbrian the word shows Plural declension, *dur* Nom., tuf Acc., tuva Nom. Acc. Neut. (On the declension of Lat. *duo*, see Neue, ii³. pp. 276 sqq.). Late compounds like *diloris*, *dinummium* are hybrid formations with Greek δι- instead of Latin *bĭ-*. The relation of I.-Eur. *dwi- to the Latin preposition *dis-*, apart, has not been established, nor yet to I.-Eur. *wi- of Dor. Gk. Ϝί-κατι, Lat. *vī-gintī*, &c., perhaps connected with O. Ind. ví, 'apart.'

§ 61. Three. I.-Eur. *tri-, Nom. Masc. *trĕyĕs (O. Ind. tráyas, Gk. τρεῖς, Cret. Gk. τρέες, O. Ir. trī, W. tri, Goth. þreis, Lith. trŷs, O. Sl. trĭje), Lat. *trēs* M., F., *tria* N. (cf. Umbr. trif or tref Acc., triia Neut.). The stem trĭ- appears in Gk. τρί-τος, τρί-πους, Lat. *tri-pes*, &c., but a stem trĕ- in Lat. *trĕ-centi*, *tre-pondo*, Lith. trẽ-czias, 'third,' O. Sl. tre-tĭjĭ, &c. The Ordinal *tĕrtius* (Umbr. tertio-) probably shows this stem trĕ- with metathesis of r; the Adverb *tĕr*, for *terr* (in Plautus scanned as a long syllable, cf. *terr-uncius*) from **ter-s*, comes from the same stem, or, like O. Ind. trís, Gk. τρίς, from the stem trĭ- (ch. iii. § 15. 8); the Adjective is *trĭ-plus* (Gk. τρι-πλός), *trĭ-plex*; the Distributive *trīnus* (see on *bīnus* above), and *ter-nus*. We find *trĭ-* and *ter-* interchanged in Compounds like *tri-gĕmĭnus* and *ter-geminus*, *tri-vĕnēficus* and *ter-veneficus*, *tri-vium* and *ter-vium* (*C. I. L.* ix. 2476), *Terventum* now Trivento; *trĭ-* and *trĕ-* in *tri-mŏdia* and *tre-modia* (Varro, *Men.* 310 B.).

§ 62. Tres. The grammarians prescribe *trēs* in the Nominative and *trīs* in the Accusative (Neue, ii³. p. 284), as is the rule in all I-stems (§§ 40, 51), though Virgil, as Gellius (xiii. 21. 10) points out, uses *tres* Acc. for the sake of variety in *A*. x. 350:

§§ 61-63.] DECLENSION OF NOUNS, ETC. NUMERALS. 413

tres quoque Threicios Boreae de gente suprema
et tris, quos Idas pater et patria Ismara mittit,
per varios sternit casus,

as he uses elsewhere *urbes* Acc. in a context where the Roman critics found that this form gave greater melody to the line (*A.* iii. 106): centum urbes habitant magnas (Gellius *l. c.* quotes the remarks of Probus on this form : hic item muta ut 'urbis' dicas, nimis exilis vox erit et exsanguis, and his reply to a caviller: noli igitur laborare, utrum istorum debeas dicere 'urbis' an 'urbes.' Nam cum id genus sis, quod video, ut sine jactura tua pecces, nihil perdes, utrum dixeris !). *Tris* Nom. is found on late inscriptions, e. g. *Eph. Epigr.* iv. 420 (other examples in *A. L. L.* vii. 65).

§ 63. **Four.** The I.-Eur. stem q^uĕtwer- had various grades, q^uetwor-, q^uetur-, q^uetru-, &c. Its Nom. Masc. *q^uetwŏres (O. Ind. catvā́ras, Dor. Gk. τέτορες, Att. τέτταρες, Lesb. πέσυρες, O. Ir. cethir, W. pedwar, Goth. fidvōr, O. Engl. fēower; cf. Lith. keturì, O. Sl. četyre) probably appears in Lat. *quattuor* (some make this an I.-Eur. Neuter *q^uetwōr, §§ 44, 45), apparently for *$quotvor(\breve{e})s$, with *t* doubled before the *w*-sound (ch. ii. § 130) and *-atv-* for *-otv-* like *-av-* for *-ov-* in *căvus*, &c. (ch. iv. § 19). The Oscan word was *petora* (so spelt by Festus 250. 33 Th., but probably better *petoro). In Compounds and Derivatives we find a stem q^uetru- (Zend caþru-, Gaul. Petru-corius; cf. Umbr. *petur-pursus* 'quadripedibus'), which in Latin is *quadru-* (with *ă* for *ĕ* by analogy of *quattuor, quartus*?), where the *d* is puzzling, for *-dr-* seems to become *-tr-* in Latin, e. g. *ātro-* for **ādro-*, *nūtrix* for **nūdrix* (ch. iv. § 113), so that *-tr-* should not change to *-dr-* [Wharton, *Etym. Lat.* p. 83 suggests that *quadra*, a square, means literally ' pointed' and comes, not from *quattuor*, but from a root q^uad-, ' to point, sharpen,' Engl. whet, the usual change of *-dr-* to *-tr-* being seen in *tri-quetrus*, triangular. *Quadra*, which retained *d* (by analogy of other words from the same root?), may have been the cause of *q^uetru- taking the form *quadru-*; cf. *K. Z.* xxxii. 565]. The Ordinal *quārtus* with its long *a* (indicated by an apex over the letter on inscriptions; see Christiansen, *de Apicibus*, p. 52) has not yet been satisfactorily explained. On an inscription of Praeneste we have *Quorta* (cf. ch. ii. § 4); the Oscan word truto- is interpreted variously as ' quartus' for *ptru-to-, and as ' certus.' The Adverb *quătĕr* stands for *q^uetrŭ-s (Zend caþruš; cf. O. Ind. catúr), as *ager* for *agrŏs, *ācer* for *ācris (ch. iii. § 16); the

Adjectives *quadrŭ-plus*, *quadrŭ-plex* show the curious change of -tr- to -dr-, remarked on above, from which *quater* is free; the Distributive *quăternus* for **quatri-nus* (like *săcerdōs* for **sacrĭdōs*, ch. iii. § 16) from **qᵘetrŭ-no-* (ch. iii. § 18), or from the Adverb *quater* with the suffix -no (see above on *bīnus*, § 59).

§ 64. Quattuor with double *t* is the spelling of the best MSS. and inscriptions, such as the Monumentum Ancyranum (see Georges, *Lex. Wortf.* s. v.). The form *quattor*, found on late inscriptions (e. g. *C. I. L.* viii. 5843; other examples in *A. L. L.* vii. 65) has been already explained from **quatt(v)órdecim*, where the *w*-sound would be dropped before the accent, as in *Jan(v)árius*, *Febr(v)árius*, &c. (ch. ii. § 54). Vulg. Lat. **quattor-decim* is indicated by the Romance words for 'fourteen,' e. g. Ital. quattordici, Fr. quatorze, but Vulg. Lat. **quattro by the words for ' four,' e. g. Ital. quattro, Fr. quatre (Sic. battor, however, from *quattor*). This Late and Vulg. Latin *quattor* can hardly be assigned to early Latin authors; so retain *quattuor* in Plaut. *Most.* 630 and scan *quattŭŏr*, like *enicăs*, *Rud.* 944 as a dactyl at the beginning of an iambic line; in Enn. *A.* 90 M. *quattŭŏr* like *virgĭnĕs A.* 102; in Enn. *A.* 609 read *ferĕ quattŭŏr partum* (?). *Petreius*, *Petrōnius* are dialectal Proper Names derived from this numeral, as *Pompeius*, *Pontius* (Lat. *Quintius*) from the numeral ' five.'

§ 65. Five. I.-Eur. **pĕnqᵘĕ* (O. Ind. páñca, Arm. hing, Gk. πέντε, πεμπ-ώβολον, Lith. penkì) shows in Teutonic assimilation of the second syllable to the first, **pempe (Goth. fimf), in Lat. and Celtic of the first to the second **qᵘenqᵘe (Gaul. πεμπε-δουλα, quinquefoil, O. W. pimp; in O. Ir. with o for e in the first syllable, cōic; cf. Umbro-Oscan pump-, *Pompeius*), Lat. *quīnque* with *e* changed to *i* before a nasal and guttural (like *tingo* for **tengo*, ch. iv. § 11), and the *i* lengthened (by analogy of *quīntus*?). The Ordinal *quīntus*, older *quīnctus*, follows the rules of Latin phonetics that *qu* becomes *c* before a consonant (ch. iv. § 137), and that in this group of three consonants the middle one is dropped (ch. iv. § 157). On the lengthening of the *i*, see ch. ii. § 144. The original form was **qᵘenc-to-* in Italic for I.-Eur. **penqᵘ-to- (or **pn̥qᵘ-to-?) (Gk. πέμπτος, Lith. peñktas, O. Sl. pętŭ; Osc. Púntiis, also Πομπτιες with -*mp*- from the Cardinal form). The Adverb is *quinquies*, older *quinquiens*, on which see § 56, the Adjective *quinquĭ-plex* [or with -*cu*- for -*quu*- (ch. iv. § 137) *quincŭ-plex*], rarely *quincuplus* or *quinquiplus*; the Distributive *quīnus* for **quinc-nus* (ch. iv. § 157).

§ 66. Quinque. The long quantity of the *i* of *quinque* is attested by the use of the tall form of the letter on inscriptions (for instances, see Christiansen, *de Apicibus*, pp. 45-46. On Vulg. Lat. *cinque* (Ital. cinque, Fr. cinq, &c.), see ch. iv. § 163).

§§ 64-70.] DECLENSION OF NOUNS, ETC. NUMERALS. 415

§ 67. **Six.** Lat. *sex* points to I.-Eur. *sĕks or *ksĕks (*M. S. L.* vii. 73), as Greek ἕξ, Ϝέξ to *sweks or *ksweks (cf. Zend xšvaš, O.Ir. sē and *fē, W. chwech). The Ordinal *sextus* has -st- in Umbro-Oscan, e. g. Umbr. sestentasiaru; *Sestius* is a dialectal byform of *Sextius*. The Adverb is *sexiēs*, older *sexiens* (see § 56); the Distributive *senus* for *sĕx-nus* (as *lūna* for *lūx-na*, ch. iv. § 162).

§ 68. **Seven.** I.-Eur. *sĕptm̥ (O. Ind. saptá, Arm. evtʻn, Gk. ἑπτά, O.Ir. secht, W. saith, Goth. sibun; cf. Lith. septyn-ì), Lat. *septem*, with Ordinal *septmo- (O. Ind. saptamá-, Gk. ἕβδομος, Pruss. septmas and sepmas), Lat. *septĭmus*, older *septumus*. The Distributive *septēnus* stands for *septen-no- (ch. ii. § 130). In later Latin we find *tt* for *pt*, e. g. *Settembris* (*C. I. L.* xi. 2885, *Setebres* 4075); cf. Ital. sette, Settembre. In Compounds we find the stem *septem-*, e. g. *septempĕdālis* Plaut., *septemplex* Virg., *septemgĕmĭnus* Catull., but *Septi-montium*, and on the restored Columna Rostrata *septe-resmos* (*C. I. L.* i. 195); *septuennis* Plaut., &c. (cf. *septuā-gintā*, below), for *septum-ennis*, shows the usual weakening of unaccented *ĕ* before *m* to *u*, and the same loss between vowels of final *m* of the first member of a compound as is seen in *circu(m)ire*, &c. (ch. iii. §§ 18 and 52).

§ 69. **Eight.** The O.-Ind. Dual form *ŏktṓ(u), cleverly explained by Fick as ' the two sets of pointed' (i. e. the fingers, without the thumbs, of both hands), from the root āk̂-, ok̂-, ' to be sharp, pointed' (O. Ind. aṣṭá and aṣṭā́ú, Arm. utʻ, Gk. ὀκτώ, O. Ir. ocht, W. wyth, Goth. ahtau, Lith. astù-n-ì) is in Latin *octō*, with Ordinal *octavus* (cf. Osc. Úhtavis 'Octavius') for *octōvus (ch. iv. § 16), and Distributive *octō-nus*. In later Latin *ct* became *tt*, *Ottobres C. I. L.* xi. 2537 (cf. Ital. otto, Ottobre), and the final -*ō* is shortened, like every final -*ō* in the poetry of the Empire, e. g. *octŏ* Mart. vii. 53. 10. In Compounds it is treated as an O-stem, e. g. *octŭ-plus*, *octŭ-plex*, *octĭ-pes*, *oct-ennis*.

§ 70. **Nine.** I.-Eur. *nĕwṇ (O. Ind. náva, Gk. ἐννέα for *ἐν-νεϝα (?), O. Ir. nōi, W. naw, Goth. niun; cf. Lith. devyn-i with d- instead of n-) is in Latin *nŏvem* with *ov* regularly enough for -ew- as in Celtic (ch. iv. § 10), but with -*em* instead of the normal *-en*. The proper Nasal appears in the Ordinal *nōnus*, older *noino-* (if the Dvenos inscription is rightly read *dienoine*, on the ninth day), from **nŏvĕno-*, where the *ō* is difficult to explain, though it seems to have a parallel in *nōn* for *noen(um)*. Failing this explanation, we may suppose that **nouno-* or **nowṇno-* was the I.-Eur. form, with the O-grade of the root, and understand Lat. *ō* as an expression of I.-Eur. ou as in *rōbus*, &c. (ch. iv. § 41). (On *nōndinum* and *noundinum*, old spellings of *nūndĭnum*, for **no(v)éndinum*, from *novem* and the root dĭn-, seen in O. Sl. dĭnĭ, 'a day,' see ch. iv. § 44.) Umbr. nuvimo- shows the form rather to be expected in Latin, **nŏvĭmo-* (O. Ind. navamá-), but in Pelign. we have Novnis 'Nonius.' The Adverb is *noviēs* (Umbr. nuvīs); the Distributive *novēnus* from **noven-no-* (ch. ii. § 130).

§ 71. **Ten.** I.-Eur. **dékm̥* (O. Ind. dáśa, Arm. tasn, Gk. δέκα, O. Ir. deich, W. deg, Goth. taihun; cf. Lith. děszim-t, O. Sl. desę-tĭ), Lat. *dĕcem*, with Ordinal *dĕcĭmus* (O. Ind. daśamá-) (cf. the proper name *Decius*), Adverb *deciēs*, and Distributive *dēnus* for which we should expect **decēnus* like *septēnus* (cf. § 74).

§ 72. **Eleven to Nineteen.** These Numerals were denoted in I.-Eur. by Compounds, expressive of the addition of the smaller unit to ten. These Compounds consist of the two Numerals themselves (not their stems) placed together, the smaller unit preceding the ten, e. g. I.-Eur. **trĕyĕs-dĕkm̥*, 'thirteen' (O. Ind. tráyō-daśa). The Latin Compounds (in which the final *-em* of *decem* sinks to *-im*, ch. iii. § 18) are, *un-decim* for **ūn(i)-decim* (on Vulg. Lat. **ŭndecim*, see ch. ii. § 147), *duo-decim*, *trē-decim* for **trēs-decim* (like *nīdus* for **nis-dus*, ch. iv. § 151), *quattuor-decim*, *quin-decim* for **quin(que)-decim* (ch. iii.§ 13), *sē-decim* (the correct spelling) for *sex-decim* (like *lūna* for **lūx-na*, ch. iv. § 162), *septem-decim*. *Octō-decim* and *novem-decim* were replaced by *duo-dē-viginti*, *un-dē-viginti* for **un(i)-de-viginti*, or by *octo et decem*, *decem novem*, a mode of expression which is found in the other numerals too, e. g. *decem duo* (Umbr. desen-*duf* Acc.), and which is used in Greek exclusively for the numbers above twelve, e. g. τρεῖς καὶ δέκα and δέκα τρεῖς, and optionally for

§§ 71-74.] DECLENSION OF NOUNS, ETC. NUMERALS. 417

twelve, δώ-δεκα or δέκα δύο. In I.-Eur. it was used for numbers above twenty, and so in Lat. *quattuor et viginti* or *viginti quattuor*, &c. The Ordinals are *undecimus, duodecimus* (O. Ind. dvādaśama-), &c.; the Adverbs *undecies, duodecies*, the Distributives *undēnus, duŏdēnus*, and so on.

§ 73. O. Lat. duovicesimus for class. *duo et vīcēsĭmus*, twenty-second, is attested by an interesting chapter of the Noctes Atticae (v. 4), which illustrates the pains taken in the Imperial period to secure correct texts of early authors. Gellius there tells us of a MS. of the Annals of Fabius : bonae atque sincerae vetustatis libri, quos venditor sine mendis esse contendebat. A grammaticus who was asked to inspect the MS., on the absolute correctness of which the bookseller was willing to stake any amount of money (grammaticus quispiam de nobilioribus, ab emptore ad spectandos libros adhibitus, repperisse se unum in libro mendum dicebat ; sed contra librarius in quodvis pignus vocabat, si in una uspiam littera delictum esset), declared that *duovicesimo anno* in Book iv. was a mistake of the copyist for *duo et vicesimo anno*, but was finally forced to admit, on being referred to other passages of ancient authors, that *duovicesimus* was a genuine Old Latin form.

§ 74. **Twenty to Ninety.** These Numerals are denoted in I.-Eur. by Neuter Compounds, 'two decades,' 'three decades,' &c., the word for 'decade' being **dekm̥-t-*, changed in Composition into **(d)k̑m̥t-* [or **(d)k̑omt-* ?; cf. Greek -κοντ- in 30–90, τριά-κοντα, τεσσαρά-κοντα, or τετρώ-κοντα, &c., which suggests that this is the plural stem, the other the dual]. In Lat. *vī-gĭntī vī-* is probably Neut. Dual Nom. of I.-Eur. **wi-*; the *-gĭntī*, with *ĭ* for *ĕ* owing to the popular accentuation **vígenti, *trígenta, *quadrágenta*, &c., which takes its *g* apparently through influence of the d of I.-Eur. **(d)k̑m̥t-* (but *vicesimus*; so Alb. -zet, 'a gross,' points to ĝ not k̑), is also Neut. Dual Nom. In *trī-gintā* the *trī-* is Neut. Plur. Nom. of the I.-Eur. stem **tri-*, the *-gintā* shows the original quantity of the Neut. Plur. suffix, which has by the time of the earliest literature been shortened in Nouns, &c. to *-ă* (ch. iii. § 43). In *quadrā-gintā* the *quadrā-* (on the form of the stem, see § 63) may correspond to Gk. τετρω- of τετρώ-κοντα (see ch. iv. § 92), or may have the Neut. Plur. ending *-ā*, an ending assumed by *quinque, sex, septem, novem* in a somewhat haphazard way in the Compounds *quinquā-gintā, sexā-gintā, septuā-gintā* (for **septu(m)āginta* ; see above on *septuennis*, § 68), *nonā-gintā*, while *octō* in *octōginta* retains its ordinary form. The Ordinals are formed with the suffix -tmo- or -t°mo- (ch. v. § 14),

E e

e. g. *vīcēsimus*, older *vicensumus* (this spelling is more frequent than *vigesimus*) for **vi-cent-tumus*, *trīcēsimus* and *trigesimus*, older *-ensumus* for **tri-cent-tumus* (O. Ind. tri-śat-tamá-); the Adverbs are *vīciēs*, older *-ens*, *trīciēs*, older *-ens* (sometimes *trīgies*), like *decies*, older *-ens* (§ 56); the Distributives *vīcēnus* (with byform *vīgēnus*), *trīcēnus* (with byform *trīgēnus*), &c., not like the abnormal *dēnus*, but like **decēnus* (§ 71).

§ 75. **Viginti, &c.** *Viginti* is spelt *veiginti* (*C. I. L.* i. 1194; x. 6009), but the *ei* may merely indicate *ī*, for the inscriptions are not of great antiquity (ch. i. § 9). The late spelling *vigenti* (*C. I. L.* v. 1645, &c.) points to *vigĭnti* (cf. *quinquagenta* xii. 482, and other examples of *-genta* quoted in *A. L. L.* vii. 69–70). In Late and Vulgar Latin the *g* was dropped (ch. ii. § 94), whence the form *vinti*; e.g. Wilm. 569:

et menses septem diēbus cum vinti duobus;

cf. Sard. vinti, Ital. venti, &c. The same thing happened to *trigĭnta*, producing the form *trienta* (*C. I. L.* xii. 5399, &c.), and in Romance, Sard. trinta, Ital. trenta, &c.; also to *quadragĭnta* (a hexameter line on a late epitaph ends, quadragintă per annos, vi. 28047), which had become *quar(r)aginta* (Fabretti, iv. 134), whence Ital. quaranta, Fr. quarante. On the accentuation of these three numerals, see ch. iii. § 11. 4. *Septŭăgintă* is the scansion required in metrical epitaphs (*C. I. L.* vi. 22251. 29426). Its analogy produced in Mediaeval Latin the form *octuaginta*, which found its way into some early editions of Latin authors (Skutsch, *Forsch.* i. 24). *Octaginta* occurs sometimes in the Edict of Diocletian (*C. I. L.* iii. pp. 810, 811) and elsewhere (see *A. L. L.* vii. 70). (For other examples of the scansion *-gintă* in late poetry, see Neue, ii³. p. 290.)

§ 76. **The Hundreds.** The I.-Eur. expression for 100 was apparently 'a decade of decades' (like the Compound later evolved in Gothic, taihuntē-hund (?)), viz. **(d)kmtŏm*, probably an old Gen. Plur. of the stem **dekṃt* (§ 46), treated as a Nom., like *sestertium, -i* Gen. for *mille sestertium*, 'a thousand of sesterces,' in Latin. This explains why the full form, and not the mere stem, is used in Compounds in Greek and Latin (e. g. ἑκατόμ-βη, ἑκατόγ-χειρος, *centum-plex*, *centum-gĕmĭnus*, *centum-pondium*); though some prefer to regard **(d)kmtŏm* as Nom. Sg. of a Neut. O-stem,' a decade,' just as O. Ind. daśati- means, (1) a decade, (2) a hundred, i. e. 'a decade (of decades'). The *d* of **(d)kmtóm* shows its influence in Latin in the presence of *g*, instead of, or along with *c*, in the expressions for the various hundreds. In O. Lat. we find Neuter Compounds, *dŭcentum* (with dŭ- the weak stem of I.-Eur. dwĕ-, a byform of dwĭ-, § 59), *trĕ-centum* (with I.-Eur. trĕ-, a byform of trĭ-, § 61),

§§ 75-78.] DECLENSION OF NOUNS, ETC. NUMERALS. 419

nongentum, &c., used with the Genitive of the thing specified,
e. g. *argenti sescentum*, Lucil. xxx. 22 M.; but these Neuter
Compounds, when referring not to a mass, but to a number of
individual things, became in course of time declined as Adjectives, *dŭ-centi -ae a*, *trĕ-centi -ae -a*, e. g. *trecentae causae* Plaut.
(cf. *nongentus*, Plin. xxxiii. 2. 31). (So in Greek YO-stem Adjectives were formed, in Att. -κόσιοι (with -σι- for -τι-), in Dor. -κάτιοι.)
They formed their Numeral Adverbs, Adjectives, and Distributives by analogy of the tens, e. g. *trĕcent-ies* (like *trīcies*), *trĕcent-ēsimus* (like *trīcesimus*), *trĕcent-ēni* (like *trīceni*). The forms *quingenti* (for **quinc-genti*, ch. iv. § 157), *septin-genti* (for **septem-genti*, **septen-genti* like *tingo* for **tengo*, ch. iv. § 11), apparently influenced *quadrin-genti* (for earlier *quadrĭ-genti*), *octin-genti*, and even *noningenti* (beside the usual *non-genti*). *Ses-centi* for **se(c)s-centi*
obeys the same phonetic law as *disco* for **di(c)-sco* (cf. *di-dic-i*;
see ch. iv. § 157. 3).

§ 77. **Centum, &c.** The stem **centŏ-* (-*ĕ*) appears in *centĭ-ceps* Hor., *centĭmănus* Hor., *centĭ-pĕda* (and *centum-peda*) Plin., &c., but *centom-* in *centumpondium* Plaut., Cato, *centumplex* Plaut. *Pers.* 560, *centum-gĕmĭnus* Virg., &c., so that the latter is the older formation. For examples of *ducentum*, &c., with Gen., from the older writers and in legal phraseology, see Neue, ii³. p. 298. The usage is confined to phrases like *ducentum auri, argenti, vini*, &c.; Plautus has *ducenti -ae -a*, &c., as in classical Latin. A transitional construction is seen in *C. I. L.* iv. 1136 *nongentum tabernae*, nine hundred shops. As to the form of the several numerals; *duocenti* is found in the late Latin of the Itala; *quadrĭgenti* is the Plautine form, though the MSS. have usually (not, however, universally in *Bacch.* 1183) changed it to *quadringenti*; for the second syllable is always short, and the Breves Breviantes Law is inoperative when a Mute and Liquid follow the short vowel, so that -*drĭ-* not -*drĭn-* must have been the second syllable of the word used in Plautus' day; *quadrigenti, quadrigenus*, &c. are probably also the classical forms (Neue, ii³. p. 297), but on Mon. Ancyr. iii. 8 *quadringenos*; of *quingentum* Festus tells us that the pronunciation before his time was *quīncentum* (Fest. 338. 19 Th. 'quincentum' et producta prima syllaba, et per c litteram usurpant antiqui, quod postea levius visum est, ita ut nunc dicimus, pronuntiari); *sescenti* is the correct spelling, not *sexcenti* (see Neue, ii³. p. 297); *septigenti* for *septingenti* occurs on the Edict of Diocletian; *nonigenti* is a late and rare form (see Neue, *l. c.*); Caper censures the form *noncenti* (104. 1 K. nongentos non 'noncentos' dicendum est), and it seems to be the rule that after *n* the voiced (*g*), and not the unvoiced (*c*) guttural is used in these words.

§ 78. **The Thousands.** The Latin *mille*, in O. Lat. a declinable Neuter Noun taking a Genitive of the things specified, e. g.
mille hominum occiditur, milli (Abl.) *passum vicerit*, is probably

unconnected with the Gk. χίλιοι, Lesb. χέλλιοι, from *ĝhĕslio-
Adj., and the O. Ind. sa-hásram from *sm-ĝhĕslom, a Neuter
Noun-compound, of which the first part is the root sem-, ' one,'
literally ' one thousand,' as Gk. ἑ-κατόν for *ἁ-κατόν (?), ' one
hundred,' ' one (decade) of decades (?).' [Some suppose that it
represents an original *sm-hesli, ' one thousand,' and that this
became *melle, *mēle, as *quaslus (cf. quăsillus) became quālus
(older quallus, ch. iv. § 162); the Plural *mēlia becoming mīlia as
*Plēnius became Plīnius (ch. iv. § 7). O. Ir. mīle would then be
a loanword from Latin, for I.-Eur. sm- would remain in Irish.]
It is cognate with the Celtic word for ' thousand ' (O. Ir. mīle,
W. mil), just as the Teutonic and Slavonic numerals are cognate,
Goth. þūsundi F., Lith. túkstantis, O. Sl. tysęšta or tysąšta F.

For the thousands, the units *duo, tria*, &c. are prefixed in Latin
as separate words, *duo milia* (on the spelling *milia* beside *mille*,
see ch. ii. § 127), *tria milia*, &c. The Ordinals and Adverbs are
formed like those of the hundreds, *mill-ēsimus, miliēs*, &c., like
cent-ēsimus, cent-iēs.

§ 79. Mille. Gellius (i. 16) quotes a number of passages to show that Cicero,
as well as the older writers of the Republic, used *mille* as a Neuter Singular
Noun, e. g. Cic. *Mil.* 53 mille hominum versabatur. So *mille passuum* (earlier
passum), a mile. [Other examples are given by Neue, ii[3]. p. 303, to which add
Plaut. *Bacch.* 928 millí (MSS. mille) cum numero náuium]. In the spelling
meilia (probably for *meillia*, for double consonants are written single on this
inscription, e. g. *redidei, tabelarios*) of *C. I. L.* i. 551 (Lucania, 132 B.C.), the *ei*
may indicate merely the long *i*-sound. Lucilius (ix. 21 M.) seems also to
recommend *ei* in both singular and plural (cf. ch. i. § 9) (so *meille* in the
Ambrosian Palimpsest, Plaut. *Stich.* 587).

§ 80. The Numerals in Romance. The Cardinals are mostly retained,
though *dŭcenti*, &c. have become Fr. deux cents, Span. doscientos, &c. But
only Italian keeps the Ordinals unchanged, primo, secondo, terzo, quarto,
&c. French has premier for *prīmus*, and for the others uses the suffix -ième.
Spanish has primero (like French) for *primus*, tercero (with the same suffix)
for *tertius*, and uses for *nōnus* noveno (the Lat. Distributive *nŏvēnus*), and
similarly for *dĕcĭmus* deceno. (For a fuller account see Meyer-Lübke, *Rom.
Gram.* ii. pp. 590 sqq.)

CHAPTER VII.

THE PRONOUNS.

§ 1. I. THE PERSONAL PRONOUNS AND THE REFLEXIVE. 1. Sing. Latin *ĕgŏ*, O. Lat. *ĕgō* represents I.-Eur. **ĕĝō* (Gk. ἐγώ), of which byforms were **egŏ* (Goth. ik, Lith. esz and àsz), **eĝōm (Gk. ἐγών), **egŏm (O. Sl. azŭ; cf. O. Ind. ahám with Aspirate instead of Media). It is strengthened by the addition of the particle *-mĕt*, e.g. *egomet*, *mihimet*, and in certain of its cases by the particle *-ptĕ* (§ 20), e.g. *mihipte*, while in the Accusative we find the Pronoun doubled for emphasis, *mēmē*. For the Genitive, *meī* is used, apparently the Gen. Sg. Neut. of the Possessive, ' of mine,' but in O. Lat. we have *mĭs* (with the Gen. ĕs-suffix?); for the Dative *mĭhĭ* (*mī*) for **mehei* or **mehoi*, with the I.-Eur. Locative ending (Umbr. *mehe*; cf. O. Ind. máhy-am) and with *mĭ-* instead of *mĕ-* because of the Pronoun's want of accent (ch. iii. § 18); for the Accusative O. Lat. *mēd*, by the time of Terence always *mē*, owing to the Latin phonetic law that final *d* was lost after a long vowel (ch. ii. § 137); this *d* is either the Ablative *d*, with a strange confusion between Acc. and Abl. functions (so in Engl. ' him' Dat. has become Acc.), or the I.-Eur. particle -id, often used in the Veda to strengthen Pronouns, **mē-id* (cf. Dor. Gk. ἐμεί Acc. for **ἐμε-ίδ*?), just as the particle **gĕ* is used to distinguish the Acc. in Teutonic (Goth. mi-k, Germ. mich; cf. Gk. ἐμέ-γε); for the Ablative, O. Lat. *mēd* from I.-Eur. **mēd (cf. O. Ind. mád from I.-Eur. **mĕd), which with *mēd* Acc., became *mē* in the second cent. B. C.; the Locative [I.-Eur. **mei or **moi, O. Ind. (Vedic) mé Loc., used also as Gen. and Dat., Gk. μοί Dat.] and Instrumental (perhaps I.-Eur. **mē or **mō) cannot be identified in Latin. On the affix -ĝh- of *mihi*, see ch. x. § 1.

§ 2. *Egŏ* is the invariable scansion of classical poetry, and the almost invariable scansion of Plautus and the early Dramatists; *egō* is found occasionally in late poetry (Neue, ii³. p. 346), where it may possibly be influenced by Gk. ἐγώ, and in Plautus (e. g. *Poen.* 1185), &c., where it must be a relic of the older quantity (Klotz, *Altröm. Metrik*, p. 51; Müller, *Plaut. Pros.* p. 30), not yet shortened by the Breves Breviantes Law (ch. iii. § 42). The preponderance of the shortened form is due to the enclitic character of the word (even *egŏmet*), for Lat. *egō* cannot represent I.-Eur. *egô, if final ŏ became ĕ in Latin (ch. iii. § 37). *Mihipte* is quoted from Cato by Fest. 144. 11 Th.; Paul. Fest. 145. 5; *mepte* occurs in Plaut. *Men.* 1059:

quin certíssumumst
mépte potius fíeri seruom, quám te umquam emittám manu.

For examples of *meme* (a somewhat doubtful form), see Neue, ii³. p. 355. *Mis* Gen. is quoted by Priscian from Ennius (*A.* 145 M.):

ingens cura mïs cum concordibus aequiperare,

and probably occurs in Plaut. in *Poen.* 1188, beginning: rebús mïs agúndis (anapaestic), and in other passages, though the MSS. have usually changed it to the more familiar *mei*. It is often mentioned as an O. Lat. form by the grammarians (see the references in Neue, ii³. p. 347), and may represent an original *mĕs, as *Salutis* is in O. Lat. *Salutes* (ch. vi. § 17). For the Dative, we have on old inscriptions *mihei* (*C. I. L.* i. 1016. 1277), and with *e* to express the *ei*-diphthong (cf. ch. iv. § 32) *mihe* (i. 1049). A still older form *mehe* (cf. *mehi* Plaut. *Men.* 925 (P.)) seems to be mentioned by Quintilian (i. 5. 21 nam 'mehe' pro m*i* apud antiquos tragoediarum praecipue scriptores in veteribus libris invenimus), though, if we retain the MSS. reading 'pro me,' we must suppose *mehe* to be a mere graphic expression of *mē*, as in Umbrian a long vowel is indicated by repeating it and inserting h, e. g. *comohota* ' commōta ' (whether this was a Latin practice is doubtful, see ch. ii. § 56). The final vowel of *mihi*, &c. had quite become a short vowel in Quintilian's time, and is described by him in the phrase commonly applied to *ĭ*, as 'a sound between *e* and *i*' (see ch. ii. § 16); and even in Plautus and the early Dramatists *mīhĭ* is the usual scansion (Leppermann, *De correptione*, p. 9). *Mihi* is often contracted to *mī*, as *nihil* to *nīl* (ch. ii. § 58), so that we have side by side in Plautus divergent treatments of this Dative, such as (1) dissyllabic *mihĭ*, e. g. *Truc.* 77 Nam míhĭ haec méretrix, &c., (2) the same with elision, e. g. *Stich.* 427 mih(i) expedi, (3) monosyllabic *mi*, e. g. (elided) *Truc.* 173 Sunt m(i) étiam. (For instances of *mi*, see Neue, ii³. 349, and on Nigidius' distinction of Gen. and Dat., Gell. xiii. 26.)

The remark of Festus (156. 6 Th.) 'me' pro mihi dicebant antiqui, illustrated by a quotation from Lucilius (*inc.* 98 M.): quae res me impendet, means, of course, merely that in O. Lat. another case was used (in this example, the Accusative; cf. Lucr. i. 326 mare quae impendent saxa), where the classical construction had the Dative; and similarly *vae te* Plaut. *Asin.* 481 (cf. *vae me* Seneca, *Apoc.* 4) is probably nothing but an unusual employment of the Accusative. The Vocative of the Possessive Pronoun *mi*, e. g. *mi fīli, mi vir*, has been regarded as a Locative-Dative by some and compared with Homer's μητέρι μοι, the Tragedians' ὦ γύναι μοι, Vedic mē gíras, 'my hymns.' But it is more likely to be a byform of *mie (with unaccented *e* sunk to *i*, ch. iii. § 18),

§§ 2–4.] THE PRONOUNS. PERSONAL. 423

as *fili* may be of *filie* (but see ch. vi. § 31), for it is always joined with a Voc., and is used in good writers only with a masculine noun (with a Fem. after Apuleius, Neue, ii³. p. 368); and this is the explanation given by the native grammarians [see below, § 12; there is no *tī (Gk. τοι, σοι) nor *sī (Gk. oἷ)]. The Accusative *med* is found on the very earliest Latin inscriptions which we possess, the Praenestine fibula (*C. I. L.* xiv. 4123), with *Manios med fefaked Numasioi*, and the Dvenos inscription (Zvet. *I.I.I.* 285, Rome), with *Dvenos med feked* (or *feced*); and in Plautus *mēd* and *mē* are doublets, in the Acc. as in the Abl., *mẹ̄* often being shortened by prosodical hiatus to *mē* before an initial vowel, while in Terence *mē*, &c. Acc., Abl. has ousted *mĕd*, &c. Whether Plautine *mē* Abl. is ever an Instrumental form, and has not lost a final -*d*, it is impossible to say; but there is no indication of its being anything but a phonetic variation of an original *mēd* (cf. ch. ii. § 137). On *mĕ-quidem* Plaut., see ch. iii. § 51.

§ 3. 2 Sing. Lat. *tū* is from I.-Eur. *tū (Hom. Gk. τύ-νη, O. Ir. tū, O. H. G. dū, O. Sl. ty), as Dor. Gk. τύ from I.-Eur. *tŭ. In the oblique cases the I.-Eur. stem was *twĕ (or *twŏ) and *tĕ (or *tŏ), &c. [e.g. Gk. σέ for Cret. τϝέ, O. Ind. (Ved.) tvá Instr., tvé Loc., tē Dat., Gen.], often enlarged by an affix -bh-, like the -ĝh- of the 1 Sing. Pron. (e.g. O. Ind. tú-bhyam Dat.). For the Genitive in Latin the Gen. Sg. Neut. of the Possessive is used, *tuī*, 'of thine' (see above, on *meī*), and a Gen. *tis* (? *tīs*) appears in O. Lat.; for the Dative, *tibī*, older *tibei*, for *tebhei (Umbr. tefe; cf. Pruss. tebbei), with *tĭ-* for *te-* owing to its unaccented character; for the Acc., as for the Abl., O. Lat. *tēd*; in the earliest literature *tēd* and *tē* appear as 'doublets' (like *mēd* and *mē*, § 2), but by the middle of the second cent. B.C. *tēd* is out of use; the Locative and Instrumental cannot be identified in Latin. A strengthened form of the Nom. is *tū-tĕ*, of the Acc. and Abl. *tē-tē*; and with addition of the particle -*mĕt* we find *tū-tĭ-met* (cf. ch. iii. § 39), *tibi-met, tē-met*.

§ 4. *Tis* (like *mĭs*, § 2) is attested for O. Lat. by the grammarians (see Neue, ii³. p. 347), and occurs in Plaut. *Mil.* 1033 (an anapaestic line):

quia tís egeat, quia té careat : ob eám rem huc ad te míssast,

where, if we keep the reading of the MSS. (the evidence of the Palimpsest is wanting), we must scan *tĭs*, unlike *mĭs*. (Shall we read quia tĭs ea egeat ?); Trin. 343 *né tis alios misereat* (so in the Palimpsest), but the other MSS. have changed the unfamiliar form to *tui*), and possibly elsewhere (see Neue, *l. c.* and add Plaut. *Cist.* 457). The Dative is spelt *tibci, C. I. L.* i. 542. 1453, but *tibe* in all the MSS. of Varro *R. R.* iii. 7. 11, and in *C. I. L.* i. 33 (one of the Scipio epitaphs in Saturnian metre, c. 180 B.C.). The Acc. is spelt *te* (probably with elision) on the same epitaph:

quáre lúbens t(e) in-grémĭum. Scípio, récipit.

Tu-met is not allowed by Priscian (i. p. 591. 5 H.). An example of *tute* is the famous alliterative line of Ennius (*A.* 108 M.) :

O Tite tute Tati tibi tanta tyranne tulisti.

(For other examples of *tute, tutimet, tibimet,* &c., see Neue, ii³. pp. 361 sqq. ; on *tŭquidem, tĕquidem,* see above, ch. iii. § 51.)

The Umbro-Oscan forms for the Accusative (and Nom.?) point to an original tīom (from *twīom as *fio* from **fwio*; or with ī for I.-Eur. ū ?), Umbr. *tiom* and *tio,* Osc. tiium (usually taken as Nom.).

§ 5. Reflexive. The I.-Eur. stem was *swĕ (or *swŏ) and *sĕ (or *sŏ), &c. (e.g. O. Ind. svá-, 'own,' Goth. svēs, O. Sl. svojĭ; Goth. si-k Acc., O. Sl. sebĕ Dat.), often with the same affix as 2 Sg. *twĕ, *tĕ (see above), viz. -bh-. The Latin Gen. is *suī*, the Gen. Sg. Neut. of the Possessive (like *mei, tui* ; see above), the Dat. *sibĭ* for *sebhei (Pelign. sef*ei*, Osc. sífeí; cf. Pruss. sebbei), with *sĭ*- for *sĕ*- owing to the unaccented use of the Reflexive; the Acc. and Abl. *sē* (O. Lat. *sēd,* which went out of use with *med, ted,* § 2), often doubled for emphasis, *sēsē.* The particle *-met* is added for the same purpose to *se, sibi,* viz. *semet, sibimet.* *Se-pse* is read in Cic. *Rep.* iii. 8. 12 : quae omnis magis quam sepse diligit.

§ 6. The spelling *sibei* is found on *C. I. L.* i. 38 (an Elegiac Scipio epitaph, c. 130 B.C.) ut sibeī me esse creatum Laetentur; i. 196 (the S. C. Bacch. of 186 B.C.) ; i. 198 (the Lex Repetundarum of 123-122 B. C.) ; i. 200 (the Lex Agraria of 111 B. C.) ; i. 205 (the Lex Rubria of 49 B. C.), &c. ; the spelling *sibe* was found (with *quase*) by Quint. (i. 7. 24) in several MSS. (sed an hoc voluerint auctores nescio), and was affected by Livy (T. Livium ita his usum ex Pediano comperi, qui et ipse eum sequebatur). Livy's spelling was probably designed to express short unaccented *i*, the sound which the grammarians describe as being 'between an *e* and an *i*' (see ch. ii. § 16). *Sibĭ* (like *mihĭ, tibĭ*) is the usual scansion in Plautus and the early Dramatists, but *sibī* is by no means rare, and is normal in the phrase *suus sibī*, 'his very own' (so *meus mihī*), e. g. suo sibi gladio hunc jugulo ; cf. O. Sl. pisachą svoją si rĕčĭ, 'scribebant suam sibi linguam'). There is no Genitive form in O. Lat., **sis,* corresponding to *mis, tis* (Priscian ii. p. 2. 29 H.). *Sed,* Acc., occurs on the S. C. Bacch., of 186 B. C. (*C. I. L.* i. 196 *inter sed*), and on the Lex Bantina of 133-118 B. C. (i. 197 *apud sed*: along with *sese, seese*); *sesed* on the inscr. of the Faliscan cooks (Zvet. *I. I. I.* 72 *a*). *Sese* is much more frequent than *mēmē* and *tētē.* (For examples of its use, see Neue, ii³. p. 355.)

The Oscan Acc. is *siom* (cf. above, § 4, on Umbro-Osc. tīom 'te'), the Umbrian Dat. *seso.*

§ 7. 1 Plur. Of the two I.-Eur. stems, *wĕ- (or *wŏ-) (e. g. O. Ind. vay-ám Nom., Goth. veis, Engl. we, Lith. vè-du Dual, O. Sl. vĕ) and *nĕ- (or *nŏ-) (e. g. O. Ind. nas, the enclitic Gen.,

Dat., Acc., O. Ir. nī, Goth. uns for *ṇs, Engl. us, O. Sl. nasŭ; Gk. νῶι Dual, O. Sl. na; with weak grade ṇs- and an affix -smĕ- in O. Ind. oblique cases, asmā́n Acc., asmā́bhis Instr., &c., Lesb. Gk. ἄμμες, Att. ἡμεῖς), the latter appears in Latin nōs Acc. (Zend nå Acc.). Nōs is also the Nominative form. The Gen. is *nostrum* (O. Lat. *nostrorum, -arum*) and *nostri*, the Gen. Plur. and the Gen. Sg. Neut. of the Possessive, 'of ours,' the Gen. Pl. being used when the idea of plurality was specially prominent, e. g. *omnium nostrum, pars nostrum*, but *amicus nostri*; the Dat., Abl. is *nōbīs* (earlier *nō-bei-s*), apparently with the plural suffix *s* added to a case suffix like that of Dat. Sg. *tibei, sibei* ; in O. Lat. *nis* seems also to have been used (Paul. Fest. 33.6 Th.), with the ordinary Dat., Abl. Plur. suffix (see ch. vi. § 48). To strengthen the pronoun, the particle -*met* is added; *nosmet* (always Nom. in Plautus), *nobismet*.

§ 8. *Enos* Acc. is found in the ancient Hymn of the Arval Brothers, preserved in a carelessly written inscription, containing the minutes of the Priesthood for the year 218 A. D. (*C. I. L.* i. 28) : *enos, Lases, iuuate*, and *enos, Marmor, iuuato*. If the lines have Saturnian rhythm, the accent must fall on the first syllable of *enos* (see ch. ii. § 141, p.128 *n.*) :

énos, Láses, iuuáte . . .
énos, Mármor, iuuáto ;

but this, and indeed every fact about the lines, is doubtful. The form *enos* is generally explained as having a particle *ĕ prefixed to *nos* (cf. ἐ-μέ). *Nosmet* is, like *vosmet*, always Subject in Plautus, but also Acc. in Terence, *Phorm.* 172, and the classical writers. The use of *nostrum* (Partitive Gen. and with *omnium*) and *nostri* is discussed by Gellius (xx. 6). For instances of *nostrorum, -ārum* for *nostrum* in Plautus, &c., see Neue, ii³. p. 359. The spelling *nobeis* is frequent in the Ambrosian Palimpsest of Plautus (see Studemund's Index, p. 505).

§ 9. 2 Plur. There are two I.-Eur. stems, *yu- (O. Ind. yūyám, Goth. jūs, Engl. you, Lith. jūs; O. Ind. yuvám Dual, Lith. jù-du) and *wĕ- (or *wŏ-) (O. Ind. vas, the enclitic Gen., Dat., Acc., Pruss. wans, O. Sl. vy vasŭ; O. Ind. vām Dual, O. Sl. va). The former, with the affix -smĕ- is found in Gk. ὑμεῖς, O. Ind. yuṣmā́n Acc., yuṣmā́bhis Instr., &c.; the latter is the stem used in Latin *vōs* Acc. (Zend vå Acc.). *Vōs* is also the Nominative form; *vestrum* (O. Lat. *vostrorum, -arum*) and *vestri* (O. Lat. *vostri*) the Gen., with the same usage and origin as *nostrum* and *nostri* (see above); *vōbīs* is the Dat., Abl., older *vobeis* (see above on *nobis*). The strengthening particle used is -*met* :

vosmet (only Nom. in Plautus, but afterwards Acc. as well), *vobismet*; and *-pte* in O. Lat. *vopte* (Paul. Fest. 578. 21 Th. ' vopte ' pro vos ipsi Cato posuit).

§ 10. For examples of Gen. *vestrum* (*vostrorum*) and *vestri*, see Neue, ii³. p. 359; and cf. *nostrum, nostrorum, nostri*, above. The spelling *vobeis* is extremely frequent in the Ambrosian Palimpsest of Plautus, and occurs in the S. C. Bacch. (*C. I. L.* i. 196. 29), the Epistula ad Tiburtes of c. 100 B. C. (i. 201), &c.

§ 11. II. THE POSSESSIVE PRONOUNS. In the I.-Eur. languages there is a close connexion between the Possessives and the Gen. of the Personal Pronouns. Thus O. Ind. (Vedic) tvá-s is Possessive 'thy,' táva is Gen., 'of thee' (I.-Eur. *tĕwĕ); Dor. Gk. τεός is Possessive, τέο (I.-Eur. *tĕ-syŏ) is Gen. Latin *tuus*, O. Lat. *tovo-* (I.-Eur. *tĕwo-) must be similarly derived from the I.-Eur. Gen. *tĕwĕ, Latin *suus*, O. Lat. *sovo-* (I.-Eur. *sĕwo-) from a corresponding Gen. *sĕwĕ, while *meus* (*meyo-) may come from the Locative-Genitive *mei (O. Ind. mē Gen., Dat.). The same connexion is seen between *cujus*, the Gen. of the Interrogative (§ 13), and *cujus -a -um* the Possessive (§ 23). Some purists objected to this Possessive, and parodied Virgil's line (*E.* iii. 1) by:

dic mihi, Damoeta, ' cujum' pecus, anne Latinum?

under the idea that *cujus -a -um* was merely a vulgar inflexion of a Gen. suffix *-us*, treated as if it had been *-us* of the Nom. Sing.

Beside the Reflexive Possessive stem *sĕwŏ- (Gk. ἑός), there was another I.-Eur. form, *swŏ- (O. Ind. svás, Gk. ὅς for *σϝος). The latter would be in Latin *so-* (ch. iv. § 68), and appears in the O. Lat. forms *sam* for *suam*, *sas* for *suas*, *sos* for *suos*, *sis* for *suis*, which must not be confounded with the Demonstrative stem *so-* on the one hand (O. Lat. *sos* for *eos*, *sum* for *eum*, &c.), nor on the other with the monosyllabic *suas, suos, suis* (pronounced *swas, swos, swis*), where, through the unaccented use of the Poss., the *ŭ* has been turned into a consonant (*w*) before a long vowel (see ch. ii. § 149), just as the *ĕ* (*ĭ*) of unaccented *meus* has been turned into *y* in monosyllabic *meas, meos, meis, meā, meō. Mieis* was the older spelling of *meis* (ch. ii. § 9), and in the Voc. Sing.

Masc. we have, besides *meus*, the form *mi*, e. g. *mi fili, mi homo, mi vir*.

For the Plural Pronouns the suffix -tĕro- (ch. v. § 16) was used (cf. Gk. ἡμέ-τερος, ὑμέ-τερος), 1 Pl. *nŏster*, 2 Pl. O. Lat. *voster*, which by the phonetic laws of Latin (cf. *vĕto* from older *vŏto*, ch. iv. § 10) became *vester* about the middle of the second cent. B. C. [Osc. nestro- (?), Umbr. vestro-.]

The Gen. Sg. Neut. of these Possessives was in classical Latin used for the Gen. of the Personal Pronouns, *mei, tui, sui, nostri, vestri*, and, where the notion of plurality was involved (as in the Partitive Genitive or with *omnium*), the Gen. Pl. *nostrum, vestrum* (in O. Lat. *nostrorum, -arum, vostrorum, -arum*) (see § 8).

The strengthening particles *-mĕt, -ptĕ* are added to the Possessives, e. g. *meamet, suismet, meapte, suopte, nostrapte*.

§ 12. The grammarians speak of an O. Lat. spelling *mius*, from which they derive Voc. *mi* (as *Laeli* Voc., *Laelius* Nom.) (e. g. Charis. p. 159. 17 K., Vel. Long. p. 77. 12 K.; other references in Neue, ii³. p. 366), though the only instance which they quote is *miis* in Ter. *Heaut.* 699 (probably a dissyllable) :

at enim ístoc nihil est mágis, Syre, miis núptiis aduérsum,

where *miis* (a spelling retained in the MSS. of Terence), like *mieis* (probably a monosyllable) on a Scipio epitaph of c. 130 B. C. (*C. I. L.* i. 38):

uirtutes generis mieis moribus accumulavi,

and *mieis* (probably a monosyllable) in Plaut. *Men.* 202 : úna uiuis mieís morigera móribus (probably *mieis, Truc.* 709, where the MSS. read *miles*), shows that spelling of *i* for *e* (I.-Eur. ey) which was the rule in Republican Latin in an unaccented syllable before *-īs* (*·eis*), e. g. *abiegnieis* (but *abiegnea* Acc.), *aesculnieis* on the Lex Parieti Faciundo of 105 B. C. (*C. I. L.* i. 577) (see ch. ii. § 9). [For other passages in Plautus where *miis* is indicated by the MSS., see Neue, *l. c.* ; in *Trin.* 822 *mis* may be Gen. Sg. of the Personal Pronoun, *mĭs* (§ 2), or Abl. Pl. of the Possessive : bonis mís quid foret aut meaé uitae (anapaestic)]. For the Vocative Sg. Masc., *meus* was used with an O-stem Noun in the Nominative form, e. g. Plaut. *Asin.* 664 :

da, méus ocellus, méa rosa, mi ánime, mea uolúptas,

Cas. 137 :

sine, amábo, ted amári, meus festús dies,
meus púllus passer, méa columba, mí lepus.

(Notice *mi lepus* in Plaut., where the Noun is not an O-stem. But Virg. has *meus sanguis*.) On the theory that *mi* is I.-Eur. *moi or *mei Loc., see § 2 above. *Mi* is not found with a Voc. Fem. Sg. or Masc. Pl. till Late and Vulgar Latin, e. g. *mi parens*, my mother, Apul. *Met.* iv. 26 ; o mi, inquit, hospites, Petron.

116, p. 82. 25 B. ; (mi homines, mi spectatores, Plaut. *Cist.* 678, should probably be *mei*, as in *Mil.* 1330 O mei oculi, O mi anime). (See Neue, ii³. pp. 368–9.) We find *tou*[*am*] for *tuam* on an old inscription (*C. I. L.* i. 1290 quei tou[am] pacem petit adiouta); *soueis* for *suis* on the Lex Repetundarum of 123- 122 B. C. (i. 198. 50, beside *suei*, *suae*, *suo*, *sua* Abl.,) and on i. 1258, i. 1297 (where it is a monosyllable :

> plouruma que fecit populo soueis gaudia nuges),

souo i. 1007 (beside *suom*, both dissyllabic :

> suóm mareitum córde dilexít souo),

souom Gen. Pl. Masc. i. 588, of c. 81 B. C.

The unemphatic Possessive is a monosyllable in the early Dramatists (by Synizesis), in iambic forms, e. g. *mĕŏs*, *sŭis*, which should probably not be scanned according to the Breves Breviantes Law *mĕŏs, *sŭis (see ch. iii. § 49). (Instances from Plaut. and Ter. in Neue, ii³. p. 371.) How far the Vulgar Latin unemphatic Possessive *mus, *mum, *ma (seen in Fr. mon, ma, and in Vulg. Ital. ma-donna, padre-mo, &c.) should be referred to O. Lat. *so-* (I.-Eur. *swo-), &c., or to these colloquial forms, is a doubtful point. (Cf. *tis* for *tuis* on a late metrical inscription, Orelli 4847 :

> cum vita functus jungar tis umbra figuris.)

O. Lat. *so-* Possess. is attested by Festus and distinguished from O. Lat. *so-* Demonstr. (*sas* Fest. 476. 17 Th. ' sas ' Verrius putat significare eas, teste Ennio, qui dicat in lib. i. :

> uirginĕs nam sibi quisque domi Romanus habet sas,

cum suas magis videatur significare, sicuti ejusdem lib. vii. fatendum est eam significari, cum ait :

> nec quisquam sapientia quae perhibetur
> in somnis uidit prius quam sam discere coepit,

idem cum ait 'sapsam,' pro ipsa nec alia ponit in lib. xvi. :

> quo res sapsa loco sese ostentatque iubetque,

et Pacuvius in Teucro :

> nam Teúcrum regi sápsa res restíbiliet ;

sis Fest. 428. 11 Th. ' sos ' pro eos antiqui dicebant, ut Ennius, lib. i. :

> constitit inde loci propter sos dia dearum,

et lib. iii. :

> circum sos quae sunt magnae gentes opulentae,

lib. vii. :

> dum censent terrere minis, hortantur *i*be sos,

lib xi. :

> contendunt Graios, Graecos memorare solent sos,

interdum pro suos ponebant, ut cum per dativum casum idem Ennius effert :

> postquam lumina sis oculis bonus Ancus reliquit ;

§ 13.] THE PRONOUNS. DEMONSTRATIVES. 429

sam Paul. Fest. 33. 6 Th. antiqui dicebant . . . 'sam' pro suam). On the other hand Festus quotes in illustration of O. Lat. *puellus* part of a line of Ennius with monosyllabic *suos* (so spelt in the MSS. of Festus 324. 17 Th. and Paulus 325. 6):

> Poeni soliti suos sacrificare puellos,

and the MSS. of Lucretius spell *suo* (monosyll.) in i. 1022, v. 420:

> ordine se suo quaeque sagaci mente locarunt,

but *sis* in his quotation of Ennius' line, just mentioned, iii. 1025:

> lumina sis oculis etiam bonus Ancus reliquit,

so that monosyllabic *sŭŏs*, &c. of everyday speech, a scansion discarded by the Augustan poets as unsuitable to the dignity of poetry, were different forms from O. Lat. *sos*, &c. We have monosyllabic *suo*, *tuā* (see ch. ii. § 65) on the dedicatory inscription of Mummius, the conqueror of Corinth (*C.I.L.* i. 542, of 146 B. C.):

> uisum animo suo perfecit, tua pace rogans te.

Gen. Pl. *meum*, *tuum*, *nostrum* are attested by Priscian (i. p. 308. 23 H.), and occur along with *suum* (cf. *souom*, *C. I. L.* i. 588, of c. 81 B. C.) in the Republican Dramatists, &c. (see instances in Neue), though an instance of *vostrum* (*vestrum*) is difficult to find. It occurs in the elegiac epitaph of Ennius quoted by Cicero, *Tusc.* i. 15. 34 :

> hic uestrum panxit maxima facta patrum.

The particle *-met* is not found with the Possessives in Cicero or Caesar, and is not common in other authors. We have *meámet culpā*, Plaut. *Poen.* 446, *suămet*, *suŏmet*, *suāmet*, *suismet* in Sallust. It was thus more a particle for Personal than for Possessive Pronouns. But *-pte* is very common, though almost exclusively with the Abl. of the Possessive, which precedes its noun, e. g. *suapte manu*, Cic.; *meopte ingenio*, Plaut.; *nostrapte culpā*, Ter. *Phorm.* 766. (See examples and references to the native grammarians, in Neue, ii³. p. 373). Still the usual method of emphatic expression was *suā ipsius manu*, *meo ipsius ingenio*, *nostra ipsorum culpa* in literary Latin, and in colloquial speech *suus sibī*, *meus mihī*, &c. (§ 6). Examples of Possessives from the Umbro-Oscan dialects are, Osc. tuvai 'tuae,' suvam 'suam,' súvad 'suā,' suveís 'sui' (perhaps Pel. SVAD 'suā,' Osc. nistrus 'nostros'); Umbr. *tua* and *tuva* 'tua,' *tuer* and *tover* 'tui,' *vestra* 'vestrā.'

§ 13. III. DEMONSTRATIVES.

There were several Demonstrative Pronoun-stems in I.-Eur., some of which appear in some languages as Adverbs and Particles only, but as Pronouns in others. Thus the stem k̑e-, (k̑o-) appears in Latin in the Adverb *ce-* of *cĕdo*, 'give here,' and in the Particle *-ce* of *hujus-ce*, *illis-ce*, &c., but in Oscan eko- is the Pronoun in common use, which corresponds to the Latin *hic*; and on the other hand the stems ĝho-, ĝhe- (cf. ĝhĭ-) of Lat. *hi-c* (O. Lat. *hĕ-c*), *ho-c* appear as particles in O. Ind. ha, hí, Gk. οὐ-χί, ναί-χι.

The Latin Demonstrative stems are:

(1) I.-Eur. sŏ-, (sĕ-), which seems to have been originally confined to Nom. Sg. Masc. and Fem., a stem tŏ- being used elsewhere (O. Ind. sá and sás M., sá F., tád N., Gk. ὁ and ὅς M., ἡ F., τό, for *τοδ, N.) So- is the stem of O. Lat. *sam* 'eam,' *sos* 'eos,' *sum* 'eum'; to- of the second element of the compound *is-te* for **is-tŏ* M. (ch. iii. § 37), *is-ta* F., *is-tud* N., from the stem *i-, *ei- (see below), though some regard the first part as the stem es- (Umbr. es-to-?), a byform of the stem so- (se-), with *i* for *e* owing to the unaccented use of the Pronoun (ch. iii. § 18). By a further reduction of the vowel *iste* became in course of time *ste*.

(2) I.-Eur. ĝhŏ- (ĝhĕ-) supplies Lat. *hĭ-c* from O. Lat. *hĕ-c* M., *haec* for **hai-ce*, *hoc* for *hocc* for **hod-c*, 'this,' all augmented by the particle *ke. The *i* of *hic* is due to its unaccented nature (see ch. iii. § 18).

(3) I.-Eur. ol- (Lat. *ŭl-tra*, *ul-timus*; see ch. ix. § 56), a grade of the root ăl- (ăl-) of Gk. ἄλλος, Lat. *alius*, &c. (§ 29), with I.-Eur. sŏ- appended. The Nom. Sg. Masc. was *ol-sŏ, O. Lat. *olle*, or *ol-sŏs, O. Lat. *ollus*, Fem. *ol-sā, O. Lat. *olla*, with *ll* by the Latin phonetic law for original ls (cf. *velle* for **vel-se*), Neut. *ol-tŏd, which should have been in Latin *oltud, *ultud, but which was adapted to the Masc. and Fem. forms and became *ollud*. In class. Lat. owing to the unaccented use of the Pronoun apparently, though the change is a curious one, the ŏ became ĭ, *ille* (*illus* being dropped), *illa*, *illud*.

(4) From I.-Eur. ĭ- (ei-) and eyo- (O. Ind. id-ám N., im-ám Acc. M., Lith. jìs M., O. Sl. -jĭ, &c.) comes the Latin 'anaphoric' pronoun (i. e. the pronoun which refers to something previously mentioned), *ĭs* M., *ea* for *eyā F., *ĭd* N. Augmented by a combination of the particle *pĕ* (ch. x. § 1) with the Pronoun-stem so-, a combination which expresses 'self,' it forms the Latin Pronoun of Identity, *ipse* M. for **i-p(e)-sŏ* (ch. iii. § 37), *ipsa* F., *ipsum* N., in the O. Lat. also *ea-pse* with flexion of the first element of the Compound only, and *ea-psa* with flexion of both elements. Augmented by the particle -*dem* (ch. x. § 1) it

expresses 'the same,' *ī-dem* for *is-dem* M. (like *audio* for *aus-dio, ch. iv. § 151), *ea-dem* F. (For a fuller list of the I.-Eur. demonstrative stems which appear in Latin, see the chapters on the Adverb and the Conjunction.)

The Declension of these stems differed originally from that of Noun-stems, though it became more and more assimilated in course of time, and in Greek had come to be almost identical. The Nom., Acc. Sg. Neut. was formed, not like O-stem Nouns in *-m*, e.g. *dōnum*, but in *-d* (often written *-t*, ch. ii. § 73), e.g. *illud*, *istud* (but *ipsum* instead of *i-ptud), *id*; the Dat. Sg. of all Genders has *-ī*, older *-ei* (*-oi*), like the Locative *-ei* (*-oi*) suffix which appears in O-stem nouns such as *Cŏrinthī*, e.g. *illī*, *istī*, *ipsī*, *huic* for O. Lat. *hoi-ce*, *ĕī*, and *eī* for *ey-ei; the Gen. Sg. of all Genders is formed by the addition to this Dative-Locative form of the Gen. suffix *-ŏs*, *-us*, as in O. Lat. *nomin-us*, e.g. *illī-us*, *istī-us*, *ipsī-us* (with shortening of vowel before vowel, *illĭus*, &c. ch. ii. § 143), *hujus* (pronounced *hŭyyus) for *hoi-us*, *ejus* (pronounced *ĕyyus) which when unaccented became in the rapid utterance of ordinary speech *illīs, *istīs, *ipsīs, *hŭis, *eīs, e.g. *illī(u)s modi* Ter. *Ad.* 441, or in one word, *illīmodi*, with *s* dropped before *m* as in *primus* for *prismus (ch. iv. § 151). The Nom. Plur. Masc. suffix of O-stem pronouns, viz. *-oi*, was in Latin (as in Greek) borrowed by O-stem nouns (see ch. vi. § 40), and so is not distinctive of the Pronoun in Latin, but the Nom. Sing. Fem. (and Nom. Acc. Pl. Neut.) in *-ai* is a feature of the pronominal declension which remains in Latin *haec* for O. Lat. *hai-ce*, *illaec* for *illai-ce, *istaec* for *istai-ce, though without the particle *-ce* the two last take the *-a* of Noun-stems, *illa*, *ista* (and so *ipsa*). Before the Dat., Abl. Plur. suffix the stem appears with an appended i (O. Ind. té-bhyas, Goth. þai-m, Lith. té-ms, O. Sl. tĕ-mŭ), e.g. Lat. *hī-bus*; cf. *ī-bus* for *ei-bus (O. Ind. e-bhyás), but *quī-bus*, not *quī-bus. There is the same difficulty with Latin Pronouns as there is with Nouns (ch. vi. § 36), in assigning any 'Ablative' forms to an original Instrumental. Thus Osc. svai puh, 'si quo' (cf. Umbr. *pu-e* 'quo'), in the sense of 'sive' (but see ch. ix. § 5), suggests that Lat. *quō* in some of its uses may be an Instrumental case form and represent an original **q^{u}ō* not **q^{u}ōd*. But

Adverbial *eā* in *praeter-ea* is shown to be an Ablative by *aruorsum ead* on the S. C. Bacch. (*C. I. L.* i. 196. 24); cf. *eod die*, xi. 4766. The Locative had also the Dat. and Gen. functions, which we found to belong to the Loc. of the Personal Pronouns, e. g. Gk. μητέρι μοι (§ 2). Its suffix in O-stems was -ei or -oi, e. g. Gk. ποῖ, Dor. πεῖ, ἐκεῖ; the former is the suffix used in Oscan, e. g. eísei, which uses in the Fem. the Ā-stem Loc. suffix, e. g. eísaí.

§ 14. O. Lat. so-. Festus (428. 11 Th.) quotes *sos* for *eos* from three lines of Ennius (see § 12); elsewhere (476. 17 Th.) he cites *sam* for *eam*, *sapsa* for *ipsa* from the same author, and (426. 2 Th.) *sum* for *eum* : 'sum' pro eum usus est Ennius lib. i. :

astu, non ui, sum summam seruare decet rem,

et lib. ii. :

ad sese sum quae dederat in luminis oras.

[The gloss (Löwe, *Prodr.* p. 350) '*soc*': *ita* is doubtful; cf. Umbr. *e-soc* 'sic.'] But neither the Demonstrative *so-* nor the byform of the Reflexive Possessive *so-* (I.-Eur. swo-) are found in the conversational language of Plautus and Terence. The Neuter *tod is preserved in an O. Lat. Adverb *topper* for *tod-per, on which see ch. ix. § 7.

§ 15. The particle -ce. This particle belongs to the stems kŏ- (kĕ-), (also k̑i- and k̑yo-) [Gk. ἐκεῖ Loc. Advb., κεῖνος, Osc. eko- (often with this particle added, e. g. ekask, ' hae '), Lat. *cĭ-ter*, *cĭ-tra*, O. Ir. cē, 'on this side,' Engl. he, him, Germ. heu-te, Lith. szìs, 'this,' O. Sl. sĭ], and appears as an Adverb or Preposition in Latin. *cĕ-do*, 'give here' (more frequent in Terence than in Plautus), (O. Ir. cit 'da' (?)), and probably in Osc. *ce-bnust*, 'huc venerit.' It is said to be employed as an enclitic in other languages too, e. g. Arm. těr-s, 'this person,' Goth. þau-h, Engl. though (?). Its widespread use with Demonstratives in Latin and Umbro-Oscan (Lat. *hĭ-c*, *ĭlle*, O. Lat. *illīc*, *iste*, O. Lat. *istīc*, Osc. eísa-k and Umbr. erak, 'eā,' Osc. ekask, 'hae,' *exac*, 'hac, íú-k, ' eā,' and so on) may be compared with the Romance forms which have prefixed Lat. *ecce* to certain Pronouns and Adverbs, e. g. Fr. çà, ' there,' from *ecce-hac*; Fr. ci, Ital. ci, 'here,' from *ecce-hīc*; Fr. ce-, Ital. ciò, 'this,' from *ecce-hoc*; Fr. celle from *ecce-illa*, Fr. cette from *ecce-ista*, &c.), (cf. *eccillum uideo* and *eccistam uideo* Plaut.). It is the same tendency of expression which has reasserted itself; and it has its equivalents in vulgar English 'this here' for 'this,' 'that there' for 'that,' and so on. The usage with these forms with -*ce* differed in early and in classical Latin; for while in early Latin they are more or less arbitrarily used, in classical Latin their use is stereotyped in most pronouns. Thus class. Lat. *illīc* is the Adverb (Locative), while *illī* is the Dative (so *istīc* and *istī*); *hae* is the Nom. Pl. Fem., *haec* the Nom. Pl. Neut.; but in Plautus *illī* and *illīc*, *isti* and *istīc*, are equally Adv. and Dat. Pron., *hae* and *haec* (*illae* and *illaec*, *istae* and *istaec*) are both used for the Nom. Pl. Fem., *illa* and *illaec* (but only *haec*, *istacc*) for the Neut., while *illīc*, *istīc*, forms not found in class. Lat., are equivalents of *ille*, *iste*, *illuc* of *illud* (but only *istuc* in Terence, and perhaps also in Plautus). Still there are rules observed even so early as

§§ 14–16.]   THE PRONOUNS. DEMONSTRATIVES.   433

Plautus' time; for example, the Nom. Pl. Masc. of *hic, ille*, is before a word beginning with a vowel *hisce, illisce*, but before a consonant *hi, illi*, and in general the forms with *-ce* are found in use before an initial vowel, *hosce, hasce, hisce* Dat.-Abl., *illisce, istisce* Dat.-Abl., though before a consonant *horúnc, harúnc* are employed when the verse-ictus has to fall on the final syllable. In the Latin of ordinary conversation, as represented by the language of Plautus' plays, the particle *-ce* has not in these pronouns the worth of a syllable, a dissyllabic *haece*, &c. being proper to a more elevated style of poetry, e.g. Ennius, *A*. 294 M. haece locutus vocat, at the beginning of a hexameter line, so that *hacetenus* and *hocedie*, quoted as O. Lat. forms by Mar. Victorinus (9. 19 K.), must come from an Epic poem, or else from some official inscription or legal document. When the interrogative particle *-nĕ* is added, the *-ce* is preserved as a full syllable, e. g. *hoc-ci-ne, si-ci-ne* with *ĭ* not *ĕ*, because the vowel has now become medial and not final (ch. iii. § 39). The full form only is used in Plautus and Terence, but in later authors we find also, e. g. *hicne* (Stat. *Theb.* i. 189; other examples in Neue, ii³. p. 422). The Interjection *em* seems always to take the forms with *-c*, e. g. *em illic, em istoc*, but not the Interjection *ecce*, e. g. *ecc-illam, ecc-istam, ecc-am* (for *ecce *ham?*, § 16). Prefixed to *quidem* the *c* is not used in *hiquidem*, &c. of the Dramatists (but *istuccquidem*, not *istudquidem*, in Plautus, as *istuc* not *istud* in the simple Pronoun).

§ 16. Hic. The old form *hec* (for *ĝhĕ-ke) appears on the earliest Scipio epitaph in Saturnian metre (*C. I. L.* i. 32):

   héc cépit Córsica Alériaque úrbe,

which has, however, *e* for original *i* in *Tempestatebus*, and in the previous line shows the spelling *hic* (probably not the Adverb, for this would naturally be spelt *heic* in so early an inscription):

   cónsol, cénsor, aidílis híc fuet a[púd uos].

The spelling *hec* seems to be a retention of the old form, due to the emphatic position of the Pronoun at the beginning of the line, if it is not merely an example of the early interchange of *ĕ* and *ĭ* in the unaccented syllable (e. g. *aidiles* for *aedilis* on the still older Scipio epitaph, i. 31; see ch. iii. § 22). The Neuter Nom.-Acc. *hoc* should be **hocc* (for **ĝhŏd-ke), but though we are expressly told that it was so pronounced before an initial vowel, as in Virgil's line: hoc erat, alma parens, &c., there is no evidence that it was ever written with *-cc*, for Priscian's statement (i. 592. 22 H.): in antiquissimis codicibus invenitur bis c scriptum, is illustrated only by the form *hoccine*. *Hoc* is always long by position in Latin poetry, as *hŏc* Abl. is long both by nature and by position (for **hŏd-ce), and *hĭc* M. is distinguished from *hĭc* Adv. in Plautus and the early Dramatists (spelt *heic* in Plautine MSS., *Merc.* 307, *Men.* 375, &c.), though, like other long syllables, *hīc*, (*hōc*) may be shortened, when unaccented, after a short syllable by the Law of Breves Breviantes (ch. iii. § 42), e. g. *quid hĭc est?*, what is here?, (*quid hŏc est?*, what is this?). But in classical poetry *hic* M. is more often scanned as a long than as a short syllable; and the grammarians assert of *hic* in a line like Virg. *A*. xi. 16 : manibusque meis Mezentius hic est, that it was pronounced **hicc* (Mar. Victor. 22. 17 K.; other references in Neue, ii³. p. 411), just as they declare *hoc erat* to have been pronounced *hocc erat*; so that it is probable that *hĭc* M. came to be pronounced **hĭcc* by the Analogy of *hoc* (for **hodc) N., which was pronounced **hŏcc*. (One

F f

theory supposes *hic* with long *i* to have been a byform of *hic*, Rev. *Philologie*, 1892.)

In the Genitive we have, e.g. *hoiusce* on the Lex Repetundarum of 123-122 B.C. (*C.I.L.* i. 198. 56), *hoiusque* (i. 603, of 58 B.C. hoiusque aedis ergo), *hoius* Plaut. *Pseud.* 271 (*holus* A, *hujus* P), *huiius Most.* 664 (A, *hujus* P). Plautus is said not to admit the form with *-ce* (*Poen.* 1257) into the colloquial language of his plays. It occurs, however, in Terence (*Andr.* 439, *Phorm.* 827), and the phrase *hujusce modi* is very common in Cicero and Sallust.

In the Dative *hoic* occurs in the Lex Bantina of 133-118 B.C. (*C.I.L.* i. 197. 26 hoice leegei). Mar. Victorinus (12. 2 K.) quotes 'ex libris antiquis foederum et legum, qui etiamsi frequenti transcriptione aliquid mutarunt, tamen retinent antiquitatem,' the form *hoic*, a form affected in pronunciation by a few in the time of Velius Longus (first cent. A.D.) (p. 76. 3 K.). In later poetry *huic* (like *cüi* in the poetry of the first cent. A.D., § 25) is scanned as a dissyllable (twice in Statius, *Silv.* i. 1. 107; i. 2. 135; and even *hüic* in Ter. Maurus, l. 1375. For other examples, see Neue, ii³. p. 415). In the Accusative the oldest spelling *hon-ce* appears in the Lex Spoletina (*C.I.L.* xi. 4766 honce loucom nequs uiolatod), *hance* in the Lex Bantina (i. 197), *hoce* for *hocce* on the S. C. Bacch. of 186 B.C., where double consonants are written single, (i. 196. 26 atque utei hoce in tabolam ahenam inceideretis) (cf. i. 1291 itus actusque est in hoce delubrum Feroniae). We have *honc* on the Scipio epitaph (i. 32), in the Saturnian line :

hónc oíno ploírume coséntiont R[ómai],

'hunc unum plurimi consentiunt Romae.' Like *hunc* from *honc* M. is *huc*(c) from *hoc*(c) N., a spelling found in an inscription of somewhat irregular orthography (i. 603, of 58 B.C., ad huc templum), and in the Falisco-Lat. *huc dederunt* (Zvet. *I.I.I.* 72 a), but in classical Latin reserved to discriminate the Adverb from the Pronoun (see ch. ix. § 10). In the Abl. we have the full form *hoce*, e.g. in the magisterial proclamation cited above for *hoce* Neut. Acc. (*C.I.L.* i. 1291 ex hoce loco ; cf. Orell. 3857), *hace* in the Lex Bantina (i. 197. 7) and throughout the Lex Repetundarum (i. 198) [cf. *hocedie* and *hacetenus*, mentioned as O. Lat. forms by Mar. Vict. (9. 19 K.)]. (For the Locative, see the Adverb *hīc*, *heic*, ch. ix. § 10). Nom.-Acc. Plur. Neut. *haice* is found in the S. C. Bacch. (*C.I.L.* i. 196. 22 haice utei in couentionid exdeicatis, 'haec uti in contione edicatis') ; *haece* has been already cited from Ennius, *A.* 294 M. haece locutus ; *hīsce* or *heisce*, the Nom. Pl. Masc. form used by Plautus before a word beginning with a vowel, occurs without the particle in two inscriptions of no great antiquity (*C.I.L.* i. 1059 heis sunt horti ; i. 1071 heis sunt duo concordes), and, according to the grammarians, in Virg. *E.* iii. 102 :

his certe, neque amor causa est, vix ossibus haerent;

we have *heisce* further in some Capua inscriptions of 108-71 B.C. (*C.I.L.* i. 565 heisce magistreis Uenerus Iouiae ; i. 566 heisce magistreis Cererus ; i. 567 heisce magistrei ; i. 569 heisce mag. ; i. 573 heisc. magistr. ; *Not. Scav.* 1893. p. 164 heisce magistreis); cf. *C.I.L.* i. 1478 (Cartagena), heisce magistris. For examples of *haec* F., see Neue, ii³. p. 417 ; e.g. Virg. *G.* iii. 305 :

haec quoque non cura nobis leviore tuendae.

The form seems to have been used both by Caesar and Cicero. In the Genitive the full form is found in Cato, e.g. *harumce* (*R. R.* 139 harumce rerum ergo), and in the old oath administered to soldiers taking furlough (ap. Gell.

§ 17.] THE PRONOUNS. DEMONSTRATIVES. 435

xvi. 4. 4 nisi harunce quae causa erit, funus familiare, feriaeve denicales, &c.). In the Dat.-Abl. *hisce* is used by Plaut. and Ter. before vowels, by Cicero, &c. before consonants too (examples in Neue, ii³. p. 419 ; cf. *heisce* in the Lex Repetundarum, *C. I. L.* i. 198. 8 de heisce, dum, &c.), and the same holds of Acc. *hosce* and *hasce* (cf. *hasce sedes, C. I. L.* iii. 7230). The stem *hŏ-* (*hĕ-*) is augmented by *i* (like the Pronoun Datives Pl., O. Ind. té-bhyas, Goth. þai-m, Lith. té-ms, O. Sl. tĕ-mŭ), in Dat. Pl. *hibus* (obsolete in Varro's time; cf. Varro, *L. L.* viii. 72), attested by Priscian, ii. p. 10. 15 H. (and Charis. p. 54. 19 K.) in Plaut. *Curc.* 506 :

eodem hércle uos pono ét paro : paríssumi estis híbus,

like *ibus* (for **eibus*) in Plaut. *Mil.* 74 (see § 19) ; it follows the analogy of Noun Ā-stems in Dat. Sg. F. *hae* in Cato (*R. R.* 14. 3 hae rei materiem ... dominus praebebit). The Nom. Pl. M. *heis-ce*, already mentioned, is, like Nom. Pl. *eis* of the stem i- (§ 19), due to the addition of the Plural suffix *-s* to the already formed plural *hei, hi*. (On the declension of *hic* in Plautus, see Studemund in Fleckeisen's *Jahrbücher*, 1876, p. 57, and on its use, Bach in Studem. *Stud.* ii). *Hic* always refers to the first Personal Pronoun in Old Latin, and means 'this that is near me, that belongs to me,' &c. ; so *hic homo* for *ego* in the Comedians. It is sometimes used for *is*, to refer to something already mentioned, in the classical historians and Epic poets, but rarely earlier, e. g. Ter. *Phorm.* 866–9 has *hic* where *ibi* would be used by Plautus :

ád fores
súspenso gradú placide ire pérrexi, accessi, ástiti,
. . . hic pulchérrumum
fácinus audiui.

The Adverb *hŏ-die* (Falisc. foied) seems to show the bare stem (cf. ch. ix. § 5). A form without the enclitic has been claimed for O. Lat. *eccum*, e. g. sed eccum Palaestrionem, 'but see, here comes P.', Plaut., though the word may be analyzed into *ecce eum* as well as into *ecce *hum* (§ 15). On Faliscan he cupat, ' here lie,' ' here lies ' (for **hei* or for **heic* ?), and on Late Lat. *hi jacet*, see ch. ix. § 10. We have Dat. *hui* in late inscriptions (Henz. 7339, Rome ; perhaps also in *C. I. L.* x. 7297, Palermo).

§ 17. Iste. Examples of the various cases of this Pronoun with *-c(e)* in Plautus and Terence are given by Neue, ii³. pp. 398 sqq., *istic* Nom. Sg. M., *istaec* F., *istuc* N., *istīc* Dat., *istunc* Acc. M., *istanc* F., *istuc* N., *istoc* Abl. M., *istac* F., *istaec* Nom. Pl. F., N., *istosci-n* Acc. Pl. M., *istaec* N., also of the later curtailed form *ste* (cf. Ital. stasera, from Lat. (*i*)*stā serā*) as in the Itala *sta nomina*; see *I. F. Anz.* ii. 153) (cf. ch. iii. § 12 a. 4). (The declension of *iste* in Plautus is treated by Studemund in Fleckeisen's *Jahrbücher*, 1876, p. 57, and its use by Bach in Studemund's *Studien* ii.) *Iste* refers to the second Personal Pronoun, 'that of yours,' as *hic* to the first and *ille* to the third. In classical Latin, but probably not in the earlier literature, it came to acquire a contemptuous sense. We find *istāce* in an old ritual mentioned by Cato (*R. R.* 132. 2): Iuppiter dapalis, macte istace dape pollucenda esto. The influence of the Noun declension is seen in Late Lat. *isto* Dat. Sg. (Apuleius), *istum* Neut. (Vulgate) ; *istae* Dat. Sg. is the reading supported by the MSS. in Plaut. *Truc.* 790 (see Georges, *Lex. Wortf.* s. v.). In colloquial Latin *ecce* is sometimes prefixed to the Acc. case of *iste*, and forms a compound, e. g. *eccistam uideo* Plaut.

§ 18. Ille. Nom. *ollus* M., *olla* F. are the words used in two ancient formulae preserved by Varro (*L. L.* vii. 42), the announcement made at a 'funus indictivum,' viz. *ollus leto datus est*, and the proclamation by the herald at the comitia, in which *olla centuria* and not 'illa c.' was used, just as we keep up the old Norman French 'oyez, oyez' in Royal proclamations. The same Nom. Fem. seems to occur in the formula, also preserved by Varro (*L. L.* vii. 8), which the augur used on the citadel in marking off a 'templum,' though the reading of the MSS. is corrupt: ullaber arbos quirquir est ... ollaner arbos quirquir est. The immediate precursor of *ille*, the Nom. Masc. *olle*, is found in the Law of Servius Tullius, quoted by Festus (290. 15 Th.): si parentem puer verberet (MS. -it), ast olle plorassit, puer divis parentum sacer esto. A very old form of the Abl. Plur., *oloes*, is cited by Paul. Fest. 14. 17 Th.: 'ab oloes' dicebant pro ab illis; antiqui enim litteram non geminabant; and in the inscription on the Columna Rostrata (a restoration made in the Imperial period) we have the Gen. Pl. *olorom* (*C. I. L.* i. 195 praesente[d Hanibaled] dictatored ol[or]om) (cf. *ollarum* on an early inscr., Marini, *Act. Arv.* p. 233). Macrobius (iii. 9. 10) quotes an old ritual with *ollis legibus*, and on the Lex Furfensis of 58 B.C. (*C.I.L.* i. 603) the same phrase occurs, *olleis legibus* (followed immediately by *illeis regionibus*), similarly on the Lex Cornelia of 81 B.C. [i. 302. (1). 6 *olleis hominibus*]. Cicero in his *De Legibus* employs in the archaic language of his laws *olli* Dat.Sg., *ollis* Dat. Pl., *olli* Nom. Pl., *olla* Neut. Pl., *ollos* Acc. Pl. In the early Dramatists the form is not found, so that it must have been already relegated to the legal style by the beginning of the second cent. B.C. Ennius in his *Annals* knows only *olli* Dat. Sg. and Nom. Pl., and *ollis* Dat.-Abl. Plur. (*illi* and *illis* are apparently not used by him), and these are the only forms of *olle* found in his imitator, Virgil, and the later Epic poëts, while Lucretius confines himself to *ollis*. Quintilian mentions *olli* among the happy archaisms of Virgil (viii. 3. 25 'olli' enim et 'quianam' et '*moerus*' et '*pone*' et '*porricerent*' adspergunt illam, quae etiam in picturis est gratissima, vetustatis inimitabilem arti auctoritatem). The old spelling may have lingered longest in these forms through the analogy of the Adverb *ōlim*, which comes from the stem *ŏl-* (Umbr. *ulo* 'illuc') a byform of *ŏl-* (ch. iv. §§ 45, 59), and does not exhibit a substitution of *ōl-* for *ŏll-* (cf. ch. ii. § 127). Servius (ad *A.* i. 254 and v. 10) mentions a theory that *olli* in these two lines of Virgil was not the Dat. Sg. of the Pronoun, but an Adverb with the sense 'tunc' (cf. the glosses *olli* 'illi ... aut tunc'; *olli* 'ibi, interdum, illi, vel illinc,' *C. G. L.* v. 229. 4-5), and *olli-c* is quoted by Paul. Fest. 231. 2 Th. as an O. Lat. form of *illic* (cf. Lucil. *inc.* 152 M.: uelut olim Auceps ille facit, where the MSS. offer *olli*). The mispronunciation, '*oli*' for *olim*, censured in Prob. App. 199. 16 K., is merely an example of the tendency of Vulg. Lat. to omit final *-m*, like the mispronunciations '*pride*,' '*passi*,' '*numqua*,' '*ide*,' censured on the same page. From *olim* was formed Late Lat. *olitanus*, 'of former time,' and the curious phrase, found in Petron. 43 p. 29. 2 B. *olim oliorum*, 'long long ago.' [Another theory connects O. Lat. *ollī*, 'then,' with O. Sl. lani, 'last summer,' and analyzes *ollo-* into **ol-no-*, not **ol-so-* (*I. F.* iii. 264).]

For instances of the addition of the particle *-ce* to *ille* in its various forms in Plautus, &c. (*illīc* Nom. Sg. M., *illaec* F., *illuc* N., *illīc* Dat., *illunc* Acc. M., *illanc* F., *illoc* Abl., *illac* F., *illisce* Nom. Pl. M. (before a vowel), *illaec* F., *illaec* Neut., *illisce* Dat.-Abl. (before a vowel), see Neue, ii[3]. p. 427. In old rituals mentioned by Cato in the *Res Rustica* we find *illiusce* (139 illiusce sacri coercendi ergo), *illāce*

(132. 1 eius rei ergo macte hac illace dape pollucenda esto), *illisce* (141. 4 Mars pater, siquid tibi in illisce suouitaurilibus lactentibus neque satisfactum est, te hisce suouitaurilibus piaculo) ; and in legal formulae in Varro's *Res Rustica*, *illosce* (ii. 5. 11 illosce boues sanos esse noxisque praestari, . . . illosce iuuencos sanos recte deque pecore sano esse noxisque praestari spondesne ?), *illasce* (ii. 4. 5 illasce sues sanas esse). The Analogy of O-stem Adjectives has produced *illum* Neut. in Late and Vulgar Latin (e. g. in the Vulgate, *S. Marc*. iv. 35), *illae* Dat. in Cato (*R. R.* 153 and 154 illae rei) and Plaut. *Stich.* 560 (filiae illae ; so the MSS.), *illo* Dat. in late authors (e.g. Apuleius) ; to the Analogy of I-stems is due *illibus*, if it be a genuine form, ascribed to O. Lat. by Serg. *in Donat.* p. 547. 37 K.

Lucilius seems to have proposed the spelling *illi* Dat. Sg., *illei* Nom. Pl. (ix. 15 M.) :

'hoc illi factumst uni' : tenue hoc facies i.
'haec illei fecere' : adde e, ut pinguius fiat,

on which see ch. i. § 9. According to Diomedes (332. 11 K.) the strengthening particle -*met* is added to *ille*, and produces *illemet*.

In colloquial Latin *ecc-* was prefixed to the Acc. case of *ille* and formed a compound, e. g. *eccillum uideo*, Plaut. By prefixing *em* [the old deictic interjection, for which *ēn* was substituted in class. Latin (ch. x. § 19)], was formed *ellum*, *ellam* of the Comedians, which survives in the exclamation used in the dialect of the Abruzzi at the present day, ello (with open *e*).

On the pronunciations *illíus* and *illīus*, see Neue, ii². 518, and cf. below, § 22.

§ 19. Is. The stem ĭ- appears clearly in *is* Nom. Sg. M., *id* N. But the encroachment of the O-declension shows itself in the numerous cases formed from a stem ĕyŏ- (e. g. *eum* for *ĕyŏm Acc. Sg. M., which ousted the old Acc. *im* ; *eis* for *eyois Dat.-Abl. Pl., which ousted the old *ībus* for *ei-bus (O. Ind. e-bhyás), with stem augmented before the Dat. Plur. suffix as in *hībus* (§ 16). Another old I-stem form may be Abl. ī- in *ī-lico*, which is used in O. Lat. in the sense of 'in loco' [' in eo loco,' Non. 325. 6 M., who quotes Accius (*Trag.* 373 R.) :

īlico, inquam, habitáto, nusquam própius],

while the class. Abl. Sg. M. is *eō* for *eyōd. *Īlĭcō* is however better explained as *in sloco*, O. Lat. for *in lŏco* (see ch. ix. § 7).

It may be owing to this stem eyo- that we find the natural Fem. *iā replaced by *ea*. The Acc. form *iam* preserved in the MSS. of Varro, *L. L.* v. 166 and viii. 44 (cf *jam*, the Adverb, ch. ix. § 10. 8 ; *ium* on a Luceria inscr., *C. I. L.* ix. 782), may be a relic of the old and correct spelling, for there is no indication that there ever existed a spelling *eiam*, of which some have supposed it to be a corruption (cf. ch. ii. § 9). (In Umbr. we find *eam* Acc. Sg. F., eaf Acc. Pl. F.)

The particle -*ce* is not added to this Pronoun-stem until Late Latin, e. g. *ejuscemodi* (Jerome, *Epist.* 82. 6) by Analogy of *hujuscemodi*. [*Posteac* in Claudius' edict on the Anauni (*Hermes*, iv. 99, l. 13) is an isolated form.] But in Oscan we have iz-ic 'is,' iú-k ' ea,' íd-ík 'id,' and in Umbrian (with intervocalic s become r) er-ec 'is,' eđ-ek ' id,' &c., as well as forms like Osc. id-ad 'ad id,' Umbr. *eo* Acc. Pl. M., eu Acc. Pl. N., &c.

The various case-forms that call for notice are these. Nom. Sg. M. *eis* appears three times beside the usual *is* on the Lex Repetundarum. It may be a Nom. formed from the strong stem ei- (cf. Dat. Pl. *ī-bus*), but is as likely to be a mere mistaken use of *ei* for *ī* as in *seine* and *leiteras* on the same inscription, an inscription not older than the last quarter of the second cent. B.C. (On *eisdem*, see § 21.) In the Dat. Sg. *iei* is written in the Lex Rubria (*C. I. L.* i. 205) of 49 B.C. (beside *ei*), by the same orthography as *mieis*, *abiegnieis*, *aesculnieis* (see ch. ii. § 9, and cf. *iei* Nom. Pl., *ieis* Dat. Pl. below). (So Umbr. ie-pru, ie-pi). The Acc. Sg. M. was in O. Lat. *im* [Charis, 133. 1 K. 'im' pro eum. nam ita Scaurus in arte grammatica disputavit, antiquos 'im,' 'ques'. . . et declinari ita: is, ejus, ei, eum vel im; Paul. Fest. 73. 29 Th. 'im' ponebant pro eum, a nominativo is; ib. 33. 7 antiqui dicebant . . . 'im' pro eum; Gl. Philox. im : αὐτόν, εἰς αὐτόν ; Gl. Cyrill. αὐτόν, τοῦτον· im (MS. eim)]. Macrobius (i. 4. 19) quotes a law of the XII Tables : si nox furtum factum sit, si im occisit, iure caesus esto, and Cicero (*Legg.* ii. 24. 60) another : cui auro dentes iuncti escunt, ast im cum illo sepelirei ureiue se fraude esto (cf. Fest. 322. 13 Th.).

This form is often given as *em*, instead of *im*, perhaps by analogy of Noun I-stems which substituted the Acc. suffix of Consonant-stems for that of I-stems, e. g. *turrem* for *turrim* (see ch. vi. § 29); so Paul. Fest. 54. 20 Th. 'em' pro eum, ab eo quod est is. Another law of the XII Tables is cited by Porphyrio in his note on the 'licet antestari ?' of Hor. *S.* i. 9. 76 : si in ius uocat, ni it, antestamino, igitur em (MSS. en) capito; and Festus (298. 15 Th.) quotes, from a speech of Cato, si em percussi. Similarly the Adverb *im* (ch. ix. § 10) (cf. O. Ind. īm, originally an Acc. of the 'anaphoric' pronoun, then a mere particle), so written in Gl. Philox. im : λοιπόν, ἤδη, is mentioned by Paul. Fest. as *em* (53. 37 Th. 'em,' tum); the Acc. of an O. Lat. derivative of *is* in the sense of *idem* is *imeum* in the Philoxenus Glossary (imeum: τὸν αὐτόν), but *emem* in Paul. Fest. (54. 2 Th. 'emem,' eundem) [cf. the form in the Glossary of Placidus, emdem (MSS. hendem) : aeque, similiter, *C. G. L.* v. 73. 19].

The Dat.-Loc. Sg. *eyei, written *eiei*[1] (along with *ei*) in the Lex Repetundarum of 123-122 B.C. (*C.I.L.* i. 198), has in Plautus and the older poetry three scansions, *ēī, ĕī* and *êi*, in Ovid and later poets one, *ĕī* (cf. *rēī* and *rĕī* Plaut., *rēī* class., ch. vi. § 19). This *ĕyĕī* is thought to have become *ēī* much as -*ĕyĕs* became -*ēs* (e. g. Lat. *trēs* for I.-Eur. *trĕyĕs*, ch. iv. § 66), which in what we may call 'ceremonious' speech would preserve its full sound, and for a time resist the Latin tendency to shorten every long vowel before another vowel (ch. ii. § 143), while after the shortening set in, *ĕī*, through its unaccented character, would in the rapid utterance of everyday life become a mere monosyllable *êi*, as *tŭī* became *tūī*, &c. (§ 12). (Priscian, ii. p. 10. 2 H. speaks as if *ei* were as much a monosyllable as *huic, cui* in the ordinary pronunciation of his time). To suppose that *eiei* was pronounced *ey-yei as *Trŏia* was pronounced *Troy-ya, *pĕjor*, *pey-yor (ch. ii. § 55), does not account for the fact that these words are always scanned with the first syllable long in poetry, while *eum* for *eyom is never scanned with its first syllable long. (See below, however, on the doubt attaching to the antiquity of the scansion *ēī*.) But the Genitive *ejus*, formed by the addition of the Gen. suffix -*us* to

---

[1] This would most naturally be explained as a Reduplication of *ei*, and some explain *ēī, ĕī* as produced in this way. But the reduplicated form of the *i*-stem had in Latin the notion of identity, e.g. *em-em* (gl. eundem). Still the theory given above is far from certain.

§ 19.]   THE PRONOUNS. DEMONSTRATIVES.   439

the already formed Locative had this pronunciation *ĕy-yus [Caesell. ap. Cassiod. 206. 6 K. 'Pompeiius,' 'Tarpeiius' et 'eiius' per duo i scribenda sunt, et propter sonum (plenius enim sonant), et propter metrum. Numquam enim longa fiet syllaba nisi per i geminum scribatur]. This pronunciation is indicated by the spelling EIIvs on inscriptions (Neue, ii³. p. 376) and MSS. (Index to Studemund's Apograph of the Ambrosian Palimpsest of Plautus). The treatment of Nom. Pl. *eyei for *eyoi and Dat.-Abl. Pl. *eyeis for *eyois is not the same as that of Dat.-Loc. Sg. *eyei ; for we have in Plautus and the older poetry no instance of *ēī, ēis, but only ĕi or êi, ī, and ĕis or êis, īs. Where ĕ is followed by a long syllable it passed in unaccented usage into y by Synizesis, e. g. ĕŏ, ĕŏs, ĕŏrum Plaut. (not ĕŏs, &c., by Law of Breves Breviantes; see ch. iii. § 49).

The old Abl. Sg. -d is seen in eod die of the Lex Spoletina (C. I. L. xi. 4766), and in Adverbial ead of the S. C. Bacch. (i. 196. 25 quei aruorsum ead fecisent, 'qui adversum eā fecissent').

In the Nom. Pl. the spelling iei is, in accordance with the orthography of the first cent. B. c. (ch. ii. § 9), found on the Lex Cornelia of 81 B. c. [i. 202. (1). 7, along with ei], on the Lex Antonia de Termessibus of 71 B. c. (i. 204, passim, never ei), on the Lex Rubria of 49 B.C. [i. 205. (1). 48], on the Lex Julia Municipalis of 45 B. c. (i. 206. 24, usually ei), and in Varro (L. L. ix. 2 and 35). We have also i in MSS. (often confused with hi), and inscriptions (examples in Neue, ii³. p. 382); and the ei of Republican inscriptions (ibid. p. 383) admits of being taken to denote the simple long i-sound. Priscian (i. 298. 9 H.) seems to distinguish monosyllabic ii (for ī) from dissyllabic ēī, and similarly iis (īs) from ēīs, dii (dī) from dēī, diis (dīs) from dēīs (see Neue, l. c.). The Nom. Pl. Masc. form used in the Lex Bantina of 133–118 B. c. (i. 197) and the Lex Repetundae of 123–122 B. c. (i. 198) is eis (cf. i. 199. 29 ?), a form which appears in the earlier spelling eeis in the S. C. Bacch. of 186 B. c. (i. 196. 5, the only occurrence of a Nom. Pl. of is on this inscr.) (possibly in i. 185 ieis), and which should be compared with his (older heis) and hisce for hi, illis (illeis) and illisce for illi (§§ 16, 18). (The reading is in Pacuv. Trag. 221 R. ap. Charis. 133. 4 K. is very doubtful). In the Gen. Pl. the form eum, mentioned by Paul. Fest. (54. 20 Th. 'eum' antiqui dicebant pro eorum), is found once (usually eorum) on the Lex Julia Municipalis of 45 B. c. [C. I. L. i. 206. 52 eum h(ac) l(ege) n(ihil) r(ogatur)]. The orthography of the Dat.-Abl. Pl. resembles that of the Nom. Pl. We have ieis on the Lex Antonia de Termessibus, the Lex Rubria, the Lex Julia Municipalis, and other inscriptions of the first cent. B. c. (see Index to C. I. L. i.), but eeis in the early spelling of the S. C. Bacch. of 186 B.C. (i. 196), while the earliest form of all, eieis, reappears on an inscr. of circ. 100 B. c., the Epistula Praetoris ad Tiburtes (i. 201 de eieis rebus af uobeis peccatum non esse. Quonque de eieis rebus senatuei purgati estis, &c.). We have also is in MSS. (often confused with his) and inscriptions (Neue, ii³. p. 383), and the eis of Republican inscriptions (see Index to C. I. L. i.) admits of being taken as an expression of the sound īs. Priscian, as we have just seen, appears to distinguish iis (pronounced īs) from ēīs, as diis (pronounced dīs) from dissyllabic dēīs.

The O. Lat. I-stem Dat.-Abl. ibus is mentioned by Nonius (486. 11 M. 'ibus' pro is minus latinum putat consuetudo, cum veterum auctoritate plurimum valeat), who quotes Plautus, Mil. 74 :

    latrónes, íbus dínumerem stipéndium,

(the MSS. of Plautus have *latronisbus* and *latronibus*), and other instances from the Comedians. The Placidus Glossary (*C. G. L.* v. 75. 9) has 'ibus,' iis, illis, with quotation of the same line of Plautus. For other lines of Plautus where some editors read *ibus*, and for Lachmann's proposal to read *ībus* (though only *ībus*, *hībus* are known in Plautus, &c.) in certain lines of Lucretius, see Neue, ii³. p. 386.

The analogy of the Ā-declension has produced *eae* Dat. Sg. F., a form found in Cato (*R. R.* 142 quo modo uilicam uti oportet, et quo modo eae imperari oportet) and probably in Plaut. *Mil.* 348: hic eae proxumust, but not in use in Varro's time (*L. L.* viii. 51); so in Late Latin *eum* for *id* (see Georges, *Lex. Wortf.* s. v.). Cato also uses *eabus* (*R. R.* 152 facito scopas uirgeas ulmeas aridas ... eabus latera doliis intrinsecus usque bene perfricato), which is quoted from Cassius Hemina (pro eis differentiae causa in feminino) by Priscian (i. 294. 4 H.).

The obscure form *necerim* mentioned by Festus (160. 21 Th,) and Paul. Fest. (161. 11 Th.), and explained by them as 'nec eum,' has been supposed by some to be a wrong reading for *nece im* (*nec eim*?), by others to contain the Pronoun-stem es- of *iste* for *este (§ 13).

The scansion ĕī is allowed by most editors of Plautus in the Dat. Sg., but a certain example is very difficult to find, except in the Prologues; and these cannot be quoted as Plautine. Thus in *Rud.* 392 where editors end the line with : ne cópia esset éi, the MSS. have *eius*; in *Bacch.* 525 : mendácium ei díxit, only the Ambrosian Palimpsest has *ei*, the Palatine MSS. have *illi* [editors similarly prefer *illis* the (probable) reading of the Palimpsest to *iis* of the other MSS. in *Rud.* 219 : neque quícquam umquam illis prófuit]; in *Curc.* 544, for which we have only the testimony of the Palatine family of MSS. :

is Summanum sé uocari díxit; ei réddidi,

ēī might be easily emended to *ĕī ego*, and so on (e. g. *Cist.* 138). But the scansion ēī in the Dat. Sg. is certain for Terence, e. g. *Andr.* 443 :

dum licitumst éi dumque aetás tulit,

and is very common in Lucretius, e. g. vi. 674 :

scilicet et fluvius quivis est maximus ei
qui non ante aliquem majorem vidit;

so that ēī (like *supera* for *supra*, ch. iii. § 15) may be a form that is not genuinely antique. The Dat. Sg. is avoided by the Augustan poets, Horace for example in his Satires and Epistles using *ejus, eum, eo* but not *ei*; but in Ovid, *Halieut.* 33, we have ĕī (see Neue, ii³. p. 378), who, however, quotes as examples of ĕī from Plautus lines where it can be scanned ĕī in prosodical hiatus, e. g. *Curc.* 603 máter ĕī uténdum dederat, like mĕī honoris, *Aul.* 463).

§ 20. **Ipse.** We have already seen the particles -*pte* and -*pse* added to various pronouns to give the sense of 'self,' 'own,' e. g. *meopte ingenio* like *meo ipsius ingenio, sepse* like *se ipsam*. These particles seem to be composed of a particle pe- (pi-), seen in *quis-piam, quippe*, &c., and the Pronoun-stems so- and to-, which alternate in the I.-Eur. Demonstrative with its Nom. *sŏ M., *sā F., *tŏd N., and its oblique cases formed from the stem to- (te-). [Lat. -*pte* should therefore not be compared with Lith. pàts, 'self,' from patìs (Lat. *potis*, Gk. πόσις, &c.)]. Similarly we find the Pronoun-stem i- augmented by -*pse* in the Latin pronoun of identity, *i-pse*, which is further strengthened in the O. Lat.

form, or forms, given by Paul. Fest. as *ipsippe* (74. 37 Th. 'ipsippe,' ipsi, neque alii), in the Glossary of Philoxenus as *ipsipte* ('ipsipti': αὐτοί, C. G. L. ii. 87. 26 and 44) and *ipsipse* ('ipsipse': αὐτός, *ib.* 91. 35), and augmented by *-pte* in *eopte* (Paul. Fest. 78. 16 Th. 'in eopte,' eo ipso). The original declension of *ipse* we may suppose to have been : Nom. Sg. *is-pse (*i-pse*) M., *ea-psa* F., *id-ptod (*i-ptod) N., Acc. Sg. *im-ptom M., &c., until the inconvenience of the alternation of -p-so- and -p-to- brought about a 'levelling' process. (*Ipsud* is not found till late Latin, see Georges, *Lex. Wortf.* s. v.) The declension of both elements of the Compound may still appear in isolated forms indicated by the MSS. of Plautus, e.g. *eapsa, Cas.* 602 [so the Ambrosian Palimpsest (A), but *ea ipsa* in the Palatine MSS. (P), as in v. 604 for *eapse* of A] ; *eaepsae, Pseud.* 833 (*eaepse* A, *eae ipsae* P) ; *eumpsum non eampsam, Truc.* 133 (eum ipsum non eam ipsam A, eum ipsum non ea ase P) ; *eumpsum, Truc.* 114 (eum ipsum A, umsum P), which have been, perhaps unnecessarily, changed by editors to *eapse, eaepse, eumpse, eampse*.

The declension of the first element appears in *eapse*, mentioned by Paul. Fest. (54. 28 Th. 'eapse,' ea ipsa), and this and similar forms are sometimes preserved in the MSS. of Plautus (e. g. *eapse, Trin.* 974, *Truc.* 24, *Curc.* 161, 534), though usually *ipse* is written for the unfamiliar *-pse* and is sometimes declined, e. g. *eumpse, Pers.* 603 (eum ipse P) ; *eampse, Poen.* 272 (eam ipse P) ; *eapse, Cas.* 604 (so A, but ea ipsa P). (On *sirempse*, see ch. ix. § 8.)

In the Nom. Sg. Masc. we have a byform *ipsus* in O. Lat. (*ipsos* in a Law of Numa quoted by Paul. Fest. 4. 29 Th.: si quisquam aliuta faxit, ipsos Ioui sacer esto), which is the form used by the Comedians before a Reflexive Pronoun, e. g. *ipsus sibi, ipsus suam rem*, &c. *Ipse* is not a development of *ipsus*. The two are separate forms, *ipse* for *-sŏ, ipsus* for *-sos*, corresponding to the I.-Eur. byforms *sŏ and *sŏs* (O. Ind. sá and sás, Gk. ὁ and ὅς) (§ 13). The influence of O-stem Adjectives produced in Late Latin *ipso* Dat. Sg. (Apul.) and *ipsae* (Apul.), of I-stems *ipsibus* Dat. Pl., ascribed to O. Latin by Serg. *in Don.* (547. 37 K.). The Plautine *ipsissumus* (*Trin.* 988), like Aristophanes' αὐτότατος, seems to have been, in the form *ipsuma* or *ipsima*, actually used in the colloquial Latin of the Empire in the sense of *domina* (Petron. 69. p. 46. 16 B. ; 75. p. 51. 23 B., &c.). (On the colloquial pronunciation *isse, issa*, for *ipse, ipsa*, see ch. ii. § 81.) *Ipsemet* is found occasionally (see Georges, *Lex. Wortf.* s. v.).

§ 21. Idem. The affix *-dem* of *ĭdem*, O. Lat. *is-dem, tantī-dem, tantum-dem*, expressing the idea of 'precisely,' 'exactly,' is thought by some to have been originally *ĭdem*, for the Oscan equivalent of Latin *ĭdem* is ís-ídum. This *ĭdem*, formed by adding the affix *-em* to the Neut. Demonstr. *id*, is used in Latin as the Neut. of the Pronoun expressing 'the same,' but in O. Ind. ĭd-ám is the Neut. of the Demonstr. 'this,' much as the Acc. Masc. with the same affix, *ĭm-em, is used in O. Ind. (imám) as the Acc. Masc. 'this,' but was in O. Lat. the equivalent of *eundem* [Paul. Fest. 54. 2 Th. emem, 'eundem' ; Gl. Philox. imeum : τὸν αὐτόν ; cf. Gl. Plac. (h)emdem, 'aeque, similiter' ; these readings leave it doubtful whether the word was formed by adding the affix *-em* to the Acc. *im*, or, as seems more likely, by doubling the Acc.]. Priscian (i. 589. 14 H.) derives *ī-dem* from *is* and *dēmum*.

The Nom. Masc. is discussed by Cicero in a passage of somewhat uncertain text (*Orat.* xlvii. 157) : 'idem campus habet' inquit Ennius, et in templis EIDEM PROBAVIT ; at 'isdem' erat verius, nec tamen 'eisdem' ut opimius : male sonabat ' isdem' ; impetratum est a consuetudine, ut peccare suavitatis causa liceret. He seems to say that *ĭdem* [also written with *ei* for the long *i*-sound (ch. i. § 9) *eidem*] was the form in use, with *s* dropped with compensatory lengthening before *d* (ch. iv. § 151), but that some purists insisted on the spelling with *s*, *isdem* or even *eisdem*. (For examples of these spellings, e. g. *eisdem C. I. L.* i. 576 ; 577. (2). 9, 11, 13 ; 1468 ; 1470, &c., see Neue, ii³. p. 390.)

In the Dat. Sg. we have *ĕīdem* and *êīdem* (like *ĕi* and *êi*, § 19), but *ēidem* is not found. On later inscriptions *idem* is very frequent (examples in Neue, ii³. p. 390), and even *isdem* (Neue, *l. c.*), a confusion with the Nom. Sg., which had the (archaic) spelling *isdem*, but the pronunciation *ĭdem*. In the Nom. and Dat.-Abl. Pl., Priscian (i. 589. 29 H.) seems to distinguish *ēī-dem*, *ēīs-dem* from *iidem* (pronounced and usually spelt *ī-dem*), *iisdem* (pronounced and usually spelt *īs-dem*). (For instances of the spelling *ī-dem* and *īs-dem*, the usual forms, see Neue, *l. c.*) The *eidem* of Republican Inscriptions (Neue, *l. c.* ; e. g. *C. I. L.* i. 197. 17 and i. 202) may represent the pronunciation *ĭdem*. Like *eis*, older *eeis*, as Nom. Plur. of *is* (§ 19), we find *eisdem* Nom. Pl. (*C. I. L.* i. 198. 27 eisdem ioudices ; often in the phrase *eisdem probauerunt*, &c., e. g. i. 1149 ; i. 1187 ; i. 1192 ; cf. i. 1143), and in later inscriptions sometimes *isdem* (Neue, p. 394). In the Dramatists, &c. with a long second syllable we find the word pronounced with Synizesis, e. g. *ĕŏdem*, *ĕŏsdem*, &c. like *ĕŏ*, *ĕŏs* (§ 19). The influence of O-stem Adjectives is seen in the Late Latin forms *eodem* Dat., *eaedem* Dat. (very rare ; see Georges, *Lex. Wortf.* s. v.).

§ 22. **The Pronominal Gen. and Dat. Sg.** In the early Dramatists we find two scansions of *illius*, *istius*, *ipsius*, &c., (1) *illĭŭs*, *istĭŭs*, *ipsĭŭs*, *alterĭŭs*, &c., (2) *illī(u)s*, *istī(u)s*, *ipsī(u)s*, but not *illĭus*, *istĭus*, *ipsĭus*, &c., as in classical poetry. Examples of the second scansion are : *istī(u)s modi* (4 syll.) in Plaut. *Most.* 746 ; *Rud.* 321 ; Ter. *Heaut.* 387, &c. Another O. Lat. form of the Gen., fully attested by Priscian (i. 196. 22 H. ; i. 226. 16 H. ; i. 266. 3 H. ; i. 303. 21 H. ; ii. 8 H.) is with -*ī*, *illi*, *isti*, *ipsi*, e. g. *illi modi* and *isti modi* (Cato), *isti modi* Plaut. *Truc.* 930 (so the MSS.). This cannot be explained as an O-stem Adjective formation, for it is found with Fem. Nouns, e. g. *toti familiae* (Afranius), *isti formae* (Terence), and a Dat. Masc. like *illo*, *isto* is not found till Late Latin. It may be a relic of the Locative form which, as we have seen, was augmented by the Gen. suffix -*us* (-*os*) to form these Pronoun Genitives in -*ius* ; but it is also conceivable that it is a doublet which has arisen out of the contracted form *illī(u)s*, *istī(u)s*, &c. in certain combinations. A word-group like *istī(u)s-modi* would be pronounced *istīmodi*, as naturally as O. Lat. *dusmus* became *dūmus*, or *prismus became *prīmus*, or *is-dem*, *īdem* ; and a large number of Priscian's examples of this Gen. in -*ī* show the Pronoun in combination with *modus*. Similarly *alī(u)s-rei* would become *alī-rei*, as *dis-rumpo* became *dīrumpo* ; cf. Priscian's examples, *aliirei causa* (Caelius), *nulli rei* (Cato). The byforms *illī*, *nullī*, &c. having been produced in such combinations would push their way into other combinations too, e. g. *tam nulli consili* (Ter. *Andr.* 608). They do not however seem to be found before a vowel initial.

The Dative in -*ī* is, as we have seen, undisturbed by the influence of the O-stem Noun declension till Late Latin, e. g. *illo*, *isto*, *ipso* (Apuleius). But a Dat. Fem. in-*ae*, attested for O. Lat. by Priscian (i. 197. 12 H. ; i. 226. 18 H.), is not unknown in early authors, e. g. *illae rei*, Cato (*R. R.* 153 and 154). (For a list of examples of these Gen. and Dat. forms, with references to the passages of grammarians dealing with them, and for a fuller discussion of the whole subject, see Luchs in Studemund's *Studien*, i. pp. 319 sqq.)

§ 23. IV. **RELATIVE, INDEFINITE, AND INTERROGATIVE PRONOUNS.** The I.-Eur. Relative-stem *yo- (O. Ind. yás, Gk. ὅς) does not supply the Latin Relative, which shows the stem *qᵘo-, a stem originally proper (with *qᵘi-, *qᵘu-) to the Interrogative and Indefinite Pronouns (O. Ind. kás, kú-tra, 'where?,' Gk. τίς, ποῦ, O. Ir. cia, W. pwy, Goth. hvas, Engl. who?, Lith. kàs, O. Sl. kŭ-to; O. Ind. cit Neut., Gk. τις, &c.), but used also as a Relative (Engl. who, &c.). I.-Eur. *qᵘo-, *qᵘi-, *qᵘu- appear in the Latin *quis?*, *si-quis*, *qui?*, *ali-cubi*, &c. (Umbro-Oscan pis, Osc. píd Neut.). We may roughly distinguish *qui* as the Relative, *quis* as the Interrogative and Indefinite Pronoun, though the stems frequently overlap, e. g. in the Latin of Cato and the earliest inscriptions *ques* is the Nom. Pl. of the Indefinite, *quī* (*quei*) of the Relative; but in class. Lat. both are *quī*. In the Italic languages (as in Celtic and elsewhere) a curious declension of the Relative (and Interrogative) was in vogue, a case-form of the Relative-stem being prefixed to a Demonstrative, like modern Gk. ποῦ τόν for ὅν in such a sentence as αὐτὸς εἶνε ὁ ἄνδρας ποῦ τὸν εἶδα, that is the man whom I saw. Thus an Abl. Sg. Fem. of the Relative is in Oscan púllad, which is compounded of the Relative-stem po- (Lat. *quo-*) (either the bare stem or a case-form) and *úllad (Lat. *ollād*), the Abl. Sg. Fem. of the Demonstrative ollo-; another is *poizad*, a similar compound with the Abl. Sg. Fem. of the Demonstrative eiso-. The old spelling of the Dat. Sg. of Lat. *qui*, viz. *quoiei*, shows it to be a compound of this kind, having for its second element the Dat. Sg. of *is* (O. Lat. *eiei*), *quō-eiei*; and Gen. Sg. *quoius* (class. *cujus*) will consequently represent *quo-eius*. Whether this method of declension was used in other cases in Latin does not appear. Another feature of the Italic Relative is its tendency to append the Pronominal particle i (cf. Gk. οὗτος-ί), e. g. Umbr. *poi* Nom. Sg. M., *porsi* (*pođi) N.; Lat. *quī* for *qᵘo-i (O. Lat. *quoi*).

The Latin Interrogative-Relative has a Possessive *cujus -a -um*, older *quoius -a -um*, which is very frequent in Plautus and Terence, and is found in Republican inscriptions (e. g. in the

444   THE LATIN LANGUAGE.   [Chap. VII.

Lex Repetundarum, i. 198. 5, 10, 29 *quoium nomen* and *quoiaue in fide*), in Cicero (e.g. *Verr.* II. i. 54. 142 *cuja res*), and Virgil (*E.* iii. 1 *cujum pecus*). Virgil's use of the word was objected to by purists, apparently through an idea that *cujus -a -um* was a vulgar inflexion of the Gen. Sg. of the Pronoun, an idea which the occurrence of the word in Cicero and in State inscriptions disproves (§ 11). It is rather formed by means of the Adjectival suffix -yo- (ch. v. § 4) from the stem *q^uo-, *q^uo-yo-, as *meus* (stem *me-yo-) from the stem *me- (§ 1). It is not till Late Latin that we find the particle *-ce* added to the Relative-Interrogative Pronoun in *cujuscemodi* (Apuleius, &c.), a word coined after the type of *hujuscemodi*.

§ 24. Stems q^{u}i- and q^{u}o-. In O. Lat. there is a usage of *quis*, possibly as a Relative, but rather in the sense of *siquis* or *quicunque*; e. g. in an old treaty quoted by Festus to illustrate O. Lat *nancitor* for *nanciscitur* (170. 25 Th.): pecuniam quis nancitor, habeto; in an old plebiscitum (Fest. 322. 11 Th.): eum quis uolet magistratus multare, dum minore parti familias taxat, liceto; on a public notice affixed to a grove at Luceria (*C. I. L.* ix. 782): quis uolet (other examples from Cato and from Cicero's laws are given by Neue, ii³. p. 430, e.g. Cato, *R. R.* 147 dominus uino quid uolet faciet). Cf. O. Lat. *necumquem* explained by 'nec umquam quemquam' (Fest. 162. 22 Th.; Paul. Fest. 163. 12 Th.). (So Umbr. *pisest totar Tarsinater* 'quisquis est civitatis Tadinatis,' Osc. *pis hafiest* 'qui habebit'). In the Dramatists *quis* is the Fem. of the Interrogative, *quae* cf the Relative (cf. Prisc. ii. 8. 21 H. quis etiam communis esse generis putauerunt vetustissimi, sicut apud Graecos τίς), e. g. Plaut. *Pers.* 200 quis haec est, quae me aduorsum incedit? (other examples in Neue, p. 441), but the distinction of *qui* Adj., and *quis* Pron. in questions, e.g. *qui homo venit?* and *quis venit?* is hardly observed, the habit of Plautus being rather to use *quis* before a vowel, *qui* before a cons. (see Neue, p. 431, and *B. P. W.* xiii. 278; similarly Cornificius seems to write *siqui* before an initial *s*, otherwise *siquis*, e.g. *siqui suadebit*, iii. 5. 8). The I-declension form of the 'Abl.' Sg. *qui*, e. g. *quicum*, is Relative as well as Interrogative and Indefinite; e. g. Ter. *Ad.* 477 psaltriam parauit, quicum uiuat; *C. I. L.* i. 200 queiue ab eorum quei emit (see Neue, pp. 455 sqq.). But the Nom. Plur. *ques*, attested by Charisius (91. 16 K. ut duces, ducibus, mores, moribus, et 'ques,' quibus; 158. 21 veteres nominatiuum pluralem 'ques' dixerunt regulam secuti, unde etiam dativus mansit in consuetudine), Festus (348. 23 Th.), Priscian (ii. 9. 13 H.) &c., seems to have been confined to the Interrogative and Indefinite use. Thus Cato began his *Origines* with the words: siques homines sunt, quos delectat populi Romani gesta describere; on the S. C. Bacch. (*C. I. L.* i. 196) we have: sei ques esent, quei sibei deicerent necesus ese Bacanal habere, 'siqui essent, qui sibi dicerent necesse esse Bacchanal habere'; and a line of Pacuvius (*Trag.* 221 R.) runs:

    ques súnt? ignoti, néscioques ignóbiles;

(other examples in Neue, p. 466).

The I-declension Neuter *quia* survives only as an Adverb or Conjunction, e.g. O. Lat. *quianam*, 'why?,' like *quidnam*; the Gen. *quium* can hardly be ascribed to Cato on the mere testimony of Servius (ad *A*. i. 95 : denique Cato in Originibus ait: si ques sunt populi. Et declinavit 'ques,' 'quium' ut 'puppes,' 'puppium'), for this remark only implies that Cato's *ques* was an I-stem formation. The I-stem Dat. *quĭbus* supplanted the O-stem *quīs* (older *queis*) in the Relative, though the O-stem form is by no means uncommon (see a long list of instances in Neue, ii³. p. 469, e.g. Plaut. *Most.* 1040 :

quis méd exemplis hódie eludificátus est).

§ 25. **Case-forms.** The original Nom. Sg. Masc. of the Relative *quo-i* (stem quŏ- with affix -i of Gk. οὗτοσ-ί, &c.) [Osc. púi(?), Umbr. *poi*; the Umbr. shows this affix also in Nom. Pl. Masc. pur-i, Acc. Pl. Fem. *paf-e*, &c.] is probably intended by the spelling *qoi* of the very ancient Dvenos inscription [Zvet. *I. I. I.* 285 qoi med mitat, 'qui me mittat (mittet)].' The weakened form *quei*, due to the unaccented use of the Relative (ch. iii. § 18), is common on inscriptions of the Republic, from the Scipio epitaph (in Saturnians) of c. 200 B. C. (*C. I. L.* i. 30) :

cónsol cénsor aidílis queí fuit apúd uos,

to the Lex Julia Municipalis of 45 B. C. (i. 206), which has *quei* far more frequently than *qui*; also in the MSS. of Plautus, &c. (see instances in Georges, *Lex. Wortf.* s. v.). The Fem. of the Indefinite Pronoun in its Adjectival use followed the Adjective Declension in taking usually the suffix -*a* in class. Latin, e. g. *siqua causa est* (but *seiquae causa erit* on the Lex Repetundarum, *C. I. L.* i. 198. 37 ; *si quae lex* on the Lex Agraria, i. 200. 41 ; and in Plautus *numquae causast quin*, &c. ; see Neue, ii³. p. 445). Gen. Sg. *quoius* appears in the Saturnian Scipio epitaph of c. 200 B. C. (*C. I. L.* i. 30) :

quoíus fórma uirtútei parísuma fúit,

in the Lex Repetundarum (i. 198), and other inscriptions, and in the MSS. of Plautus, Varro, &c. (see Georges, s. v. ; Neue, p. 450). When the *oi* sank to *ui*, the *qu* by a law of Latin phonetics became *c* (ch. iv. § 137) ; hence *cujus* (pronounced cüy-yus, ch. ii. § 55), a pronunciation indicated by spellings like *cuiius*, *cuiIus* (Neue, p. 451). (On monosyllabic *quoi(u)s* in *quoi(u)smodi*, &c., in the Dramatists, and *quoi* in *quoiquoimodi*, *cuicuimodi* in Cic., &c., see § 22). The oldest form preserved of the Dative is *quoiei* of a Scipio epitaph of c. 130 B. C. (*C. I. L.* i. 34) in a Saturnian line referring to the short life of the deceased :

quoíei uíta defécit nón honos honóre,

in the Lex Repetundarum of 123-122 B. C. (i. 198. 10, usually *quoi*), and in the Lex Agraria of 111 B. C. (i. 200. 68, usually *quoi* ; cf. *quoieique*, ll. 3. 6. 32. 45. 99) ; though the dissyllabic Dative seems not to occur in Plautus (it is read by some editors in *Trin.* 358. 558, &c. ; see Brix ad locc.), and so cannot have been used in the ordinary conversation of his time. The common form in use on Republican inscriptions is *quoi* (see Index to *C. I. L.* i.) ; the Lex Julia Municipalis, for example, of 45 B.C. (i. 206) has always *quoi*, never *cui*, as it has always *quoius*, never *cujus*, and always, except in two instances, *quei* for *qui* (so *quoi* in the Comm. Lud. Saec. of Augustus' reign). And Quintilian (i. 7.

27) tells us that in his youth *quoi* was the spelling. [Cf. Velius Longus (first cent. A. D.), p. 76. 3 K. itaque audimus quosdam plena oi syllaba dicere 'quoi' et 'hoic' pro cui et huic.] In late poetry *cui* is a dissyllable, *cŭĭ*, a scansion which is found as early as Seneca, Juvenal, and Martial, e. g. Mart. i. 104. 22 sed norunt cui serviant leones (examples in Neue, p. 454). Acc. *quem* has *-em* for *-im* (Osc. *pim*) by analogy of Noun I-stems which usually substituted the Cons.-stem *-em* for the I-stem *-im*, e. g. *turrem* (ch. vi. § 29). As to the Abl. Sg. we have not sufficient means of deciding, owing to the absence of sufficiently old inscriptions, whether and in what uses *qui*, O. Lat. for *quo*, was an Abl. (from *quĭd*), a Locative (from *quei*), or even an Instrumental (from *quī*). But the spelling *quiquam* ('in any way') on the S. C. Bacch. (l. 12), an inscr. on which original *i* and original *ei* seem to be kept distinct, goes against the Locative theory, unless indeed it is a mere mistake for *quisquam* (see § 28). The spelling *quei* on the Lex Agraria of 111 B. C. (*C. I. L.* i. 200. 17 queiue ab eorum quei emit) merely expresses the sound *quī* (see ch. i. § 9). This *quī*, byform of *quō*, *quā*, occurs in Virgil (A. xi. 822):

Accam ex aequalibus unam,
quicum partiri curas.

It was not in living use in the time of Servius (fourth cent. A. D.) (*in Donat*. p. 411. 1 K. nam dicimus 'a quo' venisti et 'a qui' venisti; sed 'a qui' in usu esse desiit). Already in Terence *quicum* is not so frequent as in Plautus. In the early authors *qui* is used: (1) as an ordinary Abl., e. g. Plaut. *Capt*. 828 qui hómine nemo uíuit fortunátior; *Bacch*. 335 sed quí praesente id aúrum Theotimó datumst?; but especially (2) as an Abl. of the instrument, e. g. Plaut *Men*. 391 quis istést Peniculus? qui éxtergentur báxeae?, 'what Mr. Brush do you mean? one to clean shoes with?'; Varro, *R. R*. ii. praef. 3 frumentum qui saturi fiamus. In this capacity it passes into a mere Adverb like *ut*, and is used even with a plural noun, e. g. Plaut. *Stich*. 292 quadrigas qui uehar; *Pseud*. 487 (uiginti minas) quas meo gnato des, qui amicam liberet; (3) as an Adverb with the sense of *quomodo*; e. g. *qui fit ut*?, a phrase in common use in classical Latin; Ter. *Adelph*. 215 qui potui melius?; (4) as an enclitic Particle, e. g *hercle qui, edepol qui, utinam qui* (Plaut.), a usage surviving in classical *at-qui*. (For a fuller list of examples, see Neue, ii³. pp. 455 sqq.; cf. below, ch. x. § 5.) The Nom. Pl. Masc. is written *quei* on Republican inscriptions (see Index to *C. I. L.* i.), this being the weakening of an original *quoi*, due to the unaccented nature of the Relative (ch. iii. § 12 a. 5), e. g. i. 196 sei ques esent, quei sibei deicerent necesus ese Bacanal habere. (On *ques* Nom. Pl. of *quis* in O. Lat., and on *queis* and *quīs*, Dat.-Abl. Plur., from *quois*, see above, § 24.)

§ 26. **The stem q^uu-.** Corresponding to Umbr. pu-fe, Osc. pu-f, 'where' (O. Ind. kúha, O. Sl. kŭde, from I.-Eur. *q^uudh-), is Lat. *-cŭbĭ* of *ălĭ-cubi*, 'somewhere,' *sī-cubi*, 'if anywhere,' *nē-cubi, num-cubi*, &c., with *cu-* instead of *quu-* by the same phonetic law of the Latin language that has made *quincu-plex* out of *quinquu-plex* (ch. iv. § 137) (cf. Vulg. Lat. *nescio-cube*, Probi App. 199. 16 K.), and clearly connected with the Interrogative, Indefinite, and Relative Pronoun-root (see ch. x. § 1, on the existence of parallel stems of Pronouns in -o, -i, -u). But apart from compounds the Latin Adverb is *ubi*. Similarly the *-cunde* of *ălĭ-cunde* (*aliquonde* is written in Plaut. *Pseud*. 317 in the Ambr. Palimps.; so Caesellius ap. Cassiod. 202. 28 K. aliquonde per quon debet scribi), *si-*

cunde, nē-cunde, wants initial *c-* in the simple form *-unde*. According to Schmidt (*K. Z.* xxxii. 405) this Latin initial *u-*, internal *cu-*, represents I.-Eur. *qʷu-, a parallel stem of qʷo-, qʷi- (cf. § 23). (For another possible explanation of this loss of the initial guttural, see Brugm. *Grundr.* i. § 431 *c*.) The Latin Interrogative and Indefinite Pronoun *üter*, 'whether of two' (on the suffix -tero-, see ch. v. § 18) shows a similar relation to O. Ind. kútra, 'whither' (stem *qʷutro-, *kutro-), Osc. potro-, ' whether of two ' (stem *qʷotro- or *kwotero- ; both derivatives of a stem *qʷe-t(e)ro- or *kwe-t(e)ro- ?). (On other Latin Adverbs beginning with *u-*, derived from the Interrogative root, and wanting an initial guttural, see ch. ix. § 10.) Ritschl's proposal [based on *Trin.* 934, where there is a manuscript corruption *cubitus* for *ubi tus* (gignitur)] to read *cubi*, &c., in some passages of Plautus, has not met with approval (*Opusc.* iii. 135).

§ 27. **The Possessive *cujus*.** The case most frequently in use in Plautus and Terence is the Nom. Sg. Fem., e. g. Plaut. *Trin.* 45 quoia hic uox prope me sonat ? ; cf. Cic. *Verr.* II. iii. 7. 16 ne is redimeret, cuja res esset ; *ib.* 27. 68 Apronius certiorem facit istum, cuja res erat. The Plural is very rare, Plaut. *Rud.* 745 :

árgentum ego pro istísce ambabus quoíae erant dominó dedi,

Trin. 533, with *quoium* for *cujorum*, Gen. Pl. (?) (*cuium* A, *quoium* B ; some read *quorum*) :

necúnquam quisquamst, quoíus ille agér fuit,
quin péssume ei res uórterit, quoiúm fuit,
alii éxolatum abiérunt, alii emórtui.

With the suffix -āti-, denoting the country of one's birth (ch. v. § 45), we have *cujās*, O. Lat. *quoiatis*, 'what countryman ? ' 'belonging to what country ? '

§ 28. **Other derivatives.** *Ălĭ-quis*, some one, is a compound of the stem *ali-*, some (connected with *ălio-*, other)[1] and the Indefinite Pronoun, like *ali-cubi*, somewhere, *ali-cunde*, &c. An O. Lat. Nom. Pl. *aliques* is mentioned by Charisius (159. 7 K.). *Ec-quis* has been explained as nothing else than *et quis*, with *c* for *t* by the same phonetic law as reduced **sit-cus* (cf. *sitis*) to *sic-cus* (ch. iv. § 159), but it is more likely to come from the pronominal stem *ĕ-* (used as a prefix in *e-nos*, Umbro-Osc. e-tanto-, &c.) with the appended particle *-ce* (without this appendage in *e-quidem*, ch. x. § 6, and in *ĕ-quis*, a byform of *ec-quis*, in Plaut.). The Neut. *ecquid* in Plautus often sinks into a mere conjunction, e. g. *ecquid placent*? *Most.* 906, &c.

Quādam for **quis-dam* (like *īdem* for *is-dem*, § 21) appends the particle *-dam* to the Indefinite Pronoun. The Nom. Plur. Masc. is not found in Plautus, and scarcely indeed in any of the older authors. We have *quesdam* Acc. Pl. in Accius, *Trag.* 477 R. *Quăvis* (cf. Umbr. *pis-her* from the verb heri-, 'to wish ') may stand for **quĭs-vis*, ' any you please,' ' whosoever you please ' (cf. O. Lat. *quis nancitor*, ' whosoever obtains,' § 24), with the same loss of *s* before initial *v* in a Compound as *dīvello* for **dīs-vello* (ch. iv. § 151), and *quĭlubet*, for **quĭs-lubet*, like *dīligo* for **dīsligo* (*ib.*), as well as for *quī-vis*, *quī-lubet*. The I-declension Abl. *quĭuis* appears in Plaut. *Stich.* 627 : quícumuis depúgno multo fácilius

---

[1] *aliquis alius* is not found in Plautus, though it occurs in Terence.

quam cúm fame. *Quī-cum-que*, O. Lat. *quei-quom-que* (*C. I. L.* i. 197. 5; 200. 50; 202, &c.), had probably a byform **quis-quom-que*, to judge from Nom. Pl. *quescumque* n Cato (*Orig.* ii. fr. 34 J. quescumque Romae regnauissent). The latter part of the word is probably the Adverb *quum* (O. Lat. *quom*), when, with the enclitic particle *-que*, so that *-cumque* means literally 'whenever' (see ch. ix. § 10. 7). In O. Lat. *quisque* is used in the sense of *quicunque*, e. g. quemque offendero, Plaut. *Capt.* 798, the particle *-que* (O. Ind. ca in kaś-ca, 'whoever,' &c., Hom. Gk. τε in ὅς τε, Goth. -h in hvō-h) giving to a word the sense of our 'ever' in 'whoever,' 'whenever,' &c. (see ch. x. § 2); but has in classical Latin the sense of 'each.' It is fem. as well as masc. in O. Lat., e. g. Ter. *Hec.* 216 quisque uostrarum; so *quemque* Acc. Sg. F. in Plaut. *Pseud.* 185. Another expression for 'whosoever' is *quisquis* (Osc. pispis, of which the Neut. *pitpit* is mentioned by Paul. Fest. 263. 8 Th.), (τίστις occurs in an Old Gk. inscr., *Mon. Antichi* i. 3. p. 594), a doubling of the Indefinite Pronoun[1]. We have *quisquis* Fem. in O. Latin, e. g. Plaut. *Cist.* 610 mulier quisquis es (cf. Nonius, 197. 30 M.). The Neuter *quicquid*, a byform of *quidquid*, shows the same assimilation of *d* (*t*) before a guttural as *accurro* for *adcurro* (ch. iv. § 160). The shortened form of the Gen. Sg. of *quis*, current in ordinary pronunciation when not specially emphasized, viz. *quoi*(*u*)*s*, *cui*(*u*)*s*, (§ 22), appears without its final *s* in Cicero's *cuicuimodi*; and the I-stem Ablative *quiqui* occurs more than once in Plautus in the phrase *cum eo, cum quiqui*, anyhow, at any cost, lit. 'with that thing or with whatsoever thing' (*Poen.* 536. 588). A curious passage, *Cas.* 523 :

> séd facito dum, mérula per uorsús quod cantat, tú colas :
> 'cúm cibo, cum quíqui' facito ut uéniant,

suggests that Roman children interpreted the alarm-note of the blackbird into the words : cum cibo, cum quiqui, *sc.* veni, 'come along! food or no food.' (*Class. Rev.* vi. 124.) *Quis* prefixed to the Adverb *quam*, *quis-quam* had the sense of 'any,' and was used especially in negative sentences. Examples of its use as Fem. in O. Lat. are Ter. *Eun.* 678 nostrarum numquam quisquam uidit ; Plaut. *Rud.* 406 :

> neque dígniorem cénseo uidísse anum me quémquam,

and of the I-declension Abl., Plaut. *Pers.* 477 nec satis a quiquam homine accepi [see § 25 on *qui-quam* Adv., 'anyhow' (?), of S. C. Bacch.: neue pro magistratud neque uirum neque mulierem quiquam fecise uelet, like *nēquī-quam*, in vain, lit. 'not anyhow,' always so spelt in the Ambrosian Palimpsest of Plautus]. Another compound of the Indefinite Pronoun, *quis-piam*, some, the formation of which was obscure to the Roman grammarians (Festus 338. 28 Th. 'quispiam' quin significet aliquis, et 'quaepiam' aliquae, similiterque alia ejusdem generis, ut dubium non est, ita unde sequens pars ejus coeperit, inveniri non potest), may be a compound of **quis-pe*, of which *quippe* for **quīpe* is an Adverbial case-form (ch. x. § 7), with *jam*, as *nunciam* of *nunc* with *jam* (ch. iv. § 67). Corresponding to *-quam*, *-piam* of Lat. *quisquam*, *quispiam* is Oscan *-um* of *píd-um* 'quidquam,' *pieis-um* 'cujuspiam.'

---

[1] So *quantus quantu's*, 'every inch of you,' Ter. *Adelph.* 394; *quantum quantum*, Plaut. *Poen.* 738; *quaequalis* in a poetical inscr., *C. I. L.* vi. 6314.

§ 29.] THE PRONOUNS. PRONOMINAL ADJECTIVES. 449

§ 29. V. THE PRONOMINAL ADJECTIVES. These are:
(1) *ălius*, I.-Eur. *ălyo- (Arm. ail, Gk. ἄλλος, O. Ir. aile,
Goth. aljis, Engl. else), Osc. allo- (on the Bantine Tablet), with
a byform *alis* in the Nom. Sg. Masc. (e. g. Catull. lxvi. 28), *alid*
in the Nom. Sg. Neut. (e. g. Lucr. i. 263). These byforms,
which are to be compared with *Cornelis*, &c. for *Cornēlius* (see
ch. vi. § 5), come into special use in the phrase *alis alium* (e. g.
ad alis alium and *cum alis alio* in the Vulgate, *alis alium*, C. I. L.
ii. 2633. 7), probably owing to the fact that the stress of the
voice in this word-group fell on the antepenultimate syllable (see
ch. iii. § 12). The deriv. Adj. *aliēnus* is for *ali-īno- (ch. iv. § 12).

(2) *alter* is formed from the root al- (al-?), seen in *alyo-, by
the addition of the suffix -tero- (ch. v. § 18), (Osc. alttro-),
while other I.-Eur. languages show a similar formation from
the root an-, seen in O. Ind. anyá- ' alius ' (O. Ind. ántara-,
Goth. an-þar, O. Engl. ōþer, Germ. ander, Lith. àn-tras). It
is often used as an Ordinal Numeral, ' second.' A stem *altro*-
appears in *altrin-secus*, *altro-vorsum* (Plaut. Cas. 555) and other
words (cf. Gk. ἀλλότριος), but in lines like Plaut. *Bacch.* 1184
alterum, &c. need not be changed into *altrum*, &c., but may be
scanned as dactyls, *altérŭm*, &c. (see Klotz, *Altröm. Metrik*, p. 59);
even in *Pers.* 226 *altra* is not certain.

(3) *ūllus* is formed by the LO-suffix (ch. v. § 21) from *ūnus*
(see ch. iii. § 15. 5), which also belongs to the Pronominal Declension, Gen. *unius*, Dat. *uni*. (With *quisque* appended we have the
word-group or compound *unus-quisque*.) The opposite of *ūllus*
is *nūllus* with the negative prefix *ně*- of *n-usquam*, *n(e)-utiquam*
(pronounced with both first and second syllable short) and the
like (ch. ii. § 149); and *ne-ullus, 'not a little one,' 'not even
one,' was probably anterior in formation to *ullus*, in which the
force of the Diminutive suffix is not so apparent. Like *nullus*,
but used properly of persons, while *nullus* was used normally
of things, is *nēmo* from *ně-hemo*. (On *hemo*, a byform of *homo*,
see ch. vi. § 1.) *Nullus* is hardly used as a substantive till Late
Latin, but *nullius* and *nullo* take the place of *neminis* and *nemine*
in class. Latin. As the Neuter of *nullus*, *nihil* is used, a compound of the negative *ně*- and *hīlum* (see ch. iii. § 52; ch. vi. § 11).

(4) *sōlus* may be connected with the Adverb *sě-, sěd-*, apart

G g

(e. g. *sēd-itio*, lit. ' a going apart ') (ch. ix. § 51), and be formed of *sō-*, a grade of *sē-* (ch. iv. § 53), with the suffix *-lo*. Some refer the word to the stem *sollo-* of Osc. sollo-, ' whole,' Lat. *soll-ers*, *soll-emnis*, but the connexion of the ideas ' alone ' and ' whole ' or 'all' is not apparent.

(5) *tōtus* is another word of uncertain etymology. Some connect it with the Umbro-Oscan word for a community, state or people, *teutā- (Osc. tovtā-, Umbr. totā-), and suppose the Latin word to exhibit another grade of the root, perhaps *touto- (see ch. iv. § 41). The word encroached on the sphere of *omnis*, and finally supplanted *omnis* in Vulgar Latin. Of the Romance languages Italian is the only one which preserves Lat. *omnis* (Ital. ogni) beside Lat. *tōtus* (Ital. tutto ; on this form, see ch. ii. § 130. p. 116).

(6) *ŭter* is one of those Latin Relative (Interrog., Indef.) forms beginning with *u-* like *ŭbi*, *ŭt* which are discussed in § 26. With the addition of *-que*, ' ever ' (see on *quis-que*, § 28), it becomes *uter-que*. The Umbro-Oscan stem is *potro- (Osc. pútúrús-píd Nom. Pl. ' utrique,' púterei-píd Loc. Sg. ; Umbr. *sei-podruh-pei* ' utroque ' Adv. is a formation like *sed-utraque* Nom. Sg. Fem., ' each separately,' Plaut. *Stich*. 106). The opposite of *uter* is *neuter*, a trisyllable (ch. ii. § 32), with the negative prefix. *Alter-uter* is a compound of *alter* and *uter*, sometimes with both elements declined, sometimes with the second only (cf. § 20 on *ipse*, Fem. *ea-psa*, *ea-pse* and *i-psa*). A form *altertra* for *alterutra* is mentioned by Paul. Fest. 6. 2 Th.

All of these take the pronominal Gen. and Dat. Sg. in *-ius*, and *-i*, but only *alius* takes the Neut. Sg. (Nom.-Acc.) in *-d*. Still they admitted more readily than *ille, iste* and the other Demonstrative Pronouns the Noun Declension forms in these cases ; e. g. *unae rei* (Gen.), Cic. *Tull*. xv. 36 ; *tam nulli consili*, Ter. *Andr*. 608 ; *coloris ulli*, Plaut. *Truc*. 293 ; *alterae legioni*, Caes. *Bell. Gall.* v. 27. 5 (see Priscian, i. 196. 18 H. and Neue, ii[3]. pp. 516 sqq.). For the Gen. Sing. of *alius* the Romans discarded *alĭus*, which was liable to confusion with the Nom., and used the Gen. Sing. of *alter* instead, *alterĭus* (in dactylic poetry, of course, only *alterĭus* is admissible, but *alterĭus* occurs in other metres, e. g. Ter. *Andr*. 628, Seneca, *Herc. Fur.* 212).

There are other Adjectives called ' Pronominal ' Adjectives, which are derived from Pronoun-stems, but which do not share

§ 29.] THE PRONOUNS. PRONOMINAL ADJECTIVES. 451

the Pronominal Declension. From the stem to- (te-) comes Lat. *tālis* (I.-Eur. *tāli- of Gk. τηλί-κος; cf. O. Sl. tolĭ Adv., 'so very,' toli-kŭ Adj., 'so great'), *tan-tus* (Osc. e-tanto-, e. g. *molto etanto estud* 'multa tanta esto'; Umbr. e-tanto-, e. g. etantu mutu adferture si 'tanta multa affertori sit') (*tantisce* pro tantis *C. G. L.* v. 155. 36), *tŏt*, older *totĭ-*, preserved in *tŏtĭ-dem* (I.-Eur. *tŏtĭ, O. Ind. táti; cf. Gk. τόσ(σ)ος for *τοτιος), and (with O-suffix) *tŏtus* (e. g. Manil. iii. 420 detrahitur summae tota pars, quota demitur). From the Relative (Interrog., Indef.) stem comes Lat. *quālis* (Gk. πηλί-κος; cf. O. Sl. kolĭ, koli-kŭ), *quantus* (Umbr. panto-), *quŏt*, older *quotĭ* (I.-Eur. *q^{u}ŏtĭ, O. Ind. káti; cf. Gk. πόσ(σ)ος for *ποτιος), and (with O-suffix) *quŏtus* (e. g. Hor. tu quotus esse velis rescribe). (On *cotti-die*, see ch. ix. § 5.) The Late Latin use of *tanti, quanti* for *tot, quot* (e. g. Tertull. nec tamen tantos inveniunt verba discipulos, quantos Christiani factis docendo), survives in Romance, e. g. Ital. quanti anni ha?, 'quantos annos habet?', 'how old is he?' (On *cē-teri*, see ch. iv. § 33.)

A Dual, like the Numeral *duo* (ch. vi. § 59), is *ambō -ae -ō* (I.-Eur. *ambhō(u), Gk. ἄμφω), Gen. *ambōrum*, &c., Dat. *ambōbus*, &c., Acc. *ambōs* and *ambō -as -ō*; in the Acc. the older *ambō* was being ousted by *ambōs* even in Plautus' time, for he uses *ambos* always before an initial consonant, and *ambō* with *ambos* before an initial vowel as the metre requires, while in Late Lat. we have *ambis* for the Dat.-Abl. Plur. e. g. *Eph. Epigr.* iv. p. 491 (cf. Caper 107. 14 K. ambobus, non 'ambis,' et ambabus; and see Neue, ii[3]. p. 279).

The Pronominal Declension has in some languages (e. g. Lithuanian and the Teutonic languages) extended itself from these Pronominal Adjectives to all Adjectives[1]. What is called in Teutonic the 'Strong Declension' of Adjectives, in Lithuanian the 'Indefinite' is really the Pronominal, e. g. Goth. blinds with Neut. blindata, 'blind,' like Neut. þata, 'that.' In Greek, on the other hand, the Pronominal Declension has lost ground, and that is why in Greek the declension of the Pronouns does not appear so unlike the declension of the Nouns as in Latin.

---

[1] We have seen (ch. vi. § 46) that in Latin the Gen. Pl. suffix of O-stems, *-ōsom*, then *-ōrom*, class. *-ōrum*, was extended from Pronouns (e. g. *olorom* 'illorum' on the Columna Rostrata) to Adjectives (e. g. *duonoro* on a Scipio Epitaph of perhaps the end of the third cent. B. C.), and in time to Nouns (e. g. *deorum* competed with *deum* in Cicero's time, ch. vi. § 47).

§ 30. **The Pronouns in Romance.** The development in the Romance languages of two series of the Personal and Possessive Pronouns, (*a*) the enclitic, e.g. Fr. me, te, mon, ton, (*b*) the accented, e. g. Fr. moi, toi, mien, tien, has been already mentioned (ch. iii. § 12 *a*, 3, and above, § 12). In Vulgar Latin *ego* became *eo*, whence the Romance forms, e. g. Ital. io, Span. yo, Sard. eo, O. Fr. eo, io, eu, jo, now je. Spanish nosotros ' we,' vosotros ' you ' represent *nos alteros, vos alteros* (cf. Fr. nous autres, &c.). The 2 Pl. Possessive remained *voster* in Vulg. Lat., whence Ital. vostro, Fr. vôtre, Span. vuestro, &c., while two rival forms competed for the 3 Pl. Possessive, *suus* (Span., Port.) and *illorum* (Ital. loro, Fr. leur).

The Demonstratives *ille, ipse* (which takes the place of *ille* in Sard. as 3 Sg. Pron. and Article, isse and issu, ' he '), *iste* had in Vulg. Lat. -*ī* in Nom. Sg., -*ui* in Dat. Sg. Masc., -*aei* in Dat. Sg. Fem., e. g. *illī* (Ital. egli, Fr. il), *illui* (*C. I. L.* x. 2654; Ital. lui, Fr. lui), *illaei* (Ital. lei, O. Fr. li). Their extension by the prefix *ecce* has been noticed in § 15, e. g. Fr. celle from *ecce-illa*. Used enclitically, *ille* has lost its first syllable in Romance, e. g. Ital. gli (from *illi*), lo (from *illum*), Span. le, Sard. li. The Definite Article in most Romance countries was supplied by *ille* (but by *ipse* in Sardinia and elsewhere), which in Roumanian is postfixed (e. g. domnu-l for *dominus ille*), and in all languages is united with a Preposition into one word, e. g. with the Preposition *ad* in Ital. al, Fr. au, &c. *Hic* survived only in word-groups, e.g. Ital. ciò from ecce hoc.

Of the Indefinite, Interrogative and Relative Pronouns *quae* and *quis* seem to have been ousted in Vulg. Lat. by *qui*; *quid* is Ital. che, and (accented) Fr. quoi, (unaccented) Fr. que.

For the Pronoun of Identity (*ipse* had become a Demonstrative) various phrases were used ; e. g. Ital. medesimo, Prov. medesme, Fr. même, Span. mismo are from *met ipsimus* ; Ital. desso from *id ipsum* (or *ad ipsum* ?) ; Ital. stesso is a compound of *iste* and *ipse*.

Alius survived in a Neuter form **alum*, whence O. Fr. el and al, O. Span. al, *alter* having taken its place (Ital. altro, Fr. autre, Span. otro). *Certus* (and *certānus*) replaced *quidam*. *Aliquis* was joined with *ūnus* into a Compound **alicunus*, whence Ital. alcuno, Fr. aucun, Span. alguno. (See Meyer-Lübke *Rom. Gram.* ii. pp. 89 sqq., 595 sqq.).

CHAPTER VIII.

THE VERB.

§ 1. I. **THE CONJUGATIONS.** The I.-Eur. Verb had two Conjugations, (1) the Thematic, in which the Person-suffixes were attached to the verb-root augmented by -ĕ- or -ŏ-, e. g. Gk. φέρ-ο-μεν, φέρ-ε-τε; (2) the Athematic, in which this vowel, the Thematic Vowel, as it is called, was absent, e. g. Gk. ἱστᾰ-μεν, ἱστᾰ-τε. In the Thematic Conjugation the 1 Sg. Pres. Ind. Act had -ō, e. g. φέρ-ω, Lat. *leg-ō*; the Subjunctive changed the Thematic Vowel of the Indicative to -ē- (and -ō-), e. g. Gk. φέρ-η-τε (φέρ-ω-μεν); the Optative changed it to -oi-, e. g. Gk. φέρ-οι-μεν, φέρ-οι-τε. In the Athematic Conjugation the 1 Sg. Pres. Ind. Act. had -mĭ, e. g. Gk. ἵστη-μι; the verb-stem was weakened in the Dual and Plural Act. and in all Numbers of the Middle, e. g. Gk. ἱστᾰ-τον, ἱστᾰ-μεν, ἱστᾰ-μαι beside Sg. ἱστη-; the Subjunctive (with strong stem) showed -ĕ- or -ŏ- between the root and the Person-suffixes, and the Optative (with weak stem) -yē- in Sg. Act., -ī- elsewhere, e. g. Gk. ἱστᾰ-ίη-ν, ἱστᾰ-ῑ-μεν (ἱσταῖμεν).

We find early Derivative Verbs like I.-Eur. tr-ā- from the root ter-, pl-ē- from the root pel- (Lat. *in-trā-re, im-plē-re*), and later Derivatives from Nouns, e. g. Lat. *curā-re* from the Noun-stem *curā-*, forming the persons of their Present Tense sometimes thematically with the suffix -yŏ- (§ 15), sometimes athematically, e. g. O. Ind. trá-yă-tē and trā-ti 3 Sg. The long vowel, with which these derivative verb-stems end, is not weakened in the Dual and Plur. Act., nor in the Middle, e. g. O. Ind. trá-sva 2 Sg. Imperat. Mid.

In Latin almost every athematic verb becomes thematic in 1 Sg. Pres. Ind., and usually in 3 Pl.; and the declension of the Pres. Ind. often shows thematic and athematic forms side by side. Thus I.-Eur. *ei-mĭ, 'I go' (O. Ind. é-mi 1 Sg., ĭ-más 1 Pl., Gk. εἶ-μι 1 Sg., ἴ-μεν 1 Pl., Lith. ei-mì) is in Latin *eo* for *ĕy-ō, a thematic form, though other Persons, e.g. 2 Sg. ī-s, older *ei-s* (*ei-s(ĭ)), are athematic; I.-Eur. *wĕl-mĭ, 'I wish' (Lith. pavelmi 1 Sg., pa-velt 3 Sg.) is in Latin thematic in 1 Sg. *vŏl-ō*, but athematic in 3 Sg. *vul-t*. The Latin Substantive Verb *sum* has best retained the features of the Athematic Conjugation, with its 1 Sg. Ind. in -*m*, its Opt. originally declined *s-iē-m*, *s-iē-s*, *s-iē-t*, *s-ī-mos*, *sī-tes*, and so on.

The four Conjugations of our Latin Grammars, (1) *amā-re*, &c., (2) *vidē-re*, &c., (3) *legĕ-re*, &c., (4) *audī-re*, &c. are, like the five Declensions (ch. vi. § 1), an unscientific classification, often bringing forms together which were of dissimilar origin, just as Modern Italian with its three Conjugations brings together in the Second forms like vendére (Lat. *vendĕre*), potére (Lat. *posse*), solére (Lat. *sŏlēre*), and in the Third dire (Lat. *dicĕre*), empire (Lat. *implēre*), apparire (Lat. *apparēre*), seguire (Lat. *sĕqui*), and venire (Lat. *vĕnīre*). We must substitute for them an enumeration of the various ways in which the Tense-stems are formed, especially the Present Tense-stem.

Of the Latin Present (i.e. Thematic Present) Tense-stems, the usual type is that which was also the most prevalent in I.-Eur., that namely in which the Present-stem shows the ordinary unweakened root (E-grade) of the Verb, e.g. Gk. πεύθ-ο-μαι from the root bheudh-, πείθ-ω from the root bheidh-, πέτ-ο-μαι from the root pet-, while the weak grade of the root is proper to the Preterite (Aorist) tense, e.g. Gk. ἐ-πῠθ-ό-μην, ἔ-πῐθ-ο-ν, ἐ-πτ-ό-μην. Latin examples (part of the 'Third Conjugation') are: *dūco*, O. Lat. *douco*, for *deuco (Goth. tiuha) from the root deu*k*-; *dīco*, O. Lat. *deico* (Goth. ga-teiha, 'I indicate') from the root deiǩ-; *veho* for *weǵh-ō (O. Ind. váh-ā-mi, Lith. vež-u, Goth. ga-vig-a, 'I move'). Another type shows a Nasal in the Present-stem (with weak grade of root) which is omitted in the other tense-stems, this Nasal being either (1) a nasal infix, e.g. Lat. *rŭ-m-po* (O. Ind. lŭ-m-pámi) from the root reup-, *fĭ-n-do*

(O. Ind. bhĭ-na-dmi) from the root bheid-, or (2) a nasal affix, e. g. Lat. *lĭ-n-o* (O. Ind. lĭ-nā-mi, O. Scand. lĭ-na) from the root lei-. Latin *meio* for *meiĝh-ō, beside *mĭngo* for *mĭ-n-ĝh-ō, is a good example of these two modes of forming the Pres.-stem; and similarly we seem to have O. Lat. *nīvo* for *(s)neíghᴺ-ō (or (s)nīghᴺ-ó? *M. U.* iv. 8), beside *nĭnguo* for *(s)nĭ-n-ghᴺ-ō, in a line of Pacuvius (*Praet.* 4 R.):

sagíttis nīuit, plúmbo et saxis grándinat.

Another affixes -yŏ- (-yĕ-) or -ĭyŏ- (-ĭyĕ-), an affix which often varied with ĭ (cf. ch. iv. § 51); e. g. in Latin (part of the Third and of the Fourth Conjugations) *farcio* (Gk. φράσσω for *φρακ-yω), with 2 Sg. *farcī-s*, from the root bhreqᴺ- (cf. *frequens*), Lat. *morior* (O. Ind. mr-iyá-tē 3 Sg.) from the root mer-. We have also a suffix -skŏ- (-skĕ-) used to form what are wrongly called 'Inceptives' (Third Conj.), with weak grade of root, e. g. *posco* for *porc-sco*, from pṛk-, the weak grade of the root prek-, 'to ask'; a suffix -ĕyŏ- (with O-grade of root) used to form Causatives (Second Conjugation), e. g. Lat. *mŏneo* for *mon-ĕyō, 'I remind,' lit. 'cause to remember,' from the root men- (cf. Lat. *me-min-i*), and so on. A very important class is the class of Verb-stems ending in a vowel (Vowel-stems), which form their 1 Sg. Pres. Ind. usually with the help of the suffix -yŏ-, e. g. in Latin (First and Second Conjugations) *no* for *(s)nā-yō (O. Ind. snā-ya-tē), *neo* for *(s)nē-yō (O. H. G. nāu), but other Persons athematically, e. g. 2 Sg. *nā-s, nē-s*, many of these Vowel-stems being Derivatives from Nouns and Adjectives (First, Second, and Fourth Conjugations), e. g. *cūro* from *cura* (stem *curā-), like Gk. τῑμά-ω from τιμά (-ή), *albeo* from *albus* (stem *albo-, *albe-), *finio* from *finis* (stem *fini-, *finei-). These various modes of forming the Present Tense-stem will be considered in later sections (§§ 6–33).

§ 2. **Traces of the Athematic Conjugation in Latin.** Of I.-Eur. verbs of the Athematic Conjugation, which retain more or less of their athematic character in Latin, the most important are the roots es-, 'to be,' ei-, 'to go,' ed-, 'to eat,' wel-, 'to wish.' ES- has in 1 Sg. *sum* (Osc. sum) with the root in weak form s-, instead of *es-* of I.-Eur. *ĕs-mĭ (O. Ind. ás-mi, Arm. em, Gk. εἰ-μί for *ἐσ-μί, Lesb. ἔμμι, Alb. jam, Goth. im, Lith. es-mì, O. Sl. jes-mĭ), though, if we may believe Varro (*L. L.* ix. 100), the older form was *esum* (sum quod nunc dicitur olim dicebatur 'esum'); 2 Sg. *es* [older es(s), scanned long by 'position' in Plautus], I.-Eur. *ĕs-sĭ (Arm. es, Hom. ἐσ-σί); 3 Sg. *es-t* (Osc.

ist), I.-Eur. *ĕs-tĭ [O. Ind. ás-ti, Gk. ἐσ-τι, O. Ir. is for *is-t, Goth. is-t, Lith. ës-ti and ĕs-t, O. Sl. (Russ.) jes-tĭ] ; 1 Pl. *sŭmus* and *sĭmus* (ch. ii. § 16), I.-Eur. *s-mes, *s-mos (O. Ind. s-más) ; 2 Pl. *es-tis* should be **s-tis*, I.-Eur. *s-tĕ (O. Ind. s-thá), but cf. Gk. ἐσ-τέ, Lith. ës-te ; 3 Pl. *sunt* (older *sont*) from *sont(i)* beside I.-Eur. *senti (Goth. s-ind), as Umbr. sent, Osc. set ; the I.-Eur. Optative *s-yē-m (*s-ĭyē-m) 1 Sg., *s-yē-s (*s-ĭyē-s) 2 Sg., *s-ī-mos 1 Pl., &c., is reproduced with some fidelity in O. Lat. *s-iē-s, s-ī-mus*, though the vowel *ī* extended itself in time over Sg. as well as Plur., class. Lat. *sim, sīs, sit* (§ 55), as in Umbr. *sir* 'sis,' *si* 'sit,' *sins* 'sint' ; in the Imperative we should expect *ĕs, the bare stem, in 2 Sg. (and *ĕs* is probably the only actual Latin form, on which see § 58), *s-tōd in 3 Sg., but we have *es-tō(d)* (cf. Gk. ἔσ-τω) ; the Inf. is *es-se*, the Loc. Sg. of an S-stem, as the Umbro-Oscan *es-om (Osc. *ezum*, Umbr. *erom*) is the Acc. Sg. of an O-stem (ch. v. § 2) ; EI- is thematic in 1 Sg. in Lat. *eo* from *ĕy-ō instead of I.-Eur. *ei-mi, but athematic in the other persons of the Pres. Ind., 2 Sg. *īs*, older *e-is*, 3 Sg. *it*, older *eit*, 1 Pl. *ī-mus*, older *ei-mus*, with strong stem *ei-* as in Lith. eī-me, eī-te, instead of weak stem ï- (possibly with a bygrade ī like O. Ind. í-mahē 1 Pl. Mid. ; but Pel. ei-te 2 Pl. Imper. points to an original ei- for Latin also), 2 Pl. *ī-tis* older *ei-tis* (with ei- again for ï-), except the 3 Plural *eunt* from *ey-o-nt(i), unless -onti was an I.-Eur. byform of -enti in the Athematic Conjugation (cf. *sunt* from *sont(i)) ; the form *int* of the Philoxenus Glossary (p. 75. 23 G. : int, πορεύονται) is too doubtful to quote as an athematic 3 Pl., for it may be a wrong reading for *ĭnunt* (cf. *prod-ĭnunt, red-inunt, ob-inunt*), although indeed the common theory of the origin of these forms presupposes an old 3 Pl. *ĭn-t* (see § 73) ; athematic too are the Inf. *īre* older *ei-re* from *ei-sĭ, Imper. *i* older *ei* (Lith. eī-k), *ĭto* older *ei-tō(d)* (with ei-, as in Umbr. ee-tu, for ï- of Gk. ἴ-τω(δ), § 57) ; ED- is thematic in 1 Sg. *ed-ō* (Gk. Fut. ἔδ-ο-μαι is a Subjunctive form, and is quite regular), but athematic in the other persons, which often show a byform ēd- (Lith. éd-mi and éd-u 1 Sg., és-t 3 Sg.) (thus Donatus ad Ter. *Andr.* i. 1. 54 distinguishes *ut una ēsset*, Subj. of *edo*, from *ut una ĕsset*, Subj. of *sum*) ; 1 Pl. *edimus*, 3 Pl. *edunt* are like *sumus, sunt* ; the Imper. *es-tō* is athematic, and the Inf. *es-se*. (On -*st*- instead of -*ss*- from I.-Eur. -dt- in *est* 3 Sg. &c., see ch. iv. § 155 ; on Imperat. *es*, § 58, below). The byforms *edĭt, edĭtis*, &c. need not be new Latin types, for there are indications that in the I.-Eur. period this root wavered between the Thematic and Athematic Conjugations (cf. Lith. éd-u for *ĕd-ō beside éd-mi ; Goth. ita for *ĕd-ō) ; WEL- was probably declined : 1 Sg. *wél-mĭ, 2 Sg. *wél-sĭ, 3 Sg. *wél-tĭ, 1 Pl.*wḷ-més or -mŏs, &c. ; Lat. *vŏlo, vult (volt)* are the normal equivalents of *wĕlō, *wĕlt(ĭ) (see ch. iv. § 10 on *ŏlīva* from Gk. ἐλαία, &c.), so that the 1 Sg. is thematic, as are possibly also the 1 Pl.[1] and 2 Pl. (cf. *sumus, sunt*), while the 3 Sg. and 2 Pl. are athematic ; for the 2 Sg. *wels, which would become *vel(l) (ch. iv. § 146), and would be probably scanned as a long syllable in Plautus [see ch. ii. § 133 on Plautine *ter(r)* for *ters* from I.-Eur. *trĭ-s], the Romans substituted the

---

[1] The -*u*- in 1 Pl. of these Athematic Verbs, *sumus, volumus*, is noticeable. *Volimus*, the reading of the Ambrosian Palimpsest in Plaut. *Pseud.* 233, *Truc.* 192 is a Late Lat. form (see Georges, *Lex. Wortf.* s. v.), due either to the Analogy of the Thematic Conj. (so Late Lat. *feris, aufere*, on which see Georges), or to the ordinary weakening of unaccented *ŭ* (so *possĭmus*, § 97, *sĭmus*, ch. ii. § 16). On the spelling *quaesumus* see below, § 33. 4.

§ 2.]   THE VERB.   CONJUGATIONS.   457

2 Sg. of a different Verb-root wei-, 'to wish' (O. Ind. vī-, with 2 Sg. vé-ṣi, Gk. ἵεμαι) [I.-Eur. wel-, wei-, weḱ- (Gk. ἑκών) all mean 'to wish,' and are probably connected]; the athematic Imper. *vĕl* (*vĕl* in Plautus too) has become a Conjunction (ch. x. § 4), while the Imper. *nolī* of the Compound, has been variously referred to a bystem of the Fourth Conjugation (I.-Eur. *wel-yō-, Goth. vilja; O. Sl. veljǫ), with Imper. *velī*, like *farcī*, § 57, and to the Optative (cf. 2 Pl. Opt. *nolītis* with 2 Pl. Imper. *nolīte*; also 1 Pl. *nolīmus*, used both in an optative and an imperative sense). The root BHER- belonged to the Thematic Conjugation (Gk. φέρ-ω, O. Ir. -biur from *ber-ō, Goth. bair-a; cf. 3 Sg. O. Ind. bhár-a-ti for *bher-e-ti, Arm. ber-ē, O. Sl. ber-e-tŭ; athematic forms however appear, O. Ind. bhár-ti 3 Sg., bhṛ-tám 2 Du.; cf. Gk. φέρ-τε 2 Pl., O. Ind. bhar-tam 2 Du.), but in Latin to the Athematic (with the usual exceptions of the 1 Sg. and probably 1 Pl. and 3 Pl. Pres. Ind.), e. g. *fer-t* 3 Sg. Pres. Ind., *fer-tis* 2 Pl. (with strong stem *fer-* instead of weak stem *for-*, I.-Eur. bhṛ-; cf. Gk. φέρ-τε), *fer* Imper., *fer-re* (for *fer-se* from *fer-sī*, ch. iv. § 146; ch. iii. § 37) Inf., while 2 Sg. *fer(r)* [this is what an original *fer-s(ĭ)* would become in Latin; cf. *ter(r)* for *ters*, ch. ii. § 133] has been brought into line with other 2 Sg. forms by the fresh addition of the 2 Sg. suffix, *fer-s*. An Optative *ferim* like *velim* and the other optatives of athematic Verbs is not found and probably never existed. (On the Pres. Part.-stems *sent-* and *sont-*, *ient-* and *eunt-*, *volent-* and *volunt-*, see § 90; and on the Optatives *sim*, O. Lat. *siem, edim, velim*, § 56; the Compounds *possum, mālo, nōlo*, &c. are discussed in § 97, *ambio* in § 46).

Of I.-Eur. athematic Verbs of the type of O. Ind. dá-ti 3 Sg. (Gk. δίδω-μι, ἵστη-μι, &c.) with root dō- (varying with the weak grade), Latin examples are: DŌ-, to give, of which 1 Pl., 2 Pl. Pres. Ind. *dă-mus, dă-tis* are the normal athematic forms with the weak root *dă-* (cf. *cătus* and *cōs*, ch. iv. § 54), while 2 Sg. *dās*, 3 Sg. *dat* (O. Lat. *dāt*, probably so scanned in Plautus, e. g. *Most.* 601, *Men.* 101), show *ā* instead of *ō*, *dō-s*, *dō-t*; the old athem. 2 Sg. Imper. *dō* (Lith. dŭ́-k) remains only in *cĕ-dŏ* (shortened under the influence of the preceding short syllable, like *havĕ, sibĭ*, ch. iii. § 42), for the ordinary form *dā* is coined on the type of the 1st Conjugation; the 2, 3 Sg. *dă-to* is however the correct athematic form, also 2 Pl. *dă-te*, and Inf. *dă-re*, older *dā-sĭ*. 1 Sg. Pres. Ind. *dō* is probably *dō-yō* (cf. O. Sl. da-jǫ), and the reduplicated Present-stem of Gk. δί-δω-μι, Pelignian dida 'det' &c. (§ 9) may appear in *reddo*, if this stands for *re-d(i)-dō*. DHĒ-, to put, appears in the Latin compounds *con-do, crē-do* (O. Ind. śrád-dhā-, lit. 'to put the heart to,' O. Ir. cretim); which are usually reckoned as ordinary thematic verbs of the 3rd Conj., like *lĕgo*, though a great many of their forms may be explained as athematic, with the weak root, Lat. -*dă-* (which at the beginning of the word would be *fă-*, ch. iv. § 114; cf. *făcio*, I.-Eur. *dhăk-yō, from DHĒ-K-, Gk. ἔ-θηκ-α, an extension of the root by addition of *k*); thus, though *condĭs, condĭt* should have *-dēs, *-det (O. Lat. *-dēt, class. *-dĕt, ch. iii. § 49), *con-dĭmus* may represent *-dămus, con-dĭtis, *-dătis, and though 2 Sg. Imper. *con-dĕ* should be *-dĕ* (Lith. dé-k), 3 Sg. *con-dĭto*, 2 Pl. *con-dĭte* may represent *-dă-tōd, *-dă-te, and Inf. *con-dĕre, *-dă-sĭ*. (On Opt. *duim* from the stem *duo*, a bystem both of DŌ- and of DHĒ-, see § 56.) The roots STĀ- and BHĀ- (Gk. ἵστη-μι 1 Sg., ἵστἄ-μεν 1 Pl.; φη-μί 1 Sg., φἄ-μέν 1 Pl.) are treated like the type trā- (a development of the root ter-; see below) and retain *ā* throughout, *stā-s, stā-mus, stā-re*, &c., *fā-tur, fā-mur, fā-ri*, &c. (cf. Gk. ἔ-στημεν, ἔ-στητε), forming the 1 Sg. Pres. Ind. with the suffix -yo, *stō* from *stā-yō (Umbr. stahu, Lith. stó-jûs, 'I station myself,' O. Sl. sta-ją; cf. Zend ā-stāyā, but see Buck, *Osk. Spr.* p. 24), *fo(r)* from *bhā-yō (Lith. bó-ju, 'I enquire,' O. Sl. ba-ją, 'I converse'; cf. O. Ind. bhā-ya-tē Pass., if this be a genuine form). The weak grade of the two roots appears in *stătus* (O. Lat. also *stătus*), *fătеоr* (cf. Osc. fatium Inf.); the reduplicated Present-stem of the former (Gk. ἵστη-μι for *σι-στη-μι), in Lat. *si-st-o*, which usurped the transitive sense that had in O. Lat. belonged to *sto*, e.g. *med Mano statod*, ' set me as an offering to Manus,' on the Dvenos inscription, ' astasent' (*leg.* -int ?) statuerunt (*leg.* -int ?) Paul. Fest. 19. 32 Th. On these Reduplicated Presents of athematic roots in Latin, *si-stĭ-mus* from the root STĀ-, *se-rĭ-mus* from the root SĒ- (Gk. ἵημι for *σι-σημι) and perhaps *re-d(i)-dĭ-mus*, see § 9. An athematic 2 Sg. Imper. from the root BHEU- (of Lat. *fui*) occurs in the Carmen Arvale, *fu* (Lith. bú-k, Umbr. fu-tu), if rightly understood in the sense of ' be ' : satur fu, fere Mars.

Of I.-Eur. athematic verbs of the type of O. Ind. prā-mi (Gk. πί(μ)πλη-μι) with root plē-, a development of root pel- (the strong grade plē- never varying with any weak grade), the Latin examples are : PLĒ- (cf. PĔL-), *im-plēre, ex-plēre*; TRĀ- (cf. TĔR-), *in-trāre*, &c. These form the 1 Sg. Pres. Ind. thematically with the thematic suffix -yo-, e.g. *im-pleo* for *-plē-yō, *in-tro* for *-trā-yō (thematic byforms with this suffix perhaps existed in the I.-Eur. period, e. g. O. Ind. trá-ya-tē beside trā-ti), but the other persons athematically, *im-plē-s, in-trā-s, im-ple-t* (O. Lat. *-ēt*), *in-tra-t* (O. Lat. *-āt*), *im-plē-mus, in-trā-mus*, &c., as also the other parts of the verb, Imper. *im-plē, im-plē-to, in-trā, in-trā-to,* Inf. *im-plē-re, in-trā-re.*

Like them were declined other verbs whose stems ended in long vowels or diphthongs, e. g. I.-Eur. *wĭd-ē- (a stem perhaps originally confined to Secondary Tenses, *wĭd-yŏ- being the stem used in the Present Tense ; see § 15), Derivative Verbs from Ā-stems, e. g. *cūrā-* from the Noun *cūra* (stem *cūrā-*, ch. v. § 2), from I-stems, e. g. *fīneī-* from the Noun *fīnis* (stem *fīneī-, fīnī-*, ch. v. § 34), but not from U-stems (e. g. *stătuo* from *status*, § 15), nor possibly (1) those from O-stems (e. g. *flāveo* from *flavus*), (2) Causatives and Intensives with 1 Sg. Pres. Ind. in -éyō (e. g. *mŏneo*, Causative of root men- ; f. *mĕmĭni*; see § 29), though these two last types have a declension which, by reason of the phonetic changes of Latin, can hardly be discriminated from the athematic declension [thus *monēs* may represent *monē-s, as well as *mon-ĕyĕ-s (cf. *trēs* for *trĕyĕs, ch. iv. § 66), *monē* Imper. may come from *monē, a stem in -ē, or *mon-ĕyĕ. In the P. P. P. however the two types are distinct, *monĭ-tus*, with I.-Eur. weak stem monĭ-, *im-plē-tus* with stem plē-, as in the Perfect Ind. Act. *mon-ui, im-plē-vi*; see § 39. 4]. Farcio (Gk. φράσσω for *φρακγω) and *făcio* both belong to the same I.-Eur. thematic type, a type in which the root has the suffix -yŏ-, varying on the one hand with -yĕ-, on the other with -ĭ- and -ī- ; the divergent roads which they have taken in Latin are perhaps due to the fact that in the declension of *facio* the weak suffix -ĭ- asserted itself (Imper. O. Lat. *face* for *facĭ, căpe* for *capĭ), in the other the weak suffix -ī (Imper. *farcī*), and this assertion of the long vowel brought with it a transference to the Athematic type, *farcĭ-re* beside *face-re* from *facĭ-se*, though the original difference between *farcio* and a Derivative like *fīnio*, is still maintained in the Perf. Ind. Act. *far-si*, for *farc-si ; beside *fīnī-vi*, and P. P. P. *far-tus*, older *farc-tus*, beside *fīnī-tus*. (On these stems with suffix -yo-, and on the Derivative Verbs and stems ending in vowels which form their 1 Sing. Pres. Ind. with the help of this suffix, see §§ 15, 21.)

§ 3.]   THE VERB. AORIST AND S-STEMS.   459

The form *cante* for *canite* quoted from the Carmen Saliare by Varro (*L. L.* vii. 27) can hardly be called an Athematic 2 Pl. (Imper.). It is rather an example of the Latin tendency to syncopate every short unaccented vowel before a single consonant, which would have destroyed most traces of the thematic vowel in the Latin Verb, if it had been allowed free play (see ch. iii. § 13 [1]).

§ 3. II. **THE TENSE-STEMS (STRONG AORIST AND S-FORMATIONS)**. The Tense-stems are formed by various modifications of the root. From the root ĝen- for example is formed by Reduplication (with ĭ as Reduplication-vowel and with weak grade of root) the Present-stem ĝi-ĝn- (Lat. *gigno*, Gk. γίγνο-μαι), expressive of continued action in Present time, 'I am producing,' and by another species of Reduplication [with ĕ as Reduplication-vowel and in the Singular (see § 39) with the O-grade of the root] the Perfect-stem ĝe-ĝon- (Gk. γέγονα) expressive of completed action, 'I have produced.' The Aorist-stem, expressive of action merely, unlimited by the idea of continuance or the idea of completeness, is in this Verb formed from the root itself ĝen- (Gk. ἐ-γεν-ό-μην), and so the O. Lat. form *genunt* (Varro, *Sat. Menipp.* 35 B. sed quod haec loca aliquid genunt; cf. Lucr. iii. 797 durare genique) might be called an Aorist (i. e. unlimited) tense-form. But the distinction between a Present-stem and an Aorist-stem is by no means so clearly marked as between a Present-stem and a Perfect-stem, and what is an Aorist-stem in one language may be used as a Present-stem in another. The stem ĝen- (with the thematic vowel ĝeno-, ĝene- as in Gk. ἐ-γενό-μην, ἐ-γένε-το) is in O. Ind. used as a Present, jána-ti 3 Sg., and the exact equivalent of Gk. ἐ-γενο- (with the Augment prefixed) is in O. Ind. not an Aorist, but the past tense of a Present-stem, in other words an Imperfect, á-jana-m, 'I was producing,' while the aorist sense is assigned to the weak grade of root, ĝn- (ĝᵉn-), a-jña-ta 3 Pl. Thus in this verb it would be more correct to say that the Present-stem was both ĝi-ĝn- and ĝen-, than to restrict the first of these to the Present, the second to the Aorist signification.

---

[1] Or is *cante*, like the other strange syncopated form quoted from the Carm. Sal. *priuicloes* 'priviculis' (p. 175), merely a trace of the older syllabic writing (ch. iii. § 14)?

Some find more exact counterparts of the Greek Strong Aorist (2nd Aorist) in Latin Perfects like *scĭdit* (O. Ind. á-chĭdă-t), *scĭd-* being the weak grade of the root *sceid-*, a root which forms its Present-stem in Latin by Nasalization, *scind-*. But, as is pointed out in § 41, *scidit* is more likely to be a Reduplicated Perfect (O. Lat. *scĭ-cĭdī*, O. Ind. cĭ-chĭdē), and to have lost its Reduplication syllable in Compounds like *disscidit* (O. Lat. *-ĭt*, *-eit*) for **dis-sci-cidit*, like *re-p-pŭlit* for **re-pe-pulit*), the Perfect having in Latin come to assume Aorist functions, e. g. *dĕdī* (1) I have given, (2) I gave. Where the Aorist-usage most shows traces of itself in Latin is in phrases like *nē attĭgas* (Subjunctive of an Aorist-stem tăg- beside the Present-stem tăng-), which suggest comparison with the Greek use of the Aor. Subj. in prohibitions, &c.

The Present-stem, as it is on the one hand occasionally indistinguishable from the Aorist-stem, so it is on the other from the Verb-stem. In a verb like Lat. *sĭno* the Nasal is clearly part of the Present-stem, and connected with the idea of continued action in present time, for it is not found in other parts of the verb (e. g. *sī-vi*, *sĭ-tum*) (cf. *tango* Pres., *tĕtĭgi* Perf., *tac-tus* Verbal Noun). But in a verb like Lat. *jungo* the Nasal is extended throughout the Verb (e. g. *junxi*, *junctum*, § 10). Similarly the 'Inceptive' suffix of *cre-sco* is properly dropped in *crē-vi*, *crē-tum*, but the same suffix is in *posco* (for **porc-sco*, I.-Eur. *pṛk-sko-) extended to Perf. *pŏposci*, &c. Some of the stems which are included in this section in the list of Present-stems are probably rather to be called Verb-stems, i. e. extensions of the root by means of a suffix to denote action, whether continued action, completed action, or momentary action; for example, the stems trĕm-, trĕs-, formed from the root ter- (O. Ind. tar-alá-, 'trembling') by means of an M-suffix (Gk. τρέμ-ω, Lat. *trĕm-o*) and an S-suffix (Gk. τρέ-(σ)-ω, Lat. *terreo* for **ters-eo*), are rather Verb-stems than Present-stems, although, for practical purposes, it is best with a view to completeness to include them in the list of Present-stem formations.

We have already spoken of the so-called Aorist (i.e. Strong Aorist) forms of the Latin Verb. Another series of forms is better considered here than assigned to any definite Tense, viz.

the S-formations, which receive further treatment in the sections dealing with the Perfect, Future, Imperfect and Pluperfect Tenses. A large number of Verb-forms, whose exact relation to each other has not yet been clearly explained, show the sibilant s in some shape or other (-ss-, -s-, -es-, &c.). We find an S-suffix in the Verb-stem just mentioned, tres-, ' to be afraid, tremble' (O. Ind. trása-ti and tar-ása-ti, Gk. τρέ(σ)ω ; cf. Lat. *terreo* for **ter-s-*); and in a stem like auk-s- of Gk. αὔξω (cf. αὐξάνω) from the root aug- (Lat. *augeo*), this S-suffix is clearly connected with the S-suffix (-es-, -os-, -s-) of the Noun *augos, *auges-os Gen. (O. Ind. ójas, 'strength'; cf. Lat. *augus-tus* like *rōbus-tus*, *fūnes-tus*, ch. v. § 71), precisely as in Derivative Verbs like Gk. τελέ(σ)-ω, Pft. Pass. τετέλεσ-ται, from the Noun τέλος, Gen. τέλε(σ)-ος; and this Noun S-suffix we shall find to be the suffix used in Infinitives like Lat. *ăgĕrĕ* for *ag̑-es-ĭ Loc. Sg., *ferrĕ* for *bher-s-ĭ Loc. Sg., *ferrī* for *bher-s-ai Dat. Sg., Gk. δεῖξαι, &c., which are nothing but cases of Verbal Nouns. Side by side with Verb-stems with an S-suffix stand Verb-stems with a suffix -syo-, e.g. O. Ind. tra-sya-ti, exactly as Present-stems in -yo- like Lat. *fŭg-io* (stem bhŭg-yo-) stand side by side with Present-stems like Gk. φεύγω (stem bheug-o-). This suffix -syo- is however usually the suffix of the Future-stem (e.g. O. Ind. dēk-ṣyā-mi from I.-Eur. deik̑-, Lith. bú-siu from I.-Eur. bheu-), but not of the ordinary Greek Futures, e. g. δείξω, φύσω, τιμήσω, which are now generally regarded as Subjunctives (the I.-Eur. Subjunctive had Future, as well as Subjunctive, force, § 55) of the S-Aorist, the difference between τιμήσομεν Fut., τιμήσωμεν Aor. Subj., δείξομεν Fut., δείξωμεν Aor. Subj. being explained by the fact that originally the Subjunctive of the S-Aorist was Athematic (§ 1), τιμήσ-ο-μεν, δείξ-ο-μεν (cf. τείσομεν Hom.), but afterwards took by analogy of Thematic Subjunctives the long vowels ω, η, and retained its proper athematic forms only in their Future Indicative usage. Gk. τιμήσω, ἐτίμησα, &c. must have had at the first double s, *τιμήσσω (-άσσω), ἐτίμησσα (-άσσα), for s between vowels in Greek disappeared when single (e. g. γένε(σ)-ος), and was reduced when double (e. g. εὗσα from the root eus-, for *εὕσσα, cf. Lat. *ŭs-si*, ch. ii. § 129), as in Latin it became *r* when single (e. g. *gĕnĕr-is*, *quaero*), and was reduced in the classical period after a long vowel or diphthong (*ib.*) when double (e.g. *quaeso*, older *quaesso, haesi*, older *haessi*). Gk. τιμήσω, older -άσσω, will then correspond to O. Lat. *amasso*, Gk. δείξω to O. Lat. *dixo* and similar forms. We have also Latin forms in *ss* used as Presents, but always with a peculiar sense (§ 33. 5), e.g. *lăcesso* (cf. *lacio, lacto*), *făcesso* (cf. *facio*), *căpesso* (cf. *capio*), *incipisso* Plaut. (cf. *incipio*), *pĕtesso* (cf. *peto*; in O. Lat. *petissere*, 'saepius petere' Fest. 250. 19 Th., *adpetissis* Accius, *Trag.* 160 R.; cf. *petīvi*), *quaeso* (cf. *quaero*), *vīso* (cf. *vĭdeo*); they have sometimes been called Latin Intensives, and compared with another S-formation in which the root is reduplicated, namely, the Desideratives (sometimes with Intensive force) of Sanscrit, e.g. pí-pā-s-āmi, 'I wish to drink,' jí-jīvā-s-āmi, 'I wish to live,' íp-sāmi, 'I wish to acquire,' and the Reduplicated Futures of Celtic, such as O. Ir. gigius 'rogabo,' gigeste 'orabitis'; their Perfects in *-īvi, lacessivi, quaesivi* (used as Pft. of *quaero*), *arcessivi*, perhaps point to parallel stems in -ss-yo-, *lacessio, *quaessio, *arcessio (cf. the I.-Eur. Fut. in -syo-, Lith. bú-siu beside Gk. φύ-σω) (on *visi*, see § 41). Other O. Lat. *s*-forms (Subjunctive or rather Optative, § 55), like *averruncassis, servassis, faxis*, used in prayers, wishes, deprecations, &c. (e.g. deos ut fortunassint precor; Juppiter, prohibessis scelus; di mactassint), have been called Latin Precatives, and compared with Sanscrit Precatives (more usual in the older literature than in classical ' Sanscrit ') such as bhū-yá-s-am from bhū-, ' to be.' These O. Lat. Fut. and Opt. forms with *ss* (corresponding to *s* after a consonant, *faxo, faxim, dixo, dixim*) are mostly found in Verbs of the first Conjugation, *-asso, -assim*, Inf. *-assere*, but sometimes in Verbs of the second, e.g. *prohĭbessis, prohibessint*. They do not occur in the Aorist (Preterite) Indicative usage of Gk. ἐτίμησα (-άσσα), ἐφίλησα (-ησσα) in Latin; but, if Umbro-Oscan tt is rightly interpreted as the equivalent of I.-Eur. ss (cf. Att. πράττω for πράσσω, this σσ being a Greek development of κy), they do occur in this usage in the other Italic languages, Osc. teremnattens ' terminaverunt,' quasi *terminassunt, prúfatted ' probavit,' quasi *probassit, duunated ' donavit ' quasi *donassit, Pel. coisatens ' curaverunt' and so on (all the examples preserved belong to the first Conjugation).

§ 3.]   THE VERB. AORIST AND S-STEMS.   463

So far we have found evidence of Verb-forms with ss after a vowel, s after a consonant, used as Aorists, Futures [in the Future use often with -(s)syo- for -(s)so-], Precatives, &c., as well as of Verb-stems with a suffix consisting of a single s (e. g. *tres- the stem of Gk. τρέω), a suffix perhaps identical with the S-suffix of Verbal Nouns. It is therefore a natural inference to explain the formations with double s as due to the addition of some S-suffix to a Verb-stem already composed by means of an S-suffix, so that Latin *amasso* would be resolved into *ama-s-so*, and possibly *dīxo* into *deic-s-so*. (On *dīxo* however, see § 55; Greek Locatives Plural also like θύρασι offer an original -ss-, which after a consonant appears as -s-, e. g. φύλαξι).

This additional S-suffix may be the same as that which seems to show the form -ĕs- in Latin Future Perfects like *vīd-ero*, *amav-ero*, *dix-ero*, and Pluperfects like *vid-eram*, *amav-eram*, *dix-eram*, and which has been identified, plausibly enough, with the Substantive verb, es-, 'to be' (it appears in the form s in *ama-rem*, *fer-rem*, *age-rem*, &c.), though some regard it as the suffix -es- of Noun-stems, comparing *vīd-ero* to Gk. εἰδέ(σ)ω, *viderīmus* Subj. to Gk. εἰδέ(σ)ιμεν Opt., and these to Gk. εἶδος, -ε(σ)-ος (similarly *ferrem*, *agerem*, &c. to *ferre*, *agere*). Others make it not only -es- but -is- or -as- (ch. iv. § 3), comparing *vīd-eram* to O. Ind. á-vēd-išam, *dixeram* to O. Ind. Aorists with -siš- such as ákšišur 3 Pl., and identify this -is- or -as-, as well as -es-, with the suffix of Noun S-stems (e. g. O. Ind. rōcíš- N., Gk. γῆρας, θέμις-, Lat. *cĭnis*), and further with Latin -*is*- of *amav-is-tis*, *amav-is-sem*, *amav-is-se*, although the *i* in these Latin Perfect-forms may be merely an example of the continuation of the vowel of the 1 Sg. Ind., &c. of the Perfect throughout the declension of this Tense, as Gk. δείξαιμι, δειξάτω, &c. continue the *a* of ἔδειξα (see §§ 67, 52, 39). The Umbro-Oscan Future forms, e. g. Osc. *didest* 'dabit,' Umbr. ferest 'feret' point to the vowel having been originally e, for the Latin weakening of unaccented vowels is almost unknown in Umbro-Oscan.

Another moot point in the analysis of the Latin Verb is the explanation of what the Roman grammarians regarded as contracted forms, such as *amassem* beside *amavissem*, *amastis* beside *amavistis*, *amarunt*, *amaro*, and *amarim* beside *amavĕrunt*, *amavero*, and *amaverim*, and also such as *invassem* beside *invāsissem*, *dixem* beside *dixissem*, *dixti* and *dixtis* beside *dixisti* and *dixistis*. There is nothing in the laws of Latin Phonetics to prevent the Contraction Theory from being right; *audivissem* would become *audissem* as naturally as *sī vīs* became *sīs*, *oblīvisci* became *oblisci* (Plaut.), *dīvīnus*, *dīnus* (Plaut.) (see ch. iv. § 70); *invasissem* would become *invassem* by that Roman practice of discarding one of two similar neighbouring syllables which reduced **arcicubii* to *arcŭbii*, *Restitutus* to *Restūtus* (see ch. iii. § 13. p. 176). Thus although the comparison of *amassem* (Ē-Subj. like *amem*) with *amassim* (Opt. like *sim*, O. Lat. *siem*), *dixem* with *dixo* and *dixim*, *amarim* with *amarem* is a very natural one, it cannot be said that the evidence is at present strong enough to warrant us in relinquishing the old explanation.

Indeed the evidence to be derived from the usage of Plautus and the other Dramatists is all the other way, for we find that Plautus and Terence treat these shorter forms exactly as they treat forms that are indubitably contracted, like *jurgo* from *jūrigo* (ch. iii. § 13); in the older poet the two are used side by side, in the later contracted have ousted the uncontracted, the latter being used only at the end of a line, i.e. only through metrical necessity. (For statistics, see §§ 48, 49.)

§ 4. 'Strong Aorist' forms in Latin. Beside the Nasalized Present-stem *tăng-* of *tango*, *attingo* we find a stem *tăg-* in O. Lat. In the Dramatists *attigas*, *attigatis* (only in prohibitions) are not uncommon, e. g. Plaut. *Bacch.* 445 ne attigas puerum istac causa (cf. Non. 75. 26 M.). A lamp discovered in the very ancient Esquiline burying-ground bears the inscription : ne atigas. non sum tua. M. sum (*Ann. Inst.* 1880, p. 260). In the simple verb we have, e. g. *si tagit*, *nisi tagam* in Pacuvius (*Trag.* 344 and 165 K.) (forms compared to *con-tigit*, *at-tigit* by Festus 540. 27 M.), and probably *tăgo* in Plaut. *Mil.* 192:

remoráre: abeo. Neque té remoror neque té tago neque te—táceo.

Similarly beside the Nasalized Present-stem *toln-* of *tollo*, *attollo* (cf. *affero*), *abstollo* (cf. *aufero*) we have *attulas*, *abstulas*, &c. (or in the older spelling *attolas*, *abstolas*) in prohibitions in the Dramatists, e.g. Novius, *Com.* 87 R. dotem ad nos nullam attulas ; Pacuv. *Trag.* 228 R. :

cústodite istúnc uos: ne uim qui áttolat, neu qui áttigat,

and in the simple verb *nisi tulat* (Accius, *Trag.* 102 R.).

Beside the Present-stem formed with the suffix -yo- (§ 15), *vĕnio-*, we find a stem *vĕn-* without this suffix in the compounds *evenat*, *advenat*, *pervenat*, &c. (e. g. Plaut. metuo ne aduenat, priusquam peruenat, utinam euenat, quomodo

§§ 4, 5.] THE VERB. AORIST AND S-STEMS. 465

euenat, &c.) These Aor. forms seem to occur only at the end of a line (the same indeed is generally, but not always, true of *attigas, attulas,* &c.), and so are licences of which the Dramatic Poets availed themselves under metrical necessity. They have been also referred to a suppression of the *i* (*y*) of *eveniat,* &c., like that of *i* (*y*) in *ăbicio* (the scansion of the Dramatists) and possibly *augŭr(i)a* of Accius (see ch. ii. § 50), on the plea that the Aor.-stem would be *vem-*, for the *n* is produced from m under the influence of the following consonantal *i* (*y*), **vem-yo* (I.-Eur. **gᵘm-yo-*, Gk. βαίνω for **βαμγω*) becoming *ven-yo, vĕnio,* as *quom-jam* became *quŏniam* (ch. iv. § 73). The root is gᵘem- (cf. Goth. qiman, 'to come'). Similarly beside *părio,* to give birth to, we have *parentes.* Beside the Reduplicated Present *gi-gn-o* from the root g̑en-, we have an O. Lat. Present *geno* (cf. Priscian, i. 528. 25 H.) of the common type of *fero* (root bher-), *veho* (root weg̑h-), *sequor* (root seqᵘ-) (see § 6). This form of the Present is frequent in Varro (e. g. *R. R.* ii. 2. 19 nam et pingues facit facillime et genit lacte; *ib.* i. 31. 4 antequam genat; *Men.* 35 B. quod genunt), and occurs in the testamentary formula ' si mihi filius genitur ' (Cic. *De Orat.* ii. 42. 141) (see Georges, *Lex. Wortf.* s. v. for examples of the word). It was a moot point among Latin grammarians whether in the phrase of the XII Tables NI ITA PACVNT, the last word was 3 Plur. of a verb **paco* (whence *păciscor*; but cf. § 28), or with the old usage of writing c both for c and for g, of a verb *pago* (an unnasalized form of *pango*; cf. *pĕpĭgi*) (see ch. i. § 6). (On *rudentes,* the ropes of a ship, see below, § 6.)

§ 5. O. Lat. forms with -ss- (-s-). The forms in -(*s*)*so* 1 Sg. may be called Future-Perfects; thus *faxo* corresponds to *fĕcĕro* in Plaut. *fr.* 62 W. :

períbo si non fécero, si fáxo uapulábo,

Capt. 695 pol si istuc faxis, haud sine poena feceris; but they are often used in the Dramatists, as the ordinary Fut. Perf. is also used, in the sense of a Future, e. g. Plaut. *Poen.* 888 nisi ero uni meo indicasso, 'I will tell my master only' (see Neue, ii³. p. 548). They have an Inf. in -*ssere,* e. g. hoc credo me impetrassere, illum confido me reconciliassere, and occur sometimes in the Passive Voice in laws, e. g. *mercassitur* (*C. I. L.* i. 200. 71); *faxitur* in an old Rogatio mentioned by Livy, xxii. 10. 6 : si antidea senatus populusque iusserit fieri, ac faxitur; *turbassitur* in a law in Cicero, *De Legg.* iii. 4. 11 ; cf. uti iussitur, 'as shall be ordered,' Cato *R. R.* xiv. 1.

The forms in -(*s*)*sim* 1 Sg. have never a reference to past time like the ordinary Perfect Subjunctive; contrast, for example, Plaut. *Capt.* 127 uisam ne nocte hac ('last night') quippiam turbauerint, with Pacuvius, *Trag.* 297 R. precor ueniám petens Ut quae égi, ago, vel áxim uerruncént bene (see *A. L. L.* ii. 223); they are frequent in Plautus, who normally uses *cave dixis, cave faxis,* &c., and not (except at the end of a line, i. e. for metrical convenience) *cave dixeris, cave feceris,* &c. (after *ne* only *dixeris,* &c.), but are much less frequent in Terence. They are generally used by Plautus in the protasis of a conditional sentence (except *ausim, faxim,* which are found in the main clause), e. g. *Aul.* 228 si locassim, and similarly in old laws, e. g. the Lex Numae (ap. Fest. 194. 21 Th.) : si hominem fulminibus occisit ; we find them also in wishes, e.g. Plaut. *Aul.* 50 utinám me diui adáxint ad suspéndium, in prayers, as in the Augural Prayer (quoted by Festus, 526. 11 Th.) : bene sponsis beneque uolueris, and with *ne* in deprecations, e. g. Plaut. *Most.* 1097 ne occupassis opsecro aram, and expressions of anxiety, e.g. Plaut. *Bacch.* 598 :

H h

mihi caútiost
ne núcifrangíbula excússit ex malís meis.

These usages mark the forms in -(s)sim as the Optative Mood of the forms in -(s)so. This -(s)s- formation appears in Vowel Verbs almost only in the first Conjugation, though we find in the second *prohĭbessit, prohibessint* and *prohibessis* occasionally, *cohibessit* (Lucr. iii. 444), *licessit* (Plaut. *Asin.* 603), &c., while for the fourth *ambissit* (MSS. *ambisset*) in the (un-Plautine ?) prologue of the *Amphitruo* of Plautus, l. 71, is quoted. In Terence these forms of Vowel Verbs are very rare, e. g. *appellassis, Phorm.* 742. In Consonant-stems of the third Conjugation they are found in poetry of all periods (*faxim* and *ausim* even in prose); examples are (Labials) *capso, accepso, incepsit,* (Gutturals) *axim, taxim, insexit, noxit,* (Dentals) *baesis* (*C. G. L.* ii. 27. 55), *incensit,* (Nasals) *empsim, surempsit* (Fest.). [For other instances, see Neue, ii². 539 sqq.; *essis* of the MSS. of Nonius (200. 30 M.) in a line of Accius [*Trag. (Praet.)* 16 R.], quoted as an example of *castra* F.: cástra haec uestra est: óptime essis méritus a nobís, seems a miswriting of *escis* (cf. below, § 33. 5); *adessint* of the Lex Repetundarum (*C. I. L.* i. 198. l. 63) may stand for *ad-essent* (cf. ch. vi. § 33); *uiolasit* (*C. I. L.* xi. 4766, with *anua*) and similar forms with *s* for *ss* belong to the period when double consonants were written single (ch. i. § 8)].

§ 6. A. Present[1]. (1) With Ĕ-grade of root and Thematic Vowel. Examples are of E-roots: I.-Eur. *sĕq^{u}ŏ-, *sĕq^{u}ĕ-, Mid., ' to be following ' (O. Ind. sáca-te 3 Sg., Gk. ἕπο-μαι, O. Ir. sechur, Lith. sekù Act.), Lat. *sequor*; I.-Eur. *weĝhŏ-, *wĕĝhĕ-, ' to be carrying ' (O. Ind. váhā-mi, Pamphyl. Gk. Fεχω(?), Lith. vežù, O. Sl. vezą, Goth. ga-viga, ' I move '), Lat. *veho.* Of EI-roots : I.-Eur. *bheidhŏ-, *bheidhĕ-, ' to be trusting ' (Gk. πείθο-μαι, Goth. beida, ' I abide '), Lat. *fīdo* from O. Lat. *feido*; I.-Eur. *deiḱŏ-, *deiḱĕ-, ' to be showing, indicating ' (Goth. ga-teiha, Germ. zeige), Lat. *dīco* from O. Lat. *deico*; I.-Eur. *meiĝhŏ-, *meiĝhĕ- (O. Ind. méhā-mi, O. Engl. mīge), Lat. *meio.* Of. EU-roots : I.-Eur. *deuḱŏ-, *deuḱĕ-, ' to be leading, drawing ' (Goth. tiuha, Germ. ziehe), Lat. *dūco,* O. Lat. *douco* for *deuḱō (ch. iv. § 37); I.-Eur. *eusŏ-, *eusĕ-, ' to be burning, singeing ' (O. Ind. óṣā-mi, Gk. εὕω for *εὔhω), Lat. *ūro,* O. Lat. **ouro* from *eusō ; I.-Eur. *plewŏ-, *plewĕ-, ' to be flowing, sailing, swimming ' (O. Ind. pláva-te 3 Sg. Mid., Gk. πλέ(F)ω, O. Sl. plovą for *plew-), Lat. *pluo* from O. Lat. *plovo* (cf. Fest. 330. 29 Th. ' pateram perplovere ' in sacris cum dicitur, significat pertusam esse; so *plovebat,* Petron. 44. p. 30. 1 B.). (The form *pluo* is proper to Compounds, e. g. *perpluo,* ch. iii. § 24.)

---

[1] For a fuller list of examples of the various Present-stem formations, see Job, *le Présent et ses dérivés dans la conjugaison latine,* Paris, 1893.

§§ 6-8.]   THE VERB. PRESENT-STEMS.   467

The weak grade of the root, which in Greek appears with the accent on the suffix, and with the Aorist sense (e. g. τραπεῖν Aor. but τρέπειν Pres., πιθέσθαι Aor. but πείθεσθαι Pres., πυθέσθαι Aor. but πεύθεσθαι Pres.), has sometimes encroached on the Pres.-stem, e.g. Dor. Gk. τράπω beside Att. τρέπω, Gk. γλύφω beside I.-Eur. *gleubhŏ- (Lat. *glūbo*, O. H. G. chliubu, Engl. cleave). Similarly Lat. *rŭdo* (O. Ind. rŭdá-mi) beside *rūdo* (O. H. G. riuzu) seems to show *rŭdŏ̄- beside *reúdŏ-, so that *rŭdentes*, the ropes of a ship, lit. ' the rattlers,' ' roarers,' might be called an ' Aorist' participle (§ 4). [In Plautus we have *rūdentes, Rud.* 1015 mítte rūdentém, sceleste, as *rūdo* in Persius, iii. 9 Arcadiae pecuaria rūdere credas. The Pft. *rudivi* (Apuleius) and Verbal Noun *ru-dītus* point to a Pres.-stem *rŭd-yŏ-, like *fŭgio*, § 15.]

Examples of Verbs which have not an E-root are: *vādo*, I am going (the weak grade *văd-* is seen in *vădum*, a ford); *caedo*, from older *caido*, I.-Eur. (s)kaidh- (Goth. skaida, cf. Engl. watershed); *ăgo*, I.-Eur. *ăĝō (O. Ind. ájā-mi, Gk. ἄγω, M. Ir. agaim, &c.; the strong stem āĝ- is seen in Lat. *amb-āges*, &c.); *scăbo*, to scrape, I.-Eur. skabh- (Goth. skaba, ' I shave'; the strong stem skābh- perhaps appears in Perf. *scābi*; see § 39).

§ 7. **Other examples.** Lat. *tego* (Gk. στέγω); *rego* (Gk. ὀ-ρέγω); *lego* (Gk. λέγω). Like O. Lat. *nīvit*, beside *nĭnguit*, for *(s)neighʰŏ- (Zend snaéžaiti, Gk. νείφει, Lith. dial. snēga) is O. Lat. *fīvo* for *dheighʰŏ-(?) (Lith. dégia Intr.), for which *fīgo* was afterwards substituted by Analogy of *fīxi*, &c. The form with *v* which, we are told, was used by Cato [Paul. Fest. 65. 19 Th. ' fivere' (apud Catonem) pro figere], reappears in the derivative *fībula* for *fīvi-bula* (cf. *fixul-ae*, Paul. Fest. 64. 7 Th. ' fixulas,' fibulas). (Lith. dygùs however points to *dhīghʰŏ-, and we have *fīgier*, not *fei-* on the S. C. Bacch.).

O. Lat. *amploctor* (veteres immutaverunt 'amploctor' crebro dictitantes, Diom. 384. 8 K.), e. g. Liv. Andr. *Odyss.*:

útrum génua amplóctens uírginem oráret,

may take its *o* from a Derivative Noun (cf. *toga* from *tego*, ch. iv. § 52, and see below, § 33. 3). The *o* of *cŏquō* for *quĕ-quō* (O. Ind. pac-, Gk. πέσσω, O. Sl. pekǫ) has been similarly referred to the influence of *cŏquus*.

§ 8. **Weak grade of root.** *Verto* is in O. Lat. *vorto* (Plaut., &c.), so that instead of showing the vowel ĕ of I.-Eur. *wĕrt-ō (O. Ind. vártatē 3 Sg. Mid., Goth. vairþa, ' I become'), it seems to show the o of the Perfect, O. Lat. *vorti* (with weak-grade of stem, wṛt-, as in O. Ind. va-vṛt-ē Perf. Mid.) and the P. P. P., O. Lat. *vorsus* for *wṛt-to (O. Ind. vṛt-tá-). But in Umbr. we find *vert-* in the Present, *vort-* in the Perfect and Verbal Noun, ku-vertu, *co-vertu* ' convertito,' ku-vurtus, 'converteris,' co-vortus, vorsum Acc. πλέθρον. The O. Lat. spelling *vorto* is in all probability a mere matter of spelling; the Present was always pronounced with *e*, *verto*, but at the time when *vo-* had come to be pronounced *ve-* (see ch. iv. § 10), it was occasionally spelt (not pronounced) *vorto*. O. Lat. *vorro* for **verso* (O. H. G. wirru, 'verwirre') may be similarly explained. In Gk. γί-γν-ο-μαι Pres., ἐ-γεν-ό-μην Aor. we find the E-root relegated to the Preterite, while a modification of the root by Reduplication is assigned to the Present (see next paragraph). In O. Lat. and O. Ind., however, the E-form, ĝen-, appears also as a Present-stem (O. Lat. *genunt*, O. Ind. ján-a-ti 3 Sg.) (see §§ 3-4). Similarly, Lat. *peto* is regarded by some as originally an Aorist-stem, the Present-stem being formed with the -YŎ-suffix (§ 15), **petio* 1 Sg., whence the Perfect *petīvi*.

Other examples of the unaccented verb-form of a Latin Compound asserting itself in the uncompounded verb are : *clūdo* for *claudo* (see ch. ii. § 36) ; *luo* for *lavo* (Sil. Ital. xi. 22) ; *spicio*, *sico* for *spĕcio*, *sĕco* (see ch. ii. § 12). (For additional instances, e. g. *plico*, see Solmsen, *Stud. Lautg.* p. 130.)

§ 9. (2) **With reduplicated root.** Latin examples are: *gigno* [I.-Eur. **ĝĭ-ĝnŏ-*, **ĝĭ-ĝn-ĕ* from root ĝen-, which also occurs with Them. Vow. as a Pres.-stem in O. Ind. and O. Lat. (§§ 3-4), Gk. γίγνομαι], *bibo* for **pibo* (ch. iv. § 163)(I.-Eur. **pĭ-bŏ-*, **pĭ-bĕ-*, O. Ind. píba-ti 3 Sg., O. Ir. ibi-d ; cf. Faliscan pipafo Fut.), *sisto* (I.-Eur. **sĭ-stŏ-*, **sĭ-stĕ-* from root stā-, O. Ind. tíṣṭha-ti 3 Sg.), *sīdo* for **sĭ-sdo* (ch. iv. § 151) (I.-Eur. **sĭ-zdŏ-*, **sĭ-zdĕ-* from root sed-, O. Ind. sída-ti 3 Sg. for **sisd-*, Umbr. *ander-sistu* 'intersidito' Imper., for **sisd(e)-tōd*). Often these Reduplicated Present-stems belong to the Athematic Conjugation, e. g. Gk. ἵστη-μι for **si-stā-mĭ* (O. H. G. sestō-m), beside Lat. *sisto*, O. Ind. tíṣṭhā-mi ; and Latin *sistĭmus*, *sistĭtis* correspond as well with the Greek ἵστᾰ-μεν, ἵστᾰ-τε, as with the thematic forms. Similarly Gk. ἵημι (I.-Eur. **sĭ-sē-*, athematic) is in Latin thematic in *sĕro* for **si-so*, though *seri-mus*, *seri-tis* may be equally referred to athematic **sisa-* as to thematic **sisŏ-*, **sisĕ-* ; I.-Eur. **dĭ-dō-*, athematic (Gk. δίδω-μι, O. Ind. dádā-mi) has in Latin lost its reduplication, except in *reddo*, if this stands for *re-d(i)do* as *reppuli*, *repperi* for *re-p(e)puli*, *re-p(e)peri*, but not in Umbro-Oscan (Pelign. dida 'det,' Umbr. *dirsa* pronounced **dĭďa* ?). All these Latin examples reduplicate with the vowel ĭ, and most belong to roots ending in a long vowel. Some Greek Aorist-stems show this reduplication with the vowel ĕ, e. g. ἔ-πεφνο-ν from root φεν-, ἐ-κέκλε-το from root κελ-, πεπῐθ-ών from root πειθ-, πεπῠθ-οιτο from root πευθ-, by analogy of which the spurious Presents πέφνω, κέκλομαι have been formed. Short *e* is also the Reduplicationvowel of the Perfect-stem (see § 39).

§§ 9, 10.]   THE VERB. PRESENT-STEMS.   469

§ 10. (3) **With root nasalized.** Of the ten conjugations under which the Hindu grammarians have classified the Sanscrit verb, three are assigned to these nasalized Present-stems, one (the seventh conjugation) showing a nasal infix, I.-Eur, -nĕ-, varying with -n-, e.g. yŭ-ná-j-mi 1 Sg., yŭ-ñ-j-más 1 Pl., yuɲk-té 3 Sg. Mid. (Lat. *jŭ-n-go*), from the root yuj- (I.-Eur. yeug-), the other two showing a nasal affix, viz. the ninth conjugation with -nā- varying with a weak grade (O. Ind. -nī-), e. g. str̥-ná-mi 1 Sg., str̥-nī-más 1 Pl., str̥-nī-tē 3 Sg. Mid. (Lat. *ster-no*), and the fifth conjugation with I.-Eur. -neu- (O. Ind. -nō-) varying with -nŭ-, e.g. r̥-n̥ó-mi 1 Sg., r̥-n̥ŭ-más 1 Pl., r̥-n̥ŭ-té 3 Sg Mid. (Gk. ὄρ-νῡ-μι). In Greek the type of Present corresponding to the Sanscrit seventh conjugation has only -n-, never -nĕ-, and has been usually modified by the addition either of a nasal affix, e.g. not *λῐ́-μ-πω (Lat. *lĭ-n-quo*) but λίμ-π-άνω (so τυ-γ-χ-άνω, λα-υ-θ-άνω, &c.), or of the -YŎ-, -YĔ- suffix, e. g. κλάζω for *κλαγγ-yω (cf. ἔ-κλαγξα) (Lat. *clango*); the Sanscrit ninth conjugation is represented by σκίδ-νη-μι 1 Sg., σκίδ-νᾰ-μεν 1 Pl., σκίδ-νᾰ-μαι Mid., πίτ-νη-μι 1 Sg., πίτ-νᾰ-μεν 1 Pl., πίτ-νᾰ-μαι Mid., &c.; the Sanscrit fifth conjugation by ἄγ-νῡ-μι 1 Sg., ἄγ-νῠ μεν 1 Pl., ἄγ-νῠ-μαι Mid., σκεδάννῡμι, πετάννῡμι, &c. In Sanscrit all these nasalized stems belong to the Athematic Conjugation, though we have thematic byforms like 3 Sg. yuñjáti, r̥nváti ; but in Greek the first type mentioned is always thematic, e. g. λιμπάνω, the others occasionally, e. g. πιτνάω, δαμνάω (byforms of πίτνημι, δάμνημι), ἰσχανάω, &c., στρωννύω, τρωννύω, ὀρίνω for ὀρινϜω, &c., while we have another type with -νεω, e. g. ἱκνέομαι, ὑπισχνέομαι, κινέω. The discrepancy between Greek and Sanscrit, the two languages in which these nasalized stems have been most fully preserved, makes it difficult to determine the original I.-Eur. types of nasalization (see *I. F.* ii. pp. 285 sqq.). In default of a better classification, we may arrange the Latin nasalized Presents in two classes, according as the nasal presents the appearance of a nasal infix or a nasal affix.

i. **With nasal infix**, e. g. *lĭ-n-quo* (O. Ind. rĭ-ná-c-mi 1 Sg., rĭ-ñ-c-más 1 Pl., Pruss. po-linka, ' he remains ' ; cf. Gk. λῐμπάνω), from root leiqᵘ- (Gk. λείπω, Lith. lëkù, Goth. leihva, ' I lend,' Germ. leihe) ; *fĭ-n-do* (O. Ind. bhĭ-ná-d-mi) from root bheid-

(Goth. beita, 'I bite'). The variation of -nĕ- and -n- seen in O. Ind. rĭ-ná-c-mi 1 Sg., rĭ-n̂-c-más 1 Pl., is not seen in other languages, where the weak grade -n- is used throughout. The Latin Presents *conquĭniscor* (Perf. *conquexus*), to stoop, and possibly *frūniscor* (cf. *fructus*), to enjoy, do however perhaps show the fuller suffix -nĕ- combined with the Inceptive suffix -s*k*o- (§ 22), if -*niscor* stands for -*nĕc-scor*, with loss of *c* (*g*) in the group -*csc*- as in *disco* for *d*ĭ*c-sco* (ch. iv. § 157), and with *i* by analogy of other Inceptives (see § 28); and Gk. κυ-νέ-(σ)-ω, Aor. ἔ-κυσ-α, may do the same. These forms with nasal infix are often augmented by the YŎ-suffix (§ 15), e.g. Gk. πτίσσω for *πτίνσ-yω, πλάζω, to beat, for *πλαγγ-yω (cf. ἔ-πλαγξα), κλάζω for *κλαγγ-yω (cf. ἔ-κλαγξα), Lith. jùng-iu, beside Lat *pinso*, *plango*, *clangó*, and *jungo*; and so in Lat. *pinsio*, *sancio* (cf. *săc-er*), *vincio* (from the root vyek-). English examples of nasal infix are: 'I spring,' from *spr̥-n-ĝhō, from the root sperĝh- (Gk. σπέρχομαι); 'I wring,' from the root werĝh- (Lith. verž-iù, 'I squeeze'). ('I stand' belongs to a rare type of I.-Eur. Present-stem in -NT, on which see Osthoff in *Versamml. Philolog.* xxi. p. 300.)

ii. **With nasal affix.** I.-Eur. lĭ-nā- (O. Ind. lĭ-nā-mi, Gk. λί-νă-μαι· τρέπομαι Hesych., O. Ir. lĕnim, 'I cling to, follow,' O. Scand. lina, 'I grow weak') is Lat. *lĭ-no*, from a root lei-, so that the I.-Eur. affix -nā- has been lost in Latin (unless *lino* represents **li-nā-ō*), and only its weak grade (O. Ind. -nī-, Gk. -vă-) remains, e.g. *lĭ-nĭ-mus* (Gk. *λῐ-vă-μεν). The -*nā*- of *aspernāri* (beside *sperno*), *consternāre*, to terrify (beside *consterno*, to strew) (but cf. ch. iii. § 19), *declīnāre* and *inclīnāre* (beside Gk. κλίνω), *destĭnāre* (beside Gk. στάνω and στανύω) cannot quite be identified with I.-Eur. -nā- (O. H. G. spor-nō-n, O. Ind. str̥-nā-ti 3 Sg., O. Sax. hli-nō-n; cf. O. H. G. stornēn, 'to be astonished,' hlinēn), for the same *ā* appears in compounds of other than nasal-stems, e.g. *occŭpāre* (beside *căpere*), *profligāre* (beside *flĭgere*) (see § 32), and the -*ĭnā*- of *la-n-c-inā-re* (cf. *lăc-er*), *coqu-ĭnā-re* (cf. *cŏquo*), which indeed suggests comparison rather with Gk. -ăvo- of λι-μ-π-άνω, ἁμαρτ-άνω, &c., than with Gk. -vā- of σκίδ-νη-μι, πίτ-νη-μι, seems to show the -*ā*- (I.-Eur. -āyŏ-) of Derivative Verbs (§ 32), like *sarcĭnatus* from *sarcĭna* (a Derivative with nasal suffix from *sarcio*, as *facĭnus* from *facio*), *runcĭnare* from *runcĭna*, *pāgĭnare* from *pāgĭna*, or *nomĭnare* from *nomen* (cf. *destĭna*, a prop). The I.-Eur. affix -neu-, -nŭ- has left very few traces in Latin: *ster-nu-o* (Gk. πτάρ-νῠ-μαι), *mĭ-nu-o* (O. Ind. mĭ-nō-mi ; cf. Gk. μῠ́-νῠ́-θω), probably for *mĭ-new-ō, &c. (cf. *dēnuo* for de *newōd, ch. iii. § 24). English examples of nasal affix are 'I spurn,' 'I shine' (Goth. skei-na), 'I fill' (with ll for ln). By rule the Nasalization should be confined to the Present Tense, and not extended to other than Present forms: e.g. *li-n-quo, re-lĭqui, re-lic-tus*; *sĭ-n-o, sĭ-vi, sĭ-tus*. But it pervades the whole verb in some cases, e.g. *jungo, junxi, junctus*. The weak grade of the root is proper to all these Nasalized Present-stems, e.g. *jungo* from root yeug-, *lĭno* from root lei-, *mĭ-nu-o* from root mei-.

§ 11. Other examples of nasal infix. Lat. *rŭ-m-po* (O. Ind. lŭ-m-pámi), from root reup- (O. Engl. berēofe, Engl. I bereave) ; *pi-n-so* (O. Ind. pĭ-ná-ṣ-mi ; cf. Gk. πτίσσω for *πτινσγω, Lat. *pinsio*) ; *sci-n-do* (O. Ind. chĭ-ná-d-mi) ; *fungor* (O. Ind. bhu-ná-j-mi); *lĭ-n-go*, from root leigh- (Gk. λείχω) (cf. O. H. G. lecchōm, from *ligh-nā-mi) ; *vĭ-n-co*, from root weik- (Goth. veiha, 'I fight'); *cla-n-go* (O. Scand. hlakka ; cf. Gk. κλαγγάνω, κλάζομαι), from root klag- (Lith. klagéti, 'to cackle') ; *pre-he-n-do* (Alb. gendem, 'I am found,' Lett. gĭdu, 'I apprehend, perceive,' for *gendu ; cf. Gk. χανδάνω, χείσομαι Fut. for *χενδ-σομαι), from root ghed- (Engl. get, Lat. *praeda* for *prae-hed-a) ; *di-stĭ-n-guo* (Goth. stigqa, 'I thrust' ; cf. Lith. sténgiu), from the root steigh- (O. Ind. téjatē, 'is sharp' ; cf. Lat. *in-stīgare*) ; *e-mŭ-n-go* (O. Ind. muñcáti, 'he releases,' Lett. múku, 'I escape,' for *munku) ; *fĭ-n-go* (O. Ir. dengaim, 'I fasten'), from root dheigh- (Goth. deiga) ; *tŭ-n-do* (Pft. *tŭ-tŭ-di*) ; *pŭ-n-go* (Pft. *pŭ-pŭg-i*) ; *accŭ-m-bo* (cf. *cŭbare*, Pft. *ac-cŭb-ui*) ; *tă-n-go* (Pft. *te-tig-i*, for *te-tăg-i, Gk. τεταγών) ; *lă-m-bo* (cf. *lăb-ium*) ; *rĭ-n-gor* (O. Sl. rẹg-nạ, augmented by -no-), beside *rictus*.

§ 12. Retention of Nasal throughout the Tenses. Like *jungo, junxi, junctum* (with possibly a Neuter Noun *jungus, -eris*, 'a team,' like Gk. ζεῦγος, in Plaut. Men. 913 : nón potest haec rés ellebori iúngere optinérier), we have *pungo, punctum* (but *pŭpŭgi* ; Priscian says the Perf. of *repungo* is *repunxi*, like *expunxi*, or *repupugi*, i. 524. 13 H.) ; *distinguo, distinxi, distinctum ; fingo, finxi* (but *fictum ; finctum*, Ter. *Eun*. 104) ; *plango, planxi, planctum ; emungo, emunxi, emunctum ; lingo, linxi, linctum ; fungor, functus* [but on plebeian inscriptions *defuctus* (C. I. L. ii. 4173), like *sactus*, e. g. *sactissimae* (vi. 15511, v. 6580), whence the Welsh loanword saith beside sant ; *nactus* and *nanctus* are equally good spellings, see Georges, *Lex. Wortf*. s. v.]. Spellings in MSS. like *corrumptus* (Neue, ii². 560), *relinqui*, Perf., are due to the same confusion. When the stem is extended by the YO-suffix, the n is retained, e. g. *vincio, vinxi, vinctum*, from root vyek-, beside *vinco, vici, victum* from root weik-, *sanctus* from *sancio*. Of roots ending in a dental we have e. g. from *tundo, tunsus* and (post-Aug.) *tusus*, and the grammarians speak of a Perf. *tunsi* (Georges, s. v.) ; but the dropping of *n* before *s* in pronunciation makes it doubtful how far the nasal was really present in such forms (see ch. ii. § 66 on *thensaurus* for θησαυρός ; cf. *mensus* from *mētior*).

472   THE LATIN LANGUAGE.   [Chap. VIII.

§ 13. Other examples of nasal affix. Lat. *sperno* (O. H. G. fir-spirni-t 3 Sg., spurnu), with Perf. *sprē-vi*, as *cerno* Perf. *crē-vi* (cf. Gk. τέμ-ν-ω, ἐ-τμή-θην) ; O. Lat. *degunere* (degustare, Paul. Fest. 50. 36 Th. ; cf. Gl. Philox. degunere: ἀπογεύσασθαι καὶ συγγνῶσαι) for *de-gus-nere from root geus- (Gk. γεύ(σ)ω, Goth. kiusa, Engl. I choose); *ap-pellāre* and *com-pellāre* for *-pel-nā-re (Gk. πίλ-νă-μαι, I approach, O. Ir. ad-ellaim), beside *pellere*, to strike ; the Compound-stem with -nā- has a peculiar sense also in *de-stĭ-nā-re, prae-stĭ-nā-re*, which in Plautus are used for 'to buy,' e. g. *Most.* 646 quid, eas quanti destinat? ; Capt. 848 alium piscis praestinatum abire (cf. Arm. sta-na-m, 'I possess, buy'), *ob-stĭ-nā-re*, to stickle for, Plaut. *Aul.* 267 :

id inhiat, ea affinitatem hanc óbstinauit grátia,

whence *obstinatus* ; there is a gloss, *gredinunda* βαδίζουσα, *C. G. L.* ii. 36. 10.

§ 14. Other Verb-stems with n. From Nasalized Present-stems we must distinguish (1) O. Lat. forms of the 3 Plur. Pres. Ind. like *dānunt, explēnunt, prodīnunt*, on which see § 73 ; (2) Derivative Ā-Verbs from Noun and Adjective Nasal-stems : e. g. *opīnor, -āri* from a Noun *opion-, connected with *praed-opiont* (MSS. praedotiont) 'praeoptant' of the Carmen Saliare (Fest. 244. 13 Th.), *optio, optare*, &c. ; *festino, -āre ; vulpīnor, -āri*, to use the wiles of a fox (Varro, *Men.* 327 B.) ; *auctiōnor, -āri ; contiōnor, -āri ; sarcino, -āre ; nomĭno, -āre* (see above); (3) Verbs in which the nasal belongs to the root, e. g. *tendo*, formed from the root ten- by means of the suffix *d* (§ 33) ; *frendo* similarly for *frem-d-o ; offendo, defendo* from the root ghᵘen-, 'to strike' (Gk. θείνω for *θενγω).

The verb *pando* is of doubtful origin. Some make it a nasalized form like *unda* (cf. Lith. vandŭ beside Goth. vatō, Engl. water ; O. Ind. udán- beside Gk. ὕδωρ); others make it a word-group, *patem-do, lit. 'I make opening,' like *vendo* and *vēnum do* [Osc. patensíns ' aperirent ' (?) has also been variously explained]. *Mando*, to chew, if connected with Gk. μασάομαι for *ματιαομαι (?), will be a parallel formation.

§ 15. With suffix -YŎ-, -ĬYŎ-. Like the Noun-suffix -yŏ-, -ĭyŏ- (ch. v. § 4) this varies with -yĕ-, -ĭyĕ- or with -ĭ-. Owing to the weakening of vowels in unaccented syllables in Latin, it is difficult to ascertain the exact form of the suffix in the various persons of the Present Tense ; but the analogy of other languages points to a declension like this of those Presents in which -yŏ- varied with -ĭ- : 1 Sg. *cup-yō, 2 Sg. *cup-i-s, 3 Sg. *cup-i-t, 1 Pl. *cup-yŏ-mos, 2 Pl. *cup-i-tes, 3 Pl. *cup-yo-nt (see Brugmann, *Grundriss*, ii. § 702).

Two classes of Present-stems with the YŎ-suffix stand out very clearly, though they occasionally overlap :

i. With E-grade of root and accent on the root, e. g. Lat. *spĕc-io* (O. Ind. páś-ya-ti, Zend spas-yẹ-iti, Gk. σκέπτομαι for *σκεπ-yo-μαι).

§§ 13–15.] THE VERB. PRESENT-STEMS. 473

ii. **With weak grade of root and accent on the suffix**, e. g. Lat. *mŏr-ior* for **mr̥-yōr* (O. Ind. mr-iyá-tē 3 Sg.), *věnio* for **gᵘm-yō* (O. Ind. gam-yá-tē, Gk. βαίνω for **βṇ-yω*). To the second belong intransitive verbs (e. g. O. Sl. sto-ją, 'I stand'); and so intimately connected is this type of the suffix with intransitive sense, that in Sanscrit its Middle is used as the Passive of all verbs, e. g. kriyé, 'I am made,' kriyáte, 'he is made,' the Passive of karómi, 'I make,' karóti, 'he makes.' In the Balto-Slavic family of languages these verbs show in the other tenses an Ē-suffix, clearly the same as the Greek Passive -η- of ἐ-μάν-η-ν beside μαίνομαι for **μṇ-yo-μαι*, a suffix likewise identified with the intransitive or passive sense. This conjugation of intransitive verbs is not found in Latin, but it has perhaps left its mark in the coexistence of Presents in -*io* and -*eo*, e. g. *jăcio* and *jăceo*, *păvio* and *păveo*. In most cases however the Ē-suffix ousted the YŎ-suffix altogether, e. g. *sĕdeo*, *sed-ē-s*, *sed-ē-mus*, &c. from an I.-Eur. Present-stem **sed-yŏ-* (Gk. ἕζομαι for **σεδ-yo-μαι*, O. H. G. sizzu for **sed-yō*), *video*, *vid-ē-s*, *vid-ē-mus*, &c. from an I.-Eur. Present-stem **wid-yŏ-* (O. Ind. vid-yá-tē, 'he is perceived,' Lith. pa-výdžiu 1 Sg. Pres.) with another (originally not a Present) stem in -ē- (Lith. pa-vydḗti Inf.). [In Goth. vitais for **widēyĕ-s*, vitaiþ for **wid-ēyĕ-t*, and in other Teutonic verbs, the same intrusion of -ē- (-ēyŏ-) into the Pres.-stem is seen as in Latin.] These Intransitive Verbs with Inf. -*ēre* constitute an important part of the second Conjugation in Latin, e. g. *călēre*, *rŭbēre*, *pătēre*; they acquire a Transitive sense by appending *făcio* to a Verb-stem in -*ē* (ch. v. § 51), e. g, *călē-făcio*, and often take as their Present-stem an 'Inceptive' formation in -*sco*, e. g. *incălesco*, *ērŭbesco* (see § 28). The association of this type with the Intransitive functions is seen in *pendeo* Intrans. beside *pendo* Trans., *mădeo* (Gk. μαδάω), *věreor* (Gk. ὁράω, ch. iv. § 10), *clueo* and *cluo* (Gk. κλύω).

Another class of Presents which show the YŎ-suffix is—

iii. **With -ā, -ē, -ō after the root**. Beside the root pel-, for example, we have the root plē-, 'to fill,' with a Present-stem **plē-yŏ-*, 'to be filling' (Lat. *im-pleo*); beside the root ter- we have the root trē-, 'to penetrate,' (cf. Gk. τρῆ-μα) with a Present-stem **trē-yŏ-* (O. H. G. drāu, Germ. drehe), as well as the root trā-,

with a Present-stem *trā-yŏ- (O. Ind. trá-ya-tē, Lat. *in-tro* for
*-trāyō) (see ch. iv. § 66). Unlike the second Conj. verbs just
mentioned, *vĭdeo, sĕdeo*, &c. with Perfects *vīdi, sēdi*, Supines *vīsum,
sessum*, and *căleo, rŭbeo*, &c. with Perfects *călui, rŭbui* and with
Supines wanting, these ē-verbs retain their *ē* throughout the conjugation, *-plēvi, -plētum*, &c. In addition to monosyllabic Verb-
stems we have such dissyllabic stems as Lat. **domā-yō, dŏmo* (O.
Ind. damā-yá-ti), and a group of onomatopoetic words, e. g. Lat.
*ul-ulā-yo, ŭlŭlo (Lith. ul-ūló-ju, and unreduplicated utó-ju, Gk.
ὑλάω for **ὑλά-yω*). Beside the Present-stems with the YŎ-suffix
we find athematic Presents from these roots with -ā, -ē, -ō (e. g.
O. Ind. trā-ti beside trá-ya-tē, Gk. πίμ-πλη-μι, τί-τρη-μι, κί-χη-μι)
which seem to have originally retained the long vowel throughout,
and not to have variation with the weak grade (e. g. O. Ind. trá-sva
2 Sg. Imper. Mid., Gk. κί-χη-μεν Pl.); and in Latin this athematic
formation appears to be used in all persons but the first, *in-trā-s,
in-trā-mus*, &c., though this cannot be proved, seeing that, e. g.
im-plēs is equally derivable from thematic *-plē-yĕ-s (cf. *trēs* for
*trĕy-ĕs, ch. iv. § 66) as from athematic *-plē-s (O. Ind. prá-si).

The YŎ-suffix played a great part in the I.-Eur. languages as
a secondary suffix, added to Verb-stems, e. g. Lat. *pinsio* beside
pinso (an already-formed Pres.-stem, § 10), Gk. ἐσθίω beside
ἔσθω, or to Noun-stems, &c. to form derivative verbs, e. g. Lat.
cūro, for **curā-yō* (Umbr. kuraia, 'curet') from the Noun-stem
*curā-, claudeo for **claudĕ-yō* from the Adjective-stem **claudĕ-,
*claudŏ-, fīnio for **fīni-yō* from the Noun-stem **fīni-, stătuo* for
*statu-yō from the Noun-stem **statu-, custōdio* for **custod-yō*
from the Noun-stem **custōd-*, and so on. But since the suffix is
in these derivatives usually maintained throughout the Latin
conjugation, *pinsītus, custodīvi, custodītus*, &c., they are better
reserved for discussion among the Verb-suffixes in § 26 (cf. Gk.
δαί-σω, δαί-νῡ-μι beside δαίω for **δα-yω*). Derivatives from
Ā-stems follow the analogy of roots with -ā (e. g. Lat. *in-tro,
in-trās, in-trāmus*, see above) in using the YO-suffix only to form
the thematic 1st Pers. Sg. of the Present Tense, while those
from U-stems use it in all persons, e. g. *stătuo, statuis, statuimus*.
For Latin athematic forms like *curā-mus* derived from stem
curā-, &c. we may compare the athematic flexion of similar

§§ 16, 17.]   THE VERB. PRESENT-STEMS.   475

Derivative Verbs in the Lesbian dialect, e. g. τίμᾱ-μεν, derived from stem τιμᾱ-, φίλη-μι, derived from stem φιλε-, στεφάνωμι, derived from stem στεφανο-. English examples of Present-stems with the YŎ-suffix are 'I lie' [O. H. G. ligg(i)u, but Pret. lag, 'I lay'], and the two Pres. Participles which have become Nouns, 'a fiend' (Goth. fijands, lit. 'hating'), 'a friend' (Goth. frijōnds, lit. 'loving').

§ 16. Ĭ in the third Conj. Presents with YŎ-suffix. We have ī often in O. Lat.; cupīs, Plaut. *Curc.* 364:

> laúdo. Laudató, quando illud, quod cupis, effécero,

facīs, *Amph.* 555 (so the MSS.); facĭt, *Curc.* 258 (?); inlicīte is the scansion required by the metre in a line of Naevius (*Trag.* 30 R.):

> sublímen altos sáltus inlicíte, ubi
> bipedés uolantes (MSS. uolucres) líno linquant lúmina ;

in 1 Pers. Plur., morīmur is attested by Priscian (i. p. 501. 16 H.) in a couplet of Ennius (*Ann.* 415 M.):

> nunc est ille dies, cum gloria maxima sese
> nobis ostendat, si uiuimus siue morimur ;

we have adgredīmur, Plaut. *Asin.* 680, *Rud.* 299; and in 3 Sg. Dep. adorītur is attested by Prisc. (*l. c.*) in a line of Lucilius (or Lucretius iii. 515 ?). The long vowel is especially common in the Inf. of the Deponent in Plautus, e. g. adgredīri, morīri, effodīri (cf. parīre). (For other examples, see Neue, ii². p. 415.) These forms can hardly be due to the false Analogy of verbs like *finio*, -īvi, -ītum, -īre, such as is seen in Late Lat. *farcī-tus* (coined on the type of *finī-tus*), for they are a feature of the older language. They rather indicate that in the period of the early literature the suffix might appear as ĭ or as ī, whereas in the classical period the usage became restricted to one or other of these forms The best explanation then of Verbs in -io 1 Sg. Pres. Ind. which belong to the third Conjugation is that they are YŎ-stems in which -ĭ- asserted itself, rather than -ī-, as the weak grade of -yŏ- (-yĕ-) ; capĕre will then stand for *capĭsĭ, cape for *capĭ. This does not however preclude the possibility of other explanations being right in particular cases, such as that a bystem without -yŏ- existed, say *fac- beside *fac-yŏ- (cf. *bene-ficent-ior* beside *faciens*), *rap- beside *rap-yŏ (cf. *rapo*, 'a robber,' Varro, *Men.* 378 B.), that -ī- belongs to a stem in -ĭyŏ-, -ĭ- to a stem in -yŏ-, e. g. spĕcio from stem *spek̑-yo- (cf. Gk. σκέπτω) with the YŎ-suffix immediately following on a consonant.

§ 17. Other examples of E-grade roots. Lat. *vĕrio, 'to close,' seen in op-(w)erio, ap-(w)erio (Lith. už-veriu, 'I shut,' àt-veriu, 'I open') (on the loss of w, see ch. iv. § 71); *ind-uo* for *indovo from *-ew-yō, to judge from Umbr. an-ovihi-mu for *and-ov-ī-mu, 'induimino' (ch. iii. § 24) from the root ew-, 'to put on.' Similarly *haurio* for *aurio* (*exaurio* is the almost invariable spelling of Latin Glossaries, Löwe, *Prodr.* p. 371 n.) from root aus- (cf. Gk. ἐξαῦσαι, 'to take out,' ἐξαυστήρ, 'a flesh-hook'); *crōc-io* (Gk. κρώζω from *κρωγ-yω, Lith. krok-iù and krog-iù).

§ 18. Of weak grade roots. i. With -*io*. Lat. *cŭp-io* (O. Ind. kup-ya-ti, 'is in agitation') ; *fŭgio* (cf. Hom. πε-φυζότες for -φυγyo-) from root bheug- (Gk. φεύγω) ; *grădior* from the root ghredh- (Goth. gridi- F., 'a step,' O. Sl. gręd̨ą, 'I come,' O. Ir. in-grennim, ' I pursue, attack,' the last two with Nasalized stem) shows the weakening of -rĕ- to -ră- mentioned in ch. iv. § 51 ; similarly *farcio* for **fracio* (Gk. φράσσω) from the root bhreqᵘ- of *frequens* (and for the connexion of 'cramming' and 'frequency,' cf. *saepe* and O. Lat. *saepissumus*, 'closely packed,' ch. ix. § 4) ; likewise *răpio*, if connected with *rĕpens*, 'sudden.'

ii. Intransitive with -*eo*. Lat. *rŭbeo* from an I.-Eur. *rŭdh-yō (O. Sl. růždą, with the ē-suffix in Inf. rŭdĕ-ti) ; *torpeo* with trp- the weak grade of the root terp- ; *stŭdeo* (cf. Gk. σπεύδω?) ; *măneo* (cf. Gk. μένω), and *păteo* (cf. Gk. πετ-άννυμι), both seem to show Lat. *ă* as a weak grade of *ĕ* (ch. iv. § 3). Like *rŭbeo* with Noun *rŭbor*, *torpeo* with Noun *torpor* and Adj. *torpĭdus* are a large number of Intransitive Verbs, *căleo* (*calor, calidus*), *plăceo* (*placidus* ; but Transitive *plāco*), *lĭqueo* (*lĭquor, lĭquidus* ; cf. *lĭquor*, third Conj.), and so on (ch. v. § 74). The *tĕneo* of *per-tineo*, lit. 'to reach through,' *trans-tineo*, 'to reach across' (Plaut. *Mil.* 468 commeatus transtinet trans parietem) is the Neuter of *tendo*.

§ 19. Alternative forms in -o and -eo. Lat. *tueor* and *tuor*, 'to look' ; *fulgeo* and *fulgo* ; *ferveo* and *fervo* ; *scăteo* and *scato* ; *abnuo* and O. Lat. *abnueo* (Diom. 382. 11 K.). In all of these the form in -*o* is the older (e. g. *contuor, intuor* Plaut., *scato* Plaut., Enn., Lucr. ; *fervit* and *fervĕre* are common in the early Dramatists, the latter often in Virgil, but to Quintilian a third Conjugation form of this verb is 'inauditum,' Quint. i. 6. 8), while the form in -*eo* is a new formation on the Analogy of the numerous Intransitives in -*eo* (cf. Caper 109. 16 K. fido non 'fideo'). We have *sordĕre* in Plaut. *Poen.* 1179. (See also below, § 33.)

§ 20. Of roots with -ā, -ē, -ō. Latin *no* for **snā-yō* (O. Ind. snā-ya-tē, and athem. snā́-ti, Lat. *nat*) ; *neo* for **(s)nē-yō* (Gk. νέω, O. H. G. nāu, Germ. nähe), *tăceo* for **tacē-yō* (Goth. þahai)þ 3 Sg. from **takē-yĕ-ti, and athem. O. H. G. dagē-s, Lat. *tacēs*) ; *flo* for **flā-yō* (cf. O. H. G. blāu from *bhlē-yō, perhaps the same word as Lat. *fleo* for **flē-yō*, Gk. φλέω, to overflow) ; *hio* for **hiā-yō* (Lith. žió-ju) from the root ĝhei- ; *jŭvo* for **juvā-yō*, I.-Eur. *dyüĝᵘā-yō, from the root dyeugᵘ- (cf. Lith. džiung-ŭ-s, 'I rejoice,' a nasalized Present) (but cf. ch. iv. § 64) ; *cŭbo* for **cub-āyō* from the root keubh- (cf. -*cumbo*, a nasalized Present). Of onomatopoetic words with 1 Sg. Pres. in -*āyō*, we have *murmuro, tintinno, unco*, to bray (Gk. ὀγκάομαι).

§ 21. Inceptives, and other Verb-stems. Though Inceptive verbs by virtue of their meaning restrict, as a rule, the inceptive suffix -skŏ- (-skŏ-) to the Present sense, e. g. *cresco*, Pft. *crēvi*; they differ from Present-stem formations like *s̆no*, Pft. *sivi*, *căpio*, Pft. *cēpi*, in this respect, that the meaning, which they express, is something more than the mere sense of action in present time, e.g. *sĕnesco* means, not 'I am old' (*sĕneo*), but 'I become old.' They are therefore better considered in a separate

§§ 18-23.] THE VERB. PRESENT-STEMS. 477

section, along with some verb-formations which are more than mere Tense-stems, such as Causatives, Intensives, Desideratives, and the like.

§ 22. **Inceptives in -skŏ- (-skŏ-)**. The root shows, as a rule, the weak grade, e. g. I.-Eur. *pṛk̂-skŏ- (O. Ind. pṛ-chā́-mi, with *-skh- for *-sk-), Lat. *posco* for *porc-sco*, from the root prek̂-. It is sometimes reduplicated in Greek, e. g. διδάσκω for *δι-δακ-σκω, but not in Latin unless *disco*, from root deik̂-, stands for *di-dc-sco*, (cf. *dĭ-dĭc-i*) and not for *dĭc-sco*. An English Inceptive is 'I wash' (O. Engl. wæsce, from a Teut. *wat-skō 1st Sg., derived from the same root as ' wet,' ' water,' Lat. *unda*, &c.).

§ 23. **Causatives and Intensives in -eyo-**. The root has the O-grade, and the accent rests on the first syllable of the suffix. Causatives of this type are a regular feature of the Sanscrit conjugation, and may be formed from any verb, e. g. mān-áyā-mi (Lat. *mŏneo* for *mon-éyō) from the root man- (I. Eur. men- ; cf. Lat. *mĕmĭni* for *me-men-i*); tarṣ-áyā-mi (Lat. *torreo*, O. H. G. derr(i)u, for *tṛs-éyō) from the root tṛṣ- (I.-Eur. ters-), so that Lat. *moneo* was literally ' to cause to remember ' [cf. Plaut. *Mil.* 49 Edepól memoria's óptima. Offaé monent; Paul. Fest. 115. 6 Th. 'monitores' qui in scaena monent histriones (our ' prompters ')], *torreo* ' to cause to be dry.' These Causatives of Sanscrit have a different accent from Derivatives in -ĕyŏ- from O-stems, in which the accent falls on the suffix -yŏ-, e. g. dēvayā́-mi, ' I honour the gods,' from dēvá-, 'a god' (an O-stem, *deiwŏ-). The same formation often has the Intensive or the Iterative sense, e. g. Gk. φορέω from I.-Eur. *bhŏr-éyō, ' I carry frequently,' from the I.-Eur. root bher-, ' to carry ' (Gk. φέρω, Lat. *fero*); Gk. ποθέω for *φοθεω from I.-Eur. *ghᴴodh-éyō (O. Ir. guidiu), ' I ask or desire earnestly,' from the I.-Eur. root ghᴴedh-, ' to ask ' (Gk. θέσσεσθαι). The P. P. P. of these verbs shows -ĭ- in some languages (O. Ind. vartĭ-tá-, Goth fra-vardi-þs), -ī- in others (cf. Lith. vartý-ti Inf., O. Sl. vrati-ti); in Lat. ĭ, e. g. *monitus*, *nocitus*; and there are indications that the I.-Eur. declension of the Present Ind. was *wortéyō 1 Sg., *wortĭmós 1 Pl., &c. (*P. B. Beitr.* xviii. p. 519). An English example is 'I lay '(Pres.), in Goth. lagja, from I.-Eur. *loghéyō; ' I lay ' is the Causative of ' I lie.'

§ 24. **Latin Desideratives in -tŭrio.** These are formed with the YŎ-suffix (§ 15), probably from Verbal Noun-stems in -tor-, e. g. *parturio* from *partor*, *scripturio* from *scriptor*, with the same change of unaccented *ŏ* to *ŭ* as in *fulgŭro*, O. Lat. *fulgŏrio* (ch. iii. § 26).

§ 25. **Latin Iteratives or Frequentatives in -*tāyŏ-** are formed from Perf. Part. Pass.-stems, or rather from the Fem. of these used as a Noun (cf. *offensa* beside *offensus*, *rĕpulsa* beside *repulsus*), with the help of the YŎ-suffix, e. g. *pulso*, older *pulto*, for *pultā-yō, from *pulsus*, older *pultus*, P. P. P. of *pello*. Sometimes the TO-suffix is doubled, e. g. *factĭto*, *ventĭto*.

§ 26. **Other Derivative Verbs with the YŎ-suffix.** The ending -āyŏ-, which properly belongs to Derivatives from Ā-stem Nouns (e. g. from *planta*, a plant, a shoot, *plantare*, to plant, lit. ' to make or turn something into a plant '), acquired a transitive sense, and was used in Latin, as in other I.-Eur. languages, with any Noun- or Adj.-stem, e. g. *clārare*, ' to make clear,' from the Adj.-stem *claro-*, *pulverare*, ' to turn something into dust,' or ' to cover with dust,' from the Noun *pulvis*, a Consonant-stem. The ending -ĕyo-, which properly belongs partly to Derivatives from O-stem Nouns or Adjectives (e. g. *claudeo*, ' to be lame,' from *claudus*, *albeo*, ' to be white,' from *albus*), partly, as a Primary suffix, to Intransitive Verbs like *rubeo*, *sedeo* (see § 32), is the corresponding intransitive formation, e. g. *clarere*, ' to be clear.' Latin Verbs in *-io* include Derivative Verbs from Consonant-stems, e. g. *custōd-io* from the stem *custod-*, and from I-stems, e. g. *inānio* from the Adj. I-stem *inani-*. This ending acquired to some extent an intransitive sense, expressing a state of body or of mind, and was in this capacity applied to other stems too, e. g. *insānio* from the Adj. O-stem *insanus*, to be mad, *saevio* from the Adj. O-stem *saevus*, to be fierce.

§ 27. **Other suffixes** commonly used in forming Verb-stems, primitive suffixes, the sense conveyed by which cannot now be detected, were (1) -dh-, e. g. Gk. κνή-θ-ω beside κνάω, (2) -d-, e. g. Gk. ἔλ-δο-μαι from root wel- (Lat. *volo*), which may be nothing

[§§ 24-28.] THE VERB. INCEPTIVES. 479

but the Verb-stems dhē-, ' to put,' and dō-, ' to give ' (cf. Lat. *crēdo*, O. Ir. cretim with O. Ind. śrád dadhāmi, lit. ' I set heart to '), as the common Latin ending *-ĭgo, -āre*, e. g. *nāvigo*, seems to be nothing else than the Verb *ăgo* (from **navigus*; cf. ch. v. § 80); (3) -t-, e. g. Gk. πέκ-τ-ω (Lat. *pecto*) and πεκτέω, beside πέκω, which seems connected with the P. P. P. suffix -to- (ch. v. § 27); (4) -s-, e. g. Gk. δέψω beside δέφω, τρέ-(σ)-ω beside τρέ-μ-ω, which seems the same as the ES-suffix of Nouns, e. g. Gk. τέλος, stem τελεσ- (Gk. τελέ(σ)ω, τε-τέλεσ-ται) (§ 3). Latin examples are: *gau-d-eo* (Gk. γήθομαι and γηθέω) for **gāvĭ-d-eo* (cf. *gāvīsus*), *sallo* for **sal-do* (Goth. salta), *plecto* (O. H. G. flih-tu, Germ. flechte) beside *plĭco, -āre* (Gk. πλέκω), *vīso*, older *vīsso, veisso* for **weid-so* (Goth. ga-veisō; cf. the O. Ind. Desiderative vi-vit-sā-mi), *quaeso*, older *quaes-so* for **quais-so*, beside *quaero* for **quaiso*, *in-cesso* for **in-ced-so* (cf. *cēdo*). Other Latin endings are: (5) *-sso*, e. g. *căpesso, incĭpisso* (Plaut.), *pĕtesso*, O. Lat. *petisso* (Fest. 250. 19 Th.) from *căpio, pĕto* (or a bystem **petio*, whence *petivi*, § 47); on these see § 3; (6) *-lo* and *-illo* of Diminutive Verbs, e. g. *conscrībillo* Catull.; (7) *-co* of *albĭco, fŏdĭco*, &c.; the last two are like Derivative Ā-verbs and belong to the first Conjugation, *conscribillare, fodicare, albicare*, like *mĕdĭcari* from *medicus*. Similarly, (8) *-ro* of *lamb-ĕro* (§ 41) is like *-ro* of the Derivative *tempĕrare* from *tempus*.

§ 28. **Other examples of Latin Inceptives.** *Misc-eo* has added the Causative ending to a lost **misco* [cf. *misc sane* for *miscĕ sane* on an old Praenestine cista (§ 58)] for **mĭk-skō* [the shortness of the *i* is seen in the Romance forms, such as Ital. (Tusc.) mesci, ' give me a drink,' the Latin *misce mĭ*] with the weak grade of the root meik-. But the E-grade is retained in O. Lat. *esco* for **es-sco*, the Inceptive of the root es-, ' to be,' used for *ero* (or rather for *sum*) in the Laws of the XII Tables : *si morbus aeuitasue uitium escit*, and *ast ei custos nec escit*, &c., and even by Lucr. i. 619 :

ergo rerum inter summam minimamve quid escit ?,

as by Ennius, *A.* 322 M. :

dum quidĕm unus homo Romanus toga superescit.

Roots extended by -ā, -ē, -ō like ĝnō- from ĝen-, keep this vowel long, as is their custom in such cases (§ 2); hence *(g)nō-sco* (Gk. γι-γνώσκω, Epir. γνώσκω), *(g)nā-scor, crē-sco, viē-sco, hiā-sco* ; and similarly Latin Intransitives in *-eo* (§ 32) and Derivatives in *-o* (for **-āyō*), *-eo, -io* (*ib.*), e. g. *rŭbē-sco, con-tĭcē-sco, īrā-scor, flāvē-sco, ob-dormī-sco, ercī-sco* [*erceiscunda* on the Lex Rubria, *C. I. L.* i. 205. (2). 55], *descīsco* (with tall form of I on Mon. Anc. v. 28, which also offers *nascerer* with an apex over the *a*); though at a later time, when the difference of quantity between vowels had become less marked, we find some uncertainty about the *e* of *quiesco* (see Gellius, vii. 15, who decides in favour of *quiēsco*, on the strength of *călēsco, nĭtēsco, stŭpēsco* and other Inceptives; cf. ch. ii. § 144). The name 'Inceptive' is unsuitable. It is only verbs of the second Conjugation uncompounded with a Preposition, such as *calesco, lĭquesco*, to which a notion of 'beginning' can be attached, and even there the notion conveyed by the suffix is rather that of passing into a state or condition, of 'becoming' than of 'beginning,' e. g. *liquesco*, 'to pass into a liquid state,' 'to become liquid.' The suffix is closely associated with Intransitive Verbs of the second Conjugation, so closely indeed that these, when compounded with the Prepositions *cum, ex, in* (Prepositions which convey the idea of 'becoming'), always form their Present-stem with this suffix in good authors, e. g. *ĕrŭbesco* (not *erubeo*), *convălesco* (not *convaleo*), *inardesco* (not *inardeo*), unless the Preposition retains its separate force, e. g. *ē-lūceo*, 'to shine out,' *co-haereo*, 'to be united with,' which have the force of *luceo ex, haereo cum*. Intransitive Derivatives from stems like *dulci-, igni-, grăvi-*, &c. are formed on this type, and take *-esco* instead of *-isco, dulcesco, ignesco, gravesco, mītesco, pinguesco*, &c; and *-āsco* of Intransitive Derivatives from Ā-stems, &c., is in Late Latin often changed to *-esco*, e. g. *gemmesco* for *gemmasco*. The spelling *-isco* for *-esco* in Late Latin, e. g. *ĕrubisco*, may often be a mere interchange of the similarly sounding vowels *ĭ* and *ē* (see ch. ii. § 14), but it may also be referred to the Late Latin importation of Verbs of the second Conjugation into the fourth (e. g. *floriet, florient* in the Itala), which has left its mark on the Romance languages, e. g. Ital. apparire (apparisco Pres.) from Lat. *appārēre* (§ 33 *a*). The *-iscor* of *ăpiscor, nanciscor*, may be referred to the old forms *apio, nancio* (whence *coepiam*, Paul. Fest. 41. 34 Th., *nanciam*, Prisc. i. 513. 17 H.), as the *-isso* of O. Lat. *pĕlisso* to a lost **petio* (whence *petivi*, § 47). 'Inceptives' from fourth Conjugation Verbs are for the most part ante-classical, e.g. *condormisco* (Plaut.), *ēdormisco* (Plaut., Ter.), *perprūrisco* (Plaut. *Stich.* 761), *persentisco* (Plaut., Ter.), but *obdormisco*, 'to fall asleep,' is used by Cicero (*Tusc.* i. 49. 117). They are mostly Compounds (except *scisco*), and the same is true of the 'Inceptives' from third Conjugation Verbs in the Republican writers, e.g. *rĕsĭpisco* (Plaut., &c.), *prŏfīciscor* (cf. *făcessere*, 'to take oneself off,' and Late Lat. *se facere*, 'to betake oneself,' e. g. intra limen sese facit, Apul.), *concŭpisco* (Cic., Sall., &c.), *implĭciscier*, to become affected (by a disease), Plaut. *Amph.* 729:

úbi primum tibí sensisti, múlier, inplicíscier?,

though in the poets and later prose writers we have *trĕmesco, gĕmesco*, &c. Inceptives' from first Conjugation Verbs found in the early writers are *ămasco* (Naev.), *hiasco* (Cat.), *lăbasco* (Plaut., Ter., Lucr.), *collabasco, permānasco, dēsūdasco*, and a few others; but this formation was not continued in the classical period, though we find Derivatives in *-asco*, derived from Noun- and Adj.-stems, e. g. *veterasco, vesperasco, gemmasco*, in which the suffix *-sco* seems to be added to change the transitive sense attaching to these Derivative Ā-verbs (e. g. *clarare*, to make clear, to clarify, § 32) into an intransitive.

It thus appears that an intransitive sense attached to the suffix *-sco-* in Latin, and that this was the reason of its close association with the Intransitive Second Conjugation. Its sense of 'passing into a state or condition' suited it for acting as the Present Tense-stem of Intransitive Verbs. A

§ 29.] THE VERB. CAUSATIVES. 481

verb with this suffix did not govern an Accusative, unless the simple verb from which it was formed governed an Accusative, e. g. *perhorrescere aliquid*, Cic., like *horrere aliquid* (a construction of *horreo, păveo*, &c., not found before Cicero's time). But in the fifth cent. A. D. the termination acquired a causative sense, e. g. *innōtescere*, to make known, inform ; *mollescere*, to make soft, not 'to become soft,' a sense which was properly expressed by the Auxiliary *facio*, e. g. *calē-facio, rubē-facio*. *Assuesco, insuesco, mansuesco*, and other compounds of *suesco* had at an earlier period assumed the sense of *assuē-facio, mansuē-facio*, and perhaps supplied the type for this new formation which was widely extended in the Romance languages (cf. § 33 *a*).

Of individual 'Inceptive' Verbs may be noticed : *callesco*, in whose Perfect Cato retained the Inceptive suffix, *callescerunt* 3 Pl. [Nonius 89. 26 M. quotes this form (MSS. calliscerunt) from Cato's speech on the Punic War : aures nobis callescerunt ad iniurias] ; *obsŏlesco* and *exŏlesco* from *sŏleo* with P. P. P. *obsolētus, exolētus; adŏlesco* and *coălesco* (*cŏl-*) from the root al- (ol-), 'to grow, nourish' (whence *indŏles, subŏles, prōles*), with P. P. P. *adultus, coalitus*.

For a list of Latin 'Inceptives,' and full details of their history, see *A. L. L.* i. 465 sqq. Umbro-Oscan examples are Umbr. pepurkurent ' rogaverint,' Osc. *comparascuster* ' consulta erit.'

§ 29. Of Latin Causatives, &c. O. Lat. *lūceo*, ' to cause to shine,' to light or kindle (e. g. Enn. *A.* 158 M. : prodīnunt famuli, tum candida lumina lucent ; Plaut. *Curc.* 9 tuté tibi puer es : laútus luces céreum ; *Cas.* 118 primum ómnium huic lucébis nouae nuptaé facem) may be a Causative form, I.-Eur. *louk-éyō (O. Ind. rōcáyā-mi), and different from *lūceo*, to shine, which seems to be an intransitive form like *sĕdeo*, with *-eo* instead of *-io*, I.-Eur. *leuk-yo (Gk. λεύσσω); *nŏceo*, I.-Eur. *nŏk-éyō (O. Ind. nāśáyā-mi) is the Causative of the root nek- (Lat. *nex*), and has in Late and Vulgar Latin the construction which we should expect, viz. with the Accusative case ; its use with the Dat. in class. Latin must be due to the analogy of *obesse, officere*, &c. The rivalry between Transitive Ā-stems and these Causative-stems, best seen in Lithuanian, where the Causatives (e. g. vartý-ti Inf.) form their Present-stems with -ā- (e. g. vartō- for I.-Eur. *wortā-), appears in Lat. *nĕcāre* beside *nŏcēre* ; *dŏmāre* may be I.-Eur. *dŏmā- (O. H. G. zamō-, 'to tame'), a byform of I.-Eur. *dŏmḗyo- (Goth. tamja, O. H. G. zemm(i)u). In O. Ind. we have examples of verbs with this suffix which have not the O-grade of root, but the weak grade, e. g. gr̥bh-áya-ti, 'he seizes.' Perhaps Latin *ci-eo* (beside *cio*) belongs to this type. But the ending *-eo* is sometimes added to other Verb-stems which have a Causative sense. Thus in Lat. *misc-eo* it is added to a stem formed already with the inceptive suffix, so that *misceo* for *mic-sc-ĕyō* has really two suffixes (cf. O. Ind. dhūnaya-ti, ' he shakes, shatters,' beside dhunā-ti and dhŭ-nó-ti, Gk. εἱλέω beside εἵλω for *ἑλ-ν-ω). And this may be the true explanation of *cieo* also. *Jŭbeo* for *yŭ-dh-eyo [from the root yeu- with the formative suffix -dh- (see § 27), cf. O. Ind. yō-dha-ti, ' is set in motion,' Lith. j-un-dù, ' I am set in motion '] is spelt in the S. C. Bacch. with *-ou-*, the diphthong always found in the perfect (*C. I. L.* i. 196, l. 27 ioubeatis, l. 9, l. 18 *iousiset* ; cf. *iousit* 547 *a*, 1166, *iouserunt* 199, l. 4, *iouserit* 198, l. 12) ; this, if not a misspelling (ch. iv. § 37), will exactly correspond with the O. Ind. causative yōdháyā-mi (I.-Eur. *youdhéyō). *Terreo*, for which we should expect *torreo, has in Umbrian the O-grade of root (Umbr. *tursitu*, O. Umbr. tusetu, ' terreto ').

I i

Other Causatives, or Transitive Verbs with the Causative -eo appended, are vĕgeo (older vŏgeo?), to rouse to life, e. g. Pomponius, Com. 78 R. animos Venus veget voluptatibus, dŏceo, suādeo, urgeo, tondeo, torqueo, mordeo, spondeo, augeo, &c.

§ 30. **Of Latin Desideratives.** These were called by the Latin grammarians 'Meditativa.' They were avoided in the higher literature and went out of use in Late Latin. They are not found in the Romance languages. Examples of Desiderative Verbs are ēsŭrio, partŭrio, emptŭrio, cēnātŭrio (see *A. L. L.* i. 408). Verbs in -urrio (-ūrio), e. g. lĭgurrio, scătŭrio, are a quite distinct class, being apparently Derivatives from Verbal Nouns in -ūris (e. g. sĕcuris) or -ūra (e. g. fĭgura).

§ 31. **Of Latin Iteratives.** The distinction of (1) 'Iteratives' in -tĭto, (2) 'Intensives' in -to, -so is untenable. The suffix in all its forms denotes repeated action ; the usual type is that of a Derivative Ā-Verb from a Perfect Participle Passive, e. g. dătare, dormītare, though from Verbs of the first Conjugation we have sometimes forms in -ĭto like clāmĭto, vŏcito, vŏlito, pointing to P. P. P. vocĭtus like crĕpĭtus (§ 92). As the to-suffix of the P. P. P. became in time so- (ch. iv. § 155), we have Iteratives in an older form, merto, pulto ('mertare' atque 'pultare' dicebant Quint. i. 4. 14 ; Plautus puns on pultem Subj. and pultem Acc. of puls in Poen. 729), and in the class. form merso, pulso. Iteratives which add the suffix to a Present-stem, e. g. sciscito Plaut., noscito Plaut., ăgĭto, are especially frequent in Late Latin, e. g. mergito Tertull., miscito Script. Gromat., while to the class of Iteratives with double suffix belong actĭto, lectĭto, cantĭto, dictĭto, haesĭto, jactĭto, ventĭto, victĭto, cursĭto, factĭto, Vulg.-Lat. *taxĭtare, whence Ital. tastare, Fr. tâter, 'to taste, try.'

Iteratives are especially used in anteclass. and postclass. Latin. They are avoided by Terence, and not much used by Cicero and Caesar, hardly at all by the Augustan writers ; in fact they seem to have been regarded as a part of the uncultured speech. In the Romance languages they have often taken the place of the parent verb, e. g. Fr. jeter (Lat. jactare), to throw (Lat. jăcio), mériter (Lat. mĕrĭtare), to deserve (Lat. mĕreo), chanter (Lat. cantare), to sing (Lat. căno). (See *A. L. L.* iv. 197.) Dŭbĭtare is the Iterative of an O. Lat. verb dubare (Paul. Fest. 47. 18 Th. 'dubat,' dubitat) ; hortari of an O. Lat. *hŏrior [attested in 3 Sg. horĭtur by Diomedes (p. 382. 23 K.) for Ennius (*A.* 465 M.): prandere iubēt horiturque], which seems to be a Deponent of I.-Eur. *ghr̥-yō (Gk. χαίρω), a byform of *ĝher-yŏ (O. Ind. hár-yā-mi, 'I delight in' ; *heriu, the Umbro-Oscan word corresponding to Lat. volo, e.g. Umbr. heris, 'vis,' Osc. heriiad, 'velit,' whence Herentas, the Oscan name of Venus) from the root ĝher- ; gŭstare is apparently an I.-Eur. Iterative of this type (O. H. G. costōn) from *ĝŭs-to-, P. P. P. of ĝeus-, 'to taste' (Gk. γεύ(σ)ειν, Goth. kiusan, 'to approve,' Engl. choose : cf. Germ. Kur-fürst) ; ĭto, -are (Gk. ἰτη-τέον) from *ĭtus P. P. P. of eo, for *ĭtāyō (Umbr. etaians, 'itent') ; pŭto, -are, to prune, to think, lit. 'to sift or cleanse often' (in Romance 'to prune,' e. g. Ital. potare), from a P. P. P. stem *pŭ-to-, 'cleansed' (Lat. pŭtus, clean, in the phrase pūrus pŭtus, e. g. Plaut. Pseud. 1200), from the root of Lat. pū-rus, for *pŭtāyō (cf. O. Sl. pytaja̧, 'I investigate,' with ū) ; dŏmĭto from domitus ; crĕpĭto from crepitus ; habĭto for habitus, which monopolized in class. Lat. the sense of 'to dwell,' 'inhabit' (cf. archaic Engl. 'to keep,' as in the *Merchant of Venice*, iii. 3 : it is the most impenetrable cur That ever kept with man), a sense which it shared

§§ 30–32.]   THE VERB.   DERIVATIVES.   483

in O. Lat. with hăbeo, e.g. Plaut. Men. 308 : nón tu in illisce aédibus Habes ? Di íllos homines, quí illic habitant, pérduint.

§ 32. Of Latin Derivative verbs with YŎ-suffix. The onomatopoetic verbs *tintinnio* (also *tinnio* and *tintinnare*), *gingrio*, to cackle, of geese (whence *gingrina*, the name of a small size of fife : genus quoddam tibiarum exiguarum, Paul. Fest. 67. 23 Th. ; cf. Gl. Philox.) have a formation analogous to the Sanscrit Intensives (e. g. nan-nam-ya-tē from the root nam-, 'to bend') and to Greek παμφαίνω for *παν-φαν-yω, μαρμαίρω for *μαρ-μαρ-yω, &c., that is to say with the suffix -yŏ- appended to the fully reduplicated root.

The suffix -yŏ-, as was remarked before (§ 10), is often added to nasalized Present-stems, especially in Greek, e. g. κλῑνω for *κλῐ-ν-yω from the root k̂lei-, and so we have : *linio*, a Late Lat. derivative from *lino*, the Present tense of the root lei- ; *pinsio* (Gk. πτίσσω for *πτινσ-yω) beside *pinso*; *vincio* from *vĭ-n-co, the nasalized Present of the root vyek- (O. Ind. vi-vyak-ti, 'he encompasses') ; *sancio* beside *săcer*. These derivatives naturally retain the nasal throughout the verb, e.g. P. P. P. *pinsītus* (but from *pinso*, *pistus*), *sanctus* (in Vulg. Lat. *sactus*, ch. ii. § 70).

Examples of Verbs in -āyŏ- from Noun Ā-stems are: *scĭntĭllo, -are* from *scintilla* ; *lăcrĭmo, -are* from *lacrima* ; *multo, -are* (Osc. *moltaum* Inf.) from *multa* ; *insĭdior, -ari, insidiae* ; *măcŭlo, -are* from *macula* ; *praedor, -ari* from *praeda* ; *mŏrari* from *mora* [in O. Lat. always transitive, 'to cause delay,' 'to detain,' whence *nil moror* (hanc rem), I do not care for, lit. 'I do not (care to) detain']. Lat. *poenio, pūnio*, from *poena*, may exhibit an alternative method of forming derivative verbs from Noun Ā-stems, viz. with the mere suffix -yŏ-, the final vowel of the Noun-stem being suppressed, as in derivative Adjectives like Gk. τίμ-ιος from τιμή ; or may follow the analogy of derivatives from I-stems, or derivatives from Consonant-stems.

Of Transitive Verbs from O-stems : *amplant*, 'pro amplificant,' Pacuv. Trag. 339 R. (ap. Non. 506. 30 M.) ; *nŏvo, -are* from *novus* ; *sāno, -are* from *sanus* ; *narro, -are* from *gnārus* (?) (ch. ii. § 132) ; *armo, -are* from *arma* Pl. ; *spŏlior, -ari* from *spolium* ; *numĕro, -are* from *numerus* ; *lŏco, -are* from *locus* ; *dōno, -are* from *donum* ; *cŭmŭlo, -are* from *cumulus* ; *damno, -are* from *damnum*. This use of the -ĀYŎ-suffix for Derivative Verbs from O-stem Nouns and Adjectives is common in all I.-Eur. languages, e. g. Goth. frijō, 'I love' (of which Engl. 'friend' is a Pres. Part.), O. Sl. prija-ją, O. Ind. priyā-yá-tē 3 Sg., all from an I.-Eur. O-stem, *priyo- (O.-Ind. priyá-, 'dear'), O. Ir. caraid, 'he loves,' from I.-Eur. karo-, 'dear' (Lat. cārus). On the use of -ātŏ- as a Participial Adjective suffix, meaning 'provided with,' 'clothed in,' &c., e. g. *armatus, dentatus, pilatus*, from *pilum, cordatus* in Ennius' egregie cordatus homo (cf. re-cordāri), see ch. v. § 28. It is probably seen in Gaulish γαισατοι [gaesati, 'Gaulish mercenaries,' C. G. L. v. 71. 23 (?)], from Gaulo-Latin *gaesum*, a spear.

The natural formation from O-stems is sometimes in -ĕyŏ-, e. g. Gk. φιλέω, to love, for *φιλε-yω, from φίλος, dear (stem φιλο- or φιλε-, ch. v. § 2), ἀδυνατέω, to be unable, from ἀδύνατος, unable ; sometimes in -yŏ- merely, e. g. Gk. μειλίσσω for *μειλιχ-yω from μείλιχος. With the latter Lat. *ūnio* from *unus*, *blandior* from *blandus* may be compared, as in Noun derivative YŎ-stems we have *somn-ium* from *somnus*, *Octāvius* from *Octavus*, &c. (ch. v. § 4) ; with the former, intransitive Verbs from second Declension Adjectives, like *claudeo* from *claudus, albeo* from *albus, clāreo* from *clarus, flāveo* from *flavus* [as in Adjective derivative YŎ-stems like *aureus* from *aurum* (ib.)], unless these follow the

I i 2

analogy of Intransitives like *sĕdeo* for I.-Eur. *sed-yō (see above, § 15), in which case their ending will be not -ĕyō but -ēyō. (The corresponding verbs in Balto-Slavic have -ēyō, e. g. Lith. kétè-ju, ' I grow hard,' from kétas, 'hard'). The same distinction between transitive -o, -āre and intransitive -eo, -ēre is seen in primary verbs like *lĭquare* and *lĭquere*. (On the proneness of Intransitive Verbs to take -eo, e. g. *ferv-eo, fulg-eo*, O. Lat. *fervo, ful-go*, see § 19.)

We have also Participial Adjectives in -ōtus, e. g. *aegrōtus* from *aeger* (stem aegro-), like Gk. μισθω-τός from μισθός, Lith. ragū́-tas from rāgas, ' a horn,' with corresponding Verb-stems in Greek and Lithuanian, e. g. Gk. μισθόω, Lith. jŭkŭ̀-ju, but no *aegrŏō or *aegrō, -ōs, -ōmus in Latin. Derivatives from I-stems have -ĭyŏ-, e. g. O. Ind. kavĭyá-tē, ' he acts like a seer,' from kaví-, ' a seer,' janĭyá-ti, ' he desires a wife,' from jáni-, ' a wife'; Gk. μητίομαι (ῐ) from μῆτις, μηνίω (ῐ) from μῆνις, κονίω (ῐ) from κόνις; Latin examples are: *finio* from *finis, lēnio* from *lenis*; they show -ĭ- in the Perfect Participle Pass., &c., e. g. Gk. ἀ-δήρῑ-τος, Lat. *finī-tus, lenī-tus, mollī-tus, insignī-tus, vestī-tus, munī-tus, stăbilī-tus, ē-rudī-tus*; from *sors*, O. Lat. *sortis*, comes *sortior*; from *pars*, stem *parti-*, comes *partior*; from *pŏtis* (O. Ind. páti-, ' lord,' Gk. πόσις) comes *pŏtior*, ' to become master of,' with an Active *potio* (e. g. Plaut. *Rud.* 911 piscátu nouó me uberí conpotíuit), which was used in Oscan as the equivalent of the Latin *possum* (Osc. putiiad ' possit,' putiians 'possint ') (§ 97). U-stem derivatives have -ŭyŏ-, e. g. O. Ind. śatrū̆-yá-ti, ' acts like an enemy,' from śátru-, ' an enemy,' Gk. δακρύω (ῠ) from δάκρυ (from Ū-stems, e. g. ἰσχύω in the Dramatists), Lat. *stătuo* from *status, mĕtuo* from *metus*, with -ū- in the Perf. Part. Pass., e. g. Gk. ἀ-δάκρῡ-τος, Lat. *statū-tus, argū-tus* (from the stem argu- of O. Ind. árju-na-, ' white,' Gk. ἀργυ-ρος), *acū-tus* (cf. *acus*, a needle)[1]. From the analogy of a number of verbs of similar meaning, which happened to be formed with one or other of these types of YŎ-suffix, a definite meaning came to attach itself in the various languages to certain suffixes. Thus in Sanscrit the ending -ĭyŏ- came to acquire a desiderative sense and was used to convey this notion, not merely in derivatives from I-stems, e. g. janĭyá-ti, ' he desires a wife,' from jáni-, ' a wife,' but in derivatives from other stems too, e. g. putrĭyá-ti, ' he desires a son,' from putrá-, ' a son ' (an O-stem). In Latin, as we have seen, the desiderative ending is -tŭriō, e. g. *parturio*, but it is possible that the ending -iō conveys this sense in *cătŭlio* from the O-stem *catulus*, *ĕquio* from *equus*.

A fact of more certainty is that Latin -ō for *-āyō was used to give a transitive sense[2], e. g. *clāro, -are*, to make clear, from the O-stem *clarus, nŏvō, -āre* from *novus* (and so in other languages, § 29, e. g. O. H. G. niuwōn, though in Greek the ending -οω ousted -αω from this usage, e. g. νεόω, to make new, from νέος, ὑγιόω, to make healthy, from ὑγιής), and Latin -eo, to give an intransitive sense, e. g. *clāreo, -ēre*, to be clear, from the same stem, *claro-*, while -io possibly had attached to it the notion of a state of body or mind, e. g. *fĕrōcio, -ire*, to be

---

[1] These Derivatives in -ŭyŏ- must be distinguished from Presents ending in -nuo, like *mĭnuo* (O. Ind. minō-mi, from I.-Eur. *mĭ-neu-mi, § 10), as well as from a Present like *pluo* (O. Lat. *plŏvo*, from I.-Eur. *plĕwō, § 6), and from *fluo, fruor*, &c., whose root has a Guttural (cf. *fluxi, fructus*, § 39. 3). *Suo* represents an I.-Eur. *syū-yō (Goth. siuja, Lett. schuju, Gk. κασσύω).

[2] On First Conjugation Deponents with intransitive sense, e. g. *aemŭlari, fluctuari* (and *fluctuare*), see §§ 62, 64.

§ 32.]   THE VERB.   DERIVATIVES.   485

haughty (Cato, &c.), *saevio, -ire*, to be fierce, *insānio, -ire*, to be insane, *dentio, -ire*, to be teething, as *-aω, -ιαω* were used in bodily ailments in Greek, e. g. ὀφθαλμιάω, ὀδοντιάω, or desideratively, e. g. τομάω. The -YŎ- suffix was the I.-Eur. suffix by which verbs were formed from Nouns and Adjectives, e. g. O. Ind. apas-yá-ti from ápas-, *ś*pas- (Lat. *opus*), Gk. ὀνομαίνω for *ὀνομη-yω from ὄνομα (Lat. *nomen*). But in Latin, denominative -yŏ- has been to a great extent supplanted by -ā-yŏ- (see below). Thus the Latin equivalents of the Sanscrit and Greek verbs, just quoted, are *ŏpĕrari* and *nōmĭnare*. This process of extending the ĀYŎ-suffix at the expense of the YŎ-suffix went on as late as the literary period. Many O. Lat. verbs of the fourth Conj. are in class. Lat. verbs of the first Conj. ; e. g. O. Lat. *fulgorio* (*fulgur-io*), from *fulgur*, used by Naevius (*Trag.* 13 R.) :

suo sónitu claro fúlgoriuit Iúppiter,

is in class Lat. *fulgŭro, -āre* ; *impetrire* is the old form of *impetrare*, consecrated to religious usage, like *porrĭcere* the old form of *projĭcere* (ch. ix. § 44) ; *artire*, Cato, &c. is in class. Lat. *artare* ; cf. *dolītus*, Varro, *Men.* 7 B. for *dŏlatus* ; *atritior*, Compar. of *atrītus*, Plaut. *Poen.* 1290 (if this is the right reading) ; *gnarivisse* quoted (apparently from Livius Andronicus) by Paul. Fest. 68. 5 Th., for *narrasse* (cf. Gl. Philox. *gnaritur* : γνωρίζεται ; *C. G. L.* v. 72. 9 *gnoritur* : cognitum sive compertum est).

The old formation remains in *custōdio* from *custos* ; *dentio*, to grow teeth (used by Plautus for 'to suffer through lack of food' in *Mil.* 34, where the parasite apologizes to the audience for his complaisance in listening to the soldier's bragging : aúribus Peraúdienda súnt, ne dentes déntiant), though *dentātus*, and not *dentītus*, is the Participial Adjective. In *dentio* we have the same -YO- or -IYO-suffix as in the Verbs indicating disease, state of body, &c. (see below), like *insānio* from *insanus*.

When a Verb is compounded with anything but a Preposition the Compound assumes the form of an Ā-Derivative, e. g. *aedificare* from *aedes* and *facio*, *sacrificare* from *sacrum* and *facio* (cf. *sacrificus*), as in Greek we have -εω of οἰκοδομέω, &c.   *Mandāre* seems to be a similar formation, as if a Derivative Verb from *manĭ-dus*, ' giving into the hand ' ; and the Derivative Verbs in *-ĭgo, -are*, e. g. *nāvigo, -are, pūr(ĭ)go, -are, jŭr(ĭ)go, -are* (on O. Lat. *purigo, jurigo*, see ch. iii. § 13) point to *navigus, &c. from *navis* and *ago*. *Mŏrĭgĕrari*, to humour, devote oneself to (also *morem gerere*), comes from the Adj. *morigero*- (Plaut. *Amph.* 1004 meo me aequomst morigerum patri esse) ; *ŏpĭtŭlari* from a stem *opi-tulo-, &c. (cf. ch. v. § 80, p. 363). (On the predominance of the Ā-type of Verb in Latin, see § 33 *a.*)

Examples of these endings are : (1) *-o, -āre* : *nōmĭno, -are* from *nomen* ; *cŏlōro, -are* from *color* ; *ŏnĕro, -are* from *onus* ; *scĕlĕro, -are* from *scelus* ; *exāmĭno, -are* from *examen* ; *prīvo, -are* from *privus* ; *ignōro, -are* to make unrecognizable, Plaut. *Men.* 468 ; *pio, -are* from *pius* ; *prŏbo, -are* from *probus* ; *săcro, -are* from *sacer* ; *grăvo, -are*, to make heavy, from *gravis* ; *cĭcuro, -are* from *cĭcur* (not *ĭ*, *Rev. Philologie*, xv. 64) ; *levo, -are*, to make light, or to lift, from *levis* ; *păro, -are*, to make equal, from *par*, Plaut. *Curc.* 506 :

eodem hércle uos pono ét paro : paríssumi estis híbus.

Ampliare, to adjourn a case, is a rough-and-ready Derivative from *amplius*, the judge's phrase in giving notice of adjournment ; similarly *compĕrendinare*, to remand for two days, from (*com**perendinus* (*dies*), Vulg. Lat. **hūcare*, to call hither (Fr. hucher), from *huc* ; some explain *nĕgare* as a Derivative of this sort from *nec* (cf. Germ. verneinen from nein), or rather from its byform *neg-* (ch. x. § 18), the byform being chosen to avoid confusion with *nĕcare*, to kill. Whether the *ā* so often seen in Verbs compounded with a Preposition, e.g. *profligare* (from *fligo*), *occŭpare* (from *căpio*), *aspernari* (from *sperno*) is due to the transitive sense of the Compound, or to derivation from lost Adjective-stems **profligo-*, **occupo-*, **asperno-*, is not clear. (On *amplio* see K. Z. xxxiii. 55.)

(2) *-io, -ire*: *raucio*, to be hoarse, from *raucus* ; *singultio* from *singultŭs* (U-stem), *blandior* from *blandŭs*, *largior* from *largus*, *prae-sāgio* from *sāgus* (an Adj. especially found in the Fem. *saga*, a go-between, e.g. Lucil. vii. 6 M. saga et bona conciliatrix).

(3) *-eo, -ēre* : *ardeo* from *āridus* [O. Lat. *ardus*, e.g. *C. I. L.* i. 577. (2). 21 ; see ch. iii. § 13], which is the Adjective corresponding to *āreo*, as *călĭdus* to *căleo*, *nĭtĭdus* to *nĭteo*, &c. (ch. v. § 74) ; *audeo*, from *ăvĭdus*, the Adj. corresponding to *ăveo*, had originally the sense of ' to be eager,' ' to have a mind to,' e.g. Plaut. *Mil.* 232 auden participare me quod commentu's, whence the colloquial *sōdes* (Terence, &c.), 'if you please,' for *si audes* (Plaut., e.g. *Trin.* 244 dá mihi hoc, mél meum, sí me amas, si aúdes) (ch. iv. § 67 . These two classes of verbs in *-eo* must be kept distinct, the Derivatives from O-stem Adjectives like *flāveo, ardeo, audeo*, and the Intransitives with Nouns in *-or* and Adjectives in *-ĭdus*, e.g. *caleo* (*calor, calidus*), *areo* (*aridus*), *aveo* (*avidus*), *niteo* (*nitor, nitidus*) (see ch. v. §§ 67, 74).

§ 33. Of other Verb-suffixes :—(1) -dh- : on *jŭbeo* with *jub-*, for **dyu-dh-*, lit. ' to set in motion,' ' rouse to action,' see § 29.

(2) -d- : *tondeo* seems to be Causative of a lost **tendo* (Gk. τένδω, to gnaw), for **tem-do* from the root tem-, ' to cut ' (Gk. τέμ-νω) ; *per-cello* for **cel-do* (cf. *clā-d-es*, Gk. κλα-ζ-άσαι· σεῖσαι, Hesych.) from a root kel- (cf. Gk. ἀπο-κλ-ά-s) ; *trūdo* (Goth. us-þriuta, 'I trouble').

Since -dh- would become *d* in Latin (ch. iv. § 114), it is impossible to determine whether the suffix -dh- or -d- appears in *cū-do* (cf. Lith. káu-ju), *fren-do* (and *frendeo*)[1] for **frem-do* (cf. *fremo*), *ten-do* from the root ten-, ' to stretch ' (cf. Gk. τείνω for **τενyω*), *of-fen-do* and *de-fen-do* from the root ghʷen- (cf. Gk. θείνω for **θεν-yω*). On *pando, mando* (third Conj.), *vendo*, see §§ 14, 95, and on *mando* (first Conj.) § 32, above.

(3) -t- : *mĕ-to* (cf. Mid. Ir. methel, 'a reaper ' ; so some explained the name *Mĕtellus*, Löwe, *Prodr.* s.v.) cannot be dissociated from Gk. ἀμάω ; nor *flec-to* from *falx*. But this formation is not so common in Latin as in Greek, though all of the numerous Gk. Verbs in *-πτω*, e.g. τύπτω, χαλέπτω may be formations with the YŎ-suffix, for -py- seems to have become *-πτ-* in Greek, **τυπ-yω*, **χαλεπ-yω*, &c. (ch. iv. § 65). The E-grade of root seems to be used with the T- as with the D-suffix, so that *plecto* (from root plek̂-, Gk. πλέκω) is the correct form, O. Lat. *-plocto* being due to false Analogy (cf. *pondus* with *o* by Analogy of *pondo-*, ch. v. § 72, and see above, § 7).

(4) -s- : *prū-r-io* shows the ending *-io* of verbs indicating bodily ailments, &c. (§ 32) attached to a lost **prūro* for **preu-so* (O. H. G. friusu, Engl. I freeze) from

---

[1] The two forms *frendo* and *frendeo* have been explained by a supposed original declension like *fren-dēs* (I.- Eur. *-dhēs*) 2 Sg., *fren-dătis* (I.-Eur. *-dhătes*) 2 Pl.

§ 33.]   THE VERB. DERIVATIVES.   487

the root preu- ; with Gk. αὔξω, a development of *αὔγω (cf. Lat. *aug-eo*, a Causative formation, § 29) with the suffix -s- (cf. I.-Eur. *auges-, *augos-, a neuter noun, O. Ind. ójas, ' strength'; cf. Lat. *augus-tus*), we may compare Lat. *aux-ilium*, and the Umbrian formula in invocations of deities *orer ose*, if this means ' his (sc. donis) macte,' *ose* being Voc. of a stem *aukso- with the sense of Lat. *auctus*. If *arcesso* is connected with *accēdo* as *incesso* with *incēdo*, the suffix must in this Verb have Causative force (cf. Lib. Gloss. ' arcesserat,' advenire compulerat; Porphyr. ad Hor. *Epp.* i. 17. 50 corvus cum accedit ad cibum, strepitu vocis alias aves arcessit), but the use of *r* for *d* before *c* is peculiar (ch. iv. § 112). *Accerso* is a metathesis of *arcesso* and belongs to colloquial Latin (e. g. Terence, Petronius), as *arcesso* to legal phraseology (see *A. L. L.* viii. 279). *Quaeso*, in older spelling *quaesso* (ch. ii. § 129), from *quai-s-s-o*, is in the earlier writers used along with *quaero* (older *quairo, C. I. L.* i. 34, from * *quai-s-o*), e. g. Plaut. *Bacch.* 178 :

mirúmst me, ut redeam, te ópere tanto quaésere,

Enn. *Ann.* 143 M. (a description of Ostia) :

Ostia munitast. idem loca nauibus celsis
munda facit nautisque mari quaesentibus uitam,

and *Trag.* 97 R. liberum quaesendum causa [1] ; in classical Latin it is found in 1 Sg. *quaeso*, 1 Pl. *quaesumus*. (On the spelling *quaesimus* in MSS. of Cic., see Neue, ii². p. 437. The spelling with *u* seems to be an affectation due to the archaic character of the word.)

(5) -ss-. These bear the same relation to the stems just mentioned as Lat. *ămasso*, &c. to *dixo, capso*. They are called ' Desiderativa ' by Priscian (i. 431. 18 H.), who explains *capesso* as ' desidero capere ' (i. 535. 10 H.). In MSS. they are often confused with ' Inceptive ' forms, e. g. *lacescentem* for *lăcessentem*, *capescit* for *căpessit* (for a list of examples, see *A. L. L.* i. 515).

(6) Verbs in -*illo*. These are hardly to be separated from Ā-Derivatives from Diminutive Nouns in -*illā*-, Adjectives in -*illo*-, &c., such as *scintillare* from *scintilla*, *stillare* from *stilla* (cf. *stiria*), *tranquillo* from *tranquillus*. They are evidently Diminutive Verbs derived in the same style from Verbs instead of Nouns. Examples are : *conscrībillare* from *conscrībo*, e. g. Catull. xxv. 11 :

ne láneum latúsculum manúsque mollicéllas
inústa turpitér tibi flagélla conscribíllent ;

Varro, *Men.* 76 B. itaque eas inceravi et conscribillavi Herculis athlis ; Varro, *Men.* 280 B. astrologi non sunt ? qui conscribillarunt pingentes caelum ; *occillare* from *occo*, Plaut. *Amph.* 183 ; *sorbillo* from *sorbeo* ; *obstringillare* from *obstringo*, e. g. Enn. *Sat.* ii. 1 M. :

. . . restitánt, occurrunt, óbstringillant, óbagitant.

(See *A. L. L.* iv. 68. 223.)
We have -*lo* in *văpŭlo, vertīlā-bundus, ventĭlo, ustŭlo*, &c.

(7) -*co* in *albico, fodico, vellico* seems to have the same Diminutive force as the preceding suffix. As the Adj. suffix -*co*- is often combined with -*lo*- in Diminu-

---

[1] *quaesere, quaesentibus, quaesendum,* cannot be the O. Lat. forms of *quaerere, quaerentibus, quaerendorum,* as *Valesius* of *Valerius,* &c., for intervocalic *s* had become *r* long before the time of Plautus and Ennius (ch. iv. § 148).

tives, e. g. *puer-cu-lus* (ch. v. § 31), so we have in Verbs *pandĭcŭlans*, stretching oneself (in yawning) Plaut. *Men.* 834 (cf. *gesticŭlari* from *gesticulus*, Dim. of *gestus*). (8) -*ro*. *Consĭdĕro* can hardly come from *sĭdus*, a star, but must with *dēsĭdero* be an extension of a Verb-stem -*sĭd*-. Other examples of this formation are *măcĕro, rĕcŭpĕro, tŏlĕro*.

(9) Other formations. Verbs in -*ĭgo*, -*are*, e. g. O. Lat. *gnarigavit*, used by Liv. Andr. for *narravit* (Paul. Fest. 68. 5 Th.), with an Auxiliary *ăgo* giving a Causative force, have been already mentioned (§ 27), and verbs in -*fĭco*, -*are* (§ 32), e. g. *amplifĭco, -āre*, in which an Auxiliary *făcio* plays the same part. *Facio* does not enter into so close composition with the Verb in *bĕnĕ facio, āre facio* (Lucr. vi. 962 sol excoquit et facit are), *călĕ facio* later *calĕfacio* with the same shortening of a final long vowel as in *havĕ* (ch. iii. § 42), *consuĕ facio* (Varro, *R. R.* ii. 9. 13 consue quoque faciunt) (on this -ĕ see § 34), *compendi facio*, to cut short (Plaut. orationis operam compendiface) ; and we have an Accusative case-form as the first element of *vēnum-do* (*vendo*), *venum eo* (*veneo*), *pessum-do, pessum eo* (on *crēdo*, see § 27 ; on *mando, -āre*, § 32 ; on *pando, mando-, -ĕre*, § 14). Other Latin Verb-suffixes are -*ut*(*t*)*io* of *balbutio*, to stammer, *friguttio*, to chirp ; -*urrio* (-*ūrio*) of *lĭgurrio, scăturio* (on which see above, § 30) ; -*cĭnor, -āri* of *patrōcinor, lēnōcinor* (cf. *patrocĭnium, lenocĭnium*), *rătiōcinor, alūcinor, tuburcinor*, &c. ; -*isso, -āre*, which is borrowed from Gk. -ιζω, e. g. *attĭcisso* (ἀττικίζω), *graecisso, patrisso* (cf. § 33 a).

§ 33 a. **The Conjugations in Romance.** In the Romance languages the Latin Conjugations are much better preserved than the Latin Declensions (ch. vi. § 1). The first Conjugation is the prevailing type. Its encroachment on the others even in the Latin period is shown by Vulg. Lat.[1] forms like *fĭdāre* (Fr. fier, Span. fiar), a Derivative from *fĭdus*, which supplanted class. *fĭdĕre*, as the Derivative *pectĭnare* supplanted *pectere* (Caper 93. 8 K. pecto caput non ' pectino,' et pexum non ' pectinatum '), as well as from the fact that Greek loanverbs appear naturally to drift into it, ὀψωνεῖν becoming *obsōnare*, προπίνειν *propĭnare*, &c., just as loanwords in French take -er (Lat. -*āre*), e. g. trinquer, and in German, -ieren, e.g. marschieren, amusieren. The freaks of false Analogy appear in Vulg. Lat. *fugīre, cupīre,* &c. (Ital. fuggire, Fr. fuir, Span. huir; Sard. kubire, Prov. cobir), with transference to the fourth Conjugation by the analogy of their 1 Sing. Pres. Ind., *fugio, cupio* ; in Vulg. Lat. *florīre, complīre* (Ital. fiorire, Fr. fleurir; Ital. compire ; cf. Fr. emplir), with a similar transference, due to the identity in Vulg. Lat. of -*eo* and -*io* (both pronounced -*yo*, ch. ii. § 149); and the confusion

---

[1] The same tendency appears at an early period. *Cēlare*, a Derivative from *cēla, concealment, has supplanted *cĕlo (cf. *occŭlo*), and the same explanation should perhaps be given of *sŏnare* (Perf. *sonui*), &c. (See § 32.)

of second and third Conjugation Verbs, which we have already remarked in the Latin of Plautus in the case of *ferveo, sordeo*, &c. (§ 19), is intensified in Romance through the approximation of the ĕ- and ē-sounds (ch. ii. § 141), so that we have Vulg. Lat. forms like *respondĕre* (Ital. rispondere, Fr. répondre), *tondĕre* (Ital. tondere, Fr. tondre), and (by Analogy of the Perfect tense *sapui*) *sapére* (Ital. sapere, Fr. savoir); so Anal. of *potui, posse* became Vulg. Lat. *potére* (Ital. potere, Span. poder), and by Anal. of *volui, velle* became *volére* (Ital. volere, Fr. vouloir). The Perfects *struxi, traxi, prostrāvi, contrīvi* have similarly produced the Vulg. Latin forms *tragere* (Ital. trarre, Fr. traire), *strugere* (Ital. struggere, Fr. dé-truire), *prostrare* (Span., Port. prostrar), *contrire* (Span., Port. curtir). Verbs of the fourth Conjugation often show the 'Inceptive' suffix in their Present, e. g. Ital. unisco Pres. Ind., unire Inf., on which see § 28. (For a fuller account of the Romance Conjugations, consult Meyer-Lübke, *Rom. Gram.* ii. pp. 137 sqq.).

Of Derivative Verb endings may be noticed (1) *-icare*, a frequent formation in Vulg. Lat., e. g. **nĭvĭcare*, to snow (Ital. nevicare, Fr. neiger), (2) *-ĭdiare* (Gk. -ιζειν), which appears in Ital. as -eggiare, in Fr. as -oyer, in Span. as -ear, e. g. Ital. biancheggiare, O. Fr. blanchoyer, Span. blanquear, (3) *-antare*, *-entare* (cf. Lat. *praesentare*), used for Factitive Verbs, e. g. **expaventare*, to terrify [(Ital. spaventare, Fr. épouvanter, Span. espantar) (*ib.* ii. pp. 604 sqq.).

§ 34. **B. Imperfect.** In Slavonic the Imperfect is formed by appending a Preterite of the Substantive Verb (1 Sg. *jachŭ from original *ēs-o-m, 'I was') to a case form (usually called an Instrumental) of a Verbal Noun. Thus of the verb 'to see,' of which the Inf. is vidě-ti (Lat. *vidē-re*), the Imperfect (1 Sg.) is vidě-achŭ, lit. 'I was a-seeing'; of the verb 'to carry,' Inf. nes-ti (from the I.-Eur. root nek̑- of Gk. ἐνεγκεῖν, &c.), the Imperfect (1 Sg.) is nesě-achŭ; of glagola-ti, 'to speak,' the Impft. (1 Sg.) is glagola-achŭ. The same method of forming an Imperfect was followed in Latin, only the Auxiliary verb chosen was not I.-Eur. es-. Lat. *vidē-bam, ferē-bam, amā-bam*, are formations consisting of a Verbal Noun-stem (probably in some case form such as the Instrumental) followed by the Preterite of an Auxiliary verb. The *b* of the Latin Imperfect is in Umbro-Oscan f (Osc. fu-fans, 'they were'), and must represent an I.-Eur. bh or dh (e. g. Lat. *ŭbi*, Umbr. pufe, Osc. puf, O. Sl. kŭde, O. Ind. kŭha from an I.-Eur. DH-suffix) (ch. iv. § 114). It can hardly be separated from the *b* of the Latin Future *vidē-bo, amā-bo*, &c. (see § 36), which is similarly in the Italic languages *f*, e. g. Fal. kare-fo ' carebo,' but whose equivalent in O. Ir., b, e. g. no charub, ' amabo ' [quasi *nu (nunc) carabo] (cf. Lat. *cārus*), shows it to represent I.-Eur. bh, not dh (which would be d in O.-Ir.). The Auxiliary verb used must then have been the I.-Eur. root bheu-, whence Lat. *fui*, O. Lat. Subj. *fuam*, &c.; and Lat. *-bam, -bās, -bat*, 3 Pl. *-bant* (Osc. -fans) may represent an I.-Eur. Preterite *bhwām, -ās, &c. (on the loss of postconsonantal w, see ch. iv. § 71), seen in O. Ir. ba (from *bām), and corresponding to the Lat. Preterite of the verb es-, *eram* (from *esām). The Verbal Noun-stem employed recurs in such formations as the Fut. *vidē-bo, arē-bo, scī-bo*, as well as in Verbs compounded with *făcio*, e. g. *arē-facio* (§ 33. 9), and in Adverbs compounded with *lĭcet*, e. g. *vidē-licet, scī-licet, ī-licet* (ch. ix. § 7)   It appears in the Acc. case in O. Ind. Perfects like vidą́-cakāra, compounded of vidám, the Acc. Sg. of a Verbal Noun (cf. Lat. *vidē-*) and cakára, the Perfect of kṛ-, ' to make ' (I.-Eur. ker-, Gk. κρ-αίνω, Lat. *creo*). Lat. *vidē-, amā-, fīnī-* might be regarded as the bare stem of the Verb without any Case-suffix, but this explanation does not suit with *legē-bam*, for the Verb-stem would here be legĕ- (legŏ-), and the only way of avoiding this difficulty [1] would be to suppose that Verbs of the third Conjugation followed the Analogy of Verbs of the second Conjugation, **legĕ-bam* becoming *legē-bam* after the fashion of *vidē-bam*, as in the third Declension of Nouns Consonant-stems followed the analogy of I-stems in their Nom. Pl., **mīlit-ĕs* becoming *mīlit-ēs* like *part-ēs* (originally -ĕyĕs, ch. vi. § 40). A similar change of their Imperfect formation was made by Verbs of the fourth Conjugation in the second century B. C., for

---

[1] Some prefer to regard the Latin Imperfect as formed of a Verbal Noun in -ĕs with an Auxiliary. In that case *legēbam* will represent **legĕs-bam* (cf. ch. iv. § 151).

§§ 35, 36.] THE VERB. FUTURE. 491

while these have -*ībam* (or -*iēbam*) in Plautus and the earlier writers, e. g. *audī-bam* (and *audiē-bam*), they follow exclusively in classical Latin the analogy of Verbs like *facio* in their Imperfect *audiē-bam* like *faciē-bam*, as in their Future *audiam* (O. Lat. *audībo* and *audiam*) like *faciam*. The Romance languages point to a Vulgar Latin Imperfect of the second and third Conjugations in -*ēam*, of the fourth in -*īam* (e. g. Sard. timia, finia, Span. vendia, Port. dormia, O. Fr. diseie ' disais,' senteie ' sentais '), while the first Conj. Impft. had -*ābam* (e. g. Sard. istava from Lat. *stābam*), but whether this may be taken as evidence that byforms **timē-am*, **finī-am*, &c. formed like *er-am*, **bhw-am*, existed in Latin from the earliest times is doubtful (see Meyer-Lübke, *Rom. Gram.* ii. p. 282 ; and cp. below, § 37).

The Imperfect Subjunctive is formed with an S-suffix which is usually referred to the Substantive Verb *es-*, appended as an auxiliary, though some explain it as a Noun-stem suffix, comparing *ăger-em* (on Subjunctive *e*, see § 55) to *ăgere* for **aĝes-ĭ*, Loc. Sg. of a Neuter S-stem **aĝos, **aĝes-os Gen., *ferr-em* for **fers-em* to *ferre* for **fersĕ*, *ămarem*, *mĕrerem*, *audirem* to *amare*, *merere*, *audire* (see § 83).

§ 35. **Fourth Conj. Impft. in -ībam.** These forms are very common indeed in the Dramatists, e. g. Plaut. *Aul.* 178 :

praésagibat mi ánimus frustra me íre, quom exibám domo,

and the Republican poets, e. g. Lucr. v. 934 :

nec scibat ferro molirier arva,

and are often used by the Augustan poets and their followers, where the ordinary form would not come into a dactylic line, e. g. *lenibat* in Virg. *A.* vi. 468 :

lenibat dictis animum lacrimasque ciebat.

From *eo*, the classical Imperfect remained *ībam*, *pĕr-ībam*, *vēn-ībam*, and from *queo*, *quībam*, *nĕ-quībam*.

Aībam, a dissyllable, is the usual form in Plautus, but we have also *aiebam*, e. g. *Rud.* 1080 quam esse aiebas (MSS. alebas). The question whether -*ībam* or -*iēbam* was the correct ending for these fourth Conjugation Imperfects was a matter of discussion among Roman grammarians. We hear of a certain Aufustius who wrote a treatise, dedicated to Asinius Pollio, to show that *veniebam* and similar forms were preferable to *venibam*, &c.

§ 36. **C. Future.** (1) In -*bō*. (I.-Eur. **bhwō*). This formation is shared by the Celtic languages [e. g. O. Ir. no charub 'amabo,' quasi ' *nu (nunc) carabo' (cf. Lat. *cārus*)], and appears in Faliscan, karefo ' carebo,' pipafo ' bibam ' in the inscription on a drinking bowl: foied vino pipafo, kra karefo ' hodie vinum bibam, cras carebo ' (*Not. Scav.* 1887, p. 262). In class. Lat. it is confined to the first and second Conjugations, *ămābo*, *vĭdē-bo*, but in the early Dramatists the fourth Conjugation Verbs show *-ĭbo* as well as *-iam* in the Future, and in the plebeian Latin of Novius' *Atellanae*, or rustic farces, we find *vivebo*, for *vīvam*, *dicebo* for *dīcam* (as in the *Atellanae* of Pomponius *paribis* for *păries*, *Com.* 20 R.). These last forms are doubtless due to the influence of the Imperfect in *-bam* (see the preceding section), a formation shared by the third Conjugation, as well as the first, second, and fourth; *vīvēbam*, *dīcēbam* called into existence *vivēbo*, *dicēbo*, on the analogy of *vĭdēbam*, *cărēbam*, which had Future forms *vidēbo*, *carēbo*. This *-bō* of the Future Tense, Falisc. *-fo*, O. Ir. -b(ō) is clearly some part of the Verb bheu- (Lat. *fui*, &c.), of which we have seen *-bam* of the Imperfect Tense to be a Preterite. The Future of Latin *sum*, *ero*, is a Subjunctive form, *es-ō, with Future meaning; a meaning which seems to have attached itself to the I.-Eur. Subjunctive (see § 55).

(2) In *-am*. For verbs of the third and fourth Conjugations in Latin the 1 Sg. of the Ā-Subjunctive (see § 55) is used for the 1 Sg. Future, though, as we have seen, in the case of Verb-stems of the fourth Conjugation, this Subjunctive did not succeed in entirely ousting the formation in *-bo* till the classical period, e.g. *lĕg-am* 1 Sg. Fut. and 1 Sg. Subj., *audi-am* 1 Sg. Fut. and 1 Sg. Subj. (but in the older literature, also *audī-bo*). For the other Persons of the Future the Ē-Subjunctive forms (see § 55) are used, *legēs*, *leget*, *legēmus*, &c., *audiēs*, *audiet*, *audiēmus*, &c. The reason of this distinction between the 1 Sg. and the other Persons of the Future Tense is not clear. It may be that the 1 Sg. Subj. had already for a long time played the part of the 1 Sg. Fut. of these verbs, as it played the part of the 1 Sg. Imperative at all periods of Latin, and still retained its place when the new Future forms, which supplanted an older *dixo*, &c. (see below), were introduced. The spellings affected by Cato *dicae*, *faciae* for *dicam*, *faciam* seem to have had nothing to do with this variation of *ā* and *ē*

in the Future of these verbs, but to be merely an attempt to express by a written symbol the weak sound of final *m* in Latin (see ch. ii. § 61)[1].

(3) In *-so*. This formation belongs to O. Lat., e. g. *dixo, faxo*. It is discussed in §§ 3 and 5. The similarity in use between *dixo*, *faxo*, *capso* on the one hand, and *ămasso*, &c. on the other, suggests that *dixo* stands for *dic-sso, *faxo* for *fac-sso, *capso* for *cap-sso. But the Umbro-Oscan Future, e. g. Osc. *deivast* 'jurabit,' *censazet* 'censebunt,' Umbr. fust ' erit,' furent ' erunt ' had only one s. In Romance the Future has been lost (but O. Fr. ier from *ero*), its place being supplied by periphrastic formations with *habeo* (the usual type), *volo*, &c. Thus Ital. canterò, Fr. chanterai represent *cantare habeo* (reduced to *hayo*) (see Meyer-Lübke, *Rom. Gram.* ii. pp. 138 and 354 sqq.).

§ 37. **Fourth Conj. Fut. in -ĭbo.** This formation is extremely common in the Dramatists, e. g. Plaut. *Asin.* 28 ut ipse scíbo, te faciam út scias, but was not adopted (as the Impft. in *-ībam* was) by the Augustan poets, though Propertius ventures on *lēnibunt*, iii. 21. 32. In Late Latin poetry it reappears, e. g. *largibor*, Juvenc. ii. 562. The existence of *audiam* beside *audībo*, and of *dicēbo* beside *dicam* may have led in Vulgar Latin to the coinage of an Imperfect without *b*, whence Romance Imperfects like Sard. timia, finia (but istava, Lat. *stabam*) (see § 34). *Red-dībo*, an O. Lat. Fut. of *reddo*, shows the Fut. of *do*, *dăbo*, e. g. Plaut. *Men.* 1038 (perhaps *reddēbo* is the spelling indicated here and elsewhere by the MSS. :

sáluom tibi ita, ut míhi dedisti, réddibo : hic me máne modo.

The Fut. of *eo* and its Compounds, as of *nĕqueo*, has *-ībo* in class. Latin as well as in the earlier period ; and it is not till Late Latin that forms like *rediet, transient* came into use (*exiet* in Hor. *C.* iv. 4. 65 : merses profundo, pulcrior evenit, is the reading of inferior MSS., and like *mollibit* of *C.* iii. 23. 19 has no probability).

Whether third Conjugation YO-stems took this form of Future (and the Imperfect in *-ībam*) is very doubtful. *Paribis* for *păries*, quoted from an *Atellana* of Pomponius (*Com.* 20 R.) may be a vulgarism. *Adgrĕdibor* is the reading of the Palimpsest in Plaut. *Pers.* 15, as against *adgredior* (*aggredior*) of the other MSS., and seems to be required by the metre ; *congrediar* of all the MSS. (AP) in Plaut. *Most.* 783 is changed by editors to *congredibor*.

§ 38. **Third Conj. Fut. in -ēbo.** *Vivebo* is quoted by Nonius (509. 3 M.) from Novius (*Com.* 10 R.) :

tíbi dum uiuebó, fidelis éro,

---

[1] Still all the instances of this spelling of Cato's seem to be 1 Sg. Fut. In MSS. of Plautus we find *-em* occasionally in 1 Sg. Fut. of Verbs in *-io* (for the references, see Neue, ii[2].

p. 447 ; and cf. above, ch. ii. §§ 1, 3, on the Vulg. Lat. change of *a* to *e* after *j*), e. g. *faciem, accipiem* ; also *sinem, Truc.* 963 (in the Palatine MSS.).

and *dicebo* by Nonius (507. 1 M.) from the same play of the same author (*Com.* 8 R.) primum quod dicebo. Plautus (*Epid.* 188) uses the phrase *exsugēbo sanguinem* :

iam ego mé conuortam in hirúdinem atque eorum éxsugebo sánguinem,

though in another passage he has the usual *exsugam* in this phrase, *Poen.* 614 :

iám nunc ego illic égredienti sánguinem exsugám procul

(in *Rud.* 1009 the correct reading is : exurgebo quidquid umoris tibist). (On Late Latin *inferebis, tremebit,* see Georges, *Lex. Wortf.* s. vv.)

§ 39. D. Perfect.

The I.-Eur. Perfect-stem, denoting completed action, was either (*a*) Reduplicated, with O-grade of an E-root in the Singular Active, and elsewhere the weak grade, ĕ being the usual Reduplication-vowel : e. g. from the root ĝen- (Lat. *gi-gn-o*) the Perfect-stem was *ĝe-ĝon-, *ĝe-ĝṇ- (Gk. γέ-γον-ε, γέ-γα-μεν; cf. O. Ind. ja-ján-a, ja-jñ-úr), or (*b*) Unreduplicated, usually with a high grade of the Stem, and that either confined to the Singular Active, or extended over all the declension : e. g. from the root weid-, 'to see, know' (Lat. *vĭd-eo*) the Perfect-stem was *woid-, *wĭd- (Gk. οἶδ-ε, ἴδ-μεν, O. Ind. véd-a, vid-má); from the root sĕd-, ' to sit ' (Lat. *sĕd-eo*), the Perfect-stem was sēd- (Goth. sēt-um, Lith. sḗd-ẹs, Partic.). Verbs beginning with vowels, e. g. root ed-, 'to eat' (Perfect-stem ēd-, O. Ind. ād-a, Goth. fr-ēt), may have been the stepping-stone between these two formations. Other Unreduplicated Perfects occur in various languages side by side with Reduplicated forms, and show the same vocalism, e. g. O. Ind. sarpa (and sa-sarpa), from the I.-Eur. root serp-, ' to creep,' Hom. δέχ-αται (beside δέ-δεκ-ται) from δέχομαι, O. Ind. skambh-ur (and caskambh-a) from the root ska(m)bh-, ' to support ' (cf. Lat. *scamnum*). In Latin both the Reduplicated and the Unreduplicated type of Perfect are found, and it is not always easy to decide whether on the one hand the Reduplication has been lost in what we may call the ' Latin period ' (e. g. *tŭli*, which is in the time of Plautus *tĕ-tŭl-i*; cf. Gk. τέ-τλαμεν), either by that Latin habit of discarding one of two neighbouring syllables with similar form [*ar(cĭ)-cŭbii*, &c.; see ch. iii. § 13. p. 176] *re-t(e)-tuli* (so *dē-tondi,* O. Lat. *de-tŏ-tondi* beside *to-tondi*), or by adaptation to other Unreduplicated forms, or whether on the other the want of Reduplication dates from what we may call the 'Indo-European period.'

The Latin Perfect had usurped the functions of the Aorist or Preterite, and denoted action in past time, as well as completed action in present time, e.g. *dĕdi* (1) I gave, (2) I have given. It thus drew within its sphere Aorist or Preterite formations, such as what is called the S-aorist, e.g. Gk. ἔ-δειξ-α, O. Ind. á-dĭkṣ-am, and gave to these its own peculiar person-endings (1 Sg. -ī from I.-Eur. -ai or -ai, O. Ind. -ē, the I.-Eur. Middle 1 Sg. suffix, so that Lat. *ded-ī* corresponds to O. Ind. da-d-ḗ, a Middle, not an Active; 2 Sg. -*istī*, and so on; see §§ 65 sqq.). Thus Lat. *dix-i* from the S-Aorist stem *deiḱ-s- (Gk. ἔ-δειξ-α) is in Latin called a Perfect, not an Aorist, and is declined like a true Perfect, *dīx-ī* (O. Lat. *deixei*, *deiḱ-s-ai), 3 Sg. *dīxit* (O. Lat. -*īt*, -*eit*) like *mĕmĭnī*, 3 Sg. *meminit* (O. Lat. -*īt*, -*eit*). Strong Aorists, both Reduplicated (e.g. Gk. ἔ-πε-φνο-ν from ghᵘen-, 'to kill') and Unreduplicated (e.g. Gk. ἐ-γενό-μην from ĝen-), may have been absorbed into the Latin Perfect with the others, but decisive evidence that will prove their existence separate from true Perfects (Reduplicated and Unreduplicated) is hard to find. Thus Lat. *fĭdī* of *dif-fĭd-ī* from *fi-n-d-o*, root bheid-, may perfectly well be a true Perfect, with Reduplication lost in the 'Latin period,' the weak grade of the stem being appropriate to the whole of the I.-Eur Middle (e.g. O. Ind. bĭ-bhĭd-ē, 1 Sg.) as well as to the Plural (and Dual) Persons of the Active Perfect (e.g. O. Ind. bĭ-bhĭd-úr, 3 Pl.). It may however be claimed for the Strong Aorist class, like O. Ind. á-bhĭda-m, Aor.; and similarly *scĭd-ī* has been called a Strong Aorist (O. Ind. á-chĭda-m) with the Latin Perfect-ending, while *sci-cĭd-ī* is the true Perfect-form; even *sci-cid-ī* might be itself ascribed to a Reduplicated Aorist-class, as *tĕtĭgī* has been identified with Gk. τε-ταγ-ών, *pĕpĭgī* with Gk. πε-παγο-ίην. It seems best to class these Latin forms merely as 'Reduplicated' and 'Unreduplicated,' without the more definite title of 'Reduplicated Perfect,' 'Unreduplicated Perfect.' To attempt a further subdivision into Reduplicated Aorist (or Preterite), Unreduplicated Aorist (or Preterite) would be to go beyond the evidence at our disposal.

There is still another formation which in Latin has the name and the person-endings of the Perfect-stem, viz. the formation adopted for Vowel-verbs (first, second, fourth Conjugations), which appends *v* (after a Consonant *u*), e.g. ămā-v-i, re-plē-v-i, audī-v-i, mŏn-u-i. This formation has not yet been satisfactorily explained (see below). The *v* disappears in *audiit* (pronounced *audīit* in ordinary speech, *audĭit* in Poetry), *audĭt*, *abĭt*, as in *ditior* from *dīvĭtior*, O. Lat. *dīnus* from *dīvīnus* (ch. ii. § 53), *sīs* for *sī vīs*.

Examples of the various types of Latin Perfect are:
(1) Reduplicated : dĕ-d-ī (O. Ind. dă-d-é, Perf. Mid.; cf. O. Ind. á-da-da-m, Impf.), Osc. de-d-ed 'dedit,' Umbr. ďeďe (on the Umbro-Oscan 3 Sg. Person-ending, see § 69), crē-dĭ-d-i (O. Ind. dă-dh-é, Perf. Mid. On *credo*, O. Ind. śrád-dhā-, 'I believe,' lit. 'put the heart to,' O. Ir. cretim, see § 27). The I.-Eur. Reduplication Vowel ĕ (in O. Ind. the vowel of the stem is often substituted) remains in class. Latin in forms like *mĕ-mĭn-i* (older *me-men-i), *pĕ-pĕr-i*, but came to be assimilated in Latin fashion (see ch. iv. § 163) to the vowel of the second syllable in *mŏ-mord-i*, *tŭ-tŭd-i* (cf. O. Ind. tu-tud-ē), &c., although in O. Lat. to the end of the Republic forms like *mĕ-mord-i* were in use.

What the Latin Stem-vowel originally was is not always to be discovered, owing to the Latin habit of weakening every vowel in a short second syllable to ĭ (ĕ) (ch. iii. § 18). *Tu-tŭd-i*, which has retained the *u*-vowel unweakened (ch. iii. § 28), shows the weak stem tŭd- of the I.-Eur. Middle and Plural Active (O. Ind. tŭ-tŭd-ē 1 Sg. Mid., tŭ-tŭd-úr 3 Pl. Act.), while *con-tŭd-it*, quoted by Priscian (i. p. 518. 13 H.) along with *con-tŭd-it* from the *Annals* of Ennius (ll. 515 and 418 M.), may be the trace of a Latin **tŭ-tūd-*, *te-taud- (O. Ind. tŭ-tód-a 1 Sg. Act., Goth. stai-staut 1 Sg. Act., stai-staut-un 3 Pl. Act., apparently from a root (s)taud-), like *ce-cīd-i* from **ce-caid-*, root (s)kaidh-. But *to-tond-i*, *spo-(s)pond-i* (O. Latin *spe-pond-i*), from the roots tend- (Gk. τένδω), spend- (Gk. σπένδω), are not necessarily derived from that form of the Reduplicated Perfect-stem which was reserved for the Singular Active in I.-Eur., the form namely with O-grade of an E-stem vowel, *te-tond-, &c.,

for their *o* may be due to the Causative Present-stems (§ 29) with which they were associated, *tondeo* (I.-Eur. *tondéyo-), *spondeo* (I.-Eur. *spondéyo-). The *or* of *mo-mord-i* (O. Lat. *me-mord-i*) is most naturally explained as the Latin equivalent of I.-Eur. ṛ, so that *me-mord-* is the weak stem, *me-mṛd-, from root (s)merd-, and *me-mord-ī* is exactly O. Ind. ma-mṛd-ē 1 Sg. Mid.; similarly the *ul* (older *ol*) of *tetŭli* will be I.-Eur. ḷ (ᵉl) (cf. Lat. *te-tul-i-mus*, Gk. τέ-τλ-α-μεν) from the root tel-.

(2) Unreduplicated: *vĭd-i*, I saw, have seen, if *vĭd-* represents I.-Eur. *woid- (ch. iv. § 10, p. 228), exactly corresponds to O. Sl. věd-ě, 'I know,' a Middle form, and perhaps the only trace of the Perfect Tense to be found in the Balto-Slavic family of languages, with the exception of the Participle, while in Latin, Celtic, and Teutonic it is the Perfect Participle which has been lost, and the other parts of the Tense retained; the Active form, I.-Eur. *woid-ă, appears in O. Ind. vḗd-a, 'I know,' Gk. οἶδ-α, Goth. vait; *sēd-i*, unless it stands for *sĕ-sd-i, as *sīdo* for *si-sd-o (§ 9)[1], shows the I.-Eur. Perfect-stem sēd- of Goth. sēt-um 1 Pl., Lith. sḗd-ęs Partic.; *ēd-i* shows I.-Eur. ēd- of O. Ind. ād-a Act., Goth. fr-ēt; *ēgi*, the Perfect of *ăgo*, does not show I.-Eur. āĝ- (O. Ind. āj-a, Gk. ἦγ-μαι, O. Scand. ōk; cf. Lat. *amb-āges*), but adopts a Latin raising of *ă* to *ē*, seen in other verbs whose root-vowel is *a*, e. g. *pēgi* from root paĝ- (Lat. *pango*) [cf. ch. iv. § 51, where it is shown that I.-Eur. ă, Lat. ă, is the weak grade of I.-Eur. ē, Lat. ē, e.g. I.-Eur. *săto- from root sē-, Lat. *sătus* beside *sē-men*, *făc-io* beside *fēc-i* (Gk. ἔθηκα) from root dhē-].

A similar absence of Reduplication appears in Umbro-Oscan, e. g. Osc. *dicust* 'dixerit' (beside Umbr. *dersicust*), Umbr. fakust 'fecerit' (beside Osc. *fefacust*), Umbr. vurtus 'verterit' and ku-vurtus 'converteris.'

(3) S-Aorist (Preterite): *dix-ī*, older *deix-ei* (Gk. ἔ-δειξ-α; cf. O. Ind. á-dĭkṣa-m) from the root deik-, a Reduplicated Perfect (Aorist?) of which appears in Umbr. *de-rsic-ust* 'dixerit' (Umbr. *rs* expresses an intervocalic d-sound, ch. ii. § 88), and apparently an Unreduplicated in Osc. *dic-ust* 'dixerit'; *ussi* (Gk.

---

[1] Umbr. pru-sik-urent 'pronuntiaverint' has certainly I.-Eur. ē (Umbr. i).

εὖσα for *εὔσσα) has a short vowel according to Priscian, i. 466. 7 H., like ŭs-tŭs which has the weak grade ŭs- of the root eus- (cf. Late Lat. ostile for ŭstile, &c., A. L. L. ii. 607). The S-Aorist forms show sometimes the weak stem, sometimes the E-grade in I.-Eur. languages, e.g. O. Ind. á-dĭkṣam just mentioned, Gk. ὤ-ρεξ-α, sometimes a still higher grade; e.g. from the root leiq^u-, O. Ind. á-rāikṣam Act. [Gk. ἔ-λειψ-α may represent -lĕiq^u- or -lēiq^u- (ch. iv. § 45), O. Ind. á-rĭkṣ-i Mid. has the weak grade]; and the same variety appears in Latin S-Perfects, e.g. dī-vīdo, dī-vīsi, but ūro, ŭssi. But it is not always possible to ascertain the quantity of the vowel in Latin, for the grammarians of the Empire are uncertain guides about the natural quantity of any vowels long by position, for which they could get no clue from the classical poets. One requires further evidence before one can fully believe Priscian (sixth cent.) (i. p. 466. 17 H.), when he posits a naturally long penult for all Perfects in -xi which have the vowel e before this ending, e.g. il-lexi from lăcio, and for no others, e.g. dux-i from dūco (so perdŭctus, Audacis exc. 359. 15 K., but dedūxerunt in the Mon. Anc. iii. 26). The use of the apex, or accent-mark, to indicate a long vowel, on inscriptions, especially on inscriptions later than 150 A.D., is also evidence of a more or less doubtful character; and even when the length of a vowel seems fairly established, e.g. rēxi (with apex over the e on an inscr. of 105 A.D., C. I. L. v. 875; also declared to have long e by Priscian, l. c.; contrast Gk. ὤ-ρεξα), there remains a further question whether the long vowel is not due to a similar phonetic law for the group g-s, as that which grammarians mention for the group g-t (in rectus, lectus, tectus, &c.), viz. that a naturally short vowel is lengthened before this Consonant-group. (On the question of the quantity of the Stem-vowel in these S-Perfects, see ch. ii. § 144, and cf. ch. iv. § 51, p. 254, where the high grade of the root is accounted for by the syncope of a short vowel, rēx- for rĕǵ-(ĕ)s-.) The vocalism of the Perfect of jŭbeo may have been altered before the end of the Republic, for the spelling jous- on old inscriptions (see C. I. L. i. Index, s. v.) proves an original diphthong ou (probably I.-Eur. eu; the root is yeudh-, O. Ind. yōdhati), and O. Lat. joussei (with s for ss before the practice of writing a double consonant came in,

§ 39.] THE VERB. PERFECT. 499

ch. i. § 8) would become naturally in classical Latin $jūsī$, as in the Perfect of *mitto* O. Lat. *meissei* became class. Lat. *mīsī* (see ch. ii. § 129). *Cēdo* has *cĕssi* (Prisc. i. 466. 6 H.). Perfects in *-ssi* often come from Verb-stems ending in *-s*, e. g. from the root eus-, *us-si*; thus *prĕmo* probably takes its Perfect *pres-si* from a lost Present **preso* [cf. Gk. τρέ(σ)ω and τρέμω; Lat. *ter(s)-eo* and *trĕm-o*, § 3]. *Fluxi* comes from the stem **bhlug^R*- (Gk. οἰνό-φλυξ), the guttural becoming *v* in *fluvo*, class. *fluo*; *co-nixi* from the root kneigh^R- (cf. *nicto*); *fixi* from the stem dheig^R-, the O. Lat. Present being *fīvo* (§ 7); *vexi* from the root weĝh-, Pres. *veho*, and so on.

The S-Aorist is not found with Vowel Verbs in Latin as it is in Greek, e. g. ἐ-τίμη-σα (Dor. -ᾱσα), ἐ-φίλη-σα (with σ apparently for σσ as in εὗσα for *εὗσ-σα, quoted above); at least it is not found in the Indicative. But in Umbro-Oscan, if tt in these languages represents an original ss (as Att. πράττω for πράσσω), we have this formation in Perfects like Pelignian coisatens ' curaverunt ' quasi *curassunt, Osc. duunated ' donavit' quasi *dōnassit, dadíkatted ' dedicavit,' prúfatted, prúfattens ' probavit, probaverunt,' teremnattens ' terminaverunt ' [all the examples preserved belong to the first Conj., and so do almost all of the Latin examples of *-ss-* forms, e. g. *amasso, amassim, amassere* (see § 5)].

(4) With *v* (*u*). This is the Perfect-stem formation of Vowel-Verbs, as of the first Conjugation, *ămāvi, nĕcā-vi*, and with the *v* (*u*) added to a stem not ending in *-ā, nĕc-ui* (so *crĕpavi* and *crĕpui, cŭbavi* and *cŭbui, dĭmĭcavi* and *dĭmĭcui,* &c.), of the second *replēvi, monui,* of the third *strā-vi, sē-vi, crē-vi, sĭ-vi,* of the fourth *audīvi, dēsĭlŭi,* and *dēsĭlīvi*. It is also found with some Consonant Verb-stems, e. g. *cŏlui, ălui, gĕmui,* and is sometimes added to a Perfect-stem already formed; e. g. *mess-ui* (but see § 51). When the stem ends in *v* (*w*), two *v*'s are not written, but the preceding vowel is lengthened, e. g. *cāvi, lāvi* (see § 47 on *fōvi*). *Statui, fui,* &c. were in O. Lat. *statŭi (statŭvi), fŭvi. Pŏsui* is a form introduced by the false apprehension of *pŏ-sĭtus* [from the Preposition *pŏ-* (Gk. ἀπό, Lat. *ab,* ch. ix. § 12) and *sĭtus* P. P. P. of *sĭno (pōno* for *pŏ-s(i)no,* ch. iv. § 151)], as if it were *posi-tus* like *mŏnĭ-tus.* The true Perfect, used by the older

K k 2

writers, is *po-sīvi*, but this could not become *posui* (*imposŭi*, Lucil. xxviii. 26 M.) by ordinary phonetic development.

Both the Perfect with *v* and the S-Perfect occasionally present shortened forms, e.g. *amasti, misti*, which are best regarded as phonetic developments of the full forms *ămāvisti, mīsisti*, due in the one case to the Roman tendency to drop intervocalic *v* (see ch. ii. § 53), and in the other to the practice of discarding one of two neighbouring similar syllables (see ch. iii. § 13, p. 176). The same shortening occurs in various parts of the Perfect-stem conjugation, e.g. *amāro* Fut. Pft., *amassem* Pluperf. Subj., and so on (see § 3).

The Perfect-stem was formed in I.-Eur. from the root of the verb, not from the Present-stem. This is the reason why a Latin Perfect often presents so different an appearance from a Latin Present. Thus *sē-vi* is formed from the root sē- (cf. *sē-men*), but *sĕro* is a Reduplicated Present, for *sĭ-s-ō (cf. Gk. ἵημι for *σι-ση-μι, § 9); *crē-vi*, I determined, *sī-vi, strā-vi* and others exhibit Nasalized Present-stems, *cer-no, sĭ-no, ster-no* (see § 10); *crē-vi*, I grew, *nō-vi, ăbŏlē-vi* and *abol-ui* have as Presents 'Inceptive'-stems *cre-sco, no-sco, abole-sco* (see § 28). But it often happened that the Perfect was influenced by the form of the Present-stem. Thus *vēni* from root gʷem- (Goth. qēmum 1 Pl.) should be **vēmi*, but takes its *n* from the Present, a YO-stem, which by the Latin Phonetic law changes its *m* to *n* before *i* (*y*), *vĕnio*.

In Oscan the Perfect Subjunctive differs from the Perf. Ind. only in its use of the Subjunctive vowel ē (§ 55), e.g. Osc. *fefacid* 'fecerit.' But in Latin the Perfect Subjunctive adds to the Perfect-stem *-ĕrim, -ĕrīs, -ĕrit*, &c. (3 Pl. *-erint*), which is generally regarded as an Optative form from the root es- (cf. *sim*) used as an Auxiliary. Others explain *vĭdĕrim*, with *vĭdĕro*, &c., as containing a Noun-stem *vidis-* (cf. *cĭnĭs-*), which is seen in its proper form in *vidis-sem* (see § 52). In the Perfect Subjunctive person-endings *ī*, not *ĭ*, is correct; scansions with *ĭ* are due to confusion with the Fut. Perf. (see Neue, ii². p. 510). In its Potential use, e.g. *dixerim*, I would say, *affirmaverim*, &c. the first Pers. Plur. is rare (e.g. *dixerimus*, Cic. *Tusc.* iii. 4. 7 ; *Nat. Deor.* i. 20. 52), and in the Deponent Conjugation this use is rare even in the Singular (e.g. *passus sim*, Ter. *Andr.* 203 ; cf. *sit passus*, Virg. *G.* iii. 141) (see *A. L. L.* i. 347).

§ 40. Other examples of Reduplicated forms : *stĕ-t-ī* (O. Ind. ta-sth-ē), *ste-tĭ-mus*, older *ste-tĕ-mos (Gk. ἔ-στα-μεν) ; *pe-pēd-i* from *pezdo (O. Engl. fist) ; *ce-cĭn-i*, older *ce-cen-ei (O. Ir. ce-chan) ; but with the Reduplication-vowel changed, *dĭ-dĭc-i*, Pres. *disco* for *dic-sco ; *pŏ-posc-ī*, O. Lat. *pe-posc-i* for *pe-pr̥k̂ (root prek̂-) with 'Inceptive'-stem suffix -sk- (§ 22) (cf. O. Ind. paprach-a, Act.), Umbr. pe-purk-urent ' rogaverint.' Peculiar to O. Lat. are : *te-tĭn-ī* (O. Ind. ta-tan-ē from tan-, I.-Eur. ten-, 'to stretch'), which was used as a Perfect of *těneo* (apud veteres 'tetini' dicitur Diom. 372. 18 K.) ; Nonius (178, 7 M.) quotes *tetinisse* and *tetinerim* from Pacuvius, *tetinerit* from Accius ; in Plaut. *Amph.* 926 we should probably read *abstinei* for *abstines* of the MSS. :

nunc quándo factis me ínpudicis ábstinei,
ab ínpudicis díctis auortí uolo,

and *tetini*, *-tini* should perhaps be read for *tenui*, *-tinui* in other passages of Plautus (*Studem. Stud.* ii. 122 n.) ; Paul. Fest. (335. 7 Th.) has preserved for us an old augural phrase, discussed by Messala in his Treatise on Augury, *purime tetinero* 'purissime tenuero' ; *scĭcĭdi* (*sciscidi*?), illustrated by Priscian (i. 517. 3 H.) with several passages from the Dramatists.

§ 41. Unreduplicated. The following, with short vowel, which are often referred to I.-Eur. strong (unreduplicated) Aorists, are more probably reduplicated forms which have lost their Reduplication, first in Compounds, then in the Simple Verb : *tŭli* (see below) ; *scĭ-di* (cf. O. Ind. ci-chid-ē Perf. Mid., á-chida-m Aor.), in O. Lat. *scĭ-cĭd-ī* (see above), cf. *ab-scidi*, *di-scidi*, *re-scidi*, &c. ; *fĭdi* (cf. O. Ind. bi-bhid-ē Perf. Mid., á-bhida-m Aor.), rare in the Simple Verb, but more frequent in the Compound *dif-fĭdi* (e.g. Virg. *A.* ix. 588 tempora plumbo diffidit ; Hor. *C.* iii. 16. 13 diffidit urbium Portas vir Macedo) ; *-cŭli* only occurs in the Compound *per-culi*, just as *-pŭli* (in the Simple Verb *pĕpŭli*) is only found in Compounds, *dispuli*, *impuli*, &c. (cf. *rep(e)puli*).

And a large number of the forms usually quoted as Unreduplicated Perfects with stem-vowel unchanged rest on very insecure foundation : *-cendi* occurs only in Compounds *ac-cendi*, *in-cendi*, &c. ; the same is true of *-fendi* of *de-fendi*, *of-fendi*, and *-hendi* of *pre-hendi*, nor can we be certain whether the *e* in these Perfects was short or long ; *lambi is attested by Priscian (i. 506. 25 H.) with the single example of a line of Lucilius (xiii. 11 M.) :

iucundasque puer qui lamberat ore placentas,

where *lamberat* is evidently Pres. of *lambero* (Plaut. *Pseud.* 743 :

eúgepae : lepidé, Charine, meó me ludo lámberas),

and is probably the very word which is quoted by Paul. Fest. 84. 30 Th. 'lamberat' scindit ac laniat ; for *psalli Priscian quotes only a line of Caesius Bassus, the friend of Persius, with *psallerat* ; of *mando* he says (i. 419. 13 H.) ejus praeteritum perfectum quidem alii mandui, alii mandidi esse voluerunt ; Livius tamen in Odyssia (a later hexameter version) :

cum socios nostros mandisset impius Cyclops;

-vĕrri (cf. Prisc. i. 532. 22 H.) is easily attested for Compounds, but not for the Simple Verb, and the same is true of -cūdi (Prisc. i. 515. 16 H.), and to a great extent of velli (Virg. Ecl. vi. 4 vellit et admonuit).

Of the remaining examples of Unreduplicated Perfect with Stem-vowel unchanged, ĭci (Pft. of īco? see Wharton, Etyma Lat. s. v.), strīdi, vīsi (an S-Aorist? ; the usual Perfect of these Present S-stems is in -īvi, e. g arcess-īvi, quaes-īvi, from arcesso, quaes(s)o, § 3), and better attested than these, păndi, prandi, scăndi, vĕrti (on sīdi, bībi, see below) ; the Verbs with Present in -ndo are sometimes credited with a Perfect in -dĭdi instead of -di (cf. condidi, but in composition abscondi, though abscondidi is quoted from the Republican Dramatists by Nonius, 75. 22 M.), e. g. descendidi, quoted from Valerius Antias and Laberius by Gell. vi. 9. 17, mandidi, a byform of mandi (Prisc. i. 419. 13 H., just cited), prandidi, censured by Diomedes, 367. 17 K. This -didi is proper to verbs compounded with do, (1) to give, (2) to put, so is applied by false analogy to de-scendo, from the I.-Eur. root skand- (O. Ind. skand-, Gk. σκανδάληθρον, O. Ir. ro-sescaind) ; the formation of păndo (cf. Osc. patensíns 'aperirent' (?)), mando, prandeo is not clear (see § 14). Verti, O. Lat. vorti (vo- became ve- in the course of the second cent. B. C., ch. iv. § 10), has probably the weak stem *wr̥t-, with which we may compare either the O. Ind. Reduplicated Perf. Mid. vavr̥tē or the O. Ind. Unreduplicated Aorist á-vr̥ta-m) ; but while the Umbrian forms ku-vurtus, co-vortus, covrtust (or courtust, for covurtust?), 'converteris' 'converterit,' ku-vertu, co-vertu 'convertito,' point to a different stem for the Present (wert- ; cf. O. Ind. vártatē) and the Perfect (wr̥t-), the O. Lat. spelling shows vort- (wr̥t-) both in the Present and in the Perfect, as well as in the Perfect Participle Passive vorsus (*wr̥t-to-, O. Ind. vr̥ttá-), so that the weak stem has the appearance of having forced its way in Latin into the Present Tense-system, leaving an identity of Stem-vowel between the Present and the Perfect. The spelling vorto may, however, have represented the pronunciation verto (see ch. iv. § 10).

The alternation of ă in Present- with ē in Perfect-stem is seen in făc-io (Umbr. façia, Osc. fakiiad 'faciat') and fēc-i (I.-Eur. dhē-k- of Gk. ἔ-θηκ-α), frăngo (root bhreg-, Goth. brikan ; see ch. iv. § 51), and frēg-i, jăcio and jēci, căpio and cēpi, pango and pēgi, ăgo and ēgi, coĕpi (Lucr.) and apere (ch. ii. § 150), it is seen also in Oscan hipid 'habuerit' (Osc. i is I.-Eur. ē), though *hēbi is unknown in Latin ; that of ŏ with ō in fŏd-io and fōd-i [the I.-Eur. root is bhedh-, Lith. bedu, 'I dig,' W. bedd, 'a grave,' varying with bhodh-, Gk. βόθρος (with β for π), Lith. badaũ, 'I prick,' O. Sl. bodą] ; of ă with ā there is one doubtful example, scăbo (with ă in scăberet, Hor. S. i. 10. 71) and scāberat, quoted as a Plupft. (with lamberat, on which see above) by Priscian from Lucil. ix. 77 M. scaberat ut porcus contritis arbore costis ; that of ĕ with ē is seen in ĕdo and ēdi, ĕmo and ēmi, lĕgo and lēgi, sĕdeo and sēdi, vĕnio (en for ºm, m̥, like Gk. βαίνω) and vēni for *vēmi (Goth. qēmum, 1 Pl.) ; the weak stem with short vowel is seen in the Present, but not in the Perfect, in fŭgio and fūgi (root bheug-), linquo and līqui (root leiqᵘ-), rŭmpo and rūpi (root reup-), vĭdeo and vīdi (root weid-), vinco and vīci (root weik-), fŭndo and fūdi.

§ 42. **Form of Reduplication.** When the root of the Verb began with a group of consonants the practice in I.-Eur. languages is to use only the first consonant of the group in the Reduplication-syllable, e. g. I.-Eur. *k̑e-k̑low-, *k̑e-k̑lu-, the Perfect-stems from the root k̑leu-, 'to hear' (Gk. κέ-κλυτε ; cf.

§§ 42-44.]   THE VERB. PERFECT.   503

O. Ind. śu-śráva, O. Ir. ru chuala from *cu-clowa, both of these last having the weak stem vowel ŭ instead of the Reduplication-vowel ĕ). This form of Reduplication appears in Latin Reduplicated Presents (see § 9) like *si-s-to* (I.-Eur. *si-st-, Zend hi-štaiti, Gk. ἵ-στημι, Umbr. se-stu). But in Latin Perfects the whole group appears in the Reduplication-syllable when the group consists of s followed by a mute, while in the stem-syllable the s is dropped (possibly sometimes retained, as in Teutonic), whereas in other I.-Eur. languages (e. g. O.-Ind., Gk.) only the mute appears in the Reduplication-syllable, e. g. Lat. *spŏ-pond-i* (*spo-spondi* is occasionally found in MSS.), *scĭ-cĭd-i* (v. l. *sciscidi*), Goth. stai-staut, O. Ind. ta-sthāú (from O. Ind. sthā-, 'to stand'). *Bĭbi* shows the ĭ of *bĭ-b-o*, the Reduplication-vowel of Present-stems, as ĕ of Perfect-stems. Similarly *dĭ-dic-i* may owe its ĭ to the fact that *disco* is a Reduplicated Present for *dĭ-dc-sco (cf. Gk. δι-δάσκω for *δι-δακ-σκω) (but see § 22). The Roman grammarians were in doubt whether the correct Perfect of *sisto* was *stĭ-t-i* or *stĕ-t-i* (see Georges, s. v.), Gellius (ii. 14) speaks of an old MS. of Cato's speeches which had the reading *vadimonium stitisses*, a reading changed by 'emend*a*tores' to *vadimonium stetisses*; the same doubt existed whether *sīdi* or *sēdi* was the Perfect of *sīdo* (*si-sd-o).

§ 43. **Assimilation of Reduplication-vowel to Stem-vowel.** Aulus Gellius, in a chapter dealing with peculiar forms of the Latin Perfect (*N. A.* vi. 9 ; cf. Nonius 140. 19 M.), says that although *poposci, momordi, pupugi, cucurri* were the forms used in his time by almost all educated men (omnes ferme doctiores), the older writers used ĕ in the Reduplication-syllable. He quotes *memordi* from Ennius (from his poem to Scipio, and referring to the rivals of his hero ?) (*Sat.* 20 M.) :

meum nón est, ut (*v. l.* at) si mé canis memórderit,

from Laberius, Nigidius, Atta, and Plautus (*Aul.* fr. 2 ut admemordit hominem), remarking that the last author used also *prae-morsisset* (the S-Aorist form), *peposci* from Valerius Antias, *pepugero* from Atta, *occecurrit* from Aelius Tubero, *speponderant* from Valerius Antias. He even assigns similar forms to Cicero and Caesar (sic M. Tullius et C. Caesar mordeo ' memordi,' pungo ' pepugi,' spondeo ' spepondi' dixerunt), although our MSS. of these authors, as of Plautus and the older writers, hardly preserve a trace of them [see Neue, ii². 465. In Plaut. *Poen.* 1074 one of the Palatine MSS. has *memordit* (D), another *me mordit* (C), another *momordit* (B)].

§ 44. **Loss of Reduplication.** This assimilation may have in some cases facilitated the loss of the Reduplication-syllable in Compounds, which was ascribed above (§ 39) to the Latin practice of discarding one of two neighbouring and similar syllables [e. g. *ar(ci)-cŭbii*, ch. iii. § 13. p. 176]. This practice of Latin [cf. Gk. ἀμ(φι)-φορεύς], along with the liability of every short second syllable to Syncope under the older law of Accentuation (ch. iii. § 13), must have operated most powerfully to the detriment of the Reduplication-syllable in Compounds, so that it is wrong to refer all Latin Unreduplicated Perfects to I.-Eur. Unreduplicated Perfect and Aorist forms. A Perfect like *tŭli*, which has in Plautus the form *tĕtŭli*, in Terence usually the Unreduplicated form, *tŭli*, as always in classical Latin, is most naturally explained as a Reduplicated form which lost its Reduplication in the second cent. B. C. The Compound *rettuli* (not *retuli*, see Georges, *Lex. Wortf.* s. v.) has a double *t*, which is clearly not due to the Preposition having had the form *red-*, but like the double *p* of *reppĕri* (beside *rĕpĕrio*), *reppŭli* (beside *rĕpello*), to the Syncope of the Reduplication-vowel, *re-t(e)-tuli*, like *re-p(e)-peri*, *re-p(e)-puli*. Other compounds, like *con-tuli*, *ob-tuli*, *at-tuli*, *sus-tuli* have precisely the form which they would have had if they, like *rettuli*, had suffered Syncope of their second syllable; only, while Syncope has left a trace of its operation in the double *t* of *rettuli*, this trace has been obliterated by the phonetic conditions of these other Compounds. **Conttuli*, **obttuli*, **atttuli*, **susttuli* are impossible forms; they must in Latin orthography be written *contuli*, *obtuli*, *attuli*, *sustuli*, so as to afford no criterion of whether the Preposition was originally compounded with *tetuli* or *tuli*. The one Compound however which does afford such a criterion pronounces for the first of these alternatives, and warrants us in asserting that an original *tetuli* has been reduced to *tuli* in the Perfect of all the Compounds of *fero* (*tollo*), and in denying the theory that they show an original *tuli*, an Aorist formation like Subj. *attulas*, &c. (see § 4). The shortened form *tuli* having thus established itself in the numerous Compounds of *fero*, words in constant use in the speech of every-day life, it may well have spread from them to the simple verb. The habitual use of *con-tuli*, *at-tuli*, *ob-tuli*, &c. would naturally lead to the preference of *tuli* for the more cumbersome *tetuli*, although by a freak of language, by the caprice of that 'usus,

quem penes arbitrium est et jus et norma loquendi,'

the shortened form *-puli* of the Compounds *re-p(e)puli*, *com-(pe)puli*, *im-(pe)puli*, &c. did not supplant the full form *pepuli* at the same time. It is the Compound Verbs which as a rule in Latin show the short form, the Simple Verbs which are most retentive of the full Reduplicated form; e. g. *dē-tondi* (*detotondi* is quoted from Varro by Priscian, i. 482. 7 H., but is declared impermissible by Servius, who lays down the law that no Compound can have a Reduplicated Perfect: 'verba quae in praeterito perfecto primam syllabam geminant, cum composita fuerint, geminare non possunt), *attondi* (in Plaut. &c.), *despondi* (Plaut., Ter., Cic.), *praecīdi* (Plaut., Cic.) beside *totondi*, *spopondi*, *cecīdi*; and this fact is additional evidence of Latin Unreduplicated forms having lost the Reduplication-syllable in Composition.

§ 45. **Co-existent Reduplicated and Unreduplicated forms.** A more certain example of an Unreduplicated form existing side by side with a Reduplicated, and not a phonetic development from the latter due to the loss of the Reduplication-syllable, is the Perfect of *pango*, *pēgi* beside *pĕpĭgi*. Both forms survived in classical Latin, the Reduplicated *pepigi* being reserved for the sense 'I have agreed,' 'stipulated,' so that it is often called by the Roman grammarians the Perfect of *păciscor*; and in addition a third Perfect is mentioned by the grammarians for the Simple Verb (not the Compounds), an S-Aorist form *panxi*, e.g. in the elegiac epitaph of Ennius (ap. Cic. *Tusc.* i. 15. 34):

hic uestrum panxit maxima facta patrum.

In the same way O. Lat. *fefaked* of the very ancient inscription on a Praenestine brooch (*C. I. L.* xiv. 4123): Manios med fefaked Numasioi, seems to be from a Perfect-stem **fe-făc-* (and similarly Osc. *fefacust* ' fecerit ' Fut. Pft., and *fefacid* 'fecerit' Pft. Subj., will have ă not ā), anterior to the weakening of unaccented vowels (see ch. iii. § 18). It would have been in class. Latin, had the form survived, **fĕfĭci*, related to *fēci* as *pĕpĭgi* to *pēgi*.

§ 46. **S-Preterite.** Examples of parallel Latin and Greek forms are *dīxi*,

§§ 45-47.] THE VERB. PERFECT. 505

O. Lat. dei- (Gk. ἔδειξα) (both Lat. *dei-* and Gk. δει- may before a consonant represent I.-Eur. dēi-, ch. iv. § 45), *rēxi* (Gk. ὤρεξα), *texi* (Gk. ἔστεξα), *clepsi* (Gk. ἔκλεψα), *mansi* (Gk. ἔμεινα for *ἔμενσα), *ussi* (Gk. εὖσα for *εὔσσα), *pexi* (Gk. ἐπεξάμην). The substitution of -*si* for -*xi* (of *sanxi, tinxi*, &c.) in *mulsi* from (1) *mulceo*, (2) *mulgeo*, *fulsi* from (1) *fulcio*, (2) *fulgeo, parsi* (and *peperci*) from *parco, sparsi* from *spargo*, &c. is due to the preceding consonants *l, r* (see ch. iv. § 157). The same Verb may use as its Perfect both the S-formation and the Reduplicated Perfect : thus *parco* has *parsi* and *peperci* ; *praemordeo* has *praemordi* and *praemorsi* (Plaut. *fr.* 120 G.) : *surgo* has *surrexi*, but in Livius Andronicus often *surregi* (in the old spelling *suregi* ; Paul. Fest. 423. 1 Th. 'suregit' et 'sortus' pro surrexit, et quasi possit fieri surrectus, frequenter posuit Livius) ; the difference between *dī-lexi, neg-lexi* (cf. *intel-lexi*) and *dē-lēgi, ē-lēgi*, &c. has been explained by referring the Perfects with *x* to a lost Present **lego* (Gk. ἀλέγω, to care for) ; *ĕmo*, to buy (cf. *redimo, coëmo*), in O. Lat. to take (Paul. Fest. 53. 26 Th. emere, quod nunc est mercari, antiqui accipiebant pro accipere) as in *ad-imo*, to take away, O. Lat. *ab-emo* with the same sense (Paul. Fest. 4. 11 Th. 'abemito' significat demito vel auferto. 'emere' enim antiqui dicebant pro accipere), *dĭr-imo, intĕr-imo, ex-imo* (cf. M. Ir. fo-emaim; 'I take,' Lith. imù, O. Sl. imą), retains in these Compounds the Perfect-formation of the Simple Verb *ēmi, redēmi, coēmi, adēmi*, &c., but in the Compounds *cōmo, dēmo, prōmo, sūmo*, in which its connexion with *emo* is obscured, it takes an S-Preterite, *compsi, dempsi, prompsi, sumpsi* (O. Lat. *suremit* however for *sumpsit* is quoted by Paul. Fest. 425. 3 Th.) ; similarly *ămĭcio*, a Compound of *jăcio*, is conjugated inconsistently with its forgotten origin *amicui* and *amixi, amictum, amicīre* (cf. *ambītum* Supine of *ambio*, a Compound of *eo*, but *amb-ĭtus*, a going round, canvassing, &c.) ; why *ēlicio* should have as Perfect *elīcui*, but *allīcio, allexi* is not clear.

§ 47. Origin of the Perfect in -vi (-ui). The *v* (*u*) of Perfects like *ămā-vi, mŏn-ŭi* has been variously explained as a case-ending of a Verbal Noun U-stem followed by the Auxiliary Verb ei-, 'to go,' as a formation on the analogy of Verb-stems which end in *v* (*u*) such as *fov-eo* (ch. iv. § 144) from the root dheghᵘ- (*fŏvi* being regarded as a Perfect formed in the same way as *fōdi* from *fŏdio*, and not in the manner stated in § 39. 4) and other even less satisfactory hypotheses. A very plausible theory supposes I.-Eur. -wĭ to have been the ending of the first and third persons singular of the Perfect of roots ending in a long vowel and compares O. Ind. ja-jñáŭ (with final unaccented ĭ dropped) with Lat. (*g*)*nōvī* (with the middle 1 Sg. ending -ai), O. Ind. pa-praŭ with Lat. *plēvī*. These O. Ind. forms are confined to the 1 and 3 Sg. of the Perfect of roots ending in a long vowel, e. g. da-daŭ, 'I have given,' 'he has given,' but da-dắ-tha, 'thou hast given,' &c., so that the original Latin paradigm may have been *plevi, plesti, plevit*, &c. There is also an explanation possible which connects these Latin Perfects with Oscan (and probably Umbrian) Perfects in -f- (-ff-), such as Osc. aa-mana-ffed 'amandavit' 'faciendum curavit,' aíkda-fed '*aequidavit' 'fines ad normam derexit,' prúf-fed 'probavit,' fufens 'fuerunt.' This Oscan f has been naturally explained, like f of Oscan fu-fans 'erant,' Falisc. kare-fo 'carebo,' as representing I.-Eur. bh, seen in O. Ir. charub 'amabo' (quasi '*carabo '). But Italic f may also represent I.-Eur. dh (see ch. iv. § 114), so that these Oscan Perfects, if separable from the Impft. fufans, may contain an Auxiliary Verb connected with the root dhē-, 'to put' (Gk. τίθημι, Lat. *crē-do*, § 27 and p. 363). Latin *v* (*u*) in the middle of a word may represent *dv* (I.-Eur. dw, as in *suāvis*, I.-Eur. *swādu-, and probably also I.-Eur. dhw), while at the beginning of a word I.-Eur. dw- is represented by Latin *b*, e. g. *bĭs* from I.-Eur. *dwĭs (Gk. δ(ϝ)ίς), so that the *v* of the Latin Perfect and the f (ff) of the Oscan may both represent the dhw- of a weak stem from the root dhē-, 'to put, place,' a stem which appears in a fuller form (the E-grade ? ch. iv. § 51) in Lat. *crē-duas*, as the numeral *duo* (see ch. vi. § 59) appears beside *bis*. If this explanation, which requires a good many possibilities, be right, Oscan -manaffed will correspond to Latin *cubavit*, &c., Oscan prúffed to Latin *cubuit*, &c., and the -ss- of *messui*, &c. will be due to the combination of the final dental of the Verb-stem with the initial dental of the Auxiliary (see below § 51).

In *cŭbui* beside *cubavi*, *crĕpui* beside -*crepavi*, the *u*-forms may be referred to the parallel Consonant-stems of *cumbere*, *crepere (*percrepis*, Varro, *Men.* 124 B.), and similarly *lāvi* (for *lavvi) to O. Lat. *lăvere*, *sŏnui* to O. Lat. *sŏnere* (cf. § 92). But Perfects in -*ui* may also come from forms in which a short vowel[1] preceded the Auxiliary *dhwai, just as *ēluo* comes from *ēlăvo*, *dēnuo* from *dē nŏvo* (*nĕwōd), *ervum* from *ĕrŏgᵘo- (cf. Gk. ὄροβος, ἐρέβ-ινθος) (see ch. iii. § 24).

Perfects in -*īvi* from Consonantal Verbs, such as *petivi* from *pĕto*, *rudivi* from *rudo*, *lacessivi* from *lăcesso*, *arcessivi* from *arcesso* (and similarly *quaesivi* for *quaessivi from *quaeso*, older *quaesso*, used as Perf. of *quaero*), probably come from parallel YO-stems, *petio, *rudio, *lacessio, &c. (cf. *sallo* and *sallio*, Perf. *sallivi*, *lino* and *linio*, Perf. *linivi*, &c., § 15).

§ 48. **Shortened forms of the Perfect in -vi.** Latin *v* was often dropped when it stood between two vowels, oftenest between two *i*'s, e. g. O. Lat. *dīnus* for *dīvīnus*, *oblisci* for *oblīvisci*, *dītem* for *dīvĭtem* (so *dis* for *dīves*) (see ch. ii. § 53), but the dropping of *u* after a consonant is not practised in the same way (ch. iv. § 71). The only Latin Perfect form without *u* is the curious *monerim* of Pacuvius, quoted as an irregular formation by Nonius (507. 23 M.) *Trag.* 30 R. :

. . . dic quid fáciam ; quod me móneris effectúm dabo,

and *Trag.* 112 R. di mónerint meliora átque amentiam áuerruncassínt tuam (parodied by Lucil. xxvi. 35 M.), which seems to be a formation from a stem *mon-* (cf. Gk. μέ-μονα ?) instead of the ordinary Perfect-stem *monu-*, unless it indicates a pronunciation *mŏn(w)erim* like *ăb(y)ĭcio* of the old Dramatists (ch. ii. § 50), and possibly *augŭr͝(y)a* in a line of Accius (*Trag.* 624 R.) (quoted by Nonius 488. 2 M., who makes the word *augura*, by some regarded as a Neut. Pl. like *rōbŏra* ; cf. O. Ind. ójas- N., 'strength ') :

pró certo arbitrábor sortis, óracla, adytus, aúgura,

and *prōgen(y)em* (? *prŏgĕnĭĕm*) in a pentameter line of a Scipio epitaph of this period (*C. I. L.* i. 38, c. 130 B. C.) :

progenie mi genui : facta patris petiei

(probably a graver's mistake for *progeniem genui*). (*Pŏsisse*, *săpisse* are shortened forms, not of *posuisse*, *sapuisse*, but of *posīvisse*, *sapīvisse*, § 39. 4). But Perfect-forms

---

[1] *Dŏmui*, which is usually explained as Perf. of *domḗyo-, a Causative by-form of *domāyo- (§ 29), is by some referred to an I.-Eur. stem ending in -ă or -ǎ (cf. Gk. ἀ-δάμᾱτος with Lat. *domĭtus*). An example of a stem in I.-Eur. -ǎ is O. Ind. vámi-mi (3 Sg. vámi-ti, but also with the Thematic Vowel, vama-ti), the equivalent of Lat. *vŏmo*, -*ĕre*.

§ 48.] THE VERB. PERFECT. 507

without *v* were extremely common ; in Cicero's time *nosse, jūdicasse*, &c. were usual (*Orat.* xlvii. 157 quid quod sic loqui, 'nosse, judicasse' vetant, 'novisse' jubent et 'judicavisse'? quasi vero nesciamus in hoc genere et plenum verbum recte dici et imminutum usitate); and in Quintilian's time the forms *audīvisse, scīvisse, conservāvisse* were scarcely heard even in public speaking [Quint. i. 6. 17–21 inhaerent tamen ei (*sc.* analogiae) quidam molestissima diligentiae perversitate ut 'audaciter' potius dicant quam 'audácter,' licet omnes oratores aliud sequantur . . . his permittamus et 'audivisse' et 'scivisse' et 'tribunale' et 'faciliter' dicere . . . sed abolita atque abrogata retinere insolentiae cujusdam est et frivolae in parvis jactantiae. multum enim litteratus, qui sine adspiratione et producta secunda syllaba salutarit ('avere' est enim), et 'calefacere' dixerit potius quam quod dicimus et 'conservavisse,' his adiciat 'face' et 'dice' et similia. recta est haec via : quis negat ? sed adjacet et mollior et magis trita]. Servius, in a note on the form *lenīit* in Virg. *Aen.* i. 451, tells us that the pronunciation of every-day life was *lenīit,* the form with the short penult being confined to poetry (sed hoc in metro ubi necessitas cogit : nam in prosa et naturam suam et accentum retentat).

Varro (*L. L.* iii. fr. p. 148 W.) mentions *amasti, nosti, abiit* as the favourite forms of his time ; and in Terence the usual forms of Perfects in -*ĕvi,* -*īvi* and of *nŏvi* are the contracted (in Plautus the uncontracted, though in the middle, not the end, of a line *sīris,* not *sīvĕris,* is used), while the uncontracted forms of Perfects in -*āvi* are used only at the end of a line (in Plautus equally with the contracted). *Eo* and its compounds have even in Plautus usually the form -*ii*- in Perfect forms, except *īvi, exīvi, ambīvi,* &c. All this indicates the forms without *v* to have been phonetic developments of the others, and to have gradually established themselves in exclusive use, the *v* being dropped earliest and most persistently in forms where it came between two *i*'s. The shortened form of -*āvit,* if it did not push itself into literary usage, must however have become, sooner or later, a part of every-day pronunciation, for the Romance forms point to a Vulgar Latin -*aut* for -*avit,* e. g. Ital. comprò from a Vulg. Lat. **comp(ă)raut*. (On *audĭt,* &c. for *audivit,* see ch. iii. § 10. 2.)

The *v* of the Perfect of verbs whose stem ends in *v* (*u*) was not dropped to the same extent ; a fact which may be explained by the different sound of -*āv*- for -*avv*- in *cāveram* (pronounced *cavveram ?) and -*āv*- in *amāveram.* But even these Perfects when *o, u* precede *v,* are contracted almost as readily as the others : e. g. *dēvōro* for *dĕvŏvĕro* in the Praetextata of Accius called 'Decius' (referring to Decius Mus) [*Trag.* (*Praet.*) 15 R.] :

pátrio exemplo et mé dicabo atque ánimam deuoro hóstibus ;

commōrat, Ter. *Phorm.* 101 ; *commŏrunt, remosse,* Lucr. ; *adjūro* (or *adjŭĕro* ?), in a passage of the eleventh book of Ennius' *Annals* (l. 386 M.) describing the Macedonian campaign of Flamininus (the words are addressed by a shepherd-guide to the Roman general) :

O Tite, siquid ego adiuro curamue leuasso,
quae nunc te coquit et uersat in pectore fixa,
ecquid erit praemi ?

and the same form (3 Sg.) in Plaut. *Rud.* 305 and Ter. *Phorm.* 537, &c. *Mŏrunt, mŏram, commŏrunt, commŏram, commossem,* &c. are not uncommon in the Augustan poets, e. g. Hor. *S.* i. 9. 48 :

dispeream ni
summosses omnis,

and *jŭĕrint* occurs in Catullus, lxvi. 18 :

   non, ita me diui, uera gemunt, iuerint

(for other examples, see Neue, ii². 533). The usage on inscriptions of the 3 Pl. Pft. forms of *cūro, prŏbo* similarly points to the forms with *v* being the older [e. g. *coraueront, C. I. L.* i. 73, *courauerunt* 1419, *coirauerunt* 565, &c. (once *coirarunt*), but *coeraverunt* and *coerarunt, curarunt*].

§ 49. Shortened forms of the Perfect in -si. A better case might be presented for the theory that the shorter forms of Perfects in *-si* (*-xi*) are really ancient forms of different origin from the full forms, for *dixti, dixem, dixe,* &c. are most found in the early Dramatists, though they are by no means uncommon in Virgil and later poets. But the explanation of this fact is rather that they were felt to belong more or less to colloquial Latin, and so were freely admitted into Comedy and Tragedy (in both of which the every-day language of cultured society was employed), but not so freely into other literature. (Quintilian ix. 3. 22 remarks on Cicero's use of *dixti* 'excussa syllaba' in the *pro Caecina,* 29. 82.) A thing that is almost conclusive proof that *dixem,* &c. are not parallel forms to *dixim, dixo,* &c. is that these shortened forms are only found with Verbs which form the Perfect in *-si* (*-xi*); we have no **capsem,* answering to *capsim,* no *axem answering to *axim.* [On the wrongness of the readings *subaxet* (for *subaxit*) in Pacuv. *Trag.* 163 R., *faxet* in Plaut. *Capt.* 712, *accepsti, Trin.* 420, 964, &c., see Neue, ii². p. 539, and for examples of the shortened forms of Perfects in *-si* (*-xi*), e. g. *vixe* and *vixem* in Varro (*Men.* 321 B. non eos optime vixe qui diutissime vixent sed qui modestissime), *misti, misse, scripsti, rescripsti* (Cic. *ad Att.* v. 9. 2), *-sumpsti, -sumpse, -cesti, -cessem, -cesse, duxti, duxe, -spexti, -spexe, vexti, traxe, emunxti,* &c. see Neue, ii². pp. 536 sqq.]

§ 50. O. Lat. Perfects in -ū(v)i. Varro declares that in the correct pronunciation of his time the *u* of verbs like *pluo, luo* was short in the Present but long in the Perfect Indicative, as in the Perfect Participle Passive of similar verbs (*L. L.* ix. 104 quidam reprehendunt, quod 'pluit' et 'luit' dicamus in praeterito et praesenti tempore, cum analogiae sui cujusque temporis verba debeant discriminare. falluntur ; nam est ac putant aliter, quod in praeteritis u dicimus longum 'plūit,' 'lūit,' in praesenti breve 'plŭit' 'lŭit' ; ideoque in venditionis lege fundi 'rūta caesa' ita dicimus ut u producamus) (but cf. *dirŭtus*). Priscian (i. 504. 22 H.) makes this pronunciation, *-ūi,* in the Perfects of Verbs in *-uo,* a feature of Old Latin, and quotes Ennius (*Ann.* 135 M):

   adnūit sese mecum decernere ferro,

while in another passage (i. 503. 14 H.) he quotes *pluvisse, pluvit* with *v* (the quantity of the *u* is not mentioned) from Livy.

Instĭtūi is the reading of the MSS. in Plaut. *Most.* 86 (in bacchiac metre, a metre in which the long quantity of a vowel preceding another vowel is often retained):

   argúmentaque ín pectus múlta institúi.

The commonest instance of *-ūi* or *-ūvi* is in the Perfect of the old verb *fuo,* viz. *fui,* used as the Perfect of *sum,* as *fūimus* in the boast of Ennius on being made a Roman citizen (*Ann.* 431 M.) :

   nos sumus Romani qui fūimus ante Rudini,

fŭit (along with *profŭit*) in Plaut. *Capt.* 555 :

   quíbus insputarí salutí fúit atque ís prófŭit,

§§ 49-52.] THE VERB. PLUPERFECT. 509

fŭerim, Mil. 1364, &c., *fŭisset* in Ennius (*Ann.* 297 M.) :

  magnam cum lassus diei
  partem fūisset de summis rebus regundis.

We have the spelling FVVEIT on an epitaph (*C. I. L.* i. 1051). (See ch. iv. § 70.)

§ 51. Some Irregular Perfects. Besides the byforms in *s* of the Perfect of *parco, -lĕgo*, &c. which are found in the older as well as the later literature (§ 46), we have some which are more recent coinages on the type of other verbs. Velius Longus (74. 4 K.) speaking of *sorpsi*, a byform of *sorbui*, says : cum recens haec declinatio a sordidi sermonis viris coeperit (cf. Caper 94. 14 K. non est... 'sorbsi,' sed sorbui), and similarly describes *terui* (for *trivi*) as a 'consuetudo nova' (*absorpsi* is used by Lucan, iv. 100). The Perfect *vulsi*, for *velli*, seems also to belong to this class of later coinages (*āvulsit* in Lucan, v. 594 ; cf. Neue, ii². 503), and *-cănui* of *concinui* (Ov., Tibull.), *occanui* (Sall.), *incinui* (Varro), &c. may be a remodelling of a Perfect with lost Reduplication *-cĭni* (*con-cini, oc-cini, in-cini*) after the pattern of *sŏnui, consonui*, &c. *Messui* (found in the older writers) is generally regarded as due to a similar addition of the ending *-ui* to an already existing Perfect **messi*, and also *nexui* (with *nexi*), *pexui* (with *pexi*), although, if the theory of the origin of the V-perfect stated in § 47 be correct, the sibilant might be referred to the influence of the dental in the auxiliary **dhwai* (cf. *ūsus* for **ut-tus, *oit-to-*, *fūsus* for **fud-tus*, &c., ch. iv. § 95. p. 281). In late inscriptions we have e.g. *reguit* (*C. I. L.* v. 923, from Aquileia : septimae qui cohortis centuriam reguit, a pentameter line), *convertuit* (viii. 2532 D b 1) ; Apuleius uses *conterui* (see Georges *Lex Wortf.* s. v.). On Heteroclite Perfects like *fui*, Perfect of *sum, tŭli* (older *tĕtŭli*) of *fĕro*, see § 97.

In Vulgar Latin, as reflected in the Romance languages, the ending *-ui* encroached still more. *Cognovit* became *cognovuit* (Ital. conobbe), *movit* became *movuit* (Ital. movve), *cecidit* was replaced by *caduit* (Ital. cadde), *stetit* by *stetuit* (Ital. stette), *venit* by *venuit* (Ital. venne), &c. [cf. § 92 on the Vulg. Lat. P. P. P. in *-ūtus*, e. g. *cadūtus*, fallen (Ital. caduto)]. The ending *-si* also extended its sphere, *respondit* passing to *responsit* (Ital. rispose), *prendit* to *pre(n)sit* (Ital. prese), *cucurrit* to *cursit* (Ital. corse), &c. (See Meyer-Lübke, *Rom. Gramm.* ii. pp. 297 sqq.)

§ 52. E. Pluperfect. The Pluperfect-stem is formed by adding to the Perfect-stem an S-suffix, probably a Preterite of the Substantive Verb *es-*, as the Imperfect in *-bam*, e. g. *ămā-bam*, uses a Preterite of the Verb *bheu-*. The *-ĕram, -ĕrās, -ĕrat* of *ămāv-eram, mĕru-eram, replēv-eram, dīx-eram, vīd-eram, pĕpĭg-eram, audīv-eram* is most naturally referred to the Imperfect of *sum*, though *vīderam* has been, with the O. Ind. á-vēdiṣ-am, analyzed into a Noun-stem in *-is* (cf. *vidis-sem*) as Gk. ᾔδεα into a Noun-stem in *-es* (see § 3). The *-is-* of the Pluperfect Subjunctive *ămāvissem, mŏnuissem, vīdissem, audīvissem* must, if the old view be correct which sees in these forms an

Auxiliary *essem* appended to the Perfect-stem, be a change of -*es*- to the I-vocalism of the Perfect, just as the *a* of Gk. δειξάτω, &c. is due to the apprehension of *a* as the appropriate vowel of the Aorist Tense.

§ 53. F. Future-Perfect. The Future-Perfect adds to the Perfect-stem -*ĕrō*, -*ĕrĭs*, -*ĕrĭt*, &c. (3 Pl. -*ĕrunt*), which seems to be nothing else than the Future (in form a Subjunctive, § 55) of *sum*, appended as an Auxiliary Verb, though those who explain the -*er*- of *vīdĕram* as I.-Eur. -is-, the suffix of a Noun-stem, see the same -is- in *vīd-ĕro* (cf. O. Ind. vēdišam) (see 3). Scansions like *fecerīmus* (Catull. v. 10), 1 Pl. of *fēcĕro*, are due to the confusion of the Future-Perfect forms with Perfect Subjunctive forms (see Neue, ii². p. 510); *aderint* is similarly used for *ădĕrunt* throughout the Lex Col. Jul. Genetivae Urbanorum of 44 B. C. (*Eph. Epigr.* ii. p. 122). The use of the Fut. Perf. in the Republican Dramatists in sentences like *mox ivero*, where it hardly differs from the Future, suggests that in its original usage the Tense was more of a Future than of a Future Perfect (see *A. L. L.* iv. 594).

In the Umbro-Oscan languages we have a suffix -us- (Umbro-Oscan u may represent I.-Eur. ō as well as I.-Eur. ŭ), which is supposed to be the termination of the Perfect Participle. Thus Osc. *fefacust* 'fecerit' will be like Gk. δεδρακὼς ἔσομαι, Umbr. fakurent like δεδρακότες ἔσονται. (On the Umbro-Oscan Perfect Participle in -us, see § 89.)

§ 54. G. Tenses formed with Auxiliary Verbs. We have seen that the suffix used to form the Imperfect Tense of all Verbs, -*bā*-, and the suffix used for the Future of Vowel Verbs, -*bŏ*- (-*bĕ*-), are nothing but parts of the Auxiliary Verb bheu- (Lat. *fui*), that the S-suffixes of the Pluperfect and Future-Perfect Indicative, and of the Imperfect, Perfect and Pluperfect Subjunctive are probably to be referred to the Auxiliary es- (Lat. *sum*), and we have seen the possibility of a similar explanation of the V-suffix of the Perfect Tense as a form of the root dhē-, 'to set, put,' used as an Auxiliary Verb. These theories receive a sanction from the proneness of the Latin and other Italic languages for Periphrastic Tense-forms. Not only was the

THE VERB. SUBJUNCTIVE.

Italic Perfect Indicative Passive a form of this kind [Lat. *ămātus sum*, (1) I was loved, (2) I am in a state of being loved, *amatus fui*, I was in a state of being loved, Osc. prúftú-set 'probata sunt,' teremnatust 'terminatus est,' Umbr. *screhto est* 'scriptum est' (the Auxiliary is joined in writing with the Participle in *frosetomest*)], and other Tenses of the Passive (Pluperfect, Lat. *amatus ĕram*, *amatus fuĕram*, Future-Perfect *amatus ĕro*, *amatus fuĕro*, Perfect Subjunctive *amatus sim*, *amatus fuĕrim*, Pluperfect Subjunctive *amatus essem*, *amatus fuissem*), but we have many other examples of Periphrastic formation. The 2 Pl. Pass. ending *-mĭnī*, e. g. *fĕrĭmĭnī*, is explained (§ 81) as the ending of a Pres. Part. Pass. (Gk. φερόμενοι) with suppression of *estis*, just as *esse* is commonly suppressed in the Fut. Inf. *dictūrus, -a, -um* (*esse*) (§ 86). Osc. manafum 'mando,' if it correspond to 'mandans sum,' is another example, showing a Pres. Part. with the Substantive Verb (cf. *C. I. L.* i. 196 senatuosque sententiam utei scientes esetis). The Auxiliary *eo* appears in the Latin Fut. Inf. Pass., e. g. *dătum* (1 Sup.) *īrī* (§ 87), the Auxiliary *hăbeo* in such phrases as *missum habeo* for *mīsi* or *dīmisi* (e. g. Plaut. *Pseud.* 602 illa omnia missa habeo, quae ante agere occepi), the Auxiliary DHĒ- (*reddo, do, făcio*, &c.) in phrases like *missum facio* for *mitto* or *dimitto* (e. g. Plaut. *Amph.* 1145), *perfectum reddo* for *perficio* (e. g. Plaut. *Asin.* 122), *factum dabo* for *faciam* (e. g. Ter. *Eun.* 212). In the Romance languages these expressions have supplanted many of the Latin tenses; e. g. *cantare habeo* (Fr. chanter-ai, Ital. canter-ò, with *habeo, habes*, &c., reduced to *hayo, has, hat, haunt*, &c.) has supplanted *cantabo*, &c., so that the Latin Future survives in Romance only in a few isolated forms, Ital. fia, O. Fr. ier from Lat. *fiam, ero*; we find a Periphrastic Perfect consisting of the Perf. Part. Pass. with *sum, sto* (Intrans.) or with *habeo, teneo* (Trans.); and for the Passive the same Participle with *sum, fio, venio*, &c. (See Meyer-Lübke, *Rom. Gram.* ii. pp. 138 sqq.)

§ 55. III. THE MOODS. A. Subjunctive. (Relics of the I.-Eur. Optative Mood in Latin.) The I.-Eur. Subjunctive had the functions of a Future (cf. Hom. *Il.* i. 262 οὐ γάρ πω τοίους ἴδον ἀνέρας οὐδὲ ἴδωμαι), as well as of a true Subjunctive; it had also Imperatival functions, and in O. Ind. while Subjunctive forms are frequent in the oldest literature, the Vedas, they survive in classical 'Sanscrit' only in Imperatival use, e. g. 1 Sg. Imper. bhar-ā-ṇi, 'let me carry.' To the unweakened stem (E-grade) was appended in the Athematic Conjugation the short vowels ĕ and ŏ, followed by either the Primary or the Secondary Person-endings (§ 65): e. g. from the Athematic Verb es-, 'to be,' we have 3 Sg. Subj. *es-e-t(i) (O. Ind. ásat(i)). In Greek these athematic Subjunctive forms are still seen in Homer (e. g. βήσομεν, τείσετε), and later in a few so-called Futures like ἔδ-ο-μαι from the Athematic Verb ed-, 'to eat,' as in Latin we have ĕro, ĕrit 3 Sg. similarly retained as a Future Tense. But in Greek, as in Latin, the athematic forms have been almost wholly supplanted by the thematic forms, which show a long vowel, sometimes ā, as in the Italic, Celtic and other languages, sometimes ē (which in Greek varies with ō, e. g. φέρ-η-τε, φέρ-ω-μεν, like athematic ε-ο in τείσ-ετε, βήσ-ο-μεν), as in the Italic and Greek languages; and this process must have begun very early, for thematic Subjunctive forms of verbs belonging to the Athematic Conjugation appear in many instances to have been I.-Eur. forms. Thus *ed-ā-, *ed-ē- must have been an I.-Eur. Subjunctive stem of ed-, 'to eat,' for we find in Lat. *edā-mus*, *edā-tis*, in Greek ἔδω-μεν, ἔδη-τε, and in O. Ind. ádā-n 3 Pl. (O. Ind. ā may represent I.-Eur. ā, ē, ō); *es-ē- from es-, 'to be,' appears in Gk. ἔη-τε, ἔω-μεν (cf. O. Ind. ásā-t 3 Sg., asā-tha 2 Pl.); and ey-ā- from ei-, 'to go,' in Lat. *eā-s*, *eā-tis* (cf. O. Ind. ayā-s 2 Sg., ayā-t 3 Sg.). The discarded athematic forms are supposed to have been utilized in Greek as Futures [the Future in -σο- (-σε-)]; thus Att. τείσομεν, τείσετε, δείξομεν, δείξετε, τιμήσομεν, τιμήσετε, &c. will not be of the same class as the ordinary I.-Eur. Future in -syo-, e. g. O. Ind. dēk-šyā-mi corresponding to Gk. δείξω, Lith. bú-siu to Gk. φύσω, but will be Subjunctives of S-Aorists; and Latin Futures in -so-, like *dixo*, *faxo*, &c., have been referred to the same source. (On this theory, see § 3.)

In Latin the ā-forms were not used for the first Conjugation, probably because a Subjunctive like *amāy-ā-s(i) 2 Sg. must have become *amās*, and so been merged in the Indicative

2 Sg. *amās*. The Ē-forms only were used for this Conjugation in Latin, e. g. *amēs* from *amāy-ē-s(i) (cf. Osc. *devaid* 'juret,' *tadait* 'censeat,' sakahíter 'sacretur'; Oscan í, in the Latin alphabet *i*, represents I.-Eur. ē, e. g. lígato- 'lēgatus,' *zicolo-* M. 'diēcula'), but in Umbrian we have Ā-forms in *kuraia* 'curet,' *etaians* 'itent.' Similarly the Ē-forms were not used for the second Conjugation in Latin, to avoid confusion between *widēy-ē-s(i), *vidēs 2 Sg. Subj., and *vidēs* 2 Sg. Ind., only the Ā-forms being allowed, e. g. *widēy-ā-s(i), *videās*. But in the other Conjugations the Ā- and Ē-forms probably existed side by side, until the latter were appropriated for the Future functions (see § 36), e. g. *ferās* 2 Sg. Subj. from *bher-ā-s(i), *ferēs* 2 Sg. Fut. from *bher-ē-s(i), *faciat* 3 Sg. Subj. (Osc. fakiiad, Volsc. façia, Umbr. façia), *faciet* 3 Sg. Fut. These Ā- and Ē-Subjunctives show in Umbro-Oscan the Secondary Person-endings (-d in 3 Sg., -ns in 3 Pl.).

The Optative must have entered into competition with the Subjunctive at an early time, for it has almost entirely ousted the Subjunctive forms in the Teutonic and Balto-Slavic families of languages, and in Latin we see the struggle still going on between the Optative-forms *edī-mus, edī-tis*, and the Subjunctive-forms *edā-mus, edā-tis* from the root ed-, 'to eat,' while in the case of the root es-, 'to be,' the Optative *sī-mus, sī-tis* have driven out of the field the proper athematic Subjunctive forms *erĭ-mus, erĭ-tis* (from *eso-, *ese-), which have been relegated to the Future function, as an *(*e*)*sē-mus*, *(*e*)*sē-tis* may lurk in the Imperfect Subjunctive ending (see § 34).

The I.-Eur. Optative had in the Athematic Conjugation the weak grade of stem, with a suffix which was in the Singular Active -yē- (-ĭyē-) and elsewhere -ī-, and with the Secondary person-endings. Thus from the root es-, the I.-Eur. Optative forms were: 2 Sg. *syē-s (O. Ind. syá-s) or sĭyē-s (O. Ind. s-ĭyá-s, O. Lat. *siēs*), 2 Pl. *s-ī-tĕ (cf. Lat. *s-ī-tis*). In the Thematic Conjugation the suffix was -oi- in Singular and Plural alike, e. g. from the root bher-, to carry, 2 Sg. *bher-oi-s (Gk. φέρ-οι-ς), 2 Pl. *bher-oi-te (Gk. φέρ-οι-τε). I.-Eur. oi of the Thematic Optative would in the unaccented syllable in Latin become -*ei*-, then -*ī*- (ch. iii. § 18), and I.-Eur. -yē- (-ĭyē-)

of the Singular Active of the Athematic Optative has been mostly replaced by -ī-, the weak form of the suffix (e. g. class. *sim* for O. Lat. *siem*, like *sīmus*, *sītis*), so that a Latin Optative form like *edīs* might equally well represent an I.-Eur. athematic *ĕd-ī-s (with E-grade of stem and with ī transferred to the Singular from the Plural, as -yē- is transferred to the Plural from the Singular in Gk. στă-ίη-μεν, a byform of σταῖμεν), and an I.-Eur. thematic *ĕd-oi-s. The probability however is that the Optative was confined to the Athematic Conjugation in Latin, and represents in every case I.-Eur. -yē-, -ī-. Again, it would be possible to argue that *stēs*, *stēmus*, &c. were representatives of I.-Eur. *stă-yē- (Gk. στă-ίης, στă-ίη-μεν), and not examples of Ē-Subjunctives. The resolution of these doubts must come from the Umbro-Oscan languages, of which the remains hitherto discovered offer too scanty material to enable us to separate with certainty Latin thematic and athematic Optatives, and Latin Subjunctives in -ē-. The use of the weak grade of the suffix -yē- in the Singular of the Optative of es- appears in these languages too, e. g. Umbr. *si* 'sis,' si 'sit, like *sins* 'sint,' Marruc. -si 'sis' or 'sit,' and has been referred to an Italic weakening of unaccented yē to ī. How far it is possible to assign an Optative force to forms like *crēduim* in the older literature, and a Subjunctive force to forms like *creduam* is doubtful. The Optative origin of the old forms in -(*s*)*sim* comes out clearly in their use in prayers (e. g. Juppiter prohibessis scelus, di mactassint, and the formula of the ancient Augural prayer: bene sponsis beneque uolueris; see § 5), but in process of time all distinctions between Optatives in -*im*, Subjunctives in -*am* and Subjunctives (possibly Optatives) in -*em* came to be effaced.

§ 56. Some O. Lat. Subj. and Opt. forms. In one of the oldest Latin inscriptions preserved, the Dvenos inscription, we have an Ā-Subjunctive *mitat* 'mittat' used as a Future, with the Optative of the root es-, *sied* 'sit,' used in the true Optative sense: qoi med mitat, nei ted endo cosmis uirco sied 'qui me mittet, ne erga te comis Virgo sit' (*asted* on the same inscr. is variously interpreted as 'adstet' and as 'ast'; see ch. x. § 5). *Siem*, *sies*, *siet* (on *sient*, see § 73; **siemus*, **sietis* have not found their way into Latin as syăma, syăta have into O. Ind.), *possiem*, &c. are by Terence used almost only at the end of a line or hemistich, i. e. through metrical necessity, but

§ 56.]   THE VERB. SUBJUNCTIVE.   515

siem, *siet* are almost invariably used in old laws (e. g. *C. I. L.* i. 196. 30 ; 197. 21 ; 198 passim ; 199. 6 ; 200 passim), and Cicero (*Orat.* xlvii. 157) says, 'siet' plenum est, 'sit' imminutum : licet utare utroque. [For statistics, see Zander, *Vers. Ital.* p. cxx, who makes -*ī*- of *sit*, &c. not the I.-Eur. I of the Plural, but a Latin weakening of -ie- as in *Cornelī* Voc. for *Cornelĭĕ* (? ch. vi. § 31)]. Besides the class. Lat. 'Subjunctives' (Optatives) in -*im*, *sim*, *ĕdim*, *vĕlim* (in Plaut. *velis* and *vis* are used as the metre requires, without difference of meaning), with its Compounds *nōlim* and *mālim* (on *noli*, see § 58), we find an O. Lat. Optative *duim*. It comes from *duo*, a bystem both of *do*, to give (root dō-) and of -*do*, to put (root dhē- of τί-θη-μι, &c.), e. g. *duitur* (v. l. *arduuitur*) XII Tab. x. 7, *interduo*, Plaut. *fr. inc.* 2 G. ciccum non interduo, *concreduo*, *Aul.* 585, *concredui*, Perf., *Cas.* 479. We have in Plautus the Optative forms *duim*, *perduim*, especially in prayers and execrations (e. g. *Most.* 668 di istum perduint), *interduim* (e. g. *Rud.* 580 ciccum non interduim), *creduim* (in phrases like *Amph.* 672 si situlam cépero, Núnquam míhi diuíni quicquam créduis post húnc diem, 'may you never trust me again'), as also the Ā-Subjunctive forms *creduam* , e. g. *Bacch.* 504 nam míhi diuini númquam quisquam créduat, Ni ego, &c.), and *accreduam* (*Asin.* 854 néque diuini néque mi humani pósthac quicquam adcréduas . . . si, &c.), while an Ē-Subjunctive form (in Future sense ?) is quoted by Paul. Fest. 20. 22 Th. *addues*, addideris (cf. *ib.* 47. 6 Th. *duis* . . . pro dederis). We have in Conditional use, e. g. *duit* in a Law of Numa (ap. Paul. Fest. 278. 9 Th.) si qui hominem liberum dolo sciens morti duit, paricidas esto ; *adduit* in a Plebiscitum de Ponderibus Publicis (ap. Fest. 322. 11 Th.) siquis . . . faxit iussitue . . . dolumue adduit, &c. Festus also quotes an old form *produit* which he explains by 'porro dederit' (284. 16 Th.). *Duim* was the form appropriate to Early Latin prayers, as in the prayer at the 'agri lustratio,' preserved by Cato (*R. R.* cxli. 3) : pastores pecuaque salua seruassis duisque bonam salutem ualetudinemque mihi domo familiaeque nostrae ; it is used even in Tiberius' letter to the Senate (Tac. *Ann.* iv. 38). There are also uncertain traces of Optative forms from other verbs, such as *coquint*, the reading of the Palatine MSS. in Plaut. *Pseud.* 819 (but *cocunt* in the Ambrosian Palimpsest), *temperint*, the reading of the same family of MSS. in *Truc.* 60, a line for which the evidence of the Palimpsest is not available (other examples, see in Neue, ii². 442 : *carint* of the Palatine MSS. in *Most.* 858 is *carent* in the Palimpsest, and the corrupt reading of the Palatine MSS. in *Men.* 984 *a*, where this line of the *Mostellaria* is wrongly inserted, *culparent* for *culpa carent*, shows *carent* to be the right form ; *verberit* of the law of the XII Tables, ap. Fest. 290. 15 Th, : si parentem puer uerberit, ast olle plorassit, is a corruption due to the fact that the words were wrongly divided in the archetype *verberetas tolle*, and the first word, being mistaken for a frequentative Verb, was changed to *verberitas*).

An O. Lat. Ā-Subjunctive is *fuam* used in the sense of *fiam*, e. g. *Bacch.* 156, in the amusing conversation between young Pistoclerus and his 'paedagogus' Lydus :

    PIST. fiam, út ego opinor Hércules, tu autém Linus.
    LYD. pol métuo magis, ne Phoénix tuis factís fuam,
           teque ád patrem esse mórtuom renúntiem,

sometimes merely in the sense of *sim*, e. g. Virg. *A.* x. 108 :

        Tros Rutulusve fuat nullo discrimine habebo.

The equivalent of *forsitan* (which is not used by Plautus, and only seldom, if ever, by Terence, ch. ix. §. 5) is in Plautus *fors fuat an*, e. g. *Pseud.* 432 :

fors fúat an istaec dícta sint mendácia.

(Cf. Ter. *Hec.* 610 fors fuat pol! ' heaven grant it may!') Nonius (478. 26 M.) quotes *volam* for *velim* from Lucil. (xxviii. 15 M.) :

eidóla atque atomus uíncere Epicurí uolam,

and Plaut. *Asin.* 109 siquid te uolam, Ubi erís? ; but in the second at least of these passages it seems to be used in the Future sense.

§ 57. B. Imperative. In the 2 Sg. Act. of the Present Imperative the bare stem of the Verb is used, e. g. Athematic *ei, from the root ei-, 'to go' (Gk. ἔξ-ει, Lat. *ex-ī* from **ex-ei*), Thematic *bhere, from the root bher-, 'to carry' (O. Ind. bhára, Arm. ber, Gk. φέρε, O. Ir. beir, Goth. bair; Lat. *age*). But a particle was often added: the particle -dhi to the 2 Sg. in the Athematic Conjugation (e. g. O. Ind. i-hí, Gk. ἴ-θι; O. Ind. vid-dhí, Gk. ἴσθι for *Fιδ-θι, O. Lith. veiz-di, O. Sl. viž-dǐ); the particle -*ki* or -*ke* in Lithuanian, e. g. eĩ-k, ' go,' dŭ-k, ' give,' bú-k, ' be'; the particle -u (cf. O. Ind. sṓ for *sou, Gk. οὗ-τος for *σου-τος) in Sanscrit to the 3 Sg. and Pl., e. g. bháratu, bhárantu; the particle -tōd to various persons both in the Athematic and Thematic Conjugations [e. g. O. Ind. vit-tā́t 2 Sg. ; Gk. ἴστω for *Fιτ-τωδ 3 Sg. ; Gk. ἔσ-τω(δ), Lat. *es-tō(d)*]. In Latin the 2 Sg. Imper. in -*tō(d)* is called the Future Imperative, because it expresses a command, not for immediate performance, but for performance after something shall have happened (e. g. Plaut. *Merc.* 770 cras petito, dabitur; nunc abi; Hor. *C.* iii. 14. 23 si per invisum mora janitorem Fiet, abito), and the same sense is attached to the O. Ind. 2 Sg. Imper. in -tāt (see Delbrück, *Altind. Syntax*, p. 363), so that it is not unlikely that this particle -tōd is nothing but the Abl. Sg. of the Demonstrative Pronoun-stem to- (ch. vii. § 13. 1), and means ' from this,' ' thereupon.' It is also found with the 3 Sg. Dual and Plur., and perhaps took with it originally the weak grade of the Verbstem (e. g. Gk. ἴ-τω 3 Sg., ὀμ-νύ-τω 3 Sg., O. Ind. kr̥-n̥ŭ-tāt 2 Sg., ' do thou'; but not in Latin *īto*, Umbr. etu, *eetu*, for *ei-tōd). In the 3 Pl. it is added to what is called the ' Injunctive' 3 Pl., viz. a form resembling an augmentless Imperfect

(I.-Eur. *bheront like Impft. *e-bheront), e.g. Gk. φερόντω for *φεροντ-τωδ, Lat. *ferunto* for *feront-tōd*. For the 1 Sg. and Plur. the Subjunctive was used, e.g. Lat. *feram, ferāmus*. In the 2 Pl. we have the 'Injunctive' form (e.g. *bherĕtĕ, O. Ind. bhárata, Gk. φέρετε, O. Ir. berid, Goth. bairiþ ; Lat. *ăgĭte* from *agete*), beside which we find in Latin a 'Future' form with -*tōte*, e.g. *estote*, apparently the addition of the 2 Plur. suffix -*tĕ* (§ 72) to the 2 Sg. 'Future' Imperative (e.g. *estō*.)

In the Latin Passive, the Injunctive form in -sŏ (e.g. I.-Eur. *bhere-sŏ, Zend bara-ŋha, Gk. φέρεο, contr. φέρου, ἐ-φέρεο, contr. ἐ-φέρου) is used, e.g. *ăgĕ-rĕ* for *age-sŏ (see ch. iii. § 38), in the 2 Sg., and in the 2 Pl. the old Passive Infinitive[1] (Dat. Sg. of a MEN-stem), e.g. *ăgĭ-mĭnī* for *aĝe-menai (Hom. Gk. ἀγέ-μεναι), *da-mini* (O. Ind. dá-manē Inf., Hom. Gk. δό-μεναι); in the 2 Sg. 'Future' Imper. and in the other persons the final *d* of -*tōd* is changed to -*r*, e.g. *ăgĭtor, dător, aguntor* (cf. Umbr. *emantur, emantu, tursiandu*). A byform for the 2, 3 Sg. is in -*mĭnō*, e.g. *prae-fāmino*, forméd apparently by Anal. of 2 Pl. -*mĭnī*. There is no Perfect Imper. in Latin, though *mĕmĭnī*, a Perfect used for a Present, has *mĕmento* for *mement-tōd (Gk. μεμάτω for *μεμη-τωδ). *Memento*, like other 2 Sg. Imperatives in -*tō*, expresses a command that usually has reference to the future, a reference naturally suggested by the command ' remember.'

§ 58. Other examples of 2 Sg. Imper. with bare stem. (1) Athematic : like athematic Ind. *im-plē-s, vidē-s, curā-s, finī-s* are Imper. *im-plē, vidē* (Lith. pa-vydé-k), *curā, finī*, &c. *Fer, vel, es* (from *sum*) are then likely to be athematic too, since their Ind. is athematic (e.g. 3 Sg. *fer-t, vul-t, es-t*; see § 2). *Fer* cannot be an Injunctive form *fer-s* (like *ter* for *ter-s* from I.-Eur. *trĭ-s, ch. vi. § 61), if, as is probable, it is in Plautus a thoroughly short syllable, capable of acting as a brevis brevians (see ch. iii. § 42), in *Curc.* 245 auférĭstaec quaeso, whereas *ter* is a long syllable in Plautus, e.g. *Bacch.* 1127. In *Mil.* 1343 however one family of MSS. reads: fĕr aequo animo, the evidence of the Ambrosian Palimpsest being unfortunately wanting, a reading which may easily be changed to fĕr animo aequo (as *Curc.* 245, for which there is similar MS. evidence, is changed by some editors to aufer quaeso istaec). The

---

[1] Or the Plural of the old Pres. Part. Passive, *agimini* for *aĝo-menoi (Gk. ἀγό-μενοι), with ellipsis of *este*, as 2 Pl. Ind. *agimini* for the same, with ellipse of *estis* (§ 82). The Inf. is used for the Imper. in Italian &c. in phrases like non parlare 'do not speak.'

small number of lines with decisive evidence on the quantity of *fer* in Plautus makes it difficult to speak with certainty. *Fer* is short in *Asin.* 672 fĕr amánti ero salútem. *Vel* is a short syllable, capable of acting as a brevis brevians in Plautus, e. g. *Amph.* 917 vél hünc rogato; *es*, 'be,' cannot be shown (like *es*, 'art') to be long by position in Plautus (see Solmsen, *Stud. Lautg.* p. 185); *es*, 'eat,' for which we should expect **ed*, beside 3 Sg. *esto*, may be coined on the type of *es*, 'be,' beside 3 Sg. *esto*, although both *es*, 'be,' and *es*, 'eat,' can also be explained as Injunctive forms (like Gk. ἐπί-σχε-s, &c.) for **es-s* and **ed-s* [1]. *Cĕ-dŏ* (with Plur. *ce-tte* for **ce-dĭte* ?), 'give me' or 'tell me,' seems to contain the Pronoun **ke* (perhaps Lith. szè, 'hither'; see ch. vii. § 15), prefixed as an Adverb or Preposition, 'here,' 'hither' (cf. Osc. *ce-bnust* 'huc venerit,' composed of **ke* and a tense of the I.-Eur. root gᵘem-, 'to come') to an athematic Imperative **dō* (Lith. dú-k; cf. Gk. δί-δω), the final vowel, shortened by the Law of Breves Breviantes after the short syllable *cĕ-*, being invariably short owing to the rapid utterance of the word in every-day talk (so *havĕ* for *avē* in the pronunciation of Quintilian's time, ch. iii. § 42).

Dā for **dō* shows the same transference to the Ā-Conjugation as Pres. Ind. *dās, dat* (O. Lat. *dăt*) (see § 2).

Another example of an athematic Imperative may be *fu* in the Carmen Arvale, if the words *satur fu, fere Mars,* are rightly interpreted 'satur esto, fere Mars.' *Fu* will be Imper. of **fuo*, like Lith. bú-k. *Nōlī* may come from a bystem of the fourth Conjugation, I.-Eur. **wel-yo-* (Goth. vilja, O. Sl. veljǫ) (see § 2). (On Late Lat. *aufere*, see Georges, *Lex. Wortf.* s. v.)

(2) *Thematic.* The thematic Imperatives O. Lat. *dīce, dūce, făce* (for **faci*, from stem *fac-yŏ-*, § 16) drop their final *-ĕ* in classical Latin owing to their frequent use in word-groups, i. e. in close connexion with a following word (like *atq(ue), neq(ue)* before consonants; see ch. iii. § 35). *Dic mihi, fac sciam* are regularly used even in O. Latin authors, and in Plautus we find *dic* in questions when the next word begins with a consonant, e. g. *dic quid est*, but *dice* is the form employed where there is anything of a pause after the word; cf. *Mil.* 256 dice, monstra, praecipe, and especially *Rud.* 124:

tu, síquid opus est díce. Dic quod té rogo.

Abdūce, addūce and other Compounds of *duco* are still found in Terence before a vowel, *abdūc*, &c. before a consonant, while *face* is the form employed at the end of a line; *ēdīce* in Virgil ('antiquitatis amans' Diom. p. 349. 30 K.) in *Aen.* xi. 463:

tu, Voluse, armari Volscorum edice maniplis.

The Compounds however of *facio*, whose short penult was not so favourable to Syncope (ch. iii. § 13. p. 173) retain the *-e, confĭce, affĭce, infĭce*, &c. Catullus has *ingermi* (xxvii. 2): inger mi calices amariores, from which we may perhaps explain *misc sane* on an old Praenestine cista with a kitchen-scene (*Mél. Arch.* 1890, p. 303) as *misc(ĕ) sane* from **misco*, an earlier form of *misceo* (see § 28). The Interjection *em* (ch. x. § 19) [e. g. *em tibi*, 'take that' (with a blow), *em ergo hoc tibi*, &c., in the Comedians] may have been originally Imperative of *ĕmo*, which in O. Lat. (§ 46) meant 'to take' (thematic **eme*, to judge from the Ind. *emis, emit*, &c.), just as the Conjunction *vel* (ch. x. § 4) was the

---

[1] *Sins* of the Carmen Arvale (quoted in ch. vi. § 55) is a very doubtful form.

§§ 59-62.] THE VERB. DEPONENT. 519

Imperative (athematic) of *vŏlo* (I.-Eur. *wĕl-mi) (cf. Umbr. heris . . . heris, 'either . . . or,' lit. 'do you wish . . . do you wish'?).

§ 59. **Other examples of Imper. in -tōd.** The final -d is retained in Oscan, e. g. 3 Sg. *deivatud* 'jurato,' *estud*, líkítud 'līcēto,' and in Early Latin inscriptions, e. g. 2 Sg. *stutod*, 'sistito' on the Dvenos bowl [a Future Imperative if we are right in interpreting *dienoine med Mano statod* 'on the ninth day set me (with an offering) for Manus']; 3Sg. *uiolatod, licetod, datod* with *exuehito, exferto, cedito* 'caedito,' on the Spoletium inscription (*C. I. L.* ii. 4766), *estod, licetod* with *fundatid, proiecitad, parentatid* on the Luceria inscr. (*C. I. L.* ix. 782); but in class. Latin, as in Umbrian, -*d* was by the phonetic laws of the language lost after a long vowel (see ch. ii. § 137), e. g. Lat. *estō, līcētō, fertō, hăbētō*, Umbr. fertu, futu 'esto,' habetu. The curious forms in -*tid* and -*tad* on the Luceria inscr. (in hoce loucarid stircus ne[qu]is fundatid neue cadauer proiecitad neue parentatid) are dialectal (Subj., with *i* for ē in -*tid*?). A Third Pl. form with -*d, suntod*, occurs on the Spoletium inscription. (On Umbrian *-tō-tā in 2, 3 Pl., see § 73.)

Deponents sometimes show -*to* for -*tor*, e. g. *nitito* (Cic. ap. Diom. 340. 1 K.), *utunto* [*C. I. L.* i. 204. (1). 8], and on the Lex Repetundarum we have the Passive *censento* (i. 198. 77).

§ 60. **Imper. Pass. 2, 3 Sg. in -mǐnō.** This is an O. Lat. form, found as 2 Sg. in Plautus (e. g. *progrĕdĭmino, Pseud.* 859: tu spectató simul,

si quo híc gradietur, páriter progredímino),

and Cato (*praefamino, R. R.* cxli. 2 Ianum Iouemque uino praefamino, sic dicito) (cf. Paul. Fest. 62. 10 Th. 'famino' dicito), and as 3 Sg. in early legal Latin; *antestamino* in XII Tables: si in ius uocat, ni it, antestamino, igitur em capito; *fruimino* in the Sententia Minuciorum of 117 B.C. (*C. I. L.* i. 199. 32 quei . . . non parebit, is eum agrum nei habeto niue fruimino); *profitemino* in the Lex Julia Municipalis of 45 B.C. (i. 206. ll. 3, 5, 8, 11). The corresponding suffix in Umbrian is -mu 3 Sg. (i. e. -mō, from -*mnōd?, ch. v. § 13), e. g. *persnihi-mu* 'precamino,' with 3 Pl. *persnihi-mumo*. In Oscan the Passive ending -*r* appears in 3 Sg. *censamur* (i. e. -mōr) 'censemino,' but the so-called Latin 2 Pl. Imper. Pass. in -*minor* is a fiction of the grammarians (see Madvig, *Opusc.* p. 239.) [Cicero in the archaic language of his laws employs *appellamino* (MSS. -*minor*) as 3 Pl. Pass. (*Legg.* iii. 3. 8), but that this is a genuine old usage may be doubted.]

§ 61. **3 Pl. Imperat.** The grammarians occasionally offer curious forms, *amento* (Sacerdos); *probunto, doceunto* (Probus; cf. 3 Pl. Ind. *mereunt*, Commod., *neunt*, Tibull.).

§ 62. **IV. THE VOICES. Deponent Verbs. Passive.** Since the Passive in Latin does not differ from the Active in the Tense-stems so much as in the Person-endings, it is best discussed here, immediately before we proceed to the consideration of the suffixes used to denote the different Persons of the Verb. In close connexion with it goes the Middle, which had originally a Reflexive force, e. g. Gk. τύπτομαι like τύπτω ἐμαυτόν, or a Neuter force, e.g. Gk. θέρομαι, ἔρχομαι. In Latin Middle Verbs are called 'Deponents,' e.g. *cingor* like *cingo me*. Thus the I.-Eur. Middle *seq^R-, 'to follow, accompany' (O. Ind. sáca-tē 3 Sg., Gk. ἕπε-ται) is in Lat. the Deponent *sequor, sequitur* 3 Sg. (O. Ir. sechur, sechethar 3 Sg.). The R-endings of the Passive and Middle or 'Deponent' in the Italic and Celtic languages are discussed in § 65, where it is suggested that the Passive R-forms may originally have been restricted to an Impersonal use in Latin, as in Umbro-Oscan and Celtic the Impersonal Passive with -r, e. g. Umbr. fera-r Subj., 'there may be carrying,' O. Ir. do-bera-r, 'there may be giving' (I.-Eur. *bherā-r), is by its absence of person-ending distinguished from the Deponent with -r, e. g. Osc. karanter 'vescuntur,' O. Ir. sechethar 'sequitur.' The Personal Passive of O. Ir. by its restriction to the Third Person indicates its Impersonal origin. A Latin phrase like *itur in antiquam silvam*, the peculiarity of which is commented on by Quintilian (i. 4. 28 : jam ' itur in antiquam silvam' nonne propriae cujusdam rationis est ? nam quod initium ejus invenias ? cui simile 'fletur') may then exemplify the oldest use of the R-Passive, except that the original form would be *ir* (*ei-r) without the 3 Sg. Person-suffix of *itur* (*ei-tŏ-r) ; and the change from the Impersonal *vitam vivitur* of O. Lat. to the Personal *vita vivitur* of class. Lat. is parallel to Horace's use of *invideor* for *invidetur mihi*, or Cato's change of *contumeliam factum itur* to *contumelia factum itur* (§ 87).

The Latin Perfect, as we have seen (§ 39), represents the I.-Eur. Perfect Middle, its 1 Sg. -ī, older -*ei*, being I.-Eur. -ai or -*ai* (O. Ind. -ē), so that a Perfect like *rĕverti* (older -*vorti*, -*vortei* ; cf. O. Ind. va-vṛtē) goes naturally with a Present *revertor*. On the other hand, the Participle in -to- (§ 92), which properly belonged to the Preterite Passive, was often used in an Active (or Middle) sense, e. g. Lat. *cēnātus, pransus, pōtus*, so that *reversus* (older -*vorsus* ; cf. O. Ind. vṛttá-), *reversus sum* are also admissible. More questionable is *vertens* as the Pres. Part. of *vertor* in the phrase : intra finem anni vertentis, 'within the current year,' *vehens* of *vehor*, &c. In the older literary period we find Active and Middle forms of the same verb side by side, but by the time of the classical writers there is less freedom of choice; *assentior*, for example, had almost wholly supplanted *assentio* in Varro's time, who tells us that Sisenna the historian still clung to the old-fashioned *assentio* in giving his vote in the senate [*L. L.* fr. ap. Gell. ii. 25. 9: 'sentior' nemo dicit, et id per se nihil est; adsentior tamen fere omnes dicunt. Sisenna unus 'adsentio' in senatu dicebat, et eum postea multi secuti, neque tamen vincere consuetudinem potuerunt; cf. Quint. i. 5. 13. Quintilian however (ix. 3. 7) allows both *assentior* and *assentio*, and the latter form is found in Cicero's *Letters* and in the *De Inventione*; see Georges, *Lex. Wortf.* s. v.]. The Middle form of *assentior* (as distinguished from *sentio*) is justified by the use of the Middle in verbs which express a state of feeling, e. g. *reor, věreor, īrascor*. For the Greek Verb-ending -ευω (e. g. κολακ-εύω), used in Derivative verbs indicating 'to play a part,' 'to act like,' we have in Latin an Ā-Middle, e. g. *aemŭl-or, -āri* from *aemulus, augŭror*, from *augur, dŏmĭnor* from *dominus, poētor* of Ennius' frank confession (*Sat.* 1 M.) :

nunquám poetor nísi sim podager,

from *poeta* and so on. Examples of Frequentative Middles are *hortor* from O. Lat. *hŏrior (3 Sg. *horĭtur* Enn.), *mědĭtor* from a lost *medor (Gk. μέδομαι), *ĭmĭtor* (cf. *ĭmāgo*), *nītor* for *nivĭtor from a root with a Guttural (cf. *nixus*, and see ch. iv. § 116).

§ 63. **Impersonal use of Latin Passive.** An example of an Acc. governed by an Impers. Pass. is Ennius, *Trag.* 190 R. :

íncerte errat ánimus, praeterprópter uitam uíuitur,

quoted by Gellius (xix. 10) in illustration of the word *praeterpropter*, 'inexactly,' 'so so,' a word which was in his time only used in plebeian Latin (nescioquid hoc praenimis plebeium est et in opificum sermonibus quam in hominum doctorum disputationibus notius) ; the same construction has been seen in Plaut. *Mil.* 24 (epityra estur), *Pseud.* 817 (teritur sinapis scelera), (but see edd. *ad locc.*), *Pers.* 577 (uēniri hanc uolo) (but cf. Plaut. *fr. inc.* l. 64 G. ego illi uenear). Without an Acc. the Impersonal Passive is very common in the older writers, e. g. Plaut. *Pseud.* 273 :

Quíd agitur, Calidóre ? Amatur átque egetur ácriter ;

Pers. 309 *ut ualetur ?*, 386 *facile nubitur*, 'marriage is easy' ; *Trin.* 580 *ibitur* ; *Capt.* 80 *quom caletur*, 'in hot weather' ; *Rud.* 1018, &c. The Latin for 'No admittance' is PRIVATVM. PRECARIO ADEITVR, a notice preserved in an inscription (*C. I. L.* i. 1215).

§ 64. **Active and Middle.** Gellius (xviii. 12) remarks on the O. Lat. use of Active Verbs like *augeo, mūto* in a Neuter sense, instead of *augeor, mutor*, and similarly of *contemplo* for *contemplor*, &c., and the seventh book of Nonius contains a host of examples from the older writers, *aucupo* for *aucŭpor, vago* for *văgor*, and so on. Quintilian (ix. 3. 6–7) remarks on the inconsistency of the Middle form of Transitive Verbs, *fabrĭcor, pūnior, arbĭtror, suspĭcor* with the Active form of a Neuter or Passive Verb, *văpŭlo*, and mentions as parallel forms *luxŭriatur* and *luxuriat, fluctuatur* and *fluctuat, adsentior* and *adsentio* (see § 62). The same uncertainty with Active and Middle forms is shown for a later period by the precepts of the grammarians, e. g. Caper (93.10 K. ructo et nausio dicendum, quamvis quidam veteres 'ructor' et 'nausior' dixerunt. non 'egeo' ... dicendum, non autem 'egeor'; 93. 21 K. suffragor non 'suffrago'; 95. 1 K. somnio dicendum, non 'somnior'). The Passive use of Deponents (e.g. vereor abs te) is discussed by Gellius (xv. 13) with examples from the older writers, and a fuller list is given by Priscian (i. pp. 379 sqq. H.). A curious instance of Attraction is seen in the use of *coeptus sum*, instead of *coepi, desĭtus sum* instead of *desii*, with a Pass. Inf., e. g. urbs coepta est aedificari (cf. mitescere discordiae coeptae, Liv.), and in O. Lat. we find *pŏtestur, poteratur, possetur* similarly used (instances in Nonius p. 508 M.), *nĕquĭtur, nequĭtum* (see Georges, s. v.). The Neuter sense of *fio* (cf. Osc. fiiet 'fiunt'), and its use as Passive of *făcio* (on the occasional use of *facior*, apparently a vulgarism, see Georges), have changed its old Inf. *fiere* to *fieri*. *Fiere* was used by Ennius (see *Gram. Lat.* v. p. 645. 9 K.), perhaps in the line in which the spirit of Homer related his experience of metempsychosis (*Ann.* 8 M.):

memini me fiere pauom (MSS. fieri),

while Cato (ap. Prisc. i. p. 377. 11 H.) used *fitur* for *fit, fiebantur* for *fiebant*. (On Imperat. *fī*, e. g. Plaut. *Pers.* 38, *Curc.* 87, *fīte Curc.* 89, 150, &c., see Georges, *Lex. Wortf.* s. v.); so *vēniri* is used for *vēnire (vēnum ire)* in Plaut. *Pers.* 577 (cf. *pereunda, Epid.* 74, *plăcenda, Trin.* 1159). As *coeptus sum* and *desitus sum* replaced *coepi* and *desii* (originally Middle formations), when these verbs were used intransitively, so Intransitive Verbs like *sŏleo, gaudeo, audeo* took a Perfect of Passive form *solĭtus sum, găvīsus sum, ausus sum*, in O. Lat. also *solui, gavisi, ausi* (Prisc. i. pp. 420, 482 H.; Non. 508. 27 M.), e. g. Liv. Andr.: quoniam audiui, paucis gauisi. On the Deponent Imperatives *nitito, utunto*, &c., see § 59.

§ 65. V. **THE PERSON-ENDINGS.** The I.-Eur. person-endings were slightly different in Primary Tenses (the Present Ind., Future Ind., &c.) and in Secondary Tenses (the Preterites Ind., the Tenses of the Optative Mood, &c.), e. g. I.-Eur. *bhĕrĕ-tĭ, 'he is carrying,' *ĕ-bhĕrĕ-t, 'he was carrying,' 'he carried,' *bhĕroi-t 3 Sg. Opt. The Tenses of the Subjunctive Mood seem to have taken sometimes the Primary, sometimes (in Umbro-Oscan perhaps always) the Secondary person-endings. In the Perfect Tense an entirely different set of endings was in use, e. g. I.-Eur. 1 Sg. *woidă, 'I know,' 2 Sg. *woit-thă, 'thou knowest,' and so on; and in the Imperative the persons are often distinguished by the addition of particles, e. g. I.-Eur. *bhĕrĕ-tōd, with the particle *tōd, Abl. Sg. of the Pronoun *to-, meaning 'from this' or 'thereupon' (§ 57).

In Passive and Deponent Verbs, Latin departs widely from the I.-Eur. scheme of Passive (or rather Middle) person-endings (contrast Lat. *feror, sequor* with Gk. φέρο-μαι, ἕπο-μαι, *ferŭmur, sequĭmur* with Gk. φερό-μεθα, ἑπό-μεθα, and with O. Ind. bhár-ē, bhárā-mahē). Latin, as well as the Umbro-Oscan languages, and the Celtic family, uses as the characteristic mark of its passive and deponent flexion the letter r (cf. O. Ir. sechur 1 Sg., sechethar 3 Sg., sechemmar 1 Pl., sechetar 3 Pl., with Lat. *sequor, sequitur, sequĭmur, sequuntur*). [In Celtic r is used in all persons of Deponents (except 2 Pl.), but only in 3 Sg., Pl. of Passives.] This r cannot be connected with the Reflexive Pronoun *swĕ- (Lat. *sē* Acc.), seeing that s between vowels does not become r in Oscan or in the Celtic languages (e. g. Lat. *sequor* might conceivably stand for *seqᵘo-sĕ, but O. Ir. sechur could not). Nor does it go well with the r of 3 Pl. suffixes in the Sanscrit Verb, and the *-runt, -re* of the 3 Pl. Pft. Act. in Latin (e. g. O. Ind. á-duh-ra, á-vavṛt-ranta, Lat. *dĕdĕrunt, dedērĕ*), since the Sanscrit r is confined to 3 Pl. suffixes, and is used in Active as well as Passive Verbs. Its original sense may have been impersonal [cf. Lat. itur in antiquam silvam, 'they go,' 'one goes'; originally without any person-ending, as in Umbro-Oscan and Celtic, e. g. Umbr. *pone esonom-e ferar*, 'when there is carrying to the sacrifice,' 'when the carrying to the sacrifice takes place,' which would be in Lat. *feratur* or *feretur*, with person-ending *-tu-* (*-tŏ-*); O. Ir. doberr or doberar, 'they give,' 'one gives,' Bret. gweler, 'they see,' 'one sees']; and the original construction of these Impersonals Passive seems to have been with an Acc. of the object (e. g. O. Lat. *vitam vivitur*; Osc., iúvilas ... sakriiss sakrafír avt últiumam kerssnaís, 'let the *jovilae* be consecrated with victims, but the last with banquets'; Welsh, Etlym gledyf coch ym gelwir, 'they call me Etlym of the red glaive,' like Lat. *me appellatur* (see § 62).

This Impersonal (Passive?) governing an Acc. has been explained as the Verb-stem with the Locative suffix r (seen in Engl. 'where,' 'there') used predicatively like the i-Locative of the

Verbal S-stem (the Latin Inf. Act.; see § 83) in such a phrase as *hostes apparere*, 'the enemy appeared' (Historical Inf.), lit. 'the enemy in the action of appearing.' On the change from, e. g. *amā-r amicos to *amantur amici*, like Horace's *invideor* for *invidetur mihi*, see above, § 62.

§ 66. (1) Active. 1 Sing. I.-Eur. Athematic Verbs ended in Primary Tenses in -mĭ (e. g. I.-Eur. *es-mi, O. Ind. ás-mi, Arm. em, Gk. εἰμί for *ἐσ-μι, Alb. jam, Goth. im, Lith. es-mì, O. Sl. jes-mĭ), Thematic in -ō (e. g. I.-Eur. *bhĕr-ō, Gk. φέρω, O. Ir. -biur for *berō, Goth. baira for *berō; Lith. vežù, ' veho'). In Secondary tenses the ending was -m (e. g. I.-Eur. *ĕ-bhĕrŏ-m, O. Ind. ábharam, Gk. ἔφερον; O. Sl. nesŭ, ' I carried,' for *nesom), after a consonant, -m̥, e. g. Gk. ἔδειξα for *ἐδειξ-m̥. The Perfect had -ă (e. g. I.-Eur. *woid-ă, O. Ind. véd-a, Gk. οἶδ-α, Goth. vait for *vaită; O. Ir. ro cechan 'cecini').

In Latin, as we have seen, Athematic Verbs form the 1 Sg. according to the Thematic Conjugation, e. g. Lat. *ĕd-ō* for I.-Eur. *ĕd-mi, *vŏl-ō* for I.-Eur. *wĕl-mi (§ 2), just as in Sanscrit Thematic Verbs take the Athematic -mi, e. g. bhárā-mi for I.-Eur. *bherō. I.-Eur. *es-mi, however, is in Latin *sum*, whether originally *sŏmĭ with Syncope of final ĭ (ch. iii. § 37) or merely *sŏm, it is impossible to determine (cf. Osc. sum). The curious 1 Sg. *inquam* [1], with the other Persons formed from a 1 Sg. *inquio*, and with Imper. *inquĕ*, resembles a Subjunctive in form, 'I should say,' or 'I shall say,' or 'let me say' (see § 55). The Secondary Tense-ending -m appears in Imperfects and Pluperfects, e. g. *ĕra-m* (cf. O. Ind. á-yā-m, 'I went,' Gk. ἔ-δρᾶ-ν, Goth. iddja, 'I went'), *ămā-ba-m* (cf. O. Ir. ba for *bām, 'I was'), *ămāvĕra-m*, in Optative forms, e. g. *si-m*, O. Lat. *sie-m* (O. Ind. siyám, syā́-m, Gk. εἴη-ν), *ămāv-ĕri-m*, *ăma-ssi-m*, *faxi-m*, and in Subjunctive, e. g. *ăme-m*, *ămāvisse-m*, *vĭdea-m*, *fĕra-m* (also used as Fut., § 36), *fīnia-m* (cf. O. Ir. do-ber for *-ram, O. Sl. berą̌, used as Pres. Ind.). But the 'Future-Subjunctives' (see § 53) take the Thematic ending, e. g. *ĕr-o* for *ĕs-ō (Zend. aɴhā,

---

[1] Explained as **ind-(s)quam* from the root seqṷ- (ch. iv. § 158), or as **ind-(ve)quam* from the root weqṷ-.

Hom. Gk. ἕω for *ἔσω), ămāv-ĕr-ō, ăma-ss-ō, fax-ō, like fĕr-ō, stō for *stāy-ō (Umbr. *stahu*).

In the Perfect, the ending of the Active Voice has been replaced in Latin by the Middle ending -ai (-*ai*), which became in the unaccented syllable -*ei*, then -*ī* (ch. iii. § 18), *tŭtŭd-ī* (O. Ind. tutud-ē), *dĕd-ī* (O. Ind. dad-é), *vīd-ī* from *veidei*, a Middle form which survives in the O. Sl. vědě, 'I know,' for *woidai (O. Lat. *fecei, poseiuei, conquaeisiuei, redidei*, all on the milestone of Popilius of 132 B.C., *C. I. L.* i. 551). Lat. *reverti, assensi*, &c. are thus really Middle forms, and go suitably with Pres. *revertor, assentior*.

§ 67. 2 Sg. The I.-Eur. endings are -sĭ (e.g. I.-Eur. *ĕ-si and *ĕs-si, O. Ind. á-si, Gk. εἶ for *ἐ-σι, which with the addition again of the suffix -s became εἶς, Hom. ἐσ-σί; I.-Eur. *ei-sĭ from the root ei-, 'to go,' O. Ind. é-ṣi, Gk εἶ for *εἰ-σι; O. Ind. bhára-si, O. Ir. beri. Goth. bairi-s), -s (e.g. I.-Eur. *ĕ-bhĕrĕ-s, O. Ind. á-bhara-s, Gk. ἔ-φερε-s, O. Ir. do-bir; O. Sl. veze 'vexisti'; and in the Present Tense, Gk. τίθη-s, Dor. φέρε-s), in the Perfect -thă (e.g. I.-Eur. *woit-tha, O. Ind. vét-tha, Gk. οἶσθα; cf. O. H. G. gi-tars-t). In Latin we have -*s* in *ĕs*, 'thou art,' for *ĕss* (scanned as a long syllable in Plautus), whether from older *ĕssĭ (ch. iii. § 37) or not, it is impossible to say, *ăgĭ-s* for *agĕ-s (if from an original *age-si, like O. Ir. beri from *bheresi, the final -ĭ must have been dropped before the fourth cent. B. C. when s between vowels became *r*; see ch. iv. § 146), *sī-s* (O. Lat. *siē-s*), *agā-s*, while in the 2 Sg. of the Perfect Tense we have -*stī*, e.g. *dĕdi-stī*, the final vowel of which (O. Lat. -*ei*, e.g. *gesistei* on a Scipio Epitaph of c. 180 B.C., *C. I. L.* i. 33), like the -*ī* of 1 Sg. *dĕd-ī* (O. Ind. dad-é), must represent an original -ai (-*ai*), while the -*s* reminds us of that -s- which so often appears in the endings of the second Person (e.g. Gk. ἔφη-σθα, τίθη-σθα, ἐθέλῃ-σθα, βάλοι-σθα). (For another theory which regards *vidis*- of *vidisti* as a Verbal Noun-stem, see § 52.)

In the Imperative, the bare stem is used, as the bare stem is used in Vocatives Sg. of Nouns, e.g. (Thematic) *age* from the Thematic Verb-stem *ăĝĕ-, *ăĝŏ-, 'to lead,' as *ăĝĕ is Voc. Sg. of the Thematic Noun-stem *ăĝĕ-, *ăĝŏ-, Gk. ἀγός, a leader,

Lat. *prōd-ĭgus*; (Athematic) ĭ for *ei from the Athematic Verb-stem ei-, 'to go' (see § 2). Sometimes the particle *tōd (Abl. Sg. of the Pronoun-stem tŏ-, 'from this,' 'thereupon') is added, when the command refers not to immediate action, but to action after something shall have happened, e. g. quum venerit, scribito, 'when he comes, write,' lit. 'write thereupon.' (So in O. Ind., e. g. 2 Sg. vit-tā́t for I.-Eur. *wit-tōd from the root weid-, 'to know'; see § 57.) The final -ĕ of O. Lat. *dūce*, *dīce*, *făce* [for *facĭ (ch. iii. § 37), from the stem *facyo-*, *facĭ-*, § 16] is dropped in classical Latin, through its frequent use in word-groups like *dic(e) mihi*, &c. So in Catullus (xxvii. 2) *inger mi* for *ingere mi* (see § 58; ch. iii. § 36).

§ 68. The athematic Sg. of *féro*, *vŏlo* would be *fers, *vels, which would become **fer(r)*, **vel(l)* (ch. iv. § 153). The former word was changed to *fer-s* by the addition of the 2 Sg. suffix -*s*, as in Greek εἶ for *ἐσι was made εἶς, thou art ; for the latter was substituted the word *vīs*, apparently 2 Sg. of a root wei-, 'to wish' (O. Ind. vī-, 2 Sg. vé-ši, Gk. ἵεμαι).

Whether *dices* of the MSS. in Plaut. *Trin.* 606 non credibile dices, is a relic of the old spelling of *dicis* is doubtful. It may be Future.

§ 69. 3 Sg. The Primary Tense-ending in I.-Eur. was -tĭ (e. g. *ĕs-ti, O. Ind. ás-ti, Gk. ἔσ-τι, O. Ir. is, Goth. is-t, Lith. ẽs-ti and ẽs-t, O. Sl. (Russ.) jes-tĭ; Dor. Gk. δίδω-τι, Att. δίδω-σι, τίθη-σι, &c.), the Secondary Tense-ending was -t (e. g. *ĕ-bhĕrĕ-t, O. Ind. á-bhara-t, Gk. ἔ-φερε for *ἔ-φερε-τ), and the ending of the Perfect -ĕ (e. g. *woidĕ, O. Ind. véd-a, Gk. οἶδ-ε, Goth. vait; O. Ir. ro cechuin 'cecinit'). In Latin all trace of the -ĭ of I.-Eur. -tĭ has been lost (e. g. Lat. *es-t*, *fer-t*, *ăgĭ-t* for *agĕ-t), but in Oscan we find -t for I.-Eur. -tĭ, and -d for I.-Eur. -t. On the very oldest Latin inscriptions we find -*d* for the Secondary ending, but certain instances of Primary endings are unfortunately wanting. Thus the Praenestine fibula has *fefaced*, 'fecit,' the Dvenos inscription has *feced*, *sied* (but *mitat*, apparently 3 Sg. Subj. used as Fut.), and in Oscan we have *deded* 'dedit,' kúm-bened 'con-vēnit,' fusí-d 'foret,' *deivaid* 'juret,' heriiad 'velit,' while Primary Tenses show -t, e. g. faamat 'habitat.' These endings had been 'levelled' to *t* in Latin before the second century B.C.; for a Praenestine cista, not of the same antiquity as the fibula just mentioned, has *dedit* beside *fecid* (*C. I. L.* i. 54 Dindia Macolnia fileai dedit. Nouios

Plautios med Romai fecid), and in all other old inscriptions we have invariably -*t*, e. g. *iousit* (ii. 5041, of 189 B. C.), *uelet* ' vellet ' *eset, fuit, censuit* (all on the S. C. Bacch. of 186 B. C., i. 196), *cepet* on the (restored) Columna Rostrata (i. 195), *fuet, cepit, dedet* on one of the oldest Scipio Epitaphs (i. 32.).

In the Latin Perfect the original ending seems to have been -*eit*, written in the very oldest inscriptions -*ed* (with that use of *e* to express the *ei*-sound which we have seen in Nom. Pl. *ploirume* on a Scipio Epitaph, Dat. Sg. *Diove Victore*, ap. Quint. i. 4. 17; see ch. iv. § 34), then -*et*, -*eit*, and in class. Lat. -*it*. Before a final -*t* a long vowel was shortened in the course of the second cent. B. C. (ch. iii. § 49), so that in class. poetry this -*it* of the Perfect is a short syllable. But in Plautus it is invariably scanned long, unless shortened in iambic words, &c. by the Law of Breves Breviantes (e. g. *dĕdĭt* may be scanned *dedĭt*, but only *vīdĭt, fēcĭt*, &c.). The long quantity is found in every type of Perfect in Plautus (see § 39), in *vīxīt, habuīt, adnumeravīt*, as well as in Perfects proper like *vicīt*. This -*eit* can hardly have been anything else than the I.-Eur. ending of the 3 Sg. Mid. of the Perfect Tense (which was, like the 1 Sg. Mid. ending -*ai*, a diphthong weakened in the unaccented syllable in Latin to -*ei*, class. -*ī*, ch. iii. § 18), augmented by the 3 Sg. Act. Secondary suffix -*t*. So that all trace of the I.-Eur. 3 Sg. Act. ending -ĕ is lost in Latin. In the Oscan Perfect, however, the ending -ed, e. g. deded ' dedit,' prúfatted ' probavit ' (quasi *probassīt, § 3), aamanaffed ' -mandavit ' (cf. δεδετ, αναΓακετ, Pel. afđed ' abiit ') is usually referred to the I.-Eur. Preterite ending -ĕt, or to the Perfect Active -ĕ augmented by -t, though whether Umbrian -d (fefure for *fefured, đeđe for *đeđed) was dropped after a short vowel, so readily as after a long vowel (like Latin -*d*) is doubtful.

In the Imperative the same form is used as the 2 Sg. 'Future' Imper. e. g. *es-tō(d)*, on which see above, § 67.

§ **70. The 3 Sg. Pft. in Latin.** We have found (ch. iii. § 49) that the shortening influence of final -*t* on a preceding long vowel is already seen in the poetry of Ennius (239-169 B. C.), who scans, e. g. *mandebăt* beside *ponebāt, splendĕt* beside *jubĕt, potessĕt* beside *essĕt*, though it probably does not appear in Plautus (c. 254-184 B. C.), that Terence (195-159 B. C.) follows the same usage as Ennius, while Lucilius (148-103 B. C.) scarcely ever allows a vowel before final -*t* to retain its original length. It is thus the versification of Plautus which must decide the original quantity of the vowel in the 3 Sg. Pft. ending -*it*. Indubitable instances of -*it* in Plautus are *ēmĭt*, *Poen.* 1059 :

emít, et is me síbi adoptauit fílium ;
vixĭt, *Pseud.* 311 :

ílico uixít amator, úbi lenoni súpplicat ;
which are the readings of both families of MSS., while we have *vĭcĭt*, *Amph.* 643 :

uicít et domúm laudis cómpos reuénit (a bacchiac line) ;
adnŭmĕrāvĭt, *Asin* 501 :

adnúmerauit et crédidit mihi néque deceptust ín eo,
where the evidence of the Ambrosian Palimpsest is wanting. (For other examples, see Müller, *Plaut. Pros.* p. 71.) The instances of -*ĭt* in Plautus, except where the Law of Breves Breviantes operates (e. g. *dĕdĭt* like *dĕdĭ*, *ăbĭ*, *ăbĭt*, *ăbĭs*, &c.), are very few and uncertain (e. g. *dixĭt*, *Pers.* 260) ; and even if it were true, as it almost certainly is not, that this scansion occurred now and then in Plautus, it would only prove that the shortening influence of final -*t* showed itself even earlier than Ennius, for there is no indication of one type of Perfect having had -*ĭt* and another type -*īt*. In other writers we have, e. g. *excĭdĭt* Naev. *Trag.* 5 R., *dĕdĭt* Ter. *Eun.* 701, *stĕtĭt*, *Phorm.* prol. 9, *crissāvĭt* Lucil. ix. 70 M., and the long quantity is found after *i* in the compounds of *eo* in Ovid, e. g. *interiĭt*, *abĭt*, *redĭĭt* (see Lachmann and Munro on Lucr. iii. 1042 ; and cf. *interieisti*, *C. I. L.* i. 1202).

The spelling in the very oldest inscriptions is -*ed* : *fefaced* on the Praenestine fibula (*C. I. L.* xiv. 4123 Manios med fefaced Numasioi, ' Manius me fecit Numerio '), *feked* (or *feced* ?) on the Dvenos bowl (Zvet. *I. I. I.* 285 Duenos med feked). This can hardly be equated with Osc. -ed, since the other spellings -*eit*, -*it* point to this early *e* being merely that symbol of the *ei*-sound which is often found in old inscriptions (ch. iv. § 34), derivable from an I.-Eur. -ai, for which in Oscan we should expect to find a diphthong rather than the simple vowel e. Other old spellings are -*et*, -*eit*, -*id*, and -*it*. Examples of -*et* are *fuet* and *dedet* (beside *cepit*) on a Scipio Epitaph, perhaps of the end of the third cent. B. C. (*C. I. L.* i. 32), *dedet* in two old inscriptions with Ablatival -*d* (i. 63 de praidad Maurte dedet ; i. 64 de praidad Fortune dedet) ; and this is the spelling adopted in the (restored) Columna Rostrata (i. 195 exemet ... cepet ... ornauet). The classical spelling -*it* occurs as early as the Scipio Epitaph, just mentioned, with *cepit* ; the dedicatory tablet of Minucius, 217 B. C., with *vovit* (i. 1503 Hercolei sacrom . M. Minuci C. f. Dictator uouit) ; a Scipio Epitaph of c. 200 B. C. (i. 30) with *fuit*, *cepit* ; the dedication of Aurelius, 200 B. C. (*Not. Scav.* 1887, p. 195), with *didit*, *probauit* ; the decree of Aemilius Paulus of 189 B. C. (*C. I. L.* ii. 5041) with *decreiuit*, *iousit* ; and the contemporary decree of Fulvius Nobilior 189 B.C. with *cepit* (i. 534 Aetolia cepit, 'took from Aetolia ') ; the S. C. Bacch. 186 B. C. (i. 196) with *censuit* ; while we have both -*it* and -*id* on the old Praenestine cista (end of third cent. ?) quoted above, with *dedit*, *fecid*. But -*eit* is not common, e. g. *probaveit* (with *coeravit*) (i. 600, of 62 B. C.), *fuueit* (i. 1051), *redieit* (i. 541, of 145 B. C.), *venieit* (i. 200. 58, &c., of 111 B. C.), so that if we had only the spellings of inscriptions to guide us, and not the versification of the early poets, we should be inclined to suppose the original form of the 3 Sg. Pft. suffix to have been -*ĕt*, -*ĕd*, which, with the usual change of unaccented *ĕ* to *ĭ*, became about the end of the third cent. -*ĭt* (-*ĭd*). It has been suggested that in some types of Perfect, e. g. *dixit* (cf. Gk. ἔδειξε(τ)), *fidit* (cf. O. Ind. á-bhid-

§§ 71-73.]   THE VERB. PERSON-ENDINGS.   529

ăt; but see § 39), the final syllable was originally short, while in other types it was long. But the versification of Plautus points to no distinction having been made between the different types in his time at least. The pronunciation of his age must have been *dixĭt*, *fĭdĭt*, *amavĭt* as well as *tutudĭt*, *vidĭt*, *fecĭt*, and this ĭ-sound can hardly be dissociated from the final -ĭ of 1 Sg. *tutudī*, &c. This -ī of *tutudi* we have seen to be the I.-Eur. -ai, the ending of the 1 Sg. Pft. Mid. (O. Ind. tutud-ē). In the 3 Sg. of the Perfect Middle, Sanscrit shows a similar form to the 1 Sg., viz. tutud-ē. We are therefore led to suppose that in Latin as in Sanscrit **tutudai* was the original form both in 1 Sg. and 3 Sg. This **tutudai*, which would become in Latin **tutudei*, then *tutudī*, was in the 3 Sg. discriminated by the addition of the 3 Sg. suffix used in Secondary Tenses in the Active Voice, -*t*, and became *tutudei-t* (written in the old orthography *tutudē-t*), then *tutudī-t*, then in the second cent. B. C. *tutudĭt*. The other types of Perfect followed in the 3 Sg., as in all other persons, the type of I.-Eur. Perfects like *tutudī*.

§ 71. **1 Plur.** In Lat. we have in all tenses the ending *-mŏs (class. -*mŭs*), while in the other I.-Eur. languages we have a variety of endings, e. g. Gk. φέρο-μεν, ἐφέρο-μεν, Dor. φέρο-μες (this I.-Eur. *-mĕs varied with *-mŏs, the Latin person-suffix), O. Ind. á-bharā-ma, Vedic vid-má. The scansion -*mūs* in Plaut. is illusory (see Müller, *Plaut. Pros.* p. 57).

§ 72. **2 Plur.** The ending -tĕ of Gk. φέρε-τε, &c. appears in Latin only in the Imperative, e. g. *fer-te*, *agi-te* for **agĕ-te*, &c. Elsewhere it was replaced by -*tĭs* (older **-tĕs*), an ending like the 2 Dual ending (with th- apparently) of O. Ind. bhára-thas, Goth. baira-ts, the use of which discriminated *agitis* Ind. from *agite* Imper., as *agis* Ind. differed from *age* Imper. Corresponding to the 2 Sg. 'Future' Imperative in -*tō* (older -*tōd*), we have a 2 Pl. 'Future' Imperative in -*tōte*, apparently composed by adding to the Sg. form the 2 Pl. suffix -tĕ, -*tōte* (e. g. *estōte*), for -*tōt-te* (ch ii. § 127).

§ 73. **3 Plur.** The I.-Eur. suffixes end with -ĭ in Primary but not in Secondary Tenses. Thus -entĭ, -ņtĭ, -nti are Primary, -ent, -ņt, -nt are Secondary, e. g. *s-ĕnti (O. Ind. s-ánti, Gk. εἰσί for Dor. ἐ-ντί, O. Ir. it, O. W. int, Goth. s-ind; so Umbr. *s-ent*, Osc. s-et for *s-ent), *bhĕrŏ-nti [O. Ind. bhára-nti, Arm. beren, Dor. Gk. φέρο-ντι, O. Ir. berit, Goth. baira-nd, O. Sl. (Russ.) berątĭ], *ĕ-bhĕrŏ-nt (O. Ind. á-bhara-n, Gk. ἔ-φερο-ν). In class. Lat. the ending both for Primary and Secondary Tenses is -*nt*, e. g. *feru-nt* (older **fero-nt*, e. g. *cosentiont* on a Scipio Epitaph,

M m

C.I.L. i. 32), *fereba-nt, fera-nt, si-nt* [Umbr. *sins*; but O. Lat. *sient*, either by analogy of Sg. *siem, sies, siet* (see § 55), or with *-ent* for *-ṇt,* *siyṇt], *s-unt* (older *sont, C.I.L.* i. 1166). But in Umbro-Oscan there is a distinction. We have -nt for I.-Eur. -ntĭ, but -ns for I.-Eur. -nt, e.g. Umbr. *sent*, Osc. set for *sent in the Ind. of the Substantive Verb, but Umbr. *sins*, in the Opt., Osc. prúfattens 'probaverunt,' so that it is likely that at some early period Latin, like the other languages of Italy, distinguished Primary -ntĭ and Secondary -nt. The 3 Pl. *tremonti* in the fragment of the Carmen Saliare, ascribed to Numa's time, is a doubtful reading [Ter. Scaur. 28. 9 K. Cum ... quoniam antiqui pro hoc adverbio ' cuine ' dicebant, ut Numa in Saliari carmine:

cuine tonas (MSS. ponas), Leucesie, prae tet tremonti (MSS. praetexere monti)],

though it is confirmed by another corrupt passage of Festus (244. 17 Th.; he is quoting from the Carmen Saliare): 'prae tet tremonti' (MSS. pretet t.) praetremunt te (MSS. praetemunt pe). In Old Latin we have a curious form in *-nunt* (older *-nont*) in the Pres. Ind. only, e.g. *dă-nunt, explē-nunt, prōdĭ-nunt, něquĭ-nont*, which has been explained on the theory that the 3 Pl. of the Pres. Ind. had once ended in *-n,* *dăn,* *explēn,* *prodĭn,* *nequĭn*, and that these forms were expanded by the subsequent addition of the Thematic Secondary ending *-ŏnt*, later *-ŭnt*, much as Gk. εἶ for *ἔσι, 2 Sg. of εἰμί, was by the addition of the Secondary suffix -s expanded to εἶ-ς, or O. Engl. sind, ' they are,' to sind-un. If it were a mere case of Nasalization like *tu-n-do, lĭ-n-o,* *stă-n-o* in *destĭno* (?), &c., Lith. einù, ' I go ' (§ 10), it is difficult to see why it should be confined to this single person, the third person plural of the Present Indicative Active. But how *danti could become *dan, *eks-plenti become *explen, has not yet been satisfactorily shown (see *I. F.* ii. 302).

I.-Eur. -ṇti, -ṇt (e.g. O. Ind. dád-ati, Gk. λελόγχ-ασι for -ṇti) does not appear in Latin, unless possibly in O. Lat. *sient* (see above). But in Umbro-Oscan -ent, -ens [I.-Eur. -ent(i) or -ṇt(i)] is as universal as *-unt* [I.-Eur. -ont(i)] in Latin, e.g. Osc. fiiet ' fiunt,' prúfattens ' probaverunt,' Umbr. furent ' erunt,' Osc. *censazet* for *-ent* ' censebunt.'

The ending of the 3 Pl. of the Latin Perfect -*ĕrunt* is to be compared with the O. Ind. 3 Pl. endings with -r- of various Tenses (e. g. á-duh-ra Pret., duh-ratē Pres., bharē-rata Opt., duh-rā́m and duh-ratā́m Imper. ; very rarely -ranta, in á-vavr̥t-ranta. The O. Ind. Perfect has in 3 Pl.' Act. -ur, e.g. dadúr, 'they have given,' and in 3 Pl. Mid. -rē, e.g. dadirē, representing probably I.-Eur. -r̥ and -rai). The byform -*ĕrĕ* is in O. Lat. -*erĭ* (*dederi*, C. I. L. i. 187, probably from Praeneste : M. Mindios L. fi. P. Condetios Ua. fi. aidiles uicesma parti Apolones dederi).

In the Imperative we have in Latin, as in Greek, the particle *tōd, 'from this,' 'thereupon,' added to a 3 Pl. form, e.g. Lat. *ferunto* for *feront-tōd*, Gk. φερόντω for *φεροντ-τωδ. The final -*d* is seen in *suntod* on the Spoletium inscription (*C. I. L.* xi. 4766). The Umbrian ending appears to have been -tōtā, e.g. etuta and *etuto* 'eunto.'

§ 74. 3 Pl. Pres. in -nunt. *Dănunt* for *dant* is quoted from the older poets by Nonius, 97. 13 M., e. g. Caecilius, *Com.* 176 R. patiére quod dant, quándo optata nón danunt (cf. Paul. Fest. 48. 18Th. 'danunt' dant); it is often used by Plautus (the references are given in Neue, *Formenl.* ii². p. 412), and is found on a Saturnian dedicatory inscription of two brothers, money-lenders, called Vertuleius (*C. I. L.* i. 1175, Sora :

dónu dánunt Hércolei máxsume méreto) ;

prodĭnunt for *prodeunt* is quoted by Festus (284. 22 Th.) from Ennius (*A.* 158 M.) :

prodinunt famuli ; tum candida lumina lucent ;

so *obinunt* for *obeunt* (id. 214. 4 Th.), *redinunt* for *redeunt* (id. 400. 12, a passage badly preserved in the MS.), quoted from Ennius [possibly with mention of *inunt* for *eunt*, so that the Philoxenus Gloss (p. 75. 23 G.), int : πορεύονται may be a corruption of inunt : πορεύονται (see § 2)] ; *nequĭnont* for *nequeunt* (Fest. 162. 24 Th.), quoted from the Odyssea of Livius Andronicus :

pártim érrant, nequínont Graéciam redíre,

and paralleled with *ferinunt* (MS. *fernunt*) for *feriunt* (MS. *fereunt*; cf. 400. 14 Th.), and *solinunt* for *solent* [rather for *solunt*, the obsolete verb of which *consulo* is a compound ; cf. Fest. 526. 14 Th. 'solino' idem (Messala) ait esse consulo] ; *explenunt* for *explent* by Paul. Fest. (56. 14 Th.) ; *inserinuntur* for *inseruntur* is used by Liv. Andr. (ap. Fest. 532. 24 Th.) : míllia ália in ísdem inserinúntur.

§ 75. 3 Pl. Perf. The isolated forms *dedro* on an old inscription of Pisaurum (*C. I. L.* i. 177 Matre Matuta dono dedro matrona ; beside *dedrot* on another inscription from the same place, i. 173 Iunone re. matrona Pisaurese dono dedrot) and *emeru* on an inscription of Cora (i. 1148 Q. Pomponius Q. f. L. Tulius Ser. f. praitores aere Martio emeru) cannot be taken as a proof that -*rŏ* was a byform of *-rĭ* in the Latin 3 Pl. Perfect. For the dropping of final consonants is a feature of the Latin of Pisaurum (see the inscriptions quoted above with *-s*, *-r* dropped; and cf. the loss of *-t* in *dede*, i. 169, and apparently of *-nt* in i. 177 M'. Curia, Pola Liuia deda), and *emeru* on the Cora inscription may be a similar dialectal variety, or merely a graphic contraction for *emerunt*. Final *-nt* often loses the dental on late inscriptions and is written *-n* or *-m*; thus we have *fecerun* and *fecerum* (also *feceru*, vi. 24649) in plebeian inscriptions of the Empire (see ch. ii. § 137). Some Roman grammarians called the form with *-re* the ' Dual ' form, a theory which is rightly rejected by Quintilian, though his own explanation, that it is a weakening of *-runt*, cannot stand (i. 5. 43 quanquam fuerunt qui nobis quoque adicerent dualem ' scripsere' 'legere': quod evitandae asperitatis gratia mollitum est, ut apud veteres pro male mereris ' male merere ') (cf. Serv. ad *A*. ii. 1). In the older writers *-runt* and *-re* seem to be used at will, e. g. Plaut. *Trin*. 535 alii éxolatum abiérunt, alii emórtui, Alií se suspendére, and Cicero (*Orat*. xlvii. 157), quoting a line of Ennius, says : nec vero reprehenderim ' scripsere alii rem ' ; ' scripserunt' esse verius censeo, sed consuetudini auribus indulgenti libenter obsequor. (Ennius, however, seems to prefer *-erunt* to *-ere* in his *Annals* ; Terence prefers *-ere*.) The older spelling *-ront*, mentioned by Quintilian (i. 4. 16), who quotes *dederont* and *probaveront*, is found on early inscriptions (see Index to *C. I. L.* i.).

The ending *-rĕ* (older *-rĭ*) seems to come from an I.-Eur. *-rĭ*, cognate with the I.-Eur. *-rai* of the O. Ind. 3 Sg. Pft. Mid. *-rē*, e. g. dadiré, ' dedere ' ; the ending *-runt* (older *-ront*), either from an I.-Eur. *-ront* (cf. O. Ind. á-vavṛt-ranta), or from a subsequent addition of the usual 3 Pl. Thematic suffix *-unt* (*-ont*) to a 3 Pl. Pft. in *-r*. Thus **dedēr* (a ' doublet ' of *dedēre* ?) would become *dedēr-unt* by the same process as we have supposed an earlier **explēn* to have become *explēn-unt*. In view of the presence of r in these O. Ind. third persons plural this is a more likely explanation than to suppose that *r* is the Latin substitute for intervocalic s.

With regard to the quantity of the *e* in *-erunt*, the short quantity, though it is in the classical and later period more prominent in Dactylic Poetry than in other verse, owing to its suitableness for the dactylic metre, is not by any means unknown in the older (and later) dramatists, e. g. in Plautus *subegĕrunt*, Plaut. *Bacch*. 928, *fecĕrunt*, *Amph*. 184 *locavĕrunt*, *Pers*. 160, *cessarunt*, *Mil*. 1432, &c.; *emĕrunt*, Ter. *Eun*. prol. 20, *conlocarunt*, *ib*. 593). Plautus appears, however, to use it only at the énd of a line or hemistich, so must have regarded its use as a licence to be resorted to under metrical necessity. It does not appear to have been used in Tragedy, nor by the earlier Epic writers, like Ennius, and not very frequently by Lucretius (e. g. *institĕrunt*, i. 406 ; see Munro's note), which points to its having been a pronunciation of colloquial Latin that won its way only gradually into the higher literature. It is generally explained as a 3 Plur. of the Auxiliary stem es-, ' to be,' and is compared with Gk. *-εσαν* of 3 Plur. Plupft., so that *dedĕrunt* from **dedesunt* would be a quite different formation from *dedĕrunt* and *dedēre*, with I.-Eur. r. Another theory makes it **dedis-ont*, the first part being a Verbal Noun-stem **dedis-* (see § 52). [On *curarunt* for *curavĕrunt* beside the older *coirauerunt* (*ĕ* ?) on inscriptions, see § 48.]

§ 76. (2) Passive (Deponent). 1 Sing. The Italo-Celtic

§§ 76-78.]   THE VERB.   PERSON-ENDINGS.   533

ending was -ōr in the Pres. Ind. [e. g. O. Lat. *sequŏr*, class. *sequŏr* (ch. iii. § 49), O. Ir. sechur], apparently an addition of Passive -r to the Active ending -ō. Those Tenses and Moods which in Latin formed their 1 Sg. Active in -*m* substitute in the Passive -*r* for -*m*, e. g. *fĕra-r* Fut. and Subj., *fereba-r* Impft., except in the Perfect group, where a periphrastic form is used, e. g. *lātus sim*, *latus essem*, not **tulerir*, **tulisser*, also *latus ero*, not **tuleror* (see § 54), though in Oscan we do find this adaptation of the Active forms in *comparascuster*, Fut. Pft. Pass. (*pon ioc egmo comparascuster* 'cum ea res consulta erit'), the Active of which would be **comparascust* (§ 89); but in Umbr. we have pihaz fust 'piatus erit,' &c.

§ 77. 2 Sing.   Since O. Ir. sechther 'sequeris' shows the I.-Eur. (athematic) ending -thēs (e. g. O. Ind. á-di-thās, Gk. ἐ-δό-θης), which is retained in the O. Ir. Imperative (e. g. cluinte, 'do thou hear,' Dep.), with the usual ending -r, we might expect to find in Latin the I.-Eur. (thematic) ending -sŏ (e. g. Zend bara-ɴha, Gk. φέρεο for *-σο, ἐ-φέρε-ο), which is retained in the Latin Imperative (e. g. *sĕquĕrĕ* for **sequesŏ*, § 57), with an appended -*r*, **sequesŏr*, in class. Lat. **sequerŭr*. But the forms actually found are (1) *sequĕrĕ*, the same as the Imperative 2 Sg. (this is the usual form in O. Lat., and even in Cicero); (2) *sequeris*, which adds to this the ending -*s* of the 2 Sg. Act., **sequerĕ-s* becoming *sequeris* (ch. iii. § 18). The addition of this -*s* discriminates the Ind. from the Imper. form as *ăgis* differs from *ăgĕ*, *ăgĭtis* from *ăgĭtĕ*. The 'Future' Imperative changes to -*r* the -d of its 2 Sg. Act., e. g. *fer-tor* 2 Sg. Pass., *fertō* from *fertōd* 2 Sg. Act. [On the O. Lat. ending for the 2, 3 Sg. Imper. -*mĭnō*, formed apparently from 2 Pl. -*mĭnī* on the type of 2, 3 Sg. Act. -*tō(d)*, see § 60, and on forms like *ūtĭto* for *utitor*, § 59.]

§ 78. For statistics of the use of -*re* and -*ris*, see Neue, ii². pp. 393 sqq. Terence uses -*re* only, Plautus both -*re* and -*ris*, but -*re* far more frequently. (He puns on *obloquere* Ind. and *obloquere* Imperat. in *Ourc.* 41.) Cicero prefers -*re* in all other tenses than the Pres. Ind., and in this tense too in Deponent Verbs. Quintilian is wrong in supposing -*re* to be a weakening of -*ris* (i. 5. 42 quod evitandae asperitatis gratia mollitum est, ut apud veteres pro male mereris 'male merere'), for -*is* did not become -*e* in Latin (ch. ii. § 137), nor can an isolated spelling like *tribunos* [*milita*]*re* for *militāris* on an old inscr. (*C. I. L.*

i. 64) be quoted as a proof of this change. The form -*rus* on a few inscriptions (*spatiarus*, *C. I. L.* i. 1220, Beneventum; *utarus*, i. 1267, Venusia; *figarus*, iv. 2082, Pompeii), none of them old, may be a mere dialectal or vulgar variety, but it may also (like -*us* in the Gen. Sg. of the 3rd Decl., ch. vi. § 22) be a genuine tradition of an older form, which arose from the addition of -*s* to *sequesŏ, &c., at a stage prior to its weakening to *sequerĕ*. Thus *spatiā-sŏ would be expanded to *spatiāsŏ-s, which would become *spatiārŏs, *spatiarus*.

§ 79. 3 Sg. The Italo-Celtic ending is -tŏr [e.g. Lat. *sĕquĭtŭr* from *seque-tŏr, O. Ir. sechethar; cf. Osc. sakarater 'sacratur,' with -ter from syncopated -t(ŏ)r as Umbr. *ager* from *agr(ŏs)], formed by adding Passive -r to the I.-Eur. Secondary ending -tŏ (e.g. O. Ind. á-di-ta, Gk. ἔ-δο-το; O. Ind. á-bhara-ta, Gk. ἐ-φέρε-το). The Imperative changes to -*r* the -d of the Particle -tōd which it appends to the bare stem in the Act., e.g. *fer-tor* Pass., *fer-to(d)* Act., *ăgĭ-tor* Pass., *agi-tō(d)* Act. (On O. Lat. -*mĭnō*, e.g. *antestamino*, 'let him take to witness,' see § 60, and on -*to* for -*tor* in *ūtĭto*, &c., § 59.)

§ 80. 1 Plur. The Italo-Celtic ending is -mŏr (e.g. Lat. *sĕquĭmŭr* for *sequo-mŏr, O. Ir. seche-mmar with a curious doubling of the m), formed by changing to *r* the s of the Active -mŏs (Lat. *fĕrĭ-mŭs* for *fere-mŏs, O. Ir. do-beram for -mŏs?).

§ 81. 2 Plur. Both the Celtic and the Italic languages depart from the ordinary procedure in this person. In O. Ir. Deponents we have the Active ending; in Latin we have the Nom. Plur. of the old Pres. Part. Passive with ellipse of *estis*, e.g. *fĕrĭmĭnī* from *fero-menoi (Gk. φερόμενοι) in the Present Tense, and analogical formations in the others, e.g. *fĕrēbā-mĭnī*, *fĕrā-mĭnī*, *ferrē-mĭnī*. The 2 Plur. Imper., though similar in form to the 2 Plur. Pres. Ind., e.g. *ferimini*, is usually explained as an old Infinitive (Dat. of a MEN-stem), for I.-Eur. *bheremenai (Gk. φερέ-μεναι) (see § 57).

§ 82. 3 Plur. The Italo-Celtic ending is -ntŏr (e.g. Lat. *sĕquuntŭr* from *sequo-ntŏr, O. Ir. sechetar; cf. Osc. karanter 'pascuntur' with -nter from syncopated -nt(ŏ)r, like 3 Sg. -ter for -t(ŏ)r; see above), formed by adding Passive -r to the I.-Eur. Secondary ending -ntŏ (e.g. O. Ind. á-bhara-nta, Gk. ἐ-φέρο-ντο. Cf. Gk. ἔμ-πλη-ντο with Lat. *im-ple-ntur*). In the Imperative the

-d of the particle -tōd appended in the 3 Pl. Act., is changed to *r*, e. g. *fĕruntor* Pass., *feruntō* from **feront-tōd* Act. (see § 57, and on O. Lat. *censento* for *censentor*, § 59).

§ 83. VI. **THE INFINITIVE**. The I.-Eur. Infinitive was merely a Case (usually Dat. or Loc. Sg.) of a Verbal Noun, and has best retained its character in the Celtic languages, where its object stands not in the Acc., as after a verb, but in the Gen., as after a Noun. The form of the Inf. varied not merely according to the case employed, but also according to the Noun-stem which was chosen. In O. Ind. we have a great variety of Infinitives, e. g. (1) Dat. of a Root-stem, a stem which was the same as the root of the Verb, e. g. -ájē, 'to drive,' lit. 'for driving' (Lat. *ăgī*; cf. Gk. χεῦ-αι?); (2) Dat. of an S-stem, e. g. ji-ṣḗ, 'to conquer' [cf. Lat. *da-rī*, O. Lat. *da-sei* (§ 85), Gk. πεῖ-σαι]; (3) Dat. of a MEN-stem, e. g. dá-manē, 'to give' (Gk. δόμεναι; Lat. *da-minī* 2 Pl. Imper. Pass., see § 57), vid-máne, 'to know' [Gk. (F)ίδ-μεναι]; (4) Loc. of a MEN-stem (without -ĭ, see ch. vi. § 37), e. g. dhár-man, 'to keep up' (cf. Gk. δό-μεν); (5) Dat. of a TU-stem, e. g. dhā́-tavē, 'to set' (cf. Pruss. dā-twei, ' to give '); (6) Acc. of a TU-stem, e. g. dhā́-tum (this is the classical or Sanscrit form of the Infinitive of every verb) (Lat. *con-dĭtum* 1st Sup., Lith. dé-tų Sup., O. Sl. dĕ-tŭ Sup.; the Balto-Slavic Supine in -tum is fused with the auxiliary verb of the same root as Lat. *fui* to form a Compound Tense, e. g. Lith. détum-bime, 1 Pl. Opt., as the Lat. 1st Supine is joined with impersonal *īrī* to form the Fut. Inf. Pass., e. g. *sublātum iri* or *sublatuiri*, see below); (7) Dat. of an I-stem, e. g. dr̥ś-áyē, ' to see,' and many others. The Teutonic Inf. is Acc. of an ONO-stem, e. g. Goth. itan, Germ. essen from **ĕd-ŏnŏ-m* (cf. O. Ind. ádanam, a Neut. Noun). The form chosen for the Latin Inf. Act. was a Loc. Sg. of an S-stem, e. g. *ăgĕ-rĕ* from **age-sĭ*, *amā-rĕ* from **ama-sĭ*, *vĭdē-rĕ* from **vide-sĭ*, *fīnī-rĕ* from **fīnī-sĭ*, *es-sĕ* from **es-sĭ*, *dĕdis-sĕ* (see § 52), *fer-rĕ* from **fer-sĭ*, *vel-lĕ* from **vel-sĭ*, the last two showing the regular change of *rs* to *rr* (cf. *torreo* from **torseyō*, ch. iv. § 153), *ls* to *ll* (cf. *collum* from **colso-*, Germ. Hals, ch. iv. § 146). For the Inf. Pass. a Dat. Sg. was chosen, either (1) of a Root-stem, e. g. *ăg-ī* (O. Lat. *ag-ei*) from **ăĝ-ai*, *mŏr-ī* (with the diphthong ai

weakened in the unaccented syllable, first to *ei*, then to *ī*, as in
ŏc-caido, oc-ceido, oc-cĭdo, ch. iii. § 18), or (2) of an S-stem, e.g.
ămā-rī (O. Lat. *ama-rei*) from *ama-sai, *vidē-rī* from *wide-sai,
fīnī-rī, O. Lat. *mŏrī-ri*, so that the Lat. Inf. Pass. differed from
the Inf. Act. only conventionally, and had no distinctive Passive
suffix. This however seems to be present in the byforms *agier,
amārier, morīrier*, though the exact origin of this *-ier, -rier* is
doubtful [1]. For the Perfect Inf. Passive the Perf. Part. Pass.
was used with the auxiliary verb *esse*, e.g. constat id factum esse,
constat ea facta esse; for the Fut. Pass. the 1st Supine with *īrī*,
Inf. Pass. of *eo*, 'to go,' e.g. constat id factum iri, constat ea factum iri. The Fut. Act., e.g. constat id eventurum (esse), is most
naturally explained as a combination of the Fut. Part. Act. with
esse, though its Old Latin indeclinable use, e.g. credo inimicos
meos dicturum (from a speech of C. Gracchus) has suggested the
theory that it is a compound of the 2nd Supine in *-tū* (e.g. *even-
tū, dictū*, Locs. of TU-stems, ch. vi. § 37) with an old byform of
esse, viz. **esom*, later **erum* (Umbr. *erom*, Osc. *ezum*, Acc. of O-
stem), *dictūrum* for **dictū-erum* being in time made personal
dicturus -a -um (the Fut. Part. Act.) in the same way as O. Lat.
'dicendum est orationem' changed to class. Lat. 'dicenda est
oratio' (Postgate in *Class. Rev.* v. p. 301). The Umbro-Oscan Pres.
Inf. Act. is the Acc. Sg. of a Verbal O-stem (e.g. Umbr. *er-om*,
Osc. *ez-um, deic-um, molt-aum* 'multare') (ch. v. § 2).

On Lat. *arē* in *arē-facio* and similar Verb-stems, see § 34.

In Vulg. Lat., as reflected in the Romance languages, the
Perf. Inf. has been lost; *esse* has become *essere* (Ital. essere,
Span. ser, Fr. être); *velle, volēre* (Ital. volere, Fr. vouloir), this
verb having been transferred (by the analogy of its Perf.
volui like *monui, habui*, &c.) to the second Conjugation, *voleo*
1 Sg. Pres. Ind. (Ital. voglio), *voleat*, 3 Sg. Pres. Subj. (Ital.
voglia), as *posse* became *potēre* (Ital. potere, Sp. poder) through
the likeness of its Perf. *potui* to the second Conjugation type.
(cf. § 33 *a*).

---

[1] Some make it an addition to *ī* of the Active Inf. ending, with Syncope of the final *ĕ*, as in *biber* for *bĭbĕre* (*A. L. L.* vii. 132). Similarly in Vulg. Lat. *esse-re* replaced *esse* (see below).

§ 84. **Pres. Inf. Act.** *Biber* for *bĭbĕrĕ* in the phrase *biber dare* (quoted by Charisius 124. 1 K. from various early authors, and censured as a mispronunciation by Caper, 108. 10 K. bibere non 'biber'), seems to be a case of syncope of final -*ĕ* (like *nec* for *nĕque*, *animal* for *ănĭmāle*, *calcar* for *calcāre*, ch. iii. § 36), though it has been also regarded as a veritably old form, a Locative without ĭ (ch. vi. § 37), like Gk. δό-μεν Inf. (see above). *Instar* may be a similar syncopated Inf. (for *instare*) used as a Noun (cf. *bustar*, an oxstall ; see ch. iii. § 36). On late inscriptions we have, e. g. *haber* (*C. I. L.* viii. 8369, of 128 A.D.) ; and on a lamp found in the oldest Esquiline cemetery (*Ann. Inst.* 1880, p. 260), Sotae sum. noli me tanger.

§ 85. **Pres. Inf. Pass.** The form in -*ier*, -*rier* belongs to O. Lat. and is employed as an archaism by the Augustan poets and their imitators (see statistics in Neue, ii². p. 409). Even in the time of Plautus it can hardly have been so current as the form in -*ī*, -*rī*, for it is confined to the end of iambic and trochaic lines, e. g. *percontarier, Most.* 963 (see Lorenz, *ad loc.*), and is never found with a short antepaenultima (except *deripier, Men.* 1006), restrictions which indicate that it was a form used only for the sake of the metre. That the -*r* of -*ri* was originally s we see from the O. Lat. form *dasi* mentioned by Paul. Fest. [48. 19 Th. ' dasi ' dari (should we read ' dasei ' or else dare ?)]. The occasional scansion of the Pres. Inf. Act. with -*ē* in Plaut. (e. g. *Pseud.* 355, 1003) has been explained as a relic of the use of -*ai* (O. Lat. -*ei* or -*ē*, ch. iv. § 34) as Active suffix (*I. F.* iv. 240). But it may be otherwise explained, as syllaba anceps before final dipody (see Müller, *Plaut. Pros.* p. 22). The theory that the ī- and ai- suffixes were in the O. Lat. period used indifferently as Act. or Pass. is plausible enough but lacks proof.

§ 86. **Fut. Inf. Act.** Gellius in the seventh chapter of the first book of his *Noctes Atticae* quotes several instances of the indeclinable use of the Fut. Inf. Act. from the older authors, in connexion with the reading: hanc sibi rem praesidio sperant futurum (Cic. *Verr.* II. v. 65. 167), found in a copy of Tiro's edition (libro spectatae fidei, Tironiana cura atque disciplina facto). This reading was defended by such examples as : credo ego inimicos meos hoc dicturum (from a speech of C. Gracchus) ; hostium copias ibi occupatas futurum, and again : deos bonis bene facturum (from the *Annals* of Claudius Quadrigarius) ; omnia ex sententia processurum esse (from Valerius Antias ; the use of *esse* is irregular) ; altero te occisurum ait (*sc.* Casina) (from Plaut. *Cas.* 693, where our MSS. are almost unanimous for *occisuram* !) ; non putavi hoc eam facturum (from Laberius, *Com.* 51 R.). Priscian (i. p. 475. 23 H.) quotes from Cato : illi polliciti sese facturum omnia ; from Lucilius (xvii. 8 M.) : nupturum te (*sc.* Penelope) nupta negas. The existence of nouns like *scriptūra, versūra, pictūra* points to the Fut. Part. *scriptūrus -a -um, versūrus -a -um, pictūrus -a -um,* &c. (formed from Ū-stems, as Gk. ἰσχῡρό-, from a Ū-stem ; cf. ch. v. § 16, ch. iv. § 60) having been an old formation (cf. *offensa* beside *offensus, rĕpulsa* beside *repulsus*), and makes it unlikely that the declinable Fut. Part. arose from this indeclinable Inf. So it may be better to regard O. Lat. *dicturum* as the Neut. Sg. of this participle used (without *esse*) impersonally, just as the Impersonal *constat*, e. g. 'constat inter omnes haec ita esse,' becomes in the Fut. Inf. Pass.

constaturum, e. g. 'spero constaturum inter omnes haec ita esse.' Similarly the Gerundive in *-ndus -a -um* seems the older form and the Gerund in *-ndum* an Impersonal use, *eundum est* being analogous to *itur* (see § 62). On the other hand the preference shown by Plautus and Terence for the omission of *esse* (for statistics, see Postgate in *I. F.* iv. 252; cf. Plaut. *Bacch.* 592 negat se iturum, with *Truc.* 85 is nunc dicitur Uenturus peregre), and the rarity of the use of the Fut. Part. in apposition (e. g. Enn. *Ann.* 412 M. carbasus alta uolat pandam ductura carinam) are quoted in support of Prof. Postgate's explanation.

§ 87. Fut. Inf. Pass. *Iri* is impersonal, like *itur* in Virgil's *itur in antiquam silvam*, so that the line of Terence (*Hec.* prol.): rumor uenit datum iri gladiatores, should be translated 'that they are going to exhibit gladiators,' 'that there is going to be a gladiatorial show.' Gellius (x. 14) quotes a curious extension of this usage from a speech of Cato, *contumelia mihi factum itur*: atque euenit ita, Quirites, uti in hac contumelia, quae mihi per huiusce petulantiam factum itur, rei quoque publicae medius fidius miserear, Quirites. This throws some light on the development of the Italo-Celtic passive from an Impersonal R-form (§ 62). (Cf. Plaut. *Rud.* 1242 mihi istaéc uidetur praéda praedatum frier.) The word-group *factum iri*, &c. seems to have become a single word in ordinary language, for we often find the Fut. Inf. Pass. written with *-tuiri* in MSS., which is frequently corrupted in later copies to *-turi* as if Nom. Pl. Masc. of Fut. Part. Act. (e. g. *sublatuiri* in Cod. A of *Bell. Alex.* xix. 2, but in other MSS. *sublaturi*; for a list of examples from Lactantius, see *A. L. L.* ii. 349). The suppression of *-m* of *sublatum*, &c. is like the suppression of *m* of *circum* in *circuit* for *circum it* (see ch. ii. § 153).

§ 88. VII. THE SUPINES. The First Supine, used after a Verb of motion, is the Acc. Sg. of a Verbal Noun, a TU-stem (e. g. *ire spectātum*, lit. ' to go to the seeing,' like *ire dŏmum*, to go to the house, *ire Rōmam*, to go to Rome), the same form as is in Sanscrit the regular Infinitive of the verb (see § 83). An O. Ind. usage like dráṣṭum á gachanti, 'they come to see,' hótum ēti, 'he goes to sacrifice' (cf. O. Sl. vidětŭ idetĭ, 'he goes to see')) (Delbrück, *Altind. Syntax*, p. 428) is what the Latin First Supine has developed from.

The Second Supine, used after an Adjective, is the Loc. Sg. of the same Verbal Noun (e. g. *ăgĭlis cursū*, nimble in running). The Loc. Sg. in *-ū* of U-stems often played the part of a Dat. (e. g. *curru* for *currui* in Virgil, see ch. vi. §§ 37, 23, 27); and we find the Second Supine used not only as a Loc., but as a Dative, e. g. (*fabula*) *lĕpĭda mĕmŏrātū*, pleasant for telling, where in the older language the Dative proper in *-ui* is used, e. g. *lepida memoratui* (Plaut.), as well as the Locative, e. g. *rīdĭcŭla audītu*

§§ 87-89.] THE VERB. SUPINES. PARTICIPLES. 539

(Plaut.), (in Plaut. *Rud.* 294 sunt nobis quaestu et cultu, this Loc. plays the part of a Predicative Dative).

This TU-stem bulks largely in the language of Plautus and the older Dramatists, e. g. opsonatu redeo (Plaut. *Men.* 288), essum vocare, ' to invite to dinner ' (*Men.* 458), nuptum dare, ' to give a girl in marriage ' (*Pers.* 383). In *Aul.* 736 *perdĭtum ire* is used almost like *perdere* :

quam ób rem ita faceres méque meosque pérditum ires líberos,

(cf. *Bacch.* 565 mi ires consultum male), and the use of the Accusative without a Preposition is paralleled by phrases like *ī mălam crŭcem* (Plaut.), *suppĕtias, infĭtias, exsĕquias ire*, &c. Like *nuptum dare* and *nuptum ire* are *vēnumdăre* or *venundare* (*vendere*) and *venum ire* (*vēnire*; but cf. O. Ind. vasna-yá-ti, 3 Sg., Gk. ὠνέομαι); *pessumdăre* or *pessumdare* and *pessum ire*. A similar Acc. of a Verbal Noun TU-stem is *asom* (class. *assum*, 1st Supine of *ardeo*) in the phrase *asom fero* on an old Praenestine cista with the representation of a kitchen scene (*Mél. Arch.* 1890, p. 303), a phrase which recurs on a Marrucine inscription, *asum . . . feret* (Zvet. *I. I. I.* 8). The 1st Supine is also found in Umbrian, e. g. *aseriato etu* ' observatum ito.' In the Romance languages the Supines have been lost.

§ 89. VIII. THE PARTICIPLES.

The I.-Eur. Participles were merely Verbal Adjectives formed with the various suffixes already mentioned in the chapter on Noun- and Adjective-stems (chap. v). Thus for the Perf. Part. Pass. the TO-suffix was used (e. g. O. Ind. -dhi-tá-, Gk. θε-τός, Lat. *crē-dĭ-tus*, Lith. dé-tas ; Goth. vaurh-ts, ' wrought'), or the NO-suffix (e. g. O. Ind. pūr-ṇá-, 'filled,' O. Engl. bund-en, ' bound-en,' O. Sl. nes-enŭ, ' carried'; cf. Lat. *plē-nus*); for the Gerundive, the YO-suffix (e.g. O.Ind. dŕś-ya-, ' seeable, worth seeing,' O.Sax. un-fôd-i, 'insatiable'; cf. Gk. ἄγ-ιος, venerable, Lat. *exĭm-ius*), or -TWO-, -TĔWO- (e.g. O. Ind. kár-tva-, ' worth doing,' Gk. διωκ-τέ(F)ος, worth pursuing), and so on. With the LO-suffix is formed the second Past Participle Act. in O. Sl., e. g. nes-lŭ, used in the periphrastic neslŭ jesmĭ, ' I have carried,' and the Aor. Part. Act. or Pass. in Armenian, e. g. gereal ' capiens, captus.'

The Pres. Part. Act. (and all Active Participles, except the

Perfect) took the suffix -ĕnt-, -nt-, -ont- (see ch. v. § 63) (e.g. O. Ind. bhárant-, Gk. φέρων, -οντος, Goth. bairands, O. Sl. bery), Lat. fĕr-ens, -entis, sĕdens (Umbr. zeđef). The Perf. Part. Act. took -wĕs- (e.g. O. Ind. ririk-vás-, Gk. λελοιπ-(ϝ)ώς, Lith. lìkęs; cf. O. Sl. mlŭz-ŭ, 'having milked'); and this formation appears in Umbro-Oscan in the Compound Tense, which corresponds to the Lat. Fut. Perf. (e.g. Osc. *fefacust* 'fecerit'), and probably in Osc. *sipus*, knowing, with full knowledge [from *sēp-wes- (?). That the *u* is long (I.-Eur. ū or ō) is inferred from the absence of Syncope, for *sipŭs, *sipŏs would become in Oscan *sips; but see ch. iii. § 16]; but in Latin the Perf. Part. Act. is not used. Neither is the Pres. Part. Middle (or Pass.), which was formed in -mĕno- (-mono-, -mno-) (e.g. O. Ind. bhára-māṇa-, Gk. φερό-μενος; cf. Pruss. po-klausi-manas, 'being heard'), though it is found in the 2 Pl. Ind. Pass., e.g. *fĕrĭmĭnī* (sc. *estis*, see § 81), and in nouns like *alumnus* (cf. Gk. ὁ τρεφόμενος, see ch. v. § 13). The Perf. Part. shows the suffix -to-, e.g. *scriptus* (Umbr. screihto-, Osc. scrifto-); the Fut. Part. Act. in *-tūrus* is probably a formation with the suffix -ro- from a TU-stem Verbal Noun, e.g. *scriptūrus*, stem *scriptū-ro-* from the stem *scriptu-* of *scriptus*, -*ūs*, *pictūrus* from the stem *pictu-* of *pictus*, -*us*, &c., like Gk. ἰσχῡ-ρός from ἰσχύς. [On its relation to the Fut. Inf. Act. in O. Lat. *scripturum*, in class. Lat. *scripturus* (-*a* -*um*) (*esse*), see § 86]. For a Participle the Latin writers, especially the poets, often substituted an Adjective, e.g. *lăcĕr* for *lăcĕrātus* (Virg. lacerum crudeliter ora), and these Adjectives or 'truncated Participles' have to some extent encroached on the Perf. Part. Pass. in the Romance languages, e.g. Ital. trovo beside trovato. (Meyer-Lübke, *Rom. Gram.* ii. p. 375.)

§ 90. **Pres. Part. Act.** The Pres. Part. Act. was liable to become in all languages an ordinary Adjective or a Noun; e.g. Goth. frijōnd-s, lit. 'loving,' assumed the sense of 'friend'; Lat. *rŭdens* (see § 6), lit. 'rattling,' assumed the sense of 'a rope, tackling'; *bĕnĕvŏlens* is a noun in Plautus, e.g. *Trin.* 46, 1148, &c. Very early examples of this seem to be Lat. *dens* (Osc. dont-?), a Pres. Part. of the I.-Eur. root ed-, 'to eat,' *sons* a Pres. Part. of I.-Eur. es-, 'to be' (cf. O. Scand. sannr, 'sooth, true,' which acquired the sense of 'truly charged,' 'guilty'). Of Pres. Parts. becoming Adjectives in Latin examples are *congruens* (beside *congruus*), *benevolens* (beside *benevolus*), *bĕnĕmĕrens* (cf. -*mĕrus* in Lucilius' *mercēdĭmĕrae lĕgiōnes*); *indĭgens*, not *indĭgus*, and *insciens*, not *inscius* (but *nescius*), are used by Plautus. The result of this close connexion of

§§ 90-92.] THE VERB. PARTICIPLES. 541

Verbal Adjectives (especially Compounds) in *-us* with Participles in *-ens*, is a Comparison like *benevolus*, *benevolentior*, *benevolentissimus*, *magnificus*, *-entior*, *-entissimus* (see ch. vi. § 55).
The O-grade of the suffix which predominates in the Greek declension, φέρων, -οντος, -οντι appears in Lat. *sons* (beside *prae-sens*, *prae-sentia*, *ab-sens*, &c.), *euntis*, *-i*, *-em*, *-es*, &c. (beside Nom. Sg. *iens*), *vŏluntas* (beside *volens*). It can hardly be due to a mere accident that all these traces of the suffix -ont- are found in verbs belonging to the Athematic Conjugation, I.-Eur. *es-mi, *ei-mi, *wel-mi (see § 2). It almost seems as if the declension of the Pres. Part. of Athematic Verbs in Latin had originally exhibited the suffix -ont-, perhaps varying with -ent- (I.-Eur -ṇt- or even -ent-), e. g. *ab-iens* Nom. Sg., *euntis* Gen., *eunti* Dat., *ientem* Acc. (see ch. vi. § 1, p. 367), or *sons* Nom. Sg., *sentis* Gen. from an I.-Eur. *sónts Nom., *sṇtós Gen. (cf. O. Ind. sánt-, satás Gen.), *sentia* Fem. (cf. *prae-sentia*) from sṇt- like Dor. Gk. ἔασσα for *ἐσηντια, the equivalent of Att. οὖσα (ch. iv. § 81). The use of *euntis*, *eunti*, &c. cannot well have been due to the dislike of the combination -ĭĕ- (*iens* has ĭĕ-, the vowel being lengthened before *ns*, ch. ii. § 144), for this combination is not objected to in other Participles, *facientis*, *capientis*, &c. The survival of the suffix *-ent-* in the struggle for existence in the Latin Present Participle, athematic and thematic, was probably aided by the Latin tendency to turn every short unaccented vowel before a consonant-group to ĕ (see ch. iii. § 18; and cf. below, § 94, on *-undus* and *-endus* in the Gerundive).

§ 91. **Perf. Part. Act.** This has been lost also in Celtic and Teutonic, but in Balto-Slavic is the only part of the Perfect Active retained. Some find traces of the formation in Lat. *cădāver*, *păpāver*, others in O. Lat. *gnārūres* Plur., 'knowing,' e. g. Plaut. *Most.* 100 :

    simúl gnarurís uos uolo ésse hanc rem mécum.

(Cf. Gloss. Placid. 'gnaruris' gnarus, sciens : Gloss. Philox. 'gnarurem' γνώριμον : 'ignarures' ἀγνοοῦντες : 'gnarurat' γνωρίζει). *Mĕmor* seems to be not a Perfect Participle, but an Adjective derived from a Perfect Participle-stem, as Gk. κεκραγμός (Eurip.) is a Noun derived from κέκρᾱγα.

§ 92. **Perf. Part. Pass.** This participle too became often an ordinary Adjective (Engl. 'cold,' 'dead,' &c. are TO-stem Participles), e. g. *cĭtus*, swift, lit. 'bestirred' (O. Ind. śī-tá-) ; *cătus*, sharp (this was the meaning of the word in the Sabine district, Varro's home, Varro, *L. L.* vii. 46), then (metaphorically) (1) piercing, of sounds, e. g. Enn. *A.* 538 M. cata signa, the shrill clarions ; (2) shrewd, of persons, literally 'sharpened,' from I.-Eur. k̂ō- (cf. Lat. *cōs*, a whetstone) (ch. iv. § 54) ; *lātus*, O. Lat. *stlātus*, broad, lit. 'extended' (cf. O. Sl. stel-ją, 'I spread, extend')[1], or a Noun, e.g. *nătus*, a son (in Plautus and Terence we have as a rule *gnatus*, a son, *natus*, born), *lēgātus*, a lieutenant, deputy. When used as an Adj. it sometimes passes into the I-declension, the favourite Adjective declension (ch. v. § 34), e.g. *fortis*, O. Lat. *forctus*, originally P. P. P. of the I.-Eur. root dhergh-, 'to establish' (O. Ind. dṛdhá-,

---

[1] Another example is *cunctus* (for *co-vinctus*?), which has still its participial sense in Plaut. *Most.*

1168 : fac istam cunctam gratiam. *Accūratus* is always a Participle in O. Lat.

'established, firm'), *in-gens*, lit. 'unknown,' from the root ĝen-, 'to know' (O. Engl. un-cūđ, 'uncouth'). When used as a Noun the Neuter often appears, e.g. *lectum* (also Masc. *lectus*, of the fourth or second decl.), *tectum*, *fātum* (the sense of 'destiny' probably originated in the phrase 'fari fatum alicui,' to lay a doom or spell on one, like the Welsh tynghu tynghed; see Rhŷs, *Proc. of Internat. Folklore Congr.* 1891, p. 150), and (especially in the case of Abstract Nouns) the Feminine, e.g. *offensa*, *rĕpulsa*.

The Participle in -to- of Intransitive Verbs has the sense of a Perfect Part. Active, e. g. *cēnātus*, having dined, *pransus*, *pōtus*, like our 'learned' in such a phrase as 'a learned man,' 'a learned judge.' Hence its use as the Perfect Participle of Deponent Verbs, e.g. *aspernātus*, *sĕcūtus*, and the coexistence of Deponent Perf. Part. and Act. Verb, e. g. *fīsus* beside *fīdo*, *maestus*, sad, beside *maereo*. These participial TO-stems from roots which have developed in Latin into Deponent Verbs often retain their true passive sense, e. g. *ābūsa* Pass. (Plaut. *Asin.* 196; cf. Pelign. oisa aetate 'confecta aetate'), so that there is a justification for Virgil's *oblīta carmina*, Horace's *dētestāta bella*, and the like.

It seems to have taken in I.-Eur. the weak grade of the Verb-root, e. g. I.-Eur. *wĭd-to- from the root weid-, 'to know' (O. Ind. vittá-, Gk. ἄ-ιστος, Goth. un-vĭs), *k̂lŭ-to- from k̂leu- [O. Ind. śrūtá-, Gk. κλῠτός, Lat. *in-clŭtus*, O. Ir. cloth for *clŭto-, O. H. G. Hlot-hari (the equivalent of Gk. Κλυτό-στρατος, cf. Germ. Heer, an army), the name 'Lothair']. In Latin this is also the rule, e. g. *dŭc-tus* from *dŭco*, *ŭs-tus* from *ūro*, *tentus* for *tṇ-tos (Gk. τατύς) from root ten-, *pŭtus* (Plaut. *Pseud.* 1200) used with its equivalent *pū-rus*. See ch. ii. § 144, where it is suggested that the long vowel of *rēctus*, &c. may be due to a Latin tendency to lengthen a vowel before the group *g-t*. The Perfect Ind. Act. too has often influenced its vocalism. The same influence caused the substitution of *-sus* for *-tus*, which spread from Dental Verb-stems, where it was due to a Latin phonetic law (ch. iv. § 155), e. g. *tensus* for *tend-tus*, *ūsus* older *ūssus*, for *ūt-tus, *oit-to-), *flexus* for *flecttus*, *salsus* for *sald-to- (cf. Goth. saltan), *perculsus* for *kḷd-to- (cf. *clādes*), to others where the Perfect has *s* (*x*), e. g. *farsus* (cf. *farsi* Perf.), *fixus* (cf. *fixi*; but *fictus* from *fingo*, *finxi*), just as the analogy of *haesi* has produced the late form *haes-ūrus*, and *hausi* (P. P. P. *haustus*), *haus-ūrus* beside *hausturus*, or as the analogy of the Present Tense is followed in O. Lat. *sortus* (*surtus*?) with *-rt-* for *-rct-*, ch. iv. § 157) for *surrectus* (Paul. Fest. 423. 1 Th. 'suregit' et 'sortus' pro surrexit, et quasi possit fieri surrectus, frequenter posuit Livius), *expergĭtus* for *experrectus* (Lucil. iii. 56 M.; Lucr. iii. 929, &c.).

On Oscan prúfto- 'probatus,' Umbr. vašeto- (from stem vakā-), &c., which have been compared with Lat. *crĕpĭtus* from *crepāre*, *implĭcĭtus* from *implicare*, see von Planta, i. p. 214. The difficulties which they offer have not yet been satisfactorily removed.

In Italian, French, and Roumanian the ending *-ūtus* (like *statūtus*, *minūtus*, &c.) has become the normal ending of the P. P. P. of the third Conjugation; e. g. Ital. venduto, Fr. vendu, Roum. vindut, point to a Vulg. Lat. *vendūtus* for *vendĭtus* (see Meyer-Lübke, *Rom. Gram.* ii. p. 370). (Cf. § 51, above, on the encroachment of the Perfect in *-ui* in Vulg. Lat.) For the Past Part. of *sum* the Italian and French languages use *status* (Ital. stato, Fr. été, &c.) (*ib.* p. 385). A Romance example of a P. P. P. which has become an Adj. is *strictus* with the sense of 'narrow' (Ital. stretto, Fr. étroit, Span. estrecho).

§§ 93, 94.] THE VERB. GERUND AND GERUNDIVE. 543

§ 93. 'Truncated' Participles. Priscian (i. 534. 6 H.) says : 'retus' pro retitus dicebant, quomodo 'saucius' pro sauciatus, et 'lassus' pro lassatus, et 'lacerus' pro laceratus et 'potus' pro potatus; Gellius (xix. 7) quotes from Laevius 'oblitteram' gentem for oblitteratam, with other novelties such as 'accipitret' for laceret, 'pudoricolorem' auroram, curis 'intolerantibus' for intolerandis.

§ 94. IX. THE GERUND AND GERUNDIVE. The Gerundive (Adj.) in -*ndo*-, Umbro-Oscan -nno- (e. g. Osc. trííbúm . . . úpsannam deded ' domum . . . operandam dedit,' Umbr. *esonir* . . . *popler anferener et ocrer pihaner* ' sacris . . . populi circumferendi et arcis piandae,' Gen. of 'Purpose') has beside it in Latin, but not, so far as we can tell, in Umbro-Oscan, a Gerund (Neut. Noun) in -*ndo*-, which seems to stand to the Gerundive in the same relation as an Impersonal to a Personal Verb, *eundum est in antiquam silvam* being Impersonal like *itur in antiquam silvam*. Until more Umbro-Oscan inscriptions with this formation have been discovered, it is rash to attempt a history of the Gerundive and Gerund on Italian soil. The evidence at present at our disposal points to the Adjectival use as having been the original one, shared by all the Italic languages, e. g. domus aedificanda, iter cognoscendae antiquitatis (ch. vi. § 20, p. 383 *n.*). In the older Latin writers when this formation is turned into finite form, i. e. when a statement is made by means of it, the usual method is to employ the Gerund with *est* governing an object, e. g. agitandum est vigilias, imperandum est servis, carendum est urbe ; but in classical Latin the Gerundive is preferred if the Verb is one which governs the Accusative, e. g. agitandae sunt vigiliae, but still as before, imperandum est servis, carendum est urbe (see Roby, *Lat. Gram.* ii[2]. Pref. pp. lxi sqq.); and the transition from the impersonal to the personal mode of expression, marked by a construction like Plautus' nominandi istorum copia (a construction allowed by Cic. with a Gen. Pl. for the sake of euphony, e. g. facultas agrorum condonandi) is like the transition from ' factum itur contumeliam ' to Cato's contumelia factum itur (§ 87).

The origin of the Gerundive suffix still remains doubtful, after all the theories that have been started to account for it (see especially Brugmann, *Grundriss*, ii. §§ 69 and 1103 ; Thurneysen, *K. Z.* xxx. 493 ; Conway, *Class. Rev.* v. 296). In the third and fourth Conjugations the form -*ĕndo*- cannot be a phonetic development of -ŏndo- through weakening of the vowel ŏ in the unaccented syllable, for we have *anfereno-* for *ămbhĭ-bhĕrĕndŏ- in Umbrian, where a weakening of this kind would not be found. Although the form -*endo*- became the approved form in classical Latin, while -*ŭndo*- (from an earlier -*ŏndo*-) was relegated to the legal and archaistic style, e.g. *rēs rĕpĕtundae*, yet the classical form is found on the earliest inscriptions. On the Senatus Consultum de Bacchanalibus of 186 B.C. (*C. I. L.* i. 196) we have *exdeicendum* 'edicendum' and *faciendam*, and on the Lex Repetundarum of 122–123 B.C. (i. 198) *tribuendei, fruendeis, fruendum*, &c. stand side by side with *legundis, scribundi, deferundo, quaerundai*, &c. The two are rather parallel endings like -*ŏnt*- and -*ĕnt*- in the Pres. Part. Act. (see § 90), although the ultimate acceptance of the Ĕ-form in both these cases may have been helped by the Latin tendency to turn a short unaccented vowel before a consonant-group into *ĕ* (ch. iii. § 18).

With the Gerundive suffix are evidently connected the suffixes of Adjectives in -*bundo*-, -*cundo*-, &c., e.g. *errā-bundus, īrā-cundus, rŭbĭ-cundus, rŏtundus* (cf. O. Ir. cruind, 'round,' ālaind, 'beautiful'?). The *b* of the first of these has been referred to the root bheu- of *fui*, &c., the *c* of the second to the suffix seen in *rŭbĭ-care, albĭ-care*, &c. (above § 27, ch. v. § 31).

§ 95. Origin of the suffix -ndo-. The suffix -*do*- of *lŭcĭ-dus*, &c. has been referred to the verb *dare*, so that *luci-dus* would really mean 'giving light' (ch. v. § 67). In the Gerundive this same suffix (cf. *Aius* from *aio, Panda* from *pando*, &c., ch. v. §§ 2, 3) may perhaps be joined not with a stem, as in *luci-dus*, but with an Accusative case, as -*dex* (from *dico*) is in *vin-dex* (ch. v. § 80), or as the finite verb is joined in composition with an Accusative in *venun-do, vendo, pessum-do*. These may be relics of a mode of expression that prevailed much more widely in the pre-literary period of Latin. The combination of Active and Passive sense, which is so peculiar a feature of the Latin Gerundive forms, e.g. 'agitandum est vigilias' Act., and 'agitandae sunt vigiliae' Pass., and 'anulus in digito subtertenuatur habendo' Act.-Pass., may then be explained from the double sense that can be attached to an expression like *rŭbōrem dare*, (1) to blush, Neut., (2) to cause to blush, Act. The Accusatives will be Accusatives of Verbal Noun-stems *rotam-dus, *laudam-dus (*laudăndus*, Audacis exc. 359. 15 K.), *rubem-dus, *habem-dus (Ital. provienda points to *habĕndus*),*ferŏm-dus (with *ferĕm-dus; cf. *ferē-bam*, § 34) (see § 34 on *rubē-facio*, &c., *ī-licet*, &c., and cf. the Zend Inf. dąm, 'to set, to give'). That -md- became -nd- in Latin, but -*nn*- (often written *n*) in Umbro-Oscan, we see from Lat. *quon-dam, quan-do*, Umbr. *ponne* and *pone*, Osc. *pon* from *qʷom-dĕ.

§ 96. Adjectives in -bundo-, -cundo-, &c. Examples of -*bundo*- from Verbs of the first Conjugation : *errā-bundus, praedā-bundus* (Sall., &c.), *populā-bundus* (Liv., &c.), *vertīlā-bundus* (Varr. *Men.* 108 B.) ; of the second : *pŭdĭ-bundus* (Aug. poets) ; of the third : *fŭrĭ-bundus, mŏrĭ-bundus, quĕrĭ-bundus, trĕmĕ-bundus* (cf. *trĕme-facio, treme-sco*), *frĕmĕ-bundus* (Accius, with *fremĭ-* ?, and Aug. poets) ; of the fourth : *lascīvi-bundus* (Plaut. *Stich.* 288 ; the quantity of the third vowel is not decided by the metre, but must be long). Examples of *-cundo-* are from the first : *fā-cundus* (cf. *fā-tus*), *īrā-cundus* (cf. *irā-tus*), *jū-cundus* (cf. *-jūtus*) ; and from the second : *fĕ-cundus* (cf. *fĕ-tus*), *vĕrē-cundus* (from Plaut. onwards), *rŭbĭ-cundus* (Ter., &c. ; cf. *rubĕ-facio*). *Rŏtŭndus* has *-ŭndo-* (cf. Ital. rotondo, Span. redondo, &c.) from *-ŏndo-* (on the spelling *rutundus*, see ch. iii. § 33). *Sŏciennus*, a Plautine word for *sŏcius* (*Aul.* 659), may be a dialectal form (Plautus was an Umbrian), of which the true Latin equivalent would be **sociendus*.

§ 97. **Some Irregular Verbs.** The irregularity of many verbs consists in their use of different stems for different tenses. The Substantive Verb shows the root ES- in some tenses (§ 2), the root BHEU- in others, e. g. Pft. *fui*[1] ; and the heteroclite conjugation of verbs like ' to be,' ' to go ' seems to date from the I.-Eur. period. Other Latin examples are *fio* (for **fwio* from bhw-, a weakened form of the root bheu- ; cf. Osc. fiiet, fiet ' fient') and *factus sum* ; *fĕrio* and *percussi* ; *fĕro* and *tŭli* (O. Lat. *tĕtŭli*, § 39), the Perfect being taken from the root of O. Ind. tul-, ' to lift,' Gk. τετλάναι, Ir. tallaim, ' I take away,' Goth. þulan, 'to endure,' Scotch thole ; *tollo* for *tol-no* (Ir. tallaim), with the Nasal Present-stem and *sustŭli* for *sustĕtŭli* (§ 44), with Preposition and Aorist- or Weak stem (§ 3) ; *vescor* and *pastus sum* ; *arguor* and *convictus sum* ; *rĕmĭniscor* and *recordatus sum* ; *mĕdeor* and *mĕdĭcatus sum* ; *surgo* differs from *surrexi* and *surrectus* in being syncopated (cf. *porgo* and *porrĭgo*) ; a contracted form of the P. P. P., *sortus*, is said by Fest. 422. 5 Th. (cf. Paul. Fest. 423. 1) to have been frequently used by Livius Andronicus ; Virgil (*A.* iv. 183) uses the full form *sub-rĭgo* in an active sense : tot subrigit aures ; on *vīs* beside *vŏlo*, see § 3. Other verbs, classed as Irregular, are the Defective Verbs : *coepi* (the Present *coepio* is found in O. Lat., see Georges, *Lex. Wortf.* s. v., e. g. Plaut. *Men.* 960 neque ego litis coepio ; *Pers.* 121 coepĕre Inf. ; on *coepi* dissyll. and *coëpi* trisyll., see ch. ii. § 150) ; *inquam* for

---

[1] *fŏret* beside *esset* seems to be a form of **fueret*, **bhwĕsēt*, like *soror-* from **swĕsōr* (ch. iv. § 10), or *Marci-por* for *-puer* ; the Oscan equivalent is fusíd, cf. Osc. fust Fut.

ind-squam (ch. iv. § 158) from the root seq^R-, 'to speak' (W. heb, O. W. hepp, 'quoth he,' &c.), the unweakened form of which appears in O. Lat. *insĕque* Imperat., *insequis*, 'narras, refers, et interdum pergis,' *C. G. L.* v. 78. 10 [or **in(d)-ve-quam* from the root weq^R-?]; *inque*, an Imperat. of *inquam*, is used by Plaut., and the 2 Sg., &c. of Pres., *inquis, inquit, inquiunt* and of Fut., *inquies, inquiet* are frequent, but *inquio* Pres. Ind. is not found till Late Lat. (cf. *inquio* 'dico,' *C. G. L.* iv. 250. 27). [On the parts in use of *inquam, ăio* for *ăgh-io (ch. iv. § 116), *infit*, see Neue ii². p. 612; *infio* is quoted from Varro by Priscian, i. p. 450. 17 H.; *ai* Imperat. (a dissyll.) is used by Naevius, *Com.* 125 R. uel aï uel nega (but *aie* 'incipe, dic,' *C. G. L.* v. 165. 7, like *infe* 'incipe, dic, narra,' *ib.* 211. 10, *infens* 'dicens,' *ib.* 211. 37); the two vowels of *aio* are sometimes united in a diphthong, e. g. *aibam* (dissyll.), *ain* (monosyll.) in a phrase like *ain vero?* 'do you really mean that?'; on the spelling *aiio*, see ch. i. § 7.]

Possum is found in the older writers in its uncompounded form *pŏtis* and *pŏtĕ sum* (examples in Georges, *Lex. Wortf.* s.v., Neue, ii². p. 600); *pote* is properly the Neuter of *potis*, e. g. *pote est* (class. *potest*), it is possible, but the Masc. (and Fem.) and Neut. forms are used of any gender and of any number, e.g. *potis est*, it is possible, Ter. *Phorm.* 379, credo equidem potis esse te, scelus, Plaut. *Pseud.* 1302; so with *potis* and *pote*, without *sum*, just as O. Ind. īśvará-, 'able,' which is used with the sense of 'can,' though generally agreeing with the subject, sometimes appears in the stereotyped form īśvarás (Delbrück, *Altind. Syntax*, p. 88). In Oscan we have a derivative verb used in this sense, putiians and putians 'possint,' putiiad and pútíad 'possit' (cf. Lat. *pŏtui*, like *mŏnui* from *moneo*), but the Latin derivative *potio* is used in the sense of 'potem facere,' *potior* (fourth and third Conj.) of 'potis fieri' [cf. *potior fieri* used in the sense of *potiri*, Plaut. *Cas.* 112 quam tu eius potior fias, like *certior* (and *certus*) *fieri*], e. g. eum nunc potiuit pater seruitutis, Plaut. *Amph.* 178; postquam meus rex est potitus hostium, *Capt.* 92; regni potiri, Cic. On *possĭmus* for *possumus* in MSS. of Virgil, *Ecl.* vii. 23 and perhaps viii. 63 : non omnia possumus omnes, also in the Verona Palimpsest of Gaius (99, 14; 101, 2), &c., see ch. ii.

§ 98.]   THE VERB. IRREGULAR VERBS.   547

§ 16. *Possem* for *potessem* has been explained by the Analogy of *possum* (for *pot(e)-sum*) beside *potis-sum*, *possim* beside *potis-sim*.

Malo, a contraction of *māvŏlo*[1], seems to come similarly from *măgĕ* (a byform of *magis*, ch. ix. § 4) united into a word-group with *vŏlo*, and *nōlo* from the Negative *nĕ-* and *volo*, though the exact process of phonetic or analogical change by which the various parts of these verbs arose is not easy to trace. Perhaps *măg(ĕ)-vŏlo* became **mavvŏlo* (written *māvolo*, as **cavvi* was written *cāvi*, § 39. 4), much as I.-Eur. g^u or gw became Lat. *v* (ch. iv. § 139). And *nĕ-vŏlo* (for the word-group cf. *ne-scio*, *nĕ-queo*, Engl. cannot) may have become **nŏvŏlo* as I.-Eur. **nĕwos* became Lat. *nŏvus* (ch. iv. § 10), and similarly **novis*, **novolt*, **novolumus*, **novoltis*, **novolunt*. By loss of intervocalic *v* (ch. ii. § 53) arose *nōlo* (the only form known to Plautus), *nōlumus*, *noltis* (ap. Diom. 386. 19 K.), *nōlunt*, while O. Lat. *nĕ-vis*, *nĕ-volt*, as well as class. *non-vis*, *non-vult*, *non-vultis* are re-formations. On Imperat. *nōlī* see § 2, and on the spellings *mallo*, *nollo*, ch. ii. § 129. Another account of *mā-volo* makes its first element the Comparative Adverb **mā, **mō (see ch. x. § 6 on *im-mo*), and not *mage*.

§ 98. **Irregular Verbs in Romance.** Of Lat. *sum* the Vulg. Lat. Inf. *essĕre* (Ital. essere, Fr. être, Span. ser), and P. P. P. *status* (Ital. stato, Fr. été), have been already mentioned (§§ 83, 92); the Pres. Subj. seems to have been *siam* (Ital. sia, Span. sea, O. Fr. soie). For Lat. *eo* various verbs were united in the Vulg. Lat. paradigm, e. g. Fr. je vais (from Lat. *vādo*), nous allons (from Lat. *ambulo* ?). Lat. *hăbeo* was, owing to its Auxiliary use, shortened to a declension like *hayo*, *has*, *hat* . . . *haunt* (Ital. ho, hai, ha . . . hanno ; Fr. ai, as, a . . . ont; Span. he, has, ha . . . han). Vulg. Lat. *voleo*, *volēre* Inf. (Ital. voglio, volere ; Fr. veux, vouloir) by Analogy of Pft. *volui*, as Vulg. Lat. *potēre* (Ital. potere, Span. poder) by analogy of *potui*, have been cited in §§ 33 *a*, 83.

---

[1] Both *mavolo* and *malo*, *mavelim* and *malim* occur in Plautus, but *malo*, *malim*, &c. are predominant later, though we have *mavolo* once at the end of a line in Terence, *Hec.* 540. *Mallem* is not found in Plautus, only *mavellem* (Solmsen, *Stud. Lautg.* p. 55.)

CHAPTER IX.

ADVERBS AND PREPOSITIONS.

§ 1. ADVERBS. Latin Adverbs are for the most part cases of Nouns, Adjectives (or Participles), and Pronouns, the cases most frequently found being the Accusative (cf. O. Ind. náktam, 'by night,' satyám, 'truly,' Acc. Sg. Neut., pratarā́m Acc. Sg. Fem., Gk. πρότερον Acc. Sg. Neut., μακράν Acc. Sg. Fem., κρύφα Acc. Pl. Neut.), Ablative (cf. O. Ind. dūrā́t, 'afar') [also Instrumental (?), cf. O. Ind. dívā, 'by day,' Gk. ἄλλῃ]¹, and Locative (cf. O. Ind. dūrḗ, 'afar,' Gk. οἴκοι, ἀναιμωτεί, ἑκοντί), and often retain case-forms which have become obsolete in the ordinary declension. Thus, *-im*, the original form of the Acc. Sg. suffix of I-stems (ch. vi. § 29), which in classical Latin was replaced by the *-em* of Consonant-stems, e. g. *partem* from the stem *parti-*, like *militem* from the stem *milit-*, is retained in Adverbs like *partim*, and in the Adverbial Accusatives of Verbal Noun I-stems, e.g. *raptim* from the stem *rapti-* (class. *raptiōn-*, ch. v. § 42), *sensim* from the stem *sensi-* (class. *sensiōn-*), *uni-versim* (Osc. úíníveresím) &c.; *nox*, an old equivalent of *noctu*, seems to be an early byform of *noctis* Gen.; *-ē* (older *-ĕd*), the suffix by which Adverbs derived from Adjective O-stems are formed in the Italic languages, is an Abl. Sg. suffix (parallel with *-ō*, older *-ōd*, ch. vi. § 33), which has been reserved for Adverbs alone. The Adverbial suffix *-tus* (I.-Eur. *-tŏs) of *fundĭ-tus, dīvīnĭ-tus*, &c., is in O. Ind. occasionally used as an Ablative suffix (Sing. or Plur.) of Nouns, e. g. mātṛ-tas, Abl. Sg. of mātár-, 'a mother,'

---

¹ In O. Ind. the Instr. Case is in the Noun Declension used to denote the sphere of motion, 'by the route of.' (Delb. *Altind. Synt.* p. 129.)

§ 1.] ADVERBS. 549

śatru-tas, Abl. Pl. of śátru-, 'an enemy'; and this close relation of Noun and Adverb suffixes makes it difficult to draw any hard and fast line between the suffixes used in the formation of Adverbs, and the suffixes used in the declension of Nouns. An example of a purely Adverbial suffix is *-iēs* (older *-iens*), by which most Numerals form their Adverbs, e. g. *sex-ies* (cf. *tŏt-ies, quŏt-ies*), or the **-mente* of the Romance languages, e. g. Fr. facile-ment, Span. facil-mente, which is nothing but the Abl. Sg. of Latin *mens*, just as the *-versus, -versum* (older *-vorsus, -vorsum*) of *quāquāversus* (*-m*), *ăliōvorsum* (contracted *aliorsum*), *retrōvorsum* (contracted *retrorsum, retrosum*), *rursus* (*-m*). for *reversus* (*-m*), &c. are nothing but the Nom. Sg. Masc. (see below) and Acc. Sg. Neut. of the P. P. P. of *verto*, to turn, or as the *-tĕnus* of *hactenus, ăliquātenus*, &c. is the Acc. Sg., employed adverbially, of the old neuter noun *tenus*, a stretching, used by Plautus in the sense of a string or snare (§ 54). The Adverbs derived from Pronouns, e. g. *ĭbi, inde, illinc*, offer special difficulty, because of our ignorance of the full number of case-suffixes used in the I.-Eur. declension of the Pronoun. Thus *-am* of *quam, tam, nam, jam* is naturally taken as Acc. Sg. Fem., but it has also been referred to an Instrumental formation with the suffix -m, -mĭ, which appears in the Instrumental case of Nouns and Pronouns in Balto-Slavic (ch. vi. § 36); and various other Latin Adverbs in *-m*, usually called Accusatives, have been referred to the same source.

Adverbs in *-ter*, e. g. *brĕvĭter*, are best explained as Nominatives Singular Masc. of stems in -tĕro-, a Stem-suffix which occurs in various pronominal and locative Adjectives, e. g. *al-ter, dex-ter*, &c. (ch. v. § 16) (*ĭ-terum* is an Acc. Sg. Neut. of a similar formation), though they have been also referred to the noun *ĭter, brev-iter* corresponding to German kurz-weg. Other examples of a Nom. Sg. Masc. Adjective stereotyped as an Adverb are probably *deinceps*, which was declined in O. Lat. like *princeps*, though it might be regarded as Acc. Sg. Neut. (cf. exordium princeps), *demus* an O. Lat. byform of *dēmum*; more certainly *adversus, rursus*, &c., the byforms of *adversum, rursum*, and other compounds of *versus* (*-m*), &c.

Examples of Acc. Sg. Neut. forms are, beside the Adverbs in

-*tim* (-*sim*) just mentioned, Adverbs in -*um* like *ĭ-terum*, another time (Acc. of *itero-, O. Ind. ítara-, 'other,' from the Pronoun-stem i-, ch. vii. § 13, with the suffix -tero-, ch. v. § 16), *cē-terum* (ch. x. § 5), *commŏdum* (beside *commode*), *multum*, *părum* (§ 7), *plērum-que* (p. 559), *vērum*, *tantum*, along with some Superlatives like *mĭnĭmum* (usually *minime*), *potissimum*, *insānum* (not *insane* in Plaut.) 'very,' and occasional Adverbs from I-stem Adjectives, e.g. *făcĭlĕ*, *difficile*, *sublīmĕ* (though -*iter* is the usual suffix, e. g. *breviter*, *fĭdēliter*, the formation in -*ĕ* being reserved for poetry, e. g. dulce ridentem . . . dulce loquentem, Hor.). The comparative degree of the Adverb is always the Acc. Sg. Neut. of the Comparative Adjective, e. g. *longius*, *facilius*, *brevius*. Accusatives Sing. of Nouns used Adverbially are *vĭcem*, *id gĕnus*, &c., to which we may add an Acc. Pl. *fŏrās*, which is only used with verbs of motion towards (*foras ire*, like *rus ire*, *domum ire*), and seems to be Acc. Pl. of *fora (Gk. θύρα), a door. Of Acc. Pl. Neut. forms we have *ceteră* (Virg. *A*. ix. 656 cetera parce puer bello), *omnia* (Virg. *A.* iv. 558 omnia Mercurio similis; *C. I. L.* vi. 1144 omnia magno Constantino), possibly the O. Lat. forms *contră* [for which *contrā*, an Abl. Sg. Fem., was used in class. Lat., and *contrud*, an Abl. Sg. Neut. (cf. Lat. *contrō-versia*), in Oscan], and *frustră* (class. *frustrā*).

Of Ablatives we have for O-stems, beside the *ēd*-suffix already quoted (a suffix used to form the Superlative Degree of Adverbs, e. g. *facillĭme*, O. Lat. *facilumed*, *brevissĭme*), the ordinary *ōd*-suffix (ch. vi. § 33), e. g. *certo* (beside *certe*), *vero* (beside *vere*), *assĭduo* (usually *assidue*), *explōrāto* (and *explorate*), *mĕrĭto* and *immerito* (neither of these are Adverbs in Plautus, for they are used with *meo*, *tuo*, &c.), *festīnāto* (also *festinatim*), *fortuīto* (also *fortuitu*; see ch. v. § 49). Examples of Ablatives Sg. Fem. are *dextĕrā* (scil. *parte*), *rectā* (scil. *via*), *eādem* (scil. *opĕra*), *extrā*, *suprā*. As was pointed out before (ch. vi. § 36), the loss of final *d* after a long vowel at the beginning of the 2nd cent. B. C. makes it impossible to be certain that some of these 'Ablatives' (e. g. *ūna*, *omnīno*) are not really Instrumentals (e. g. Gk. λάθρᾱ, κοινῇ?); for it is natural to suppose that the Instrumental suffix, whose existence in the Latin declension of Nouns is difficult to establish (ch. vi. § 36), may have survived in Latin as an Adverbial suffix. The shortening of -ō (by the Law of Breves Breviantes, ch. iii. § 42) in cĭtŏ, mŏdŏ, and of -ē in bĕnĕ, mălĕ, is no proof that these words ended originally in -ŏ, -ĕ (Instr.) and not in -ōd, -ēd (Abl.), but should be referred to their greater use in every-day speech (cf. hăvĕ beside mŏnē, &c. in Quintilian's time, ch. iii. § 42), and their more frequent occurrence in word-groups, e. g. *bene-rem-gĕras, male-sānus* (cf. *diĕquinti* beside *fĭdē*, ch. iii. § 44). It is only rarely that the occurrence of an Adverb on an old Latin inscription, or on inscriptions written in Oscan, or some other dialect which retained -*d*, enables us to decide, e. g. O. Lat. *meritod (meretod), porod, extrad, suprad*, Osc. *contrud*, Falisc. rected, which are Abl. forms, Osc. suluh, 'wholly,' from the stem *sollo-*, all, whole, which is called an Instrumental form (but see ch. vi. § 36). The third Declension 'Abl.' (originally a Consonant-stem Locative, ch. vi. § 37) appears in *fortĕ, spontĕ, rĕpentĕ* (O. Lat. *dĕrepente*), &c., and the Plural Abl. (Instr. Loc.) in *grātīs* (older *gratiis*), 'for mere thanks' (cf. Ter. si non pretio, at gratiis), *ingratiis (ingratis), fŏrīs* (used with verbs of rest, e. g. foris manere, occasionally with verbs of motion from, e. g. foris venire), *alternis*. Examples of Locatives of U-stems are *hŭmi* (first found in Terence, Andr. 726), *postrī-diē, die crastĭnī, noctū* (cf. O. Ind. aktā́ú) (see ch. vi. §§ 37–38).

Pronominal Adverbs show various suffixes: (1) -*bī* (older -*bei*) with locative sense, e. g. *ĭbī, ŭbī*, also *ibĭ, ubĭ*, with final vowel either shortened by the Breves Breviantes Law (ch. iii. § 42), or originally short (cf. Osc. puf); (2) -*ī* (older -*ei*), the Locative O-stem suffix, e. g. O. Lat. *illi, isti*, there, which in classical Latin always have the particle -*c(e)* appended, *ill-ī-c, ist-ī-c*; (3) -*ō*, to indicate motion to a place, e. g. *eō, quō, istō, aliō*, apparently Abl. forms like *porrō* (O. Lat. *porod*); O. Lat. *hoc, istoc, illoc* may represent **hŏd-c(e), *istŏd-c(e), *illŏd-ce*, Acc. Sg. Neut., for in class. Lat. we have *huc, istuc, illuc*; (4) -*ā*, to indicate direction, manner, &c., e. g. *qua, ea*, which like *quo, eo* are Abl. forms (O. Lat. *arvorsum ead*), not Instrumental like Greek πῆ, ταύτῃ, πάντῃ (afterwards confused with Dative -ῃ); (5) -*im*, to indicate motion from a place, e. g. *illim, istim*, which in class. Lat. always append the particle -*ce, illinc, istinc* (cf. *hinc, dehinc*); (6) -*nde*, with similar sense, in *unde, inde*; this *inde* is shortened by syncope of the final vowel to -*in* in the Compounds *proin, dein*,

552   THE LATIN LANGUAGE.   [Chap. IX.

exin, &c. (ch. iii. § 36). Other endings like *-dam* of *quondam* (cf. *quidam*), *-dem* of *quĭ-dem*, *tan-dem*, with the sense of 'exactly,' 'precisely' in *ibi-dem*, *tantī-dem* (cf. *īdem*, ch. vii. § 21), *-tem* of *ĭ-tem*, *-ta* of *ĭ-ta*, are apparently case-forms of pronominal stems, as *-quam* of *un-quam*, *us-quam* (cf. *quis-quam*), appears to be Acc. Sg. Fem. of the stem *q^{u}o-. (See ch. x. on the Conjunctions.) Other Adverb formations are (1) in *-fāriam*, indicating division, e.g. *bĭ-fariam*, *quadrĭ-fariam* (cf. Gk. -φάσιος from -φατιος, e.g. τρι-φάσιος); (2) in *-sĕcus*, indicating motion from a place; this *secus* is an Adverbial Noun, and is appended to Adverbial forms in *-im*, e.g. *extrin-secus*, *intrin-secus*, *altrin-secus*, as *-tenus* to Abl. Sg. Fem. forms, e.g. *quā-tenus*, *aliquā-tenus*, *eā-tenus*; it is derived from the root seq^u-, 'to follow,' and must be distinguished from (1) the Adverb *sĕcus*, otherwise (O. Ir. sech, 'beyond,' W. heb, 'without'); (2) the Adverbial Noun *sĕcus*, a Neuter byform of *sexus*, used in phrases like: trecenti occisi sunt virile secus, '300 were killed of the male sex' (see § 50 on the Preposition *secus*). The Abl. *fīnī* (*fīnĕ*) occurs in O. Lat., like *tenus*, after an Abl., e.g. senem osse fini dedolabo, Plaut., oleas operito terra radicibus fini, Cato; but came to take a Genitive, e.g. amphoras nolito implere nimium, ansarum infimarum fini, Cato; fine inguinum ingrediuntur mare, Sall.

Instances of Adverbial word-groups are *ad-fătim*, sufficiently, lit. 'to weariness,' *ad-mŏdum*, *quem-ad-modum*, *quā-rē*, *quam-ob-rem*, *dē-nuō* for *de nŏvo*, *sē-dŭlō* for *se dolo*, *ī-līcō* perhaps for *in sloco* (old form of *lŏco*), *ī-licet*, *scī-licet*, *vĭde-licet*, *im-prīmis*, *dumtaxat*, &c.

In the Romance languages Lat. *mente* (p. 549) is the favourite Adverbial suffix, though Lat. *-ō* (*-um*) is not uncommon, e.g. Vulg. Lat. *altō* or *altum* (Ital. alto, Fr. haut, Span. alto) (*-iter* has been lost). *Mente* (Abl. of *mens*) retains a trace of its independence in usages like Span. temeraria y locamente, O. Fr. humle e dulcemente. So firmly has it established its footing as Adverbial suffix that it is even added to already formed Adverbs, e.g. Ital. quasimente, O. Fr. ausiment. (For fuller details of the formation of Adverbs in Romance, see Meyer-Lübke, *Rom. Gram.* ii. pp. 637 sqq.).

§ 2.] ADVERBS. 553

§ 2. **Nominative Adverb-forms.** *Breviter*, &c. are better considered Nom. Sg. Masc. than Acc. Sg. Neut. for **brevi-terum*, since the loss of *-um* seems only to occur in a few words of constant use, such as *noenum*, *ni(hi)lum*, which came to be employed exclusively in that doublet-form which the words assumed before a vowel, e. g. *no(e)n(um) est, ni(hi)l(um) habeo* (ch. iii. § 52). *Iterum* did not become **iter*, nor *ceterum*, **ceter*. The crystallizing of the Nom. Sg. Masc. of the Adjective as an Adverb, used with any number or gender, finds a parallel in the extension of *pŏtĭs*, properly Nom. Sg. Masc., Fem. only, e. g. *potis sum, potis es, potis est ille, potis est illa*, to all persons and numbers of the Verb, e. g. *quî istuc potis est fieri?*, Plaut., with Neuter subject (see ch. viii. § 97). The Adverbs (Prepositions) *praeter, propter*, &c. might be similarly explained ; *praeter it ille*, **praetera it illa*, **praeteri eunt illi* became *praeterit, praetereunt* without distinction of gender or number (but see p. 554). *Nūper* (Superl. *nuperrime*) appears to be Nom. Sing. Masc. of the Adjective *nupĕro-* (Plaut. *Capt.* 718 recéns captum hominem, núperum, nouícium) for **nŏvĭ-pĕro-*, 'newly acquired,' unless it is Acc. Sg. Neut. of an I-stem Adj. (ch. v. § 34) for **nupere*. *Făcul* (Paul. Fest. 61. 32 Th. 'facul' antiqui dicebant et 'faculter' pro facile ; Fest. 266. 20 Th. 'perfacul' antiqui, et per se 'facul' dicebant, quod nunc facile dicimus ; Non. 111. 21 M. 'facul' pro faciliter, huic contrarium est 'difficul'), a word used by Lucilius in his description of the Roman patricians (vi. 2 M.) :

peccare inpune rati sunt
posse, et nobilitate facul propellere iniquos,

is better regarded as Neut. Sg. for *facile*, with syncope of *-ĕ*, as in *volup* for *volupe*, Neut. of **volupis* (ch. iii. § 36), than as Nom. Sg. Masc. of an Adj.-stem *faculo-* (cf. *sacri-ficulus*), since the reduction of *-lŏs* to *-l* seems to be dialectal only (e. g. Oscan *famel*) (ch. vi. § 4), and not, like the reduction of *-rŏs* to *-r* (e. g. Lat., Umbr. *ager*, Gk. ἀγρός), shared by Latin. We have *difficŭl* Nom. Sg. Neut. in Varro *Men.* 46 B. :

quod utrúm sit magnum an párvum, facile an díffícul.

Sĭmŭl (older *semol, C. I. L.* i. 1175, in MSS. of Plautus *semul*, e. g. *Rud.* 760, *Men.* 405) (Umbr. sumel?) may be Acc. Sg. Neut. of *sĭmĭlis*, unless it rather shows the L-suffix of O. Sl. ko-li, ko-lĕ, ' when,' to-li, to-lĕ, ' then,' &c. ; *simul* and *simulter* (a byform of *similiter*, used by Plaut. *Pseud.* 382) correspond to *facul* and *faculter*. *Deinceps* was declined like *princeps* in O. Lat. (Paul. Fest. 53. 1 Th. 'deincipem' antiqui dicebant proximo quemque captum, ut principem primum captum ; cf. *ib.* 50. 5), and may have been associated with *princeps* in a fragmentary line on the Lex Repetundarum (*C. I. L.* i. 198. 79) : iudex deinceps faciat pr[incipe cessante]. *Dēmus* (cf. Gk. τῆμος) was used by Livius Andronicus (Paul. Fest. 49. 27 Th.) ; it is the reading of the Palatine family of MSS. in Plaut. *Truc.* 245 : qui dé thensauris íntegris demús danunt (demum oggerunt A), and is required by the metre in *Trin.* 781. In the Adverbial compounds of *versus* the terminations *-us* and *-um* compete in the early literature, e. g. *rursum* and *rursus* (also *russum, rusum*, &c., ch. ii. § 104; *rursum* appears to be used in Plaut. after Compounds with *re-*, e.g. redeo rursum, and at the end of the line), *prorsum* (with local sense in Plaut. *Pers.* 677 simulato quasi eas prorsum in navem ; *Mil.* 1193, &c.) and *prorsus* (cf. *prosa oratio*), *sursum* and *sursus*, but in the classical period one of the rival forms often has the monopoly, e.g. *rursus, prorsus, sursum* (for statistics, see Ritschl, *Opusc.* ii. 259 ; Neue, *Formenl.* ii³. 743). These compounds show other adverbial suffixes in *ūniversim* (Osc. úiníveresím), *ūnōse* for **unō-vorse* (Pacuv. *Trag.* 213 R. óccidisti, ut múlta paucis uérba unose obnúntiem). On the Preposition *versus*, see § 58. Adverbs in *-ter* are in classical Latin almost confined to Adjectives of the third Decl. (Cicero in his earlier writings uses *hūmāniter*, but finally discarded it for *hūmānē*), but in the older literature are often formed from O-stem Adjectives [Priscian, ii. 70. 20 H. gives a list of these from the older writers, e. g. *ămīcĭter, maestĭter*, Plaut., and the eleventh book of Nonius is devoted to obsolete Adverb forms, especially (1) Adverbs in *-ter* from O-stem Adjs., (2) in *-ĕ* from I-stem Adjs, e. g. *cĕlĕre, fĭdēle*, (3) in *-tus*, e. g. *mĕdullĭtus, largĭtus, commūnĭtus*]. The NT-stems have *-nter*, e. g. *vehementer, impŭdenter*, instead of *-nt-ter* (cf. 3 Pl. Imper. *fĕruntō* for **feront-tōd*, ch. viii. § 57), by dissimilation, some say, for **-nt-i-ter* (ch. iii. § 13, p. 176). From *audāx* we have *audacter* (less commonly *audācĭter*; see Georges, *Lex. Wortf.* s. v.), but from *fallāx, fallāc--ĭter*, from *lŏquāx loquācĭter*, from *prŏcāx procācĭter*, &c. *Difficulter* is more usual than *difficĭlĭter* (see Georges); *făculter* is mentioned by Paul. Fest. (61. 32 Th. 'facul' antiqui dicebant et 'faculter'), but *făcĭlĭter* (see Georges) was the form that competed with *facilē* (cf. Mart. Cap. iii. 325 cum difficulter dicamus, cur 'faculter' dici non potest?); *simulter* is quoted from Plaut. *Pseud.* 382 by Nonius 170. 19 M. Quintilian condemns both *audaciter* and *faciliter* [i. 6. 17 inhaerent ei (*sc.* analogiae) quidam molestissima diligentiae perversitate, ut 'audaciter' potius dicant quam audacter, licet omnes oratores aliud sequantur, et 'emicavit' non emicuit, et 'conire' non coire; his permittamus et 'audivisse' et 'scivisse' et 'tribunale' et 'faciliter' dicere], regarding *audacter* and *facile* as the true Latin forms.

Other Adverbs that might be called Nominative forms are: *ēmĭnus* and *commĭnus* (the spelling *co-minus* is due to the analogy of *ē-minus*; see Georges s. v.), which may be Nom. Sg. of Compound Adjectives (cf. Gk. αὐτό-χειρ, e. g. Soph. *Ant.* 1175 Αἵμων ὄλωλεν, αὐτόχειρ δ' αἱμάσσεται); *rĕcens* (used with a Perfect Participle, e. g. Lucr. vi. 791 nocturnumque recens extinctum lumen), which is equated with *lĭbens* by Charisius (114. 21 K.): utimur sic 'recens venit,' quod est pro adverbio nomen, ut 'libens dixit.' (Similarly *rĕpens* comes very near *rĕpentĕ* in phrases like Liv. xxii. 8. 1: repens alia nuntiatur clades); *prō-tĭnus* (also *prō-tĕnus*), 'stretching forward,' may be the Nom. Sg. of an O-stem, as the (somewhat doubtful) form *prō-tenis* (Afran. *Com.* 107 R. cómissatum prótenis rectá domum Digredimur) may be the Nom. Sg. of an I-stem (ch. v. § 34); *sĕcus* in *intrin-secus*, &c., has been sometimes explained as Nom. Sg. of an Adj. **seco-*, lit. 'following from within.' But these, and indeed all the Adverbs cited as Nominatives, are capable of other explanations; *recens* (like *deinceps*) as Acc. Sg. Neut.; *cominus, eminus* [with the other Adverbs in *-s, rursus* and other compounds of *versus* (*vorsus*)] as augmented with the same particle *-s* (p. 573) as appears in Greek μέχρι(ς), ἀμφίς (and ἀμφί), εὐθύ(s), &c. (with *dēmus* cf. Gk. ἦμος, τῆμος, and for *-tenus, -secus*, see above); *praeter, propter, subter* are best explained as suffixless Locatives (ch. vi. § 37) like O. Ind. prā-tár, 'early,' sanu-tár, 'away,' Lat. *super* and Gk. ὑπέρ (cf. O. Ind. upár-i, with the Locative suffix), Lat. *inter* and O. Ind. antár (but antári-kša-), though they are also capable of being referred to the O. Ind. ending of local Adverbs, *-tra* (I.-Eur. *-trĕ*?); e. g. tátra, 'there,' yátra, 'where,' anyátra (Lat. *ălĭter*?), 'elsewhere,' **prai-trĕ*, &c. becoming by syncope **prai-ter*, &c.; *prŏcul* has been similarly explained as **pro-tle* (ch. iv. § 105), by Dissimilation from **pro-tre* (ch. iv. § 84), or as Acc. Neut. Sg. of a compound Adjective, whose second element

§§ 3, 4.] ADVERBS. 555

is from the same root, qʉel-, as Gk. τῆλε, πάλαι, but it is more naturally referred to some extension of the Preposition *prŏ* by a *co*-suffix (cf. *rĕcĭ-prŏcus* from *re-co-* and *pro-co-*, O. Sl. pro-kŭ) ; *nūpĕr* (Superl. *nuperrime*) may have as its second component the Preposition *per* of *antio-per* (§ 7), *sem-per* (?), Osc. *pert* in *petiro-pert* ' quater,' and as its first the adverbial particle *nŭ (O. Ind. nú, ' now,' Gk. νῦ-ν, νῠ, Lat. *nu-dius tertius*, &c., ch. x. § 10). The existence of Adverbs in Latin derived from Nom. Sing. case-forms is thus at once natural to imagine and difficult to prove.

§ 3. **Genitive Adverb-forms.** Examples of *nox*, used for *noctū*, in O. Lat. are XII Tab. : si nox furtim faxit ; Enn. *Ann.* 439 M. :

si luci, si nox, si mox, si jam data sit frux ;

(cf. Plaut. *Asin.* 598, and see Gell. viii. lemm. 1). In Lucil. iii. 22 M. it is qualified by *mediā*, as if *nocte* :

hinc media remis Palinurum peruenio nox.

The parallel Adverbs in other I.-Eur. languages, e. g. Gk. νυκτός, O. Ind. aktós, ' by night,' vástōs, ' by day' (cf. Germ. nachts), suggest that it is a Genitive form (see however ch. iii. § 16). *Dius*, in O. Lat. ' by day,' may then be likewise a Genitive form (I.-Eur. *dĭw-os was the Gen. of the word for ' day,' O.-Ind. divás Gen., Gk. Διfός Gen.) and *inter-dius*. They have also been explained as suffixless Locatives (ch. iv. § 37), like O. Ind. sa-dívas, ' at once,' pūrvē-dyús, ' early in the morning ' (so *pĕnĕs* may be a suffixless Loc. of *pĕnus* Neut. § 37). Examples of *dius* are, Plaut. *Merc.* 862 noctu neque dius ; Titin. *Com.* 13 R. noctu diusque. *Interdius* is more common, e.g. Plaut. *Asin.* 599 : nunc enim ésse

negótiosum intérdius uidélicet Solónem ;

(other instances in Georges, *Lex. Wortf.* s. v.), just as *interdiū* became the usual word for ' by day,' while *diū* [formed on the analogy of *noctū*, a U-stem Loc. (ch. vi. § 37), according to one theory] is seldom found in this sense. (It is found only in conjunction with *noctu*, at least in the older writers). Nonius (98. 20 M.) gives as examples Plaut. *Cas.* 823 (apparently anapaestic) :

noctúque et diu ut uiro súbdola sis ;

Aul. fr. 4 nec noctu nec diu ; Titin. *Com.* 27 R. (in his play about the life of the *fullones*) :

nec nóctu nec diú licet fullónibus quiéscant.

[On *diu*, for a long time, see ch. x. § 12 ; we have *quandius* for *quamdiu* in the epitaph of a litter-bearer (*C.I.L.* vi. 6308), *quamdius* (vi. 13101)]. *Mox* has been, like the Adverb *nox*, explained as an old Genitive-form, or a form with the Adverbial suffix -s (a variety of -sŭ, -sĭ, the suffix of the Loc. Plur.?, cf. Gk. πέριξ and μεταξύ) ; its cognates are O. Ind. makṣū́, ' soon, quickly,' an Adverb from the Adjective makṣú-, ' quick,' O. Ir. mos- (e. g. mos-ricub, 'I will soon come'), moch, ' early.' *Vix* (connected with *vicem* ?) must be of similar formation. *Per-nox* is an Adj. (e. g. lunā pernocte, Ov.), so in Late Lat. *pernox et perdius, -a, -um.*

§ 4. **Accusative Adverb-forms.** The Adverbial use of the Accusative Case was a feature of I.-Eur. syntax. In addition to the Latin examples already given (*vĭcem, id gĕnus, sĕcus* in *vĭrīle secus*, &c.), may be mentioned *partem* (e. g. *magnam partem, maximam partem*), *principĭum* (e.g. Cato, *R. R.* 157. 1 de brassica pythagorea, quid in ea boni sit salubritatisque, principium te cognoscere oportet). When used alone as an Adverb, the Acc. Sg. *partem* retains its old form *partim* (see Gell. x. 13 on *partim hominum venerunt* and Cato's *cum partim illorum erat*). If *saltem* is Acc. Sg. of **salti-*, a leap, lit. 'with a leap,' 'swiftly, easily, assuredly,' it has taken -*tem* by analogy of *au-tem*, *i-tem*, &c. [*saltim*, e.g. C. G. L. v. 146. 13, is, according to Georges, *Lex. Wortf.* s. v., a late spelling, like *decim* for *decem* (ch. ii. § 8; cf. B. P. W. xiii. 310], for the other Adverbial Accusatives of Verbal Nouns retain, in addition to the old Stem-suffix *-ti-* (class. *-tiōn-*, ch. v. § 42), the old form of the Case-suffix, *-im*. Other examples of these Verbal Adverbs are *dătātim* from the Frequentative *dătăre*, whence *datatim ludere*, to play at ball (Plaut. *Curc.* 296), a phrase used in the famous description of the coquette (' Naev.' *Com.* 75 R.) : quasi in choro

<blockquote>
ludéns datatim dát se et communém facit.
aliúm tenet, alii ádnictat, alibí manus
est óccupata, álii peruellít pedem,
alií dat anulum áspectandum, á labris
alium ínuocat, cum álio cantat, áttamen
aliís dat digito lítteras ;
</blockquote>

praesertim from *sero*, lit. 'in the front row' (cf. *dīsertim* O. Lat. for *diserte*) ; *tŏlūtim*, at a trot (see Nonius, 4. 1 M.), connected with *tollo* ; *strictim* (e.g. *strictim tondere*, as opposed to *per pectinem tondere*, Plaut. *Capt.* 268) from *stringo*, to graze, touch the surface ; *pĕdĕtemptim*, cautiously, like *sensim*, lit. 'feeling,' (Nonius quotes a byform *pedepressim*, 29. 1 M.) ; *passim* from *pando* ; *cursim*, hastily, for which Virgil and others use *cursu* [Abl. Sg. of the Verbal Noun-stem *cursu-*, like the Comedians' *curricŭlō* (fugere, abire, percurrere, &c.), Abl. Sg. of *curriculum* (cf. Plaut. *Trin.* 1103, *Stich.* 337)] ; *stătim*, at once, lit. 'standing,' 'on the spot' (like *īlĭcō*, § 7), is the Acc. Sg. of the Verbal Noun *stăti-* (class. *stătiōn-*), while O. Lat. *stătim* (for the *ā*, see Nonius, 393. 5 M. ; Donat. in *Phorm.* v. 3. 7), comes from a bystem *stāti-* (cf. *stătu-* and *stātu-*) ; in Plautus the word has the sense of 'standing to one's ground,' e.g. Plaut. *Amph.* 239 néc recedít loco quín statim rém gerat ; *ib.* 276 ita statim stant signa ; it does not mean 'at once' till Afranius' time (Langen, *Beitr.* pp. 16 and 337). Parallel with the Adjectives in *-āto-* derived from Nouns, e. g. *togatus* from *tŏga*, and, like them, not postulating the existence of a verb in *-are* (e.g. **togare*) (ch. v. § 28), are Adverbs in *-ātim* like *assulatim*, from *assŭla*, a splinter (e.g. Plaut. *Capt.* 832 áperite hasce ambás foris, Príus quam pultando ássulatim fóribus exitium ádfero), *guttatim* from *gutta*, *ostiatim* from *ostium*, *vicatim* from *vīcus*, *gradatim* from *grădus*, &c., also *paulatim*, *pauxillatim*, *nostratim* from *noster* ; cf. *nostrates*), and from proper names, *tongiliatim* (tongiliatim loqui, ... a Tongilio parasito, qui ... salutatus convicio responderet ; see Löwe, *Prodr.*), *zopyriatim*, Lucil. ix. 74 M. *Vir* forms its Adverb with *-ītim*, *vĭritim* (so *proprītim* Lucr. ii. 975). *Confestim* comes from a stem **festi-*. a byform of which, **festiōn-*, is indicated by the Verb *festīno*, from which Virgil (*A.* ix. 488) coined the Adj. *festīnus*. These Adverbs in *-tim* (*-sim*) were more frequent in early than in classical Latin (Gellius xii. 15 remarks on their frequency in the historian Sisenna), but returned into fashion at a later period (see A. L. L. viii. 98). *Vicissim* (which some derive from **vic-essi*, a Loc. Plur. of **vix*, Acc. *vicem*) is an abnormal form. In O. Lat. we have also *vicissatim*, with that substitution of *-atim* for *-im*, *-m*, which we see in two forms mentioned by Paul. Fest. 79. 12 Th., *interatim* for *intĕrim* and *interduatim* (cf. Plaut. *Truc.* 882?) for *interdum*. *Prō-tĭnus* (also spelt *prō-tenus* ; see Georges, *Lex. Wortf.* s. v.) meant (1) forward, onward (of

§ 4.]   ADVERBS.   557

space or time), e.g. en ipse capellas Protenus aeger ago, Virg.; sic vives protinus, Hor.; (2) without interval of space, e. g. Virg. *A.* iii. 416 cum protinus utraque tellus Una foret, of the traditional connexion of Italy with Sicily; (3) without interval of time, forthwith (its usual sense); *quā-tenus* (also spelt *qua-tinus*; see Georges), whose earlier form *quatenos* is quoted by Festus (346. 34 Th.) from a speech of Scipio Africanus, meant originally (1) 'as far as,' of space, then (2) 'as long as,' of time, then acquired a causal sense like our 'in so far as,' a usage found first in Lucr. ii. 927, &c., but avoided by the classical prose writers, as well as by Virgil; in later Latin it took also (4) the sense of 'quomodo,' 'qua ratione,' (5) the final sense of 'ut,' (6) the consecutive sense of 'ut,' (7) the force of an Acc. before an Inf., and was very widely used (see *A. L. L.* v. 399). (On the Prep. *tenus*, see § 54.) Adverbs in *-am* are usually called Accusatives Sing. Fem., though a new theory makes them relics of the old Ā-stem Instr. Sg. in -ām, of which -ā was a byform, and explains Gk. Adverbs in -ă like τάχα, ὦκα, κρύφα as Instrumentals in -m; see *I. F.* i. 17). Other examples quoted are: *perpĕram*, falsely, wrongly, said to be Acc. Sg. Fem. of *perperus* (cf. *C. G. L.* iv. 141. 19 'perperum,' perversum), sc. *viam*, an Adjective used by the Dramatist Accius in his poem on stage technique (*Pragmaticon*, fr. inc. i. M.), a precursor of Horace's *Ars Poetica*:

 discribere in theatro pérperos
popularis,

along with the derivative noun *perpĕritūdo* (fr. inc. ii. M.):

 ét eo plectuntúr poetae quám suo uitio saépius
 dúctabilitate ánimi nimia uéstra aut perperitúdine;

protinam, forth, forward, an O. Lat. Adverb, used always of motion forward from a place of rest (Langen, *Beitr.* p. 163), e. g. Plaut. *fr.* 16 G. dare pédibus protinam sése ab his regiónibus, and sometimes wrongly written *protinus* in MSS. of Plautus and Terence (e. g. Ter. *Phorm.* 190), seems to be an Acc. Sg. Fem. of an Adjective-stem **prŏtĭno-*, as *contīnuō* is Abl. Sg. Neut. of the Adjective-stem *continuus*; *prō-miscam* (e. g. Plaut. *Pseud.* 1062 ut meá laetitia laétus promiscám siet; cf. Paul. Fest. 281. 1 Th.) is similarly related to the usual *pro-miscue* (also *promisce*).

Of Accusative Plural, *ălĭās* (sc. vices), at other times, *altĕrās* quoted (apparently from Cato) by Paul. Fest. 20. 8 Th., *utrasque*, on both occasions, used by the historian Cassius Hemina (ap. Non. 183. 25 M.: in Hispania pugnatum bis. utrasque nostri loco moti), and by the comedian Caecilius Statius (*Com.* 225 R.:

 atque hércle,
utrásque. te, cum ad nós uenis, subfárcinatam uidi),

have been called Locative Plural forms like Gk. θύρασι, and the occasional use of *fŏrās* in the sense of *fŏrīs* (better explained as a vulgarism, e. g. Petron. 30, p. 21. 10 B.. III et pridie Kalendas Januarias C. noster foras cenat, the entry on the engagement-tablets of the wealthy parvenu, Trimalchio; cf. *ib.* 47, p. 32. 4 B.) has been referred to the same source; *contra* is an Adverb, not a Preposition (but *Pers.* 13 contra me astat; cf. *Pseud.* 156), in Plautus and Terence, e. g. *tueri contra* (cf. Liv. i. 16. 6 and ix. 6. 8 contra intueri), *auro contra vendere*, &c., and has the final vowel short like *frustrā* (for the quantity *-ă*, see Brix, *Trin.*[3]

introd. p. 20) [*ne frustrā sis*, 'don't mistake,' is frequent in Plaut.. but *frustra sum* (cf. *ita sum, bene sum*, &c.) is avoided by classical writers (*A. L. L.* ii. 3), though *frustra* in Plautus usually occurs with this verb (with other verbs *nequiquam*)]. *Contrā* can hardly be anything else than Acc. Plur. Neut. (cf. Gk. ἀντία Pl., ἀντίον Sg.) of **con-t(e)ro-* (ch. v. § 16) ; and *frustrā* may be the same case of a stem **frustro-*, whence *frustrari* [cf. Liv. ii. 31. 9 neque frustrabor cives meos neque ipse frustra dictator ero; Ennius in one of his *Saturae* (inc. 84 M.) plays on the words *frustra* and *frustrari* for four lines consecutively : nám qui lepide póstulat álterum frustrári, Quém frustratur frústra· eum dícit esse frústra, and so on, somewhat in the style of the Schoolmaster in the *Merry Wives of Windsor*] ; *torvā tueri* and similar adverbial Accusatives Pl. Neut. belong, like *dulce ridentem*, to the language of poetry. (Servius ad *Aen.* iii. 594 cetera Graius, &c., quotes from Sallust *sanctus alia* ; cf. Tac. *Ann.* xii. 3 juvenem et alia clarum, and see *A. L. L.* ii. 90).

The Comparative Degree of the Adverb is in Latin (as in Greek) expressed by the Acc. Sg. Neut. of the Adjective (the Superlative in Greek, but not in Latin, by the Acc. Pl. Neut.), e. g. *pejus* (Superl. *pessime*), *longius* (Superl. *longissime*). The Adverb corresponding to the Compar. Adj. *major* (pronounced ˙măj-jor,' ch. ii. § 55) is not **majus* but *măgis* ; this *magis*, properly **ma(h)is* (Osc. *mais*), takes its *g* from *magnus*, as *figūra* for **fīhura* (ch. iv. § 116) takes its *g* from *fingo*, and represents either I.-Eur. **mais* (**mais* ?), (Goth. mais), from a stem mā-, seen in O. Ir. mār (mōr), 'great,' or more probably **maĝhis* from a stem magh-, seen in O. Ind. máh-, 'great' (cf. the Oscan name Mahio-). In either case the suffix is -is, the weak grade of the Comparative suffix -ios, seen in Superlatives like Gk. πλε-ῖσ-τος, Goth. ma-is-ts, &c. (ch. vi. § 52), just as the -ιν of Att. πλεῖν, a byform of πλεῖον and πλέον, is the weak grade of -ion (see on these weak grades ch. iv. § 51, and on the Compar. suffix, ch. vi. § 53, and cf. *magis-tro-, minis-tro-*, Osc. mins-tro-). This *-is* seems to have been confused by the Romans with *-is*, the Nom. Sg. ending of I-stem Adjectives, like *facilis, potis*, so that from *măgis*, regarded as a Nom. Sg. Masc. or Fem., was formed *măgĕ*, a Nom. Sg. Neut., as *pŏtĕ* from *pŏtis* (cf. Serv. ad *Aen.* x. 481 nunc mage sit, &c. : 'mage '... propter metrum dictum est pro magis, sicut etiam 'pote ' pro potis, . . . quod adeo in usum venit ut etiam in prosa inveniatur ; Cicero in Frumentaria : mage condemnatum hominem in judicium adducere non posse), whence *māvŏlo* (pronounced **mavvolo*?, ch. viii. § 97) for *mag(e)-volo* ; *nĭmĭs* did not produce a parallel Neuter in *-ĕ*, **nime*, perhaps because there existed already a cognate Neuter in *-ium, nimium* (Neut. of the Adj. *nimius*) with Comparative sense, ' too much ' ; but *sătĭs*, a Noun meaning ' sufficiency ' (cf. *fătis*, § 7), and properly used in sentences like *satis est mihi divitiarum*, then extended as an Adverb to sentences like *satis divitiarum habeo, satis dives sum*, developed a Neuter **sate*, curtailed to *sat*[1]) ; *plus*, if *plous* on the S. C. Bacch. (*C. I. L.* i. 196, of 186 B. C.) be merely an expression of the sound *plūs* (as *plouruma, Cloul[i]* on the epitaph of the actor, i. 1297, seem to show for *ū*,

---

[1] Another explanation of *sat* makes it Neut. Sg. of a stem satu- (cf. Lith. sotùs, 'satisfying'), whence, with addition of the suffix -ro-, was formed the Latin Adj. *sătŭr* (stem satu-ro-). *Paene* may similarly represent **paenŭ* (cf. *pēnūria*). Satin (with the Interrog. Particle -nĕ) is used in questions, e. g. *satin abiit?* 'has he gone?' Terence puns on *satin* and *satis* in *Phorm.* 683 : Satin ést id ? Nescio hércle : tantum iússus sum.

§ 5.]   ADVERBS.   559

ch. iv. § 37), will have, like *magis* and *nimis*, the comparative suffix *-is*, and will represent **plo-is* [cf. *ploera*, 'plura,' an archaism used by Cicero in his laws (*Legg.* iii. 3. 6), *plo-ir-ume*, 'plurimi,' on one of the oldest Scipio epitaphs (i. 32, end of the third cent. B. C. ?)], with root plo-, a variety of the root ple- of Greek πλείων, πλεῖστος (ch. vi. § 55). That forms like *mage*, &c. are not mere expressions of a tendency to drop final *s* in pronunciation (ch. ii. § 137), we see from a line like Plaut. *Poen.* 461 : conténtiores máge erunt atque auidí minus, where the final of the word is elided (cf. ch. viii. § 78 on *-rĕ* and *-ris* in 2 Sg. Pass.).

For *plērum-que*, *plerum* is used in a passage of the historian Sempr. Asellio (ap. Prisc. i. p. 182. 13 H. ut fieri solet plerum, ut in victoria mitior mansuetiorque fiat), an Acc. Sg. Neut. of the O. Lat. Adjective *plerus*, used for example by Pacuvius, *Trag* 320 R. :

periére Danai, pléra pars pessúm datast.

Other examples of the Adverbial Acc. Sg. Neut. of I-stem Adjectives are : *vŏlŭp* for *volupĕ* (ch. iii. § 36) ; *impūnĕ* from *impunis*, a compound of *in* and *poena* ; *vīlĕ*, an Adverb in common use in the time of Charisius (116. 7; 187. 7 ; 183. 14 and 18 K.) ; *fĭdēlĕ*, quoted from Plaut. *Capt.* 439 (fac fidele sis fidelis) by Nonius, 512. 59 M. ; *sublīmĕ*, aloft. For this last we often find *sublimen*, as in the Plautine expressions *sublimen rapere*, *ferre*, *auferre*, which is nothing but an Adverbial word-group *sub limen*, ' under or up to the lintel ' (on the confusion in MSS. between *sublime*, *sublimem* and *sublimen*, see Ritschl, *Opusc.* ii. 462) ; *saepĕ*, Neut. of an old Adj. **saepis* (whence *saepio*) of which the Superl. is possibly to be read in Plaut. *Pers.* 633 :

úbi rerum omniúm bonarum cópiast saepíssuma,

'the most closely packed store,' ' the densest store ' (*frĕquens* seems to be connected with *farcio* by a similar transference of meaning).

Gellius (x. 1) says that Pompey consulted various authorities, and finally Cicero, on the question whether he should write *tertium* or *tertio* consul in the dedicatory inscr. on the temple of Victory, and by his advice wrote merely *tert.* The distinction between the two words is a slight one, ' during the third year' and 'in the third year.'

§ 5. **Ablative (Instr.) and Locative Adverb-forms.** The normal formation of Adverbs from O-stem Adjectives was in *-ē*, older *-ēd* (e. g. *facilumed* on the S. C. Bacch., *C. I. L.* i. 196 ; cf. Falisc. rected, Osc. *amprufid* ' improbe,' Umbr. rehte, *totce* ' publice '), a suffix which in classical Latin was distinctive of O-stems as -(*i*)*ter* of I- and Consonant-stems. The ending *-ō* (the Abl. suffix, originally *-ōd* ; possibly in some words the Instrumental suffix, originally *-ō*, but see below) competes, as we have seen, with *-ē* in some Adverbs formed from O-stem Adjectives, and is exclusively used by good writers in *sŭbĭto* (cf. O. Lat. *desubito*), *omnīno*, *mĕrĭto* (*meritod*, *C. I. L.* i. 190), the Abl. of *meritum*, desert (cf. Plaut. *Asin.* 737 meritissimo ejus), &c. Charisius seems to say that the use of *-o* for *-e* in Adverbs was a feature of some dialects of Latin (193. 16 K. non quia negem ultra Safinum interque Vestinos Teatinis et Marrucinis esse moris e litteram relegare, o videlicet pro eadem littera claudentibus dictionem). Adverbs formed from O-stem Nouns have *-ō*, e. g. *mŏdŏ*, with Adverb or Preposition prefixed in *postmodo*, *prŏpĕmodo* [these are not early forms; *postmodo* is indeed read in Ter. *Hec.* 208, but *propemodum* is the only form used in the old Drama. Asinius Pollio (Cic. *Fam.* x. 33. 1) seems to have introduced the form *postmodo* into prose, and Livy prefers it to *postmodum* (see Neue, ii³. p. 600)] ; O. Lat. *antigerio* (antiqui pro valde dixerunt, Paul. Fest. 6. 18 Th. ; vel admodum vel imprimis, Gl. Placid. ; cf. Gl. Philox.), a word described by Quintilian (viii. 3. 25 ; cf. i. 6. 40) as quite obsolete in his day, apparently Abl. Sg. of a Verbal Noun, an IO-stem (ch. v. § 4), *anti-gerium* from *antĕ* and *gĕro*, a carrying in front ; O. Lat. *nŭmĕro*, quickly, or too quickly, e. g. Plaut. *Men.* 287 numero huc aduenis ad prandium, whence Varro (ap. Non. 352. 32 M.) derives the name *Numerius*, 'prematurely born,' a Beneventan name first introduced into the Roman aristocracy, according to the tradition, by a Fabius who married the daughter of a rich citizen of Beneventum (Fest. 178. 32 Th.) ; *numero*, probably used originally with Verbs of motion, may mean ' with musical note or rhythm,' like Germ. nach Noten ; *vulgo* from *vulgus*; *princĭpio* (rarely Acc. Sg. *principium*) ; *impendio* (Abl. of *impendium*, outlay), used as an Adverb (Gell. xix. 7. 10 translates it by *impense*) by the Republican Dramatists, especially with *magis*, *minus*, e. g. Ter. *Eun.* 587 impéndio magis ánimus gaudebát mihi. Instead of *fortĕ*, the Nom. *fors* is sometimes used (e. g. Virg. *A.* ii. 139) with an ellipse of *sit an* [cf. *forsĭtan* (first in Terence¹) and *forsan* (first in Lucr.), often written *forsitam* and *forsam* (see Ritschl, *Opusc.* ii. 570) by Anal. of Advbs. in *-am*? cf. p. 69], while *fortasse* and *fortassis* (in O. Lat. followed by Acc. and Inf, e. g. Plaut. *Asin.* 36 ubi fit polenta, té fortasse dícere, but also; e. g. *Rud.* 140 fortásse tu huc uocátus es ad prándium) seem to be parts of a verb **fortare*, to assert. affirm, derived from O. Lat. *forctus*, strong, as *af-firmare* from *firmus*. *Opĕrĕ*, ' Abl.' of *opus*, appears in a great many Adverbial expressions, e. g. *magnŏpere*, *tantŏpere* for *magn(ō) opere, tant(ō) opere* (cf. Plaut. *Mil.* 75 me opere orauit maxumo). *Ritĕ* is a similar formation from **ris*, a by-form of *rītus* (cf. O. Ind. r̥tú-, 'the fitting time,' esp. for a sacrifice, r̥tá-, 'fitting, suitable,' P. P. P.. r̥tĕna, 'fitly, duly,' Adv. (Instr.)].

Tĕmĕrĕ (on the quantity of the final *e*, see *A. L. L.* iv. 51) is either the Loc. Sg. of a lost Noun **temus* (cf. O. Ind. támas-, ' darkness'), lit. ' in the dark,' or Acc. Sg. Neut. of a lost Adj. **temeris*, lit. 'darkly, blindly' (cf. O. Lat. *tĕmĕrĭter*). On the adverbial Locative cases of Nouns in common use, *hŭmī*, *dŏmī*, *militiae*, &c., see ch. vi. §§ 37-38. *Diē* whether with original *-ē* (cf. *eod die*, *C. I. L.* xi. 4766, an inscr. where *-d* is not invariably written after a long vowel ; *die noine* or *dze noine*, ' on the ninth day,' on the Dvenos inscr., if this reading be the correct one) or with original *-ēd* [cf. Falisc foied, apparently ' hodie ' (*Not. Scav.* 1887, pp. 262 and 307): foied vino pipafo kra karefo ' hodie vinum bibam, cras carebo'] occurs in a great many Adverbial word-groups, e. g. *postrī-die* (cf. *die crastini*), *prī-die*, *cottī-die* and *cotī-die* (spelt *quotidie* only by precisians, Quint. i. 7. 6), *pĕrendie*, *hŏ-die*, *mĕrī-die* (see ch. iv. § 112), from which was formed the Noun *merīdies*. *Cotti-die* can hardly represent anything but a compound of *dies* and the word *quot* in some form or other (cf. *quot Kalendis*², Plaut. *Stich.* 60 ; *quotannis*, and in Late Latin *quot diebus* and *quot dies*) with *co-* written for *quo-*, its equivalent in sound (ch. iv. § 137), but what that form was is not easy to say. Some make it *quō-tus*, a correlative of *tōtus* (cf. totos dies, Plaut. *Aul.* 73 ; totis horis, *Mil.* 212);

---

¹ Whether *forsitan* really occurs in Terence is doubtful. (*Fleck. Jahrb.* 1894, p. 284.)

² *cotidie*, the reading of the MSS. in Plaut. *Stich* 165, is changed by editors to *quot dies*.

others postulate a *quot-tus* (beside *quŏ-tus* from *quo-*) formed from *quot-* with that TO-suffix which is used in Ordinal Numerals, *quar-tus*, *quin-tus*, &c., just as *quot-umus* (Plaut. *Pseud.* 962. 1173) is formed on the type of *septumus*; others again suppose *quŏt(ĭ)tus* (O. Ind. katithá-) to have been a byform of *quŏtus*; *peren-die*, the day after to-morrow, is connected with Osc. *perum*, without (originally 'beyond'; cf. Gk. πέρᾱ), of the phrase *perum dolom mallom* 'sine dolo malo,' and means literally 'on the beyond day'; *hŏ-die* seems to join to *die* the bare stem *hŏ-* (but see ch. iii. § 51 on *sĭ-quidem*). (For other Abl. and Loc. Adverb-forms, see ch. vi. § 38.)

Eādem, at the same time, always with the Fut. or Fut. Pft. in Plautus, e. g. *Trin.* 577:

i hac, Lésbonice, mécum, ut coram núptiis
dies cónstituatur; eádem haec confirmábimus,

is occasionally found without ellipse of *ŏpĕrā*, e. g. *Capt.* 449:

séquere me, uiáticum ut dem á tarpezitá tibi:
eádem opera a praetóre sumam sýngraphum;

ūnā may, in some uses at least, have sprung from a similar phrase; cf. *Pseud.* 318:

quia pol quá opera credám tibi,
úna opera alligém canem fugitíuam agninis láctibus.

Of Adverbs in *-ē* from O-stems may be noticed: *valde* [the full form *vălĭde* is found in Plautus, *Pseud.* 145 (A.P), &c.] from *validus*; Cicero was the first to use it with an Adj.; *fĕrē* and *fermē* are related as Positive and Superl. (cf. p. 185).

§ 6. Adverbs in -tus. The best established in classical usage were *antīquĭtus*, *dīvīnĭtus*, providentially, *fundĭtus*, lit. 'from the ground,' 'from the bottom' (derived from *fundo-*, O. Ir. bonn, Gael. bonn, 'the sole, the ground or base'; cf. O. Ind. budhná-, Gk. πυθμήν and πύνδαξ, the bottom of a vessel, O. Engl. botm), *pĕnĭtus*, lit. 'from within' (see § 37 on *pĕnĕs*), *rādīcĭtus*, *intus*. *Intus* is used not only of motion from within, e. g. Plaut. *Men.* 218 euocate intus Culindrum, but also like Greek ἐντός (cf. ἐκτός), of rest within, e. g. *Capt.* 192 ibo intro atque intus súbducam ratiúnculam; cf. Lucil. ix. 59 M., who explains the distinction between *ad* and *apud* as the same as that between *intrō* and *intus*:

intro nos uocat ad sese, tenet intus apud se.

Quintilian declares the use of *intus* in the sense of *intro* (motion to within) to be a solecism (i. 5. 51). (The suffix *-tus*, when added to another preposition, *sub*, has the same variety of meaning; for *subtus*, like *intus*, denotes not merely motion from, but also rest in, e. g. uti subtus homo ambulare possit, Cato, R. R. xlviii. 2). But in the older and the later literature many other of these Adverbs occur. Nonius in his eleventh book, which deals with the Adverb forms of the older writers, cites *commūnĭtus*, *publĭcĭtus*, *pugnĭtus*, with the fist, *hūmānĭtus*, *immortālĭtus*, *largĭtus*, 'pro large'; and elsewhere mentions *ănĭmĭtus*, *germānĭtus*, *mĕdullĭtus* [from the *Saturae* of Ennius (l. 7 M.):

Enní poeta, sálue, qui mortálibus
uersús propinas flámmeos medúllitus],

ŏcŭlĭtus, prīmĭtus, sollemnĭtus, &c. From the Adverb *penitus* Plautus coined the Superlative Adj.-*penitissumus* (see Varro, *Men.* 522 B. ut ait Plautus 'penitissumae'), which is common in Late Latin. He uses in one passage an Adj. *penitus* (*Asin.* 40 usque ex penitis faucibus), which also found currency in the late literature (cf. *penitē* Adv., Catull. lxi. 178).

§ 7. Adverbial word-groups and compounds. *Antioper* πρὸ τούτου, Gloss. Philox., seems, if the reading is right, to represent **antia* [Acc. Pl. Neut. of **antio*-, Gk. ἀντίος : cf. *antiae* (sc. *comae*), front curls], with the Preposition *per* (on *o* for *u* after *i* in the unaccented syllable, e. g. *filiolus*, see ch. iii. § 18), as *părum-per* represents *părum* (Acc. Sg. Neut. of **par-o-*, little, a byform of *par-uo-*, *parvus*) with the same Preposition (cf. the Umbro-Oscan Numeral Adverbs, Umbr. triiu-per, 'three times,' Osc. *petiro-pert*, four times; on the form *pert*, see § 38). *Topper*, a word quite obsolete in Quintilian's day (i. 6. 40 ab ultimis et jam oblitteratis repetita temporibus, qualia sunt 'topper' et 'antigerio' et 'exanclare' et 'prosapia,' et Saliorum carmina vix sacerdotibus suis satis intellecta) seems to be a similar word-group with an Acc. Sg. Neut. **tod* (from the Pronominal-stem to-, ch. vii. § 13; cf. *is-tud*) governed by the Preposition *per*; according to the Roman grammarians (see Festus, p. 532 Th.) the word had two meanings, (1) 'cito, celeriter, temere,' e. g. Liv. Andronicus (a translation of Homer, *Od.* viii. 138 sq.):

> námque núllum peíus mácerat humánum
> quámde máre saéuom, uís et cui sunt mágnae;
> tópper córpus confríngent inportúnae úndae,

and in his translation of Bk. xii. 17:

> tópper cíti ad aédis uénimus Circái,

and of Bk. x. 395:

> tópper fácit hómines ut príus fuérunt;

(2) 'fortasse,' a later sense, e. g. Pacuvius (*Trag.* 424 R.):

> tópper tecum sít potestas fáxit si mecúm uelit,

and the historian Caelius Antipater (cotemp. of C. Gracchus): eadem re gesta, topper nihilo minore negotio acto, gratia minor esset. *Sem-per* may likewise have as its first element an Acc. Sg. Neut. **sem* (Gk. ἕν), and as its second the Preposition *per* (*sempiternus*[1] may then be a formation on the analogy of *aeviternus*; but see *Suppl. Arch. Glott. Ital.* i. 58). These examples suggest that in *paulis-per*[2], *tantis-per*, *aliquantis-per* the first element may be a Neuter-stem in *-is*, possibly a weak grade of Comparative *-ius* (cf. *măgĭs*, p. 558), and not, as is usually thought, an Abl. (Loc. Instr.) Plural form, *paulis*, 'by littles,' 'little by little.' The *-per* of these words however may be the Greek *-περ* of ὥσπερ, καθάπερ, &c. (ch. x. § 1). (On *nuper*, see § 2.) *Impraesentiārum* is more naturally analyzed into *in praesentia rerum* (a phrase which actually occurs in

---

[1] Explained as **sempe(r)ternus* with loss of *r* by Dissimilation (ch. ii. § 103).

[2] *Paulisper*, with the tall form of I to indicate the long quantity, occurs in *C. I. L.* vi. 27788.

§ 7.]   ADVERBS.   563

its full form ; see *A. L. L.* iv. 11), with suppression of one of two similarly sounding syllables (see p. 176), than into *in praesentia harum*, with ellipse of *rerum*. Another adverbial word-group, consisting of a Preposition with its Noun, is *affătim*, for *ad-fatim* from a lost noun *fatis, weariness (cf. *fatīgo*), e. g. Liv. Andr. *Com.* 5 R. affatim edi, bibi, lusi; Plaut. *Poen.* 534 bibas ... usque affatim, where *affatim* (perhaps better written *ad fatim*, for an early *affatim* would have become *affetim) means 'abundantly' ; it is also used with a Gen. in the sense of 'abundance,' e. g. Plaut. *Men.* 457 affatim hominumst.   Paul. Fest. 8. 34 Th. says : Terentius ' affatim' dixit pro eo quod est ad lassitudinem, which shows that the grammarians of the Empire still realized that *affatim* was a combination of the Preposition *ad* with a Noun (like *ad saturitatem*, Plaut. *Rud.* 758; *ad rāvim*, *Aul.* 336, *Cist.* 304 ; *praeconis ad fastidium*, Hor. *Epod.* 4. 12).   Indeed from the words of Gellius (vi. 7) we gather that in the second century A. D. the Adverb was divided in spelling and pronunciation into two words *ad fatim*, for he speaks of the pronunciation *áffatim* (like *ádmodum*) as unusual, only to be defended on the supposition that the phrase was one word and not two (quod 'affatim' non essent duae partes orationis, sed utraque pars in unam vocem coaluisset). It was possibly this pronunciation *ad fătim* that gave rise to the curtailed Adverb *fatim*, which was in use in the time of Servius (4th cent. A. D.) (Serv. ad *Aen.* i. 123 ' fatim ' enim abundanter dicimus). *Ămussim* (Paul. Fest. 5. 3 Th.), Accus. of *amussis*, a carpenter's rule, may be a similar late curtailment of *ad amussim*, though we find *examussim* as early as Plautus. Another word-group of the kind is *sēdŭlō*, from *sē*, a Preposition used in O. Lat. in the sense of its cognate *sine* (§ 51), and *dŏlus*. From the Adverb *se-dulo* (with *ŭ* for *ŏ* in the unaccented syllable, ch. iii. § 26) was formed the Adjective *sedulus*. That this is the true account of *sedulo* is clear from *se dulo malo* of the Lex Agrária (*C. I. L.* i. 200. 40), and from the comparison of phrases like Plaut. *Trin.* 90 *haud dicam dolo*, 480 *non tibi dicam dolo*, *Men.* 228 *non dicam dolo*, with *Capt.* 886 *quod ego dico sedulo*, Ter. *Phorm.* 453 *ego sedulo hunc dixisse credo* (but *sedulo* is commoner with *facio* than with *dico*) ; though the confusion of *sedulo* with an Adverb from an Adjective-stem *sedulo*- must have been very early, for the byform *sedulum* is found in a line of 'Plautus' (*fr.* 41 G.) *sedulum est*, and in a plebiscitum about weights and measures quoted by Festus (322. 3. Th.) : ex ponderibus publicis, quibus hac tempestate populus oetier qui solet, uti coaequetur sedulum, uti quadrantal uini octoginta pondo siet, congius uini decem pondo siet, &c. (cf. later *sedule*). The Roman grammarians usually explained the word in this way ; Acron however, in his commentary on Terence, derived the word from an Adjective-stem *sedulo*-, as *falso* from the Adj. *falso*- (ap. Charis. 192. 30 ; 219. 5 K.). Another combination of Preposition and Noun is *ob-viam*, which has its literal sense in Plautus (usually with *esse*, *ire*, *venire*, &c.) ; thus in *Capt.* 791 the parasite Ergasilus, who is hurrying to give Hegio news of the arrival of his son, cries out :

éminor intérminorque néquis obstiterit óbuiam,

'that no one stand in my way'; it has not the sense of *praesto* in Plautus nor in Terence. From *obviam* was formed the Adjective *obvius* (but cf. *pervium*, *pervius*), as from *sedulo*, *sedulus*. Like *obviam* (and *inter-vias* with *vias* Acc. Pl.) is *obiter*, a word regarded with suspicion by purists, though Augustus gave it his sanction, and reproved Tiberius for using *per viam* instead. The Emperor Hadrian seems to have reversed his predecessor's decision (Charis. 209. 12 K.

'obiter' divus Hadrianus Sermonum I quaerit an Latinum sit . . . quanquam divus Augustus reprehendens Ti. Claudium ita loquitur : scribis enim 'per viam' ἀντὶ τοῦ obiter). *Ilicō* is explained by Charisius (201. 17 K.) as *inlŏco* (the length of the initial *ī* could be accounted for by the old form *sloco*, ch. iv. § 150), and has often this sense in Old Latin authors (for examples, see Charisius, l. c. and Nonius, 325. 6 M.) (in Plautus the local sense is not nearly so common as the temporal, and is found only with verbs of rest, e. g. *Rud*. 878 *ibidem ilico manete* ; 836 *illic astate ilico*) : Nonius (l. c.) makes it the equivalent of 'in eo loco,' but the sense of *ibi* is foreign to *ilico*, a fact which tells against its derivation from **ī*, an old Abl. Sg. of *is*, and *locus*. *Ilico* has not the sense of 'on that spot,' but of 'on the spot' (e. g. ilico hic ante ostium, Plaut. *Trin*. 608), and its change from a local to a temporal meaning finds an exact counterpart in our phrase 'on the spot,' which may be used in the sense of 'immediately,' 'without delay.' Curiously enough the O. Lat. adverbial word-group *īlicet*, which in the Comedians has the sense of *īre lĭcet* (e. g. Plaut. *Capt*. 469 :

ilicet parasiticae arti máxumam malám crucem,

'the profession of diner-out may go hang itself on the highest possible gallows'), from which by an easy transition it acquired that of *actum est* [e. g. Plaut. *Cist*. 685 perii, opinor, actumst, ilicet, was brought again into fashion by Virgil in the sense of *ilico*, e. g. *Aen*. xi. 468 :

ilicet in muros tota discurritur urbe.

[Charisius quotes the note of a commentator on this line : (ilicet) nunc pro ilico, id est statim. antiqui pro eas licet,' and mentions a somewhat similar use of the word in a line of Afranius (*Com*. 215 R.) : an tu eloquens ilicet?, 'have you become an orator all at once?']. By another freak of language the confusion of *ilicet* with a word of similar sound was repeated some centuries later, when it was used (e. g. by Sidonius Apollinaris, fifth cent. A. D.) in the sense of *scilicet* (cf. Paul. Fest. 74. 22 'ilicet,' sine dubio). A verbal group like *ilicet* is *vidēlicet*, which in the earlier period occurs with the construction of *vidēre licet*, e. g. Plaut. *Asin*. 599 :

nunc enim ésse
negótiosum intérdius uidélicet Solónem,

Lucret. i. 210 :

esse videlicet in terris primordia rerum,

also *scilicet*, construed like *scīre licet* in such a line as Plaut. *Pseud*. 1179 : scilicet solitum esse, 'of course he used to' (on these verbal Noun stems *i-*, *vide-*, *sci-*; see ch. viii. § 34). *Sīs* (for *sī vīs*, ch. ii. § 53), *sultis* Plur., similarly takes an Inf. in Plaut. *Asin*. 309 sís amanti súbuenire fámiliari fílio.

The word *mŏdus* enters into several adverbial word-groups. Besides *admodum*, *propemodum* (and later *propemodo*), *postmodum* (and *postmodo*), which have been already mentioned, we have *quemadmodum*, *quōmodō* [cf. *cujusmodī*, *hujusmodi*, *ejusmodi*, &c., which in Plautus are scanned as cretics or the equivalents of cretics (ch. vii. § 22), *cuicuimodi* (perhaps not in Plautus)], *quōdammodo*, *tantummodo* and (in Late Latin) *solummodo*, &c. (cf. the compounds *omnĭ-modis*, *multĭ-modis*, on which see Neue, ii³. pp. 609 sq.). We find *rēs* in *quā-rē*, *quam-ob-rem*, &c., *dies* in *in-dies*, *prope-diem*.

A Preposition with a Noun (or Adj.) appears also in *dē-nŭō*, for *de nŏvo* (with

§ 8.]					ADVERBS.					565

u for unaccented *ov*, ch. iii. § 24), like *de integro*, *ex-templo* (in Plaut. also *ex-tempulo*), from *templum* in its O. Lat. sense of *locus* (e. g. *Acherusia templa*, Enn.), *in-cassum*, lit. 'into the empty' (cf. *cassa nux*, Plaut.), like its synonyms in Late Lat. *in vanum* and *in vacuum* ; *im-prīmīs*, *cum-primis* (cf. *apprimē*, used with an Adj. in the sense of a Superlative in ante-classical and post-classical Latin). A verbal phrase is seen in *dum-taxat* [*taxat* is Pres. Subj. of **taxo*, a byform of *tango*, as *viso* of *video*, *quaeso* of *quaero* (ch. viii. § 33. 4) for **tag-so*], a legal phrase whose original sense appears in O. Lat. laws like *C. I. L.* i. 197. 12 : sei quis magistratus multam inrogare uolet, [quei uolet, dum minoris] partus familias taxsat, liceto, ' so long as he assigns a fine of the smaller portion of his property,' ' of less than half of his property' (for *dumtaxat* the Oscan expression is *ampert* from the Negative particle an- and the Preposition pert, ' beyond ' ; thus on the Tabula Bantina : *in*[*im*] *svae pis ionc fortis meddis moltaum herest*, *ampert minstreis aeteis eituas moltas moltaum licitud* ' et siquis eum fortius (? forte) meddix multare volet, dumtaxat minoris partis pecuniae multas multare liceto ') (Zvet. *I. I. I.* 231. 12). *Actū-tum* is merely *actū*, lit. ' on the act,' followed by *tum*, then.

§ 8. **Other Adverbs.** One of the puzzles of Latin etymology is the O. Lat. Adverb *sĭmītū*, the equivalent of *simul*, found as an archaism on some inscriptions of the Empire in the forms *simitu* (*C. I. L.* vi. 7578), and certainly once (possibly twice) *simitur* (vi. 9290, a slave-girl's epitaph of 13 B. C., and read by Ritschl in x. 174, an epitaph in illiterate verse). Nonius mentions *simitu* (175. 16 M.) with three examples from Lucilius and Plautus ; so that this form is well established. Plautus elides the last syllable in *Stich.* 249 mecúm simitu ut íres ad sesé domum. The later (plebeian) form *simitur* can hardly be due to a change of *-d* to *-r* like that seen in O. Lat. *apor*, *apur* for *apud* (§ 19) ; it is more likely to be a corruption caused by confusion with the Impersonal *itur*, 3 Sg. Pass. of *eo*, to go. *Simitu* has been explained as a Compound of the root sem- (ch. vi. § 57) in some form or other with *ītū*, the Abl. Sg. of the Verbal Noun *ītus*, a going.

Another puzzle is *ĭgĭtur* (the quantity of the final syllable cannot be determined in Plautus), the oldest sense of which is ' then,' ' thereupon ' (cf. Non. 128. 14 ' igitur' positum pro postea), e. g. the first clause of the XII Tables: si in ius uocat, ni it, antestamino : igitur em capito, a clause well known to Roman schoolboys of the first cent. B.C. as the beginning of one of their most formidable lesson-books (cf. Cic. *Legg.* ii. 4. 9 a parvis ... Quinte, didicimus ' si in ius vocat' atque alia ejus modi ' leges' nominare); Plaut. *Cas.* 215 móx magis quom ótium ét mihi et tíbi erit, Ígitur tecúm loquar: núnc uale ; *Mil.* 772 quándo habebo, igitúr rationem meárum fabricarúm dabo ; *igitur tum* (e. g. *Most.* 689), *igitur deindĕ*, *igitur dēmum* are all frequent in Plautus. This makes unlikely the theory that *igitur* is a curtailment of *quid igitur* ?, a form of *quid ăgĭtur* ?, with *ă* weakened to *ĭ* in the unaccented syllable of the word-group *quid-agitur* ? Another theory connects it with Lith. -ktu of tŏktu, ' so,' kŏktu, 'as,' or with O. Sl. -gda of togda, ' then,' igda, ' hitherto.' It has also been resolved into the three Pronominal-stems i- (ch. vii. § 13), ko- [*ib.* ; *digitus* is quoted as a parallel case of the change of *-icit-* to *-igit-* ; others make the particle **gĕ* (Gk. γε) the second element of *igitur*], and to- (*ib.*) ; the last with the ending -r, seen in O. Ind. tár-hi, ' then,' kár-hi, ' when,' &c.). Its use varies in different authors ; thus it is placed normally as first word of the sentence in Sallust and Tacitus, but almost never in Cicero's speeches ; and it is avoided by purists like Terence (except in his earliest plays), Lucilius, Caesar, and the older and the younger Seneca (for statistics, see *A. L. L.* iii. 560). Its formation evidently seemed to the Romans to have something irregular about it (cf. Quint. i. 5. 39 ex quo genere an sit 'igitur' initio sermonis positum dubitari potest, quia maximos auctores in diversa fuisse opinione video, cum apud alios sit etiam frequens, apud alios numquam reperiatur). Another Adverb (?) of uncertain etymology is *siremps* in the formula found on old laws, *siremps lex esto*, 'the same law shall hold' (*C. I. L.* i. 197. 12 ; 198. 73 ; 200. 27 ; 202. (1). 38, (2). 1, &c. ; see Georges, *Lex. Wortf.* s. v.), and in the form *sirempse* (which Charisius calls the Ablative of *siremps*, 93. 24 ; 146. 1 K.) in the (un-Plautine?) prologue of the *Amphitruo* of Plautus, l. 73 :

sirémpse legem iússit esse Iúppiter.

One theory declares it to be composed of *sis* (*si vis*) and *empse*, the old Acc. Sg. Masc. of *ipse* (ch. vii. § 20), and to have originally meant 'the aforesaid' (person), but to have been in course of time wrongly associated with *lex esto* (*Wien. Stud.* 1891, p. 296).

Sētius, less (esp. *non setius, nihilo setius*, also *quo setius* like *quo minus*), is the correct spelling, not *sēcius*, which is not found till the period when *ti* began to be confused with *ci* (see ch. ii. § 90, and Fleckeisen, *Fünfzig Artikel*, p. 28), so that the word cannot be equated with Gk. ἧσσων (for *ἧκγων ; cf. ἥκιστος). Though treated by the Roman grammarians as the Comparative of the Adverb (Preposition) *sĕcus* and as a byform of the normal comparative *sĕquius* (e. g. Afranius 293 R. sín, id quod non spéro, ratio tális sequius cécideriț) (from the root sequ-, 'to follow,' Gk. ἕπομαι ; lit. 'following,' hence 'inferior'), it seems impossible to connect *setius* with *secus* (see § 1) or with *sequius*. Gellius (xviii. 9. 4), describing a controversy he had heard over the spelling of the O. Lat. verb *insĕco* (*insequo*), to narrate (Gk. ἔνισπον), mentions as an argument adduced by one of the disputants, that the form *sectius* was found in Plaut. *Men.* 1047 (our MSS. in this line of Plautus, a line unfortunately undecipherable in the Ambrosian Palimpsest, vary between *setius quam, sed usquam*, and *secus quam*) :

haéc nihilo esse míhi uidentur sétius quam sómnia,

and that this *sectius* was connected with the O. Lat. *insectiones* 'narrationes,' so that the line really meant 'nihilo magis narranda esse quam si ea essent somnia.' On the strength of this very questionable authority, it has been attempted to connect *sētius* with the root sequ-, 'to follow,' by the theory that *sĕctius* was the oldest form (from *secto-*, a participial-stem from *sequor* ; cf. *secta*, *sector*), which became *sĕttius*, then *sētius*. But even granting the existence of this form *sectius*, a form most probably due to an error in the copy of Plautus used, the change of *ct* to *tt* is a late one (ch. ii. § 95), and the substitution of *ēt* for *ĕtt* too doubtful (ch. ii. § 130) to make this theory at all convincing. It is much more likely that *setius* and *secus* were entirely different words (like *mĕlius* and *bĕnĕ, pejus* and *mălĕ*), associated as Comparative and Positive owing to their similarity of meaning.

Oppĭdō is another of the problems of Latin etymology. The most likely theory is that *oppĭdum*, a town, meant originally the part on the plain (*ob-*pedum* ; cf. Gk. πεδίον) as opposed to the *arx*. This distinction seems to be expressly made in the Titulus Aletrinas (*C. I. L.* i. 1166) in a passage referring to the water supply of a town : aquam in opidum adqu[e] arduom. The

Adverbial Abl. *oppido* will then be exactly similar to *plānē*. In Plautus it goes usually with a Verb, but in Terence only with an Adj.

§ 9. Numeral Adverbs in -ies (see ch. vi. § 56).

§ 10. Pronominal Adverbs. (On the Relative Adverbs which show initial *u-* in the simple word, but as the second element of a compound *-cu-*, e. g. *ŭbi, sĭ-cubi, unde, sĭ-cunde,* see ch. vii. § 26).

(1) With suffix *-bi* (Umbr. -fe, Osc. -f, e. g. Umbr. pufe, Osc. puf, 'ubi,' Umbr. ife). The Umbro-Oscan forms point to *-fī* as their original suffix, with f representing I.-Eur. bh (Gk. -φι), as in the Dat. Sg. of the Personal Pronouns (e. g. Osc. sífeí 'sibi,' I.-Eur. *sebhei, ch. vii. § 5), or more probably dh (Gk. -θι; cf. O. Sl. kŭde, O. Ind. kúha). Latin *-bi* is in O. Lat. *-bei* [e. g. *ubei* on the S. C. Bacch. (*C. I. L.* i. 196); other examples in Georges, *Lex. Wortf.* s. v.; on the spelling *ube*, e. g. Varro *R. R.* i. 4. 4, see ch. vii. § 6], and is in poetry scanned as a long or as a short syllable (similarly *ibĭdem*), a variation of quantity which is most naturally explained by supposing that the last syllable was originally long (representing I.-Eur. -ei), and was in time shortened through the influence of the short first syllable (*avĕ* from *avē*, &c., ch. iii. § 42). The Oscan form however suggests that the short final vowel may not be a late development (cf. *utĭ-* and *utei*, ch. x. § 11). Latin examples of this formation are *u-bĭ, si-cubĭ, num-cubi*, &c., *ubī-que, ibĭ, ibĭdem* (rarely *ibīdem* in Plaut.), *in-ibi* [*inibi esse* like *in eo esse (ut)*, 'to be on the point of'], *intĕr-ibi* (often used by Plautus for *intereā, interim*), *post-ibi* (used sometimes by Plautus for *postea*), *ălĭbi* and the less usual *aliubi* (as early as the Lex Agraria of 111 B. C., *C. I. L.* i. 200. 86 : aliubeiue aliterue), *utrŭbi, utrubique* and *utrobique* (on these spellings, see Georges s. v.), *neutrubi*.

(2) With suffix *-ī* (older *-ei*). In the language of Plautus *illī* or *illīc* (older *ollīc*, Paul. Fest. 231. 2 Th.), *istī* or *istīc* may be Dat. Sg., 'to him,' or Adverb (Loc. Sg.), 'there.' The scribes of our MSS. however have gone on the principle of correcting *illi, isti,* 'there,' to *illic, istic*, usually (e. g. *Capt.* 278, where the metre requires *illi*), and almost always *illic, istic,* 'to him,' to *illi, isti,* so that the relative frequency of the two forms of the Adverb in Plautus, or other writers, cannot well be determined. The Adverb from the pronoun *hic* seems to have had the enclitic *-c(e)* at all periods of the literature, *hīc*, older *heic* (*C. I. L.* i. 551. 590. 1007. 1009) ; *heicei* on the epitaph of an actor, i 1297:

> Protogenes Cloul[i] suauei heicei situst mimus,
> plouruma que fecit populo soueis gaudia nuges,

may be a graver's error, for the orthography of the inscription is erratic; *heice* (i. 1049 me heice situm inmature). But on late inscriptions we occasionally find *hi* (e. g. ii. 3244 hi jacet). [Faliscan he, hei in the formula he (hei) cupat 'hic cubat, -ant' may owe the suppression of its -c to the initial c- of the following word ; cf. Zvet. *I. I. I.* 66.] From the Pronominal-stem *so- (ch. vii. § 13) we have *si,* and with the enclitic *-c(e), sic*[1] (cf. Umbr. i-sek

---

[1] For an example of the older spelling *seic* we may take this touching epitaph of a girl called Flavia Amoena [*Mitth. (röm.)* viii. 150] :

ut rosa amoena homini est quom
primo tempore floret,
quei me viderunt, seic ego Amoena
fui

'item'); from the Relative (Interrog., Indef.) the Adverb *qui* (which is perhaps rightly regarded as an Instr. (cf. O. Engl. hwī, O. Sl. čimĭ) from a stem *qui-*, ch. vii. § 25), and with the suffix *-n(e), quin* (ch. x. § 16), as well as the compounds *alio-qui* and *alio-quin, cetero-qui* and *cetero-quin, nē-qui-quam* (ch. vii. § 28), and perhaps *quippe* (if for *quĭ-pe*) and *quippiam* (*quĭpiam*) (see ch. x. § 7; ch. vii. § 28).

(3) With suffix *-ō*, e. g. *eo, eo-dem* (*id-eo* has only the later sense of purpose, not the earlier of motion towards, 'that for that purpose,' 'and that indeed with that object'), *quo, quo-cunque, ălĭquo, ălio, utro, utroque, neutro*. These have the same sense as Adverbs formed with *-versum, -s* (older *-vorsum, -s*), and often have this participle added, e. g. *aliōvorsum* and *aliorsum*, Plaut. (for the suppression of *v* between the two vowels, see ch. ii. § 53), *quorsus, -m*. The Preposition *ad* is appended in *quo-ad*, and prefixed in *ăd-eo* (used in a literal sense in the older literature, e. g. Cato, *R. R.* xl. 3 surculum artito usque adeo quo praeacueris ; cf. adeo res rediit, 'things have reached such a pass,' in the Comedians), and *ad-quo*, a variety of *quoad*, 'so far as,' for which Nonius (76. 6 M.) cites two lines of Afranius, *Com.* 278 R. :

and 249 R. :
ut scíre possis ádquo te expediát loqui,
irátus essem adquó liceret.

We have the same suffix *-ō* in Adverbs indicating motion towards, formed from Prepositions by means of the *tro-* (*ro-*) suffix, *rĕ-tro, cĭ-tro, ul-tro, por-ro* ; and that this *-ō* represents earlier *-ōd*, the Ablative case-ending of O-stems, we see from the spelling *porod* on an old Praenestine cista (*Mél. Arch.* 1890, p. 303). Oscan adpúd in a Capua inscr. (*Rhein. Mus.* 1888, pp. 9 and 557; adpúd fiiet) seems to be the equivalent of Latin *quoad* (cf. Afranius' *adquo*) and to have the sense of 'so long as,' Lat. quoad fient. In Umbrian, where, as in Latin, final -d is dropped after a long vowel, we find *ar-ni-po* with another sense of *quoad*, 'until,' followed by a Future Perfect, *sersitu arnipo . . . pesnis fust* 'sedeto quoad precatus erit' (the *-ni-* of *arnipo* seems to be like the *-ni-* of Latin *dō-ni-cum*, ch. x. § 12, and *-po* may represent *pŏm rather than *pŏd) ; the Adverb corresponding to Latin *quo* is *pu-e* with that suffix -i (?) (Gk. οὗτοσ-ί) written -i, -ei, -e, which is added not merely to the Nom. Sg. Masc. of the Umbrian Relative, *po-i,* or *po-ei*, or *po-e* (Lat. *quī* for *quo-* with *ī*, ch. vii. § 25), but to other parts of its declension, e. g. Acc. Pl. Fem. *paf-e* ; the Adverb from O. Lat. *sēd-ūter-que* (Plaut.), 'each separately,' is in Umbrian *sei-podruh-pei*, with *uh* expressive of the long *o*-sound (a close *o*, nearly or altogether *u* ; see ch. ii. § 20). The fact that the O-stem Abl. shows -u in Umbr. has been used as an argument that Umbr. *ulo* 'illuc,' *postro* 'retro,' &c. are Instrumentals. Similar formations from *ille, iste* are found at all periods of Latin, *illō* (cf. Umbr. ulu, *ulo*), *istō* (for examples, see Georges), but the Adverbs generally used are *illuc, istuc*, with final syllable scanned long in poetry, and similarly from *hic* we have *huc*, hither, *ad-huc*, hither-to (is *hō indicated by the form *horsum* for *hovorsum* ?). In the earlier literature the forms with the enclitic *-c(e)* end in *-oc*, with final syllable again scanned long, e. g. *hoc* (as in Plaut. *Capt.* 480, where the parasite is touting for a dinner :

quís ait. 'hoc'? aut quís profitetur ?),

an archaic form employed by Virgil, *A.* viii. 423 (see the note of Servius on the passage) :

hoc tunc Ignipotens caelo descendit ab alto

§ 10.]   ADVERBS.   569

[for other examples, see Georges, *Lex. Wortf.* s. vv. ; statistics of the spelling *hoc* and *huc* in Plaut., &c. are given in *Fleck. Jahrb.* (Suppl.) 1891, p. 293 *n.*]. This *-uc* has been referred to an earlier *-oi-ce* with the Locative suffix *-oi*, which is used in Adverbs of motion towards in Greek, ποῖ, ὅποι, &c., but it seems unnatural to regard it as anything but a phonetic development of the earlier *-oc.* If the vowel in these endings be naturally long, it must have been originally ou (ch. iv. § 41), and the parallel Adverbs in Greek will be not ποῖ, ὅποι but ποῦ, ὅπου, which mean in Greek 'where,' not 'whither.' But it may have been naturally short ; for the metrical value of the syllable can be explained by the fact that *c* really represents *cc*, from an earlier *dc*, **hod-c(e)*, **is-tod-c(e)* (ch. iii. § 51), so that the forms would be really Accusatives Sing. Neut. (cf. however O. Lat. *illuc, istuc*, and class. *hoc*, Acc. Sg. Neut.), and not Ablatives.

Quo, eo, &c. have also other senses in Latin, as with Comparatives *eo major, eo minor* (cf. Lith. jů with Comparatives ; Welsh po, 'by how much the'), *quo major, quo minor*, &c., from which comes the use of *quo* for *ut* in final sentences with a Comparative, e. g. quo facilius haec fieri possint, and the word-group *quōmĭnus*, lest, e. g. quominus haec fieri possint ; also *quo*, whereby, &c. These too are Ablative forms, originally **quōd*, **eōd*, as we may see from Osc. *pod . . . mins* 'quominus' in the Tabula Bantina (Zvet. *I. I. I.* 231. 10): *nep fefacid pod pis dat eizac egmad min*[s] *deivaid dolud malud* 'neve fecerit quo quis de ea re minus juret dolo malo'; Osc. *svaepod . . . svaepod* 'sive . . . sive,' Umbr. *svepo* ; Umbr. *eso* (*iso*) from the stem **ek-so-*, also *esoc* (*issoc*) for **ek-sok* 'sic' ; with the last, cf. the Latin gloss : *soc*, ita (Löwe, *Prodr.* p. 350, a doubtful form). In a leaden execration tablet (Zvet. *I. I. I.* 129), written in Oscan (presumably not the best Oscan), we have svai puh (h indicates the length of a vowel in Umbrian), a spelling which, if found on a magisterial proclamation, or any carefully written inscription, might establish the existence of an Oscan *pō* (pū), an Instrumental form, beside *pōd* (pūd), the Ablative form. But the character of this inscription diminishes the value of the evidence of this, as well as of the other 'Instrumental' Adverb, which occurs on the same tablet, suluh 'omnino' (from the stem sollo-, 'all, whole') ; besides it is doubtful whether h indicates vowel-length in Oscan. In another Oscan execration scroll (*I. F.* ii. 435), we have the form sullud (the last letter somewhat doubtful), but the fragmentary state of the inscription makes it impossible to determine satisfactorily that sullud is an Adverb.

(4) In *-ā*, e. g. *qua*, 'in which direction' (cf. *qua . . . qua*, 'both . . . and '), *ne-qua-quam, haud-qua-quam, qua-propter* (cf. Plaut. *Amph.* 815 qua istaec propter dicta dicantur mihi), *ea* (often appended to Adverbs, *propter-eā, praeter-eā, post-eā, ant-eā*, and on the S. C. Bacch. *arvorsum ead* in the sentence : sei ques esent, quei aruorsum ead fecisent, quam suprad scriptum est), *ea-dem, alia, aliqua, hac* (appended like *ea* to Adverbs, *post-hac, ante-hac, praeter-hac*, and in a plebiscitum ap. Fest. 322. 8 Th. *adversus hac* ; cf. Osc. *post exac* 'posthac'), *illac, istac*. With *tĕnus* appended these Adverbs indicate distance : *quatenus*, 'how far' (on the subsequent development of meanings, see § 4), *hactenus*, 'thus far' (cf. Hor. est quadam prodire tenus). The formation is evidently the same as that of Adverbs derived from Prepositions with the suffix *-tro-* (*-ro-*), e. g. *extra* (*exstrad* S. C. Bacch.), *supra* (*suprad* S. C. Bacch.) (cf. Oscan púllad 'qua,' an Adverbial Ablative Sg. Fem. of the Relative, formed by adding the Abl. Sg. Fem. of the Oscan Demonstr. stem ollo- (Lat. *illo-*, older *ollo-*, ch. vii.

§ 18) to the Relative stem po- (ch. vii. § 23) ; [p]úllad víú uruvú íst 'quā via flexa (?) est,' Zvet. *I. I. I.* 136. 56). *Qua-ad* is found for *quo-ad* on late inscriptions, and is a not uncommon variant in good MSS. (see Georges).

(5) In *-im, ŭtrim-que, illim* (found in Cicero as well as in the older writers, whereas *istim* is doubtful ; see Georges, *Lex. Wortf.* s. vv.), but usually *illinc*, as *istinc, hinc*. The same suffix is found in the forms to which the Adverb *sĕcus* is appended, *intrin-secus, altrin-secus, extrin-secus,* and apparently in *exim, intĕrim* and *ŏlim,* though in two at least of these three last words, it has not its usual sense of motion from. *Intĕrim* is equivalent to *intĕr-eā, inter-ibi* (Plaut.), while *olim,* from meaning 'at that time' (often answering to *quum* in Plautus, e. g. olim quom caletur maxime, *Truc.* 65), came to mean 'at any former time,' ' formerly,' ' once upon a time,' then ' at any time,' ' occasionally' (e. g. Lucil. iii. 4 M. uiamque Degruma*tus* uti castris mensor facit olim), and to be used even of future time (e. g. Hor. : non si male nunc, et olim Sic erit). *Olim* can hardly come directly from the Pronoun-stem *ollo-* of O. Lat. *ollus, olle* (class. *ille*), best analyzed into *ol-so- (ch. vii. § 13), for *ŏll-* would not become *ōl-* (ch. ii. § 130); it is rather to be derived from the stem ōl-, a grade of the OL- (AL-) stem, without the suffix so- (cf. Umbr. *ulo* 'illuc' with *u* the equivalent of Lat. *ō*). The origin of the suffix *-im* has not yet been satisfactorily explained.

(6) In *-ndĕ*. This suffix seems to be the suffix *-m* (hardly the Acc. Sg. suffix) augmented by the particle *-de*. As the Adverbs meaning 'thence,' *ille, iste* added to *-im* the particle *-c(e)*, the corresponding Adverbs from *is, qui* add to *-m* the particle *-de* (cf. Gk. ἐνθέν-δε), which, like *-ce*, was liable to be curtailed of its final short vowel in every-day pronunciation (ch. iii. § 36). Thus we have *inde* (which should not be derived from the Preposition *in,* but must go with *unde*), *indĭ-dem,* and with prefixed Adverb *de-inde* (curtailed to *dein*), *pro-inde* (and *proin*), *ex-inde* (and *exin,* a different word from *exim* ; see Georges, *Lex. Wortf.* s. v.), &c., *unde, sĭ-cunde, nĕ-cunde, undĭ-que, aliunde, ălĭcunde.* For *ŭtrinde,* quoted from a speech of Cato by Charisius (224. 14 K. utrinde factiones tibi pares) we should expect *utrunde.*

(7) In *-um* (*-om*), the Acc. Sg. Neuter, e. g. *tum* and with the enclitic *-c(e), tunc* (cf. *nunc* and *etiam-num*), *quum,* older *quom,* with appended *jam* in *quŏn-iam* (ch. x. § 13), and appended *-dam* in *quon-dam* (cf. *qui-dam,* ch. vii. § 28), *dum* (ch. x. § 12), *dū-dum* (*ib.*), *non-dum.* From the Pronominal-stem i- (Lat. *is*) an Adverb in *-m* was in use in O. Lat. in the sense of 'then,' variously written as *im* and *em* (ch. vii. § 19) ; and from the Relative-stem seen in *u-bi,* &c. we have the *um-* of *un-quam* (cf. O. Lat. **umquis* of *necumquem* 'nec umquam quemquam' Fest. 162. 22 Th.), and with negative *nĕ-* prefixed, *nun-quam* (*ne umquam* is the reading of the MSS. of Plaut. *Most.* 307) ; though some make this originally to have ended in *n,* not in *m,* and find the form with initial *c* (like *si-cubi, si-cunde*) in the *-cun-* of *qui-cun-que* (ch. x. § 2), *ne-cun-quem* (so interpreting the O. Lat. word mentioned by Festus), which they compare with Goth. *-hun-* of ni hvas-hun, 'none so ever.'

(8) In *-am,* apparently the Acc. Sg. Fem., though some make it an Instrumental case (suffix -m or -mĭ, ch. vi. § 36). If Festus is right in quoting *tame* as an O. Lat. form of *tam* from the Carmen Saliare (Fest. 546. 1 Th. 'tame' in Carmine positum est pro tam), all these Adverbs in *-am* may have originally ended in a short vowel. From the Relative Pronoun we have *quam,* the correlative of which is taken from the Pronoun to- (ch. vii. § 13), not from the Pronoun i-, *tam.* The two are united in *tan-quam.* Whether *jam,* now (cf.

§ 10.]   ADVERBS.   571

Lith. jaŭ, 'already'), is the corresponding formation from the stem i- is not certain. The indeclinable Adj. *nē-quam* may be a colloquial compound of *quam*, as the Adverb *nē-quaquam* is of *quāquam*, so that *nequam* would literally mean 'a no-how' (cf. O. Lat. *nequalia* 'detrimenta' Fest. 162. 23 ; Paul. Fest. 163. 13 Th.). Another compound is *perquam*, exceedingly (cf. *admodum quam*, Plaut.). The addition of the Preposition *dō* (§ 27) to *quam* gives the Adverb *quandō* (ch. x. § 12), originally temporal, then causal (cf. *quandōquidem, ălĭ-quando, quandō-que* (Umbr. *panu-pei*) (cf. O. Sl. kądu, 'qua, unde'?), while O. Lat. *quam-dē* is a byform of *quam*, than, as in a passage of Livius Andronicus (quoted in § 7) : peius . . . quamde mare saeuom, and Lucr. i. 640 quamde gravis inter Graios qui vera requirunt. Other derivatives are *ălĭquam* in *aliquam-diu*, &c., *quam-vīs* (rarely with Subj. in Plautus, and always with an Adj. or Adv. ; not in Terence), and *quam-quam* (cf. *tam-quam*), *n(e)-ŭtĭ-quam, nē-qua-quam*, &c.

From the pronominal-stem *no-* (O. Ind. ná-nā, 'in various places or ways,' lit. 'there and there,' 'thus and thus'), connected with the stem *eno-* (*ono-) (O. Ind. ana-, 'this,' Lith. anàs, 'that,' O. Sl. onŭ) we have *nam* used in emphasizing a question, e. g. quid cerussā opus nam ? Plaut. (hence *quis-nam*, who ?, O. Lat. *quiă-nam*, why?), and in the sense of 'for' ; from the stem *do-*, *-dam* of *quon-dam* (cf. *qui-dam*).

(9) With other suffixes : of *t*-suffixes we have (*a*) *-ta* in *ĭ-tă*, so (Umbr. itek), *i-tă-que*, therefore (ch. x. § 8) ; *uta*, as, may be inferred from O. Lat. *ali-uta* (cf. *ali-ubi*, p. 564), otherwise, quoted from the Laws of Numa by Paul Fest. [4. 27 Th. si quisquam aliuta faxit, ipsos Ioui sacer esto ; cf. the gloss *aliutea* (leg. *aliuta*), aliud, amplius, Löwe, *Prodr*. 432]. The final *a* was no doubt originally long, if every final short vowel became *-ĕ* in Latin (ch. iii. § 37), but there are no traces of this quantity in *itaque* in the older poetry (on *itaque* in the Saturnian epitaph of Naevius, see ch. x. § 8), and probably none in *ita* either. So that the shortening of the final vowel under the influence of the preceding short syllable must have established itself in this word of common use at a very early date.

(*b*) *-tem* in *ĭ-tem, au-tem* (cf. O. Ind. *-tham* of ka-thám, 'how,' &c. ?).

(*c*) *-t* (originally with a short final vowel, probably ĭ ; cf. O. Ind. i-tĭ, 'thus') in *ŭt, ŭtĭ-nam, uti-que*. The Umbro-Oscan equivalents of Latin *ut* show an *s* after the *t*, Umbr. puze, *puse*, ending originally in -tsĭ or -tsĕ, Osc. puz (*pous* on the Bantine tablet must surely mean *ou* for *ŭ*), which in Latin appears in the local Adverbs *us-quam, nus-quam*.

Ūs-que is a different word, derived from the I.-Eur. Preposition ud-, as *abs-que* from *ab* (see § 57 for *ūsque*).

The suffix *t* appears also in *aut*, which probably ended originally in a short *-i* (Gk. αὖ-τε has τε for I.-Eur. *-qŭĕ, ch. x. § 2), as we see from Umbr. *ote*, Osc. avti. The long *-i* of *utī* is probably Loc. *-ei* (§ 11).

Of *d*-suffixes, besides (*a*) *-dam* of *quon-dam* (temporal Adv. of *quī-dam*) and (*b*) *dum*, with idea of time in *dū-dum, non-dum, vix-dum, inter-dum* already mentioned, we have (*c*) *-dem* in *qui-dem* (ch. x. § 6), and with the sense of 'exactly,' 'just' (cf. *is demum, ibi demum*) in a large number of Adverbs, such as *tantĭ-dem, ibĭ-dem, indĭ-dem, ĭtĭ-dem, tŏtĭ-dem* (from *toti, the older form of *tot*, ch. vii. § 29), as well as in the Pronoun of Identity, *ī-dem* (ch. vii. § 21), with its curious derivative *ĭdentĭdem*, repeatedly (explained as 'idem ante idem' or 'idem tum idem'), also with the idea of time (cf. *dum* in *inter-dum, non-dum*) in *tan-dem* (cf. *demum*), *prī-dem*.

§ 11. **PREPOSITIONS.** Prepositions are Adverbs, which came to be specially used in connexion with certain cases of the Noun, or in composition with a Verb. In the early stage of a language the cases alone were sufficient to indicate the sense, but as the force of the Case-suffixes became weakened, or as the necessity for clearer definition was more recognized, the Case-suffix was strengthened by the addition of an Adverb. Thus *ire monte* might mean 'to go out of the mountain' or 'to go down from the mountain.' To indicate the first sense, the Adverb *ex* was used, *ire monte ex* ; to indicate the second, the Adverb *de, ire monte de*; or *ex-ire monte, *de-ire monte*. These Adverbs which, owing to their meaning, are most frequently associated with particular cases of Nouns, or are used in composition with Verbs, are called Prepositions ; and the process, by which Latin Adverbs became Prepositions, may be seen in operation at various periods of the language. Thus *contra*, which has hardly passed the Adverb stage with Plautus and Terence, is a Preposition in classical Latin and governs an Accusative Case ; *coram* is not a Preposition till Cicero's time ; *simul* in Augustan poetry and Silver Age prose; *retro* not till Late Latin (e.g. *vade retro me*, S. Marc. viii. 33, *Vulgata*). It is customary now in writing Latin to write the Preposition and the Verb in one word, e.g. *exire*, but not the Preposition and the Noun, e.g. *ex monte* ; and this practice is justified by the fact that a Verb compounded with a Preposition had, so to speak, a separate life of its own in its compound form. *Exĭgo*, for example, was a different word from *ăgo*, and so suffered weakening of the vowel *a* in the unaccented syllable ; *pōno* ceased to be recognized as a compound of *po-* (see § 12) and *sĭno*, and changed its Perfect *pŏ-sīvi* to *posui* (ch. viii. § 39. 4) ; *summitto* shows that assimilation to which the internal consonants of a word were liable. On the other hand a Noun with a Preposition is as a rule not so treated (although there are not wanting examples like *sedulo* for *se dolo*, § 7), unless a Compound Adjective is formed of the Preposition and the Noun, e.g. *pĕrĕgre*, Loc. of **peregris* compounded of *per-* and *ager* (ch. vi. § 38). Still it must be remembered that in the Roman pronunciation the Preposition and the Noun formed a word-group (e.g. *circum-lĭttora*, ch. iii. § 12 *a*. 6), and in the Roman orthography they were usually written together (e.g. *ingalliam, initaliam*, Mar. Victorin. 23. 12 K.), sometimes with consonant-assimilation, (e.g. *summănus* for *sub manus*, Plaut. *Pers.* 450). This close union of the Preposition with its Verb and Noun must have led at a very early time to the syncope of a final short syllable of Prepositions; and it is possible that byforms like Gk. ἐνί and ἐν may be doublets of very ancient date, representing the forms assumed by the word when used independently and in composition (cf. Engl. 'by' and 'be'-witch, Germ. 'bei' and 'be'-leben, similarly 'off' and 'of,' 'too' and 'to' are doublets, one of which is used as Adv., the other as Prep.). Tmesis, or the separation of the prepositional part of a Compound, from the other part, is a feature of the older stage of every language; and is common in O. Lat. (e.g. *sub uos placo* was the archaic phrase for *supplĭco* retained in Latin prayers; *transque dato* and *endoque plorato* are legal archaisms for *trādĭtoque* and *implōrātoque*, Fest. 444. 30 Th.). An arrangement like *sub uos placo, ob uos sacro* (for *obsecro vos*) (cf. Vedic ví nō dhēhi, 'lend us') became the rule in the Celtic languages, thus in O. Ir. at-om-aig 'adigit me' the Pronoun is 'infixed' between the Preposition and the Verb, as if we had in Latin 'ad me agit.'

In the later stages of a language the use of Prepositions increases more and more. In Latin this culminated in the loss of Case-suffixes, and the use of Prepositions in their place, as we see in the Romance languages. As early as the first cent. A.D. a grammarian points out that *in manus aqua* is the phrase in vogue instead of the older *aqua manibus* (Caper 92. 8 K.). New distinctions of prepositional meaning were expressed by compounding Prepositions with one another, e.g. *de-ex, de-sub,* &c. [cf. *abante, C. I. L.* xi. 147, Fr. avant], a process which may have begun at a very early stage; for I.-Eur. Prepositions often show an appended particle (Pronoun and Adverb), such as (1) -s(ĕ), Gk. -σε, e.g. ἄψ, ἐξ, Lat. *abs, ex, sus-*; (2) -d(ĕ), Gk. δόμον-δε, e.g. Lat. *postid, antid, prod-* (cf. O. Sl. -dŭ of prĕ-dŭ-, 'before'); (3) -tĭ, e.g. O. Ind. práti, Zend patiy, Gk. προτί, ποτί, Osc. pert-; (4) -n(ĕ), e.g. Lat. *pōne* for **pos-ne* (cf. Germ. von, O. H. G. fona and fon). These particles, whose original form is not always recognizable (thus a Latin -*d* from -*dĕ* might come from an original *dĕ, *dĭ, *dŏ, *dŭ, &c., ch. iii. § 37), cannot be separated from the pronominal stems mentioned in § 10, ch. x. § 1 (e. g. the 'Adverbial' -δε of Gk. δόμονδε from the 'pronominal' -δε of Gk. ő-δε); and it is doubtful how far there was originally any real distinction between them. In Latin their original form is especially obscured by the Latin tendency to syncopate a short second syllable (ch. iii. § 13), a process which may have led to the confusion of the Preposition *endŏ-*, *indŭ-* with the different Preposition *en-*, *in-*, in such words as *indŭ-grĕdi*, *in-gredi*, *indŭ-pĕrator*, *im-perator*, and ultimately to the disuse of *endo*, *indu*, in favour of *en*, *in*. (In Terence *inaudio* alone is used for earlier *ind-audio* and *in-audio*. A similar confusion of I.-Eur. *endo and *en may have taken place in Celtic).

And the tendency of a Latin Preposition, because unaccented, to be obscured brought about that confusion of *ob-* and *ab-*, *de-* and *di-* (*dis-*) in Compounds which we see in Late Latin, and which even in the earlier centuries of the Empire attracted the notice of the grammarians (Vel. Long. 64. 19 K., &c., on *de-* and *di-*; in Romance *abdurare*, *abaudire*, *abtenere* have supplanted *obdūrare*, *obaudire*, *obtĭnēre*). A much earlier opportunity of confusion was afforded by Prepositions which represented different developments, case-forms, &c. of the same root, e.g. Lat. *per*, through, and Umbro-Osc. per, 'on behalf of, before,' the equivalent of Lat. *pro* (both I.-Eur. *per and *pro being derived from the same root per-, on which see § 38); and this confusion is very hard to trace. The readiness too with which a Preposition changes its meaning is an obstacle in the way of identifying its cognates in other languages. Oscan úp, *op* governs the Abl. with the sense of Lat. *apud*, while Latin *ob* (governing the Acc.) has passed from that sense (§ 35) to its classical sense of ' on account of '; O. Ind. ā́ with Abl. following has the sense of ' to,' but with Abl. preceding might be translated ' from '; examples which show that a difference of meaning between a Preposition in one language and in another is not a valid proof that the two words were not originally identical. Much less is the difference of case governed to be taken into account. In the earlier stage of every language the Prepositions must have been used with great elasticity, sometimes with one case, sometimes with another (cf. O. Lat. *in potestatem esse*, &c.), the fixing down of Prepositions to a particular case being always a feature of an advanced stage of language. [Servius may thus be right in saying (ad *Ecl.* i. 29 *longo post tempore*) that *post, ante, circum* were used also with the Abl. in earlier times : antiqui enim ' post ' ' ante ' ' circum ' etiam ablativo jungebant, quod hodie facere minime possumus; Pompeius (278. 21 K.) attributes *ante templo* and *propter homine* to Pacuvius]. It should be noticed that in Umbro-Oscan local Prepositions, indicating rest in a place, &c., go with the Locative case, not the Abl. as in Latin. Their position too varied in course of time. In classical Latin a Preposition, especially a monosyllabic Preposition, precedes the noun (hence ' Pre-position '), except in particular circumstances (e. g. metu in magno, &c.; see Neue, ii³. pp. 942 sqq. for statistics), but in the older literature often follows it; and in Umbro-Oscan postposition is common, e.g. Umbr. asam-ađ, ' ad aram,' *termnom-e* ' in terminum.' (So our ' in here ' was earlier ' here in '). In I.-Eur. the Preposition seems to have preceded the Verb, but to have followed the Noun, while between the Prep. and the Verb a Particle or Enclitic Pronoun (ch. iii. § 12) might be inserted (cf. O. Lat. *anti-d-eo*, § 18 ?, *sub vos placo*, p. 569).

On the Vulgar Latin treatment of Prepositions in composition with Verbs, as it is reflected in the Romance languages, see Meyer-Lübke *Rom. Gram.* ii. pp. 617 sqq. To the ordinary Prepositions were added *foris*, e. g. Vulg. Lat. *foris-facere* (Fr. forfaire, Ital. fuorfare), and other words.

§ 12. **Ab, ap-, po-, abs, ā-, au-, af, absque.** *Ăb*, from, is I.-Eur. *ap (Goth. af, Engl. of, off), a curtailed form of *ăpŏ (O. Ind. ápa, Gk. ἄπο, e.g. O. Ind. apa-i-, ' to go away,' Gk. ἄπ-ειμι, Lat. *ab-eo*; cf. Lat. *ăpŭd* for *apo-d*, see below), of which another curtailment was *po (O. Sl. po-, Lith. pa-), found in Lat. *pŏ-sĭtus, pōno* for *po-s(i)no* (with Pft. *pŏ-sīvi* changed to *pŏs-ui* owing to a false apprehension of *po-situs* as if it were *posi-tus* like *mŏnĭ-tus*). (*Po-lubrum*, a wash-basin, *pŏ-lire*, and Germ. vo-n, O. H. G. fo-na and fo-n, have also been referred to this I.-Eur. form, § 39). The form *ăp-* appears in *ăp-ĕrio*, and was no doubt the shape assumed by the word in such collections as *ab templo*; *ab* is due to the same

Latin preference for -*b* rather than -*p*, as substituted *ob* for *op* (Osc. *op* ; cf. Lat. *op-erio*), *sub* for *sup (ch. ii. § 73). The form *abs* (pronounced and often written *aps*, see ch. ii. § 80), in which the Preposition is augmented by the particle *-s(ĕ) (Gk. ἄψ), is used in Composition before Tenues, e. g. before *t, c* in *abs-traho, abs-condo*, while before *p* it is, by a law of Latin phonetics (ch. iv. § 157), reduced to *as-*, e. g. *as-porto* for *aps-porto, *as-pello* for *aps-pello ; it appears also in the O. Lat. phrase *absque me (te*, &c.*) esset (foret)*, equivalent to ' si sine me esset,' where *que*, like its O. Ind. equivalent ca in the Rig-Veda, seems almost to have the sense of ' if ' (cf. O. Engl. an for and); at a later period *absque me*, &c. was used without the verb, and *absque* came to take the sense of *sine*, without (*A. L. L.* vi. 197). That *ā* (Osc. aa-manaffed ' amandavit,' Umbr. aha-, aa-, a-, e. g. *aha-vendu* beside *pre-vendu*) is another form of *ab*, as *ē* of *ex* (see below), is generally believed, though it is difficult to see why *ob* and *sub* did not develope corresponding forms *ō, *sū; it may be an entirely different word, associated with *ab* because of its resemblance in meaning, form, and usage [1]. *Au-* of *aufŭgio*, *aufĕro*, &c. is an example of an association of this kind. It has not been produced from *ab* by any phonetic process, but represents a different I.-Eur. preposition, *aw(ĕ) (O. Ind. áva, Pruss. au-, e. g. O. Ind. ava-bhr- ' au-fero '), which was brought into requisition in these Compounds before an initial *f* to avoid confusion with the compounds of *ad*, e. g. *affero*. (On the confusion between *āfluo* and *affluo*, see Nettleship, *Contrib. Lat. Lex.* s.v.). A curious Preposition *af*, used in Cicero's time occasionally in account-books, with the name of the person from whom money had been received, occurs on a few inscriptions, and in O. Lat. *afvolant* for *āvŏlant*. Whether it is a dialectal form (cf. Pelign. af-ďed ' abiit ' ?) with *f* representing some I.-Eur. aspirate (cf. O. Ind. ádhi, ' on,' used with Abl. in the sense of ' from '), or a Latin variety of *ab* (or *au* ?) with *f* produced originally under the influence of some following consonant (most probably *v*), it is impossible to say. It may be a mere (Greek ?) trick of writing, with the symbol F employed to denote the *u-* or *w-* sound, like the Greek digamma (cf. Prisc. i. 35. 17 H.).

---

[1] Lat. *ā* and W. Teut. ō are referred to I.-Eur. *ā by Buck, *Osk. Spr.* p. 25.

§ 13. **Ab, abs, a.** In Plautus *ab* is used before vowels and *j, s, r* ; *ā* before *b, p, m, f, v, c, q, g* (Labial and Guttural sounds); *abs* (and *a*) before *tu, tuus*, &c.; *ab* and *a* before *t, d, l, n*; in class. Lat. *ab* is used before vowels and *l, n, r, s, j; ā* before *b, p, f, v* ; '*abs* before *c, q, t* (Cicero began with *abs te*, but discarded this expression for *a te*) ; in Late Latin *ab* is used before vowels, *ā* before consonants (see Langen, *Beitr.* 331 ; Georges, *Lex. Wortf.* s. v. ; *A. L. L.* iii. 148). The usage of *ā* in the older period allows of its being a mere phonetic development of *ab*, for *ā bello* may be simply an expression of the sound *abbello* (ch. ii. § 130), and so the shortening of *ā* by the Law of Breves Breviantes in Plautus, e. g. *quid ă béllo portat?*, will not be a case of the shortening of a naturally long vowel by this law (see ch. iii. § 34).

§ 14. **Af.** Cicero's words are (*Orat.* xlvii. 158) : una praepositio est 'af,' eaque nunc tantum in accepti tabulis manet, ne his quidem omnium, in reliquo sermone mutata est ; nam 'a-movit' dicimus et 'ab-egit' et 'abs-tulit,' ut jam nescias 'a' ne verum sit an 'ab,' 'abs.' Quid si etiam 'au-fugit,' quod 'ab-fugit' turpe visum est et 'a-fer' noluerunt, 'aufugit' et 'aufer' maluerunt. Quae praepositio praeter haec duo verba nullo alio in verbo reperietur. Velius Longus (60. 13 K.), who refers to this passage of Cicero, gives as an illustration of the now obsolete use of *af* in receipts, *af Longo* (his own name); Paul. Festus (19. 31 Th.) mentions *afvolant* as an actual form used by an ancient writer. On an inscription of Amiternum (*Not. Scav.* Oct. 1891) we have *af vinieis, af villa* (beside *ab castello, ab segete*) ; on the Epistula ad Tiburtes (*C. I. L.* i. 201, of c. 100 B. C.) *af uobeis* ; on the milestone of Popillius (i. 551, of 132 B. C., from Lucania) *af Capua* (besides *ab Regio*) ; on a bilingual (Greek and Latin) inscription ascribed to c. 81 B. C. (i. 587) *af Lyco* ; on an inscription of Praeneste (i. 1143) *af muro*, and so on.

§ 15. **Ad**, at, to, I.-Eur. *ad (O. Ir. ad, e. g. at-om-aig ' adigit me,' lit. ' ad me agit,' Goth. at, Engl. at ; cf. Goth. at-tiuha with Lat. *ad-dūco*, Goth. at-baira with Lat. *ad-fĕro*) is a different word from the Conjunction *at*, I.-Eur. *at (Goth. aþ- in aþ-þan, ' but '), though often confused with it in Roman spelling (ch. ii. § 76). On the old form *ar*, e. g. *arfuerunt, arvorsum*, due to the phonetic change of *d* to an *r*-sound before *f, v*, see ch. iv. § 112. This Preposition, which governs the Acc. in Umbro-Oscan as in Latin, is found augmented with the particle *s(e) in Oscan, e.g. az húrtúm 'ad hortum' ; but also ad, e. g. adpúd 'adquo' 'quoad,' idad ' ad id.' In Umbrian we have *ař*, e. g. *ař-fertur* 'adfertor,' *ařputrati* 'arbitratu ' (ch. iv. § 112), postfixed to Nouns, e. g. asam-*ař* ' ad aram,' written *ar*- in *arnipo* ' quoad ' (§ 10. 3).

§ 16. **Ambĭ-**, around, on each side, I.-Eur. *ambhĭ (Gk. ἀμφί; cf. O. Ind. abhí, Gaul. ambi-, O. Ir. imme, imb-, W. am-, O. Engl. ymb, O. Sl. obi-), a Locative of the same stem as I.-Eur. *ambhō, ' both '

(Gk. ἀμφω, Lat. *ambo* ; cf. O. Ind. ubhá-, Goth. bai, baj-ōþs, Lith. abù, O. Sl. oba), appears in Latin compounds in the forms, (1) *amb-* before a vowel, e. g. *amb-arvāle* (sacrificium) ' quod arva ambiat victima ' (Serv. ad *Ecl.* iii. 77), *amb-urbiales* (hostiae) ' quae circum terminos urbis Romae ducebantur ' (Paul. Fest. 4. 15 Th.), *amb-ustus* ' circumustus ' (*ib.* 4. 17), whence by false analogy *comb-ustus*, instead of *com-ustus (unless this rather represents *co-amb-ustus*), *amb-ĭtus* ' circuitus ' (*ib.* 4. 18); (2) *am-* before a consonant, e. g. *am-ter-mini* (oratores), a phrase of Cato's ' qui circa terminos provinciae manent ' (Paul. Fest. 13. 9 Th.; Macr. i. 14. 5; Gl. Philox.), *am-plector*, *am-pendices* ' quod circumpendebant ' (Paul. Fest. 16. 3 Th.), *am-segetes* ' quorum ager viam tangit ' (*ib.* 16. 1 ; Charis. 231. 11 K. seems to quote a similar *amfines*), *ăm-ĭcio* for *am-jicio*. The form *ambĭ-* in compounds bears the sense of ' both ' in *ambĭ-dens* (ovis) ' quae superioribus et inferioribus est dentibus ' (Paul. Fest. 4. 9 Th.), *ambi-lustrum* ' quod non licebat nisi ambos censores post quinquennium lustrare civitatem ' (' Serv.' ad *Aen.* i. 283), *ambi-vium*. In Umbro-Oscan the word appears with an *r*-suffix (cf. *inter*), Osc. amfr-et ' ambiunt,' Umbr. ambr-etuto ' ambiunto,' but also e. g. Osc. am-núd ' circuitu,' am-víanud ' vico,' Umbr. *an-ferener* ' circumferendi.'

§ 17. **An-**, a curtailment of I.-Eur. *ănă, ' on ' (Zend ana, Gk. ἀνά, Goth. ana, Engl. on, O. Sl. vŭ for *ŏn) (cf. I.-Eur. *ănŭ), (O. Ind. ánu, Zend anu) may appear in *ăn-hēlus* (also derived from the root an-, ' to breathe,' whence *ănĭmus*, &c.), *an-quīro* [by some explained as **amb(i)-quiro*], *an-tennae*, *an-testari* (or for *ante-tennae, *ante-testari, ch. iii. § 13, p. 176). Its presence is more certain in Umbro-Oscan, e. g. Osc. ava-Faκετ ' consecravit,' *an-getuzet* ' proposuerunt,' Umbr. an-tentu ' intendito,' am-pentu ' impendito,' unless indeed it is here some variety of Lat. *in*, as an- the Umbro-Oscan negative prefix (ch. iv. § 81) is of Lat. *in-*.

§ 18. **Antĕ**, before, I.-Eur. *antĭ (O. Ind. ánti, ' opposite, near,' Gk. ἀντί, opposite, instead of, Goth. and, ' towards,' Engl. an-swer, Lith. añt, ' on '), a Locative Sing. of some stem connected with Lat. *antes*, rows, O. Ind. ánta-, ' vicinity, end,' Goth. and-eis, ' end,' of which Gk. ἄντα, opposite (cf. ἄντην), is another case. In Oscan the Preposition (governing the Acc. as in Latin) appears without the final short vowel (this loss of a final ĭ is common in Oscan), e. g. ant púnttram 'ante pontem;' but in Latin, though *poste* was reduced to *post* (see below), *ant* is not written for *ante* [in Plaut. *Rud.* 509, if the reading of the MSS. is right, we must pronounce *ant(e)positast*, a quadrisyllable:

> quam quaé Thyestae quóndam antepósitast Téreo.

On *antenna* and *antestor*, see above]. With the particle *dĕ appended, as in *postid*, is the form *antĭd-* in O. Lat. *antĭd-eo* (e. g. Plaut. *Trin.* 545 sed Campans genus Multo Surorum iam antidit patientiā), *antĭd-hac* (used by Plautus when three syllables are required by the metre, *antehac* being a dissyllable; cf. *antĭdit*, &c. and *anteit*, &c.), *antĭd -eā* (Liv. xxii. 10. 6 in the Vow of the Ver Sacrum; *antea* is not found in Plautus, and only once in Terence, viz. *Andr. 52*). In *antid-* the -ĭ of I.-Eur. *anti, not being final, does not sink to ĕ (cf. *anti-stes*, &c., ch. iii. § 39).

§ 19. **Apud,** which is also spelt *aput*, seems to be the I.-Eur. Preposition *ăpŏ (of which Lat. *ab* is a curtailment; see above), augmented by the particle *d(e), or *t(ĭ), and must have been originally *apo-d*, or *apo-t* (cf. Dor. ποτί). An old form *apor*, with that change of -*d* to an *r*-sound (before *f*, *v*) seen in *arfue-runt*, *ar-vorsum*, &c. (ch. iv. § 112), is quoted by Paul. Fest. 19. 34 Th. (cf. *apur finem* on a Marsic inscr., Zvet. *I. I. I.* 45; *apur* is quoted by Mar. Vict. 9. 17 K.). On the spelling *aput*, like *at, set* for *ad, sed*, see ch. ii. § 76. In Oscan úp, *op* (Lat. *ob*) is used with the Abl. in the sense of Lat. *apud*, e. g. *op tovtad* 'apud populum,' úp eísúd sakaraklúd 'apud id sacellum.'

§ 20. **Circum, circā, circĭter.** *Circum*, around, is the Adverbial Acc. Sg. of *circus* (Gk. κρίκος, a ring; cf. O. Engl. hring, with nasalization), which had in O. Lat. the sense of class. *circulus* (Dub. Nom. 573. 4 K; cf. above, ch. v. § 24), and is used, for example, by Accius of the moon's orbit (*Trag.* 100 R.):

> quot lúna circos ánnuo in cursu ínstitit.

In the early literature *circum* is the only form, whether Adverb or Preposition, but in class. Lat. a byform *circā* appears, first found in Cicero (who uses it in three passages of the Verrine orations, but afterwards seems to have discarded it), possibly never in Caesar, but much affected by Livy. *Circā* is a formation on the type of *suprā, extrā,* &c., perhaps originally employed with verbs like *esse* (Cicero's three examples of the words are : *Verr.* II. i. 51. 133 canes esse circa se multos; i. 48. 126 canibus, quos circa se haberet; iv. 48. 107 Henna, quam circa lacus sunt plurimi), owing to a feeling that *circum* was suitable only for verbs of motion, e. g. legatos circum civitates mittere, 'to send ambassadors a tour of the states,' ire circum urbem, ' to go a circuit of the city ' (*A. L. L.* v. 295). *Circiter*, an adverbial formation like *breviter*, O. Lat. *amiciter* (see § 1), came to be restricted to the logical sense of ' about,' ' almost,' e. g. Plaut. *Cist.* 677 loca haec circiter. The form *circo* appears in the Adverb *id-circo*, as *circa* in *quocirca*, with the same logical sense (cf. Osc. *amnud*, 'because of,' in *egm*[*as tovti*]*cas amnud* 'rei publicae causa,' an adverbial Abl. Sg. Neut. of amno-, a formation with the suffix -no- from the Preposition am- [Lat. *am-, ambi-*], as comno- ' comitium ' from the Prep. com-).

Cīs, cĭtrā, on this side (cf. Umb. çimu, *šimo*, 'retro'?), are formed from the I.-Eur. pronominal root ḱi-, 'this' (Gk. -κι of οὑκί, πολλάκι, Goth. hi-na, ' this,' Engl. he, Lith. szìs, O. Sl. sĭ), exactly as their opposites *uls, ultra*, on that side, from the I.-Eur. pronominal root ol-, 'that' (ch. vii. § 13), the first by the addition of the particle **s(e) (p. 573 ; on *uls* for **oll*, see § 56), the second (an Abl. Sg. Fem.) by the suffix -tero- (ch. v. § 16). The Adverb *citrō* (Abl. Sg. Neut. or Masc.) corresponds to *citrā* as *ultrō* (e. g. ultro citroque) to *ultrā*.

§ 21. Clam, clancŭlum. *Clam*, an Adverbial Acc. Sg. Fem. (?) from the root *k*el-, ' to hide ' (Lat. *cēlō, occŭlo,* &c.), had in O. Lat. a byform *clam-de, clande* (written *clade* in the MSS. of Placidus 15. 32 G.; but cf. *quamde* from *quam*, ch. x. § 11), whence was formed the Adj. *clandestīnus.* Another O. Lat. form written *callim* in the MSS. of Paul. Fest. 33. 6 ('callim ·̇ antiqui dicebant pro clam, ut 'nis' pro nobis, ' sam ' pro suam, ' im ' pro eum) is more difficult to explain. (Should we read *calam*, and refer the form to the Analogy of *pălam* ? It may be merely the coinage of some grammarian to support his etymology of *clam*). *Clam*, which governs the Acc. always in Plaut. and Ter., and perhaps never the Abl. at any period of Latin (Langen, *Beitr.* p. 230), has in the Comedians another, apparently a Diminutive form, *clancŭlum* (but cf. *procul*, § 2), used as a Preposition by Terence, Adelph. 52 *clanculum patres*. Cf. the glosses: *clanculae* 'absconsae' (*C. G. L.* v. 277. 58); *clanculum* 'occultum' (*ib.* 278. 1).

§ 22. Cŏm-, (cŭm), with, and co- (e.g. *cōgo* for *cŏ-ăgo*), I.-Eur. **kŏm* and **kŏ* (?) (with palatal or with guttural *k* ?) (O. Ir. com-, co, W. cyf-, cy, Osc. *com, con, co-*, Umbr. *com, -co, co-*) is in early inscriptions written *quom* (Bersu, *Gutturale*, p. 42), like the Relative Adverb *quom*, when, because *quo-* had the same sound as *co-* (ch. iv. § 137). The *o* of *com* became *u* in the unaccented use of the word (ch. iv. § 20), and before certain initial consonants (ch. ii. § 22), and *cum* became the recognized spelling of the simple Preposition, though in compounds, e.g. *com-es*, the *o*-form was retained. On the form *co-*, e.g. *co-eo* (Quint. i. 6. 17), O. Lat. *co-ventionid*, and the like, see ch. ii. §§ 61, 65. Its original difference from *com-* is not certain. Osc. *com*, with, governs the Abl., and is prefixed in *compreivatud, conpreivatud* 'cum privato' on the Tabula Bantina (cf. Umbr. *com prinvatir* 'cum legatis'), but Umbr. *kum, com* is postfixed in the sense of 'apud,' 'juxta,' e.g. asa-ku, 'juxta aram,' *veris-co* (opposed to *pre verir* and *post verir*), at the gates.

§ 23. Contra (see §§ 1, 4). Osc. *contrud* in the phrase on the Bantine Law: *svae pis contrud exeic fefacust* 'si quis contra hoc fecerit,' is followed by the Adverb (Locative) *exeic*, as Lat. *arvorsum* in the S. C. Bacch. by the Adverb (Abl. Fem.) *ead*: sei ques esent, quei aruorsum ead fecisent. It is Abl. of an O-stem (cf. Lat. *contrō-versia*), as *contrā* of an Ā-stem.

§ 24. Cōram, in presence of (not a Preposition till Cicero's time), seems to be connected with *ōs*, Gen. *ōris*, the face, perhaps being an Adverbial Acc. Sg. Fem. of a stem **cōso-* (**cōro-*), compounded of the preposition *com-* (*cum*) and this noun (cf. O. Ind. sākṣād). *Incoram* with a Gen., e.g. incoram omnium, is found in Apuleius.

§ 25. Dē, down from, concerning (Fal. de in the phrase: de zenatuo sententiad, Zvet. *I.I.I.* 70); O. Ir. dī, O. W. dī; cf. O. Ir. di-mōr, 'very great,' with Lat. *de-magis*, &c. corresponds to Osc. *dat* (e.g. *dat senateis tanginud* 'de senatus sententia'), which seems to have the particle -t(i) affixed, as per-t, Lat. *per* (§ 38), unless the -t stand for -d, in which case **dad* may be an Ablative (Lat. *dē* for **dēd*?). The Umbrian Preposition is da (with final -d or -t dropped in Umbrian fashion), if *da-etom* on the Eugubine Tables (vi. A 28) stands for Lat. *demptum* (cf. Osc. da-did 'dedat,' da-díkatted 'dedicavit').

§ 26. **Dĭs-**, apart, is most naturally referred to some byform of the root dwo-, dwi-, 'two' (Goth. tvis-, e.g. tvis-standan, 'to separate'), wanting the w (see ch. iv. § 71). With the w the same formation expressed the Numeral Adverb **dwĭs* [O. Ind. dvís, Gk. δ(ϝ)ίς, M. H. G. zwis], and is in Latin *bis* (ch. iv. § 68). Before a vowel *dis-* becomes, by the phonetic law of Latin, *dir-* (ch. iv. § 148), e. g. *dĭr-ĭmo*, and before voiced consonants (see ch. iv. § 151) *dī-*, e. g. *di-mŏveo* (*dis-mota* on the S. C. Bacch., *C. I. L.* i. 196).

§ 27. **Endŏ**. (Cf. O. Ir. ind-., e. g. ind-riuth, 'I attack,' Gaul. ande-?), also under the form *indu*, the *i* and *u* being apparently weakening of *e* and *o* due to the unaccented use of the Preposition. It corresponds in meaning to *in* (both with Abl. and Acc.), and was in classical Latin replaced by *in*, e. g. class. *im-pĕrātor*, O. Lat. *indu-perator*, class. *in-grĕdi*, O. Lat. *indu-gredi*. It seems to represent an I.-Eur. **en-dŏ* (Gk. ἔνδο-θι, ἔνδο-θεν, ἔνδον), compounded of the Prep. **en* (Lat. *in*) and the Prep. **dŏ* (cf. Lat. *dō-nec*; O. Ir. do, Engl. to, Lith. do, O. Sl. do), the last element being connected with the Adverbial particle **d(e)* (Gk. δόμον-δε). The final -ŏ has been preserved from becoming -ĕ in Latin (ch. iii. § 37) by the frequent use of the word as the first element in a compound. (So **prŏ* remains *pro* in Latin and does not in unaccented use become **prĕ*, owing to compounds like *prŏ-ficiscor*, &c.). Traces of the same confusion of I.-Eur. **endo-* and I.-Eur. **en-* are seen in Celtic.

Endo and indu. The form *endo* occurs, e. g. in the epitaph of Ennius, quoted by Cicero, in his *De Republica* (ap. Sen. *Epp.* 108. 34):

 si fas endo plagas caelestum ascendere cuiquam est,
  mi soli caeli maxima porta patet,

in a clause of the XII Tables (ap. Fest. 452. 6 Th.): si caluitur, pedemue struit, manum endo iacito, 'if he deceives, or attempts to run away, the prosecutor may arrest him,' a clause alluded to by Lucilius, xvii. 10 M.:

 si non it, capito, inquit, eum, et si caluitur, endo
 fertŏ manum,

§§ 26-29.] PREPOSITIONS. 583

and in other laws, and is one of the archaisms used by Cicero in drawing up his code of laws (*Legg.* ii. 8. 19); it is employed too by Lucretius (vi. 890) endŏ mari [cf. the glosses: *endoclusa* ἐγκεκλεισμένη; *endo festabat*; *endo rivum κατὰ ῥεῖθρον*; *endodicarit μηνύσει* (*C. G. L.* ii. 61. 35); *endogenia* (*-ua* ?) 'naturaliter amoena'; *endoriguum* 'irriguum' (*C. G. L.* v. 193. 25)]. The form *indo-* appears in a line of Ennius, referring to Romulus and Remus (*Ann.* 59 M.):

indotuetur ibi lupus femina, conspicit omnis;

the form *indu*, e. g. in Ennius, *Ann.* 298 M. indu foro lato sanctoque senatu (cf. Lucil. *inc.* 17 indŭ foro); in Lucr. v. 102 nec jacere indu manus (cf. ii. 1096 indu manu), as well as in the compounds *induperator* Enn., Lucr., *indupedio* Lucr., *indugredior* Lucr., &c. By the time of Plautus the word seems to have dropped out of ordinary usage, for it occurs in his plays only in compounds like *ind-audio* (Terence knows only *in-audio*), *ind-ĭpiscor* (cf. class. *ind-ĭgeo, indĭ-gĕna, ind-ŏles*, &c.); and though it occurs at the end of Varro's *Res Rusticae* (iii. 17. 10): ille inde endo suam domum, nos nostram, the phrase is a quotation from Ennius' curious experiment in language, mentioned by Ausonius (*Techn.* 18) and others: endo suam do, with *do*, an apocopated form of *dŏmum*, after the type of Homer's δῶ.

§ 28. **Ergā, ergō.** *Ergā*, originally local (e. g. Plaut. *Truc.* 405 tonstricém Suram Nouístin nostram quae érga aedem seséd habet?, if the MSS. reading be right), must be connected with *ergō*, on account of, in O. Lat. a preposition or rather postposition, governing the Genitive, e. g. funeris ergo, XII Tab. Whether the two words have been differentiated on the type of *ultrā* and *ultrō, intrā* and *intrō*, or whether they came originally from two different stems, it is impossible to say. *Ergo* has been explained as a compound of the Preposition *ē* and the Abl. Sg. of a stem **rego-* (from the root reĝ-, 'to stretch'), meaning 'direction,' so that its change of meaning would resemble that of German wegen (originally von wegen). *Ergā* might similarly represent *e *rĕgā*, like *e rĕgiōne*, opposite. It is not restricted to the expression of friendly feeling in Plautus, e. g. *Pseud.* 1020 ne málus item erga mé sit, ut erga illúm fuit; *Cas.* 618 aut quód ego umquam erga Uénerem inique fécerim.

§ 29. **Ex, ec-, ē,** out of. I.-Eur. **eks* (Gk. ἐξ, Gaul. ex-, O. Ir. ess-, W. es-; cf. Lith. isz?) appears to be a compound of a Preposition **ek* and the particle **s(e)*, as Gk. ἄψ, Lat. *abs*, append the same particle to **ap*, a curtailment of **apo* (§ 12). In Latin compounds the Preposition often appears before the letter *f* in the form *ec-* in MSS. (cf. Ter. Scaur. 26. 14 K. effatus, non 'exfatus' nec 'ecfatus,' ut quidam putaverunt; Ter.

Maur. l. 949 K. muto vel partem prioris, si fit hirtum, syllabae, 'ecfer' ut dicam, vel illud, 'hoc tibi effectum dabo'), e.g. *ecfŏdio, ecfĕro, ecfāri* (for examples, see Neue, ii³. p. 870), often corrupted to *haec* and to *et* (see *Class. Rev.* v. 295; *Fleck. Jahrb.* 1890, p. 771). (*Et* is often a corruption also of *ex*, owing to the fact that the symbols for these words in minuscule writing were very similar.) This *ec-* may be merely a phonetic development of *ex* before *f*, as *ē* of *ex* before *d* (e.g. *ē-dūco*; cf. *sē-dĕcim*), *m* (e.g. *ē-mitto*; cf. *sē-mestris*), &c. (ch. iv. § 151). Corresponding to Lat. *ē* we find in Osc. ee-stínt (apparently with a different sound from I.-Eur. ē, which is in Osc. i, í, e.g. *ligud* 'lege'), eehiianasúm 'e(ve)hiandarum,' Umbr. ehiato- 'evehiato-,' easa 'ex ara,' &c. (see ch. ii. § 6).

Extrā. (O. Lat. *extrad*; cf. the S. C. Bacch., *C. I. L.* i. 196 exstrad urbem) is an Abl. Sg. Fem. of an extension of *ex* by the suffix -t(e)ro- (ch. v. § 16), like *in-tra, cĭ-tra, ul-tra*, &c. Oscan ehtrad (with *ht* for *ct*, as in Uhtavis, the Oscan form of *Octavius*), O. Ir. echtar may represent an original stem *ek̂(s)-tero- or *ek̂-tero-.

§ 30. **Ĭn**, in, the unaccented form of O. Lat. *en* [cf. *énque*, but *ináltod* on the (restored) Col. Rostrata (*C. I. L.* i. 195)] is I.-Eur. *ĕn (Gk. ἐν, O. Ir. in, W. yn, Goth. in, Lith. į̃). The same form is used in Latin and other languages with the two senses, (1) in, (2) into [whereas in Greek the second is distinguished by the addition of the particle *s(e), ἐνς, Att. εἰς], and appears to be a Locative case, formed without the case-suffix -ĭ (ch. vi. § 37). (The Greek byform ἐνί shows this case-suffix; but cf. above, § 11). Before labial consonants *in* became *im* by the Latin phonetic law (ch. iv. § 78), e.g. *im-pleo, im-mitto, imbello* (in war), *C. I. L.* iii. 4835, &c. On the derivative Prepositions *endo, inter*, see §§ 27, 32.

Osc. en (ín), Umbr. en, have with Acc. and Loc. (not Abl.) the two senses of Lat. *in*, but are postfixed, e.g. Osc. *exaisc-en ligis* 'hisce in legibus,' Pel. eite uus pritrom-e, 'do ye go past or forward,' Umbr. arvam -en 'in arvum,' arven 'in arvo,' fesner-e 'in fanis.' Osc. -en with the Abl. imad-en 'ab ima (parte),' *eisuc-en ziculud* 'ab eo die (*dieculo),' which has the sense of Lat. *ab*, has been referred to Lat. *inde* (but see § 10. 6).

§ 31. **Infrā** (*infera*, C.I.L. i. 1166), an Abl. Sg. Fem. like *suprā, citrā, intrā*, connected with the Adj. *infĕrus* (on which see ch. v. § 16).

§ 32. **Intĕr**, between (O. Ind. antár, O. Ir. ētar ; e. g. O. Ind. antár-chid- 'inter-scindo'), is formed from *in* by the addition of the suffix -tero- (see ch. v. § 16), like *intĕrior* (cf. *intrō, intrā*), as *ex-tero-*, &c. from *ex*. The Oscan form is anter (with Acc., but once with Abl.-Loc. Plur.), the Umbrian form is anter, *ander* (governing the Acc.), both with an- corresponding to Lat. *in-*, the Preposition, as to Lat. *in*, the Negative, e. g. Umbr. an-takro- 'in-tegro-.'

§ 33. **Intrā, intŭs**. *Intrā* is an Abl. Sg. Fem. like *extrā*, class. *contrā* (while *intro* is an Abl. Sg. Neut. like Osc. *contrud*, Lat. *contrō-versia*) (cf. Osc. Entra-, the name of a goddess). *Intus* (Gk. ἐν-τός with the I.-Eur. affix -tŏs, implying usually motion from, § 1) wavers between an Adverb and a Preposition in such a phrase as Virgil's *tali intus templo*, 'in such temple, within' or 'within such temple' (cf. Lucr. vi. 798).

§ 34. **Juxtā**, which is first used as a Preposition by Caesar, is Abl. Sg. Fem. of a stem **juxto-*, whether this be P. P. P. of a verb **juxo* formed from *jungo* as *viso* from *video*, *quaeso* from *quaero* (ch. viii. § 33. 4), or a Superlative with the I.-Eur. Superlative suffix -isto- (Gk. πλε-ῖστος, &c.). The Adv. *juxtim* is found as early as Livius Andronicus (*Trag.* 11 R.).

§ 35. **Ŏb**, I.-Eur. **op(i)*, apparently a variety of **epi* (Gk. ἐπί, on, to, ὄπι-σθεν, behind, O. Ind. ápi, 'by,' Lith. api-, 'around'; cf. Lith. ap-szvĕsti, 'to make light,' with Lat. *ob-caeco*, to make dark), is in Oscan *op* (with the sense of Lat. *ăpud*, governing the Abl., e.g. *op tovtad* 'apud populum,' úp eísúd sakaraklúd 'apud id sacellum'), and often retains its *-p* in Latin spelling in compounds like *op-tĭneo* (e.g. *optenui* on a Scipio Epitaph, C.I.L. i. 38; cf. Quint. i. 7. 7), *op-ĕrio*, though in the simple word the Latin usage substituted the Media for the Tenuis as the final consonant (cf. *ab* for *ap*, *sub* for *sup*, and see ch. ii. § 76). In classical Latin it has the sense of 'before,' e.g. *ob oculos ponere*, to describe, or 'on account of'; but in the earlier literature it had other shades of meaning; cf. Paul. Fest. 193. 7 Th.

ob praepositio alias ponitur pro circum, ut cum dicimus urbem
'obsideri,' ... 'obvallari,' ... alias pro ad, ut Ennius:

<small>ob˙Romam noctu legiones ducere coepit;</small>

Servius tells us that many interpreted *ob Italiam* in Virgil, *Aen.*
i. 233 as 'juxta Italiam,' with the old sense of *ob* : ob enim
veteres pro juxta ponebant. (This variety of meanings has been
explained by the theory that Lat. *ob* represents, not only I.-Eur.
*epi, *opi, but also an *ebhi, seen in O. Ind. abhí.) By the addition of the particle *s(e), as *ab* became *abs* (e.g. *abs te, abstineo*),
so *ob* became *obs*, a form occasionally found in compounds before
t-, e.g. *obstinet* (Fest. 228. 6 Th. o. dicebant antiqui, quod nunc est
ostendit), *obstrudant* (Paul. Fest. 221. 3 Th. ' avide trudant'; Fest.
220. 14) (so Umbr. *os-tendu* 'ostendito'). (On *ŏmitto*, see ch. iii. §34.)

§ 36. **Pălam**, like its opposite, *clam*, an Acc. Sg. Fem. (but
see § 1) of some stem, perhaps connected with the Plautine
verb *dispalesco* (*Bacch.* 1046):

<small>periisse suáuiust
quam illúd flagitium uólgo dispaléscere</small>

(from the root of *pālari*, to wander, be dispersed abroad). Others
connect it with *palma*, the hand, and make it mean literally ' in
the hand.' Besides the Adv. *palam* we have *prō-palam*, as early
as Plautus, but *palam* is not a Prep. till the Augustan Age.

§ 37. **Pĕnĕs** (governing the Acc., usually of a person), represents some case of *penus, -oris* N., or a kindred stem, from the
root pen- of *penĭ-tus* (§ 1), *penĕ-tro*, &c., a suffixless Locative
according to some (cf. Dor. αἰές), a Loc. Pl. according to others,
who offer a similar explanation of *vĭcissi-m* (ch. ix. § 4), *sēmissi-,
vix, mox* (cf. § 3). The final syllable may have been prevented
from being weakened to -*is* by the fact that the stress of the
voice fell on it in the common phrases *penés-me, penés-te, penésnos, penés-vos*, &c. (ch. iii. § 12 *a.* 3). *Penes* is used only with
Pronouns in Plautus.

§ 38. **Pĕr**, through (Goth. fair-, Lith. peř), connected with
I.-Eur. *perō, ' I transport, bring or pass through' (O. Ind. pr̥-,
O. Sl. perą; cf. Gk. πείρω, πεῖρα, Lat. *ex-pĕrior*, &c.),
corresponds to Osc. *per-* of *peremust*, Fut. Pft. of a verb used

apparently in the old sense of Lat. *perĕmo* (Fest. 266. 31 Th. 'peremere' Cincius in libro de Verbis Priscis ait significare idem, quod prohibere: at Cato in libro qui est de Re Militari pro vitiare usus est), though the commoner form of the Oscan Preposition is pert (with the suffix -tĭ of Gk. προτί, § 11), e.g. *comono pertemest* 'comitia peremet,' *am-pert*, 'not beyond' (used like Lat. *duntaxat*, § 7), *petiro-pert*, 'four times' (cf. Lat. *sem-per*, § 7), and to Umbr. per, pert, e.g. *per-etom* 'peremptum,' *trio-per*, 'three times,' which with the Abl. has the sense of Lat. *pro*, e.g. *nomne-per* 'pro nomine.' The intensive sense of *per-* in *per-magnus*, *per-quam*, &c. (often separated from the qualified word, e.g. per pol quam paucos reperias, Ter. *Hec.* 58; hence *per-taesus* did not become *per-tīsus*, ch. iii. § 23), is seen in Lith. per-saldùs, 'very sweet'; cf. Gk. περι-μήκης, very long, &c. (cf. Engl. 'through' and 'thorough'). Again Lat. *per-* approaches the usual sense of Gk. περί, about, around, in *pertĕgo, perungo, pervŏlito*. The sense of 'past,' 'beyond' (cf. Osc. *am-pert*, pert víam 'trans viam,' Umbr. pert spinia 'trans spinam' (?)) appears in *per-go*, &c.; and with the implication of wrong or injury (cf. Gk. παρα-βαίνω, παρ-όμνυμι), in *per-jūrus* [from which *pejĕro, perjero* (see Georges, *Lex. Wortf.* s. v.), can hardly be separated, though the *ĕ* is hard to explain], *per-do, per-fĭdus*, and of difference in *perĕgrē* It thus appears that *per* represents a considerable variety of meanings, and this variety is increased if we take into account Umbro-Oscan per, pert. For besides the sense of Lat. *pro*, on behalf of, seen in Umbr. *nomne-per*, &c. in the Eugubine Liturgy: (*tio . . . ocre-per Fisiu, tota-per Iovina, erer nomne-per, erar nomne-per . . . subocau* 'te pro arce Fisia, pro populo Iguvino, pro ejus (M.) nomine, pro ejus (F.) nomine, subvoco,' estu esunu fetu fratrus-per Atiiedie 'ista sacra facito pro fratribus Atiediis'), once written -pert in the phrase: Petruniapert natine ' pro Petronia natione,' it has the local sense of Latin *pro-*, forward, in front, in the words, Umbr. *per-ne*, per-naio-, opposed to *post-ne* (Lat. *pōne*, behind), post-naio-, Osc. Perna-, the name of a goddess [cf. I.-Eur. *per- in *per-ŭt(ĭ), from *wĕtos-, ' a year,' O. Ind. parut, ' in the former year,' Gk. πέρυσι, Dor. πέρυτι). The reason of this is that the I.-Eur. root per- produced a large number of Prepositions, representing different case-forms, &c., *pérĭ Loc.

(O. Ind. pári, 'around,' Gk. περί), *pᵉrós Gen. (O. Ind. purás, 'before,' Gk. πάρος), *pérm (O. Ind. páră, 'beyond'; cf. párā, Gk. πέρᾱ; Lat. *perem-* of *peren-die,* Osc. *perum dolom mallom* 'sine dolo malo'), and so on. The weak grades of the root, pr̥-, pr-, seen in Gk. παρά, Goth. faura, faur, Engl. be-fore, appear in Lat. *por-* of *por-tentum,* &c., Umbr. pur-titu, *pur-ditom* (unless this be merely a metathesis of *prŏ*), and in Lat. *prŏ,* Umbr. *pro,* pru, Osc. *pro,* pru, as well as in Lat. *prae* from *prai (Pel. prai-, Osc. *prae,* Umbr. pre), perhaps a Dative form (cf. Gk. παραί, O. Ind. paré).

§ 39. **Pŏ-,** retained only in a few Compounds, *po-situs, po-lubrum, porceo,* &c., as Teut. *miþ, 'with' (Goth. miþ, Germ. mit, like Gk. μετά) is in English retained only in the compound 'midwife' (see under *ab,* § 12).

§ 40. **Post, pōnĕ.** *Post,* behind, from **posti,* O. Lat. *poste, posti-d* (with the particle *d(e)), adds the suffix -tĭ (§ 11) to I.-Eur. *pos (Lith. pàs, &c.), which seems to be derived from *pŏ- (Lith. pa-, 'under,' O. Sl. po, 'about'), a curtailment of *ăpŏ (see § 12). In certain collocations the -*t* was dropped by the Latin phonetic law (ch. iv. § 157), e.g. *C. I. L.* i. 1454 postempus; of Virg. *Aen.* iii. 1 Marius Victorinus says (22. 11 K.): posquam res Asiae, non 'postquam'; and this *pos* might be further reduced (before *m,* &c., ch. iv. § 151) to *pō-,* e.g. *pō-merium* (so spelt, not *pomoerium*), quod erat post murum 'post-moerium' dictum, Varro *L. L.* v. 143.

Pone (Plaut., &c.) adds the suffix -*nĕ* (§ 11) to *post* (Umbr. *postne,* opposed to *perne*; cf. pustnaio-, pusnao- Adj., opposed to pernaio-).

Umbrian *post* is joined with the same case as *pre* (Lat. *prae*), e.g. *post verir Treblanir* and *pre verir Treblanir,* in O. Umbr. pusveres Treplanes and preveres Treplanes, and similarly Osc. púst feíhúís ' post fines,' while Osc. *post exac* corresponds to Lat. *posthac.*

In Umbro-Oscan we find a Preposition postin governing the Acc. case with the sense of Lat. *secundum,* e.g. Umbr. pusti kastruvuf, 'according to their lands,' Osc. pústin slagím, 'according to the locality (?).'

§§ 39-43.] PREPOSITIONS. 589

§ 41. Poste, posti-d, pos, pō-. *Poste*, which shows the regular change of -ĭ when final to ĕ (ĭ not final is retained, e. g. *posti-d*, see ch. iii. § 39), is found in a fine line of Ennius, *Ann.* 244 M., an exhortation to rowers :

poste recumbite, uestraque pectora pellite tonsis,

frequently in Plautus, e. g. *Asin.* 915 (see Ritschl, *Opusc.* ii. 541 sqq.), and probably in Terence, *Eun.* 493 (see *A. L. L.* ii. 140). Its reduction to *post* is like that of *animalĕ* to *animal, nequĕ* to *nec*, &c. (ch. iii. § 36). The Adverb *postid* is not unfrequent in Plautus (e. g. *postid locorum, Poen.* 144, &c.), as also *postid-eā* (cf. *antid-eā, antid-hac*), compounded with the Adverbial Abl. Sg. Fem. of *is* (§ 10. 4) (e. g. *postidea loci, Stich.* 758, &c.), and has on account of its exclusively adverbial use been regarded as a compound of *post(e)* with *id*, the (adverbial) Acc. Sg. Neut. of *is* (cf. *post-eā, ad id locorum*, Sall., Liv.), though this explanation requires us to see in *postidea, antidea*,&c. a pleonastic repetition of the pronouns, *post-id-eā, ant-id-eā*. Cicero (*Orat.* xlvii. 157 ; cf. Vel. Long. 79. 3 K.) says that he preferred *posmeridianas* (quadrigas) to *postmeridianas*, while Quintilian (ix. 4. 39) seems to mention the form *pomeridiem*. (On the spelling *pos* for *post* in MSS. of Plautus, see Ritschl, *Opusc.* ii. 549 ; of Virgil, see Ribbeck, *Prolegg.* p. 442 ; of other authors, see Georges, *Lex. Wortf.* s.v.). The evidence points to Lat. *pos-* being not I.-Eur. *pos, but a syncopated form of I.-Eur. *pos-tĭ (see Stolz, *Beitr.* p. 21).

§ 42. Prae, before, I.-Eur. *prai (Lith. prẽ; cf. O. Ir. rē or ria, with a dropped final nasal). In O. Lat. also *pri*, according to Paul. Fest. 282. 27 Th. (cf. *pris-cus, pris-tĭnus, primus* for *prĭs-mo-*, Pelign. Prismā-, pri-stafalacirix ' prae-stabulatrices '), probably I.-Eur. *prĭ (Lith. pri, O. Sl. pri, Goth. fri-), connected with I.-Eur. *prŏ, ' before,' and with Gk. πάρος, O. Ind. purás, purá, Goth. faura, Engl. be-fore (*B. B.* xvii. 17), possibly a Dative formation from the root per- (see above, § 38). The Preposition is found with the same use as in Latin, but with prominence of the idea 'before' (often for Lat. *ante*), in the Umbro-Oscan languages ; Pel. prai-cim, Osc. prai, *prae-sentid* ' praesente ' (with the usual sense of Lat. *praesens* ; in the Columna Rostrata we have *praesens* in its older sense : praesente[d] . . . dictatored ol[or]om, ' being in command,' *C. I. L.* i. 195), *prae-fucus* ' praefectus,' Umbr. *pre verir Treblanir* ' ante portas Treblanas,' *pre-pa*, ' priusquam,' lit. ' prae-quam,' pre-habia ' praebeat.'

§ 43. Praetĕr, past, except, is formed from the preceding by means of the suffix -tero- like the Adverbs *brĕvĭ-ter*, &c. (§ 2), as from I.-Eur. *prĭ is formed Pelignian pritro- (in an epitaph, Zvet. *I. I. I.* 13 eite uus pritrome ' ite vos praeter ' quasi ' praeterum in '). (Cf. Umbr. pretro- ' prior.')

§ 44. **Pro, por-.** *Prŏ*, before, forth, is I.-Eur. *prŏ (O. Ind. prá, Gk. πρό, O. Ir. ro-, used like the Greek augment with preterite tenses, Goth. fra-, Lith. pra-, O. Sl. pro). The long vowel seems to be the vowel of the Oscan preposition (or I.-Eur. *prŭ, Gk. πρύτανις, &c.), e.g. *pru-hipid* ' prohibuerit,' *pruter-pan* ' priusquam,' and may have been I.-Eur. (Gk. πρω-ί, early, O. H. G. fruo, Lett. prû-jam, ' forth '). These Oscan forms suggest that Lat. *prō* was not originally **prōd*, an Abl. form (which would be in Oscan *prud-, not pru-), so that the *prōd-* of *prōd-est, prōd-ire*, may be a form augmented by the particle *-d(e) like *anti-d-*, *posti-d, r-ed-*, &c. In Late Latin the form *prode* (cf. Charis. 236. 29 K.) is common, especially with *esse* (cf. Charis. 237. 8 K., and see Neue, ii³. p. 662) (*prodius* : ulterius, longius, a prodeundo, quoted by Nonius 47. 10 M. from Varro, is generally corrected by editors to *propius*). The *por-* of *por-rĭgo* or *porgo, porrĭcio* for **por-jicio, por-rō* (O. Lat. *porod*), &c. is either a metathesis of *prŏ-*, or represents an I.-Eur. by-form *pṛ (cf. Gk. παρά) (see ch. iv. § 92). In Umbrian we have *pro-* for Lat. *pro*, before, e.g. *procanurent* 'procinuerint,' affixed in ie-pru (cf. promo- 'primus'), and *pur-* in a verb corresponding in sense to Lat. *porricio* and in form apparently to Lat. *prō-do*, with P. P. P. *pur-ditom*, Imper. *pur-dovitu.*

§ 45. **Prō- and prŏ-.** The variety *prō-* and *prŏ-* in Compounds (the simple preposition has always the long vowel) is seen more in the early literature than in the stereotyped usage of the classical age : *prŏvehat atque prŏpellat*, Lucr. iv. 194 and vi. 1027 ; Lucr. *prŏpagare* ; O. Lat. *prŏ-tinam*. *Prō-* almost ousts *prŏ-* in class. Latin, but *prŏ-* is normal before *f-*, e. g. *prŏ-ficiscor, prŏ-fundo*, except in *prō-ficio* (for *prōde-facio*, as in Late Latin ?) ; but Catullus (lxiv. 202) has *prŏfudit*; Plautus (*Men.* 643) and Ennius (*Trag.* 293 R.) *prŏfiteri* ; Plautus (*Trin.* 149) *prŏfecturus*. The Greek πρόλογος is *prŏlogus* in the Comedians (cf. *prŏpola*, Lucil. v. 28 M.), προπίνω is *prŏpinare*. Even in classical poetry we have *prŏcuro*. O. Lat. *prŏ-tervus* might be similarly explained, were it not for the fact that there are indications of an old form *proptervo-* (so in the MSS. of Plaut. *Bacch.* 612, and in the Ambrosian Palimpsest in *Truc.* 256 : see Löwe, *Gloss. Nom.* pp. 142, 184, who connects the form with Gk. προπετής). *Prŏbus* (cf. O. Ind. prabhú- 'preeminent') apparently adds to *prŏ* the same formation (from the root bheu- 'to be ' ?) as *super-bus* (cf. Gk. ὑπερφυής) to *super.*

§ 46. **Prŏcŭl** is formed from *prŏ by the suffix -ko- [a suffix often attached to adverbs, e.g. Lat. *postī-cus, antī-cus* (ch. v. § 31), *rĕcĭprŏcus* from **reco-* and **proco-*, § 49], and some L-suffix (see § 2). It is used as a Prep. as early as Ennius (*Trag.* 220 R.)

§ 47. **Prŏpĕ** (e. g. Plaut. *Curc.* 97 prope me est) adds to I.-Eur. *prŏ the particle -pe (ch. x. § 1. 4). The sense 'nearly' is perhaps later than Plautus (*A.L.L.* ix. 165). For Superl. *proxime* we should expect *prop-(i)s-ime*, ch. vi. § 54).

§ 48. **Proptĕr**, near, on account of (in Plautus this latter sense is always expressed by *propter*, not by *ob*, when a person is spoken of), is formed from the Adverb *prope* by means of the suffix -tero-, as *praeter* from *prae* (§ 43), *circiter* from *circum* (§ 20).

§ 49. **Rĕ-**, back, has in O. Lat. a byform *rĕd-*, with the addition of the particle *d(e) (§ 11; cf. *anti-d, posti-d*), which in class. Lat. remains in *red-eo, red-do*, &c. (*redi-vīvus* is peculiar), but is before a consonant usually discarded for *rĕ-*, e. g. *rĕ-dūco* (O. Lat. *red-duco*, but perhaps only *re-dux*), (before a vowel, not till Late Latin, e. g. *reaedifico*; see *A. L. L.* viii. 278). From *re-* was formed the Adverb *rĕ-trō* (like *in-trō, ci-trō, ul-trō*), which in Late Lat. became a Preposition, e. g. vade retro me, S. Marc. viii. 33, *Vulgata*. An Adjective-stem *rĕco-* from this Preposition (ch. v. § 31) is seen compounded with a stem *prŏco-* from the Prep. *prŏ-* in the word *reci-procus*. In Umbrian this Prep. appears in two Compound Verbs, re-vestu 'revisito' and re-statu 'restituito.'

§ 50. **Sĕcundum, sĕcŭs**. *Secundum*, according to, close behind, &c. is the Adverbial Acc. Sg. Neut. of *secundus*, following (§ 4). In plebeian Latin *secus* was used for *secundum* (Charis. 80. 18 K. id quod vulgus usurpat, 'secus illum sedi,' hoc est secundum illum, et novum et sordidum est; cf. Caper. 103. 12 K.; so on plebeian inscriptions, *secus merita ejus, secus viam*, &c., but also in O. Lat. authors, for Charis. (220. 14 K.) quotes *hoc secus*, 'soon after this,' from the historian Sempr. Asellio), which may be Nom. Sg. Masc. of an Adj.-stem (cf. *heres secus*, 'h. secundus,' *C. I. L.* iii. 387), or Acc. Sg. of a Neuter S-stem *secus*, like *tenus* (§ 54). Apparently connected with the Prep. *secus* are O. Ir. sech, 'past,' W. heb, 'without,' from a stem *seq^{u}o-; and the Latin Adv. *secus* appended to Adverbs in -im, e.g. *extrin-secus* (§ 10. 5), as well as the *secus* of phrases like *secus accidit, non secus atque* (Comp. *sequius*) has been also referred to our Preposition on the theory that this Adverb meant originally 'following but coming short of,' 'less,' as O. Ir. sech meant 'following and going past,' 'more than' (see § 8).

§ 50 a. Sĭmŭl, used as a Prep. in Augustan and later poetry, and in Silver Age prose, is perhaps Acc. Sg. Neut. of *similis* (see § 2).

§ 51. Sĭnĕ, sē. *Sine*, if connected with O. Ind. sanu-tár (cf. sani-túr), M. H. G. sun-der (which have the suffix -tero-), must represent I.-Eur. *sᵉnĭ (*sᵉnŭ), and must have been in O. Lat. **sene*, the change from *e* to *i* being due to the unaccented use of the word, as in *mihi* for **mehi* (ch. vii. § 1). The spelling *seine* on the Lex Repetundarum (*C. I. L.* i. 198. 54) is best explained, like *leiteras* on the same inscription, as a case of *ei* wrongly used for *ĭ* (ch. ii. § 130).

In O. Lat. there is another Preposition of the same meaning, *sē(d)* (as an Adverb meaning 'apart'), which became obsolete except in Compounds like *sēd-ĭtio*, lit. ' a going apart,' *se-orsum (-s)* (a dissyll. as early as Plautus), *sē-dŭlō* from *sē dolo* (whence the Adj. *sēdulus*, § 7), *sē-cūrus*, *sē-cēdo*, *sē-cerno* ; it is evidently connected with the Conjunction *sĕd* (ch. x. § 5); the *d* of *sēd-ĭtio*, &c. need not be the Abl. Case-suffix, but may be the particle *d(e) (cf. *re-d-*, § 49). This Preposition occurs in the legal phrase *se fraude*, 'without hurt,' free from penalty, written *sed fraude* on the Lex Repetundarum of 123–122 B.C. (*C. I. L.* i. 198), and on the Lex Agraria of 111 B.C. (i. 200, ll. 29 and 42, but *se dulo malo* l. 40) (cf. Paul. Fest. 500. 6 Th. 'sed ' pro sine inveniuntur posuisse antiqui). The compound *sed-ŭterque* (cf. Umbr. *sei-podruhpei*) occurs in the Nom. Sg. Fem. in Plaut. *Stich.* 106 sedutraque ut dicat mihi. This *sē(d)* has been plausibly connected with the I.-Eur. Reflexive Pronoun-stem *swe- (Lat. *sē* Acc.), and explained as originally meaning ' by oneself.' The Old Slavonic Prepositions své-ně, své-nĭ, své-nje, ' except, without,' in which this root swe- appears with an N-suffix, suggests that Lat. **se-ne* may also be connected with the Reflexive Pronoun. The first part of the Compound Verb *sol-vo*, and the Adjs. *sō-brius* (cf. *ē-brius*, according to Charis. 83. 16 K. from *bria* ' vas vinarium '), *sō-cors* (cf. *secordis* ' stultus, fatuus,' *C. G. L.* iv. 282. 52), is of kindred origin. Festus quotes *nesi* ' pro sine positum' from an inscription on the temple of Diana on the Aventine, but the fragmentary condition of the MS. of Festus for this passage (nesi pro sine positum ... Dianae Aventinen ... , 166. 26 Th.) makes it doubtful whether the word is not really the conjunction *nisi,* used in a context which gave it the force of *sine.*

§ 52. Sŭb, subtĕr, subtŭs. *Sub,* under, is I.-Eur. *ŭpŏ (O. Ind. úpa, 'to,' Gk. ὐπό, under, for ὐπό, O. Ir. fo, W. gwo-, go-, Goth. uf). The initial *s-*, which is found also in the Umbrian Preposition su(b), e. g. *subocau,* 'subvoco,' su-tentu 'subtendito,' as well as in *super* (§ 53), is generally explained as a curtailment of prefixed *ex* (I.-Eur. *eks), so that *sub* would represent an I.-Eur. compound Preposition *eks-upo, but is as likely to be the particle -s(e) (§ 11). This particle -s(e) is postfixed in the form *sus-* for *sub-s,* e. g. *sus-tineo, sus-que de-que* (in the O. Lat. phrase *susque deque fero, habeo* (Plaut. *Amph.* 886), explained by Gell. xvi. 9 as meaning 'aequo animo sum'), apparently used by wrong analogy in old forms of *sumpsit* and *sumpserit* quoted by Paul. Fest. 425. 3 Th., *suremit* and *surempsit.* *Sub-ter* is a formation like *prae-ter* (§ 43), and *sub-tus* like *in-tus* (§ 33). The diminutive sense of Lat. *sub* in *sub-absurdus,* &c. is shared by Gk. ὐπό (e. g. ὐπόλευκος) and O. Ir. fo (e. g. fo-dord, 'a murmur').

§ 53. Sŭpĕr, sŭprā, insuper, supernĕ. *Super* is I.-Eur. *ŭpĕr, *ŭpĕrĭ (O. Ind. upári, Gk. ὐπέρ for ὐπέρ, O. Ir. for, O. W. guor-, Goth. ufar) with a prefixed *s-* as in Lat. *sub,* just mentioned. Umbr. super governs the Loc., e. g. super kumne 'super comitio.' *Sŭprā* is an Abl. Sg. Fem. (*suprad* on the S. C. Bacch.) like *in-trā, ci-trā,* &c. The form *supera* is quoted by Priscian (ii. 30. 3 and 55. 23 H.) from Cicero's poems, and is found in Lucretius as well as on *C. I. L.* i. 1011. (2). 11 (see p. 181). The Umbrian equivalent is *sobra,* governing the Acc., e. g. *sobra tudero* 'supra fines.' *Super-nĕ* (also *supernĕ,* Adv. of *supernus*) is formed from *super* as *pōnĕ* from *post* (§ 40). It is not used as a Preposition in Latin, at least in classical Latin, but is so used (governing an Acc.) in Umbrian, *superne adro* 'super atra (vascula).' *Insuper* is a Prep. as early as Cato (*R. R.* xviii. 5).

§ 54. Tĕnŭs, apparently the Adverbial Acc. Sg. of a Neuter S-stem *tenes-, from the root ten-, 'to stretch' (cf. *tenus* N., 'a cord,' in Plaut. *Bacch.* 793 pendébit hodie púlcre; ita intendí tenus) is used as a Preposition as early as Ennius. It takes the Abl. Sg., e.g. Tauro tenus, Cic. (originally 'from T. in a line,' then used for 'usque ad'), and the Gen. Pl., e.g. crurum tenus, Virg., and in Late Latin the Acc., e.g. Tanain tenus, Val. Flacc. It is not found in prose till the Silver Age (see *A. L. L.* i. 415). *Tenus* is appended to Adverbs in -*ā* (older -*ād* Abl. Sg. Fem.) in the sense of 'as far as,' lit. 'stretching from,' e.g. *aliqua-tenus, hac-tenus* (on which see § 10. 4; cf. *prō-tinus*, § 4).

§ 55. **Trans**, across (Umbr. *traf, trahaf*), is either the Pres. Part. of **trāre, in-trare, pĕnĕ-trare* (probably the Nom. Sg. Masc. crystallized in Adverbial usage; cf. § 2), or is an extension of an obsolete Preposition **tram* (an Acc. Sg. Fem. from the same root) by the same particle **s(e) as appears in the Prepositions of kindred meaning, *ul-s, ci-s*. It is clearly connected with O. Ir. tré or tria, trī, trem-, tar, W. trwy, trach, O. Ind. tirás, all from the root ter-, 'to go through, drive through' (O. Ind. tr̥-, 'to bore,' Gk. τείρω, Lat. *tĕro*, &c.). The *-ans*, pronounced *-as* (ch. ii. § 66), of *trans* became before voiced consonants *ā* by the Latin phonetic law (ch. iv. § 151), e.g. *trā-do* (but *transdo C. I. L.* i. 198, ll. 54, 58, &c.), *trā-mitto* (and *trans-mitto*). Umbr. *traf, trahaf* (i.e. träf), tra governs the Acc. with a verb of motion, e.g. *traf sahatam etu* 'trans Sanctam ito,' the Loc. with the idea of rest, e.g. *trahaf sahate vitla trif feetu* 'trans Sanctam vitulas tris facito.'

§ 56. **Uls, ultrā,** beyond, on the other side, came from the same root, I.-Eur. ol- (whence Lat. *ille*, O. Lat. *olle* for **ol-sŏ, ch. vii. § 13), the first being augmented by the particle **s(e) (§ 11), the second (an Abl. Sg. Fem.) by the suffix -tero- (ch. v. § 16). The *ŏ* has become *ŭ* before the combination *l* with a consonant by the Latin phonetic law (ch. iv. § 20), but the original vowel appears in *oltimus* (Osc. últiumo-) in Ennius' description of Servius Tullius (*A*. 337 M.):

<blockquote>
mortalem summum fortuna repente
reddidit ut summo regno famul oltimus (MSS. optimus) esset.
</blockquote>

(The *ovis* of the MS. of Varro *L. L.* v. 50 is a scribe's emendation of *vis*, the same mis-writing of *uls* as occurs later in v. 83, or is due to the correction of *ols* to *uls*, and should not be printed *ouls*, which would imply *ūls*. The shortness of the vowel is proved by the Romance forms of *ultra*; cf. Gell. xii. 13. 8 on the extension of *in, cis, uls* to *intra, citra, ultra*: quoniam parvo exiguoque sonitu obscurius promebantur, addita est tribus omnibus eadem syllaba. It is a mistake to suppose that there is an accent to indicate length over the first vowel of *ultra* in Claudius' tablet at Lyons.) An original *ol-s(e) must have become *oll* in Latin; the form *uls* is due to a later re-addition of *s* on the analogy of *ci-s*, &c. (cf. ch. viii. § 68 on *fer-s*).

§ 57. Usquĕ, with long *u*, to judge from Romance forms like O. Fr. usque, Fr. jusque for *de usque* (for Lat. *ŭ* would be represented by o, see ch. ii. § 26), is formed from the I.-Eur. Preposition *ud, 'out, up out' (O. Ind. úd, Goth. ūt, Engl. out) in the same way as *absque* from I.-Eur. *ap(o) (§ 12), so is not connected with *usquam* (§ 10. 9).

The Prepositional use of this Adverb (see § 11), e. g. usque quintum diem, Cels. (in Cic. only 'usque Romam,' &c.; so Ter. Ad. 655 Miletum usque, but Cato R.R. xlix. 2 usque radices persequito), is due to a curtailment of the proper phrase *usque ad*, much as in Attic Greek ὡς (for ὡς εἰς) came to be used as a Preposition, e. g. ὡς τὸν βασιλέα ἰέναι. The Latin grammarians point out that *usque*, unlike other Prepositions (cf. p. 573), can take a Preposition as prefix, e. g. *abusque, adusque* (Expl. in Donat. 517. 22 K. nemo enim dicit 'de post forum,' nemo enim 'ab ante'; at vero dicimus 'ab usque' et 'ad usque'); *ab usque* was a poetic inversion of Virgil's which found its way into Silver Age prose (*A.L.L.* vi. 80); *ad usque* (first in Catull. iv. 24) is likewise a phrase of Augustan poetry and Silver Age prose (*A.L.L.* vii. 107).

58. **Versus, versum, adversus, adversum, exadversus, exadversum.** *Versus* apparently a Nom. Sg. Masc., as *versum* is an Acc. Sg. Neut., of the P. P. P. *versus*, corresponds to the Celtic Preposition meaning 'towards,' 'against' (O. Ir. frith, fri, W. wrth, O. W. gurt). On its Adverbial use, see § 2.

CHAPTER X.

CONJUNCTIONS AND INTERJECTIONS.

§ 1. CONJUNCTIONS. As Prepositions are hardly separable from Adverbs of Locality, so Conjunctions are closely connected with pronominal Adverbs. These pronominal Adverbs, as we have seen (ch. ix. § 10), are not always capable of being referred to their proper case-form (e.g. ĭbĭ̆, ŭbĭ̆), owing to our imperfect knowledge of the declension of the I.-Eur. pronoun. Nor is it easy to find their cognates in the various I.-Eur. languages; so rapidly does the meaning of a Conjunction alter. Thus Latin *ĕnim*, which in the older literature is a particle of asseveration, 'indeed,' had by the classical period appropriated the sense of 'for'; and in French, pas (Lat. *passus*) and point (Lat. *punctum*) have acquired a negative sense from their use in the phrases ne . . . pas, ne . . . point. A feature of I.-Eur. Conjunctions is their tendency to append other Conjunctions or conjunctive Particles (e.g. ὡς in Greek may append δή, περ, &c., ὡς δή, ὥς περ); and this habit puts another obstacle in the way of identifying cognate Conjunctions in different languages, for in one language they may appear extended by one particle, in another language by another. The exact form of these conjunctive Particles is also a difficult thing to ascertain; we often see parallel stems in -o, -i, -u, &c. (e.g. *q^{u}o-, *q^{u}e-, *q^{u}i-, *q^{u}u- are all various forms of the Relative and Interrogative Pronoun-stem, ch. vii. § 23; -tĕ and -tĭ appear in O. Ind. u-tá, Gk. αὖ-τε, O. Ind. í-ti, Gk. ἔ-τι), and parallel forms with long and with short vowel (e.g. Negative *nĕ and *nē appear in O. Ind. ná and ná̄, Lat. *nĕ-* and *nē-*; I.-Eur. *wĕ, 'or,' O. Ind. vā, Lat. -*vĕ*); and the tendency was always

§ 1.]   CONJUNCTIONS.   597

present to adapt the ending of one Conjunction to the ending of
another Conjunction of similar meaning (e. g. Lat. *saltem* for
saltim, adapted to *au-tem*, *ĭ-tem*?, ch. ix. § 4). It will therefore
be best to designate these conjunctive Particles according to their
consonants, as, for example, (1) the T-particle of Lat. *tam, ĭ-tem,
u-t(ĭ)*, Gk. αὖ-τε, O. Ind. u-tá(-ấ), í-ti, 'so,' O. Sl. te, ·and'; (2) the
D-particle of O. Ind. i-dấ, 'now' (Lat. *ĭdō-neus*?); *dum, ĭbĭ-dem*,
Gk. δή, δέ, ὅ-δε; (3) the DH- particle of Gk. ἔν-θα, O. Ind. kú-ha,
'where,' O. Sl. kŭ-de, 'where;' (4) the P-particle of Lat.
quip-pe, nem-pe, Lith. kaĩ-p, 'how, as,' szeĩp . . . teĩp, ' so . . . so ';
(5) the N-particle of Lat. *nam, num, nem-pe, quis-nam*, O. Ind.
hi-ná, 'for,' O. Sl. tu-nŭ, ' then.' These particles are not easily
distinguished on the one hand from the particles affixed to Prepositions (e. g. *-tĭ of O. Ind. prá-ti, Gk. προ-τί, Osc. per-t ; *-ně
of Lat. *pō-ne*, Umbr. *post-ne*, Germ. vo-n), as has been already
mentioned (ch. ix. § 11), nor on the other are they always to be
distinguished from Case-suffixes. Indeed the usage of the oldest
Indian literature, where, for example, the particle kám is often
added to a Dativus Commodi or to a Dative of Purpose (see
Delbrück, *Altind. Syntax*, p. 150), and other particles are more or
less allotted to special cases, suggests that the Case-suffixes may
have at the first originated in this way, just as Gk. ἄν came in
time to be a sign of a Mood of the Verb. Thus not only has
the -s of the Nom. Sg. Masc. been with great probability
referred to the pronominal-stem *so- (*se-) (ch. vii. § 13), but also
the Abl. -d to the suffix *dě expressive of motion, joined with
an Accusative, in the sense of motion towards, in Gk. δόμον-δε,
Gen. -s (which in Greek and other languages has the function
of an Abl.) to the similar *sě of Gk. ἄλλο-σε. The person-
suffixes of Verbs may often have had a similar origin. The
*-dhĭ of the 2 Sg. Imper. in O. Ind., Gk. &c., e.g. ἴ-θι, is the
asseverative particle *dhĭ, joined to Imperatives, as Lat. *dum* in
ăgĕ dum ; the *-tōd of the 2 Sg. Fut. Imper., e. g. quando uidebis,
dato, Plaut., is the Adverbial Abl. Sg. Neut. of the Pronoun *to-,
from this,' ' thereupon ' (ch. viii. § 57). And in the declension of
the Pronouns themselves we have clear instances of the progress of
appended particles to case-suffixes in *gě (Gk. γε) used as the sign
of the Acc. Sg. in Goth. mi-k, Germ. mi-ch, *g̑hĭ (O. Ind. hí,

Gk. ναί-χι) as the sign of the Dat. Sg. in O. Ind. má-hy-am, ch. vii. § 1). The -*d* of the Acc. Sg. of the Personal Pronouns in Latin has been similarly explained as the particle *ĭd, so common in the oldest Indian literature, where it is used to emphasize a preceding word, so that Lat. *tēd* was originally **tē id* (cf. tuám íd in the Ṛig-Veda) (see ch. vii. § 1).

§ 2. (1) **Conjunctive.—Que, et, atque, ac, quoque, etiam.** -*Quĕ*, I.-Eur. *-$q^u\breve{e}$ (O. Ind. ca, Gk. τέ, Goth. -h, e.g. ni-h 'ne-que'), apparently the bare stem of the Relative *q^uo-(*q^ue-) (ch. vii. § 23), is in Latin, as it was in I.-Eur., an enclitic appended to the first word of the sentence. Through Syncope, to which final -*ĕ* was always liable in Latin (ch. iii. § 36), it has become -*c* in *nec* (*neque*), *ac* for **at-c* (*at-que*), &c., and probably often had this sound before an initial consonant in the rapid utterance of every-day life. In some lines of Plautus (*Stich.* 696, *Capt.* 246, *Poen.* 419, &c.) we must, if the reading of the MSS. be right, scan: dúmq(ue) se exórnat; pérq(ue), cōnséruitiúm commúne, &c. (Skutsch, *Forschungen*, i. p. 151). I.-Eur. *-$q^u\breve{e}$ gave a relative and indefinite sense to pronouns, and so in O. Latin, though in the classical period the fuller ending -*cunque* (O. Lat. -*quomque*, e.g. queiquomque, *C.I.L.* i. 197. 5; 198, &c.; see Georges, *Lex. Wortf.* s.v.) is preferred, e.g. *quem-que* Plaut. for *quem-cunque* (O. Ind. kaś-ca, Hom. Gk. ὅς τε, Goth. hvō-h F.); so *quis-que*, each (cf. O. Ir. cā-ch, W. pawb, O. W. paup, apparently from I.-Eur. *q^uō-$q^u\breve{e}$ or *q^uā-$q^u\breve{e}$). This -*cunque* seems to be nothing but *cum-que*, ' whenever' (Hor. *C.* i. 32. 15), though some connect it with O. Ind. caná (with ka-, &c, 'whoever,' &c.), and others make the -*cum*- (-*cun*-) a byform of *um*- (*un*-) of *um-quam*, &c. (ch. ix. § 10. 7). The corresponding particle in Oscan is -píd (O. Ind. -cit), e.g. pokka-píd 'quandoque.' Lat. *quŏ-quĕ* is composed of some part of the Pronoun-stem *quo*- (*que*-) and the enclitic -*que* (perhaps the bare Pronoun-stem; cf. O. Ind. kva-ca,' anywhere, in any case,' from kvà, 'where,' and ca, Lat. -*que*). Similarly, *at-quĕ*, of the Preposition (Adverb) *ad* and the enclitic, lit. 'and to,' 'and further'; in O. Lat. it often signifies 'forthwith,' e.g. Plaut. *Most.* 1050:

quóniam conuocáui, atque illi me éx senatu ségregant.

§§ 2-4.]   CONJUNCTIONS.   599

Umbrian *ape*, when, also spelt api, appei, may be the same formation as Lat. *atque*. The Umbro-Oscan equivalents of Lat. *nĕquĕ*, Osc. nep, neip, nip, Umbr. neip, *nep*, have -p for I.-Eur. *-q^{u}ĕ. *Ĕt* is the I.-Eur. Adverb *ĕtĭ (O. Ind. áti, 'over,' Gk. ἔτι, further), used in Latin, as in Gothic (iþ, 'and '), for the copula. It may be that it gradually encroached on the sphere of the older -*quĕ*, for it is noticeable that only -*que*, not *ĕt*, is found in the (restored) inscription on the Columna Rostrata (*C. I. L.* i. 195). The Umbrian copula is also et, but in Oscan íním, a word related to Lat. *enim* (see below).

In *ĕt-iam*, *et* is associated with the Adverb *jam*, now, the *i* (*y*) becoming vocalic by the Latin phonetic law in the middle of a word, as in *mĕdius* (I.-Eur. *médhyos, O. Ind. mádhyas, Gk. μέσ(σ)ος, &c.) (ch. iv. § 67).

§ 3. **Atque, ac.** On Republican Inscriptions the rule is that *atque* be used before an initial vowel, *ac* before an initial consonant, and so in the MSS. of Terence. But in the MSS. of Plautus *atque* is sometimes used before a consonant, where the metre requires the pronunciation *ac* (e. g. *Epid.* 522), and in the MSS. of Cato *atque* is the prevailing spelling (whatever Cato's pronunciation may have been) before initial consonants and vowels alike. The classical authors, as well as Plautus, seem to avoid *ac* not only before vowels, but also before *c-, g-, q-* (see Georges, *Lex. Wortf.* s. v. ; Skutsch, *Forsch.* i. 52 ; *B. P. W.* xiii. 312). *Atque* is the spelling in Republican inscriptions ; *adque* occurs in the Res Gestae of Augustus (once), and is in later inscriptions very frequent, as well as in good MSS. (see Neue, ii³. 953). *Atque atque* seems to mean 'nearer and nearer' in Ennius, *Ann.* 519 M. :

atque atque accedit muros Romana iuuentus.

§ 4. (2) **Disjunctive.**—Ve, aut, vel, sive, seu. -*Vĕ* is I.-Eur. *-wĕ, (O. Ind. vā, e. g. náktam vā dívā vā, ' by night or by day,' Hom. Gk. ἠ-(ϝ)έ), probably a curtailment of an I.-Eur. Adverb *ăwĕ (O. Ind. áva, 'away'). The I.-Eur. particle had also the sense of ' as,' ' like,' seen in Lat. *ce-u*, O. Ind. i-va, ' as,' e-vá, ' thus,' later e-vám.

Aut is compounded of I.-Eur. *au [Gk. αὖ, again, Goth. au-k, 'also' (quasi *αὖ-γε), Engl. eke], another curtailment of the same Adverb (cf. *au-fŭgĭo, auf-ĕro*, ch. ix. § 12), and the particle -tĭ (§ 1). Similar are Umbr. *ote*, Osc. *avti* and avt, though the latter Oscan form has generally the sense of Latin *autem*.

Vĕl is the old 2 Sg. Pres. Imperative of *vŏlo* (ch. viii. § 58), lit.

'choose,' as Germ. wohl (e. g. Homer, wohl der grösste Dichter, 'Homerus vel summus poeta') was originally Imper. of wollen.

Vel can hardly represent *vell* for *vels, an old 2 Sg. 'Injunctive,' for it is so thoroughly a short syllable in Plautus as to be capable of acting as a Brevis Brevians (ch. iii. § 42), e. g. *Poen.* 827 uél ĭn lautumiis, uél ĭn pistrino, although Umbr. heris... heris, e. g. heris vinu heri puni 'vel vino vel posca,' is 2 Sg. Ind. of heri-, ' to wish' (whence Herentas, the Oscan Venus). Other instances of Imperatives used as Particles are *pŭtă*, for example, Hor. and *ăgĕ*; *em*, the Interjection, probably represents *ĕmĕ*, 2 Sg. Imper. of *emo*, I take (§ 19).

Sīvĕ is compounded of *sī*, older *sei*, and *-ve*. Before *-u*, the curtailed or syncopated form of *-ve* (as *-c* of *-quĕ*, *-n* of Interrogative *-nĕ*, &c.), the *ei*-diphthong was by the Latin phonetic law (ch. iv. § 66) reduced to *ĕ* (as in *deus* from *deiu(u)s*, ch. iv. § 33). Lat. *si* was in Umbrian sve (Osc. svaí), and the Umbrian equivalent of Lat. *sive* is *sve-po* 'siquō.'

§ 5. (3) **Adversative.**—At, ast, sed, autem, atqui, tamen, ceterum, verum, vero. *Ăt* is the I.-Eur. Adverb *ăt(ĭ) (O. Ir. aith-, 'back,' Lith. at-, O. Sl. otŭ, 'from'), used in Latin, as in Gothic (aþ-þan, 'but'), as a Conjunction. On its confusion in spelling with the Preposition *ad*, see ch. ii. § 76.

Ast is a Conjunction found in old laws in various senses (Charis. 229. 30 K. 'ast' apud antiquos variam vim contulit vocibus, pro atque, pro ac, pro ergo, pro sed, pro tamen, pro tum, pro cum, ut in glossis antiquitatum legimus scriptum), especially (1) 'if further,' 'and if moreover,' e. g. Lex Serv. Tull.: si parentem puer uerberet, ast olle plorassit, puer diuis parentum sacer esto; (2) 'if,' e. g. XII Tab. 10. 8 (in the curious law referring to the use of gold in dentistry): ... neue aurum addito, at cui auro dentes iuncti escunt, ast im cum illo sepeliet uretue, se fraude esto), and occasionally in the early writers, e. g. with the sense of 'if further,' Plaut. *Capt.* 683:

si ego hic peribo, ast ille ut dixit nón redit,

with the sense of 'further' or 'but,' Accius, *Trag.* 260 R.:

idem splendet saépe, ast idem nímbis interdúm nigret.

It may be a formation from *ad*, and stand for *ad-s-tĭ as *post* for *po-s-tĭ (ch. ix. § 40), so that its original signification would be 'further,' 'moreover,' though, owing to the custom of using it in the added clause of the protasis in conditional sentences, it came to acquire the notion of 'if further,' and even of 'if.' It is one of the archaisms used by Cicero in drawing up his code of laws (*Legg.* ii. 8. 19, &c.), who gives it the senses of (1) 'if further,' (2) 'if' (so on the law relating to the Ludi Saeculares of Augustus' reign, *ast quid est* 'siquid est'), (3) 'further' (so in Cicero's translation of Aratus's *Prognostica*, l. 160). The Augustan poets revived the use of the word, as a substitute for *at*, where the metre required a long syllable, and in the second cent. A.D. it passed into prose. If *asted* on the Dvenos inscription (usually explained as *adstet*) be really *ast*, it is a byform with the particle -*d*(*e*) like *postid* (ch. ix. § 40).

Sĕd, if we may believe the statement of some grammarians (Charis. 112. 5 K.; Mar. Victorin. 10. 13 K.; Ter. Scaur. 12. 8 K.; Isid. *Orig.* i. 26. 24), who argue against the spelling *set* (ch. ii. § 76), was at some early period *sedum*. The word can hardly be separated from the Preposition (Adverb) *sē* (*sēd*), 'apart' (ch. ix. § 51), and may be a compound of *sĕ, a byform of *sē*, with the Conjunctive particle *dum* (see below).

Autem adds the particle -*tem* (cf. *ĭ-tem*) to the I.-Eur. Adverb *au [Gk. αὖ, again, Goth. au-k, 'also' (quasi *αὖ-γε), Engl. eke], which is probably identical with the Preposition *au-* of Lat. *au-fero, au-fŭgio* (ch. ix. § 12), and cognate with the I.-Eur. Conjunction *wĕ (see under Lat. -*ve*). The Oscan equivalent of *autem* is avt, apparently a 'doublet' of avti, the equivalent of *aut* (§ 4). The older usage of *autem* is seen in passages like Plaut. *Merc.* 118:

et cúrrendum et pugnándum et autem iúrigandumst in uia,

(cf. *sed autem, Rud.* 472; *et autem, Poen.* 841).

Atquī adds to the Conjunction *at* the particle *quī*, which is much used by the early Dramatists as a mere particle of emphasis [e.g. Plaut. Hercle qui (*Pseud.* 473), utinam qui, ut qui (*Trin.* 637)], and which is either the Abl., Loc. or Instr. Sg. of the Relative (ch. vii. § 25). *Atquin* (on this spelling, see Georges, *Lex. Wortf.* s. v.) has the particle -*n*(*e*) appended (§ 1, above).

Tămĕn however, 'none the less,' is clearly related to *tam* (ch. ix.

§ 10. 8), so, 'equally much,' which was often used in the sense of *tamen* in O. Lat. (Fest. 548. 3 Th. antiqui 'tam' etiam pro tamen usi sunt, with examples from Naevius, Ennius, and Titinius; for examples in Plautus, see Seyffert, *Stud. Plaut.* p. 14) (cf. class. *tam-etsī* and *tamen-etsi*). Some see in *tam-en* a relic of the earlier usage, retained in Umbro-Oscan, of putting the Preposition *in* (older *en*) after the word it governs, e. g. Umbr. arvamen 'in arvum,' Pel. pritrom-e 'praeter' quasi 'praeterum-in' (ch. ix. § 30); others suppose that the particle *-nĕ* (of *quando-ne*, &c., § 1), appended to *tam*, produced *tam-i-ne* or *tamen(e)*, and quote Plaut. *Mil.* 628, where the MSS. reading points to *tamine*, as a proof that interrogative *-ne* appended to *tam* produced this same form:

tám capularis? támne tibi diu uídeor uitam uíuere.

On the other hand *tanne* is mentioned by Festus 542. 26 Th. as the O. Lat. form of *tam* with interrogative *-ne*, and exemplified by Afranius, *Com.* 410 R.: tanne árcula Túa plena est aránearum? Festus also quotes *tame*, as an old form of *tam*, on which see ch. ix. § 10. 8.

Cētĕrum is the adverbial Acc. Sg. Neut. of the stem *cētero-* (Nom. Pl. *cēteri*), as *cetera* in such a line as Virg. *A.* ix. 656: cetera parce puer bello, 'for the rest—you are a boy—deal sparingly with war,' is an adverbial Acc. Pl. Neut. *Ceterum* of Plautus' *Truc.* 847, &c. is exactly parallel to *unum* of Plautus, *Mil. Glor.* 24 nisi únum epityra *ei* éstur insanúm bene, 'but— one thing,—&c.' The root of the word is the I.-Eur. pronominal *k̂e, which shows the short vowel in the Latin enclitic *-ce* of *hujus-ce*, &c. (ch. vii. § 15), the long vowel in Lat. *cē-teri*, &c. (see § 1 on the variation of quantity in pronominal *wĕ, *nĕ, &c., and cf. ch. iv. § 33).

Vērum is similarly an adverbial Acc. Sg. Neut. of the Adj.- stem *vero-*, true, and *vērō* an adverbial Abl. (Instr.?) Sg. Neut. of the same stem.

§ 6. (4) **Limitative and Corrective.—Quidem, immo.** The formation of *quĭdem* has not yet been satisfactorily explained. The *quĭ-* may be the bare stem of the Pronoun (see § 2 on *quŏ-*

quĕ); or if *ĭdem* represents *ĭd-dem, *quidem* may be the Neuter Pronoun with the suffix *-dem* (§ 2) *quĭd-dem (but see ch. vii. § 21 on *ĭdem*).

Equĭdem might be similarly explained as *et-quidem* [cf. Plaut. *Pers.* 187 *et quidem* (A), *eq.* (P)], but is better referred to the pronominal prefix *ĕ-* of *e-nos*, Umbro-Osc. e-tanto-, &c., augmented by the particle *-ce* in *ec-quis*, and in *ecce* (see § 19). Its association with the first Personal Pronoun in Cicero and other good writers (see Neue, ii³. p. 963) shows that to a Roman the first syllable suggested a reference rather to *ego* than to *et* (cf. Prisc. ii. 103. 5 H.; *ecce* in Plautus very often refers to the person speaking, *A. L. L.* v. 18). The exact truth regarding its use in Plautus is not easy to ascertain, for the MSS. frequently write it for *et quidem* (e. g. *Pers.* 187), and editors often substitute it for *quidem* after *tu, me*, &c. to avoid the scansion *tŭ quidem*, *mĕ quidem* (like *sĭquidem*, ch. iii. § 51), or the division of a dactyl between two words in iambic and trochaic metres, e. g. *atque quidem*.

Immō (not *imo* [1], according to Brambach, *Hülfsbüchlein*, s. v.) has the scansion of a pyrrhic (◡ ◡) according to the MSS. in passages like Terence, *Phorm.* 936:

<blockquote>immo uéro uxorem tú cedo. In ius ámbula,</blockquote>

a scansion which has not yet been accounted for. Nor is the derivation of the word at all clear. One theory makes it Adverbial Abl. Sg. Neut. of *īmus*, another analyzes it into *in-mō*, 'in magis,' supposing *mō to be an I.-Eur. Comparative 'more,' whence comes Gaul. -mā-rus of Virdo-mārus, O. Ir. mār, mōr, 'great,' &c.

§ 7. (5) Explanatory.—Enim, nam, namque, quippe, nempe, nemut. *Enim*, in O. Lat. an asseverative particle merely (cf. class. *enim-vero*), a usage imitated by Virgil, e.g. *A.* viii. 84:

<blockquote>quam pius Aeneas tibi enim, tibi, maxima Juno,
mactat sacra ferens,</blockquote>

is most naturally referred to I.-Eur. **eno-* (**ene-*) (cf. O. Ind. aná, 'indeed,' 'for'), another form of I.-Eur. **no-* (**ne-*) (§ 1), (cf. *illim* from *ille*, *istim* from *iste*, ch. ix. § 10. 5). The weak point of this etymology is that it prevents us from connecting the word

---

[1] *Imo* occurs in the Aes Italicense of 176-180 A.D. (*C. I. L.* ii. 6278, l. 20).

directly with *einom* 'igitur,' of the Dvenos inscription, Pel. inom (?), 'et,' Osc. ínim, 'et' Umbr. *enom* (enum-ek, inum-ek, with the particle *-ce* of Lat. *hujus-ce*, &c.), also *enem* 'tum,' which all show the Pronominal root i- of Lat. *is* (ch. ix. § 19) prefixed to a form (-nim, -nom) of the root no- (ne-). Lat. *enim* (from *e-no-) will stand to O. Lat. *einom* of the Dvenos inscr. (from *ei-no- ; cf. O. Ind. ēna-, 'he,' ēná, 'so, here'), as O. Ind. asā-ú, 'this' (from *e-so-) to O. Ind. ēṣá-, 'this' (from *ei-so-).

Nam, often used in O. Lat. in questions, e.g. 'quid cerussa opus nam?' 'why, what is the use of paint?' Plaut. (cf. *quisnam*), without that definite sense of 'for,' 'because' to which the word is restricted in classical literature (but cf. *uti-nam*), is the same case-form of the Pronominal-stem *no- (§ 1) as *quam* of *q^{u}o-, *tam* of *to- (Acc. Sg. Fem. ?, ch. ix. § 10. 8).

Namque adds to *nam* the enclitic *-quĕ* (§ 2). It is used only before an initial vowel in Plautus and Terence.

Quippĕ appends the particle *-pĕ* (§ 1) to some case of the Relative or Interrogative or Indefinite Pronoun, either the Acc. Sg. Neut. *quippe* for *quid-pe* (cf. *quippini* equivalent to *quidni*), or (if *-ipp-* can represent *-īp-* in Latin; cf. *ipsippe* 'ipsi neque alii' Paul. Fest. 74. 37 Th., and see p. 116 *n.*), the Loc. Instr. Sg., *quippe* for *quī-pe*, or else the Abl. Sg. *quippe* for *quīd-pe*.

Nempĕ appends the same particle to a form *nem* (the same case-form of the Pronominal-stem *no-, as *-tem* of *autem* is of the stem *to-). This form *nem* appears also in O. Lat. *nemut* 'nisi etiam vel nempe' (Fest. 160. 28 ; Paul. Fest. 161. 13 Th.). On the pronunciation *nemp(e)* before initial consonants, see ch. iii. § 35.

§ 8. (6) Conclusive.—Ergo, itaque, igitur.

Ergō has already been explained, in connexion with its use as a Preposition, e.g. *funeris ergo* (ch. ix. § 28), as possibly standing for ē *rŏgo (cf. *e rĕgione*), 'from the direction,' and has been compared with German wegen, M. H. G. vonwëgen.

Ĭtăquĕ, compounded of *ĭtă* (ch. ix. § 10. 9), and *-quĕ* (§ 2), seems, like *ita*, never to have *ā* even in the earliest poetry. We should scan the Saturnian line of the epitaph of Naevius (ap. Gell. i. 24. 2):

> Ĭtăque póstquam est Órcho tráditus thesaúro (see p. 128 *n.*).

The grammarians of the Empire distinguish *ităque*, therefore, from *ităque*, and so, 'et ita,' (e.g. Serv. *in Don.* 427. 13 K. tunc corripitur media cum una pars fuerit orationis, tunc vero producitur cum duae), but short *a* is invariably shown in the Dramatists in both senses of the word. The grammarians' rule about *itaque* resembles their rule for the penultimate accentuation of *pleráque*, *utráque*, Nom. Sg. Fem. (cf. ch. ii § 93 on Late Lat *áqua*, *acqua*).

Igitur had in O. Lat. the sense of *tum* (Paul. Fest. 74. 29 Th. 'igitur' nunc quidem pro conpletionis significatione valet, quae est ergo. Sed apud antiquos ponebatur pro inde et postea et tum), as in Plaut. *Mil.* 772:

quándo habebo, igitúr rationem meárum fabricarúm dabo,

or in the first law of the XII Tab.: si in ius uocat, ni it, antestamino. igitur em capito. The etymology of the word, one of the most puzzling in Latin, is discussed in ch. ix. § 8.

§ 9. (7) **Optative.**—**Ut, utinam.** *Ut*, in wishes, e.g. Juppiter ut Danaum omne genus pereat, is the Conjunction *ŭt*, that (older *ŭtĭ*, ch. iii. § 36), with suppression of the idea 'I wish' or 'do thou grant.'

In *ŭtĭnam* the final *ĭ* of *ut(ĭ)* is retained, and *nam* has its older sense of a strengthening particle, 'indeed' (§ 7).

§ 10. (8) **Interrogative.**— -**Ne, nonne, num, utrum, an, anne, cur, quare, quianam.** In class. Latin -*nĕ* is the general interrogative particle, while *nonnĕ* is limited to questions which expect an affirmative, *num* to those which expect a negative, answer. This distinction is unknown to Plautus, who uses *nonne* hardly at all (e.g. *Trin.* 789), (-*ne* being used instead, e.g. *Trin.* 178, *Men.* 284, or *nōn*, e.g. *Stich.* 606), and *num*, *numquis* without a negative sense occasionally, e.g. *Most.* 999. (A list of examples of the Interrogative Particles in Plautus and Terence is given in *Amer. Journ. Phil.* vol. xi. 1890.) It is easy to see how these meanings came to be attached to *non-ne*, 'is ... not,' and *num*, 'now' [Gk. νυν; cf. *nunc* for *num-c(e)*, ch. ix. § 10], e.g. *nonne haec ita sunt?*, 'is not this the case?'; *num haec ita sunt?*, 'now is this the case?' (with emphasis on the word 'is').

-*Ne* is probably I.-Eur. *nĕ (Zend -na, appended to Interrogatives, e.g. kas-nā, 'who then?'; cf. O. H. G. na weist tu na, 'nescisne?'), though it might also represent I.-Eur. *nŭ (ch. iii. § 37) (O. Ind. nŭ, in the phrase: kathā́ nú, 'how then?'; cf. Hom. τί νύ μοι μήκιστα γένηται;). On its reduction by Syncope to -n, e.g. vĭdĕn, audīn, see ch. iii. § 36.

Ūtrum is the adverbial Acc. Sg. Neut. of ŭter, like Gk. πότερον. Ăn (Goth. an; cf. Gk. ἄν, in that case) belongs to the I.-Eur. pronominal root seen in Lith. añs, 'that,' O. Sl. onŭ, &c. Cūr (O. Lat. quōr) is I.-Eur. *q^{u}ōr [Lith. kuř, 'where,' for *kŭr (I. F. ii. 420); cf. O. H. G. hwār, 'where?', from I.-Eur, *q^{u}ēr, and O. Ind. kár-hi, 'when?', from I.-Eur. *q^{u}ŏr], with a change of ō to ū in a monosyllable before final -r (ch. iv. § 16) that has a parallel in fūr from *fōr (Gk. φώρ). It may also represent I.-Eur. *q^{u}ou- (Gk. ποῦ, where?) with the suffix -r. (On O. Lat. ō, class. ū for the I.-Eur. diphthong ou, see ch. iv. § 41.)

Quārē, which must not be connected with cur, since the length of the final vowel makes the idea of Syncope impossible (calcarĕ becomes calcar, but avarē could not become *avar), is the Ablative of Cause, just as cui rei Plaut. Truc. 394 (quoi rei te adsimulare retulit?) is the Dative of Purpose, of the word-group quae res? (cf. quamobrem?). Plautus uses cur or quamobrem, quoi rei, but perhaps not quare. (Epid. 597 quare filiam Credidisti nostram? is bracketed by Goetz.)

Quĭănam, in O. Lat. poetry (Fest. 340. 25 Th.; 'Servius' ad Virg. A. x. 6) (not in Comedy, so not colloquial; Langen, Beitr. p. 326), and adopted as an archaism occasionally by Virgil (A. v. 13 and x. 6), is the adverbial (I-stem) Acc. Pl. Neut. of quis-nam (ch. vii. § 28), as quid-nam is the adverbial Acc. Sg. in such a phrase of Plautus as: quid tu, malum, nam me retrahis?, 'plague on you, why do you pull me back?'

§ 11. (9) Comparative.—Ut, uti, quasi, ceu, quam.

Ŭt, of which the final short vowel is preserved in ŭtĭ-nam, ne-utĭ-quam, [pronounced n(e)utiquam with first, as well as second, syllable short], ŭtĭ-que, is one of those Relative Particles that appear in Latin with initial u, but in the Umbro-Oscan dialects with an initial p-, which is their usual equivalent for an I.-Eur. labiovelar guttural (see ch. iv. § 135). The Umbro-Oscan forms are discussed in ch. ix. § 10. 9.

§ 11.] CONJUNCTIONS. 607

Ŭtī is in O. Lat. *utei* (e. g. on the S. C. Bacch. of 186 B.C., *C. I. L.* i. 196).

Quăsĭ. It is difficult to derive *quasi* from *quam si*, though the two expressions were undoubtedly equivalents : e. g. in the Republican Laws *quasei* is the usual form, as in the Bantine tablet of 133-118 B.C., *C. I. L.* i. 197. l. 12, in the Lex Repetundarum of 123-122 B.C., i. 198. l. 41 (cf. l. 73), but *quansei* occurs in the Lex Agraria of 111 B.C., i. 200. l. 27 ; and in Plautus we have (1) *quam si* in the sense of the usual *quăsĭ* in *Poen.* 241 item ... quam si, (2) *quăsĭ* in the sense of ' than if,' (*quam si*) in *Mil.* 482, &c. (see Brix's note on *Trin.* 265). For the first syllable of *quasi* was so thoroughly short that it acted as a 'Brevis Brevians' and made the normal quantity of the final vowel of -*si* short as early as the time of Plautus, whereas the combination *ns* (*ms*) properly lengthens a preceding vowel in Latin (ch. ii. § 144). We are thus driven to suppose that *quam* (adverbial Acc. Sg. Fem.) and *quă* (adverbial Acc. Pl. Neut.) were two equivalent Conjunctions which were joined with *si* to denote (1) as, (2) than if, and that the classical usage made a differentiation of them, assigning the sense of 'as' to the combination *qua-si* and the sense of 'than if' to the combination *quam-si*.

Ceu, which is restricted to the Epic and Lyric Poets and a few Silver Age prose writers (the elder Pliny, &c.), is compounded of the Pronominal-stem **ko- (k̑e-), 'this' (ch. vii. § 15) and the particle **wĕ, 'as, like' (§ 4). It has been supposed that as *seu* is a syncopated form of *sive* [*sei-w(ĕ), § 4], *ceu* must come from a fuller form **k̑ei-w(ĕ), the Locative Case of the Pronoun with the particle **wĕ. But of this fuller form there is no trace, so it is better explained as **cē-ve (cf. *cē-teri*) (ch. iv. § 33).

Quam is the Acc. Sg. Fem. of the Relative, as *tam* of the Demonstrative (ch. ix. § 10). The two words are combined in *tanquam*. Its Oscan equivalent is *pan* (Zvet. *I. I. I.* 231. 6 *mais egm*[*as tovti*]*cas amnud pan pieisum brateis* ' magis rei publicae causa quam cujuspiam gratiae ') or *pam* (*ib.* 231. 16 *pruter pam medicatinom didest* ' priusquam judicationem dabit '). In O. Lat. we have a form augmented by -*dĕ, quamde*, e. g. Liv. Andr. ap. Fest. 532. 8 Th. :

        námque núllum péius mácerat humánum
        quámde máre saéuom uís et cui sunt mágnae,

(a translation of Hom. *Od.* viii. 139). This *quamde, quande* (Umbr. pane) would probably become **quan* (Osc. *pan*?), as *deinde* became *dein* (ch. ix. § 10. 6), and would be merged in *quam*.

§ 12. (10) **Temporal.—Quum, quando, dum, donec, ut, ubi.** *Quum*, O. Lat. *quom*, is most simply explained as an Adverbial Acc. Sg. Neut. of the Relative, an I.-Eur. *q^uom. Terentius Scaurus (28. 9 K.) mentions an old form of the word (MSS. *cuine*, for which editors read *quomne* or *cume*), and quotes a couplet from the Carmen Saliare; but unfortunately the passage in the MSS. is so corrupt that little certain has hitherto been made of the lines (see ch. viii. § 73). The Umbrian word *ponne, pone* and the Oscan pún, *pon* seem to be compounded of I.-Eur. *q^uom and a particle -dĕ [cf. O. Lat. *quamde* for *quam* (Umbr. pane, Osc. *pan*) § 11; and see below on *quan-do*].

Quandō seems to be the Acc. Sg. Fem. of the Relative with the I.-Eur. Preposition *dŏ, 'to,' or with some form of the particle *-de* of O. Lat. *quamde*, than (§ 11). The Faliscan form cuando (cu- or cv-) (Zvet. *I. I. I.* 70 cuando datu) affords presumption that the word did not end originally in *-d*, so that *-dō* would not be an Abl. The 'Preposition' -do, 'to' (ch. ix. § 27) would give a suitable sense, ' to what' (*sc.* time), for in Plautus the Conjunction is mainly temporal, though in Terence it is mainly causal, as *quandŏquĭdem* is at all periods of the literature (see *Studemund's Studien*, ii. pp. 85 sqq.). Varro mentions its use for *quum*, 'when,' as a feature of the dialects of Formiae and Fundi (ap. Charis. 111. 23 K.). In *quandone* (*C. I. L.* vi. 25048 nequa ei loci controversia quandone fieret; 25905 con qua reliquias meas quandone poni volo) we have the suffix further augmented by the particle *-ne* (cf. *dō-nĭ-cum* and see ch. ix. § 10; O. Sl. kŭ-da-no 'quando,' beside kŭ-da 'quando' shows another form of the N-suffix), and in *quandō-quĕ*, whenever, by the particle *-quĕ*, 'ever' (§ 2). *Quandoc*, quoted from the XII Tab. by Festus 346. 3 Th. (cf. Paul. Fest. 345. 4, 7 Th.) seems to be a syncopated form of *quandoque* as *nĕc* of *nĕquĕ*. The scansion *quandŏquidem*, found as early as Plaut. (*Trin.* 991 sáluos quandoquidem áduenis; some would scan *quandōc'dem*) seems to be like *sĭquidem* (see ch. iii. § 51).

§ 12.]   CONJUNCTIONS.   609

Dum, which is often a mere asseverative particle, e. g. *ăgĕ dum* (Gk. ἄγε δή), *quīdum*, how so? *prīmumdum*, first of all, is an Acc. Sg. Neut. from the Pronominal-stem **do-*, as *tum* from **to-*, *quum* from **qᵤo-* (Gk. δή is another case-form of the same stem). The phonetic laws of Latin hardly allow us to connect it with *diū*, *diēs*, which come from the root dyew-, diw-; but the first part of *dū-dum*, often referred to *diu* and *dies*, may come from a stem **du-*, a byform of **do-*, whence Gk. δήν for **δϝᾱν*, O. Sl. davĕ, 'olim' (*I. F.* ii. 250). Similar parallel stems were **no-* and **nu-*; and as Latin *num* may stand for **no-m* from the first or **nu-m* from the second, so Lat. *dum* may stand for **do-m* or **du-m*. The temporal sense is clearly seen in the particle *-dum* in *non-dum*, *etiam-dum*, *inter-dum*, &c. On late plebeian inscriptions we find a form *dunc*, while, e. g. *C. I. L.* vi. 25063 :

> ad tu ne propera simili qui sorte teneris,
> dunc annos titulo nomina ut ipse legas;

apparently an extension of *dum* by the particle *-c(e)*, on the type of *nunc*, *tunc* (ch. ix. § 10. 7). The connexion of the two meanings 'while' and 'until' is seen in archaic Engl., e. g. *Macbeth*, iii. 1. 143 while then, God be with you.

Dōnĕc must be considered in connexion with the byforms *dōnĭcum* and *dōnĭquĕ*. *Dōnĭcum* is mentioned as an O. Lat. form by Charisius (197. 15 K.), who quotes Livius Andronicus:

> íbi mánens sedéto dónicum uidébis
> mé carpénto uehénte meám domum uenísse,

as well as Plautus and Cato. It is naturally resolved into **do-ne* (the Preposition **do*, ch. ix. § 27, and the affix -ne, § 1), and *cum* the temporal Adverb, 'to when,' 'till when' (cf. Umbr. *ar-ni-po* and its Latin equivalent *quo-ad*. Some explain *donec* as a form of *donicum* with the last syllable dropped, but the loss of final *-um* in Latin is confined within strict limits [on *nihil(um)*, *no(e)n-(um)*, see ch. iii. § 52], and would hardly be allowed in *donecum*. *Donec* is more naturally explained as the syncopated form of *doni-que* (cf. *nec* and *neque*, § 18), and *doni-que* as **done* augmented by the particle *-que*, 'ever' (cf. *quando*, when, *quandoque*, whenever; also *dē-nique*); but the weak point in this account is that *donique* is not found till Lucretius, and so is later than *donec*. Perhaps the true explanation is that *donicum* was appre-

R r

hended as *donec cum*, and so with omission of *cum* became *donec*, while Lucretius coined a *donique* on the analogy of *nec* and *neque*. Whether Fr. donc and the cognate Romance words come from *donec* is doubtful [see Körting, *Lat.-rom. Wörterb.* s. v.; *donec* in Petronius 40 (see Friedl. *ad loc.*) and 55 need not be translated 'then.']

Ut (see § 9). *Ubi* (see ch. ix. § 10. 1).

§ 13. (11) **Causal.—Quum, quoniam, quod, quia, quippe.**
Quum (see ch. ix. § 10. 7).

Quŏnĭam is a compound of *quum* (*quom*) and *jam*, the *j* (*y*) becoming vocalic by the law of Latin phonetics in the middle of a word (so I.-Eur. *médhyos, O. Ind. mádhyas, Gk. μέσ(σ)ος, &c., became *medius* in Latin, ch. iv. § 63). Its oldest sense is temporal 'when now' (with Pres Ind., the Pres. tense being required by the *jam*), e. g. Plaut. *Trin.* 112:

> quoniam hínc iturust ípsus in Seleúciam,
> mihi cónmendauit uírginem ;

and it is possible to trace its gradual development from a temporal to a causal sense in the course of Latin Literature (see Luebbert, *Gramm. Stud.* ii.).

Quŏd. I.-Eur. *q^{u}ŏd (Lith. kad, 'that,' after verba declarandi, &c., also used in the sense of 'if') is the Acc. Sg. Neut. of the Relative O-stem, used like Homeric ὅ in such a line as *Od.* i. 382:

> Τηλέμαχον θαύμαζον ὃ θαρσαλέως ἀγόρευε.

In Plautus it is always, or almost always, subject or object of a relative sentence, e. g. *Capt.* 586 :

> fílium tuum quód redimere se aít, id ne utiquam míhi placet;

from the second cent. A.D. it is used with verba declarandi, &c. e. g. Apul. *Met.* x. 7 asserere incipit quod se vocasset.

Quĭă is an Acc. Plur. Neut. of the Relative I-stem (Slov. či, 'if,' Bulg. ὲι, 'that, because'), and has the same double meaning as *quod*, (1) that, (2) because. With appended *-nam* it had interrogative meaning 'why?' (see § 10) like *quid? quidnam?*

Quippĕ (see § 7). (On *quatenus* see ch. ix. § 4.)

§ 14. (12) **Conditional.—Si, nisi, ni, sin, sive, seu, modo, dummodo.** *Sĭ*, O. Lat. *sei*, is a Loc. Sg. of the Pronoun *so-, seen in Lat. *ip-se, ip-sa* (ch. vii. § 20), as Lith. jéi, 'if,' of the Pronoun seen in Lat. *is, ea* (ch. vii. § 19). Greek εἰ has been connected by some with the Latin, by others with the Lith. conjunction. *Sic*, so, is the same word with the enclitic -*c(e)* appended (ch. vii. § 15). Osc. svaí, Umbr. sve come from a stem *swo- (whence Goth. sva, 'so '), of which O. Lat. *suad* 'sic,' quoted from an augural prayer by Festus (526. 15 Th. suad ted 'sic te ') is an Abl. Sg. Fem., as the Umbro-Oscan forms are Loc. Sg. Fem.; but Volscian se shows the same stem as Latin. The stems *so-, *swo- were no doubt originally connected like the two stems of the second Sg. Personal Pronoun *twe- and *te- (ch. vii. § 3). (On sw- see ch. iv. § 68.)

Nĭsĭ is a compound of the negative *ně* (§ 18) with *si*, 'not if.' It is probably this word which is quoted in the form *nesi* (ch. ix. § 51) in a defective passage of Festus, who explains it as *sine* (166. 26 Th.); it is spelt *nisei* on the S. C. Bacch. and the Lex Repetundarum, and *nise* (with *e* for the *ei*-diphthong, ch. iv. § 34) on the Lex Rubria. The change of *ĕ* to *ĭ* in the first syllable is due to the unaccented use of the word (as *sĭne* for *sĕ-ne*, *mihi* for *mehei*) (ch. iii. § 18).

The Umbro-Oscan forms have *swai instead of *sei (Lat. *si*), as their second component, the Negative being represented in Oscan by the Loc. Sg. form *nei (Osc. *nei svae*), in Umbrian by a form no (Umbr. *nosve*). In that very old Latin inscription, known as the Dvenos inscription, we find the Negative in another Loc. form *noi* (is this a mere graphic variety of *nei*?), if *noisi* is rightly interpreted 'unless.' With the first part of *nisi* we may compare Osc. *ne pon* 'nisi quum' (Zvet. I. I. I. 231. 14 *izic comono ni hipid ne pon*, &c. ' is comitia ne habuerit nisi quum,' &c.).

Nĭ, I -Eur. *nei, perhaps *ně with the deictic particle -ῑ of Gk. οὑτοσ-ί, &c. (ch. vii. § 23), had originally the sense of *nōn* or *nē*, as in *quid-ni, quippi-ni* [Lith. neĩ, 'not at all'; Osc. *svae pis censtomen nei cebnust* 'si quis in censum non venerit,' *nei-p mais pomtis com preivatud actud* 'neve magis (quam) quinquies cum privato agito,' *nei svae* 'nisi,' svai nei-p 'si non' 'si nec'], and still retains this sense in some passages of O. Lat., e. g. Cato: caueto ni quam materiem doles, and in Virgil's line: ni teneant cursus. It came however to acquire the sense of *nisi* from its use in such phrases as si in ius uocat, ni it, XII Tab., 'if he summons him (and) he does not go,' id ni fit, pignus dato Plaut., 'lay me a wager in the event of that not happening,' lit. 'that does not happen, lay me a wager.' (See O. Brugmann, *Gebrauch des Cond.* '*Ni*,' 1887.)

Sin is usually said to represent *sī-nĕ*, 'if not,' with the same syncope of the negative particle as in *quīn*, lest (§ 16), or as of the interrogative particle in *audin* for *audis-ne*, &c. (§ 10); and this explanation exactly suits its use in sentences like Cic. *Epp. Famm.* xii. 6. 2 qui si consecutus erit, vicimus ; sin —, quod di omen avertant, omnis omnium cursus est ad vos. But this negative sense of *sin*, 'if not,' is hardly attached to the word in the time of Plautus. The Plautine use of *sin* has been explained by the O. Lat. habit of attaching interrogative -*ne* to the first word of the relative clause, instead of to the first word of the main clause [e.g. Ter. *Phorm.* 923 quodne ego discripsi? instead of: quod ego discripsi, illudne rescribam?], so that, e. g. Plaut. *Trin.* 309 si animus hominem pepulit, actumst . . . sin ipse animum pepulit, uiuit, might more properly be written : sin ipse animum pepulit? uiuit. It is however unnecessary to regard the *n* of *sin* as either the Interrogative or the Negative Particle -*ne*; for it may be merely that Demonstrative suffix -*ne* seen in *alioquin*, &c. (§ 16) [*Quin* (see § 16) represents (1) *quî* with Negative -*ne*, (2) *quî* with Interrogative -*ne*, (3) *quî* with Demonstrative -*ne*]. The older spelling *sein* occurs, for example, on an epitaph, much affected by the Romans [1] (*Not. Scav.* 1887, p. 180):

<blockquote>
mortua heic ego sum, et sum cinis, is cinis terrast ;
sein est terra dea, ego sum dea, mortua non sum.
</blockquote>

Sīve and *seu* (see ch. iv. § 33).

Mŏdŏ is the adverbial Abl. (Instr.?) Sg. of *mŏdus*, measure, limit (cf. Hor. quis desiderio sit pudor aut modus?), 'only'; *dum-modo*, 'while only.' A common sense of the word is the temporal sense, 'only a little while ago' (cf. Caper 96. 15 K. 'modo' praeteriti est temporis, et ideo dicendum 'modo scripsi,'

---

[1] This is a translation of Epicharmus' epigram (ap. Schol. Hom. *Il.* x. 144) :
εἰμὶ νεκρός, νεκρὸς δὲ κόπρος, γῆ δ' ἡ κόπρος ἐστίν.
εἰ δέ τε γῆ νεκρός ἐστ', οὐ νεκρός, ἀλλὰ θεός.

'modo feci' non 'modo scribo,' 'modo facio'; quamvis quidam veteres et praesentis putaverint), emphasized in the Praenestine dialect by the addition of *tam* (tam modo, inquit Praenestinus, Plaut. *Trin.* 609). The shortening of the final *-o* is due to the influence of the preceding short syllable (see ch. iii. § 42 on the Law of Breves Breviantes), like *dătŏ* (originally *datōd) Plaut., *hăvĕ, bĕnĕ, mălĕ,* &c.

§ 15. (13) Concessive.— Etsi, quamquam, quamvis, licet. The formation of all these words is evident: *et-sī*, 'even if,' *quam-quam* (reduplicated), *quam-vīs*, 'how you wish' (like *quantum-vis*, 'however much you wish' or *quam-lĭbet*, 'how you please'), *lĭcet*, 'it is allowed,' 'granted.'

§ 16. (14) Final.—Ut, quo, quominus, quin, ne, neve, neu, nedum. *Ut* (see § 11).

Quō is the Abl. (Instr.?) Sg. Neut. of the Relative, used with Comparatives, *quo facilius* like *eo facilius. Quōmĭnŭs* adds to *quo* the Comparative *mĭnŭs*, 'less,' used in a negative sense (cf. *mĭnĭmē*, 'by no means'; *părum sciens*, 'ignorant').

Quĭn is composed of *quī*, how (Abl.? Loc.? Instr.?), and the negative particle *nĕ* (§ 18), and is found with *-ne* (or perhaps *nē*, 'lest') in unsyncopated form in Ter. *Andr.* 334 : efficite qui detúr tibi ; Égo id agam mihi quí ne detur, and in a fragment from some comedy (*Com.* inc. 47 R.) :

haúd facile est defénsu qui ne cómburantur próxumae.

In some instances it represents *qui* (Nom. Sg. Masc.) with *-ne*, e. g. nemo fuit quin sciret (qui nesciret); and a construction like nulla mulier fuit quin sciret, nil tam difficile est quin exquiri possit, is best explained as a universalizing of *qui* Masc., as of *potis* Masc. in *potis est* (ch. ix. § 2), though some regard the *qui* of this usage as the Adv., and compare it to that Mod. Gk. use of ποῦ τόv for ὅν mentioned in ch. vii. § 23 (*I. F.* iv. 226).

It is used also in other ways than as a Final Conjunction (the manifold uses of *quin* were a favourite theme of Latin grammarians; see Gell. xvii. 13). *Quin* in affirmations, e. g. hercle quin recte dicis, Plaut., may be merely the Adverb *qui* of *hercle qui,* &c. with the Demonstrative suffix *-ne* (so *atquin* and *atqui, alioquin* and *alioqui, ceteroquin* and *ceteroqui*; see on these forms Georges, *Lex. Wortf.* s. vv.); *quin* in commands, originally with Ind. (and so usually in Plautus), e.g. quin dicis?, then by 'constructio ad sensum' with Imper. (so usually in Ter.), e.g. quin dic, is the Adverb *qui* with the Interrogative particle *-ne*, 'how not?' 'why not?'; *quin* in a sentence like Plaut. *Trin.* 360: quin comedit quód fuit, quod nón fuit? (i.e. eumne dicis qui, &c.), is *qui* Nom. Sg. with the same particle (cf. *Mil.* 13 quemne ego seruaui? 'you mean the man whose life I saved?' (see above, § 14 on *sin*).

Nē is I.-Eur. *nē, 'not' (O. Ind. ná, O. Ir. nī), a variety of I.-Eur. *nĕ, 'not' (Lat. *nĕ*-, § 18). In O. Lat. *nī* (I.-Eur. *nei, Osc. *nei*) was used in the sense of *nē* (§ 14). In Umbro-Oscan i corresponds to I.-Eur. ē (Lat. *e*), so that Osc. *ni* in *ni hipid* 'ne habuerit,' *ni fuid* 'ne fuerit,' Marruc. *ni* in *nita[g]a* 'ne tangat' exactly correspond to Lat. *nĕ*.

Nĕvĕ adds to *nē* the enclitic *-vĕ*, or, which in *neu* is reduced by syncope (cf. *sive* and *seu*, § 14).

For *nedum* (especially used by Livy, also by Cicero, but rarely by the other authors) *ne* alone is occasionally found (*Journ. Phil.* xx. 177). An early instance of the word, which is not employed by Plautus, is Ter. *Heaut.* 454:

> satrapa sí siet
> amátor, numquam súfferre eius sumptús queat;
> nedúm tu possis,

lit. 'ne(dum) tu te posse credas dico satrapam non posse,' 'satrapa non potest, nondum tu potes,' with which we may compare Plaut. *Amph.* 330:

> uíx incedo inánis, ne ire pósse cum onere exístumes.

Nedum is related to *ne*, as *vixdum* to *vix, nondum* to *non*; cf. Liv. xxiv. 4. 1 puerum vixdum libertatem, nedum dominationem modice laturum. On the construction and use of the word, see *Harv. Stud.* ii. pp. 103 sqq.

§ 17 (15) **Asseverative Particles.—Ne** (nae), -ne. *Nē* is the spelling indicated by the references to the word in the Roman grammarians, for they speak of it as the same in form with prohibitive *ne* (Charis. 189. 2 K.; Diom. 394. 21 K.), and is also the spelling of the best MSS. (Georges, *Lex. Wortf.* s.v.), though there is no reason why there should not have been in Latin two separate affirmative particles *nē* and *nae*, as there were in Greek νή and ναί (cf. δή and δαί), representing an original *nē and *nai, a Loc. Sg. Form (cf. Osc. svaí, 'if,' § 14). The form *nĕ corresponds to *nĕ of the affirmative suffix -*nĕ* found in the Dramatists with Personal and Demonstrative Pronouns; cf. O. Scand. þēr-na 'tibimet' (e.g. Plaut. *Mil.* 565:

> égone si post húnc diem
> muttíuero, etiam quód egomet certó sciam,
> dato éxcruciandum mé;

for other examples, see *Amer. Journ. Phil.* ii. 51), as *wĕ to *wē, 'or,' *dĕ to *dē, &c. (§ 1).

§ 18. (16) **Negatives.—In-, ne-, nec, non, haud, ve-.** *Nĕ-* (I.-Eur. *nĕ, O. Ind. ná, &c.) is prefixed, not only to Verbs, e.g. *ne-scio*, O. Lat. *ne-vis*, *ne-parcunt*, &c. (cf. O. Engl. nille, nolde; O. Sl. něsmǐ, &c.), but also to other parts of speech, e.g. *nĕ-fas*, *n(e)-utiquam*, *neüter* (*nē-*, I.-Eur. *nē, O. Ind. ná, &c., appears in *nēquīquam*, &c.); *in-* (I.-Eur. *n̥, O. Ind. an-, a-, Gk. ἀν-, a-, &c.) and *vē-* (I.-Eur. *wĕ, O. Ind. vă-; cf. O. Sl. u-bogŭ, 'poor'), a curtailment of I.-Eur. *ăwĕ-, O. Ind. ava-, ch. ix. § 12) only to Adjectives, &c. (but see Langen, *Beitr.* p. 181 on *imprŏbare*, *infĭteri, ignoscere*, &c.). I.-Eur, *n̥- (Lat. *in-*, older *en-*, ch. iv. § 81), the weak or unaccented grade of I.-Eur. *nĕ (ch. iv. § 51), is represented in Umbro-Oscan by an-, e.g. Umbr. antakres 'integris,' Osc. *amprufid* 'improbe.'

Nōn is generally supposed to represent **noen*(um), the 'doublet' of *noenum* (usually explained as **nĕ-oinom*, 'not one') before an initial vowel, as *nihil*, *nīl* was the similar doublet of *nihilum* (ch. iii. § 52); though the absence of a satisfactory parallel for the change of *oe* to *ō* (instead of the usual *ū*) has led many to see in the first part of the word some other form of the Negative stem (cf. Umbr. *no-sve* 'nisi,' § 14), leaving the final *n* to be explained as the particle (negative or demonstrative, § 1) *-nĕ (or *-nŭ; cf. O. Ind. na-nú, Hom. οὔ νυ, and see ch. iii. § 37).

Noenŭ (e.g. Lucr. iii. 199 noenu potest) should be written *noenus*, and represents **ne-unus* as *noenum*, **ne-unum* (cf. *dēmus* and *dēmum*, ch. ix. § 2) with suppression of *-s* in pronunciation (ch. ii. § 126). The other theory makes it differ from *noenum* in appending **nŭ* instead of *num* (§ 10).

Haud, which is confined within narrower limits than *non* in O. Lat., being used especially with Adjectives and Adverbs, usually immediately before the negated word, and never in questions, has been referred (along with Gk. οὐ) to I.-Eur. **ăwĕ-*, 'away' (see above on *vē-*), so that it would properly be spelt **aud*. The Roman grammarians preferred the spelling *haud* to *haut*, e.g. Charis. 112. 8 K. haud ... d littera terminatur. οὐ enim Graeca vox d littera terminari apud antiquos coepit), and were probably right in doing so; for the byform *hau* seems to be the 'doublet' (ch. ii. § 136) before an initial consonant [Mar. Vict. 15. 25 K. cum (sequens) verbum a consonanti incipit, d perdit, ut ' hau dudum ' et ' hau multum ' et ' hau placitura refer '], e.g. *C. I. L.* i. 1007 heic ést sepulcrum hau púlcrum pulcrai féminae. (On the spellings *haud, haut, hau*, see Georges, *Lex. Wortf.* s. v.) The initial *h-* must have been used as a distinguishing mark to differentiate the word from *aut* (cf. Prob. *Inst. Art.* 145. 9 K. 'aut' si sine aspiratione scribatur et in t litteram exeat, erit conjunctio; si vero 'haud' cum aspiratione scribatur et in d litteram exeat, erit adverbium).

Nĕc in O. Lat. has the sense of *non*[1] [Festus 162. 14 Th. quotes XII Tab.: ast ei custos nec escit, and Plautus 'in Phasmate ' (*Most.* 240) nec recte si illi dixeris], like Osc. neip (svai neip dadit 'si nec dedat'), Umbr. neip (*sve neip portust issoc pusei subra screhto est* 'si nec portarit ita uti supra scriptum est '). The *g* of *nĕg-ōtium, neg-lĕgo* (often spelt *neclego* in MSS.; see Georges, *Lex. Wortf.* s. v.), &c. is variously explained as a phonetic change of the *-c* (**q^{u}ĕ*) of *nec* (see ch. ii. § 73), or as the particle **gĕ* (Gk. γε) of **nĕ-g(ĕ)* (cf. Lith. nè-gi, ne-gu), a different formation from **nĕ-q^u(ĕ)*.

§ **19. INTERJECTIONS.** Interjections, being for the most part onomatopoetic words, do not come under the phonetic laws

---

[1] Catullus (lxiv. 83) uses the phrase *funera nec funera* to express the Greek τάφοι ἄταφοι.

of a language; their analysis and etymology offer little difficulty. The Latin interjections need not therefore detain us long. *Oh!* *ah! st!* are more or less the same sounds that we ourselves use to express astonishment and surprise, and to enforce silence; and they require no discussion. Many are borrowed from the Greek, especially the exclamations used at musical or other entertainments, e. g. *euge* [in the Dramatists *eugē* (*eugae*) with a lengthening of the final syllable[1] like our 'bravo,' 'hallo'], *sŏphōs, pălĭn*, as ours come from the Italian or French, e.g. bravo, da capo, encore. But some are peculiarly Latin and offer points of interest. *Em* (not to be confused with *hem*, an Interjection of terror, grief, &c.), which is used by the Republican Comedians, where *ēn* (Gk. ἤν) is used by the classical writers (in the Comedians *ēn* is used only in rhetorical questions, e. g. *enunquam?*, Plaut. *Men.* 142, 925), seems to be the Imperative of *ĕmo*, lit. 'take,' a sense which suits well in phrases like *em tibi*, 'take that!' 'there's for you!' (in giving a blow), e. g. Plaut. *Asin.* 431 em ergo hoc tibi. Others make it Adverbial Acc. of *is*, O. Lat. *em*, 'tum' (Paul. Fest. 53. 37 Th.), which is also, perhaps properly, spelt *im* (ch. vii. § 19). Joined with *ille* (in the Acc. Case) it produces *ellum* [ello (with open *e*) is still heard in the Abruzzi], *ellos*, &c. So *ecce* (O. Sl. ese and se) from the Pronominal stem *eke- (*eko-) (ch. vii. § 15) either with appended -*ce*; [cf. Osc. eko-, 'this,' usually with appended -k (Lat. -*ce*), ekak 'hac,' ekkum 'item'], or else with doubling of consonant (as in *att-at*) produces *eccillum*, *eccillos*, &c., whence the Romance forms, Fr. celui, Ital. quello, &c. (see ch. vii. § 15). *Eccum* has been explained as *ecce* *hum (the enclitic -*ce* not being appended to the Pronoun because it exists already in the Interjection, just as *ecceillunc, &c. is never found); and this analysis is preferred to *ecce eum*, because the word is used by the Dramatists only when the person referred to is present on the stage, whereas *is* is the Pronoun used of persons who have been recently mentioned. Still *ecce eum might be explained as a parenthesis, e. g. Amphitruo eccum exit foras, 'A. —see him— has come out.' *Eccum* is the original of the Italian

---

[1] *Heiă*, the usual scansion, as in this refrain of a Late Lat. boating-song (*Poet. Lat. Min.* iii. p. 167 B.):

heia, viri, nostrum reboans echo sonet heia!,

appears as *heiā* in Plaut. *Merc.* 998.

interjection ecco, and in Plautus often comes very near *ecce,* e. g. *Mil.* 25 ubi tu es? Eccum, *Poen.* 279 assum apud te eccum.

Prō (not *proh,* see Neue, ii³. p. 985) seems to be merely the Preposition (Adverb) *prō,* forth, lit. ' away with it ! '

Vae, I.-Eur. *wai (Goth. vai, Lett. wai), borrowed in late Greek, οὐαί, is the same word as our Noun ' woe.'

Ăgĕ is, like *em,* an Imperative used interjectionally, in Plautus and Terence often with the enclitic *dum* appended, *agedum* (like Gk. ἄγε δή, § 1). The interjectional use of Imperatives is a feature of all languages; our ' lo ' is the Imperative of ' to look,' and we have in modern Italian vie (for *veni*), tie or te (for *tene*), guar (for *guarda*).

The names of deities occur in *hercle, me-hercules* (*sc.* juvet, Paul. Fest. 90. 11 Th.), *me-hercle, me-castor, me-dius fidius* ('the god of good faith,' with *dius* for *deus* because the first syllable is unaccented ?), *pol* (a curtailment of *Pollux*), *ecastor* (better *eccastor,* for the first syllable is long, but not long by nature, since it is shortened by the Law of Breves Breviantes in the Dramatists; see ch. iii. § 34). The last might represent *et Castor,* but *ĕdĕpol* can hardly represent *et deus Pollux,* although the irregular forms assumed by many of the English interjections, ' zounds,' ' sblood,' ' marry ' (for ' Mary '), show us the difficulty of tracing curtailed phrases of the kind back to their origin by the ordinary methods. *Eccĕrē* is either an invocation of Ceres or *ecce re,* ' lo indeed.'

INDEX[1]

(The numbers refer to the pages; *i* and *j*, *u* and *v* are treated as identical.)

A, pronunciation, 13 sqq.; phonetic changes, 219 sqq.; in weak grade of Ō-root, 258 sq.; of Ē-root, 258 sq.; of Ĕ-root, 261; varying with ŏ, 259; with ā, 259 sq.; Lat. ă for I.-Eur. ă (ə), 221 sqq.; for ĕ, 222; for *au* in *Agustus*, &c., 38, 41 sq.; in lă, ră, mă, nă, 222; for ŏ, 234 sq.; Lat. ā for ă lengthened, 220; for ō, 220; in lā, rā, nā, 219 sq.; not weakened to ē, 199; *aa* written for ā, 10.
-ā, shortening of, 210 sq.; in Nom. Sg., 210 sq., 373; of *qua*, Adv., &c., 551.
Ā-Subjunctive, 512 sqq.
a, ab, abs, Prep., 575 sqq.; *ab-* confused with *ob-*, 574.
abante, 573, 595.
abĕst, the scansion, 214 sq.
ăbicio, 45.
abiĕgnus, pronunc. of, 138.
Ablative (see Declension), Adv. use of (see Cases).
Ablaut (see Gradation).
abnuo and *abnueo*, 476.
abolevi and *abolui*, 500.
abscīsio and *abscĭssio*, 112.
abscondi and *abscondidi*, 502.
absida, 79.
absinthium, 79.
absque, 576.
abstinei (?), 501.

Abstufung, 367.
abstulas, 464.
abusque, 595.
abȳssus, the scansion, 156.
ac (see *atque*).
Acca Larentia, 118 *n*.
accēdo, 194.
Accentuation, 148 sqq.; studied at Rome, 151 sq.; Early Law, 157 sqq.; I.-Eur., 157 sqq., 165 sqq.; of *făcĭlĭŭs*, &c., 158; of Sentence, 165 sqq.; Secondary, 158 sqq., 161; Paenultima Law, 160 sqq.; of Word-Groups, 161 sqq., 169 sq.; of *-ās*, 163; of *addūc*, &c., *audīt*, &c., 163; of *illōc*, &c., 163; of *tantōn*, &c., 163; with *-qu(e)*, &c., 163; of Gen., Voc. Sg. of IO-stems, 163 sq.; of Interj., 164; Vulg. Lat., 164 sq.; of *-ĭĕrem*, *-ĭŏlum*, 164; with Mute and Liquid, 164; of Comp. Vb., 164; of Numeral, 165; and Ictus in Plaut., 166 sqq.; of *sum*, 167; of Pron., 167 sq.; of Prep., 167 sqq.; of Adv., 168 sq.; of Conj., 169; of Auxiliary, 169.
accentus, meaning of, 152, 154.
accepsti (?), 508.
acceptor for *accipiter*, 115.
accerso, 487.
Accheruns, Plaut., 58.
Acchilles, Plaut., 58.
accipiter, 259.

---

[1] If a word is not found in this Index, the ending or suffix of the word should be looked for. Thus the reference for *furibundus*, *fremebundus*, &c., will be found under *-bundus*, the reference for *commenticius*, &c., under *-ticius*.

Accius, doubling of vow., 8 sqq.; *gg* for *ng*, 10 sq.; *ei* for *ī*, 9 sq.
acclinis, 275.
accubuo, 323.
accuratus, 541 *n.*
Accusative (see Declension), Adv. use of (see Cases).
ăcer, 260, F. 371; *-ris*, M., 371.
ăcerbus, 180.
acertas for *acritas*, 365.
acetum, 335.
-āceus (see Suffix *-KO-*).
Achivi, 196.
acies, acisculus, 347.
acredula, 353.
acrufolius, spelling, 364.
āctito, pronunc. of, 134; of *actum*, 139.
Active, endings (see Verb).
actus, Noun, 344.
actutum, 565.
acuo, 260
acupedium, 259.
-ācus (see Suffix *-KO-*).
Acute Accent, 153 sqq.
ad, Prep., 576; spelling of, 76 sq.; *ar*, 288, 99.
adagio, 291.
addues, 515; *-it*, 515. (See *arduuitur*.)
adeo, Adv., 568; accent. of, 166.
adeps, alipes, 287.
adessint (?), 466.
adgredīmur, the scansion, 475.
adgretus, 285.
Adjectives, dist. of Gender (see Gender); Decl. of (see Declension); Compar. of (see Comparison); form of (see Suffixes); Numeral (see Numerals); Pronom. (see Pronouns); used as Part., 540, 543; from Part., 540 sqq.
adjuro (-jue-), Fut. Pft., 507.
adnūit, Perf., 508.
adolesco, 481.
adorītur, the scansion, 475.
adpetissis, 462.
adquo, 568.
adsum, pronounced *ass-*, 313.
advenat, 464.
adventicius, 337.
Adverbs, 548 sqq.; Nom. forms, 553 sqq.; in *-ter*, 553 sqq.; Gen. forms, 555; Acc. forms, 555 sqq.; Compar. of. 557 sq.; Abl., Instr.,

Loc. forms, 559 sqq.; in *-tus*, 561; in *-tim*, 548; in *-e*, 548; word-groups, 562 sqq.; *-mente*, 552; of doubtful origin, 565 sqq; Num. (see Numerals); Pronom., 567 sqq.; Compound, 360 sq.
adversus (-m), Prep., 595.
adulescens, spelling of, 197.
aduncus, 259.
adusque, 595.
ae, pronunc. of, 37 sqq.; and *e*, 42, 242; for *au*, 42; for Gk. η, 42 sq.; for *ā*, 242 (see also AI).
Aecetiai, 188.
aedes, 241, 346.
aedīlis, 340; *aidīles*, Nom. Sg. 376.
aedituumus (-tuus), 405.
aegrotus, 484.
-aei- for *-ai-*, 242.
aemidus, 258.
Aenea, Nom., 373.
aequanimus (-itas), 123, 364.
aequipero, 192.
aequus, pronunc. of, 42.
-aes in Gen. Sg., 381 sq.
aes, 157.
Aesculapius, 242; spelling, 198.
aetas, 173.
aevum, 241, 251, 348.
af, Prep., 576 sq.
affatim, 563.
afluo and *affluo*, 576.
age, 600, 618.
ager, 221.
agilis, 332.
Agma, 10 sq., 60, 65.
agmen, 292.
agnomen, 294.
agnus, 235; F., 370.
ago, 221; *egi*, 497; *actum*, pronunc., 139; *age*, 600, 618; *axim*, 465 sq.
agoeā (?), the scansion, 373 *n.*
agricola, 317.
Agrigentum, 197.
agulum, 334.
Agustus for *Aug-*, 38, 41 sq.
Ahala and *Ala*, 54.
Ahenobarbus, 364.
ahenus, 265; spelling of, 55, 57.
AI, phon. changes of, 241 sq.; ĀI, 251 sq.; *ai* on inscrr., 242.
-ai of Gen. Sg., 381 sq.; Dat., 386.
aio, 546, 265; pronunc., 53; spelling

INDEX. 621

aiio, 8; *ai*, *aie*, Imper., 546; *aibam*,
aiebam, 491; pronunc. of *ai-*, 43.
-al- from I.-Eur.], 279.
ala, 293.
alacer, pronunc. of, 18; *-ris*, M., 371;
  -ecer, 18, 198.
albeus for *alv-*, 51.
albico 488.
albogalerus, 361, 364.
Albsi for *Albensi*, 177.
albus, 223.
alebris, 334.
Aleria, 197.
ales, 351.
Alexander, *-ter*, *Alixentrom*, Acc., 73.
Alfius, dial. for *Alb-*, 80.
aliā, Adv., 569.
alias, Adv., 557.
alibi and *aliubi*, 567.
alica (*hal-*), 56.
alicunde, 570.
alienus, 449.
alio, Adv., 568.
alioqui (*-n*), 568, 614.
aliorsum, 549.
aliquamdiu, 571.
aliquando, 571.
aliquantisper, 562.
aliquis, 447.
aliquo, Adv., 568.
-ālis (see Suffix -LI-).
aliter, 554; cf. 553.
alitus and *altus*, 335.
ālium, *all-*, 115; *-eum*, 22. (See *alum*).
aliunde, 570.
alius, 449; *-is*, 375.
aliuta, 571.
allexi, 505.
alnus, 309.
alo, 223.
Alphabet, 1 sqq., 5; Gk. letters, 4, 11 sq.;
  Claudius' reforms (see Claudius).
alter, 449, 452; *-ĭus*, Gen., 450.
alteras, Adv., 557.
*alternas (?), Nom. Pl., 398.
alternis, Adv., 551.
alteruter, 450; *-rtra*, 450.
alucinor, 488; spelling of, 117.
alum, 333. (See *ālium*.)
alumnus, 327.
-am of *quam*, *tam*, &c., 549.
am-, Prep., 578.
amarus, 259.

amasius, 305.
ambages, 345 sq., 221.
ambegna (*-igna*), 229.
ambi-, Prep., 577.
ambio, 505; *-issit*, 466.
ambo, 451.
ambulo, 547.
amendo (*-ando*), 200.
amicio, 505, 578.
amicus, 337.
amitto (*amm-*), 109, 114.
ammentum, spelling of, 114.
amnego for *abn-*, 80.
amnis, 282.
amnuo for *abn-*, 80.
amo, 274; *-ento*, 3 Pl., 519.
amoenus, 246.
ampendices, 578.
amplant, 483.
amplector 578; *-oct-*, 467.
amplio, 485.
amsegetes, 578.
amtermini, 578.
amurca, 33, 75.
amussim, 563.
amygdala, *-iddula*, 198.
an, Conj., 606.
an-, Prep., 578.
Anaptyxis (see Parasitic Vowel).
anas, 274.
ancaesus (*-īsus*), 198.
anceps, older, *-cipes*, 178.
ancilia, 287.
anclabris, 334
ancora, 155, 190; *-ch-*, 59.
anculus, a servant, 178; *-cilla*, 333.
ancunulentae, 196.
ancus, 259.
angina, 326.
ango, 271: *-ustus*, 223, 356.
anguila (*-illa*), 115.
anguis, 338.
anhelo, 199, 578; *alen-*, 98; *-ll-*, 112.
animadverto, 362.
animus, *-ma*, 223.
annus, 117, 314.
anquina, 247.
anquiro, 578.
anser, 272.
antae, 274.
ante, 578; *ant(e)positus*, 579; *antea*,
  579, 569; *antehac*, 569; *antid-*, 579;
  antidhac, 579.

antennae, 578.
antes, 578.
antestamino, 519, 578.
antiae, 562.
anticus, 337.
antideo, 575, 579.
antigerio, 560.
antioper, 562.
antiquus, 337.
antistes, 350.
antruo, -dr, 289.
anuis, Gen., 384.
-ānus (see Suffix -NO-).
ānus, 333.
Aorist (see Tense-Stems).
aper, 222.
aperio, 475.
Apex, over long vow., 4, 129, 134, 161 sq.
apinae, 58.
apio, Vb., 480.
apiscor, 480.
aplustrum, 96.
Apocope, 203 sqq.; accent in, 153, 161.
appello, 472; -amino, 519
Appenninus (Ape-), 117.
Appius (see Claudius).
apprime, 565.
apricus, 178.
Aprilis, 178.
aprugnus, -unus, 294.
apud, 579; -or, -ur, 288.
aqua, 223; trisyll. (?), 87; ā-, acq-, 87; -aï, Gen., 382.
aquīlā, the scansion, 210.
Aquilonia, 286.
-ar- from I.-Eur. ṛ, 279.
ar for ad, Prep., 288, 99.
ara, asa, 305.
*aramen for aeramen, 201.
aranea, 292.
aratrum, 330.
arbiter, 288.
arbor, 290; -os, 356; -osem, Acc., 305.
arboretum (-bustum), 306, 335.
arbutum (-itum), 197.
arceo, 223.
arcesso, 487; -ivi, 506; accerso, 487.
arcubii, 176.
arcus, 300; decl. of, 344; F., 344.
ardea, 279.
ardeo, 486.
ardus, 184.
arduuitur (?), xii Tab., 288, 515.

are-(facio), 490; arf-, 184.
arena (see harena).
argentum, 296.
arger for agg-, 288.
Argiletum, accent of, 161 sq.
argumentum, 336.
argutus, 484.
aries, 261; -jete, 144.
-āris (see Suffix -RI-).
arispex, 29.
-ārius (see Suffix -IO-); ousted by -āris, 321.
armus, 279.
aro, 223.
arquites, 300.
ars, 341.
artena, 172.
Article, Def., 452; Indef., 410
Articulation, Basis of, 30.
artio, 485.
artus, 343.
Aruncus for Aur-, 42, 40.
arvum, 323; -uus, 323.
-ās (see Suffix -TI-); accent of, 163.
-as, Nom. Pl., 398; Gen. Sg., 381.
aser, blood, 261.
asinus, 305.
asom fero, 539.
asp- for absp-, 310.
asper, aspr-, 185.
aspergo (-argo), 200.
aspernor, 470, 486.
Aspirates, phon. changes of, 279 sqq.;
Gk. in Lat. orth., 4, 11 sq., 54, 57 sqq., 72, 99 sq.; Tenues (see Tenues Asp.).
asporto, 210.
assentior (-o), 521.
Asseverative Particles, 614.
Assibilation (see Palatalization).
assidue (-o), 550.
Assimilation, of Cons., 311 sqq.; of Prep., 312 sq.; of unacc. vow., 201; of final cons. (see Sandhi).
-asso, Vb.-forms in, 462 sqq.
assulatim, 556.
ast, 600 sq.
asted, Dven. Inscr., 514.
-aster, -ast(r)inus (see Suffix -TERO-, Suffix -D-).
at, Conj., 600; spelling, 76 sq.
Atella, 312.
ater, 81.

INDEX. 623

Athematic, Conjug. (see Verb) ; Pres. Part. Act., 541.
-*atim* of Adv., 556.
atque (*ac*), 598 sq., 122 ; spelling, 599 ; *atque atque*, 599.
atqui (*-n*), 601, 614.
atrītus, 485.
atrox, 259, 354.
attat, 617 ; accent of, 164.
attigas, 464.
attulas, 464.
-*atus*, e.g. *dentatus*, P.P.P., 483.
AU, phon. changes of, 242 sq. ; pronunc., 37 sqq. ; weak grade of ŌU-root, 261 ; -*au*- for *ăvĕ*, 243 ; ĀU, 252.
au-, Prep., 576.
au, Interj., 38.
aububulcus, 235.
auceps, 180.
audacter (*-iter*), 554.
audeo, 486 ; -*si*, 522 ; -*sus sum*, 522 ; -*sim*, 465 ; *aussus*, 112.
audio, 307.
ave (see *have*).
Avernus, 197.
averruncassis, 462.
averta, 197.
Aufidus, 250.
augeo, 482, 243.
augur, -*ger*, 198 ; -*ra*, Accius, 48.
avillus, 235.
aula (*olla*), 41 ; *aulla*, 112.
Aulius, 267.
aureae, 261.
aurichalcum, 41.
auriga, 261.
auris, 243.
Aurora, 243, 356.
aurugo (*-igo*), 37.
aurum, 243.
aus- (*os*-) in *osculor*, &c., 41, 262.
aus for *avus*, 52.
ausculto, 243 ; *asc*-, 41.
auspex, 180.
aussus, 112.
austerus, -*ris*, 338.
austium, 262.
aut, 599.
autem, 601, 571.
autor for -*ct*-, 89, 119.
autumo, 180, 235.
avunculus, *aunç*-, 49, 172 ; *anc*-, 172.

Auxiliary Vbs., 511 ; accent., 169.
auxilla, 333.
Avyayībhāva, Compd., 360 sq.
-*āx* (see Suffix in Gutt., -*KO*-.
-*ax*, e. g. *aureax*, 355.
axim, 465 sq.
axis, 305, 338.
axites (*-tiosi*), 352.

B, pronunc., 78 sqq. ; for Gk. φ, 11 ; for *v*, 47, 49 sqq. ; phon. changes of, 282 ; for dw-, 265, 268 ; for bh, 282 sq. ; for dh, 289 sq. ; *br* for sr. 303, 308.
baca, spelling of, 116 sq.
Bahuvrīhi, Compd., 360 sq.
balbus, 282, 358.
balbutio, 488.
*baliolus (?), 287.
ballaena, 48, 58 ; spelling, 117.
balneum, *balin*-, 173.
-*bam* of Impft., 489 sqq.
barba, 283.
barbactum for *verv*-, 52.
barbar(*us*), 374.
barca, 184.
basilica, *bass*-, 115 ; *basis*, *bass*-, 115
Basis of Articulation, 30.
batillum (see *vat*-).
battuo, spelling of, 113.
beatitudo (*-tas*), 341.
Belena (?), 48.
bellum, O. Lat. *duellum*, 268.
bellus, 326.
bene, -*ĕ*, 551 ; *ben*(*e*), 184 ; -*merens*, Adj, 540 ; -*volens*, 352 ; and -*lus*, 540 ; -*ficus* for *venē*-, 51.
benīgnus, pronunc. of, 138.
Benuentod, 184.
*berbix for *vervex*, 52.
bessi-, 409.
BH, phon. changes of, 282 sq.
bhā-, 'to speak,' 457.
bher-, 'to carry,' 457.
bheu-, 'to be,' 458.
-*bi* of *ibi*, &c., 551, 567.
bi- of *bidens*, &c., 411.
bibo, Vb., 468 ; -*i*, Perf., 503 ; -*er*(*e*), Inf., 537.
bicorpor, 376.
bigae, 196.
-*bilis* (see Suffix -DHLO-).
bimus, 144, 294.

bini, 411.
bipinnis for -pen-, 23.
bis, 411.
blasfēmus, the scansion, 156.
blatta, 314.
-bo of Fut., 491 sqq.
bonus, 326 ; Compar., 406.
bos, 253 ; bobus, bu-, 250.
-br- for mr, 269 sqq.
-bra (see Suffix -DHRO-).
braca, spelling of, 116.
bracchium, 58 ; spelling of, 117.
Breathing, Gk. in Panhormus, &c., 57.
Breath-Stops (see Tenues).
Breves Breviantes, 210, 126, 129 sq., 201 sq.
brevis, 227, 292
breviter, 553.
Britanni (Britt-), 115.
Broken Reduplication, 358.
Bruges for Phryg-, 36, 58.
-brum (see Suffix -DHRO-).
bruma, 407.
Bruttii (-ri-), 29.
-bs-, -bt-, pronunc. of, 79.
bucetum, 335.
bucina, spelling of, 117.
bulba for vulva, 50.
-bulum (see Suffix -DHLO-).
-bundus, e. g. errabundus, 545.
Burrus for Pyrrh-, 36, 75.
burrus, 75.
-bus, Dat. Pl., scansion of, 404.
bustar (bo-), 205, 250.
bustar (cf bustum), 250.
butīrum, the scansion, 156.
*butis (-tt), 116.
Butrio, 33.
buxus, 75.

C, the letter, 2, 6 sq., 76 ; pronunc., 84 sqq. ; palatalization of, 87 sq. ; for qu, 299 sqq., 315 ; cl for tl, 283 sq.
cadaver, 541.
caduceus, 288.
caducus, 337.
cadui for cecīdi, 509.
Caecilius, Cec-, 42 ; Caeic-, 242.
caecus, 242.
caedes, 346.
caedo, 242 ; cecīdi, 496 ; cedre, 184.
caelebs, 48.

caeles, 352.
caelum, the spelling coe-, 44.
caementum, 285 ; -ta, F., 400.
caeruleus, 275.
calamitas, 286 ; kad-, 286.
calamitosus, 353.
calandae for cale-, 23.
calcar, 203.
caldus for -lid-, 173.
cale-(facio), 490 ; calf-, 173, 184.
calicare, 95.
caligo, 355.
callescerunt, Cato, 481.
callim (?), 580.
*calmus for -lam-, 198.
calor, N., 356.
calumnia, calvor, 327.
calvus, 323.
calx, heel, 355.
calx, lime, 95 ; -ls, 107.
Calypsōnem, 155.
camellus for -ēlus, 115.
Camena, 308.
camera (·mar-), 197.
Camerina (-mar-), 197.
Camillus, 308.
cammarus (ga-), 74.
Campans for -nus, 182.
campester, 330.
cancer, 96.
canes, Nom. Sg., 346 ; -nĕs, Pl., 399.
canicula, 347.
cano, 223 ; -nte, Carm. Sal., 459 ; Perf., 501, 509.
Canopus, 75.
canus, 307.
capax, 355.
caper, 276.
caperro, spelling of, 117.
capesso, 462.
capiclum for -tulum, 83.
capio, 298 ; cepi, Perf., 502.
capis, bowl, 83.
capistrum, 331.
Capito, 349.
Caralis, -lar-, 93 ; -rar-, 93.
Carda (-dea), 317.
Cardinal Numerals (see Numerals).
cardus for -duus, 174.
carictum (?) for -rec-, 23.
cārint (?), 515.
carmen, 271 sqq. ; C. Saliare, 5, 245, 459 n.

INDEX. 625

Carna, 317.
căro, 278, 273, 349.
carpatinae, 75.
carpo, 279.
cartilago, 279.
Carvilius Ruga, letter G, 7.
carus, 491.
cascus, 307.
Cases, 366 sqq. ; Strong and Weak, 367 ; suffix ousted by Prep., 573 ; Adv. use of, 548 sqq. ; of Nom., 553 sqq. ; of Gen., 555 ; of Acc., 555 sqq. ; of Abl., Instr., Loc., 559 sqq. (See Declension.)
cassis, -ida, 354 ; *casila*, 286.
cassus, empty, 565.
Castōrem, 155.
casus, -ss-, 110 sq.
Cato (Elder), *-ae* for *-am*, 61, 493 *n*.
catulio, 484.
catus, 258, 541.
cavaedium, 362.
cauculus for *-calc-*, 96.
cauda, 41.
caveo, 235 ; *cave*, accent, 169 ; pronunc., 49 ; *cavi*, 499.
Cauneas (*cave ne eas*), 169.
Caurus, 258.
causa, -ss-, 110 sq.
Causative Vbs., 477, 481 sq.
causis (*cave sis*), 49.
cavus (*cov-*), 234 sq.
-ce, Particle, 432 sq.
cĕdo, 432, 518 ; *cette*, 284.
cĕdo, Perf. *cessi*, pronunc., 111.
cedre for *caedere*, 184.
cedrus, 289.
celer, 351 ; *-rissimus*, 407.
-cello, 486.
celo, 488 *n.*, 227.
celox, 354.
celsus, 229.
cena, 277 ; *-atus*, P. P. P. ; 520, 542 ; *-oe-*, 44, 277.
-cendi, Perf., 501.
censeo, 273 ; *-ento*, Pass., 519.
centum, 418 sq. ; *-plex*, 418 sq. ; *-tussi-*, 409 ; *-centum* for *-ti*, 418 sq. ; *-tesimus, -tensu-*, 418 sq.
cerebrum, 296 ; *-ber*, 370.
ceresium, cherry, 18.
cerno, 472 ; *crevi*, 500.
certo (*-e*), 550.

cervix (Sg., Plur.), 355.
Cerus, 329.
cesaries for *caes-*, 43.
cetero-, 244 ; *-rum*, Conj., 602 ; *-ra*, Adv., 602 ; *-roqui* (*-n*), 568, 614.
cette, 284.
-cetum, 335.
ceu, 607.
-ch- (Gk. χ), *-cch-*, Plaut., 58.
Change of unaccented vowel (see Weakening).
Chersonensus, the spelling, 136 *n*.
Chi (see Aspirates).
Chius (Adj.), scansion of, 132.
-ci- and *-ti-*, 82 sqq.
cibus, decl. of, 344.
cicindela, 333.
ciconia, Praen. *conea*, 22.
cicur, quant. of *i*, 485.
*cĭcus for *-icc-*, 116.
cieo (*cio*), 481 ; *cītus*, 335, 541.
cincinnus, 315.
cinctutus, 335.
cingo, -nxi, -nctus, pronunc., 140.
cinis, 357.
-cinor (*-cinium*), 488.
circes, 352.
circo-, -um, Prep., 579 ; *-ā*, 579 ; *-iter*, 580.
Circumflex Accent, 153 sqq., 161.
cis (*citra*), 580, 432 ; *-ter*, 432.
cistella, 333.
citera for *-thar-*, 190.
citrus, 289.
citus, 541 ; *cī-*, 335 ; *-tŏ*, Adv., 551.
civicus, 337.
-cl- for *-tl-*, 81.
clades, 219.
clam (*clanculum*), 580 ; *clamde*, 580.
clamo, 279.
clandestinus, 580.
clango, 471.
clarare (*-ere*), 484.
Claudius (App.), reforms alph., 6, 105 ; (Emp.), reforms alph., 3 sqq., 36, 47 sq., 79 (see also *Clo-*).
claudo, 180, 252 ; *clu-*, 40, 196.
clavis, 347.
clavus, 298.
clepo, 298 ; *-psi*, 505.
cliens (*clu-*), 29.
clipeus (*clu-*), 29.
clivus, 275, 323.
cloaca (*clu-*), 37.

626   THE LATIN LANGUAGE.

Clodius, 41 ; *Cla-*, 42.
Cloelius, 250 ; *Cloul*[*i*], 246.
Close Syll., quant. of vowel, 133 sqq.
clueo (*-uo*), 473, 295.
-clum (*-culum*, q. v.) (see Suffix -LO-).
clunis, 250.
Clutĕmestra, the scansion, 202.
co- for *quo-*, 300.
-co of *albico*, &c., 479.
coa (from *coeo*), 318.
coalesco, 481.
coculum, 300.
coelum for *cael-*, 44.
coemptionalis senex, 143.
coena for *ce-*, 44, 277.
coepio, 545 ; *-pi*, 502 ; scansion of, 143 ; *-plus sum*, 522.
coero, *coi-*, for *curo*, 248.
coetus, 142, 39.
cogito, 143.
cognatus, spelling of, 114.
cognomen, 294.
cognosco, *con-*, 294 ; Perf., 509.
cogo, 143.
cohibeo, scansion of, 143.
cohors, 183.
co(*h*)*um*, 235.
cojicio, pronunc. of, 53.
coinquo, 311.
colina (?), the spelling, 236.
Collective, Compd., 360 sq., 365 ; Noun, 399.
collega, 318 ; *-gius* for *-m*, 370.
collis, 271.
collum, gender of, 369.
cōllum for *-l-*, 112.
cŏlo, 227 ; spelling of, 300.
colober for *-lub-*, 37.
coloephia for *-ly-*, 36.
colonia, 321.
columen (*culm-*), 185.
columna, pronunc., 69 ; *-lom-*, 37, 69 ; C. Rostrata, 7 ; *-mella*, 69.
colurnus, 97.
colus, 300.
com- (*cum*) (*co-?*), Prep., 580 ; bef. *v-*, *f-*, 50 sq., 66, 99 sqq. ; bef. *n-*, *gn-*,. 114 ; bef. *s-*, *f-*, 136 sqq. ; *quom*, 581 ; *cum* bef. *n-*, 121 ; *c. eo c. quiqui*, 448.
combretum, 227.
comburo, 578, 144.
comes, 350.
comis, 307.

commendo (*-man-*), 200.
commentus, 335.
comminus, 554 ; *-m-*, 115.
commircium, the spelling, 229.
communis, 247.
como, *-mpsi*, 505.
compages, 346.
Comparison, of Adj., 404 sqq. ; Compar., 404, 406 ; Superl., 405, 407 ; irreg., 407 sq. ; of Adv., 550.
compellare, 472.
Compensation, length by, 314.
comperendinare, 486.
compesco, 192.
compitum, 194.
complere, in Romance, 489.
Compounds (Noun and Adj.), 358 sqq. ; accent of, 161 sqq. ; Ā-stems, 363 sq. ; O-stems, 364 ; I-stems, 364 ; U-stems, 364 ; N-stems, 364 ; R-stems, 365 ; Dent., Gutt. Stems, 365 ; S-stems, 365 ; in Pacuv., 360 ; in Lucr., 360 ; in Plaut., 362 ; (Verbs), 362 sq. ; accent of, 164 ; influence on Simple Vb., 468 ; (Adv.) (see Adverbs) ; (Prep.) (see Prepositions).
concapit, xii Tab., 379.
concino, *-ui*, 509.
conditio, 341 ; *-cio*, 88.
conea, Praen., 22.
conesto for *cohon-*, 143.
confestim, 556.
confeta (*sus*), 318.
confuto, 309.
conger (*go-*), 74 ; *gu-*, 33.
congius, 280.
congruens (*-uus*), 540.
conitor, spelling of, 114.
coniveo, 302 ; *-nixi*, 499.
Conjugations (see Verb).
Conjunctions, 596 sqq. ; accent, 169 ; variety of meaning, 596 ; of stem, 596 ; of vow.-quant., 596 ; Conjunctive, 598 sq. ; Disjunctive, 599 sq. ; Adversative, 600 sqq. ; Limitative, 602 sq. ; Explanatory, 603 sq. ; Conclusive, 604 sq ; Optative, 605 ; Interrog., 605 sq. ; Compar., 606 sqq. ; Temp., 608 sqq. ; Causal, 610 ; Condit., 610 sqq.; Concessive, 613 ; Final, 613 sq. ; Assev., 614 sq. ; Neg., 615 sq.

INDEX. 627

conjux (-nx), 69, 358.
conquaeisivei, 242.
conquiniscor, 470.
consacro for -sec-, 200.
conscribillo, 479, 487.
considero, 488.
consilium, 286; -sid-, 286.
consiptus, 195.
Consiva, 199.
Consonant, lost in group, 309 sqq.;
Stems and I-stems, 338, 341 (see
Suffixes).
consternare, 470, 192.
consul, pronunc. of, 136 sq.
contages, 346.
contamino, 292, 294.
conterere, in Romance, 489.
conticinium, 194.
continuo, 557.
contio, 67; pronunc., 141; covent-, 250;
-nct-. 310.
contra, 581; -ă, 557.
Contraction, e. g. cra for cera, 177;
e. g. mg for magnus, 125; Contr. Vb.-
forms (see Verb).
controversia, 581.
contubernium, spelling of, 193.
contŭdit, 496.
contumelia factum itur, 538.
conubium, spelling of, 114.
conucella, 273.
convicium, 225.
conviva, 318.
convollo (-vell-), 228.
copia, 144; copis, Adj., 144.
copula, 143.
coquino, 470.
coquo, 467; -int (?), 515.
coquus, 291; spelling of, 299.
cor, 279; scansion, 122, 215.
corallium (curali-), 34.
coram, 581.
corbus for -vus, 51.
cordatus, 483.
corigia for corr-, 114.
Cornelis, 372.
cornicen, 192.
Corniscas, 404.
cornix, 347.
cornu, 279.
cornus, cornel, 279.
corolla, 333.
corona, 59; spelling of, 59.

corruptus, cŏr-, 114; -mpt-, 471.
Corus, 258.
cos, 259.
cosentiont, Scipio Epit., 529.
cosmis, Dvenos inscr., 307.
cothurnus, 33.
cotonea, 75.
cottidie, 560; spelling, 227 sq.
coventio, S. C. Bacch., 250.
courauerunt, 246.
coxa, 298.
crabro, 220.
cracli for clatri, 97.
crapula, 197.
Crasis, 142 sqq.
Crassus, story of, 169.
crastinus, 325.
crates, 219, 279.
crebesco for -br-, 95.
credo, 479; -duam, -im, 514.
creo, 329.
crepa for capra, 98.
crepo, -ui, -avi, 499, 506; -itus, P. P. P.,
542.
crepus, 98.
crepusculum, 273.
cresco, 479; -ēvi, 500.
cretariae for cet-, 96.
creterra, 118.
cribrum, 330.
crimen, 336.
crinis, 339.
crista, 339.
crocio, 476.
crudelis, 340.
crudus, 298.
cruentus, 352.
cruor, 298.
crustum, pronunc. of, 141; -trum, 96;
-tlum, clustr-, 97.
Crustuminus (Cl-), 93.
-ct- for Gutt. with t, 291, 293.
-ctum, e. g. virectum, 335.
-cu- for quu, 86 sq., 300.
-cubi, 446.
cubiculum, scansion of, 175.
cubo, -ui (-avi), 506, 499.
cuculus, 290; -ullus, 115.
cudo, 486; -di, 502.
cui (see qui, quis); cui rei?, 606.
cuicuimodi, 445, 564.
cujus, Poss., 443, 447; cujâs, 447.
cujuscemodi, 444.

2 S S

culfus (κόλπος), 59.
-culi, Perf., 501.
culmen, 235; (colum-), 185.
culmus, 328.
-culo-, Dim. (see Suffix -LO-).
culpa, col-, 236.
-culum, scansion of, 146, 175 sqq. (see -clum).
cum (see com-).
cumbo, 471.
cumprimis, 565.
cunae, 258.
cunchin for co-, 33.
cunctus, 541 n.
-cundus, 544 sq.
cunila (?), 155.
-cunque, 598.
cuntellum for cull-, 97.
cupa (-pp-), 116.
cupio, 476; -īs, 475.
cur, 606.
cura, 247; coi-, coe-, 248; cou-, 246.
curbus for -rv-, 51.
curia, 180.
curiosus, 353.
curriculo, 556.
curro, 239; cecurri, 503; Perf. in Romance, 509.
cursim, 556.
curtina for co-, 34.
curtus, 239.
custos, 308.
-cutio (quatio), 196.
cutis, 260.
cygnus, 292; ci-, 36.

D, pronunc., 80 sqq.; and -t in at, ad, &c., 76 sq.; phon. changes of, 285 sqq.
D-particle (see Particles).
-d, Abl., 391 sq.
Dalmatia (De-), 17.
-dam of quidam, &c., 552.
Dama, spelling of, 117.
damma, spelling of, 117.
damnas esto, 183.
damnum, 328.
Danubius for -uv-, 51.
danunt, 531.
dapsilis, 340.
dasi (?), O. Lat Inf., 537.
datatim, 556.
Dative (see Declension).

dautia, 286.
-de of inde, &c., 570.
de, Prep., 581; confused with di-, 574.
deabus, 403.
debeo, scansion of, 143.
debil for -lis, 376.
debilito, 176.
decem, 416; -cim, 19, 21, -cimus, 416, Decius, 416.
decimanus, 326.
Declension (Noun, Adj.), 366 sqq.; Nom. Sg., 371 sqq.; Gen., 379 sqq.; Dat., 385 sqq.; Acc., 387 sq.; Voc., 388 sqq.; Abl., 390 sqq.; Instr., 392 sqq.; Loc., 395 sqq.; Nom. Pl., 397 sqq.; Gen., 401 sq.; Dat., Abl., Loc., Instr., 402 sqq.; Acc., 404; (Pron.) Pers., 421 sqq.; Demonstr., 431 sqq.; Rel., 443 sqq.; Pron. Adj., 450 sqq.; (Verb) (see Verb).
declino, 470.
decor, M., -us, N., 356; decorus Adj., 356.
decreiuit, 22.
decussi-, 409.
dedro, 531; -ot, 531.
defendo, 486.
defrudo, the spelling, 196, 40.
defrătum, 261; -fri-, 197.
defuctus, 471.
degener, 356.
Degrees of Compar. (see Comparison).
degunere, 472.
Dehnstufe (see Gradation).
deinceps, 553.
deinde, 570; dein, 122.
delenio (-lin-), 199, 225.
delicatus, 287.
delico, 286.
delirus (-ler-), 199, 22.
delubrum, 331.
-dem of idem, &c., 441; of tandem, &c., 552.
demo, -psi, 505.
Demonstratives (see Pronouns).
demum, 549; -s, 553.
Denominative (see Derivative).
dens, 540.
Dentals, phon. changes of, 283 sqq.
dentio, 485.
denuo, 564.
Deponent, 519 sqq.; Past Part. of Act. Vb., 520, 542; Perf. of Neut. Vb., 522; bef. Pass. Inf., 522; Act.

INDEX.

Perf., 520; Pres. Part., 520; Act. by-form, 521 sq.; Pass. use of, 522, 542; *-ari* like Gk. *-ενειν*, 521.
deprensa, 336.
derbiosus, 268.
Derivative Verbs, 478, 483 sqq.
descendidi, 502.
desciso, pronunc. of, 479.
deses, 358.
Desideratives, 478, 482, 484.
desidero, 488.
desilui (*-ivi*), 499.
desitus sum, with Pass. Inf., 522.
destino, 470, 472.
Determinative Comp., 360 sq.
detestatus, Pass., 542.
detondi (*-tot-*), 504.
devas Corniscas, 404.
deunx, 409.
devŏro, Fut. Perf., 507.
deus (cf. *div-*), 244; *dei*, *di(i)*, Nom. Pl., 399, 21; *deum*, *-orum*, Gen., 402; *deis*, *diis*, Dat., 21; *diibus*, 404; *-dius* (?), 618.
dextans, 409.
dexter, 285; *-timus*, 405; *-tera*, Adv., 550.
DH, phon. changes of, 289 sq.
DH-particle (see Particles).
dhē-, 'to put,' 457.
di- (see *dis-*) for *de-*, 574; for *bi-*, 412; *di* for *z*, 105.
dicae for *-am*, 492.
dicax, 355.
dicis, Gen., 358.
dīco, 243; *-ces* (?), 2 Sg., 526; *-c* (*-ce*), Imper., 518; *-xi*, 495, 497, 504; *-xo*, 463; *-xim*, 465; *-xerŏ*, 212; *dicebo*, 492, 494; *dicturum*, O. Lat., 537.
-didi, Perf., 496, 502.
dienoine, Dvenos inscr., 560.
diequinti, 397; pronunc., 212.
dies, 252; pronunc., 24, 30, 133; gend., 369 *n*.; Nom. Sg., 377; Gen., 382; *dii*, 382; in word-group, 169; in Comp. Adv. 560; *dienoine*, Dvenos inscr., 416.
Diespiter, decl. of, 364.
difficul, N., 205; *-lter* (*-liter*), 553.
Digamma, Lat. F., 2, 5; for *v*, 8.
Digentia, 287.
digitus, 76; *-ct-*, 185.
dignus, 293; pronunc., 138 sq.

dīlexi, Perf., 505.
diloris, 412.
dimico, 194; *-avi* (*-ui*), 499.
dimidius, 409, 159; *de-*, 30.
Diminutives, 333, 336 sq.
dimminuo, the spelling, 314.
dingua, O. Lat. for *lingua*, 286.
dinummium, 412.
dinus for *divin-*, 52.
Diovem, 263 sq.
Diphthongs, phon. changes of, 239 sqq.; pronunc., 37 sqq.; shortened bef. cons., 251 sq.; when final, 213; Gk. in Lat. orth., 43 sq.; Gk. *ει*, 244.
dirimo, 582.
dirrumpo, the spelling, 314.
dis-, Prep., 582.
discerniculum, 333.
disciplina, 176; *-plic-*, 97.
disco, 477; *didici*, 501.
disertim, 556.
dispalesco, 586.
dispennite for *-nd-*, 64.
Dissimilation of *l*, *r*, 275; syll. lost by, 176.
dissipo, 304; spelling of, 193.
distennite for *-nd-*, 64.
distinguo, 471; spelling of, 301 sq.
Distributives (see Numerals).
Dite, Voc., 389.
diu, 555; *-tinus*, 325.
dives, *dis*, 408; Compar., 408.
divisi, Perf., 498.
Division of Syll., 124 sqq.
divissio, the spelling, 110 sq.
dius, Adv., 555.
divus (cf. *deus*), 244; *devas*, 404.
dixeram illis, pronunc. of, 123.
-dō of *cupido*, &c. (see Suffix -N-).
-do, Vbs. in, 486; Perf., 502; of *condo*, &c., 457.
do, I give, decl. of, 457; *da*, Imper., 518; *dedi*, 495 sq.; *dedro* (*-t*), 531, 124; *datus*, 222 (see *duo*).
doceo, 259, 482; *-eunto*, 3 Pl., 519.
dodrans, 409.
Dolabella, 331.
dolĭtus, 485.
dolus, 318.
domnus for *-min-*, 185.
domo, Vb., 474, 481; *-ui*, 506 *n*.
domus, 258; decl., 344; *-mos*, Gen., 380, 384.

630   THE LATIN LANGUAGE.

donec, 609; -icum, 609; -ique, 609.
donum, 232.
dorsualis, 340.
dos, 341.
dossum for -rs-, 96.
Double Cons., pronunc. of, 108 sqq.;
 for Single, 113 sqq.; written, 3, 8;
 II, 7 sq.; VV, 7; Vow., 3, 9 sq.
Doublets, 120 sqq, 204.
drachuma, 145.
Dropping (see Loss).
drua for tr-, 289.
Drusus, 289.
Dual, traces of, 366, 400.
Dvandva, Comp., 360 sq., 365.
dubito, 482.
dubius, 411.
dūcenti, 419; -tum, O. Lat., 418 sq.
duco, 466; duc, Imper., 518; -xi,
 pronunc., 498; ductus, pronunc., 542.
duellum, 268.
Dvenos Inscr., 2.
duicensus, 411.
duidens, 411.
Dvigu, Comp., 360 sqq.
duis, O. Lat. for bis, 411.
dum, 609, 570.
*dumpa, 286.
dumtaxat, 565.
dumus, 237.
dunc, 609.
duo for do, 515; -im, 515.
duo, Num., 410 sq.; scansion, 411;
 -um, Gen. Pl., 412; -a, Neut. Pl.,
 412; -decim, 416; -centi, 419; -vice-
 simus, 417; -deviginti, 416.
Duodecim Tabb. (see Twelve Tables).
duonus, 268.
duplex (-us), 411.
dupundius (-on-), 197.
-dus, e. g. pallidus, 353 sq.
Dusmius, 237.
dw-, phon. change of, 265 sqq.

E, pronunc., 18 sqq.; for oe, 44; for
 ae, 42 sq.; for i in hiatus, 19,
 22; in atonic syll., 25, 30; ĕ for ĭ,
 25, 29 sq.; phon. changes of, 223
 sqq.; for short vow. in atonic syll.,
 191 sq., 194; for a after j, 17; for ĭ
 after i, 230, 232; for -ĭ, &c., 205 sq.;
 ē for ĕ lengthened, 224; for -ĕyĕ-,
 -ĕhĕ-, 224; in grade of ĕ-root, 260;

not weakened to ĭ, 199; shortening
 of -ē, 211 sq.; O. Lat. ē for ei, 244
 sq.; Gk. (see Eta).
-ĕ, loss of, 204 sq.; 'Dat.' in, 387;
 with -ī in Abl. Sg., 390 sqq.
-ē of Adv., 548.
ē, ex, Prep., 583; ec-, 583.
E-grade of Root (see Gradation).
Ē-Subjunctive, 512 sqq.
eādem, Adv., 561.
eapse (-ā?), 441.
-ebam of legebam, &c., 490.
-ebo, Fut., 3 Conj., 493.
-ebris of funebris, &c., 196.
ebrius, 592.
ecastor (ecc-), 618.
ecce, 617; -cere, 618; -um, 617, 435;
 -illum, -istum, 432.
eclesia, the spelling, 115.
ecquis, 447.
Ecthlipsis, 309 sqq.
ecus for equus, 86.
edepol, 618.
edice, Imper., 518.
ĕdo, Vb., decl. of, 456; ēdi, 497; -am,
 -im, 512; Imper., 518; essus, the
 spelling, 112; -tus, 309.
-ĕdo, -ēdula (see Suffix -D-).
edulis, 340.
edus for haedus, 42.
egestas, 326.
ego, decl., 421 sqq.; scansion, 422;
 mihi, scansion, 422.
egregius, Voc. of, 389.
egretus, O. Lat., 285.
EI, on inscrr., 244 sq.; for ĭ, 9; for
 ĭ, 245, 22; for ē, 22; phon. changes
 of, 243 sqq.; for atonic ai, oi, 243
 sq.; ĒI, 252; O. Lat. ē for ei, 244 sq.
ei-, 'togo,' 456.
ejero, 199.
einom, Dvenos inscr., 604.
-eis, Nom. Pl., O-stem, 398.
ejulo, pronunc. of, 53.
-eius, Prop. Names in, 320.
ejuscemodi, 437.
-el-, phon. change of, 228 sq.
-ēla (see Suffix -LO-).
elicui, Perf., 505.
-ēlis (see Suffix -LI-).
Elision, 144 sq.; of -m, 61 sq., 144;
 -s, 123; -i of -āi, -ēi, 381, 383 (see
 Hiatus).

INDEX. 631

elixus, 293.
-ella (-us), -ĕl-, 112 sqq., 115.
ellum, 617.
-ellus (see Suffix -LO-).
-em- for I.-Eur. m̥, 273 sq.
-em, -im, Acc. Sg., 388; for -am, Fut., 493 n.
em, Interj., 617.
em, ' tum,' 438 ; ' eum,' 438.
emem, 'eundem,' 438.
eminus, 554.
emitor for im-, 30.
emo, 505 ; emi, 502 ; -psi, 505 ; -ptus, spelling of, 70 ; emeru, 531 ; -psim, 466.
-endus, -undus, Ger., 544.
emungo, 471.
-ēmus of supremus, &c., 407.
-en- for I.-Eur. n̥, 273 sq.
en, Prep. (see in).
en, Interj., 617.
Enclitics, 165 sqq.
endo, indu, 582 sq.; and in-, 583 ; endoque plorato, 573.
eneco, spelling of, 194.
enim, 603 ; -vero, 603.
Ennius, introduced double cons., 3, 8.
enocilis, 197.
enos, Carm. Arv., 425.
-ens (see Suffix -NT-).
-ens- for Gk. ησ (?), 136 n.
ensis, 274.
-entia, -ium (see Suffix -NT-).
-entior, Compar., 407.
enubro- (-nib-), 191.
enunquam, 617.
-ēnus (see Suffix -NO-).
eo, Adv., 568 sq.
eo, Vb., decl. of, 456 ; eunt-, Part., 541 ; -ŭt, Perf., 214.
Epirus, accent of, 155.
epulonus, 348.
eques, 336.
equidem, 603.
equifer, 361.
equio, 484.
equus, 226 ; spelling, 300; pronunc. of e-, 42.
-er- for rĭ, 231 sq. ; for -ŏr- in faeneris, &c., 34 (see also E).
-er, from -ros, 374 ; M., -ris F., 371.
ercisco, pronunc. of, 479.

erĕmus, the scansion, 156.
erga, 583.
ergo, Prep., 583, ; Conj., 604 ; accent, 166 ; -ŏ, 212.
erro, 308.
erugo, -cto, 298.
erumna for aer-, 43.
-ĕrunt, -ēre, 3 Pl., 531 sq.
ervum, 196.
ĕs, ĕst (see edo, decl. of).
ĕs, ĕst (see sum, decl. of).
-es (see Suffix -T-) ; -es, -is, Acc. Pl., 404 ; Nom. Pl., 399 ; O-stems, 398.
esca, 310.
esco, 479.
-ēsimus, -ensumus, 418.
essere for esse, 536.
essis (?), 466.
-esso, Vb.-forms in, 462 sqq.
(e)st, (e)s, Procope of, 121.
-ester (see Suffix -TERO-).
et, Conj., 599.
Eta (Gk.), Lat. ae, 42 (see -ens-).
ctiam, 599 ; -dum, 609 ; -num, 570 ; -nunc (-nn-), 62, 69, 121.
etsi, 613.
-etum, e. g. arboretum, 335.
EU, pronunc. of, 39 sqq.; phon. changes, 245 sq.; EU, 252.
evenat, 464.
euge (-ae), 617 ; accent, 164.
-eus, -eum (see Suffix -IO-).
-ĕx of remex, &c., 358.
exadversus (-m), Prep., 595.
examen (-agm-), 292.
examussim, 563.
exaurio, the spelling, 475.
exemplum, 271.
exfuti, 309.
exiet (?), Fut., 493.
eximius, 319.
exinde, 570.
exolesco, 481.
expergitus, 542.
expers, 192.
explenunt, 531.
explodo, 196.
explorato (-e), 550.
exsugebo, 494.
exta, 311.
extemplo, 565.
extinguo, spelling of, 301 sq.
extispica, 358.

extra, 584.
exuo, 475.
F, the letter, 2, 5, 291; pronunc., 98 sqq.; for Gk. φ, 11; from I.-Eur. bh-, 282 sq.; -bh-, 283; dh-, 289 sq.; -dh-, 289; ĝhw, 297; ghu, 302; for h, 294 sq., 56; b, 78, 80.
Fabaris, 95.
fabula, 334.
facesso, 462.
facetus, 335.
faciae for -am, 492.
facies, 345; -is, 347.
facilis, -cūl, N. (Adv.), 553; -cile, Adv., 554; -ciliter, -culter, 553; -cilumed, S. C. Bacch., 559.
facio, 457; decl. of, 458; cal\e\f., &c., 183 sq., 488; -is, -it, 475; feci, 497, 502; fac(e), 518; faxo (-im), 465; -xet (?), 508; fefaked, Praen. fib., 504; feked, Dvenos inscr., 528.
facundus, 545.
faenisicia (fen-), 42.
faenus (fen-), 42.
fagus, 221.
falla, 355.
falx, 486.
fama, 328.
fames, 345.
famex, 355.
familia, 193; -ā (?), Nom., 211; -as, Gen., 381.
famul for -lus, 374.
fanum, 307.
far, 357.
farcio, 476; decl., 458; -rsus, 542.
-fariam, 552.
farina, 357.
farnus, 279, 294.
farreus, 277.
fastidium, 176.
fastigium, 277.
fastus, decl. of, 344.
fatigo, 563.
fatim, 563.
fatum, 542; -us, 370.
Fatuus, 324.
fatuus, 324.
favilla, 235.
favor, 357.
faux, 355.
febricula, 333.

fecundus, 545.
fefaked, Praen. fib., 504.
fel, 295.
feles, 346.
felix, 354.
fello, 225.
femina, 225, 327.
Feminine (see Gender).
femur, decl. of, 349 sq.
-fendo, Vb., 486; -di, Perf., 501.
fere, ferme, 561, 185.
feriae, 307.
ferio, percussi, 545; ferinunt, 531.
fero, decl. of, 457; fer, 517; tuli, 545, 494, 503; tetuli, 494, 497.
ferox, 354.
fertum, a cake, 310.
ferveo (-vo), 476; -bui, 51.
ferus, 297.
fescemnoe (?), 398.
festino, Vb., 472; -us, Adj., 556; -ato (-im), Adv., 550.
festus, 307.
fetigo for fat-, 18.
fetus, 344.
fiber (feb-), 229.
fibula, 467.
ficedula (-cella ?), 353.
fidele, Adv., 559.
fidelia, 290.
Fidenae, the scansion, 127 n.
fides, 345; -ēi, Gen., 383.
fidicina, 358.
fido, 243; in Romance, 488.
fiducia, 337.
fidus for foed-, 356; fidustus, 356.
Fifth Decl. (see Suffix -YĒ-, -Ē-).
figel for -ulus, 375.
figlina, 184.
figo, 467; -xi, 499; -xus, 542; figarus, 534.
figura, 291.
filius, 225, 22; -ie, -i, Voc., 389 sq.; filiabus, 403.
filix (fĕ-), 229.
Final, Cons., pronunc. of, 119 sqq.; -d, 122; -m, 67 sq., 123; -nt, 124; -r, 97; -s, 108, 123; -t, 123; double cons., 119, 122; Vowel, short, 203 sqq.; long, 207 sqq.; syll. in -m, 216 sq.
findo, 469; fidi, 495, 501.
fingo, 297; -nxi, pronunc., 140; -nctus, 471.
fini (-e), Adv., 552.

INDEX. 633

finitimus, 405.
flo, 545, 522; *fi*, 522; *fieri*, 132; O. Lat. *-re*, 522; *fitur*, 522.
firmus, pronunc. of, 141.
First, Pers. Sg., ending, 524 sq.; Pl., 529; Syll., accent. of, 157 sqq.
fivo, O. Lat. for *figo*, 467.
fixulae, 467.
flagro, 222; confused with *fragro*, 92.
flamen, a blast, *-mm-*, 118.
flavus, 279.
flecto, 486.
flemina, 258.
fleo, 476.
flexuntes (?), 352.
flo, 476.
Flora, 356.
florere, in Romance, 489.
flos, 258.
fluentum, 352.
fluo, 484 n.; *-xi*, 499.
foculum, 289.
fodico, 488.
fodio, *-odi*, Perf., 502.
foedifragus (*-erif-*), 365.
foedus, N., 356; *fid-*, 356.
fons, pronunc. of, 136.
for, decl. of, 457; *fari*, 221.
foras, 550, 557.
forceps, 178.
forcilla, the spelling, 239.
forctus, O. Lat., 182 sq., 541.
forem, 545 n.
foris, 551; in Vb. Comp., 575.
forma, pronunc. of, 141.
formidolosus, spelling of, 197.
formonsus for *-os-*, 69.
formus, 302.
fornax, 239.
fors, 278; Adv., 560; *forsan*, *-m*, 560; *forsitan*, *-m*, 560; *f. fuat an*, 516; *forte*, 560.
fortasse (*-is*), 560.
Fortes and Lenes, 71 sqq.
fortis, 541; *-rct-*, 342.
fortuito (*-u*), 550.
forum, 289.
Foslius, 307.
fovea, 295.
foveo, 289, 302.
Fourth Decl., blends with Second, 343 sq.
fr- for *mr-*, 269 sqq.

fraces, 270.
Fractions (see Numerals).
fragro and *flagr-*, 92; *fragl-*, 92.
fragum, 306.
frango, 222; *fregi*, 502; *fractus*, pronunc. of, 139.
frater, 221.
fraxinus, 279.
frendo, 486; (*-deo*), 486 n.; *fressus*, the spelling, 115.
frequens, 559.
Frequentatives, 478, 482 sq.
frigidus, *frid(d)-*, 30, 119; *-gd-*, 185; *-aria*, 172.
frigus, 306.
fviguttio, 488.
frugi, 407; Compar., 408.
frumentum, *-mint-*, the spelling, 23.
frundes for *-ond-*, 31, 33.
fruniscor, 470, 237.
fruor, 484 n.; *-imino*, 519.
frustra, (*-ă*), 557; *-au-*, 40; *-or*, Vb., 558.
frustrum for *-tum*, 96.
fuga, 239.
fugio, 476; *fugi*, 502.
fui (see *fuo*).
fulgeo (*-go*), 476; *-lsi*, 505
fulgorio, 485.
fulica, (*-lc-*), 236.
fulmentum, 310.
fulvus, 235.
fuma, 'terra,' 295.
fumus, 237.
funambulus, 364.
Fundanius, Gk. mispronunc. of, 58, 99.
fundatid, Luceria inscr., 519.
funditus, 561.
fundo, *fudi*, 502; *exfutus*, 309.
funera nec funera, 616 n.
funerus (?), 356.
fungor, 471.
funtes for *-ont-*, 33.
fuo, *-am*, 515; *fu*, 518; *fui*, Perf., 545; scansion, 132, 508 sq.
fur, 233; scansion, 215.
furca, 239.
furnus, 239; *fur-*, 239.
furo, 297.
furvus, 306.
fuscus, 306.
Fusio-, 305.
fussus, the spelling, 113.
futtilis, 309; spelling of, 117.

634   THE LATIN LANGUAGE.

Future (see Tense-stems); Fut. Perf. (do.); Fut. Imper., 516 sqq.

G, letter, 2 sq., 6 sq.; pronunc., 84 sqq.; from I.-Eur. Gutt. Asp., 291, 296 sq., 298, 302; Gutt. Ten., 292 sqq.; g̒, 301 sq.; for *gu*, 301 sq.; *c-*, 72, 74 sqq.; Ĝ, phon. changes of, 296; G, 298; Ĝ̒, 301 sq.
gaesum, 305; spelling of, 112.
Gaius, 252; pronunc., 53.
gallicinium, 194.
gallina, 370.
garrio, 277.
gaudeo, 479; *gavisi*, 522; *-us sum*, 522.
Gaulish, mispronunc. 27.
gelu, 296, 261.
gemma, 273.
Gender, 368 sqq.; of N-stems, 349; in Adj., 370 sq.; Fem. O-stems, 369; Masc. and Neut. O-stems mixed, 369 sq.; Fem. Ā-stems and Neut. O-stems, 400; disuse of Neut., 369 sq.
gener, 271.
genetrix, 191; *-nit-*, 200.
genista, 195.
Genitive (see Declension); IO-stem, accent, 163 sq.; Gerund. of Purpose, 383 *n.*
geno for *gigno*, 459, 465.
gens, 341.
genu, 296; *-nva*, the scansion, 144.
genuinus, 326.
genus, 225.
germen, 271 sqq.
Gerund, &c., 543 sqq.
gesticulor, 488.
-gg- written for *ng*, 10 sq.
ĜH, phon. changes of, 296 sq.; GH, 298; Ĝ̒Hu̒, 302.
ĝhe- (ĝho-), Dem. Pron., 430.
gigno, 468; *geno*, 459, 465.
gingrina, 483; *-rio*, Vb., 483.
-gintā, the scansion, 418.
glaber, 290.
glacies, 261.
glans, 302.
glarea, 288.
*glerem for *-lir-*, 30.
globus, *-mus*, 80.
glos, 296.

glosa, spelling of, 112.
gluma (*glubo*), 282.
-gm-, pronunc. of, 89; *-gn-*, 64, 70.
Gnaeus, 294.
gnar- (Adj.), *-us*, 220; *-uris*, 541; (Vb.) *-itur*, 485; *-ivisse*, 485; *-igavit*, 488.
gnatus (*nat-*), 541.
gnoritur, 485.
Gnosus, spelling of, 117.
-gnus (see Suffix -NO-).
-gō (see Suffix -N-); for *-guo*, 301 sq.
gobius, 74.
goerus for *gy-*, 36.
gorytus (*co-*), 74.
grabattus, 118.
Gracchus, Varro's deriv., 93.
Gradation of Vowels, 253 sqq.; Weak grade, 255 sqq.; of yĕ, wĕ, 256; E-grade, 255 sq.; O-grade, 255 sq.; ĕ-ŏ, 258; ē-ō, 258; ō-ă, 258 sq.; ē-ă, 258 sq.; ă-ŏ, 259; ā-ă, 259 sq.; ĕ-ō, 260; ĭ-ī, 260; ŏ-ō, 260; ŭ-ū, 260 sq.; ĕ-ă, 261; ŏu-au, 261 sq.
gradior, 476.
gradus, 222.
grallae, 285.
gramae, *-mmosus*, 118.
grando, 297.
granum, 219 sq.
grates, 341.
gratis (*-iis*), 403, 551.
gratus, 279.
gravastellus, 330.
Grave Accent, 153 sqq.
gravedo (*-īdo*), 23, 353.
gravis, 301; *-iā*, 210; *grevis, 18.
Greek, Aspirates (see Asp.); Diphthongs (see Diph.); Letters (see Alphabet); Loanwords, parasitic vow., 70 sq.; accent, 155 sq.; for nuances of feeling, 182; for exclamations, 617; Mispronunc. of Lat., 27, 45, 58, 114 sq.; Orthography, influence on Lat., 12, 576; Phonetics, infl. on Lat., 28, 32, 152 sq.; Transcription of Lat., ch. ii. passim, 135; Lat. of Gk. (see under Gk. name of letter, e. g. Eta, also Aspirates, Diphthongs, Breathing, Tenues).
Grimm's Law, 31.
groma, 96.
grus, 298.

INDEX.   635

-gu- for guu, 86 sqq., 301 sq. ; pronunc., 84 sqq.
guberno, 74.
gulfus (see cul-).
gummi, 74.
-guo (-go) in Vbs., 301 sq.
gurges, 301, 358.
gurgulio, 275.
gusto, Vb., 482 ; -us, Noun, 296.
Gutturals, letters, 2 sq., 6 sq., 10 sq. ; phon. changes of, 290 sqq. ; three series, 290 sqq. ; Proper (or Velar), 297 sq.
gutus (-tt-), 116.
gyla, the spelling, 29, 36.
gyrus (goe-), 36 sq.

H, pronunc. of, 53 sqq. ; to denote vowel-length, 54 ; hiatus, 265 ; for *f*, 56, 294 sq. ; dropped bet. vow., 54, 294 ; from ĝh, 296 sq. ; from gh, 298.
habeo, 280 ; scansion of Comp., 143 ; 'to dwell,' 483.
habito, 482.
hacetenus, 433.
haedus, 242 ; *faed-*, 56 ; *ed-*, 42.
haereo, 242 ; -ssi, the spelling, 112 ; -surus, 542.
Half-long Vowel, 127.
halica (al-), 56.
halo, 220.
hanser (see anser).
harena, spelling of, 56.
hariolus, spelling of, 56 ; *far-* (?), 56.
haruspex, arisp-, 29.
hasta, 308.
haud, 616 ; hau, 120, 122 ; -quaquam, 569.
havĕ, pronunc. of, 49, 56, 127 n.
haurio, 475 ; -ssi, the spelling, 112 ; -surus, 542.
hebes, 351.
hec, O. Lat., 433.
Hecoba, O. Lat., 197.
hedera, haed-, 43.
Hedonei, Gen., 381.
heia, 617 n.
helvus, 276, 229.
hem, Interj., 617 ; pronunc. of, 61.
Hercules, spelling of, 197.
Herentas, 482.
heri, 264, 396 ; (-e), 25 sq. ; -sternus, pronunc. of, 135.
heries (heriem Junonis), 345.

Heteroclite, Nouns, 367 ; locus, -ca, 400 ; Vbs., 545 (see Comparison, irreg.).
heu, Interj., 39.
Hiatus, 144 sq. (see Prosodical H.)
hibernus, 269 sq.
hic, Pron., decl. of, 430 sqq. ; pronunc., 433 ; huic, pronunc., 44.
hic, Adv., 567, 433.
Hidden Quantity (see Close Syllable)
hiems, 358, 297 ; -mps, 70.
hilaris, 338 sq. ; -rus, 182.
hilaritudo (-tas), 341.
Hiluria for Illyr-, 36, 115.
hinnuleus, pronunc. of, 118.
hio, 476.
hiquidem, 433.
hircus, spelling of, 56.
hirrio, 90.
hirsutus, hirtus, 229.
hiulcus, 337.
hoc (Adv.), O. Lat., 568.
hocedie, 433.
hodie, 561 ; pronunc., 84.
holus (hel-), 228 sq. ; -atrum, 362.
homicida, 364.
homo, 349 ; hem-, 367 ; hum-, 33, 236 ; -ullus, 333 ; -uncio, 337 ; -unculus, 337.
hordeum, 298.
horitur, Enn., 482.
horreo, 277.
horsum, 568.
hortor, 482.
hortus, 296.
hospes, 178, 298.
hosticapas, 187, 371, 373.
hosticus, 337.
hostis, 298, 341.
huc, Adv., 568.
*hucare, 486.
hui, Interj., 39.
hujuscemodi, accent. of, 162.
humane (-iter), 554.
humerus (see um-).
humilis, 338.
humus, 236 ; decl., 344.
Hydruntum, 289.

I, the letter, 3, 7 sq. ; written for II, 7 sq. ; tall form, 4, 8 sqq., 47, 133 sq., 137 n. : doubled in aiio, &c., 8, 47, 53 ; symbols of long, 9 ; pronunc., 23 sqq. ; phon. changes, 230 sqq. ;

Lat. *ĭ* for atonic vow., 193 sqq.; for *ĕ* bef. *ng, gn,* &c., 225 sq., 229 sq.; in hiatus, 19, 21 sqq.; in *tuncine,* &c., 206 sq.; for *ŭ* in *optimus,* &c., 189, 23 sqq.; *i-* prefixed to *st-,* &c., 102, 105 sqq.; *-ĭ* dropped, 204 sq.; Lat. *ĭ* for *ē* in *filius,* &c., 224 sq.; for atonic ai, oi, 243 sq.; for ei, 243 sqq.; for *ĭ* lengthened, 230; varying with *ĭ,* 260; -*ī* shortened, 213.

J, the letter, 7; pronunc., 44 sqq.; I-Eur. Y, phon. changes of, 262 sqq.; Lat. *j* for ĝhy, 263 sqq.; for dy-, 263 sq.; dropped bef. accented vow., 144.

I-stems, mixed with Cons.-stems, 338, 401 (see Suffix -I-).

Ī-Subjunct. (Opt.), 513 sqq.

-*ī*- in Fut. Perf., 510; Perf. Subj., 500; 3 Conj. Vbs. in *-io,* 475.

ĭ-ŭ, ŭ-ĭ, in *stupila,* &c., 37.

ja- pronounced *je-*, 15, 17.

jacio, jaceo, 473; *jeci,* 502.

jaculum, 332.

jajentaculum, 17.

jajunus, 17.

iam, 'eam,' Acc. Sg., 437.

jam, 570.

jandudum for *-mdă-,* 66, 121.

janitrices, 274.

janto, 17.

janua, 264; *jen-,* 17.

Januarius, pronunc. of, 15; *Jen-,* 17.

Janus, decl. of, 344; *-is,* Carm. Sal., 339.

-ibam, -iebam, Impft., 491.

ibi, 567; *-dem,* 571, 567.

-ibo, Fut., 493.

-īc of *illic,* &c., 551.

-icanus, e. g. *Afr-,* 327.

ici, Perf., 502.

-ĭcius (see Suffix -KO-).

Ictus, and accent. in Plaut., 165 sqq.

-ĭcus (see Suffix -OK-).

idcirco, 580; *icc-,* 314.

idem, 431; decl. of, 441 sq.

identidem, 571.

ideo, 568.

idolatria, 176.

idōlum, the scansion, 150.

-ĭdus, e. g. *pallidus,* 353 sq.

je- for *ja-,* e. g. *jecto* for *jacto,* 15, 17.

jecur, decl. of, 349; *joc-,* 41.

-ieis, old spelling of *-eis,* Dat. Abl. Pl., 19, 21.

jejunus (jaj-), 17; pronunc., 53.

-ie(n)s of Numeral Adv., 408.

iens, euntis, Gen., 541.

jento (ja-), 17; *jejent-,* 17.

-ier, Inf. Pass., 536 sq.

-iĕrem, accent of, 164.

igitur, 565, 605; accent., 169.

Ignatius for *Egn-,* 229.

ignis, 229.

ignoro, 485.

ignosco, 363, 615.

-igo of *navigo,* &c., 479.

-īgo (see Suffix in Gutt.).

-iit of *abiit,* &c., 528; of *audiit,* &c., 132.

ilicet, 564.

ilico, 564.

ilignus, 293, 229.

-ilis (see Suffix -LI-); *-ilis,* of Pass. Adj. (do.).

illac, Adv., 569.

ille, 430, 436 sq.; pronunc., 122; accent., 167; *-ui,* Dat. Sg., 452.

illĕx and *illēx,* 135 *n.*

illex, the spelling, 112.

illic (-i), Adv., 567, 432.

illicio, -exi, pronunc. of, 498, 139.

illim, Adv., 570.

illimodi, 431.

-illo of Dim. Vbs., 479, 487 sq.

illuc, Adv., 568.

-illus (see Suffix -LO-); (*-ilus*), 115.

illustris, 293.

-im of *sensim,* &c., 548; of *illim,* &c., 551; (*-em*) Acc. Sg., 388.

im, 'eum,' 438.

imago, 521.

imbilicus for *umb-,* 29.

imeum (?), 'eundem,' 438.

imitor, 521.

immanis, 339.

immo, 603.

impendio, 560.

Imperative (see Moods); as Particle, 600; accent of *addŭc,* &c., 163.

Imperfect (see Tense-stems).

impero, 192.

Impersonal Pass., 520 sq.

impetrio, 485.

impleo, 473.

INDEX. 637

impliciscor, 480.
implicitus, P. P. P., 542.
Imporcitor, 279.
impraesentiarum, 562.
imprimis, 565.
improbo, 615.
impudenter, 554.
impune, 559.
-imus of Superl. (see Comparison).
imus, infimus, 407.
in (en), Prep., 584 ; *im, im-*, 50 sq., 66, 69, 99 sqq., 121 ; bef. *s-, f-*, 136 sqq.
in-, Neg., 615 ; with Vb., 615, 363.
-ina (see Suffix -N-).
incassum, 564.
Inceptives, 476 sq., 479 sqq.; *-ēsco*, 134.
incipisso, 462.
incitega, 197.
inclino, 470.
inclutus (-lit-), 239 ; spelling of, 197.
incogitabilis, 334.
incoho, spelling of, 57.
incolomis, the spelling, 192.
incoram, 581.
incubus (-bo), 348.
incurvicervicus, Accius, 360.
indaudio, 583.
inde, 570 ; pronunc., 122 ; *-didem*, 570 sq.
Indefinite Pron. (see Pronouns).
Indeterminate Vow., 257.
indigena, 583.
indigeo, Vb., 583 ; *-us (-ens)*, Adj., 540.
Indo-European, languages, 218 ; prototype of word, 218 ; alph., 218 sqq.
indoles, 345, 583.
indu (see *endo*).
indugredior, 583.
induo, 475.
induperator, 583.
industrius, 189.
inebrae aves, 191.
infans for *infandus*, 182.
inferebis, 494.
inferus, -fer, 374 ; *-fra*, Prep., 585 ; *-fera*, 181 ; *infimus, imus*, 407.
Infinitive, 535 sqq.; as Imper., 517 ; Pres. Act., 535, 537 ; Pass., 536 sq.; Fut. Act., 536 sq.; Pass., 536, 538 ; Perf. Act., 536 ; Pass., 536 ; Hist., 524.
infit, 546.
infiteor, 615.
ingens, 274, 541.

inger, Imper., 526.
ingratis (-iis), 551.
inibi, 567.
inipite (?) 198.
Initial Syll. (see First Syll.).
inlicite, the scansion, 475.
inpeirator, 22.
inquam, 524 ; Conj. of, 545 sq.
inquies, -etus, 182.
inquilinus, 227.
insane, -um, 550.
insciens, -us, 540.
insequo, -co, 566 ; decl., 545.
inserinuntur, Liv. Andr., 531.
insons, pronunc. of, 136.
insperatas, Nom. Pl., Pompon., 398.
instar, 205.
instigo, 284, 471.
institūi, Perf., 508.
Instrumental, 548 (see Declension) ; Adv. use of, 559 sqq.
insuper, 593.
int (?), 3 Pl., 456.
intellexi, Perf., 505.
intemperies, Sg., *-ae*, Pl., 347.
inter, 585.
interatim, 556.
interdiu (-s), 555.
interduatim, 556.
interdum, 609.
interduo, 515 ; *-im*, 515.
interealoci, accent. of, 162.
interibi, 567.
Interjections, 616 sqq.; from Gk., 617; Imper., 618 ; accent. of, 164.
interim, 570.
Interrogative, Particles, 605 sq. ; Pron. (see Pronouns).
intervias, 563.
intolerans for *-andus*, Laev., 543.
intra, Prep., 585 ; *-tro*, Adv. 561.
intrare, 474.
intus, Adv., 561 ; Prep., 585.
inventio, 274.
invito, Vb., *-us*, Adj., 299.
-inum for *-ēnum*, 23.
inunt, 3 Pl., 531.
involucrum, 329.
-ĭnus (see Suffix -NO-).
jocus, 264.
-ŏlum, accent. of, 164.
-ior (see Comparison).

Iotacismus, 27.
Ioues (Dvenos Inscr.), 264.
ipse (*-us*), 430, 440 sq. ; *isse,* 79 ; *ipsima,*
 -issumus, ipsippe (*-pse, -pte*), 441 ;
 eapse (*-a*), 441.
ira, spelling of, 245.
iri in Fut. Inf. Pass., 538.
Irregular Verbs, 545 sqq.
-is of *Cornelis,* &c., 375.
is, Pron., 430 ; decl. of, 437 sqq. ;
 ejus, pronunc. of, 53.
-isco for *-esco,* Incept., 480.
Issa, 79.
-issimus, Superl. (see Compar.).
-isso, Vb., 488.
istac, Adv., 569.
iste, 430 ; decl., 435 ; pronunc., 122 ;
 accent., 167.
istīc (*-i*), Adv., 567.
istuc, Adv., 568
-it, 3 Sg. Perf., 527 sq.
ita, 571 ; *-idem,* 571.
Italia, the scansion, 127 n.
-itānus, e. g. *Abder-,* 327.
itaque, 604 sq., 571 ; scansion, 604.
itare, 482.
item, 571.
-iter, Adv., 549, 553.
iter, decl. of, 349.
Iteratives, 478, 482 sq.
iterum, 330 ; 550.
-itia (*-um*) (see Suffix -IO-).
itur, Impers., 520.
ju- pronounced *ji-,* 15.
jubeo, 481 ; *jussi,* pronunc. of, 110 sq. ;
 O. Lat. *joussei,* 498.
jucundus, 545.
judex, 182.
Jugatinus, 325.
jugis, 338.
jugmentum, -gum-, 336, 292.
juger-, 245 ; *iugra* for *-era,* LexAgr., 184.
jugum, 237 264.
Julius, 250.
ium, ' eum,' Luceria inscr., 437.
jumentum, 336.
jungus (?), 471.
junior, 408.
juniperus (*-pir-*), 374, 192 ; *ji-,* 35.
junix, 345.
Jupiter (*-pp-*), 246, 389 ; spelling, 116 ;
 decl., 377 ; *Jov-,* 263 sq.
jurigo, O. Lat., 173.

jus, ' broth,' 237 ; ' law,' 264.
-ius, Compar., scansion of, 406 n.
jusjurandum, 358.
justus, 356.
juvenalis, -ilis, 340.
juvencus, 264.
juvenis, 239 ; Compar., 408.
juventa, 334 n. ; *-tas* (*-tus*), 341.
juvo, 476 ; *juerint,* 508.
juxta, 585.
-ix of *felix,* &c. (see Suffix -KO-, Gutt.) ;
 of *cornix,* &c. (see Suffix -Ĭ-)

K, the letter, 2, 6 sq ; pronunc., 84
 sqq. ; phon. changes of I.-Eur. K̑,
 295 sq. ; of K, 297 sq.
kadamitas, 286.
Kappa in Lat., 72.
Karmadhâraya, Comp., 360 sq.
k̑e- (k̑o-), Dem. Pron., 429 sqq.

L, pronunc. of, 89 sqq. ; bef cons.,
 96 sq. ; I.-Eur. L, phon. changes
 of, 275 sq. ; Ļ, 278 sq. ; Lat. *l* for *d,*
 80, 82, 285 sqq. ; for *r,* 92 sq. ; for
 n, 96 ; for *ll,* 109 sqq.
l- for *tl-,* 283 sq.
-l, vow. shortened bef., 213 ; decl. of
 Nouns in, 376.
Labials, phon. changes of, 281 sqq.
Labiovelar Gutt., phon. changes of,
 299 sqq. (see Qu, Gu, GHu).
labes, 345.
labium, 261.
labo, 303.
lābrum, 180.
lac, spelling of, 122 ; *lact* (*-te*), 378.
lacca, 307.
lacer for *-ratus,* 540.
lacesso, 462.
lacio, 191.
lacrima, 223 ; spelling, 57 sq.
lacus, 301.
lacusta for *loc-,* 201.
laevus, 242.
lambero, 479.
lambo, 471 ; *-bi* (?), Perf., 501.
lambrusca for *lab-,* 65.
lammina, -mn- (*-nn-*), 184.
lana, 279.
lancino, 470.
langueo, 306.
lanius (*-io*), 348.

INDEX. 639

lanterna (*-mpt-*), 70.
lapis, 353.
larignus, 293.
Larinum, 288.
larix, 286.
larva (*-rua*), 46.
lassus, 258.
latex, 355.
laticlavus, 361.
Latona, 349.
lātus, 219 sq., 541.
lavo, 235; *-vi*, 499; *lautus, lo-*, 250; *-luo* in Compounds, 196.
laurus, 286.
lautia, 286.
lector, pronunc. of, 139.
lectum (*-s*), 542; pronunc.. 139.
Legato Pronunciation, 131.
legatus, 541.
legirupa (*-ger-*), 373, 192.
legitimus, 405.
lego, 260; *lēgi*, 502; *lectum*, pronunc., 139.
Lenes and Fortes, 71 sqq.
Length (see Long Cons., Vow.)
Lengthening, by Position (see Pos.); by Compensation, 314; bef. *nf, ns*, 136 sqq.; *gn, gm*, 138 sq.; *ct, x*, 139 sq.; *nct, nx*, 140; *r* with cons., 140 sq.; *s* with cons., 141.
lenibat, 491; *-ibunt*, 493.
lenocinor, 488.
-lens (*-lentus*) (see Suffix -NT-).
lentus, 252.
lepesta, 286.
leptis for *nep-*, 96.
Letters (see Alphabet).
Levana, 326.
Leucesie, Carm. Sal., 245.
levir, 200, 242.
lĕvis, 292.
lēvis, 244.
lex, 260.
-lexi (*-legi*), Perf., 505.
-lĭ-, syncopated after cons., 171.
libertabus, 403.
libet (*lub-*), 29.
libra, 289.
licet, 613.
lien, 349.
ligula, 272.
ligurrio, 291, 482.
limitrophus, 176.

limus, mud, 328.
lingo, 471.
lingua, 229, 286.
lingula, 272.
linio, 483.
lino, 470.
linquo, 469; *liqui*, 502.
linter (*lun-*), 29.
liquare, -ere, 484.
liquor, 268.
lira, 199.
littera, spelling of, 117; l. canina, 90.
litus, spelling of, 117.
lixa, 293; *-ivus*, 323.
-ll- for ld, ln, ls, 275; dl, 285; nl, 271; rl, 277.
Locative (see Declension); Adv. use of, 559 sqq.
locus, -ca, Pl., 400; O. Lat. *stlocus*, 303, 307, 564; in wordgroup, 170.
Loebasius, 248.
loedus, O. Lat., 248.
Long, Cons., orth. of, 3, 109; Vow., 3 sq., 9 sq. (see Quantity).
longus, spelling of, 236.
loquella, the spelling, 112 sqq.
loquor, 284.
Losna, 292.
Loss, of Cons. in Group, 309 sqq.; of final syll. in *-m*, 216 sq.
lotus, 250.
lubricus, 306.
lubs, Marso-Lat., 12, 177.
luceo, 481.
lucerna, 237.
luci claro, 396.
Lucilius, *i* and *ei*, 9, 27; *g* for *gg*, 11; *a* for *ă*, 10, 14; *e* and *ae*, 42; *r*, 90; *pellicio*, 97; *numeri*, Gen., 383 *n*.; *mille*, 420; *illi*, 437.
Lucipor, 183.
Lucretius, use of Compounds, 360.
luctus, pronunc. of, 135.
lucus, 250.
ludus, 287; *loed-*, 248.
lues, 345.
lumbus, 290.
luna, 292.
lupus, 291; F., 370.
lurco, 179.
**lŭr(i)dus* for *lūri-*, 37.
lŭstra, lūstra, 141.
lustro, 293.

lutra, 289.
lux, 276 (see *luci*).
lympha, 286 ; spelling, 11, 36.

M, the letter, 7 ; pronunc, 60 sqq. ; final dropped, 68 sq., 123 ; assimilated, 121 ; L.-Eur. **M**, phon. changes of, 268 sqq. ; **M**, 273 sq. ; Lat. *m* for *n*, 269 ; bef. *v-*, *f-*, 50 sq., 66, 99 sqq. ; for *p*, 281 ; for *b*, 282 sq. *-m*, vow. shortened bef., 213 ; final syll. dropped, e. g. *nihil(um)*, 216 sq. ; of 1 Sg., 524.
macer, 223.
macero, 488.
madeo, 223, 473.
maereo, maestus, 306, 542.
magis (*-e*), 558.
magister, 232.
magistratus, 343.
magnanimus, 364.
magnopere, 362.
magnus, 261.
Maia, -ii-, 8 ; *-di-*, 105.
major, 292, 408 ; pronunc., 53.
malĕ, 551 ; *mal(e)-*, 184 ; *-ficus*, 51.
malignus, pronunc. of, 138.
mālo, 547 ; *-ll-*, 111 sqq. ; *malim*, 515.
malogranatum, 364.
mālus, 307.
Mamers, 95.
mamilla, 113.
mamma, 118 *n.*, 363.
mamor for *marm-*, 95.
mamphur (?), 197.
mandare, 485.
mandere, 472 ; Perf. of, 501.
mane, 396.
maneo, 476 ; *-nsi*, 505.
mani- (*-no-*), 183 ; *Manes*, 339.
manico-, a handle, 337.
manifestus (*-nuf-*), 193.
maniplus, pronunc. of, 94.
mansues (*-tus*), 182.
mantele (*-llum*), 117.
manualis, 340.
marcerat for *-cidat*, 288.
mare, 338.
maredus for *-didus*, 288.
maritimus, 405.
Marius, 320.
marmor, 18 ; pronunc., 95.
Marpesius (*-pessos*), 117.

Marpor, 185.
marsuppium (*-p-*), 117.
Marsus, 84.
mascel, 375.
Masculine (see Gender).
Maspiter, 278.
massa, 104.
mateola, 19.
mater, 219.
matertera, 405.
matruelis, 340.
*mattinus for *-tut-*, 184.
mattiobarbulus, 197.
mattus, 185, 309.
maturrime, 407.
mavolo, 547.
maximus, 407 ; pronunc., 139.
Media Prosodia, 161.
Mediae, pronunc. of, 71 sqq. ; M., Tenues and Asp., phon. changes of, 279 sqq.
mediastinus (*-tri-*), 330.
medioximus, 407.
medipontus (*-l-*), 287.
meditor, 521, 287.
Meditrina, 347.
medius, 226.
medius fidius, 618.
medullitus, 561.
mehe, O. Lat., 422.
mehercle (*-cules*), 618.
mejo, 466.
mel, scansion of, 122.
meles, 346.
Melica for *Med-*, 287.
melior, 406.
meltom (?), 406.
melum for *māl-*, 18.
membrum, 270.
memini, 270 ; *-mento*, 517.
memor, 541.
mendicus, spelling of, 245.
mendum, N. (*-da*, F.), 400.
menetris, for *meretrix*, 96.
mens, 274 ; *-mente*, Adv., 549, 552.
mensa, pronunc. of, 67.
mentiō, the scansion, 212.
-mentum (see Suffix -TO-).
mercedimerae, 540.
mercennarius (*-n-*), pronunc. of, 118.
merda, 306.
mereo, -eunt 3 Pl., 519 ; *merēbatur*, the scansion, 202.

INDEX. 641

meretrix, 347 ; menetris, 96.
merga, 351.
merges, 351.
mergo, 285.
meridies, 288; med-, 288.
merito, 559.
mers for -rx, 107.
merto for -so, 482.
merula, 288.
messis, 340.
-met of egomet, &c., 421, 423 sq., 429.
Metathesis of r, l, 91, 97 sq.
Metellus, 486.
metior, mensus, 471.
mĕto, 486 ; -ssui, 499.
metuculosus, 333.
metus, F. (O. Lat.), 343, sq.
meus, 426 sqq. ; mi, Voc., 427.
Mezentius, Med-, 104.
mica, 306.
migro, 302.
miles, 287; scansion, 119, 215; -ex, 108.
mille, 419 sq. ; milia, spelling of, 112 sq.
milvus (-uos), 46.
mina (μνᾶ), 64 ; in word-group, 169 sq.
minerrimus, 407.
Minerva, 306, 190.
mingo, 455
-mini, 2 Pl., Ind., 534 ; Imper., 517.
minimus, 407 ; -me (-mum), Adv., 550.
miniscitur, 200.
minister, 232.
-mino, Pass., 517, 519.
minor, 407.
mi(n)sterium for -nist-, 173, 202.
minuo, 471.
Mircurios, Praen. inscr., 229.
mis, Gen., 421 sq.
misceo, 479 ; mixtus, -stus, 107.
misellus, -serulus, 333.
miser, 306 ; my-, 29.
mitto, pronunc. of, 117 ; misi, O. Lat. meissei, 499, 112.
mitulus, myti-, 37.
ml, phon. change of, 270 sq.
-mn-, pronunc. of, 64, 69 sq.
mo- for meo-, Poss., 426.
moderor, 356.
modestus, 356.
modo, 612 ; -ŏ, 551 ; Comps. of, 559.

modus in word-groups, 169, 564.
moe-, O. Lat. for mu- in moerus, &c., 248.
moles, 345 sq.
mollibit (?), 493.
monedula (-er-), 288.
moneo, 477 ; moneris, -int for monu-, 506.
-mōnium (-ia) (see Suffix -IO-).
Monosyllables, shortening of, 215 sq.
monstrum, 331.
Months, Gender of, 369.
monumentum, -nom-, 201 ; -tus, 370.
Moods, 511 sqq.; Subj., 511 sqq. ; Opt., 511 sqq. ; Imper., 516 sqq.
mordeo, 303, 482; Perf. of, 505; momordi, 497; mem-, 503.
morigeror, 485.
morior, 473; -īmur, -iri, 475; -tuus, 324 ; -tus, 174.
moror, 483.
mors, 278.
morvus for -bus, 52.
mostellum, 331.
moveo, Perf, in Romance, 509.
mox, 555.
mr, phon. change of, 270 sq.
-ms-, phon. change of, 270.
mucus (-cc-), 116.
mulceo, -lsi, 505.
mulgeo, 296 ; -lsi, 505 ; -lctus, 279.
mulier, 287 ; -ĭĕrem, accent. of, 164.
multimodis, 362.
multus, Compar., 408.
Mummius, dedicatory inscrr., 11.
-mungo, Vb., 471.
munus, 247.
-mur, 1 Pl. Pass., 534.
*murca for am-, 107.
muriola, spelling of, 117.
murmur, 315.
-mus, 1 Pl. Act., 529 ; scansion, 529.
mus, 237.
musca, 239.
muscipula, 365.
musimo, 71.
Mutation of Vowels (see Gradation).
Mute and Liquid, vow. lengthened bef., 94 ; accent. of penult with, 164.
muto, 247 ; for -tor, 522.
muttus, 58.
mutuus, 324.
myser for mis-, 29.

N, pronunc. of, 60 sqq. ; I.-Eur. N.,

T t

phon. changes of, 271 sqq.; Ņ, 273 sq.; Lat. *n* for *l*, 96; for *m*, 270; for *gn-*, 292, 294.
N-particle (see Particles).
Naepor, 183.
Naevius, 294.
Nahartis, *Nart-*, 54.
nam, 604, 571.
Names, of birds, &c., changed by Anal., 201; Proper, form of Italic, 319 sq.; in *-o*, 348 sq.; in *-is*, 375.
namque, 604.
nanciscor, 261, 480; *-cio*, 480; *-ctus* (*-nctus*), 471.
naris, 272.
narro, 483; pronunc., 118; *-r-*, 118 sq.
Nasal, pronunc. of, 60 sqq.; Gutt., 10 sq., 60, 65; Vb., 469 sqq.; 3 Pl., e. g. *danunt*, 530 sq.
nassiterna, the spelling, 112.
nasus, 259; *-ssum*, 112.
nātrīx, 355.
natus (*gn-*), 541, 219 sq., 294.
naufragus, 180; *-ium*, 252.
navis, 221, 252.
-nct-, pronunc. of, 64, 70.
-nd-, pronunc. of, 64, 70.
-nde of *unde*, &c., 551.
-ndo-, of Gerund, 543 sq.
-ne, Interrog., 605 sq.
-ne, Affirm., 615.
nĕ-, Neg., 615.
nē, *nae*, Affirm., 614 sq.
nē, Neg., 614; accent. of, 166.
nebula, 226.
nec, 'non,' 616.
nec (see *neque*).
necerim, 'nec eum,' 440.
neco, 481; *-avi* (*-ui*), 499.
necto, *-xui*, 509.
necubi, 446.
necumquem, 570.
nedum, 614.
nefas, 615.
Negatives, 615 sq.
neglego, 616; *-xi*, 505.
nego, 486.
negotium, 616.
nemo, 449.
nempe, 604; scansion, 63; pronunc., 122.
neo, 476, 225; *neunt*, 519.
nepos, 351, 272; *-us*, 32.
neptis, 351; *lept-*, 96.

nequalia, 571.
nequam, 571.
nequaquam, 569.
neque (*nec*), 122.
nequeo, 547; *-quinont*, 531; *-quitur*, 522.
Nero, 271.
nescio, 547.
nesciocube, 446.
nesi, 592.
neve (*neu*), 614, 122.
Neuter (see Gender); in *-r*, decl. of, 349; in *-es*, 355 sq.
neuter, 450; pronunc., 143.
neutiquam, pronunc. of, 143.
-nf-, lengthening of vow. bef., 136 sqq.
ni, 611.
nicto, 293.
Nigidius, on *h*, 55; Agma, 65; accent of *Valeri*, 163, 390.
nihil (*nīl*), 216 sq., 144, 57.
nimis (*-ium*), 558.
nisi, 611; *-se*, 25.
nitedula (*-ella*), 333, 353.
nītor, Vb., 521; *-tito*, 519; *-xus*, 294.
nittio for *-ct-*, 89.
nivit, Vb., Pacuv., 455.
nix, 272.
-nm-, phon. change of, 271 sqq.
no, 476.
nobilis, 334.
noceo, 481; *-ivus*; Adj., 323.
noctu, 555.
noenum (*-ŭ*), 615.
nola (from *nolo*), 318.
nolo, decl. of, 547; *-ll-*, 111 sqq.; *-lim*, 515.
nomen, 294; *-clator*, 364.
Nominative (see Declension): Adv. use of, 553 sqq.
non, 615, 216 sq.
nonaginta, 417.
nondum, 570, 609.
nongenti (*noning-*), 419.
nonne, 605.
nonus, 416.
*noptia for *nuptiae*, 37.
nos, decl. of, 424 sq.; *-ss*, 112.
nosco, 479; *gn-*, 294; *-vi*, 500.
nostrās, &c., accent. of, 163.
*noto for *na-*, 15, 17.
nōtus, (*gn-*), 233.
novem, 415 sq.; *-decim*, 416; *-venus*, 416.

INDEX. 643

Novensiles (-d-), 286.
novicius, 338.
novitas, 341.
novus, 226.
nox, 234 sq.; Adv., 555.
-ns-, pronunc. of, 63 sq., 69; for s after long vow., 69; from -nss-, 112; vow. long bef., 136 sqq.
-ns of triens, sextans, &c., 409.
-nt, 3 Pl., 529; -nto, 531; -ntor, 535; -ntur, 534.
nubes, 346 nubs, 182.
nudipes, 361.
nudius tertius, 260, 377.
nudus, 260, 235, 179.
nullus, 449; pronunc., 113.
num, 605.
Numasioi, Praen. fib., 305.
Number, 366; Dual (see Dual).
Numerals, 408 sqq.; Fractions, 409; accent. of, 165.
Numerius, 560; -ri, Gen., 383 n.
numerus, 270; numero, Adv., 560.
nummum, Gen. Pl., 402.
nunc, 570.
nuncubi, 446.
nundinae (nond-. nound-), 251, 180.
nunquam, 570.
-nunt, 3 Pl., e. g. danunt, 530 sq.
nuntius, 180; novent-, nont-, 250 sq.; pronunc., 141.
nuper, Adv., -rus, Adj., 180, 553.
nurus, 239; -ra, 343; no-, 37.
-nus, e. g. facinus, 356.
nusciosus (-citiosus), 96.
nutrio, 249.

O, pronunc. of, 30 sqq.; phon. changes of, 232 sqq.; ŏ in e-roots, 258; ō in ĕ-roots, 258; ŏ-ō, 260; ŏ-ă, 259; Lat. ō for lengthened ŏ, 233; Lat. ŏ for a, 17 sq.; for e with w, l, 225 sqq.; for atonic vow. bef. Lab., 192 sqq.; after qu-, 300; Lat. ō for au, 40 sq.; for ou, 248 sqq.; not weakened to ū, 199.
O-stems, blend with U-stems, 343 sq. (see Suffix -O-, -YO-, &c.)
-ō, 1 Sg., 524; of Rufo, &c., 348 sq.; of quo, Adv., &c., 551; of vero, Adv., &c., 550; for -ĕ in Adv., 559; shortening of, 212 sq.
ob (obs-), Prep., 585; ousted by ab-, 574.

ob vos sacro, 573.
obinunt, 531.
obiter, 563.
oblitterus for -atus, 543.
obliviscor, -lisc-, 52; -litus, Pass., 543.
oboedio, 196, 246.
obrussa, 198.
Obscure Vowel, 185 sqq., 257.
obsequium, 321.
obsolesco, 481.
obsono, 488.
obstetrix, 191.
obstino, 472; obstinatus, 310.
obstringillo, 487.
obtineo, spelling of, 78 sq.
obviam (-us, Adj.), 563.
occanui, Perf., 509, 198.
occĭdamus (?) for -cēd-, 199.
occillo, 487.
occulo, 227; oquoltod, S. C. Bacch., 227.
occupo, 470, 486.
ocior, 259, 406.
ocris, 259.
octo, 415; -decim, 416; -ginta, 417 sq.; -tag-, 418; -tuag-, 418; -tingenti, 419; -tavus, 220.
oculus, 234.
odium, 259.
odor, 235.
OE, pronunc. of, 39 sqq.; spelling, 246. (See OI.)
oenus, 248, 410.
ofella, 113.
offendices, 272.
offendo, 486; -sa, Noun, 542.
officina, 174, 349.
OI, phon. changes of, 246 sqq.; ŌI, 252 sq.; OI, OE on inscrr., 247 sq.
oiei, Interj., 39.
oinos, 410.
Oinumama, 193.
oinuorsei, 178.
-ol- from el, 228 sq.; l, 278 sq.
ol-, Dem. Pron., 430.
olentica, 337.
oleo, 287.
olim, 570; o. oliorum, 436; olitanus, 436.
oliva, 228; -um (oleum), 196.
olla (aula), 41.
olle (-us), 436; oloes, olorom, 436.
Olympus, accent. of, 155.
Omega, Lat. transcr. of φ, 44.

Omicron, Lat. transcr. of, 33.
omitto, 113 sq., 202.
ommento, 80.
omnimodis, 362.
omnis, 450; *omnino*, 325.
Onomatopoetic Verbs, 483, 476.
-onssus (*-ōsus*), 353.
-ont, 3 Pl., O. Lat., 529.
-ōnus, O. Lat. for *-ō*, 348 sq.
onustus, 306.
opera, 400.
-opere, Adv., 560.
operio, 475; for *ap-*, 18.
operor, 485.
opificina, 174.
opilio (*up-*), 34.
opinor, 472.
opiparus, 192.
Opiter, 180.
opitulor, 485.
opituma, 174.
oppido, 566.
opportunus, opor-, 114.
Optative (see Moods).
optimus, 406.
optio, 369.
opulens (*-lentus*), 352.
opus, 485.
oquoltod, S. C. Bacch., 227.
-or- from I.-Eur. ṛ, 278 sq.
-or, 1 Sg. Pass., 533; Nom. Sg., e. g. *calor* (see Suffix -S-).
Orata, as a nickname, 40.
orbis, 239; *orbs*, 182.
orbus, 258.
orca, 239.
ordia prima for *primord-*, 362.
Ordinal Numerals (see Num.).
ordo, pronunc. of, 141.
oreae, 261.
orichalcum, 202.
oricla for *auricula*, 40 sq.
orno, 33, 310; pronunc., 141.
-orum (*-um*), Gen. Pl., 402.
-os, Nom. Sg., e. g. O. Lat. *colos*, 356.
os, mouth, 358.
os, bone, 405.
os- (*aus-*), e.g. *osculor*, 41.
Oscus, 310.
ostendo, 310.
ostium, 262; *ust-*, 34.
-ōsus (*-ossus, -onssus*), 112, 353.
OU, phon. changes of, 248 sqq.; ŌU,

253; Lat. *ou* for *eu*, 245 sq.; on inscrr., 246; written for *ŭ*, 246; for *ū*, 246.
-ov- for *-uv-*, 33.
ovifer, 361.
ovis, 235.
*ŏvum for *ōv-*, 34.
-ōx (see Suffix in Gutt.).
oxime, 407.

P, pronunc. of, 78 sqq.; phon. changes of, 281 sq.; dial. from qᵘ, 299 sq.; not final, 77; bet. *m-n*, &c., 70.
P-particle (see Particles).
pacunt or *pag-*, xii Tabb., 465; *paciscor*, 465; *-peciscor*, 200.
Pacuvius, use of Compds., 360.
paedora for *-res*, 356.
Paelignus, pronunc. of, 138.
paene, 558 *n.*
paeninsula, 360.
paenula, 197.
Paenultima Accent.-Law, 160 sqq.
pagina, 326.
palam, 586.
Palatal Gutt., phon. changes of, 295 sqq. (see K̂, Ĝ, ĜH).
Palatalization of Cons. bef. *y*, 263; of *t*, 81 sqq.; of *c*, 87 sq.; *l*, 91, 98; *r*, 91, 98.
palea, 279.
palma, 279, 328.
palor, 586.
palpebra (*-tra*), 331.
palumbes, 346.
pălus, -ŭs, the scansion, 214.
pālus, 293.
Panda, 318; *-āna porta*, 318.
pandiculor, 488.
pando, 472; *-di*, Perf., 502.
pango, 259; Perf. of, 504; *panxi*, 504; *pegi*, 497; *pepigi*, 495.
panis, 339.
pannucia, 337.
panus, pannus, 117.
papae, accent. of, 164.
papaver, 541.
Papirius Crassus, his use of *r* for *z*, 6.
Parasitic Vowel, 145 sqq.; with *l, r*, 93 sqq.; in Gk. loanwords, 70 sq.; *u* bef. *l*, 193 sq., 197 sq.
parcarpus (?) for *panc-*, 273.

INDEX. 645

paroepromus, 360.
parco, Perf. of, 505 ; *-rsi*, 505.
parcus, 318.
parentatid, Luceria inscr., 519.
parentes, 465.
paret (*-rr-*), 117.
paricidas, 371, 373, 117 sq.
pario, 279 ; *-īre*, 475 ; *-ibis*, 492 sq.
paro, to equalize, 485.
pars, 278 ; *partem*, Adv., 555.
Participles, 539 sqq. ; Pres. Act., 540 ; Fut., 540 ; Perf., 541 ; Pres. Pass., 540 ; Perf., 541 sq. ; *-tus* (*-sus*), 542 ; truncated, 543 ; used as Adj., 540 sq.
Particles (see Conjunctions) ; T-, 597 ; D-. 597 ; DH-, 597 ; P-, 597 ; N-, 597 ; *-ce*, 432 sq. ; relation to Case-suffix, 597 sq. ; to Pers.-suff., 597 ; Imper. used as, 600.
partim, 556.
parum, 562 ; *parumper*, 562.
parvus, 562 ; Compar., 406 sq.
pasco, pastum, 310.
passar for *-er*, 201.
passim, 556.
Passive, 519 sqq. ; Impers., use, 520 sq., 523 ; with Acc., 521 ; Person-endings (see Verb) ; Inf. (see Inf.) ; Part. (see Participles).
pastillus, 339.
pateo, 476, 222.
pater, 222 ; *p. familias*, 381.
Patricoles, 197.
patrisso, 488.
patrocinor, 488.
patronus, 349.
patruelis, 340.
paucus, 243.
paveo, pavio, 473.
paulatim, 556 ; *-lisper*, 562 ; *-lum*, spelling of, 111 sq.
pax, 259.
-pe, Particle, 597.
pecten, 349.
pectino, 488.
pecto, 479 ; *-xi*, 505 ; *-xui*, 509.
pecu, 281 ; *pecus*, 354.
pedepressim, -temptim, 556.
peditaster, 330.
pēdo, 307 ; *pepedi*, 501.
pejero, 48, 199 ; *perj-*, 313, 587.
pejor, pronunc. of, 53.

pelegrinus for *per-*, 93.
pellex for *pael-*, 115.
pello, 472 ; *pepuli*, 504.
pelluviae, 285.
pendeo, pendo, 473.
penes, Prep., 586.
penetro, 586, 594.
penitus, Adv., Adj., 561 sq. ; *-te*, Adv., 562.
penna, 313.
penuria, 558 n.
penus, 586.
-per, e.g. *paulisper*, 562.
per, Prep., 586 sqq.
peragro, pronunc. of, 94.
percello, 486 ; *-culsus*, 542.
percussi, Perf., 545.
peregre, 396.
peremne, 191.
peremo, 587.
perendie, 560, 588, 192.
perendino (see *comperendino*).
peres for *ped-*, 81.
perfacul, 198.
Perfect (see Tense-stems) ; quant. of penult of S-perf., 134 sq. ; accent of *-ĭt*, &c., 163 ; scansion *-iĭt*, 214.
perfidus, 587.
pergo, 587.
periculum, scansion of, 175 sq.
perjero (see *pej-*).
Periphrastic Tenses, 510 sq.
perna, 251.
pernix, 354 ; *pĕrn-*, 141.
pernox, 361, 555.
perperam, 557.
perplovere, 466.
perquam, 571.
Personal Pron. (see Pronouns).
Person-endings (see Verb).
perstroma, 172.
pertineo, 476.
pertisus, 195.
pervenat, 464.
pervicus, 317 sq.
pes, 286.
pesna (?), 313.
pessum, 539.
petesso, -isso, 462.
petiolus (?), 76.
peto, 468 ; *-ivi*, 506.
petorritum, 300.
Petreius, 300.

petulcus, 337.
phalerae, 190.
phasellus, *-ll-* for *-l-*, 115.
Phi (see Aspirates).
Philippus, accent. of, 155.
Pi, Lat. transcr. of, 75.
piaculum, 333 ; O. Lat. *-colom*, 193.
pidato (*pedatu*), 19, 21.
pigmentum, pronunc. of, 139.
*pilla for *pīla*, 115.
pilleus (*-l-*), 117.
pilumnoe poploe, Carm. Sal., 398.
pinaria for *pen-*, 200.
pinguis, 292.
pinna, 229.
pinso, 471 ; *-io*, 470.
pirus, 374.
piscis, 232.
piscosus, 353.
Pitch-Accent, 148 sqq.
pituita, pronunc. of, 52.
pius, 265 ; scansion, 131.
placenta, 190.
plăga, 318.
Plancus, 179.
plango, 471.
plaudo, *plodo*, 41.
plaustrum, *plostrum*, 41.
Plautus, use of Compds., 362 ; dial.
   Plotus, 242.
plebes, 376.
plecto, 486.
plenus, 324.
-pleo, to fill, 458, 473, 223.
pleoris (?), Carm. Arv., 408.
plerumque, *plerus*, Adj., 559.
plico, 200, 468.
Plinius, 225.
plisima (?), Carm. Sal., 408.
plodo, 41.
*plopus for *pŏpulus*, 98.
plostrum, 41.
pluo (*plovo*), 466.
Pluperfect (see Tense-stems).
plurimus, 408.
plus, 408, 558 ; *-ra* (*-ria*), 401.
pŏ-, Prep., 575, 588.
podex, 307.
poella for *pu-*, 37.
poena, 246 sq.
Poenus, 246.
poeta, 373.
pol, 618.

polio, 575.
Polla, 41.
pollen, *polenta*, 367.
Pollio, spelling of, 112 ; *-ŏ*, 212.
Pollux, 179, 182 ; *-luces*, O. Lat., 245.
polubrum, 575, 331.
pomerium, 588.
Pompeius, 300.
pondo, 258.
pondus, 356.
pone, Prep., 588.
pono, 178 ; *posui* (*posivi*), 499 ; *-ss-*, 115.
Pontius, 300.
popina, 300.
populus, scansion of, 146 ; *-loi Romanoi*,
   O. Lat., 387.
pōpulus, in Romance, 98.
-por for *puer*, 183, 185.
por-, Prep., 590.
porca, 279.
porceo, 588.
porcus, 277.
porricio, 485.
porrigo, *porgo*, 545, 178.
porro (O. Lat. *porod*), 568.
porrum, 279.
Porsena, spelling of, 23.
posco, 477 ; *poposci*, 501 ; *pep-*, 503.
Position, length by, 129 sqq. ; bef.
   Mute and Liq., 94, 129 sqq.
Possessive, Compd., 360 sq. ; Pron.
   (see Pron.).
possum, decl. of, 546 ; Inf. in Romance,
   536 ; *potestur*, 522.
post, *pos*, *pō-*, *poste*, *postid*, 588 sq. ;
   postea, 569 ; *posteac*, 437 ; *posthac*,
   569 ; *postibi*, 567 ; *postmodum* (*-o*),
   559.
posterior, N., 378.
posticus, 337.
postmeridianus, spelling of, 589.
postridie, 560.
Post-tonic, Syncope (see Syncope) ;
   Vow.-change (see Weakening).
postulo, 179.
postumus (*-remus*), 407.
*poteca for *apoth-*, 107.
Potina, 349.
potior (*-io*), 484, 546.
potis, 233.
potis (*pote*) *sum*, 546.
poto, 232.
potus, 520, 542.

INDEX. 647

-*pp*- for *p*, 116.
prae, 589; *prae let tremonti*, Carm. Sal., 530.
praebeo, scansion of, 143.
praecipes (-*ceps*), 182.
praeco, 180, 187.
praecox (-*coquus*), 358.
praeda, 143.
praedopiont, Carm. Sal., 189, 472.
praefamino, 517.
praefiscini, 192; -*ne*, 396.
praemium, 143.
Praenestine, *conea*, 22, 106, 177; *tam modo*, 613; Sync., 177; *fibula*, 188.
praes, 180, 187.
praesagio, 259, 486.
praesens, 589.
praesertim, 556.
praestigiae, 95.
praestino, 472.
praesto (-*tu*), 178.
praestolor (-*tul*-), 34.
praeter, 589; -*ea*, 569; -*hac*, 569.
praeterpropter, 521.
praetor, 350.
prandeo, -*di*, Perf., 502; -*sus*, 520, 542.
pratus for -*m*, 370.
precor, 296.
precula for *perg*-, 76, 97.
prehendo, 471, 42, 132; -*di*, 501; *prendo*, 57, 143; Perf. in Romance, 509.
prelum, 307.
premo, 307; -*ssi*, 499.
Prepositions, 572 sqq.; written with Noun, 168, 572; oust Case-suff., 573; Compound, 573; with many Cases, 574; assim. in Comp. Vb., 312 sq.; accent., 167 sqq.
Present (see Tense-stems).
Pretonic, Syncope (see Syncope); Vowel-change (see Weakening); ĕ, ŏ changed to ă (?), 159, 222.
pri, Prep., 589.
pridie, 560.
primilegium for *priv*-, 52.
primordia, 362.
primus, 410; *primumdum*, 609.
princeps, 178; pronunc., 141.
principio (-*ium*), Adv., 560.
prior, N., 378.
priscus, 337.
pristinus, 325.
pristris for *pristis*, 96.

privicloes, Carm. Sal., 403.
privignus, 181, 325; pronunc. of, 138.
pro, Prep., 590; -ŏ, 590.
pro, Interj., 618.
probunto, 519.
probus, 590; -*boum*, 246.
procapis, 182.
procestria, 191.
Procope, 107; (*e*)*st*, 121.
procul, 590.
procus, 258.
prōd-, Prep., 590; *prodius*, 590.
prodigium, 291.
prodinunt, 531.
produit, 515.
profestus, 199.
proficio, 590.
proficiscor, 480.
profitemino, 519.
profligare, 470, 486.
progenies, 345 sqq.; *progenie* (Scip. Ep.), 48, 506.
progredimino, 519.
prohibeo, scansion of, 143; -*bessis*, 462.
proiecitad, Luceria inscr., 519.
proinde, 570; *proin*, 122.
proles, 345.
prolixus, 293.
prologus, 590.
promenervat, Carm. Sal., 194.
promiscam, 557.
prompsi, Perf., 505.
promunturium, spelling of, 197.
pronis for -*nus*, 339.
Pronominal, Adverbs, 567 sqq.; in -*bi*, 567; -ī, 567; -ŏ, 568 sq.; -*ā*, 569; -*im*, 570; -*nde*, 570; -*um*, 570; -*am*, 570; T-suffix, 571; D-suff., 571; Adjectives, 449 sqq.
Pronouns, 421 sqq.; Pers., Refl., 421 sqq.; Poss., 426 sqq.; Dem., 429 sqq.; Rel., Indef., Interrog., 443 sqq.; Decl. of (see Declension); accent. of, 167 sq.; *illôc*, &c., 163.
Pronunciation, 13 sqq.
pronus, 326; -*nis*, 339.
propages, 346.
propagmen, 292.
prope, 591; -*modum* (-*o*), 559.
Proper Names, Italic, 319 sq.
properus, 374.
propino, 590, 488.

propinquus, 358.
propitius, 194.
propius for *-pri-*, 95.
propritim, 556.
propter, 591, 179; *-ea*, 569.
proptervus, 590.
prorsus (*-m*), 553; cf. 549.
prosa, 553.
Proserpina, 98; *Prosepnai*, (not *-ais*) 382, 184.
Prosodical Hiatus, 132, 144 sq., 209 sq.
prosperus, 257.
prosternere, in Romance, 489.
Prosthetic *i*, 102, 105 sqq.
prosum, Vb., 590.
protervus, 590.
protinus (*-tenus*), 554, 556, 200; *-am*, 557; *-is*, 554.
protulum for *prothyr-*, 190.
proximus, 591.
prurio, 487.
*psalli, Perf. (?), 501.
-pse, *-pte*, Particles, 440.
puber, 356.
pubes, 346.
Publicola (*Popli-*), 76.
publicus, 287.
Publius, 287.
puer, *-re*, Voc., Fem. in O. Lat., 374; *-por* in Compd., 183, 185.
puertia (*-rit-*), 174.
pugil, 376.
pulcer, spelling of, 12, 59 sq.
puleium (*-egi-*), 48, 292.
pulenta for *pol-*, 33.
pulex, 355.
-puli of *impuli*, &c., 501; *pulsus*, 278.
pulto (*-so*), 482.
pulvis, 235.
pŭmex for *pūm-*, 37.
pumilio (*pom-*), 34.
pungo, 471; *pepugi*, 503; *punctus*, pronunc., 140.
pupa (*-pp-*), 116.
purus, 542; *purime*, 407.
pusillus, 305.
puter, 260; *puteo*, 260.
puto, 482; *-tă*, 211, 600.
putrefacio, scansion of, 212.
pūtus, 542.

Q, the letter, 3, 7; *qu*, pronunc.,

84 sqq.; length by Position, 87; I.-Eur. Q^u, phon. changes of, 299 sqq.
q^{u}o-, q^{u}i-, q^{u}u-, Pron. stems, 443 sqq.
qoi (Dvenos inscr.), 445.
qua, Adv. (*quaad*), 569 sq.
quadra, 413.
quadraginta, 417 sq.; accent., 165; *quarr-*, 418.
quadrans, 409.
quadrigae, 196.
quadrigenti (*-ing-*), 419.
quadruplex (*-plus*), 414.
quaequalis, 448 *n*.
quaero, 487; *-sivi*, 506.
quaeso, 462, 487; *-umus* (*-imus*), 487 *-ss-*, 112.
qualis, 451.
quallus, the spelling, 112.
quam, 570, 607; of *unquam*, &c., 552; *quamde*, 570, 607; *-libet*, 613; *-vis*, 613; *-obrem*, 606; *quamquam*, 613.
quando, 608, 571; *-ŏ*, 213; *-que*, 571; *-quidem*, 571, 608; *quandoc*, 608; *quandone*, 608.
quansei, 607.
Quantity, 126 sqq.; overmastered by accent, 129 (see Shortening, Lengthening, Scansion); changed bef. cons.-group, 133 sqq.; of vow in close syll., 133 sqq.
quantus, 451; *-mvis*, 613.
quapropter, 569.
quare, 606.
quartus, 413.
quasi, 607; *-se*, 25.
quasillus, 305.
quatenus, 557.
quater, 413; *-nus*, 414.
quatio, *u* in Comp., 196.
quattuor, 413 sq.; spelling, 414, 113; *-ttor*, 414; *-decim*, 416.
que, 598 sq.; enclitic, 166 sq.; *qu(e)*, 598.
queistores, 242.
quercus, 291; *-nus*, 294.
querella, the spelling, 112 sqq.
queror, 227.
querquera, 315.
quetus for *quie-*, 142 sq.
-qui- for Gk. κυ, 36.
qui, Pron., 443 sqq.; pronunc., 39,

INDEX.

44 ; *cui*, pronunc., 39, 44, 446 ;
  spelling, 87.
qui, Adv., 446, 568 ; *-qui (-n)*, 613 ;
  -dum, 609.
quia, 610 ; *-nam*, 606.
quicumque, 448 ; *-dam*, *-libet*, *-vis*, 447.
quidem, 602 ; *siq-*, *tüq-*, &c., 216.
quies, 182.
quiesco, pronunc. of, 134 ; *quetus* for *quie-*, 142 sq.
quin, 613.
quinque, 414, 229 ; pronunc., 414 ;
  -ndecim, 416 ; *-n(c)tus*, 70 ; pronunc.,
  140, 414 ; *-ngenti*, 419 ; *-ncentum*,
  O. Lat., 419 ; *-nquaginta*, 417 ;
  -ncunx, 300 ; *-nus*, 414.
quippe, 604 ; pronunc., 122.
quirquir, 288.
quis, 443 sqq. ; pronunc., 85 ; *-que*,
  -piam, *-quam*, *-quis*, 448.
quisquiliae, 315.
quo, Adv., 568 ; Conj., 613 ; *-ad*,
  568 ; *-circa*, 580 ; *-modo*, *-ŏ*, 212.
quod, Conj., 610.
quoiatis (cujas), 447.
quoiei, Dat., 445.
quoiquoimodi, 445.
quom for *cum*, Prep., 581.
quominus, 569, 613.
-quomque (-cunque), 598.
quondam, 571.
quoniam, 610.
quoque, 598.
quorsus (-m), 568.
Quorta, 413.
quot, 451 ; *-annis*, 560 ; *-idie* (see *cott-*).
quotumus, 561.
quotus, 451.
quum, 608, 570.

R, pronunc. of, 89 sqq. ; I.-Eur. R,
  phon. changes of, 276 sqq. ; Ṛ, 278
  sq. ; Lat. *r* for *s*, 303 sqq., 101,
  105 ; for *d*, 285, 288, 80 sqq. ; for *l*,
  92 sq. ; for *n*, 96 ; dropped in *prae-st(r)igiae*, &c., 91, 95 ; bef. cons., 97.
-r, long vow. shortened bef., 213 sq. ;
  of Passive, 523, 533.
rabies, 347 ; *-es*, Gen., 383.
rabo for *arrabo*, 177.
rabula, 177.
racemus, 306.
radix, 220.

Raius for *Rav-*, 252.
ramentum, 312.
rapio, 476.
rapŏ, a robber, 475.
ratio, 340.
ratiocinor, 488.
ratis, 307.
ratus, 259.
ravastellus, 330.
raucus, 180.
Raudus for *-vid-*, 185.
raudus, 248 sq.
-re, 2 Sg. Pass., 533 ; Inf. Act., 535 sqq.
re-, *red-*, Prep., 591.
reccidi, Perf., 504.
recens, Adv., 554.
recidivus, 322.
reciprocus, 337.
Recomposition, 199 sq. (see Reformation).
recordor, 483.
recta, Adv., 550.
recupero, 488.
reddo, 468, 114 ; *reddibo*, 493.
red(d)uco, 114 ; *redux*, 591.
rederguo for *-arg-*, 198.
redinunt, 531.
redivia, 286.
redivivus, 591.
Reduction (see Weakening, Shortening).
reduncus, 259.
Reduplicated, Present, 468 ; Perfect,
  496 sq., 501 sqq. ; form of red.,
  502 sq. ; assim. of red. vow. to
  stem-vow., 503 ; loss of, 503 sq. ;
  Noun, 358, 363.
Reflexive Pron. (see Pronouns).
refriva faba, 178.
regina, 370.
regnum, pronunc. of, 138.
rego, 296 ; *rexi*, 505 ; pronunc. of, 139, 498.
regula, 318.
Relative Pron. (see Pronouns).
reliquus, pronunc. of, 323 ; *-cuos*, O. Lat., 46.
reluvium, 286.
remex, 358.
remulcum, pronunc. of, 142.
ren, 264.
reor, *ratus*, 259.

repandirostro-, Pacuv., 360.
rĕpens, 268; Adv., 554; -nte, 551.
repo, 307.
repperi, Perf., 504.
reppuli, Perf., 504.
repulsa, 542.
requies, decl. of, 346.
res, 252, 225; in word-group, 169.
reses, 358.
respondeo, Perf. in Romance, 509.
Res(ti)tutus, 176.
retro(r)sum, 549.
rettuli, Perf., 503 sq.
retus for retitus, 543.
reverti, Perf. of, -tor, 520.
reus, 244.
rex, 260, 276.
Rho, Lat. transcr. of, 12, 59.
-rĭ-, syncop. after cons., 171, 179 sq.
-ri, Inf. Pass., 535 sqq.; -rier, 536 sq.
rien, 264.
rigor, 306.
ringor, 471.
-ris, 2 Sg. Pass., 533; and -er in Adj. M., F., 371.
rite, 560.
ritus, 560.
rivalis, 244.
Rivers, gender of, 368.
rius for rivus, 52.
-rl-, pronunc. of, 97.
-rm- for nm, 271 sqq.
-ro, e. g. lambero, 479.
robigo, 348; rub-, 34.
robur (-or), 356, 379; -us, 379.
robus, Adj., 248.
rodus, 248 sq.
Roma, 307.
ropio, 76.
Rostrata Columna (see Col. Rostr.).
rota, 258.
rotundus, 544 sq.
Rough Breathing (Gk.) (see Breathing).
-rr- for rs, 277 sq.
-rs-, pronunc. of, 91, 96.
rubeo, 476.
ruber, 239.
rubicundus, 545.
rubigo for rob-, 34.
rubus, 307.
rubustus for rob-, 34.
ructo (see eructo).

rudentes, 467.
rudis, 249, 338.
rŭdo, 307.
rudus, 248 sq.
rues, 345.
rufus, 248.
Ruga (see Carvilius).
rumen, 307.
rumentum, 'abruptio,' 314.
Rumina ficus, Rumon, 307.
rumpia, 33.
rumpo, 471; rupi, 502; -mptus (see corruptus).
rupes, 346; -pp-, 118.
ruri (-e), 396.
rursus (-m), (rus-), 549, 553.
-rus, 2 Sg. Pass., 534.
Rustic Latin, ĕ for ĭ, 19, 25, 30; veha, 22; ē for ī, 24 sq., 29 sq.; frundes, 31, 33; tundo, 33; o for au, 40 sq.; e for ae, 42 sq.
rusticus, 337.

S, voiced written z, then r, 6; pronunc. of, 101 sqq.; phon. changes of, 303 sqq.; Lat. s for ss, 305 sq., 109 sqq.; for ns, 136 sq.; for th in Not. Tir., 58; O. Lat. s, class. r, 305; dial. s, 305.
S-Perf., Vb.-forms (see Tense-stems).
s- from ps-, ks-, 303.
-s, O. Lat., e. g. colos, 356; 2 Sg., 525.
sabulum, 304.
sacena (scena), 261, 184.
sacerdos, 179 sq.
săcri-, săcro-, 183.
sactus for sanct-, 70.
saepe, 559.
saepes (se-), 42.
Saeturni, 242.
Saguntum, 104.
sagus, 259 sq.
sal, 223.
Saliare Carmen (see Carmen Sal.).
salignus, 293.
salio, 223.
salix, 278, 223.
sallo, 285, 479.
saltem, 556.
*salvaticus for silv-, 201.
sambucus (sab-), 65.
Sanates, 183.

INDEX. 651

sancio, 470 ; *sanctus*, pronunc., 140 ;
  sact-, sant-, 70.
Sandhi, 120 sqq.
sanguis (-en), 377.
saplutus, 104.
sarcina, 326.
sarmentum, 310.
satis (sat), 558 ; *satin*, 558 n.
satur, 558 n.
satura (-ira), 197.
Saturnian Metre, 128 n., 132 n., 159.
satus, 222.
saucius for *-atus*, 543.
savium, 268.
*sauma for *sagma*, 89.
saxum, 261.
sc- lengthens final vow., 131 ; *isc-*
  (see Prosthetic *i*).
scabellum (-mill-), 283.
scabo, 223, 281, 259 ; *-bi*, Perf., 502.
scaena (sce-), 42.
scaeptrum (sce-), 42.
scaevus, 242.
Scaliger's Law, 361, 363, 365.
scalpo, 279.
scalprum, 333.
scamnum, 283.
scando, -di, Perf., 502.
Scansion, traditional, 127 n. ; errors
  in late literature, 128 sq. (see
  Shortening).
Scaptensula, the spelling, 136 n.
scateo (-to), 476.
scaturio, 482.
scauria for *sco-*, 41.
scelerus (?), 356.
scelus, 229.
scena, a priest's knife, 184, 261.
scena, (σκηνή), *scae*, 42.
scheda, sc(h)i-, 23.
scilicet, 564.
scindo, 280, 471 ; *scicidi*, 495, 501 ;
  scisc- (?), 503 ; *scidi*, 495, 501.
Scipio Afr. (Min.), *ve-* for *vo-*, 228.
sclis (stl-), 307, 83.
scloppus, 307.
-sco, Incept., 477.
scobis, 259, 338.
scopulus, 197.
scoriscus for *corusc-*, 29.
scriba, 318.
scribo, 282.
scrobis, 306.

scrofa, 80.
scrupulus (scrip-), 29.
sculna, 184.
sculpo, 279.
sē-, 'to sow,' 224.
se, Pron., 424.
se (sed), Prep., 592 ; *se fraude*, 592.
secespita, 261.
secius (see *set-*).
seco, 298 ; *si-*, 23.
Second Pers., Sg. ending, 525 sq. ;
  Pl., 529.
Secondary Accent, 158 sqq., 161.
secordis, 592.
secratum for *sacr-*, 18.
secta, 566.
sectius (?), 566.
secundum, Prep., 591.
secundus, 411.
securus, 592.
secus, Noun, 552 ; Adj., 591 ; Adv.,
  552 ; Prep., 591.
-secus, 552, 554.
sed, O. Lat., 'himself,' 424.
sed, Conj., 601.
sedda for *-ll-*, 287.
sedecim (sexd-), 416.
sedeo, 285 sq., 473 ; *sedi*, 497, 502.
sedes, 345 sq.
seditio, 592.
sedulo, 563 ; *-us*, Adj., 563.
sedum, 601.
sedutraque, 450.
seges, 351.
segmentum, 293.
selinum, the scansion, 156.
seliquastra, 287.
sella, 287.
semel, 410, 229.
semermis, 364.
semi-, 409, 225.
se(mi)modius, 176.
semissi-, 409, 586.
semper, -iternus, 562.
semptem for *sept-*, 66.
senatus, decl. of, 343 ; *-ti*, Gen., 380,
  384 ; *-tuos*, Gen., 384.
seneca, 337 ; *senecio*, 337.
senecta, 334 n.
senex, 271, 354 ; decl. of, 367.
Sentence-Accent, 148 n., 165 sqq.
sententia, 352.
senus, 415.

seorsum, 592.
septem, 415; -decim, 416; -tuaginta, 417 sq.; -tingenti, 419; -timus, 415; -tenus, 415; -tuennis, 415; sempt-, 66.
septentriones, 269.
Septidonium for Septiz-, 104.
septimus decimus, accent of, 163.
sepulcrum, 334; spelling of, 57, 59 sq.
sequius, 566.
sequor, 520.
Serena for Sir-, 30.
serius, Adj., 267.
serpillum, 197.
serpo, 277.
serra for sera, 115.
sero, 468; sevi, 500; satus, 222.
sesamum, spelling of, 198 sq.
sescenti, 419.
sescentoplagus, 364.
sescuncia, 300; -onc-, 236.
sesqui-, 409.
sesse for sese, 112.
sestertius,409; -ium, Gen. Pl., 402; 418.
setius, 566.
Setus (Ζῆθος), 104.
seu, sive, 122.
severus, 226 sq.
sex, 415; sexaginta, 417.
sextans, 409.
Sextius (-st-), 415.
Sh^{e}va, 257.
Short Vowel (see Quantity).
Shortening, of vow. bef. vow., 131 sqq.; bef. n with cons., 141 sq.; bef. l with cons., 142; bef. -l, -m, -r, -t, 213 sq.; of final vow., 207 sqq.; of final syll. long by position, 215 sq.; of monosyll., 215 sq.; after short syll. (see Breves Breviantes); of long diphth. bef. cons., 251 sq.
si, 610.
sibi, 424; -e, 25.
Sibilants, phon. changes of, 302 sqq.
sibilo, 78; -f-, 80; su-, 30.
sic, 567; pronunc., 121 sq.; sicine, 433.
siccus, 447.
Sicilicus, mark of double cons., 4, 8.
sicubi, 446.
sido, 468; sidi (sedi), 503.
sidus, 267.
siem, 514 sq.
*sifilo for sib-, 30, 78, 80.
signum, pronunc. of, 138 sq.

silenta for -tia, Neut. Pl., Laev.,401,352.
silicernium, 287.
-sim, Subj., 465.
simila, 286.
similis, 338.
simitu (-tur), 565.
simplex (-plus), 410.
simpludiarea funera, 410.
simul, Adv., 553; Prep., 592.
simulter, 553.
simus for sumus, 29.
sin, 612.
sinatus for sen-, 200.
sincinia, 410.
sinciput, 141.
sine, 592; sei-, 592.
Single Cons. for Double, 113 sqq.
singnifer for sign-, 66.
singuli, 410.
sino, 471.
sins, Carm. Arv., 518 n.
siquidem, the scansion, 216.
sis for si vis, 52; sultis, Plur., 181.
siremps(e), 566.
sisto, 468; Perf. of, 503.
sive (seu), 122, 600.
-so, Vb.-forms in, 462 sqq.
so- (se-), 'this,' 430.
so- for suo-, Poss., 426 sqq.
so-, O. Lat. Demonstr., 430, 432.
sobrinus, 303.
sobrius, 592.
soc (?), 'ita,' 432.
socer, 192, 227; -erus, 374.
sociennus, 545.
sociofraudus (-uf-), 364.
socius, 262.
socors, 592.
socrus, 344; -a, 343.
sodes, 265, 486.
Sofia, scansion of, 150.
sōl, the scansion, 215.
soldus for -lid-, 185.
solea, 287.
solemnis for -ll-, 111.
solerare, 'solidare,' 288.
solinunt, 531.
solitaurilia, 8.
solitus sum, Perf. Dep., 522.
solium, 287.
sollemnis (-nn-),70; -mpn-, 70; sole- 111.
sollicitus, 361.
sollistumus, 407.

INDEX. 653

sollo-, 8, 16.
sollox, 354.
solum, 287.
solvo, 592; *-lui* for *-lvi*, 48; *-lutus*, 260.
solus, 449.
somnium, 319.
somnolentus, spelling of, 192.
somnus, 227.
Sonant L, M, N, R (see L̥, M̥, N̥, R̥).
sonivius, 323.
sono, 488 n.; *sonui*, 506.
sopor, 227.
sorbeo, 283; *-psi* for *-bui*, 509; *-billo*, 487.
sordēre, *-ĕre*, 476.
sordes, 345.
soror, 227.
sortus, P. P. P., 542.
sp- lengthens final vow., 131; *isp-* (see Prosthetic *i*).
sparsi, Perf., 505.
spatiarus, 534.
species, decl. of, 346.
specio, 472; *spi-*, 23.
sperno, 472.
spes, 257, 345 n.
spica, *spe-*, 25.
Spiritus (see Breathing).
spondeo, 482; *spopondi*, 496; *spe-* (*sposp-* ?), 503.
spongia (*-ea*), 22.
spuo, 264.
-ss- for tt, 304, 309; for *x*, 102; reduced to *s*, 110 sqq.
-ssere, Inf., 465.
-(s)sim, Subj., 465.
-(s)so, Vb.-forms in, 462 sqq.; Perf. of, 506.
stā-, 'to stand,' 457.
Staccato pronunciation, 131.
stagnum, pronunc. of, 138.
stătim, 556; *ste-*, 15.
Statina, 349.
statod (Dven. inscr.), 519.
status, 221; as P. P. P. of *sum*, 542.
ste for *iste*, 435, 167.
stelio (*-ll-*), 117.
stella, pronunc. of, 112.
Stem, Noun and Adj., 316 sqq.; suffix (see Suffixes); interchange of U- and O- stems, 343 sq.
sterĭlus, 338.
sterno, 470, 219; *stratus*, 219, 306.

sternuo, 471.
sterquilinium, the spelling, 301.
stetim for *stat-*, 15.
-sti, 2 Sg. Perf., 525.
stilicidium, spelling of, 112.
stilla, 487.
-stinguo, 471.
stipendium, 116.
stircus for *-erc-*, 20, 229.
stl-, O. Lat., *Stlaborius*, *Stlaccius*, *stlembus*, *stlis*, *stlocus*, *stloppus*, 307.
stlattarius, 219.
stlis (*scl-*), 83, 307.
sto, decl. of, 457; *steti*, 501; Perf. in Romance, 509; *status*, 221, 542.
stolidus, 235.
storax, 37.
stramen, 279; *stratus*, 219.
strenna for *-n-*, 116.
strenuus, 323; *-nn-*, 113.
Stress-Accent, 148 sqq.
strictim, 556.
stridi, Perf., 502.
stringo, 229; *strictus*, 542.
stritavus, O. Lat. for *trit-*, 196.
Strong, Cases, 367; Root-grade (see Gradation).
strues, 345.
strufertarii, 361.
struo, in Romance, 489.
struppus (*-opp-*), 58.
studeo, 476.
stultus, 235.
stupa (*-pp-*), 116.
stupila for *stipula*, 37.
suad, 'sic,' 611.
suadela, spelling of, 115.
suadeo, 482, 259; pronunc., 53.
Svarabhaktic Vowel (see Parasitic).
suavis, 221; pronunc., 53.
suavisaviatio, 361.
sub, *sus-*, Prep., 593; *sub vos placo*, 572.
subaediani, spelling of, 195.
subaxet (?), 508.
**subilo* for *sib-*, 30.
Subjunctive (see Moods).
sublimen, 559; *-us*, 338.
suboles, 345.
Subordinate Words, 165 sqq.
subrigo, 545.
subrimii haedi, 193.
subsicivus, 323.

subtel, 199, 213.
subtemen (-egm-), 292, 70.
subter, 593; *-tus*, 561; Prep., 593.
subverbustus, 306.
subula, 334.
succidaneae porcae, 195.
sucerdae, 260.
sucus, 76; spelling of, 116.
sudus, 307.
suesco, 481.
suffio, 267.
Suffixes (Noun, Adj.), 316 sqq.; -O-, -A-, 316 sqq.; -IO-, 318 sqq.; -UO-, 322 sqq.; -NO-, 324 sqq.; -MENO-, 327 sq.; -MO-, 328; -TEMO-, 328 -RO-, 328 sqq.; -TERO-, 329 sq.; -*cro*-, 329; -TRO-, 329 sqq.; -DHRO-, 329 sqq.; -LO-, 331 sqq.; -TLO-, 332 sqq.; -DHLO-, 332 sqq.; -TO-, 334 sqq.; -KO-, 336 sqq.; -I-, 338 sqq.; -NI-, 339; -MI-, 339; -RI-, -LI-, 339 sq.; -TI-, 340 sqq.; -TIŎN-, 340 sqq.; -TĀT(I)-, 341 sq.; -TŪT(I)-, 341; -U-, 342 sqq.; -TU-, 343 sq.; -YĔ-, -Ĭ-, -Ĕ-, 344 sqq.; -EN-, 348 sq.; -YEN-, 348 sq.; -WEN-, 348 sq.; -MEN-, 348 sq.; -R-, 349 sq.; -ER-, -TER-, 350; -T-, 350 sqq.; -NT-, 352; -WENT-, 352 sq.; -D-, 353 sq.; Gutt., 354 sq.; -S-, 355 sqq.; -ES-, 355 sqq.; -YES-, 357; -*issa*, 365; -*ia*, 365; -*itto*-, 365.
Suffixless Stems (Noun. Adj.), 357 sq.
**sufilo* for *sib*-, 30.
sugo, 76.
Sulla, *Sy*-, 29, 36.
sultis, for *si vultis*, 181.
sum, 237; decl. of, 455 sqq.; enclitic, 167; Perf., 545; *es*, Imper., 518; *sim*, 514; *simus* for *sŭmus*, 29; *ero*, 492; *eram*, 490; *forem*, 227, 545 *n.*; (*e*)*st*, Procope, 121.
summosses, Hor., 507.
summus, 407; -*opere*, 362.
sumo, -*psi*, 505; *suremit*, 505, 593; *surempsit*, 593.
suo, 264, 484 *n.*
suovitaurilia, 361.
supellex, decl. of, 367; -*erl*-, 97; -*pp*-, 118.
super, Prep., 593; Adj. (-*rus*), 374.
superbus, 590.
supercilium, 195.

Superlative Degree (see Comparison); *i* for *u* in, 189.
superne, 593.
superus (-*per*), 374.
Supines, 538 sq.
supparum (*sip-*) 29.
Suppression of Syll., e. g. *ar*(*ci*)*cubii*, 176 sq.
supra, 593; -*pera*, 181, 593.
suremit, 505, 593; -*psit*, 593.
surgo, 178; *surrexi*, 545, 505; *suregit*, 505; *sortus*, 542.
surpui, Perf., 178; *surptus*, 178.
sursum (-*s*), 549, 553.
-*sus* (-*tus*), P. P. P., 542.
sus-, Prep. (see *sub*); *susque deque*, 593.
sus, sow, 260.
suspicio, 225.
sustuli, Perf., 545.
suus, 426 sqq.; monosyll., 426 sqq.; O. Lat. *so*-, 426 sqq.
swĕ-, phon. change of, 227.
Sylla, 29.
Syllable, Close (see Close Syll.); Division, 124 sqq.; First (see First Syll.); Suppression of (see Suppression; Syncope); Syllabic Writing, 12, 177.
sylva, the spelling, 11, 29.
Syncope, 170 sqq., 150 sqq.; Praenestine, 177; by old Accent-Law, 178 sqq.; final syll., 181 sq.; pretonic, 183 sq.; post-tonic, 184 sq.; final vow. (see Apocope); vow. in final syll., 203 sqq.
Synizesis, 142 sqq.

T, pronunc. of, 80 sqq.; and *d*, final, 76 sq.; phon. changes of, 283 sq.; for *d* bef. *r*, 285, 289.
T-particle (see Particles).
-*t*, 3 Sg., 526 sqq.; vow. shortened bef., 214.
-*ta* of *ita*, &c., 552.
tabes, 346.
Tables, Twelve (see Twelve).
taceo, 476.
taeter, 289.
talis, 451.
talus, 293.
tam, 570; -*me*, Carm. Sal., 570; -*etsi*, 602; *tanne*, 602, 69.
tamen, 601; -*etsi*, 602.

INDEX.   655

tango, 471 ; tago, 464 ; tetigi, 495.
tanquam, 570.
tantus, 451 ; -tidem, 571 ; -tisper, 562 ;
    -tummodo, 564.
Tarentum, accent of, 155, 197.
tarpessita, 104.
tata, 118 n., 363.
Tatpurusha, Comp., 360 sq.
*taxilare, 482.
-te, 2 Pl. Imper., 529.
tector, pronunc. of, 139 ; -tum, 542.
Tecumessa, 64, 71, 145 sq.
ted, 423.
teges, 351.
tego, 303 ; texi, 505 ; pronunc. of, 139.
tegula, 318.
tela, 293.
Telesia, 287.
Telis for Thetis, 75.
telum, 293 ; -ll-, 112.
-tem of item, &c., 552.
temere, 560.
temperi, spelling of, 192, 356.
temperies, 344.
temperint (?), 515.
tempestas, 342 ; -tus, O. Lat., 342.
templum, 565.
Tempsa, Temese, 181.
tendo, 486 ; -sus, 542.
tenebrae, 270.
teneo, 476 ; -tus, 542 ; tetini, 501.
tenor, tenus, 355.
Tense-Stems, 459 sqq. ; Aor. and S-,
    459 sqq. ; Pres., (1) Them. E-grade,
    466 sqq. ; (2) Redupl., 468 ; (3)
    Nasal, 469 sqq. ; (4) YO-,' 472 sqq. ;
    (5) Inceptives, 476 sq., 479 sqq. :
    (6) Causatives, 477, 481 sq. ; (7)
    Desideratives, 478, 482, 484 ; (8)
    Iteratives, 478, 483 sqq. ; (9) Deri-
    vatives, 478, 483 sqq. ; Stem-suf-
    fixes, 478 sq., 486 sqq. ; Impft. (Ind.
    Subj.), 489 sqq. ; Fut., 491 sqq. ;
    Perf. (Ind. Subj.), 494 sqq. ; (1)
    Redupl., 496 sq., 501 sqq. ; (2) Un-
    redupl., 497, 501 sqq. ; (3) S-, 497
    sqq., 505, 508 ; (4) V-, 499 sq.,
    505 sqq. ; (5) irreg., 509 ; Plupft.
    (Ind. Subj.), 509 sq. ; Tenses with
    Auxil., 510 sq.
tento for -mpt-, 70.
Tenues, (Lat.) pronunc. of, 71 sqq. ;
    (Gk.) Lat. transcr. of, 74 sq. ;

(I.-Eur.) phon. changes of, 279
    sqq. ; Ten. Asp., 280, 308.
tenuis, 274; pronunc., 46, 174 ; -via, 144
tenus, Prep., 593 ; hactenus, &c., 569.
tenus, Noun, 355.
-ter, Adv., 549, 553.
ter, 412 ; scansion, 119 ; ternus, 412.
terebra, 331.
teres, 351.
tergus, 302.
-terior (see Comparison).
terminus, 269 ; termo, 327.
tero, terui for trivi, 509.
terreo, 481.
terrimotium, 362.
terruncius, 412.
tertius, 412 ; -o (-um), Adv. 559.
tesca (-qua), 337.
tesera for -ss-, 115.
testamentum, 277.
tetini, Perf., 501.
tetuli, Perf., 494, 497.
-th- for s, 58.
Thelis, for Thetis, 286.
Thematic, Conj. (see Verb) ; Vowel,
    453.
thensaurus for thes-, 69, 136 n.
Theta (see Aspirates).
Third Pers., Sg. ending, 526 sqq. ;
    Pl., 529 sqq.
-ti- and -ci- confused, 82 sqq.
tibi, spelling of, 423 (see tu).
tibicen, 364.
-ticus (see Suffix -KO-).
tilia, 225.
-tim, Adv., 548.
tingo, 225 ; tinctus, pronunc., 140.
tinnio, pronunc. of, 118 ; tintinnio (-no),
    483.
-tinus, Adj. (see Suffix -NO-) ; Adv.
    (see tenus).
-tis, 2 Pl., 529.
tis, Gen., 423.
-tivus (see Suffix -UO-).
Tmesis, 187, 573.
-tō, Fut. Imper., 516.
to-, 'this,' 430.
toga, 255.
Toitesiai, Dvenos inscr., 305.
tolero, 488.
tollo, sustuli, 545.
tolutim, 556.
tondeo, 486 ; totondi, 496.

Tone-Accent, 148 sqq.
tongere, 259.
tongiliatim, 556.
topper, 562.
-tor, Imper. 'Pass., 533 sq.
torculus, 300.
-tōrium (see Suffix -IO-).
tormentum, 310.
torpedo (-ĭdo), 23.
torpeo, 476.
torqueo, 482; torsi, 310; tortus, 310.
torreo, 477.
torris, 339.
tot, 451; totidem, 451, 571.
-tōte, Fut. Imper., 517.
tōtus, 450; -tt-, 116.
tŏtus, 451.
-tr- for dr, 81, 289.
-tra, Adv., 569.
trā-, ' to go through,' 458.
trabes (-bs), 376.
trado, -nsd-, 594.
trahea for -ha, 318.
traho, in Romance, 489.
tramitto, -nsm-, 594.
trans, trā-, Prep., 594.
transmarinus, 362.
transtineo, 476.
Trasumennus for Tars-, 97.
Trees, gender of, 368.
tremo, 499; tremebit, 494; tremonti, 530.
tres, 412 sq.; trĕ-, trĭ-, 412; tredecim, 416; trecenti (-um), 418 sq.; triginta, 417 sq.; accent., 165; trienta for trigi-, 418; tricenus (-g-), 418; tricies (-g-), 418; trinus, 412; triplex (-us), 412.
tribunal(e), 205.
tricae, 58, 116.
tric(h)ilinium for tricl-, 94.
triens, 409.
triginta dies, accent. of, 169.
tripodare, 256.
*trippa, 119.
tristus for -is, 368.
tritavus (strit-), 196.
triumphus, spelling of, 59.
-tro, Adv., 568.
Troja, pronunc. of, 53.
*trono for tono, 95.
trudis, 338.
trudo, 486.
-trum, (see Suffix -TRO-); with ĕ, 191.
-tt- for ct, 86, 89; by Sync., 284.

tu, decl. of, 423 sq.
-tu, 2 Sup., 538 sq.
tuber, 270.
tuburcinor, 488.
tudes, 351.
-tudo (see Suffix -TŪT(I)-, -D-).
tueor (-uor), 476.
-tuiri, Fut. Inf. Pass., 538.
-tulas, attulas, 464.
tuli (see fero).
-tum, 1 Sup., 538 sq.
tum, 570; tunc, 570.
tumba, 36.
tundo, tutudi, 496; tunsi (?), 471; tunsus, tusus, 471; tundo for tondeo, 33.
-tur, 3 Sg. Pass., 534.
turba, 239.
turbinĕs, the scansion, 399.
turdus, 308.
-turio, Desider., 478.
turnus for to-, 31, 33.
-turo-, Fut. Inf., 537; Part., 540.
turtur, 363.
-tus, -sus, P. P. P., 542; of funditus, &c., 548.
tus, 58.
Tuscus, 278.
tutĕ, Pron., 423 sq.
tutela, spelling of, 115.
tuus, 426 sqq.; monosyll., 426 sqq.
Twelve Tables, 7, 565.
tympanum (typ-), 272.
Tyrannio, taught Accent., 151, 154.

U, V, the letter, 3, 7 sq.; V and VV, 267 sq.; 52; uu for ū, 10; Gk. (see Upsilon); U, pronunc., 34 sqq.; V, 44 sqq.; ü-sound, 25 sqq.; I.-Eur. Ū, phon. changes of, 237 sqq., 260 sq.; V (W), 265 sqq.; Lat. ŭ for o, 235 sqq., 31 sqq.; for atonic vĕ-, 196; in weak-grade of root with labiovel., 239; for atonic vow. bef. lab., 192 sqq.; for ō, 33 sq.; Lat. ū for ō, 233; for ŭ lengthened, 237; for eu, 245 sq.; for ou, 248 sq.; Lat. v from gu, 301 sq.; for b, 47, 49 sqq.; dropped bet. vowels, 52; dropped after cons., 52 sq., 144.
-ŭ, shortening of, 213; of cornŭ, &c., scansion, 377 sq.
ŭ-ĭ and ĭ-ŭ, e. g. stupila, 37.
V-perfect (see Tense-stems).

INDEX. 657

U-stems, blend with O-stems, 343 sq. (see Suffix -U-).
vădo, 467.
vadum, 467.
vae, 618.
valde, 561 ; -lid-, 174.
Valeri (Voc., Gen.), accent. of, 164.
vapor, 299.
vapulo, 522.
Variation of Vowels (see Gradation).
varix, 279, 355.
Varro, ī and ei, 9 ; deriv. of Gracchus, 147 n. ; on dirus, 244.
vas, a surety, 290.
vas, a vessel ; vassa, Pl., 112.
vates, 346 sq., 221 ; O. Lat. vatius, 375.
vatillum, spelling of, 51.
ubba for obba, 33.
uber, 290, 250.
ubi, 567 ; -e, 25.
-ubris, e.g. lugubris, 196.
-uc, Adv., 551.
-ūcus (see Suffix -KO-).
udus, 180.
-ve, Conj , 599 ; enclitic, 166 sq.
ve- for vo-, 228.
vē-, Prefix, 615.
veclus for -tul-, 83
vectis, 341.
vegeo, 482, 296.
vegetus, 296, 335.
veha for via, 22.
vehemens, vē-, 54, 57; -ter, Adv., 554.
veho, 226 ; -xi, 499.
vel, 599 sq.
Velar Gutt. (see Gutt. Proper, Labio-velar).
velatura, 308.
velim (see volo).
vella for vi-, 29.
vellico, 488.
vello, older vo- (?), 228 ; -li, 502 ; vulsi, 509.
vellus, 266
velox, 354.
veltrahus for -rtrag-, 93.
velum, 333 ; -ll-, 112.
vendo, 472, 488 ; -ditus, in Romance, 542.
veneficus, bene-, 51.
venenum, 326.
veneo, 488, 539 ; -iri, 522.
venio, 473; veni, 500; Perf. in Romance, 509 ; -venat, 464 ; -ventio, 274.
ventus, 251.

venum, 539 ; -do, 472.
Venus, 356.
vepres, 346.
Verb, 453 sqq. (see Tenses, Moods, Pass., Dep., Inf., Part., Sup., Ger.) ; Conjugations, 454 ; Athem. Conj., 453 sqq. ; Them. Conj., 453 sqq. ; Contracted forms, 463 sq. ; Person-endings, 522 sqq. ; 3 Conj. Vbs. in -io, 475 ; atonic form of Simple Vb., 468 ; in -o, -eo, 476 ; -urrio, 482 ; -uo, 484 n. ; Onomat., 483 ; Compound, 485; in -uttio, 488 ; -cinor, 488 ; -isso, 488 ; 1 Conj. predominant, 488 ; Noun-stem in -ē-, 490 ; Irreg., 545 sqq. ; Contracted Perf.-forms, V-perf., 506 sqq. ; S-perf., 508.
verberit (?), 515.
verbum, 290
verēcundus for -ē-, 202.
vereor, 473 ; verēbamini (?), 202.
Vergilius, spelling of, 23.
vermina, 310.
vermis, 339.
Verner's Law, 157.
vernus, 324.
vero (-e). 550.
verres, 277.
verro, 468 ; vo-, 228 ; -ri, Perf., 502.
verruca, 277, 337.
Verrugo, 337.
-versus (-m), Adv., 549.
versus (-m), Prep., 595.
Verticordia, 361.
verto, 266 ; vo-, 228 ; -ti, Perf., 502.
Vertumnus, 327.
veru, 301.
verus. 266 ; -m, -o, Conj., 602 ; -o (-ē), Adv., 550.
vespa, 266.
vesperi, 396.
vesperna, 324
vestis, 305, 341.
veto, 288 ; vo-, 228.
vetranus, for -ter-, 184.
Veltö, the scansion, 212.
vetus, 356 ; Compar., 407 ; veter, 356 ; -tustus, 407.
Ufentina, 250.
-ūgo (see Suffix in Gutt.).
-ui (-avi), Perf., 506.
UI, pronunc. of, 39, 44 ; vĭ-, pronunc., 29.

U u

-vĭ-, Syncope of, 171 sq., 180 sq.
vibix, 355.
vicem, Adv., 550.
vicenus (-g-\ 418; -cesimus,417; -cies,418.
viciniae, Loc., 397.
vicissim, 556, 586 ; -satim, 556.
viclus for -tul-, 83.
victrix, N., 371.
vicus, 295.
videlicet, 564.
video, 473. 266, 232; -di, 502, 497;
    viden, pronunc., 163 ; vissus, spelling, 112.
viduus, 268.
vieo, 266.
vigeo, 229.
vigil, 376.
vigilandŏ, the scansion, 213.
viginti, 417 sq. ; accent., 165 ; vinti, 418.
vile, Adv., 559.
vilicus, the spelling, 112 sq.
villa, pronunc. of, 112 sq. ; ve-, 29.
villum, 333, 179.
villus, 229.
vinarius, 321.
vincio, 470.
vinco, 471, 298 ; vici, 502.
vindemia, 178.
vindex, 362.
vinea (-ia), 22.
Vinnius, pronunc. of, 118.
vinolentus, spelling of, 192.
violens (-tus\ 352.
vir, 260 ; pronunc., 29; -um, Gen. Pl., 402.
virdis, &c., for -rid-, 171, 185.
virectum, 335.
vireo, 260.
viritim, 556.
virus, 267.
vis, Noun, 230 ; vis, Plur., 399 345, n.

vis, 2 Sg. (see volo, decl. of).
viso, 462 ; -si, 502 ; visso, 112.
vissit for vixit, 107.
vita, 179 ; vitam vivitur, 521.
vitex, 230.
vitis, 266, 341.
vitus, 344.
viveradix, 192, 361.
vivo, 301 ; vivebo, Nov., 492 ; vixi, 499 ;
    -ss-, 107 ; vivitur vitam, 521.
vivus, 230.

vix, 555 ; -dum, 614.
-ul- for lĭ, 232 ; from l, 278 sq.
ulciscor, ultus, 310.
uligo, 287.
-ūlis (see Suffix -LI-).
-ullus (-ūlus), 115.
ullus, 449 ; pronunc., 113.
ulmus, 279.
ulna, 260, 179.
uls, ultra, 594 sq. ; pronunc., 142 ; ol-
    timus, 236.
ulula, 363.
ululo, 474.
Ulysses (Ulixes), 286, 200.
-um (-orum), Gen. Pl , 402.
umbilicus, 283 ; imb-, 29.
umbo, 283.
umerus, 236 : spelling, 56.
unā, Adv., 561.
Unaccented Vow., weakened (see
    Weakening) ; Syncope of (see Syncope).
unco, 476.
uncus, 259.
unde, 570 ; pronunc., 122.
undecim, 416 ; pronunc., 141.
undeviginti, 416.
undique, 570, 206.
-undus (-endus), Ger., 543.
unguis, 293.
unguo, 301 ; -nctus, pronunc., 140.
unicus, 337.
universus, 178 ; -sim, 554 ; oinuorsei,178.
Unomammia, Plaut., 364 ; Oinumama 193.
unose, 554.
unquam, 570.
unus, 409 sq. ; -quisque, 449.
vo-, O. Lat. for ve-, 228.
-vo- atonic changed to vu, 267.
-uo, Vbs. in, 484 n.
Vocative (see Declension) ; of IO-
    stems, accent., 163 sq.
*vocitus, empty, 18.
vocivus, 18 ; voco for va-, 15, 18.
voco, 228.
Voices (see Passive, Deponent).
Voice-Stops (see Mediae).
Volaterrae, 228.
-vollo (?) (ve-), 228.
volo, I wish, decl. of, 456 sq. ; accent.,
    169 ; velim, 515 ; volam, 516 ; volĭmus,
    456 n. ; Inf. in Romance, 536.

INDEX. 659

volturus, 374.
Volumnus, 327 ; -*nius*, 228.
voluntas, 541.
volup, 553.
voluptas, 342.
vomo, 267, 506 n, 228.
ropte, 426.
roro, 301, 228.
vorro (*ve*-), 468, 228.
vorto (*ve*-), 467, 228.
vos, decl. of, 425 sq.
Vowel, Grades (see Gradation);
Quantity (see Quant., Shortening,
Lengthening).
vox, 358.
upilio (*op*-), 34.
Upsilon, Lat. transcr. of, 4, 11, 36, 248.
upupa, 315, 363.
urbanus, 325.
urbs, 239 ; spelling, 78 sq.
urceus, 239.
urgeo, 239, 482.
urna, 310.
-*urnus* (see Suffix -NO-).
uro, 466 ; *ussi*, 497 ; pronunc., 111 ;
ustus, pronunc., 255.
-*urrio*, Vbs. in, 482.
ursus, 239.
-*us*, Gen., e.g. *Venerus*, 384 ; decl. of
Neuts. in, 355 sq. (see -*rus*, 2 Sg. Pass.).
usque, 571, 595.
ustium for *ost*-, 34.
usurpo, 173.
ut, 606, 605 ; accent., 166 ; *uti*, 607.
uter, Noun, 289.
uter, Pron., 450 ; -*que*, 450.
uterus (-*um*), 369.
Utica, 37.
utinam, 605.
utor, 247 ; *utarus*, 534 ; *ūssus*, 112 ;
utunto, 519.
utrasque, Adv., 557.
utrimque, Adv., 570.
utrinde, Adv., 570.
utro, Adv., 568.
utrubi, Adv., 567.
utrum, Conj., 606.
-*ut*(*t*)*io*, Vbs. in, 488.

-*utus*, P. P. P., 542.
-*uu*- written for *ū*, 10.
-*ū*(*v*)*i*, Perf., 508 sq.
vulgo, 560.
vulnus, spelling of, 236.
vulpes, 346.
vulpinor, 472.
vultur, *volturus*, 374.
-*uus* (see Suffix -UO-).
uxor, written *voxor* in MSS., 5.
vy- for *vi*-, e. g. *vyr*, 29.

W, Lat. expression of, 7 sq. ; I.-Eur.
W, phon. changes of, 265 sqq.
Weak, Cases, 367 ; Grade of Root
(see Gradation).
Weakening, of Atonic Vowel, 185
sqq.,148 sqq.; syll. long by Position,
191 sq. ; short syll., 194 sq. ; bef.
r, 192 ; bef. Lab., 192 sqq. ; of
Diph , 195 sq. ; of Diph. in Hiatus,
196 ; of *jĕ*, *vĕ*, 196 ; *o*, *u*, *i*, 196 sq. ;
Gk. loanwords, 197 sq. ; long vow.
unweakened, 199 ; short, 198 sq. ;
re-formation, 199 sq. ; weakening
in pretonic syll., 200 ; by Assimilation, 201 ; in final syll., 203 sqq.
wel-, ' to wish,' 456 sq.
Wharton's Law, 159, 222.
Winds, gender of names, 369.
Word-Groups, 361 sq., 365 ; accent.,
161 sqq., 169 sq.

X, the letter, 2, 5 ; written *xs*, *cx*,
&c., 5 ; pronunc. of, 101 sqq. ; -*ss*-
for, 102, 107 ; for Gutt. with *s*, 291,
-*x* (see Suffixes in Gutt.).

Y, the letter, 4, 11 ; Gk. (see Upsilon) ; Lat. expression of *y*-sound,
7 sq. ; pronunc of Lat. *y*, 34 sqq. ;
I.-Eur. Y, phon. changes of, 262
sqq. ; Lat. *y* for *i*, *u*, 29 (see U).

Z, the letter, 4, 5 sq ; Gk. (see Zeta);
pronunc. of, 101 sqq. ; I.-Eur. Z,
phon. changes of, 303 sqq. ; Lat. *z*
for *j*, 49.
Zabulus, for *diabolus*, 105.
Zeta, Lat. transcr. of, 4, 11, 101, 104.

THE END.

ADDENDA ET CORRIGENDA

p. vii. Prof. Stolz has now published a *Lautlehre der lateinischen Sprache* (Leipz. 1894), giving the phonetic laws of Latin, (cf. chap. iv of this book) along with a general introduction to the study of the language.

p. 344, § 95. The new number of the *American Journal of Philology* (vol. xv. p. 194) has a paper by Mr. L. Horton-Smith, in which this view of the origin of the Gerundive *-ndo-* is supported by a strong array of arguments.

p. 153, l. 12	for	*illīc*	read	*illĭc*.
p. 198, l. 3	,,	*Ann. Epigr.*	,,	*Ann. Épigr.*
p. 235, l. 7 ab im.	,,	*on-*	,,	*ŏn-*.
p. 238, l. 9 ab im.	,,	*orbs*	,,	*orbis*, late Lat. *orbs*.
p. 242, l. 14	,,	*dĕverī*	,,	*dĕverī*.
p. 276, l. 8	,,	*cālāre*	,,	*calāre*.
p. 291, l. 11 ab im.	,,	**qĕnqᵘĕ*	,,	**pĕnqᵘĕ*.
p. 356, l. 4	,,	**modes-*	,,	**modes-* (whence *moderōr*).
p. 415, l. 6	,,	*sĕnus*	,,	*sĕnus*.
p. 420, l. 3	,,	**egŏ*	,,	**eĝŏ*.
l. 4	,,	**egŏm*	,,	**eĝŏm*.
p. 528, l. 22	,,	fefaced	,,	fefaked.
p. 551, l. 19	,,	U-stems	,,	Vow.-stems.

LaVergne, TN USA
26 January 2011
214093LV00002B/7/P